The Dickens Bibliographies

General Editor
Duane DeVries
Polytechnic University

AMS Studies in the Nineteenth Century
Number 22

ISBN 0-404-64452-X

GENERAL STUDIES
OF CHARLES DICKENS AND HIS WRITINGS
AND COLLECTED EDITIONS
OF HIS WORKS

An Annotated Bibliography

Volume One
Bibliographies,
Catalogues, Collections, and
Bibliographical and Textual Studies
of Dickens's Works

GENERAL STUDIES
OF CHARLES DICKENS AND HIS WRITINGS
AND COLLECTED EDITIONS
OF HIS WORKS
An Annotated Bibliography

Duane DeVries
Polytechnic University

Volume One

Bibliographies,
Catalogues, Collections, and
Bibliographical and Textual Studies
of Dickens's Works

AMS PRESS, INC.
NEW YORK

LIBRARY OF CONGRESS CATALOGING-IN-PUBLICATION DATA

DeVries, Duane.
  General Studies of Charles Dickens and His Writings and
  Collected Editions of His Works: An Annotated
  Bibliography / Duane DeVries
     p. cm. – (AMS Studies in the Nineteenth Century; no. 22)
     Includes bibliographical references and index.
     Contents: v.1 Bibliographies, checklists, catalogues,
     collections, and bibliographical and textual studies.
     ISBN 0-404-64452-X (alk. paper)
     1. Dickens, Charles, 1812-1870—Bibliography. 2. Dickens,
     Charles, 1812-1870—Criticism and interpretation—
     Bibliography.   I. Title.   II. Series.
  Z8230.D48   2004
  [PR4581]
  016.823'8—dc21   99-086395
                                                           CIP

All AMS books are printed on acid-free paper that meets the guidelines
for performance and durability of the Committee on Production
Guidelines for Book Longevity of the Council on Library Resources.

AMS Press, Inc.
Brooklyn Navy Yard, Bldg. 292, Suite 417, 63 Flushing Ave.
Brooklyn, New York 11205
U.S.A.

Manufactured in the United States of America

TABLE OF CONTENTS

To JoAnne
my wife and bibliographical companion
without whom none of this
would have been possible

ACKNOWLEDGMENTS

If I do these acknowledgments in roughly chronological order, my first thanks must go to Theodore Grieder. Ted was the person who first convinced me to consider bibliography as an option when he asked me, more than twenty-five years ago, to serve as associate editor for the American Literature, English Literature, and World Literatures in English Information Guide Series, published by Gale Research Company. Ted, long retired, died in New Mexico this August. This volume must serve as what I have to offer as his memorial.

Thanks are also due to Robert L. Patten, Rice University, who recommended me to Garland Publishing in 1978 as someone who might be interested in developing a series of Dickens bibliographies. I agreed to head the project, and eleven volumes were published as The Garland Dickens Bibliographies between 1981 and 1993. In 1997 the series was transferred to AMS Press as The Dickens Bibliographies. Two volumes and an update of a volume in the Garland series have since been published.

All bibliographies are built upon previous ones, so I am indebted to my predecessors in the field. I have scoured your works and absconded with your references shamelessly. Since this is, of course, how bibliographies get compiled, we are fellow sharers of information in this bibliography business.

In seeking out works beyond those in these bibliographies and in verifying and annotating all entries, I have worked principally at the New York Public Library, the Brooklyn Public Library, the New York University Library and the Fales Collection there, the Columbia University Library, the Library of Congress, the British Library, and the library of the Dickens House (now the Dickens Museum), London. I wish to thank the librarians and assistants who have made research easier for me, particularly former curator David Parker, present curator Andrew Xavier and assistant curator Florian Schweizer at the Dickens House and their marvelous and caring staff, who have always made working there a pleasure, as have former and current officers of the Dickens Fellowship, who frequently passed through–Cedric Dickens, Alan S. Watts (and Mrs. Watts), Michael Slater, Tony Williams, and Anthony Burton. Thanks also to John Grigg, who has been instrumental in surveying the Dickens House collections in preparation for further cataloguing of the collections there. I am grateful to the Polytechnic University Library for providing access to other libraries.

I am indebted to the National Endowment for Humanities for a Travel to Collections grant (1988), and to J. H. A. Lokin, Haarlem branch, Dickens Fellowship; to Lee Biondi, Heritage Book Shop, Los Angeles, CA; to Gareth Cordery, University of Canterbury, Christchurch, New Zealand; and to Joel J. Brattin and Rodney G. Obien, Worcester Polytechnic Institute, for materials.

I particularly want to thank Don Richard Cox, University of Tennessee, and Leon Litvack, The Queen's University of Belfast, fellow editors in The Dickens Bibliographies series, for reading the manuscript of this bibliography. Their suggestions have been invaluable. I must also thank Michael Slater, Birkbeck College, University of London, now retired, for reading the introduction and being constantly helpful, informative, and caring.

In compiling and annotating this bibliography, I have found myself frequently using a number of works on Dickens—*Forster*, *Forster-Ley*, *Pilgrim Letters*, and *Johnson* (see the list of abbreviations, below), of course, but also *The Dickens Index*, edited by Nicolas Bentley, Michael Slater, and Nina Burgis (**140**); *Dickens and Dickensiana*, the catalogue of the Gimbel Collection, by John B. Podeschi (**1509**); the volumes by my fellow editors in The Dickens Bibliographies and the Garland Dickens Bibliographies (**12, 13**); and the *Oxford Reader's Companion to Dickens*, edited by Paul Schlicke (**2309**). For more general references I have relied heavily on James L. Harner's *Literary Research Guide* (**1147**) in particular, as well as Robert Balay's *Guide to Reference Books* (**1133**), Michael J. Marcuse's *A Reference Guide for English Studies* (**1152**), and William A. Wortman's *A Guide to Serial Bibliographies for Modern Literatures* (**1162**).

For the preparation of this volume for publication, I am deeply indebted to Gabriel Hornstein, president of AMS Press, for taking on this project, and to Jack Hopper, editor, and the staff at AMS Press, for following through. All have provided advice and expertise. It has been a joy to work with these kind, intelligent, and generous people. Also thanks to the editors of *Dickens Studies Annual*, who were eager to publish a variant of my introduction as "A Survey of Bibliographical and Textual Studies of Dickens's Works," in volume 33 (2003), especially Stanley Friedman, who read it and liked it.

I must not forget colleagues at Polytechnic University and other friends and family for encouragement and support. Polytechnic University granted me two sabbaticals that enabled me to devote a considerable amount of time to the bibliography that I would not otherwise have had.

One person I have not yet mentioned has been my mainstay and support, my bibliographical companion, from the very beginning, and that is my wife JoAnne Keller DeVries. She has encouraged me in this project, worked with me in libraries, helped to take notes, read the manuscript more than once, and collaborated in compiling the index. I have dedicated this volume to her, but I do not think that is anywhere near sufficient. It will have to do for now.

ABBREVIATIONS

Note: I have kept abbreviations to the minimum in this bibliography so that the user will not find himself or herself turning back constantly from text to these introductory pages. A few works are referred to often enough, however, to merit abbreviated reference. They follow.

DeVries DeVries, Duane. *General Studies of Charles Dickens and His Writings and Collected Editions of His Works: An Annotated Bibliography*. New York: AMS Press, 2003- . To be published in four volumes—Vol. 1: *Bibliographies, Catalogues, Collections, and Bibliographical and Textual Studies of Dickens's Works* (the present volume); Vol. 2: *Autobiographies, Biographies, Letters, Obituaries, Reminiscences, and Biographical Studies*; Vol. 3: *General Critical Studies*; Vol. 4: *General Special Studies and Collected Editions*.

Forster Forster, John. *The Life of Charles Dickens*. 3 vols. London: Chapman & Hall, 1872-74 (actually published November 1871, November 1872, and December 1873); revised ed., 2 vols. Library Edition. London: Chapman & Hall, 1876.

Forster-Ley Forster, John. *The Life of Charles Dickens*. Ed. J. W. T. Ley. London: Cecil Palmer, 1928, passim.

Hogarth-Dickens Letters [Hogarth, Georgina, and Mamie, or Mary, Dickens, eds.]. *The Letters of Charles Dickens*. Edited by His Sister-in-Law and His Eldest Daughter. In 2 vols.: Vol. I: *1833 to 1856*; Vol. II: *1857 to 1870*. London: Chapman and Hall, 1880 (actually published 21 November 1879); also Vol. III: *1836 to 1870*. London: Chapman and Hall, 1882 (actually published 2 November 1881); revised ed. 2 vols. London: Chapman and Hall, 1882; 3rd ed. London and New York: Macmillan, 1893.

Johnson   Johnson, Edgar. *Charles Dickens: His Tragedy and Tri-
                            umph.* 2 vols. New York: Simon and Schuster, 1952.

Nonesuch Letters   Dexter, Walter, ed. *The Letters of Charles Dickens.* 3 vols.
                            Nonesuch Edition. Bloomsbury [London]: Nonesuch
                            Press, 1938.

Pilgrim Letters   House, Madeline, Graham Storey, et al., eds. *The Let-
                            ters of Charles Dickens.* The Pilgrim Edition (vols. 8-12:
                            The British Academy: The Pilgrim Edition). 12 vols.
                            Oxford: Clarendon Press, 1965-2002.

PREFACE

This volume has been long in the making. It began back in 1978, when Larry Davidow, then of Garland Publishing, asked me to serve as editor of a series of Dickens bibliographies along the lines of Garland's Shakespeare bibliographies then in process of publication. In designing the series, I proposed fifteen volumes devoted to individual Dickens novels, a sixteenth volume of the Christmas Books, Christmas Stories, and Dickens's other shorter fiction, a seventeenth of his nonfictional, theatrical, and poetic writings, and a final eighteenth volume that would contain general bibliographical, textual, biographical, critical, and special studies of Dickens. The series has since been taken over by AMS Press. My original plan was to avoid at all costs undertaking a volume in the series myself. I found editors for the first seventeen volumes fairly quickly; but, when the three people I considered most qualified to do the eighteenth volume quickly (and probably wisely) turned me down, I had no alternative but to take on the task myself.

In the process of accumulating lists of works to be covered, and reading and annotating them, it soon became clear that I had enough material for first two, then three, and then finally four volumes, all of considerable length. The basic structure of the work has remained constant from the beginning, however—the four areas of Dickens scholarship are bibliographical and textual studies (volume 1), biographical studies (volume 2), critical studies (volume 3), and a wide variety of special studies (volume 4). The present volume (*DeVries*, I, to use one of my abbreviations), comprising bibliographies and bibliographical and textual studies, has gone through two major re-organizations and, in the process, become more complex as I searched for logical subdivisions of the more than 2,500 works that fall into these categories. I have, as I point out in my introduction, below, been greatly aided by the guidelines established by Philo Calhoun and Howell J. Heaney in their "Dickensiana in the Rough" (**1392**), a review of William Miller's *The Dickens Student and Collector: A List of Writings Related to Charles Dickens and His Works, 1836-1945* (**1005**). I have also heeded the advice of James L. Harner in the first and, later, in the second edition of his *On Compiling an Annotated Bibliography* (New York: The Modern Language Association of America, 1985, 2000).

From the beginning the editors of the other volumes in these series and I have aimed at completeness, at least where English language studies of Dickens are concerned. Most have not included foreign language studies because Dickens's world-wide fame has produced translations and critical studies in so many languages as to make inclusion of all in an annotated bibliography a near impossibility. In this volume I have included a number of foreign language bibliographies because these, at least, will enable a researcher to begin the process of seeking out translations and studies in other languages. My main title indicates that these four volumes will contain only "general studies," since the other volumes in the Garland and AMS bibliographies deal with the individual works, and this restriction will certainly apply in volumes two through four. In volume one, however, I have included bibliographies and bibliographical and textual studies of individual works of Dickens because I believe it is important, and certainly useful, to have all of these studies in one place in order to give a complete picture of the bibliographical and textual work done to date on Dickens. This involves some redundancy, it is true, but the bibliographer and the student of Dickens's texts will, I know, be pleased that I have done so. Others can easily ignore the bibliographies and studies of individual works since I have placed them in their own sections.

Part One of the present volume is devoted to bibliographies and bibliographical studies of Dickens's works; cumulatively they establish the canon of Dickens's works and track attempts to determine which of a number of anonymous works attributed to Dickens were actually written by him. Part Two lists and annotates a variety of bibliographies and bibliographical studies of adaptations of Dickens's works–translations by others; readings Dickens himself made from his works; dramatic and other adaptations by others; plagiarisms, imitations, continuations, parodies, and forgeries; and, finally, a different kind of adaptation or supplement–original and later illustrations of Dickens's works. Part Three contains bibliographies and checklists of Dickens studies, including general, serial, and specialized bibliographies, as well as bibliographies of studies of individual works and commentaries on bibliographies and bibliographical studies. Part Four covers library catalogues and catalogues of Dickens collections, including guides to collections, scrapbooks in them, guides to Dickens museums, and commentaries on collections and library accessions. Part Five lists catalogues of Dickens exhibitions and exhibitions concerning others that contain significant Dickens items, as well as reports and reviews of the exhibitions and their catalogues. Part Six covers a relatively unknown side of Dickens scholarship–auction and booksellers' catalogues and published records and reports of these sales. It also contains a section listing books and articles about collecting Dickens, from first editions to Royal Doulton pottery figurines and postcards. Finally, Part Seven focuses on Dickens at work on his novels and other writings. It includes studies of textual changes in his manuscripts, number plans, page proofs, and the editions over which he had control. Again, there is a section concerned with Dickens at work on individual works.

Works are listed alphabetically within sections and parts throughout. In sections dealing with individual works, the works are also listed alphabetically rather than chronologically, though one or two of the readers of the manuscript would have preferred it otherwise, and I was myself sometimes inclined in that direction. I decided, however, that works would be easier to locate if arranged alphabetically.

I have included reviews of the more major studies and certainly of all full-length bibliographies and bibliographical and textual studies. If only a portion of a work on Dickens is included, such as a short bibliography in a critical study, reviews of the critical study are not listed here, though they will be included when the critical study is listed in *DeVries*, III. I have also included brief commentary from the reviews.

In compiling this bibliography, I have consulted all of the works listed in Part Three, Dickens Studies, as well as works in other parts of the bibliography that contain bibliographies of Dickens studies. I have tried always to be as complete as possible. While a number of works are listed here for the first time in any Dickens bibliography, I have also made certain to include all relevant bibliographies and bibliographical and textual studies listed in any previous Dickens bibliography, even hopelessly outdated items and ones of the most minor significance—if only because they have been listed in previous bibliographies and are therefore part of the record of Dickens studies. The annotation will make their insignificance clear.

As an aid to readers, I have included a number of cross-references in the body of the work, though I have tried to keep these at a reasonable level. As in other bibliographies in the two Dickens bibliographies series, cross references are indicated in bold-faced numbers (usually within parentheses) that refer to the entry numbers in the bibliography.

The index will be of greater value, I believe. Many of the items in this bibliography could have been listed in more than one part of it. Sometimes I *have* put part of a work in one section and part in another, where this seemed particularly warranted. But more often than not, I have used the index as the ultimate cross reference. In headnotes to the various sections of the bibliography I have given the relevant index entries to consult. Like the cross-reference numbers in the text, these are boldfaced. For example, in the headnote to section 3A, General Bibliographies of Dickens Studies, I refer the reader to the index entry **Bibliographies of Dickens studies, general bibliographies**, in part 2 of the subject index, where the reader will find listed by reference number general bibliographies of Dickens studies located in other parts of the bibliography.

As for the index itself, I have divided it first into an author and a subject index. Part 1 of the author index lists by title all of the works in the bibliography that were published anonymously. Too often such works simply never make it into an index. Part 2 of the author index lists the authors of record, as well as reviews they authored. Cross-references to authors are also listed here.

The subject index is likewise divided into two parts. Part 1, which is concerned with Dickens's works, is divided into 1) individual works: fiction; 2) individual works: attributions and collaborations, nonfiction, poetry, public readings, speeches, and theatrical works; 3) abridgements, anthologies, editions, and collected editions; and 4) Dickens's personal writings (autobiographies, diaries, letters, and notebooks). These are not complete lists of Dickens's works and editions; they identify only works and editions mentioned in this bibliography. Part 2 of the subject index is the more conventional subject index.

As now planned, volume four of the *General Studies of Charles Dickens and His Writings* (*DeVries*, IV) will contain a supplement that updates the first three volumes and a cumulative index. I will be happy to hear of any omissions from the current volume and any new publications that should be listed in a supplement. At present my e-mail address is ddevries33@aol.com or ddevries@duke.poly.edu, and my address is 423 Atlantic Avenue, Apt. 2G, Brooklyn, NY 11217. Letters may also be addressed to the publisher.

Duane DeVries

INTRODUCTION

More books have been written about Dickens than any other English novelist, and a distressingly large number of them have not been worth reading. Amid this mass of memoirs, biographies, introductions, critical commentaries, and miscellaneous studies, there is even more that is unreliable. . . . The great difficulty of writing about Dickens remains that hardly anything that has been written before about 1950 can be taken on trust; and yet the moment one turns back to the original sources there is the danger of being completely overwhelmed.

–K. J. Fielding, *Charles Dickens* (London: National Book League, 1953), p. 3.

Although Fielding omitted Dickensian bibliographical and textual studies from his list of suspect works, this may simply have been an oversight. The dour pessimism of his observation certainly seems far-reaching enough. But there is enough truth in his criticism to give a prospective bibliographer pause. Venturing into the minefield of Dickens studies to catalogue, organize, understand, and evaluate it has been a daunting experience—fascinating certainly, more often frustrating, and even confusing, and seemingly endless, like Tristram Shandy's attempting to write his life and finding that the more he advances the further behind he gets. And yet, ultimately, there is an end, perhaps arbitrary, but ideally after *almost* everything has been seen.

I began the present work, of which you have only the first of four volumes in your hands, in the early 1980s and worked on it over the next twenty years with greater or lesser intensity, depending on my teaching and administrative duties, until early retirement in 1995 made it possible to devote much more time to the completion of the work. Looking back, it has at times seemed a Shandean kind of progress, but here *is* the first volume at last, an annotated bibliography of bibliographies, catalogues, collections, and bibliographical and textual studies of Dickens's works, designed to serve as the base for all future Dickens studies.

Volume 2, which should, if this aspect of Shandyism does not further prevail, appear well before another two decades roll around, will deal with biographies, letters, and biographical studies of Dickens. Volume 3 will cover general critical studies of Dickens's works, and volume 4 general specialized studies of Dickens and his works. Volume 4 will also list and annotate collected editions and other compilations of Dickens's writings.

Anyone intrepid enough—some might say foolish enough—to tackle Dickensian bibliography had also better pay sufficient attention to Philo Calhoun and Howell J. Heaney's "Dickensiana in the Rough" (**1392**), their devastating critique of William Miller's *The Dickens Student and Collector: A List of Writings Relating to Charles Dickens and His Works, 1836-1945* (**1005**), which they published in the *Papers of the Bibliographical Society of America* in 1947. One would have liked Miller's ambitious bibliography, published a year earlier, to have been better. Miller was one of the great Dickensians of the twentieth century, and one of the leaders in the exploration of Dickensian bibliographical and textual study centered at the *Dickensian*, which he had helped found. Robert H. Haynes, who wrote the introduction to Miller's bibliography, offers something of an apologia for Miller in noting that he completed his bibliography in the Harvard Library during the Second World War, where he was "separated by the Atlantic from his accumulation of materials," which made the "verifying of many of his references . . . arduous and, in some cases, . . . impossible." Even in 1946 the volume of Dickens material was formidable, though nothing to what it was to become later, and Miller largely omitted newspaper articles to keep his bibliography from becoming too bulky. It ended up being 351 pages long, but seventy of those pages comprised the index.

Miller saw his work as an updating of F. G. Kitton's *Dickensiana: A Bibliography of the Literature Relating to Charles Dickens and His Writings* (**996**), published in 1886. Kitton's work listed and annotated 584 biographical, critical, poetical, anthological, musical, dramatic, plagiaristic, and miscellaneous items, with extensive excerpts from the biographical and critical studies. It was the most comprehensive bibliography for its time. However, as Haynes points out, by 1946 Kitton's bibliography was "more or less obsolete because of new material which has made its appearance during the period which has elapsed and because of numberless previously unrecorded items which have been brought to light." Now, another fifty-five or so years later, I might make the same claim, or rather, the more than twenty authors of volumes in the two series of Dickens bibliographies (**12, 13**), of which the present volume is but one of twenty-one proposed and one of fourteen published to date, might make that claim. Obviously in twenty-one volumes, we will be filling a great many more pages and including a great many more references than Miller imagined in his wildest dreams. In 1946 the Dickens factory was scarcely beginning to tool up after the Second World War, though Edmund Wilson had already written the essays he combined as "Dickens: The Two Scrooges" in his *The Wound and the Bow: Seven Studies in Literature* (Boston: Houghton, Mifflin, 1941), a study that would revolutionize Dickens studies for decades to follow.

Calhoun and Heaney acknowledged that in 1946 a new bibliography was long overdue, and they conceded that Miller's own "unique collection" of Dickensiana, on which much of his volume was based, at least "merited a catalogue" and that "the rest of the book is at least a memorial to the good taste and scholarly instincts of a lifetime." "If its results are faulty and incomplete," they rather condescendingly asserted, "that too is part of a leisurely cultural tradition which, until recently, has held itself aloof from modern standards of utility and thoroughness." Their principal complaint was lack of thoroughness in the work. They found that Miller missed many items recorded not only in standard serial bibliographies and indexes but also in Kitton's *Dickensiana*, Charles F. Carty's supplement to it (953), published in 1902, and T. W. Hill's catalogue of Miller's own collection of music based on Dickens's works (1473), published in 1940. There is "no important source," they concluded, "which does not note a substantial number of books, portions of books or articles of more than trivial interest, which ought to be and are not included in Miller."

Calhoun and Heaney also deplored the arrangement of the bibliography. Although Miller followed Kitton's divisions, Calhoun and Heaney found this grouping "so mussy and confusing, it is difficult to be entirely coherent in criticising it," though they tried. Nor did they find Miller's extremely limited annotations useful. They would have liked more accurate details of editions and other publication information to begin with, but they also proposed that the ideal bibliographer should include annotation that would contain "something in the nature of a critical appraisal of his material." Such commentary, they believed, would "at least have contributed a degree of warmth and color to his basic structure." Their final criticism was of Miller's inadequate index, "one of the most thoroughly irritating examples of that fine art which either of us has yet encountered."

Doing it right, Calhoun and Heaney concluded, "is worth doing." They never attempted the task themselves, however, nor has anyone else—until the present series of Dickens bibliographies. Our constant and continuing aim is to do it right, and we hope that, for ourselves as well as for future generations of Dickens students and scholars, we are making some success of it.

I have three purposes in writing this introduction. The first is to provide something of a history of Dickensian bibliography, though not all of the sections that follow are amenable to this approach. I also want to aid students and researchers of Dickens's works by sometimes indicating how to proceed in using the bibliographies and other guides and studies listed here and sometimes revealing which of these are more important and more useful than others. On the other hand, I do not mean to prevent the future bibliographer, or the researcher, for that matter, from searching every nook and cranny of this bibliography. For the mind so swayed, this can be infinitely pleasurable, but for the researcher it can also be valuable, even necessary. The slightest reference may contain just the information needed or generate the spark that will flame into a major discovery or insight. The third purpose is equally important: to stress the value and significance of bibliographical and textual work. Too often it is seen—even, disturbingly, in academic settings—as second-rate scholarship, inferior to literary criticism. It is never that. Bibliographical and textual investigation is where all other scholarly and critical work must begin. Without it, criticism rests on weak or nonexistent foundations, producing brilliant flights of fantasy, perhaps, but nothing more than that. In Dickens's case, bibliographical and textual work establishes both canon and text, or, more frequently, texts and its variants, upon which criticism can build. Through studies of manuscript, number plans and memoranda, and proofs, it deals with basic craftsmanship, development of techniques and insight, the importance of influence, and the nature of artistry and genius. Catalogues of collections, auction sales, and booksellers' offerings provide an accumulation of materials (manuscripts, letters, documents, relics, and other literary and personal artifacts) that biographers and critics will find essential and that will uncover the richness of a life and a career. Bibliographies of studies of the author's life and works will help to place a critic's work in historical perspective, provide a foundation for his or her work, reveal past critical dead ends, and suggest new approaches.

Bibliographies of Dickens's Works

The bibliography of Dickens's works (**19**) that John Forster appended to the third volume of his biography of Dickens, published in December 1873, three and a half years after Dickens's death, was the first serious effort to catalogue information about the publication of Dickens's works. Forster lists Dickens's writings year by year, beginning with *Sketches by Boz* and including all separately published works. He indicates as well the monthly and weekly serial publication of the novels and nonfictional works, Dickens's contributions to the Christmas numbers of *Household Words* and *All the Year Round* (but not his journalistic pieces in these two weekly magazines), and some details about the volumes published in the Cheap Edition, the Library Edition, the "Authorized French Translation of the Works of Dickens," and the Charles Dickens Edition of the collected works, all published in Dickens's lifetime. Generally speaking, Forster gets the basic details of publication correct, though his listing of lesser works is not complete, useful details are lacking, and there are some errors.

James Cook's *Bibliography of the Writings of Charles Dickens* (**10**), published in 1879, the next serious attempt at a bibliography of Dickens's works, was quite detailed for its time. Cook obviously used Forster's bibliography, for he points out that he lists Dickens's chief works separately from the "minor and miscellaneous productions," to avoid the "strictly chronological arrangement observed" by Forster. But he indicates that, nevertheless, he made his compilation "with the aid of a set of various Works as they were originally published, in parts or volumes." If Forster's intent was essentially informational, Cook's was to provide "necessary" particulars for "the Bibliophilist or Collector," a new personage already on the scene only nine years after Dickens's death. Cook's annotations thus needed to be more detailed than Forster's. For example, he frequently quotes information about the writing of a work from Dickens's prefaces, and, where Forster merely noted the original illustrators of the novels, Cook includes much information about the original illustrations, additional plates that were made, and extra illustrations published later, matters that would particularly interest a collector.

Where bibliographical details rather than collecting points are concerned, Cook also modifies and expands upon Forster. He itemizes the *Household Words* and *All the Year Round* articles that Dickens collected in *Reprinted Pieces* (1858) and the three series of *The Uncommercial Traveller* (1861, 1866, 1875 [posthumously]) and devotes a separate section to the Christmas Books. Cook also includes separate sections on *Household Words* and *All the Year Round.* In addition, he provides much bibliographical information about the collected editions that Dickens published in his lifetime (he even itemizes the volumes in the Cheap Edition and the Charles Dickens Edition) and several published after 1870–the Household Edition (1871-79), the Illustrated Library Edition (1873-76), the Shilling series (1877), the Sixpenny series (1878), and the Popular Library Edition (then in process of publication), all by Chapman and Hall. He lists several minor works not mentioned by Forster–the early play *Is She His Wife?* (1837); "In Memoriam," Dickens's eulogy for Thackeray (1864); the Mudfog Papers from *Bentley's Miscellany* (1837-38; first collected 1880); the prologue to J. Westland Marston's *The Patrician's Daughter* (1842); and the introduction to Adelaide Anne Procter's *Legends and Lyrics* (1866)–as well as the People's Edition of Dickens's works (1865), a reissue of the Cheap Edition in green paper boards.

The bibliographical work of Richard H. Shepherd received mixed reviews from his contemporaries. But his 1880 *Bibliography of Dickens* (**42**) is a full-scale attempt to establish the basic details of Dickens's works. This bibliography appeared in various stages of minor revision through 1885, principally in sections not involving Shepherd's list of Dickens's printed works, a list that remained pretty constant through the 1882 and 1884 revisions. The Dickens House Museum, London, has a copy of the 1880 edition with corrections written into it by A. Wallis, with an introduction in his hand, as unfair as it is vehement, criticizing Shepherd as "one of those literary ghouls who thrive best upon dead authors" and complaining that the bibliography is "of not the least value to anyone above the rank of a mere novice." The bibliography would, however, hold its own for many years thereafter. Because of its fuller listing of Dickens's works and editions of them published in Dickens's lifetime and because of its greater supply of details about those works, it is much more informative than the bibliographies of Forster and Cook. It contains, for example, the earliest attempt to list the original publication of the early writings that Dickens collected as *Sketches by Boz*, missing only nine of sixty. Shepherd also identifies several additional minor works for the first time.

Shepherd's bibliography contained three other sections–Letters, Speeches, and "Ana" (containing reviews of Dickens's works and a number of bibliographical and critical studies)–all of which he updated in the revised versions. The first two volumes of *The Letters of Charles Dickens*, edited by Georgina Hogarth and Mamie Dickens, were published in London by Chapman and

Hall in November 1879, just a few months prior to Shepherd's bibliography, and he had time to list the letters in it, note a number not included, and compile a four-page list of errata for the two volumes. In subsequent editions, he omitted the list of letters in the *Hogarth-Dickens Letters*, but included a revised list of published and unpublished letters *not* found there, though he entirely ignored excerpts from Dickens's letters published in Forster's *Life of Dickens*. His list of errata in the *Hogarth-Dickens Letters* grew, and he accompanied this list with a legitimate complaint that few of the errors noted in his first edition had been corrected in a two-volume revised edition of the letters published in 1882. The number of Dickens's speeches that Shepherd itemized remained at fifty-nine throughout the revisions, but he expanded the "Ana" section.

There is evidence that Shepherd consulted the bibliographies of Forster and Cook; both appear in Shepherd's "Ana" section. Although Shepherd makes no comment on Forster's bibliography, he is surprisingly critical of Cook's volume: "For the more recondite matters which give the chief if not the sole value to a compilation of this kind, the reader will search this bulky *brochure* in vain. Nor is the record of more commonly known and accessible details anywhere thoroughly reliable either as to accuracy or completeness. . . . The pamphlet is also disfigured by a considerable number of *errata*, which should be corrected in a future edition."

Shepherd was more interested in providing bibliographical information for posterity than in serving the new Dickens collectors, but the next group of bibliographies and bibliographical commentary is very much collector-oriented—John F. Dexter's "Hints to Dickens Collectors" (**2216**), published in *Dickens Memento* (**1948**) in 1884; Charles P. Johnson's *Hints to Collectors of Original Editions of the Works of Charles Dickens* (**27**), published in 1885; and John H. Slater's chapter on Dickens in his *Early Editions: A Bibliographical Survey of the Works of Some Popular Modern Authors* (**44**), published a decade later in 1894. Dexter's work is not a bibliography but rather advice to collectors on which editions one should collect, how much they will cost, and how to determine their authenticity. Johnson's small volume (56 pages) is the most thorough of the lot, but also, as his title indicates, for the collector. In his introduction, he finds both Shepherd and Dexter "useful," but adds that he knows of "no volume that will enable a collector or dealer to tell, at a glance, whether any particular volume offered to him is of the genuine, first edition throughout, with the plates in the first state." This, he asserts, "has been my object in preparing these 'Hints to Collectors.'" It is evident from Johnson's comments, written a mere decade and a half after Dickens's death, that the Dickens industry is booming. Not only have book dealers and auction houses entered the picture, but dishonest ones as well, for Johnson needs to warn his readers of the disreputable practice of passing off later editions as first editions. Thus, his plan, he announces, "has been to compare several copies of each work . . . ; to collate them; to note the smallest variations in title-pages, or plates; and to put the information thus gathered in a compact and intelligible form." This plan results in fuller collations of pages and illustrations than had been attempted previously, with commentary on variations in editions, information about the color of cloth bindings in the one-volume editions, and the earliest examination of the different states of the first edition of *A Christmas Carol.* Johnson also includes sections on dramatizations of Dickens's novels, portraits of Dickens (73 items), and Dickensiana. Slater mentions Johnson and Cook in his introduction, but, apart from lengthy annotations for some of Dickens's works, there is not much new in his chapter on Dickens, except for the then current prices for various editions of individual novels.

One other bibliography belongs to the 1884-94 decade, John P. Anderson's "Bibliography," included in Frank T. Marzial's *Life of Charles Dickens* (**1**), published in 1887. Unlike the others, it is not collector-oriented, and it includes editions of Dickens's collected works, selected works, individual works, and miscellaneous works published between 1870 and 1887 as well as earlier. The information provided about each entry is relatively brief, approximately what one finds in Forster's bibliography. It is, however, historically more important for its listing of studies of Dickens, and so is discussed more fully in the section on bibliographies of Dickens studies, below.

Hard upon the heels of Slater and Anderson came Frederic G. Kitton. An artist, writer, and Dickens collector, he helped to found the Dickens Fellowship in 1902. He died two years later, but his Dickens library eventually became the foundation of the library at the Dickens House in 1926. His earliest bibliography, *Dickensiana: A Bibliography of the Literature Relating to Charles Dickens and His Writings* (**996**), was published in 1886 and was the first major bibliography of writings about Dickens. This was followed a number of years later by *The Novels of Charles Dickens: A Bibliography and Sketch* (**29**) in 1897 and the companion volume *The Minor Writings of Charles Dickens* (**154**) in 1900. Although the former seems more a study of the conception, writing, and publishing of Dickens's major works than a full-fledged bibliography, it does contain the essential bibliographical information, usually in a paragraph or two hidden in the midst of the chapter on each novel. In the twenty-page chapter on *Bleak House*, for example, after commenting on Dickens's initial ideas for his new novel, listing titles (included with the manuscript bequeathed by John Forster to the Victoria and Albert Museum) that Dickens contemplated using before settling on *Bleak House*, discussing Dickens's views on the Court of Chancery, and printing excerpts from Dickens's letters describing both the difficulties and joys of writing the novel, Kitton provides, midway through, the basic bibliographical information:

> "Bleak House" was issued by Messrs. Bradbury and Evans in twenty monthly parts, demy octavo, green wrappers, at one shilling each, commencing in March, 1852, and ending in September, 1853, Parts 19 and 20 forming a double number. The work contained forty etched illustrations by H. K. Browne, and was dedicated, "as a Remembrance of our Friendly Union. To my Companions in the Guild of Literature and Art." The complete story was published in September 1853, in one volume, cloth, at a guinea—*Collation*, pp. xvi., 624. It

has often been reissued in the same form, with or without a date, the first
Cheap Edition, with a frontispiece by H. K. Browne, appearing in the Second
Series (Messrs. Bradbury and Evans, 1858), cloth, at five shillings.

The original MS and the corrected proofs of "Bleak House" are at South
Kensington. A copy of the first edition in parts, as issued, is valued at £2, and
in cloth from £1 to £2.

Following this, in the remaining pages of the chapter, Kitton mentions the
popularity of the novel (it sold 30,000 copies in March, 40,000 in November),
examines its contents (the character of Jo, the repulsive burial ground at St.
Mary-le-Strand, the prototype for Mr. Jarndyce's Bleak House, the models for
Boythorn and Skimpole), and discusses the attacks on Dickens's portrayal of
Chancery and overseas charity. These are obviously not bibliographical matters. Although Kitton makes a minor concession to the book collector in announcing then current prices for first editions in parts and volume form, his
bibliographical details are not sufficient for the collector trying to avoid
inauthentic copies of the work, and the richness of the chapter lies more in
the non-bibliographical than the bibliographical information it provides.

In *The Minor Writings of Charles Dickens* the bibliographical details are of
greater importance, and, in the preface, Kitton acknowledges his indebtedness
to the bibliographies of Cook, Shepherd, Johnson, and Dexter (in contrast, in
the preface to *The Novels of Charles Dickens*, he notes his indebtedness to John
Forster's *Life of Charles Dickens* and the *Letters of Charles Dickens* compiled by
Georgina Hogarth and Mamie Dickens). But he also indicates the original
work he has done in preparing this volume, including "the compilation of a
complete list of Dickens's ephemeral contributions to periodical literature,
notably to those journals of which he himself was editor." Since almost all of
these articles were published anonymously, Kitton relied on internal evidence,
the endorsement of Charles Dickens, Jr., autograph manuscripts in the Forster
Collection at the Victoria and Albert Museum, and the "office" set of *All the
Year Round* with the authors of the articles "inscribed against each article," a
set that has since disappeared, though it was then, according to Kitton, in the
possession of W. H. Howe, a Dickens collector.

Comparing Kitton's list of Dickens's journalistic writings with the "Complete Listing of Dickens's Known Journalism, December 1833-August 1869"
in Michael Slater and John Drew's **The Uncommercial Traveller** and *Other Papers* (**161**), published in 2000, is instructive. Kitton misses a number of items
since identified: a few early theater reviews and election and other reports for
the *Morning Chronicle*, 1834-36 and 1844; several essays in the *Morning Chronicle*
and the *Carlton Chronicle*, 1834-36, later included in *Sketches by Boz* (most of
these were not identified until 1933 and a few even later); a number of book
and theater reviews in the *Examiner*, 1837-49; "The Spirit of Chivalry in Westminster Hall," published in *Douglas Jerrold's Shilling Magazine*, August 1845; several articles in *Household Words*; and three, mostly debatable, pieces in *All the
Year Round*. On the other hand, Kitton identifies a small number of Dickens's

writings that Slater and Drew miss, pieces published principally in *Bentley's Miscellany* and the *Daily News*, as well as a few other minor items.

Kitton has chapters on *Sketches by Boz*, *American Notes*, *Pictures from Italy*, *Hard Times* (inexplicably included here rather than in the earlier volume), the Christmas Books, Miscellaneous Prose Writings (*Sunday Under Three Heads*, *Sketches of Young Gentlemen*, *Sketches of Young Couples*, *A Child's History of England*, and, to some extent erroneously, *The Loving Ballad of Lord Bateman*), and other chapters on works Dickens edited or for which he wrote introductions; Dickens's plays; his poems, songs, and other rhymes; and an appendix on plagiarisms of Dickens's novels and "unauthorised continuations, etc.," of *Edwin Drood*. For the chapters dealing with Dickens's full-length "minor" works, Kitton follows pretty much the procedure he used in *The Novels of Charles Dickens* in providing bibliographical information about each work. With *A Christmas Carol* and *The Battle of Life* he does note that there are various issues of the first edition of each work but is not particularly precise about the sequence of publication. These matters would be left for later bibliographers to work out. Kitton's work on the minor writings is a major bibliographical contribution. In addition, Kitton collected a number of Dickens's journalistic pieces in his editions of Dickens's *Old Lamps for New Ones and Other Sketches and Essays Hitherto Uncollected* (**418**) in 1897, *To Be Read at Dusk and Other Stories, Sketches and Essays, Now First Collected* (**418**), in 1898, and *The Poems and Verses of Charles Dickens* in 1903 (**419**).

The *Household Words* Contributors' Book turned up shortly thereafter in the possession of R. C. Lehmann, a great-nephew of W. H. Wills, Dickens's subeditor on *Household Words* and *All the Year Round*, and was used with Lehmann's permission by B. W. Matz in editing the two volumes of *Miscellaneous Papers, Plays and Poems* (**425**), published in 1908, in the National Edition of Dickens's Works. This collection also represented the culmination of Matz's and F. G. Kitton's work to identify and recover Dickens's anonymous newspaper and magazine articles. The result was the addition, as Matz notes in his introduction, of "some eighty or so hitherto unknown writings" and two poems to the Dickens canon. This was supplemented in turn by the *Collected Papers* in the Nonesuch Edition (**460**), published in two volumes in 1937, edited by Arthur Waugh, Hugh Walpole, Walter Dexter, and Thomas Hatton, which added newer discoveries by Dexter and others (Matz had died in 1925). These included seven articles, one play (the fragment from "O'Thello," a musical burlesque Dickens wrote in 1833), six poems, eight speeches, and *The Loving Ballad of Lord Bateman*, to the last of which Dickens's contribution was minor but definite—see Dexter (**325**) and Haight (**475**). Occasionally over the post-Kitton years other individual pieces have been identified or found to be misattributed—see pp. xxxiii-xxiv, below, and section 2 of part 1 of the subject index.

After Kitton, the next attempt at a full bibliography of the Dickens canon was Joseph C. Thomson's *Bibliography of the Writings of Charles Dickens* (**48**), published in 1904. In a brief introductory note, Thomson modestly announces that he "makes no claim to originality" but hopes that, by coordinating the "labours" of other bibliographers, he can produce "a list of the writings of Dickens to which with some reasonableness the term 'complete' may be applied." Using the chronological approach of Forster and Shepherd, Thomson provides a much fuller account than either, seeming to include every bit of information about each work from virtually every Dickens bibliography published to date, and he includes a section on "Value" under each work in which, using, as he notes in his introductory statement, "the admirable *Book-Prices Current*" (**2061**), he comments at some length on then current and auction prices of various editions and sets of extra illustrations.

Thomson's work was followed by John C. Eckel's *The First Editions of the Writings of Charles Dickens and Their Values: A Bibliography* (**16**), published in 1913, with a revised edition in 1932. Eckel's work still stands, despite criticism of its writing style and its errors, as the standard modern bibliography of Dickens's writings, though one directed more toward collectors than scholars. Dickens "is essentially a collectors' author," he writes in the introduction to the 1913 edition, "for the reason that his books in their original state make an irresistible appeal." To satisfy this "appeal," Eckel includes, for the first time in Dickensian bibliography, collations that give "a permanent idea of the physical side of a first edition." Although Eckel claims in the introduction to the 1932 edition that the reception of his first edition "was more than flattering," and quotes then recent auction prices to show how valuable it already was as an out-of-print book, critics were not always as happy with either edition as Eckel suggests they were of the first. The *Times Literary Supplement* reviewer (**16**) of the second edition found the volume ultimately "disappointing" in its scholarship and writing.

One can easily see why the volume is both praised and criticized. On the one hand, it provides far more information about the works it considers than any previous bibliography had, and it covers the entire range of Dickens's works, from the major novels to the smallest contribution to *Household Words*, with information on advertisements in the monthly parts of all the serialized novels and a collation of the advertisements and information on the inside and outside of the back wrappers. On the other hand, the information provided is not always full, not always accurate, and not always consistent from one work to the next. As one might expect, the minor works are given shorter shrift than the major works. But for the major works, the extent of the collation varies from work to work, in accordance, one supposes, with Eckel's perception of the needs of collectors and booksellers. Thus, *Pickwick Papers* is given forty-two pages, with detailed information about the illustrations (particularly the "first state" of the plates, since many of them were re-etched after the original plates became too worn) and the advertisements in each monthly issue, about the eleven "points" that indicate one has a "perfect," or "prime," set of the original parts, and about auction prices of sets in differing condition. Eckel also includes a briefer collation of the first bound volume of the novel. But all this information is scattered throughout the chapter; it is difficult to pull it together sufficiently to get a clear picture of what makes a "prime Pickwick in parts." It is easier to follow the information in the three-page chapter on *Bleak House* in the 1932 edition, but here all Eckel chooses to give the reader is a short general collation of the parts issue, a little bit of information about illustrations that were duplicated, a vague statement about the advertisements, and brief details about the advertisements for four of the issues. In the chapters on *A Christmas Carol* and *The Battle of Life*, Eckel does discuss the various states of their first editions.

Not more than a year after the publication of the second edition of Eckel's bibliography, Thomas Hatton and Arthur H. Cleaver published *A Bibliography of the Periodical Work of Charles Dickens: Bibliographical, Analytical, and Statistical* (**24**). They limit their study to the thirteen works that Dickens published in monthly parts, though the monthly publications included of *Sketches by Boz, Master Humphrey's Clock* (containing *The Old Curiosity Shop* and *Barnaby Rudge*), *Oliver Twist*, and *A Tale of Two Cities* were not their first editions. They include full part by part collations of each of these editions, with additional commentary on any peculiar or unique aspects of text, plates, wrappers, and advertisements. One is impressed by the fullness of the content and the logicality of the arrangement of material. Brian Lake, a proprietor of Jarndyce Antiquarian Booksellers, London, and a bibliographer in his own right, calls the Hatton and Cleaver volume "the near-definitive bibliography of the 'part' issues" in a lukewarm review (**45**) of Walter E. Smith's two-volume bibliography of *Charles Dickens in the Original Cloth* (see below). However, had Hatton and Cleaver included the novels first published in weekly installments as well, the work would have been much more satisfying and useful.

The Dickens sections of the first two editions of *The Cambridge Bibliography of English Literature*, compiled by F. J. H. Darton in 1940 (**11**) and by Philip Collins (as *The New Cambridge Bibliography of English Literature*) in 1969 (**8**), follow next, with no significant bibliography of Dickens's works in between, and with the Collins section obviously updating the Darton section. They are more expansions on Anderson than on Eckel or Hatton and Cleaver in the information they provide, and therefore more designed for the researcher than the collector. They contain lists of "principal" editions of individual and collected editions, as well as editions of imitations and sequels, dramatizations, and sets of extra illustrations for a few of the novels. The two editors also list collections of Dickens's letters and speeches and, in a very limited way and using an inexplicable selection process, individual letters and speeches.

Walter E. Smith's two-volume *Charles Dickens in the Original Cloth: A Bibliographical Catalogue of the First Appearance of His Writings in Book Form in England with Facsimiles of the Bindings and Titlepages* (**45**, **46**), with *Part One: The Novels with* **Sketches by Boz**, published in 1982, and *Part Two: The Christmas Books and Selected Secondary Works*, published in 1983, is the essential supplement to Hatton and Cleaver, dealing specifically with the first clothbound editions of all of the novels and *Sketches by Boz* in the first volume and the Christmas Books and other principal nonfictional works in the second. Brian Lake (**45**) rightly criticizes volume 2 of Smith's bibliography for incompleteness. Smith covers only *Sketches of Young Gentlemen, Sketches of Young Couples, American Notes, Pictures from Italy, A Child's History of England, The Uncommercial Traveller,* and *The Life of Our Lord* in the volume, in addition to the five Christmas Books, leaving scholar, bookseller, and collector still dependent upon Eckel for the theatrical and shorter journalistic and fictional works.

Most of the bibliographies mentioned so far have been concerned with the English first editions of Dickens's works. The American editions, bibliographically speaking at least, first came to the attention of William Glyde Wilkins, whose *First and Early American Editions of the Works of Charles Dickens* (**61**), published in 1910, revised and expanded the information in two of his earlier articles in the *Dickensian* (**60, 62**). Wilkins's work was followed by that of Herman L. Edgar and R. W. G. Vail in their *Early American Editions of the Works of Charles Dickens* (**17**) in 1929. They list only editions in an exhibition (but obviously a superb one) held at the New York Public Library in 1929 and so add to but do not quite supersede Wilkins. Edgar and Vail include nearly every edition in Wilkins's volume that was published in Philadelphia and New York, but, in most cases, they do not list editions published in Boston. They include additional but sometimes conflicting details, and list a few editions that are not in Wilkins. Wilkins, for example, misses Harper & Brothers's 1844 New York edition of *A Christmas Carol* and does not list any editions of *Cricket on the Hearth, The Battle of Life, The Haunted Man and the Ghost's Bargain, A Child's History of England, Hard Times,* and *The Uncommercial Traveller.* Sometimes, as with editions of *American Notes* and *The Chimes,* the two bibliographies disagree about the order of publication as well. Wilkins lists a few volumes of selections from Dickens's works published after 1870; the Edgar and Vail list ends with an 1871 edition of *A Child's Dream of a Star,* which is in Wilkins, too. Wilkins also identifies a number of American plagiarisms and parodies. Neither bibliography is adequate on early collected editions. Section D, "Books: Collected Editions & Selections," pp. 244-99 of *Dickens and Dickensiana* (**1509**), John B. Podeschi's catalogue of the Richard Gimbel Collection in the Yale University Library, published in 1980, lists far more early American editions of collected works.

Two more recent and more monumental attempts to catalogue American publications, Dickens's among them, seemed initially promising. The first, *A Checklist of American Imprints for 1820[-],* edited by Richard H. Shoemaker et al. (**87**), is now up to 1846 (published in 1997), and so lists American editions of Dickens's works through *Pictures from Italy* and *The Battle of Life.* In the second, *Bibliography of American Imprints to 1901,* compiled by the American Antiquarian Society and the Research Libraries Group (**65**), volume 46 (published in 1993) contains American editions of Dickens's works. Unfortunately, neither of these publications is as complete as its title suggests, and both must be used cautiously. They miss editions recorded in Wilkins and in Edgar and Vail, and make strange errors, such as listing an edition of *A Christmas Carol* with illustrations by Arthur Rackham, as being published in Philadelphia in 1843 when it was actually published in 1915. A useful feature (barring such errors) of the *Bibliography of American Imprints to 1901* is that it lists editions published to 1901. Also see Peter S. Bracher's "A Check List of Dickens' Works Published by Harper & Brothers, 1842-70 (**5**), in his "Harper & Brother: Publishers of Dickens" (**174**), published in 1976, and his "The Early American Editions of *American Notes*: Their Priority and Circulation" (**379**), published in 1975, both more specialized studies, and Newbury F. Read's "The American Editions of Pickwick" (**131**), published in the *Dickensian* in 1936, which lists 127 editions published in the United States, 1836-1936.

Towards the close of the twentieth century, three important bibliographical projects began publication, all aimed more at the researcher than the collector. The first is *The Nineteenth Century Short Title Catalogue*. The English and American editions of Dickens's works published between 1836 and 1870 will be found in volume 12 of *Nineteenth Century Short Title Catalogue. Series II. Phase I, 1816-1870* (**15**), published in 1988. While the title of the series suggests that the editors are aiming at nothing short of completeness, the publications listed are actually those that are in eight libraries: the Bodleian Library, the British Library, Harvard University Library, the Library of Congress, the Library of Trinity College (Dublin), the National Library of Scotland, the Cambridge University Library, and the University of Newcastle Library. These are, of course, fine libraries, and the final list should be reasonably, if not quite, complete. Of particular concern is the potentially incomplete representation of American editions of Dickens's novels, many fugitive at best, published in Philadelphia and Boston as well as in New York, and even in less populated cities. A number of these may not have made their way to the shelves of these libraries, as a comparison of entries with those in Wilkins and Edgar and Vail will quickly reveal, and others may not be readily identifiable because publishers are not given in the short title catalogue.

The second important project is the third edition of *The Cambridge Bibliography of English Literature*, of which one volume has been published. Fortunately for our purposes, this was the volume for 1800-1900, published in 1999, for which Paul Schlicke did the section on Dickens (**41**). This is a selective bibliography, one must remember, but in the preface the general editor, Joanne Shattock, announces that the "emphasis is on primary material" and that the aim is to include "all significant English language editions, and where known, American and continental editions." What Schlicke has produced, building of course on his predecessors in the first and second editions (see p. xxiii, above), is most impressive. One would not go to the volume for a complete listing of early American editions, but the cataloguing of English editions is sound, and modern editions are well represented. A list of the more important collected editions is also useful.

The third major project is more specialized, though, it is hoped, more comprehensive: *The Garland Dickens Bibliographies* (**13**), and its successor *The Dickens Bibliographies* (**12**), published by AMS Press, of which the present volume is one and the present writer the general editor. Thirteen of twenty-one projected volumes and one update have already been published. Eleven were published in the Garland Dickens Bibliographies: the volumes on *David Copperfield*, by Richard J. Dunn (**103**), published in 1981; *Our Mutual Friend*, by Joel J. Brattin and Bert G. Hornback (**120**), published in 1984; *Hard Times*, by Sylvia Manning (**110**), published in 1984; *Dickens's Christmas Books, Christmas Stories, and Other Short Fiction*, by Ruth F. Glancy (**98**), published in 1985; *Oliver Twist*, edited by David Paroissien (**118**), published in 1986; *Great Expectations*, by George J. Worth (**109**), published in 1986; *Barnaby Rudge*, by Thomas J. Rice (**93**), published in 1987; *The Old Curiosity Shop*, edited by Priscilla and Paul Schlicke (**117**), published in 1988; *Pickwick Papers*, edited by Elliot Engel (**125**), published in 1990; *Martin Chuzzlewit*, by Robert E. Lougy (**113**), published in 1990; and *A Tale of Two Cities*, by Ruth F. Glancy (**138**), published in 1993. Three have been published in The Dickens Bibliographies series (AMS Press)—*The Mystery of Edwin Drood*, by Don R. Cox (**115**), published in 1998; *Dombey and Son*, by Leon Litvack (**106**), published in 1999; and the present bibliography—as well as the update of *David Copperfield*, edited by Richard J. Dunn and Ann M. Tandy (**104**), published in 2000. Robert Hanna's *Dickens's Non-Fictional, Theatrical, and Poetical Writings: An Annotated Bibliography* is in hand and scheduled for publication in 2004.

Other updates of volumes in the Garland Dickens Bibliographies will be published over the next few years in *Dickens Studies Annual*, with some being published separately by AMS Press. Robert Heaman's update of Brattin and Hornback's *Our Mutual Friend* bibliography will be published in *Dickens Studies Annual* in volume 33 (2003), as will a version of the introduction you are now reading. Ruth Glancy's update of her bibliography of the Christmas works and other short fiction and David Paroissien's of *Oliver Twist* are tentatively scheduled for publication in 2004. AMS Press also plans to reprint volumes published in the earlier series. While the authors of the Garland and AMS Press bibliographies do not include detailed collations of the earliest editions of Dickens's works, they do list and annotate all the important English and American editions of a particular work from the first to the most recent.

Also useful is the bibliographical material in the introductory matter and appendices of the volumes in the Clarendon Dickens, yet another major Dickens project, nine of which have been published to date—*Oliver Twist*, edited by Kathleen Tillotson (**119, 2474**), published in 1966; *The Mystery of Edwin Drood*, edited by Margaret Cardwell (**114, 2434**), published in 1972; *Dombey and Son*, edited by Alan Horsman (**105, 2376**), published in 1974; *Little Dorrit*, edited by Harvey P. Sucksmith (**111, 2420**), published in 1979; *David Copperfield*, edited by Nina Burgis (**102, 2359**), published in 1981; *Martin Chuzzlewit*, edited by Margaret Cardwell (**112, 2423**), published in 1982; *Pickwick Papers*, edited by James Kinsley (**128, 2493**), published in 1986; *Great Expectations*, edited by Margaret Cardwell (**107, 2381**), published in 1993; and *The Old Curiosity Shop*, edited by Elizabeth M. Brennan (**116, 2460**), published in 1997. In addition, each volume contains a section titled "Descriptive List of Editions," specifically those published in Dickens's lifetime and under his supervision. These are brief rather than full collations, useful for the scholar if not for the collector.

The best bibliography of Dickens's manuscripts is to be found in volume 4 of Barbara Rosenbaum and Pamela White's *Index of English Literary Manuscripts* (**40**), published in 1982. The compilers have located 333 manuscripts, not including letters. Their annotations briefly describe each manuscript, indicate its present location, and note whether or not a transcript exists or whether or not the manuscript has been published in whole or in part.

Bibliographical Studies

Bibliographical studies of Dickens's works abound and range from important work on the states of the first edition of *A Christmas Carol* to reports on Dickens exhibitions and book sales, from sales figures for Dickens's novels to the identifying of essays that Dickens published anonymously, from studies of translations and dramatic adaptations of Dickens's works to scrapbooks in the Dickens House library. Here is an enormous body of research work that in many instances backs up and supplements the bibliographies already noted above. A number of these works are of great value to Dickens studies. One important field is the identification of Dickens's lesser-known works. The earlier bibliographers mentioned above established relatively quickly the important bibliographical information about Dickens's volume-length works. But identification of many of Dickens's journalistic pieces was slow in coming. Still, one would have thought the identification of the nonfictional, theatrical, and poetical works in *Collected Papers* in the Nonesuch Edition (**460**) was definitive (see p. xxvii, above), as no doubt Arthur Waugh and his colleagues did. But it was soon discovered that this was not the case. Since 1937, K. J. Fielding and Alec W. Brice have identified a number of Dickens's anonymous pieces, most of them published in the *Examiner* (**383-86, 406-07, 409-10**). William J. Carlton has identified fifteen *Morning Chronicle* dramatic reviews (**388**), and Patrick J. McCarthy (**428**) and Charles VanNoorden (**458-59**) have identified other pieces by Dickens in the *Morning Chronicle*, 1835-36. Philip Collins has located still other pieces (**391-94**), and K. J. Fielding, in his edition of *The Speeches of Charles Dickens* (**408**), published in 1960 and with additions in 1988, has located more speeches that Dickens gave and better versions of others previously published. Other short pieces were identified by Walter Dexter (**396-97, 399-400**), William Long (**421**), and Graham Storey (**452**). Harry Stone, in his *Charles Dickens' Uncollected Writings from **Household Words** 1850-*

1859 (**449**), published in two volumes in 1969, has identified numerous short pieces and parts of articles by Dickens in *Household Words*.

Another concern has been the identification of the first publication in magazines and newspapers of the pieces Dickens collected as *Sketches by Boz*. Shepherd, as mentioned above, compiled the earliest list and thought, as did Kitton and Eckel (even in his second edition), that twelve of the pieces were written especially for *Sketches by Boz*, when actually, as it has turned out, only four were. In 1933, Hatton and Cleaver (**24**), closely followed by Walter Dexter (**363**), identified five of the eight published earlier. Hilmer Nielsen identified a sixth in 1938 (**372**). The remaining two were identified by William J. Carlton in 1951 (**390**) and Graham Mott in 1984 (**371**). With the exception of Mott's identification of the final previously published piece, Duane DeVries's "The Publication History of *Sketches by Boz*" (**132**), published in 1976, is the fullest record of previously published pieces and the arrangement of these and the pieces written specifically for the collected edition in the first and subsequent editions published in Dickens's lifetime.

Identifying Dickens's collaborations with other authors and pieces attributed to Dickens but written by others has also occupied scholars, as has identifying authors of articles in *Household Words* and *All the Year Round* not written by Dickens. Anne Lohrli's **Household Words: A Weekly Journal, 1850-1859,** *Conducted by Charles Dickens* (**155**), published in 1973, and Harry Stone's *Charles Dickens' Uncollected Writing from* **Household Words**, *1850-1859* (**449**), are particularly helpful in identifying authors of articles in Dickens's *Household Words*. Ella A. Oppenlander, in *Dickens'* **All the Year Round:** *Descriptive Index and Contributor List* (**158**), published in 1984, has done comparable work with Dickens's contributions to *All the Year Round*, but many authors of articles in the latter remain unidentified. For accounts of the *Household Words* Office Book used by Lohrli, see her study, of course, and also her article, "*Household Words* and Its 'Office Book'" (**514**), published in 1964. For an account of the *All the Year Round* letter book used by Oppenlander, see her account but also Philip Collins's in *Victorian Periodicals Newsletter* (**494**), published in 1970. A number of studies of Dickens's collaborations with other authors, of incorrect or dubious attributions to Dickens, and of authorship of articles in the two magazines will be found in sections 1F and 1G, below.

Other bibliographical studies are concerned with the primacy of issues of first editions, particularly of *A Christmas Carol*. Ruth Glancy's "Commentary on the First Issue Problem" in her bibliography of *A Christmas Carol* (**260**) summarizes the controversy and draws sensible conclusions. Important earlier publications on this issue are E. Allen Osborne's *The Facts about* **A Christmas Carol** (**279**), published in 1937; Philo Calhoun and Howell J. Heaney's "Dickens' *Christmas Carol* after a Hundred Years: A Study in Bibliographical Evidence" (**252**), published in 1945; and Richard Gimbel's *Charles Dickens's* **A Christmas Carol.** *Three States of the First Edition* (**258**), published in 1955, and his "The Earliest State of the First Edition of Charles Dickens' *A Christmas*

Carol" (**259**), published in 1958. There has also been considerable discussion over the years about what makes up a "Prime Pickwick in Parts"—that is, a set of the monthly numbers of *Pickwick Papers* with the original printing of each part (only 500 copies of Part 2 were printed originally, for example, compared to 20,000 to 40,000 of the later numbers), the earliest etchings of illustrations, and the original advertising inserts. Among the best of these studies are George W. Davis's *The Posthumous Papers of the Pickwick Club: Some New Bibliographical Discoveries* (**342**) and John C. Eckel's *Prime Pickwicks in Parts. Census with Complete Collation, Comparison and Comment* (**124**), both published in 1928, and William Miller and E. H. Strange's "The Original *Pickwick Papers*: The Collation of a Perfect First Edition," reprinted as the "The Bibliography" in their *A Centenary Bibliography of the Pickwick Papers* (**129**), published in 1936.

Still other bibliographical studies concern publishers' agreements and other publication matters and the characteristics of particular early or later editions of Dickens's works. For publishers' agreements and the publishing history of Dickens's works, see Robert L. Patten's *Charles Dickens and His Publishers* (**224**), published in 1978, a mass of information about the writing, printing, and publication of Dickens's works; Newbury F. Read's "On the Writing of *Barnaby Rudge*" (**244**), published in 1934, on the tangled history of the writing and publication of *Barnaby Rudge*; Gerald Grubb's "On the Serial Publication of *Oliver Twist*" (**327**), published in 1941; and Kathleen Tillotson's "*Oliver Twist* in Three Volumes" (**336**), published in 1963. For the difficulties of editing Dickens's works, see particularly John Butt's "Editing a Nineteenth-Century Novelist (Proposals for an Edition of Dickens)" (**175**), published in 1961, sage advice to a prospective editor; Butt and Tillotson's "Preface by the General Editors" to the Clarendon Edition of Dickens's works (**176**), first published in 1966; and Sylvère Monod's "'Between Two Worlds': Editing Dickens" (**246**), published in 1978, on the editing of the Norton Critical Edition of *Bleak House* (**2327**).

Bibliographies and Surveys of Translations, Readings, Dramatic Adaptations, Plagiarisms and Imitations, and Illustrations

There is no full bibliography of translations of Dickens's works, though numerous bibliographies and surveys of varying thoroughness and age have been published (**549-640**). The only person who seems to have tried to collect translations was Marie Roche, Lady Dickens, the wife of Dickens's son Henry. Her collection is now in the British Library (**1456**) and obviously quite outdated. For more modern editions, a variety of bibliographies may be consulted, most dealing with translations into a particular language, although the *Index Translationum* (**583**), an international bibliography of translations, has tried to cover the field since 1932, gradually increasing the number of countries represented over the years from six at the beginning to over seventy today, according to James Harner's *Literary Research Guide* (**1147**).

In "A First Bibliography of the Reading Editions of Charles Dickens's Works" (663), published in 1921, John Stonehouse compiled the earliest list of the readings that Dickens abridged from some of his novels and used for his reading tours of Great Britain and the United States. Since then, however, they have become, if not quite exclusively, the scholarly property of Philip Collins (644-55), and in 1975 he published the definitive edition of them (652), with a long introduction containing everything one would want to know about them and headnotes and sometimes endnotes to each reading providing additional information. Collins also published facsimile editions of Dickens's readings of *A Christmas Carol* (649) and *Sikes and Nancy*, from *Oliver Twist* (650), in 1971 and 1982, respectively, both with useful notes. John D. Gordan published a facsimile of *Mrs. Gamp*, from *Martin Chuzzlewit* (659) in 1956, with elaborate commentary. Two important studies are of readings Dickens prepared but never performed in public, Jean Callahan's "The (Unread) Reading Version of *Great Expectations* (643), published in 1999, and Michael Slater's "*The Bastille Prisoner:* A Reading Dickens Never Gave" (662), published in 1970.

Dramatic adaptations of Dickens's works have been pretty thoroughly covered by bibliographers and other scholars, particularly film and stage adaptations. Most of the major bibliographies in this area are still relatively up to date. H. Philip Bolton's *Dickens Dramatized* (676), published in 1987, is an impressive, full-scale work, even though Bolton modestly insists that his handlist of some 3,000 items, covering nearly 400 pages, is "by no means a complete listing" of dramatic performances for stage, film, radio, and television. For film versions alone, Ana L. Zambrano's earlier study and bibliography *Dickens and Film* (823), published in 1977, is quite detailed, as is Michael Pointer's even more recent "Catalog of Film, Television, and Video Productions" in his *Charles Dickens on the Screen: The Film, Television, and Video Adaptations* (788), published in 1996. In addition, one may consult numerous general bibliographies of stage and film productions that include adaptations of Dickens's works, such as the impressive, if as yet incomplete *The American Film Institute Catalog of Motion Pictures Produced in the United States* (667), begun in 1971, with six volumes published to date, or the Dickens items located on the Internet Movie Database Web site, http://us.imdb.com (697).

Among classic studies of Dickens and the drama are T. Edgar Pemberton's *Charles Dickens and the Stage. A Record of His Connection with the Drama as Playwright, Actor, and Critic* (784), published in 1888; S. J. Adair Fitz-Gerald's *Dickens and the Drama, Being an Account of Charles Dickens's Connection with the Stage and the Stage's Connection with Him* (707), published in 1910; Alexander Woollcott's *Mr. Dickens Goes to the Play* (819), published in 1922; J. B. Van Amerongen's *The Actor in Dickens. A Study of the Histrionic and Dramatic Elements in the Novelist's Life and Works* (809), published in 1926; and F. Dubrez Fawcett's *Dickens the Dramatist: On Stage, Screen and Radio* (704), published in 1952, all of which contain sections, now considerably outdated obviously, on dramatic adaptations of Dickens's works.

Many bibliographies and surveys of dramatic productions of individual Dickens works have been published, including, among the more recent and more scholarly, Richard P. Fulkerson's "*Oliver Twist* in the Victorian Theatre" (**713**), published in 1974; Ana L. Zambrano's "*David Copperfield*: Novel and Film" (**821**), published in 1977; H. Philip Bolton's "*Bleak House* and the Playhouse" (**675**), published in 1983; Paul Sammon's The "*Christmas Carol*" *Trivia Book: Everything You Ever Wanted to Know About Every Version of the Dickens Classic* (**796**), published in 1994; Elizabeth Brennan's "Little Nell on Stage, 1840-1841 (**677**), published in 1997; a number of entries in Paul Schlicke's *Oxford Reader's Companion to Dickens* (**798**), published in 1999; and Fred Guida's "Filmography" in his *"A Christmas Carol" and Its Adaptations* (**720**), published in 2000.

Some work has been done on the imitations and continuations of Dickens's works. Louis James calls them all "plagiarisms" in his account of them in the *Oxford Reader's Companion to Dickens* (**838**), published in 1999, and in his earlier "The Beginnings of a New Type of Popular Fiction: Plagiarisms of Dickens" (**837**), published in 1963, and I have used "plagiarisms" as the lead term in the heading for section 2D, below, in this bibliography. Paul Schlicke lists a number of them in the third edition of the *Cambridge Bibliography of English Literature* (**41**). J. Cuming Walters, in his The Complete **Mystery of Edwin Drood**. *The History, Continuations, and Solutions (1870-1912)*, published in 1912 (**849**), and, more recently, Steven Connor in the new Everyman Edition of *The Mystery of Edwin Drood* (**831**), published in 1996, have tracked the numerous completions of the novel by others and the various proposed solutions to the mystery. Paul Hoggart has located a number of travesties of Dickens works (**836**), and William Glyde Wilkins has identified American parodies of *American Notes* (**850**). One should also mention the well-known forgery by Thomas J. Wise of Dickens's minor work *To Be Read at Dusk*—see John Carter and Graham Pollard's *An Inquiry into the Nature of Certain Nineteenth Century Pamphlets* (**830**), published in 1934.

Scholars have thoroughly catalogued the illustrations in the parts editions of Dickens's works—the "original" illustrations. They are listed part by part in the elaborate collations in Hatton and Cleaver's *Bibliography of the Periodical Works of Charles Dickens* (**24**), where every plate is itemized by title, and are discussed in detail in Jane R. Cohen's *Charles Dickens and His Original Illustrators* (**864**), published in 1980. However, these are not the only illustrations included in Dickens's works published in his lifetime. In the first volume of *Charles Dickens in the Original Cloth* (**45**), Walter E. Smith supplements Hatton and Cleaver by itemizing the plates in the original volume editions of *Sketches by Boz* and *Oliver Twist* and the illustrations inserted in the text in the serial publication of *Master Humphrey's Clock*. In his second volume (**46**), Smith itemizes the illustrations for *Sketches of Young Gentlemen, Sketches of Young Couples,*

Pictures from Italy, and *A Child's History of England* (only frontispieces for each of the three volumes). He is, however, less specific about the illustrations for the five Christmas Books, merely listing the number of illustrations by each of several artists for each volume, and *The Life of Our Lord*, noting only that eight of the twelve illustrations are paintings, that three are facsimiles of pages of Dickens's manuscript, and that the frontispiece is a portrait of Dickens. Thomas Hatton's list, "A Bibliographical List of the Original Illustrations to the Works of Charles Dickens, Being Those Made Under His Supervision," in *The Nonesuch Dickens: Retrospectus and Prospectus* (**218, 885**), published in 1937, itemizes the 877 plates made for Dickens's works during his lifetime. These are printed in the volumes of the Nonesuch Dickens, and each set of the collected edition contained one of these plates in a separate boxed volume. J. A. Hammerton's *The Dickens Picture-Book. A Record of the Dickens Illustrators* (**884**), published in 1910, not only reproduces (though in considerably reduced size) 600 of the original illustrations to Dickens's novels but comments on illustrators of later editions of Dickens's works and on sets of extra illustrations, reproducing a number of these as well. Also see Frederic G. Kitton's *Dickens and His Illustrators* (**894**), published 1899, for facsimiles of some of the original drawings, lists of illustrators of post-1870 editions of his novels, and sets of extra illustrations, as well as his supplementary *Dickens Illustrations, Facsimiles of Original Drawings, Sketches and Studies for Illustration in the Works of Charles Dickens*, published 1900.

Some of the earlier bibliographies mentioned above list sets of extra illustrations to Dickens's novels, several done during Dickens's lifetime and others done after his death. See the subheading **extra illustrations** under **Illustrations for Dickens's works** in part 2 of the subject index. There is, however, no bibliography of illustrations for Dickens's works published after 1870, though reference to illustrated editions of individual works may be found in the Dickens Bibliographies published by Garland and AMS Press (**12, 13**).

Some studies have focused on the illustrations for individual works and on individual illustrators–see particularly Percy Fitzgerald's "Concerning the Plates and Extra Plates and 'States' of Pickwick" in his *Pickwickian Manners and Customs* (**881**), published in 1897; Joseph Grego's *Pictorial Pickwickiana* (**883**), published in 1899; Joan Stevens's "'Woodcuts Dropped into the Text': The Illustrations in *The Old Curiosity Shop* and *Barnaby Rudge*" (**933**), published in 1967; Sarah A. Solberg's "'Text Dropped into the Woodcuts': Dickens' Christmas Books" (**928**), published in 1980; Albert Johanssen's *Phiz: Illustrations from the Novels of Charles Dickens* (**892**), published in 1956; and George S. Layard's studies of plates that were suppressed for several of Dickens's works (**900**), published in 1899 and 1907.

Bibliographies of Dickens Studies

Here there is richness, particularly in the form of duplication, much that is inevitably outdated, and, to compensate for the outdated, a plethora of serial bibliographies that, in their online versions, at any rate, are quite up to date, if not ever complete. Historically, the interest in compiling lists of Dickens studies began with Cook's 1879 bibliography (**10**). At the end of his list of Dickens's works, Cook threw in lists of plagiarisms and continuations; portraits, paintings, and sets of extra illustrations; biographies; and a few studies of Dickens. Shepherd (**42**) includes an "Ana" section that grew from sixty-four in his 1880 bibliography to seventy-nine in the 1884 revision, with a "Supplementary Ana" section of an additional twenty-three studies supplied by W. R. Hughes. Both Dexter and Johnson (**2216, 27**) include small sections of ana, but it was F. G. Kitton who pulled the material together in his *Dickensiana: A Bibliography of the Literature Relating to Charles Dickens and His Writings* (**996**) in 1886 in a 511-page edition containing 584 numbered and heavily annotated items, though some of these–in sections labeled Poetical, Anthological, Musical, Dramatic, and Plagiaristic, Etc.– are not biographical or critical, and a few are reviews of John Forster's *Life of Charles Dickens* and *The Letters of Charles Dickens*, edited by Georgina Hogarth and Mamie Dickens. Still, that leaves 374 biographical and critical studies and reviews of individual works published by 1885, Kitton's cut-off date for entries. This figure does not include Kitton's summary of a number of items (unnumbered) published in *Notes and Queries* or his section entitled "Omniana," which he characterizes as "Brief Notes, selected principally from ephemeral literature, relating to Charles Dickens and his Writings." In his introduction, Kitton asserts that the quantity of studies of Dickens is the "surest indication of the nature and extent" of Dickens's popularity and, Kitton suggests, of his enduring fame.

To do something of an analysis of Kitton's bibliography, twenty-six of the biographical and forty-four of the critical studies, as well as seventy-six reviews of individual works by Dickens, for a total of 146, were published before Dickens's death (1840-June 1870). This leaves 105 biographical and sixty-eight critical studies, as well as thirty-two reviews of individual works, for a total of 205, that were published in the fifteen years following Dickens's death. To Kitton's totals, Charles F. Carty, in his "Some Addenda to Kitton's 'Dickensiana'" (**953**), published in 1902, added sixty-eight numbered items and four unnumbered ones, carried forward to 1901. Only one of these is a pre-1870 biographical sketch, and four are pre-1870 critical studies. Three are biographies published between 1870 and 1885 and five are critical studies. Fifty-three are post-1885 publications and represent what Carty was able to locate for the next fifteen years. Yet, as he acknowledged, he had "missed many."

Hard upon Kitton's bibliographical heels came John P. Anderson's bibliography (**1**) with twenty-four double-columned pages of appendices to his bibliography of Dickens's works, with subsections labeled "Biographical, Critical, Etc.," "Dramatic" (plays based on Dickens's works), "Musical," "Parodies and Imitations," "Poetical," and "Magazine and Newspaper Articles." Since Anderson lists Kitton's volume, he obviously was indebted to it, but, in some respects, the two works are complementary. Items in one are not necessarily in the other. In comparing, for example, the book-length biographical and critical studies listed in the two works, there are approximately twenty works in Kitton that are not in Anderson and forty or so in Anderson that are not in Kitton, but most are in both.

The next attempts at full-scale bibliographies of Dickens studies would come much later. In the meantime, the earliest serial literary bibliographies began to record the annual (and sometimes monthly, quarterly, and semiannual) production of Dickensiana–*Poole's Index to Periodical Literature, 1802-81* (**1049**) was published in 1882, revised in 1891, and added five supplementary volumes, 1888-1908, for 1882-1907. The series was continued as the *International Index to Periodicals*, 1907-65; the *Social Sciences and Humanities Index*, 1965-74; and the *Humanities Index*, 1974-). *Poole's Index* was complemented by the *Readers' Guide to Periodical Literature*, 1900- (**1046**), and that in turn by the retrospective *Nineteenth Century Readers' Guide to Periodical Literature, 1890-1899, with Supplementary Indexing, 1900-1922* (**964**), published in 1944. In the meantime, the *Dickensian* began publication of "Dickensiana Month by Month" from 1905-18 and then "Dickensiana of the Quarter," to reflect its new publication schedule, from 1919 to 1941, followed by "Recent Dickensiana" or "Dickensiana" from 1941 to 1968 (**1043**), and "The Year's Work in Dickens Studies" from 1968-83 (**1052**). The listings are particularly valuable for the earlier decades of the century as a complement to the *International Index to Periodicals* and the *Readers' Guide to Periodical Literature*.

By the 1920s, scholarly literary journals were multiplying, and the new serial bibliographies, created to record their output, were gearing up for the great work ahead. The British Modern Humanities Research Association's *Annual Bibliography of English Language and Literature* (**1039**) first appeared in 1921 (for the year 1920), and the following year the "American Bibliography" in *Publications of the Modern Language Association of America* (**1042**) appeared (for 1921), though until 1956 it listed only works by American scholars. The "Victorian Bibliography" first appeared in 1933 (for 1932), in *Modern Philology* and, from 1958 on, in *Victorian Studies* (**1058**), with cumulative volumes for 1932-44, 1945-54, 1955-64, 1965-74, and 1975-84, edited, respectively, by W. D. Templeman (**1025**), Austin Wright (**1033**), Robert C. Slack (**1022**), Ronald E. Freeman (**978**), and Richard C. Tobias (**1026**). This twentieth-century triumvirate of scholarly serial bibliographies was joined in 1970 by "The Dickens Checklist," compiled by Alan M. Cohn and others for the *Dickens Studies Newsletter* and its successor *The Dickens Quarterly* (**1037**), and, even more recently, in 1976, by the Canadian *Annual Bibliography of Victorian Studies* (**1036**), using the Literary Information and Retrieval Database (LITIR). It is edited by Brahma Chaudhuri and was first published, annually, in 1980 (for 1976), and in various cumulative gatherings (1976-1980, 1970-1984, 1975-1989, 1945-1969). It is also available on CD-ROM (1970-1999), and online at the Victorian Database Online Web site, http://www.victoriandatabase.com (**1234**). To these one should add the *Essay and General Literary Index* (**1051**), begun by Minnie E. Scars and Marian Shaw in 1934 (for 1900-33), and the *Subject Index to Periodicals* (**1041**), begun in 1916 (for 1915) by the Library Association, London, which was published as the *British Humanities Index* after 1962. Both of these are still being published, too.

A study by Abigail A. Loomis, "Dickens Duplications: A Study of Overlap in Serial Bibliographies in Literature" (**1413**), published in 1986, concludes that there is no one serial bibliography in the humanities, and particularly in literature, that "provides ongoing comprehensive coverage," despite the need for such. Loomis analyzed the 1980 Dickens entries in the MLA and MHRA bibliographies, *The Year's Work in English Studies* (**1054**), "Recent Dickens Studies" in *Dickens Studies Annual* (**1047**), "The Year's Work in Dickens Studies" in the *Dickensian*, "The Dickens Checklist" in *Dickens Studies Newsletter*, and the "Victorian Bibliography" in *Victorian Studies*. She found that none located all the Dickens studies published in a given year. The *Dickens Studies Newsletter* contained the largest number of entries and the shortest time lag (though about half the entries were published prior to 1980), and, because highly selective, the *Dickensian* and the *Year's Work in English Studies* the smallest number. Loomis also found a high rate of duplication, or overlap, and percentages of unique entries ranging from eight to fifteen percent in the less selective bibliographies. Obviously it is important for a scholar to consult all of these each year.

To return to our history, William Miller's *The Dickens Student and Collector: A List of Writings Relating to Charles Dickens and His Works, 1836-1945* (**1005**), published in 1946, with supplements in 1947 and 1953, was the first major bibliography of Dickens studies to appear since Kitton's *Dickensiana* sixty years earlier. It was severely criticized by Philo Calhoun and Howell J. Heaney in their "Dickensiana in the Rough," published in *Papers of the Bibliographical Society of America* in 1947 (**1392**), as discussed at the beginning of this introduction. Miller's bibliography was, nevertheless, in 1946, the most inclusive bibliography of Dickens studies ever, and not all reviewers condemned it.

Joseph Gold's *The Stature of Dickens: A Centenary Bibliography* (**982**), published twenty-five years later in 1971, and largely covering the period 1870-1968/69, with a few earlier works, was intentionally a selective bibliography, a "presentation," as Gold explains, of what he found to be "of lasting scholarly value or interest." R. C. Churchill claims in the preface to his *A Bibliography of Dickensian Criticism, 1836-1975* (**956**), published in 1975, that his is "the most comprehensive" bibliography of Dickens criticism "yet attempted," but "criticism" is the key word here, for Churchill pretty much excludes any work that is not critical, such as bibliographies, biographies, and bibliographical, textual, and biographical studies. Reviewers have generally found the volume verging toward the eccentric—in its selection of material and its structure in particular.

Other bibliographies of Dickens studies, though intentionally of more limited scope, have been ambitious. Among these are the three editions of the

Cambridge Bibliography of English Literature (the second edition was called *The New Cambridge Bibliography of English Literature*). While the listing of works by English authors in these volumes attempt to be exhaustive, the secondary literature is quite selective. The Dickens section in the first edition (**11**) was compiled by F. J. H. Darton, with the "Bibliographies and Catalogues" and the "Biography and Criticism" sections covering only six and one-half double-columned pages of books and chapters in books published through 1937, with approximately another page of studies of individual novels. A supplementary volume by K. J. Fielding (**18**) added another seven pages of entries, 1936-55, a majority of which were journal articles. The Dickens section in the second edition (**8**), published in 1969, was compiled by Philip Collins and was far more elaborate than the first. By then the Dickens industry was in full swing, and it must have been difficult to put together even a representative selection of biographical and critical studies. The columns in these editions were longer and wider, about doubling the amount of information per page. Collins not only expanded the pre-1955 entries (though a few lesser items disappear), but also extended the bibliography through 1967. The main sections of studies were expanded in number as well as in length, filling thirteen pages (roughly equivalent to twenty-six pages in the first edition), and including a good many journal articles. Of course it was all highly selective. Compare Collins's two-page list of bibliographies and auction catalogues with the present volume to see the difference between selectivity and near comprehensiveness.

The huge section on Dickens in the third edition (**41**), published in 1999, and compiled by Paul Schlicke, is both impressive and something of a disappointment, though the latter is not of Schlicke's making. The introductory section on manuscripts, bibliographies, reference works (including Web sites), and studies of manuscripts and editions is, if selective, a useful updating of this section in the earlier editions. It is followed by section 1, which lists editions and studies of individual works, including letters and speeches, with subheadings (where needed) of bibliographies, editions, Dickens's reading adaptations, commentary on the text, imitations, dramatizations, reviews, and studies and appreciations. Section 2 lists personal recollections and memoirs, obituaries, and studies of special periods and aspects, bibliographies and adaptations, Dickens's illustrators and their illustrations, and biographies. The entries are essentially short-title ones, and there are no annotations. The organization throughout is chronological. Section 2 also lists critical and topographical studies, but only those published before 1920. This new and assuredly controversial policy for these two parts of the third edition gives the bibliography a curiously dated look, particularly since the second edition contained critical and topographical studies through 1967–and the first edition publications through 1938. Ironically, one needs to go to the first and second editions to begin to update the third. The justification for this has some sense to it, one must acknowledge. In her "Editor's Preface," Joanne Shattock, editor of the volume (Vol. 4: *1800-1900*), states that the "availability of comprehensive bibliographies of secondary material, both in electronic and volume form," at least back to 1920, meant that the CBEL did not need to "provide a selective list of secondary criticism for each author, as had previously been the case" in the first two editions.

Other selective bibliographies of note or bibliographies limited in scope are George H. Ford and Lauriat Lane, Jr.'s "Bibliography," a twenty-three page list in *The Dickens Critics* (**977**), published in 1961, "a selection," they point out, "from the impossibly enormous body of material written about Dickens before 1960" that seemed to them to be, "in whole or in part, 'criticism.'" The list contains principally post-1935 studies (though there are some earlier works going back to 1840) and so largely reflects the influence of Edmund Wilson on modern Dickens criticism. Ada Nisbet's bibliographical essay on Dickens in *Victorian Fiction: A Guide to Research* (**1013**), published in 1964, is highly selective but an invaluable guide to Dickens studies prior to 1964, and a testament to what she characterizes as the "phenomenal rise in the number of ardent scramblers over Dickensian terrain" since 1918. Philip Collins provides the supplementary essay in *Victorian Fiction: A Second Guide to Research* (**959**), published in 1978, covering the next thirteen years (1962-75) of what he terms the "continuing boom" in Dickens studies. J. Don Vann published an intervening update of Nisbet's guide in his "A Checklist of Dickens Criticism, 1963-67" (**1028**), published in *Studies in the Novel* in 1969, and Lauriat Lane, Jr.'s "Dickens Studies, 1958-1968: An Overview" (**998**) covers essentially the same period. John J. Fenstermaker published his *Charles Dickens, 1940-1975. An Analytical Subject Index to Periodical Criticism of the Novels and Christmas Books* (**973**) in 1979, in an attempt to make sense out of "post-Wilsonian" criticism of Dickens's novels, but his work, as the title indicates, is restricted to journal articles and excludes the important and rapidly growing body of full-length studies of Dickens's novels.

The last two major bibliographies of limited scope are Alan M. Cohn and K. K. Collins's *The Cumulated Dickens Checklist: 1970-1979* (**958**), published in 1982, and the Dickens section of Brahma Chaudhuri's *Annual Bibliography of Victorian Studies*, published as *Charles Dickens, a Bibliography: 1970-1986* (**954**) in 1988. Cohn and Collins's bibliography covers a mere ten years, though thoroughly), and is a cumulation and re-ordering of the checklists published quarterly in the *Dickens Studies Newsletter*. They intended their volume as a supplement to Gold's bibliography, though theirs is far more comprehensive. Since the checklist continued to appear quarterly in the *Dickens Studies Newsletter*, and continues now in the *Dickens Quarterly*, the bibliography remains up to date, in varying degrees of thoroughness, listing editions of Dickens's works, books, articles, reviews, dissertations, miscellaneous items, and, more recently, "Web Sites of Note." This bibliography (and its continuations) is paralleled by Chaudhuri's, which covers only a few more years of work, and is part of an Internet database that has been published in various printed formats as well (see **1036**). Like many Internet databases, it is not always as accurate as one might like, but it is reasonably thorough in its coverage, though not as thorough as the Cohn and Collins bibliography, which has more entries for a shorter period of time. Like Cohn and Collins, the bibliography stays updated by the continuing database.

There are many other useful bibliographies, more general or more specialized in scope, that supplement and, equally as often, duplicate the ones listed here. Some are thematic, some concerned with studies of individual Dickens works (as already noted), some with the works of a particular country or those written in a particular language. Admittedly, any one of these might, at any given time, suit the purposes of a researcher better than the ones singled out here. The bibliographies noted above are the principal sources of studies of Dickens for the modern scholar. Here is a sampling, however, of some of the useful specialized bibliographies; these and others will be found in section 3C and 3D in this bibliography: William A. Wortman's *A Guide to Serial Bibliographies for Modern Literatures*, 2nd edition (**1162**), published in 1995; James L. Harner's "Databases" and "Internet Resources," in his *Literary Research Guide*, 4th edition (**1145-47**), published in 2002; T. H. Howard-Hill's multi-volume *Index to British Literary Bibliographies* (**1148**), published 1969- ; Frank T. Dunn's *A Cumulative Analytical Index to **The Dickensian**, 1905-1974* (**1165**), published in 1976; Kathryn Chittick's *The Critical Reception of Charles Dickens, 1833-1841* (**1259**), published in 1989; George H. Ford's "Appendix: Dickens' Awareness of Reviews," in his *Dickens and His Readers: Aspects of Novel-Criticism since 1836* (**1261**), published in 1955; and, for individual Dickens works, the volumes in the Garland Dickens Bibliographies and The Dickens Bibliographies published by AMS Press (**12, 13**). For more selective bibliographies of individual Dickens works, see section 3C of this bibliography.

For the twenty-first-century researcher there is now a steadily increasing number of Dickens and Victorian Web sites, each with links to each other and to still other Web sites (surely, a new form of bibliographic resource). Among the best are The Active Portal Project, University of Wisconsin (**1221**), which provides access to "7200 links to pages found on 467 sites" concerning Dickens (as of 17 April 2003); David Perdue's Charles Dickens Page (**1225**); The Dickens Fellowship Web site (**1226**); The Dickens Page Web site, created by Mitsuharu Matsuoka (**1227**); The Dickens Project Web site, University of California, Santa Cruz (**1228**); the Victorian Research Web, Indiana University (**1233**); George Landow's Victorian Web Web site (**1235**); and the Voice of the Shuttle Web site (**1236**). Many of these provide links to the texts of Dickens's novels and to a variety of essays, bibliographies, chat rooms–almost anything one could want. There was also, until summer 2003, a valuable Web site, Concordances of Great Books, perhaps not technically a bibliographical reference, at www.concordance.com (**1224**), which contained the texts of fifty-five Dickens works, many from the Project Gutenberg and The Online Books Page Web sites, but following the death of William A. Williams, Jr., its webmaster, it was discontinued. It has to some extent been replaced by Alex

Catalogue of Electronic Texts, conducted by Eric Lease Morgan. South Bend, Indiana, at http://www.infomations.com/alex, which is described on its home page as "a collection of public domain documents from American and English literature as well as Western philosophy." As of 7 September 2003, the user can display the text of twenty Dickens works, but these do not include all of the principal novels. It is hoped, obviously, that Mr. Morgan will continue to add Dickens texts to his Web site.

Library Catalogues and Catalogues of Dickens Collections

These must not be overlooked in working with or locating manuscripts (including letters) and editions of Dickens's works, translations, adaptations, extra illustrations, and book-length studies of Dickens and his works. Of particular value are catalogues of collections specializing in Dickens, such as the collections given or sold to the Dickens House (**1457**), the Dexter Collection in the British Library (**1436, 1527**), the VanderPoel Dickens Collection at the University of Texas (**1445**), the Cruikshank and Dickens portions of the library of William Andrews Clark, Jr., at UCLA (**1453**), the Elkins Collection in the Free Library of Philadelphia (**1464**), the J. Pierpont Morgan Library in New York (**1478**), the Berg Collection in the New York Public Library (**1499**), the Gimbel Collection in the Yale University Library (**1509**), Dickens letters in the Henry E. Huntington Library (**1514**), Harry Smith's "Sentimental Library" (**1525**) since dispersed at auction (**1918**), the Widener Collection at Harvard University (**1518**), the Suzannet Collection (**1529-30**), now scattered, but a significant portion of which was donated to the Dickens House (**1524**), and the Forster Collection of manuscripts, page proofs, letters, and other items in the Victoria and Albert Museum, London (**1538-43**). These as well as a number of lesser collections contain valuable manuscripts and rare printed matter and are accessible to the scholar with the necessary credentials.

There is always a thrill in holding in one's hands a beautifully bound manuscript of a Dickens work, whether it is a multi-volume set of the manuscript of a major Dickens novel in the Forster Collection of the Victoria and Albert Museum or a slim article for *All the Year Round* in the Rare Books Division of the New York Public Library. Of course "holding in one's hands" is a bit of a euphemism, since the manuscript is usually placed on a special book rack, and one turns the pages timorously under close supervision of an alert librarian. As Annette Low explains, in "The Conservation of Dickens' Manuscripts" (**2304**), published in 1993, an illustrated report on the recent rebinding of the manuscripts in the Forster Collection, the pages are now hinged at one edge into "blank books of alkaline paper," with the other edge being "held down with a strip of Bondina across the corners." Such binding allows for flex and expansion and contraction, with "generous support leaf margins" preventing any handling of the manuscript pages themselves.

Of equal importance are the Dickens sections of the major national library and union catalogues–The British Museum and Library (**1435-42**), the American Library of Congress (**1481**) and National Union Catalogue (**1482**), the French Bibliothèque Nationale (**1431-33, 1493**), the Italian *Catalogo Cumulativo* (**1446**)–and of major city and university libraries, such as the New York Public Library (**1495-1501**) and the Houghton and the Widener Libraries, Harvard University (**1469-72**). The entries in these catalogues are not as fully described as in the often elegant and beautifully illustrated catalogues of special Dickens collections; indeed, they are generally unannotated and without illustrations, and their online catalogue entries are sometimes even more Spartan.

In lieu of handling and searching the typically large volumes of printed library catalogues, one can do the equivalent online at three incredible Web sites: Libweb (**1484**), at http://sunsite.Berkeley.edu/Libweb, providing access to the catalogues of 6,500 libraries in more than 115 countries; LibDex, the Library Index Web site, edited and compiled by Peter Scott (**1522**), at http://www.libdex.com, which offers access to the online catalogues of 18,000 (as of 1 April 2003) public, university, and other libraries, as well as links to numerous other interesting sites; and the OCLC WorldCat Web site (**1503**), at http//www.oclc.org/worldcat, which is a database of over 48,000,000 entries from the merged catalogues of innumerable libraries worldwide, available, however, only through subscribing libraries. The advantage of WorldCat is that it is essentially a union catalogue, locating libraries that contain the volume in which one is interested. If one is trying to locate a particular edition of a Dickens novel, say, or a rare bibliographical item, the WorldCat Web site is the one to use, as are two other powerful consortium catalogues available online. The first is the *Catalog collectif de France* (**1431**), at http//www.ccfr.bnf.fr, which accesses more than 14,000,000 documents from the Catalogue des fonds des bibliothèques municipales rétroconvertis and the Catalogue du système universitaire de documentation, in addition to the Catalogue BN-OPALE PLUS of the Bibliothèque Nationale. The second is the COPAC Web site of the Consortium of University Research Libraries (**1452**), which will be found at http://copac.ac.uk/copac and provides access to "the merged online catalogues of 22 of the largest university research libraries in the UK and Ireland *plus* the British Library."

Various guides have also been published which list and describe major and minor Dickens collections–see particularly, Lee Ash and William G. Miller's *Subject Collections: A Guide to Special Book Collections and Subject Emphases as Reported by University, College, Public, and Special Libraries and Museums in the United States and Canada* (**1552**), the latest edition published in 1993; Barbara L. Bell's *An Annotated Guide to Current National Bibliographies* (**1553**), published in 1986; Donald L. DeWitt's *Guide to Archives and Manuscript Collections in the United States: An Annotated Bibliography* (**1555**), published in 1994; Robert B. Downs's *American Library Resources: A Bibliographical Guide* (**1557**), published in 1951, with later supplements, and his and Elizabeth C. Downs's *British and Irish Library Resources: A Bibliographical Guide* (**1558**), published in 1981; James L. Harner's section on "Research Libraries" in his *Literary Research Guide* (**1560**), published in 2002; Philip M. Hamer's *A Guide to Archives and Manuscripts in the United States* (**1564**), published in 1961; Bonnie R. Nelson's *A Guide to Published Library Catalogs* (**1565**), published in1982; Keith W. Reynard's *The Aslib Directory of Literary and Historical Collections in the UK* (**1566**); and Moelwyn I. Williams's *A Directory of Rare Books and Special Collections in the United Kingdom and the Republic of Ireland* (**1570**), published in 1985 and revised by B. C. Bloomfield and Karen Potts in 1997.

Exhibition Catalogues

These catalogues, too, can be the source of valuable information about Dickens bibliography. The earliest track Dickens's post-1870 reputation and the attempts, particularly by the Dickens Fellowship, formed in 1902, to maintain and build that reputation. The first four Dickens exhibitions, held in London between 1903 and 1909, were sponsored by the Fellowship. The Dickens Exhibition held at Memorial Hall for three days in March 1903 (**1806**), was, as its compiler, Frederic G. Kitton, points out in his introduction to the catalogue, the first exhibition "absolutely restricted to Dickens"; it included manuscripts, autograph letters, original editions, translations, relics, portraits, original drawings, and other items. The *Athenaeum* reviewer (**1806**) called the exhibition "an excellent piece of bibliography, which may well become important to collectors," and the London *Times* reviewer (**1851**), waxing a little more eloquent, asserted that it provided "convincing evidence of Dickens's immense hold upon the feelings and the hearts of the people." The second Dickens exhibition, held at the New Dudley Gallery, 22 July-28 August, only five years later (**1789**), was compiled by two other early Dickensians, B. W. Matz and J. W. T. Ley, the latter of whom asserts in the illustrated catalogue's introduction that "today Dickens is the most popular and most beloved novelist" and that he and Matz had tried to make the exhibition "as comprehensive as possible." The third exhibition was also held at the New Dudley Galleries the following year, 7 August-30 September (**1813**), with a brief introduction to the illustrated catalogue written this time by Percy Fitzgerald, yet another early Dickensian. Intervening between the first and second exhibitions was the first Pickwick exhibition (**1788**), also at the New Dudley Galleries, 22 July-28 August 1907. Its illustrated catalogue was compiled by Matz and Ley, and is a 116-page listing of the Pickwickiana in the exhibition—English, American, and other foreign editions and translations of the novel; plagiarisms, parodies, plays, playbills, and music; relics and mementos; political cartoons and caricatures; postcards, calendars, posters, advertisements; portraits and biographies of Dickens; autograph letters; and a number of other items.

London celebrated 1912, the centenary of Dickens's birth, with a major exhibition at the Victoria and Albert Museum, running from March to October. It was the museum's first Dickens exhibition, based on its Forster Collection, the manuscripts, page proofs, number plans, and other items that John Forster had bequeathed to the museum. The V&A issued a nicely descriptive and illustrated catalogue (**1828**). A photograph of part of the exhibition can be seen in Trevor Blount's review of 1970 exhibitions (**1837**). There was also an exhibition at the Franklin Club, St. Louis, Missouri, 7-12 February 1912 (**1792**), which issued a 49-page catalogue, and one the following year, close enough to count, perhaps, as a centenary exhibition, at the Grolier Club in New York (**1802**), 23 January-8 March 1913, which issued a 256-page illustrated catalogue, and included the manuscript of *A Christmas Carol*, thirty-two pages of the manuscript of *Pickwick Papers*, and manuscripts of lesser works, as well as editions, sketches, extra illustrations, letters, playbills, relics, and other items.

Between 1912 and 1970, the centenaries of Dickens's birth and death, there were a number of exhibitions of lesser importance devoted almost entirely to specific collections. Interest in Dickens, or at least in Dickens exhibitions, waned between 1913 and 1936, as to a large extent scholarship did, except for continuing activity in the Dickens Fellowship and in the pages of the *Dickensian*. The only notable exhibition during this period seems to have been of the Howard Duffield collection of items associated with *Edwin Drood* (**1459**), mounted at the Grolier Club, New York, in 1932. The year 1936, the centenary of the beginning of the serialization of *Pickwick Papers*, produced at least three exhibitions, however. In London, a second major Pickwick exhibition by the Dickens Fellowship was mounted, this time at the Dickens House (**1787**), March-April 1936. There were other Pickwick exhibitions of lesser import at the Southwark Public Libraries and Cuming Museum, London (**1820**), and at the Public Library, Museums, and National Gallery of Victoria, in Melbourne, Australia (**1817**), for which catalogues were issued. An exhibition was also held in 1936, and an illustrated catalogue issued (**1790**), of the Charles J. Sawyer collection of Dickens's manuscripts, letters, presentation copies, parts editions, and Dickensiana. In 1941, the Henry W. & Albert A. Berg Collection at the New York Public Library produced its first Dickens exhibition, but its catalogue was only four pages long (**1814**). In 1946, the William M. Elkins collection at the Free Library of Philadelphia was featured in an exhibition, June-July 1946, for which an illustrated catalogue (**1793**) was issued, and in 1949 and 1958 exhibitions at the New York Public Library featured items from the Berg Collection. The earlier presented first editions of first books by English writers, including *Sketches by Boz*, and the later exhibited prompt books of Dickens's public readings and related materials, with catalogues for both by John D. Gordan (**1798, 1800**). In February 1962, items from the Richard Gimbel collection were exhibited in the Sterling Memorial Library, Yale University (**1797**), and Gimbel's entire Dickens collection went to Yale University at his death eight years later.

The year 1970, however, was another matter. If interest in Dickens, or at least in major Dickens exhibitions, waned after 1913, with a brief revival in 1936, the centenary of Dickens's death certainly renewed it. A flurry of exhibitions opened in 1970, most in England, but there were also exhibitions in the

United States at Loras College in Dubuque, Iowa (**1783**), at the University of Texas (**1796**), at the University of California in Los Angeles (**1831**), at the Pierpont Morgan Library in New York (**1834, 1848**), and in the Berg Collection, New York Public Library (**1823**). At the New York Public Library, there were also a smaller exhibition of "Dickens in America" and one of illustrations of Dickens's characters by a number of artists (**1834**). In Belgium, the University of Liège sponsored an exhibition organized by the British Council (**1784**).

In England, Malcolm Andrews reported in the *Dickens Studies Newsletter* (**1833**), there were "seventy or more exhibitions mounted by libraries." He names only the major ones, but does single out as "one of the most interesting" an exhibition at Liverpool University on "Pickwick and Pickwickiana" based on the "extensive holdings of an anonymous local collector," whom Michael Slater (**1884**) identifies as F. S. Bradburn, and whose catalogue, Richard A. Vogler (**1888**) finds, from an examination of it (**1811**), to be "not necessarily of a wealthy, but certainly of a devoted and astute collector." G. Chandler, the librarian at the Liverpool Central Library also reports on an exhibition there (**1844**). Another, smaller exhibition was held at Knebworth House in Hertfordshire (**1807**) of letters and other items associated with the friendship of Dickens and Edward Bulwer-Lytton. And Trevor Blount, in a review of centenary exhibitions for the *Dickensian* (**1837**), describes an exhibition in Eastgate House in Rochester of "various items from the Percy Fitzgerald Collection."

Exhibitions in London were numerous. Trevor Blount describes an exhibition in the King's Library in the British Museum (**1781**) as a "notable assemblage of material" from the John F. Dexter Collection. Several reviewers liked the exhibition on "Dickens and Medicine" at the Wellcome Institute of the History of Medicine (**1795**); Blount, for example, found it "a relatively small exhibit but an informative one" and "a great pleasure to visit." The British Council held a small "centenary book exhibition" in London (**1780**).

The major London exhibitions, however, were at the Dickens House and the Victoria and Albert Museum. The Dickens House featured, as the title of its catalogue, compiled by Michael Slater (**1819**), indicates, *Treasures from the Dickens Collection Formed by the Late Comte Alain de Suzannet* of letters, playbills, drawings and sketches, rare editions, manuscripts, and other materials donated to it by Suzannet between 1930 and 1950 and by his widow in 1966 and 1971. Many of the items are now on permanent exhibition in the two Suzannet Rooms in the museum. The Victoria and Albert Museum exhibition (**1827**) was nothing less than sensational, if one can say this about a museum exhibition. It was the first major Dickens exhibition at the museum since its 1912 show. Running from 10 June-20 September, it was designed by Christopher Firmstone to reflect the purpose announced by John Pope-Hennessey, museum director, in the foreword to the catalogue: "to portray one of the greatest creative artists of the nineteenth century against the background of the life and social history of his time." The exhibition twisted and turned theatrically like a Dickensian street, and the earlier portions of it were confined and dim, as Dickens imagined his childhood to be, with the spaces lightening and opening up as his career developed. The manuscripts of ten of his novels, page proofs, letters, editions of his works, playbills, drawings, paintings, photographs, relics, and a plethora of other items were worked into the dramatic physical structure. As I said in my review of the exhibition (**1827, 1834**), the museum, "apart from mounting a major exhibition exciting in itself, has provided a great service for scholars in showing the range and depth of the material available, much of it relatively unexplored to date, for further investigation into the life and works of a great author."

The history of Dickens exhibitions pretty much ends here, at least for the time being. The Dickens exhibition scene has been relatively quiet since 1970, but will no doubt come alive again in 2012, the bicentennial of Dickens's birth.

I have included in this bibliography the numerous reports on Dickens exhibitions, collections, and library accessions of Dickens material, as well as Dickens scrapbooks (most at the Dickens House) and Dickens museum guides (see parts 5B, 4E, 4C, and 4D, respectively, below). The reader will find many of these as interesting in themselves as they are informative and useful.

Auction and Booksellers' Catalogues

One last area of bibliographical significance needs to be covered. Occasionally auction and booksellers' catalogues have shown up in Dickens bibliographies, principally in the three editions of the *Cambridge Bibliography of English Literature*, and there very selectively, and to an even lesser extent in the volumes of T. H. Howard-Hill's *Index to British Literary Bibliography* (**1148**). Though such catalogues are by no means error-proof, a perusal of the more important of them will quickly reveal their value to Dickens scholarship. The editors of the *Pilgrim Letters* used them extensively, for at least two important reasons. First, since lists of purchase prices (occasionally with the names of purchasers) printed after the sale are often inserted in sale catalogues deposited in libraries, and just as frequently written in by a collector or curator who was at the auction, it is sometimes possible to locate the current owners. A number of sale catalogues in the British Library are auctioneers' copies, with manuscript notes and prices, that were apparently donated by the principal London auction houses. Major collections of auction catalogues will also be found in the New York Public Library and the Library of Congress, as well as, according to David Pearson in his *Provenance Research in Book History: A Handbook* (London: British Library, 1994), pp. 144-46, in the Cambridge University Library, the Bodleian Library at Oxford University, and the National Art Library in the Victoria and Albert Museum. Second, most sale as well as booksellers' catalogues will give excerpts from letters or manuscripts

or even print or include a photographic facsimile of a letter, a page of manuscript, a book cover, or a title page. Having even the partial text of a letter that
has disappeared after an auction or been subsequently destroyed is of inesti-
mable value to the scholar. At one point in working on this bibliography, out
of curiosity I examined the letters in the first ten volumes of the *Pilgrim Letters*,
then all that had been published, to see what sources the editors had used for
the text of letters for which the autograph manuscripts were unavailable.
Some of these letters had been published in books and articles, but the text of
a far greater number, in the vicinity of 900, came from auction and booksellers' catalogues. Unfortunately, and uncharacteristically for this thoroughly
scholarly enterprise, many of the catalogues are so inadequately identified as
to make locating of them impossible.

James Harner, in the fourth edition of his *Literary Research Guide* (**1147**),
pp. 612-13, rightly declares that booksellers' and auction catalogues "are
among the most underutilized scholarly resources." They are valuable, he
adds, for "identifying hitherto unrecorded printed works, editions, or manuscripts," for "finding descriptions (and sometimes reproductions or transcriptions) of unique items no longer locatable," for "tracing the provenance of a
copy (and thus possibly locating it)," and for "reconstructing an individual's
library." Michael Hunter, in his "Auction Catalogues and Eminent Libraries,"
Book Collector, 21 (1972), pp. 471-88, also holds that auction catalogues "are
mainly interesting for showing what books eminent men owned" but cautions
that the listings in catalogues are not always complete since many volumes in a
collection may not be offered in a sale.

Auction catalogues do indeed provide a record of some great Dickens collections, and frequently give detailed descriptions of important items in the
collection, from elaborate collations of prime Pickwicks in parts to itemizing
of large collections of letters. These should find a place among the catalogues
of great Dickens collections mentioned, particularly since these were dispersed at auction rather than donated intact to a library, and the auction catalogue remains the sole published record of a great collector's library, even if
incomplete. A few of the more important sale catalogues are those of the collections of George McCutcheon (**1903**); William F. Gable of Altoona, Pennsylvania (**1904**); Mr. and Mrs. Edward Daoust (**1905, 1910**); George Ulizio, of
Pine Valley, New Jersey (**1913**); Ogden Goelet, New York (**1916-17**); Harry B.
Smith, New York (**1918**); Augustin Daly (**1919**); Edwin M. Lapham, Chicago
(**1922**), best known for his set of prime Pickwick in parts, the Lapham Pickwick; Edwin W. Coggeshall, New York (**1925, 1931**); Ralph T. Jupp, London
(**1929, 2056**); Jerome Kern, New York (**1934**); Theodore N. Vail, New York
(**1937**); Lewis A. Hird, Englewood, New Jersey (**1963**); Comte de Suzannet,
Lausanne, Switzerland (**1976-77**), and see also his published catalogues (**1529-
30**); H. W. Bruton, Gloucester (**2012**); William Wright (**2008**); Richard Manney
(**2018**); and, most recently, Horace N. Pym (**2016**).

Other dispersed libraries are of interest for other reasons. First there are the catalogues of the sale of Dickens's property–the furnishings and other effects of Gad's Hill, his last residence, in 1870 (**2019**); his pictures and objets d'art, also in 1870 (**1943**); and his library (**2055**), in 1878. In 1939, Lady Dickens (his son Henry's wife) and her children sold the manuscript of *Life of Our Lord* (**1981**), and, very recently, in 1999, a collection of valuable legal papers then still held by the Dickens family (**2014**) and termed the" Dickens Archive" by Sotheby's was offered at auction. In a disappointing sale, few items found purchasers, but, fortunately, the bulk of the archive eventually ended up in the British Library, as reported by Malcolm Andrews in the *Dickensian* in 2001 (**1589**). Also interesting are sales of the property of old friends or publishers of Dickens–Samuel Rogers (**1941**), including eleven of Dickens's novels, three of which were presented to Rogers by Dickens; William Macready (**1945**), including eight novels, five of which were presented to Macready or his wife; Angela Burdett-Coutts (**1996**), including presentation copies, the autograph manuscript of *The Haunted Man, and the Ghost's Bargain*, and a collection of "upwards of 600 letters" from Dickens, and others from members of the Dickens family and circle; Edmund Yates (**2002**), including letters from Dickens to Yates, one of his writers for *All the Year Round*; and Richard Bentley (**1952**), including correspondence between Dickens and Bentley, one of his earliest publishers, and seven publishing agreements. Still other catalogues reveal the collections of prominent Dickens scholars–for example, John C. Eckel (**1909**), William Glyde Wilkins (**1930**), Herman LeRoy Edgar (**1967**), A. Edward Newton (**1970**), and Thomas Hatton, who sold his collection in parts over the years (**1906, 1972, 1978-79**).

Book auction records can sometimes be helpful. The most useful is probably *Book-Prices Current* (**2061**), which was published from 1888 (for 1886/87) to 1957 (for 1955/56), giving the auction house, the date of the sale, the price, and frequently the purchaser of numerous Dickens items, manuscripts as well as books, from 1921 on and American as well as English sales from 1916 on. *Book-Auction Records* (**2060**) lists the auction house and price but not the purchaser or specific date of sale from 1903 on, beginning with just London houses and gradually increasing its range to include all British, then American, and then houses of other countries (the last since 1968). *American Book-Prices Current* (**2065**) gives prices of Dickens items but not the sellers or purchasers, and so is less useful.

Supplementing the sale and booksellers' catalogues and the auction records are innumerable reports of these sales (**2071-2197**) in such publications as the *Times Literary Supplement*, the London *Times*, and the *New York Times* (though not so much in recent years). These help to identify important sales and, where catalogues are not easily located, at least give some idea of what was in the sale.

Many books have been published as guides for the beginning collector of books, some of which contain brief sections on collecting Dickens's works.

A few of the earliest are mentioned above in the section on bibliographies of Dickens's works. More recent or interesting ones are Charles J. Sawyer and J. Harvey Darton's *English Books, 1475-1900: A Signpost for Collectors*, an introduction to book collecting, with a chapter on Dickens (**2265**), published in 1927; Allen and Patricia Ahearn's *Collected Books: The Guide to Values, 1998 Edition* (**2199**), published in 1997; Colton Storm and Howard Peckham's *Invitation to Book Collecting, Its Pleasures and Practices* (**2274**), published in 1947; and John T. Winterich and David A. Randall's *A Primer of Book Collecting*, 3rd edition (**2278**), published in 1966. Others are more personal, such as William H. Arnold's *Ventures in Book Collecting* (**2200**), published in 1923; Percy Fitzgerald's *The Book Fancier, or The Romance of Book Collecting* (**2229**), published in 1886; A. Edward Newton's *The Amenities of Book Collecting, and Kindred Affections* (**2250**), published in 1918; Horace N. Pym's *A Tour Round My Book-Shelves* (**1710**), published in 1891; A. S. W. Rosenbach's *A Book Hunter's Holiday: Adventures with Books and Manuscripts* (**2260**), published in 1936; and Walter T. Spencer's chapter on "Dickensiana" in his *Forty Years in My Bookshop* (**2271**), published in 1923.

Biographies or biographical studies of the great Dickens collectors are always fascinating—see, for example, Leslie A. Morris's "Harry Elkins Widener and A. S. W. Rosenbach: Of Books and Friendship" (**2249**), published in 1995; Edwin Wolf, 2nd, and John F. Fleming's *Rosenbach, a Biography* (**2281**), published in 1960; and sketches of Rosenbach (**2247**), Widener (**2248**), George Ulizio (**2237**), Jerome Kern (**2270**), Charles Sessler (**2238**), Harry B. Smith (**2253**), and William Andrews Clark, Jr. (**2263**), in *American Book-Collectors and Bibliographers*, edited by Joseph Rosenblum in two series (**2261-62**), published in 1994 and 1997. Also see "Collecting Charles Dickens," a special issue, published September 1997, of *Firsts: The Book Collector's Magazine* (**2202**), which contains five articles by Lee Biondi, proprietor of The Heritage Book Shop, Los Angeles, written from a bookseller's point of view. In "Strategies of Collecting" (**2203**), pp. 24-39, he begins with the premise that "a nice 'Dickens Collection' is do-able at various paces and price levels, and with a reasonable degree of difficulty," and then surveys the problems and difficulty of collecting the principal works. Three of the other articles look at bibliographical matters concerning the collecting of editions of *Great Expectations*, *Pickwick Papers*, and *Sketches by Boz* (**298**, **341**, **359**), while the remaining piece, "The Charles Dickens Reference Shelf" (**1137**), is an annotated list of Dickens reference works.

Studies of Manuscripts and Textual Changes/Dickens at Work

One might say that the study of Dickens's manuscripts, page proofs, and number plans, as well as the significance of textual changes between manuscript and published text began with John Butt and Kathleen Tillotson's *Dickens at Work* (**2291**) in 1957, so important and valuable, such a classic, has this study become in modern Dickens scholarship. The volume was based to a considerable extent on work both authors had done in the late 1940s and early 1950s (**2286, 2288-89, 2360-61, 2373, 2378**); also see **2287, 2290,** and **2377** for three later studies. Scholarly interest in the manuscripts goes back, however, to the nineteenth century. As early as 1874 articles were appearing in the United States (**2480, 2483-85, 2487**) describing the manuscript of *Our Mutual Friend*, which was then in the possession of George W. Childs, a Philadelphia publisher and collector and former acquaintance of Dickens. Surprisingly, Dickens had given the manuscript and the number plans to E. S. Dallas, a literary critic, whose qualification for such a gift seems to have been that he had written a favorable review of the novel for the London *Times*. The manuscript and its number plans had passed through two other owners before Childs purchased them from the second of these. Then the only major Dickens manuscripts in the country, they are now in the Pierpont Morgan Library, New York.

It was John Forster who, in his *Life of Charles Dickens* (**19, 2298**), published in 1871-73, first emphasized the importance of the manuscripts, number plans, and proofs to an understanding of Dickens's craftsmanship and artistry. He included facsimiles of a page each of the number plans for *David Copperfield* and *Little Dorrit*, as well as facsimiles of the last page of the manuscripts of *Edwin Drood* and *Oliver Twist*. In the biography, Forster also indicated a number of changes, mainly minor ones, that Dickens made in preparing his novels for publication and printed some manuscript material, including Dickens's extant fragment of his autobiography and the original ending for *Great Expectations*. He mentioned in passing that a number of Dickens's manuscripts, page proofs, and number plans were in his possession, but he did not discuss textual changes and their significance.

At Forster's death in 1876, the manuscripts, number plans, and page proofs of the thirteen Dickens manuscripts in his possession went to the South Kensington Museum, now the Victoria and Albert Museum, where scholars soon had access to them. In 1877, in "Charles Dickens's Manuscripts," *Chambers's Journal* published a description of them for its readers (**2292**), an article sufficiently popular to be reprinted in the *Eclectic Magazine*, *Littell's Living Age*, and *Potter's American Monthly*, the last of which added a paragraph criticizing the way in which the manuscripts and page proofs were displayed in cases in the library. In 1880 the museum published a *Handbook of the Dyce and Forster Collections in the South Kensington Museum* (**1541**) in which the manuscripts and proofs were described. In 1885, J. A. H. Murray pointed out in a *Notes and Queries* piece (**2413**) that he had discovered variant readings in editions of *Hard Times* and wondered whether or not there were any more such variants in other Dickens works. In 1896, J. Holt Schooling published an article, "Charles Dickens's Manuscripts," in the *Strand Magazine* (**2310**), centered on twenty-six illustrations of pages from the manuscripts, page proofs, number plans, and original illustrations, in which he commented on some of the interesting alterations that Dickens had made in the course of composing his novels.

F. G. Kitton, too, was fascinated by the manuscripts and what they revealed about Dickens's creativity. He published a facsimile of the manuscript of *A Christmas Carol* in 1890 (**267**) and included descriptions of a number of the manuscripts in *The Novels of Charles Dickens* (**29**) in 1897 and in *The Minor Writings of Charles Dickens* (**154**), in 1900. The bibliographical notes he wrote for the six novels published in the Rochester Edition (**2302**), 1900-01, contained information about the manuscripts, and he described the manuscripts of the Christmas Books in an article in the *Library Review* (**2344**) in 1893.

Over the years, in the first half or so of the twentieth century, a series of commentaries on cancellations in and additions to the manuscripts and page proofs kept interest in the subject of Dickens's craftsmanship alive. As early as 1910, M. H. Spielmann, in "How Dickens Improved His Style: His Tell-Tale Manuscripts" (**2312**), commenting on a group of accompanying photographic facsimiles of pages from the manuscripts of *Oliver Twist*, *Martin Chuzzlewit*, *David Copperfield*, and *Bleak House*, found that the increasingly smaller, cramped hand and the increasingly larger number of corrections showed "the more careful craftsman." Between 1951 and 1955, Leslie C. Staples, then editor of the *Dickensian*, printed a number of passages that, largely because of his self-imposed length restrictions (exactly thirty-two full pages per number), Dickens canceled in page proof (**2313**). Most articles, however, concentrated on a single novel, sometimes, as in Alain de Suzannet's "The Original Manuscript of 'The Pickwick Papers'" (**2497**), published in 1932, locating scattered pages of the novel, or, as in William Miller's "The Manuscript of *Oliver Twist*" (**2472**), published in 1915, locating portions of the work. Other studies, such as Gerald G. Grubb's "Dickens's Marchioness Identified" (**2465**), published in 1953, showed how cancellations or additions in manuscript or page proofs modified or deepened a character, or, as in Albert A. Dunn's "The Altered Endings of *Great Expectations*: A Note on Bibliography and First-Person Narrative" (**2386**), published in 1978, changed the emphasis of an ending. In his *Dickens romancier*, published in Paris in 1953 (**2307**), Sylvère Monod was the first biographer/critic to use the manuscripts, number plans, and page proofs extensively to study, as he expressed it in his 1968 English translation of his work, how the novels were "conceived, constructed, and written." These materials, Monod concluded, "provide evidence of Dickens' earnest, conscientious, even anxious work, and particularly of his passionate, lifelong interest in language and style."

But scarcely anyone else paid any attention to the number plans, except for *Edwin Drood* scholars who were, from virtually 1870 on, desperately seeking out solutions to the "Mystery," and looking everywhere. This led W. Robertson Nicoll, in his *The Problem of "Edwin Drood": A Study in the Methods of Dickens* (**2448**), published in 1912, to print, "now for the first time" the complete number plans for parts 1-6, as well as a page in Dickens's hand containing characters' names and proposed titles for the novel. Percy Carden printed facsimiles of the number plans for *Drood* in 1931 (**2431**). The immediate predecessor of Butt and Tillotson was Ernest Boll, who printed, in "The Plotting of *Our Mutual Friend*" (**2476**) in 1944, a transcription of the number plans for Dickens's last complete novel, and, as Butt and Tillotson were to do, used the number plans to reveal Dickens's working methods, craftsmanship, and artistry in "the weaving of the story." Corrections in Boll's transcription were noted by Joan D. Winslow in 1978 (**2491**).

The importance of Butt and Tillotson was not so much that they extensively explored the number plans, page proofs, and manuscripts of Dickens's novels, because they did not do that much of this—they sampled rather than feasted. Their purpose, as they stated in the preface, was to represent "different stages of [Dickens's] career and different kinds of work." It was their approach to Dickens as a working craftsman rather than an inspired genius that was the astonishing and innovative element of their approach, "the process," as they put it, "rather than the result," the "craft" rather than the "art." Yet they also insisted that "the inspiration and justification of our work is none the less a conviction of Dickens's greatness as a creative artist." In the heyday of the New Criticism, they dared to suggest, and illustrate convincingly, that, like Shakespeare, Dickens had control of his craft, and this control became the art of writing the novel, or at least the specific form at which Dickens excelled, the novel in parts. A careful study of Dickens's letters, particularly those to John Forster, and of his manuscripts, page proofs, and number plans would reveal this in great detail, they were convinced, and would prove to be as valid an approach to understanding Dickens critically as ignoring an author's background and working methods and letting the works, and words, speak for themselves.

While Butt and Tillotson looked particularly closely at the number plans for *Dombey and Son*, *David Copperfield*, and *Hard Times*, with other novels they approached the study of Dickens's craftsmanship from a variety of perspectives—see the annotation for **2291**. Thus, much more remained to be mined in the archives of the Victoria and Albert Museum and in the other museums holding number plans, manuscripts, and page proofs. It took eight to nine years after the publication of *Dickens at Work*, however, for scholars to publish further investigations into this rich lode of unpublished material. Tillotson followed up her work on *Dickens at Work* with her edition of *Oliver Twist* (**2474**), published in 1966. It was the first volume in the Clarendon Dickens, of which she and Butt served as general editors. The Clarendon Edition, as they announced in a "Preface by the General Editors (**176**), which is printed in all the volumes in the series, would establish a critical text, one "free of the numerous corruptions that disfigure modern reprints, with an apparatus of variants that will exhibit Dickens's progressive revision." See below under my commentary on textual studies of individual Dickens works for *Oliver Twist* and other volumes published in the Clarendon Edition. One of the earlier studies to deal with the manuscripts more generally was Harvey P. Sucksmith's *The Narrative Art of Charles Dickens: The Rhetoric of Irony and Sympathy in His Novels* (**2315**), published in 1970, and related, obviously, to Sucksmith's earlier work on *Bleak House* (**2332**). In this full-length study, Sucksmith makes frequent use of textual variants to study Dickens's "conscious and rhetorical art." Burt Hornback, in his *"The Hero of My Life": Essays on Dickens* (**2301**), published in 1981, likewise studies Dickens's craftsmanship through frequent reference to manuscript materials. Joel J. Brattin was later to publish several textual studies of individual novels (see below), growing out of his doctoral dissertation, "Reading between the Lines: Interpreting Dickens's Later Manuscripts" (**2285**), completed in 1986. In his "A Map of the Labyrinth: Editing Dickens's Manuscripts," which he published in *Dickens Studies Annual* in 1985 (**2284**), Brattin makes a case for using the manuscript of a Dickens novel as the copy-text for the most authoritative edition of the novel and contemplates the difficulties and desirability of actually making transcripts of the manuscripts.

Susan Shatto's series, The Dickens Companions (**2311**), designed to provide elaborate notes on individual novels, is now well along, with notes on *Our Mutual Friend* by Michael Cotsell (**2482**), published in 1986; *The Mystery of Edwin Drood* by Wendy S. Jacobson (**2444**), published in 1986; *Bleak House* by Susan Shatto (**2331**), published in 1988; *A Tale of Two Cities* by Andrew Sanders (**2508**), published in 1988; *Oliver Twist* by David Paroissien (**2473**), published in 1992; *Hard Times* by Margaret Simpson (**2415**), published in 1997; *Great Expectations* by David Paroissien (**2398**), published in 2000; and *Martin Chuzzlewit*, by Nancy A. Metz (**2426**), published in 2001. Notes in these useful volumes contain the number plans (where they exist) as well as textual variants. Significant textual variations are also noted in the elaborate annotations in *The Annotated Dickens* (**2299**), two large volumes edited by Edward Guiliano and Philip Collins, published in 1986, containing the texts of *Pickwick Papers, Oliver Twist, A Christmas Carol, Hard Times, David Copperfield, A Tale of Two Cities*, and *Great Expectations*. In his 1987 doctoral dissertation, "Proof Revisions in Three Novels by Charles Dickens: *Dombey and Son, David Copperfield,* and *Bleak House*" (**2297**), Philip A. Everson closely studies the revisions Dickens made in the three novels to show that "as his novels became more complex, his proof revisions became increasingly significant."

Where the number plans are concerned, Harry Stone's beautifully produced *Dickens' Working Notes for His Novels* (**2314**), published in 1987, is the masterwork. It contains photographic facsimiles, as well as Stone's transcriptions, of all the number plans and other memoranda for *The Old Curiosity Shop* (three pages of notes for the closing chapters of the novel), *Martin Chuzzlewit* (pages of trial titles and two pages of number plans, for No. IV, chapters 9 and 10, and No. VI), *Dombey and Son* (a complete set of number plans, a title page, and a sheet of memoranda, both sides filled), *David Copperfield* (several pages of trial titles and a complete set of number plans), *Bleak House* (several pages of trial titles and a complete set of number plans), *Hard Times* (a double page of memoranda and a full set of number plans divided into weekly and monthly parts), *Little Dorrit* (two pages of memoranda for the concluding double number and a complete set of number plans), *Great Expectations* (three pages of memoranda concerning dates, general notes, and titles), *Our Mutual Friend* (a complete set of number plans, with a page of notes on the back of the plan for No. XIX/XX), and *The Mystery of Edwin Drood* (a page of notes and the number plans for Nos. I-VI, those completed at his death).

Finally, Paul Schlicke's *Oxford Reader's Companion to Dickens* (**2309**), published in 1999, is filled with textual information. The highlighted sections on the individual novels and other works (all written, incidentally, by Schlicke himself) contain information about the manuscripts, number plans, and page proofs, as well as other textual information. Also included is an entry by Joel J. Brattin, "Composition, Dickens's Methods of" (**2283**), that is a concise, knowledgeable description of Dickens at work. The number plans, manuscripts, and page proofs in the Forster Collection, Victoria and Albert Museum, are available on microfilm, a set that should be available in major research libraries (**1539**). A color microfilm of the manuscript of *Great Expectations* in the Wisbech and Fenland Museum, Cambridgeshire, England, has also been produced, though George Worth, in his bibliography of the novel (**109**), complains that it "is almost impossible to read" and Anny Sadrin (**2405**) that it is "blurred and unreadable." In their bibliography of *Our Mutual Friend* (**120**), Brattin and Hornback indicate that a microfilm of the manuscript of the novel is available from the Pierpont Morgan Library, New York.

A number of the important textual studies published from the 1960s on were concerned with individual works, often closing gaps left by Butt and Tillotson. It is best to look at these studies work by work.

Sketches by Boz

No manuscripts or memoranda exist for Dickens's earliest work. Two major studies of this work were published in the 1970s, Virgil Grillo's ***Sketches by Boz***: *End in the Beginning* (**2502**) in 1974 and Duane DeVries's *Dickens's Apprentice Years: The Making of a Novelist* (**2499**) in 1976. Both study the revisions that Dickens made when he collected his early newspaper and magazine sketches and tales as *Sketches by Boz* and those he made in later editions of the work. DeVries does this perhaps more thoroughly than Grillo, if only because he devotes more space to his analysis; the second half of Grillo's book is concerned with Dickens's later works. Cary D. Ser's 1974 doctoral dissertation, "*Sketches by Boz*: A Collated Edition" (**2505**), deserves notice, though one might question his use of the 1839 edition as copy-text rather than the first edition of 1836-37. Also valuable are Michael Slater's introduction and headnotes to his edition of *Dickens's **Sketches by Boz** and Other Early Papers, 1833-39* (**2506**), published in 1994.

Pickwick Papers

Only forty-six pages of the manuscript of *Pickwick Papers* are extant, identified in Elliot Engel's bibliography of *Pickwick Papers* (**125**), pp. 14-16. There are no number plans, other memoranda, or proofs. Given the ease and spontaneity with which Dickens wrote in the 1830s (the evidence is in the manuscripts, which are only lightly corrected), one would not expect number plans this early. Dickens seems first to have used them in writing *The Old Curiosity Shop*. James Kinsley's introduction to the Clarendon Edition of *Pickwick Papers* (**2493**) is the principal study of what is known about the composition of *Pickwick Papers*. Kinsley comments at length on the initial scheme for *Pickwick Papers* and Dickens's development of the work, on textual variations in the editions published in Dickens's lifetime, and on the location of the extant fragments of the manuscript. In "The Original Manuscript of 'The Pickwick Papers'" (**2497**), published in 1932, Alain de Suzannet identifies and describes the extant manuscript pages of the novel.

Oliver Twist

The manuscript of *Oliver Twist* is incomplete, and a brief history of what remains and what was lost will be found in David Paroissien's bibliography of the novel (**118**), p. 6, as will a list of commentaries on textual matters, pp. 27-34. No memoranda or proofs are extant. There are two important examinations of textual matters concerning *Oliver Twist*. The earliest is Kathleen Tillotson's lengthy and valuable introduction to the Clarendon Edition of the novel (**2474**), published in 1966, in which she comments on the composition, publication, and reception of the work, examines textual variations in the editions published in Dickens's lifetime, and describes the incomplete manuscript of the novel. Although Burton M. Wheeler, in "The Text and Plan of *Oliver Twist*" (**2475**), published in 1983, disagrees with the belief of Tillotson and others that *Oliver Twist* was planned as a novel from the beginning, his study is textually important because he looks particularly at Dickens's revision of the novel when he published the work, which he had been serializing in *Bentley's Miscellany*, in a three-volume edition in 1838. He looks at a number of "significant deletions" that show that the work was "the product of a radical change of plans" on Dickens's part as he struggled, after the fourth installment, and over the next three installments, with the need to change what started as a "short serial" into a full-fledged novel. Also see Philip Horne's Penguin Classics Edition of the novel (**2469**), published in 2002, for textual variants.

Nicholas Nickleby

According to Paul Schlicke, in *The Oxford Reader's Companion to Dickens* (**2309**), p. 405, "only fragments survive" of the manuscript of this novel, and nothing else. Michael Slater has done some valuable work on the textual variants, in his *The Composition and Monthly Publication of **Nicholas Nickleby*** (**2456**), published in 1973, and in his Penguin English Library Edition of the novel (**2457**), published in 1978, where he also gives the locations of the six extant chapters of the novel. In his World's Classics Edition of the novel (**2455**), published in 1990, Paul Schlicke examines some of the textual variations in editions published in Dickens's lifetime, as does Mark Ford in his Penguin Classics Edition (**2453**), published in 1999.

The Old Curiosity Shop

As Priscilla and Paul Schlicke note in their bibliography of this novel (**117**), pp. 5-7, the complete manuscript (including the *Master Humphrey's Clock* chapters), the corrected proofs for chapters 33-67, and other notes are in the Forster Collection, Victoria and Albert Museum, as are the number plans for chapters 66-72 ("the first extant number plans for a Dickens novel"), and galley proofs for chapters 29-31 and 37 are in the Dexter Collection, British Library, London. The principal textual study of the extant number plans, manuscript, and proofs is Angus Easson's impressive "*The Old Curiosity Shop*: From Manuscript to Print" (**2464**), published in 1970. The changes Easson analyzes show, he asserts, the way Dickens's "imagination was fired," as well as his active creativity and the developing comedic element in the work. They also indicate, he concludes, that Dickens was hampered by serial publication and that he wrestled with "the Protean shape of his material." In "'The Story-Weaver at His Loom': Dickens and the Beginning of *The Old Curiosity Shop*" (**2467**), published in 1970, Robert Patten uses Dickens's textual changes between manuscript and published text, as well as Dickens's letters, to show how he modified his original plans for *Master Humphrey's Clock* as he expanded the story of Little Nell and her grandfather from a short tale to a long serial novel. In his article entitled "Some Old Curiosities from *The Old Curiosity Shop* Manuscript" (**2459**), published in 1990, Joel J. Brattin hypothesizes about why Dickens made a large number of cancellations and revisions in manuscript and page proof. Elizabeth Brennan covers similar territory in the Clarendon Edition and the Oxford World's Classics Edition of the novel (**2460-61**), published in 1997 and 1998, respectively.

Barnaby Rudge

The complete manuscript and the corrected proofs for chapters 17 and 18 are in the Forster Collection, Victoria and Albert Museum, as Thomas J. Rice notes in his bibliography of the novel (**93**), pp. 4-6. Also see his section on the "History of *Barnaby Rudge*'s Composition and Publication," pp. 10-24. The only important study of textual matters, apart from the chapter in Butt and Tillotson, is Joel J. Brattin's "'Secrets Inside . . . to Strike Your Heart': New Readings from Dickens's Manuscript of *Barnaby Rudge*, Chapter 75" (**2318**), published in 1991, which concerns the fifteen percent of text for chapter 75 that Dickens deleted in order to make the chapter exactly twelve pages long.

Martin Chuzzlewit

As Robert Lougy indicates in his bibliography of *Martin Chuzzlewit* (**113**), pp. 6-8, the complete manuscript, some pages of preliminary notes, the number plans for parts IV and VI, and corrected proofs for parts I and V are in the Forster Collection, Victoria and Albert Museum, and small portions of proofs are elsewhere. The only significant commentaries on textual matters will be found in chapter two, "The Text and Its Variations," of Sylvère Monod's study of the novel (**2427**), published in 1985; in Margaret Cardwell's editions of the novel, the Clarendon Edition (**2423**) and the World's Classics Edition (**2422**), published in 1982 and 1984, respectively, and in Patricia Ingham's Penguin Classics Edition (**2425**), published in 1999.

The Christmas Books

As noted earlier, the entire manuscript of *A Christmas Carol*, now a star attraction of the Pierpont Morgan Library, New York, was first published in facsimile in 1890. It has been reproduced more than twice since, most recently by Frederick B. Adams, Jr., in 1967 (**2334**), with brief commentary on the manuscript, and by John Mortimer in 1993 (**2346**). In his introduction, "Meeting the Manuscript," Mortimer comments on what the manuscript revisions reveal about Dickens's working methods. In *The Annotated Christmas Carol* (**2340**), published in 1976, Michael P. Hearn comments on the writing and publication of the novel and includes textual commentary in his marginal notes. The manuscript of *The Chimes*, Dickens's second Christmas Book, is in the Forster Collection, Victoria and Albert Museum, with "proof copies" in the Forster Collection and in the Dexter Collection in the British Library, as noted in Ruth F. Glancy's bibliography of *Dickens's Christmas Books, Christmas Stories, and Other Short Fiction* (**98**), pp. 144-45. Michael Slater has done the principal textual work on this novel—see his "Dickens (and Forster) at Work on *The Chimes*" (**2354**), published in 1966, based on his 1965 doctoral dissertation, "*The Chimes*: Its Materials, Making, and Public Reception" (**2353**), and see appendices in his edition of *The Christmas Books* (**2352**), published in 1971, which include six passages of political satire that Dickens deleted in the manuscript at John Forster's suggestion. The manuscript of *The Cricket on the Hearth*, Dickens's third Christmas Book, is in the Pierpont Morgan Library, and a facsimile reproduction of it and two leaves on which Dickens tried out titles and names of characters was published in 1981, along with a brief note on the manuscript by Verlyn Klinkenborg (**2345**) and a more elaborate introduction by Andrew Sanders (**2350**), commenting on the origin, writing, publication, and reception of the work. Glancy also describes the manuscript (**98**), p. 194. The manuscript of the fourth Christmas Book, *The Battle of Life*, is likewise in the Pierpont Morgan Library—see Glancy (**98**), p. 240. The only important textual study to date of this work is Glancy's "The Shaping of *The Battle of Life*: Dickens' Manuscript Revisions" (**2339**), published in 1988, which compares the manuscript with the first edition to reveal what changes Dickens made in the non-extant proofs. The manuscript of *The Haunted Man, and the Ghost's Bargain*, the last Christmas Book, is in the Carl H. Pforzheimer Library, New York, as Glancy (**98**), pp. 266-67, indicates, and, again, Glancy has done the only important textual work on the novel. Her "Dickens at Work on *The Haunted Man*" (**2338**), published in 1986, is a fascinating study of Dickens's planning and writing of the work, based on his letters, the three pages of notes he made for the story, and the manuscript itself. Also see Glancy's sections in her bibliography (**98**) on "Commentary on the Manuscript, Publication, Textual Matters, Illustrations" for each of the five Christmas Books, pp. 7-9, 146-49, 195-97, 240-42, 267-68.

Dombey and Son

As Leon Litvack notes in his bibliography of the novel (**106**), pp. 7-10, this is "the first of Dickens's novels for which a detailed series of preparatory notes survive." There is also a complete manuscript and "various portions of four sets of proof" for the novel. All of these are in the Forster Collection, Victoria and Albert Museum. Also see Litvack's section on "Scholarship Concerning Composition and Publication," pp. 13-22, for a number of textual studies. The principal post-1957 research on *Dombey and Son* is that of Paul D. Herring, in his "The Number Plans for *Dombey and Son*: Some Further Observations" (**2374**), published in 1970. Herring's essay is intended as a supplement to the chapter on *Dombey and Son* in Butt and Tillotson, but it is also valuable because Herring prints for the first time a full transcription of the number plans, with interspersed commentary on how Dickens used them in crafting his novel. The plans are not as structured as later number plans, Herring indicates, but they show Dickens's "growing awareness of the necessity for skillful craftsmanship in the planning and composition of his novels." In "New Readings in *Dombey and Son*" (**2377**), published in 1968, Kathleen Tillotson examines in detail Dickens's revisions in the manuscript and proofs of one installment of the novel. Alan Horsman, in the Clarendon Edition of the novel (**2376**), published in 1974, provides further commentary on the writing and design of the novel, describes the manuscript and the page proofs, and examines textual differences in the various editions published during Dickens's lifetime.

David Copperfield

The manuscript, number plans, pages of titles Dickens considered, galley proofs for the first three numbers, and page proofs for the rest are extant in the Forster Collection, Victoria and Albert Museum, as Richard Dunn points out in his bibliography of *David Copperfield* (**103**). Also see his section on "Commentary on the Text," pp. 6-13. The number plans are reproduced in full in Butt and Tillotson. Philip Gaskell, in his "The Textual History of *David Copperfield*" (**2365**), published in 1972, examines at Dickens's writing, proofreading, and publishing of the novel through the six editions published in his lifetime, a process he repeats in his "Dickens, *David Copperfield*, 1850" (**2364**) in 1978. Nina Burgis does the same in the Clarendon Edition (**2359**) and the World's Classics Edition (**2358**) of the novel, published in 1981 and 1983, respectively, as does Jerome H. Buckley in the Norton Critical Edition (**2357**), published in 1990. In "'Let Me Pause Once More': Dickens' Manuscript Revisions in the Retrospective Chapters of *David Copperfield*" (**2356**), published in 1998, Joel J. Brattin investigates the manuscript revisions in the four chapters in which David "looks back over significant phases of his life." Also see George Ford's Riverside Edition of the novel (**2363**), published in 1958, for passages Dickens cancelled in the monthly proof sheets.

Bleak House

In his *Oxford Reader's Companion to Dickens* (**2309**), p. 48, Paul Schlicke notes that the "manuscript, trial titles, and corrected proofs" are in the Forster Collection, Victoria and Albert Museum, but so are the complete number plans. Harvey P. Sucksmith printed the first transcription of the number plans for *Bleak House* in his "Dickens at Work on *Bleak House*: A Critical Examination of His Memoranda and Number Plans" (**2332**) in 1965. Sucksmith was particularly interested in showing how Dickens used them in planning and writing his novel to create pathos, "moral sympathy," and irony in the novel, a theme he was to take up again in his *The Narrative Art of Charles Dickens* (**2315**), published in 1970. In "Dickens at Work on Manuscript and Proof: 'Bleak House' and 'Little Dorrit'" (**2333**), published in 1976, J. L. Watson studies the manuscript, number plans, and page proofs of *Bleak House* and *Little Dorrit* to show Dickens's strong "sense of artistic control." The Norton Critical Edition of the novel, edited by George H. Ford and Sylvère Monod (**2327**) and published in 1977, recorded a number of the textual variations from the manuscript to the 1868 edition, as well as reprinting the number plans and the various titles Dickens wrote down for the novel. These will also be found in Duane DeVries's Crowell Critical Library Edition of the novel (**2324**), published in 1971. An interesting article by Sylvère Monod, "'When the Battle's Lost and Won . . . ': Dickens *v.* the Compositors of *Bleak House*" (**2329**), published in 1973, concerns Dickens's corrections in proof of over 700 errors made by at least forty different compositors who set the novel into type (and Dickens missed 159 other errors). Monod also discusses errors made in later editions of the novel.

Hard Times

In her bibliography of *Hard Times* (**110**), p. 6, Sylvia Manning indicates that the manuscript, number plans, and sets of proofs are in the Forster Collection, Victoria and Albert Museum. Also see the section on "Commentary on the Text," pp. 7-9. Ford and Monod also produced the Norton Critical Edition of *Hard Times* in 1966 (**2411**), with textual notes, and in it transcribed for the first time the complete number plans for the novel. In a 1968 essay in the *Dickensian*, "Dickens at Work on the Text of *Hard Times*" (**2412**), Monod reflects on his work with the text of the novel for the Norton Edition.

Little Dorrit

In his *Oxford Reader's Companion to Dickens* (**2309**), p. 336, Paul Schlicke points out that the number plans, manuscript, and most of the corrected proofs are in the Forster Collection, Victoria and Albert Museum, while other proofs are in the Dexter Collection of the British Library. Paul D. Herring printed the first transcription of the number plans in 1966 in his "Dickens' Monthly Number Plans for *Little Dorrit*" (**2418**) and also commented on how Dickens used the month by month plans to develop and keep track of the "interlocking plots" and the numerous characters he needed for his portrayal of society as a world of imprisonment. In the Clarendon Edition of the novel (**2420**), Harvey P. Sucksmith provides considerable information about textual variants between manuscript and the 1868 edition of the novel. Stephen Wall and Helen Small in the Penguin Classics Edition (**2421**), published in 1998, and Angus Easson in the Everyman Dickens Edition (**2417**), published in 1999, comment on textual matters, and Wall and Small include a transcription of the number plans as well. Also see J. L. Watson under *Bleak House*, above.

A Tale of Two Cities

There are no number plans or proofs for this novel. The manuscript is in the Forster Collection, Victoria and Albert Museum, as Ruth Glancy notes in her bibliography of the novel (**138**), p. 7. Also see her section "Commentary on the Manuscript, Publication, Textual Matters, Illustrations," pp. 7-11. David Tucker's "Dickens at Work on the MS of *A Tale of Two Cities*" (**2509**), published in 1979, is the only major commentary on textual matters for this novel. He examines three passages that Dickens cancelled in manuscript by pasting slips of paper over them. The revisions, Tucker believes, were "a considerable improvement" over the original drafts and are evidence that Dickens "took considerable pains" with the novel.

Great Expectations

The manuscript, working notes, and other memoranda are in the Wisbech and Fenland Museum in Cambridgeshire, George J. Worth notes in his bibliography of *Great Expectations* (**109**), pp. 4-6, while galley proofs for chapters 1-4 and 51-58 are in the Forster Collection, Victoria and Albert Museum, and for the entire novel in the Pierpont Morgan Library, New York. Also see the "Commentary on the Text" section of Worth's bibliography, pp. 6-15. A considerable amount of textual work has been done on this novel since 1965, much of it centering on Dickens's original ending and later, happier variations on it. See the ninety-three entries in Worth's index under "Conclusion" for commentary on the ending of the novel up to 1986. There have been more studies since. The working notes, two pages of "Names" and two of "General Mems," were first printed by John Butt in "Dickens at Work" (**2286**) and "Dickens's Plan for the Conclusion of *Great Expectations*" (**2378**) in the late 1940s. Much of the textual commentary has come from Edgar Rosenberg, beginning with his "A Preface to *Great Expectations*: The Pale Usher Dusts His Lexicons" (**2402**), published in 1972, and concluding with his recent and long anticipated Norton Critical Edition of *Great Expectations* (**2401**), published in 1999. A substantial portion of the "Backgrounds" and "Contexts" sections of this annotated edition is the culmination of his textual studies of the novel, an impressive compilation of material, and supersedes his previous publications as well as those of other scholars, though Margaret Cardwell's textual work in the Clarendon Edition (**2381**) and the World's Classics Edition (**2380**), published in 1993 and 1994, respectively, is also valuable, as are the appendices in Angus Calder's Penguin English Library Edition of the novel (**2379**), published in 1965.

Our Mutual Friend

As Joel J. Brattin and Bert G. Hornback indicate in their bibliography of *Our Mutual Friend* (**120**), pp. 6-7, the manuscript and number plans of the novel are in the Pierpont Morgan Library, and the page proofs are in the Berg Collection, New York Public Library. Also see the section on "Commentary on the Text" in the Brattin-Hornback bibliography, pp. 22-28. As noted above, Ernest Boll published the transcription of the number plans in 1944 (**2476**). Since then, the principal textual studies have been by F. X. Shea and Brattin. Shea began his work on the novel in his 1961 doctoral dissertation, "The Text of *Our Mutual Friend*: A Study of the Variations between the Copy Text and the First Printed Edition" (**2490**), and followed it with "No Change of Intention in *Our Mutual Friend*" (**2489**), published in 1967, on what the notes and manuscript reveal about Dickens's characterization of Mr. Boffin, and with "Mr. Venus Observed: The Plot Change in *Our Mutual Friend*" (**2488**) in 1968. In "Dickens' Creation of Bradley Headstone" (**2477**), published in 1985, Brattin examines what the number plans and the manuscript revisions reveal about Dickens's gradual development of the character Bradley Headstone. In "'I Will Not Have My Words Misconstrued': The Text of *Our Mutual Friend*" (**2478**), published in 1998, Brattin analyzes the different kinds of variants he has found between the first edition (1864-65) and the Charles Dickens Edition (1868) of the novel, a total of 2,203 "corrections, alterations, and mistakes." He concludes, however, that probably most of these changes were made by someone other than Dickens and are, therefore, not particularly significant. Also see Brattin's Everyman Dickens Edition of the novel (**2479**), published in 2000, for a further study of the textual variants and Dickens's use of his Book of Memoranda (**2530**) and the number plans in constructing the novel.

The Mystery of Edwin Drood

As Don R. Cox notes in his bibliography of the novel (**115**), pp. 7-10, the manuscript (with one page missing), number plans, list of projected titles, the "Sapsea Fragment," and the proofs for part 5 of *Edwin Drood* are in the Forster Collection, Victoria and Albert Museum. A complete set of corrected proofs, with some additional pages of proofs, is in the Gimbel Collection, Yale University Library, and a set of proofs for the third monthly number (chapters 10-12) is in the Houghton Library, Harvard University. Also see the section on "Textual Issues, Illustrations, Editing Problems," pp. 13-42, in Cox's bibliography. W. Robertson Nicoll, as mentioned above, printed a transcription of the number plans in his *The Problem of "Edwin Drood,"* published in 1912 (**2448**), and *Drood* scholars have continued over the years since to use the number plans, manuscript, and proofs, and whatever else they could find, including Dickens's letters and entries in his Memoranda Book (**2530**), to speculate about how Dickens intended to end the novel.

Butt and Tillotson wisely did not attempt to do anything with the novel in their *Dickens at Work*, but since the 1950s other scholars have. Felix Aylmer, in *The Drood Case* (**2428**), published in 1964, reprints the number plans and examines them, the manuscript, the monthly cover, and the illustrations in once again confronting the "Mystery" in the work. In "The *Drood* Remains" (**2436**), published in 1966, Arthur J. Cox studies changes Dickens made in the manuscript to show problems he had with writing to length. In the introduction (**2434**) to the Clarendon Edition of the novel, published in 1972, Margaret Cardwell compares the manuscript with the published version and describes the manuscripts and the proofs and records textual variants in footnotes to the text. She also uses some of this material in the World's Classics edition of the novel (**2433**), published in 1982. Arthur J. Cox covers roughly the same ground in two editions he edited, the Penguin English Library Edition (**2437**) in 1974, and the Folio Society Edition (**2438**) in 1982, as does Steven Connor in the new Everyman Library Edition (**2435**), published in 1996. William M. Burgan, in "The Refinement of Contrast: Manuscript Revision in *Edwin Drood*" (**2430**), published in 1977, studies Dickens's revisions in the manuscript of the novel. They show, he asserts, that Dickens was primarily "engaged in augmenting rather than curbing his initial ideas." In "*Edwin Drood* and the Mystery of Apartness" (**2429**), published in 1984, John Beer uses Dickens's notes and textual revisions in examining where critics from John Forster on thought Dickens meant to go with the plot of the novel. Don R. Cox's "The *Every Saturday* Page Proofs for *The Mystery of Edwin Drood*" (**2439**), published in 1994, is an important supplement to Cardwell's introduction to the Clarendon Edition. Cox describes and gives the provenance of a previously unnoted, if incomplete, set of page proofs in the Harvard University Library, that Dickens sent to Boston as advance sheets for the serialization of the novel in *Every Saturday*. The proofs, Cox concludes, "verify some of the changes we know took place between the first version" of the text and the final printed version.

Shorter Fiction, Nonfiction, Theatrical and Poetical Works, the Book of Memoranda

Ruth Glancy's bibliography of *Dickens's Christmas Books, Christmas Stories, and Other Short Fiction* (**98**) is useful in locating manuscripts of Dickens's Christmas stories and the other shorter fiction and identifying what few textual studies of these have been published. Likewise, Michael Slater, in the four volumes he edited (the last with John Drew) in the Dent Uniform Edition of Dickens's Journalism (**2506, 2521-23**), published 1994-2000, locates existing manuscripts and occasionally notes manuscript revisions and textual variations, as does Harry Stone in his two-volume *Charles Dickens's Uncollected Writings from* **Household Words**, *1850-1859* (**449**). Robert Hanna will also do this in his forthcoming bibliography of Dickens's nonfictional, theatrical, and poetical writings (**12**). However, not a great deal of textual scholarship has been devoted to individual minor works. Richard F. Batterson has done a thorough study of "The Manuscript and Text of Dickens's 'George Silverman's Explanation'" (**2336**), published in 1979. David Paroissien compared the text of "Travelling Letters, Written on the Road" with the first edition of *Pictures from Italy* in his 1968 doctoral dissertation (**2519**), in an article obviously based on his dissertation, "Dickens's 'Pictures from Italy': Stages of the Work's Development and Dickens's Methods of Composition" (**2520**), published in 1971, and in "A Note on the Text," in his 1973 edition of *Pictures from Italy* (**434**). Walter E. Smith also itemizes textual variants, in side by side columns, between the *Daily News* pieces and the first bound edition in Part Two of his *Charles Dickens in the Original Cloth* (**46**), published in 1983. Also see Kate Flint's Penguin Classics Edition of the work (**1124**), published in 1998.

In their Penguin English Library Edition of *American Notes* (**2524**), published in 1972, John S. Whitley and Arnold Goldman include textual notes identifying changes that Dickens made in the Cheap Edition, published in 1850, and the Charles Dickens Edition of the work, published in 1868—as does Patricia Ingham in her Penguin Classics Edition of the work (**2515**), published in 2000. Finally, though technically not a published work of Dickens, the Book of Memoranda that Dickens kept between 1855 and sometime in the 1860s was reproduced in photographic facsimile, accompanied by a printed transcription, by Fred Kaplan in 1981 (**2530**). In his introduction, Kaplan describes the notebook, gives its provenance, and lists the previous publication of excerpts from the manuscript. He also includes nearly thirty pages of elaborate editorial notes and comments on how Dickens used memoranda entries in his writings. Kathryn Chittick, in "The Meaning of a Literary Idea: Dickens's Memoranda Notebook" (**2526**), published in 1982, intelligently explores Dickens's creative use of the memoranda notes in writing his later works.

It has been a long journey to this point. Obviously a great deal of important scholarly work has been done for both the researcher and the collector in compiling bibliographies of Dickens's works, translations of them, and every variety of adaptation of them. Bibliographical studies are more than numerous, and bibliographies of studies of Dickens's works fill library shelves, and are sometimes quarterly, or semiannually, and always yearly updated by an impressive list of serial bibliographies. Equally useful work has been done in recording union, national, and public and private library collections of Dickens's works and Dickensiana, as well as in cataloguing and reporting on important exhibitions. Numerous auction and booksellers' catalogues document major and minor private collections (unfortunately usually after the demise of the collector) and often contain transcriptions of Dickens letters, or at least portions of them, that even the alert editors of the *Pilgrim Letters* have occasionally not managed to locate. Textual studies of Dickens's number plans and other memoranda, manuscripts, and page proofs are verifying his craftsmanship and his artistry and asserting the importance of this approach to an understanding of his creativity. Surely there is not much more to be done.

I suppose, however, that nothing is ever sufficiently complete for the scholar/researcher. K. J. Fielding, quoted at the beginning of this introduction, had it both right and wrong, at least where bibliographical and textual scholarship is concerned. Unfortunately bibliographical work is inevitably Shandean, out of date from the moment it is published, and even then at least a year or two behind. Still, it is generally reliable in the recording of data, if usually annoyingly incomplete, but, in the mass, it is cumulative and, where necessary, corrective. Many of the individual Dickens bibliographies, it is true, are, in themselves, quite outdated by now. This is particularly true of bibliographies of translations of Dickens's works—because these were often one-time events that have not been updated. From a collector's or bookseller's point of view, some of the basic bibliographical work remains to be done on the minor works and that on the major works needs to be reexamined, if not much at this point corrected or updated. Bibliographers were somewhat slow to understand the complexities of Victorian mass publication and of the relationship of Dickens's serialization of his works to their volume publications, but these matters are now pretty much understood, though the question of what constitutes a true first edition or the best copy-text remains a matter of perennial debate. Bibliographies of Dickens studies, on the other hand, have never been as complete, as detailed, and as informative as Calhoun and Heaney desired, even bibliographies published after their cautionary "Dickensiana in the Rough" appeared more than half a century ago. I hope they would have liked this present volume and the others in the Garland Dickens Bibliographies and the Dickens Bibliographies currently being published by AMS Press, two series designed to comprise, together, the most comprehensive, and annotated, bibliography of Dickens's works and Dickens studies ever attempted.

While a number of important textual studies have been published, spurred on by the outstanding work of John Butt and Kathleen Tillotson, much remains to be investigated—and used in creative, insightful studies of the relationships between text, creativity, inspiration, and genius. Now, at least, a number of primary documents are available for significant textual and critical work. The editors of the *Pilgrim Letters* have just completed the twelve volumes of known Dickens letters, and plans are in place for publishing in the *Dickensian* new letters that turn up. Michael Slater has recently published (1994-2000) the four volumes in the Dent Uniform Edition of Dickens's Journalism, as noted above, the last volume with John Drew. The Clarendon Edition of Dickens's works is in progress, providing more authoritative texts for the scholar to use. The Dickens Companion series, also in progress, is supplementing the strictly textual notes in the Clarendon volumes with explanatory as well as additional textual notes. The manuscripts themselves, at least of the novels, have been available on microfilm for a number of years.

A new century, a new millennium for that matter, has begun. In numerous books and journal articles, scholars have been examining the bibliographical and textual evidence—manuscripts, number plans and other memoranda, page proofs, letters, editions, exhibition and auction and booksellers' catalogues, Dickensiana, and ephemera that make up Dickens's personal, public, and creative lives and the scholarly survey of them. The computer and the Internet have begun to revolutionize publishing and scholarship, and are opening up new approaches to bibliographical and textual scholarship. The 200th anniversary of Dickens's birth is rapidly approaching. The museum and library directors are undoubtedly beginning to plan their 2012 exhibitions. These exhibitions will take advantage of all this scholarly activity and show us a Dickens more creative, more troubled, something of a victim of the intense perusal of his life and writings that has been going on, but a Dickens whose reputation remains not only intact but considerably more enhanced than earlier.

It now remains for young Dickens scholars and critics, and perhaps even some older ones, to use this newly accumulated body of information and these new electronic tools to gain and disseminate a better understanding of Dickens's artistry and genius for a new age.

Duane DeVries
September 2003

GENERAL STUDIES
OF CHARLES DICKENS AND HIS WRITINGS
AND COLLECTED EDITIONS
OF HIS WORKS
An Annotated Bibliography

VOLUME ONE

Bibliographies,
Catalogues, Collections, and
Bibliographical and Textual Studies

PART ONE: THE DICKENS CANON, EDITIONS, ATTRIBUTIONS

1A. BIBLIOGRAPHIES OF DICKENS'S WORKS

Note: A number of entries in this section also contain secondary studies. They have been placed here because a significant portion of each work is concerned with editions of Dickens's works. A number of entries in sections 4A and 5A, particularly library and union catalogues and some exhibition catalogues, as well as some sale catalogues in section 6A of comprehensive Dickens collections, might also have been placed here; these should be consulted for manuscripts and editions of Dickens's works. Also see "Charles Dickens's Manuscripts" (2292) and **Bibliographies of Dickens's works** in part 2 of the subject index for other entries.

1. Anderson, John P "Bibliography." In *Life of Charles Dickens.* By Frank T. Marzials. Great Writers series. London: Walter Scott, 1887; reprinted Folcroft, PA: Folcroft Library Editions, 1973, pp. i-xxxiii.

Includes collected editions and selections, single works (the volume, not the parts, editions), biographical and critical studies (including magazine and newspaper articles), dramatizations of Dickens's works by others, musical selections, parodies, and poetical tributes.

2. Ba[ruch], G[ertrud], W[alter] Kl[uge], and J[erôme] v[on] Ge[bsattel]. "Charles Dickens." In *Kindlers neues Literatur Lexikon.* Ed. Walter Jens. 20 vols. München, Ger.: Kindler, 1988-92, IV, 634-55.

Provides brief commentary in German on the novels and *Sketches by Boz* in alphabetical order, with a list of general book-length studies (principally in English) at the beginning (pp. 634-35) and, at the end of commentary on each individual work, lists of important English editions, translations into German, and studies (books and articles), principally in English, of the work.

3. Block, Andrew. "Dickens, Charles." In his *The English Novel, 1740-1850: A Catalogue Including Prose Romances, Short Stories, and Translations of Foreign Fiction.* London: Grafton, 1939, pp. 61-62; 2nd ed., London: Dawsons of Pall Mall, 1961; Dobbs Ferry, NY: Oceana Publications, 1962, pp. 59-60.

Lists and provides basic publication information about Dickens's novels through *David Copperfield*, as well as about the Christmas Books, *Sketches by Boz*, and *The Pic Nic Papers*.

4. Bloom, Harold. "Books by Charles Dickens." In *Charles Dickens's **A Tale of Two Cities***: *Bloom's Notes*. Ed. Harold Bloom. A Contemporary Literary Views Book. Broomall, PA: Chelsea House, 1996; reprinted as *Bloom's Reviews, Comprehensive Research and Study Guides: Charles Dickens's **A Tale of Two Cities***. Ed. Harold Bloom. Broomall, PA: Chelsea House, 1996, pp. 66-70; also reprinted in *Charles Dickens's **Great Expectations***: *Bloom's Notes*. Ed. Harold Bloom (**1086**), pp. 69-73.

A basic list of Dickens's works in volume form (titles, dates, and numbers of volumes only). The list includes some collected works, as well as collections of letters, speeches, and minor writings.

5. Bracher, Peter S. "A Check List of Dickens' Works Published by Harper & Brothers, 1842-70." In his "Harper & Brothers: Publishers of Dickens" (**174**), pp. 332-35.

Includes separate publication of Dickens's novels in monthly parts and volume form by Harper & Brothers, as well as the serialization of his novels and the reprinting of his pieces from *Household Words* and *All the Year Round* in *Harper's New Illustrated Monthly Magazine* and *Harper's Weekly*.

6. B[rown], G[eorge] A. "Dickens." In *The Cambridge History of English Literature*. Ed. A[dolphus] W. Ward and A[lfred] R. Waller. Vol. 13. *The Nineteenth Century, II*. Cambridge, Eng.: Cambridge University Press, 1916, 1922 (new impression), etc., pp. 530-44.

A selected list of 1) Dickens's manuscripts (those in the Victoria and Albert and the British Museums, not elsewhere), bibliographies, and biographies; 2) editions of Dickens's collected works; 3) editions of the individual novels and other works, with information about serial publication and associated Dickensiana; 4) collections of illustrations to the novels; and 5) critical and special studies (mainly books) to 1912. This bibliography, by then considerably outdated, was excluded from the Cheap Edition of *Cambridge History of English Literature* (1932), which is "text only," and all later reprints.

7. "Charles Dickens: A Select Bibliography." In *Charles Dickens*. By K[enneth] J. Fielding. Writers and Their Work, 37. London: Published for the British Council and the National Book League by Longmans, Green, 1953, pp. 39-47 (to 1952); revised 1960, 1963, 1969; reprinted with additions to the bibliography, 1966 and later (1971?), pp. 39-51 (to 1970); also in *Dickens: The Early Novels*. By Trevor Blount. Writers and Their Work, 204. Lon-

don: Longmans, Green, 1968, pp. 41-52 (through 1967), and in *Dickens: The Later Novels*. By Barbara Hardy. Writers and Their Work, 205. London: Published for the British Council and the National Book League by Longmans, Green, 1968, pp. 41-52 (through 1967).

A peripatetic short-title list of Dickens's individual works and principal collected editions and a selective listing of bibliographies and biographical and general critical studies. This bibliography is not identical to Handley's (**22**).

8. C[ollins], P[hilip] A. W., comp. "Charles Dickens, 1812-70." In *The New Cambridge Bibliography of English Literature*. Vol. 3: *1800-1900*. Ed. George Watson. Cambridge, Eng.: Cambridge University Press, 1969, cols. 779-850; reprinted separately as *A Dickens Bibliography*. By Philip Collins. [London]: Dickens Fellowship, by arrangement with the Cambridge University Press, 1970, cols. 779-850.

A considerable expansion and updating of the Dickens bibliography in the *Cambridge Bibliography of English Literature*–see Darton (**11**)–with occasional omissions. Collins includes journal articles and book-length studies, making this volume considerably more useful than its predecessor. It is unfortunately marred by a number of errors occasioned by the haste with which the entire volume was prepared. The "Introduction" section to the period, cols. 1-158, and the section on "The Novel: General Works," cols. 657-66, by other compilers, are also valuable. See the *Index* to *The New Cambridge Bibliography of English Literature*, vol. 5, ed. J. D. Pickles (Cambridge, Eng.: Cambridge University Press, 1977), p. 133, for additional references to Dickens and to Charles Dickens, the Younger, his eldest son. For the third edition, see Paul Schlicke (**41**).

9. Collins, Philip. "Dickens, Charles (John Huffam)." In *Reference Guide to Short Fiction*. Ed. Noelle Watson. St. James Reference Guides. Detroit: St. James Press, 1994, pp. 156-59.

Includes a bibliography of Dickens's works (emphasizing the shorter fiction) and of book-length bibliographical and critical studies.

10. Cook, James. *Bibliography of the Writings of Charles Dickens, with Many Curious and Interesting Particulars Relating to His Works*. London: Frank Kerslake; Paisley, Scotland: J. and J. Cook, 1879. 88 pp.

Not always correct on details but gives considerable information about the publication of Dickens's major and minor works, collected editions published through 1878, and periodicals. Cook also lists and comments on eight plagiarisms and continuations, fourteen portraits and other paintings as well as sets of extra illustrations, biographies, and a few additional works about Dickens. He gives then recent prices of original editions of Dickens's works, locates some of Dickens's manuscripts, comments on the sale of Dickens's library and other matters, and reprints several poetical addresses to Dickens. His purpose, he announces, is "to give the Bibliophilist or Collector a thorough knowledge of the peculiarities of the several editions hitherto published, or in course of publication." An "Addenda," pp. 81-88, adds a number of items to the various sections of the bibliography, as well as several studies of Dickens, 1856-76, and four more portraits.

Reviews: *Academy*, 16 (1879), 226 ("likely to prove a standard of reference for its special topic"); *Notes and Queries*, 5th ser, 12 (1879), 460 (useful, but needs index).

11. D[arton], F. J. H., comp. "Charles Dickens (1812-1870)." In *The Cambridge Bibliography of English Literature*. Vol. 3: *1800-1900*. Ed. F. W. Bateson. Cambridge, Eng.: Cambridge University Press, 1940, pp. 435-55.

Developed out of a need to supply "a modern equivalent" of the individual author bibliographies placed at the ends of chapters in *The Cambridge History of English Literature*–see Brown (**6**)–as F. W. Bateson, the general editor of *The Cambridge Bibliography of English Literature* points out in his preface to volume 1. This five-volume bibliography (including Supplement) lists in more or less chronological order the works of English authors and a selection of secondary studies. In the section on Dickens, Darton includes publications through 1938, organized under the headings 1) Bibliographies and Catalogues, 2) Collected Works, 3) The Novels, 4) Christmas Books and Christmas Numbers, 5) Minor Works and Reprinted Papers, 6) Plays and Poems, 7) Works Associated with or in Part by Dickens, 8) Letters and Speeches, and 9) Biography and Criticism. The sections on Dickens's works are subdivided not only into the individual works but further into editions and studies and sometimes additional categories. Articles by Dickens not reprinted are excluded. The list of secondary works is highly selective and, thus, far less useful than the listings of primary works. The "Introduction" section to the period (pp. 3-155) and the section on "Prose Fiction: Bibliographies, Histories and Critical Studies" (pp. 364-66), by other compilers, are also useful. The brief Dickens entry in the *Concise Cambridge Bibliography of English Literature, 600-1950*, ed. George Watson (Cambridge: Cambridge University Press, 1958; 2nd ed., 1965), pp. 170-72, is not worth the time of a serious Dickens student. Also see volume 4 (*Index*), of *The Cambridge Bibliography of English Literature*, p. 72, for other Dickens items, as well as Fielding (**18**), Collins (**8**), Watson (**59**), and Schlicke (**41**).

12. DeVries, Duane, gen. ed. *The Dickens Bibliographies*. New York: AMS Press, 1998- .

A continuation of the Garland Dickens Bibliographies (**13**). The first volume in this new series, Don R. Cox's *Charles Dickens's **The Mystery of Edwin Drood**: An Annotated Bibliography* (**115**), was published in 1998, and the second,

Leon Litvack's *Charles Dickens's **Dombey and Son**: An Annotated Bibliography* (**106**), in 2000. The next volume scheduled is the one you now hold in your hands, with volumes to follow on biographies, letters, and biographical studies (Duane DeVries), critical studies (Duane DeVries), special studies and collected editions of Dickens's works (Duane DeVries), *Nicholas Nickleby* (Paul Schlicke), *Bleak House* (Angus Easson), *Little Dorrit* (Tony Williams), and the nonfictional, theatrical, and poetical writings (Robert C. Hanna), the last of which will be published in 2004. Over the next few years AMS Press is also planning to issue reprints of the volumes in the Garland Dickens Bibliographies, along with updates, the latter of which will first appear in issues of the *Dickens Studies Annual* and then, perhaps, as separate publications. The update of Richard J. Dunn's bibliography of *David Copperfield* (**103**) by Dunn and Ann M. Tandy appeared in volume 28 of *Dickens Studies Annual* and has since been published separately (**104**). Robert Heaman's update of the volume on *Our Mutual Friend* (**120**) originally compiled by Joel J. Brattin and Bert G. Hornback will be published in volume 33 of *Dickens Studies Annual* in 2003. This will be followed in succeeding years by David Paroissien's update of his *Oliver Twist* bibliography (**118**) and Ruth Glancy's update of her volume on the Christmas Books, Christmas Stories, and other short fiction (**98**).

13. DeVries, Duane, gen. ed. *The Garland Dickens Bibliographies.* 11 vols. New York and London: Garland Publishing, 1981-93.

A series of annotated Dickens bibliographies cut short before completion. As planned, each of the first fifteen volumes was to be devoted to an individual novel, another to the Christmas works and short stories, yet another to the nonfictional, theatrical, and poetical writings, and a final four to the general bibliographical, textual, biographical, critical, and special studies of Dickens. Together, the volumes were intended to comprise the fullest, most authoritative bibliography of works by and about Dickens in English ever compiled. Eleven were published: those on *Pickwick Papers*, by Elliot Engel (**125**); *Oliver Twist*, by David Paroissien (**118**); *The Old Curiosity Shop*, by Priscilla Schlicke and Paul Schlicke (**117**); *Barnaby Rudge*, by Thomas J. Rice (**93**); the Christmas Books, Christmas Stories, and other short fiction, by Ruth F. Glancy (**98**); *Martin Chuzzlewit*, by Robert E. Lougy (**113**); *David Copperfield*, by Richard J. Dunn (**103**); *Hard Times*, by Sylvia Manning (**110**); *A Tale of Two Cities*, by Ruth F. Glancy (**138**); *Great Expectations*, by George J. Worth (**109**); and *Our Mutual Friend*, by Joel J. Brattin and Bert G. Hornback (**120**). The series is being continued as *The Dickens Bibliographies*, published by AMS Press—see DeVries (**12**).

Review: J. K. Bracken (**1139**), pp. 73-74 (volumes in this series "offer the most comprehensive coverage of editions and criticisms of Dickens's individual works," with "descriptive and extensive" annotations, and "supersede all previous bibliographies of Dickens criticism").

14. Dibelius, Wilhelm. "Versuch einer Dickensbibliographie." In his *Charles Dickens*. Leipzig and Berlin: B. G. Teubner, 1916, pp. 479-504; 2nd ed., 1926, pp. 479-505.

A fairly extensive listing, updated in the second edition, of collected editions, miscellaneous works, letters and diaries, manuscripts, bibliographies, biographies, studies of Dickens's ancestors and family, and critical, biographical, and special studies of Dickens's works in general and of specific novels and other writings. These are largely works published in England and America, but included are some German and other foreign language studies.

15. "Dickens, Charles." In *Nineteenth Century Short Title Catalogue. Series II. Phase I. 1816-1870*. Vol. 12. Newcastle-upon-Tyne, Eng.: Avero, 1988, pp. 109-50.

Lists editions of Dickens's collected works, smaller collections, letters, speeches, single works, selections, translations, readings, dramatic and other adaptations, works edited, and doubtful and supposititious works published through 1870 in England, America, and Europe. There are also a two-item bibliographical appendix and a short general appendix of works concerning Dickens published through 1870. The items listed are extracted from the catalogues of the Bodleian Library, the British Library, the Harvard University Library, the Library of Congress, the Library of Trinity College Dublin, the National Library of Scotland, and the University Libraries of Cambridge and Newcastle (a letter code identifies which libraries contain which editions). Also see entries for Catherine Dickens, p. 109, and Charles Dickens, the Younger, p. 150. There is also a title index, volumes 44-53. For fuller details see Harner (**1147**), pp. 290-91. Harner also notes that this work is available on CD-ROM. A third series, to cover the years 1871-1919, is in progress. According to David McKitterick, in the *Times Literary Supplement*, 4 July 1997, p. 11, it is being published in fourteen "enhancements," on CD-ROM, the earliest of which look "distinctly provisional," in the "throes of creation."

16. Eckel, John C. *The First Editions of the Writings of Charles Dickens and Their Values: A Bibliography*. London: Chapman and Hall, 1913; reprinted Folcroft, PA: Folcroft Library Editions, 1973; Havertown, PA: R. West, 1976; Norwood, PA: Norwood Editions, 1976. xviii + 296 pp.; 2nd ed., revised and enlarged as *The First Editions of the Writings of Charles Dickens, Their Points and Values: A Bibliography*. New York: Maurice Inman; London: Maggs Brothers, 1932; reprinted New York: Haskell House, 1972. xvi + 272 pp.

Both editions of this major bibliographical work fully describe the first editions in parts and volume form of Dickens's works, and sometimes later editions, with detailed collations (particularly for *Pickwick Papers* in parts), and comment on variants, the illustrations, and other special circumstances of publication. Eckel includes chapters on "The Important Novels" (including, surprisingly, *Sketches by Boz*), "The Secondary Books" (including *Hard Times, A Christmas Carol,* and the other Christmas Books), "Books in Which Dickens Had Only a Limited Interest," "Plays," "Contributions to Newspapers and Periodicals," "Wrongly Ascribed Writings," "Miscellaneous and Unclassified," "Unusual and Costly Dickensiana," "Speeches," and, in the second edition, "Association Books" and "Collation of Back Wrappers." Both editions have fairly extensive indexes. There are some variations in the illustrations in the two editions (thirty-seven in the first, twenty-nine in the second). The revised edition considerably reduces the "Values" section, which deals with prices, adds a few minor works, modifies general descriptions and some details, and takes advantage of new scholarship, particularly in reference to *Pickwick Papers* and *A Christmas Carol.* For further evaluation of this bibliography, see the introduction to the present volume, pp. xxxvii–xxix. A "large paper" edition limited to 250 copies signed by Eckel was also issued in 1913.

For an updating, see "A New Dickens Bibliography" (**36**). For corrections, see Davis (**1400**), Dexter (**1401**), "Dickens Part-Issues" (**1402**), and Muir (**1420**).

The British Library's *Charles Dickens: The J. F. Dexter Collection* (**1436**) lists the page proofs of the 1913 edition of this work (Dex.295), with manuscript notes by John F. Dexter and insertions, including an undated manuscript letter to Arthur H. Cleaver from W. E. Cleaver, and press cuttings—also noted in *The British Library General Catalogue of Printed Books to 1975* (**1438**), vol. 91, p. 247.

The Berg Collection, New York Public Library, contains a number of holograph and typescript manuscripts and other material connected with the editions of this work: 1) the holograph manuscript of the first edition; 2) a typescript of the first edition with some manuscript additions and with editorial markings, used, it is noted, by the printer to set the work into type; 3) the holograph and typescript manuscript for the 1932 revised edition (a number of printed pages from the first edition are pasted in where no changes were to be made); 4) the uncorrected page proofs (labeled "For Indexing"), original signed contracts, letters from the publishers (most from B. W. Matz on both Chapman and Hall stationery and *The Dickensian* stationery) concerning the setting up and printing of the edition and providing bibliographical information to be included in the edition, corrected proof of Chapman and Hall's announcement of the edition, and financial returns, 1912-14, telling the story of the production and sales of the first edition of the bibliography; and 5) the galley proofs for the revised edition (a note indicates that these are the "First Corrected Proof Sheets and Directions for the Printer for the Revised Edition of the Dickens Biblio., 1932").

Reviews, 1913 edition: *Athenaeum,* 29 November 1913, p. 621 (invaluable for collectors, though not always phrased clearly); *Notes and Queries,* 11th ser, 8 (1913), 478-79 ("carefully prepared," "perfect"); *Spectator*, 111 (1913), 1087-88 ("some very slight defects" in a "compilation of great interest," with "fascinating" and useful illustrations).

Reviews, 1932 edition (and reprints): P. Brooks, *New York Times Book Review*, 2 October 1932, p. 20 (a "handsomer volume" than the first edition; a work of "solid merit"); E. Gleaves, *American Reference Books Annual, 1974* (5th ed., Littleton, CO: Libraries Unlimited, 1974), pp. 517-18 (surveys disparaging criticism of the revised edition—though sees some improvement in the revised over the first edition); A. de Suzannet, *Dickensian*, 29 (1932/33), 117-19 (congratulates Eckel on "several notable additions and improvements," but criticizes him for uncorrected errors from the first edition and other flaws, only a few of which Suzannet enumerates); *Times Literary Supplement*, 26 January 1933, p. 64 (comments on the additions to the revised edition, but finds the volume ultimately "disappointing" in its scholarship and writing, some examples of which are provided), and 2 February 1933, p. 80 (a letter from Walter Dexter seconding the reviewer's disappointment and pointing out other defects of the revision).

17. Edgar, Herman L., and R. W. G. Vail. "Early American Editions of the Works of Charles Dickens." *Bulletin of the New York Public Library*, 33 (1929), 302-19; reprinted in the two-part publication *Charles Dickens: His Life as Traced by His Works*. By Cortes W. Cavanaugh [and] *Early American Editions of the Works of Charles Dickens*. By Herman Edgar and R. W. G. Vail. New York: New York Public Library, 1929, pp. 14-31.

Edgar and Vail list American editions of Dickens's books, as well as articles and stories in journals, giving descriptions of the original covers and providing other standard bibliographical information regarding publication. But they list only items in an exhibition at the New York Public Library, 1 May-31 August 1929, from the collections of the Pierpont Morgan Library, C. W. Cavanaugh, Herman L. Edgar, Richard Gimbel, Dr. A. S. W. Rosenbach, and Dr. Howard Duffield, of Dickens's manuscripts, letters, published works, plays, playbills, relics, and other Dickensiana, or that are to be found in the New York Public Library though not included in the exhibition. Other items in the exhibition are discussed and listed in Cavanaugh's section of this two-part publication. As Edgar and Vail point out, their list needs to be supplemented by items in Wilkins (**61, 1930**), Grolier Club (**1802**), McCutcheon (**1903**), Daoust (**1905**), and Eckel (**16**). Illustrated.

18. F[ielding], K[enneth] J., comp. "Charles Dickens (1812-1870)." In *The Cambridge Bibliography of English Literature*. Vol. 5: *Supplement: A. D. 600-1900*. Ed. George Watson. Cambridge, Eng.: Cambridge University Press, 1957, pp. 623-30.

Updates Darton (**11**) to ca. 1954/55, listing a number of journal articles as well as book-length studies. See the "Introduction" section to the nineteenth century (pp. 519-47) and the section on nineteenth-century "Prose Fiction: Bibliographies, Histories, and Critical Studies" (pp. 614-15) by other compilers for additional useful studies related to Dickens. See also Collins (**8**), Watson (**59**), and Schlicke (**41**).

19. Forster, John. "Appendix. I. The Writings of Charles Dickens." In his *The Life of Charles Dickens*. 3 vols. London: Chapman & Hall, 1872-74 (actually published November 1871, November 1872, and December 1873), III, 505-15; slightly revised as "Appendix. The Writings of Charles Dickens, Published During the Period Comprised in This First Volume" and "Appendix. I. The Writings of Charles Dickens, Published During the Period Comprised in This Second Volume." In his revised *The Life of Charles Dickens*. 2 vols. Library Edition. London: Chapman & Hall, 1876, I, 525-28; II, 522-25.

Lists the major and minor writings of Dickens in chronological order (in editions through 1870), providing names of illustrators and publishers, dates of prefaces and of the publication of parts of the novels, and sometimes additional bibliographical information. The collected editions to 1870 are also included. The bibliography is only slightly expanded in the 1876 revision, the principal addition being the first edition of Forster's biography, with the note that the three volumes of the first edition were actually published in November 1871, November 1872, and December 1873, respectively, rather than, as their title pages indicate, in 1872, 1873, and 1874.

20. Geissendoerfer, J. Theodor. "Zweiter Teil." In his *Dickens' Einfluss auf Ungern-Sternberg, Hesslein, Stolle, Raabe und Ebner-Eschenbach*. Americana Germanica, 19. [Philadelphia]: University of Pennsylvania, 1915, pp. 28-51.

A bibliography of single and collected editions of Dickens's works published in English in Germany and translations of Dickens's works into German, along with a brief list of German critical studies.

21. Hammerton, J[ohn] A. "Bibliography." In his *The Dickens Companion: A Book of Anecdote and Reference*. Vol. 18 of the Charles Dickens Library. London: Educational Book Company, [1910], pp. 595-607.

A 1910 bibliography of Dickens's writings, arranged chronologically.

22. Handley, Graham, comp. "Selected Bibliography." To accompany Barbara Hardy's "Charles Dickens." In *British Writers*. Vol. 5: *Elizabeth Gaskell to Francis Thompson*. Ed. Ian Scott-Kilvert, under the Auspices of the British Council. New York: Scribner's, 1982, pp. 70-74; updated as "Charles Dickens: A Select Bibliography." In Barbara Hardy's *Charles Dickens: The Writer and His Work*. A *Writers and Their Work* Special. Windsor, Eng.: Profile Books, 1983, pp. 95-107.

A list of collected editions and editions of individual works; a more highly selective listing of bibliographies, biographies and biographical studies, and general critical studies; and a listing of one or two critical studies of each of the individual novels. Handley's bibliography is not identical to "Charles Dickens: A Select Bibliography" (**7**), above.

23. Hardwick, Michael, and Mollie Hardwick. "Chronology of Charles Dickens's Works." In their *The Charles Dickens Companion*. London: John Murray, 1965; New York: Holt, Rinehart and Winston, 1966; reprinted as a Dutton paperback, New York: E. P. Dutton, 1968; London: John Murray, 1969, pp. xi-xiii.

A brief listing of Dickens's works in chronological order, with basic publication information.

24. Hatton, Thomas, and Arthur H. Cleaver. *A Bibliography of the Periodical Works of Charles Dickens, Bibliographical, Analytical, and Statistical*. London: Chapman and Hall, 1933; reprinted New York: Haskell House, 1973; Cambridge, MA: Maurizio Martino, [1992]. xix + 384 pp.

A highly detailed collation of text, wrappers, illustrations, and advertisements of each number of the works Dickens issued in parts: *Pickwick Papers*, *Sketches by Boz* (1837 39), *Nicholas Nickleby*, *Master Humphrey's Clock* (including *The Old Curiosity Shop* and *Barnaby Rudge*), *Martin Chuzzlewit*, *Oliver Twist* (1846), *Dombey and Son*, *David Copperfield*, *Bleak House*, *Little Dorrit*, *A Tale of Two Cities* (1859), *Our Mutual Friend*, and *The Mystery of Edwin Drood*. In their introduction, Hatton and Cleaver point out that their work contains "every bibliographical detail known" to them about these thirteen works. Thirty-one illustrations. But there are some errors; for corrections and cautions, see Carter (**1393**), "Dickens Part-Issues" (**1402**), Haynes (**1409-10**), Miller and Suzannet (**1418**), and Strange (**1426**).

Reviews, 1933 edition: J. K. Bracken (**1139**), p. 74 ("the authoritative guide to the first appearance of Dickens's novels"); J. Carter, *Publisher's Weekly*, 125 (1934), 1303-06 ("definitive"); M. Sadleir, *Dickensian*, 30 (1933/34), 147-50 (commends the "general arrangement" of the work and comments on the difficulty of the task Hatton and Cleaver set themselves and the "admirable clarity" with which they fulfilled it; a "monumental work"); *Times Literary Supplement*, 22 March, 1934, p. 220 (finds that it compares favorably to Eckel's revised edition [**16**] for its "greater detail," its "greater clarity of expression," and its "more convincing arguments" and comments on a number of points made by Hatton and Cleaver), and 12 April 1934, p. 268 (a letter from A. de Suzannet, who likewise praises the bibliography but argues with the reviewer's belief that the inserted advertising slips in the parts issues of Dickens's works are not important in "determining priority of issue"; Suzannet also thinks Hatton and Cleaver do not give enough importance to "the various states of the illustrations" in determining priority of issue).

Review, 1973 reprint: *American Reference Books Annual*, 5 (1974), 519 (finds the reprint "a boon to Dickens collectors").

25. Heichen, Paul. "Bibliographie." In his *Charles Dickens, sein Leben und seine Werke*. Naumburg, Ger.: Verlag von Albin Schirmer, [1898], pp. 9-48.

A bibliography of Dickens's works and writings about his life and works, with all English titles translated into German. The bibliography includes selections, musical pieces, dramatizations, parodies, imitations, poetical appreciations, biographical and critical works, and articles in German magazines (only five items). The 723-page work itself is divided into biographical (pp. 49-302) and critical (pp. 303-590) sections, followed by an alphabetical list of the characters in Dickens's novels with brief descriptions (pp. 610-715).

26. Hollington, Michael. "Bibliography: Chronology of Dickens's Major Works." In *Charles Dickens: Critical Assessments.* Ed. Michael Hollington. 4 vols. Helm Information Critical Assessments of Writers in English. Mountfield, Eng.: Helm Information, 1995, I, 25-26.

A brief list of Dickens's works published in volume form. Also see Hollington (**990**).

27. Johnson, Charles P. *Hints to Collectors of Original Editions of the Works of Charles Dickens.* London: George Redway, 1885. 56 pp.

A descriptive bibliography and an early attempt to straighten out the publication history of Dickens's works for the benefit of those already beginning to collect first editions. Johnson states that he has examined several copies of all the works, with the exception of one minor work, collated them and noted variations. He also gives the market value of the works in 1885. In characterizing the editions, he provides all title-page information, descriptions of original bindings of the first and some later volume editions of the works, and some details about the parts issues. He also includes some "Dickensiana," a list of thirty-six plays based on Dickens's novels, and a list of seventy-three woodcuts, etchings, lithographs, and engravings of portraits of Dickens.

28. Johnson, E. D. H. "Chronology of Novels" and "Bibliographical Note." In his *Charles Dickens: An Introduction to His Novels.* New York: Random House, 1969, pp. 167-68, 169-71.

The "chronology" gives the dates for the serial publication of individual Dickens novels (though not noting missed issues). The bibliographical note is a brief, evaluative survey of what are, in Johnson's opinion, the best collected editions of Dickens's works, the best editions of a few of the individual novels, the most important collections of letters and speeches, the two best biographies, and the fifteen best specialized and critical studies.

29. Kitton, Frederic G. *The Novels of Charles Dickens: A Bibliography and Sketch.* The Book-Lover's Library. London: Elliot Stock, 1897; reprinted New York: AMS Press, 1975. ix + 245 pp.

Not technically a bibliography. Kitton devotes separate chapters to each of the novels (except for *Hard Times*), providing useful information about the writing and publication of each, including its illustrators, publishing agreements, royalties, price, number of copies sold, and reception by the critics. He also provides information useful to the collector of first and rare editions and information about the manuscripts. Altogether the work provides a detailed history of Dickens's writing and publication of his works, to be supplemented and corrected, of course, by later studies—see Patten's *Charles Dickens and His Publishers* (**224**), for example—but for its time it is an amazing collection of information, even though Kitton modestly notes in the preface that much, though not all, of the information is from *Forster* and the *Hogarth-Dickens Letters*.

Reviews: *Academy*, 51 (12 June 1897), Fiction Supplement, p. 14 ("a pleasant compilation of the facts concerning the writing, publication, and characters of Charles Dickens's novels"); P. Aronstein, *Englische Studien*, 26 (1899), 96-97 (in German—favorable); *Notes and Queries*, 8th ser, 12 (1897), 59 ("carefully compiled," valuable, with a "remarkably good index").

30. "A List of the Principal Works of Dickens." *Dickensian*, 24 (1927/28), 328-29.

Gives titles, dates, and sometimes prices, but no other publication details, of Dickens's principal works. Illustrated.

31. [Matz, B. W.]. "Charles Dickens." In his *The Works of Charles Dickens and of Thomas Carlyle. With Full Particulars of Each Edition and Biographical Introductions*. London: Chapman and Hall, [1900], pp. 3-20; the listing of Dickens's works is reprinted in his *Charles Dickens: Some Notes on His Life and Writings*. London: Chapman and Hall, [1901]; reprinted Norwood, PA: Norwood Editions, 1978, pp. 41-48; it is updated in "The Various Complete Editions of the Works of Charles Dickens." In his *Two Great Victorian Writers: Dickens the Novelist; Carlyle the Philosopher* (**33**), pp. 17-35.

Following a brief survey of Dickens's life and career, considerably expanded in *Charles Dickens: Some Notes on His Life and Writings*, Matz lists and describes the collected editions of Dickens's works published by Chapman and Hall: the Gadshill, Authentic, Illustrated Library, Crown, Half-Crown, Cabinet, "Charles Dickens," Shilling, and Two-Shilling editions. Matz also notes an edition of the Christmas Stories and a few miscellaneous volumes. Illustrated. The text of *Two Great Victorian Writers* is different and the list updated slightly, but many of the illustrations used are the same. Also see Matz (**33**).

32. Matz, B. W. "Editions of Dickens, and the Books They Have Inspired." Special Dickens Number. *T. P.'s Weekly*, 19 (2 February 1912), 139.

A bibliographical sketch, mentioning the four collected editions published in Dickens's lifetime, the twenty-eight editions published by Chapman and Hall to 1912 (though not itemizing them), and other editions, as well as commenting briefly on a selection of biographical and critical studies of Dickens and several studies of *Pickwick Papers* and *The Mystery of Edwin Drood.*

33. Matz, B. W. "The Various Complete Editions of the Works of Charles Dickens." In his *Two Great Victorian Writers: Dickens the Novelist; Carlyle the Philosopher.* London: Chapman and Hall, [1905], pp. 17-35.

A listing of the contents, illustrations, and other special features of the individual volumes in the various collected editions of Dickens's works published by Chapman and Hall: the Gadshill, Authentic, Biographical, Oxford India Paper, Dickens Fellowship, Fireside, Crown, Half-Crown, "Charles Dickens," Shilling, and Two-Shilling editions, and editions of the Christmas Books and Christmas Stories. Illustrated. Also see Matz (**31**).

34. Miller, William, and T. W. Hill. "Charles Dickens's Manuscripts." *Dickensian*, 13 (1917), 181-85, 217-19.

Briefly describes the state and extent of completeness of the manuscripts of Dickens's novels and a few other works, and lists (pp. 217-19) extant manuscripts and proofs of the novels and a number of other book-length works, articles, and stories—and their location in 1917. Also contains facsimiles of a page each of the manuscripts of "O'Thello," *Pickwick Papers* (p. 170), and *The Old Curiosity Shop.*

35. Myers, Robin, ed. "Dickens, Charles (1812-70)." In his *A Dictionary of Literature in the English Language, from Chaucer to 1940.* 2 vols. Oxford: Pergamon Press, 1970; 2nd ed., 1980 [1979], I, 250-52.

A concise listing of Dickens's individual works, collected editions, selected collections of letters and speeches, and selected bibliographies.

36. "A New Dickens Bibliography." *Dickensian*, 39 (1942/43), 99-101 (*Dombey and Son*), 149-53 (*David Copperfield* and *Martin Chuzzlewit*), 173-75 (*Bleak House*); 40 (1943/44), 36-37 (*Nicholas Nickleby*), 76-78 (*Our Mutual Friend* and *The Old Curiosity Shop*), 143-45 (*Little Dorrit*); 41 (1944/45), 82-83 (*A Tale of Two Cities*), 206-07 (*The Mystery of Edwin Drood*).

Intended as "a guide to the collection of First Editions of Dickens" and as an updating and correction of the first and second editions of Eckel's bibliography (**16**). The bibliography is incomplete–*Pickwick Papers, Oliver Twist, Barnaby Rudge, Hard Times,* and *Great Expectations* are missing, as well as *A Christmas Carol* and the other Christmas Books. For each work included, the bibliography provides details of Dickens's writing of the work, location of manuscript and proofs, number of illustrations, the dedication, publishing details, number of prefaces, reading editions, a fairly simple collation of the work in volume form but not in monthly parts, and a few other matters. Usually the cover of the monthly wrapper is reproduced and also the illustrated and the regular title pages.

37. Nowell-Smith, Simon. "The 'Cheap Edition' of Dickens's Works (First Series) 1847-1852." *Library*, 5th Ser., 22 (1967), 245-51.

Provides numerous details and full bibliographical information about the publication in numbers, parts in wrappers, and volumes of the nine works in the first series of the Cheap Edition. Illustrated.

38. Orton, Robert M., comp. "Dickens, Charles." In his *Catalog of Reprints in Series, 1940[-71]*. New York: H. W. Wilson, 1940-57; Metuchen, NJ: Scarecrow Press, 1958-72, passim.

Lists Dickens's works by individual titles published in various series, such as the World's Classics, the Everyman Library, and the Modern Library, giving series, year of publication, publisher, pages, price, and, where relevant, the author of the introduction. This series went through twenty-one editions, with a page or two devoted to Dickens's works in each, most editions including a supplement with further Dickens entries.

39. Pierce, Gilbert A. "Alphabetical Order of Dickens's Novels and Minor Tales, with the Date of Their First Publication." In his *The Dickens Dictionary: A Key to the Characters and Principal Incidents in the Tales of Charles Dickens. With Additions by William A. Wheeler*. Boston: J. R. Osgood, 1872; reprinted, Boston: Houghton, Osgood [later, Houghton Mifflin], The Riverside Press, Cambridge, 1878, etc.; London: Chapman & Hall, 1878, etc.; and New York: Haskell House, 1972, pp. xiii-xv; completely revised and expanded as "A Condensed Bibliography of the Writings of Charles Dickens." In his *The Dickens Dictionary: A Key to the Plot and Characters in the Tales of Charles Dickens. With Copious Indexes and Bibliography. With Additions by William A. Wheeler*. A new and revised edition, illustrated. Standard Library Edition of *The Writings of Charles Dickens*. With Critical and Bibliographical Introductions and Notes by Edwin Percy Whipple and Others. Vol. 32. Boston and New York: Houghton Mifflin, The Riverside Press, Cambridge, 1894; reprinted, Boston and New York: Houghton Mifflin, 1914, etc.; 1914 edition reprinted New York: Kraus Reprint Corp., 1965, pp. 588-94; reprinted, London: Chapman and Hall, 1897, 1923, etc.; Boston and New York: Houghton Mifflin, 1926 (pagination varies).

The 1872 list of Dickens's works is not very useful, simply providing the title and year of publication (or years for the novels published in parts) although it gives the contents and the date of original publication for the essays in *Reprinted Pieces* and the contents of *Sketches by Boz* and *Sketches of Young Couples* (but omits *Sketches of Young Gentlemen*). The bibliography of Dickens's works in the 1894 and later editions arranges the works by year of publication and is more bibliographically detailed and extensive.

40. Rosenbaum, Barbara, and Pamela White, comps. "Charles Dickens, 1812-1870." In their *Index of English Literary Manuscripts*. Vol. 4: *1800-1900*. Part I. *Arnold-Gissing*. London and New York: Mansell, 1982, pp. 705-42.

A valuable account of the "wealth of surviving Dickensiana" and collections of the same, written by Pamela White, precedes the actual listing of 333 manuscripts, from the holograph manuscripts of the novels and accompanying proofs and notes to Dickens's early poetic effusions. Letters are not included. Dickens items are arranged alphabetically under these headings: Verse, Prose (subdivided into Titled Works, Miscellaneous and Untitled Works, Public Readings, and Speeches), Dramatic Works, Diaries and Notebooks, Marginalia in Printed Books and Manuscripts, and Miscellaneous (subdivided into Prompt-Books and Scenes for Amateur Theatricals and Dickens as Editor). Annotation for each item provides a brief description of the manuscript and indicates its present location, when a transcript exists, and whether the work has been published in whole or in part. Includes a photographic facsimile of the first page of the manuscript of *Great Expectations*.

41. S[chlicke], P[aul]. "Charles Dickens 1812-70." In *The Cambridge Bibliography of English Literature*. Vol. 4: *1800-1900*. 3rd. ed. Ed. Joanne Shattock. Cambridge, Eng.: Cambridge University Press, 1999, cols. 1181-1273.

The large impressive section on Dickens in this new and massive edition of a major bibliographical work begins with an introductory section on manuscripts, bibliographies, reference works (including Web sites), collected editions, and studies of manuscripts and editions. It is followed by section 1, which lists editions and studies of individual works, including letters and speeches, with subheadings (where needed) of bibliographies, editions, Dickens's reading adaptations, commentary on the text, imitations, dramatizations, reviews, and studies and appreciations.

Section 2 lists personal recollections and memoirs, obituaries, general critical studies up to 1920, and studies of special periods and aspects, bibliographies and adaptations, Dickens's illustrators and their illustrations, topographical studies to 1920, and biographies. The entries are essentially short-title ones and there are no annotations. The organization throughout is chronological. The cutoff date of 1920 for critical and topographical studies, a new policy for the third edition, gives the bibliography a curiously dated look, particularly since the second edition contained critical and topographical studies through 1967–and the first edition publications through 1938. Shattock explains this limitation in her "Editor's Preface": "The availability of comprehensive bibliographies of secondary material, both in electronic and volume form, and the back-dating to 1920 of two major bibliographies, the Annual Bibliography of English Language and Literature and the Annotated Bibliography of English Studies, make it clear that it would be an unnecessary duplication for the third edition of CBEL to provide a selective list of secondary criticism for each author, as had previously been the case [in the first two editions]." For the sections on Dickens in earlier editions of this work, see Darton (**11**) and Collins (**8**).

Also see several more general sections in this volume by others: Book Production and Distribution, cols. 1-94; Literary Relations with the Continent, cols. 95-206; The Novel, General Works, cols. 859-69; and Newspapers and Languages, cols. 2849-2978. There are also sections on a variety of background information (History, Political Economy, Religion, etc.), some listings in which should be relevant to Dickens. See the index for a few references to Dickens elsewhere in this volume.

42. [Shepherd, Richard H.]. *The Bibliography of Dickens: A Bibliographical List Arranged in Chronological Order of the Published Writings in Prose and Verse of Charles Dickens (from 1834 to 1880)*. Manchester, Eng.: A. Ireland; London: Elliot Stock, [1880]; reprinted Folcroft, PA: Folcroft Press, 1970; Norwood, PA: Norwood Editions, 1976; Philadelphia, PA: R. West, 1977. viii + 107 pp.; 2nd ed., revised and enlarged as *The Bibliography of Dickens: A Bibliographical List Arranged in Chronological Order of the Published Writings in Prose and Verse of Charles Dickens (from 1833 to 1882)*. [London: Printed for private circulation, 1882]. 70 pp.; also included as "The Bibliography of Dickens: A Bibliographical List Arranged in Chronological Order of the Published Writings in Prose and Verse of Charles Dickens (from 1833 to 1882)," in *The Plays and Poems of Charles Dickens, with a Few Miscellanies in Prose. Now First Collected*. Ed. Richard Herne Shepherd. 2 vols. London: W. H. Allen, 1882 (and reprinted unchanged, 1885), II, 337-406; further revised as "The Bibliography of Dickens: A Bibliographical List of the Published Writings in Prose and Verse of Charles Dickens from 1833 to 1883 (Including His Letters)," in *The Speeches of Charles Dickens (1841-1870), With a New Bibliography Revised and Enlarged*. Ed. Richard Herne Shepherd. London: Chatto and Windus, 1884, pp. 325-73.

An important, if not always quite accurate, early bibliography. Shepherd lists and describes the parts issues and magazine serializations as well as the first and sometimes later volume editions of the novels and many of the minot works, including magazine and newspaper pieces. He itemizes by name of correspondent letters of Dickens in the first two volumes of the *Hogarth-Dickens Letters* and also letters published elsewhere or unpublished and in various library collections. In addition, he includes four pages of errata for the *Hogarth-Dickens Letters*. He also lists fifty-nine speeches, most published in *Speeches Literary and Social,* compiled by Shepherd and John Camden Hotten (London: John Camden Hotten, [1870]), and itemizes sixty-four secondary items under "Ana." In his *Dickensiana* (**996**), F. G. Kitton points out that Shepherd incorporates Cook's bibliography (**10**) into his while at the same time condemning it for not being sufficiently "recondite," accurate, or complete.

Shepherd's earliest attempt at a bibliography of Dickens's writings, "A Bibliography of the Writings of Charles Dickens, Arranged in Order of Publication," was included in *Speeches Literary and Social* (**43**), pp. 358-65. Compared to the 1880 version, this is quite brief and incomplete, without any information about Dickens's letters or speeches or an "Ana" section, but it seems to have served as the base for the later work, which is also more fully annotated.

In the 1882 revision, the bibliography is updated, revised "throughout and considerably enlarged." Shepherd includes an even more extensive list of errata for the *Hogarth-Dickens Letters,* the list now including additional errors found in volumes 1 and 2, as well as errors in volume 3 (1882) and the two-volume revised edition of 1882. He legitimately complains that few of the errors noted in the 1880 edition of his bibliography were corrected in the revised edition of the letters, and new ones incurred. He no longer lists the letters in the *Hogarth-Dickens Letters,* but instead includes a revised list of known correspondence, published and unpublished, not included there; this is considerably revised, since letters that were included in volume 3 of the *Hogarth-Dickens Letters* are now excluded, of course. While the number of speeches identified remains the same as in the 1880 bibliography, there are now seventy-nine items in "Ana" and an additional twenty-three in a "Supplementary Ana" supplied by W[illiam] R. Hughes, many of them early reviews of Dickens's works. The separately published bibliography was a privately published edition of fifty copies, one copy of which, in the Dexter collection (Dex. 29) in the British Library, London, contains manuscript notes by J. F. Dexter, in which he provides a more detailed description of *Sunday under Three Heads* (1836), lists pieces in *All the Year Round* by Dickens, lists Edmund Yates's contributions to *Household Words* from a list supplied by Yates himself, lists obituaries of Dickens from 1870, and adds a few items to the "Ana" section. In his *Dickensiana* (**996**), F. G. Kitton notes that the 1882 edition of *The Plays and Poems* was withdrawn a few weeks after publication because it contained copyrighted material and reissued in 1885 without it; the bibliography, however, remained unchanged. Minor revisions were made in it in the 1884 edition of the speeches.

The Dickens House Museum has a copy of the 1880 edition with addenda and corrections written in, apparently in the hand of A. Wallis (see a letter inserted in this copy) and with a brief handwritten introduction surely unfairly criticizing Shepherd as "one of those literary ghouls who thrive best upon dead authors" and whose bibliography is "of not the least value to anyone above the rank of a mere novice." The Dickens House Museum also has two other copies of the 1880 edition with nearly identical addenda and corrections on interleaved pages, both in the hand of Shepherd, according to a note on the inside cover of one. These were meant, obviously, for a projected third edition in 1884 since the subheading has been changed to read "(from 1833 to 1884)." In the bibliography in the 1884 edition of *The Speeches of Charles Dickens*, Shepherd omits the errata for the *Hogarth-Dickens Letters*, the list of speeches, and the "Supplementary Ana"; adds and corrects occasional details; and adds a few letters published elsewhere–three to Thomas Heaphy, one to Thomas Hood, and two to James Planché.

Review: "The Bibliography of Dickens." *Cope's Tobacco Plant*, January 1881, pp. 571-73 (more a history of Dickens's literary career than a review of the work at hand).

43. [Shepherd, Richard H.]. "A Bibliography of the Writings of Charles Dickens, Arranged in Order of Publication." In *Speeches Literary and Social. By Charles Dickens. Now First Collected. With Chapters on "Charles Dickens as a Letter Writer, Poet, and Public Reader."* [Compiled by John Camden Hotten and Richard H. Shepherd]. London: John Camden Hotten, [1870], pp. 358-65.

The earliest attempt at a bibliography of Dickens's writings. It is quite brief and incomplete compared to Shepherd's next version (42), published in 1880. The 1870 volume of Dickens's speeches was reprinted in the Mayfair Library (London: Chatto and Windus, 1881) from the original plates, but with the bibliography omitted. When Shepherd published *The Speeches of Charles Dickens [1841-1870]. With a New Bibliography Revised and Enlarged* (London: Chatto & Windus, 1884) three years later, the "new bibliography" appended to it (42) was revised and enlarged from his 1880 bibliography. The American edition of *Speeches Literary and Social*, entitled *Speeches, Letters, and Sayings of Charles Dickens* (New York: Harper & Brothers, 1870) did not contain the bibliography in the London edition.

44. Slater, J[ohn] H. "Charles Dickens." In his *Early Editions: A Bibliographical Survey of the Works of Some Popular Modern Authors*. London: Kegan Paul, Trench, Trübner, 1894, pp. 76-106.

In this volume intended for collectors, Slater, ignoring Shepherd's work (42), notes that, despite the researches of Charles P. Johnson (27), James Cook (10), and F. G. Kitton (29, 154), "a very great deal yet remains to be said about the works of Dickens" and about the imitations and parodies of them.

Slater identifies some thirteen imitations and provides a list of Dickens's works, noting details about text and illustrations of genuine first and important subsequent editions and various sets of extra illustrations to the novels. He also gives some then current prices paid at sales.

45. Smith, Walter E. *Charles Dickens in the Original Cloth: A Bibliographical Catalogue of the First Appearance of IIis Writings in Book Form in England with Facsimiles of the Bindings and Titlepages. Part One: The Novels with* **Sketches by Boz***.* Los Angeles: Heritage Book Shop, 1982. xvi + 120 pp.

A bibliographical catalogue for book collectors, dealers, and librarians of Dickens's works in their original cloth bindings, noting the rarity of this form and the variety of cloth bindings used for Dickens's works, though all such bindings, Smith concedes, are "plain and unappealing." In this handsomely produced volume, the bibliographical entries give title page text, binding information and description, collation, contents, internal flaws (usually typographical errors or peculiarities), and illustrations, with extensive notes by Smith, for the two series of *Sketches by Boz* and each of the novels. Smith also includes a list of "Related Publications" and numerous photographic facsimiles of cloth bindings and title pages. See the second volume (**46**), below. Also see Jarndyce Antiquarian Booksellers (**2033**).

Reviews: *AB Bookman's Weekly*, 70 (1982), 3206-07; *American Notes and Queries*, 21 (1982/83), 196 (definitive; detailed bibliographical descriptions; an "essential" work); B. Lake, *Antiquarian Book Monthly Review*, 9 (1982), 229-31 (asserts that Smith "has succeeded in bringing together much of the information which has up to now only been available from a dozen or more sources," and, for "the general reader, or the bookseller who needs fairly simple and straight-forward information," this volume "will be useful and certainly a great improvement over Eckel" [**16**], but complains that Smith has not clearly answered the question of what defines a first edition and, particularly in the then forthcoming part 2, has been less than complete in his coverage); R. Patten, *American Book Collector*, 3, vi (1982), 52-56 (finds this a valuable book in some respects but sees that there are greater complexities in defining a first edition of Dickens's works than Smith confronts, involving the parts issues, the state of the illustrations, and other matters, revealing "how much more we need to know" about the subject), and *Papers of the Bibliographical Society of America*, 77 (1983), 209-17 (compares sometimes favorably, sometimes unfavorably to Podeschi [**1509**]); J. Stephens, *Dickensian*, 79 (1983), 118-19 (notes new bibliographical information provided by Smith but feels more questions are raised than answered by "the rich mass of material presented"). Also see reviews below (**46**).

46. Smith, Walter E. *Charles Dickens in the Original Cloth: A Bibliographical Catalogue of the First Appearance of His Writings in Book Form in England with Facsimiles of the Bindings and Titlepages. Part Two: The Christmas Books and Selected Secondary Works.* Los Angeles: Heritage Book Shop, 1983. xvi + 95 pp.

Identical in scope to the first volume (**45**), above, and covering the five Christmas Books, *Sketches of Young Gentlemen*, *Sketches of Young Couples*, *American Notes*, *Pictures from Italy*, *A Child's History of England*, *Uncommercial Traveller* (1861), and *The Life of Our Lord*. Also see Jarndyce Antiquarian Booksellers (**2033**).

Reviews: *AB Bookmen's Weekly*, 73 (20 February 1984), 1317 (very useful for dealers, collectors, and librarians); M. P. Hearn, *American Book Collector*, ns 5 (January-February 1984), 65 (in both volumes the editions in "original cloth" are "expertly described," each entry "a detailed bibliographical essay," but Hearn wishes Smith had been more complete in his coverage; in part 2 the "thorny publishing history of *A Christmas Carol* is particularly well handled"); B. Lake, *Antiquarian Book Monthly Review*, 11 (1984), 62-63 (finds that part 2 is "rather more satisfactory" than part 1 and that Smith has "done a good job" on the states of the first edition of *A Christmas Carol* and *The Battle of Life*, but still laments the incompleteness of Smith's work, concluding overall that it was "a wasted opportunity"); J. Pace-Mann, *Antiquarian Book Monthly Review*, 11 (1984), 153 (letter to the editor about an early issue of *A Christmas Carol*, with reply by B. Lake, p. 195); R. Patten, *Papers of the Bibliographical Society of America*, 78 (1984), 521-26 (put together "more perfunctorily" than part 1; not the "full-scale descriptive bibliography" that Dickens scholarship needs, but "we must be grateful" for what Smith adds to our knowledge of Dickens bibliography).

47. Sucksmith, Harvey P. "Bibliography." In his *The Narrative Art of Charles Dickens: The Rhetoric of Sympathy and Irony in His Novels* (**2315**), pp. 359-61.

Lists the extant manuscripts and proofs and first volume editions of Dickens's novels and a few collections of his works and letters.

48. Thomson, J[oseph] C. *Bibliography of the Writings of Charles Dickens*. Warwick, Eng.: J. Thomson; New York: G. E. Stechert, 1904. 108 pp.

A detailed bibliography, drawn, as Thomson notes, from *Forster*, the *Hogarth-Dickens Letters*, Kitton's writings (see **29, 154**), and *Book-Prices Current* (**2061**), with considerable annotation and arranged chronologically. Thomson includes the plays, the early sketches and tales (incomplete), newspaper and magazine articles (including Dickens's articles in *Household Words* and *All the Year Round*), some speeches, and introductions to books by others, as well as the novels and principal nonfiction works. For editions of the novels in particular, Thomson provides information about their conception, critical reception, and then current monetary value. Inevitably, there are some errors and omissions and inclusion of a few pieces not by Dickens, but for its time this work was surprisingly thorough and detailed. Compare Shepherd (**42**), Cook (**10**), Anderson (**1**), Forster (**19**), Kitton (**29, 154**), and Slater (**44**). For commentary on Thomson's bibliography, see Muir (**1420**), Prideaux (**1423**), and Pierpont (**436**).

49. Topp, Chester W., comp. *Victorian Yellowbacks & Paperbacks, 1849-1905*. Vol. 1: *George Routledge*. Denver, CO: Hermitage Antiquarian Bookshop, 1993, passim.

Lists and provides extensive year by year bibliographical details about various Dickens works reprinted by George Routledge, 1853-1903. Topp also provides information about earlier editions of these works published by others. The information is based on Topp's own collection but goes, obviously, far beyond it.

50. Topp, Chester W., comp. *Victorian Yellowbacks & Paperbacks, 1849-1905.* Vol. 2: *Ward & Lock.* Denver, CO: Hermitage Antiquarian Bookshop, 1995, passim.

Lists and provides impressive year by year bibliographical details about various Dickens works published by Ward & Lock, London, 1877-92. Illustrated.

51. Topp, Chester W., comp. *Victorian Yellowbacks & Paperbacks, 1849-1905.* Vol. 3: *John Camden Hotten and Chatto & Windus [and] Chapman & Hall.* Denver, CO: Hermitage Antiquarian Bookshop, 1997, passim.

Lists and provides impressive year by year bibliographical details about various Dickens works published by Chapman and Hall, London, 1849-1897. Topp also itemizes two relevant publications by John Camden Hotten, 1870. Illustrated.

52. Topp, Chester W., comp. *Victorian Yellowbacks & Paperbacks, 1849-1905.* Vol. 4: *Frederick Warne & Co.; Sampson Low & Co.* Denver, CO: Hermitage Antiquarian Bookshop, 1999, passim.

Lists and provides impressive year by year bibliographical details about various Dickens works published by Frederick Warne & Co., 1882-93. Illustrated.

53. Turner, John R. *The Walter Scott Publishing Company: A Bibliography.* Pittsburgh Series in Bibliography. Pittsburgh, PA: University of Pittsburgh Press, 1997, passim.

Provides in passing bibliographical descriptions of editions of individual Dickens works published by this company, 1884-1913. See the index to locate these editions. Illustrated.

54. Turner, Michael. *Index and Guide to the Lists of the Publications of Richard Bentley & Son, 1829-1898.* Bishops Stortford, Eng., and Teaneck, NJ: Chadwyck-Healey, 1975, passim.

This index is meant to accompany the lists themselves, which are available on microfiche. The Dickens items are briefly noted on p. 65.

55. Vann, J. Don. "Charles Dickens (1812-70)." In his *Victorian Novels in Serial.* Index Society Fund Publications. New York: Modern Language Association, 1985, pp. 61-75.

Lists each part number, its date of publication, and the chapters it contains of *Pickwick Papers, Oliver Twist, Nicholas Nickleby, The Old Curiosity Shop* and

Barnaby Rudge (in *Master Humphrey's Clock*), *Martin Chuzzlewit, Dombey and Son, David Copperfield, Bleak House, Hard Times* (in weekly numbers of *Household Words*), *Little Dorrit, A Tale of Two Cities* and *Great Expectations* (in weekly numbers of *All the Year Round*), *Our Mutual Friend,* and *The Mystery of Edwin Drood.* Vann also notes which later editions of these works indicate the parts issues in the text. Vann's introduction deals with Dickens's practices of serialization and his editorial policies for serial publication.

56. "The Various Editions of Dickens." In "Charles Dickens." *Literature,* 9 (1901/02), pp. 583-85.

A chronological listing of collected editions, with brief comments about contents, artists, and other matters, from the Cheap Edition (1847-52) through the Imperial Edition of 1901, some twenty-seven editions.

57. Villalobos, Carlos. "Bibliografía de Charles Dickens." In *Charles Dickens, 1812-1870: Homenaje en el primer centenario de su muerte.* Ed. María E. González Padilla et al. Mexico City: Universidad Nacional Autónoma de México, Facultad de Filosofía y Lettras/Departamento de Lettras Inglesas, 1971, pp. 193-204.

Lists selective bibliographies, collected editions, editions of separate works, and critical studies of Dickens to 1967–principally English editions, with a very few Spanish and Mexican editions and studies.

58. Ward, K. Anthony. "Dickens, Charles (1812-1870)." In his *First Editions: A Field Guide for Collectors of English and American Literature.* Aldershot, Eng.: Scolar Press; Brookfield, VT: Ashgate, 1994, pp. 92-97.

For "the serious book collector," this work lists and provides fairly detailed publication information about the first editions and sometimes early issues of first editions of Dickens's works, though the finer details of works with more complicated publication histories, such as *A Christmas Carol,* are not thoroughly discussed.

59. Watson, George, ed. "Dickens, Charles, 1812-70." In *The Shorter New Cambridge Bibliography of English Literature.* Cambridge, Eng., London, New York, etc.: Cambridge University Press, 1981, cols. 900-08.

The section of primary works is considerably reduced from that by Philip Collins in *The New Cambridge Bibliography of English Literature* (8). The entries for *Pickwick Papers,* for example, here occupy one-eighth of a column as opposed to four and one-half columns in the *NCBEL,* and those for minor works are completely omitted. Biographies and critical studies have been reduced from forty-eight columns in the *NCBEL* to one column, though the editor brings the few works listed forward to 1979 for biographies and to 1973 for critical studies.

60. Wilkins, William Glyde. "First and Early American Editions of the Works of Charles Dickens." *Dickensian*, 3 (1907), 186-88.

Provides information about the publication of Dickens's works in America. F. Corder, p. 249, corrects several details. See also Wilkins's response, p. 277. Also see Wilkins (**61, 62**).

61. Wilkins, William Glyde. *First and Early American Editions of the Works of Charles Dickens.* Cedar Rapids, IA: Privately Printed [Torch Press], 1910; reprinted New York: Burt Franklin, 1968. 51 pp.

A considerable expansion in the listing of editions and in details about editions previously noted in his *Dickensian* articles (see **60, 62**), which Wilkins hopes now makes the bibliography "reasonably complete." He has also added some information about American parodies and imitations of Dickens's works, anthologies, collected editions, and editions illustrated by American artists. Reproductions of several covers, title pages, and illustrations for the novels are included.

Review: C. V[an] N[oorden], *Dickensian*, 6 (1910), 274 ("the last word on the subject").

62. Wilkins, William Glyde. "More about Early American Editions of the Works of Dickens." *Dickensian*, 4 (1908), 190-91.

A follow-up to his earlier article (**60**). Lists several more editions–of *David Copperfield*, *Dombey and Son*, *The Old Curiosity Shop*, *Barnaby Rudge*, *American Notes*, *Mrs. Gamp and the Strolling Players*, and *Mrs. Lirriper's Lodgings*. Also see p. 250 for Wilkins's identification of two more editions in parts of *Dombey and Son*. See also Wilkins (**61**).

63. Wing, George. "Bibliography." In his *Dickens*. Edinburgh: Oliver and Boyd, 1969, pp. 106-16.

A selected bibliography of primary and secondary works, the latter of which are predominantly book-length studies and essays in books.

64. Yaakov, Juliette, and John Greenfieldt. "Dickens, Charles, 1812-1870." In their *Fiction Catalog*. 13th ed. New York and Dublin: H. W. Wilson, 1996, pp. 170-74.

Lists a specific edition or two of each of Dickens's novels and some shorter tales, with brief plot summaries by way of annotation. The first edition (Minneapolis: H. W. Wilson, 1908) was edited by Isabel S. Monro and revised in 1931; subsequent editions (with supplements) were issued more frequently by various editors, and every five years from 1971 (eighth edition, edited by Estelle Fidell), on, now with annual supplements. In the preface to the eighth edition (New York: H. W. Wilson), Fidell points out that the first edition listed about 2,000 titles of "the best fiction of all time," presumably for use by libraries in building their collections for adults; the thirteenth edition lists 5,461. See Harner (**1147**), p. 105, for complementary lists of selected fiction.

1B. GENERAL AND LITERARY BIBLIOGRAPHIES AND LITERARY CHRONOLOGIES

Note: Also see **Bibliographies, general and literary (with sections on Dickens)** and **Chronologies, literary (with sections on Dickens)** in the subject index.

65. American Antiquarian Society and the Research Libraries Group, Inc. "Dickens, Charles, 1812-1870." In *Bibliography of American Imprints to 1901: Author Index.* Vol. 46. New York, Munich, London, Paris: K. G. Saur, 1993, pp. 246-53, and passim.

Gives title, place of publication, publisher, and date of publication only for individual works and collected editions of Dickens's works. For example, eleven editions of *Bleak House,* thirteen of *Pickwick Papers,* and twenty collected editions published to 1901 are listed. Works by Dickens's descendants will be found on pp. 253-54. This volume is one of ninety-two volumes. Volumes 1-42, *Main Part,* contain an alphabetical list of individual titles, including those of Dickens's works. Here the entries are reasonably detailed, with some bibliographical annotation. The *Author Index,* in which volume 46 appears, occupies volumes 43-56. Volumes 57-71 comprise the *Subject Index,* volume 61 of which (p. 1) lists 77 studies, including biographies, of Dickens. There are also a *Place Index,* volumes 72-82, and a *Date Index,* volumes 83-92. The listings are by no means complete, as is acknowledged, the editors announcing the multivolume work as "a beginning or contribution toward a complete listing of American imprints," since their databases, though large, are limited. For Dickens, the editors have obviously not used Edgar and Vail (**17**) or Wilkins (**61**); several editions listed there are not here. In addition, works published after 1901 have mysteriously found their way into the bibliography. For example, an edition of *A Christmas Carol* illustrated by Arthur Rackham and published in Philadelphia in 1915 is listed as published in 1843, twenty-four years before Rackham was born.

66. *American Book Publishing Record: Cumulative, 1876-1949: An American National Bibliography. A Cumulation of American Book Production for the Years 1876-1949, as Catalogued by the Library of Congress and the National Union Catalog. Arranged by Subject According to Dewey Decimal Classification and Indexed by Author and Title with a Separate Subject Guide.* 15 vols. New York: R. R. Bowker, 1960, passim; reprinted 1980; continued for *1950-1977.* 15 vols. New York: R. R. Bowker, 1978; for *1975-1979.* 5 vols. New York and

London: R. R. Bowker, 1981, and for *1980-1984*. 5 vols. New York and London: R. R. Bowker, 1985; annually thereafter, as well as monthly, passim.

Use the author, title, and subject indexes to locate Dickens items. See Harner (**1147**), p. 472, for details about the range of this series. Harner indicates that this series is available on microfiche for 1876-1981 and that, despite being neither comprehensive nor totally accurate, it is still "the most convenient source for keeping abreast of new works, editions, or reprints published since 1876" in the United States. Also see Jones (**76**).

67. *Books in Print.* New Providence, NJ: R. R. Bowker, 1948- , passim.

A standard volume in checking on editions of Dickens's works distributed in the United States and in print in any given year. The latest edition seen, *Books in Print, 2000-2001* was published in nine volumes—*Authors*, volumes 1-4; *Titles*, volumes 5-8; and *Publishers*, volume 9. A good many editions of Dickens's works are listed in I, 2741-44. Individual titles can easily be found in that section of the series. *Books in Print* is also available in various electronic formats—see the list in I, vii. The latest subject index available is *Subject Guide to Books in Print, 2000-2001*, published in six volumes. For the huge number of Dickens studies in print, see II, 4226-28. All entries are brief and unannotated. For details of supplemental volumes, *Children's Books in Print* (1969-), *Forthcoming Books* (1966-), and *Publisher's Trade List Annual* (1873-), see Harner (**1147**), p. 484.

68. *The British National Bibliography: Cumulated Subject Catalogue, 1951-1954. A Subject List of British Books Published During the Years 1951-1954, Based upon the Books Deposited at the Copyright Office of the British Museum and Classified According to the Dewey Decimal Classification.* Ed. under direction of A. J. Wells. 2 vols. London: Council of the British National Bibliography, British Museum, 1958, passim, and *The British National Bibliography Cumulated Index 1950-1954. An Index to the Five Annual Volumes of the British National Bibliography for the Years 1950-1954 in One Alphabetical Sequence of Authors, Titles and Subject References, Covering the British Publications of Those Years Deposited at the Copyright Office of the British Museum.* Ed. under the direction of A. J. Wells. London: Council of the British National Bibliography, British Museum, 1955, passim; also cumulated *1955-1959*, 3 vols. + *Cumulated Index.* Ibid., 1963, passim; published annually 1960-75, with various cumulated indexes; from 1976 on cumulated annually in 2 vols., vol. 1 being the *Subject Catalogue* and vol. 2 the *Indexes* (Author, Title, and Subject), passim.

There are numerous Dickens items, both new editions of his writings and secondary studies. One must use the indexes to locate them. Currently the bibliography is kept nearly up-to-date by weekly publication, with monthly and quarterly cumulations and with monthly indexes. See Harner (**1147**), p. 320, and Marcuse (**1152**), p. 40, for details about the range of this series.

69. Butler, Marian, ed. *Canadian Books in Print: Author and Title Index, 2002.* Toronto, Buffalo, NY, and London: University of Toronto Press, 2002, passim, and *Canadian Books in Print: Subject Index, 2002.* Toronto, Buffalo, NY, and London: University of Toronto Press, 2002, passim.

Very few Dickens works and studies are to be found in the latest volumes of this series. The author section lists only three editions of individual Dickens novels, and one needs to check the "Literature" headings in the subject guide to locate the occasional Dickens study published in Canada. Harner (**1147**), p. 512, notes that this work has been issued quarterly since 1967 with an annual cumulation, one weakness being that it "excludes most French-language titles."

70. *Catalog of the "A. L. A." Library: 5,000 Volumes for a Popular Library Selected by the American Library Association and Shown at the World's Columbian Exposition.* Compiled at the New York State Library under the supervision of Mrs. S. C. Fairfield, and the selection made by American Library Association. Washington, D. C.: Government Printing Office, 1893, passim; revised as *A. L. A. Catalog: 8,000 Volumes for a Popular Library, with Notes.* Ed. Melvil Dewey, and prepared by the New York State Library and the Library of Congress under the auspices of the American Library Association Publishing Board. Washington, D. C.: Government Printing Office, 1904, passim; further revised as *A. L. A. Catalog, 1926: An Annotated Basic List of 10,000 Books.* Ed. Isabella M. Cooper. Chicago: American Library Association, 1926, passim.

Intended, among other purposes, as a guide for readers, librarians, and booksellers. Dickens's novels, Christmas Books, major nonfiction works, and letters are included, and even occasional biographies. Supplements appeared in 1912 and 1923 (updated to 1921). Later supplements appeared in 1933 (covering 1926-31), 1938 (covering 1932-36), 1943 (covering 1937-41), and 1952 (covering 1942-49).

71. Cox, Michael, ed. *The Oxford Chronology of English Literature.* 2 vols. Oxford: Oxford University Press, 2002, passim. Also on CD-ROM.

In volume 1, entries are listed by year and then alphabetically by author. Basic publication information is provided for volume publication, though brief notes following the listings also give dates for publication in parts. For Dickens's works in volume 1, see pp. 395-467 (1836-70) and p. 490 (*The Mudfog Papers*, first published in 1880). Volume 2 contains the author index, which lists works included in volume 1; for Dickens's works, see p. 59. There is also a title index in volume 1.

72. Ghosh, J. C., and E. G. Withycombe, comps. *Annals of English Literature, 1475-1925: The Principal Publications of Each Year Together with an Alphabetical Index of Authors with Their Works.* Oxford: Clarendon Press, 1935, passim; corrected, 1936, passim; 2nd ed., published as *Annals of English Literature, 1475-1950: The Principal Publications of Each Year Together with an Alphabetical Index of Authors with Their Works.* Comp. R. W. Chapman and W. K. Davin. Oxford: Clarendon Press, 1961, passim; reprinted with corrections, Oxford: Clarendon Press, 1965, passim.

For Dickens's publications, see 1836-70, 1880, 1882.

73. Gray, Martin. *A Chronology of English Literature.* Harlow, Eng.: Longman; Beirut: York Press, 1989, passim.

Gives a brief historical background for each year and works published, by genre (prose, drama, poetry), including Dickens's works.

74. *Guide to Microforms in Print.* Englewood, NJ: Microcard, 1961-77; Westport, CT: Microform Review, 1978-81; Westport, CT: Meckler, 1982-90; Munich, Ger.: K. G. Saur, 1991- , passim.

Annually lists a number of Dickens editions and studies in its author-title and subject (the latter arranged by Dewey Decimal classification) indexes.

75. *International Books in Print, 1979[-]: English-Language Titles Published in Africa, Asia, Australia, Canada, Continental Europe, Latin America, New Zealand, Oceania, and the Republic of Ireland.* München, Ger.: K. G. Saur, 1979- , passim.

Annually lists a small number of editions of Dickens's works in the author-title index and studies of Dickens in the subject index (arranged by Dewey Decimal classification) and in the Persons index. Harner (**1147**), p. 503-04, indicates that this work is also available on CD-ROM and as a part of *Bowker-Whitaker Global Books in Print Plus* on CD-ROM.

76. Jones, Lynds E., comp., under the direction of F. Leypoldt. *The American Catalogue: Author and Title Entries of Books in Print and for Sale (Including Reprints and Importations), July 1, 1876.* 2 vols. New York: R. R. Bowker, 1880, passim; supplementary vols. published for *July 1, 1876-June 30, 1884; July 1, 1884-June 30, 1890; July 1, 1890-June 30, 1895; July 1, 1895-Jan. 1, 1900.* 2 vols. each (vol. 1: *Authors & Titles,* vol. 2: *Subjects*). New York: R. R. Bowker, 1885, 1891, 1896, 1901, passim; published in single volumes with combined author/title/subject/series index, *1900-1905, 1905-1907, 1908-1910.* New York: R. R. Bowker, 1905, 1908, 1911, passim; all vols. reprinted New York: Peter Smith, 1941, passim.

Intended as "a more methodical, continuous and comprehensive system of trade bibliography" than previous publishers' trade list annuals by including "all books (with certain exceptions) published in the United States which were in print, and for sale to the general public," on the date or the inclusive dates indicated. For Dickens's individual and collected works, *The American Catalogue* gives title, date of publication, publisher, price, and size. Also see Kelly (**77**). Harner (**1147**), p. 472, states that the *American Book Publishing Record* (**66**) supersedes this series.

77. Kelly, James, comp. *The American Catalogue of Books (Originals and Reprints), Published in the United States from Jan., 1861, to Jan., 1866, with Date of Publication, Size, Price and Publisher's Name.* . . . New York: Wiley & Son, 1866, passim; a second volume, covering January 1866 to January 1871, was published in 1871, passim; both reprinted New York: Peter Smith, 1938, passim.

A continuation of Roorbach's *Bibliotheca Americana* (**85**), Kelly's volumes list American editions of Dickens's works. Individual works and volumes in collected editions are also listed under their titles. Also see *American Book Publishing Record* and Jones (**66** and **76**). See Harner (**1147**), p. 473, for details about the range of this series.

78. Lenrow, Elbert. *Reader's Guide to Prose Fiction: An Introductory Essay, with Bibliographies of 1,500 Novels Selected, Topically Classified, and Annotated for Use in Meeting the Needs of Individuals in General Education.* New York and London: Appleton-Century, 1940, passim.

Twelve of Dickens's novels are listed in the index. Annotations are dreadful—*Bleak House,* for example, is described as a "humorous chronicle of an interminable suit in chancery."

79. *Paperbound Books in Print.* . . . New York: R. R. Bowker, 1955- , passim.

For paperback editions of Dickens's works, check first in the author index or title index and then in the subject index under Literature. Information is given about edition and price. Unfortunately, books about Dickens are not indexed under his name in either of the indexes. Issued monthly since 1965 with cumulative issues thrice yearly.

80. Peddie, Robert A., and Quinton Waddington [et al.], eds. and comps. *The English Catalogue of Books (Including the Original "London" Catalogue), Giving in*

One Alphabet, under Author, Title and Subject, the Size, Price, Month and Year of Publication, and Publisher of Books Issued in the United Kingdom of Great Britain and Ireland, 1801[-1968]. Published annually, and cumulated as follows: London: S. Low, Marston (vols. 1-6, for 1835-63, 1863-72, 1872-80, 1881-89, 1890-97, 1898-1900), 1864, 1873, 1882, 1891, 1898, 1901; Published for Publishers' Circular by S. Low, Marston (vol. 8, for 1906-10, and the vol. for 1801-36), 1911, 1914; Publishers' Circular (vol. 7, for 1901-05, and vols. 9-21 for 1911-68), 1906, 1916-69; reprinted in 9 vols. (to 1915), New York: Kraus Reprint, 1963, passim; also on microfiche as *The Publishers' Circular, 1837-1900, including the English Catalogue of Books.* Ed. Simon Eliot and John Sutherland. Cambridge, Eng.: Chadwyck-Healey, 1988, passim. Also see *Index to the English Catalogue of Books.* Comp. Sampson Low [et al.]. 4 vols. (1837-57, 1856-76, 1874-80, 1881-89). London: S. Low, 1858, 1876, 1884, 1893, passim.

Useful for confirming publication information about Dickens's novels and book-length secondary studies published in the United Kingdom through 1968 (London: Publishers Circular, 1969), when publication ceased. Each volume or cumulative volume contains an alphabetical list of Dickens's works published during the dates indicated and giving title, size, price, date of publication, as well as publisher and date of publication for the latest published edition listed. Each See Harner (**1147**), pp. 289-90, and Marcuse (**1152**), p. 40, for details about the range of this series. Harner points out that this is "the most complete record of books published in Great Britain during the nineteenth century." He adds that from 1874-1961 *A Reference Catalogue of Current Literature* (**83**) "is an important supplement," though after 1924 "more thorough coverage of works published or issued in Great Britain is provided by *Whitaker's Cumulative Book List* (**92**) and after 1950 by the *British National Bibliography* (**68**).

81. Potter, Marion E., [et al.], comps. "Dickens, Charles." In *The United States Catalog: Books in Print 1899[-1928].* Minneapolis (and later New York): H. W. Wilson, 1900-28; simultaneously with and continued by *The Cumulative Book Index: 1898[-]: A World List of Books in the English Language.* Ed. Marion E. Potter [et al.]. Minneapolis (and later New York): H. W. Wilson, 1899- , passim.

The section on Dickens lists editions of the individual novels and collected editions, with prices, as well as books about Dickens. *The United States Catalog* was published monthly, annually, and in cumulations for varying numbers of years to 1928. *The Cumulative Book Index* is also published, monthly, annually, and in cumulations for varying numbers of years. It attempts to include all books published in the English language, wherever published. See Harner (**1147**), p. 55, for details about the range of this series. He indicates that *International Books in Print* (**75**) "offers more extensive international coverage."

82. *Publishers' Circular and Booksellers' Record of British and Foreign Literature.* Vols. 1-172. London: Sampson Low, etc., 1837-April 1959, passim; succeeded by *British Books.* Vols. 173-79. Croyden, Eng.: *Publishers' Circular,* May 1959-December 1962, March 1963-66, passim; absorbed by *The Publisher* (London). Vols. 180-83. London: *The Publisher,* February 1967-April 1970, passim.

Records first and later editions of Dickens's works. The bibliographical information in the listing above gives little indication of title and publisher changes over the nearly 150 years of this first semi-monthly and then weekly listing of newly published books in England and usually America. The information supplied varies, too, but usually includes author, title, publisher, publication date, size, number of pages, and price. In his *Some Patterns and Trends in British Publishing, 1800-1919* (London: Bibliographical Society, 1994), Simon Eliot stresses (p. 26) the importance of this catalogue in recording works published during the years indicated.

83. *A Reference Catalogue of Current Literature, Containing the Full Titles of Books Now in Print and on Sale, with the Price at Which They May Be Obtained of All Booksellers.* London: Joseph Whitaker; New York: Scribner, Welford & Armstrong, 1874-1939, 1952-61 (no volumes were published 1940-51), passim; continued as *The Reference Catalogue of Current Literature (British Books in Print),* then as *British Books in Print.* London: Whitaker, 1962-87, passim, and then as *Whitaker's Books in Print: The Reference Catalogue of Current Literature.* London: J. Whitaker & Sons, 1988- , passim. Updated monthly as *British Books in Print Microfiche.* 1978- , passim.

This reference can be used to locate books by Dickens and works whose titles begin with Dickens. According to Harner (**1147**), p. 320, it "cumulates and updates the weekly list in *Bookseller,* 1858- ." At least in the earlier years, the compilation consisted principally of catalogues issued by United Kingdom publishers—but with an unannotated index at the beginning to the works listed in these catalogues. The latest edition seen, *Whitaker's Books in Print 2000: The Reference Catalogue of Current Literature* (London: J. Whitaker & Sons, 2000) is a five-volume combined author-title index. The Dickens entries, II, 3105-07, include dramatizations and other adaptations of Dickens's works as well as the numerous editions of Dickens's works in print. Also see Peddie and Waddington (**80**).

84. Rogal, Samuel J. *A Chronological Outline of British Literature.* Westport, CT, and London: Greenwood Press, 1980, passim.

Lists births, deaths, historical events, and literary works, including Dickens's, published for each year.

85. Roorbach, O[rville] A., comp. *Bibliotheca Americana, Including Reprints and Original Works, from 1820 to 1848, Inclusive*. New York: O[rville] A. Roorbach, 1849; With Supplement [for 1850], New York: G. P. Putnam, 1850, passim; revised as *Bibliotheca Americana: Catalogue of American Publications, Including Reprints and Original Works, from 1820 to 1852, Inclusive*. New York: O[rville] A. Roorbach, 1852; reprinted New York: Peter Smith, 1939, passim. Supplements: *October, 1852, to May, 1855*. New York: O[rville] A. Roorbach, Jr., 1855, passim; *May, 1855, to March, 1858*. New York: Wiley & Halsted; London: Trubner, 1858, passim; *March, 1858, to January, 1861*. New York: O[rville] A. Roorbach; London: Trubner, 1861, passim.

Gives author, title, price, publisher, and sometimes the year of publication. In the original volume, under "Dickens, Chas.," pp. 155-56, Roorbach lists works published by Harper & Brothers, J. Wiley, Carey & Hart, B. Getz & Co., and Lea & Blanchard. For continuation of *Bibliotheca Americana*, see Kelly, *The American Catalogue of Books* (**77**). Harner (**1147**), pp. 472-73, characterizes *Bibliotheca Americana* as "incomplete, frequently inaccurate, and inconsistent," though "the most comprehensive general list of works published in the country during the period." He notes that it is "gradually being superseded" by Shoemaker et al., *A Checklist of American Imprints* (**87**), in progress.

86. Ryland, Frederick. *Chronological Outlines of English Literature*. London and New York: Macmillan, 1890, etc. (to 1914); reprinted New York: B. Franklin, 1968, passim.

While not really useful for the scholar, this volume briefly lists Dickens's works in Part I, "General Outline" (see pp. 194-224 for 1836-70), which includes—in addition to literary works published—biographical dates, foreign literature published, and historical events for each year. Dickens's works are also listed in Part II, "Authors and Their Works" (see pp, 267-68). Later editions contain two changes in the dating of Dickens's works.

87. Shoemaker, Richard H., [et al.], comps. *A Checklist of American Imprints for 1820[-]*. New York and London: Scarecrow Press, 1964- , passim.

A series, in process of publication, to update, correct, and expand Roorbach's *Bibliotheca Americana* (**85**), listing American editions of Dickens's works and identifying libraries containing these volumes. The latest volume seen, for 1846 publications, was compiled by Carol Rinderknecht and Scott Bruntjen (Lanham, MD, and London: Scarecrow Press, 1997). As one might anticipate, Dickens first makes his appearance in the volume for 1836 publications. See Harner (**1147**), p. 473-74, for details about the range of this series. Also see Carol Rinderknecht, comp., *A Checklist of American Imprints for 1830-1839: Author Index* (Metuchen, NJ, and London: Scarecrow Press, 1989), p. 45, for the Dickens items, and Carol Rinderknecht, comp., *A Checklist of American*

Imprints for 1830-1839: Title Index, 2 vols. (Metuchen, NJ, and London: Scarecrow Press, 1989), passim.

88. Smallwood, P. J. *A Concise Chronology of English Literature.* Totowa, NJ: Barnes and Noble Books, 1985, passim.

Lists births, deaths, historical events, and literary works published, for each year, including Dickens's.

89. Sutherland, John. "Victorian Fiction: Reprints and Critical Commentary." *British Book News*, December 1984, pp. 711-14.

A survey of reprints of editions and collections of critical commentary on Dickens and other Victorian novelists, followed by a list of some recent critical studies of Victorian fiction.

90. Tanselle, G. Thomas. *Guide to the Study of United States Imprints.* 2 vols. Cambridge, MA: Belknap Press of Harvard University Press, 1971, passim.

Lists several studies that deal with American editions of Dickens's works—see the index under Dickens.

91. Todd, William B., and Ann Bowden. *Tauchnitz International Editions in English, 1841-1955: A Bibliographical History.* New York: Bibliographical Society of America, 1988, passim.

Largely a listing of Tauchnitz's publications, a number of which were of Dickens's works, with connecting historical narrative. See the index and the Author-Title Register for convenient listings of Dickens's works. Illustrated.

92. *Whitaker's Cumulative Booklist: The Complete List of All Books Published in the United Kingdom during the Period, Giving Details as to Author, Title, Sub-Title, Size, Number of Pages, Price, Date, Classification, Standard Book Number, and Publisher of Every Book, in One Alphabetical Arrangement under Author, Title and Subject, Where This Forms Part of the Title, [1923-86].* London: J. Whitaker & Sons, 1924-87, passim; continued by *Whitaker's Book List, [1987-].* London: J. Whitaker & Sons, 1988- , passim.

Issued quarterly and cumulated annually, with some five-year cumulations, 1939-43 to 1963-67, compiled from the weekly listings in *The Publisher and Bookseller*, superseded by *The Bookseller*. Check under Dickens in the index to find the section (usually Fiction) in which Dickens's works are listed. For fuller details and related works, see Marcuse (**1152**), p. 40. Also see Peddie and Waddington (**80**).

1C. BIBLIOGRAPHIES OF INDIVIDUAL DICKENS WORKS

Note: Several bibliographies in section 1A, above, contain either lists of editions of individual Dickens works or detailed collations of parts issues of individual works. See particularly Collins (**8**), Darton (**11**), Eckel (**16**), Hatton and Cleaver (**24**), Schlicke (**41**), and Smith (**45, 46**). For other bibliographies of individual Dickens works, see **bibliographies of editions** under the individual work in part 1 of the subject index.

Barnaby Rudge

93. Rice, Thomas J. *Barnaby Rudge: An Annotated Bibliography*. Garland Dickens Bibliographies, 6; Garland Reference Library of the Humanities, 630. New York and London: Garland Publishing, 1987. xxxvii + 351 pp.

One in a series of extensively annotated Dickens bibliographies—see DeVries (**13**). This volume covers the various manuscript materials, editions, adaptations, and textual, bibliographical, critical, and special studies of *Barnaby Rudge*, Dickens's fifth novel, through 1986, including doctoral dissertations and major foreign-language studies. It also contains a "Historical Chronology, 1751-1848" of events relevant to Dickens's first historical novel, a chronology of Dickens's works, and full author, title, and subject indexes (pp. 315-51). Of special interest is a central section entitled "*Barnaby Rudge*: The Context," which lists and annotates works by Dickens and others related to the novel, historical materials, topical materials, and bibliographical guides to these materials. This section, Rice notes in his introduction, "will provide the necessary backgrounds for future investigation" of this novel. In a preface, Rice points out that only in the past twenty-five years have scholars paid much attention to *Barnaby Rudge* and that he has thus designed this bibliography more as "a guide *for* research" on *Barnaby Rudge* than as "a guide *to*" studies of it. Rice's introduction comments convincingly on why this novel should not have been as neglected as it has been, notes some of the features that "make it unique among Dickens's creations," and examines some of the early and often perceptive criticism of this novel, as well as more recent critical approaches.

Reviews: R. A. Aken, *Choice*, 25 (1987/88), 1224 (a "valuable primer for further research"); I. Crawford, *Dickensian*, 84 (1988), 182-83 (an "impressive, diverse array of materials," valuable annotations, "highly judicious" assessments; "another outstanding contribution to Garland's invaluable series"); J. J. Fenstermaker, *Dickens Quarterly*, 8 (1991), 85-88 (praises the "full and extensively cross-referenced" annotations and the introductory "historical survey"); B. F. Fisher, IV, *Literary Research*, 13 (1988), 53-54 (commends highly as a reference work that makes "readily accessible the great author and the plenty written about him," and finds the index useful); M. B. Lambert, *American Reference Books Annual*, 19 (1988), 487-88 (praises highly; finds Rice "very knowledgeable").

Bleak House

Note: See DeVries (**12**) and entries in 1A.

Christmas Books, Christmas Stories, and Other Shorter Fiction

Note: Also see Collins (**9**), Smith (**46**), and Kitton (**154**).

94. Burns, Landon C. "A Cross-Referenced Index of Short Fiction [Antho-
   logies] and Author-Title Listing." *Studies in Short Fiction*, 7 (1970), v-vi, 1-
   218, and supplements.

   A listing of anthologies of short fiction published principally in the 1950s
and 1960s itemizing the contents of each volume, followed by a listing of the
contents by author and title. The first supplement to this list was published as
"The 1970 Supplement to a Cross-Referenced Index of Short Fiction Anthologies and Author-Title Listing," *Studies in Short Fiction*, 8 (1971), 351-409; the
second supplement was published in volume 13 (1976) and supplements were
published annually thereafter in the spring issue of the journal. Various co-
editors have helped with the supplements. Dickens's stories are frequently
listed.

95. Chicorel, Marietta, ed. *Chicorel Index to Short Stories in Anthologies and Collec-
   tions.* Chicorel Index Series, 12. New York: Chicorel Library Publishing
   Corp., 1974, pp. 517-20, and *Chicorel Index to Short Stories in Anthologies and
   Collections, 1975/76: 1977 Annual.* Chicorel Index Series, 12, 1977 Annual.
   Ibid., 1977, p. 172.

   Dickens's five Christmas Books, the Christmas Stories from *Household
Words* and *All the Year Round,* his other stories, and descriptive essays, principally from *The Uncommercial Traveller* and *Reprinted Pieces,* are included in the
listings.

96. Cook, Dorothy E., and Isabel S. Monro, comps. "Dickens, Charles,
   1812-1870." In their *Short Story Index: An Index to 60,000 Stories in 4,320
   Collections.* New York: H. W. Wilson, 1953, pp. 350-54.

   A short-title list of Dickens's stories published in various short story collections through 1949. Supplements were issued for 1950-54, 1955-58, 1959-63,
1964-68, and 1969-74—and then annually, by various compilers, with five-year
cumulations. The latest volume seen, *Short Story Index, 1994-1998: An Index to
Stories in Collections and Periodicals* (New York: H. W. Wilson, 1999), was edited
by John Greenfieldt and Juliette Yaakov. Also see *Short Story Index: Collections
Indexed, 1900-1978,* ed. Juliette Yaakov (New York: H. W. Wilson, 1979).
Cook and Monro's 1953 volume supersedes the *Index to Short Stories,* compiled
by Ina Ten Eyck Firkins (White Plains, NY: H. W. Wilson, 1915); 2nd and

enlarged edition (New York: H. W. Wilson; London: Grafton, 1923), with supplements in 1929 and 1936.

97. Davis, Paul. "A Chronological List of Some Noteworthy Versions of the Carol." In his *The Lives and Times of Ebenezer Scrooge.* New Haven, CT, and London: Yale University Press, 1990, pp. 259-70.

An unannotated list of editions, dramatizations, facsimile reproductions of the manuscript, imitations, cartoons, parodies, films, readings, sound recordings, musical compositions, drawings, etc., of *A Christmas Carol,* beginning with the first edition and ending with the 1988 film *Scrooged,* starring Bill Murray.

98. Glancy, Ruth F. *Dickens's Christmas Books, Christmas Stories, and Other Short Fiction: An Annotated Bibliography.* Garland Dickens Bibliographies, 4; Garland Reference Library of the Humanities, 479. New York and London: Garland Publishing, 1985. xxxiii + 610 pp.

One in a series of extensively annotated Dickens bibliographies—see DeVries (**13**). This volume covers the various editions, manuscript materials, adaptations, and textual, bibliographical, critical, and special studies of Dickens's five Christmas Books, the nine Christmas Numbers for *Household Words,* the nine Christmas Numbers for *All the Year Round,* and four other works of short fiction, as well as various selected and collected editions of the Christmas works and other stories. This volume of 2,201 numbered entries includes foreign studies and dissertations and a full name/subject index (pp. 555-610). In her introduction, Glancy notes that, though Dickens's shorter works of fiction have been unduly neglected by modern critics, this "was not always the case," as the thickness of this 610-page volume illustrates. She also examines the popularity of Dickens's Christmas works and records the "academic battles" over their literary quality. Glancy is currently preparing an update to this bibliography.

Reviews: S. Ebershoff-Coles, *American Reference Books Annual,* 17 (1986), 457-58 (praises quality and length of annotations); D. A. Thomas, *Dickens Quarterly,* 3 (1986), 139-42 (notes a few "minor slips," finds the organization "a bit confusing," but characterizes the work as a "major scholarly achievement" for its thoroughness, "exceptionally detailed" annotation, and an introduction that exhibits the author's "command of the vast amount of information included in her bibliography"); *Wilson Library Bulletin,* 60, iii (November 1985), 61 ("this thorough bibliography should encourage graduate students and scholars to examine the works' critical legacy anew and to build upon it").

99. Hearn, Michael P. "Bibliography." In Dickens's *The Annotated Christmas Carol.* Ed. Hearn (**2340**), pp. 174-80.

Lists works by Dickens in chronological order, "notable" editions of *A Christmas Carol* and the Christmas Stories and other Christmas Books, translations of *A Christmas Carol,* studies of Dickens and his writings (highly selective), and a few studies of John Leech, the original illustrator of *A Christmas Carol*. For textual matters taken up in this volume, see Hearn (**2340**).

100. "Secutor" (pseud.). "Early Issues of First Editions: Dickens' Christmas Books." *Bookman's Journal*, 2 (1920), 23, 41.

Itemizes the various issues of the first editions of Dickens's five Christmas Books.

David Copperfield

101. Bauer, Matthias. "Literaturverzeichnis." In his *Das Leben als Geschichte: Poetische Reflexion in Dickens' "David Copperfield."* Anglistische Studien, 10. Köln and Wien, Ger.: Böhlau Verlag, 1991, pp. 320-37.

A three-part unannotated bibliography of 1) Dickens's works (listing some modern editions of several of the novels, collected letters, and other works), 2) related works, and 3) secondary literature, a fairly extensive list of books and articles with particular relevance to *David Copperfield*.

102. Burgis, Nina. "Descriptive List of Editions 1849-1867." In the Clarendon Edition of Dickens's *David Copperfield* (**2359**), pp. lxiii-lxv.

Provides bibliographical descriptions with collation, information about the plates, and notes on the printing and publication of editions of *David Copperfield* published in Dickens's lifetime.

103. Dunn, Richard J. *David Copperfield: An Annotated Bibliography*. Garland Dickens Bibliographies, 8; Garland Reference Library of the Humanities, 280. New York and London: Garland Publishing, 1981. xxv + 256 pp.

One in a series of Dickens bibliographies—see DeVries (**13**). This volume is an extensively annotated bibliography (778 numbered entries) of the editions, manuscript materials, letters, illustrations, adaptations, and critical, special, biographical, and bibliographical studies of *David Copperfield*, with a full author-subject index (pp. 227-56). Dunn excludes non-English language studies and translations. In his introduction (pp. xi-xxiv), he comments intelligently on Dickens's closeness to this novel and on the novel's language, portrayal of memory, first-person narration, and problems of structural unity. He also warns the reader of "the uneven quality of the biographical, topographical, and textual studies" of *David Copperfield*. For a supplement to this volume, see Dunn and Tandy (**104**).

Reviews: *American Notes and Queries*, 21 (1982/83), 196 (notes contents); *Choice*, 19 (1981/82), 1376 ("authoritative" introduction; a "model reference work throughout"); J. J. Fenstermaker, *Dickens Studies Newsletter*, 14 (1983), 72-74 (notes some "minor blemishes," finds the introduction "occasionally wanting," but assesses the work as overall an "invaluable resource," with "substantial" and "judiciously complete" annotations); E. S. Gleaves, *American Reference Books Annual*, 13 (1982), 672-73 ("extraordinarily rich compilation," with "generous and readable" annotations; the "most extensive compilation now available" of *David Copperfield* studies); D. Paroissien, *Dickensian*, 79 (1983), 165-67 ("exemplary," and serving a wide audience); R. Patten, *Papers of the Bibliographical Society of America*, 77 (1983), 209-17 (praises Dunn's "recovery of fugitive, dispersed, and little known comments" about *David Copperfield* and the "soundness" of his annotations; "exemplary in format, scope, and judgment").

104. Dunn, Richard J., and Ann M. Tandy. "*David Copperfield*: An Annotated Bibliography. Supplement I–1981-1998." *Dickens Studies Annual*, 28 (1999), 345-467; published separately, The Dickens Bibliographies, AMS Studies in the Nineteenth Century, 23. New York: AMS Press, 2000. xx + 117 pp.

An update of Dunn's earlier bibliography of *David Copperfield* (**103**), with entries through early 1998. The format of the earlier volume is pretty much retained and the entry numbers (779-1140) are continuous from that volume. The introduction in *Dickens Studies Annual* comments intelligently on shifts in critical approaches to the novel since 1981. In the separately printed volume, this introduction becomes the preface and a new, longer introduction by Dunn, "A Life of *David Copperfield*," pp. xi-xx, is added. In it, he comments on the critical fortunes of *David Copperfield*, "a book with brilliant surfaces and intriguing depths"; on this novel as an important "mid-century cultural document"; on its autobiographical elements; and on the *David Copperfield* bibliography (and its supplement) as comprising "A Life of *David Copperfield*" in its own right. A useful author-subject index is included in both versions of the supplement.

Dombey and Son

105. Horsman, Alan. "Descriptive List of Editions 1846-1867." In the Clarendon Edition of Dickens's *Dombey and Son* (**2376**), pp. xlvii-xlix.

Provides bibliographical description with collation, information about the plates, and notes on the printing and publication of editions of *Dombey and Son* published in Dickens's lifetime.

106. Litvack, Leon. *Charles Dickens's **Dombey and Son**: An Annotated Bibliography*. The Dickens Bibliographies, AMS Studies in the Nineteenth Century, 19. New York: AMS Press, 1999. xxxv + 399 pp.

One in a series of extensively annotated Dickens bibliographies—see DeVries (**12**). This volume covers the various editions, manuscript materials, adaptations, illustrations, and textual, bibliographical, critical, biographical, and special studies in English of *Dombey and Son*, with a full author/subject index. In his introduction, Litvack intelligently and extensively surveys the scholarly and critical studies of the work. "The future," he concludes, "looks bright for continued study of this fascinating novel," the "first work of Dick ens's artistic maturity."

Reviews: S. E. Kelsey, *Choice*, 38 (2000/01), 302 ("informative, insightfully annotated citations"; "highly recommended for academic libraries"); V. Purton, *Dickensian*, 96 (2000), 247-48 ("a wonderful book" to be "used and enjoyed," with "delights and discoveries everywhere," and a "richly informative" index and excellent, judicious annotations); C. Ringelheim, *American Reference Books Annual*, 32 (2001), 515 (largely descriptive; recommends for "university and college collections").

Great Expectations

107. Cardwell, Margaret. "Descriptive List of Editions 1861-1868." In the Clarendon Edition of Dickens's *Great Expectations* (**2381**), pp. lxiv-lxvii.

Provides bibliographical descriptions, with collation, information about the plates, and notes on the printing and publication of editions of *Great Expectations* published in Dickens's lifetime.

108. Sadrin, Anny. "Appendix 2: Editions of *Great Expectations* during Dickens's Lifetime." In her *Great Expectations*. Unwin Critical Library. London: Unwin Hyman, 1988, pp. 278-80.

A simple listing of these editions. For other supplementary material in this edition, see Sadrin (**661, 1093, 2405**).

Reviews: M. Cardwell, *Dickensian*, 85 (1989), 50-51 ("an invaluable, even indispensable, handbook for the serious student"); T, J. Cribb, *Review of English Studies*, 45 (1994), 123-24 (dislikes Sadrin's critical approach though finds the scholarly apparatus "well enough" achieved), J. Dobrinsky, *Etudes anglaises*, 44 (1991), 350 (in French; "excellent"); D. Gervais, *Modern Language Review*, 86 (1991), 181-82 ("meticulously done," with a useful introduction, though Sadrin is "more reliable as a guide to specific problems than when she is being speculative"); R. Mason, *Notes and Queries*, ns 36 (1989), 525-27 ("a detailed and complex consideration of a detailed and complex work of art"); S. Monod, *Victorian Studies*, 33 (1989/90), 513-15 ("intelligent, informative, well-organized," and "delightfully" readable); D. Paroissien, *Dickens Quarterly*, 10 (1993), 223-27 (an "exceptionally useful book").

109. Worth, George J. *Great Expectations: An Annotated Bibliography*. Garland Dickens Bibliographies, 5; Garland Reference Library of the Humanities, 555. New York and London: Garland Publishing, 1986. xxii + 346 pp.

One in a series of extensively annotated Dickens bibliographies—see DeVries (**13**). This volume covers the various manuscript materials, editions, adaptations, and textual, bibliographical, critical, and special studies in English of *Great Expectations*, including doctoral dissertations, through 1983. This volume of 1,114 entries includes full name and subject indexes (pp. 313-46). In his introduction, Worth assesses the novel's critical fortunes, finding that, for most of the twentieth century, *Great Expectations* has ranked "near if not at the top among Dickens's novels in critical and popular favor," though its nineteenth-century reputation was mixed. He attributes the more recent respect for this novel to changing critical emphases.

Reviews: J. J. Fenstermaker, *Dickens Quarterly*, 5 (1988), 33-36 (would prefer a more elaborate subdivision of the entries and a lengthier introduction, but finds the annotations "useful" and the bibliography generally warranting "approval and gratitude"); L. Lane, Jr., *Newsletter of the Victorian Studies Association of Western Canada*, 13, ii (1987), 15-21; J. M. Parker, *Choice*, 24 (1986/87), 750 (a "thorough and useful compilation" with "informative annotations" and an excellent introduction); E. Patterson, *American Reference Books Annual*, 18 (1987), 463 (high praise for an "extraordinary collection of writings about Dickens's *Great Expectations*").

Hard Times

Note: Also see Kitton (**154**).

110.   Manning, Sylvia. *Hard Times: An Annotated Bibliography*. Garland Dickens Bibliographies, 3; Garland Reference Library of the Humanities, 515. New York and London: Garland Publishing, 1984. xxiii + 296 pp.

One in a series of extensively annotated Dickens bibliographies—see DeVries (**13**). This volume covers the various editions, manuscript materials, adaptations, and textual, bibliographical, critical, and special studies of *Hard Times* in English through 1982, including doctoral dissertations, with a full subject index and index of proper names (pp. 263-96). Manning's introduction trenchantly surveys the critical response to *Hard Times*, from its neglect well into the twentieth century (more often than not it was not even listed among Dickens's works or, at best, tagged as a minor work) to its resuscitation by F. R. Leavis in his "The Novel as Dramatic Poem (1): *Hard Times*," *Scrutiny*, 14 (1947), 185-203; reprinted as chapter 5, "*Hard Times*: An Analytic Note," in his *The Great Tradition* (London: Chatto & Windus, 1948), and its subsequent rehabilitation as an important novel in the Dickens canon.

Reviews: A. M. Cohn, *Dickens Quarterly*, 3 (1986), 135-36 (offers a few additions and emendations, but finds the work "a welcome addition to the Dickens reference shelf," with an "informative introduction"); J. Rettig, *American Reference Books Annual*, 16 (1985), 401 (well annotated—an "invaluable source"); J. G. Watson, *Notes and Queries*, ns 34 (1987), 558-59 (praises the introduction, annotations, and index, as well as the "light" the volume throws on the critical history of *Hard Times*).

Little Dorrit

111.   Sucksmith, Harvey P. "Descriptive List of Editions 1855-1868." In the Clarendon Edition of Dickens's *Little Dorrit* (**2420**), pp. l-lii.

Provides bibliographical description with collation, information about the plates, and notes on the printing and publication of editions of *Little Dorrit* published in Dickens's lifetime.

Martin Chuzzlewit

112.   Cardwell, Margaret. "Descriptive List of Editions 1843-1867." In the Clarendon Edition of Dickens's *Martin Chuzzlewit* (**2423**), pp. lxi-lxii.

Provides bibliographical descriptions with collation, information about the plates, and notes on the printing and publication of editions of *Martin Chuzzlewit* published in Dickens's lifetime.

113. Lougy, Robert E. *Martin Chuzzlewit: An Annotated Bibliography.* Garland Dickens Bibliographies, 6; Garland Reference Library of the Humanities, 1033. New York and London: Garland Publishing, 1990. xxx + 290 pp.

One in a series of extensively annotated Dickens bibliographies—see DeVries (**13**). This volume covers the various editions, manuscript materials, adaptations, and textual, bibliographical, critical, and special studies of *Martin Chuzzlewit* in English, including dissertations, through 1987/88, with a full author/subject index (pp. 263-90). A special section on "Dickens in America: Background, American Topography, American Characters" is also included. In a preface, Lougy indicates his initial surprise at the "good amount of attention" that he discovered has been devoted to *Martin Chuzzlewit*, since his belief had been that it had remained "for so long in the shadow of Dickens's other novels." His introduction looks particularly at the American section of the novel and its anticipated unfavorable reception in the United States, but also at its mixed British reception. Yet, he points out, it was frequently dramatized for the stage, and two of its characters in particular, Mrs. Gamp and Mr. Pecksniff, fascinated Dickens's contemporaries—and later critics as well. Lougy concludes that no one critic or critical approach can ever answer all the questions about this novel, fully assess its strengths and weaknesses, or exactly pinpoint its continuing appeal. Nevertheless, he asserts, it is one of those powerful works of fiction that continue to fascinate us because "they contain within them a secret, a mystery or elusive center, that defies any critical solution, and yet teases us into critical responses."

Reviews: M. Y. A[ndrews], *Dickensian*, 88 (1992), 173-75 (a valuable aid to research and "profile of Dickens's artistic reputation," disproving the belief that this novel has "received relatively little attention from critics and scholars"); M. A. Beck, *American Reference Books Annual*, 22 (1991), 486 (praises the "engaging" introduction and the "informative and evaluative annotations"; a "useful work").

The Mystery of Edwin Drood

Note: Also see Kitton (**154**).

114. Cardwell, Margaret. "Descriptive List of Editions 1870-1875." In the Clarendon Edition of Dickens's *The Mystery of Edwin Drood* (**2434**), pp. li-liii.

Provides bibliographical descriptions with collation, information about the plates, and notes on the printing and publication of editions of the unfinished novel in the five years after Dickens's death.

115. Cox, Don R. *Charles Dickens's* **The Mystery of Edwin Drood***: An Annotated Bibliography.* The Dickens Bibliographies. AMS Studies in the Nineteenth Century, 17. New York: AMS Press, 1998. xxxvi + 669 pp.

One in a series of extensively annotated bibliographies—see DeVries (**12**). This volume covers the various editions, manuscript materials, adaptations, illustrations, and textual, bibliographical, critical, biographical, and special studies of *The Mystery of Edwin Drood* principally in English through 1997, including doctoral dissertations, with a full author/subject index. In his introduction, Cox comments perceptively on the great interest generated by Dickens's unfinished novel, manifested in the numerous attempts to complete the novel and the ongoing discussion about how Dickens intended to end it. He also surveys the critical response to the work, from 1870 on.

Reviews: C. Forsyte [Gordon Philo], *Dickensian*, 95 (1999), 161-63 (a "monumental work"); W. S. Jacobson, *Dickens Quarterly*, 17 (2000), 249-54 (would have liked the volume to be more selective, more concise, but praises its cross referencing and indexing and particularly the sections on manuscript and textual materials, as well as Cox's "reliable and scholarly work"); S. E. Kelsey, *Choice*, 36 (1998/99), 288 ("clearly organized" and "comprehensive"; for "all academic libraries"). Also see Stewart (**1107**).

Nicholas Nickleby

Note: See DeVries (**12**) and entries in 1A.

The Old Curiosity Shop

116. Brennan, Elizabeth M. "Descriptive List of Editions." In the Clarendon Edition of Dickens's *The Old Curiosity Shop* (**2460**), pp. xcvi-ciii.

Provides bibliographical descriptions with collations, information about the illustrations, and notes on the printing and publication of editions of *The Old Curiosity Shop* in Dickens's lifetime, including early translations.

117. Schlicke, Priscilla, and Paul Schlicke. *The Old Curiosity Shop: An Annotated Bibliography.* Garland Dickens Bibliographies, 9; Garland Reference Library of the Humanities, 708. New York and London: Garland Publishing, 1988. xxi + 495 pp.

One in a series of extensively annotated Dickens bibliographies—see DeVries (**13**). This volume covers the various manuscript materials, editions, adaptations, illustrations, and textual, bibliographical, critical, and special studies published in English of Dickens's fourth novel, including doctoral dissertations, with a full, useful index (pp. 453-95). In the preface, the authors point out that, in contrast to other bibliographies in the series, theirs includes "a large number of decidedly non-scholarly, non-intellectual, and even unintelligent responses to Dickens's work" because *The Old Curiosity Shop* "was nothing if not a popular work of art, and one crucial measure of that popularity" was its impact outside intellectual circles. Their introduction tracks the novel's early popular success and critical acclaim (for its pathos, moral elevation, and comic elements) as well as its later critical decline, reflecting "a widespread change in sensibility among readers." They also note, however, recent reexaminations of the novel's "dark" side and new and promising historical approaches.

Reviews: M. Y. A[ndrews], *Dickensian*, 88 (1992), 173-75 (a valuable aid to research and "profile of Dickens's artistic reputation," with an "impressive number of entries and sections"); I. Campbell, *Aberdeen University Review*, 53 (1989), 165-66 (an "admirable bibliography," a "model of thorough research," with "exemplary presentation"); B. F. Fisher, IV, *Literary Research*, 13 (1988), 53-54 (commends highly as a reference work that makes "readily accessible the great author and the plenty written about him" and finds the index useful); J. R. Ivey, *American Reference Books Annual*, 20 (1989), 445 (basically descriptive of the wide-ranging scope of this bibliography).

Oliver Twist

Note: Also see Bentley (**144**).

118. Paroissien, David. *Oliver Twist: An Annotated Bibliography*. Garland Dickens Bibliographies, 2; Garland Reference Library of the Humanities, 385. New York and London: Garland Publishing, 1986. xxxi + 313 pp.

One in a series of extensively annotated Dickens bibliographies—see DeVries (**13**). This volume covers the various manuscript materials, editions, adaptations, illustrations, and textual, bibliographical, critical, and special studies in English of *Oliver Twist* (808 entries) with full author and subject indexes (pp. 297-313). Paroissien also includes sections on *Oliver Twist* and the Newgate novel and on the English poor laws and other background topics. An appendix on "Dickens's Involvement with *Oliver Twist*" contains a chronological side by side listing of events in Dickens's life, his publications relevant to *Oliver Twist*, and political and social events, 1822-69. Paroissien's introduction, pp. xiii-xxix, examines the reasons for the appeal of the novel to Victorian and to modern readers, though he also points out that some contemporary criticism of the novel complained that it romanticized criminality, against which Dickens defended the novel's reality. Paroissien also surveys twentieth-century views and criticisms of the novel. He is currently preparing an update to this bibliography.

Reviews: J. J. Fenstermaker, *Dickens Quarterly*, 5 (1988), 33-36 ("a distinguished achievement," with full annotations that are "lucid and balanced," other useful aids, and an "interesting, valuable, and informative" introduction); C. H. Kullman, *American Reference Books Annual*, 18 (1987), 463 ("a valuable addition to the Garland Dickens Bibliographies"); S. A. Parker, *Choice*, 24 (1986/87), 286 (an "essential contribution to Dickens studies," a "reference tool to captivate and engage").

119. Tillotson, Kathleen. "Descriptive List of Editions 1838-1867." In the Clarendon Edition of Dickens's *Oliver Twist* (**2474**), pp. xlviii-lvi.

Provides bibliographical description with collation, information about the plates, and notes on the printing and publication of editions of *Oliver Twist* published in Dickens's lifetime.

Our Mutual Friend

120.   Brattin, Joel J., and Bert G. Hornback. ***Our Mutual Friend: An Anno-tated Bibliography.*** Garland Dickens Bibliographies, 1; Garland Reference Library of the Humanities, 481. New York and London: Garland Publishing, 1984. xxi + 197 pp.

One of a series of extensively annotated bibliographies—see DeVries (**13**). This volume covers the various editions, manuscript materials, adaptations, illustrations, and textual, bibliographical, critical, and special studies of Dickens's last complete novel, excluding studies of the novel not in English. The introduction, pp. xii-xxi, notes the widely divergent opinions of this novel, from the contemporary reviews to the most recent criticism, though pointing out that interest in *Our Mutual Friend* has "continued to accelerate." The authors also suggest "some future directions" for the study of this novel. The bibliography contains 683 entries, and there is a full author/subject index (pp. 175-97). Robert Heaman is currently preparing an update to this bibliography.

Reviews: M. Cotsell, *Dickens Quarterly*, 3 (1986), 136-39 (notes a few omissions, and misplacements, dislikes some organizational decisions, but generally finds the authors have not "missed a great deal"); C. H. Kullman, *American Reference Books Annual*, 16 (1985), 401 (praises the quality of the annotations in this "easy-to-use resource guide"); R. B. Meeker, *Choice*, 22 (1984/85), 960 ("thorough, accurate, and generally excellent," with "superb, informative annotations"); J. Rettig, *Wilson Library Bulletin*, 59 (1984/85), 358 (a brief, mainly descriptive review; a "helpful bibliography").

Pickwick Papers

121.   "Books of Selections from 'Pickwick.'" *Dickensian*, 32 (1935/36), 140.

A list of twenty-six books, 1861-1931.

122.   *Collation of the Famous Lapham-Wallace Pickwick.* New York: Privately printed by Harry F. Marks, n. d. 8 pp.

A detailed bibliographical description of a well-known collation of *Pickwick Papers* in parts. The Harvard University Library online catalogue identifies the author as Albert A. Hopkins and the date of publication as "ca. 1925."

123.   Craig, Clifford. *The Van Diemen's Land Edition of the Pickwick Papers: A General and Bibliographical Study with Some Notes on Henry Dowling.* Hobart, Tasmania: Cat and Fiddle Press, 1973. 65 pp.

Provides some background information about and a detailed description of the parts of a serialized edition of *Pickwick Papers* published without Dickens's permission in Van Diemen's Land (now Tasmania) by Henry Dowling, 1838-39. It was published in twenty-five parts of twenty-four pages each, without illustrations. A comparable description of the bound volume (1839) of the parts issues, containing 20 illustrations based on the original illustrations for the London edition, is also included. Illustrated.

124. Eckel, John C. *Prime Pickwicks in Parts. Census with Complete Collation, Comparison and Comment.* New York: E. H. Wells; London: C. J. Sawyer, 1928. [xii] + 91 pp.

Eckel discusses the history and collations of fourteen "good copies" of *Pickwick Papers* in parts, reaffirms the eleven "points" that he established in his bibliography of 1913 (**16**) for a "prime" collation of the novel, itemizes the requirements for the original plates, examines part by part and in great detail the advertisements in the Bruton copy of *Pickwick Papers*, and compares some of its points with those of other well-known collations. By way of conclusion, to his original eleven points Eckel adds four textual points, another concerning the imprint, a number concerning the illustrations, and nine concerning the advertisements. This work contains eleven plates and a foreword by A. Edward Newton.

The Berg Collection, New York Public Library, contains 1) galley proofs for this edition, with minor corrections only (labeled "Revised Proofsheets of 'Prime Pickwicks'"; 2) a corrected make-up dummy of the front matter for the volume, with holograph suggestions in the hand of A. E. Newton (he wrote the foreword) and with an accompanying letter from Eckel to Julius S. Weyl of Edward Stern & Company, the Philadelphia printers who set up the work; and 3) a later make-up dummy for the entire volume set up on large brown-paper sheets, with pieces of proof pasted on and with some corrections, queries, and notations.

Review: *Times Literary Supplement*, 25 October 1928, p. 788 (a brief descriptive notice).

125. Engel, Elliot. **Pickwick Papers:** *An Annotated Bibliography.* Garland Dickens Bibliographies, 7; Garland Reference Library of the Humanities, 568. New York and London: Garland Publishing, 1990. xxxii + 345 pp.

One in a series of Dickens bibliographies—see DeVries (**13**). This volume is an extensively annotated bibliography (665 numbered items) of the editions, manuscript materials, letters, adaptations, illustrations, and critical, special, biographical, and bibliographical studies of Dickens's first novel, with full author/subject index (pp. 287-345) compiled by Duane DeVries. The bibliography includes doctoral dissertations but not non-English language studies and translations. In his introduction, Engel traces in some detail the history of criticism of the novel, stressing that neither the earlier appreciations nor the more recent scientific analyses of "structure, unity, social criticism, and the dark implications of the interpolated tales" have "done full justice" to this novel. Modern critics, he concludes, "would do well to remember" that *Pickwick Papers* is "a glorification of the foolishness and frivolity within the human soul—and its desperate need for both."

Reviews: M. Andrews, *Dickensian*, 88 (1992), 173-75 (a valuable aid to research, with "judicious and illuminating" annotations, but too selective in entries); A. F. Dalbey, *Choice*, 28 (1990/91), 281-82 (informative introduction, comprehensive annotations, "useful and complete index"); J. J. Fenstermaker, *Dickens Quarterly*, 8 (1991), 85-88 (notes some weaknesses but has high praise for the introductory "historical survey"); C. H. Kullman, *American Reference Books Annual*, 22 (1991), 485-86 (praises annotations; a "useful resource").

126. "The English Editions of Pickwick." *Dickensian*, 32 (1935/36), 126-28.

Lists ninety-five editions of *Pickwick Papers* from the first edition to the "News Chronicle" edition of 1934. This article is attributed by Gold (**982**) to Walter Dexter but treated as an anonymous piece in Frank T. Dunn's *A Cumulative Analytical Index to **The Dickensian**, 1905-1974* (**1165**). It is included in the Dickens Fellowship's *Catalogue of a Pickwick Exhibit Held at the Dickens House* (**1787**), arranged by William Miller.

127. Fitzgerald, Percy. "Bibliography of 'Pickwick.'" In his *The History of Pickwick: An Account of Its Characters, Localities, Allusions, and Illustrations, with a Bibliography*. London: Chapman and Hall, 1891; reprinted Folcroft, PA: Folcroft Library Editions, 1977, pp. 357-75.

Provides extensive information about the parts publication of *Pickwick Papers* as well as a listing of later editions, translations, imitations, sets of illustrations, and critical and other studies. For errors in this work, see Marshall (**1414**).

128. Kinsley, James. "Descriptive List of Editions 1837-1867." In the Clarendon Edition of Dickens's *The Pickwick Papers* (**2493**), pp. lxxxvi-xc.

Provides bibliographical description with collation, information about the plates, and notes on the printing and publication of editions of *Pickwick Papers* published in Dickens's lifetime.

129. Miller, W[illiam], and E. H. Strange. *A Centenary Bibliography of the Pickwick Papers*. London: Argonaut Press, 1936. 223 pp.

"The Bibliography," pp. 1-65, an elaborate collation of "a perfect copy" of *Pickwick Papers* in parts, is reprinted from Miller and Strange, "The Original *Pickwick Papers*: The Collation of a Perfect First Edition" (**130**), including the illustrations. In "Contemporary Criticism," pp. 67-185, the authors also reprint a number of early reviews of *Pickwick Papers*. In "The Seymour Controversy," pp. 186-223, they reprint Mrs. Robert Seymour's *An Account of the Origin of the "Pickwick Papers"* (London: Printed for the Author, [1854?]) and letters to the *Athenaeum*, 19 March, 28 March, 29 March, and 3 April 1866, by Seymour's son, Dickens, and Henry G. Bohn, on the subject of Seymour's influence on the novel.

Review: *Times Literary Supplement*, 28 March 1936, pp. 249-50 (principally reviews two other works; mentions but does not review this work).

130. Miller, William, and E. H. Strange. "The Original *Pickwick Papers*: The Collation of a Perfect First Edition." *Dickensian*, 29 (1932/33), 303-09; 30 (1933/34), 31-37, 121-24, 177-80, 249-59; 31 (1934/35), 35-40, 95-99, 219-22, 284-86; reprinted as "The Bibliography." In their *A Centenary Bibliography of the Pickwick Papers* (**129**), pp. 1-65.

In offering advice on how to collect a prime *Pickwick* in parts, Miller and Strange give a full bibliographical description of the work, based on the notes of John F. Dexter, and including variants in the text. They also reproduce many variant plates for the illustrations, including Plates 1 and 2 as done by Seymour and later by Hablot K. Browne ("Phiz").

131. Read, Newbury F. "The American Editions of Pickwick." *Dickensian*, 33 (1936/37), 21-26.

Lists 127 American editions (1836-1936) and thirty-five editions "printed in England for the American market" but with an American imprint (1880-1932), and two editions for the blind, one in braille (1930), one a "talking book" (1935).

Sketches by Boz

Note: Also see Smith (**45**) and Kitton (**154**).

132. DeVries, Duane. "Appendix A: The Publishing History of *Sketches by Boz*." In his *Dickens's Apprentice Years: The Making of a Novelist* (**2499**), pp. 147-57.

A bibliography of the first publication of Dickens's tales and essays collected as *Sketches by Boz*, along with a listing of the changing arrangement of contents in editions of *Sketches by Boz* through the Charles Dickens edition of 1868. Note that the date of the original publication of No. 11, "The Old Bailey," in the *Morning Chronicle* was 23 October 1834, *not* 1835. Also see Mott (**371**) for an addition to DeVries's bibliography.

133. Grillo, Virgil. "*Sketches by Boz*, In Order of Their Publication Chronologically" and "Periodical Groups of the *Sketches by Boz*." In "Chapter Five:

Revisions for Synthesis." In his *Charles Dickens' **Sketches by Boz**: End in the Beginning* (**2502**), pp. 87-92, 95-96.

Lists chronologically the first publication in magazines and newspapers of Dickens's early writings that comprise *Sketches by Boz* and then rearranges them in a second list by the periodicals and newspapers in which they appeared. Grillo also traces, through comparable lists, the arrangement of the pieces in the first editions of the two series of *Sketches by Boz* and their rearrangement in the monthly parts reissue, 1837-39.

134. House, Madeline, and Graham Storey. "[Appendix] F. First Publication of Dickens's Sketches" and "[Appendix] G. The Lord Chamberlain's Copies of Dickens's Plays." In *Pilgrim Letters*, I, 692-94, 695-700.

Appendix F is a listing of the original publication of Dickens's early tales and essays–slightly updated by DeVries (**132**) and Mott (**371**). Appendix G describes the fair copies, now in the British Library, London, of Dickens's three early plays, *The Strange Gentleman, The Village Coquettes,* and *Is She His Wife?* The verses of two songs from *Is She His Wife?* are given, as are five songs from *The Strange Gentleman* not printed in its published edition.

135. Sawyer, John E. S., and F. J. Harvey Darton. "Appendices: I. The First Editions [of *Sketches by Boz*], A Bibliography; II. The Plates." In Darton, *Dickens: Positively the First Appearance* (**2498**), pp. 129-45.

A bibliography of the early editions of *Sketches by Boz,* 1836-39, including a fairly extensive collation of the 1837-39 edition in parts and a listing of the plates that Cruikshank did for these editions.

136. Slater, Michael. "The First Publication of Dickens's Sketches in Serial and Volume Form." In his edition of Dickens's ***Sketches by Boz** and Other Early Papers, 1833-39* (**2506**), pp. xxiii-xxvi.

The most up-to-date listing of the first publication of the individual sketches that comprise Dickens's *Sketches by Boz,* though not as bibliographically detailed as the listing in DeVries (**132**). For more details about the original writing and publishing of the sketches, see Slater's "Introduction" (**2506**).

137. Walder, Dennis. "Appendix A: The First Publication of the *Sketches* in Periodical Volume and Number Form" and "Descriptive Headings, 1868 Charles Dickens Edition." In Dickens's *Sketches by Boz.* Ed. Dennis Walder. Penguin Classics. London, New York, etc.: Penguin Books, 1995, pp. 567-73, 574-82.

In the first appendix, lists the first publication of Dickens's magazine and newspaper sketches collected as *Sketches by Boz* and, in the second, gives the page headlines that Dickens created for the Charles Dickens Edition of the novel.

A Tale of Two Cities

138. Glancy, Ruth F. *A Tale of Two Cities: An Annotated Bibliography*. Garland Dickens Bibliographies, 12; Garland Reference Library of the Humanities, 1339. New York and London: Garland Publishing, 1993. xxviii + 236 pp.

One in a series of extensively annotated Dickens bibliographies—see DeVries (**13**). In its 672 items this volume covers the various manuscript materials, editions, adaptations, illustrations, and textual, bibliographical, critical, and special studies published in English of Dickens's *A Tale of Two Cities*, including doctoral dissertations, with a full name and subject index (pp. 213-36). Translations of the novel have not been included, Glancy indicates, and the bibliography contains "a limited number of foreign articles." In her introduction, Glancy surveys the "wildly diverging opinions" of the critics, "opinions that over the years have remained conflicting rather than showing a progression in attitudes or approaches" and have been "surprisingly personal" in their responses to the novel. She also looks at studies of the characters in the novel and the novel's sources and notes the "recent huge increase in critical interest" in the novel.

Reviews: N. Page, *Dickensian*, 90 (1994), 50-51 ("an admirably comprehensive bibliography," an "addition to the useful Garland series . . . to be warmly welcomed"); J. Rettig, *American Reference Books Annual*, 25 (1994), 513 (a "thorough," helpful bibliography); D. A. Thomas, *Dickens Quarterly*, 11 (1994), 148-51 ("a very good introduction, extensive and thorough annotation, and comprehensive coverage"); J. G. Watson, *Notes and Queries*, ns 42 (1995), 508-09 ("organized with meticulous care"; a "good and useful bibliography" that "has the somewhat rare quality of inspiring one to reread the novel it deals with").

Nonfictional, Theatrical, and Poetical Works

Note: Also see Chicorel (**95**), Smith (**46**), and the section on *Sketches by Boz* (**132-37**), above.

139. Arnott, James F., and John W. Robinson. *English Theatrical Literature, 1559-1900: A Bibliography, Incorporating Robert W. Lowe's* **A Bibliographical Account of English Theatrical Literature**, *Published in 1888*. London: Society for Theatre Research, 1970, pp. 282-83, 257.

Arnott and Robinson list and provide bibliographical annotation for ten editions of *Memoirs of Joseph Grimaldi*, 1838-1968, but this work is useless otherwise for Dickens: under "Dickens, Charles (1812-1870)," they list only Pemberton's *Charles Dickens and the Stage* (**784**).

140. Atkinson, David. "Appendix: Dickens's Journalism." In *The Dickens Index*. By Nicolas Bentley, Michael Slater, and Nina Burgis. Oxford and New York: Oxford University Press, 1988, pp. 302-06.

Only lists articles by Dickens that first appeared in the *Examiner* (1838-49), *Household Words* (1850-59), *All the Year Round* (1859-69), and elsewhere (1834-69) and that were reprinted in the two volumes of Dickens's *Collected Papers* in the Nonesuch Dickens (**460**). For bibliographies of Dickens's journalism that go beyond this limited list, see Collins (**146**), Lohrli (**155**), Oppenlander (**158**), Slater (**159-61**), and Stone (**449**). Also see Fitzgerald (**152**).

141. Beetz, Kirk H. "Collins's Collaborations with Charles Dickens." In his *Wilkie Collins: An Annotated Bibliography, 1889-1976*. Scarecrow Author Bibliographies, 35. Metuchen, NJ, and London: Scarecrow Press, 1978, pp. 62-64.

An unannotated listing of editions of their collaborations: *The Lazy Tour of Two Idle Apprentices, No Thoroughfare, The Perils of Certain English Prisoners*, and *The Wreck of the Golden Mary*. Beetz does not list *The Frozen Deep* and the dramatization of *No Thoroughfare* as collaborations. Also see Beetz (**1292-93**).

142. Bentley, Richard, & Son. *A List of the Principal Publications Issued from New Burlington Street during the Year 1836*. London: Richard Bentley & Son, 1893, pp. [32]-[33], [36]-[40].

Provides publication details and other bibliographical and textual information about Dickens's early play *The Village Coquettes* and *Bentley's Miscellany*, including a list of original contributors to the magazine that Dickens edited and reproduction of an etching by Hablot K. Browne of Dickens on the publishing day of the magazine.

143. Bentley, Richard, & Son. *A List of the Principal Publications Issued from New Burlington Street during the Year 1837*. London: Richard Bentley & Son, 1894, pp. [2]-[7].

Provides further publication details and other bibliographical and textual information about *Bentley's Miscellany* while Dickens was its editor, including a list of contributors and their contributions to numbers 1-13 of the magazine.

144. Bentley, Richard, & Son. *A List of the Principal Publications Issued from New Burlington Street during the Year 1838*. London: Richard Bentley & Son, 1894, pp. [10]-[11], [42]-[43], [46]-[47], [55]-[59].

Provides publication details and other bibliographical and textual information about Dickens's *Memoirs of Joseph Grimaldi*, the first and second editions of *Oliver Twist* in three volumes, and *Bentley's Miscellany*, volumes 3 and 4. The letter of George Bentley, son of Richard Bentley, to the London *Times*, 7 December 1871, is reprinted; in it the son takes exception to John Forster's characterization of his father in volume 1 of *Forster* and reviews the relationship of Dickens and his father.

145. Bentley, Richard, & Son. *A List of the Principal Publications Issued from New Burlington Street during the Year 1839*. London: Richard Bentley & Son, 1894, pp. [38]-[39].

Provides information about *Bentley's Miscellany*, volumes 5 and 6, and notes Dickens's resignation as editor early in 1839.

146. Collins, P[hilip] A. W. *Dickens's Periodicals: Articles on Education, an Annotated Bibliography*. Vaughan College Papers, 3. Leicester, Eng.: University of Leicester, 1957. 36 pp.

An annotated bibliography of the articles on education in *Household Words* and *All the Year Round*, some by Dickens himself, illustrating Dickens's concern with education. With "few exceptions," Collins notes, these articles are "well-informed and sensible, and provide a fair conspectus of mid-Victorian Radical opinion on these issues." Where possible, Collins identifies the authors of the articles, all published anonymously. Entries are arranged under these headings: Educational Policies, Schools for the Poor, Middle-Class Schools, Universities and Other Advanced Training, Adult Education, and Miscellaneous (Special Schools, Naval and Military Education, and Teachers). Introductory sections to each summarize Dickens's views on main and subtopics in the bibliography. A brief appendix lists some ten works that reprint some of the essays, including Dickens's own *Reprinted Pieces*, *The Uncommercial Traveller*, *Christmas Stories*, and *Miscellaneous Papers* (**425**). Also see Lohrli (**155**) and Oppenlander (**158**).

147. Connolly, L. W., and J. P. Wearing. "Dickens, Charles, 1812-70." In their *English Drama and Theatre, 1800-1900: A Guide to Information Sources*. American Literature, English Literature and World Literatures in English: An Information Guide Series, 12. Detroit, MI: Gale Research, 1978, pp. 149-57 and passim.

Lists and lightly annotates Dickens's plays as well as bibliographic, biographic, and critical studies relevant to Dickens's dramatic interests—all briefly annotated. See the index for still other references to Dickens.

148. "Dickens's Contributions to *Household Words*." *Dickensian*, 35 (1938/39), 203-04.

Lists forty-six works that Dickens co-authored, often with W. H. Wills, in *Household Words*, 1850-58, as identified in the *Household Words* office book, also used by Lohrli (**155**). Also see Atkinson (**140**), Collins (**146**), Fitzgerald (**152**), Slater (**160-61**), and Stone (**449**).

149.   Ellis, James, with Joseph Donohue, comps. *English Drama of the Nine-teenth Century: An Index and Finding Guide.* New Canaan, CT: Readex Books, 1985, pp. 76-77.

Lists nine editions of six plays by Dickens. For adaptations of Dickens's works by others, one would need to know the adapters' names.

150.   Fielding, K[enneth] J. "Notes on Texts and Sources." In his *The Speeches of Charles Dickens* (**408**), pp. 423-43.

Essentially a valuable listing of the sources Fielding used to compile the texts of the speeches included.

151.   Firkins, Ina T. E., comp. "Dickens, Charles, 1812-1870." In her *Index to Plays, 1800-1926.* New York: H. W. Wilson, 1927; reprinted New York: AMS Press, 1971, 1979, p. 46; also *Index to Plays: Supplement.* New York: H. W. Wilson, 1935, passim.

Lists a few reprintings but usually not the original editions of Dickens's plays, including those he wrote with Wilkie Collins. See the subject index in both volumes for a couple of plays *about* Dickens.

152.   Fitzgerald, Percy. "Appendix B: Dickens's Own Contributions to His Two Journals." In his *Memories of Charles Dickens. With an Account of "Household Words" and "All the Year Round" and of the Contributors Thereto.* Bristol: J. W. Arrowsmith; London: Simpkin, Marshall, Hamilton, Kent, 1913; reprinted New York: Benjamin Blom, 1971; New York: AMS Press, 1973, pp. 365-71.

Fitzgerald lists Dickens's writings in *Household Words* and *All the Year Round* based on the office books for the two magazines. B. W. Matz's collection of Dickens's *Miscellaneous Papers, Plays and Poems* for the National Edition (**425**), including his articles for *Household Words* and *All the Year Round*, contains more pieces for *Household Words* than are in Fitzgerald's list, though for *All the Year Round* Fitzgerald lists a couple of pieces Matz did not include. For more recent updatings, see Atkinson (**140**), Collins (**146**), Lohrli (**155**), Oppenlander (**158**), and Stone (**449**).

153. Hanna, Robert C. "Charles Dickens' 'The Life of Our Lord' as a Primer for Christian Education." *Dissertation Abstracts International*, 56 (1995/96), 2183A (University of North Carolina, Greensboro, 1995).

The abstract notes that an appendix "contains the first annotated bibliography of book and magazine editions" of the work.

154. Kitton, Frederic G. *The Minor Writings of Charles Dickens: A Bibliography and Sketch.* The Book-Lover's Library. London: Elliot Stock, 1900; reprinted New York: Haskell House, 1970; New York: AMS Press, 1975. xi + 260 pp.

Intended as a companion volume to *The Novels of Charles Dickens* (**29**), provides the first detailed, if sometimes incomplete and occasionally inaccurate, information about *Sketches by Boz, American Notes, Pictures from Italy, Hard Times,* the Christmas Books, *Sunday Under Three Heads, Sketches of Young Gentlemen, Sketches of Young Couples, A Child's History of England,* articles, short stories, works edited by Dickens, plays, poems, songs, and rhymes. An appendix deals with plagiarisms and the continuations of *The Mystery of Edwin Drood.* While Kitton did not know of the *Household Words* Office Book—see Lohrli (**155**)—or the *All the Year Round* Letter Book—see Oppenlander (**158**)—he did have access to an "office" set of *All the Year Round* with authors' names written in and to manuscripts in Dickens's hand in the Forster Collection, Victoria and Albert Museum, London, of articles published in the *Examiner* not previously identified as Dickens's. In expository form, Kitton provides information about the conception, contents, publication, editions, auction prices, and a variety of other matters concerned with these works. Index.

Reviews of 1970 reprint: J. Gold, *Dickens Studies Newsletter*, 3 (1972), 14-16 (complains that the index "incomplete and unreliable" but finds the bibliographical information thorough and descriptions of content done with admirable "clarity and good humor"); P. A. Winkler, *American Reference Books Annual*, 3 (1972), 521 (a basic, useful source).

155. Lohrli, Anne. *Household Words: A Weekly Journal, 1850-1859, Conducted by Charles Dickens: Table of Contents, List of Contributors and Their Contributions, Based on the Household Words Office Book in the Morris L. Parrish Collection of Victorian Novelists, Princeton University Library.* Toronto and Buffalo, NY: University of Toronto Press, 1973. x + 534 pp.

The principal matter of this book is not a transcription of the Office Book, which would also have been welcomed by Dickens scholars, but a tabulation of the contents of each issue of *Household Words*, 30 March 1850 to 28 May 1859, giving the title, length in columns, payment, and, where known, the contributor's name for each article (pp. 58-193), as well as brief sketches of many of the contributors and a listing of their articles in *Household Words*, with date, volume number, pagination, and some indication of content. In an introduction, pp. 3-50, Lohrli surveys in considerable detail the variety of topics with which *Household Words* articles were concerned, the established tone of the magazine, the format of issues, the level of payment for articles, the diversity of the staff and other contributors, and other relevant matters concerned with Dickens's weekly magazine. She notes that of 355 occasional contributors she has not been able to identify "more than one hundred." She also describes the *Household Words* Office Book, which for each article lists the author(s), title, date of publication, date and amount of payment, along with occasional memoranda, almost entirely in the hand of W. H. Wills, the subeditor. Lohrli also includes a title index, bibliography of works consulted, and four illustrations. See corrections in Cheney (**493**). Also see Oppenlander (**158**).

Reviews: A. W. C. Brice, *Dickens Studies Newsletter*, 6 (1975), 56-58 (despite a number of reservations, finds the work "a very good one"); *Choice*, 11 (1974/75), 913-14 (an "important resource for scholars"); P. Collins, *Victorian Periodicals Newsletter*, 7, iii (September 1974), 30-32 (finds the work an "admirably devised and splendidly executed compilation," with an informative introduction; Collins identifies a further contributor to *Household Words*); S. Curran, *Studies in English Literature, 1500-1900*, 14 (1974), 657 ("adds greatly to our knowledge" of the periodical); K. J. Fielding, *Yearbook of English Studies*, 6 (1976), 308-10 (a highly valuable volume, much more than "a glorified table of contents"); A. Laude, *Review of English Studies*, ns 26 (1975), 232-34 ("of considerable value," "a remarkable feat by a very able scholar and literary detective," but with some "tiny blemishes"; the introduction is "very satisfyingly dense with facts"); P. F. Morgan, *English Studies*, 56 (1975), 367-68 (a "fine" volume); H. Stone, *Dickensian*, 70 (1974), 209-11 (finds the title misleading but contents "enormously useful," though notes several deficiencies); R. H. Tener, *Ariel: A Review of International English Literature*, 5, iv (October 1974), 82-83 (a "handsome," "excellent," thorough work, a "model of its kind," with a "richly detailed introduction"); *Times Literary Supplement*, 19 April 1974, p. 410 (of "great value").

156. Nayder, Lillian. "The Collaborations of Dickens and Collins." In her *Unequal Partners: Charles Dickens, Wilkie Collins, and Victorian Authorship*. Ithaca, NY: Cornell University Press, 2001, pp. xi-xii.

Lists eleven works on which the two authors collaborated, principally Christmas numbers of *Household Words* and *All the Year Round*, but also *The Frozen Deep* and *The Lazy Tour of Two Idle Apprentices*.

157. Nicoll, Allardyce. *A History of Early Nineteenth Century Drama, 1800-1850*. Vol. 2: *Hand-List of Plays, 1800-1850*. Cambridge: Cambridge University Press, 1930, p. 295; 2nd ed., as *Early Nineteenth Century Drama, 1800-1850*. Vol. 4 of *A History of English Drama, 1660-1900*. [2nd ed.]. Cambridge, Eng.: Cambridge University Press, 1955, etc., p. 305.

Lists four Dickens plays written before 1850. Also see Nicoll (**778-79**).

158. Oppenlander, Ella A. *Dickens' **All the Year Round**: Descriptive Index and Contributor List*. Troy, NY: Whitston, 1984. 752 pp.

A companion volume to Lohrli (**155**). Basing her work largely on the *All the Year Round* letter-book in the Huntington Library, San Marino, CA, and on the earlier researches of Philip Collins, some published (**181, 391, 494**), much of it unpublished, according to her "Acknowledgements," Oppenlander identifies a number of the anonymous contributors to *All the Year Round*, but by no means all. She provides this information in four computer-generated lists: 1) an issue by issue table of contents, listing title, author (where known), pagination, and number of columns in length of each piece through 4 June 1870; 2) an author index, listing the known contributors and their articles by volume, date, and pagination; 3) a title index, containing some 2,500 entries; and 4) a key-word index, followed by a list of sources. In an introduction (pp. 1-61), Oppenlander traces the dissolution of Dickens's marriage and of *Household Words*, the origin and establishment of *All the Year Round*, and the characteristics, format, audience, staff, policies, business practices, and influence of *All the Year Round*. This is a useful compilation but it is limited by the incompleteness of the letter-book itself, by the missing office-book, and by the disappearance of a once extant office set of *All the Year Round* with contributors identified used by Kitton in *The Minor Writings of Charles Dickens* (**154**). As a result, only eighty-three authors are listed; the authors of about seventy-five percent of the articles remain unidentified. The work originated, obviously, from her doctoral dissertation: "Dickens' *All the Year Round*: Descriptive Index and Contributors List." *Dissertation Abstracts International*, 39 (1978/79), 6781A (University of Texas at Austin, 1978), the abstract of which reads pretty much like the above annotation.

Reviews: E. M. Casey, *Victorian Periodicals Review*, 20 (1987), 70-72 (wishes the author had included more information about the articles and gone beyond mere computer listings, though concedes this is "a much welcome addition to the growing bibliographical resources for the study of Victorian periodicals"); E. M. Eigner, *Yearbook of English Studies*, 18 (1988), 345-46 (favorable); R. B. Meeker, *Choice*, 22 (1984/85), 1620 (a "credible job" of compilation); S. Monod, *Etudes anglaises*, 39 (1986), 224-25 (in French; finds the faults "nombreuses et graves"); D. Paroissien, *Dickens Quarterly*, 3 (1986), 142-44 (sees the work as an "important contribution" to *All the Year Round* studies, though, because of presumably lost records, only one-quarter of the contributors can be identified; also finds the key word index and the introduction valuable); P. Preston, *Notes and Queries*, ns 35 (1988), 545-48 (a "valuable" and "serviceable" volume that "throws a new light on Dickens as a periodical editor"); J. Rettig, *American Reference Books Annual*, 17 (1986), 458 (useful and informative); A. Sanders, *Dickensian*, 82 (1986), 180-81 ("the best guide so far to Dickens's work as a journalist and editor").

159. Slater, Michael. "Appendix B: Complete Listing of Dickens's Known Journalism, December 1833-June 1851." In his edition of Dickens's *"The Amusements of the People" and Other Papers: Reports, Essays and Reviews, 1834-51* (**2521**), pp. 372-78.

A list of Dickens's journalistic writings for the eighteen years indicated, giving date of publication, title of work, and newspaper or periodical in which it appeared, including his known theater and book reviews and reports of political events and dinners, as well as his newspaper and magazine sketches, tales, and articles, though, as Slater notes, most "Letters to the Editor and editorial addresses to Dickens's readers have not been included." Slater includes in the list all the pieces collected in the two series of *Sketches by Boz* that were previously published in newspapers and magazines but not the four pieces first published in *Sketches by Boz*–"A Visit to Newgate," "The Black Veil," "The Great Winglebury Duel," and "The Drunkard's Death." Nor does he list the seven pieces originally published in the *Daily News* in early 1846 under the title "Travelling Letters Written on the Road" that formed the core of *Pictures from Italy* (1846).

160. Slater, Michael. "Appendix C: Complete Listing of Dickens's Known Journalism (All in *Household Words*), July 1851-January 1859." In his edition of Dickens's *"Gone Astray" and Other Papers from **Household Words**, 1851-59* (**2522**), pp. 509-11.

Lists only the title and date of publication in *Household Words* of articles by Dickens and his collaborations with others, the latter as identified by Harry Stone in his *Charles Dickens' Uncollected Writings from "Household Words" 1850-1859* (**449**). Slater does not, however, include the weekly parts of *Child's History of England* (published in *Household Words*, 1852-53), which might legitimately have found a place in this list, though he does mention the serialized work in his introduction.

161. Slater, Michael, and John Drew. "Appendix D: Complete Listing of Dickens's Known Journalism, December 1833-August 1869." In their edition of Dickens's ***The Uncommercial Traveller** and Other Papers, 1859-70* (**2523**), pp. 436-46.

A list of Dickens's journalistic writings from December 1833 on, incorporating the lists in volumes 2 and 3 of the Dent edition of Dickens's journalism (**159, 160**), giving only date of publication, title of work, and newspaper or periodical in which it appeared. As Slater and Drew note, most "'Letters to the Editor' and editorial addresses to Dickens's readers have not been included." The new additions to the list, 1859-69, are from *All the Year Round*, with the exception of Dickens's "In Memoriam: W. M. Thackeray," from *Cornhill Magazine*, and "On Mr. Fechter's Acting," from *Atlantic Monthly*. Also see Slater and Drew (**2523**). For earlier bibliographies of Dickens's journalism, some supplementary to Slater and Drew's list, see Atkinson (**140**), Collins (**146**), Fitzgerald (**152**), Lohrli (**155**), Oppenlander (**158**), and Stone (**449**).

1D. GENRE BIBLIOGRAPHIES

Note: Also see **Bibliographies of genres (with sections on Dickens)** in the subject index.

162. Adamson, Lynda G. *World Historical Fiction: An Annotated Guide to Novels for Adults and Young Adults.* Phoenix, AZ: Oryx Press, 1999, passim.

Lists most of Dickens's novels under "The British Isles, 1789-1859" (their "historical" period) and *Barnaby Rudge, Master Humphrey's Clock* (for *Barnaby Rudge*), and *A Tale of Two Cities* under the previous historical period. See the index. The annotation for each work gives basic publication information and one-sentence plot summaries that are close to laughable—for example, *Little Dorrit*: "Little Dorrit grows up in Marshalsea prison where her father is confined for his debts, and she helps to feed the family with her needlework until her father receives an inheritance when she is in her teens, and more problems ensue."

163. Baker, Ernest A. "Dickens, Charles, 1812-1870." In his *History in Fiction: A Guide to the Best Historical Romances, Sagas, Novels, and Tales.* [Vol. 1:] *English Fiction.* London: George Routledge & Sons; New York: E. P. Dutton, 1907, p. 117; considerably expanded as *A Guide to Historical Fiction.* London: George Routledge & Sons; New York: Macmillan, 1914; reprinted [New York]: Argosy-Antiquarian, 1968; New York: Burt Franklin, 1969, pp. 154-55.

In both versions, lists Dickens's novels (excluding *Barnaby Rudge* and *A Tale of Two Cities*) and principal editions of his collected works. In the revised edition Baker refers to these two excluded novels briefly on pp. 124 and 282 as examples of historical novels. In the original edition, Baker lists *Barnaby Rudge* separately (on p. 95) but not *A Tale of Two Cities*. In both editions, Baker comments that Dickens's novels are "the finest, and on the whole, the truest existing picture of the classes of society lower than those portrayed by Thackeray" and an "invaluable record of innumerable phases of life that have passed away."

164. Bleiler, Everett F. "Dickens, Charles (John Huffam) (1812-1870)." In his *The Guide to Supernatural Fiction: A Full Description of 1,775 Books from 1750 to 1960, Including Ghost Stories, Weird Fiction, Stories of Supernatural Horror, Fantasy, Gothic Novels, Occult Fiction, and Similar Literature.* Kent, OH: Kent State University Press, 1983, pp. 155-57.

Lists nine Dickens works—from *Pickwick Papers* to *The Lazy Tour of Two Idle Apprentices*—and briefly indicates the supernatural elements in each.

165. Brussel, I[sidore] R. "Charles Dickens." In his *Anglo-America: First Editions 1826-1900: East to West. Describing First Editions of English Authors Whose Books Were Published in America before Their Publication in England.* Bibliographia Series, 9. London: Constable; New York: Bowker, 1935, pp. 75-86.

Lists and provides basic bibliographical information about some nineteen works of Dickens first published in book form (generally unauthorized) in the United States. Most are minor works—"Public Life of Mr. Tulrumble," "The Tuggs's at Ramsgate," and "Pantomime of Life," for example—included in anthologies of essays or stories or separately published Christmas Stories.

166. Contento, William G., and Martin H. Greenberg. "Dickens, Charles." In their *Index to Crime and Mystery Anthologies.* Boston: G. K. Hall, 1990, pp. 141-42.

Includes Dickens's shorter works and excerpts from his novels concerning crime and mystery—with the anthologies in which they appear.

167. Fisher, Benjamin F., IV. "The Residual Gothic Impulse: 1824-1873." In *Horror Literature: A Core Collection and Reference Guide.* Ed. Marshall B. Tymn. New York and London: R. R. Bowker, 1981, pp. 176-220.

Lists and summarizes the plots of *Bleak House*, *A Christmas Carol*, *Little Dorrit*, *Martin Chuzzlewit*, *The Mystery of Edwin Drood*, and *Our Mutual Friend* as examples of horror literature (pp. 202-04). In the introduction to his list, which also includes the works of other authors, Fisher notes Dickens's lively interest in the Gothic and his fascination with crime, criminals, and the supernatural (pp. 186-87).

168. McGarry, Daniel D., and Sarah H. White. *Historical Fiction Guide: Annotated Chronological, Geographical and Topical List of Five Thousand Selected Historical Novels.* New York: Scarecrow Press, 1963, passim; 2nd ed. as *World Historical Fiction Guide: An Annotated, Chronological, Geographical and Topical List of Selected Historical Novels.* Metuchen, NJ: Scarecrow Press, 1973, passim.

See the index first. The authors provide basic publication details and very brief descriptions of *Barnaby Rudge*, *David Copperfield*, *Hard Times*, *Little Dorrit*, *Nicholas Nickleby*, *Oliver Twist*, and *A Tale of Two Cities.* The second edition adds *A Christmas Carol*, but otherwise the text is unchanged.

169. Palmegiano, E. M., comp. *Crime in Victorian Britain: An Annotated Bibliography from Nineteenth-Century British Magazines.* Bibliographies and Indexes in World History, 31. Westport, CT, and London: Greenwood Press, 1993, pp. 25-34, 34-36, 85-92, and passim.

Lists articles on crime, including some by Dickens, found in *All the Year Round,* 1859-95; *Bentley's Miscellany,* 1837-68; *Household Words,* 1850-59, and many other magazines. Palmegiano gives a brief indication of the contents of each article.

170. Trautmann, Joanne, and Carol Pollard. *Literature and Medicine: Topics, Titles & Notes.* Hershey, PA: Department of Humanities, Hershey Medical Center, 1975, pp. 69-71; revised as *Literature and Medicine: An Annotated Bibliography.* Contemporary Community Health Series. Pittsburgh, PA: University of Pittsburgh Press, 1982, pp. 74-75.

An annotated list of literary works with medical components, including Dickens's *Bleak House, David Copperfield, Dombey and Son, Great Expectations, Martin Chuzzlewit, The Old Curiosity Shop, Pickwick Papers,* and two pieces from *The Uncommercial Traveller.* The annotations comment on medical elements (including types of deaths) in the works. The Dickens entries are unchanged in both editions.

1E. GENERAL BIBLIOGRAPHICAL STUDIES OF DICKENS'S WORKS

Note: Also see **Bibliographical studies of Dickens's works, general studies** in the subject index.

171. Altick, Richard D. "Appendix B: Best-Sellers" and "Appendix C: Periodical and Newspaper Circulation." In his *The English Common Reader: A Social History of the Mass Reading Public 1800-1900*. Chicago: University of Chicago Press, 1957; 2nd ed. Columbus: Ohio State University Press, [1998], pp. 381-90, 391-96.

In Appendix B Altick gives (pp. 383-84) casually gathered sales figures for some of Dickens's novels in parts and three of the Christmas Books. In Appendix C, he gives (pp. 394-95) initial and average sales figures for *Household Words* and *All the Year Round*.

172. Altick, Richard D. *The Art of Literary Research*. New York: W. W. Norton, 1963; revised ed., 1975; 3rd ed., revised by John Fenstermaker, 1981; 4th ed., by Richard D. Altick and John J. Fenstermaker, 1993, passim.

The first and later editions comment in passing on modern editions of Dickens's novels. The third edition also touches upon Harry Stone's contribution to the Dickens canon in his *Charles Dickens' Uncollected Writings from **Household Words** 1850-1859* (**449**), on the collection of Dickens manuscripts in the Victoria and Albert Museum (London), and on some textual studies of Dickens's works. See the index. The fourth edition somewhat updates the references to Dickens in the third edition. Also see Altick (**1587**).

173. Ballou, Ellen B. *The Building of the House: Houghton Mifflin's Formative Years*. Boston: Houghton Mifflin, 1970, passim.

Provides a fascinating look at the maneuvering and jostling among certain American publishing houses in the 1860s to publish collected editions of Dickens's works, shorter pieces, and *The Mystery of Edwin Drood*. In chapter 3, a "detailed examination" of Dickens and his "authorized American publishers," Ballou touches upon the publication problems and sales of the Household Edition of Dickens's works, planned by Henry Houghton for Sheldon and Company in the early 1860s; this was, she notes, not an edition approved by

Dickens and thus a "pirated edition" (pp. 37-38, 50-58). In chapter 4, "The Mystery of Edwin Drood," pp. 59-95, Ballou examines the publishing business of Ticknor and Fields, ca. 1864, and Hurd and Houghton, particularly concerning the 1865 lawsuit over the Household Edition and the competition of the two firms with Harper's over the right to publish Dickens's works in a period before international copyright laws. The result was the Household Edition, with illustrations by F. O. C. Darley and John Gilbert (ultimately fifty-three volumes, with four publishers, the last Hurd and Houghton), the Riverside Edition (26 vols, New York: Hurd and Houghton, 1867), and the Diamond Edition (12 vols., Boston: Ticknor and Fields, 1867). T. B. Peterson also entered the race, Ballou notes, with a seven-volume edition and Hurd and Houghton with another (the Globe Edition, 13 vols.), and they had also taken over the Household Edition as a result of the law suit. Ballou's publication details, particularly concerning the number of volumes in editions, differ somewhat from those in Podeschi (**1509**), pp. 257-59, which are more detailed and undoubtedly more accurate. Ballou also points out that James R. Osgood, working for Ticknor and Fields, had some success from a visit to Dickens in 1867, which produced "A Holiday Romance," but Dickens was talking with other publishers, too. This led, later in the year, to Dickens's second American visit and publication by Fields in the *Atlantic Monthly* of "George Silverman's Explanation." The chapter concludes with a look at the negotiations of the newly-formed Fields, Osgood, & Company over the advanced sheets for *The Mystery of Edwin Drood*, the disagreements with Dickens, and the general mess of the serialization of the novel in America in *Every Saturday*, but pirated in *Appleton's Journal* and *Harper's Weekly*.

174. Bracher, Peter S. "Harper & Brothers: Publishers of Dickens." *Bulletin of the New York Public Library*, 79 (1975/76), 315-35.

A richly detailed history of Dickens's relationship with an American publisher of unauthorized editions of his major and many of his minor writings, 1842-1852, and authorized (with payments for the "rights" to his works) thereafter. Bracher appends "A Check List of Dickens' Works Published by Harper & Brothers, 1842-70" (**5**), pp. 332-35.

175. Butt, John. "Editing a Nineteenth-Century Novelist (Proposals for an Edition of Dickens)." In *English Studies Today: Second Series. Lectures and Papers Read at the Fourth Conference of the International Association of University Professors of English Held at Lausanne and Berne, August 1959*. Berne, Switz.: Francke Verlag, 1961, pp. 187-95; reprinted in *Art and Error: Modern Textual Editing*. Ed. Ronald Gottesman and Scott Bennett. Bloomington and London: Indiana University Press, 1970, pp. 155-66.

Necessary reading for anyone undertaking the editing of a Dickens novel. Butt's essay is a valuable survey of the materials the editor of an authoritative,

definitive edition of a work by Dickens would need to consider in establishing
the text, listing textual variants, and rounding out the edition with valuable
supplementary information such as the running heads from the Charles Dickens
Edition and Dickens's number plans. Butt discusses manuscripts, corrected page proofs, and editions in which Dickens made changes. This information is accompanied by a fascinating variety of suggestions and warnings.
Butt's criteria were used by himself and Kathleen Tillotson in their planning
of the Clarendon Edition of Dickens's works (Oxford: Clarendon Press,
1966-), though Butt died in November 1965, a few months before the publication of the first volume in the edition but after the "Preface by the General
Editors" (**176**) was completed.

176.   Butt, John, and Kathleen Tillotson. "Preface by the General Editors."
    In Dickens's *Oliver Twist*. Ed. Kathleen Tillotson (**2474**), pp. v-vii.

In commenting on the characteristics of the Clarendon Edition of Dickens's works, of which *Oliver Twist* was the first volume published, Butt and
Tillotson indicate that for each volume "a critical text is established, a text free
from the numerous corruptions that disfigure modern reprints, with an apparatus of variants that will exhibit Dickens's progressive revision, and accompanied by all such assistance as Dickens himself supplied in the shape of prefaces, descriptive headlines, illustrations, and cover designs from the wrappers
of the monthly parts issues, which often foreshadow the drift of the novel as
Dickens originally conceived it." They note that a "very substantial" amount
of material is available, including the autograph manuscripts from *The Old Curiosity Shop* on, with "about 45 leaves of *Pickwick Papers*, about 160 leaves of
Nicholas Nickleby, and 480 leaves (about two-fifths) of *Oliver Twist*," as well as
many sets of proofs, mostly for the works after *The Old Curiosity Shop*. The
general editors also discuss the textual apparatus of the Clarendon Edition
and Dickens's methods for revising proofs. This "Preface by the General Editors" is reprinted in each of the volumes issued to date in the Clarendon Edition—see Elizabeth M. Brennan on *The Old Curiosity Shop* (**2460**); Nina Burgis
on *David Copperfield* (**2359**); Margaret Cardwell on *Great Expectations* (**2381**),
Martin Chuzzlewit (**2423**), and *The Mystery of Edwin Drood* (**2434**); Alan Horsman
on *Dombey and Son* (**2376**); James Kinsley on *Pickwick Papers* (**2493**); Harvey P.
Sucksmith on *Little Dorrit* (**2420**); and Kathleen Tillotson on *Oliver Twist*
(**2474**)—with brief additional comments relevant to the volume in question.
Each volume in the series contains the original illustrations, extra illustrations
(often photographic facsimiles of pages of the manuscript, number plans, and
cover designs for the wrappers of monthly parts), a descriptive list of editions
published in Dickens's lifetime, and various appendices.

177.   Carter, John. *Binding Variants in English Publishing, 1820-1900*. Bibliographia: Studies in Book History and Book Structure, 6. London: Constable; New York: Ray Long & Richard R. Smith, 1932, pp. 106-09 and passim; reprinted in his *Binding Variants and More Binding Variants in English Publishing, 1820-1900*. New Castle, DE: Oak Knoll Books, 1989, pp. 106-09 and passim (each of the two books combined here is reproduced exactly as originally published).

For purposes of bibliography as well as of book publishing, Carter examines the way and the materials in which books were bound, 1820-1900, with a few examples from Dickens's works, most specifically *The Memoirs of Joseph Grimaldi*, *Oliver Twist* (3 vols., 1838), and *Edwin Drood*, pointing out variants in binding not noted elsewhere. Also see Carter and Sadleir (**306**).

178. Carter, John. *Publishers's Cloth: An Outline History of Publisher's Binding in England, 1820-1900*. New York: Bowker; London: Constable, 1935, passim.

Notes in passing that the "phenomenal success" of *Pickwick Papers* in parts "raised the fictional part issue from its 'servants' hall' status" and made the publication of novels in parts popular for "thirty years and more." As to binding the completed parts, Carter points out that other novels, such as those by William Harrison Ainsworth, were bound in "richly pictorial" covers, an influence of the illustrator, but that Dickens's novels always appeared in plain cloth binding.

179. "Charles Dickens." *Bookseller* (London), no. 150 (1 July 1870), 573-78.

In lieu of a conventional obituary/eulogy, provides a surprisingly detailed account of "the order and sequence" of the publication of Dickens's works, including information about their serial publication, in addition to other bibliographical details. The author also mentions some of Dickens's pre-*Pickwick* sketches, *Sunday Under Three Heads*, and two early plays and corrects accounts that Dickens began his journalism career on the *Morning Chronicle* by mentioning his earlier work on the *Mirror of Parliament* and the *True Sun*.

180. "The Clarendon Dickens." *Bookseller*, 8 October 1966, pp. 1928-29.

Describes the editorial guidelines for this edition in progress of Dickens's works—whose aim is "to present the text as Dickens meant his readers to see it, free from the corruptions that have taken place during a century and more."

181. Collins, Philip. "Dickens's Weeklies." *Victorian Periodicals Newsletter*, no. 1 (January 1968), pp. 18-19.

Notes the bibliographical problems connected with needed research on the authorship of articles in *Household Words* and *All the Year Round*.

182. Collins, Philip. "Dickensian Errata." *Times Literary Supplement*, 20-26 November 1987, p. 1278.

In commenting on the then recent reprinting of the Oxford Illustrated Dickens (21 volumes, London and New York: Oxford University Press, 1987), Collins notes the number of errors in the text, particularly when compared with the text of the volumes of the Clarendon Edition published to date. He also notes the accumulating errors in the editions printed in Dickens's own lifetime, the text of the Charles Dickens Edition (1867-[75]) being the worst. Unfortunately, he points out, that is the one on which the Oxford Illustrated Dickens claims to be based. He also comments unfavorably on the text of the Everyman Edition and the Penguin Edition, though he designates the latter as "collectively the best buy" of available editions. He is happy with the texts of the Clarendon Edition and the World's Classics Edition (which is based on the Clarendon),and has particular praise for the text and textual apparatus in the volumes of *David Copperfield*, edited by Jerome H. Buckley (**2357**) and *Bleak House*, edited by George Ford and Sylvère Monod (**2327**) for the Norton Critical Editions. A letter from Peter Rowland in the 11-17 December issue, p. 1377, recommends the "elegant" Heron Edition of the works and notes an error corrected in the Oxford Illustrated Edition of *Edwin Drood*. In the 18-24 December issue, on p. 1403, Collins responds, also praising the Heron Edition and noting still other errors in the Oxford Illustrated Dickens. Finally, in the 1-7 January 1988 issue, David Attwooll, a representative of the Oxford University Press, writes to point out that the Press's intent was to produce an inexpensive hardback edition, not a scholarly one, and that only specific textual errors called to its attention are changed in the subsequent reprintings of volumes in the Oxford Illustrated Dickens.

183. "Completion of the National Edition of Dickens's Works." *Dickensian*, 4 (1908), 130.

Notes that, with the publication of *Forster* in two volumes, the National Edition is complete, the "most sumptuous edition ever published" from both a "typographical and bibliographical point of view." Also see Philip (**435**).

184. Dexter, Walter. "The 'Library,' 'People's' and 'Charles Dickens' Editions." *Dickensian*, 40 (1943/44), 186-87.

Provides brief details about three of the collected editions published in Dickens's lifetime: the Library Edition, People's Edition, and Charles Dickens Edition.

185. Dickens, Charles, the Younger. Introductions. In *The Works of Charles Dickens*. [Macmillan Edition]. 21 vols. London: Macmillan and Co., 1892-1925, passim.

The title page of most of the volumes in this edition indicate that it is "a reprint of the first edition, with the illustrations, and an introduction, biographical and bibliographical, by Charles Dickens the Younger." The edition contains the fifteen novels, as well as *American Notes, Pictures from Italy, Sketches by Boz, Christmas Books, Stories from the Christmas Numbers, Reprinted Pieces, The Lazy Tour of Two Idle Apprentices, The Uncommercial Traveller, A Child's History of England, Letters,* and shorter pieces. The introductions by Dickens's eldest son contain biographical and bibliographical material from what one must accept as an authoritative source, though the information provided is not always as accurate as such a source would seem to indicate. The nature of the information provided varies from introduction to introduction but usually includes details about the writing of the particular work, editions published in Dickens's lifetime, dramatizations of the work by others, and the manuscript where extant.

186. "Dickens's Dealings with Americans." *American Literary Gazette and Publishers' Circular*, 8, xii (15 April 1867), 348-49.

Asserts that, though Dickens "has always been loud in his complaints against what he calls the 'piracy' of American publishers," he "has derived a considerable part of his income from moneys paid him for advance sheets of his various works" by American publishers—as far back as Harper Brothers' edition of *Pickwick Papers.* Some of these transactions are noted, with the further opinion that Dickens "knew how to drive a pretty hard bargain" with American publishers. Also see Lea (205), "Notes on Books and Booksellers: The Dickens Controversy" (220), "Important Announcement from Charles Dickens" (196), and "Notes: Literary," in *Nation* (219).

187. Dreyfus, John. *A History of the Nonesuch Press.* London: Nonesuch Press, 1981, pp. 80-87.

Briefly describes the preparations for and publication of the Nonesuch Dickens in 1937-38 and the controversy at the Nonesuch Press over the decision by John Macy, the director, to include one of the 877 original plates purchased from Chapman and Hall in each set of the edition. Dreyfus also mentions the extensive advertising of the edition, particularly through *Nonesuch Dickensiana* (218), and calls the edition "a most notable piece of book design." Also see McKitterick, Rendall, and Dreyfus (207), below.

188. *An Evening with Charles Dickens and the Story of the Charles Dickens Library.* [London: Educational Book Co., 1910?]. 48 pp.

An elaborate, illustrated brochure advertising the Charles Dickens Library (London: Educational Book Company, 1910), a collected edition of Dickens's works, edited by J. A. Hammerton. The brochure contains "Of Authors the

Best Beloved," by Hammerton, about the edition, pp. 1-2; "The Revival of Dickens," by Coulson Kernahan, with praise of the edition, pp. 5-10. It also contains "How I Illustrated Dickens," by Harry Furniss, pp. 13-19, who did 500 illustrations for the edition; and a sample introduction (for *Nicholas Nickleby*) and excerpts from *The Dickens Picture Book: A Record of Dickens Illustrators*, volume 17 of the edition (**884**), and *The Dickens Companion: A Book of Anecdote and Reference*, volume 18 of the edition (**21**), both by Hammerton.

189. Exman, Eugene. *The Brothers Harper: A Unique Publishing Partnership and Its Impact upon the Cultural Life of America from 1817 to 1853*. New York: Harper & Row, 1965, pp. 155-57, 163, 309-10.

Comments briefly on Dickens's crusade for an international copyright agreement with the United States in 1842 and on Harper's serial publication of *Martin Chuzzlewit* in 1843 and of *Bleak House* in 1852-53.

190. Feather, John. *Publishing, Piracy and Politics: An Historical Study of Copyright in Britain*. London: Mansell, 1994, passim.

Comments in passing on Dickens's unsuccessful attempts to protect the copyrights of his novels against American publishing practices, 1842-70, and on his son Charles's attempts after 1870.

191. Fielding, K[enneth] J. "The Monthly Serialisation of Dickens's Novels." *Dickensian*, 54 (1958), 4-11.

Summarizes Dickens's comments on the challenge and craftsmanship of monthly serialization, the format he used for initial publication of most of his novels (except for *The Old Curiosity Shop, Barnaby Rudge, Hard Times, Great Expectations*, and *A Tale of Two Cities*), and lists the number divisions of the monthly parts for *Pickwick Papers, Oliver Twist, Martin Chuzzlewit, Dombey and Son, David Copperfield, Bleak House, Little Dorrit, Our Mutual Friend*, and *The Mystery of Edwin Drood*. Fielding accidentally omitted *Nicholas Nickleby*, an error caught by Levy (**321**).

192. Fielding, K[enneth] J. "The Weekly Serialisation of Dickens's Novels." *Dickensian*, 54 (1958), 134-41.

Gives the number divisions of Dickens's novels that were serialized weekly (*The Old Curiosity Shop, Barnaby Rudge, Hard Times, Great Expectations*, and *A Tale of Two Cities*) by part, chapter, and date, preceded by comments on Dickens's difficulty in writing for weekly publication, though Fielding points out that the three later works show increasing mastery of the form.

193. Fitzgerald, Percy. "Dickens Curios." *Gentleman's Magazine*, 276, ns 52 (1894), 443-58.

Comments on the joy and difficulty of collecting editions of Dickens's works, particularly in parts, and, in this regard, particularly in parts of *Pickwick Papers*. In addition, Fitzgerald lists series of extra illustrations done for *Pickwick Papers* by a number of artists. He also describes and comments on the variants in editions of the Christmas Books (particularly the points of the earliest issues of *A Christmas Carol*), *Master Humphrey's Clock, Sketches by Boz, Oliver Twist,* the questionable *The Loving Ballad of Lord Bateman*, a number of single-edition rarities among minor publications (some incorrectly attributed to Dickens), and other items. For other commentary on the states of the first edition of *A Christmas Carol*, see Calhoun and Heaney (**252**) and the cross references listed there.

194. Hardwick, Michael, and Mollie Hardwick, comps. "The Works." In their *The Charles Dickens Encyclopedia*. Reading, Eng.: Osprey; New York: Scribners, 1973, pp. 1-31; reissued London: Macdonald Futura Publications, 1976; revised, London: Futura Publications, 1990; Ware, Eng.: Wordsworth, 1992; reissued as a Citadel Press Book, Secaucus, NJ: Carol Publishing Group, 1993, pp. 17-61.

Includes bibliographical information, the background of the writings, and brief summaries of Dickens's writings in chronological order.

195. H[ill], T. W. "The Universal Dickens." *Dickensian*, 9 (1913), 261-62; 10 (1914), 68-69.

In the first piece, Hill praises the first three volumes (*Sketches by Boz, Pickwick Papers*, and *Oliver Twist*) of Chapman and Hall's Universal Edition of Dickens's works. He notes that Chapman and Hall have issued "scores of complete editions of Dickens's writings—they have nearly twenty today—and the various issues have ranged in size from pocket size 12mo up to royal octavo and quarto 'library' editions—paper wrappers, cloth boards, half-morocco bindings have all been requisitioned—while prices have varied from sixpence up to twenty-one shillings a volume." In the later piece Hill indicates that the collected edition will be completed in April 1914 and calls it a "handsome set." The edition consisted of twenty-two volumes, as noted on back cover advertisements of issues of the *Dickensian* for 1914, where further information about the edition may be found.

196. "Important Announcement from Charles Dickens." *American Literary Gazette and Publishers' Circular*, 9, iii (1 June 1867), 84-85 (and subsequent issues).

A Ticknor and Fields advertisement for its three new editions of Dickens's works: the Diamond Edition, the Charles Dickens Edition, and the Illustrated Library Edition, published with the authorization of Dickens. The advertisement gives particulars of the editions but also prints four letters to Ticknor and Fields from Dickens: 1) 2 April 1867, announcing his agreement with the firm; 2) 2 April 1867, stating his pleasure with the illustrations for the three editions; 3) 8 April 1867, thanking the firm for the moneys involved; and 4) 16 April 1867, the letter printed in "Notes on Books and Booksellers: The Dickens Controversy" (**220**), which appeared in the editorial matter of the 1 June 1867 issue. Also see "Notes: Literary," in *Nation* (**219**).

197. Ives, Maura. "Descriptive Bibliography and the Victorian Periodical." *Studies in Bibliography: Papers of the Bibliographical Society of the University of Virginia*, 49 (1996), 61-94.

In commenting on the drawbacks of scholars' not being as bibliographically descriptive of periodicals and the articles in them as of books, Ives uses *Household Words* as an example of a periodical that was issued in "several impressions" and a "series of printings" (p. 69).

198. Kaser, David, ed. *The Cost Book of Carey & Lea, 1825-1838*. Philadelphia: University of Pennsylvania Press, 1963, passim.

Gives the costs for publication of Carey & Lea's early Dickens titles (through *Oliver Twist*). See p. 336 of "Index to the Entries," for the Dickens items.

199. Kaser, David. *Messrs. Carey & Lea of Philadelphia: A Study in the History of the Book Trade*. Philadelphia: University of Pennsylvania Press, 1957, pp. 111-14.

Comments on Carey & Lea's publication of works by Dickens, beginning with the first series of *Sketches by Boz* in May 1836. Kaser notes that, when Henry Carey wrote Dickens on 14 June 1837 (the letter was addressed to "Mr. Saml. Dickens"), enclosing a bank draft for £25 and pointing out that this was "not as a compensation, but as a memento of the fact that unsolicited a bookseller has sent an author, if not money, at least a fair representation of it." Such an action, Kaser indicates, was unheard of at the time. Dickens refused the bank draft in a letter of 26 October 1837, asking only for a copy of the American edition. Carey, Kaser reports, "packed a box of the Dickens titles that the firm had published" and sent them to Dickens, who acknowledged their arrival in a letter of 18 July 1838.

200. Kennethe, L. A. [Walter Dexter]. "The Cheap Edition." *Dickensian*, 39 (1942/43), 112-14.

Briefly gives some details of the weekly and monthly publication in parts of volumes in the Cheap Edition and of the clothbound volumes of complete novels.

201. Kilgour, Raymond L. *Estes and Lauriat: A History, 1872-1898, with a Brief Account of Dana Estes and Company, 1898-1914.* Ann Arbor: University of Michigan Press, 1957, passim.

Describes the People's Edition, the University Edition, and the Cambridge Edition of Dickens's works published by Estes and Lauriat, ca. 1880, as well as its Handy Large Type Edition, 1884 (pp. 139-40), and the Illustrated Sterling Edition, an "édition de luxe," 1890 (pp. 159, 166, 177).

202. Kitton, F[rederic] G. "American Edition of Dickens." *Notes and Queries*, 9th ser., 10 (1902), 96.

In response to a query by C[harles] W[elsh] in *Notes and Queries*, 9th ser., 9 (1902), 387, about a forthcoming expensive American edition of Dickens's works on parchment, Kitton replies that the collected edition, to be published by G. D. Sproul, New York, would be limited to fifteen sets of about 150 volumes each and designated the "St. Dunstan" Edition, the niceties of which he further describes, adding that the volumes would be sold for $1,000 each, or £30,000 ($146,280) for the set. This edition was apparently never published—see Carr (**1445**) and Kitton (**2303**). Shaylor (**228**) lists the price of the projected St. Dunstan Edition as £26,000.

203. Kitton, F[rederic] G. Reviews of volumes in the Macmillan Edition of Dickens's Works. *Library Review*, 1 (1892/93), 158-60, 228-31, 360-66, 494-500, 562-67, 705-17, 778-84; 2 (1893), 17-21, 75-79.

Uses what are ostensibly reviews of volumes in the Macmillan Edition of Dickens's works with introductions by Charles Dickens, Jr., to comment briefly on biographical, bibliographical, and critical aspects of each work (*Pickwick Papers, Oliver Twist, Nicholas Nickleby, Martin Chuzzlewit, The Old Curiosity Shop, Barnaby Rudge, Dombey and Son*, the Christmas Books, *Sketches by Boz, David Copperfield, American Notes*, and *Pictures from Italy*).

204. Kline, Barbara. "The Author as Book Designer." In *A Miscellany for Bibliophiles*. Ed. H. George Fletcher. New York: Grastorf & Lang, 1979, pp. 189-219.

Points out, pp. 193-95, that Dickens "constantly took an interest in the design, format, and illustration of his books." Where illustrations were concerned, Kline indicates, Dickens "was the sole ultimate arbiter of what would and would not do," and, with *A Christmas Carol,* "completely controlled" the production of the volume. Illustrated.

205. Lea, Henry C. "American Editions of Dickens." *American Literary Gazette and Publishers' Circular,* 9, ii (15 May 1867), 36-37.

In a letter to the publisher (George W. Childs), in response to a statement in "Notes on Books and Booksellers" **(219)** in the previous issue, Lea provides interesting information about the publication of Dickens's novels in America by Carey, Lea & Blanchard, beginning with *Pickwick Papers,* for which the firm sent him a remittance of £50 in 1838 "in acknowledgment of the success of his work" and negotiated unsuccessfully with him for other early novels, though he believes another American publisher paid Dickens for *The Old Curiosity Shop* and *Barnaby Rudge.* Dickens "refused to countenance any American editions of his works," for many years after his visit to America in 1842, Lea indicates, and refused the firm's offer for *Martin Chuzzlewit.* Accordingly, it printed that novel and *David Copperfield* without authorization. Lea also notes that the practice of paying for advance sheets of works by English authors was "of very old date." Also see "Dickens's Dealings with Americans" **(186),** "Notes on Books and Booksellers: The Dickens Controversy" **(220),** and "Important Announcement from Charles Dickens" **(196).**

206. "Library Notes: The Nonesuch Dickens." *Serif,* 1, i (April 1964), 29-30.

Praises the high quality of the Nonesuch Press Edition of Dickens's works **(460),** 1937-38, singling out the reproduction of the illustrations and Francis Meynell's design of the edition.

207. McKitterick, David, Simon Rendall, and John Dreyfus. "The Nonesuch Dickens . . . ." In their "Descriptive Catalogue of the Books & Prospectuses." Appended to Dreyfus **(187),** pp. 238-43.

A bibliographical description of the Nonesuch Edition of Dickens's works, with emphasis on the illustrations and binding of each volume. The text was based on the Charles Dickens Edition of Dickens's works, except, obviously, for works not printed in that edition, the editors note. They also comment on the extensive advertising done for the edition, particularly the *Retrospectus and Prospectus* **(218)**; note that sixty-six sets were destroyed by German bombs in 1940 and that, in October 1938, individual volumes were sold; and discuss the nature of the steel plates and wood engravings used in the edition and the controversy over the breaking up of the set of 877 plates in order to include one plate with each collected edition sold. Also see Dreyfus **(187)** for commentary on some of these matters.

208. Meckier, Jerome. "The Everyman Dickens." *Dickens Quarterly*, 14 (1997), 165-78.

A review essay on the first eight volumes of the new Everyman Dickens, under the general editorship of Michael Slater. Meckier notes that "nearly a dozen more" volumes are "slated for production before the year 2000." He finds the series a major publishing event in the history of Dickens scholarship, a series that "aspires to be scholarly as well as popular" and that will ultimately displace "the increasingly dated Dickens volumes in the Penguin English Library." Meckier takes a number of pages to comment fairly critically on the introductions to the individual volumes.

209. Meckier, Jerome. "Health and Money." In his *Innocent Abroad: Charles Dickens's American Engagements*. Lexington: University of Kentucky Press, 1990, pp 183-236.

Examines Dickens's arrangements with American publishers to publish editions of his novels, particularly Ticknor and Fields.

210. Meynell, Sir Francis. *A Note on the Format*. Bloomsbury [London]: Nonesuch Press, 1937. 5 pp.

On the mechanics of preparing the Nonesuch Edition of Dickens's works (23 volumes, Bloomsbury [London], The Nonesuch Press, 1937-38)—type size and character, version of plates used, page size, page headings, character and thickness of paper, and binding. Also see Nonesuch Press (**217, 218**).

211. Moss, Sidney P. "Charles Dickens and Frederick Chapman's Agreement with Ticknor & Fields." *Papers of the Bibliographical Society of America*, 76 (1981), 33-38.

On the mutually satisfactory publication agreement made between Dickens and Frederick Chapman of Chapman and Hall on one side and Ticknor & Fields, a Boston firm, on the other on 15 April 1860. Moss prints for the first time the full text of the agreement, which, among other considerations and rights and privileges, gave Ticknor & Fields exclusive rights to the publication of Dickens's works in America.

212. Moss, Sidney. "The Lure of America." In his *Charles Dickens' Quarrel with America*. Troy, NY: Whitston, 1984, pp. 212-29.

Comments on Dickens's relationships with American publishers of his books, particularly Ticknor & Fields.

213. Mott, Frank L. "Dickens and the Pirates." In his *Golden Multitudes: The Story of Best Sellers in the United States.* New York: Macmillan, 1947, pp. 79-88.

A brief history of the publication of Dickens's works in the United States during and after his lifetime. Mott concludes that Dickens's great popularity in the States was to some extent "due to the publishers, who, pirates and price-cutters though many of them were, gave Dickens such an audience as no other single author has ever had in any country."

214. Muir, P. H. "Note No. 55. Dickens and Tauchnitz." *Book Collector,* 4 (1955), 329.

Indicates that Bernhard Tauchnitz, a Leipzig publisher, "was regularly supplied with the parts issues of novels" by both Dickens and Thackeray and that *Martin Chuzzlewit, Dombey and Son, David Copperfield, Bleak House, Little Dorrit,* and *Our Mutual Friend* were all published in volume form by Tauchnitz as the novels were being serialized in England. Also see Muir (**291**).

215. "The National Edition of the Works of Charles Dickens." *Dickensian,* 2 (1906), 248.

Briefly describes the then forthcoming National Edition (40 volumes, London: Chapman and Hall, 1906-08).

216. "A New Edition of Dickens's Illustrations from the Original Plates." *Times* (London), 8 June 1937, p. 13.

Notice of the publication of the first volume in the Nonesuch Edition of Dickens's works (see **210**), with all of the original illustrations, and a description of this collected edition.

217. Nonesuch Press, Bloomsbury [London]. *The Nonesuch Dickens. A Prospectus and a Portrait.* Bloomsbury [London]: Nonesuch Press, [1937]. 16 unnumbered pages.

An advertising pamphlet giving favorable critical responses to the edition proposed in *The Nonesuch Dickens: Retrospectus and Prospectus* (**218**) and to the "sample copy" of *Pickwick Papers* sent to the press. This pamphlet also includes two specimen pages from that novel and a reiteration of the features of the forthcoming edition—text, illustrations, paper, binding, price, etc. Also see Meynell (**210**).

218. Nonesuch Press, Bloomsbury [London]. *The Nonesuch Dickens: Retrospectus and Prospectus.* Bloomsbury [London]: The Nonesuch Press, 1937. 130 pp.

This volume is sometimes referred to as *Nonesuch Dickensiana* because the cover and the half title page give this as the title, and the title is sometimes listed as *Retrospectus and Prospectus: The Nonesuch Dickens* because of the arrangement of the two halves of the title on the title page. However the title is given, the volume consists of four parts. Part I, "Charles Dickens and His Illustrators," by Arthur Waugh, pp. 9-52, comments on Dickens's relations with his illustrators. Part II, "A Bibliographical List of the Original Illustrations to the Works of Charles Dickens, Being Those Made under His Supervision," compiled by Thomas Hatton (**885**), pp. 55-78, is "a Census of all the illustrations to the Works of Charles Dickens which were made during his lifetime," in the possession of the Nonesuch Press. Part III, "Retrospectus: Editions of Dickens's Works," pp. 81-122, reviews the more important editions of Dickens's works with "specimen pages" from them, including the monthly parts editions, the Charles Dickens Edition (1867-[75]), the Illustrated Library Edition (1873-76), the Gadshill Edition (1897), and the National Edition (1906-08). Part IV, "Prospectus: The Nonesuch Dickens," pp. 125-30, gives a brief description of the "unique" Nonesuch Edition, designed and planned by Francis Meynell, with the text printed under the supervision of a committee composed of Arthur Waugh, Walter Dexter, and Thomas Hatton, and with illustrations reproduced from all the original plates purchased from Chapman and Hall. A few details about fonts, binding, and other technical matters are also provided. Also see McKitterick, Rendall, and Dreyfus (**207**).

Reviews: R. Straus, *Dickensian*, 33 (1936/37), 211-13 (a "document of real bibliographical importance"); E. L. Tinker, *New York Times Book Review*, 29 August 1937, p. 20 (contains "a delightfully told" chronicle of Dickens's collaboration with his illustrators).

219. "Notes: Literary." *Nation* (New York), 4, xciv, xcv, xcix (18 April, 25 April, 23 May 1867), pp. 308, 328, 408.

In connection with articles published and subsequently published in the *American Literary Gazette and Publishers' Circular* (**186, 196, 205, 220**), the 18 April article comments on Dickens's receipt of money for individual works from Harper & Brothers, T. B. Peterson & Brothers, and others, and whether for manuscripts or advance sheets. The 25 April article, in providing a "bit of literary history" on Dickens and his American publishers, claims that prior to the publication of *Dombey and Son* Dickens "had never received anything" from American publishers for his works and notes that, in the competition between Harper's and the *International Magazine* for advance sheets of *Bleak House*, Harper's had won out by sending a representative directly to Dickens to negotiate for them, whereas *International Magazine* went to his publishers and got nowhere. The 23 May article also reports that Dickens had just declared Ticknor & Fields to be "his only authorised publisher in America," and notes that this publishing company had just announced a "Charles Dickens Edition" to be published in thirteen or fourteen volumes. The 25 April article was reprinted in "Notes on Books and Booksellers," *American Literary Gazette and Publishers' Circular*, 9, i (1 May 1867), 5-6.

220. "Notes on Books and Booksellers: The Dickens Controversy." *American Literary Gazette and Publishers' Circular*, 9, iii (1 June 1867), 68-69.

Prints Dickens's letter to Ticknor & Fields, 16 April 1867 (see *Pilgrim Letters*, XI, 352-53), noting that, apart from his association with them, he has received payment for his works published in America only from Harper's (through Sampson Low, their London agent) for advance sheets of *A Tale of Two Cities*, *Great Expectations*, and *Our Mutual Friend* and from Hurd & Houghton for 100 impressions of the illustrations for *Pickwick Papers*. *American Literary Gazette* finds this statement "almost next of kin to dishonesty," in connection with which it notes that Harper & Brothers had also paid Dickens for *Bleak House* and *Little Dorrit*, and it reprints a letter from Sampson Low to the *Pall Mall Gazette*, dated 7 May 1867, stating that, as agent for Harper & Brothers, he had paid Dickens "many thousands of pounds for and on account of his works, when no other publishing house had paid anything." The magazine also prints a letter from T. B. Peterson & Brothers to George W. Childs, publisher of the *American Literary Gazette*, complaining of Dickens's cold shouldering of the firm when it thought it had purchased "the equitable right" to publication of Dickens's works in America from other American publishers. Earlier announcements concerning the Ticknor and Fields editions will be found in *American Literary Gazette and Publishers' Circular*, 8, vi (15 January 1867), 191-92, 201; 8, vii (1 February 1867), 216, 226; and 8, viii (15 February 1867), 254. For announcements of T. B. Peterson's National Edition of Dickens's works, see *American Literary Gazette and Publishers' Circular*, 8, vii (1 February 1867), 216, 230; for announcements of Hurd & Houghton's Globe Edition, Household Edition, and Riverside Edition of Dickens's works, see the same journal, 8, xi (1 April 1867), pp. 321, 335. Advertisements usually continue in some subsequent issues. For earlier comments in this magazine on Dickens's relations with his American publishers, see "Dickens's Dealings with Americans" (**186**), Lea (**205**), "Important Announcement from Charles Dickens" (**196**), and "Notes: Literary," in *Nation* (**219**).

221. Nowell-Smith, Simon. "Editing Dickens: For Which Reader? From Which Text?" *Times Literary Supplement*, 4 June 1970, pp. 615-16.

Reviews the problems and choices that confront a modern editor of a Dickens novel, opting, quite generally, for "a text as close as possible to what the author intended, or would have wished, at one moment in time." Nowell-Smith also believes in a "clean text," with textual changes noted but no explanatory notes, an influence he claims to have had on the format of the Clarendon Edition of Dickens's works. In a letter to the editor, 11 June 1970, p. 638, Geoffrey D. Hargreaves, in disagreement, insists on the supremacy of the manuscript in determining textual authenticity.

222. Nowell-Smith, Simon. "Firma Tauchnitz, 1837-1900." *Book Collector*, 15 (1966), 423-36; revised and expanded in his *International Copyright Law and the Publisher in the Reign of Queen Victoria*. Oxford: Clarendon Press, 1968, pp. 42-50.

Comments on Bernhard Tauchnitz's publication of Dickens's works in Germany in his "Collection of British Authors" series, from 1841 on, and the bibliographical significance of these publications.

223. Page, Norman. *A Dickens Companion*. London: Macmillan; New York: Schocken Books, 1984, passim.

For bibliographical and textual commentary, the sections on the individual novels and other writings in "Dickens' Writings," pp. 53-277, provide information about the best texts, Dickens's writing of the works, and their publication details. Page also includes useful bibliographies of critical studies, illustrations, film versions, and early dramatizations of Dickens's novels (**781-82, 915, 1014**), as well as biographical and critical commentary. Also see "Appendix D: The Berg Notebook" (**2531**), pp. 349-51. Illustrated.

224. Patten, Robert L. *Charles Dickens and His Publishers*. Oxford: Clarendon Press, 1978, passim.

In this magnificently detailed scholarly study of Dickens's relationships with his several publishers, one finds a great deal of information about the writing, printing, and publication of Dickens's works from *Sketches by Boz* to *Edwin Drood*. Much of this is based on the account books of Dickens's two main publishers, Bradbury and Evans and Chapman and Hall; see the valuable appendices drawn from these: "A. Sales and Profits of Dickens's Works, 1846-70," pp. 349-416; "B. The Printing History of Dickens's Monthly Serials, 1846-70," pp. 417-57; "C. Income from Dickens's Works for Dickens, Bradbury and Evans, and Chapman and Hall, 1846-70," pp. 458-61; and "D. Income from *Household Words* and *All the Year Round*," pp. 462-64. There is also a useful "Select Bibliography," pp. 465-83 (**1182**). Illustrated.

225. Peyrouton, N. C. "A Postscript on Pirates." *Dickensian*, 56 (1960), 179-81.

Describes the piracy of several literary works (including Dickens's) in 1850-51 in *The Australasian*, published in Melbourne, Australia. Dickens's let-

ter, 27 June 1851, to the periodical condemning the practice–here published
for the first time–was, as Peyrouton points out, "mild indeed," considering
letters Dickens wrote condemning English and American piracies of his
works.

226.   *Prospectus of the Autograph Edition of the Complete Writings of Charles Dickens
       in Fifty-Six Volumes.* New York: George D. Sproul; London: Chapman
       & Hall, 1903. 28 pp.

Announces that the Autograph Edition is intended to be the definitive one
for "both the general reader and the book collector," that general editor F. G.
Kitton would be contributing a bibliographical essay on each novel and "pro-
fuse topographical notes," that eminent critics (listed) would write the introductions to each novel, that the edition would contain not only the original
illustrations but all those done since, including some specifically for this edition (the first volume, *Pickwick Papers*, would thus contain 447 illustrations),
and that the edition would also include *Forster*, the letters and speeches, volumes of Dickensiana, and volumes on the artists by Kitton. Each of the 250
sets would also contain an authentic autograph or other piece of writing by
Dickens. The prospectus also contains brief biographical sketches of the artists contributing new illustrations to the edition. Unfortunately, only fifteen
volumes, containing *Pickwick Papers* (vols. 1-3), *David Copperfield* (vols. 4-6), *The
Old Curiosity Shop* (vols. 7-8), *Reprinted Pieces* (vol. 9), *Barnaby Rudge* (vols. 10-
12), and *Dombey and Son* (vols. 13-15), were published. Also see Kitton (**2303**).

227.   R[ussell], N[orman]. "Advertising in and of Dickens's Work." In *Oxford
       Reader's Companion to Dickens.* Ed. Paul Schlicke (**2309**), pp. 4-5 (pp. 5-6
       in the 2000 paperback edition).

Discusses the advertisements that appeared in the monthly numbers of
Dickens's novels, as well as the ways in which Dickens's publishers promoted
his novels.

228.   Shaylor, Joseph. *The Fascination of Books, with Other Papers on Books &
       Bookselling.* London: Simpkin, Marshall, Hamilton, Kent, 1912, pp. 346-
       47.

Comments on two "magnificent" collected editions of Dickens's
works–the St. Dunstan Edition (130 volumes, selling for £26,000, of which
only fifteen copies "are being printed") and the Autograph Edition (fifty-six
volumes, selling for £336). Unfortunately, only fifteen volumes (containing six
works) of the Autograph Edition were published and none of the St. Dunstan
Edition–see Kitton (**2303**), Carr (**1445**), and *Prospectus of the Autograph Edition*
(**226**). Shaylor also comments on the popularity of Dickens's Christmas Books
and the Christmas numbers of *Household Words* and *All the Year Round*–and on

Thackeray's imitations of them (pp. 49-52). Kitton (**202**) lists the projected price of the St. Dunstan Edition as £30,000.

229. Shillingsburg, Peter L. "Nineteenth-Century British Fiction." In *Scholarly Editing: A Guide to Research*. Ed. D. C. Greetham. New York: Modern Language Association of America, 1995, pp. 331-50.

In discussing textual scholarship concerning various collected editions and individual works of Victorian novelists, Shillingsburg makes passing references to those of Dickens's novels, noting the importance of the Clarendon Edition (**176**) of Dickens's works (still in progress), though criticizing the volumes already published for not being perfectly clear, where cancellations are concerned, about "what was *added* as replacement text, and what was already part of the text when the cancellation was made."

230. S[horter], C[lement] K. "A Literary Letter." *Sphere*, 17 (2 April 1904), 22.

Notes that the St. Dunstan Edition (known as the Millionaire's Edition—fifteen copies on parchment in 130 volumes), the Bibliophile's Edition (fifty copies on handmade paper in 112 volumes), and the Autograph Edition (250 copies in fifty-six volumes) published in New York by Sproul and in London by Harrap have the same text. However, despite Shorter's statement, only fifteen volumes (containing six works) of the Autograph Edition were published, and apparently none of the volumes in the other two editions—see Kitton (**2303**) and Carr (**1445**). Shorter also comments more generally, about Dickens, "the one great Victorian writer who has appealed alike to the most cultivated and the least cultivated mind, to gentle and simple, to educated and uneducated, to people of all classes and all ranks." Also see *Prospectus of the Autograph Edition* (**226**) for the sudden cancellation of these editions, and Shorter (**231**).

231. S[horter], C[lement] K. "A Literary Letter: The Millionaire's Dickens." *Sphere*, 37 (1909), 236.

Comments briefly on various collected editions of Dickens's works and notes that "the best edition of Dickens that has ever been placed upon the market is "The Millionaire's Edition" published by George Sproul in three forms, the St. Dunstan's Edition, the Bibliophile's Edition, and the Autograph Edition. He comments favorably upon the Autograph Edition for its "perfect typography," for containing "all the illustrations that have ever been made," and the valuable introductions. Illustrated. But see *Prospectus of the Autograph Edition* (**226**) for the sudden cancellation of these editions. Only fifteen volumes (containing six works) of the Autograph Edition were ever published and apparently none of the other two editions—see Kitton (**2303**) and Carr (**1445**). Also see Shorter (**230**).

232. Southton, J. Y. "Matters for Dickensian Research. I. Dickens Publishes Two Almanacs." *Dickensian*, 7 (1911), 15-17.

Proposes as subjects for fruitful research the *Household Words* Almanacs for 1856 and 1857 and reprints an advertisement for them in *Household Words*. See Miller (**430**) for further details.

233. Stange, G. Robert. "Reprints of Nineteenth-Century British Fiction." *College English*, 21 (1959/60), 178-83.

Evaluates, generally unfavorably, a small number of modern reprints of Dickens's novels then available in paperback editions—nine volumes of six titles: *Bleak House, David Copperfield* (3), *Great Expectations, Hard Times, Oliver Twist*, and *A Tale of Two Cities* (2).

234. Tanselle, G. Thomas. "Problems and Accomplishments in the Editing of the Novel." *Studies in the Novel*, 7 (1975), 323-60; reprinted with corrections in his *Textual Criticism and Scholarly Editing*. Charlottesville, VA, and London: Published for the Bibliographical Society of the University of Virginia by the University Press of Virginia, 1990, pp. 179-217.

In this article emphasizing textual matters in editing editions of American novels in the Center for Editions of American Authors, Tanselle points out that the special problems with editing novels are their length, a belief that individual variants in a novel lack the significance of variations in a poem or a shorter work, and the expense of reproducing all the textual variants. He also looks at the Wesleyan Edition of Henry Fielding's works and series of Clarendon editions, among which he mentions the Clarendon Dickens in progress. Tanselle finds Kathleen Tillotson's argument (**2474**) for choosing the 1846 edition of *Oliver Twist* as the copy-text "not fully convincing" and does not find her handling of the textual apparatus, Margaret Cardwell's of *The Mystery of Edwin Drood* (**2434**), or Alan Horsman's of *Dombey and Son* (**2376**) entirely satisfactory. He generally prefers the author's manuscript as the copy-text in accordance with principles laid down in W. W. Greg's "The Rationale of Copy-Text," *Studies in Bibliography*, 3 (1950/51), 19-36. The reprint corrects "some dozen and a half errors."

235. Tebbel, John. *A History of Book Publishing in the United States*. 4 vols. New York and London: R. R. Bowker/Xerox, 1972-81, passim.

Check the index to each volume for the references to the American publication of Dickens's works and for Dickens's campaign for an international copyright.

236. Thomas, Gilbert. "Publishing Dickens 60 Years Ago." *Bookseller*, no. 3356 (18 April 1970), 2042-43.

Writes of his work for Arthur Waugh in the firm of Chapman and Hall, 1908-14, and briefly comments on the firm's editions of Dickens's works as the last of the copyrights were running out.

237. Tillotson, Geoffrey. "The English Scholars Get Their Teeth into Dickens." *Sewanee Review*, 75 (1967), 325-37.

Ostensibly a review of *Pilgrim Letters*, I, and Kathleen Tillotson's edition of *Oliver Twist* (**2474**) but more a personal account of the origin of the edition of Dickens's letters and the Clarendon Edition of Dickens's works.

238. V[ann], J. D[on], and A[nny] S[adrin]. "Editions." In *Oxford Reader's Companions to Dickens*. Ed. Paul Schlicke (**2309**), pp. 204-09 (pp. 207-14 in the 2000 paperback edition).

Concise, highly detailed accounts of collected editions over which Dickens had control (Vann), collected editions published after Dickens's death (Vann), and foreign English-language individual and collected editions (Sadrin).

239. Winship, Michael. "The Transatlantic Book Trade and Anglo-American Literary Culture in the Nineteenth Century." In *Reciprocal Influences: Literary Production, Distribution, and Consumption in America*. Ed. Steven Fink and Susan S. Williams. Columbus: Ohio State University Press, 1999, pp. 98-122.

Provides (pp. 106-07) some financial details concerning Ticknor and Fields's authorized edition of Dickens's collected works in 1858, published through an agreement with Chapman and Hall, Dickens's London publishers. This was Chapman and Hall's Library Edition, for which the London company, according to Patten (**224**), "supplied special American title-pages and vignettes."

1F. BIBLIOGRAPHICAL STUDIES OF INDIVIDUAL DICKENS WORKS

Note: For other comments on editions of individual Dickens works, see section 7B, below, and **Bibliographical studies of Dickens's works** and **bibliographical studies** under the individual work in part 2 of the subject index.

Barnaby Rudge

240. Bede, Cuthbert [Edward Bradley]. "Charles Dickens's Novel 'Gabriel Vardon.'" *Notes and Queries*, 6th ser., 5 (1882), 387.

Asks where *Gabriel Vardon* appears in the Dickens canon. In an appended note, the editor points out that there are similar characters in this work and in *Barnaby Rudge*. A response by J. W. Jarvis, 6th ser., 6 (1882), 13-14, notes an advertisement for the novel in a copy of the second series of *Sketches by Boz* (December 1836), followed by one for *Barnaby Rudge* in *Bentley's Miscellany* in 1839, but does not make a connection between the two.

241. Gibson, Frank A. "Dickens's Unique Book: A Bibliographical Causerie." *Dickensian*, 44 (1947/48), 44-48.

Describes the appearance and format of, advertisements and errors in, and other bibliographical information about the monthly parts of *Master Humphrey's Clock*.

242. "Lord Jeffrey's Autograph Volumes of Dickens." *Dickensian*, 7 (1911), 37-40.

Reprints and reproduces in photographic facsimile Dickens's inscriptions in presentation copies to Lord Jeffrey of *The Old Curiosity Shop* and *Barnaby Rudge*.

243. Parrish, M[orris] L. "[Query] 272. Dickens: Gabriel Vardon (Barnaby Rudge)." *Bibliographical Notes and Queries*, 2, x (April 1938), 9.

In reference to an advertisement for *Gabriel Vardon* in John Macrone's catalogue at the back of his edition of Dickens's *Sketches by Boz*, second series, queries why Dickens changed the title from *Gabriel Vardon* to *Barnaby Rudge* and why Chapman and Hall finally published it rather than Macrone.

244. Read, Newbury F. "On the Writing of *Barnaby Rudge*." *Dickensian*, 30 (1933/34). 53-57.

Traces in considerable detail the "chequered and stormy career," 1836-41, of the work that started as *Gabriel Vardon* and ended as *Barnaby Rudge*, including the "tangle of agreements" Dickens made with John Macrone and Richard Bentley before he published the work as part of *Master Humphrey's Clock* in 1841.

Bleak House

Note: See Exman (**189**).

245. Easson, Angus. "Paperback Editions of *Bleak House*." *Dickens Quarterly*, 1 (1984), 12-18.

Evaluates ten paperback editions of *Bleak House*, selecting the Norton Edition, edited by George Ford and Sylvère Monod, 1977 (**2327**) as front runner, followed by the Crowell Edition, edited by Duane DeVries, 1971 (**2324**), and, in third place, the Penguin Edition, edited by Norman Page, 1971 (**2330**).

246. Monod, Sylvère. "'Between Two Worlds': Editing Dickens." In *Editing Nineteenth-Century Fiction: Papers Given at the Thirteenth Annual Conference on Editorial Problems, University of Toronto, 4-5 November 1977*. Ed. Jane Millgate. New York and London: Garland Publishing, 1978, pp. 17-39.

As an introduction to a discussion of editing decisions made by George Ford and himself in editing *Bleak House* (**2327**) for a largely American audience and by himself (for the Bibliothèque de la Pléiade Edition) for French readers, Monod notes that an editor's principal task is "to make our author *genuinely accessible*."

247. Petrullo, Helen B. "Sinclair Lewis's Condensation of Dickens's *Bleak House*." *Yale University Library Gazette*, 45 (1970/71), 85-87.

On a condensation of *Bleak House* done by the American novelist in 1942 for the Readers Club but never published. The work, which was to emphasize the importance of Inspector Bucket in the novel, was to be entitled *The Inspector Bucket Edition of Bleak House by Charles Dickens, Edited with Certain Remarks on Detective Stories by Sinclair Lewis*. Petrullo briefly looks at Lewis's changes, which would have reduced the novel by one-third. "Detective Stories and Mr. Dickens," the introduction that Lewis wrote, is printed for the first time immediately following this article, pp. 88-92.

248. Shillingsburg, Peter L. "Editorial Problems Are Readers' Problems." *Browning Institute Studies*, 9 (1981), 43-57.

In commenting on editorial problems in various then recent and ongoing collected editions of Victorian authors, Shillingsburg identifies certain textual problems in *Bleak House*, disagreeing in part with Monod (**246**) on editorial practices. Shillingsburg also notices that while the Tillotson edition of *Oliver Twist* in the Clarendon Edition (**2474**) gives deletions made by Dickens in the novel, it does not record Dickens's additions.

249. Wall, Stephen. "Annotated English Novels?" *Essays in Criticism*, 32 (1982), 1-8.

In favor of the fullest explanatory annotation in new editions of Victorian novels, Wall criticizes the Clarendon Edition of *Dombey and Son* (**2376**) for only including textual notes and praises the Norton Edition of *Bleak House* (**2327**) for having both (and costing significantly less).

Christmas Books, Christmas Stories, and Other Shorter Fiction

Note: Also see Brennan (**323**), Davis (**471**), Gibson (**241**), Howe (**476**), Johnson (**417**), Kitton (**418**), Kline (**204**), Matz (**517**), Robinson (**483**), Stone (**449-51**), Thomas (**538**), Weaver (**461**), and *Sketches by Boz*, below. For other commentary on the states of the first edition of *A Christmas Carol*, see **A Christmas Carol, states of the first edition**, in part 1 of the subject index.

250. Allbut, Charles. "A Misapprehension." *Dickensian*, 5 (1909), 105, 132-35.

In a letter to the editor, Allbut notes that the hymn in *The Wreck of the Golden Mary*, the Christmas number for *Household Words*, 1856, was written by Harriet Parr, not Dickens. A second letter reconfirms the first.

251. Ardagh, J. "Some Notes on 'A Christmas Carol.'" *Dickensian*, 20 (1924), 204.

Briefly comments on the first and later editions of *A Christmas Carol*, artists who illustrated the work, dramatizations of it, and other such basic information.

252. Calhoun, Philo, and Howell J. Heaney. "Dickens' *Christmas Carol* after a Hundred Years: A Study in Bibliographical Evidence." *Papers of the Bibliographical Society of America*, 39 (1945), 271-317.

A pleasantly written account of how *A Christmas Carol* came to be written that also surveys scholarship connected with the perplexing question of the bibliographical points of the first and succeeding issues of the first edition, particularly with reference to colors and date on the title page, the heading of the first chapter, and the color of the end papers. This involved not only some chemical tests but also an examination of Dickens's letters of the time and a census of presentation copies, the results of which are presented in a series of

appendices. The appendices list the textual changes in the first to third edi
tions, give full collation for what Calhoun and Heaney see as the first state of
the first issue, describe all the known presentation copies and a few other copies, and characterize the various states of the first and second editions.
Calhoun and Heaney differ with Eckel (**16**) and Osborne (**279**) in several respects in defining the first issue of the first edition of the novel–in giving priority to yellow end papers, the red and blue 1843-dated title page, and the first
chapter heading of "Stave I."

253. Carter, John. "'The Battle of Life': Round Three." *Antiquarian Bookman*,
    33 (1964), 2203-05.

Reports on a meeting of experts that determined that Eckel's (**16**) 1913
description of the earliest state of the first edition of *The Battle of Life* (Round
One) was authentic and not a forgery, as it was called in a catalogue of a
Sotheby sale of 27 February 1962 (Round Two)–see Sotheby & Co. (**1988**).
Also see *Antiquarian Bookman*, 33 (1964), p. 2319, for further comment on this
issue, and Todd (**286**). Illustrated.

254. "The Christmas Number of 'All the Year Round.'" *Dickensian*, 3 (1907),
    299.

Asserts that when the Christmas numbers of *All the Year Round* were published, it was not known who wrote the individual stories in each. In a reply,
4 (1908), 48-49, Robert Pierpont notes that a collected edition of the stories in
All the Year Round was published as *The Nine Christmas Numbers of All the Year
Round* (London: *All the Year Round* Office, n. d.), which identified the authors
of the individual pieces. He provides the names of some of these authors.

255. Davies, H. Neville. "The Tauchnitz Extra Christmas Numbers of *All
    the Year Round.*" *Library*, 5th ser., 33 (1978), 215-22.

Points out that the three volumes (Leipzig, 1862, 1867, 1867) in the
Tauchnitz paperback series of "Collections of British Authors" containing
Dickens's Christmas numbers of *All the Year Round* (1859-66) also contain the
first identification of the authors of the stories. The earliest British edition
identifying them was published in 1868. The attributions from both sources
are similar, Davies notes, with only minor variations in the forms of names, as
his itemized comparison shows.

256. "A Dickens Inscription." *Saturday Review of Literature*, 34, li (22 Decem-
    ber 1951), 23.

Prints an inscription by Dickens to a Frank Powell in a copy of *A Christmas Carol,* dated 13 Mar 1844, commenting comically on Powell's having been refused admittance to Dickens.

257. Frank, Jerome P. "Deluxe Dickens." *Publishers Weekly,* 224, iv (22 July 1983), 80.

Deals with the technical details of the design and production of an elegant edition of *A Christmas Carol* (New York: Holiday House, 1983), illustrated by Trina Schart Hyman, whose six color plates and four black-and-white tailpieces are found to capture "the essence of the work" in depicting "the emotional highs of the book in classic Dickensian style."

258. Gimbel, Richard. *Charles Dickens's **A Christmas Carol**. Three States of the First Edition.* N.p.: Privately printed, 1956 [1955]. 8 pp.

Detailed bibliographical descriptions of the first edition (three states), second edition, and "Mixed, Trial and Odd Copies" of *A Christmas Carol.* A "Notice" on the last page states that this small pamphlet was "Presented for Discussion by Colonel Gimbel at a Meeting of the Colophon Club of Princeton University, 6 December 1955."

259. Gimbel, Richard. "The Earliest State of the First Edition of Charles Dickens' *A Christmas Carol.*" *Princeton University Library Chronicle,* 19 (1957/58), 82-86.

Contends that the first issue of the first edition has the title page printed in red and green (not red and blue), its end papers green (not yellow), its half title and verso of the title page printed in green (not blue), and the text, uncorrected, headed "Stave I" (not "Stave One"). The changes in all but the last item, Gimbel states, characterize the *second* state and were made because the green ink and the green end papers proved unsatisfactory some time early in the printing of the first edition. Illustrated.

260. Glancy, Ruth F. "Commentary on the First Issue Problem [of *A Christmas Carol*]." In her *Dickens's Christmas Books, Christmas Stories, and Other Short Fiction: An Annotated Bibliography* (**98**), pp. 10-16.

Lists in chronological order and summarizes twenty-nine attempts to characterize the first and other issues of the first edition of *A Christmas Carol.* In her introductory comment to this section of her bibliography, Glancy notes that the problem exists because "there seems to be no end to the combinations" in which variations in "title page, end pages, date, stave numbering, and text" occur. She offers a convincing analysis of the situation–Dickens experimented with the appearance of the work during the initial publication, and, while changes were being made, the printers "anxious not to waste valuable paper, used all the available title pages and endpapers quite randomly."

261. Hamilton, Doris H. "Christmas Autographs." *Hobbies*, 65, x (December 1960), 110-11.

Includes bibliographical details and the provenance of the manuscript for *A Christmas Carol*, now in the Pierpont Morgan Library, New York.

262. Hancher, Michael. "Reading the Visual Text: *A Christmas Carol.*" *Yale University Library Gazette*, 74 (1999/2000), 21-40.

Comments intelligently on the physical details of the first edition of the work–binding, cover decoration, color of end papers, illustrations, and page layout. Illustrated.

263. Iacone, Salvatore J. "Inscribed Books and Literary Scholarship." In *A Miscellany for Bibliophiles*. Ed. H. George Fletcher (**204**), pp. 47-65.

Notes in passing (p. 57) that the investigations of Calhoun and Heaney (**252**) indicated that dated inscriptions by Dickens in copies of *A Christmas Carol* presented to his friends helped determine that copies with yellow end papers preceded those with green end papers.

264. Johnson, Edgar. "Bibliographical Note." In Dickens's *A Christmas Carol* (**265**), pp. vii-xii.

Comments intelligently on disagreements among bibliophiles over the characteristics of a true first issue of the first edition of *A Christmas Carol*. Johnson holds with Calhoun and Heaney (**252**) and Gimbel (**258-59**) that there were three "successive stages" of the edition involving color of end papers, color of title page text, and a few other matters, but that the publisher threw nothing out, so that variants of every kind exist, all with the thirty-nine typographical errors that were not corrected until the second edition.

265. Johnson, Edgar. "Introduction." In Dickens's *A Christmas Carol: A Facsimile of the First Edition*. Illustrated by John Leech. Ann Arbor, MI: A Giniger Book published in association with University Microfilms Library Services, 1967, pp. iii-xii.

Describes the writing and reception of *A Christmas Carol*, surveys the bibliographical scholarship on the various editions and states of the first edition, and criticizes an earlier 1922 facsimile edition (London: Cecil Palmer, 1922) as being that of the second edition, with thirty-nine typographical errors silently corrected. The last part of the introduction is a brief bibliographical note (**264**).

266. Jonas, Maurice. "'The Chimes,' 1845." *Notes and Queries*, 9th ser., 11 (1903), 27.

Notes an error in the attribution of the engravers in the list of illustrations in this edition.

267. Kitton, F[rederic] G. "Introduction." In Dickens's *The* [sic] *Christmas Carol: A Facsimile Reproduction of the Author's Original Manuscript*. London: Elliot Stock; New York: Brentano, 1890, pp. iii-viii.

Although Kitton briefly discusses the history of the manuscript itself, his introduction is concerned largely with the publishing history and reception of *A Christmas Carol*. Kitton points out that the novel in its original red cloth cover had (by 1890) gone through some twenty-five editions, the last of which had been published in 1885.

268. Lloyd-Blood, J. K. "Bibliographical Notes: *A Christmas Carol*." *Times Literary Supplement*, 12 December 1936, p. 1040.

A query about the "Eleventh Edition" of *A Christmas Carol* (Bradbury and Evans, 1846).

269. M[atz], B. W. "Books Presented by Dickens to Ainsworth and His Daughter." *Dickensian*, 12 (1916), 157-58.

Comments briefly on the occasions on which Dickens gave presentation copies of *The Haunted Man* to William Harrison Ainsworth and *Peter Parley's Tales about Christmas* to Blanche, Ainsworth's daughter. Includes facsimiles of the two inscriptions.

270. [Matz, B. W.]. "When Found." *Dickensian*, 17 (1921), 171-74.

In responding, p. 171, to an article by J. Pennell in *Bookman's Journal* (**282**), Matz concludes that the question of whether the original end papers of the first issue of the first edition of *A Christmas Carol* were yellow or green "will never be definitely settled" because the binder very likely "did some with yellow end papers and some with green."

271. McGuire, Patrick. "Collecting Christmas Books." *American Book Collector*, 6, vi (November/December 1985), 3-10.

Briefly comments on editions of Dickens's Christmas Books and Christmas Stories but offers little for the collector.

272. Newton, A[lfred] Edward. "The Greatest Little Book in the World." *Atlantic Monthly*, 132 (1923), 732-38; reprinted in *The Greatest Little Book in the World and Other Papers*, Boston: Little, Brown, 1925, pp. 408-23.

Comments digressively on, among other aspects of *A Christmas Carol*, occasional bibliographical matters concerning its writing and publication.

273. Newton, A[lfred] Edward. "Introduction." In Dickens's *A Christmas Carol in Prose, Being a Ghost Story of Christmas*. Boston: Atlantic Monthly Press, 1920. pp. v-ix; reprinted as "Introduction to *A Christmas Carol*." In *Praise from Famous Men: An Anthology of Introductions*. Ed. Guy R. Lyle. Metuchen, NJ: Scarecrow Press, 1977, pp. 131-35.

A generally appreciative introduction with emphasis on the bibliographical details of the first edition. The edition itself is a photographic reproduction of the first edition.

274. "Notes on Sales: 'Christmas Books' by Dickens and Others." *Times Literary Supplement*, 20 December 1923, p. 900.

Provides basic publishing information about Dickens's Christmas Books and about several imitations of them, including those by Thackeray.

275. "Notes on Sales: Dickens's 'Christmas Carol.'" *Times Literary Supplement*, 23 December 1920, p. 880.

Summarizes Eckel's (**16**) views on the principal "points" for a first issue of the first edition of *A Christmas Carol*, but describes "another hitherto totally unrecognized variant [that] has turned up," with the bookplate of Bartholomew Molière Tabuteau. The reporter also gives details of the provenance of the manuscript of *A Christmas Carol*, then already in the Pierpont Morgan Library, New York City. See a letter to the editor, from "L. A. W.," 30 December, p. 892, for a bit of information about Tabuteau.

276. "Notes on Sales: Dickens's Christmas Numbers." *Times Literary Supplement*, 25 December 1924, p. 888.

Provides bibliographical details about the Christmas numbers of *Household Words* and *All the Year Round* and the republication of Dickens's contributions to them in various forms and gives some information about imitations of the Christmas Stories by others. In a reply, 8 January 1925, p. 24, Robert Pierpont notes that the names of the contributors to the *All the Year Round* Christmas numbers were published around 1868 in a collected edition of them (London: Chapman and Hall), though he further clarifies the authorship of the stories in several instances and adds a few more details about the Christmas numbers.

277. "Notes on Sales: 'Pickwick' and 'A Christmas Carol.'" *Times Literary Supplement*, 14 January 1932, p. 32.

A note about the sale of Thomas Hatton's important set of *Pickwick Papers* in parts at Sotheby's (**1978**), the publication of the first six parts of the Lombard Street *Pickwick Papers* (**2492**), and points made by E. Allen Osborne in his article "The Variants of 'The Christmas Carol'" (**280**), with which the anonymous writer agrees.

278. Osborne, E. A[llen]. "'A Christmas Carol.'" *Times Literary Supplement*, 30 October 1937, p. 808.

In connection with his then forthcoming bibliographical study of *A Christmas Carol* (**279**), asks readers for documentary evidence of various issues and "trial" copies of the book.

279. Osborne, E. Allen. *The Facts about A Christmas Carol.* London: Printed for the Author by The Bradley Press, 1937. 33 pp.

In this limited edition of 55 copies, Osborne provides numerous bibliographical and other details and conjectures about the writing and publication history of *A Christmas Carol.* Osborne finds that he disagrees on almost every point of bibliographical detail with the revised Eckel bibliography (**16**) and resolves to his own satisfaction the question of the order of publication of issues and editions of this novel in chapters on "The History of the *Carol*," "The Bibliography of the *Carol*," and "Conjectures about the *Carol*." He includes useful appendices: 1) a list of Dickens's corrections in the proof copy; 2) an account of the sales of *A Christmas Carol*, 1843-1844; 3) a list of the distinguishing characteristics of the various early editions (through 1873) of the novel; and 4) a chart of the textual variants in these editions. The volume also contains colored reproductions of the title pages of the red and green and the red and blue 1844 issues. See Osborne's earlier examination of *A Christmas Carol* (**280**).

Reviews: A. de Suzannet, *Dickensian*, 34 (1937/38), 128 ("does not appear to have established any new 'facts' of importance," and those "he has gathered are marshalled, as a rule, without order or clarity, and his reasoning is not always convincing"); *Times Literary Supplement*, 11 December 1937 (Osborne "is long on enthusiasm and perseverance, but short on lucidity and sometimes on judgment"; still, "he has assembled a quantity of useful evidence").

280. Osborne, E. A[llen]. "The Variants of 'The [sic] Christmas Carol.'" *Bookman* (London), 81 (1931/32), 192-94.

Comments on the "conception and production" of *A Christmas Carol* and describes and lists the variations in text, title and half title pages, the colored plates, the end papers, and the binding, as well as the variant issues and editions. Illustrated. Expanded and updated in Osborne's *The Facts about **A Christmas Carol*** (279).

281. Parrish, Morris L. "[Query] 196. Dickens: *A Christmas Carol.*" *Bibliographical Notes and Queries*, 2, vi (July 1936), 6.

Asks about a particular state of an issue of the first edition of *A Christmas Carol*. There was no response to the query.

282. Pennell, J. "The Real First Issue of 'A Christmas Carol.'" *Bookman's Journal and Print Collector*, 4 (1921), 207-08.

Gives bibliographical details for early issues of *A Christmas Carol* and decides that the genuine first issue has yellow end papers. For the customary debate following upon such an assertion, see correspondence in subsequent issues from W. Marchbank and Walter G. Crombie, p. 220; Charles J. Sawyer and E. G. Sykes, p. 236; Albert M. Cohn, p. 252; Sawyer, 5 (1921/22), 104; Cohn, 141; Sawyer, 170; and finally Pennell, 6 (1922), 34, who reaffirms his belief in the yellow end papers and, by way of review, lists the bibliographical points for the early issues of *A Christmas Carol*.

283. Prideaux, W. F. "Dickens's 'Christmas Carol.'" *Notes and Queries*, 7th ser., 12 (1891), 45.

On the precedence of the issues of the first edition—in response to F. G. Kitton's comments on the matter in his introduction to a facsimile edition of the manuscript (**267**). In responding, J. Cuthbert Welch, p. 217, points out one discrepancy in Prideaux's analysis, a correction accepted apologetically by Prideaux, p. 452. The subject is further commented on by J. S. Udal in "First Editions," *Notes and Queries*, 8th ser., 1 (1892), 427-28.

284. Sadleir, Michael. "'A Christmas Carol.'" *Times Literary Supplement*, 28 January 1932, p. 60.

Responding to "Notes on Sales: 'Pickwick' and 'A Christmas Carol'" (**277**), Sadleir comments on the chalkiness given off by the green end papers for *A Christmas Carol* and notes that in other works (not by Dickens) published about the same time, chalkiness did not seem to be a problem.

285. Southton, J. Y. "Authorised Leipzig Edition of Dickens." *Dickensian*, 8 (1912), 181-83.

Comments on editions of *A Christmas Carol* (1843), *The Chimes* (1845), and *The Cricket on the Hearth* (1846) issued by Bernhard Tauchnitz at Leipzig, with the words "Edition Sanctioned by the Author" on the title page. Southton speculates that Dickens must have sent proofs to Leipzig because the volume of *A Christmas Carol* has "Stave I" (rather than "Stave One"), with the other staves in Roman numerals, too.

286. Todd, William B. "Dickens's *Battle of Life*. Round Six." *Book Collector*, 15 (1966), 48-54.

A follow-up on the conference of experts described in Carter (**253**), leading, after further investigative trips (rounds 4 and 5), to the conclusion that the precedence listed in Eckel (**16**) "is essentially correct." Todd's article is a highly technical discussion of the controversy over the precedence of the states of the issues of *The Battle of Life*, based on an examination of eighty-three copies of this Christmas Book. Illustrated.

287. Todd, William B. "Note 170. Dickens's *Christmas Carol*." *Book Collector*, 10 (1961), 449-54.

Further technical arguments on the various states of the first edition of *A Christmas Carol*.

David Copperfield

288. Coustillas, Pierre, ed. "Gissing's Introduction to the Autograph Edition of 'David Copperfield.'" *Gissing Journal*, 33, i (January 1997), pp. 10-19.

In his introduction to the first reprinting of George Gissing's introduction to *David Copperfield* in the ill-fated Autograph Edition, published in New York by George Sproul (see **226** and **2303**), Coustillas points out that Sproul published *David Copperfield* in three volumes in 1903 but "went bankrupt very shortly afterwards," and the "300 sets that had been printed were not disposed of before he went out of business." Since a number were not bound as well, the book, as a result, Coustillas reports, "is now extremely rare and very few people have had a chance of reading Gissing's introduction to it." Also see Coustillas (**1397-98**) and Dunn (**1405**).

289. Dexter, Walter, and Kentley Bromhill [T. W. Hill]. "'The *David Copperfield* Advertiser.'" *Dickensian*, 41 (1944/45), 21-25.

The authors provide details about the advertising "inserts," entitled "Advertiser," in the monthly numbers of *David Copperfield*.

290. Moore, John H. *Wiley: One Hundred and Seventy-Five Years of Publishing*. New York, etc.: John Wiley & Sons, 1982, p. 44.

Makes passing remarks on editions of *Dombey and Son* (1846-48) and *David Copperfield* (1849-50) published by Wiley & Putnam.

291. Muir, P. H. "Note No. 53. The Tauchnitz *David Copperfield*, 1849." *Book Collector*, 4 (1955), 253-54.

Points out that the first two of the three volumes of the Bernhard Tauchnitz Edition (Leipzig) were published prior to completion of the serialization of *David Copperfield* in England and must, therefore, have been based on the parts issues. Also see Muir (**214**).

292. Parrish, M[orris] L. "[Reply to Query] 241. Dickens: *David Copperfield*." *Bibliographical Notes and Queries*, 2, ix (January 1938), 3.

Provides bibliographical notes on an edition in parts of *David Copperfield* published by John Wiley in America.

Dombey and Son

Note: Also see Moore (**290**) and Wall (**249**).

293. Bland, D. S. "The 'Lost' Sentence in *Dombey & Son* Once More." *Dickensian*, 52 (1955/56), 142-43.

Notes that the missing sentence from the end of chapter 16 that Tillotson (**297**) refers to actually also appeared in three post-1859 editions based on the first edition–the Macmillan Edition of 1892-95, the Glasgow Edition (n. d.), and the Imperial Edition (1912). Unlike Tillotson, Bland thinks the sentence should continue to be omitted, even though a later reference to it in the novel might prove to be confusing.

294. L., S. "The First Edition of *Dombey and Son*." *Times Literary Supplement*, 22 January 1920, p. 52.

A query about a typographical error in *Dombey and Son*, leading to the question of identifying the true first edition of the novel. Among the responders to the query, Harry B. Poland, p. 68, straightens out the matter and notes errors in the illustrations for *Dombey and Son*; William Sinclair, p. 68, points out another error in the illustrations; and W. J. Garnett, p. 87, asserts that the first edition of *Dombey and Son* "swarms with errors" (some of which he notes), as do other novels of Dickens, several of whose errors he also itemizes.

295. Levine, Richard A. "Reviews–Paperback Editions: *Dombey and Son*." *Dickens Studies Newsletter*, 3 (1972), 53-57.

Compares three paperback editions of *Dombey and Son*, preferring either the Dell or Penguin Edition over the Signet.

296. Patten, Robert L. "The Fight at the Top of the Tree: *Vanity Fair* Versus *Dombey and Son.*" *Studies in English Literature, 1500-1800,* 10 (1970), 759-73.

Using the account books of Bradbury and Evans (discovered in 1969), who published both novels, Patten compares the writing and the sales of the two novels and the popularity of the two authors.

297. Tillotson, Kathleen. "A Lost Sentence in *Dombey and Son.*" *Dickensian,* 47 (1950/51), 81-82.

Notes that Miss Tox's remark at the end of chapter 16 (the end of monthly number 5) about Dombey and son being "a daughter after all!" appeared in the first edition and its reissues and in the Cheap Edition (1858) but not in the Library Edition (1859) and presumably not in any edition thereafter. The remark, Tillotson believes, was probably deliberately removed by Dickens, and she speculates about his reasons for doing so. For a response, see Bland (**293**).

Great Expectations

298. Biondi, Lee. "Great Complications." In his "Collecting Charles Dickens" (**2202**), pp. 54-57.

Comments on the publishing history of *Great Expectations*, the bibliographical problems involved in collecting editions of it, and the revised ending. Illustrated.

299. Brattin, Joel. "Frustrated Expectations: The Clarendon *Great Expectations.*" *Dickens Quarterly,* 11 (1994), 138-47.

In this review article of Margaret Cardwell's edition of *Great Expectations* (**2381**), Brattin finds his own expectations "disappointingly unfulfilled" by Cardwell's editorial decisions, including her choice of the three-volume 1861 edition as copy-text over the manuscript and the serialized version. He also criticizes her "far from complete" textual apparatus.

300. Calhoun, Philo. "Rarity of *Great Expectations.*" *New Colophon,* 1, iv (October 1948), 402.

Queries why the three-volume edition of *Great Expectations* is so rare. A reply, presumably by David A. Randall, 2, v (January 1949), 84-85, notes that there are varying theories as to why this is so—suggesting himself that it was a small edition to begin with and that unsold copies of it were overprinted with the words "second" to "sixth edition." He asks readers for more information. John Carter reports, 2, vii (September 1949), 278-79, that he has examined copies of the first five editions and found errors uncorrected but minor deterioration of type, leading him to suspect that Randall's theory is correct.

301. Davis, Paul B. "Dickens, Hogarth, and the Illustrated *Great Expectations.*" *Dickensian*, 80 (1984), 130-43.

Discusses the influence of Hogarth on Dickens's writing, particularly on *Great Expectations*, and notes several editions of *Great Expectations* that were illustrated. Davis points out that neither the serialization of the novel in *All the Year Round* nor the first English edition and American editions of the work were illustrated. Davis finds that the "most successful illustrations are probably those by F. W. Pailthorpe (1885), Gordon Ross (1937), and Harry Furniss (1910)." Illustrated.

302. DeVries, Duane. "Reviews–Paperback Editions: *Great Expectations.*" *Dickens Studies Newsletter*, 5 (1974), 56-61.

Compares and evaluates twelve paperback editions of *Great Expectations*, not finding the "ideal, fully scholarly edition" among them, but noting merits of the Penguin Edition, the Odyssey Press Edition, and the Bobbs-Merrill Edition.

303. Dundek, John M. "Note 551. A New First American Edition of *Great Expectations.*" *Book Collector*, 43 (1994), 298-99.

Asserts that the edition of *Great Expectations* published by James G. Gregory (New York, 1861) is a "new claimant to the title of first American book edition" of this novel, being issued as part of Gregory's collaborative effort with three other publishers of the American "Household Edition" of *Works of Charles Dickens*. Dundek also comments on known later editions of *Great Expectations*.

304. H., F. M. "Rare Books, Autographs and Prints." *Publishers' Weekly*, 98 (1920), 201-02.

Comments on and gives details of a controversy between Edward K. Butler and John C. Eckel over the points of a first edition of *Great Expectations*.

305. Lake, Brian. "Publication History of *Great Expectations.*" *Dickensian*, 90 (1994), 47.

In this letter to the editor, Lake praises Appendix D of Margaret Cardwell's Clarendon Edition of *Great Expectations* (**2381**) for at last straightening out the printing history of the states of the first edition of this novel, there being "five different printings, all from standing type"–1,000 published on 6 July, 750 on 5 August, 750 on 17 August, 5,000 on 21 September, and 750 on 30 October 1861, with "identifiable variations" between each impression.

Hard Times

306. Carter, John, with Michael Sadleir. *More Binding Variants*. Aspects of Book-Collecting. London: Constable; Toronto: Macmillan, 1938, pp. 7-8; reprinted in *Binding Variants and More Binding Variants in English Publishing, 1820-1900*. By John Carter. New Castle, DE: Oak Knoll Books, 1989, pp. 7-8 (each of the two books combined here is reproduced exactly as originally published, though the new title page for the combined volumes lists only Carter as the author).

Supplementing Carter's *Binding Variants in English Publishing, 1820-1900* (**177**), Carter and Sadleir describe four variants of binding for *Hard Times* and add information about the binding of *Oliver Twist*.

307. Smith, Anne. "Reviews–Paperback Editions: *Hard Times*." *Dickens Studies Newsletter*, 4 (1973), 115-22.

Compares and evaluates seven paperback editions of *Hard Times*, giving high praise to the Norton Edition, edited by George Ford and Sylvère Monod (**2411**).

308. Terauchi, Takashi. "For a Better Norton Critical Edition of *Hard Times*." *Studia Anglistica (Tennoji)/Studies in English: A Journal of Graduates of English Language and Literature at Osaka University of Education*, no. 2 (September 1982), 13-36.

Although Terauchi praises the Norton Edition of *Hard Times* (**2411**) for noting many of Dickens's changes in text, he still finds it "not quite satisfiable" and offers eighteen pages of recommended modifications, often going back to editions earlier than the Charles Dickens Edition, on which, he believes, Ford and Monod relied too heavily, preferring himself the first complete edition (1854) as the better copy-text for an authoritative edition.

309. Terauchi, Takashi. "On the Significance of a Cancelled Passage from *Hard Times*." *Studia Anglistica (Tennoji)/Studies in English: A Journal of Graduates of English Language and Literature at Osaka University of Education*, no. 1 (February 1982), 21-35.

On minor confusion caused by later references in the novel to earlier passages cancelled by Dickens in page proofs, instances clarified, Terauchi indicates, in the textual notes in the Norton Critical Edition of *Hard Times* (**2411**). In their second edition of this novel, Ford and Monod acknowledge Terauchi's help in revising and correcting the textual notes.

Little Dorrit

310. Burgan, William. "Reviews—Paperback Editions: *Little Dorrit.*" *Dickens Studies Newsletter*, 3 (1972), 22-24.

Compares the Penguin Books and the Odyssey Press paperback editions of *Little Dorrit*.

311. Ker, William P. "A Misprint in 'Little Dorrit.'" *Times Literary Supplement*, 19 September 1918, p. 441.

Ker corrects an error that he notes has appeared in almost every edition of *Little Dorrit* since the Library Edition (1859).

Martin Chuzzlewit

Note: See Exman (**189**).

312. C., M. "[Query] 242. Dickens: *Martin Chuzzlewit.*" *Bibliographical Notes and Queries*, 2, ix (January 1938), 3.

A query about the back wrapper of part 19/20 of the novel. See reply by G. W., 2, xi (November 1938), 4.

313. Nisbet, Ada B. "The Mystery of 'Martin Chuzzlewit.'" In *Essays Critical and Historical Dedicated to Lily B. Campbell*. By Members of the Department of English, University of California. University of California Publications, English Studies, 1. Berkeley and Los Angeles: University of California Press, 1950, pp. 201-16.

On the publication and unexpectedly poor sales of *Martin Chuzzlewit*.

The Mystery of Edwin Drood

314. Doyle, Arthur Conan. "The Alleged Posthumous Writings of Known Authors: Oscar Wilde—Jack London—Lord Northliffe—Dickens—Conrad—Jerome." In his *The Edge of the Unknown*. London: John Murray; New York: G. P. Putnam's Sons, 1930; reprinted [Alexandria, VA]: Time-Life Books, 1991, pp. 133-55.

In the section of this essay devoted to Dickens, pp. 149-54, the author of the Sherlock Holmes stories notes that in the original version of this essay, which was published in the *Fortnightly Review*, 128 (1927), 721-35, as well as in *Bookman* (New York), 66 (1927/28), 342-49, he "devoted some space" to a continuation of *The Mystery of Edwin Drood* by T. P. James, who claimed it had been written by Dickens from the grave. But Doyle indicates his mixed response to this claim, finding the work "like Dickens gone flat." He also describes in some detail his being present when Florizel von Reuter and his mother communicated with Dickens by way of a board and pointer about the ending to *Edwin Drood.*

315. Fisher, Benjamin F., IV. "Reviews–Paperback Editions of *The Mystery of Edwin Drood." Dickens Studies Newsletter,* 8 (1977), 19-22.

Compares three paperback editions of *Edwin Drood,* finding that the Penguin Edition, edited by Arthur J. Cox (**2437**), despite lamentable typographical errors, is "by far the best" edition, including as it does Dickens's notes and number plans for the novel.

316. Forsyte, Charles [Gordon Philo]. "Charles Dickens Junior, Harold Macmillan, and *Edwin Drood." Notes and Queries,* ns 37 (1990), 35-36.

On Dickens's son's assertion (from conversations with his father) in his introduction to the English Macmillan Edition (1923) of *The Mystery of Edwin Drood* (**2295**) that Dickens intended Drood to be murdered. Forsyte here asserts that, while Dickens's son had written the introduction much earlier, copyright restrictions prevented him from republishing the novel (with his introduction) until 1923. Forsyte provides more accurate information in a subsequent article (**317**).

317. Forsyte, Charles [Gordon, Philo]. "Charles Dickens Junior, Harold Macmillan, and *Edwin Drood." Notes and Queries,* ns 41 (1994), 353-54.

On the Macmillan American and English editions of *The Mystery of Edwin Drood* (**2295**), which contain an introduction by Charles Dickens, Jr., with his comments on his father's acknowledgment to him that Drood was murdered. The English edition could not be published before 1920 (it was published in 1923), when the copyright ran out, Forsyte notes, but the American edition, with the son's introduction, was published at the back of the volume for *A Tale of Two Cities* in 1896. This corrects information in his earlier article on the subject (**316**).

318. Goldman, Arnold, J. S. Whitley, and Stanley Bayliss. "Dickens Editions." *Times Literary Supplement,* 18 August 1972, p. 970.

The authors comment on textual choices made in two editions of Dickens's works–the Penguin English Library Edition of *American Notes,* edited by Whitley and Goldman (**2524**), and the Clarendon Edition of *The Mystery of Edwin Drood* (1972) edited by Margaret Cardwell (**2434**). See responses by "Your Reviewer," 25 August 1972, pp. 996-97, and by James Cochrane and Arnold Goldman, 15 September 1972, p. 1060.

319. [Harrison, William H.]. "An Alleged Post-Mortem Work by Charles Dickens." In *"Rifts in the Veil." A Collection of Inspirational Poems and Essays Given Through Various Forms of Mediumship; Also of Poems and Essays by Spiritualists.* [Ed. William H. Harrison]. London: W. H. Harrison, 1878, pp. 31-60.

Comments on the completion of *Edwin Drood* by T. P. James, Brattle-borough, Vermont, in 1873. Harrison quotes extensively from newspaper accounts that described James's séances with the deceased Dickens, séances that, James claimed, enabled him to complete the work. In the introduction, pp. 9-13, Harrison indicates that the contents of *"Rifts in the Veil"* are collected in "large measure from the back volumes of *The Spiritualist* newspaper" (which, to a modern reader, accounts for its naive acceptance of the spiritualist source of the continuation). The British Library copy contains an autograph letter from Harrison indicating that he is the editor of this volume (and presumably author of the sections not attributed to others).

Nicholas Nickleby

320. Dexter, Walter. "When Found—Dedication Copies." *Dickensian*, 38 (1941/42), 186.

Identifies and gives the provenance of two dedication copies, one of *Nicholas Nickleby* (to William Macready, the actor) and one of *The Village Coquettes* (to J. P. Harley, the actor, who performed in this comic opera).

321. Levy, H. M., Jr. "An Omission Unnoticed: *Nickleby* Forgotten." *Dickensian*, 63 (1967), 41.

Points out that, in his listing of the monthly parts publication of Dickens's novels, K. J. Fielding (**191**) omitted *Nicholas Nickleby*, the details for which Levy here supplies.

322. R., D. A. P. "Nicholas Slips." *Dickensian*, 41 (1944/45), 84-86.

Compares errors in the first edition of *Nicholas Nickleby* with their corrections by Dickens in the Charles Dickens Edition (as incorporated in the National Edition, 1906).

The Old Curiosity Shop

Note: Also see Gibson (**241**), "Lord Jeffrey's Autograph Volumes of Dickens" (**242**), and "Hampstead" (**346**).

323. Brennan, Elizabeth M. "Appendix C: Contents of *Master Humphrey's Clock*, 1840-41." In Dickens's *The Old Curiosity Shop*. World's Classics Edition (**2461**), pp. 574-77.

Itemizes the contents of *Master Humphrey's Clock*, 1840-41, part by part.

Oliver Twist

Note: Also see Tillotson (**2474**), Carter (**306**), and Shillingsburg (**248**).

324. "Delta" (pseud.). "Rare Editions of Dickens." *Birmingham Daily Mail*,
6 March 1912, p. 4.

Asserts that the most rare collectors' items are those that were printed after
Dickens made changes in the edition, such as substituting illustrations by
"Buss" in *Pickwick Papers*, using "Veller" rather than "Weller" on the title page
of that novel, or using the so-called "fireside plate" in the original version of
Oliver Twist.

325. D[exter], W[alter]. "Author and Artist: The Claims of George
Cruikshank Definitely Refuted after One Hundred Years and the Discovery of a New Work by Dickens." *Dickensian*, 34 (1937/38), 97-100.

Indicates that some in a series of forty-three letters from Dickens to Cruikshank show the falsity of Cruikshank's claim to have been largely responsible
for *Oliver Twist*. Dexter quotes briefly from some of the letters in which Dickens's control of the story and the subjects for illustrations seems particularly
evident. Two of the letters, Dexter points out, indicate that Dickens (*not*
Thackeray) had "certainly had a hand" in *The Loving Ballad of Lord Bateman*,
"revised it for publication, and definitely wrote the humorous notes which
accompanied it." See also Johnson (**477**), Lucas (**480**), Ritchie (**531**), Spencer
(**535**), and particularly Haight (**475**), who resolves the issue of attribution.

326. Fore, A. T. "For the Dickens Collector: Some Interesting Facts about
Oliver Twist." *Dickensian*, 22 (1926), 163.

Gives brief details of the various editions of the novel. See addendum in a
letter from F. O. Hutchinson, *Dickensian*, 23 (1926/27), 59.

327. Grubb, Gerald G. "On the Serial Publication of *Oliver Twist*." *Modern
Language Notes*, 56 (1941), 290-94.

Straightens out details of the monthly publication of *Oliver Twist* in *Bentley's
Miscellany*, noting that there were *three* interruptions of the story, not one, and
that it concluded in the April, not the March, 1839 issue of the magazine.

328. Kaplan, Fred. "Table of Installments and Chapter-Division in Different
Editions of *Oliver Twist*." In **Oliver Twist** *Authoritative Text, Backgrounds
and Sources, Early Reviews, Criticism*. Norton Critical Edition. Ed. Fred
Kaplan. New York: Norton, 1993, pp. 379-81.

These concern the weekly serialization of the novel in *Bentley's Miscellany*, the 1838-41 edition in monthly parts, and the 1846 edition.

329. Lauterbach, Charles E., and Edward S. Lauterbach. "The Nineteenth Century Three-Volume Novel." *Papers of the Bibliographical Society of America*, 51 (1957), 263-302.

The authors point out, pp. 270-71, that Dickens signed a contract with Richard Bentley in 1836 to write a three-volume novel and that *Oliver Twist* was indeed eventually published in such a format in 1838 though Bentley "had to do some padding to eke out his three volumes of 320 pages each." Also see the statistical tables, pp. 285-302, which include *Oliver Twist*.

330. "News for Bibliophiles." *Nation*, 86 (1908), 551-52.

Comments on and provides basic bibliographical information about American editions of two of Dickens's works not included in any prior bibliographies: *Public Life of Mr. Tulrumble, Once Mayor of Mudfog, and Oliver Twist; or the Parish Boy's Progress* (New York: N. p., 1837), which includes no more than the first two chapters of *Oliver Twist*, and *Travelling Letters, Written on the Road* (New York: Wiley & Putnam, 1846), containing the first three letters from the *Daily News* (London), 21, 24, and 31 January 1846.

331. Nowell-Smith, Simon. "[Query] 197. Dickens: *Oliver Twist* (1838)." *Bibliographical Notes and Queries*, 2, vi (July 1936), 6.

Queries the states of the various issues of the first edition of the 1838 three-volume edition of *Oliver Twist*. In a reply, 2, xi (November 1938), 3, M[orris] L. Parrish quotes from three contradictory descriptions of the first state of the edition regarding whether it was published with or without a list of illustrations. Also see Parrish (**332**).

332. Parrish, M[orris] L. "Oliver Twist." *Times Literary Supplement*, 14 May 1938, p. 344.

Because of conflicting statements in bibliographical sources, Parrish asks whether or not the first issue of the three-volume edition of *Oliver Twist* (1838) contained a list of illustrations. In a reply, 11 June 1938, p. 408, Joseph C. Thomson announces that, in his revision of his *Bibliography of the Writings of Charles Dickens* (**48**), then nearing completion (but never published), he will indicate, among other points, that in some copies the list is pasted in, which would suggest that a copy without the list was earlier. However, the true test of a first issue, he asserts, is that it contains the so-called "Fireside Plate," which was replaced in the second issue. Also see Nowell-Smith (**331**).

333. Patten, Robert L. "Reviews–Paperback Editions: *Oliver Twist.*" *Dickens Studies Newsletter,* 3 (1972), 84-92.

Compares and evaluates eight paperback editions of *Oliver Twist,* finding the Rinehart Edition the "least objectionable," but none wholly satisfactory.

334. Patten, Robert L. "When Is a Book Not a Book?" *Biblion: The Bulletin of the New York Public Library,* 4, ii (Spring 1996), 35-63.

Explores the many social, cultural, and aesthetic ramifications of the serial publication of *Oliver Twist* in *Bentley's Miscellany* as opposed to its publication in three-volume form six months before its conclusion in the magazine. To ignore its serial publication–and that of many other similarly constructed novels–is, Patten asserts, "a significant distortion of the history of the book." To the question "When is a book not a book?" Patten answers, "When it is a Serial," adding "And that can make all the difference." Handsomely illustrated.

335. Schweitzer, Joan. "The Chapter Numbering in *Oliver Twist.*" *Papers of the Bibliographical Society of America,* 60 (1966), 337-43.

Points out that the number of chapters varied in different editions of *Oliver Twist* published by Dickens–the *Bentley's Miscellany* serialization, the 1846 single-volume edition, and the Charles Dickens Edition contained fifty-three chapters, while the 1838, 1839, and 1841 editions contained fifty-one chapters. Schweitzer examines Dickens's revisions in this regard.

336. Tillotson, Kathleen. "*Oliver Twist* in Three Volumes." *Library,* 5th ser., 18 (1963), 113-32.

A full study of how the three-volume "third edition" of *Oliver Twist* was planned and brought to fulfillment, 1838-41. Tillotson uses Dickens's agreements with Richard Bentley, his letters during the period, the twenty-two chapters of the autograph manuscript, and the advertisements, in addition to comparing the text of this and earlier editions, to "investigate the printing history and bibliographical features of *Oliver Twist* in three volumes"–all done with Tillotson's meticulous bibliographical scholarship and in fascinating detail.

Our Mutual Friend

337. Fisher, Benjamin F., IV. "Reviews–Paperback Editions: *Our Mutual Friend.*" *Dickens Studies Newsletter,* 5 (1974), 87-90.

Compares three paperback editions of *Our Mutual Friend*–the Modern Library, New American Library, and Penguin editions–finding virtues in all.

Pickwick Papers

Note: Also see Carter (**178**), "Delta" (**324**), and "Notes on Sales: 'Pickwick' and 'A Christmas Carol'" (**277**).

338. Austin, Roland. "'Pickwick Papers,' First Edition." *Notes and Queries*, 11th ser., 10 (1914), 153.

On two sets of prime Pickwicks in parts.

339. B., C. C. "'Pickwick Papers': Printers' Errors in First Edition." *Notes and Queries*, 11th ser., 4 (1911), 248.

Notes an error in the list of errata in the first edition of Dickens's first novel, as well as an omission from the list. Replies concern how to detect a first issue from later ones by Robert Pierpont, pp. 292-93; Charles S. Burdon, p. 293; W. F. Prideaux, pp. 352-53; Roland Austin, p. 353; and "F. Verisopht" (pseud.), p. 353.

340. Bay, J. Christian. *The Pickwick Papers, Some Bibliographical Remarks*. Chicago: Privately printed, 1936. 7 pp.; revised and expanded as *The Pickwick Papers, Some Bibliographical Remarks: An Address Delivered before the Caxton Club, January Sixteenth, 1937*. Chicago: Caxton Club, 1938. 29 pp.; reprinted in his *The Fortune of Books: Essays, Memories and Prophecies of a Librarian*. Chicago: Walter M. Hill, 1941, pp. 223-37.

Discusses the Dickens-Seymour controversy over the origin of *Pickwick Papers*, some of the points for a prime *Pickwick* in parts, the miscellaneous character of the installments of *Pickwick Papers*, and this novel's "fabulist," non-realistic nature. In *The Fortune of Books*, Bay notes that this lecture was originally presented at the annual meeting of the Minnesota Library Association in 1936 (2 October) and 150 copies were distributed at the meeting; it was reprinted twice in 1936, "with some expansion," and was then read at the Caxton Club on 16 January 1937 and published in its "permanent form" by the Caxton Club in 1938. The 1938 text is largely that of 1936 (the difference in total pages is misleading), but the text is somewhat expanded as well as refined, somewhat more detailed, with parts rearranged, a new introduction added, and one section omitted.

341. Biondi, Lee. "Rise to Fame: *Pickwick* Triumphant." In his "Collecting Charles Dickens" (**2202**), pp. 47-50.

In what he describes as a "brief introduction to the mysteries and pleasures of *Pickwick*," Biondi intelligently examines the origination and publication history of Dickens's first novel and the history of its illustrations (through three artists). He also comments on collecting the original parts of the novel and the virtual impossibility of putting together a "prime" *Pickwick* in parts. Illustrated.

342. Davis, George W. *The Posthumous Papers of the Pickwick Club: Some New Bibliographical Discoveries*. London: Marks & Co., 1928; reprinted Folcroft, PA: Folcroft Press, 1971; New York: Haskell, 1972; Folcroft, PA: Folcroft Library Editions, 1973; Norwood, PA: Norwood Editions, 1976; Philadelphia, PA: R. West, 1977. 20 pp.

Concerned largely with textual points and the states of illustrations that determine the earliest issues of the installments of *Pickwick Papers*.
Review: *Times Literary Supplement*, 13 December 1928, p. 996 (favorable).

343. D[exter], W[alter]. "The Pickwick Dedications and Prefaces." *Dickensian*, 32 (1935/36), 61-64.

Provides facsimile reproductions of Dickens's inscription in his presentation copy of *Pickwick Papers* to Serjeant Thomas Noon Talfourd, to whom he dedicated the novel, and of a corrected proof of a page of Dickens's preface to the 1847 Cheap Edition in which he describes both the origin of *Pickwick Papers* and his posting of the manuscript of his first story ever to be published. Dexter also prints the full dedication to Talfourd, some five paragraphs in length, which, he points out, appeared only in early editions of the novel.

344. Fitzgerald, Percy. "Pickwickiana." *Gentleman's Magazine*, 282, ns 58 (1897), 178-202.

In an essay on the continuing popularity of Dickens's first novel, Fitzgerald comments on "the flood of commentary, dissertation, pictures, dramas, topographical inquiries, and even critical *exegesis*" it has generated, identifying and often itemizing the various editions, translations, selections, dramatic versions, imitations, commentaries, criticisms, topographical studies, commentaries on the illustrations, and the original and extra illustrations of the novel. Fitzgerald also prints the original announcement of the forthcoming publication of *Pickwick Papers* describing the projected adventures of the Pickwick Club. Finally, he comments not only on the illustrations for the novel but also on the original plates for the novel and the variations in subsequent re-engravings of them.

345. Gresh, Richard H. "Query 343. Charles Dickens, *The Posthumous Papers of the Pickwick Club* 1836-7." *Book Collector*, 30 (1981), 101.

Gresh announces that he is conducting a census and collation of prime *Pickwick* in parts and requests information about the Frederick Corder-Herman LeRoy Edgar copy and the Ida O. Folsom-Frank J. Hogan copy.

346. "Hampstead" (pseud.). "A Dickens Discovery." *Bookman* (London), 76 (1929), 195-96.

Identifies the publication of thirteen extracts from early chapters of *Pickwick Papers* in a rare Leipzig magazine, *The Englishman and Spirit of the English Journals in Literature and Science*, the first appearing in no. 53 (5 July 1837) and the last in no. 86 (28 October 1837). In a reply, in *Bookman*, 77 (1929/30), 320-22, Thomas Schreiner describes a serialization of *The Old Curiosity Shop* in *The British Museum*, vol. 5 (1841), also apparently published in Germany, to which "Hampstead" in an accompanying note denies any great bibliographical significance, pointing out that piracies and imitations of Dickens's works were quite common.

347. Harries, J. M. "'Pickwick Papers': A Bibliographical Curiosity." *Notes and Queries*, ns 20 (1973), 100.

Asks for further information about an edition of *Pickwick Papers* with the imprint "Published by C. Boardman, Stratford, E." P. G. Scott, p. 341, provides information about this and related editions.

348. Newton, A[lfred] Edward. *Bibliography and Pseudo-Bibliography*. The A. S. W. Rosenbach Fellowship in Bibliography, 5. Philadelphia: University of Pennsylvania Press; London: Oxford University Press, 1936, passim.

Newton comments on the bibliographical problems connected with publication of a novel in parts–in reference to *Pickwick Papers*.

349. Newton, A[lfred] Edward. *The Format of the English Novel, with Reproductions of Title-Pages from Books in the Author's Library*. Cleveland, OH: Rowfant Club, 1928; reprinted New York: Burt Franklin, 1971, pp. 19-28.

In a brief discussion of publishing novels in parts, mentions *Pickwick Papers* and *Sketches by Boz*. Illustrated.

350. "100 Years of Publishing: Centenary of Chapman and Hall. Mr. Waugh's Retirement. How the 'Pickwick Papers' Began." *Observer* (London), 22 December 1929, p. 7.

A clear, presumably accurate account of how Dickens came to be chosen to write *Pickwick Papers*, with financial details of the agreement between publishers and author. Rendall (**353**) finds this a more accurate account than that in *Forster*.

351. "The *Pickwick* Advertisements and Other Addresses to the Public." *Dickensian*, 32 (1935/36), 86-90.

Provides facsimile reproductions of the descriptive advertisement for *Pick-wick Papers* in the *Athenaeum*, 26 March 1836, and of a one-inch advertisement in the London *Times*, 26 March 1836, and reprints a number of addresses to the public in various monthly numbers of the novel.

352. R[endall], V[ernon]. "An American 'Pickwick.'" *Notes and Queries*, ns 4 (1957), 123-24.

Refers to his copy of a pirated edition of *Pickwick Papers* published "about 1840" by T. B. Peterson in Philadelphia, in his "uniform edition of Dickens' Works," with illustrations by three different artists, none as good as Phiz, Rendall reports, and with a five-page dedication to Serjeant Talfourd, M. P., which Rendall reprints here because it "will be new to most readers and was doubtless dropped early by Dickens."

353. R[endall], V[ernon]. "Dickens: Pickwickiana." *Notes and Queries*, 158 (1930), 96.

Among a variety of notes on *Pickwick Papers*, mentions that an offprint by Arthur Waugh on Chapman and Hall from the *Observer*, 22 December 1929 (**350**), gives information about the publishing of *Pickwick Papers* more accurate than that in *Forster*.

354. Roe, F. Gordon. "Pickwick in Australia." *Connoisseur*, 106 (1940), 126-27.

Provides details about the first Australian edition of *Pickwick Papers*, published by Henry Dowling in Launceston, Van Diemen's Land, in twenty-five weekly parts in colored paper wrappers, August-December 1838, and in volume form, July 1839. Illustrated.

355. Shillingsburg, Peter L. "Reviews–Paperback Editions: *The Pickwick Papers*." *Dickens Studies Newsletter*, 3 (1972), 119-23.

Compares and evaluates five paperback editions of *Pickwick Papers*, preferring the Penguin Edition, edited by Robert L. Patten (**2496**) for critical apparatus but none of the five for textual accuracy.

356. "Tiny Tim" (pseud.). "'The Pickwick Papers.'" *Notes and Queries*, 6th ser., 6 (1882), 29.

Queries whether "Veller" or "Weller" on a signboard in the title page vignette of the first edition of *Pickwick Papers* indicates an earlier issue of the edition. A response by W. Stavenhagen Jones, 6th ser., 7 (1883), 135, notes that this variant was probably caused by duplicate plates necessitated by the demand for the novel (but Jones gives no indication of which version was the earlier).

357. "A Unique Pickwick." *Dickensian*, 9 (1913), 206-07.

Describes a seven-volume, extra-illustrated copy of *Pickwick Papers* assembled by W. Glyde Wilkins.

358. Wilkins, W[illiam] G[lyde]. "A Unique Pickwick." *Dickensian*, 13 (1917), 133-34.

Describes an "exceedingly rare," profusely illustrated American edition of *Pickwick Papers*, Carleton's Royal Edition (New York: G. W. Carleton, 1880).

Sketches by Boz

Note: Also see Newton (**349**) and Carlton (**390**).

359. Biondi, Lee. "In the Beginning . . . Charles Dickens Makes a Pseudonym for Himself: A Bibliographical Background to Dickens' *Sketches by Boz*." In his "Collecting Charles Dickens" (**2202**), pp. 40-46.

In list form, Biondi gives the publishing history of *Sketches by Boz* through the "New Edition, Complete," of 1839, though he confuses the details about the two sketches that Dickens combined to produce "The Last Cab Driver and the First Omnibus Cad" for the Second Series of *Sketches by Boz*—see DeVries (**2499**)—and misses the original publication of "Our Next-Door Neighbours" in the *Morning Chronicle* and the *Evening Chronicle*—see Mott (**371**)—and of "Sentiment" in *Bell's Weekly Magazine*—see Nielsen (**372**). He includes the correct collation for the illustrations by George Cruikshank in the first and second series of the work and in the 1839 edition and, by way of an introduction, briefly surveys the publishing history of the work. Illustrated.

360. Brumleigh, T. Kent [T. W. Hill]. "Journalistics." *Dickensian*, 48 (1951/52), 82-89.

Summarizes information about the publication history of *Sketches by Boz*, *Reprinted Pieces*, and *The Uncommercial Traveller*. The article contains some errors, obviously those of Hill's sources. See also an Erratum, p. 133.

361. Carlton, William J. "Dickens's Debut in America." *Dickensian*, 55 (1959), 55-56.

Clarifying a confusing remark by Horace Greeley about the publication of two of Dickens's early tales (later collected in *Sketches by Boz*) in *The New-Yorker*, Carlton points out that "Horatio Sparkins" was published in the

29 March 1834 issue and "Some Passages from the Life of Mr. Watkins Tottle" in two parts in the 21 February and 28 March 1835 issues.

362. Cohn, Albert M. *A Few Notes upon Some Rare Cruikshankiana.* London: Karslake, 1915, passim.

Comments briefly on two Dickens-related items: the rarity of *The Loving Ballad of Lord Bateman*, with illustrations by George Cruikshank, and the little-known drawing Cruikshank did in 1837 for the wrapper of the revision of *Sketches by Boz* that was finally issued in twenty monthly parts in 1839. The original, reproduced by glyphography (engraving on a waxed copper plate), with a date of 1837, is printed, facing p. 22. Cohn points out that, when Chapman and Hall took over the publication of the book, the glyphographic reproduction was found to be unsatisfactory, so the drawing "was slightly altered by Cruikshank, and it was re-engraved by Jackson," with a new date of 1839. Illustrated.

363. Dexter, Walter. "The Genesis of *Sketches by Boz.*" *Dickensian*, 30 (1933/34), 105-11.

A detailed, if incomplete, account of where and in what order Dickens published the tales and sketches (1833-36) that he collected as *Sketches by Boz* (1836). For earlier attempts to identify the original publication of these pieces, see Shepherd (**42**), Kitton (**154**), Thomson (**48**), and Eckel (**16**). For later compilations, see Hatton and Cleaver (**24**), House and Storey (**134**), Grillo (**133**), DeVries (**132**), and Slater (**136**). For addenda to Dexter's list see Nielsen (**372**), Carlton (**390**), DeVries (**2499**), and Mott (**371**), all incorporated, finally, in Slater's list.

364. D[exter], W[alter]. "Macrone and the Reissue of *Sketches by Boz.*" *Dickensian*, 33 (1936/37), 173-76.

When John Macrone, who had purchased the copyright of *Sketches by Boz* from Dickens for £100, planned to publish the work in monthly parts in 1837/38, Dickens and Chapman and Hall purchased the copyright back for £2,000 and published the work serially themselves. Dexter prints "in full for the first time" an angry letter from Dickens to John Forster on Macrone's intent, as well as Dickens's letter (printed in *Forster*) announcing the latter purchase.

365. Dexter, Walter. "When Found—The Pirates." *Dickensian*, 30 (1933/34), 239.

Identifies the almost immediate republication of Dickens's first story, "A Dinner at Poplar Walk" (first published in the *Monthly Magazine*, December

1833, and collected in *Sketches by Boz* as "Mr. Minns and His Cousin"), in the *London Weekly Magazine*, 7 December 1833, formerly known as *The Thief*.

366. "Dickens Published Here Early in 1834. Richard Gimbel Finds 6 Stories Printed Months before Hitherto Earliest Known Date." *New York Times*, 15 April 1935, p. 21.

Notes the discovery, by a well-known Dickens collector, of the 1834 reprinting in *The Albion*, a New York weekly, of six of the stories Dickens originally published in the *Monthly Magazine*, 1833-34.

367. Houtchens, Carolyn W., and Lawrence H. Houtchens. "Contributions of Early American Journals to the Study of Charles Dickens." *Modern Language Quarterly*, 6 (1945), 211-17.

The authors note that the New York *Albion*, 7 February and 21 March 1835) reprinted the original version of "Passage in the Life of Mr. Watkins Tottle" from the *Monthly Magazine*, including passages that were later excised by Dickens.

368. Hughes, T. Cann. "Charles Dickens: 'Our Parish.'" *Notes and Queries*, 150 (1926), 64.

A bibliographical query about the parts of this series of articles in *Sketches by Boz*. No responses followed, but see DeVries (**132**).

369. Jarvis, John W. "'Sketches by Boz,' Second Series, London, Macrone, St. James's Square, 1836." *Notes and Queries*, 6th ser., 6 (1882), 148.

Notes that his copy of the second series of *Sketches by Boz* lists and contains ten plates rather than the twelve listed in other copies of this edition and wonders whether or not his is an earlier issue. Podeschi (**1509**), pp. 5-6, indicates that the first edition of the Second Series contains ten plates, while the second edition contains twelve.

370. Matz, B. W. "*Sketches by Boz*–A Bibliographical Note." *Dickensian*, 1 (1905), 64-65.

Outdated comments on basic bibliographical matters.

371. Mott, Graham. "The First Publication of 'Our Next Door Neighbours.'" *Dickensian*, 80 (1984), 114-16.

Notes for the first time that the essay published in *Sketches by Boz* as "Our Next Door Neighbour" (the plural changed to the singular) was originally published in both the *Morning Chronicle* and *Evening Chronicle* for 18 March

1836, an important addendum to Biondi (**359**), DeVries (**132**), Grillo (**133**), and House and Storey (**134**).

372.   Nielsen, Hilmer. "Some Observations on *Sketches by Boz.*" *Dickensian*, 34 (1937/38), 243-45.

Records his discovery that Dickens's early story, entitled "Sentiment" in *Sketches by Boz*, was originally published under the heading "Original Papers" in *Bell's Weekly Magazine*, 7 June 1834. Nielsen also comments on the writing of other early sketches by Dickens, notes the influence on Dickens of eighteenth-century and early-nineteenth-century essayists, mentions several stories and sketches by others that were like those Dickens was writing 1833-36, and speculates about another title Dickens might have considered for *Sketches by Boz*.

A Tale of Two Cities

373.   McMaster, R. D. "Reviews–Paperback Editions: *A Tale of Two Cities.*" *Dickens Studies Newsletter*, 3 (1972), 16-22.

Compares and evaluates thirteen paperback editions of *A Tale of Two Cities*, and in the process sets standards for classroom texts of Dickens's novels. While McMaster finds "no altogether satisfactory editions" of *A Tale of Two Cities*, he singles out the Signet Classic Edition, with an "Afterword" by Edgar Johnson (New American Library, 1963), and the Penguin Edition (1970), edited by George Woodcock, as "worthy of attention," the former for its text, indication of weekly and monthly parts, and the historical emphasis of its afterword, and the latter for its "perceptive and well-integrated" introduction and its notes.

374.   Review of the Nonesuch Edition of *A Tale of Two Cities*. *Times Literary Supplement*, 21 August 1937, p. 611.

Queries why certain items peripheral to the text were not included or not treated properly in the first volumes of the Nonesuch Edition. In "Bibliographical Notes: The Nonesuch Dickens," in the 28 August issue, p. 628, Harry G. Carter, representing the Nonesuch Press, is quoted in response, with a further comment by the anonymous reviewer, who feels Carter did not quite answer all his queries.

375.   Sanders, Andrew. "Appendix A: The Serialization of *A Tale of Two Cities* in 1859." In Dickens's *A Tale of Two Cities*. Ed. Andrew Sanders. World's Classics. Oxford and New York: Oxford University Press, 1988, pp. 467-68.

Gives details of the novel's publication in *All the Year Round*.

376. Todd, William B. "Note 94. Dickens, *A Tale of Two Cities*, 1859." *Book Collector*, 7 (1958), 80.

Notes three states of the first monthly number.

Nonfictional, Theatrical, and Poetical Works

Note: Also see "Charles Dickens" (**179**); Goldman, Whitley, and Bayliss (**318**); "News for Bibliophiles" (**330**); Dexter (**320**); and the section on *Sketches by Boz* (**359-72**), above.

377. B., C. T. "'Quiz.'" *Notes and Queries*, 3rd ser., 12 (1867), 130-31.

Asks for the author of *Sketches of Young Ladies*, "said to be by 'Quiz,'" and *Sketches of Young Gentlemen*, which C. T. B. believes was "obviously written by the same person." A response by A. M., "Quiz's 'Sketches of Young Ladies,'" pp. 219-20, is ambiguous about the authorship. In "'Sketches of Young Ladies': 'Sketches of Young Gentlemen,'" *Notes and Queries*, 4th ser., 9 (1872), 23, C. T. B. correctly concludes that, as *Forster* indicates, Dickens was the author of *Sketches of Young Gentlemen* and also of *Sketches of Young Couples*, but not of *Sketches of Young Ladies*.

378. Bentley, Nicolas. "A First Edition Mystery: Some Fancy Forensic Spade-Work." *Antiquarian Book Monthly Review*, 4 (1977), 48-50.

Compares the text of Dickens's *Travelling Letters, Written on the Road* (published in New York by Wiley and Putnam, 1846, in the form of two pamphlets containing the seven letters by Dickens first published in the London *Daily News*) to two editions of *Pictures from Italy*: the first edition (London: Bradbury & Evans, 1846) and the Illustrated Library Edition (1874). The study shows that the text published by Wiley and Putnam is identical to that of the *Daily News* letters but somewhat more abbreviated than the comparable text of *Pictures from Italy*. Bentley concludes that there is "a remarkably strong case" for assuming that the American edition constitutes "a true first edition of *Pictures from Italy*." One should, however, keep in mind that, as Paroissien points out in his edition of *Pictures from Italy* (**434**), only "about one-third" of the text of *Pictures from Italy* was published in the *Daily News*. Illustrated.

379. Bracher, Peter. "The Early American Editions of *American Notes*: Their Priority and Circulation." *Papers of the Bibliographical Society of America*, 69 (1975), 365-76.

A virtually day by day, even hour by hour history of the publication of *American Notes* in the United States from 7 November 1842 (the English edition had arrived by ship the evening before) to 8 November, by which date four different editions, three in New York and one in Philadelphia, had been published. Bracher provides the number of sales, price, and other publishing information.

380. Bracher, Peter. "The Lea & Blanchard Edition of Dickens's *American Notes*, 1842." *Papers of the Bibliographical Society of America*, 63 (1969), 296-300.

Gives the history of the publication of an obscure Philadelphia edition (not the first in America) of *American Notes*, based on the publisher's cost book, newspaper advertisements, and other sources. A copy is owned by the Philadelphia Historical Society, Bracher notes, and he provides a bibliographical description of this copy and edition.

381. Bracher, Peter S. "The New York *Herald* and *American Notes*." *Dickens Studies*, 5 (1969), 81-85.

Points out that, contrary to accepted belief, James Gordon Bennett's *New York Herald* did not bring out two editions of *American Notes* (in 1842 and 1867). Instead, it "never printed more than a generous selection of 'racy extracts'" from the book.

382. Bracher, Peter. "Thwarting the Pirates: Timing the Publication of *American Notes*." *Dickens Studies Newsletter*, 7 (1976), 33-34.

Points out that Dickens delayed the publication of *American Notes* in England until 19 October 1842 in order to prevent copies being sent on the *Caledonia*, which sailed at noon on that date, thus delaying its publication by American printers until 7 November.

383. Brice, Alec W. "'Ignorance and Its Victims': Another New Article by Dickens." *Dickensian*, 63 (1967), 143-47.

Comments on and reprints "Ignorance and Its Victims," an anonymous article in the *Examiner*, 29 April 1848. Brice convincingly attributes this article to Dickens, mainly through its linkage to "Ignorance and Crime," which Dickens had published anonymously in the *Examiner* the previous week. Also see Brice's doctoral dissertation, "Dickens and *The Examiner*: Some Newly Identified Articles" (University of Edinburgh, 1968). Also see Fielding and Brice (**410**).

384. Brice, Alec W. "'A Truly British Judge': Another Article by Dickens." *Dickensian*, 66 (1970), 30-35.

Reprints "A Truly British Judge," from the *Examiner*, 19 August 1848, and argues that it is "almost certainly" by Dickens, particularly because of its style and tone.

385. Brice, Alec W., and K. J. Fielding. "A New Article by Dickens: 'Demoralisation and Total Abstinence.'" *Dickens Studies Annual*, 9 (1981), 1-19.

The authors attribute to Dickens and reprint (pp. 4-14) "Demoralisation and Total Abstinence," an anti-abstinence article in the *Examiner*, 27 October 1849. Brice and Fielding think the article is "perhaps" not only Dickens's best contribution to the *Examiner* but "perhaps the clearest and the most complete statement of his social philosophy that he was to write outside his fiction." The attribution relies largely on stylistic and circumstantial evidence–and on "the impossibility of its having been written by anyone else in the same circle." Its conclusion Brice and Fielding find to be "even more demonstrably Dickensian."

386. Brice, Alec W., and K. J. Fielding. "On Murder and Detection–New Articles by Dickens." *Dickens Studies*, 5 (1969), 45-61.

The authors propose that Dickens was likely the author of three articles in the *Examiner* in 1849 on the murder investigation, trial, and execution of James Blomfield Rush. They believe that it is "highly probable" that Dickens wrote "False Reliance" (2 June 1849), which they reprint completely; that "it appears likely" that he wrote "Rush's Conviction" (7 April 1849), reprinted in part; and that he "could possibly" have written "Capital Punishment" (5 May 1849), also reprinted in part.

387. Buckler, William E. "'Household Words' in America." *Papers of the Bibliographical Society of America*, 45 (1951), 160-66.

Prints letters to Dickens and to Bradbury and Evans from New York publishers seeking Dickens's favor in the republication of *Household Words* in the United States and offering a variety of schemes and incentives in the absence of an international copyright law. These letters provide some interesting details concerning the magazine's publication in New York.

388. Carlton, William J. "Charles Dickens, Dramatic Critic." *Dickensian*, 56 (1960), 11-27.

From internal evidence and references in letters and other sources, identifies and reprints fifteen *Morning Chronicle* drama reviews (1835-36) as definitely or probably by Dickens.

389. Carlton, William J. "Dickens or Forster? Some *King Lear* Criticisms Re-Examined." *Dickensian*, 61 (1965), 133-40.

Provides convincing evidence that John Forster, *not* Dickens, was the author of "The Restoration of Shakespeare's Lear to the Stage" in the *Examiner*, 4 February 1838, contrary to the attribution by B. W. Matz in the *Miscellaneous*

Papers (**425**). Dickens was, however, Carlton asserts, the author of a later unsigned review of a performance of *King Lear* in the *Examiner*, 27 October 1849, the holograph manuscript of which is in the Forster Collection, Victoria and Albert Museum, London. The first page of this manuscript is reproduced on p. 138. For reprintings of this review, see Staples (**448**) and Van Noorden (**459**).

390. Carlton, William J. "'The Story Without a Beginning': An Unrecorded Contribution by Boz to the *Morning Chronicle*." *Dickensian*, 47 (1950/51), 67-70.

Reprints, with explanatory notes, a political allegory by Dickens published in the *Morning Chronicle*, 18 December 1834, and identifies the earliest publication of Dickens's "Brokers' and Marine Store Shops" (*Sketches by Boz*) in the *Morning Chronicle*, 15 December 1834.

391. Collins, P[hilip]. A. W. "Dickens as Editor: Some Uncollected Fragments." *Dickensian*, 56 (1960), 85-96.

Comments on and reprints twenty-one editorial comments, supplementary footnotes to articles, and notices by Dickens in his weekly magazines, *Household Words* and *All the Year Round*, not previously reprinted. These are, Collins acknowledges, "not . . . very important examples of Dickens's writings, though one or two of them contain interesting observations."

392. Collins, Philip. "Dickens on Ghosts: An Uncollected Article, with Introduction and Notes." *Dickensian*, 59 (1963), 5-14.

Points out that in a then unpublished letter to Emile de la Rue, 29 February 1848 (since published in *Pilgrim Letters*, V, 253-56), Dickens refers to himself as author of an unsigned review of a book on ghosts. The review, of Catherine Crewe's *The Night Side of Nature; or, Ghosts and Ghost Seers*, Collins notes, appeared in the *Examiner*, 26 February 1848. It is reprinted here with a few explanatory notes.

393. Collins, Philip. "Some Uncollected Speeches by Dickens." *Dickensian*, 73 (1977), 89-99.

Gives transcriptions or paraphrases of a "dozen or so gleanings" of speeches not in Fielding's edition (**408**), most "small and of only minor interest."

394. Collins, Philip. "Some Unpublished Comic Duologues of Dickens." *Nineteenth-Century Fiction*, 31 (1976/77), 440-49.

Prints the text of a hitherto unpublished manuscript in the D. Jacques Benoliel Collection, Free Library of Philadelphia, of a series of short comic duologues in Dickens's hand. This was material, Collins points out, intended "for a pair of stand-up comedians—mostly in cross-talk form," and, from internal evidence, written at some time in the 1860s, though the material in one sketch appeared in a letter Dickens wrote in July 1851. Because there is no reference to the duologues as such in any Dickens letter, Collins speculates that Dickens probably never performed them.

395. Darwin, Bernard. "New Discoveries of Charles Dickens: His Earliest Writings in Maria Beadnell's Album." *Strand Magazine*, 89 (1935), 574-79.

Reproduces three drawings by Henry Austin and Dickens's poetic contributions to Maria Beadnell's album (then in the possession of the Comte de Suzannet and now in the Dickens House Museum, London), as well as excerpts of contributions by other friends from the early 1830s. Darwin also prints two letters from Dickens to Ella Maria Winter, Maria's daughter, dated 13 March 1855 and 15 December 1858. Dickens's poems include "Acrostic," "The Devil's Walk," "The Churchyard," and "Lodgings to Let."

396. Dexter, Walter. "'Bentley's Miscellany.'" *Dickensian*, 33 (1936/37), 232-38.

Provides numerous details of Dickens's involvement with *Bentley's Miscellany*—quotations from reviewers of the magazine, information about contributors, and a reprinting of Dickens's various editorial addresses, notes, and prefaces. A reproduction of the cover of the first number of the magazine is included.

397. D[exter], W[alter]. "A New Contribution to 'The Monthly Magazine' and an Early Dramatic Criticism in 'The Morning Chronicle.'" *Dickensian*, 30 (1933/34), 223-25.

Identifies Dickens's review of John Buckstone's play *The Christening*, which was based on Dickens's tale, "The Bloomsbury Christening", in the 14 October 1834 issue of the *Morning Chronicle* (and later published in *Sketches by Boz*). The review is reprinted here, along with two protests that appeared in the *Monthly Magazine* for May 1834 about Buckstone's unauthorized borrowing, at least one of them obviously by Dickens.

398. Dexter, W[alter]. "A Stage Aside: Dickens's Early Dramatic Productions." *Dickensian*, 33 (1936/37), 81-85, 163-69, 254-56; 34 (1937/38), 36.

Comments on and provides some bibliographical details about four of Dickens's plays: *The Strange Gentleman* (1836), *The Village Coquettes* (1836), *Is She His Wife?* (1837), and *The Lamplighter* (1838).

399. [Dexter, Walter]. "An Unpublished Prologue." *Dickensian*, 37 (1940/41), 5.

Prints a poetic prologue by Dickens, probably written, Dexter speculates, to precede a performance of Douglas Jerrold's *The Housekeeper*, though this, Dexter warns, should not be taken as an indication that Dickens was involved in any other way with the performance.

400. Dexter, Walter. "When Found—Early Verses by 'Boz.'" *Dickensian*, 28 (1931/32), 1-3.

A facsimile reproduction of "A Fable (Not a Gay One)," an early poetic effort by Dickens written in Maria Beadnell's album in 1834. The album, then in the collection of the Comte de Suzannet, is now in the Dickens House Museum, London.

401. Dexter, Walter. "When Found—The Life of Our Lord." *Dickensian*, 31 (1934/35), 1.

Refers to letters from Lady Dickens (the widow of Sir Henry Fielding Dickens) pointing out that she did not think Charles Dickens had given any title to the work published as *The Life of Our Lord* (1934) since the title on her late husband's copy of the manuscript was written in by Georgina Hogarth and differs from that on the Mark Lemon copy—see Winifred Matz (**427**).

402. "Dickens's First Contribution to 'The Morning Chronicle.'" *Dickensian*, 31 (1934/35), 5-10.

Reprints Dickens's first newspaper article, a report of a dinner honoring Earl Grey in Edinburgh, from the *Morning Chronicle*, 17 September 1834.

403. "The Extraordinary Gazette." *Dickensian*, 34 (1937/38), 45-47.

Reprints a three-page advertising leaflet for the second number of *Bentley's Miscellany* containing an illustration by Phiz (Hablot K. Browne) and text by Dickens.

404. "Family Votes to Publish Dickens['s] 'Life of Our Lord.'" *New York Times*, 21 January 1934, p. 1.

Brief front-page notice that, following the death of Sir Henry Fielding Dickens on 21 December 1933, and in accordance with his will, the Dickens family had voted to publish *The Life of Our Lord*, which Dickens had written for his children.

405. Fenn, George M. "A Lost Play by Dickens." *Athenaeum*, no. 3847 (20 July 1901), 104.

Responding to Walter T. Spencer's article (**447**) about the publication of Dickens's early play *Is She His Wife?*, Fenn writes that he possesses "the undoubted MS. copy" of the play in a "coarse brown-paper wrapper" with the title "Is She His Wife? I One Act" written on it. However, he notes that, on the first page of the manuscript, the title is given as "Something Singular I in One Act I a Comic Burletta," with "St. James's Theatre I 1837" written beneath. He adds that the copy, which he points out is not in Dickens's hand, contains notes by the stage manager and cast, stage directions, and two added lines of dialogue. Also see Grubb (**412**), Pierpont (**436**), and Shepherd (**444**).

406. Fielding, K[enneth] J., ed. "A New Article by Dickens: Scott and His Publishers." *Dickensian*, 46 (1949/50), 122-27.

Using a comment Dickens made in a letter to John Forster in 1838, Fielding identifies Dickens as the author of an anonymous review that appeared in the *Examiner*, 2 September 1838, of *Refutation of the Misstatements and Calumnies Contained in Mr. Lockhart's Life of Sir Walter Scott, Bart., Respecting the Messrs. Ballantyne* (1838), written by James Ballantyne's trustees and son. The review is reprinted on pp. 123-27.

407. Fielding, K[enneth] J. "Re-reading *The Examiner*, 1832-55." *Victorian Periodicals Newsletter*, 1 (1968), 24-25.

Fielding notes that he and A. W. C. Brice are working on John Forster's association with the *Examiner*, 1832-55, and on identifying Dickens's contributions to that paper. See Brice (**383, 384**). Brice and Fielding (**385, 386**), and Fielding and Brice (**410**).

408. Fielding, K[enneth] J. "Textual Introduction," "Notes on Text and Sources," and Headnotes. In *The Speeches of Charles Dickens*. Ed. K[enneth] J. Fielding. Oxford: Clarendon Press, 1960, pp. xv-xviii, 423-43, and passim; reprinted, with an additional introduction, "Revised Edition: 1988." In *The Speeches of Charles Dickens: A Complete Edition*. Ed. K[enneth] J. Fielding. Hemel Hempstead, Eng.: Harvester/Wheatsheaf; Atlantic Highlands, NJ: Humanities Press International, 1988, pp. xv-xviii, xxv-xxxii, 423-43, and passim.

In his original introduction, Fielding criticizes Shepherd's editions of 1870 and 1884 of Dickens's speeches (**42, 43**) and notes that in editing the speeches he himself went back to the original and often better sources for text than Shepherd did. In headnotes to the 115 speeches or reports or summaries of speeches—as opposed to the fifty-six included in Shepherd's editions, fifty-eight in the National Edition (volume 38, London: Chapman and Hall, 1908), and sixty-five in the second of two volumes of *Collected Papers* the Nonesuch Edition (**460**)—Fielding points up the significance of each speech, describes the occasion, comments on the reception by the press, and provides other valuable background information. He also includes explanatory footnotes. "Notes on Text and Sources" identifies his sources for the text of the speeches. There is a useful twelve-page index.

The 1988 "Complete Edition" reprints the 1960 edition without change, adding to the original introductory material only a new introduction that contains an additional speech (given at the Royal Academy Banquet, 3 May 1862), a speech that Dickens wrote for Madame Celeste [Eliott] to give at her farewell benefit as manager of the Lyceum Theatre on 31 March 1860; several brief remarks that Dickens made at his public readings; and notes on two unrecorded speeches that Dickens gave on more private occasions—as chair at a Shakespeare birthday dinner at the Garrick Club, 22 April 1854, and at a farewell dinner for Thackeray, 11 October 1855. Fielding also mentions a few additional sources of text of Dickens's speeches. For a speech not included here, see Long (**421**).

409. Fielding, K[enneth] J. "Two Prologues for the Amateur Players." *Dickensian*, 56 (1960), 100-02.

Comments on and reprints excerpts from two prologues, one by Serjeant Thomas Noon Talfourd and the other by Edward Bulwer-Lytton, written for productions by Dickens's company of amateur actors in 1847.

410. Fielding, K[enneth] J., and Alec W. Brice. "Charles Dickens on 'The Exclusion of Evidence.'" *Dickensian*, 64 (1968), 131-40; 65 (1969), 35-41.

In reference to Brice's earlier reprinting (**383**) of the anonymous article "Ignorance and Its Victims," there argued to be by Dickens, Fielding and Brice look at three other articles published in the *Examiner*, 1849-1850, opposed to the court practice of determining whether or not a child was qualified to give evidence (i. e., properly educated) by asking questions from the Church Catechism. One of these articles, "The Exclusion of Evidence," 12 January 1850, might possibly be by Dickens, but there is no conclusive evidence of this, they state. Even if not by Dickens, the articles, they conclude, "remind us of what the world of Dickens was like" and give some idea of the reformist attitudes of journalists Dickens associated with, whom he influenced, and who influenced him. See also a letter to the editor by

W. J. Carlton, *Dickensian*, 65 (1969), 111, for additional details about an alderman mentioned in "The Exclusion of Evidence."

411. Grubb, Gerald G. "The American Edition of 'All the Year Round.'" *Papers of the Bibliographical Society of America*, 47 (1953), 301-04.

Notes that the American edition of *All the Year Round* was not a pirated edition. Dickens signed an agreement with Thomas Coke Evans to print the magazine in America from stereotype plates provided by the London publishers, though problems ensued from the poor American sales.

412. Grubb, Gerald G. "An Unknown Play by Dickens?" *Dickensian*, 46 (1949/50), 94-95.

Refers to a letter from Dickens to John Pritt Harley, undated but written before 1837, about a one-act play entitled "Cross Purposes" that Dickens wrote, as he puts it, "long before I was Boz," that "would admit of the introduction of any Music." The editors of *Pilgrim Letters*, I, 226, date the letter [?21 January 1837], and believe that the play referred to was performed and published as *Is She His Wife? or, Something Singular*. Also see Fenn (**405**), Pierpont (**436**), and Shepherd (**444**).

413. H., W. B. "Charles Dickens." *Notes and Queries*, 12th ser., 9 (1921), 48.

Believes a satirical announcement in the 3 September 1859 issue of *All the Year Round* about postal regulations governing periodicals is by Dickens. Also see p. 249 for an explanatory comment by W. B. H. on the content of the announcement.

414. Hanna, Robert C. "*The Life of Our Lord*: New Notes of Explication." *Dickensian*, 95 (1999), 197-205.

Surveys the small number of editions and studies of *The Life of Our Lord*. Accompanied by an illustration by "Artelius" that appeared in the first Swedish edition (1934) of the work.

415. "The Hatton Garden Philanthropist." *Dickensian*, 37 (1940/41), 167-68.

Reprints a short piece from the *Monthly Magazine* for March 1834 criticizing Allan S. Laing, whom Dickens would later satirize as Mr. Fang in *Oliver Twist* for his conduct in court. The author believes that the tone and content suggest that the article may have been written by Dickens.

416. Husk, W. H. "Charles Dickens and the 'Memoirs of Grimaldi.'" *Notes and Queries*, 4th ser., 6 (2 July 1870), 2-3.

Points out that Dickens was the editor, not the author, of the work and that Grimaldi's manuscript had originally been given to Thomas Egerton Wilks for editing. As the second editor, Dickens merely condensed the work further and made "some trifling alterations in it, and wrote the preface." In a response, 29 July 1870, p. 81, Richard Bentley points out that he was the publisher of the work and that Dickens "*did write a good deal of the work*" (Bentley's emphasis), as autograph letters in his possession would prove. He states that he placed the manuscript edited by Wilks in Dickens's hands, and "whatever is good in it was the result of the corrections, alterations, and in many instances the re-writing the narrative." Dickens, he adds, "did everything that was possible to improve it, but it was not possible to make it a book on which he could look with pleasure."

417. Johnson, Charles P. "'To Be Read at Dusk,' by Charles Dickens." *Athenaeum*, 97 (1891), 636.

A brief note pointing out that Dickens's tale, originally published in *The Keepsake* for 1852, was also published separately in a nineteen-page pamphlet *To Be Read at Dusk* (London: G. Barclay, 1852). But see Carter and Pollard (**830**), above, for evidence that this pamphlet was a forgery by T. J. Wise.

418. Kitton, Frederick [sic] G. "Introduction." In Dickens's *Old Lamps for New Ones and Other Sketches and Essays Hitherto Uncollected.* New York: New Amsterdam Book Co., 1897, pp. v-vii; revised as "Introduction." In Dickens's *To Be Read at Dusk and Other Stories, Sketches and Essays, Now First Collected.* London: George Redway, 1898, pp. xi-xxiii.

In the American edition (introduction dated October 1897), Kitton asserts that, in this collection of previously unreprinted "fugitive pieces" by Dickens, many were "apparently unknown to bibliographers as the productions of the great novelist." Kitton provides bibliographical information about a number of the forty-six essays included. The English edition (introduction dated December 1897) also contains forty-six essays, but only thirty of them are also in the American edition. In the introduction, which is extensively revised, Kitton notes that twenty-four of the essays "have never been included in any Dickens Bibliography, the discovery and identification of these being the result of much investigation and research on my part."

419. Kitton, F[rederic] G., ed. *The Poems and Verses of Charles Dickens.* London: Chapman and Hall; New York: Harper & Brothers, 1903; reprinted Kennebunkport, ME: Milford House, 1974. 206 pp.

Prints Dickens's poems and verses with background and bibliographical notes on their writing and publication.

420. Ley, J. W. T. "A Charles Dickens Fragment: Story of a Noble Effort in Good-Doing. Appeal to Unfortunates. First Reprint of a Letter in Great Britain." *Western Mail & South Wales News* (Cardiff), 11 March 1930, p. 8.

Prints the text of Dickens's "Appeal to Fallen Women," in letter form, and claims that it is here "reprinted for the first time in this country and only for the second time in the world." It was first printed in Edward F. Payne and Henry H. Harper's *The Charity of Charles Dickens. His Interest in the Home for Fallen Women and a History of the Strange Case of Caroline Maynard Thompson* (Boston: Bibliophile Society, 1929). Ley further comments on Dickens's friendship with Angela Burdett-Coutts and notes that *Forster* has very little to say about the Home for Fallen Women at Shepherd's Bush, for which Dickens produced the letter and which he helped Miss Coutts establish.

421. Long, William F. "Dickens and the Coming of Rail to Deal: An Uncollected Speech and Its Context." *Dickensian*, 85 (1989), 67-80.

Identifies and prints, from the *Railway Times*, 3 July 1847, the fullest account of a previously unrecorded speech by Dickens, 30 June 1847, at a dinner celebrating the opening of the South-Eastern Railway (SER) Company branch line from Minster to Deal in Kent, as well as other less full accounts of the speech and the dinner. This speech is not included in K. J. Fielding's edition (**408**) of Dickens's speeches. Long also provides something of an account of Dickens's life at the time, he and his family being settled for the summer at nearby Broadstairs. Long notes that, while Dickens "is said to have regarded the SER as 'his own special' and 'favourite' line," it was, ironically, the SER on which he was travelling that wrecked at Staplehurst on 9 June 1865 and "destroyed his ability to enjoy rail travel" thereafter. Illustrated with a map of railways into Kent, 1847, on p. 66.

422. Low, Donald R. "The Speeches, Lectures, and Readings of Charles Dickens and William M. Thackeray in the United States, 1842-1868." *Dissertation Abstracts International*, 16 (1956), 2555-56 (Northwestern University, 1956).

As he notes in his abstract, Low identifies and examines the speeches that Dickens made on his first visit to the United States in 1842 and the speeches he made and the readings he gave on his second visit in 1867-68.

423. "Makrocheir" (pseud.). "Charles Dickens as a Poet." *Notes and Queries*, 4th ser., 5 (25 June 1870), 591.

Queries whether a collection of Dickens's "fugitive pieces," such as a poem (published the previous week in the London *Daily News*) from one of Lady Blessington's annuals, might not be "acceptable to the public."

424. "A Manuscript of Dickens. 'Life of Our Lord' to Be Published." *Times* (London), 22 January 1934, p. 12.

Quotes from Henry Fielding Dickens's will, where he gives permission to his wife and children to publish the manuscript of "Life of Our Lord." The article notes that they have decided to publish it.

425. Matz, B. W. "Introduction." In Dickens's *Miscellaneous Papers, Plays and Poems*. Ed. B. W. Matz. Vols. XXXV and XXXVI. The National Edition. London: Chapman and Hall, 1908, XXXV, ix-xvii.

Comments on the sources used, including the "Contributors' Book" for *Household Words* and the "office" set of *All the Year Round* (the latter now lost), which identified contributors to these two magazines, to put together this collection of Dickens's newspaper and magazine pieces and his plays and poems, almost all of which are here reprinted for the first time. A few were first reprinted in the *Dickensian*, vols. 2-4 (1906-08), undoubtedly under the supervision of Matz, who was then editor.

426. Matz, B. W. "An Untraced Article by Dickens." *Athenaeum*, no. 4158 (6 July 1907), 15.

A query as to where the article by Dickens was once published, the galley proof for which, entitled "The Spirit of Chivalry at Westminster Hall," Matz indicates, is in the Forster Collection, Victoria and Albert Museum, London. It has, Matz notes, corrections in Dickens's hand. The query was not answered in a later issue of the *Athenaeum*, but Matz obviously located it, for he points out, in volume 34, *Reprinted Pieces, Sunday Under Three Heads and Other Tales, Sketches, Articles, Etc.* (London: Chapman and Hall, 1908) of the National Edition of Dickens's works, which he edited, that it appeared in somewhat condensed form in *Douglas Jerrold's Shilling Magazine*, August 1845. In volume 34, it is printed "in its complete form from the galley proof."

427. Matz, Winifred. "My Copy of 'The Children's New Testament.'" *Dickensian*, 30 (1933/34), 89.

Gives the title ("The Children's New Testament: An Abstract of the Narrative of the Four Gospels for the Use of Juvenile Readers, Written by Charles Dickens Exclusively for His Own Children in 1846") and the opening and concluding paragraphs of a previously unpublished work of Dickens—one that he did not want published during the lifetime of his children. With the death of Sir Henry Fielding Dickens, his last surviving child, on 22 December 1933, publication of the complete work was due shortly (as *The Life of Our Lord* in 1934). Matz quotes, she points out, from a typescript copy made by her father, B. W. Matz, from Mark Lemon's copy, with the permission of Kate Dickens Perugini, more than twenty years earlier. Also see Dexter (**401**).

428. McCarthy, Patrick J. "Dickens at the Regent's Park Colosseum: Two Uncollected Pieces." *Dickensian*, 79 (1983), 154-61.

Comments on and reprints two generally favorable notices by Dickens published in the *Morning Chronicle*, one (8 July 1835) on the opening of the 1835 exhibition at the Colosseum, the other (10 July 1835) on the "grand opening fête" that accompanied it.

429. Mead, H. R. "Some Dickens Variations." *Papers of the Bibliographical Society of America*, 41 (1947), 344.

Traces minor bibliographical variations in three copies of *Sketches of Young Gentlemen* in the Huntington Library, San Marino, CA.

430. Miller, W[illiam]. "The Household Words Almanac." *Dickensian*, 7 (1911), 44.

Describes the rare almanacs for 1856 and 1857. See Southton (**232**).

431. "The New Dickens Writings." In "Special Dickens Number." *Bookshelf*, 2, viii (February 1908), pp. 166-68.

Comments on the two volumes of *Miscellaneous Papers* in the National Edition of Dickens's works (**425**) and the recent publication of other little-known works by Dickens.

432. "A Newly Discovered Dickens Manuscript." *John o' London's Weekly*, 8 (1922/23), 364.

Reproduces in facsimile and comments on the one-page manuscript "just come to light" of Dickens's prologue to Wilkie Collins's *The Lighthouse*, first acted on 29 June 1855.

433. "Olybrius" (pseud.). "Verses on Leigh Hunt by Southey and Dickens." *Notes and Queries*, 166 (1934), 79.

Prints verses by Robert Southey and by Dickens written in a copy of Hunt's *Abou Ben Adhem* and transcribed in a book catalogue of Barnet J. Beyer, Inc., New York (not located). The six-line poem attributed to Dickens is signed "Boz" and is quite undistinguished.

434. Paroissien, David. "A Note on the Text." In Dickens's *Pictures from Italy.* Ed. David Paroissien. London: André Deutsch, 1973; New York: Coward, McCann & Geoghegan, 1974; reprinted London: Robinson, 1989, pp. 244–46.

Provides details about the original publication of *Pictures from Italy* as "Travelling Letters Written on the Road" in the London *Daily News,* 21 January–11 March 1846, and the expanded published editions of the work. Paroissien also comments briefly and generally on the revisions and additions Dickens made when he published the *Daily News* pieces in book form. Unfortunately, Paroissien's notes, pp. 250-57, do not touch upon the particulars of Dickens's revisions. A small bibliography (**1127**) is also included.

435. Philip, Alex J. "The Newly Discovered Writings of Dickens." *Dickensian,* 4 (1908), 89-91.

Comments on Dickens's periodical pieces, most reprinted for the first time in the two volumes of *Miscellaneous Papers* in the then recently published National Edition (**425**). Among other things, they show, Philip states, the consistency, continuity, and firmness of Dickens's views on various subjects and are useful reflections of the novels themselves.

436. Pierpont, Robert. "Bibliographical Notes on Dickens and Thackeray." *Notes and Queries,* 10th ser., 3 (1905), 337-38.

In reply to an article by W. F. Prideaux (**1423**), Pierpont refers to errors in dating the first publication of Dickens's early play *Is She His Wife?* It was published, Prideaux notes, in the late 1830s, not the early 1870s. In a further reply, Robert Walters, p. 377, comments on the rarity of the first edition of *Is She His Wife?* Full particulars of this publication can be found in Shepherd's much earlier 1885 introduction to *The Plays and Poems of Charles Dickens* (**443**). Also see Fenn (**405**), Grubb (**412**), and Shepherd (**444**).

437. Piret, Michael J. "Charles Dickens's 'Children's New Testament': An Introduction, Annotated Edition, and Critical Discussion." *Dissertation Abstracts International,* 52 (1991/92), 3613A (University of Michigan, 1991).

Following an introduction on the history of the text of Dickens's *Life of Our Lord,* written in 1846, which Piret believes should be entitled *The Children's New Testament,* Piret provides, as his summary indicates, "the first scholarly edition" of the text, based on Dickens's manuscript, with headnotes and footnotes connecting the text to its Biblical sources. Additional chapters of commentary deal with what Dickens's modifications of the Biblical account reveal of "the unorthodoxy of his religious views."

438. "The Proposed Benefit for Leigh Hunt: An Unpublished Pamphlet."
　　　Dickensian, 36 (1939/40), 31-32.

Prints from a proof copy in the Huntington Library, San Marino, CA, a
pamphlet apparently never published, an appeal by Dickens for two theatrical
benefits to be given in London in July 1847 for Leigh Hunt. The performances were cancelled when Hunt was awarded a government pension; however, as is pointed out, other performances to benefit Hunt and also John
Poole were given later in the month in Manchester and Liverpool.

439. "[Query No.] 92. Dickens: *Remarks on Ventilation.*" *Bibliographical Notes
　　　and Queries*, 2, i (January 1936), 3.

Notes that a four-page pamphlet by Henry A. Gouge, *Supplement to the
"New System of Ventilation." With Remarks on Ventilation by Charles Dickens* (New
York, June 1875), contains a previously unknown article by Dickens, pp. 2-3.
An introductory note indicates that Dickens wrote the piece on ventilation for
Stephen English, editor of the *Insurance Times* and an "intimate friend of Mr.
Dickens in England," when he was in America in 1867/68, provided that
English "would not announce his name as the author." The article was origi-
nally published anonymously in the *Insurance Times* in August 1869. It was pub-
lished under Dickens's name for the first time by Gouge with English's per-
mission.

440. Roos, David A. "Dickens at the Royal Academy of Arts: A New Speech
　　　and Two Eulogies." *Dickensian*, 73 (1977), 100-07.

Reprints Dickens's response (about 350 words) to the toast to "The Interests of Literature" at the annual banquet, 3 May 1862–as reported in the London *Times* two days later. This is incorporated into Fielding's 1988 edition of
The Speeches of Charles Dickens (**408**), pp. xxv-xxvi. Roos also reprints two eulogies of Dickens himself at later RAA dinners, one by Anthony Trollope on
29 April 1871, the other by John Forster on 4 May 1872.

441. Sabin, Frank T. "Dickensiana." *Athenaeum*, 97 (1891), 765.

Notes the discovery of a privately published and possibly unique copy of
Mr. Nightingale's Diary, 1851. The edition was mentioned in *Forster* but no copy
was previously known. This one, Sabin reports, has Wilkie Collins's signature
on the title page and markings in the text in his hand, including a brief addition not in the 1877 American edition.

442. Seawim, G. "A Newly Discovered Dickens Fragment." *Dickensian*, 54
　　　(1958), 48-49.

Prints a previously unpublished fragment from *Bentley's Miscellany*, 2 (February 1837), 152, entitled "Theatrical Advertisement, Extraordinary." For a commentary on this piece and an attempt to identify the theatrical managers in it referred to as "Messrs. Four, Two and One," see Malcolm Morley, "Messrs. Four, Two and One," *Dickensian*, 57 (1961), 78-81 (illustrated).

443. Shepherd, Richard H. "Introduction." In his edition of *The Plays and Poems of Charles Dickens* (**42**), I, 7-96.

Includes bibliographical information about the publication of Dickens's plays, descriptions of the plays and actors who performed in them, and various previously published letters from Dickens to his theatrical collaborators and friends. Shepherd also comments on the various productions of plays by others that Dickens directed and acted in and on Dickens's ability as an actor.

444. Shepherd, Richard H. "A Lost Work of Charles Dickens." *Pen*, 1 (1880), 311-12.

On *Is She His Wife?*–a play not mentioned in *Forster*. Shepherd reproduces a playbill that clearly identifies "Boz" as author of the play. Also see Fenn (**405**), Grubb (**412**), and Pierpont (**436**).

445. Simon and Schuster, publishers. "Foreword." In *The Life of Our Lord. Written for His Children during the Years 1846 to 1849 by Charles Dickens and Now First Published*. New York: Simon and Schuster, 1934, pp. 3-8.

Gives something of a history of Dickens's writing of the manuscript for his children and not intending it for publication. It was kept "as a precious family secret" for some eighty-five years, the publishers note, and ultimately published by the wife and children of Dickens's son Henry. The opening page of the manuscript is reproduced in photographic facsimile.

446. Smith, Wilbur J. "Boz's *Memoirs of Joseph Grimaldi*, 1838." *Book Collector*, 16 (1967), 80.

In response to Stott (**453**), describes an edition of the *Memoirs* in the library of the University of California at Los Angeles and refers to Richard Bentley & Son's *A List of the Principal Publications Issued from New Burlington Street During the Year 1838* (**144**), which "contains two pages on the history of the book's publication." Also see Strange (**454**).

447. Spencer, W[alter] T. "A Lost Play by Dickens." *Athenaeum*, no. 3846 (13 July 1901), 72.

From a copy in his possession, verifies that Dickens's *Is She His Wife?* was printed in twenty-two pages with a printed wrapper but without indication of date of publication and printer's or publisher's name. See the response by George M. Fenn (**405**).

448. Staples, Leslie C. "Dickens and Macready's *Lear.*" *Dickensian*, 44 (1947/48), 78-80.

Reprints a most favorable review of a performance by William Macready, the famous actor, in *King Lear* that originally appeared in the *Examiner*, 27 October 1849. The review, Staples asserts, is clearly by Dickens, as evidenced by a manuscript of the piece in his hand. This piece was earlier reprinted by Van Noorden (**459**). Also see Carlton (**389**).

449. Stone, Harry, ed. *Charles Dickens' Uncollected Writings from* **Household Words** *1850-1859.* 2 vols. Bloomington and London: Indiana University Press, 1968; as *The Uncollected Writings of Charles Dickens:* **Household Words**, *1850-1859.* 2 vols. London: Allen Lane, Penguin Press, 1969. xx + 359 pp; xii + pp. 361-716.

An important collection of previously uncollected pieces. Stone reprints for the first time seventy-eight articles, announcements, notes, introductions, and several conclusions (to Christmas numbers) solely by Dickens himself or in collaboration with other authors, all of which appeared anonymously in *Household Words*. These represent, Stone points out, "some quarter of a million published words from Dickens' prime." Stone's introduction deals at length with the editorial demands Dickens made on himself and the other writers for *Household Words*, with the variety of subjects covered by the articles and representing Dickens's views and interests, and with the "new shadows and new highlights" they provide to the canon of Dickens's writings. Stone also gives something of a history of Dickens's experiences as an editor, from *Bentley's Miscellany* to *All the Year Round*, focusing on *Household Words*, whose plan, staff, management, "conductorship" by Dickens, content, fortunes, and dissolution Stone discusses at some length. He also treats of Dickens's handling of a manuscript from arrival to publication, with many examples of his editorial revisions and practices, and discusses the ways in which Dickens collaborated with other authors. Appendices contain examples of Dickens's editing of an article by someone else and one by himself based on extant page proofs in the former and an earlier manuscript version in the latter case; biographical notes on Dickens's collaborators; Dickens's instructions to prospective contributors to "The Holly-Tree Inn" and "The Wreck of the Golden Mary" Christmas numbers; and a "'Household Words' Volume, Issue, and Date Conversion Table." There are also a selected bibliography (**1129**), index, and 132 illustrations. Also see Collins (**391**). Stone briefly describes this work and his introduction to it in "Dickens," *Victorian Periodicals Newsletter*, no. 7 (January 1970), 8.

Reviews: J. Bayley, *New York Review of Books*, 8 October 1970, pp. 8-12 ("a service for Dickensians"); R. C. Carpenter, *Journal of Popular Culture*, 4 (1970/71), 540-49 ("handsomely put together," a "worthwhile contribution" to Dickens studies, with a "useful introduction" about *Household Words* and Dickens's editorial practices, though some questionable attributions to Dickens); J. A. Carter, *Dickens Studies Newsletter*, 2 (1971), 45-47 (praises Stone's "patient research and careful evaluation of stylistic evidence" for establishing Dickens's contributions but notes that a number of attributions are speculative and disagrees with Stone's assertion that the passages he has identified as Dickens's are "prime Dickens"); P. Collins, *Dickensian*, 66 (1970), 42-49 (a major and predominantly laudatory review by a knowledgeable reviewer, who sees the new attributions as "a very considerable and exciting achievement," even though two-thirds of the writings may actually be by Dickens's collaborators; Collins finds the introduction "the most useful and comprehensive account yet written of Dickens's plan for his periodical and his mode of conducting it" and praises Stone for his extensive annotations and his often convincing defense of his attributions–though he has some qualifications and notes one "serious omission"); R. Cutforth, *Listener*, 82 (1969), 894 (comments on Dickens as editor and finds Stone's introduction illuminating and "a model of lucid compression"); K. J. Fielding, *Victorian Studies*, 13 (1969/70), 216-17 ("soundly edited and elegantly produced," the pieces revealing "Dickens the editor, the imaginative writer, and the reporter of his times"); T. J. Galvin, *Library Journal*, 94 (1969), 760 ("an edition of major importance to the Dickens canon"); J. Hagan, *Nineteenth-Century Fiction*, 24 (1969/70), 361-66 (praises the work as "handsome, profusely annotated, and lavishly illustrated," with an introduction that is "the most thorough account to be found anywhere of Dickens's editorial principles and practices," but finds the "yield of Stone's immense labors" disappointing); J. Holloway, *Encounter*, 34, vi (June 1970), 63-68 (comments on but does not evaluate the edition), and *Spectator*, 223 (1969), 750-51 (Holloway principally comments on the contents of the pieces included, finding these writings to be mainly Dickens's editorial work, his revisions of the writings of others); S. Monod, *Etudes anglaises*, 23 (1970), 219-22 (in French; finds Stone "un *editor exemplaire*" and the two volumes "magnifiques"); V. S. Pritchett, *New Statesman*, 78 (1969), 865-66 ("a scholarly exposition of how Dickens worked as an editor with his team, how he planned and cut the stories and articles he commissioned and wrote in lines here and there of his own"; Pritchett also comments on Dickens's "enormous energy" and desire for "absolute power" as an editor); *Times* (London), 29 November 1969, Books, p. v (an "excellent anthology" that "brings to light the fantastic combination of technical skill and creative energy in Dickens"); *Times Literary Supplement*, 13 November 1969, p. 1319 ("useful"; the pieces "provide further evidence about Dickens's views on social questions of the day"); G. Wing, *Ariel: A Review of International English Literature*, 1, iv (October 1970), 56-66 ("The pieces are fascinating in themselves and the work of detection on them even more so," requiring "the erudition and discrimination of a fine scholar").

450. Stone, Harry. "Dickens Rediscovered: Some Lost Writings Retrieved." In "The Dickens Centennial" issue. *Nineteenth-Century Fiction*, 24, iv (March 1970), 527-48; reprinted separately as *Dickens Centennial Essays*. Ed. Ada Nisbet and Blake Nevius. Berkeley, Los Angeles, and London: University of California Press, 1971, pp. 205-26.

In discussing what had then not been identified or collected of the Dickens canon, Stone looks particularly at Dickens's Christmas issues for *Household Words* and *All the Year Round*. He notes that in putting these together Dickens wrote more than the stories that have been identified as his and did his usual thorough editing of those written by others. Even in collecting his own stories, Dickens cut passages from them and added others, Stone indicates. Where seven of these are concerned, Stone points out, the changes Dickens made in collecting them are in his hand on the numbers themselves in the Berg Collection, New York Public Library, New York (**1499**). More than one-half of the article is devoted to identifying and reprinting previously unnoted passages that Dickens contributed to *A Message from the Sea* (1860) and discussing what they reveal of Dickens's craft and imagination.

451. Stone, Harry. "The Unknown Dickens: With a Sampling of Uncollected Writings." *Dickens Studies Annual*, 1 (1970), 1-22, 275-76.

Comments on, identifies, and reprints portions of "The Haunted House," the first extra Christmas number of *All the Year Round* (1859), not previously identified as by Dickens. These include various introductory paragraphs to the individual tales in the issue, transitions, and the final section, "The Ghost in the Corner Room." More generally, Stone comments on these and other "lost writings" of Dickens, pointing out that to supplement the pieces collected in his own *Charles Dickens' Uncollected Writings from "Household Words" 1850-1859* (**449**) various early writings and pieces or fragments from *All the Year Round* still remain to be identified as part of the Dickens canon, particularly from the Christmas numbers of *All the Year Round*. Illustrated.

452. Storey, Graham. "An Unpublished Satirical Sketch by Dickens." *Dickensian*, 74 (1978), 6-7.

Prints a previously unpublished manuscript of about 300 words entitled "Opinion," signed "J. Buzfuz," and dated 8 January 1859. Now in the Pierpont Morgan Library, New York, the manuscript (in Dickens's hand) is a satiric treatment of the Crimea, Storey points out. He offers various reasons why it was never published; it was, for example, written nearly three years after the end of the Crimean War and at a time when the Crimea and post-war commentaries on it were not particularly newsworthy.

453. Stott, R. Toole. "Note 277. Boz's *Memoirs of Joseph Grimaldi* 1838." *Book Collector*, 15 (1966), 354-56.

Examines the question of whether or not there were two states of the first edition of the *Memoirs*. See response by Smith (**446**) and see Strange (**454**).

454. Strange, E. H. "The Memoirs of Grimaldi: A Bibliographical Note." *Dickensian*, 33 (1936/37), 239-40.

Lists the bibliographical points of the first issue of the first edition. See Stott (**453**) and Smith (**446**).

455. Suzannet, A[lain] de. "Maria Beadnell's Album." *Dickensian*, 31 (1934/35), 161-68.

Reproduces four pages from the album kept, 1827-1859, by Dickens's first sweetheart. Two of these pages contain holograph poems written by young Dickens, one original ("Acrostic" on M-A-R-I-A-B-E-A-D-N-E-L-L), the other a transcription of Thomas Moore's "Written in an Album." Suzannet's text describes and quotes from other entries by Dickens ("The Devil's Walk," "The Churchyard," and "Lodgings to Let"). Suzannet also describes entries by other friends and relatives of Maria Beadnell. A letter to the editor from Arthur Jenkins, *Dickensian*, 32 (1935/36), 72, mentions an earlier poem entitled "The Devil's Walk" (London, 1831), apparently written by Robert Southey and Samuel Taylor Coleridge and illustrated with ten drawings by Thomas Landseer, brother of Edwin, the more famous artist, of which Dickens's poem seems to be an imitation.

456. Turner, Godfrey. "'Boz' and the Play." *Theatre* (London), 17, ns 5 (1885), 171-73.

Comments briefly on the original publication of Dickens's plays.

457. Tyson, Moses, ed. "A Review and Other Writings by Charles Dickens, Edited from the Original Manuscripts in the John Rylands Library." *Bulletin of the John Rylands University Library*, 18 (1934), 177-96; also printed separately, Manchester: Manchester University Press; Librarian, John Rylands Library, 1934. 22 pp.

Prints and comments on several letters from Dickens in the John Rylands Library collection, all reprinted in *Nonesuch Letters* and *Pilgrim Letters*. Tyson also prints and comments on a manuscript in the John Rylands Library of a review by Dickens of a pamphlet by Charles William Stewart, Lord Londonderry, entitled *A Letter to Lord Ashley, M. P., on the Mines and Collieries Bill*, with Dickens's cancellations in manuscript noted. The article, Tyson comments, was presumably written for the *Morning Chronicle*, of which Mackay was then acting assistant subeditor, but not printed there. Actually it *was* printed there, as Dexter (**1612**) and, more specifically, the editors of *Pilgrim Letters*, III, 351, note, on 20 October 1942. For more details, about Dickens's views on the Mines and Collieries Bill and his review of Londonderry's pamphlet, see *Pilgrim Letters*, III, 278-85, 309, 351-52. Tyson appends "A List of the Letters and Manuscripts of Charles Dickens which are Now in The John Rylands Library," pp. 192-96 (**1534**). Illustrated. For further details of the Gaskell Collection, see John Rylands University Library (**1658**), Lingard (**1671**), "Notes and News [Gaskell Collection]" (**1694**), Quinn (**1511**), and Tyson (**1533**).

458. Van Noorden, C[harles]. "Dickens as a Reporter." *Bookman* (London), 47 (1914/15), 148-49.

Reprints Dickens's report in the *Morning Chronicle*, 2 May 1835, of the by-election of Lord John Russell for South Devon. Van Noorden identifies the report on the basis of a comment by Dickens in a speech at the Newspaper Press Fund Dinner in May 1865 about his reportorial days. "One is glad," Van Noorden concludes, "to discover any example of Dickens's reporting days." Illustrated.

459. Van Noorden, C[harles], ed. "A New Bit by Dickens: A Dramatic Critique Which Has Never Been Reprinted Until Now." *Book Monthly*, 15 (1920), 231-32.

Reprints Dickens's review of Macready's *King Lear*, which originally appeared in the *Examiner*, 27 October 1849, from the manuscript of it in the Forster Collection, Victoria and Albert Museum, London. For a later reprinting of this review, see Staples (**448**). Also see Carlton (**389**).

460. W[augh], A[rthur], H[ugh] W[alpole], W[alter] D[exter], and T[homas] H[atton]. "Introduction." In their edition of Dickens's *Collected Papers*. 2 vols. The Nonesuch Dickens. Bloomsbury [London]: Nonesuch Press, 1937, I, v-vi.

The editors announce that they have included "about a hundred and twenty minor writings" of Dickens, most of which were published earlier by B. W. Matz in his two volumes of *Miscellaneous Papers, Plays and Poems* (**425**), but which include writings discovered since then, in addition to Dickens's plays, poems, and speeches. In the table of contents the pieces not in Matz's volumes are identified by an asterisk. These include seven articles, one play (the fragment from "O'Thello"), six poems, eight speeches, and *The Loving Ballad of Lord Bateman*, on which, they note, Dickens exercised an editorial hand.

461. W[eaver], H. F. "Dickens: A Bibliographical Query." *Bookman's Journal and Print Collector*, 2 (1920), 248.

Queries whether or not the Bernhard Tauchnitz Edition of *Hunted Down; A Story. The Uncommercial Traveller: A Series of Occasional Papers*, Collection of British Authors, volume 536 (Leipzig, 1860) was the earliest edition of Dickens's "Hunted Down" and *The Uncommercial Traveller*.

462. Wilkins, William Glyde. "First American Edition of 'American Notes.'" *Dickensian*, 5 (1909), 210-11.

Points out Dickens's displeasure at the earliest publication of *American Notes* in the United States—as an "Extra Number" of *Brother Jonathan*, 7 November 1842. Illustrated.

463. Wilkins, William Glyde. "First Collected Edition of 'Travelling Letters Written on the Road.'" *Dickensian*, 6 (1910), 17.

Points out that the original letters in the *Daily News* (London), collected as *Pictures from Italy*, were reprinted in two parts in New York in 1846 by Wiley & Putnam, in a series entitled "Wiley & Putnam's Library of Choice Reading."

Collaborative Pieces

Note: Also see Dexter (**325**) and Stone (**449-51**).

464. Andrew, R[ay] V. "Bibliography." In his *Wilkie Collins: A Critical Survey of His Prose Fiction, with a Bibliography*. A Garland Series: The Fiction of Popular Culture. New York and London: Garland, 1979, pp. 338-58.

At the end of this printing of a doctoral dissertation from Potchefstroom University, South Africa, 1959, Andrew lists Collins's *Household Words* and *All the Year Round* articles, noting ones on which he collaborated with Dickens—and also includes a "Selected List of Books Consulted."

465. Baker, William. "The Manuscript of Wilkie Collins's *No Name*." *Studies in Bibliography: Papers of the Bibliographical Society of the University of Virginia*, 43 (1990), 197-208.

Concentrates on the changes made by Collins between manuscript and serial publication in *All the Year Round* but also comments on Dickens's involvement, as editor, in Collins's revisions. For an earlier paper on this subject, see Baker's "Wilkie Collins, Dickens, and *No Name*," *Dickens Studies Newsletter*, 11 (1980), 49-52.

466. Brannan, Robert L. "Introduction." In his *Under the Management of Mr. Charles Dickens: His Production of "The Frozen Deep."* Ithaca, NY: Cornell University Press, 1966, pp. 1-88.

Brannan surveys the genesis, staging, and performances of the play for which Wilkie Collins wrote the original draft, though the idea for the play seems to have been largely Dickens's, and examines Dickens's extensive revisions of the script. He also comments on Dickens's compelling performance as Richard Wardour. And the effect doing so had on Dickens himself. Brannan prints the 1857 script, labeled by Dickens "The Prompt-Book," of which about forty pages of "stage directions, instructions for the prompter, and dialogue are in Dickens's handwriting." He also includes "Note on the Text of the Play," pp. 89-90, and a "Bibliography" (**1123**), pp. 161-73. Illustrated. See his doctoral dissertation, *"The Frozen Deep*: Under the Management of Mr. Charles Dickens." *Dissertation Abstracts International*, 26 (1965/66), 5429 (Cornell University, 1965).

467. Collins, Philip. "Dickens on Chatham: An Uncollected Piece, with Introduction and Notes." *Dickensian*, 59 (1963), 69-73.

Reprints Dickens's contributions to "One Man in a Dockyard," a description of the Chatham dockyards, published in *Household Words*, 6 September 1851, a piece on which Dickens collaborated with R. H. Horne.

468. Collins, Philip. "Dickens on Keeley the Comedian: An Uncollected Piece, with Introduction and Notes." *Dickensian*, 60 (1964), 5-10.

Identifies "Robert Keeley," an article in *All the Year Round*, 10 April 1869, as by Dickens—except for the opening references to Charles Lamb written by Herman Merivale. Collins quotes from an unpublished letter by Dickens to Georgina Hogarth, 8 April 1869, in which Dickens acknowledges his authorship and comments further on Keeley's acting. Collins reprints all but the section by Merivale. Illustrated. See Merivale (**521**).

469. Crum, Margaret. *English and American Autographs in the Bodmeriana.* Cologny-Genève, Switz.: Fondation Martin Bodmer, 1977, p. 31.

Refers to a double-leaf manuscript in the Bibliotheca Bodmeriana, Cologny-Genève, in Dickens's hand, of a preface to a publication of summaries of essays entered for a competition for working men who were to respond to eight or more questions relating to income. Crum notes that Dickens mentions this preface in a letter to Angela Burdett-Coutts dated 4 December 1856. For the letter, see Edgar Johnson's *The Heart of Charles Dickens, as Revealed in His Letters to Angela Burdett-Coutts, Selected and Edited from the Collection in the Pierpont Morgan Library* (New York: Duell, Sloan and Pearce; Boston: Little, Brown, 1952), pp. 329-30, which does not explain the reference. The letter is reprinted in *Pilgrim Letters*, VIII, 230-31, where the editors explain that the preface was to Miss Coutts's *A Summary Account*, new edition (1857), presumably written by Coutts, with help from Dickens, since he writes, "I have gone over the additional MS, and hope I have made it quite plain. I enclose my draft," and notes a specific change he has made. This preface is not included in *Miscellaneous Papers* in the National Edition (**425**) or in the Nonesuch Edition's *Collected Papers* (**460**). For further information, see Fielding (**500**).

470. "A Curious Dance Round a Curious Tree." *Dickensian*, 23 (1926/27), 207.

A photographic facsimile of the first page of a ten-page manuscript in Dickens's hand comprising 217 of the 393 lines of "A Curious Dance Round a Curious Tree," published in *Household Words*, 17 January 1852. The facsimile shows, the anonymous author asserts, that, despite the reprinting of this work in W. H. Wills's *Old Leaves: Gathered from Household Words* (**487**), a collection of his writings, it was clearly by Dickens. See also Matz and Thomson(**520**) and Muir (**523**).

471. Davis, Nuel P. *The Life of Wilkie Collins*. Urbana: University of Illinois Press, 1956, passim.

Much of this biography deals with the close, complex personal friendship and literary relationship of Dickens and Collins, begun in March 1851. Davis also examines their collaborations on *The Lazy Tour of Two Idle Apprentices* and *The Perils of Certain English Prisoners*, *A Message from the Sea*, and other Christmas numbers, as well as on a number of other projects, and Collins's work with Georgina Hogarth and Mamie Dickens to produce the *Hogarth-Dickens Letters*.

472. "Dickens and Wilkie Collins." *New York Times*, Saturday Review of Books and Art sect., 4 September 1897, p. 4.

Based on an article in the *Pall Mall Gazette* (**484**) containing excerpts from some then unpublished letters from Dickens to W. H. Wills about the editing of *Household Words* and *All the Year Round*. The *New York Times* author comments on some details of Dickens's collaboration with Wilkie Collins referred to in the letters, noting that, while the "master mind [of Dickens] invariably asserts itself," Collins nevertheless "seems to have been a very useful man" in regard to the publication of the two magazines, particularly in the reading of submitted manuscripts.

473. Drew, John M. L. "Charles Dickens, Traducteur? A New Article in *All the Year Round*." *Dickensian*, 93 (1997), 116-25.

Offers evidence that Dickens may have composed "Dress in Paris" (*All the Year Round*, 28 February 1863), a "critique of the female slavery to fashion evident in the Paris of the Second Empire" out of passages "selected and translated from [Eugène] Pelletan's controversial publication [*La Nouvelle Babylone, lettres d'un provincial en tournée à Paris*, 1862], interspersed with brief linking sentences of his own."

474. Firman, Frederick B. "Dickens or Wilkie Collins?" *Notes and Queries*, 10th ser., 3 (1905), 207.

A tempest in a teapot. Firman queries the authorship of *The Lazy Tour of Two Idle Apprentices*, noting that an incident described at length in it appears also under the title of "The Dead Hand" in Collins's *Queen of Hearts* (1859). Walter Jerrold replies, p. 278, that, as *Forster* indicates, *The Lazy Tour* is a joint work by the two authors but "separating the two shares is not possible." Robert Pierpont, responding in 4 (1905), 255, simply quotes from R. H. Shepherd's *Bibliography of Charles Dickens* (**42**), where Dickens's contributions to the work are specifically identified.

475. Haight, Anne L. "Charles Dickens Tries to Remain Anonymous . . . Notes on the Loving Ballad of Lord Bateman, Together with a Reprint of the Ballad." *Colophon*, New Graphic Series, no. 1 (March 1939), 39–66; reprinted separately under same title, [London]: Printed for The Colophon, 1939. 28 unnumbered pp.

Haight asserts that a newly discovered "packet of letters from Dickens to George Cruikshank" in a sale at Hodgson's, 10 December 1937 (**1953**), clarifies the problem of authorship of this work, which was illustrated by George Cruikshank. Two of the letters, undated but written between 1 May and 1 September 1839, "prove unquestionably," that Dickens "was the sole author of the Preface and the Notes and that he altered the verses of the ballad as set down by Cruikshank, and wrote the last verse." The two letters, originally published by Dexter (**325**), are republished here. The editors of *Pilgrim Letters* assign them dates of [?May 1839] and [3 July 1839]), I, 552, 559. Haight also comments on the ill-feeling that developed between Dickens and Cruikshank, growing out of Dickens's unfavorable comments on Cruikshank's works in "Whole Hogs" (*Household Words*, 23 August 1851) and "Frauds on the Fairies" (1 October 1853). In addition, she gives a full bibliographical collation for the two issues of the first edition of *The Loving Ballad of Lord Bateman*, notes later editions, reprints Dickens's preface and notes, and provides facsimiles of the pages of the poem with the accompanying illustrations. The article, which is handsomely produced, also contains other illustrations. See Johnson (**477**), Lucas (**480**), Ritchie (**531**), and Spencer (**535**) for earlier speculation about Dickens's involvement in the volume. A letter from Thackeray to Cruikshank, (May? 1839), provides further evidence that Thackeray had no hand in the volume—see *The Letters and Private Papers of William Makepeace Thackeray*, collected and edited by Gordon N. Ray, 4 vols. (Cambridge, MA: Harvard University Press, 1945–46), I, 380–81.

476. Howe, Winona R. "Writing a Book in Company: The Collaborative Works of Charles Dickens and Wilkie Collins." *Dissertation Abstracts International*, 53 (1992/93), 503A–04A (University of California, Riverside, 1991).

Studies the works that Dickens and Collins wrote in collaboration, particularly extra Christmas numbers of *Household Words* and *All the Year Round*, and concludes that the collaboration was beneficial to both.

477. Johnson, Charles P. "'The Loving Ballad of Lord Bateman.'" *Athenaeum*, 91 (1888), 86.

Reviews the controversy and conflicting evidence over whether Thackeray or Dickens had a hand in this volume illustrated by George Cruikshank, concluding that it was more probable that "Thackeray, not Dickens, wrote the preface and notes in question," citing as his strongest evidence the then unpublished drawings, later published by Anne Thackeray Ritchie (**531**), and accompanying text of the poem that was at least partly in Thackeray's hand. Also see Dexter (**325**), Lucas (**480**), Spencer (**535**), and Haight (**475**), who finally resolves the issue in Dickens's favor.

478. Johnson, Charles P. "An Unknown (?) Pamphlet by Dickens." *Athenaeum*, 94 (1889), p. 674.

Suspects that an eleven-page pamphlet entitled *Drooping Buds*, "Printed for Private Circulation by the Royal Infirmary Dorcas Society To Awaken Interest in an Hospital for Sick Children in Glasgow" in 1866, identified as by Dickens and originally printed in *Household Words*, 3 April 1852, may have been written by someone else under Dickens's direction. It was written by Henry Morley, both Kitton (**510**) and Matz (**519**) believed, but more recent investigation by Harry Stone shows that Dickens wrote portions of the article. Stone reprints it in *Charles Dickens's Uncollected Writings from "Household Words" 1850-1859* (**449**), pp. 401-08, and identifies the portions he believes were written by Dickens. Lohrli (**155**) also allocates the article to Morley and Dickens.

479. Lohrli, Anne. "Wilkie Collins and *Household Words*." *Victorian Periodicals Review*, 15 (1982), 118-19.

Notes that, though Collins's name did not appear with the serialization of his *The Dead Secret* in *Household Words*, 3 January to 13 June 1857, he was announced in the Christmas number of 1856 (6 December) and in the issues of 20 and 27 December 1856 as the author of the forthcoming multi-part story.

480. Lucas, E. V. "A Wanderer's Notebook: Authenticated Boz." *Sunday Times* (London), 24 April 1938, p. 16.

Asserts that Walter Dexter in the "current" *Dickensian* (**325**) has authenticated Dickens's contribution to *The Loving Ballad of Lord Bateman* and comments on Dickens's involvement with the poem. Also see Johnson (**477**), Ritchie (**531**), Spencer (**535**), and particularly Haight (**475**), who resolves the issue of attribution.

481. Mitgang, Herbert. "1857 Story Is Attributed to Dickens." *New York Times*, 21 June 1988, p. C19.

Reports on Harry Stone's attribution of an interpolated story in *The Lazy Tour of Two Idle Apprentices*, a collaboration of Dickens and Wilkie Collins, to

Dickens. Stone, Mitgang reports, has named the untitled story "The Bride's Chamber" and quotes Stone as stating that the story "reveals a great deal about Dickens's extramarital yearning" for Ellen Ternan. Steven Marcus and Richard Dunn (here misspelled Dunne) offer supportive statements. Stone has since republished the story as *The Bride's Chamber* (Santa Monica, CA: Waxwing Editions, 1996).

482. Peek, Laura. "Cookbook Reveals Dickens Nakedly as a Chef." *Times* (London), 22 December 2001, p. 15.

Claims that a newly discovered scrap of paper reveals that Dickens had a hand in writing *What Shall We Have for Dinner?* (1851), formerly attributed to his wife. On the scrap of paper, Peek indicates, Betty Lemon, a daughter of Mark Lemon, describes how the two Dickenses cooked meals in the Lemon kitchen and then retired afterwards to Lemon's study, where various recipes "were discussed and eventually a cooking book was compiled." Also see an editorial–"Cooking the Book: What the Dickens Is the Recipe for This Victorian Stew?"–in the same issue of the *Times*, p. 19, which comments on Dickens's involvement with the book and his love of food. Illustrated.

483. Robinson, Kenneth. *Wilkie Collins: A Biography.* London: The Bodley Head, 1951; New York: Macmillan, 1952; reprinted Westport, CT: Greenwood Press [1972]; London: Davis-Poynter, 1974, passim.

Robinson traces in considerable detail the literary relations of Dickens and Collins, including their collaborations on several Christmas stories, plays, and *The Lazy Tour of Two Idle Apprentices.* He also covers Dickens's publication of other works by Collins in *Household Words* and *All the Year Round,* including his novels *The Woman in White* (1859) and *No Name* (1862-63).

484. "Some More Unpublished Dickens." *Pall Mall Gazette,* 19 August 1897, p. 3.

Comments on some then unpublished letters at which the author had been allowed to look, nearly all from Dickens to Wilkie Collins, dealing with the editing of *Household Words* and *All the Year Round.* Brief excerpts from the letters concern the contributions of Collins and George A. Sala.

485. Stone, Harry. "Dickens and Composite Writing." *Dickens Studies,* 3 (1967), 68-79.

In this earlier version of the introduction to his then unpublished collection of the uncollected writings of Dickens (**449**), Stone looks at Dickens's method of "composite" writing–articles written in collaboration with others. The results, he points out, were mixed: some of these pieces were among Dickens's "most carefully planned and polished writings" while others were "hasty efforts and salvage attempts." Stone finds three categories of "composite" articles: 1) those planned as composites from the start, 2) those written by someone else but substantially modified by Dickens, and 3) dull, slack, long, technical, or badly written pieces by others on which Dickens performed fairly extensive but minor editorial surgery. Stone concludes that the composite writings "offer unique opportunities to study how Dickens saw the world and how he incorporated that vision into his writings" and reveal how Dickens's editorial gifts often turned journalism, the "revisions of the moment," into art.

486. Stone, Harry. "New Writings by Dickens." *Dalhousie Review*, 47 (1967), 305-25.

Comments on the variety in content and style in the articles Dickens wrote for *Household Words* in collaboration with other writers and not hitherto recorded in the canon, noting particularly the range of social concerns and the childhood reminiscences in them. This article is reprinted with minor revisions and two excisions as parts 12-14 of Stone's introduction to *Charles Dickens' Uncollected Writings from "Household Words" 1850-1859* (**449**), I, 53-68.

487. Wills, W[illiam] Henry. Dedication. In his *Old Leaves: Gathered from Household Words*. London: Chapman and Hall; New York: Harper & Brothers, 1860, introductory page.

The dedication, obviously to Dickens, reads "TO THE OTHER HAND, whose masterly touches gave to the OLD LEAVES here freshly gathered, their brightest tints, they are affectionately INSCRIBED," in tribute to Dickens's editing of Wills's pieces, or, in a few cases, his collaboration with Wills—on "A Plated Article," for example, which Wills publishes here, pp. 325-34, and which Dickens published as his own in *Reprinted Pieces* (1858). Wills indicates in a footnote on page 1 that portions of articles whose titles are preceded by a small graphic of a hand with pointing finger "are by another hand," presumably Dickens's. A good many of the articles in Wills's volume are preceded by this hand, but there are no indications within the articles themselves which portions are by Wills and which by Dickens.

1G. INCORRECT, DUBIOUS, OR SHARED ATTRIBUTIONS; AUTHORSHIP OF ARTICLES IN MAGAZINES EDITED BY DICKENS

Note: This may seem like a forced combination of subjects for one section, but, in fact, most of the incorrect attributions of articles to Dickens were to pieces published anonymously in *Household Words* and *All the Year Round*. Identifying the authors of articles in these two journals thus goes a long way toward straightening out the Dickens canon—see particularly Collins (**146**), Lohrli (**155**), and Oppenlander (**158**). Also see Carlton (**389**), Cohn (**362**), Dexter (**325**), Fitzgerald (**1284**), and Matz (**425**), as well as **Attributions, incorrect or dubious attributions, collaborations** in section 2 of part 1 of the subject index.

488. B., G. F. R. "Dickens: 'Pincher Astray.'" *Notes and Queries*, 6th ser., 11 (1885), 165.

Notes that, as Edmund Yates points out in his *Edmund Yates: His Recollections and Experiences*, 2 vols. (London: Richard Bentley and Son, 1884), II, 111n, he was the author of "Pincher Astray" (in *All the Year Round*, 30 January 1864), which Shepherd (**42**) and others attributed to Dickens. In a response, p. 254, Charles J. Clark points out that, in a complete set of *All the Year Round* in his possession that has the author's name attached to each article, the article is attributed to Yates.

489. B., I. X. "Authors of Quotations Wanted." *Notes and Queries*, 11th ser., 5 (1912), 90.

Asks for the author of a poem about Dickens beginning "And God did bless him." John T. Page, p. 154, answers that the author was Coulson Kernahan. Page reprints the complete poem and notes that it was originally published in the *Graphic* (no date given) as by "C. K.," and reprinted in the Dickens Number of *Household Words*, ns 14, no. 21 (14 June 1902) in "Charles Dickens as Others See Him," pp. 493-94, under the heading "Mr. Coulson Kernahan," p. 494. Kernahan himself notes there that the poem had been attributed to Charles Kent at the time but that he himself was its author.

490. Bede, Cuthbert [Edward Bradley]. "Did Charles Dickens Contribute to 'Figaro in London'?" *Notes and Queries*, 7th ser., 7 (1889), 3.

Notes that the 1884 Jarvis catalogue (**2043**) mentions that the periodical *Figaro in London* contained "chatty, racy anecdotes and jokes, said to be written by Charles Dickens and Gilbert à Beckett," and wonders if this is so. Bradley adds that he finds, however, no such attribution in James Cook's bibliography (**10**). A response by Ja[me]s B. Morris, p. 153, notes that *Figaro in London* was published 10 December 1831-31 December 1838 and that in volume 3, p. 67, an article, "Movements of the Middle Men," contains names that are a lot like those used by Dickens in *Sketches by Boz*.

491. Carlton, William J. "Dickens Periodicals." *Times Literary Supplement*, 22 September 1961, p. 629.

Queries the whereabouts of the office set of *All the Year Round*, with the contributors' names written in. Oppenlander (**158**) notes (p. 60) that more recent efforts to locate this set were not successful. See G. F. R. B. (**488**), Kitton (**508**), Matz (**425**), Suddaby (**536**), and Thomas (**538**).

492. Carlton, William J. "Who Wrote 'Mr. Robert Bolton'?" *Dickensian*, 54 (1958), 178-81.

Presents documentary evidence that this piece in *Bentley's Miscellany* (August 1838) was *not* by Dickens but by John H. Leigh Hunt, probably the second son of Leigh Hunt, though Dickens may have rewritten part of it or made some changes in it.

493. Cheney, David R. "Correction of the Misattribution of a Poem in 'Household Words.'" *Notes and Queries*, ns 24 (1977), 15-16.

Provides evidence that the poem "Moonrise," published anonymously in *Household Words*, 24 September 1853, and attributed by Lohrli (**155**), p. 115, to Adelaide Anne Procter, is really by Edmund Ollier.

494. Collins, Philip. "The *All the Year Round* Letter Book." *Victorian Periodicals Newsletter*, no. 10 (November 1970), 23-29.

Describes the manuscript Letter Book for *All the Year Round* in the Henry E. Huntington Library, San Marino, CA, kept by W. H. Wills, subeditor and general manager of the magazine, as "a small ledger of wafer-thin paper (10 ¼ x 8 ½ inches) of 494 pages," with a copy of a letter or two on almost every page, many illegible because copies were often made, Collins points out, by a process whereby the manuscript letter "was (it would seem) treated with some liquid preparation and was them pressed onto the verso of a page in the letter," though sometimes a clerk simply transcribed a letter. It also contains an index of correspondents–nearly 300, Collins indicates. The letters date from 1859 to 1877, though there are significantly smaller numbers of them for 1861-70, which leads Collins to believe that Wills must have kept records of those letters elsewhere. In the 200 or so pages from Dickens's tenure (though predominantly from 1859 to 1862), there are, Collins reports, over 200 copies of letters, almost all signed by W. H. Wills. The rest, from 1871-77, are signed by Charles Dickens, Jr. The letters show, Collins indicates, how much Wills contributed to the running of the weekly magazine and also reveal some "interesting details . . . about the organization and publishing" of it, of which Collins provides a number of examples. He also points out that, while most of the letters from 1859 to 1869 are by Wills (ending with his retirement), six are by Dickens and a few by other staff members.

495. Collins, Philip. "Dickens and Conolly." *Times Literary Supplement*, 18 August 1961, p. 549.

Corrects two passing attributions of articles to Dickens in "Dickens and [John] Conolly: An Embarrassed Editor's Disclaimer," by Richard A. Hunter and Ida Macalpine, in *Times Literary Supplement*, 11 August 1961, pp. 534-35, and comments on the care that must be taken in authorial attribution of articles in *Household Words* and *All the Year Round*. Collins notes, however, that "Dickens can generally be assumed to approve of whatever was published in the magazines he 'conducted.'"

496. Collins, Philip. "'Inky Fishing Nets': Dickens as Editor." *Dickensian*, 61 (1965), 120-25.

Accompanied by a photographic facsimile of a page of proof for a work by Percy Fitzgerald, with the text nearly obscured by Dickens's editorial ink marks, this article is a fascinating look at the extent of Dickens's editorial revisions of works contributed to *Household Words* and *All the Year Round*.

497. De Ternant, Andrew. "Dickens's French Contributor." *Notes and Queries*, 164 (1933), 189.

Asks if Antonin Roche might be the author of "numerous anonymous articles on French literature and manners" that appeared in the 1850s and 1860s in *Household Words* (and presumably *All the Year Round*). Neither Lohrli (**155**) nor Oppenlander (**158**) lists Roche as a contributor to Dickens's magazines.

498. Dickinson, Charles M. *The Children and Other Verses*. New York: Cassell; London: Sampson Low, Marston, Searle, & Rivington, 1889, p. 141.

A footnote to the poem "The Children" reprints a letter from Charles Dickens, Jr., to Dickinson, the author, indicating that the work has "often been erroneously attributed" to his father, but that it was definitely not written by him. Also see Williamson (**1548**).

499. Edwards, P. D., comp. *Edmund Yates, 1831-1894: A Bibliography.* Victorian Fiction Research Guides, 3. St Lucia: Department of English, University of Queensland, 1980, 1982, passim.

Lists Yates's contributions to *All the Year Round*, as well as his other works. Edwards also lists biographical and critical sources for Yates, pp. 66-73, 78-79, and locates manuscripts of his letters. The introduction, pp. 1-37, a sketch of Yates's life and literary career, makes passing references to the Garrick Club Affair (Yates's infamous argument with Thackeray) and Dickens's involvement in it. The 1982 edition contains "Addenda and Corrigenda (Consolidated List, Oct. 1982)," pp. 73-79.

500. Fielding, K[enneth] J. "'Women in the Home': An Article Dickens Did *Not* Write." *Dickensian*, 47 (1950/51), 140-42.

Points out that Dickens did not write the article attributed to him in the *Dickensian* (**548**), even though the manuscript is in his hand. Fielding identifies it as part of a preface that Angela Burdett-Coutts wrote, and Dickens revised, for the second edition of her book *A Summary Account of Prizes for Common Things, Offered and Awarded by Miss Burdett Coutts at the Whitelands Training Institution* (London: Hatchard, 1856).

501. Gluchowski, Krzysztof. "Dickens and Poland." *Dickensian*, 98 (2002), 44-51.

Lists sixteen articles in *All the Year Round*, referring to Poland, identifies the author of three of them, and speculates about the authors of the others. Gluchowski also quotes from three of Dickens's letters in which he comments on Polish exiles in London.

502. Gomme, G. J. L. "T. B. Aldrich and 'Household Words.'" *Papers of the Bibliographical Society of America*, 42 (1948), 70-72.

Notes that "The Flight of the Goddess," a poem written in 1867 by Thomas Bailey Aldrich, an American author, was printed in the 1868 reissue of the first volume of *Household Words* (1850) from the original stereotyped plates by Ward, Lock, & Tyler (subsequent volumes of *Household Words* were also reissued, 1868-70). Gomme notes that, in the London *Athenaeum*, 10 October 1868, Aldrich protested this unauthorized publication of his poem, which was followed by a reply from S. O. Beeton of the publishing company in the 17 October issue. While this is bibliographically interesting, it should also serve as a warning to Dickens scholars that there may be other such inserts to fill up blank pages in these reissues.

503. Grubb, Gerald G., and Leo Mason. "Dickens and Joseph C. Neal's *Charcoal Sketches.*" *Dickensian*, 46 (1949/50), 37-41.

In response to Leo Mason's earlier article, "Poe-Script," *Dickensian*, 42 (1945/46), 79-81, on the possible influence of Dickens on Neal, an American journalist and essayist, Grubb points out that Dickens had nothing to do with the incorporation of Neal's *Charcoal Sketches* as volume 3 of *The Pic Nic Papers* (1841), which Dickens edited, and broke with Colburn over the piracy. Mason, pp. 38-41, agrees with Grubb's information and adds a few notes on the publishing history of *The Pic Nic Papers*.

504. Houtchens, Carolyn W., and Lawrence H. Houtchens. "Three Early Works Attributed to Dickens." *Publications of the Modern Language Association of America*, 59 (1944), 226-35.

Notes three pieces in the *New-York Mirror* identified as by "Boz": 1) "My First Song," a humorous sketch (14 October 1837); 2) "Reminiscences of a Good-Natured Man," a serious essay (20 April 1839); and "Hobbledchoys," a 64-line poem (7 August 1841). The Houtchenses print the first and the third, which they believe "bear the strongest indications of authenticity" and an excerpt from the second, but note that "all the evidence" of Dickens's authorship "is internal." These works have not been accepted into the Dickens canon.

505. Houtchens, Lawrence H. "The *Spirit of the Times* and a 'New Work by Boz.'" *Publications of the Modern Language Association of America*, 67 (1952), 94-100.

Gives details of a hoax perpetrated by the American journal, *The Spirit of the Times*, to avenge itself on cheap journals that pirated its articles. It widely announced and then published in its issue of 29 February 1840 the first installment of what it claimed was a "New Work by Boz," which it entitled *Marmaduke Myddleton*. When *The Spirit of the Times* announced its hoax, Houtchens reports, a number of other journals were caught "red-handed" reprinting the installment—and making quite obviously false claims about the authorship and their source for the manuscript.

506. Huff, Lawrence. "The Lamar-Dickens Connection." *Mississippi Quarterly*, 40 (1987), 113-15.

A note about a story in *Household Words*, "Colonel Quagg's Conversion," early attributed to Dickens but actually by George Sala, though perhaps, Huff suggests, showing Dickens's editorial hand. The story was based, Huff points out, on a story by John Basil Lamar, a Georgia (USA) planter and author. Lohrli (**155**) also attributes the piece to Sala.

507. Hughes, T. Cann. "'The Picnic Papers.'" *Notes and Queries*, 163 (1932), 296.

Provides some details and has some queries about the authorship of the forty pieces published in *The Pic Nic Papers* (the correct title), which Dickens edited (1841). T. O. Mabbott, p. 463, comments further on the publication and on Edgar Allan Poe's review of it in *Graham's Magazine*, November 1841.

508. Kitton, F[rederic] G. "Dickens's 'Household Words.'" *Notes and Queries*, 8th ser., 9 (1896), 327.

Indicates that he has rediscovered the home of the office set of *All the Year Round* (though he does not say where, and it has not since been located) in which the names of the authors of the articles are written in. Kitton asks whether or not a similar set is extant for *Household Words*. Such a set does exist, though no one answered Kitton's query at the time. It is now in the Princeton University Library and was used by Anne Lohrli as the basis for her ***Household Words: A Weekly Journal, 1850-1859, Conducted by Charles Dickens*** (**155**). Kitton used the set of *All the Year Round* in writing his *The Minor Writings of Charles Dickens: A Bibliography and Sketch* (**154**). It was then, as he notes (p. vii), in the possession of W. H. Howe. In establishing Dickens's writings for *Household Words* and *All the Year Round*, Percy Fitzgerald (**152**) claimed to have seen the office sets of both journals, but that for *All the Year Round* has vanished, as Oppenlander indicates in her *Dickens' **All the Year Round**: Descriptive Index and Contributor List* (**158**), for which she had use only of the *All the Year Round* Letter Book. Also see G. F. R. B. (**488**), Matz (**425**), Suddaby (**536**), and Thomas (**538**).

509. Kitton, F[rederic] G. "A Pseudo-Dickens Item." *Notes and Queries*, 9th ser., 1 (1898), 144-45.

Notes that the "Remarks" in *Methods of Employment . . . With Remarks by Charles Dickens, Esq.* (London: Privately printed, 1852) were quoted from *Household Words* but not written by Dickens.

510. Kitton, F[rederic] G. "Pseudo-Dickens Rarities." *Athenaeum*, no. 3646 (11 September 1897), 355-56.

Dispels the book collector's belief that *More Hints on Etiquette for the Use of Society at Large, and Young Gentlemen in Particular* (1838), *Sergeant Bell and His Raree Show* (1839), *Lizzie Leigh* (1850–actually by Elizabeth Gaskell), *A Curious Dance Round a Curious Tree* (1852), and *Drooping Buds* (1866) were written in whole or in part by Dickens. For further discussion of the authorship of *Sergeant Bell and His Raree Show*, see Prideaux (**527**), Shepherd (**533**), and Van

Noorden (**542**). For comments on *A Curious Dance*, see Matz and Thomson (**520**). For the authorship of *Drooping Buds*, see Johnson (**478**) and Matz (**519**).

511. Lamb, Virginia K. "Notes et Documents: Nerval, Dickens et . . . Sala." *Revue de Littérature Comparée*, 53 (1979), 84-86.

Points out that an article entitled "Key of the Street," published in *Household Words*, 6 September 1851, that Gérard de Nerval used as a model, convinced it was by Dickens, was actually by George A. Sala, as indicated by Harry Stone in his *Charles Dickens's Uncollected Writings from "Household Words" 1850-1859* (**449**), II, 409, where Stone quotes from a letter Dickens wrote to W. H. Wills that he had "delicately altered" Sala's "very remarkable piece of description."

512. "'Lines Written on the Sands,' Attributed to Dickens." *Dickensian*, 4 (1908), 238.

Attributes a poem of dubious distinction to Dickens. But see a letter to the editor by Arthur J. Prentice, p. 303, for the suggestion that the poem is probably by A. A. Procter.

513. Lohrli, Anne. "Greek Slave Mystery." *Notes and Queries*, ns 13 (1966), 58-60.

Comments on but does not answer the question of how a poem, "Hiram Power's Greek Slave," sometimes attributed to Dickens but clearly by Elizabeth Barrett Browning, came to be published anonymously in Dickens's *Household Words*, 26 October 1850.

514. Lohrli, Anne. "*Household Words* and Its 'Office Book.'" *Princeton University Library Chronicle*, 26 (1964/65), 27-47.

This richly detailed study describes the appearance of the *Household Words* "Office Book" in the Morris L. Parrish Collection, Princeton University Library, comments on how the entries were recorded, and points out some problems of attribution. The book is, Lohrli points out, a "working record," kept by W. H. Wills, the subeditor, with the "occasional omission and errors," on many of which Lohrli remarks. For her important work on the contributors to *Household Words*, based on the Office Book, see Lohrli (**155**). Material from this essay, somewhat revised, Lohrli reports in the acknowledgments to that work, "forms the basis of the section of the Introduction titled 'The *Household Words* Office Book.'"

515. Lohrli, Anne. "*Household Words* Anthologies for American Readers." *Dickens Studies Annual*, 14 (1985), 205-40.

On the various anthologies of articles from *Household Words* published in the United States, most of whose pieces were not by Dickens himself. Lohrli provides the relevant bibliographical information and lists the contents of anthologies published by George Putnam, Bunce & Brother, John E. Beardsley, and H. C. Peck & Theo. Bliss, 1852-54. Illustrated.

516. M[atz], B. W. "A Child's Hymn in 'The Wreck of the Golden Mary.'" *Dickensian*, 12 (1916), 128-30.

In reexamining a work sometimes attributed to Dickens, sometimes to Harriet Parr (writing under the pen name of "Holme Lee"), Matz supports Parr as the author, largely on the evidence that the hymn appeared in "Poor Dick's Story," which she wrote. A letter to the editor by J. T. Page, pp. 192-93, offers further support for Matz's view. Lohrli (**155**) also supports this view, pp. 395-96, where she reviews evidence for this attribution. Stone (**449**), however, seems to think that Dickens wrote the poem (p. 564).

517. [Matz, B. W.]. "Dickens's Christmas Numbers. His Anonymous Contributors Identified." *Daily Graphic* (London), 22 November 1906, p. 12.

Provides new information and corrects misconceptions about contributors to the *Household Words* Christmas numbers.

518. Matz, B. W. "'Dickensiana.'" *Times Literary Supplement*, 25 May 1916, p. 249.

In a letter to the editor, Matz points out that, though "Sister Rose in Seven Chapters," published anonymously in *Household Words*, 7-24 April 1855, is sometimes attributed to Dickens, it was actually written by Wilkie Collins. Matz mentions three other anonymously published pieces sometimes attributed to Dickens that were not by him—Elizabeth Gaskell's "Lizzie Leigh" (*Household Words*, 30 March, 6 and 13 April 1850), William Howitt's "The Miner's Daughters" (*Household Words*, 4-18 May 1850), and "Fortune Wildred, the Foundling" (whose author Matz does not know). Also see Matz (**519**).

519. Matz, B. W. "Writings Wrongly Attributed to Dickens." *Chambers's Journal*, 7th ser., 14 (1924), 603-06; reprinted in *Dickensian*, 21 (1925), 128-32.

Identifies a number of works written by other authors and willfully, wrongly, or mistakenly attributed to Dickens, particularly pieces originally published in *Household Words*. Matz uses as examples "Fortune Wildred, the Foundling," "Lizzie Leigh" (actually by Elizabeth Gaskell), "The Miner's Daughters" (William Howitt), "Sister Rose" (Wilkie Collins), "A Suburban Romance" (W. H. Wills), "The Daily Governess," a series of papers entitled

"Abuses of the Law" (by various authors), "A Curious Dance Round a Curious Tree" (W. H. Wills–but see **520**), "A Plated Article" (W. H. Wills and Dickens), "Drooping Buds" (Henry Morley), "Foreigners' Portraits of Englishmen" (W. H. Wills and Eustace Murray), "'Household Words' and English Wills" (W. H. Wills), "Epsom" (W. H. Wills), "Douglas Jerrold" (Wilkie Collins), and "By Rail to Parnassus" (Henry Morley). Lohrli (**155**) attributes "Drooping Buds" to Morley and Dickens, "Epsom" to Wills and Dickens, and "Foreign Portraits of Englishmen" to Wills, Murray, and Dickens. Stone (**449**) reprints and identifies where possible Dickens's contributions to "Foreign Portraits of Englishmen," I, 143-50; "Epsom," I, 296-310; "A Curious Dance Round a Curious Tree," II, 381-91; and "Drooping Buds," II, 401-08. Stone also reprints "'Household Words' and English Wills," though conceding it may be "possibly entirely by Wills" (I, 182) and "By Rail to Parnassus," though finding "little of Dickens' work" in the piece. The *Dickensian* reprint of Matz's article contains minor variations and the omission of a paragraph in which Matz faults himself for having credited Dickens, in the original edition of *Miscellaneous Papers, Plays, and Poems* (**425**) in the National Edition of Dickens's works with the authorship of two poems, "Hiram Power's Greek Slave," accredited by Lohrli to Elizabeth Barrett Browning, and "Aspire" (no attribution in Lohrli). Also see Matz (**518**).

520.   Matz, B. W., and J. C. Thomson. "A Curious Dance Round a Curious Tree." *Athenaeum*, no. 4064 (16 September 1905), 370.

Matz and Thomson really get the argument going about the authorship of "A Curious Dance Round a Curious Tree," published in *Household Words*, 17 January 1852, though the dispute actually began in a review of Luther S. Livingston's *Auction Prices of Books*, vol. 2 (1905), in the *Athenaeum*, no. 4061 (26 August 1905), 264-65 (**2064**), where the anonymous reviewer points out that, although Livingston attributes "A Curious Dance" to Dickens, it was really by W. H Wills, as noted by F. G. Kitton in the *Athenaeum*, 11 September 1897 (**510**). In "Literary Gossip," in no. 4062 (2 September 1905), 308-09, a correspondent, Lewis Johnson, is quoted as pointing out that the work *was* written by Dickens, for he had seen the manuscript, then in the possession of Thomas J. Wise. In a brief letter to the editor in the 16 September issue, B. W. Matz, then editor of the *Dickensian*, speculates about the authorship, suggesting that Dickens undoubtedly had an editorial hand in the revision of the piece but adding that he would like to see the manuscript, and J. C. Thomson points out that, in a note in *Old Leaves Gathered from Household Words* (**487**), in which the piece was reprinted, W. H. Wills indicates that portions of his *Household Words* articles published therein were "by another hand," most obviously Dickens's. Thomson finds it "almost inconceivable" that Wills would have claimed the work as his own had it not been. Under the same title in no. 4066 (30 September 1905), p. 437, H. Buxton Forman writes that obviously it was a case of joint authorship but that only the parts by Dickens (about one-half the work, he estimates) are "worth reading." He notes, however, that the manuscript is no longer in Wise's possession, though he had been given a chance while it was to examine the portion of it in Dickens's hand, and it was filled with erasures and corrections and clearly Dickens's original work. In "Literary Gossip," in no. 4067 (7 October 1905), 472-73, J. J. Hays writes that he knows the two women who were at the charity event at St. Luke's described in the article, and they noticed that both Dickens and Will, who were also there, "were keenly observant of everything." Finally, in no. 4083 (27 January 1906), 108-09, Percy Fitzgerald reaffirms that both Dickens and Wills must have had a hand in the writing of the piece. Stone (**449**), II, 381-91, reprints "A Curious Dance Round a Curious Tree," identifying it as "primarily by Dickens" and pinpointing the portions that Dickens wrote from an extant ten-page portion of the manuscript in Dickens's hand in the Berg Collection, New York Public Library. He also comments on revisions Dickens may have made in Wills's portion of the article, discusses the "heavily canceled and interlineated" manuscript itself, and includes a photographic reproduction of a page of the manuscript. See further "A Curious Dance Round a Curious Tree" (**470**), Kitton (**510**), Matz (**519**), and Muir (**523**).

521. Merivale, Herman. "With the Majority." *Temple Bar*, 80 (1887), 181-95.

Prints a letter he received from Dickens, dated 3 March 1869, accepting an article by Merivale, "Last of the Low Comedians," for *All the Year Round* if he did not object "to its being much condensed, and narrowed into a remembrance of [Robert] Keeley," with whom most of the article was concerned (it was published as "Robert Keeley," 10 April 1869). Dickens worked hard on the essay, Merivale reports, adding information from his own experience and pruning and editing it fairly drastically, including the addition of "a page and a half at the end, so carefully and skilfully interwoven with my own work and the tone of it that one might well be puzzled where the link was forged."

522. Moss, Sidney P. "Did Forster Write the *Foreign Quarterly* Article on 'American Poetry'?" *Papers of the Bibliographical Society of America*, 80 (1986), 461-68.

Argues that John Forster did not write the article that was highly critical of American poetry that appeared in the January 1844 issue of *Foreign Quarterly Review* and that was subsequently condemned by William Cullen Bryant, Park Benjamin, and Edgar Allan Poe, who was himself convinced that Dickens had written it—see Gerald G. Grubb's "The Personal and Literary Relationships of Dickens and Poe (Part Two: 'English Notes' and 'The Poets of America')," *Nineteenth-Century Fiction*, 5 (1950/51), 101-20. Moss, however, provides no evidence to support Dickens, or anyone else for that matter, as the author.

523. Muir, P. H. "Note 295. *A Curious Dance Round a Curious Tree*." *Book Collector*, 17(1968), 80-81.

For the bibliophile, comments on the manuscript and published version (in *Household Words*, 17 January 1852) of this piece, which was written by Dickens and W. H. Wills, 217 out of 393 lines of the printed text being in Dickens's hand in the manuscript. For the controversy over the authorship of this piece, see Matz and Thomson (**520**).

524. Peters, Catherine. "*All the Year Round*: An Attribution." *Notes and Queries*, ns 37 (1990), 36-37.

In an addendum to Oppenlander (**158**), provides evidence that Frances Eliot was the author of "The Old Cardinal's Retreat," a story published in *All the Year Round*, 8 January 1870.

525. Peterson, Linda H. "Mother-Daughter Productions: Mary Howitt and Anna Mary Howitt in *Howitt's Journal, Household Words*, and Other Mid-Victorian Publications." *Victorian Periodicals Review*, 31 (1998), 31-54.

Touches upon the series "Bits of Life in Munich," written by Anna Mary Howitt and, as here indicated, edited by her mother Mary Howitt, for *Household Words*, 1850-51. The daughter is identified as the author of these articles in Lohrli (**155**).

526. Pierpont, Robert. "Mrs. Marsh, Authoress of 'The Valley of a Hundred Fires.'" *Notes and Queries*, 10th ser., 8 (1907), 149.

Notes (incorrectly) that Mrs. Marsh was also the author of "His Portmanteau" and "His Hat Box," two stories in *Somebody's Luggage*, Dickens's Christmas Number for *All the Year Round*, 1862, and asks for her full name. The replies, pp. 150 and 253, do not concern her work for Dickens but note that the author of these stories was more likely a Mrs. Stretton. Oppenlander (**158**) identifies Julia Cecilia Stretton as the author of the two pieces. According to Lohrli (**155**), Marsh's first name was probably Anne.

527. Prideaux, W. F. "'Serjeant Bell and His Raree Show.'" *Notes and Queries*, 9th ser., 12 (1903), 306-07.

Asserts that there is "absolutely no evidence to show that Dickens had any share whatever in the production of this work, negotiations between Dickens and Thomas Tegg, the publisher, over it having fallen through."

528. Ratchford, Fannie E. *Letters of Thomas J. Wise to John Henry Wrenn: A Further Inquiry into the Guilt of Certain Nineteenth-Century Forgers*. New York: Alfred A. Knopf, 1944, pp. 259-60 and passim.

In a letter dated 8 May 1902, Wise offers Wrenn a copy of Dickens's *To Be Read at Dusk* (forged by Wise with a fake publication date of 1852), noting its rarity and its good price. In other letters to Wrenn, Wise comments occasionally on collecting Dickens.

529. Reed, A[lfred] H. "Introduction." In *From the Black Rocks, on Friday, and A Gold Digger's Notes*. Edited (or Written?) by Charles Dickens. Wellington, NZ: A. H. and A. W. Reed for the Dunedin Public Library Association, 1950, pp. 9-16.

Reed notes that the author of "From the Black Rocks, on Friday," a story about New Zealand, published in *All the Year Round*, 17 May 1862, is unknown, but he believes that the story "owes a great deal of its charm to Dickens himself," perhaps through Dickens's editorial revisions of someone else's work. Dickens may have been interested in it, Reed suggests, because two of his sons had emigrated to Australia and he was himself in 1862 "on the point of accepting an invitation to undertake an eight months' reading tour of Australia for a fee of £10,000, and this would no doubt have brought him to New Zealand." The proposal, however, "fell through." In his brief introduction to "A Gold-Digger's Notes," p. 42, Reed states that Dickens probably left this piece "pretty much as it came to him." Also see Reed (**1717**), pp. 57-61. Oppenlander (**158**) gives no author for either work, but see Ross and Bagnall (**532**), who identify the author of the two works as Reverend Robert Carter.

530. Reeves, David W. "Boz in the Black Country?" *Blackcountryman*, 10, ii (Spring 1977), 68.

Reeves prints what he claims to be an excerpt from "a collection of sketches and essays supposedly from the pen of Charles Dickens," written in Blackcountry dialect from the coal and iron-producing districts in Warwickshire and Staffordshire. The excerpt, however, is surely spurious or, more likely, creative.

531. Ritchie, Anne Thackeray. "Lord Bateman: A Ballad. With Hitherto Unpublished Drawings by William Makepeace Thackeray: Comment." *Harper's New Monthly Magazine*, 86 (1892/93), 124-29.

Prints previously unpublished drawings her father did to accompany *Lord Bateman: A Ballad* and comments on the "delightful notes" appended to a then modern edition of the poem published with George Cruikshank's illustrations (originally published, with the notes, in 1839). These notes, as Ritchie indicates, have been variously attributed to Cruikshank, Dickens, and her father. They "*sound* like Mr. Dickens's voice," she states, "and the ballad like my own father's," though she admits that she has "absolutely no foundation" for these impressions. After reviewing what Georgina Hogarth, Charles Johnson (**477**), and others have had to say on the subject, she concludes that the matter remains a mystery. See Dexter (**325**), Lucas (**480**), and Spencer (**535**), for further speculation about the authorship of the notes, and Haight (**475**), who finally resolves the issue of attribution in Dickens's favor in 1939 on the evidence of two letters from Dickens to Cruikshank. A letter from Thackeray to Cruikshank (May? 1839), further indicates that Thackeray had no hand in the volume—see *The Letters and Private Papers of William Makepeace Thackeray*, ed. Gordon N. Ray, 4 volumes (Cambridge, MA: Harvard University Press, 1945-46), I, 380-81.

532. Ross, R[uth] M., and A. G. Bagnall. "'From the Black Rocks on Friday': More than a Bibliographical Footnote." *Turnbull Library Record*, 16 (1983), 45-53.

In reference to A. H. Reed's 1950 republication of two stories from *All the Year Round*, the first of which was "From the Black Rocks on Friday" (**529**), Ross and Bagnall point out that Dickens was *not* the author of this work. They identify the author of the two pieces as the Reverend Robert Carter of New Zealand, who was living in Lincolnshire at the time.

533. Shepherd, Richard H. "A Forgotten Children's Book of Charles Dickens." *Walford's Antiquarian*, 12 (1887), 33-37; reprinted as "Sergeant Bell's Raree Show." *Gentleman's Magazine*, 267, ns 43 (1889), 596-99.

Believes it "more than probable that a considerable portion" of *Sergeant Bell and His Raree Show*, a children's book, was by Dickens, but that he withdrew from the project before finishing the work, but see Kitton (**510**) and Van Noorden (**542**), who point out the fallacy of such attribution.

534. Spackman, M. L. "A Cookery Book." *Notes and Queries*, ns 1 (1954), 38.

Asks about a cookbook compiled by Dickens's wife. In reply, C. A. T., p. 180, provides the title of the fifty-five page work published in 1851, with a new edition in 1852: *What Shall We Have for Dinner?* by Lady Maria Clutterbuck, Catherine Dickens's pseudonym.

535. Spencer, Walter T. "'Loving Ballad of Lord Bateman,' 1839." *Times Literary Supplement*, 2 May 1935, p. 288.

A letter to the editor that describes an incident that Spencer thinks may have been the source of the inaccurate information that Dickens was author

of the poem *The Loving Ballad of Lord Bateman*. In response, A. M. Cohn
(p. 313) offers some verses from about 1790 that he thinks may have been the
"inspiration" for the poem, Spencer (p. 364) amplifies upon his original remarks, S. Hodgson (p. 380) speculates that Dickens may have done the verse
and Thackeray (rather than Cruikshank) the drawings, and M[orris] L. Parrish,
12 December 1936, p. 1035, comments on a proof copy of an edition of the
poem containing additions in Cruikshank's hand. See Dexter (**325**), Johnson
(**477**), Lucas (**480**), Ritchie (**531**), and particularly Haight (**475**), who resolves
the issue of attribution.

536. Suddaby, John. "Dickens's 'The Blacksmith' Song." *Dickensian*, 11
      (1915), 163.

A letter to the editor giving details of a musical setting by J. L. Hatton,
published in *Musical Cabinet No. 170* (London and New York: Boosey & Co.,
n. d.), for a poem from *All the Year Round* that Suddaby assumes to be by
Dickens. A letter from William Miller, pp. 194-95, warns that the poem may
be by Dickens's friend, B. W. Procter ("Barry Cornwall"), as indicated in the
"office" set of *All the Year Round*. Suddaby replies, pp. 250-51, by reviewing
the frequent attribution (originally in *Forster*) of the song to Dickens and adding that he himself "should be happy if the song be either a Dickens or a
Dickensian one." Oppenlander (**158**), p. 64, lists both Dickens and Procter
(with a question mark for each) as possible author of "Trade Songs: The Blacksmith," published in the issue for 30 April 1859.

537. Thomas, Deborah A. "A Christmas Story Dickens Never Wrote." *New
      York Times*, 11 February 1972, p. 36.

In a letter to the editor, Thomas points out that "What Christmas Is in the
Company of John Doe," reprinted in the *New York Times*, 25 December 1971,
p. 1, from *Harper's New Monthly Magazine*, February 1852, and attributed there
as well as in the *New York Times* reprint to Dickens, was actually written by
George Augustus Sala and was originally printed in *Household Words*, in the
extra Christmas number for 1851. Thomas chides the *New York Times* for misleading its readers in several respects.

538. Thomas, Deborah A. "Contributors to the Christmas Numbers of
      Household Words and *All the Year Round*, 1850-1867." *Dickensian*, 69
      (1973), 163-72; 70 (1974), 21-29.

Uses the account book for *Household Words* (now in the Princeton University Library, Princeton, NJ) and other sources for *All the Year Round*, since its
Office Book has disappeared, to identify the writers of the various stories in
Dickens's Christmas numbers of these magazines. These are listed year by
year, with explanatory comments.

539. Tillotson, Kathleen, and Nina Burgis. "Dickens at Drury Lane." *Dickensian*, 65 (1969), 80-83.

The authors reprint an anonymous review of an adaptation of Donizetti's *La Favorita* and a farce, *My Wife's Come* (by Edward and John Maddison Morton), in the *Examiner*, 21 October 1843. They believe the review is by Dickens and "unmistakeably" in his style.

540. Tillotson, Kathleen, and Nina Burgis. "Forster's Reviews in the *Examiner*, 1840-1841." *Dickensian*, 68 (1972), 105-08.

Tillotson and Burgis itemize John Forster's reviews in the *Examiner*, 1840-1841, based on his underlining of items in the paper's indexes for those years. These items include some fifty reviews, many substantial, and some twenty theatrical notices done over fifteen months, not all previously identified as Forster's. Where Dickens is concerned, Tillotson and Burgis provide confirmation that Forster wrote reviews of *The Old Curiosity Shop* and *Barnaby Rudge* but not the short notice of the third edition of *Oliver Twist* (1841). See also Brice (**1390-91**) and Collins (**1395**).

541. Todd, William B. "A Handlist of Thomas J. Wise." In *Thomas J. Wise: Centenary Studies*. Ed. William B. Todd. Austin: University of Texas Press, 1959, pp. 80-122.

A list of Wise's publications, indicating which are forgeries. There are five Dickens items, pp. 89-90, one of which, *To Be Read at Dusk* (with a false date of 1852), is identified as a forgery.

542. Van Noorden, C[harles]. "'Sergeant Bell and His Raree Show.'" *Dickensian*, 5 (1909), 224.

A letter to the editor pointing out that the actual author of this work was George Mogridge (1787-1854) using the pseudonym of "Peter Parley." Also see Kitton (**510**) and Shepherd (**533**).

543. Welch, J. Cuthbert. "'More Hints on Etiquette.'" *Notes and Queries*, 8th ser., 2 (1892), 26.

Notes that the London bookseller, Walter T. Spencer, advertised a copy of *More Hints on Etiquette, for the Use of Society at Large* (London: Tilt, 1838) as having been written by Dickens and George Cruikshank—on the basis of the handwritten manuscript then in the possession of William Wright. Also see Kitton (**510**), who argues that Dickens was not the author of the work.

544. Wells, Charles. "The World of Books: Contributors to H. W." *Bristol Times and Mirror*, 3 June 1916, p. 24.

Comments on the account book that W. H. Wills kept for *Household Words*, which provides the names of contributors of articles.

545. Wells, Charles. "The World of Books: Not D." *Bristol Times and Mirror*, 3 June 1916, p. 24.

Points out that "Sister Rose in Seven Chapters," then being offered for sale in New York, is, as B. W. Matz has indicated (**519**), by Wilkie Collins and not by Dickens.

546. "Who Wrote Dickens?" *Macmillan's Magazine*, 54 (1886), 112-15.

Pretends to describe the theories of an American group of "Spencerians" who purportedly believed that Dickens's works were written by Herbert Spencer since someone with Dickens's lack of education could not possibly have done so and since there are similarities between the ideas of Dickens and Spencer.

547. "Who Wrote Dickens's Novels?" *Cornhill Magazine*, 58, ns 11 (1888), 113-21; also in *Eclectic Magazine*, ns 48 (1888), 540-44.

In this parody of those who think Sir Francis Bacon wrote Shakespeare's plays, attributes Dickens's writings to William Gladstone for roughly comparable reasons.

548. "Women in the Home." *Dickensian*, 23 (1926/27), 106-07.

Reprints a brief essay presumed to be by Dickens on "the question of Education and the influence of Women in the Home" from a manuscript, with the comment that it is not known where the original was published. See Fielding (**500**) for a denial of the attribution of this piece to Dickens.

PART TWO: TRANSLATIONS, READINGS, ADAPTATIONS, PLAGIARISMS AND IMITATIONS, AND ILLUSTRATIONS

2A. BIBLIOGRAPHIES AND SURVEYS OF TRANSLATIONS OF DICKENS'S WORKS

Note: In most countries an equivalent to *Books in Print* (**67**) is published, usually annually; such volumes list editions of Dickens's works published and available in these countries, principally translations, as well as studies of Dickens (see, where available, their subject indexes). Unfortunately, many of these are not available in any but the largest research-oriented libraries and even there are not always up to date. The British Library, for example, contains such works for Belgium, Canada, Cuba, India, Mexico, Russia, Switzerland, and Yugoslavia, among others. Only the most major of these are included below (see **550, 563, 592-93, 595, 635**). But see *Index Translationum* (**583**) for translations of Dickens's works into many languages. Also see **Translations of Dickens's works** in part 2 of the subject index.

549. Anikst, Alexander. "Dickens in Russia." *Times Literary Supplement*, 4 June 1970, p. 617.

In addition to commenting on Dickens's influence on Russian writers and critics, Anikst briefly evaluates Russian translations of Dickens's novels.

550. Associazione Italiana Editori. "Dickens, Charles." In *Catalogo dei libri in commercio, 2002: Librie opere multimediali*. 6 vols. Milano: Editrice Bibliografica, 2002, *Autori*, I, 917-18; *Saggetti*, I, 868.

This latest edition of the Italian equivalent of *Books in Print* (**67**), lists 131 editions of Dickens's works, most in Italian translation, in the Author section. The subject index lists nine studies of Dickens in Italian.

551. Axon, William E. A. "Dickens in Welsh." *Notes and Queries*, 9th ser., 3 (1899), 225.

Mentions that the first translation of a Dickens work into Welsh was "A Child's Dream of a Star," by W. C. Davies (London, 1875).

552. Bachman, Maria. "Dickens Plagiarisms in Poland." *Kwartalnik Neofilolo-giczny*, 21 (1974), 227-31.

Comments on the "wide interest" in Dickens in Poland in the second half of the nineteenth century, most of the translations of his works into Polish being done 1862-87. Bachman lists and summarizes a number of plagiarisms—that is, imitations of Dickens's works.

553. Bathurst, Robert B. "Dickens's Liberal Russian Readers." *Dissertation Abstracts International*, 38 (1977/78), 5448A (Brown University,1977).

Analyzes the influence of Dickens on Russian authors, particularly Tolstoy and Dostoevsky, and finds that Russian readers generally have paid more attention to Dickens the social critic than to Dickens the humorist, seeing his characters "as essences, almost as emblems of social evils," rather than as examples of "psychological truth." "Reading the Russian Dickens," Bathurst concludes, "is a lesson in the problems of cultural transfer," showing "the degree to which art, interpretation and criticism can be shaped by translation, politics and cultural norms."

554. Bębenek, Stanisław, gen. ed. *Bibliografia literatury tłumaczonej na język polski wydanej w latach 1945-1976.* [Vol. 1]. Warsaw: Czytelnik, 1977, pp. 308-11; *1977-1980.* [Vol. 3]. Warsaw: Czytelnik, 1983, p. 68.

The first volume of this bibliography of literature from other countries translated into Polish contains forty-nine Dickens entries; volume 3, its supplement, lists only two Dickens items.

555. *"Biblio" 1934[-1970]: Catalog des ouvrages parus en langue française dans le monde entier.* Paris: Service Bibliographique des Messageries Hachette, 1935-71; earlier volumes reprinted New York: Kraus Reprint Corporation, 1962; continued in quarterly and annual issues, the latter as *Les livres de l'année–Biblio: Bibliographie générale des ouvrages parus en langue française, 1971[-1979].* Paris: Circle de la Librairie, 1972-80, passim.

Covers works in French published world wide. There are author, title, and subject indexes, but, since there is no heading for Dickens in the subject index, only editions of Dickens's works can be located easily. The title of this series varies. For fuller details of the ins and outs of these works, see Marcuse (**1152**), p. 45.

556. Bick, Wolfgang, Bärbel Czennia, and Sybille Rohde-Gaur. "Bibliographie der deutschen Übersetzungen der Romane von Charles Dickens." *Anglia*, 107 (1989), 65-88, 430-51.

A bibliography of German translations of Dickens's novels from 1837/38 (*Die Pickwickier*) to 1987 (*Hard Times*), showing that *Oliver Twist* has been the most frequently translated of Dickens's novels into German with seventy-four editions, *David Copperfield* second with fifty-one, and *Pickwick Papers* third with forty-five.

557. Bielecka, D[aniela]. "Dickens in Poland." *Dickens Studies Annual*, 17 (1988), 195-223.

In the first part of her study, "The Novels," Bielecka identifies some translations of Dickens's works into Polish, and her footnotes provide bibliographical information about a number of the Polish critical studies of Dickens's works that she mentions. In the second part, "Stage Adaptations," Bielecka surveys and comments on stage adaptations of Dickens's novels in Poland from World War I on and includes photographs of some of the productions. Also see Daniela Bielecka, "Dickens in Poland," in *Literatura angielska i amerykańska: problemy recepcji* [English and American Literature: Problems of Reception], ed. Anna Zagórska and Grażyna Bystydzieńska (Lublin: Uniwersytet Marii Curie-Skłodowsklej, 1988), pp. 119-35.

558. Brittain, W. H. "German Edition of the 'Pickwick Papers.'" *Dickensian*, 6 (1910), 193.

In a letter to the editor, Brittain notes publication of a German translation of *Pickwick Papers* (3rd ed., Leipzig: H. Roberts, 1842) as *Die Pickwickier* . . . –the full title being given in a reproduction of the title page of this edition.

559. Brown, James W. "Charles Dickens in Norway: 1839-1912." *Dissertation Abstracts International*, 30 (1969), 273A (University of Michigan, 1968).

This study of Dickens's reception in Norway shows, as Brown indicates in his abstract, that Dickens "was the most popular and influential non-Scandinavian novelist in Norway during the latter half of the nineteenth-century," culminating in 1912 with new translations of his works and "long commemorative articles written by outstanding critics who praised both the man and his writings." Dickens first became known in Norway in 1842, Brown points out, but was not well-known until the 1850s, when the first "Dano-Norwegian translations of his works began to appear and the pages of Norwegian magazines and newspapers were filled with articles and stories from *Household Words*." Brown also discusses Dickens's impact on Norwegian writers.

560. Caneschi, Luigi. "Bibliografia." In Dickens's *Impressioni d'Italia* [Pictures from Italy]. Translated by Luigi Caneschi. 2 vols. Lanciano, Italy: R. Carabba, 1911, pp. 11-18.

A selective short-title listing (to 1909) of Dickens's works in English, collected English editions, translations of Dickens's works into Italian (the only useful section of this bibliography), and critical and biographical studies (principally English but with some foreign-language books and articles, including Italian ones). See Izzo (**584**) for a continuation and see Piscopo (**614**).

561. Carlton, W[illiam] J. "Dickens in Shorthand." *Dickensian*, 44 (1947/48), 205-08.

Lists editions of shorthand versions of Dickens's novels and of anthologized passages from the novels in shorthand.

562. Casotti, Francesco M. "Italian Translations of Dickens." *Dickensian*, 95 (1999), 19-23.

Surveys the publication of translations of Dickens's works into Italian, largely from 1990 on. Casotti notes that many of Dickens's works "are in print and can easily be found in bookshops" and have "always proved best-sellers" in Italy, though he admits that the translations are not always good and the critical reception of Dickens has not been particularly enlightened. Even so, Dickens's works were "always widely reviewed in the main Italian dailies and periodicals," and generally favorably, and the translations sold well. Casotti adds that, though "many critics and influential scholars," such as Mario Praz, "discouraged, or even prevented, the study and appreciation of Victorian fiction and of Dickens's works in particular," Dickens still remains popular in Italy today. Over 100 Dickens titles are currently in print, Casotti points out, and Dickens is frequently mentioned in the press and in public forums, an indication that he has also become "a permanent feature of the Italian cultural background." The footnotes provide bibliographical information about many of the recent translations and about a number of serious critical studies of Dickens's works by Italian scholars, 1968-96.

563. *Cátalogo dos Livros Disponíveis, 1985[-]*. Lisbon, Port.: Associação Portuguesa de Editores e Livreiros, 1985, passim.

This Portuguese Books in Print contains author, title, and subject indexes. In the latest edition seen, *Livros Disponíveis, 1999* (for 1998), the author index lists twenty-three titles of individual Dickens novels in Portuguese. The subject index, however, uses such broad headings that it is extremely time consuming to locate any studies of Dickens's works.

564. *Charles Dickens. Bibliography of the Romanian Translations Published in Volume (1898-1966)*. Bucharest: Romanian Institute for Cultural Relations with Foreign Countries, 1967. 32 pp.

An introduction, "Charles Dickens in Romania," pp. 3-4, indicates that the volume "is meant to show the spreading of Dickens' work" translated and published in Romania, from *A Christmas Carol* in 1898, the first work translated, to *David Copperfield* in 1965, although it is noted that some of the earlier translations were made from French or German translations of Dickens's novels. The author also mentions Dickens's increased fame in Romania after World War II. The translations are listed by year of publication on pp. 7-18. Also included are an annotated list of "Writings on Charles Dickens's Life and Work" by Romanian authors and translations into Romanian of studies by non-Romanian authors, pp. 19-24; "Romanian Translations Published in Magazines and Newspapers" (beginning with the 1884 translation of "The Black Veil" from *Sketches by Boz*), pp. 25-26; and indices of translated titles, of translators, illustrators, and authors of secondary works, and of translations published since 1949 with the number of copies printed, pp. 27-32. Also see Duțu (**571**) and Duțu and Alexandrescu (**572**).

565. Chéron, M. Paul. *Catalogue général de la librairie française au XIXe siècle*. Vol. 3. Paris: P. Jannet, 1858, pp. 962-63.

Lists Dickens's works published in France in various languages, principally French, 1837-55. Also see Lorenz (**596**).

566. *Clio: Catalogo dei libri italiani dell' Ottocento (1801-1900)/Catalogue of Nineteenth Century Italian Books (1801-1900)*. 19 vols. Milan: Editrice Bibliografica, 1991, II, 1602-03.

Lists forty-eight translations of Dickens's works into Italian, more than are in Pagliaini (**611**), and locates one Italian library, principally the Biblioteca Nazionale in Florence, in which each work may be found, but it does not have a subject catalogue, which Pagliaini does.

567. Delattre, Floris. "II.–Dickens en France: Traducteurs et critiques." In his *Dickens et la France: Étude d'une interaction littéraire Anglo-Française*. Paris: Librairie Universitaire, 1927, pp. 43-88, 179-92.

Comments on some of the early translations of Dickens's works into French and the critical response in France to his novels.

568. *Deutsche Bibliographie, 1945-1950: Verzeichnis aller in Deutschland erschienenen Veröffentlichungen und der in Österreich und der Schweiz im Buchhandel erscheinenen deutschsprachigen Publikationen sowie der deutschsprachigen Veröffentlichungen anderer Länder*. 4 vols. Frankfurt: Buchhändler-Vereinigung GmbH, 1953-60, passim; continuations published annually and then semi-annually in multi-volume editions, and in five-year cumulations to date.

This bibliography of works in German published in Germany, Austria, Switzerland, and other countries includes works by Dickens and studies of his works. For the former, see under "Dickens," in Part I; for the latter, see under "Dickens" in the subject index. The latest cumulation seen covers 1991-95, in twelve volumes to date (through "Mari"), published 1998-2000. The latest semi-annual publication seen is for January-June 1999, in six volumes.

569. Devonshire, M[arian] G. "Dickens" and "Dickens (1848-1870)." In her *The English Novel in France, 1830-1870.* London: University of London Press, 1929; reprinted London: Frank Cass; New York: Octagon Books, 1967, pp. 289-97, 312-29.

In chapter 17 (pp. 289-97), Devonshire includes a list of translations into French of Dickens's novels, 1838-1847 (p. 290), and quotes from the mixed reviews they received. Chapter 19 (pp. 312-29) continues the list of translations through 1870 and lists the serial publication of Dickens's tales and novels in French magazines for the same period (pp. 313-16). The translations are also listed in two appendices, "Tales and Serials in French Periodicals (1848-1870)," pp. 449-53, passim, and "Index of Authors with Works," pp. 454-79 (see pp. 460-61).

570. Dontchev, Nicolaï. "Dickens en Bulgarie." Special Dickens Number. *Europe*, no. 488 (December 1969), 130-35.

Briefly surveys translations, dramatizations, and the few critical studies of Dickens published in Bulgaria.

571. Duţu, Alexandru. "Dickens in Romania." *Studii de literatură universală*, 16 (1970), 45-51.

In a bibliographical essay (in Romanian), Duţu notes that "The Drunkard's Death" (*Sketches by Boz*) was the first work of Dickens translated into Romanian, though he and Alexandrescu (**572**) had earlier claimed it was "The Black Veil" (also *Sketches by Boz*). Duţu identifies other translations and critical studies, almost all later than 1878, and comments on Dickens's influence on such writers as Alexandru Vlahuţă and I. L. Caragiale and the growing interest in Dickens in Romania. An English summary, from which the above information is taken, is on p. 51. Also see *Charles Dickens. Bibliography of the Romanian Translations* (**564**).

572. Duţu, Alexandru, and Sorin Alexandrescu. *Dickens in Rumania: A Bibliography for the 150th Anniversary.* Bucharest: National Commission of the Rumanian People's Republic for UNESCO, 1962. 6 pp.

Contains unannotated (and untranslated) listings of translations into Romanian, studies and references, "Chronicles on Various Dramatization[s]," and an Index of Translations giving novels and dates of their translations. According to the authors, *Barnaby Rudge, Little Dorrit, Bleak House, A Tale of Two Cities,* and *Our Mutual Friend* have never been translated into Romanian. They claim that the first work translated was "The Black Veil" from *Sketches by Boz* in 1884–but see Duţu (**571**)–and that the first novel translated was *The Old Curiosity Shop* in 1886. Illustrated. Also see *Charles Dickens. Bibliography of the Romanian Translations* (**564**).

573. Dyboski, Roman. "Dickens w Polsce" [Dickens in Poland]. In his *Charles Dickens: Życie i twórczość* [Charles Dickens: Life and Works]. Lwów-Warszawa:Książnica-Atlas, 1936, pp. 103-07.

A bibliography of Polish translations of Dickens's works and of some Polish critical studies. The volume itself, written in Polish, seems to be more a critical than a biographical study.

574. Fridlender, I. V. [*Charles Dickens . . . 1838-1945*]. Leningrad: Publičnaia Biblioteka, 1946. 127 pp.

A preliminary bibliography of translations, critical studies, biographies, reviews, and other books and articles on Dickens in Russian. See Fridlender and Katarsky (**575**) for a much fuller bibliography.

575. Fridlender, I. V., and I. M. Katarsky. [*Charles Dickens: Bibliography of Russian Translations and Critical Literature in Russian, 1838-1960*]. Moscow: Vsesoiuznaia Gosudarstvennaia Biblioteka Inostrannoi Literatury, 1962. 327 pp.

This volume is a considerable updating of Fridlender's 1946 bibliography (**574**), with an English summary (pp. 25-27) of Katarsky's introduction and an English table of contents, though the rest is in Russian. Katarsky notes that the items in this "attempt at compiling a complete Russian 'Dickensiana'" are arranged chronologically to trace "the history of Russia's growing acquaintance with Dickens' writings" and the "changing opinions of Russian literary critique to his artistic heritage." The bibliography contains 2,256 items; 1,172 are translations of Dickens's works (collected editions, individual works and magazine pieces, letters, etc.), and the rest are critical studies, bibliographical indexes and reviews, biographies, critical reviews, and dramatic versions of the novels. An extensive appendix (pp. 235-90) contains brief literary, historical, and bibliographical notes by Katarsky and others on Dickens and Russian culture. There is also an extensive index (pp. 293-322).

576. Gattégno, Jean. "Les premières traductions françaises des romans de Dickens." In special issue: "Studies in Charles Dickens." *Cahiers victoriens et edouardiens*, no. 20 (October 1984), 107-14.

Comments on some early French translations of Dickens's works.

577. Gilenson, Boris. "Dickens in Russia." *Dickensian*, 57 (1961), 56-58.

In addition to commenting on Dickens's reception by Russian authors and the Russian public, Gilenson reports that, from the October Revolution up to World War II, the general circulation of Dickens's works amounted to two million copies and, during the twelve years following the war, this figure grew to 7,500,000. The most popular works, he points out, were *Dombey and Son* (eighteen editions), *David Copperfield* and *Pickwick Papers* (seventeen editions each), and *Oliver Twist* (fourteen editions). Six editions of Dickens's collected works were published by 1961, the last, a nineteen-volume edition published in 1957, selling 600,000 copies. Gilenson does not, however, itemize these numerous editions.

578. Harper, Kenneth E., and Bradford A. Booth. "Russian Translations of Nineteenth-Century English Fiction." *Nineteenth-Century Fiction*, 8 (1953/54), 188-97.

The authors provide evidence that all the major and many of the minor nineteenth-century English novelists were extensively translated into Russian. They note that Dickens was "perhaps as widely read in Moscow and Leningrad as in London and New York" and, in a footnote, give some amazing sales figures.

579. Hornát, Jaroslav, and Ian Milner. "Dickens in Czechoslovakia, 1842-1976." *Acta Universitatis Caroliniae: Philologica*, 19 (1991), 21-55.

A study of Dickens in Czechoslovakia listed in the Modern Language Association's *MLA Bibliography* (**1042**) for 1992.

580. Howlett, B. Y. "Cultural Transfer in Translation, with particular Reference to Russian and Chinese Translations of Dickens' *David Copperfield*." *Index to Theses* (**1188**), 46 (1997), A8 (University of Leeds, 1996).

As indicated in the abstract, this is "an examination of the issue of cross-cultural transfer in translation based on a comparative study of various Russian and Chinese translations" of *David Copperfield*, "illustrating how different translators, working at different times, for widely different audiences, both pre- and post-revolutionary, have attempted to render English social and cultural relia in their respective target-language versions."

581. Hung, Eva. "The Introduction of Dickens into China (1906-1960): A Case Study in Target Culture Reception." *Perspectives: Studies in Translatology*, 4, i (1996), 29-41.

Points out that Dickens was "one of the first major English writers to be introduced into China," the first recorded mention of his work occurring in 1906. The earliest references to Dickens stressed his social criticism, Hung reports, and translations in classical Chinese by Lin Shu in collaboration with Wei Yi followed–*Nicholas Nickleby* in 1907, *David Copperfield* in 1908, and *Dombey and Son* in 1909–but little or nothing more for decades, though Dickens was often mentioned in Chinese criticism as "one of the best known foreign writers in China." After 1949, when a Communist government was established in China, Dickens was criticized for failing to "pinpoint the cause of social evil" as "an exploiting class empowered by Capitalism," Hung reports. There were, however, translations of Dickens's works in the 1940s and 1950s, she indicates, though "simplified or abridged translations far outnumbered complete works, and, despite Communist criticism, Dickens remained very popular, "one of the twelve most popular western authors in China," between 1949 and 1960.

582. H[utchinson], B[en]. "Dickens in Germany." *Book Collecting and Library Monthly*, no. 31 (November 1970), 230.

Notes that "at least two German publishers"–Frederick Fleisscher and Bernhard Tauchnitz–"were issuing Dickens in English before British copyright was recognised by some German states in 1846."

583. *Index Translationum. Repertoire International des Traductions. International Bibliography of Translations*, no. 1 (1932)-no. 31 (1940), published quarterly. Paris: International Institute of Intellectual Cooperation, 1932-40, passim; the first thirty-one numbers reprinted, 4 vols., Vaduz, Liechtenstein: Kraus Reprint, 1964, passim; continued as ns 1 (1948)-39 (1986), published annually. Paris: UNESCO (United Nations Educational, Scientific and Cultural Organization), 1948-92, passim; also on CD-ROM, 1994- , and on the Internet, passim.

Lists translations, by country, of works published around the world. Begun modestly in 1932 with translations from six countries, the *Index Translationum* in its most recent volume, ns 39 (for 1986), published in 1992, included translations from over sixty countries. See the author index for the numerous Dickens entries. Also see *Cumulative Index to English Translations, 1948-1968*. Boston: G. K. Hall, 1973, I, 232, for translations included in *Index Translationum* that were published in English-speaking countries (only four are listed for Dickens's works, however). The online database, available in libraries, announces that it "contains cumulated bibliographical information on books translated and published in about a hundred of UNESCO's Member States since 1979" and is updated quarterly. A search on 16 January 2003 produced 1,362 records for translations of Dickens's works from 1977 on, including nine for *Bleak House*, 163 for *A Christmas Carol*, and 182 for *David Copperfield*.

584. Izzo, Carlo. "Bibliografia Generale." In his *Autobiografismo di Charles Dickens*. Collezione di Varia Critica, 11. Venice: Neri Pozza Editore, 1954, pp. 173-90.

In addition to a listing of Dickens's works and studies of Dickens (largely book-length), contains a list of translations, abridgements, and adaptations in Italian, 1844-1954. The volume itself is a biographical and critical study of Dickens in Italian. See Caneschi (**560**) and Piscopo (**614**).

585. Kayser, Christian G., [et al.], eds. *Novus Index Locupletissimus Librorum . . . . Neues Bucher-Lexicon . . . , 1833-1840[-1910]*. Leipzig: Verlag von Ludwig Schumann, 1841-1911, passim; continued as *Deutsches Bücherverzeichnis: eine Zusammenstellung der im deutschen Buchhandel erschienenen Bücher, Zeitschriften und Landkarten. Nebst Stich- und Schlagwortregister Bearbeitet von der Bibliographischen Ableitung des Börsenvereins der deutschen Buchhändler zu Leipzig . . . 1911 bis 1914[-]. . . .* Leipzig: Verlag des Börsenvereins der deutschen Buchhändler zu Leipzig, 1916- , passim.

Lists books in English and German by Dickens from 1840 on. Published in multi-volume, multi-year (principally five-year) cumulations. The latest seen, for 1981-85 (volumes 80-90, published 1987-90), contained three Dickens entries. The publisher changed over the years, as did the title, but Leipzig was always the place of publication.

586. Kimura, Yuriko. "Some Problems in Translating Christian Terminology: English Victorian Novels in Japan." In *ICLA '91 Tokyo: The Force of Vision, VI: Inter-Asian Comparative Literature*. Ed. Earl Miner, Toru Haga, et al. Tokyo: International Comparative Literature Association, 1995, pp. 199-204.

Listed in the Modern Language Association bibliography (**1042**) for 1996.

587. Kogztur, Gizella. "Dickens en Hongrie." Special Dickens Number. *Europe*, no. 488 (December 1969), 124-30.

Surveys Hungarian translations of Dickens's novels and the small amount of Dickens criticism published in Hungary.

588. Kong, Haili. "Dickens in China." *Dickens Quarterly*, 4 (1987), 39-41.

Notes that the first translations of Dickens's works into Chinese (*The Old Curiosity Shop, David Copperfield,* and *Oliver Twist*) were published in China in 1907 and 1908. They were very loose translations, Kong indicates, because Lin Shu, the translator, did not know English and relied on a friend who did. Kong points out that studies of Dickens began to appear in the 1930s and 1940s, but were largely on Dickens's life or his "fictional world"; later studies, however, up to 1966, at the start of the Cultural Revolution, often referred to individual novels, though they "concentrated on Dickens's political attitudes and on his social criticism." Studies of Dickens and his works resumed in 1977, including translations of biographies from other languages, Kong reports, and translations of all of Dickens's novels, some short stories, and *Johnson* are planned. Dickens, now a "popular foreign writer" in China, has had a great influence on almost all Chinese writers, Kong points out, with more scholarly activity in the offing.

589. Lann, Eugeny. "Dickens' Early Style and the Translation of the 'Posthumous Papers of the Pickwick Club.'" *The Literary Critic* or *Literatura ir kalba* (Vilnius), 1 (1940), 156-71.

Listed in the Modern Humanities Research Association bibliography (**1039**) for 1940 and in Gold (**982**).

590. Lary, N[ikita] M. "Select Bibliography." In his *Dostoevsky and Dickens: A Study of Literary Influence.* London and Boston: Routledge and Kegan Paul, 1973, pp. 162-65.

In addition to listing English studies of Dickens's influence on Dostoevsky, the select bibliography lists a number of critical studies in Russian that were published in Russia (the titles are not translated, unfortunately), and seven translations of individual Dickens works into Russian (while noting that "the complete list of translations available to Dostoevsky is much longer").

591. Leighton, Lauren G. *Two Worlds, One Art: Literary Translation in Russia and America.* DeKalb: Northern Illinois University Press, 1991, passim.

See the index for occasional passing comments on Russian translations of Dickens's works.

592. *Libros en Venta en América Latina y España, 2000.* 11th ed. 3 vols. San Juan, PR: NISC Puerto Rico, 2000, I, 552.

Lists fifty-eight editions of Dickens's works in Spanish published in Latin America, Mexico, and Spain. Earlier editions were published in 1964, 1974, 1985, 1988, 1990, 1992, 1993, and annually since 1997, in various places, by various publishers, and with the title *Libros en Venta en Hispanoamérica y España* for the first through seventh editions. There are author, title, and subject (by Dewey Decimal listing) indexes.

593. *Libros españoles en venta, 1983[-].* Madrid: Agencia Española del ISBN, Ministerio de Cultura, Centro del Libro y la Lectura, 1983/84- , passim.

Balay (**1133**), p. 92, notes that this catalogue of Spanish books in print is published irregularly. The latest edition seen, for 1996, was published in five volumes, with a three-volume author-title index and a two-volume subject index. Eighty-four translations of works by Dickens are listed under his name in the *Autor-Titulo* index, I, 1107-08. Fifteen additional works are included in a 1997 *Addenda,* seventeen in a 1998 *Addenda,* and seventeen in a 1999 *Addenda.* Balay indicates that this continues *Libros españoles: catalogo ISBN* (1973) and *Libros españoles ISBN* (1974-82).

594. Lindblad, Ishrat. "Dickens in Swedish." *Stockholm Papers in English Language and Literature,* Publication 4 (April 1984), 1-68.

In his first chapter, Lindblad notes that Dickens was introduced to Sweden through Germany and that the first translation of Dickens into Swedish, extracts from *Sketches by Boz* and *Pickwick Papers,* was published in 1839 and the first complete novel, *Nicholas Nickleby,* in 1842, with all of the novels being published in Swedish translation by 1880, except for *The Mystery of Edwin Drood,* which was not translated until 1957. Lindblad also traces Dickens's now up, now down, reputation in Sweden and, more briefly, his influence on several Swedish writers. In chapter 2 Lindblad comments on the Swedish translations as well as on editions of Dickens's works published in English in Sweden, pointing out that *David Copperfield, A Tale of Two Cities,* and *Great Expectations* were Dickens's most popular novels in Sweden. Later chapters are concerned with bibliographies, biographies and letters, and critical studies. In a concluding chapter, Lindblad asserts that, despite the ups and downs of Dickens's reputation in Sweden, "there have been continual signs of an interest in Dickens," with only Shakespeare, among English authors, having "made a greater or more enduring impact" on Sweden. Dickens's novels, he concludes, "will remain a part of Sweden's cultural heritage," with a "handful of his major novels" continuing "to be loved and read." Lindblad also includes a "Bibliography of Translations," pp. 53-68, listed by individual work, with the translators and other publication information provided, and comments on three works in Swedish that are concerned with Dickens's reputation in the country. The first is Paul Brandberg's doctoral dissertation, "Dickens och Sverige" (Uppsala, 1945), which "contains an account of the reception of Dickens in the Swedish press especially the critics who contributed to *Aftonbladet* during the 1850's" and also describes "at some length" Dickens's influence on Emilie Flygare-Carlén. The second work Lindblad describes is Märta Eneberg's *Charles Dickens I sin samtids Finland, skrifter utgivna av Svenska litteratursällskapet I*

Finland: Historiska och litteraturhistoriska studier 35 (Helsinki, 1960), which is "a survey of Dickens's reputation in Finland during his lifetime," though it is "somewhat limited by the fact that it does not take into account his reception in neighbouring countries like Sweden, Denmark and Germany, which exercised a definite influence on Finnish cultural life during that period." The third work is Gunnel Tottie's *Dickens I Sverige, studier I Dickens mottagande I Sverige 1839-74 samt hans betydelse för August Blanches författarskap* (Stockholm, 1960), which "covers some of the same ground as Brandberg's, but goes far beyond it in scope and thoroughness" in discussing "the rise of interest" in the English novel in Sweden and tracing "the ups and downs of Dickens' reputation in Sweden during his lifetime." According to Lindblad, Tottie also surveys "some of the most important contemporary Swedish critics and suggests that the writer Auguste Blanche was greatly influenced by Dickens."

595. *Livres disponibles, 2001/French Books in Print: Ouvrages disponibles publiés en langue française dans le monde. Liste des éditeurs et liste des collections de langue française.* 6 vols. Paris: Electre, 2000, passim.

Contains two volumes each of *Auteurs, Titres,* and *Sujets.* The author index, I, 1230, lists fifty-five editions of individual Dickens novels, principally in French translation. The subject index is based on the Dewey Decimal classification, and Dickens novels as well as studies of Dickens can be found in the appropriate categories.

596. Lorenz, Otto H., [et al.]. *Catalogue général de la librairie française, pendant 25 ans (1840-1865)[-1922-1925].* 34 vols. Paris: O. Lorenz [and, later, other publishers], 1867-1931/45; reprinted Nendeln, Liechtenstein: Kraus Reprint, 1967-70, passim; continued as *La Librairie français: Catalogue général des ouvrages en vente au 1er Janvier 1930.* 3 vols. Paris: Au Cercle de la Librairie, 1931-32, passim, with supplements of varying years' duration to 1946/56, and then annually with subtitle *Les Livres de l'année* and, later, the title *La Librairie française: Les Livres de l'année: Catalogue général des ouvrages parus en langue française* through 1970, and then as *Les Livres de l'année–Biblio: Bibliographie générale des ouvrages parus en langue française,* 1971-78, and finally as *Les Livres du mois* to date, passim; also, to fill in the missing years, *Catalogue général des ouvrages en langue française, 1926-1929.* 9 vols. München, New York, London, Oxford, Paris: K. R. Saur, 1987, passim.

Lists translations of Dickens's works into French. Also see Chéron (**565**).

597. Łyżwińska, Maria, and Andrzej Weseliński. "Dickens in Poland: 1839-1981." In *Anglica: Studies in English and American Literature.* Warsaw: Wydawnictwa uniwersytetu Warsawskiego, 1988, pp. 123-40.

The authors comment on Dickens's impact on Polish "literary life and critical scholarship," noting that twelve of his novels and several lesser works have been translated into Polish. As early as the 1840s, they indicate, there was "a steady increase of information about Dickens in Polish newspapers and periodicals," with critical notices emphasizing the social criticism in his works, as was true of later "modernist" critics. Interest in Dickens decreased in the first decade of the twentieth century, they point out, but grew in the second decade with a new translation of *Pickwick Papers* (1910) and a critical evaluation (in Polish, 1912) by Andrzej Tretiak that "anticipated some of Edmund Wilson's views on Dickens's novels"; however, the first book-length study of Dickens, R. Dyboski's *Karol Dickens*, did not appear until 1936. In surveying post-World War II Polish criticism of Dickens, the authors find that it, too, emphasized Dickens's social criticism, though more recent criticism (after 1965) is more comprehensive in scope. The authors do not include a bibliography of Polish translations or criticism, but their footnotes contain references to a number of studies and translations.

598. M., H. E. "Table-Turning Extraordinary." *Notes and Queries*, 8th ser., 12 (1897), 145-46.

From a St. Petersburg writer, brief commentary on the difficulties of translating Dickensian metaphors into Russian, with examples from a passage in *Dombey and Son*.

599. Manini, Luca. "Meaningful Literary Names: Their Forms and Functions, and Their Translation." *Translator*, 2 (1996), 161-78.

Dealing in part with Italian translations of Dickens's novels, Manini notes problems in translating proper names that are meaningful in themselves, what he calls "semantically loaded names."

600. Matsumura, Masaie. "Dickens in Japan." In *Charles Dickens: Our Mutual Friend: Essays from Britain and Japan*. Tokyo: Nan'Un-Do, 1983, pp. 173-204.

Provides something of a history of Japanese scholarly interest in Dickens and other Victorian novelists, the first translation of Dickens into Japanese being, apparently and surprisingly, *Sketches of Young Couples* in 1882. Matsumura finds the "awakening of Dickensian interest in Japan" to be marked by two centennial issues of *Eigo Seinen* [Rising Generation], 1 and 15 February 1912, and the Dickens number of *Eigo Kenkyu* [Study of English], April 1929. Most of this bibliographical essay is a detailed survey of Japanese critical studies of Dickens's novels, beginning with the *Eigo Seinen* numbers of 1912, and of translations of critical studies by Western scholars into Japanese, beginning with Stefan Zweig's *Drei Meister: Balzac, Dickens, Dostoievsky* (1920) in 1935. Matsumura particularly honors the more recent studies by Tadao Yamamoto and several centennial collections of essays published in 1970 in special issues of *Eigo Seinen* and in *Dikenzu no Bungaku to Gengo* ("The Literature and Language of Dickens"), edited by Michio Masui and Matsami Tanabe, but also notes a number of major individual studies, most of them journal articles published before and after 1970. Matsumura also comments on Dickens's influence on Japanese writers, which, he notes, has not been as strong as that of such writers as Turgenev, Dostoevsky, de Maupassant, and Zola. Matsumura appends a "Bibliography of Translations" of Dickens's works into Japanese, pp. 202-04, based on his survey of the translations in his "Dickens in Japan,"in *Michi* (**601**), 34-48, and in a footnote lists his own articles on Dickens.

601. Matsumura, Masaie. "Dickens in Japan." *Michi, a Journal for Cultural Exchange*, 1, i (Spring 1978), 34-54.

In a running, evaluative commentary, identifies English editions and translations into Japanese of Dickens's works. In a second section, Matsumura comments on Dickens's impact on Japanese writers, finding the influence strongest on a few late nineteenth- and early-twentieth-century writers.

602. Mikdadi, F. H. "*David Copperfield* in Arabic." *Dickensian*, 75 (1979), 85-93.

Identifies four available translations into Arabic of *David Copperfield*, one a version for children, one for young people. All four are abridged, however, Mikdadi points out, which gives a false impression of the novel. Mikdadi offers a number of examples of the evils of abridgement, including the omission of characteristic Dickensian description in order to get the story told briefly, "vast differences in language, culture, and readership" that lead to textual modification, and passages translated *too* literally.

603. Monod, Sylvère. "'N. D. T.' ou: Le Traducteur annotateur." *Franco-British Studies: Journal of the British Institute in Paris*, no. 5 (Spring 1988), 25-37.

In a part of this essay dealing with the "Note du traducteur" (N. D. T., or translator's note), Monod comments on his annotations for his 1979 French translation of *Bleak House*, the first volume of the la Bibliothèque de la Pléiade series published by Gallimard in Paris. He acknowledges his indebtedness to the notes in his and George Ford's edition of the novel for Norton (**2327**) but points out that in the French edition he also needed to comment on the significance of Dickens's names for his characters, as well as on the wordplay, pronunciation of words (as in Chadband's "Terewth" for "Truth"), and various accents (such as what Monod terms Mademoiselle Hortense's "franglais à l'envers," her reverse Franglais).

604. Monod, Sylvère. "Translating Dickens into French." In *Dickens, Europe and the New Worlds.* Ed. Anny Sadrin. Basingstoke, Eng.: Macmillan; New York: St. Martin's Press, 1999, pp. 229-38.

Finds all existing French translations of Dickens's works "grievously imperfect" and comments on the difficulties of translating Dickens–and any great writer of English words–and his humor into French. Given these difficulties, the ideal approach, for Monod, is what he calls "identity of effect," in a translation "an impression as closely similar as possible to that produced on the English reader by the original text."

605. Munch-Peterson, Erland. "Dickens, Charles." In his *Bibliografi over oversaettelser til dansk 1800-1900 af prosafiktion fra de germanske og romanske sprog* [A Bibliography of Translations into Danish 1800-1900 of Prose Fiction from Germanic and Romance Languages]. Copenhagen: Rosenkilde og Bagger for the Kongelige Bibliotek, Nationalbibliografisk afdeling [Rosenkilde and Bagger for the Royal Library, Department of National Bibliography], 1976, pp. 74-84.

A list of Danish translations of Dickens's works.

606. Naumov, Nićifor. *Dikens kod Srba i Hrvata.* Philological Faculty of Belgrade University Monographs, 9. Belgrade: Philological Faculty of Belgrade University, 1967. 174 pp. (doctoral dissertation, University of Belgrade, 1963).

No English summary is included with this study of Dickens in Serbia and Croatia. According to Edgar Rosenberg, who reviewed it for the *Dickensian*, 66 (1970), 52-54, part 1 covers the early development of Dickens's reputation in Serbia and Croatia from 1852 on; parts 2 and 3 give the history of translations of Dickens's novels, 1865-1960; part 4 concerns dramatizations of Dickens's novels but "is almost entirely dominated by a discussion of *The Cricket on the Hearth*"; and part 5 traces Dickens's influence on a "handful" of nineteenth-century Serbo-Croatian novelists. The volume is evidence, Rosenberg concludes, that "the Slavs have been among the briskest of Dickens's foreign brokers." Naumov includes a bibliography, pp. 155-68, of Serbo-Croatian translations of Dickens's works, translations of biographical and critical studies originally published in English, and studies of Dickens by Serbo-Croatian authors (but with no English translations of titles).

607. Nielsen, Jørgen E. "Charles Dickens in Denmark." In *Proceedings from the Second Nordic Conference for English Studies* (Helsinki, 19-21 May 1983). Ed. Håkan Ringbom and Matti Rissanen. Meddelandan från Stiftelsens för Åbo Akademi Förskningsinstitut (Publications of the Research Institute of the Åbo Akademi Foundation), 92. Åbo, Finland: Åbo Akademi, 1984, pp. 489-96.

A study of Dickens's reception in Denmark, 1837-1983. Nielsen notes that "Making a Night of It," from *Sketches by Boz*, was, in 1837, the first translation of a work by Dickens into Danish, followed by a translation of *Nicholas Nickleby* (1839-41 in installments, but from a German translation) and *Pickwick Papers* and *Oliver Twist* (both in 1840). From then on, Nielsen points out, "Dickens's success was immediate and indisputable." From 1850 on, most translations were by Adam Ludwig Moltke, Nielsen notes, and appeared "simultaneously with the appearance of the original in monthly parts." Unlike some of the other Danish translators, Moltke, whose translations were largely "responsible for the impression Dickens has created on Danish readers," avoided numerous omissions of text, and was "extremely loyal" to the original text, Nielsen indicates, but his "slavish imitation" often resulted in "clumsiness, perhaps longwindedness." Nielsen points out that there have been some excellent recent translations of Dickens's novels, particularly by Eva Hemmer Hansen. He also comments on a number of critical studies.

608. Nielsen, Jørgen E. "The Danish Translations of *A Tale of Two Cities*." In *A Literary Miscellany Presented to Eric Jacobsen*. Ed. Graham D. Caie and Holger Nørgaard. Copenhagen, Den.: University of Copenhagen, 1988, pp. 388-405.

Describes and evaluates twenty-two editions of Danish translations of *A Tale of Two Cities*, 1859-1959, and their translators and compares and contrasts various translations of particular passages.

609. Nielsen, Jørgen E. "Lexicography and the Establishment of Translation Norms." In *Symposium on Lexicography III*. Ed. Karl Hyldgaard-Jensen and Arne Zettersten. Lexicographica Series Maior, 19. Tübingen, Ger.: Max Niemeyer, 1988, pp 355-64.

Examines some Danish translations of Dickens's novels, particularly those of Adam Ludwig Moltke, the principal early translator of Dickens's works into Danish, by focusing in on how "translation norms" are determined—that is, how certain terms and phrases in the original language not traditional or obvious in the second language are eventually established in the second language, such as "casualty ward," "Circumlocution Office," and "Barkis is willin'." More difficult, Nielsen indicates, are matters of dialect. Cockney English, for example, he points out, is handled in Danish by introducing occasional grammatical errors and by printing the spoken language phonetically, as Dickens did when he used "wot" instead of "what." Nielsen also discusses the problem of how to convey in translation the English notion of "gentleman" and legal terms and titles.

610. Nielsen, Jørgen E. *Den Samtidige engelske litteratur og Danmark, 1800-1840* [Contemporary English Literature in Denmark]. 2 vols. Publications of the Department of English, University of Copenhagen, 3-4. Copenhagen: Nova, 1976, I, 170-71, 452-54, and passim; II, 205.

In Danish, though Cohn and Collins (**958**) note that both an English and a Danish abstract were issued separately. The references to Dickens in the text in volume 1 are relatively few–and brief. The references to Dickens in the bibliography, which occupies volume 2, fill less than a page.

611. Pagliaini, Attilio, comp. "Dickens, Carlo." In *Catalogo Generale della Libreria Italiana dall'anno 1847 a tutto il 1899.* 3 vols. Milan: Associazione tipografico-librarià italiani, 1901-03; reprinted Vaduz, Liechtenstein: Kraus Reprint, 1964, I, 794-95; also see supplements for 1900-1910, 1911-1920, 1921-1930, 1931-1940, passim.

This author catalogue lists forty-six Italian translations of Dickens's works (the 1931-40 supplement lists fifty-six). A subject catalogue, 3 vols., 1900-20, lists all of two titles concerning Dickens. Also see *Clio* (**566**).

612. Parchevskaya, B. M. List of Russian translations of Dickens's works and publications about Dickens, 1960-80. In *Taina Charl'za Dikkensa.* By E[katerina] Y. Genieva. Moscow: Izd-vo "Knizhnaia patata," 1990, pp. 62-123, 490-511.

In Russian. According to N. Diakonova (**1272**), in addition to translations and studies of Dickens's works, Parchevskaya also includes "a list of Russian works of fiction, tales, and poems, where Dickens either is in one way or other mentioned or presented."

613. Petrie, Graham. "Dickens in Denmark: Four Danish Versions of His Novels." *Journal of European Studies,* 26 (1996), 185-93.

Comments principally on four film versions in Danish of Dickens's novels made by the Nordisk Company, 1921-24, and directed by A. W. Sandberg, but also remarks on a few earlier, very short English films, most brief excerpts from the novels concerning individual characters, 1898-1920. The four Sandberg films–*Great Expectations* (1921), *Our Mutual Friend* (1921), *David Copperfield* (1922), and *Little Dorrit* (1924)–were silent 10-11-reelers (about two hours) and were circulated widely, Petrie reports, in England, America, and Europe, where they were favorably received, though present-day Danish critics view them "much less favourably."

614. Piscopo, Ugo. "Dickens en Italie." Translated from the Italian by Camille Sinaï. Special Dickens Number. *Europe*, no. 488 (December 1969), 116-24.

Surveys Italian scholarly and critical studies of Dickens and his works, 1918-59. For bibliographies of Italian publications of Dickens's works and critical and scholarly publications in Italian about Dickens, see Caneschi (**560**) and Izzo (**584**).

615. Poyatos, Fernando. "Aspects, Problems and Challenges of Nonverbal Communication in Literary Translation." In *Nonverbal Communication and Translation: New Perspectives and Challenges in Literature, Interpretation and the Media*. Ed. Fernando Poyatos. Amsterdam and Philadelphia: John Benjamins, 1997, pp. 17-47.

Uses a number of examples from Dickens's works.

616. Prades, Juana de José. "Los Libros de Dickens en España." *El Libro Español*, 1 (1958), 515-24.

A bibliography of Spanish translations of Dickens's works, both collected editions and individual works, as well as seven biographies, four translated from other languages.

617. Prager, Leonard. "Charles Dickens in Yiddish (A Survey)." *Jewish Language Review*, no. 4 (1984), 158-78.

Comments on some translations of Dickens's works into Yiddish, the earliest being *David Copperfield* in 1894 and the latest (an example of "bitter irony," Prager indicates) *Great Expectations* in 1939. Prager also looks at Dickens's influence on writers in both Modern Yiddish and Modern Hebrew, but he finds that there has been "little original Dickens scholarship or criticism in Yiddish." He includes a "Checklist of Translations," pp. 170-73, which lists translations of *Oliver Twist, Barnaby Rudge, A Christmas Carol, The Cricket on the Hearth, Dombey and Son, David Copperfield, A Tale of Two Cities, Great Expectations*, and *Doctor Marigold's Prescriptions*.

618. Quérard, J.-M. *La littérature française contemporaine, XIX siècle.* [Vol. 1]. Paris: G.-P. Maisonneuve & Larose, [1857?]; continued by Charles Louandre and Félix Bourquelot as *La littérature française contemporaine, 1827-1844*. Vols. 2-6. Ibid., [1857]; reprinted in facsimile, 6 vols. Mayenne: Joseph Floch, 1965, III, 261-62.

Lists Dickens's earlier works published in France in both English and French.

619. Sadrin, Anny. "Traductions et adaptations françaises de *A Tale of Two Cities*." In *Charles Dickens et la France: Colloque international de Boulogne-sur-Mer, 3 Juin 1978*. Ed. Sylvère Monod. Lille, France: Presses Universitaires de Lille, [1981], pp. 77-91.

Notes only eight versions of the text of *A Tale of Two Cities* in French (as opposed to about forty of *David Copperfield*), four of which are adaptations, one an unacknowledged abridged and simplified version, and only three full translations. Sadrin also comments on a successful dramatized version of the novel in Paris in 1936.

620. S[adrin], A[nny]. "Translations of Dickens." In *Oxford Reader's Companion to Dickens*. Ed. Paul Schlicke (**2309**), pp. 567-69 (pp. 578-80 in the 2000 paperback ed.).

A concise, selective survey.

621. Sadrin, Anny. "'The Tyranny of Words': Reading Dickens in Translation." In *Dickens: The Craft of Fiction and the Challenges of Reading, Proceedings of the Milan Symposium, Gargano–September 1998*. Ed. Rossana Bonadei et al. Milano: Edizioni Unicopli, 2000, pp. 273-81.

Comments intelligently on the difficulties of translating Dickens into another language and offers a number of examples, including some engrossing contrasts in three French translations of *Great Expectations*.

622. Schmuck, Hilmar, and Willi Gorzny, gen. eds. "Dickens, Charles." In their *Gesamtverzeichnis des deutschsprachigen Schrifttums (GV), 1700-1910*. Vol. 28. München, New York, London, and Paris: K. G. Saur, 1981, pp. 387-96; also Gorzny, Willi, and Reinhard Oberschelp, gen. eds. "Dickens, Charles." In their *Gesamtverzeichnis des deutschsprachigen Schrifttums (GV), 1911-1965*. Vol. 27. München: Verlag Dokumentation, 1977, pp. 36-53.

In these catalogues of German publications, the editors list editions of Dickens's works published in Germany in both German and English.

623. Sherif, Nur. *Dickens in Arabic (1912-1970)*. Beirut, Lebanon: Beirut Arab University, 1974. 36 pp.

Notes that Dickens was first translated into Arabic with *A Tale of Two Cities* in 1912, when the novel itself "was an unknown genre in Arabic literature" and publishing "shoddy translations of English and French works" was the order of the day. Sherif adds that very little appeared either in translated novels or biography and criticism through the 1930s and into the 1940s. From the late 1940s on, he finds "a slowly developing interest" in Dickens. He discusses and evaluates the complete translations of Dickens's works that were brought out then for the first time and the critical essays that began appearing.

624. Soto Vázquez, Adolfo L. *El inglés de Charles Dickens y su traducción al español.* Monografías, 16. La Coruña, Spain: Universidade da Coruña, Servicio de publicacións, 1993. 221 pp.

A study, in Spanish, of the difficulties of translating Dickens into Spanish, especially (as determined by chapter headings) in regard to dialect, jargon and professional terminology, and malapropisms. Soto Vasquez includes a useful bibliography, pp. 209-21, that includes a list of Spanish translations of Dickens's works (pp. 210-12), as well as a list of Dickens's works in English, studies of Dickens (mainly in English), and studies (in various languages) of translating, stylistics, sociolinguistics, and dialects.

625. Special issue on Dickens in Europe. *Dutch Dickensian*, 14, xxiii (July 1993), 1-41.

Prints four lectures presented at the annual international conference of the Dickens Fellowship in Haarlem, the Netherlands, on 14 June 1992, on the reception of Dickens in Europe. Illustrated. These are preceded by an address, "Immortal Memory," pp. 4-8, by the president of the fellowship, J. H. A. Lokin, also president of the Haarlem branch.

In "Dickens in Germany," pp. 9-19, Heinz Reinhold comments on the relatively rare references to Germany in Dickens's works, on Bernhard Tauchnitz's publications in Germany of Dickens's works in English and on the pleasant relationship of the two men, and, at much greater length, on the generally "humdrum" and "often incorrect" translations of Dickens's works into German. Only the translations of Gustav Meyrink, a well-known novelist, done prior to World War I, got "very near the original," Reinhold concludes, "and no serious attempt at surpassing this achievement has since been made." He also summarizes Dickens's influence on a number of nineteenth-century and a few twentieth-century German writers and surveys the critical reception of Dickens in Germany and its decline after World War I, caused largely, he believes, by the "era of naturalism" in German literature and thought.

In "Dickens in Russia," pp. 20-25, Andrew Sanders touches upon early translations of Dickens's works by Irinarch Ivanovich Vvedensky (mis-identified, he notes, in *Forster* as Trinarch Ivansvitch Wredenskii) and upon the influence of Dickens on Tolstoy and Dostoevsky.

In "Dickens in France," pp. 26-33, Sylvère Monod notes Dickens's "lifelong and affectionate relationship with France" and his somewhat tentative relationship with French acquaintances. However, he devotes most of his paper to providing a "few choice examples" of what he terms the "very complex and in part obscure" history of French translations of Dickens's novels—a "garbled version" of *Pickwick Papers* by Eugénie Niboyet (1898); Amédée

Pichot's translation of *David Copperfield* (1851), the "first complete and authorized French edition of Dickens's works" ([1857]-74), published by Louis Hachette (though Hachette's translators, Monod adds, were a "rather haphazardly chosen" lot); and the more recent nine volumes of the Bibliothèque de la Pléiade *Oeuvres de Dickens*, edited by Pierre Leyris and himself. Monod also reviews the favorable French critical response to Dickens's works, that of Hippolyte Taine in the nineteenth century and of Floris Delattre, Louis Cazamian, André Maurois, Alain Chartier, Jean Gattégno, and Anny Sadrin, as well as his own, in the twentieth.

In "Dickens in the Netherlands," pp. 34-41, Bernt Luger briefly surveys the rise and fall of Dickens's reputation in the Netherlands in the nineteenth century and something of a revival in the twentieth. He notes the complete translation of Dickens's works in the 1950s by the Utrecht publishing house Het Spectrum, the work of Godfried Bomans as both translator and critic, and the Dickens Fellowship in the Netherlands. In the notes at the end of the article, Luger lists several surveys and studies of Dickens's reception in the Netherlands, most in Dutch, but including his own survey in English of the first fifty years of Dickens's reception in Holland, "Dickens in Holland: A Short History of Appreciation," *Haarlem Dickensian Gazette*, July 1991 (not seen).

626. Suzannet, A[lain] de. "The First German Translation of *Nicholas Nickleby*." *Dickensian*, 28 (1931/32), 60-62.

Describes the serialization and reproduces an illustration of the cover of *Leben und Abenteuer des Nicolaus Nickleby* (Brunswick, Ger.: George Westermann, 1838-39).

627. *Titel-Katalog, mit Sigelung der Firmen Kohn, Neff & Co. GmbH, Koehler & Volckmar GmbH, Könemann GmbH & Co. KG, Umbreit GmbH & Co., Wehling GmbH, Koch, Neff & Oetinger & Co., Verlagsauslieferung GmbH, A-G.* Stuttgart, Ger.: K. F. Koehler Verlag GmbH, 2001, pp. 1269-71.

Lists over 100 editions of individual Dickens works, principally in German, available for purchase.

628. Tschumi, Raymond. "Bibliography." Appended to his "Dickens and Switzerland." *English Studies*, 60 (1979), 456-61.

A listing of Swiss publications of translations of Dickens's works into German, French, Italian, and Romansh, a Swiss dialect; editions and anthologies in English; influences; bibliographies; biographies; and critical and special studies of Dickens's works. In the study itself, Tschumi's comments on Dickens and Switzerland.

629. Uhrström, W. "*Pickwick* in Sweden." *Dickensian*, 32 (1935/36), 117-18.

Identifies and comments on five Swedish translations of *Pickwick Papers* (1861, 1871, 1925, 1927, 1929) and gives a few details about two Swedish dramatizations of the novel (1889, 1932).

630. van Kessel, J. C. "Dickens in het Nederlands." *Dutch Dickensian*, 6, xv (December 1976), 31-51.

A bibliography of translations of Dickens's works into Dutch, 1840-1975, preceded by a brief commentary.

631. Vereş, Grigore. "Ch[arles] Dickens' Writings in Nineteenth Century Romanian Periodicals." *Synthesis: Bulletin du Comité National de Littérature Cmparée de la République Socialiste de Roumanie* (Bucharest, Romania), 7 (1980), 165-76.

Asserts that in the nineteenth century Dickens's works continued to remain "alien" to Romanian readers and critics because "they offered none of the romantic scenes and situations nor the social themes that would have attracted a people going through a process of national revival," and the novel of urban life did not evolve in Romania until the end of the nineteenth century. Until then, Vereş believes, the "language of the novel" was not sufficiently mature to allow for more than translating of Dickens's shorter fiction, and the impetus for this came mainly through Dickens's popularity in Germany and through "the great number" of German translations. The first work translated into Romanian was "The Drunkard's Death" (from *Sketches by Boz*) in 1844 by Iosif Many. The next published translation did not appear until1883. It was Ion and Sofia Nădejde's translation of "The Black Veil," another story from *Sketches by Boz*. They also translated and published parts of *The Old Curiosity Shop* in 1886, and Sofia Nădejde translated *Hard Times*, the first complete Dickens novel in Romanian. It was published in 120 consecutive issues of the magazine *Lumea nouă*. A few other translations of stories followed in the 1890s, Vereş points out.

632. Vereş, Grigore. "Dickens and His Romanian Readers: A Tentative Approach." *Analele Stiintifice ale Universitatii "al. i Cuza" din Iasi*, ns 24, section 3f, Literatură (1978), 109-13.

Notes that, in the nineteenth century, Romanian readers knew Dickens mainly through French translations of his novels, particularly the volumes published by Hatchette. Vereş comments–not very precisely and not in much detail–on some of the translations of Dickens's novels into Romanian in the 1890s, usually from French or German translations, and on Dickens's influence on Romanian writers. Since 1944, he notes, translations of Dickens's works into Romanian have increased considerably, and now almost all of his works are available in Romanian.

633. Vereş, Grigore. "Dickens Criticism in Romania before World War II." *Synthesis: Bulletin du Comité National de Littérature Comparée de la République Socialiste de Roumanie* (Bucharest, Romania), 8 (1981), 269-79.

Despite his title, in the first part of his essay, Vereş comments on translations of Dickens's works into Romanian. The first translation of a novel, *Hard Times*, did not appear until 1894-96, he indicates. The next novels to be translated, *Pickwick Papers* (an incomplete version) and *David Copperfield*, appeared in the 1920s, with a full version of *Pickwick Papers* in the late 1930s and *Oliver Twist* in 1944. In the second and longer part of the essay, Vereş examines the critical response to Dickens's works, noting that the first "perceptive and well-documented study about Dickens' art," did not appear until 1883, a few others shortly thereafter, more around the turn of the century, and a number in 1912. From brief quotations given, these seem to have been more appreciative studies than critical analyses, with Dickens recognized as "a writer with an authentic art and a humanistic message," though, as it is noted, other Romanian critics disagreed with this assessment. One critic, Paul Rareş (a pseudonym, probably for N. Porfiri, according to Vereş), in an essay published in 1922, showed an interest in Dickens's later works and his darker vision of life. More essays on Dickens appeared in the 1930s, up to the outbreak of the Second World War, and "bear witness to the constant attention that was paid to the ethical values, the democratic spirit, and the humanistic message found in the great English novelist's work," Vereş concludes.

634. Vereş, Grigore. *Opera lui Charles Dickens în România.* Bucharest, Romania: Editura Minerva, 1982. 315 pp.

In Romanian. The English summary, pp. 287-302, notes that this is a "study of the fortune and reputation of Dickens' works in Romania," more specifically, in chapter 1, the "peculiar features of Dickens's literary reputation and his reception in some European countries"; in chapter 2, "the conditions in Romanian society and culture, which influenced the attitude toward Dickens' works, the significance of some early contacts with this work before translations were made, and then the activity of translating Dickens viewed chronologically"; in chapter 3, "an analysis of the contemporary translations"; and, in chapter 4, "a survey of Dickensian criticism in Romania," pretty much an updating of his earlier "Dickens Criticism in Romania before World War II" (**633**). By 1982, Vereş adds, over two million copies of translations of Dickens's works into Romanian had been issued, with thirteen of the fifteen novels translated, as well as the sketches and some Christmas books and stories. In terms of the critical reception, Vereş points out that Dickens's entry into Romania was through the socialist press, with an emphasis on *Hard Times*. See his doctoral dissertation, "The Reception of Charles Dickens' Works in Romania" (Babeş-Bolyai University, Cluj-Napoca, Romania, 1975).

Reviews: R. Albu, *Analele Stiintifice ale Universitatii "al. i Cuza" din Iasi*, ns 29, Sect. 3f. Literatură (1983), 98-100; S. Avadenei, *Cronica*, 28 May 1982, p. 10; R. Bales, *Dickensian*, 79 (1983), 119-20 (a "kaleidoscopic jumble" of quite "unfamiliar and fascinating things," with "very rich footnotes"); V. Stanciu, *Steaua*, 33, vii (1982), 39, 44.

635. *Verzeichnis Lieferbarer Bücher/German Books in Print, 2002/2003. Autoren Titel Stickwörter.* 32nd edition. 12 volumes. Frankfurt am Main: MVB Marketing- und Verlagsservice des Buchhandels GmbH, 2002, III, 3297-98.

This annual author-title list of German books in print (first published in 1971/72) notes numerous editions of individual Dickens works in German and English. Also see the *Schlagwort-Verzeichnis* portion (**1279**) of this major publication.

636. Wellens, Oscar. "The Earliest Dutch Translations of Dickens (1837-1870): An All-Inclusive List." *Dickensian*, 93 (1997), 126-32.

A more or less chronological account (not really a list) of Dutch translations of Dickens's works, 1837-70. Wellens includes information about translators, titles, publishers, and dates of publication.

637. Wilkins, W[illiam] Glyde. "Early Foreign Translations of Dickens's Works." *Dickensian*, 7 (1911), 35-37.

Describes various German, French, and Dutch translations of Dickens's early novels—*Pickwick Papers, Oliver Twist, Barnaby Rudge, Martin Chuzzlewit*—and their illustrations.

638. Zentella Mayer, Arturo. "Carlos Dickens en México." In *Charles Dickens, 1812-1870: Homenaje en el primer centenario de su muerte*. Ed. María E. González Padilla (**57**), pp. 161-82.

In addition to surveying the responses of Mexican critics (principally in the nineteenth century) to Dickens, Zentella Mayer comments on several Spanish translations of Dickens's works published in Mexico. Illustrated with reproductions of a few title pages.

639. Zhang Ling and Zhang Yang. "Dickens in China." *Dickens Quarterly*, 16 (1999), 191-98.

A historical survey of translations of Dickens's works into Chinese and of Chinese biographical and critical studies of Dickens. The earliest translations, 1907-09, of five novels—*The Old Curiosity Shop, Nicholas Nickleby, David*

Copperfield, Oliver Twist, and *Dombey and Son*—were, the authors point out, by Lin Shu in classical Chinese. Further translations, most of poor quality, appeared in the Nationalist Republican period, from the 1920s to the end of the 1940s, the Zhangs indicate, but new and better translations of more than half of Dickens's major works were published in the 1950s and 1960s during the New Republic. Now, after the Cultural Revolution (when Dickens could only be read secretly, and was, they note), all of Dickens's novels "are available in Chinese versions and in many different editions," and numerous biographical and critical studies of Dickens have been published and various English, American, French, and Russian studies translated. "It can be seen from all these developments," the authors conclude, that Dickens is "an everlasting evergreen tree that has taken root deeply in the thick yellow soil of China."

640. Zhang Yu. "Chinese Translations of 'David Copperfield': Accuracy and Acculturation." *Dissertation Abstracts International*, 53 (1992/93), 485A (Southern Illinois University, Carbondale, 1991).

Studies five Chinese translations of *David Copperfield*, each reflecting "the social and literary awareness of the translator," published in 1907, 1943, 1950 (two), and 1980.

2B. BIBLIOGRAPHIES AND BIBLIOGRAPHICAL STUDIES OF DICKENS'S READING VERSIONS OF HIS WORKS

Note: Also see **Public readings** in section 2 of part 1 of the subject index and **reading version** under individual titles in part 1 of the subject index.

641. Byerly, Alison. "From Schoolroom to Stage: Reading Aloud and the Domestication of Victorian Theater." In *Culture and Education in Victorian England*. Ed. Patrick Scott and Pauline Fletcher. Lewisburg, PA: Bucknell University Press; London and Toronto: Associated University Presses, 1990, pp. 125-41, an issue of *Bucknell Review*, 34, ii (1990).

Comments on Dickens's career as a public reader of his own novels, noting that, when Dickens edited his work for public reading, the changes he made were for greater theatricality.

642. Calhoun, Philo. "Introduction." In Dickens's *The Little Carol, Being A Christmas Carol in Prose*. Ed. Philo Calhoun. Waterville, ME: Colby College Press, 1954, pp. ix-xxii.

Comments generally on Dickens's shortening of the text of *A Christmas Carol* between 1853 and 1867 for his public readings of the work. The text included here is, however, Calhoun's own condensation of the work for reading aloud. Illustrated.

643. Callahan, Jean. "The (Unread) Reading Version of *Great Expectations*." In Dickens's *Great Expectations: Authoritative Text, Backgrounds, Contexts, Criticism*. Ed. Edgar Rosenberg (**2401**), pp. 543-56.

After commenting generally on Dickens's public readings and their popularity, Callahan looks more closely at Dickens's reading version of *Great Expectations*, one of five readings he prepared but never performed. In its present state, Callahan points out, it would have taken over three hours to read. Even so, she notes, in emphasizing the Pip-Magwitch plot, including Joe Gargery, Dickens ended the reading with Magwitch's death and completely eliminated Estella, Biddy, Trabb and Trabb's boy, Orlick, and others, and at least thirty of the novel's fifty-nine chapters. Callahan also looks at the ways in which Dickens further reduced the text, including condensation and suppression of social commentary, conflation of scenes, and "the purging of all feminine influence in Pip's story," a number of examples of which she analyzes.

644. Collins, Philip. "Appendix C: Dickens's Readings from the *Christmas Books*." In Dickens's *The Christmas Books*. Ed. Michael Slater (**2352**), II, 355-58.

Concise commentary on Dickens's readings and prompt-copies of *A Christmas Carol* (by far the most popular reading), *The Cricket on the Hearth*, *The Chimes*, and *The Haunted Man and the Ghost's Bargain* (the last never performed).

645. Collins, Philip. "Christmas All Year Round–Philip Collins Discusses Dickens's Public Readings." *Listener*, 82 (25 December 1969), 881-83.

This transcription of a radio talk is more historical and critical than bibliographical, but Collins does more or less itemize the readings. He comments on Dickens's theatrical inclinations and the emphasis in the readings on comedy rather than social criticism–except, obviously in *Sikes and Nancy*, his reading from *Oliver Twist*. In a review in *Dickens Studies Newsletter*, 2, i (March 1971), 25-28, of "Dickens Special Number," *Eigo kenkyu: The Study of English*, Supplementary Issue, June 1970, Masaie Matsumura indicates that this transcription was translated into Japanese by Akira Takeuchi, pp. 98-100.

646. Collins, Philip. "The Dickens Reading-Copies in Dickens House." *Dickensian*, 68 (1972), 173-79.

Describes and assesses the bibliographical importance of the reading-copies added to the Dickens House collection as a gift of the Comtesse de Suzannet in 1971. These, Collins points out, consist of six of the "earliest surviving versions" of the twenty-one readings prepared by Dickens (the other fifteen are in the Berg Collection, New York Public Library): *The Haunted Man* (never performed), *The Story of Little Dombey*, *Mr. Bob Sawyer's Party* (from *Pickwick Papers*), *The Bastille Prisoner* (from *A Tale of Two Cities*), *Nicholas Nickleby at the Yorkshire School*, and *Mr Chops, the Dwarf* (from "Going into Society," Dickens's contribution to *A House to Let*, the Christmas number of *Household Words*, 1858). Collins notes that the comtesse's gift also included such associated items as the "Billington" copy of *Sikes and Nancy* (**650**) into which Adeline Billington, to whom Dickens gave this privately printed copy of the reading, copied the "textual alterations and performance-signs" from Dickens's own copy, and an unpublished typescript eyewitness account (written in 1930) by Rowland Hill, a journalist, of Dickens's reading of *A Christmas Carol*. Illustrated.

647. Collins, Philip. "Dickens Reading-Copies in the Beinecke Library." *Yale University Library Gazette*, 46 (1971/72), 153-58.

Points out that the Gimbel bequest to Yale University (see **1509**) contains three of the privately printed scripts that Dickens used in his public readings—*Little Dombey* (very similar to the copy in the Suzannet Collection at the Dickens House—see **646, 1457A** and **1524**—but with some variations), *Great Expectations* (one of two copies, the other being in the Berg Collection, New York Public Library [**1499**], prepared but never performed, and with no autograph textual revisions in the printed text of either copy), and *Nicholas Nickleby at Dotheboys Hall* (one of several copies of a shortened version of his popular reading *Nicholas Nickleby at the Yorkshire School*). Collins provides considerable bibliographical detail about these volumes, distinguishing them from other known copies of these readings. Also see Podeschi (**1509**), pp. 166, 204, and 322.

648. Collins, Philip. "Dickens' Public Readings: Texts and Performances." *Dickens Studies Annual*, 3 (1974), 182-97, 242-44.

A paper from a Dickens Conference held at the University of Alberta, 1-2 October 1970. Collins provides examples of Dickens's modifications in turning parts of his novels into the public reading versions. Collins also gives excerpts from a number of eyewitness accounts and favorable reviews of the readings. For reports on the conference, see Norman Page, *Dickensian*, 67 (1971), 43-44, and Robert L. Patten, *Dickens Studies Newsletter*, 1 (1970), 22-24.

649. Collins, Philip. "Introduction." In Dickens's *A Christmas Carol: The Public Reading Version. A Facsimile of the Author's Prompt-Copy*. Ed. Philip Collins. New York: New York Public Library, 1971, pp. ix-xxiii.

Provides an engrossing description of how Dickens prepared the reading copy of his most popular public reading and modified it over a period of time as it went from a three-hour to a two-and-one-half-hour to an eighty-to-ninety-minute reading. Collins also comments on the audience response, as described in various accounts of Dickens's reading of this work and in Dickens's own comments. The facsimile reproduced here is the prompt-copy of the reading in the Berg Collection of the New York Public Library. Collins's extensive textual and explanatory notes, pp. 171-206, fully reveal the evolution of the text.

Review: L. C. S[taples], *Dickensian*, 68 (1972), 127-28 (praises Collins's "excellent" notes, his recording and explanations of manuscript emendations, and his "admirable" introduction).

650. Collins, Philip. "Introduction." In Dickens's *Sikes and Nancy: A Facsimile of a Privately Printed Annotated Copy, Now in the Dickens House, Presented by Dickens to Adeline Billington*. Ed. Philip Collins. London: Dickens House, 1982, pp. iii-vi.

Collins describes Dickens's preparation of this reading from *Oliver Twist* and the particular copy of the "second edition," the later version of the reading, into which Dickens's "own underlinings and stage-directions have been copied," probably, as Collins indicates, by its recipient, the actress Adeline Billington, from Dickens's own copy, which has disappeared. The text itself shows underlining for emphasis, stage directions ("Shudder," "Pause," "Look around with Terror"), alerts ("XXMurder comingXX"–double underlined), and one cancelled passage.

651. Collins, Philip. "Introduction." In Dickens's *Sikes and Nancy and Other Public Readings*. Ed. Philip Collins. World's Classics. Oxford and New York: Oxford University Press, 1983, pp. vii-xx and passim.

Provides information about Dickens's readings and about his textual preparation of his prompt-copies of them. Collins's headnotes to the twelve readings included in this edition also contain some textual commentary, and his extensive footnotes are concerned largely with textual matters and Dickens's underlining of passages and inserting of other stage directions for himself.

652. Collins, Philip. "Introduction," Headnotes, Endnotes, and Footnotes. In *Charles Dickens: The Public Readings*. Ed. Philip Collins. Oxford: Clarendon Press, 1975, pp. xvii-lxix and passim.

In this first complete edition of the texts of Dickens's public readings, all transcribed from Dickens's own copies, Collins's long introduction provides extraordinarily detailed information about the history of the readings, the performances, Dickens's preparation of his prompt-copies, the later history of these prompt-copies, and the various published editions of the readings. Collins also discusses other Victorian one-man shows, comments on Dickens's talent as a performer, and quotes numerous contemporary descriptions of the readings. Each reading is also preceded by an often lengthy and valuable head note and sometimes an additional endnote, giving that reading's particular history. Collins includes numerous textual and explanatory footnotes, though he has not attempted to trace the history of Dickens's revisions, identifying only major deletions and the more significant changes. He also includes photographic facsimiles of Dickens's annotated text of two pages of *Sikes and Nancy* and an illustration of Dickens reading.

653. Collins, Philip. "'Sikes and Nancy': Dickens's Last Reading." *Times Literary Supplement*, 11 June 1971, pp. 681-82.

Comments on two reading copies of *Sikes and Nancy*, one in the Berg Collection, New York Public Library, with marking in Dickens's hand, and a later one, in the Dickens House, known as the "Billington copy," with markings in Mrs. Adeline Billington's hand.

654. Collins, Philip. "The Texts of Dickens' Readings." *Bulletin of the New York Public Library*, 74 (1970), 360-80.

Points out that the texts of the twenty-one readings prepared by Dickens take three different forms: prompt-copy, "trade" edition, and collected edition. Collins locates most of the prompt-copies (sixteen, he indicates, are in the Berg Collection, New York Public Library) and provides details about each of the twenty-one readings. Two illustrations show Dickens's holograph revisions. See also Collins (**646-47**) and New York Public Library (**1499**).

655. Collins, Philip. "The Texts of Dickens' Readings: A Postscript." *Bulletin of the New York Public Library*, 75 (1971), 63.

An addendum to Collins (**654**) identifying one more prompt-copy, noting the changing ownership of others, and correcting a few errors in his earlier report.

656. Dickens, Cedric C. "A Reading Edition of the 'Carol.'" *Bookseller*, 30 October 1965, pp. 2016-17.

More for publicity's sake than anything else, Cedric Dickens comments on his edition of the reading version of *A Christmas Carol* (London: Dickens House, 1965), printed to aid the Dickens House.

657. Eckel, John C. "The Reading Edition of Dickens' *Great Expectations*." *Bookman's Journal and Print Collector*, ns 11 (1924/25), 93.

Corrects a statement in the September 1924 issue—see "Books in the Sale Rooms," ns 10 (1924), 212-14—to the effect that only two or three copies of the reading edition of *Great Expectations* are known and that this edition is not mentioned in any bibliography by noting indignantly that four pages are devoted to it in his 1913 bibliography (**16**).

658. Fielding, K[enneth] J. "Charles Dickens and Thomas C. Evans. A Proposed Reading Tour in the U. S. A.–1859." *Notes and Queries*, 196 (1951), 123-24.

Describes and comments on a recently-discovered copy in Dickens's hand of a detailed conditional agreement from 1859 with an American publishing agent, Thomas C. Evans, for giving public readings from his works in America for £10,000. The agreement, printed here, provides details of the proposed itinerary and other conditions. "Nothing came of the agreement," Fielding points out, and offers possible reasons why, noting that Dickens, in letters to John Forster and Wilkie Collins, offered a different explanation from Evans's, in his *Of Many Men* (New York: American News Co., 1888), pp. 1-41, as to why the trip never took place.

659. Gordan, John D. "Introduction," "A Guide for Readers," "Notes on the Text," and "Appendix." In *Mrs. Gamp by Charles Dickens: A Facsimile of the Author's Prompt Copy.* New York: New York Public Library, 1956, pp. 1-18, 20, 81-114, 115-20.

In his "Introduction" Gordan comments on Dickens's revisions in both the original manuscript of *Martin Chuzzlewit* and in this reading, as well as on Dickens as a public reader generally and specifically in regard to this reading. He also compares the two reading versions of *Mrs. Gamp* (the original of 10,000 words, the final version of 4,000), the Berg copy being the original version with the "corrections, deletions and additions which Dickens made in the text between 1858 and 1868" that make up the shorter final version, to show how Dickens put together and modified the reading version for greater, more unified effect. Gordan also notes that thirteen (including *Mrs. Gamp*) corrected prompt-copies of the seventeen readings that Dickens actually performed and two of the four he prepared but never read are in the Berg Collection, New York Public Library. "A Guide for Readers" tells how to follow the text for the original and for the final versions of the reading. "Notes on the Text" helps, as Gordan indicates, to trace the gradual development of the reading and provides various technical details about the textual revisions and the state of the manuscript. The "Appendix" contains Gordan's comments on and a photographic facsimile of two pages of manuscript that "appear to be [a fragment of] the copy from which the type was set for the private printing" on which the Berg copy is based. Also see "Foreword" by Monica Dickens, who expresses the Dickens family's appreciation to the New York Public Library for the "fine quality" of this facsimile reproduction and remarks on the "hours of patient work" that Dickens put into this reading.

660. Kennethe, L. A. [Walter Dexter]. "The Unique Reading Books." *Dickensian*, 39 (1942/43), 75-78.

Briefly describes copies of the volumes Dickens actually used in his public readings of his writings and gives recent sale prices for some. Dexter includes photographic facsimiles of a page of Dickens's handwritten additions to *Sikes and Nancy* and another to *The Story of Little Dombey.*

661. Sadrin, Anny. "The Public Reading Version." In her *Great Expectations* (**108**), pp. 26-29.

Briefly describes Dickens's preparation of the reading version. For other supplementary bibliographical and textual material in this edition, see Sadrin (**1093, 2405**).

662. Slater, Michael. "*The Bastille Prisoner*: A Reading Dickens Never Gave." *Etudes anglaises*, 23 (1970), 190-96.

Describes and comments on Dickens's revisions in the reading he condensed from Book I of *A Tale of Two Cities* and had privately printed in preparation for a public reading of the work that never took place–based on extensive handwritten revisions in the copy then in the Count de Suzannet's library. Slater speculates that Dickens never gave the reading because it was "so wholly deficient in comedy."

663. Stonehouse, John H. "A First Bibliography of the Reading Editions of Charles Dickens's Works." In Dickens's *Sikes and Nancy: A Reading.* Ed. John H. Stonehouse. London: Henry Sotheran, 1921, pp. 49-57.

Lists twenty-two published and unpublished editions of individual readings, including four not used by Dickens, and two collected editions of readings, with some annotation.

664. "'Up to Cheerfulness': Facsimile of Dickens' Prompt-Copy of *A Christmas Carol.*" *Bulletin of the New York Public Library,* 75 (1971), 336.

Announces the then forthcoming publication of Dickens's prompt copy of *A Christmas Carol* (**649**) and comments on its uniqueness, Dickens's use of it in all his readings of the story, and the virtues of this particular edition of it, for which Philip Collins wrote the notes and introduction.

2C. BIBLIOGRAPHIES AND BIBLIOGRAPHICAL STUDIES OF DRAMATIC AND OTHER ADAPTATIONS OF DICKENS'S WORKS

Note: See **Adaptations of Dickens's works** in part 2 of the subject index and the sections on adaptations of individual novels in the volumes of the Garland Dickens Bibliographies (**13**), The Dickens Bibliographies (**12**), and under individual titles in part 1 of the subject index. Studies of individual adaptations have generally not been included here though studies of multiple adaptations of individual works have been.

665. Allingham, Philip V. "Dramatic Adaptations of the Christmas Books of Charles Dickens, 1844-8: Texts and Contexts." *Dissertation Abstracts International*, 49 (1988/89), 3728A-29A (University of British Columbia, 1988).

Focuses on "the degree of Dickens' participation in the officially sanctioned dramatisations of his Christmas Books, 1844-8, by such prolific early Victorian playwrights as Edward Stirling and Mark Lemon." Allingham looks at the methods used by the adapters, critically studies "the plays and their contexts," and makes textual comparisons of the printed texts of the novels with the manuscripts and final texts of the plays. He also prints the texts of the adaptations, two for the first time.

666. Allombert, Guy. "Dickens au cinéma" and "Essai de filmographie de Dickens." Special Dickens Number. *Europe*, no. 488 (December 1969), 42-50, 51-54.

The first essay briefly surveys several major film versions of Dickens's novels; the second lists silent films (1909-24), sound films (1933-68), and television productions (1961-69) of Dickens's works, giving cost, director, length, and other production information.

667. *The American Film Institute Catalog of Motion Pictures Produced in the United States.* 1971- , passim.
   Vol. A: *Film Beginnings, 1893-1910: A Work in Progress*. Ed. Elias Savada. 2 parts. Metuchen, NJ, and London: Scarecrow Press, 1995.
   Vol. F1: *Feature Films, 1911-1920*. Ed. Patricia K. Hanson. 2 parts. Berkeley: University of California Press, 1988.
   Vol. F2: *Feature Films, 1921-1930*. Ed. Kenneth W. Munden. 2 parts. New York: Bowker, 1971.

Vol. F3: *Feature Films, 1931-1940.* Ed Patricia K. Hanson and Alan Grevinson. 3 parts. Berkeley: University of California Press, 1993.

Vol. F4: *Feature Films, 1941-1950.* Ed. Patricia K. Hanson and Amy Dunkleberger. 3 parts. Berkeley, Los Angeles, and London: University of California Press, 1999.

Vol. F6: *Feature Films, 1961-1970.* Ed. Richard P. Krafsur. 2 parts. New York: Bowker, 1976.

The first volumes in what seems destined to be a lengthy series. The second (or third) part of each of the volumes in this series is an index, which should be consulted for a list of films based on Dickens's works included in the volume. The entries themselves contain production details, including casts, a plot summary, information about other theater and film versions, and reviews of the productions.

668. [Andrews, Malcolm]. "Editorial." *Dickensian,* 94 (1998), 83-84.

Andrews has nothing against the numerous adaptations of Dickens's works (even Dickens did it with his reading adaptations, he indicates) and notes that we "continue to measure [Dickens's] posthumous success by the ceaseless flow of adaptations, good, bad, and indifferent." Still, Andrews concludes, Dickens "will survive his adapters."

669. Aros, Andrew A. (as conceived by Richard B. Dimmitt). *A Title Guide to the Talkies, 1964 through 1974.* Metuchen, NJ: Scarecrow Press, 1977, passim; *1975 through 1984.* Metuchen, NJ, and London: Scarecrow Press, 1986, passim.

These two volumes supplement Dimmitt (**700**) and give production details of a few more films based on Dickens works.

670. Baker, H. Barton. *The London Stage: Its History and Traditions from 1576 to 1888.* London: W. H. Allen, 1889, passim; revised and expanded as *History of the London Stage and Its Famous Players (1576-1903).* London: George Routledge and Sons; New York: E. P. Dutton, 1904; reprinted New York: Benjamin Blom, 1969, passim.

Mentions in passing a number of dramatic versions of Dickens's novels, significantly more in the revised edition. See the index under "Dickens." Both editions comment briefly on Dickens's own plays (see pp. 144-45 in the 1889 edition and pp. 157-59 in the 1904 edition).

671. Baker, R. "The Dramatization of Dickens's Novels." *American Magazine,* 16, ns 6 (1900/01), 545-49.

Baker comments on some of the earlier dramatizations of Dickens's novels, pointing out that, generally, Dickens's novels "do not lend themselves very well to the adapter's skill, for his characters are more often descriptive than dramatic," the dramatic adaptations by others giving but "a faint idea" of Dickens's strength and genius.

672. Baskin, Ellen. *Serials on British Television, 1950-1994.* Aldershot, Eng.: Scolar Press; Brookfield, VT: Ashgate, 1996, passim.

Use the "Index of Authors of Original Works" to locate the thirty-three serials based on Dickens's works. The entries themselves, arranged chronologically, give production information, including casts and brief plot summaries.

673. Baskin, Ellen, and Mandy Hicken, comps. *Enser's Filmed Books and Plays: A List of Books and Plays from Which Films Have Been Made, 1928-1991.* Aldershot, Eng., and Brookfield, VT: Ashgate, 1993, passim.

For a list of films made from Dickens's works, with production information, see pp. 475-77 of the "Author Index," but also consult the "Film Title Index," which contains additional entries.

674. Billington, Michael. "Dickens on the Screen." *Illustrated London News*, 257 (28 November 1970), 19-21.

A week before the London premier of the film musical *Scrooge*, with Albert Finney, Billington briefly reviews some of the film versions of Dickens's novels, noting that, while the best have captured Dickens's "narrative vitality, his exuberant characterization," and his humor, they have not conveyed "his dark Dostoievskyan side, his often surrealistic strangeness, his ability to build a whole book (as in *Bleak House*) around a great chain of metaphor." Accompanied by two pages of photographs from the films.

675. Bolton, H. Philip. "*Bleak House* and the Playhouse." *Dickens Studies Annual*, 12 (1983), 81-116.

Includes a chronologically ordered "Handlist of *Bleak House* Dramas," pp. 98-115, giving authors and titles, number of acts, places and dates of first performances, and sources of information of some forty-eight dramatizations of *Bleak House*. In the earlier portion of the article, Bolton comments on a number of these dramatizations.

676. Bolton, H. Philip. *Dickens Dramatized.* London: Mansell; Boston: G. K. Hall, 1987. xviii + 501 pp.

An impressive compilation and study. This work is, as Bolton points out in his preface, "both a calendar of dramatic performances" of plays for stage, film, radio, and television and "a bibliography of published texts and unpublished manuscripts derived from the novels and stories of Charles Dickens." Only dramatic readings from the works, including Dickens's own, are excluded. Bolton also modestly notes that, although he has identified "some 3,000 dramatic productions and publications," this is "by no means a complete listing." In a long introduction, pp. 1-63, Bolton gives a history of the dramatization of Dickens's works and Dickens's own collaborations on plays with Wilkie Collins, as well as something of a history of the dramatization of novels on the stage and, more specifically, of Victorian dramatizations of Victorian novels. He also surveys the authors of dramatizations of Dickens's novels and stories and comments on the actors and actresses who performed in them. The "Handlists" that follow, pp. 65-458, list the dramatizations of each of the novels (in chronological order), with introductions to each section. The entries under each novel are also listed chronologically by date of publication or first performance, along with whatever details Bolton unearthed about the title, playwright, date and place of performance or broadcast, manuscript or publication, the sources of such information, and commentary on casts and other matters. A useful index, pp. 459-501, appears to be quite comprehensive. Illustrated.

Reviews: B. Bell, *Theatre Research Internationale*, 13 (1988), 60-61 ("an unsatisfactory book on a number of levels," though there is "a great richness of material here for scholars" and "much that is good"); J. S. Bratton, *Dickensian*, 84 (1988), 50-51 ("an immensely suggestive and exciting collection of material which triggers new speculation at every glance"–the "best kind of bibliographic book"); G. U. de Sousa, *American Reference Books Annual*, 19 (1988), 545 (praises highly for completeness and detail; a "major reference work on Dickens"); J. Ellis, *Nineteenth Century Theatre*, 16 (1988), 68-72 (finds that the work "offers the most substantial proof ever assembled of the broad and abiding popularity of Dickens as it extended far beyond a reading public," though notes a few errors and omissions); S. J[ames], *Library Review*, 36 (1987), 295-96; J. M. Parker, *Choice*, 25 (1987/88), 451-52 (a "welcome addition to Dickens studies"); A. Sanders, *Times Literary Supplement*, 21 August 1987, p. 908 (fascinating in "the very density of the variety" charted); P. Schlicke, *Theatre Notebook*, 43 (1989), 44 (the "most abundant and accurate evidence of Dickensian adaptations ever collected"); A. Shelston, *New Theatre Quarterly*, 5 (1989), 306 (a "remarkable compilation of information," of "infinite usefulness," and with an introductory essay that is "never less than informative"); G. J. Worth, *Victorian Studies*, 32 (1988/89), 255-57 (finds the work "a bountiful record of how dramatic versions of his works have spread Dickens's . . . fame," but reminds the reader of Bolton's own cautions about the reliability of some of his information).

677. Brennan, Elizabeth M. "Appendix K. Little Nell on Stage, 1840-1841." In Dickens's *The Old Curiosity Shop*. Clarendon Edition (**2460**), pp. 630-34; reprinted as "Appendix E: Little Nell on Stage, 1840-1841." In Dickens's *The Old Curiosity Shop*. Oxford's World Classics (**2461**), pp. 580-84.

Describes and comments on early dramatizations of *The Old Curiosity Shop*.

678. Butler, Ivan. "Dickens on the Screen (with a Glance at Other Victorian Novelists)." In *Film Review, 1972-73*. South Brunswick, NJ, and New York: A. S. Barnes, 1972, pp. 18-25.

A brief survey. Butler gives the title, year, director, and principal actors for a number of film versions of Dickens's novels (pp. 19-21). Illustrated with stills of some of the productions.

679. Castelli, Louis P., and Caryn L. Cleeland. "Annotated Guide to Writings about David Lean." In their *David Lean: A Guide to References and Resources*. Boston: G. K. Hall, 1980, pp. 103-15 and passim.

Includes studies of Lean's two Dickens films, *Oliver Twist* and *Great Expectations*. Synopses, credits, and notes for these two films will be found on pp. 74-76 and a list of reviews of them on pp. 98-99.

680. Cavanagh, John. "Dickens, Charles (1812-1870)." In his *British Theatre: A Bibliography, 1901 to 1985*. Motley Bibliographies, 1. Mottisfont, Eng.: Motley Press, 1989, pp. 339-40.

Lists principal book-length studies and dissertations dealing with Dickens and the theater. Harner (**1147**), p. 190, notes that a revised edition extending coverage to 1990 is in progress. Also see Arnott and Robinson's bibliography (**139**), for which Cavanagh, according to Harner, p. 189, is apparently also preparing a revised edition.

681. Chicorel, Marietta, ed. *Chicorel Theater Index to Plays for Young People in Periodicals, Anthologies, and Collections*. Chicorel Index Series, 9. New York: Chicorel Library Publishing Corp., 1974, pp. 84-86.

An unannotated list of thirty-seven plays based on Dickens's works.

682. Chicorel, Marietta, ed. *Chicorel Theater Index to Plays in Anthologies, Periodicals, Discs, and Tapes*. 3 vols. [Chicorel Index Series, 1-3]. New York: Chicorel, 1970-72, passim; continued as *Chicorel Theater Index to Plays in Anthologies and Collections, 1970-76*. Chicorel Index Series, 25. New York: Chicorel, 1977, passim.

See under "Dickens" and individual titles of his works for unannotated listings of dramatizations of Dickens's works.

683. Colby, Robert A. "Thackeray and Dickens on the Boards." In *Dramatic Dickens*. Ed. Carol H. MacKay. Houndmills, Eng.: Macmillan; New York: St. Martin's Press, 1989, pp. 139-51.

Comments on a number of dramatizations of works by Dickens and Thackeray. Colby asserts that in these plays "Dickens's novels in general were exploited for their sensational, lachrymose, or farcical elements, which came to be magnified under the glare of gaslight." His characters were generally reduced "to mere silhouettes" or, for the sake of the comic lead actor in a company, the comic characters were "disproportionately enlarged" over the plot line.

684. Coleman, Edward D. "The Jew in English Drama [*Oliver Twist*]: An Annotated Bibliography." *Bulletin of the New York Public Library*, 44 (1940), 432-34; also published in his *The Jew in English Drama: An Annotated Bibliography*. New York: New York Public Library, 1943; reprinted New York: New York Public Library and KTAV Publishing House, 1970, pp. 68-70.

Itemizes, with bibliographical annotations and lists of reviews, thirty-six dramatic adaptations of *Oliver Twist*. For the full bibliography in *Bulletin of the New York Public Library*, see 42 (1938), 827-50, 919-32; 43 (1939), 45-52, 374-78, 443-58; 44 (1940), 361-72, 429-44, 495-504, 543-68, 620-34, 675-98, 777-88, 843-66. The 1970 reprint appends two supplementary lists, by Edgar Rosenberg and by Flola L. Shepard, but neither of these includes any dramatizations of Dickens's works.

685. Connor, Billie M., and Helene G. Mochedlover. *Ottemiller's Index to Plays in Collections: An Author and Title Index to Plays Appearing in Collections Published between 1900 and 1985*. 7th ed., revised and enlarged. Metuchen, NJ, and London: Scarecrow Press, 1988, p. 67.

Lists only five adaptations of Dickens's works. Earlier editions going back to 1943, edited by John H. Ottemiller until his death in 1968, exist but are not as inclusive.

686. Cooke, Alistair. "Charles Dickens: *Our Mutual Friend, Dickens of London*." In his *Masterpieces: A Decade of Masterpiece Theatre*. New York: VNU Books International/Alfred A. Knopf, 1981, pp. 67-78.

Pretty much a heavily illustrated coffee-table book. Though noting that many film-makers are eager to film Dickens's novels, Cooke begins with the assertion that "the only person who might have successfully translated Dickens to the screen is Walt Disney, in his early inventive prime" because, like Dickens's, his characters "are built on idiosyncrasy and drawn as beings more alive and less human than humans in the flesh." Cooke comments briefly on Masterpiece Theatre's *Dickens of London* (1977) and *Our Mutual Friend* (1978), the former of which he sees as "a brave attempt, by Yorkshire Television, to dramatize the first thirty-two years of Dickens's life as recalled by Dickens himself on his last reading tour of America." The pages of this chapter are mainly taken up with large color and black and white photographs of shots from principally these two films.

687. Cooper, F[rederick] Renad. *Nothing Extenuate: The Life of Frederick Fox Cooper.* London: Barrie and Rockliff, 1964, passim.

Provides information about dramatic adaptations by Cooper of a number of Dickens's works, often quoting from reviews of them. Illustrated.

688. Costello, Tom, ed. *International Guide to Literature on Film.* London, etc.: Bowker-Saur, 1994, pp. 66-69.

Where Dickens is concerned, a limited list, with minimal information, comprising thirty-two films of eleven novels and two Christmas Books.

689. Cox, Philip. "The Professional Writer: Adaptations of Dickens's Early Novels." In his *Reading Adaptations: Novels and Verse Narratives on the Stage, 1790-1840.* Manchester, Eng., and New York: Manchester University Press, 2000, pp. 121-62.

Examines a few of William Thomas Moncrieff's dramatic adaptations of Dickens's early novels, particularly *Pickwick Papers* and *Nicholas Nickleby*, notes Dickens's disparagement of them, but observes that, nevertheless, they "made an enormous contribution to his fame and currency as a writer."

690. Daisne, Johan. "Dickens, Charles." In his *Dictionnaire filmographique de la littérature mondiale/Filmographic Dictionary of World Literature.* . . . 2 vols. Gand [Ghent], Belg.: Story-Scientia, 1971-75, I, 106-08; *Supplement.* Ibid., 1978, p. 169.

Lists sixty-one film adaptations of Dickens's novels, 1903-70, principally English and American but also a few French and Danish, and gives the director and cast for each. The supplement adds only two more to the list, both from 1970.

691. Davis, Jim. "*The Only Way* and the Other Way: A Dickens Adaptation for the 1890s." In *British Theatre in the 1890s: Essays on Drama and the Stage.* Ed. Richard Foulkes. Cambridge and New York: Cambridge University Press, 1992, pp. 59-70.

Briefly comments on earlier dramatic adaptations of *A Tale of Two Cities* but devotes most of the study to *The Only Way*, first performed in 1899, and written "ostensibly by the Revd Freeman Wills and the Revd Canon Langbridge, but shaped and developed also by John Martin Harvey [who played Sydney Carton] and his wife." Illustrated.

692. Denman, Kamilla L. "Haunted Screens and Shadowed Texts: Film Adaptations of British Victorian Prose Fiction." *Dissertation Abstracts International*, 57 (1996/67), 2047A (Harvard University, 1996).

The abstract indicates that this study examines "the many levels on which Victorian British prose fiction has been adapted to film—semiotic, cultural, historical, aesthetic, cognitive, and generic" and includes a "film index of 1031 film and television adaptations of Victorian British prose fiction." Dickens is, obviously, included.

693. [Dexter, Walter]. "Dickens on Screen and Stage." *Dickensian*, 31 (1934/35), 215-18.

On four then recent dramatizations of Dickens's novels, with quotations from various reviews of them, to some of which Dexter takes exception.

694. "Dickens and the Drama." *T. P.'s Weekly*, 6 (1905), 398.

Comments on a few adaptations of Dickens's works.

695. "Dickens & the Stage. The Famous Novelist's Unrealized Ambition to Win Reputation as an Actor." *Everybody's Weekly*, 8 July 1911, pp. 609-10.

In addition to describing Dickens's acting, comments on the dramatizations of Dickens's works.

696. "Dickens as Filmed in England and America: Old Friends with New Faces." *Illustrated London News*, 185 (1934), 1100-01.

Two pages of illustrations from then recent films based on Dickens's novels—*David Copperfield* (MGM, with Freddie Bartholomew, Frank Lawton, Maureen O'Sullivan, and W. C. Fields), *The Old Curiosity Shop* (British International Pictures, with Elaine Benson, Hay Petrie, and Ben Webster), and *Great Expectations* (Universal Pictures, with Phillips Holmes, Jane Wyatt, and Henry Hull).

697. "Dickens, Charles." The Internet Movie Database Web site. http://us.imdb.com/Name?Dickens,+Charles#11920(IMDb).

Lists 133 films based on Dickens's novels and stories, 1897-2000. Clicking on a title provides a brief plot outline, cast list, and other production information. There are also user comments and ratings, message boards, and recommended sites to visit.

698. "Dickens on the Stage." *Times* (London), 16 January 1915, p. 11.

Commentary on dramatic adaptations of Dickens's works, largely based on Frederic G. Kitton's list in his *Dickensiana* (**996**) and comments in *Forster*.

699. "Dickens on the Stage: The First Performances." In *The Dickens Souvenir of 1912*. Ed. Dion C. Calthrop and Max Pemberton. London: Chapman and Hall, 1912, pp. 29-33.

Lists casts for the first performances of five plays based on Dickens's novels (*Pickwick Papers, Barnaby Rudge, Martin Chuzzlewit, A Christmas Carol,* and *A Tale of Two Cities*), the information taken, as noted, from S. J. Adair Fitz-Gerald's *Dickens and the Drama* (**707**).

700. Dimmitt, Richard B. *A Title Guide to the Talkies: A Comprehensive Listing of 16,000 Feature-Length Films from October, 1927, until December, 1963*. 2 vols. New York and London: Scarecrow Press, 1965, passim.

Lists fourteen films based on Dickens's works and provides basic production information. For continuations, see Aros (**669**).

701. Duffield, Howard. "Edwin Drood." *Times Literary Supplement*, 31 May 1934, p. 392.

Queries about and comments on a dramatization of *The Mystery of Edwin Drood* by W. Stephens and asks for the source of Wilkie Collins's assertion that he had been asked to complete Dickens's unfinished novel and had refused. In a response, 14 June, p. 424, Percy T. Carden points out that Collins made such a statement in a letter to J. Cuming Walters, 4 December 1878, which is printed here. Carden also comments briefly on several dramatizations and continuations of *Edwin Drood*.

702. Emmens, Carol A. *Short Stories on Film*. Littleton, CO: Libraries Unlimited, 1978, pp. 88-89; 2nd ed., as *Short Stories on Film and Video*. Ibid., 1985, pp. 79-80.

The 1978 edition lists and provides details of eight versions of *A Christmas Carol*, two of *Cricket on the Hearth*, and one of "The Signalman" (from *Mugby Junction*, Dickens's Christmas Number for 1866). The 1985 edition adds three versions of *A Christmas Carol*. Adaptations for video may be found in both editions.

703. Epstein, Norrie. *The Friendly Dickens: Being a Good-Natured Guide to the Art and Adventures of the Man Who Invented Scrooge.* New York: Viking, 1998, passim.

In what is essentially a miscellany, Epstein comments on a variety of topics, biographical and critical, proceeding in more or less chronological fashion with sidebars and with quotations from a number Dickens scholars. A number of the sections are concerned with adaptations of Dickens's works: "Adapting *Nickleby*: Interview with David Edgar," pp. 106-09; "Playing Nicholas [Nickleby]: Interview with Roger Rees," pp. 110-13; "Masterpiece Theatre: Interview with David Lodge" (concerning an adaptation of *Martin Chuzzlewit*), pp. 167-70; "Reading *Carol*: Interview with Patrick Stewart" (concerning his readings of *A Christmas Carol*), pp. 193-97; "Dickens's Women: Interview with Mariam Margolyes" (concerning her one-woman shows on Dickens's women), pp. 288-92, and "*Miss Havisham's Fire*: Interview with Dominick Argento" (concerning his opera based on *Great Expectations*), pp. 341-44. Also see "A Select Filmography," pp. 383-405, which lists and comments on seventy-five film and television versions of Dickens's works, 1897-1998. Illustrated.

704. Fawcett, F[rank] Dubrez. *Dickens the Dramatist: On Stage, Screen and Radio.* London: W. H. Allen, 1952. xiii + 278 pp.

While there are introductory chapters on dramatic elements in Dickens's own works and on his own dramatic writings, chapters 3-6 comprise a history of dramatic adaptations of his fiction in the nineteenth and twentieth centuries. In addition, chapter 7 examines Dickens's activities as an actor-manager of amateur dramatic productions, chapter 8 deals with Dickens's public readings, chapter 9 with readings by others from his works, chapter 10 with film versions of his works, chapter 11 with radio dramatizations, and chapter 12 with actors famous for portraying characters from Dickens's works. In "Appendix A: Plays and Adaptations of the Works of Charles Dickens for Stage, Screen and Television," pp. 232-54, Fawcett provides title, type of drama, adapter, and place and year of first performance of nearly 300 plays and adaptations for the stage, screen, and early days of television. Appendix B lists "Characters Played by Dickens in Amateur Theatricals" (including, strangely, a list of Dickens's public readings), and Appendix C lists "Some Nineteenth-Century Theatres Associated with Dickens." "Appendix D: Dickens on the Gramophone" pp. 262-63, is an outdated listing of eleven recordings of readings from and dramatizations of Dickens's works. Many of the illustrations that accompany the text are production photographs.

705. Finlay, Ian F. "Dickens in the Cinema." *Dickensian*, 54 (1958), 106-09.

A list of films inspired by Dickens's novels, 1902-58. See corrections and additions by Edward Wagenknecht, p. 192.

706. Fitz-Gerald, S. J. Adair. "David Copperfield on the Stage." *Dickensian*, 10 (1914), 228-34.

Comments on a number of nineteenth- and early-twentieth-century dramatizations of *David Copperfield*, giving information about casts, theaters, and adapters. An accompanying illustration is on p. 226. See added details in a letter to the editor from A. E. Brookes Cross, pp. 278-79.

707. Fitz-Gerald, S. J. Adair. *Dickens and the Drama, Being an Account of Charles Dickens's Connection with the Stage and the Stage's Connection with Him*. London: Chapman and Hall, 1910; reprinted New York: Benjamin Blom, 1971. xxiii + 352 pp.

Following an account of Dickens as dramatist and amateur actor, pp. 1-72, are chapters on dramatizations by others of each of Dickens's novels and information about performances of these, including cast lists (pp. 73-322). Numerous illustrations.

Review: C. T. Rhode [W. Dexter], *Dickensian*, 7 (1911), 18 (a "dramatic feast," "admirably" arranged, nicely detailed).

708. Fitz-Gerald, S. J. Adair. "Dickens and the Stage." *Dickensian*, 13 (1917), 124-26; reprinted in *Living Age*, 294 (1917), 177-79.

Fitzgerald asserts that, among the more than 200 stage dramatizations of Dickens's novels he has unearthed, there are a number of successful versions, largely because Dickens was himself influenced by the drama but also because his characters are so fully described that they are easily adapted to the stage. However, Fitzgerald finds Dickens's plots, with their "innumerable miniature dramas," too elaborate to be easily adapted.

709. F[itz-Gerald], S. J. A[dair]. "'Oliver Twist' on the Stage in 1838." *Notes and Queries*, 11th ser., 2 (1910), 129.

Asks for the name of the adapter of and the actors in a dramatization of *Oliver Twist* performed at the St. James's Theatre in London, 27 March 1838. John T. Page, p. 191, quotes from the *Dickensian*, August 1905, about various adaptations of *Oliver Twist*, but the earliest noted there was from 21 May 1838. Robert Walters, p. 191, however, quotes from a review of the dramatization that appeared in the *Literary Gazette*, 31 March 1838, disparaging the play but praising the actors, whom Walters identifies from the review. W. Scott, p. 215, refers to and gives a few details about a dramatization of *Oliver Twist* performed in Edinburgh in 1840. Alfred F. Robbins, p. 234, mentions other dramatic versions of the work produced later in 1838 and also productions in 1868, 1869, 1903, and 1905.

710. Fitz-Gerald, S. J. Adair. "The Stage History of 'David Copperfield.'" *Era*, 23 December 1914.

Listed in "Dickensiana Month by Month" in the *Dickensian* (**1043**), 11 (1915).

711. Fulkerson, Richard. "*David Copperfield* in the Victorian Theatre." *Victorians Institute Journal*, 5 (1976), 29-36.

Comments on four nineteenth-century adaptations.

712. Fulkerson, Richard P. "The Dickens Novel on the Victorian Stage." *Dissertation Abstracts International*, 31 (1970/71), 3502A (Ohio State University, 1970).

In the abstract Fulkerson points out that all of Dickens's novels were dramatized for the Victorian stage—over 150 plays were produced on the London stage alone, of which the texts of about fifty are extant. Fulkerson examines a number of these plays and concludes that studying them "produces some indirect evidence about Dickens's relation to the Victorian audience and about the dramatic features of his novels." The plays, Fulkerson notes, ignored the social criticism in the novels and emphasized the melodrama and humor; the later novels, heavy with social criticism, were, accordingly, less popular with the dramatists.

713. Fulkerson, Richard P. "*Oliver Twist* in the Victorian Theatre." *Dickensian*, 70 (1974), 82-95.

Comments on various dramatic adaptations of the novel and their productions. Illustrated.

714. Giddings, Robert, Keith Selby, and Chris Wensley. "The Classic Serial Tradition." In their *Screening the Novel: The Theory and Practice of Literary Dramatization*. Basingstoke, Eng.: Macmillan, 1990, pp. 43-53.

Deals in part with the difficulty of making films of Dickens's novels, with chapters on "The Classic Novel: *Great Expectations*," pp. 54-78, and "The Screening of *Great Expectations*," pp. 79-93, which focus on David Lean's film of the novel. There are also passing references in these and other chapters to films of other Dickens novels—see the index.

715. Gifford, Denis. *The British Film Catalogue, 1895-1970: A Reference Guide.* New York, etc.: McGraw-Hill, 1973, passim; revised and expanded as *The British Film Catalogue, 1895-1985: A Reference Guide.* New York and Oxford, Eng.: Facts on File, 1986, passim.

Claims to be "the first complete catalogue of every British film produced for public entertainment since the invention of cinematography." Films are listed chronologically, but there is a title index that will help one locate films based on Dickens's novels that have the same titles. Production information provided includes cast lists. Entries for 1971-85 in the 1986 revision are appended to a corrected reprint of the 1973 edition as "The British Film Catalogue, Part Two: 1971-1985," with its own index. Decidedly brief plot summaries are included (for a 1983 production of *Oliver Twist*, with George C. Scott as Fagin: "Rich man saves orphan from criminal gang").

716. Gifford, Denis. "Dickens, Charles." In his *Books and Plays in Films, 1896-1915: Literary, Theatrical and Artistic Sources of the First Twenty Years of Motion Pictures.* London: Mansell; Jefferson, NC: McFarland, 1991, pp. 45-47.

Lists sixty early silent films based on Dickens's works, giving title, production company, date of release, and length.

717. Glavin, John. *After Dickens: Reading, Adaptation and Performance.* Cambridge Studies in Nineteenth-Century Literature and Culture, 20. Cambridge and New York: Cambridge University Press, 1999. xiii + 226 pp.

With reference to several adaptations that he staged for the annual conference of the Dickens Project, University of California, Santa Cruz, which adaptations themselves were influenced by the theory and practice of Jerzy Grotowski, Glavin develops an approach to reading Dickens that involves exploration of the theatrical and anti-theatrical elements in his works. But he also explores ways of adapting Dickens's works for theatrical performance and occasionally comments on various recent commercial adaptations of Dickens's novels. He includes his script for a portion of *Our Mutual Friend* (pp. 194-206) and comments on his adaptations of *Bleak House* and *Little Dorrit*—see particularly "How to Do It," pp. 155-88, for his comments on his dramatization of *Little Dorrit*.

Reviews: *Forum for Modern Language Studies*, 37 (2001), 342 (a "playwright's book"; Glavin's "raids upon the texts" of Dickens's novels, "as daringly opportunistic as Dickens's himself, yield valuable booty"); L. James, *Theatre Notebook*, 54 (2000), 125-27 (a "firmly postmodernist" approach); J. John, *Dickens Quarterly*, 18 (2001), 91-95 (finds much to object to, or, rather, finds much that others will object to in the work; concludes that it is "a more rewarding book in retrospect than it seems during the reading process"); R. E. Remshardt, *Victorian Studies*, 43 (2000/01), 671-73 ("challenging and rewarding"); A. Sadrin, *Etudes anglaises*, 53 (2000), 219-20 (in French; written "avec virtuosité et avec suffisance"); P. Schlicke, *Review of English Studies*, 51 (2000), 154-56 ("brilliant, erudite, and engagingly written" but "above all perverse"); G. Smith, *Dickensian*, 96 (2000), 56-57 (unfavorable: "the silly and the serious jostle each other" in this book, "often on the same page").

718. Goble, Alan, ed. *The International Film Index, 1895-1990.* 2 vols. London, etc.: Bowker-Saur, 1991, passim.

Lists some 232,000 films by title in volume 1, *Film Titles*, including films based on Dickens's works, but there is no index of authors. Volume 2 deals with directors.

719. Gooch, Bryan N. S., and David S. Thatcher. "Dickens, Charles John Huffam." In their *Musical Settings of Early and Mid-Victorian Literature: A Catalogue.* Garland Reference Library of the Humanities, 149. New York and London: Garland Publishing, 1979, pp. 202-35.

Lists some 352 songs, instrumental pieces, musicals, film music, operas, and other musical forms alphabetically by title of the Dickens work concerned, with a "Miscellanea" section at the end.

720. Guida, Fred. *"A Christmas Carol" and Its Adaptations: A Critical Examination of Dickens's Story and Its Productions On Screen and Television.* Jefferson, NC, and London: McFarland, 2000. xi + 264 pp.

As Guida notes in his introduction, Part One is "a survey of the literary, historical, and personal forces that were brought to bear on Dickens as he sat down to write the *Carol*, in the closing weeks of the year 1843"; Part Two is "a survey of the audiovisual *Carols*, primarily film and television, that have proliferated over the years"; and Part Three deals with Dickens's other Christmas Books and Christmas Stories and references to Christmas in his other works. Guida includes a "Filmography" and a "Bibliography," pp. 171-231, 245-49. The filmography is "a chronological listing of film, television, and video adaptations of *A Christmas Carol*," giving production details, excerpts from reviews, cast lists, etc., 1901-98. The bibliography consists of a listing of studies "On Dickens, History and/or Literature," "On Christmas," and "On Film, Television, Radio, Theatre and/or Recordings." Illustrated. Also see Guida's Web site for this work: http://www.dickensachristmascarol.com. (**1229**).
Reviews: G. Petrie, *Dickens Quarterly*, 19 (2002), 106-07 ("a labor of love and a work of serious scholarship," with "a valuable and detailed 60-page filmography"); G. Smith, *Dickensian*, 96 (2000), 156-58 (an "entertaining and useful" volume, the "Annotated *Carol* Filmography" being "the heart of the work").

721. Halliwell, Leslie. *Halliwell's Film Guide.* 16th ed. Ed. John Walker. [London]: HarperCollins, 2000, passim.

Provides basic casting and production information about, as well as a brief evaluation of, each film listed. The films are arranged alphabetically by title.

Compared to listings in other bibliographies of Dickens's films, Halliwell's volume is quite incomplete. Earlier editions were published every other year from 1977 to 1991, and yearly thereafter.

722. Harlow, Nancy R. "Dickens' Cinematic Imagination." *Dissertation Abstracts International*, 35 (1974/75), 7307A (Brown University, 1974).

The abstract notes that "Appendix A contains all available data on the 94 film versions made from Dickens' Fiction."

723. Hudson, Virginia O'R. "Charles Dickens and the American Theatre." Doctoral Dissertation, University of Chicago, 1926. *Abstracts of Theses, Humanistic Series., University of Chicago*, 4 (1925/26), 329-32.

Examines the different versions of dramatizations of Dickens's novels and stories performed principally New York and Chicago theaters, 1837-1900, and Boston theaters to 1880.

724. "The Humanity of Charles Dickens Caught by the Cinema: Scenes from Three of the Great Master's Greatest Novels." *Graphic*, 106 (1922), 406-07.

On three films by Thomas Bentley—*Barnaby Rudge* (1915), *The Old Curiosity Shop* (1914), and *Pickwick Papers* (1921)—and some filming difficulties in connection with them. Illustrated.

725. Irwin, Joseph J. "Dramatizations of English Novels on the Nineteenth-Century English Stage." Doctoral dissertation, University of Iowa, 1942.

Listed in Altick and Matthews (**1187**).

726. Kael, Pauline. *5001 Nights at the Movies: A Guide from A to Z*. New York: Holt, Rinehart and Winston, 1982, 1985 (Owl Book Edition), passim; revised, New York: Henry Holt, 1991, passim.

See under "Dickens" in the index for the films based on his novels, for which Kael provides concise evaluations and some production details.

727. Keller, Dean H. *Index to Plays in Periodicals*. Revised and expanded edition. Metuchen, NJ, and London: Scarecrow Press, 1979, pp. 176-78, and *Index to Plays in Periodicals, 1977-1987*. Metuchen, NJ, and London: Scarecrow Press, 1990, p. 70.

In the earlier volume, lists seventeen and, in the later volume, seven adaptations of Dickens's works. An earlier edition was published in 1971.

728. Kitton, F[rederic] G. "Dickens on the Stage." *Household Words*, 45, ns 3 (14 March 1903), 150.

Deals briefly with dramatic versions by others of Dickens's novels and with Dickens's passion for the stage.

729. Klein, Michael, and Gillian Parker. "Selected Filmography: Film Adaptations of English Novels, 1719-1930s." In *The English Novel and the Movies*. Ed. Michael Klein and Gillian Parker. New York: Frederick Ungar, 1981, pp. 323-47.

Some sixty film versions of Dickens's novels are listed, with their directors and dates, on pp. 329-33. Also see the "Selected Bibliography," pp. 352-68, an unannotated listing of general film adaptation studies and studies of individual films, directors, and novelists.

730. Lauritzen, Einar, and Gunnar Lundquist. *American Film-Index, 1908-1915*. Stockholm: Film-Index, 1976, passim, and *American Film-Index, 1916-1920*. Stockholm: Film-Index, 1984, passim.

Films, including those based on Dickens's works, are listed alphabetically by title, with production details.

731. Lazenby, Walter S., Jr. "Stage Versions of Dickens's Novels in America to 1900." *Dissertation Abstracts International*, 23 (1962/63), 2250 (Indiana University, 1962).

Studies dramatizations of Dickens's novels produced in the United States. Early on, Lazenby's abstract indicates, these were versions imported from Britain, but by 1848 "Americans were providing their own adaptations." Lazenby also examines the techniques of adaptation, the characterizations, the actors and productions, and the eventual decline of productions around 1900.

732. Leese, Betty, comp. "Dickens Filmography." Unpublished typescript in British Film Institute Library, London.

Mentioned in Pointer (**788**).

733. Leiter, Samuel L., and Holly Hill, eds. *The Encyclopedia of the New York Stage, 1920-1930*. 2 vols. Westport, CT, and London: Greenwood Press, 1985, I, 175, 487-88; II, 705-06, 987, and Leiter, Samuel L., ed. *The Encyclopedia of the New York Stage, 1930-1940*. New York, Westport, CT, and London: Greenwood Press, 1989, p. 486.

For 1920-30, the editors list and comment on four productions—*The Cricket on the Hearth* (1925) in Russian, *The Lady Dedlock* (1928), *Pickwick* (1927), and

When Crummles Played (1928). For 1930-40, they refer to *The Cricket on the Hearth* (1937). *The Encyclopedia of the New York Stage, 1940-1950* (Westport, CT, and London: Greenwood Press, 1992), contains no Dickens reference.

734. Leonard, William T. *Theatre: Stage to Screen to Television.* 2 vols. Metuchen, NJ, and London: Scarecrow Press, 1981, I, 293-303; II, 1137-50, 1510-16.

Comments on stage, film, and television versions of *A Christmas Carol, Oliver Twist,* and *A Tale of Two Cities,* as well as an opera based on *A Christmas Carol,* giving various production details and brief excerpts from critical reviews.

735. Library of Congress, Copyright Office. *Dramatic Compositions Copyrighted in the United States, 1870 to 1916.* 2 vols. Washington, D. C.: Government Printing Office, 1918, passim.

The plays are listed by title, with useful cross-references; thus, under *Bleak House* one finds not only plays with that title but also cross references to dramatizations of the novel entitled *The Dedlock Secret, Jo, the Waif of the Streets,* and *Tom All Alone's.* Also see under "Dickens" in the index in volume 2 for references to dramas based on his works.

736. Library of Congress, Copyright Office. *Motion Pictures, 1912-1939; Motion Pictures, 1940-1949; Motion Pictures, 1950-1959; Motion Pictures, 1960-69.* Catalog of Copyright Entries, Cumulative Series. Washington, D. C.: Library of Congress, 1951, 1953, 1960, 1971, passim.

See the indexes to these volumes for nineteen works based on Dickens's novels and stories, listed by title, with principal production information, though no cast lists. For motion pictures produced 1894-1912, see Howard L. Walls (**811**).

737. Lynch, Richard C. *Broadway, Movie, TV, and Studio Cast Musicals on Record: A Discography of Recordings, 1985-1995.* Discographies, 68. Westport, CT, and London: Greenwood Press, 1996, pp. 27-28, 63-64, 117-19.

Gives publishing details and lists casts and songs, with composer, librettist, and other relevant information, about three musicals based on Dickens novels: *A Christmas Carol* (1994), *Great Expectations* (1995), and *Oliver!* (1960, 1963).

738. Magill, Frank N., ed. *Magill's Survey of Cinema: Silent Films.* 3 vols. Englewood Cliffs, NJ: Salem Press, 1982, passim.

See Tanita C. Kelley's "*Oliver Twist*," II, 821-24; Joan I. Cohen's "*Oliver Twist*," II, 825-27; and Lennox Sanderson, Jr.'s "*A Tale of Two Cities*," III, 1088-90. Each two to three page essay gives production information on a particular film adaptation but also refers to other film versions of the same novel.

739. Magill, Frank N., ed, with Patricia K. Hanson and Stephen L. Hanson, assoc. eds. *Magill's Survey of Cinema: English Language Films.* 1st ser. 4 vols. Englewood Cliffs, NJ: Salem Press, 1980, passim.

Includes cast and filmmaker lists, a description, and an evaluation of four films based on Dickens's novels: "*A Christmas Carol*" (1951, with Alistair Sim), by James Ursini, I, 336-38; "*Oliver!*" (1968, with Mark Lester, Ron Moody, and Oliver Reed), by Nick Roddick, III, 1252-55; "*Oliver Twist*" (1951, with John Howard Davies, Alec Guinness, and Robert Newton), by DeWitt Bodeen, III, 1256-58; and "*A Tale of Two Cities*" (1935, with Ronald Colman and Basil Rathbone), by DeWitt Bodeen, IV, 1667-70.

740. Manchel, Frank. "Dickens in the Film: The Adaptation of Three Books." In his *Film Study: A Resource Guide.* Rutherford, Madison, and Teaneck, NJ: Fairleigh Dickinson University Press, 1973, pp. 149-56.

Comments on David Lean's adaptation of *Great Expectations* (1947), the 1935 version of *A Tale of Two Cities* (David Selznick), and George Cukor's adaptation of *David Copperfield* (1935). According to "The Dickens Checklist," *Dickens Studies Newsletter*, 6, i (March 1975), 34, this study was condensed and slightly revised in *Exercise Exchange*, 19 (Fall 1974), 20-28.

741. Marsh, Joss L. "Inimitable Double Vision: Dickens, *Little Dorrit*, Photography, Film." *Dickens Studies Annual*, 22 (1993), 239-82.

While largely concerned with Christine Edzard's film version of *Little Dorrit* (1987), in a final section, "Dickens, Cinema, and the Culture of the Country," pp. 273-77, Marsh comments on filmic elements in Dickens's novels, as well as on several English film adaptations of other Dickens novels.

742. Mawson, Harry P. "Dickens on the Stage." *Theatre* (New York), 15 (1912), 46-49, viii.

Comments on the success or failure of various dramatizations of Dickens's works and some of the well-known actors who performed in them. Illustrated with numerous photographs and drawings of scenes from dramatizations of Dickens's novels.

743. McCracken-Flesher, Caroline. "The Incorporation of *A Christmas Carol*: A Tale of Seasonal Screening." *Dickens Studies Annual*, 24 (1996), 93-118.

On the "transmutation" of *A Christmas Carol* "into a tool for corporate enrichment," its being "co-opted for corporate culture"–in advertising, television, and film versions. Illustrated.

744. McPharlin, Paul. "Plays from Dickens." *Notes and Queries*, 157 (1929), 132.

Asks if anyone has compiled a list of dramatic adaptations of Dickens's novels. In response, H. M. Cashmore, p. 304, refers McPharlin to F. G. Kitton's *Dickensiana* (**996**), pp. 362-82; Reginald Clarence's [H. J. Eldredge's] *"The Stage" Cyclopaedia: A Bibliography of Plays* (London: "The Stage," 1909); Firkins's "Index to Plays, 1800-1926" (**151**); and issues of the *Dickensian*.

745. Millard-Anderson, Barbara S. "Cultural Transformations of 'Nicholas Nickleby': From the Book to the Boards." *Dissertation Abstracts International*, 56 (1995/96), 3139A (University of South Carolina, 1995).

An examination of nineteenth- and twentieth-century "stage productions, children's literature, public readings, and film" based on *Nicholas Nickleby*.

746. Miller, W[illiam]. "Henry Burnett and 'The Ivy Green.'" *Dickensian*, 10 (1914), 96.

Describes a volume of songs set to music by Burnett, Dickens's brother-in-law, entitled *Miscellaneous Vocal Music* (London: C. Jefferys, n. d.), and prints a hitherto unknown musical setting for Dickens's poem "The Ivy Green." A letter to the editor from Robert H. Baker, p. 164, identifies yet another (a seventh) setting of the poem by Arthur Crump, 1898.

747. Miller, W[illiam]. "Pickwick Music." *Dickensian*, 32 (1935/36), 70.

A list of twenty-six published musical pieces based on *Pickwick Papers*, from 1838-1908, but many are undated.

748. Miller, W[illiam]. "Plays from Pickwick." *Dickensian*, 32 (1935/36), 36.

A list of twenty-nine published plays, 1837-1934, based on *Pickwick Papers*.

749. Miller, William. "A Unique Dickens Item." *Dickensian*, 7 (1911), 94-96.

On a piece of music, "Lucie Manette, a Dramatic Overture."

750. Montgomery, George E. "Dickens on the American Stage." *American Magazine*, 8 (1888), 190-203.

Asserts that, while the dramatizations of Dickens's novels have been quite inferior to the novels themselves, "no novelist has been more popular or more interesting on the stage" than Dickens, and "few novelists have offered as rare and extraordinary opportunities to the actor." Montgomery also provides information about a number of dramatizations of Dickens's novels for both the English and American stage, as well as about some of the American actors who made their characterizations famous. Illustrated.

751. Morley, Malcolm. "*All the Year Round* Plays." *Dickensian*, 52 (1955/56), 128-31, 177-80.

A history of the dramatizations of the Christmas numbers of *All the Year Round*, 1860-1938. Morley notes how Dickens and Collins used a printed list of characters and scenes (though they never wrote a dramatic version) in *A Message from the Sea*, the Christmas number for 1860, to secure, if but briefly, the rights to the work, a practice, Morley indicates, that Dickens also used for *Great Expectations*. Illustrated.

752. Morley, Malcolm. "Apt Adaptations of Dickens." *Dickensian*, 59 (1963), 61.

A review of three published dramatizations of Dickens's works written by Eric Jones-Evans and published by G. P. Wilson (Southampton, Eng.): *The Haunted Man* (1962), *Scrooge and the Miser* (1962), and *The Death of a Lawyer* (1962), based on *Bleak House*.

753. Morley, Malcolm. "*The Battle of Life* in the Theatre." *Dickensian*, 48 (1951/52), 76-81.

Provides much information about stage versions, 1846-47 and late-nineteenth- and early-twentieth-century, of *The Battle of Life*. Illustrated.

754. Morley, Malcolm. "*Bleak House* Scene." *Dickensian*, 49 (1952/53), 175-82.

A history of the dramatizations of *Bleak House*, 1853, 1875-76, and later—to 1950. Illustrated. See a correction, *Dickensian*, 50 (1953/54), 42.

755. Morley, Malcolm. "'The Cricket' on the Stage." *Dickensian*, 48 (1951/52), 17-24.

Comments on stage versions of *The Cricket on the Hearth*, 1845-46 and later to 1941. Illustrated.

756. Morley, Malcolm. "Curtain Up on *A Christmas Carol.*" *Dickensian*, 47 (1950/51), 159-64.

Comments on stage versions of *A Christmas Carol*, 1844 and later. Illustrated.

757. Morley, Malcolm. "Early Dickens Drama in America." *Dickensian*, 44 (1947/48), 153-57.

Gives details of performances of dramatizations, 1837-42, of early Dickens works (from *Pickwick Papers* to *Barnaby Rudge*) in the United States. Illustrated.

758. Morley, Malcolm. "Early Dramas of *Oliver Twist.*" *Dickensian*, 43 (1946/47), 74-79.

Comments on a number of dramatizations of *Oliver Twist*, mainly produced 1837-39 but a few produced 1905-12. Illustrated.

759. Morley, Malcolm. "Enter *Dombey and Son.*" *Dickensian*, 48 (1951/52), 128-33.

A history of stage versions of *Dombey and Son*, 1847-48 and 1860-1946. Illustrated.

760. Morley, Malcolm. "Enter *Our Mutual Friend.*" *Dickensian*, 52 (1955/56), 39-43.

A history of stage versions of *Our Mutual Friend* to 1954. Morley notes that, although Dickens took care to protect *Great Expectations* and *A Message from the Sea* from publishing pirates and dramatizers, he did not do so for *Our Mutual Friend*; as a result, the first dramatic adaptation appeared in 1866, only seven months after he completed the novel in November 1865. Illustrated. See Morley (**751, 774**).

761. Morley, Malcolm. "*Hard Times* on the Stage." *Dickensian*, 50 (1953/54), 69-73.

A history of stage versions of *Hard Times*, 1854-1939. Morley also mentions two farces based on Dickens's involvement with *Household Words*, produced in 1858 and 1859, and the "editorial upheavals" when Dickens ended *Household Words* and began *All the Year Round*. Illustrated.

762. Morley, Malcolm. "*Little Dorrit* On and Off." *Dickensian*, 50 (1953/54), 136-40.

A history of the small number of dramatizations of *Little Dorrit*, 1856-57, 1864, 1870, 1905-06 (German), and 1953 (Russian). Illustrated.

763. Morley, Malcolm. "*Martin Chuzzlewit* in the Theatre." *Dickensian*, 47 (1950/51), 98-102.

Comments on dramatizations of *Martin Chuzzlewit*, mainly 1844-46, but a few later ones. Illustrated.

764. Morley, Malcolm. "*Nicholas Nickleby* on the Boards." *Dickensian*, 43 (1946/47), 137-41.

Comments on dramatizations of *Nicholas Nickleby*, 1838-48. Illustrated.

765. Morley, Malcolm. "*No Thoroughfare* Back Stage." *Dickensian*, 50 (1953/54), 37-42.

On the difficulties Wilkie Collins and Dickens had in dramatizing their joint Christmas Story for 1867. Morley gives details of the first production of the dramatic version (London, 1867). He also identifies a French translation (*L'Abîme*) in 1868 and an American translation of that (also 1868), as well as later productions of *No Thoroughfare* to 1903. Illustrated.

766. Morley, Malcolm. "Pepper and *The Haunted Man*." *Dickensian*, 48 (1951/52), 185-90.

A history of the dramatizations of Dickens's last Christmas Book, 1848-1908. Also see *Dickensian*, 49 (1952/53), 85, for the correction of a date. Illustrated.

767. Morley, Malcolm. "Plays and Sketches by Boz." *Dickensian*, 52 (1955/56), 81-88.

A superficial history of Dickens's own dramas and later productions of them, as well as dramatizations by others based on stories in *Sketches by Boz*. Illustrated.

768. Morley, Malcolm. "Plays from the Christmas Numbers of *Household Words*." *Dickensian*, 51 (1954/55), 127-32, 169-73.

A history of productions of plays based on Dickens's Christmas Stories, beginning with *The Seven Poor Travellers* in 1855. Illustrated.

769. Morley, Malcolm. "Plays in *Master Humphrey's Clock*." *Dickensian*, 43 (1946/47), 202-05.

On dramatizations of *The Old Curiosity Shop* and *Barnaby Rudge*, 1840-41 and later.

770. Morley, Malcolm. "Ring Up *The Chimes.*" *Dickensian*, 47 (1950/51), 202-06.

On dramatizations of *The Chimes* in 1844-46, 1872-73, and 1910. Illustrated.

771. Morley, Malcolm. "Stage Appearances of *Copperfield.*" *Dickensian*, 49 (1952/53), 77-85.

A history of dramatizations of *David Copperfield*, 1850-51 and 1866-1945. Illustrated.

772. Morley, Malcolm. "Stage Solutions to the Mystery." *Dickensian*, 53 (1957), 46-48, 93-97, 180-84.

Comments on a number of dramatic versions of *The Mystery of Edwin Drood* and their conclusions, 1870-1956. Illustrated.

773. Morley, Malcolm. "The Stage Story of *A Tale of Two Cities.*" *Dickensian*, 51 (1954/55), 34-40.

A history of dramatizations of *A Tale of Two Cities*, 1860-1936. Illustrated.

774. Morley, Malcolm. "Stages of *Great Expectations.*" *Dickensian*, 51 (1954/55), 79-83.

In this history of stage productions of *Great Expectations*, Morley notes that Dickens registered a dramatic version of *Great Expectations* by himself (more a list of characters and scenes than anything else; he never wrote the play) as a means of forestalling others from dramatizing the work, although this did not prevent American productions of the work in 1861-62 and 1867; on the other hand, the first London production did not occur until 1871, after Dickens's death. Morley also mentions several later productions—to 1947. Illustrated.

775. Mullin, Donald, comp. *Victorian Plays: A Record of Significant Productions on the London Stage, 1837-1901.* New York, Westport, CT, and London: Greenwood Press, 1987, passim.

Lists a number of dramatizations of Dickens's works by others, among them Charles Dickens, Jr. Of Dickens's own plays, only *Is She His Wife?* and *No Thoroughfare* (largely by Wilkie Collins) are included, but Mullin identifies the theaters in which each was performed and gives cast lists for the latter.

776. Nash, Jay R., and Stanley R. Ross. *The Motion Picture Guide*. 12 vols. Chicago: Cinebooks, 1985-87, passim.

See the index (volumes 11-12) for the twenty-one sound and the twelve silent films of Dickens's works listed. The entries themselves provide production details, including cast lists and comments on and evaluations of the films and the performers, sometimes briefly, sometimes at length. Volumes 1-9 cover 1927-84; volume 10, by Robert Connelly, is *Silent Film, 1910-1936*. Harner (**1147**), p. 647, notes that there is also an annual supplement: *The Motion Picture Guide Annual* (New York: Cinebooks, 1987-) and that the work is also available on CD-ROM.

777. Newton, H. Chance. "Dramatisers of Dickens, and How He Foiled a Few." *Household Words*, 49, ns 7 (1905), 1769.

Comments on several dramatizations of Dickens's novels and their authors.

778. Nicoll, Allardyce. *A History of Early Nineteenth Century Drama, 1800-1850*. 2 vols. Cambridge: Cambridge University Press, 1930, I, 96-99, 146-47, 209-10; II, passim; as *Early Nineteenth Century Drama, 1800-1850*, Vol. 4 of *A History of English Drama, 1660-1900*. [2nd ed.]. Cambridge: Cambridge University Press, 1955, etc., pp. 96-99, 146-47, 209-10, and passim.

Comments on some of the adaptations by others of Dickens's novels for the stage as well as on Dickens's own dramatic works, which Nicoll characterizes as "operatic farces." In Vol. 2: *Hand-List of Plays, 1800-1850* (**157**), dramatic adaptations by others of Dickens's plays are listed by dramatist, and there is no easy way to locate them; however, Nicoll does identify some of them in the index for volume 1 of this work.

779. Nicoll, Allardyce. *A History of Late Nineteenth Century Drama, 1850-1900*. 2 vols. Cambridge: Cambridge University Press, 1946; reprinted 1949, I, 80, 93; as *Late Nineteenth Century Drama, 1850-1900*. Vol. 5 of *A History of English Drama, 1660-1900*. [2nd ed.]. Cambridge: Cambridge University Press, 1959, etc., pp. 80, 93.

Includes brief notices of some of the dramatic adaptations of Dickens's novels. In Vol. 2: *Hand-List of Plays, 1850-1900*, p. 344, lists three plays by Charles Dickens, Jr., two of which are dramatic adaptations of *The Battle of Life* and *The Old Curiosity Shop*. The third, mistakenly attributed to the son rather than the father, an error not caught in the revision, is *No Thoroughfare* (1867), which Dickens wrote in collaboration with Wilkie Collins. Dramatic adaptations by others of Dickens's plays are listed by dramatist, and there is no easy way to locate them; however, Nicoll does identify some of them in the index for volume 1 of this work.

780. Odell, George C. D. *Annals of the New York Stage*. 15 vols. New York: Columbia University Press, 1927-49, passim.

In this enormously detailed history of the New York stage, 1699-1894, Odell makes fairly frequent reference to stage performances of Dickens's works (from 1842 on), to his public readings (1867-68) and those of his son Charles (1887-88), readings from his works and public lectures by others, and even Dickens parties. Odell's comments can be most easily traced through the index in each volume, but one needs to be careful here, and check not only the entries under "Dickens" but also under the titles of his individual novels.

781. Page, Norman. "Early Dramatizations of Dickens' Works." In his *A Dickens Companion* (**223**), pp. 325-28.

A selective list of dramatizations.

782. Page, Norman. "Filmography." In his *A Dickens Companion* (**223**), pp. 319-23.

Lists films based on Dickens's novels with brief information about each.

783. Parsons, Coleman O. "The Friendship of Theodore Martin and William Harrison Ainsworth." *Notes and Queries*, 166 (1934), 435-39.

Comments in passing (p. 438) on *Sam Weller; or, The Pickwickians* (1837), William T. Moncrieff's adaptation of *Pickwick Papers*. It was, Parsons notes, "ill received by press and by author, who satirised him in 'Nicholas Nickleby' as the 'literary gentleman' at the farewell supper given to Mr. Vincent Crummles—an adapter of two hundred and forty-seven novels as fast as they came out, some even faster." Parsons also comments briefly on both Moncrieff's adaptation of *Nicholas Nickleby*, which appeared when the novel was only three-quarters finished, and Edward Stirling's adaptation of it (1838), a performance of which Dickens actually attended.

784. Pemberton, T. Edgar. "Chapter V. Adaptations and Impersonations." In his *Charles Dickens and the Stage. A Record of His Connection with the Drama as Playwright, Actor, and Critic*. London: Redway, 1888, pp. 136-85.

Provides details of a number of dramatic adaptations of Dickens's novels, principally ones performed during Dickens's lifetime, including Dickens's usually negative reactions to them. Pemberton also comments on the performances of a number of the actors who portrayed Dickens characters in them.

785. Petrie, Graham. "Silent Film Adaptations of Dickens, Part I: From the Beginning to 1911," "Part II: 1912-1919," and "Part III: 1920-1927." *Dickensian*, 97 (2001), 7-21, 101-15, 197-213.

Not so much bibliographically oriented as a commentary on the nature, extent, and focus of a number of early silent film adaptations of Dickens's works, which the author has obviously viewed, though Petrie does give dates and some production details of these films. He notes in passing that "most published filmographies seriously misrepresent the actual number of films made" but finds that Michael Pointer's *Charles Dickens on the Screen* (**788**) is "by far the most reliable published compilation yet," and in agreement, with a couple of exceptions, to his own lists. Illustrated.

786. Pierce, Dorothy. "Special Bibliography: The Stage Versions of Dickens' Novels." *Bulletin of Bibliography and Dramatic Index*, 16 (1936/39), 10, 30-32, 52-54.

Provides information about the authors, places and dates of the first performances, and publications of dramatizations of Dickens's novels in English and other languages.

787. "Plays from Dickens's Books: Some Notable Performances Given in New York." *New York Sun*, 22 October 1911, third sect., p. 8.

Complains that in the then forthcoming centenary year no plays based on Dickens's works were scheduled for the American theater. In a long article, the anonymous author reviews a number of the actors who portrayed Dickens characters earlier on the American stage in productions of most of Dickens's works from 1837 (*Pickwick Papers*) on, in the process giving information about the plays and their authors.

788. Pointer, Michael. *Charles Dickens on the Screen: The Film, Television, and Video Adaptations*. Lanham, MD, and London: Scarecrow Press, 1996. vii + 207 pp.

As Pointer notes in his introduction, this is "an attempt to survey and record" as many cinema and television versions of Dickens's works "as it is possible to trace." The first half of the volume is a detailed survey in some twelve short chapters of Dickens's works "on the Screen," 1897 to date. The second half contains a "Catalog of Film, Television, and Video Productions," pp. 115-94, which claims to be the "most comprehensive catalog of such dramatizations ever published." Pointer nowhere acknowledges the earlier work of Ana Zambrano (**821-23, 1370-71**), however, although he does list the work of H. Philip Bolton (**676**) and Paul Davis (**97**) in his "Bibliography" (**1366**), pp. 195-97, and mentions there an unpublished typescript, "Dickens Filmography," by Betty Leese, in the British Film Institute Library, London (**732**). Pointer's catalogue is divided into Silent Films, Sound Films, and Television and Video Productions, and the entries are listed chronologically in each division. Each entry provides, where available, production details and cast lists. Pointer finds that the theatricality of Dickens's characters and plots in particular stimulated film treatments of his novels, as did, obviously, earlier stage versions. Illustrated with numerous film stills.

Reviews: B. Rosenberg, *Dickens Quarterly*, 14 (1997), 46-49 ("performs its scholarly service well" in giving the reader "all the available information about when, how, and to what effect Dickens's works have been adapted and re-created in film," though "a more theoretically ambitious study" would have been welcome); G. Smith, *Dickensian*, 93 (1997), 143-44 (finds the "Catalog" in part 2 of "immense value" as a reference tool and source of basic information but the study of Dickens on the screen in part 1 lacking in scholarship and careless in details). Also see Petrie (**785**).

789. Poole, Mike. "Dickens and Film: 101 Uses of a Dead Author." In *The Changing World of Charles Dickens*. Ed. Robert Giddings. London: Vision Press; Totowa, NJ: Barnes & Noble, 1983, pp. 148-62.

Points out that the treatment of Dickens's works in film is perhaps more "a history of that culture itself" than anything else—the "ability of film and television to assimilate, re-make and recycle any literary entity in their own image." Poole does not necessarily find this "debasing" but rather a means of making Dickens "*usable* again to audiences who would not otherwise encounter him."

790. Powell, Dilys. "Postscript: Dickens on Film." In *Dickens and Fame 1870-1970: Essays on the Author's Reputation*. Ed. Michael Slater. Centenary Number of *Dickensian*, 66, ii (May 1970), pp. 183-85.

Brief commentary on some filmed versions of Dickens's novels, concluding that "the truly gigantic Dickens eludes the screen, however wide." Also see Riley (**793**).

791. Rand, Frank H. *Les adaptations théâtrales des romans de Dickens en Angleterre (1837-1870)*. Paris: Librairie Lipschutz, 1939. 204 pp. (doctoral dissertation, Université de Paris, Faculté des lettres, 1939).

In part 1, provides details about a number of adaptations of Dickens's novels produced between 1838 and 1870 in England. Part 2 is a critical study of these adaptations. A bibliography, pp. 185-99, lists the adaptations, with author where known (pp. 185-94), followed by a list of general studies and studies of Dickens relevant to the subject. Rice (**93**) finds Rand's information "more accurate" than that in Fawcett (**704**).

792. Reynolds, Ernest R. *Early Victorian Drama (1830-1870)*. Cambridge, Eng.: W. Heffer & Sons, 1936; reprinted New York: Benjamin Blom, 1965, pp. 142-44.

Reynolds lists nineteenth-century dramatizations of Dickens's novels but asserts that Dickens was not as major an influence on mid-nineteenth-century drama as S. J. Adair Fitz-Gerald (**707**) indicates he was.

793. Riley, Michael M. "Dickens and Film: Notes on Adaptation." *Dickens Studies Newsletter*, 5 (1974), 110-12.

Takes exception to Powell (**790**), pointing out that a Dickens film "is not a Dickens novel, and if it succeeds it must do so on its own artistic terms."

794. Rogers-Harper, Wendy. "Great Adaptations: David Lean's Encounters with the Novel." *Dissertation Abstracts International*, 52 (1991/92), 3754A-55A (University of South Florida, 1991).

Examines "critical issues and creative strategies of six novels and of the films adapted from them" by Lean, including *Great Expectations* and *Oliver Twist*.

795. Roman, Robert C. "Dickens's 'A Christmas Carol.'" *Films in Review*, 9 (1958), 572-74.

A superficial survey of films based on Dickens's first Christmas Book from 1908, 1910, 1913, 1914, 1916, 1935, 1938, and 1951, with some production details. Illustrated.

796. Sammon, Paul. *The "Christmas Carol" Trivia Book: Everything You Ever Wanted to Know About Every Version of the Dickens Classic*. Secaucus, NJ: Carol Publishing Group, 1994. xvii + 237 pp.

Lists and evaluates various film (including cartoon) and television versions, musicals, dances, spoken word recordings, and other versions of *A Christmas Carol*, pp. 29-186. In chapter 17, "Credits and Video Sources," pp. 187-201, Sammon lists all such sources, with information about director, actors, length, etc.; in chapter 18, "Bibliography," pp. 202-04, he lists his sources of information; and in chapter 19, "Carols on Tape," pp. 205-08, he lists companies that may have some of the versions on video and audio tape, as well as stills from various productions. Chapter 1, "The Author," pp. 1-9, is a biographical sketch of Dickens. Chapter 2, "The Story," pp. 10-28, superficially discusses the writing and publication of the work.

797. Saunders, Mary. "Dickens and Film: A Survey of Filmographical, Bibliographical, and Critical Materials." *Victorians Institute Journal*, 20 (1992), 303-13.

Surveys the limited ways then available for tracking film and television versions of Dickens's works and comments on several scholarly studies of Dickens and film. Saunders also briefly evaluates some of the then recent films and television versions of Dickens's works.

798. Schlicke, Paul, ed. Entries on Adaptations of Dickens's Works. *Oxford Reader's Companion to Dickens* (**2309**), passim.

Contains several entries by various contributors on adaptations of Dickens's works, all concise, selective surveys of their subjects. See in particular A[lan] S. W[atts], "Abridgements of Dickens's Works," pp. 1-2, "Adaptations of Dickens's Works," p. 4, and "Sequels and Continuations," pp. 513-14; G[illian] A[very], "Children's Versions of Dickens," pp. 92-93; H. P[hilip] B[olton], "Dramatizations and Dramatizers of Dickens's Works," pp. 195-99; G[rahame] F. S[mith], "Films and Film-Makers of Dickens," pp. 233-36, and "Television Adaptations of Dickens," pp. 548, 554; and R[obert] T. B[ledsoe], "Dickens's Works," pp. 385-86. The pagination varies somewhat in the 2000 paperback edition—see, respectively, pp. 1-2, 4-5, 525-26, 96-97, 198-202, 241-44, 565, and 394-95.

799. "Second Thoughts on First Nights. On Some Acting Editions of that Favorite Author, Mr. Charles Dickens." *New York Times*, 1 November 1914, section 8, p. 8.

Cursory remarks on some dramatic adaptations of Dickens's novels.

800. Sibley, Brian. "You Have Never Seen the Like of Me Before!" and "Nice Story, Mr. Dickens!" and "Hear Dickens, and Die!" and "The End of It." In his ***A Christmas Carol: The Unsung Story***. Oxford: Lion Publishing; Sutherland, Austral.: Albatross Books, 1994, pp. 141-56, 157-75, 176-86, 187-96.

In these four chapters accompanying a printing of Dickens's major Christmas Book, Sibley comments, respectively, on imitations and dramatic and musical adaptations, film adaptations, reading versions by Dickens and others, and parodies of *A Christmas Carol*.

801. Slater, Michael. "The Centenary on Radio, Stage and Screen." *Dickensian*, 66 (1970), 237-39.

Comments on a number of adaptations of Dickens's works performed in 1970, the centenary of Dickens's death. Also see a response by Philip Collins, *Dickensian*, 67 (1971), 42, concerning his own readings from Dickens's works.

802. Slide, Anthony, ed. *Selected Film Criticism, 1896-1911*; *Selected Film Criticism, 1912-1920*; *Selected Film Criticism,1921-1930*; *Selected Film Criticism, 1931-1940*; *Selected Film Criticism, 1941-1950*; *Selected Film Criticism: Foreign Films, 1930-1950*; and *Selected Film Criticism, 1951-1960*. Metuchen, NJ, and London: Scarecrow Press, 1982, 1982, 1982, 1982, 1983, 1984, 1985, passim.

These volumes contain fairly substantial excerpts from reviews of the films listed, including several based on Dickens's works. There is an alphabetical table of contents listing the films, but, except for the last two volumes, no indexes.

803. Stephens, John R. *The Profession of the Playwright: British Theatre, 1800-1900*. Cambridge, New York, etc.: Cambridge University Press, 1992, pp. 97-98 and passim.

Makes several passing comments on Dickens and the theater and on dramatic piracies of Dickens's works by William Thomas Moncrieff and Colin Hazlewood.

804. Suddaby, John. "Hull's Early Plays of Dickens." *Hull Museum Publications*, no. 51 (March 1908), 13-23; no. 53 (June 1908), 31-37.

Notes that "some 70 playbills relating to the first and other early productions" of dramatizations of Dickens's novels in Hull, England, "have recently come to light," covering 1837-50. Suddaby also provides details of a number of these. The contents of no. 51 were reprinted in somewhat abbreviated form as Chapter X, "Hull's Early Plays of Dickens," in Thomas Sheppard's *Evolution of the Drama in Hull and District* (Hull, Eng.: A. Brown, 1927), pp. 83-98.

805. "Table-Talk." *Appleton's Journal*, 4 (1870), 263-64.

Comments on some American dramatic productions of Dickens's novels.

806. T[homson], P[eter]. "Dickens, Charles (John Huffam) (1812-70)." In *The Cambridge Guide to World Theatre*. Ed. Martin Banham. Cambridge, New York, etc.: Cambridge University Press, 1988, p. 279; updated as *The Cambridge Guide to Theatre*. Cambridge: Cambridge University Press, 1992, p. 279; revised ed., 1995, p. 296.

A brief entry, largely on the influence of the theater on Dickens's writings. Thomson devotes one sentence to Dickens's own plays and several to adaptations of his works by others and famous actors who played roles in them. In the revised edition only minor emendations are made.

807.   Tibbetts, John C., and James M. Welsh, eds. *The Encyclopedia of Novels into Film*. New York: Facts on File, 1998, pp. 59-61, 79-81, 156-57, 307-09, 323-25, 404-06.

Contains a list of film versions, followed by brief essays by various authors on the novel and film versions, of, respectively, *A Christmas Carol* (by Frank Thompson), *David Copperfield* (by Gene D. Phillips, S. J.), *Great Expectations* (by C. Kenneth Pellow and John C. Tibbetts), *Oliver Twist* (by Kathryn Osenlund), *Pickwick Papers* (by Ben Furnish), and *A Tale of Two Cities* (by Michael W. Given). In an introduction, pp. xiii-xx, Tibbetts and Welsh comment, pp. xiv-xv, on Dickens's effective use of what would later be seen as cinematic techniques.

808.   Tupper, Lucy. "Dickens on the Screen: His Books Have Been Used for Some All-Time Best Pictures." *Films in Review*, 10 (1959), 142-52.

Comments on a number of film versions of Dickens's novels, 1908-58. Illustrated.

809.   Van Amerongen, J. B. "Appendix: Dickens on the Stage." In his *The Actor in Dickens. A Study of the Histrionic and Dramatic Elements in the Novelist's Life and Works*. London: Cecil Palmer, 1926; New York: D. Appleton, 1927; reprinted New York: Benjamin Blom, 1969; New York: Haskell House, 1970, pp. 261-73, 295-96 (doctoral dissertation, University of Amsterdam, 1926).

Discusses a selected group of dramatic adaptations by others of Dickens's novels. Illustrated.

810.   Wagner, Geoffrey. *The Novel and the Cinema*. Rutherford, Madison, and Teaneck, NJ: Fairleigh Dickinson University Press; London: Tantivy Press, 1975, passim.

Makes only passing references, none significant, to films based on Dickens's novels.

811. Walls, Howard L. *Motion Pictures, 1894-1912, Identified from the Records of the United States Copyright Office*. [Washington, D. C.]: Copyright Office, Library of Congress, 1953, passim.

See the index for works based on Dickens's novels and stories. This volume was published outside the series produced by the Library of Congress (**736**) covering motion pictures, 1912-69, but is consistent with that series.

812. Walsh, Jim. "Dickensiana on Cylinders and Discs." *Hobbies*, 63, x (December 1958), 106, 108-09; xi (Jan. 1959), 106, 108, 124.

Identifies, describes, and provides bibliographical information about some early and more recent recordings of songs, recitations, and dramatizations, 1897-1913 (part 1) and 1913-58 (part 2), based on Dickens's works. Illustrated.

813. Walsh, Ulysses. "Dickens on Discs." *Dickensian*, 43 (1946/47), 42-45.

Refers to early phonograph recordings of Dickens's works, 1903-15, and comments on songs mentioned in Dickens's works.

814. Wearing, J. P. *The London Stage, 1890-1899: A Calendar of Plays and Players*. 2 vols. Metuchen, NJ: Scarecrow Press, 1976; *1900-1909*. 2 vols.; *1910-1919*. 2 vols.; *1920-1929*. 3 vols.; *1930-1939*. 3 vols.; *1940-1949*. 2 vols.; *1950-1959*. 2 vols. Metuchen, NJ, and London: Scarecrow Press, 1981, 1982, 1984, 1990, 1991,1993, passim.

A chronological listing of first-night productions, with cast lists and other production information. See the index under "Dickens" for plays based on his works.

815. West, Dorothy H., and Dorothy M. Peake, comps. *Play Index, 1949-52: An Index to 2616 Plays in 1138 Volumes*. New York: H. W. Wilson, 1953, passim.

Look under Dickens for an unannotated list of published adaptations of his works. Eight continuations have been published to date—for 1953-60, ed. Estelle A. Fidell and Dorothy M. Peake (1963); for 1961-67, 1968-72, and 1973-77, ed. Estelle A. Fidell (1968, 1973, 1978); for 1978-82, ed. Juliette Yaakov (1983); for 1983-87, 1988-92, and 1993-97, ed. Juliette Yaakov and John Greenfieldt (1988, 1993, 1998). The full title of the latest volume is *Play Index, 1993-1997: An Index to 4,617 Plays*.

816. West, Russell. "English Nineteenth-Century Novels on the German Stage: Birch Pfeiffer's Adaptations of Dickens, Brontë, Eliot and Collins." In *Beitrage zur Rezeption der britischen und irischen Literatur des 19. Jahrhunderts im deutschsprachigen Raum*. Ed. Norbert Bachleitner. Atlanta, GA: Rodopi, 2000, pp. 293-316.

Includes Pfeiffer's adaptation of *The Old Curiosity Shop*. Listed in the Modern Language Association bibliography (**1042**) for 2000.

817.   Williams, Tony. "Fellowship Forum: Imitating the Inimitable?–Dickens and Adaptation." *Dickensian*, 97 (2001), 74-76.

Comments on the difficulty of adapting Dickens's works for film or stage but asserts that the "constant re-invention in the context of different ages" is what keeps Dickens alive.

818.   Wilstach, Paul. "Dramatisations of Dickens." *Bookman* (New York), 14 (1901/02), 52-62.

Provides details about various English and American dramatizations of Dickens's works, accompanied by a number of drawings and photographs of characters from productions.

819.   Woollcott, Alexander. "The Dramatizations of Dickens." In his *Mr. Dickens Goes to the Play*. New York and London: G. P. Putnam's Sons, 1922; reprinted Port Washington, NY: Kennikat Press, 1967, pp. 221-36.

Comments on some of the adaptations by others of Dickens's works. Illustrated.

820.   Workers of the Writers' Program of the Work Projects Administration of the City of New York, comps. "Adaptations from Fiction." In their *The Film Index: A Bibliography*. Vol. 1: *The Film as Art*. New York: H. W. Wilson, 1941, pp. 303-26.

See under titles of individual works by Dickens for films based on these works and reviews of them.

821.   Zambrano, Ana L. "*David Copperfield*: Novel and Film." *University of Hartford Studies in Literature*, 9 (1977), 1-16.

In addition to commenting on a number of film adaptations of *David Copperfield*, appends a list of film versions, 1911-70.

822.   Zambrano, Ana L. "Feature Motion Pictures Adapted from Dickens: A Checklist–Part I" and "Feature Motion Pictures Adapted from Dickens: A Checklist–Part II." *Dickens Studies Newsletter*, 5 (1974), 106-09; 6 (1975), 9-13; adapted as "Feature Motion Pictures Adapted from Dickens: A Chronological Checklist." In her *Dickens and Film* (**823**), pp. 399-41.

Gives detailed information about the cast, director, producer, writers, length, and other relevant matters for numerous films of Dickens's works.

823. Zambrano, A[na] L. "Modern Film Adaptations of the Novels of Dickens." In her *Dickens and Film*. Gordon Press Film Series. NY: Gordon Press, 1977, pp. 241-379.

In chapter 4 of her study, Zambrano examines the success with which filmmakers have adapted Dickens's novels to film, decade by decade. Zambrano also deals with how the film adaptations "help us reevaluate Dickens, see him anew, refreshed," and confirm the "modernity of Dickens's vision." She appends "Feature Motion Pictures Adapted from Dickens: A Chronological Checklist" (**822**), pp. 399-441. Illustrated. *Dickens and Film* is adapted from her doctoral dissertation, "The Novels of Charles Dickens and the Modern Film: A Study in the Aesthetics of Visual Imagination," *Dissertation Abstracts International,* 33 (1972/73), 3682A (University of California, Los Angeles, 1972); Ann Arbor, MI: University Microfilms, 1972.

2D. BIBLIOGRAPHIES AND BIBLIOGRAPHICAL STUDIES OF PLAGIARISMS, PIRACIES, IMITATIONS, CONTINUATIONS, PARODIES, AND FORGERIES OF DICKENS'S WORKS

Note: "Plagiarism" is used rather loosely in the references below. Sometimes it means an imitation, sometimes a continuation, sometimes a parody, sometimes an unauthorized publication of a Dickens work, and sometimes all of the above. Also see **Continuations of and sequels to Dickens's works, Forgeries of Dickens's works, Parodies of Dickens's works, Piracies of Dickens's works**, and **Plagiarisms, imitations, etc., of Dickens's works** in part 2 of the subject index.

824. Barker, Nicolas, and John Collins. *A Sequel to "An Inquiry into the Nature of Certain Nineteenth Century Pamphlets" by John Carter and Graham Pollard: The Forgeries of H. Buxton Forman and T. J. Wise Re-Examined.* London and Berkeley, CA: Scolar Press, 1983; reprinted Aldershot, Eng.: Scolar Press; New Castle, DE: Oak Knoll Books, 1992, passim.

Makes passing references to Wise's lithographic facsimile (1884) of Dickens's *Sunday under Three Heads* and to his forgery of *To Be Read at Dusk* (1852).

825. Baughman, Roland. "Some Victorian Forged Rarities." *Huntington Library Bulletin*, no. 9 (April 1936), 91-117; also reprinted separately, [Cambridge, MA?]: Reprinted for private circulation, [1936?].

Points out that fifty-four of the fifty-five forgeries identified in Carter and Pollard (**830**) are in the Huntington Library, San Marino, CA, including an 1852 *To Be Read at Dusk*, a bibliographical description of which is provided on p. 104 of the "Appendix: Huntington Library Copies of Books Questioned by Carter and Pollard," pp. 102-17. Baughman notes that "paper evidence" provides proof of the Dickens forgery.

826. Becker, May L. "The Reader's Guide." *Saturday Review of Literature*, 1 (1924/25), 653.

Surveys and reviews continuations of *The Mystery of Edwin Drood*.

827. "Bogus Pickwickiana." *Dickensian*, 41 (1944/45), 56, 74-76.

Provides information about plagiarisms of *Pickwick Papers* and reproduces the covers of four such publications.

828. Carlton, William J. "A *Pickwick* Lawsuit in 1837." *Dickensian*, 52 (1955/56), 33-38.

Reports details of the unsuccessful lawsuit of Chapman and Hall against Edward Lloyd to restrain him from publishing *The Penny Pickwick*. Illustrated.

829. Carter, John. "Note 184. T. J. Wise and the Technique of Promotion." *Book Collector*, 12 (1963), 202.

Makes a brief reference to a Wise forgery (the separate publication of Dickens's "To Be Read at Dusk" from *The Keepsake* for 1852) listed in Thomson (**48**). See also Carter and Pollard (**830**).

830. Carter, John, and Graham Pollard. "Part III. Dossiers: Charles Dickens." In their *An Enquiry into the Nature of Certain Nineteenth Century Pamphlets*. London: Constable; New York: Charles Scribner's Sons, 1934; reprinted New York: Haskell House, 1971, pp. 183-87; 2nd ed., as *An Enquiry into the Nature of Certain Nineteenth Century Pamphlets, with an Epilogue*. Ed. Nicolas Barker and John Collins. London and Berkeley, CA: Scolar Press, 1983, pp. 183-87 and p. 15 of added section.

An investigation of the forgeries of Thomas J. Wise. The section on Dickens concerns specifically the separate publication of *To Be Read at Dusk* in 1852. An analysis of the paper on which this edition was published shows it could not have been manufactured before 1861, Carter and Pollard conclude, so "there can be no doubt that it is a forgery." See index for other passing references to Dickens. The second edition adds a further note.

831. Connor, Steven. "Appendix C: Unfinished Business: The History of Continuations, Conclusions and Solutions." In Dickens's *The Mystery of Edwin Drood*. Ed. Steven Connor (**2435**), pp. 286-307.

Provides a history of and comments on the various attempts after Dickens's death to complete the novel.

832. "Dickens and the Pirates." *New York Times*, 18 January 1926, p. 20.

An editorial response in praise of F. Gordon Roe's article about *The Penny Pickwick* and other plagiarisms of *Pickwick Papers* (**847**).

833. Fitz-Gerald, S. J. Adair. "Pickwick Piracies." *Dickensian*, 6 (1910), 323-24.

Attempts to identify one of the "theatrical pirates" who did an unauthorized dramatization of *Pickwick Papers* and whom Dickens treated, in a letter to John Forster, 7 September 1837, with scathing sympathy. Fitz-Gerald believes it was J. P. Prest (actually T. P. Prest, Thomas Peckett Prest) rather than Edward Stirling, W. T. Moncrieff, or George Almar. In a letter to the editor, *Dickensian*, 7 (1911), 21-22, W[illia]m Douglas opts for Moncrieff as the author and criticizes Fitz-Gerald for other statements as well.

834. Hamilton, Walter. "Charles Dickens." In his *Parodies of the Works of English and American Authors*. Vol. 6. London: Reeves & Turner, 1889; reprinted New York and London: Johnson Reprint, 1967, pp. 215-28.

Prints nine brief parodies of Dickens's works, pp. 215-24, followed by an annotated list of forty-three other parodies, pp. 224-26, and a list of sixty-five "Plays Founded upon the Novels of Charles Dickens," pp. 226-28, based on Anderson (**1**), but with "more entries and fuller details," Hamilton claims.

835. Hoggart, Paul. "The Pirates of Charles Dickens." *Times* (London), 28 March 1981, p. 6.

Comments on plagiarisms and piracies of *Pickwick Papers* and on Dickens's "sporadic attempts" to fight the plagiarists of his works, particularly Edward Lloyd and George Reynolds.

836. Hoggart, Paul. "Travesties of Dickens." In *English and Cultural Studies: Broadening the Context. Essays & Studies, 1987*, ns 40 (1987). Ed. Michael Green. Atlantic Highlands, NJ: Humanities Press; London: John Murray, 1987, pp. 32-44.

Surveys a few of the contemporary imitations of *Pickwick Papers*.

837. James, Louis. "The Beginnings of a New Type of Popular Fiction: Plagiarisms of Dickens." In his *Fiction for the Working Man, 1830-50: A Study of the Literature Produced for the Working Classes in Early Victorian Urban England*. London: Oxford University Press, 1963, pp. 45-71; Harmondsworth, Eng., and Baltimore, MD: Penguin, University Books, 1974, pp. 51-82.

Identifies and briefly comments on the numerous plagiarisms, imitations, abridgements, and unauthorized portfolios of illustrations of Dickens's works from *Pickwick Papers* to *Dombey and Son*. James notes that, though "comparatively few lower-class readers" actually read Dickens's works, they read the cheaper imitations, thus giving Dickens "a central place in the development of cheap popular literature." The chapter in the 1974 edition is slightly revised. Illustrated.

838. J[ames], L[ouis]. "Plagiarisms of Dickens." In *Oxford Reader's Companion to Dickens.* Ed. Paul Schlicke (**2309**), pp. 443, 452-54 (pp. 457-60 in the 2000 paperback edition).

Comments on the numerous plagiarisms of Dickens's works.

839. Lindsay, C. L. "Continuation of 'Edwin Drood.'" *Notes and Queries*, 8th scr., 6 (1894), 472.

Prints a letter in which Wilkie Collins, writing to George B. Smith, 4 December 1878, remarks that he was asked to finish *Edwin Drood* after Dickens's death but *"positively refused"* and gives Smith permission to "publicly contradict" any rumors to the contrary.

840. Looker, Samuel J. "Supplements to Classic Works." *Notes and Queries*, 181 (1941), 97-98.

Mentions sequels to *Pickwick Papers, Dombey and Son,* and *David Copperfield* written by others, though Looker finds all such continuations "odious and to be reprehended."

841. [Matz, B. W.]. "The Mystery of Edwin Drood: Its 'Completions' and 'Solutions.'" In "Special Dickens Number." *Bookshelf*, 2, viii (February 1908), pp. 162-64.

A brief history of the attempts to complete Dickens's last novel.

842. [Matz, B. W.]. "Plagiarisms of Dickens." *T. P.'s Weekly*, 9 (1907), 265, 302, 333, 365.

Surveys the various plagiarisms of Dickens's works published in his lifetime and Dickens's unsuccessful attempts to "put an end to them."

843. McGowan, Mary T. "Pickwick and the Pirates: A Study of Some Early Imitations, Dramatisations and Plagiarisms of *Pickwick Papers.*" *Index to Theses* (**1188**), 30, ii (1977), 7 (Birkbeck College, University of London, 1975).

No abstract is provided, but Engel (**125**), p. 41, reports that this is an "impressively thorough examination of the numerous plagiarisms, imitations, and sequels" of the novel.

844. Miller, W[illiam]. "G. W. M. Reynolds and Pickwick." *Dickensian*, 13 (1917), 8-12; reprinted in *Living Age*, 294 (1917), 239-41.

Provides bibliographical details about Reynolds's *Pickwick* imita-tions—*Pickwick Abroad, Noctes Pickwickianae,* and *Pickwick Married*—and reprints Reynolds's criticism of Dickens's sentimentality and praise for his humorous characters that appeared in the *Teetotaler,* 4 July 1840.

845. Miller, W[illiam]. "Imitations of Pickwick." *Dickensian,* 32 (1935/36), 4-5.

Lists twenty-six imitations of *Pickwick Papers,* 1837-40, and three more re-cent ones.

846. "Notes on Sales: The 'Penny Pickwick.'" *Times Literary Supplement,* 19 December 1929, p. 1088.

Comments principally on one of Edward Lloyd's *Pickwick* imitations but also on other such spinoffs of Dickens's first novel.

847. Roe, F. Gordon. "The Pirate Boz: Thomas Peckett Prest, an Impudent Imitator of Dickens." *Bazaar, Exchange and Mart,* 21 Aug 1934, pp. 1, 4.

A bit on the background of Prest, who, as "Bos," produced *The Penny Pick-wick,* which Roe calls "the grossest crib" of *Pickwick Papers* and which he briefly describes. Prest was also responsible, he notes, for *Sam Weller's Budget of Recitations* (1838), *The Pickwick Songster,* and possibly other imitations of Dick-ens's first novel. Roe further mentions *The Sketch Book,* a "travesty" of *Sketches by Boz; Nikelas Nickelberry,* a "parody" of *Nicholas Nickleby;* and *Mister Humfrie's Clock,* *"Bos" Maker,* and lists a number of Prest's non-Dickensian works. Illus-trated.

848. Sewell, C. W. H. "'Edwin Drood' Continued." *Notes and Queries,* 9th ser., 12 (1903), 389.

Asks who finished *Edwin Drood* after Dickens's death, with a response by the editor that the first completion was the anonymous *John Jasper's Secret.* Sev-eral respondents comment on this and other continuations of the novel: John T. Page, p. 510, and, in 10th ser., 1 (1904), W. C. B., p. 37; T. N. Brushfield, p. 37; and H. Snowden Ward, pp. 331-32. Also see responses in 11th ser., 1 (1910), by O. S. T., p. 69; John T. Page, p. 153; and W. B. H., p. 394. For more details, see the section on "Continuations, Conclusions, Sequels, and Alternate Versions" in Cox (**115**), pp. 166-92.

849. Walters, J. Cuming. "The Sequels and Solutions." In his *The Complete Mystery of Edwin Drood. The History, Continuations, and Solutions (1870-1912)* (**1108**), pp. 205-54.

Summarizes a number of continuations of *Drood*, which he then charts in "Conclusions of 'Edwin Drood' Tabulated" (a fold-out chart, facing p. 254).

850. Wilkins, W[illiam] Glyde. "American Parodies on Dickens's 'American Notes.'" *Dickensian*, 4 (1908), 214-18.

Comments on *Change for the American Notes, by an American Lady* (actually written by an English gentleman, Wilkins notes), *English Notes* by "Quarles Quickens," and *Some Notes on America to Be Rewritten*, a pamphlet. Excerpts from these works are included.

2E. BIBLIOGRAPHIES AND BIBLIOGRAPHICAL STUDIES OF ILLUSTRATIONS FOR DICKENS'S WORKS

Note: Also see **Illustrations for Dickens's works** and **Illustrators of Dickens's works** in part 2 of the subject index and **illustrations** under titles of individual works in part 1 of the subject index.

851. Alderson, Brian. *Edward Ardizzone: A Preliminary Hand-list of His Illustrated Books, 1929-1970*. Pinner, Eng.: Private Libraries Association, 1972, pp. 12, 30.

Provides bibliographical information about publication of and Ardizzone's illustrations for three Dickens works: *Great Expectations* (New York: Heritage Club, 1939); *Bleak House*, abridged by Percy S. Winter (Oxford: Sheldon Library, Oxford University Press, 1955); and *David Copperfield*, abridged by Stanley Wood (Oxford: Sheldon Library, Oxford University Press, 1955).

852. Allingham, Philip V. "The Original Illustrations for Dickens's *A Holiday Romance* by John Gilbert, Sol Eytinge and G. G. White, as These Appeared in *Our Young Folks, an Illustrated Magazine for Boys and Girls*, Vol. IV." *Dickensian*, 92 (1996), 31-47.

The article is largely devoted to descriptions and evaluations of the nine plates that were included in the American publication of Dickens's children's story but that were not printed in the English publication in *All the Year Round* or in any edition of the work until the 1995 Everyman Edition of Dickens's *Holiday Romance and Other Writings for Children*. Allingham includes photographic facsimiles of the nine plates, with bibliographical information about each, pp. 44-47.

853. Baker, Charles, ed. *Bibliography of British Book Illustrators, 1860-1900*. Birmingham, Eng.: Birmingham Bookshop, 1978, passim.

Lists Dickens's works illustrated by Charles E. Brock, Henry M. Brock, W. Cubitt Cooke, Frederic G. Kitton, Henry M. Paget, and Fred Pegram.

854. Bates, William. "Bibliographiana." In his *George Cruikshank: The Artist, the Humourist, and the Man, with Some Account of His Brother Robert: A*

Critico-Bibliographical Essay. 2nd ed. London: Houlston and Sons; Birmingham, Eng.: Houghton and Hammond, 1879, pp. 77-94.

Lists books, reviews, and magazine and newspaper articles about Cruikshank and his works; pamphlets, letters to the *Times* (London), etc., written by him; and obituaries and eulogies. "Bibliographiana" was not included in the first edition (1878) of this work.

855.   Bland, David. *Bibliography of Book Illustration. The Book,* no. 4. London: Published for the National Book League by the Cambridge University Press, 1955, passim.

Lists a number of studies that contain information about Dickens's illustrators.

856.   Bolton, Theodore. *American Book Illustrators: Bibliographic Check Lists of 123 Artists.* New York: R. R. Bowker, 1938, passim.

Lists works by Dickens or containing selections by Dickens illustrated by five American artists–Reginald Bathurst Birch, F[elix] O. C. Darley, Arthur Burdett Frost, Thomas Nast, and Jessie Wilcox Smith.

857.   Browne, Edgar. *Phiz and Dickens as They Appeared to Edgar Browne.* London: James Nisbet, 1913; New York: Dodd, Mead, 1914; reprinted New York: Haskell House, 1972, pp. 74-89, 244-305, and passim.

Browne's recollections of his father, Hablot K. Browne, one of Dickens's principal illustrators, whose pseudonym was "Phiz." In chapter 5, "Dickens and Some of His Illustrators," pp. 74-89, Browne discusses Dickens's request for changes in the drawings by various of his illustrators, quoting from a number of his letters to them, including letters to his father. In chapter 16, "Phiz the Illustrator," pp. 244-305, he writes in considerable detail about his father's success as an illustrator of Dickens's *Pickwick Papers, Nicholas Nickleby, Master Humphrey's Clock* (*The Old Curiosity Shop* and *Barnaby Rudge*), *Martin Chuzzlewit, Dombey and Son, David Copperfield, Bleak House, Little Dorrit,* and *A Tale of Two Cities* and prints two previously unpublished letters from Dickens to Hablot K. Browne, 29 June and 6 July 1853, relative to the final numbers of *Bleak House.* There are brief quotations from Dickens's letters throughout. Illustrated

858.   Bruce, D. J. "Collecting Cruikshank." *Antiquarian Book Monthly Review,* 19 (1992), 394-404.

Mentions the rarity both of one plate by George Cruikshank for the three-volume *Oliver Twist* (1838) and of *Cruikshank's Magazine.* The second number of this journal (February 1854) contained Cruikshank's reply to Dickens's criticism of his Fairy Library, on which Bruce comments. Bruce also quotes and discusses Cruikshank's claim to have been the originator of two of Dickens's works. Illustrated.

859. Buchanan-Brown, John. *Phiz! The Book Illustrations of Hablot K. Browne*. Newton Abbot, Eng.: David & Charles; published as *Phiz! Illustrator of Dickens' World*. New York: Charles Scribner's Sons, 1978, passim.

Among the 216 plates that occupy most of the volume, will be found some of Browne's preliminary pencil sketches for Dickens's novels, from *Pickwick Papers* and *Sunday under Three Heads* to *Bleak House* and *Little Dorrit* (though not for *A Tale of Two Cities*, which he also illustrated). Also see the "Check List of Books Illustrated by Hablot Knight Browne," pp. 195-98, a short-title list of books illustrated by Browne, including several Dickens novels.

860. Butt, John. "Notes to Illustrations: I. Dickens's Instructions for *Martin Chuzzlewit*, Plate XVIII." *Review of English Literature*, 2, iii (July 1961), 49-50.

Notes that Dickens's manuscript instructions to Hablot K. Browne for Plates XVIII, XXXVII, and XXXVIII of *Martin Chuzzlewit*, as well as for the frontispiece and title page vignette, are in the Henry E. Huntington Library, San Marino, CA, and prints Dickens's detailed instructions for Plate XVIII. The text is accompanied by photographic facsimiles of the manuscript and by Browne's first drawing and final engraving of this plate.

861. C., F. "Tenniel's Book Illustrations." *Notes and Queries*, ser. 12, 4 (1918), 237-38.

A list of books illustrated by John Tenniel, including Dickens's *The Haunted Man and the Ghost's Bargain* (1848), with five illustrations by Tenniel–but no descriptions of or other details about them.

862. Cardwell, Margaret. "A Newly Discovered Version of a Collins Sketch for *Edwin Drood*." *Dickensian*, 70 (1974), 31-34.

Adds a seventh sketch by Charles Collins to the six noted by Lehmann-Haupt (**901**), a variation on the two published previously of a group of "Cathedral" figures, and which Cardwell conjectures may be the latest drawn of the three. The sketch, she points out, was discovered by Barry Pike, a London schoolteacher, in a second-hand bookshop. It is reproduced here along with the two earlier drawings. Also see Raven (**920**).

863. Chambers, C[harles] E. S., comp. *A List of Works Containing Illustrations by John Leech*. Edinburgh: William Brown, 1892, passim.

Includes Dickens's Christmas Books and the drawing Leech submitted in applying unsuccessfully as Robert Seymour's replacement as illustrator for *Pickwick Papers*, first published in the Victoria Edition of *Pickwick Papers* (2 vols., London: Chapman and Hall, 1887, I, facing p. 203).

864. Cohen, Jane R. *Charles Dickens and His Original Illustrators*. Columbus: Ohio State University Press, 1980, passim.

In this elaborate study of Dickens's original illustrators, Cohen makes frequent reference to original drawings, revised illustrations, and Dickens's comments on illustrations. Many original sketches, revised illustrations, unused sketches, etc., are reproduced in the volume. Also see Cohen's doctoral dissertation, "Charles Dickens and His Original Illustrators" (Harvard University, 1968).

865. Cohn, Albert M. *A Bibliographical Catalogue of the Printed Works Illustrated by George Cruikshank*. London and New York: Longmans, Green, 1914, pp. 68-71.

Brief bibliographical descriptions of the books that Cruikshank illustrated for Dickens.

866. Cohn, Albert M. *George Cruikshank: A Catalogue Raisonné of the Works Executed during the Years 1806-1877, with Collations, Notes, Approximate Values, Facsimiles, and Illustrations*. London: From the Office of "The Bookman's Journal," 1924, pp. 25-26, 75-81.

Lists and provides bibliographical descriptions of editions of the several Dickens works illustrated by Cruikshank, with a listing of his illustrations.

867. Cordery, Gareth. "Bibliography: Harry Furniss (1854-1925)." *Imaginative Book Illustration Society Newsletter*, no. 20 (Spring 2002), 29-48.

A descriptive bibliography of books illustrated by Furniss, including several of Dickens's, particularly the 500 illustrations for the Charles Dickens Library (ed. J. A. Hammerton, 18 vols., London: Educational Book Company, 1910). For the Dickens entries, see part 1, no. 33, and part 2, nos. 42, 44, 46, and 47. Cordery is currently preparing an expanded bibliography of Furniss's Dickens illustrations. Also see Cordery (868) and Hammerton (188, 884).

868. Cordery, Gareth. "Furniss, Dickens and Illustrations (Part One)" and "Furniss, Dickens and Illustrations (Part Two)." *Dickens Quarterly*, 13 (1996), 34-41, 98-110.

In Part One Cordery comments on Harry Furniss (1854-1923) as an illustrator, particularly of 500 illustrations for the Charles Dickens Library Edition (**188**). Cordery argues that, though Furniss never met Dickens, he "was particularly suited to illustrate" his works because there were "close parallels" in their aesthetics as well as in their lives and personalities. In Part Two Cordery looks at Furniss as an illustrator, noting the influence of Dickens's original illustrators, particularly George Cruikshank and Hablot K. Browne, on his iconography, especially when he reworked specific illustrations they had done. Only in the twenty-four illustrations Furniss did for *Great Expectations* and the one he did for *Hard Times*, both of which novels were originally published without illustrations, was he completely free of these influences, Cordery observes. Illustrated. Also see Cordery (**867**) and Hammerton (**884**).

869. Cox, Don R. "'Can't You See a Hint?': The Mysterious Thirteenth Illustration to *Edwin Drood*." *Dickensian*, 92 (1996), 5-18.

Describes a set of preliminary sketches by Luke Fildes for *Edwin Drood* in the Gimbel Collection, Yale University Library, and focuses in on one of them, convincingly arguing that it is not a preliminary drawing (the thirteenth illustration) for the next number Dickens was to write, forestalled by his death, but a discarded drawing of Rosa Bud and Edwin Drood at the gate of the Nuns' House for a scene in chapter 3 of the novel. Also see a "Letter to the Editor" from Charles Forsyte [Gordon Philo], pp. 127-29, who agrees that it depicts Rosa and Edwin but suggests that it illustrates the final scene between the two in chapter 13. In a further letter in *Dickensian*, 93 (1997), 206, Forsyte decides in favor of Cox's conclusions—in the light of both personal correspondence with Cox and a further article by Cox on the *Drood* sketches (**870**).

870. Cox, Don R. "'Mr. Grewgious Experiences a New Sensation': How *Edwin Drood* Was Illustrated." *Dickensian*, 93 (1997), 13-26.

Describes and comments on the more than fifty preliminary drawings for *Edwin Drood* by Luke Fildes in the Gimbel Collection, Yale University Library (**1509**) and his twelve final drawings in the Houghton Library, Harvard University. Cox points out that the only reference to the latter collection is in the catalogue of the Widener Dickens collection (**1518**). Cox also traces one drawing, "Mr. Grewgious Experiences a New Sensation," through its stages of development, including the final stage—its engraving by Charles Roberts, who made numerous refinements in Fildes's final drawing. Also see a letter to the editor from Charles Forsyte [Gordon Philo], 93 (1997), 206, providing further comment on Cox's article and on a letter he wrote about one of Fildes's sketches in connection with an earlier article by Cox (**869**). Illustrated.

871. Crewdson, William H. P. "C. E. Brock." *Antiquarian Book Monthly*, 24, vi (June 1997), 28-31.

A biographical sketch of the artist who illustrated a set of Dickens's Christmas Books (mentioned in passing), among other Dickens works. Brock illustrated twelve of Dickens's works altogether between 1900 and 1932, all of which are included in an accompanying list of works illustrated by Brock. Illustrated.

872. D., F. W. "'Pickwick,' First Edition." *Notes and Queries*, 7th ser., 2 (1886), 508.

Asks about the number of engravings made for the title page for the first edition of *Pickwick Papers*. In responses in 7th ser., 3 (1887), Ja[me]s. B. Morris, C. E., and Jonathan Dipps (p. 75), G. F. Blandford (p. 175), and J. B. Morris and F. W. D. (p. 257) comment on variations in the engraved title page in various copies of the first edition.

873. Davies, Russell. "Bibliography." *Ronald Searle: A Biography*. London: Sinclair-Stevenson, 1990, pp. 189-90.

Provides basic bibliographical information about three editions of Dickens's works illustrated by Searle: *A Christmas Carol* (London: Perpetua; New York [sic; actually Cleveland, OH]: World, 1961); *Great Expectations*, abridged by Doris Dickens, a great-granddaughter of Dickens (London: Michael Joseph; [New York]: Norton, 1962); and *Oliver Twist* (London: Michael Joseph; [New York]: Norton, 1962), as well as *Scrooge*, by Leslie Bricusse (Nashville, TN: Aurora Publications, 1970), and *The Humour of Dickens*, ed. R[obert] J. Cruikshank (London: News Chronicle Publications, [1952]). Davies also comments on Searle's "superb drawings" for these works. Also see "Documentation" (**877**).

874. "Dickens Stamps." *Dickensian*, 66 (1970), 193-94, 263.

Lists stamps from various countries issued in 1970 in commemoration of the centenary of Dickens's death, with a photograph on p. 263 of the British stamps issued.

875. "Dickens's Instructions to 'Phiz' for the *Pickwick* Illustrations." *Dickensian*, 32 (1935/36), 266-68, 283.

Comments on and reproduces four drawings by Hablot K. Browne with Dickens's remarks on them.

876. Dobson, Austin. "Illustrated Books." In Andrew Lang's *The Library. With a Chapter on Modern English Illustrated Books by Austin Dobson* (**2240**), pp. 123–78.

Dobson glances at illustrations by George Cruikshank, Hablot K. Browne, and John Leech for Dickens's works (pp. 155–56).

877. "Documentation." In *Ronald Searle*. New York: Andre Deutsch, Mayflower Books, 1978, pp. 231–34.

Identifies four editions of Dickens's works illustrated by Searle, the three indicated in Davies (**873**) and *A Tale of Two Cities*, Outlook through Literature, Part 6 (Chicago: Scott Foresman, 1964). This volume, largely a collection of Searle's humorous drawings, contains "Some Biographical Notes," pp. 17–31, and a chronology of Searle's life, but, unfortunately, it makes no mention of his illustrations for these Dickens works, nor are any of the illustrations included in this collection of drawings.

878. Douglas, R[ichard] J. H. *The Works of George Cruikshank Classified and Arranged, with Reference to Reid's Catalogue and Their Approximate Values.* London: Printed by J. Davy & Sons at the Dryden Press, 1903, passim.

Provides detailed bibliographical descriptions with some commentary on editions of works by Dickens that Cruikshank illustrated and, in an appendix, itemizes the plates that Cruikshank did for the first series and the 1839 edition of *Sketches by Boz*. A copy of this work is in the John F. Dexter Collection, British Library (**1436**), with manuscript notes by Dexter (Dex. 197). Also see Reid (**1512**).

879. E., A. C. "Charles Green, R. I." *Notes and Queries*, 196 (1951), 392.

Asks for the whereabouts of a series of illustrations of scenes from Dickens's novels by Green, a "fine artist of the old school." In response to A. C. E., Gerald G. Grubb, 198 (1953), 499, points out that a set of fourteen illustrations was commissioned from Green by William Lockwood, Apsley Hall, Nottingham, and traces their provenance through 1912. He adds that Green also did thirty-two illustrations for the Household Edition of *The Old Curiosity Shop*, the wrapper for *Pickwick Papers* in the Crown Edition, ten illustrations for the Gadshill Edition of *Great Expectations*, and several sets of illustrations for *Pears' Annual*—twenty-seven for *A Christmas Carol* (1892), twenty-nine for *The Battle of Life* (1893), thirty for *The Chimes* (1894), and thirty for *The Haunted Man and the Ghost's Bargain* (1895).

880. F., P. "Pickwick and 'Phiz.'" *Notes and Queries*, ns 1 (1954), 498.

An unanswered request for the source of thirty-two illustrations for *Pickwick Papers* in the style of "Phiz" (Hablot K. Browne) published as *Thirty-Two Illustrations to the Posthumous Papers of the Pickwick Club: Engraved on Steel by Various Humorists, from Sketches at the Times and Places, by Mr. Samuel Weller* (London: Gratton and Gilbert, n. d.). As Podeschi (**1509**) points out, Thomas Onwhyn was an artist who used "Sam Weller" or "Peter Palette" as his pseudonym. Podeschi lists, pp. 461-63, various editions of Onwhyn's drawings for *Pickwick Papers* (though not the particular edition referred to here), the earliest published by an E. Grattan (spelled thus) in 1837.

881. Fitzgerald, Percy. "Concerning the Plates and Extra Plates and 'States' of Pickwick." In his *Pickwickian Manners and Customs*. London: Roxburghe Press, n. d. [1897]; reprinted Folcroft, PA: Folcroft Library Editions, 1974; New York: Haskell House, 1974; Norwood, PA: Norwood Editions, 1976; Philadelphia: R. West, 1978, pp. 91-128.

Provides some information about the different states of the original plates of the illustrations for *Pickwick Papers*. Illustrated. For errors in this work, see Marshall (**1415**).

882. Gordon, Catherine M. "Subjects from the Novels of Charles Dickens, 1838-1870." In her *British Paintings of Subjects from the English Novel, 1740-1870*. New York and London: Garland, 1988, pp. 359-68.

A chronological list of paintings based on subjects from Dickens's novels, 1838-70, a few of which are reproduced in black and white (plates 199-204). The volume itself is a printing of an unrevised doctoral dissertation, Courtauld Institute of Art, University of London, 1981. Gordon comments in the text itself about paintings based on Dickens's novels.

883. Grego, Joseph, ed. *Pictorial Pickwickiana. Charles Dickens and His Illustrators*. 2 vols. London: Chapman and Hall, 1899. xxiii + 493 pp; xii + 509 pp.

The title page indicates that this work contains 350 drawings and engravings by Dickens's original and later illustrators, with "Notes on Contemporary Illustrations and 'Pickwick' Artists." While reproduction of these illustrations is the principal thing here, there are chapters on Dickens's relationships with the original illustrators of *Pickwick Papers* and on their illustrations, as well as sections on later illustrators of the novel. In "Pickwick on the Stage," II, 7-35, Grego comments on a number of productions of dramatizations of the novel and reproduces illustrations of actors in *Pickwick* roles. In "'Bos' Piracies," II, 37-81, he discusses several piracies and includes illustrations from them. In "Pickwickiana," II, 83-100, he looks at and reproduces illustrations from various *Pickwick* songbooks, sketches of *Pickwick* characters, etc.

884.   Hammerton, J. A. *The Dickens Picture-Book. A Record of the Dickens Illustrators.* Vol. 17 of the Charles Dickens Library. London: Educational Book Company, [1910]. viii + 466 pp.

A collection of some 600 of the original illustrations to Dickens's novels, work by work, in considerably reduced size and therefore not very well reproduced, with accompanying commentary on the illustrators. Hammerton also comments on the illustrators of later editions of Dickens's works and on sets of "extra-illustrations" to the novels up to 1910 and reproduces some of these illustrations as well. There is a separate chapter on the art of Harry Furniss, who did 500 plates for the Charles Dickens Library of Dickens's works of which this and its companion volume, *The Dickens Companion: A Book of Anecdote and Reference* (**21**) are part, and on "Dickens in Art," in which Hammerton reproduces paintings of scenes and characters from Dickens's novels, as well as provides a list (pp. 47-50) of such art.

885.   Hatton, Thomas, comp. "A Bibliographical List of the Original Illustrations to the Works of Charles Dickens, Being Those Made under His Supervision." In *The Nonesuch Dickens: Retrospectus and Prospectus* (**218**), pp. 55-78.

A "Census of all the illustrations to the Works of Charles Dickens which were made during his lifetime," in the possession of the Nonesuch Press, totalling 877 items, here numbered, the etched plate of one to be included in each of the 877 sets printed in the edition.

886.   Hodnett, Edward. "A Selective Catalog of Illustrators and Illustrated Books." In his *Five Centuries of English Book Illustration.* Aldershot, Eng.: Scolar Press, 1988, pp. 311-56.

A list of illustrators, with the books they illustrated and books and articles about these artists. For Dickens, see Edward Ardizzone, John Austen, Frederick Barnard, Charles Edmund Brock, Hablot K. Browne, George Cattermole, George Cruikshank, Richard Doyle, Luke Fildes, Barnett Freedman, Harry Furniss, Blair Hughes-Stanton, John Leech, Daniel Maclise, James Mahoney, Samuel Palmer, Arthur Rackham, Ronald Searle, Steven Spurrier, William Clarkson Stanfield, and Marcus Stone.

887.   Houfe, Simon. "Bibliography of the Works of John Leech" and "Bibliography." In his *John Leech and the Victorian Scene.* Woodbridge, Eng.: Antique Collectors' Club, 1984, pp. 245-59, 260.

The first bibliography lists the illustrations Leech did for Dickens's Christmas Books as well as other drawings and paintings, including two of himself and Dickens in costume for the amateur production of Ben Jonson's *Every*

Man in His Humour (reproduced on p. 88) and an illustration he submitted for *Pickwick Papers* when applying to replace the deceased Robert Seymour, the original illustrator. See items 7-8, 46-47, 67-68, 75-76, and 90. The second bibliography is a list of books and articles about Leech.

888. Hudson, Derek. "Books Illustrated Wholly by Arthur Rackham." In his *Arthur Rackham: His Life and Work*. New York: Charles Scribners' Sons, 1960, pp. 166-73.

Lists and provides basic bibliographical information about *A Christmas Carol* (1915) and *The Chimes* (1931). Also see Latimore and Haskell (**898-99**).

889. Hunnisett, Basil. *Engraved on Steel: A History of Picture Production Using Steel Plates*. Brookfield, VT: Ashgate, 1998, pp. 192-203.

Comments on the use of and innovations in engravings by George Cruikshank, Hablot K. Browne, and John Leech, particularly for Dickens's novels. Illustrated.

890. J., W. "'Memoirs of Grimaldi.'" *Notes and Queries*, 6th ser., 12 (1885), 427.

Queries the number of plates that this work edited by Dickens should have. In responses, G. F. R. B. and F. W. Cosens (p. 500) itemize the plates in the first edition (1838) of the work. In 7th ser., 1 (1886), J. M. M. provides further information and an additional query about the illustrations (p. 36); W. F. P. asks about additional notes in the 1846 edition by Charles Whitehead (pp. 312-13); George Bentley, son of Richard Bentley, who published the work, provides authoritative information about the various editions of the work (p. 378); J. M. M. asks if Bentley can answer his previous query and comments further on the plates of the 1846 edition (p. 473). In 7th ser., 2 (1886), George Bentley (p. 35) gives more details about the illustrations in answer to J. M. M.'s earlier query; and there are further contributions by E. T. Evans (p. 117), William Tegg (p. 134), W. J. Lawrence and George Bentley (pp. 211-12), Alex. E. Burnett (p. 297), and H. T. Mackenzie Bell (pp. 456-57). A. H. Christie adds a further comment in 7th ser., 3 (1887), 114.

891. Jerrold, Blanchard. "List of the Principal Works Illustrated by George Cruikshank." In his *The Life of George Cruikshank, in Two Epochs*. 2 vols. London: Chatto & Windus; New York: Scribner and Wolford, 1882, II, 239-65; as "Bibliographical List of the Principal Works Illustrated by George Cruikshank." New Edition (1 vol.), London: Chatto & Windus, 1883, etc.; reprinted as New Edition with Eighty-Four Illustrations. London: Chatto & Windus, 1898, pp. 347-76.

Includes Dickens's *Sketches by Boz*, *Oliver Twist*, and *Memoirs of Grimaldi*, to which Jerrold devotes separate chapters in the biography.

892. Johannsen, Albert. *Phiz: Illustrations from the Novels of Charles Dickens.* Chicago: University of Chicago Press, 1956; Cambridge: Cambridge University Press, 1957. xi + 442 pp.

Prints all of Hablot K. Browne's illustrations for Dickens's novels (*Pickwick Papers, Nicholas Nickleby, Martin Chuzzlewit, Dombey and Son, David Copperfield, Bleak House, Little Dorrit*), including the different etchings of a single plate and even, in some instances, a retouched plate, with notes on "some of the more easily recognizable variations" between etchings of the same illustration. Johannsen also gives a brief sketch of Browne's life and career (p. xi) and includes an introductory section to the plates for each novel on the history of the etching of the illustrations for that novel.

Reviews: B. Corrigan, *Victorian Studies*, 1 (1957/58), 99-100 (a "beautifully produced record of one of the most famous of all associations between author and illustrator"); *Nineteenth-Century Fiction*, 12 (1957/58), 92-93 (important for the scholar as well as the collector; given the limitations imposed by Johannsen, "a better job of pictorial reproduction and editorial commentary could hardly have been done"); L. C. S[taples], *Dickensian*, 53 (1957), 116 (of considerable value "to the Dickensian collector and bibliographer"; a "monumental and unusually shaped volume," though the over 500 reproductions of Phiz's plates are not of the best quality); *Times Literary Supplement*, 29 March 1957, p. 190 (finds the book "a most pleasant possession" and notes that Phiz's illustrations are "a necessary complement" to Dickens's text).

893. Kelly, C. M. "[Appendix] VI: Books Illustrated by the Brocks." In his *The Brocks, a Family of Cambridge Artists and Illustrators.* London and Edinburgh: Charles Skilton, 1975, pp. 158-71 and passim.

Lists individual Dickens works illustrated by C. E. and H. M. Brock, brothers, between 1900 and 1932. An illustration by H. M. Brock for *The Old Curiosity Shop* is on p. 81, and one by C. E. Brock for *Martin Chuzzlewit* is in a set of plates between pp. 112 and 113.

894. Kitton, Frederic G. "Appendix I: Illustrators of Cheap Editions," "Appendix II: Concerning 'Extra Illustrations,'" and "Appendix III: Dickens in Art." In his *Dickens and His Illustrators: Cruikshank, Seymour, Buss, "Phiz," Cattermole, Leech, Doyle, Stanfield, Maclise, Tenniel, Frank Stone, Landseer, Palmer, Topham, Marcus Stone, and Luke Fildes. With Twenty-Two Portraits and Facsimiles of Seventy Original Drawings Now Reproduced for the First Time.* London: George Redway, 1899; reprinted Amsterdam: S. Emmering, 1972; New York: Abner Schram, 1972; New York: AMS Press, 1973, pp. 219-26, 227-40, 240-42.

Appendix I provides bibliographical details of works illustrated by Frederick Barnard, F. O. C. Darley, Sol Eytinge, Sir John Gilbert, Charles Green, A. Boyd Houghton, Charles R. Leslie, George J. Pinwell, Fred Walker,

Thomas Webster, and others and a few biographical details about these artists. Appendix II lists, by artist, editions of extra illustrations of Dickens's works. Appendix III lists paintings of scenes and characters from Dickens's novels by thirty-three artists, with comments on some of the paintings. Also see Kitton's *Dickens Illustrations, Facsimiles of Original Drawings, Sketches and Studies for Illustration in the Works of Charles Dickens* (London: George Redway, 1900, viii pp. + 30 plates).

895. Kitton, Fred[eric] G. *John Leech, Artist and Humourist: A Biographical Sketch.* London: George Redway, 1883. 67 pp.; new edition, revised, London: George Redway, 1884. 131 pp.

In this sketch of Leech's life and career, Kitton prints previously unpublished letters from Leech to John Forster, three of which deal with problems about the illustrations for *The Cricket on the Hearth* (12, 16, and 18 November 1846). Kitton also includes a "Chronological List of Works Illustrated Wholly or Partly by John Leech," pp. 64-67. Illustrated. In the revised edition, Kitton makes only minor revisions of phrasing in the text, but omits a section containing eight letters from Leech to John Forster, the ten plates of Leech's illustrations (only a few simple line drawings remain), and the list of works illustrated by Leech.

896. Latimer, Louise P., comp. "Dickens, Charles." In her "A Bibliography of Authors." In *Illustrators of Children's Books, 1744-1945.* Ed. Bertha Mahony, Louise P. Latimer, and Beulah Folmsbee. Boston: Horn Book, 1947, pp. 467-68 and passim.

Lists illustrators of individual novels of Dickens—who can then be investigated more fully in Latimer's "A Bibliography of Illustrators, and Their Works," pp. 383-448, and, where applicable, in "Brief Biographies of Living Illustrators," pp. 267-76.

897. Latimer, Louise P. "Illustrators: A Finding-List." *Bulletin of Bibliography*, 13 (1926/29), 27-29, 46-48, 74-75, 94-95; reprinted as Bulletin of Bibliography Pamphlet, 27; revised as *Illustrators: A Finding List.* Useful Reference Series, 39. Boston: F. W. Faxon, 1929, passim.

A list prepared "to meet the need of the Young People's Department of the Public Library of the District of Columbia," its aim "to include American and foreign illustrators whose work, in books for boys and girls, seems of sufficient merit to warrant inclusion." Some illustrators of Dickens's works are included, among them Fred Barnard, Frances D. Bedford, Charles E. Brock, Hablot K. Browne, George Cattermole, Frederick Simpson Coburn, George Cruikshank, Harvey T. Dunn, Charles Green, Gertrude Remain Hammond, John Leech, James Mahoney, Arthur Rackham, Ernest H. Shepard, Marcus

Stone, Donald Teague, F. H. Townsend, Rowland Wheelwright, and Patten Wilson—with lists of the books illustrated and their publishers (but no dates).

898. Latimore, Sarah B., and Grace C. Haskell. *Arthur Rackham: A Bibliography.* Los Angeles: Suttonhouse, 1936, pp. 44-45, 67.

Provides full bibliographical details of two works by Dickens illustrated by Rackham: *A Christmas Carol* (London: William Heinemann; Philadelphia: J. B. Lippincott, 1915) and *The Chimes* (London: George W. Jones for Members of the Limited Editions Club, 1931).

899. Latimore, Sarah B., and Grace C. Haskell. "A Bibliography of Children's Books Illustrated by Arthur Rackham." *Horn Book Magazine,* 16 (1940), 197-213.

Gives full bibliographical details of an edition of *A Christmas Carol* (London: Heinemann; Philadelphia: J. B. Lippincott, 1915) illustrated by Rackham but does not list the illustrations (p. 206).

900. Layard, George S. "Suppressed Plates: The Suppressed Portrait of Dickens, 'Pickwick,' 'The Battle of Life,' and 'Grimaldi'" and "Suppressed Plates: III.–Dickens['s] Cancelled Plates: 'Oliver Twist,' 'Martin Chuzzlewit,' 'The Strange Gentleman,' 'Pictures from Italy,' and 'Sketches by Boz.'" *Pall Mall Magazine,* 17 (1899), 254-60, 341-48; reprinted with minor additions as "The Suppressed Portrait of Dickens, 'Pickwick,' 'The Battle of Life,' and 'Grimaldi'" and "Dickens's Cancelled Plates: 'Oliver Twist,' 'Martin Chuzzlewit,' 'The Strange Gentleman,' 'Pictures from Italy,' and 'Sketches by Boz.'" In his *Suppressed Plates, Wood Engravings, &c., Together with Other Curiosities Germane Thereto, Being an Account of Certain Matters Peculiarly Alluring to the Collector.* London: Adam and Charles Black, 1907, pp. 26-42, 43-58.

Comments on and prints changes in, cancellations of, and substitutions for certain illustrations designed for several of Dickens's works, as well as a portrait of Dickens from 1837, that were "suppressed" rather than published. Illustrated.

901. Lehmann-Haupt, C. F. "New Facts Concerning 'Edwin Drood.'" *Dickensian,* 25 (1928/29), 165-75.

Points out that, on the testimony of Lady Dickens, the wife of Sir Henry Dickens, Dickens's eighth child, Charles Collins designed and drew the original monthly cover for *Edwin Drood.* However, he fell ill, and it was finished by Luke Fildes. The finished cover and Collins's original drawing for it are reproduced side by side. Lehmann-Haupt also reproduces six drawings by Collins intended for the early monthly numbers and comments on what a comparison of them with Fildes's published illustrations "teach us about the development in Dickens's mind of the plot of his novel." Also see Cardwell (**862**) and Raven (**920**).

902. "A List of Books Illustrated by Arthur Rackham and Considered Suitable for Children (Modern Reprints)." *Arthur Rackham Society Newsletter*, no. 6 (March 1991), pp. 5-6.

Lists *A Christmas Carol* (New York: Children's Classics, 1987) as well as *A Christmas Carol*, retold by Jane Parker Resnick (Philadelphia: Running Press, 1990).

903. Lister, Raymond. *Catalogue Raisonné of the Works of Samuel Palmer*. Cambridge, New York, etc.: Cambridge University Press, 1988, pp. 120-36, 150-51.

Lists the five designs Palmer did in 1846 for *Pictures from Italy* (one of which was not used), reproduces them, and provides details about them, including their provenance. See pp. 120-36 for works Palmer did in Italy, 1837-39, particularly numbers 288, 305, 314, and 315, which were early versions of some of the 1846 illustrations.

904. Marchmont, Frederick [Hugh A. Torriano]. *The Three Cruikshanks: A Bibliographical Catalogue, Describing More than 500 Works . . . Illustrated by Isaac, George and Robert Cruikshank*. London: W. T. Spencer, 1897. pp. 1-8, 51-57.

Lists (pp. 51-57) the various editions of Dickens's works that George Cruikshank illustrated: *Sketches by Boz, The Pic-Nic Papers, Oliver Twist*, and *Memoirs of Joseph Grimaldi*, as well as some then thought to be by Dickens—*Sergeant Bell and His Raree Show, More Hints on Etiquette*, and *The Loving Ballad of Lord Bateman*—and an item of Dickensiana, *Sam Weller, a Journal of Wit and Humour*, ed. Sam Slick (1837). The introduction, pp. 1-8, praises some of George Cruikshank's illustrations for *Oliver Twist* but admits that others show characteristics that "have alienated from him the admiration of artists and critics"—that is, too much melodrama, too much mechanical "technical accomplishment" in the etchings, and, thus, a "minimum of charm and freshness."

905. Matthews, Maleen. "Illustrators of Dickens's 'Chimes.'" *Country Life*, 160 (1976), 1626-27.

Briefly comments on Dickens's writing of the work and on its original illustrators—John Leech, Daniel Maclise, Clarkson Stanfield, and Richard Doyle. Matthews also mentions several illustrators of later editions published through 1935–Anne Anderson, Francis D. Bedford, Harold Copping, and Hugh Thomson. Illustrated.

906.   Matthews, Maleen. "Seen Through Various Eyes: Illustrators of *The Cricket on the Hearth.*" *Country Life*, 162 (1977), 1604, 1606.

Briefly comments on Dickens's planning of the work and on his choice of its original illustrators–John Leech, Daniel Maclise, Richard Doyle, Clarkson Stanfield, and Edwin Landseer. Matthews also mentions illustrators of later editions of the work, through 1927, including Fred Barnard, Francis D. Bedford, C. E. Brock, Harold Copping, L. Rossi, Hugh Thomson, and Gilbert S. Wright. Illustrated.

907.   McLean, Ruari. *Victorian Book Design and Colour Printing.* London: Faber and Faber, 1963, passim; 2nd ed., London: Faber and Faber; Berkeley: University of California Press, 1972, passim.

Makes passing references to illustrations for Dickens's works in parts. Illustrated.

908.   Meister, Debra. "Collectors' Corner: A Twelve Year Old Dream Comes True." *Arthur Rackham Society Newsletter*, no. 8 (February 1992), pp. 5-6.

Describes finding (and purchasing) an original charcoal sketch by Arthur Rackham that served as part of the end paper and also appeared on the slipcase of the Limited Editions Club's edition of *The Chimes* (1931). It is reproduced on the cover of the *Newsletter.*

909.   Miller, George E. "Postcard Dickensiana, 1900-1920." *Dickensian*, 71 (1975), 91-99.

Points out that "postcards and other related items of paper ephemera," 1900-1920, interest collectors because they reproduce "in an inexpensive and highly collectable form some of the best work of many illustrators of Dickens's novels," as well as "photographic and 'oilette' views of the 'Dickens Country' and of some of the more famous stage productions and character impersonations of the time." Illustrated. Cohn and Collins (**956**) note that his article was reprinted in *Deltiology*, 15, vi (1975), 1, 3; 16, i (1976), 3.

910.   Nuhn, Roy. "Charles Dickens's Post Cards: A Dickens of a Collectible." *Barr's Post Card News* (Lansing, Iowa), 7 April 1986, pp. 1, 48; 5 May, pp. 50, 87; 9 June 1986, pp. 41, 76.

"The Dickens Checklist," *Dickens Quarterly*, 3 (1986), 150, indicates that these articles include checklists of post card sets.

911. Nuhn, Roy. "Dickens Christmas Postcards." *Collector's Showcase*, 14 (January 1994), 28.

Listed in "The Dickens Checklist," *Dickens Quarterly*, 12 (1995), 37.

912. Nuhn, Roy. "The World of Charles Dickens: An Analysis of the Dickens Postcards." *American Postcard Journal*, 6, v (October 1980), 25-33.

A bibliographical checklist of sets of postcards printed 1900-16 containing illustrations from Dickens's novels. Numerous illustrations.

913. O'Hea, Michael. "Hidden Harmony: Marcus Stone's Wrapper Design for *Our Mutual Friend*." *Dickensian*, 91 (1995), 198-208.

Examines the differences between the original sketch by Marcus Stone for the wrapper design for the monthly serialization of *Our Mutual Friend* and the printed wrapper (photographs of both are provided), connecting these to Dickens's comments on the original design in letters to Stone.

914. Olmsted, John C., and Jeffrey E. Welch. *Victorian Novel Illustration: A Selected Checklist, 1900-1976*. Garland Reference Library of the Humanities, 164. New York and London: Garland, 1979, passim.

An annotated bibliography of books and articles about illustrations for Victorian novels arranged chronologically by year, 1901-76, with many references (among a total of 319 items) to Dickens and his illustrators. See the introduction, pp. xi-xv, which deals almost entirely with Dickens and his illustrators.

915. Page, Norman. "Dickens' Illustrators." In his *A Dickens Companion* (**223**), pp. 279-91.

Both lists and appraises the original–but not later–illustrations of Dickens's works.

916. Parker, Derek. "In Keeping: Drawing the Line on the Complete Dickens." *Times* (London), 4 June 1981, p. 12.

On the over 1,000 drawings being done by Charles Keeping for the Folio Society's complete edition of Dickens's works (1981-88). Illustrated.

917. [Partlow, Robert B., Jr., and Robert L. Patten]. "Opportunities for Research." *Dickens Studies Newsletter*, 1, i (March 1970), 6-7.

Lists some of the relatively unexplored collections of photographs, illustrations, and other visual materials that Dickens scholars should know about.

918. P[atten], R[obert] L. "Illustrators and Book Illustration." In *Oxford Reader's Companion to Dickens*. Ed. Paul Schlicke (**2309**), pp. 288-93 (pp. 290-96 in the 2000 paperback edition).

A concise, selective history of the illustrating of Dickens's works.

919. Poppe, Arthur. "Dickens on Post Cards." *Barr's Post Card News* (Lansing, Iowa), 15 November 1984, pp. 36, 46.

Listed in "The Dickens Checklist," *Dickens Quarterly*, 3 (1986), 151.

920. Raven, Robert. "Some Observations on Charles Collins's Sketches for *Edwin Drood*." *Dickensian*, 96 (2000), 118-26.

Believes that the sketches produced by Charles Collins for *Edwin Drood* and reproduced in two earlier articles–see C. F. Lehmann-Haupt (**901**) and Margaret Cardwell (**862**)–were drawn "prior to any of the text being written." Raven reproduces five of the seven sketches, none of which was ever used because Collins withdrew from the project. Raven speculates about the order in which the five sketches he reproduces were drawn and what they reveal about "the first thoughts of Dickens concerning the early chapters of the novel."

921. Riall, Richard. *A New Bibliography of Arthur Rackham*. Bath: Eng.: Ross Press, 1994, pp. 124-25, 173.

Includes Rackham's illustrations for *A Christmas Carol* (twenty drawings and the end papers, London: William Heinemann; Philadelphia: J. B. Lippincott, 1915) and *The Chimes* (six full-page and fourteen smaller black and white drawings, London: Limited Editions Club, 1931), with full bibliographical descriptions of the editions, though there is no itemization or description of individual drawings.

922. Roe, F. Gordon. "Pickwick and the Pirates." *Connoisseur*, 79 (1927), 78-82.

Comments on, describes, and reproduces illustrations from a number of ephemeral imitations, continuations, and plagiarisms of *Pickwick Papers*, 1836-41.

923. *Sanders, Andrew. "Appendix 2: The Illustrations to *Dombey and Son*." In Dickens's *Dombey and Son*. Ed. Andrew Sanders. Penguin Classics. London, New York, etc.: Penguin Books, 2002, pp. 950-57.

When Dickens was writing the earlier parts of this novel, he was living in Lausanne, Switzerland, while his illustrator, Hablot K. Browne, remained in London. As a result, Sanders points out, Dickens had considerable correspondence about the illustrations with Browne and John Forster, Dickens's good friend, who "acted as a go-between and as a filter for a series of often sharp observations and suggestions for alterations." Sanders prints a number of the comments and directions from Dickens to Forster and to Browne. Along with the illustrations to *David Copperfield*, he concludes, the illustrations for *Dombey and Son* represent "the peak of the harmonious collaboration between a great novelist and a talented, but inevitably subservient, illustrator."

924. [Sargent, George H.]. "The Bibliographer: Errors in 'Nicholas Nickleby.'" *Boston Evening Transcript*, 24 January 1917; reprinted in *Dickensian*, 13 (1917), 105.

On a misprint and an alteration in the captions for two of the plates in *Nicholas Nickleby* in parts. In a letter to the editor, *Dickensian*, 14 (1918), 134, Morris F. Cook points out other variations in several of the illustrations.

925. Sketchley, R[ose] E. D. "Bibliography." In her *English Book-Illustration of Today: Appreciations of the Work of Living English Illustrators, with Lists of Their Works*. London: Kegan Paul, Trench, Trübner, 1903, pp. 121-73.

Lists and provides publication information about Dickens's works illustrated by Charles E. Brock, Henry M. Brock, W. Cubitt Cooke, F. G. Kitton, H. M. Paget, and Fred Pegram–to September 1901.

926. Slater, Michael. "Appendix: The Extra Illustrations to *Nicholas Nickleby*." In his *The Composition and Monthly Publication of* **Nicholas Nickleby** (**2456**), p. 43; reprinted 1982, I, xxxv.

Describes two sets of extra illustrations for the novel, one by Thomas Onwhyn, under the pseudonym of "Peter Palette," and the other by Kenny Meadows, published during the serialization of the novel. Some of these illustrations accompany the text.

927. Snell, Tricia. "Extra Illustrations to the Novels of Charles Dickens: Background and Analysis (1837-97)." Typescript manuscript. April 1987. 51 pp. + 40 reproductions of illustrations + 8 pp. of charts and index. In Dickens House, London.

Examines the practice in the nineteenth century of publishing collections of text and graphics and graphics alone, including plagiarisms or "other forms of interpretations" of published works (many such were inspired by Dickens's works, Snell points out). She focuses in on extra illustrations to Dickens's works, examining them both in their relation to the original illustrations, whose character conceptions were usually adhered to, and in their own right, either as illustrations produced for "binding in" or for framing separately in "limited edition sets" or "presentation folios." Snell notes, however, that "the market for extra illustrations fell away after 1841," with "virtually no extra illustrations recorded" until several years after Dickens's death. Charts at the end record the extra illustrations published to 1870 for *Pickwick Papers, Nicholas Nickleby, Oliver Twist, Martin Chuzzlewit, Dombey and Son,* and *Master Humphrey's Clock (The Old Curiosity Shop* and *Barnaby Rudge),* as well as for the Cheap Edition, and the extra illustrations published 1870-97.

928. Solberg, Sarah A. "'Text Dropped into the Woodcuts': Dickens' Christmas Books." *Dickens Studies Annual,* 8 (1980), 103-18.

On how the illustrations (most of which were woodcuts, Solberg points out) were used in the original editions of the Christmas Books, with bits of text worked into them, a "more sophisticated relationship" than that used in *Master Humphrey's Clock*–see Stevens (**933**). Solberg notes that in later editions of the Christmas Books, even ones including the illustrations, this technique was not reproduced. Illustrated. Also see her doctoral dissertation, "Dickens and the Illustration of His Work" (University of Edinburgh, 1979).

929. [Staples, Leslie C.]. "The 'Phiz' Plates to *Nickleby.*" *Dickensian,* 53 (1957), 144.

Briefly notes that Albert Johannsen, author of *Phiz: Illustrations from the Novels of Charles Dickens* (**892**), had written to question the existence of a third set of steel engravings for plates 3-6 of *Nicholas Nickleby* mentioned in works by David C. Thomson (**935**) and by Hatton and Cleaver (**24**).

930. Steig, Michael. "Appendix: A Checklist of the Work of Hablot Knight Browne, 1836-1859." In his *Dickens and Phiz.* Bloomington, IN, and London: Indiana University Press, 1978, pp. 317-22.

Lists the works Browne illustrated with the number of illustrations per work (but not the titles of individual illustrations), including the works he illustrated for Dickens. The text is accompanied by 126 predominantly full-page illustrations, pp. 173-298, many from Dickens's works, including some preliminary drawings side by side with the finished etchings.

931. Steig, Michael. "*Martin Chuzzlewit's* Progress by Dickens and Phiz." *Dickens Studies Annual,* 2 (1972), 119-49, 360-62.

In this study of the illustrations for the monthly parts of *Martin Chuzzlewit,* Steig includes some of Dickens's instructions (for plates 37-40) to Hablot K. Browne concerning the illustrations. Steig notes occasional contrasts in details between Browne's preliminary pencil drawings and the published plates. Illustrated.

932. Stephens, Frederic G. "A Chronological List of the Principal Books Illustrated by George Cruikshank." In his *A Memoir of George Cruikshank and an Essay on the Genius of George Cruikshank by William Makepeace Thackeray.* Illustrated Biographies of the Great Artists. London: Sampson Low, Marston, Searle & Rivington, 1891, pp. 132-42.

A simple list that includes the works that Cruikshank illustrated for Dickens.

933. Stevens, Joan. "'Woodcuts Dropped into the Text': The Illustrations in *The Old Curiosity Shop* and *Barnaby Rudge.*" *Studies in Bibliography*, 20 (1967), 113-34.

Examines the significance of the placing of the illustrations in the text of the two novels Dickens published within the framework of *Master Humphrey's Clock* and in later, separate editions of these novels. Stevens concludes that Dickens "not only planned which aspects of his story should be given visual emphasis, often writing with pictorial possibilities in mind, but selected also the positions in which the 'woodcuts dropped into the text' would be most effective," even sometimes indicating the shape he wanted for a particular illustration. Later editions, Stevens adds, were published either without illustrations (until 1861) or with separate plates, often quite misplaced. Eight illustrations.
Review: *Times Literary Supplement*, 27 April 1967, p. 362 ("an admirable paper").

934. Strange, E. H. "The Original Plates in *Nicholas Nickleby.*" *Dickensian*, 29 (1932/33), 227-28.

Points out that, because of the large sale of the novel, Hablot K. Browne "etched as many as four different plates" for some numbers of *Nicholas Nickleby*. Strange also comments on some of the variants this produced.

935. Thomson, David C. *Life and Labours of Hablôt [sic] Knight Browne, "Phiz."* London: Chapman and Hall, 1884, passim.

Much of the volume discusses Browne's work, including the many illustrations he did for Dickens's works, and is illustrated with a number of Browne's preliminary sketches as well as finished illustrations for Dickens. See particularly chapter 2, "The Original Drawings for Dickens's Works," which includes some of Dickens's notes and letters to Browne on his drawings. Some of the correspondence between the two survives, Thomson points out, but Browne destroyed many of his letters from Dickens. He prints one previously unpublished letter from Dickens, 15 March 1847, that did survive, criticizing a sketch that Browne had done for *Dombey and Son*, then in progress. Thomson also traces the provenance of many of Browne's drawings up to 1884. Also see chapter 13, "Hints to Collectors of the Works of 'Phiz,'" pp. 227-31.

Chapter 14, "Method of Work and Position as an Artist," pp. 232-39, contains an interesting table by Browne on the time needed to prepare an etching for a Dickens novel and other relevant information about Browne's working methods.

936. Wark, Robert R. "The Curious Case of Joseph Clayton Clark[e]." *Huntington Library Quarterly*, 59 (1997/98), 551-55.

An attempt to identify the corpus of "witty, slick, and technically accomplished pen-and-watercolor drawings of characters from the novels of Charles Dickens" by Joseph Clayton Clarke (1856 [or 1857]-1937), who used the pseudonym "Kyd." Wark thinks that the drawings, which he places in the caricature tradition of George Cruikshank, "may number in the thousands, representing, with numerous repetitions, about four hundred different Dickens characters." Collections of his drawings, Wark states, may be found in the British Museum, the Humanities Research Center at the University of Texas, and the Huntington Library. The Huntington, he adds, has the largest collection, about 840 drawings, "scattered through 16 extra-illustrated sets," all of which have been photographed by the library for purposes of easy comparison. Having made such an examination, Wark points out that "there are two readily distinguishable styles in which the drawings were created." Dated watermarks on the paper reveal, he indicates, that the first type of drawing, that "constructed primarily in watercolor with little visual dependence on outlines, although details of faces and hands are executed in what appears to be a fine, wiry, ochre pen line," was created mainly in the early 1880s. The second type, in which characters "are constructed in calligraphic-like pen work, with watercolor used only as a tinted wash," was created primarily in the first decade of the twentieth century. From close examination, Wark hypothesizes that both sets began as tracings, "presumably from a master set Clark[e] retained for this purpose," but that the drawings in Kyd's later style required two rather than three steps for their completion, a "significantly faster" process than the first, which enabled him to produce the quantity of drawings demanded of him later in his career. Illustrated.

937. Wark, Robert R. "The Gentle Pastime of Extra-Illustrating Books." *Huntington Library Quarterly*, 56 (1993), 151-63.

Briefly comments on late-nineteenth- and early-twentieth-century sets of extra illustrations of Dickens's novels in the Henry E. Huntington Library, San Marino, CA (p. 163).

938. Weitenkampf, Frank. "American Illustrators of Dickens." *Boston Public Library Quarterly*, 5 (1953), 189-94.

Comments on the poor quality of the copies of the etchings of George Cruik-shank and Hablot K. Browne made by American engravers for American editions of Dickens's novels as late as 1906. Weitenkampf also points out that by the 1860s American artists began doing original illustrations for Dickens's works. He surveys and evaluates the work of these American illustrators, particularly praising the works of F. O. C. Darley in the late 1860s and, to a lesser extent, of Sol Eytinge, Jr., and a few others, while indicating that the rest (among them Thomas Nast, the political caricaturist) were quite unsuccessful. Illustrated.

939. Weitenkampf, Frank. "Illustrators in Masquerade: A Short Chapter in Dickens Bibliography." *Bulletin of the New York Public Library*, 49 (1945), 423-26.

Lists a number of nineteenth-century American editions (an admittedly incomplete list) of Dickens's works with annotations on "the strange misstatements on the title pages regarding the illustrations." Sometimes, as Weitenkampf points out, not all the artists are listed, sometimes incorrect ones are given (not necessarily unintentionally), and sometimes the names are partially inaccurate. He provides correct details about the illustrations and illustrators.

940. Wilkins, William Glyde. "Variations in the Cruikshank Plates to *Oliver Twist*." *Dickensian*, 15 (1919), 71-74.

Lists the plates that were touched up for the 1846 edition and reproduces the original sketch by Cruikshank for one of the illustrations.

PART THREE: DICKENS STUDIES

Note: Also see especially **Bibliographical studies of Dickens's works, Bibliographies of Dickens studies, Biographical studies of Dickens, Biographies of Dickens, Critical and appreciative studies of Dickens, Specialized studies of Dickens's works**, and **Textual studies of Dickens's works** in part 2 of the subject index and similar headings under individual works in part 1 of the subject index. Bibliographies are not included here that are listed in book-length studies of Dickens unless they are intended as independent bibliographies and not simply as lists of works cited—with a few important exceptions, as in Ackroyd (**942**). Some of the volumes in this section contain lists of Dickens's works but are included here because such lists are incidental to the lists of secondary studies in them and are not of serious bibliographical import, though they are listed under **Bibliographies of Dickens's works** in part 2 of the subject index. A number of references in Section 1A, **Bibliographies of Dickens's Works**, above, contain important bibliographies of secondary works and should be consulted. See **Bibliographies of Dickens studies** in part 2 of the subject index. Many of the more general works listed here are analyzed and evaluated more fully in such guides as those by Balay (**1133**), Harner (**1147**), Marcuse (**1152**), Wortman (**1161**), and Chalcraft, Prytherch, and Willis (**1140**); in most instances only the extent to which these general bibliographies provide information about Dickens has been recorded. Surveys of criticism of Dickens's works will be found in the forthcoming volume three, *General Critical Studies of Dickens's Works*, of DeVries.

3A. GENERAL BIBLIOGRAPHIES OF DICKENS STUDIES

Note: Also see **Bibliographies of Dickens studies, general bibliographies**, in part 2 of the subject index.

941. Abernethy, Peter L., Christian J. W. Kloesel, and Jeffrey R. Smitten, comps. "Charles Dickens." In *English Novel Explication, Supplement 1*. London: Bingley; Hamden, CT: Shoe String Press, 1976, pp. 52-66; Kloesel, Christian J. W., and Jeffrey R. Smitten, comps. "Charles Dickens." In *Supplement II*. Hamden, CT: Shoe String Press, 1981, pp. 59-75; Kloesel, Christian J. W., comp. "Charles Dickens." In *Supplement III*. Hamden, CT: Shoe String Press, 1986, pp. 89-115; *Supplement IV*. Hamden, CT: Shoe String Press, 1990, pp. 67-82; *Supplement V*. Hamden, CT: Archon Books, 1994, pp. 80-98; and *Supplement VI*. Hamden, CT: Archon Books, 1998, passim.

An unannotated listing of articles and studies in books, supplementing Bell and Baird (**948**) and Palmer and Dyson (**1015**) for 1972-74, 1975-79, 1980-85, 1986-first half of 1989, second half of 1989-first half of 1993, and second half of 1993-early 1997.

942. Ackroyd, Peter. "Notes on Text and Sources" and "Bibliography." In his *Dickens*. London: Sinclair-Stevenson; New York: HarperCollins, 1990; London: Minerva Press, 1991 (paperback), pp. 1084-1142, 1143-53.

The first is a valuable record of the sources Ackroyd used, chapter by chapter, in writing his biography, essentially a survey of Dickens biographical scholarship. Particularly valuable are his evaluations of these sources. The second is a list of the principal book-length studies of Dickens.

943. Altick, Richard D. Supplementary note for footnote 1 on p. 1344 of the first edition of Samuel C. Chew's "Dickens, Collins, and Reade" (in *A Literary History of England*, ed. Albert C. Baugh [New York: Appleton-Century-Crofts, 1948], pp. 1344-54). In *A Literary History of England*. Ed. Samuel C. Chew and Richard D. Altick. 2nd ed. New York: Appleton-Century-Crofts, 1967, n. p.

While the bibliographical listing for Dickens in the first edition is quite brief, Altick's updated note in the supplement in the second edition (attached to a reproduction of the text of the first edition), on unnumbered pages, is much lengthier and his occasional annotations more evaluative.

944. American Library Association. "Dickens, Charles." In *The A. L. A. Index: An Index to General Literature, Biographical, Historical, and Literary Essays and Sketches, Reports and Publications of Boards and Societies Dealing with Education, Health, Labor, Charities and Corrections, Etc., Etc.* Comp. by William I. Fletcher. Boston and New York: Houghton, Mifflin, The Riverside Press, Cambridge, 1893, pp. 81-82; 2nd ed., 1901, pp. 161-62; also *A. L. A. Index to General Literature: Supplement 1900-1910: A Cumulation of the Index to General Literature Sections of the Annual Literary (Library) Index, 1900 to 1910 Inclusive, to Which Have Been Added Analytic Entries to 125 Books Heretofore Unanalyzed in Print.* Chicago: American Library Association, 1914, p. 69.

The 1893 edition lists some thirty-two essays on Dickens in books and collections of essays. The second edition, "greatly enlarged and brought down to January 1, 1900," includes these as well as some thirty-four additional essays published since the first edition. The 1914 supplement adds others, as indicated in the title. Continued, with some overlapping with the 1914 *Supplement*, as *Essay and General Literature Index* (**1051**).

945. Andrews, M[alcolm]. Y. "Charles Dickens: British Publications in the 1960s." *British Book News*, June 1970, pp. 427-29.

A brief evaluative survey of some thirty books and editions published or, in a few cases, republished in the 1960s.

946. Bateson, F. W. "Charles Dickens (1812-1870)." In his *A Guide to English Literature*. London: Longmans, 1965; Chicago: Aldine; New York: Doubleday (An Anchor Original), 1965; 2nd ed., London: Longmans, 1967; Chicago: Aldine Publishing, [1968]; Garden City, NY: Anchor Books, 1968, pp. 174-75; revised, with Harrison T. Messerole, as *A Guide to English and American Literature*. 3rd ed. London and New York: Longman; New York: Gordian Pr., 1976, pp. 179-80.

A highly selected listing of book-length critical studies and of recommended editions of a few of Dickens's novels—updated in the 1976 edition.

947. Beene, Lynn D. "Dickens, Charles." In her *Guide to British Prose Fiction Explication: Nineteenth and Twentieth Centuries*. New York: G. K. Hall; London, etc.: Prentice Hall, 1997, pp. 138-219.

An unannotated list of articles and chapters in books containing critical studies, mainly from 1960 and later, of the individual novels and stories.

948. Bell, Inglis F., and Donald Baird. "Dickens, Charles." In their *The English Novel, 1578-1956: A Checklist of Twentieth-Century Criticisms*. Denver, CO: Alan Swallow, 1958, pp. 32-40.

Bell and Baird list from two to eleven items for each of Dickens's novels from a limited list of book and journal sources. The result is a strange and decidedly incomplete mixture of the significant and the insignificant. Bell and Baird make too frequent reference to a small group of works—*Johnson*, Edwin P. Whipple's *Charles Dickens: The Man and His Work* (Boston and New York: Houghton Mifflin, 1912), Butt and Tillotson (**2291**), G. K. Chesterton's *Appreciations and Criticisms of the Works of Charles Dickens* (London: J. M. Dent, 1911), George Gissing's *Critical Studies of the Works of Charles Dickens* (ed. Temple Scott, New York: Greenberg, 1924), and Edmund Wilson's *The Wound and the Bow* (Boston: Houghton, Mifflin, 1941). Valuable though these works may be, their repeated listing drastically limits the number of other entries included. For example, the only references listed for *A Tale of Two Cities* are *Johnson* and Whipple. For a continuation and its supplements, see Palmer and Dyson (**1015**) and Abernethy, Kloesel, and Smitten (**941**).

949.   Bloom, Harold. "Bibliography." In *Modern Critical Views: Charles Dickens.* Ed. Harold Bloom. New York, New Haven, CT, and Philadelphia: Chelsea House, 1987, pp. 343-51.

A selected list of critical studies–books and articles–most from 1950-85, with a few of earlier date.

950.   Bloom, Harold. "Bibliography." In *Victorian Fiction.* Ed. Harold Bloom. Critical Cosmos Series. New York and Philadelphia: Chelsea House, 1989, pp. 479-500.

Contains a "General" section of critical studies, as well as sections on individual novelists, including "Charles Dickens," pp. 486-88, which lists some seventy-five works, mainly books. The selection of articles is eccentric.

951.   Bloom, Harold. "Works about Charles Dickens." In *Charles Dickens. Comprehensive Research and Study Guide, Bloom's Major Novelists.* Ed. Harold Bloom. Broomall, PA: Chelsea House, 2000, pp, 116-18.

A highly selective checklist containing fifty-four works about Dickens.

952.   Camberwell Public Libraries. *Dickens and His Times.* Books & News, 22. [London]: H. H. Greaves, [1963]. 8 pp.

A handlist of books by and about Dickens for library patrons, with some annotation and commentary.

953.   Carty, Charles F. "Some Addenda to Kitton's 'Dickensiana.'" *Literary Collector,* 5 (1902/03), 12-14, 43-46.

In addition to a listing of chief works by Kitton, itemizes some sixty-eight works Kitton missed in his *Dickensiana* (**996**), mainly American in origin, and refers, in a closing commentary, to a number of related items.

954.   Chaudhuri, Brahma, comp. and ed. *Charles Dickens, a Bibliography: 1970-1986.* Bibliography on Demand Series. Edmonton, Can.: LITIR Database, 1988. xii + 223 pp.

A listing, with brief annotations for many items, of Dickens studies published 1970-86. The bibliography proper, pp. 1-84, is divided into 1) General Works, 2) Bibliographies, 3) Biographies, Letters and Diaries, and 4) Critical Studies. Users should be advised that these are not precise headings; there are occasional, often obvious, errors in the entries in the continuing database from which this bibliography was compiled (see Chaudhuri, **1036**). Although there is no section listing editions of Dickens's works, a number of editions of Dickens's writings will be found under Dickens's name in sections 1 and 4.

This Dickens bibliography contains 2,228 entries as opposed to Cohn and Collins's 2,987 entries for only 1970-79 (**958**), supplemented in the quarterly issues of *Dickens Studies Newsletter* and *Dickens Quarterly* (**1037**), and the attempts to indicate book reviews are rudimentary, whereas Cohn and Collins are quite thorough in this regard. The larger portion of this volume is devoted to full and useful subject, author, and title indexes, though there are errors here, too, and omissions. Presumably updated volumes are or will be available, but there has been no notice or advertising about updates.

955. [Childers, Joseph]. "Dickens, Charles. 1812-1870." In *The Reader's Adviser*. Vol. 1: *The Best in Reference Works, British Literature, and American Literature*. 14th ed. Ed. David S. Kastan and Emory Elliott. New Providence, NJ: R. R. Bowker, 1994, pp. 347-51.

Following the briefest of comments on Dickens's life and novelistic accomplishments, Childers lists, with modest annotation, recommended modern editions then in print of Dickens's novels, a few collections of his letters and works, and forty recommended studies of Dickens in print, through 1993—with prices. In general, volume 1 of *The Reader's Adviser* (published in six volumes, with Marion Sader as Series Editor) is a wide-ranging bibliography, listing and lightly annotating general and period reference works as well as those addressed to specific English and American authors. For scattered references to Dickens, see volume 6, *Indexes*, p. 70. Earlier editions go back to 1921 (all published by R. R. Bowker, New York), when the work, edited by Bessie Graham, was entitled *Bookman's Manual*. Graham published four more editions (1924, 1928, 1935, and 1941), before the work was taken over by Hester R. Hoffman, who published three revised editions as *Bessie Graham's Bookman's Manual* (1948, 1954, 1958). She then edited two more editions under the titles *The Reader's Adviser and Bookman's Manual: A Guide to the Best in Print in Literature, Biographies, Dictionaries, Encyclopedias, Bibles, Classics, Drama, Poetry, Fiction, Science, Philosophy, Travel, History* (New York: R. R. Bowker, 1960) and *The Reader's Adviser: An Annotated Guide to the Best in Print in Literature, Biographies, Dictionaries, Encyclopedias, Bibles, Classics, Drama, Poetry, Fiction, Science, Philosophy, Travel, History* (2 vols., New York: R. R. Bowker, 1964). The eleventh edition, *The Reader's Adviser: A Guide to the Best in Literature* (2 vols., New York and London: R. R. Bowker, 1968), was edited by Winifred F. Courtney. With the twelfth edition (1974-77), there is a different editor for each volume in the three-volume series, now entitled *The Reader's Adviser: A Layman's Guide to Literature*, and one is principally concerned with volume 1: *The Best in American & British Fiction, Poetry, Essays, Literary Biography, Bibliography and Reference*, ed. Sarah L. Prakken (New York: R. R. Bowker, 1974). For the thirteenth edition (New York and London: R. R. Bowker, 1986), Fred Kaplan served as editor of volume 1. For all the editions, however, the Dickens entries are basically as described above for the fourteenth edition, with occasional rearrangement and expansion (or contraction) of contents, and, obviously, in turn, an updating of available editions of Dickens's works and studies of his life and works.

956. Churchill, R. C. *A Bibliography of Dickensian Criticism, 1836-1975.* London: Macmillan; Garland Reference Library of the Humanities, 12. New York and London: Garland Publishing, 1975. xiv + 314 pp.

Churchill claims in his preface that this is "the most comprehensive" bibliography of Dickens criticism "yet attempted." While he lists a few bibliographies, biographies, collections of letters, and anthologies, his concern is with critical studies of Dickens's works. Many, but by no means all, of the items in this bibliography are annotated, largely with direct quotations expressing their authors' critical viewpoints, and arranged chronologically within sections. The bibliography is difficult to use—works are scattered under too many subtopics, page numbers are not given for articles, and cross-referencing is more confusing than helpful. Publishing information is scanty (only author, title, and publication date for books; no volume or page numbers for magazines). The bibliography's main headings are 1) Introduction (bibliographies, biographies, etc.), pp. 1-8; 2) General Criticism: Nineteenth Century, pp. 9-18; 3) General Criticism: Twentieth Century, pp. 19-37; 4) Criticism of Particular Works, pp. 38-122; 5) Aspects of Dickens (with thirty-six subheadings), pp. 123-228; 6) Critical Comparisons, pp. 229-79; and 7) Index, pp. 280-314. Also see Hunt (**1412**).

Reviews: *British Book News,* April 1976, pp. 297-98 (a "somewhat eccentric volume" but still useful, with some hidden values); *Choice,* 12 (1975/76), 1550 (generally unfavorable review); A. M. Cohn, *Dickens Studies Newsletter,* 7 (1976), 120-22 (finds the bibliography far more selective than Churchill's claim for it); P. Collins, *Dickensian,* 72 (1976), 108-10 (a "useful, unusual, engaging, sometimes amusing, sometimes irritating book," emphasizing critical studies over biographical and other studies), with Churchill's response, 73 (1977), 113 (defends himself against Collins's additional charge that there is too much of Churchill himself in the work); A. Easson, *Literature & History,* no. 7 (Spring 1978), 121-22 (highly unfavorable); K. J. Fielding, *Modern Language Review,* 72 (1977), 924-25 ("useful," "puzzling," "personal," with strange omissions and inclusions, with examples of some given); G. W. Kennedy, *Victorian Studies,* 20 (1976/77), 343-45 (not a "truly comprehensive Dickens bibliography" and one whose "standards of selection remain a mystery"; "a helpful reference book, but one to be used with caution"); P. Koda, *Book Collector's Market,* 3, ii-iii (March/April-May/June 1977), 34-35 ("a rich book for Dickensians," but one with some inaccuracies in the text); C. Mann, *American Reference Books Annual,* 7 (1976), 613-14 (some criticism but finds it "a fascinating book for scanning and dipping"); A. Samuels, *Library,* 5th ser., 32 (1977), 82-84 (criticizes the structure, intent, and content of the work); M. Seydoux, *Bulletin de Documentation Bibliographique* (Part 2 of *Bulletin des Bibliothèques de France*), 22 (1977), 70 (in French; a useful, if not exhaustive work); M. Zack, *Library Journal,* 100 (1975), 1810 ("meticulously prepared and arranged," the "most complete listing thus far published," with "generously annotated" citations).

957. Cockshut, A. O. J. "Dickens, Charles (John Huffam)." In *Great Writers of the English Language: Novelists and Prose Writers.* Ed. James Vinson and D. L. Kirkpatrick. New York: St. Martin's Press, 1979, pp. 327-31; reprinted in *The Novel to 1900.* Great Writers Student Library, 8.

Ed. James Vinson and D. L. Kirkpatrick. New York: St. Martin's Press, 1980, pp. 78-82; reprinted as *The Novel to 1900*. St. James Reference Guide to English Literature, 4. Chicago and London: St. James Press, 1985, pp. 78-82; reprinted with revisions in *Reference Guide to English Literature*. Ed. D. L. Kirkpatrick. 2nd ed. 3 vols. St. James Reference Guides. Chicago and London: St. James Press, 1991, I, 480-83.

This well-travelled listing of bibliographies and critical studies of Dickens, as well as of Dickens's works and modern editions of them, is followed by a commentary on Dickens's greatness. In the 1991 edition, the list of book-length critical studies is considerably expanded, and it and the list of editions of Dickens's works updated to 1990.

958. Cohn, Alan M., and K. K. Collins, comps. *The Cumulated Dickens Checklist: 1970-1979*. Troy, NY: Whitston, 1982. vi + 391 pp.

This impressive, valuable bibliography is based on the quarterly checklists in *Dickens Studies Newsletter* (**1037**) and intended as an extension of Gold (**982**). The editors have included works from 1969 not in Gold and have also included some works from 1980. Its only shortcoming is the limited explanatory annotation. It is divided into five main parts, with a number of subdivisions: 1) Dickens's Works, 2) Secondary Sources, 3) Reprints, 4) Doctoral Dissertations, and 5) Miscellaneous (audiovisual materials, adaptations, plays and scripts, recordings, etc.). An appendix lists the contents of several collections of Dickens criticism, and there are several indexes, including author and subject ones. The thoroughness of the bibliography is little short of amazing—see Paroissien (**1421**) for some explanation of Cohn's method of procedure. The bibliography contains *at least* 1,000 (81 under "S" alone) references not included or not specifically cross-referenced to Dickens in any of the standard serial bibliographies—Modern Humanities Research Association (**1039**), Modern Language Association of America (**1042**), and Victorian (**1058**)—and an extensive listing of reviews and reprints of editions. Where Ph.D. listings are concerned, Cohn and Collins miss perhaps at most six dissertations—usually general studies—picked up by one or another of the serial bibliographies (usually the Modern Humanities Research Association), but it contains by far the most complete listing of dissertations devoted in whole or in part to Dickens for the period covered. While there are some errors, particularly in cross-reference numbers and spelling, the monumentality of the work far outweighs these minor flaws.

Reviews: J. J. Fenstermaker, *Dickens Quarterly*, 1 (1984), 24-26 (sees the bibliography as a "virtually comprehensive gathering of . . . Dickensiana" for 1970-79, though finds the index and cross references "not wholly satisfactory"); L. Hartveit, *English Studies*, 65 (1984), 225 (done with "exemplary care" and shows "how persistent and widespread Dickens's presence is"); S. Monod, *Etudes anglaises*, 38 (1985), 470-72 (in French; an indispensable bibliographic tool—full and excellently organized); S. Monod, *Yearbook of English Studies*, 16 (1986), 321-22 (finds the organization "convenient, intelligent, and thoughtful" and the volume coming "very near perfection"); P. Preston, *Notes and Queries*, ns 33 (1986), 252-55 (praises the high standard of accuracy and the elaborate and "beautifully clear" index); *Times Literary Supplement,* 4 February 1983, p. 120 (a "convenient guide"); T. Wortham, *Nineteenth-Century Fiction,* 37 (1982/83), 619-21 (an "intelligently arranged table of contents and an extensive index make the task of locating pertinent items relatively easy").

959. Collins, Philip. "Charles Dickens." In *Victorian Fiction: A Second Guide to Research.* Ed. George H. Ford. New York: Modern Language Association, 1978, pp. 34-113.

A sequel to Nisbet (**1013**), further documenting the "continuing boom" in Dickens criticism and scholarship. Collins methodically surveys the field, 1962 to ca. 1975, under the headings Manuscripts and Catalogues, Bibliographies and Other Aids, Editions, Biography, General Criticism, Studies of Special Aspects (with fourteen subheadings), and Studies of Individual Novels. He concludes with recommendations for directions future Dickens scholarship and criticism should take. See the Index for references to Dickens in other chapters of this volume and also the chapter "General Methods," by Richard D. Altick, pp. 1-20, for useful general studies of Victorian fiction.

960. Combs, Richard E. "Dickens, Charles." In his *Authors: Critical and Biographical References: A Guide to 4,700 Critical and Biographical Passages in Books.* Metuchen, NJ: Scarecrow Press, 1971, pp. 44-45; expanded as "Dickens, Charles." In *Authors: Critical & Biographical References.* Ed. Richard E. Combs and Nancy R. Owen. 2nd ed. Metuchen, NJ: Scarecrow Press, 1993, pp. 72-75.

The first edition lists forty and the second 170 works containing critical and biographical references to Dickens.

961. Cook, Christopher, ed. "Recent Research on Dickens." *Pears Cyclopaedia, 1991-92: A Book of Background Information and Reference for Everyday Use.* Centenary Edition. London: Pelham Books, 1991, pp. M56-57.

Covering the period 1940-90, briefly surveys criticism, editions of Dickens's works, and "Standard Biographies" from *Forster* on, including Peter Ackroyd's *Dickens* (**942**), which is termed one of "the most remarkable books of 1990." There is also brief commentary on film, stage, and television adaptations, 1980-90, on the Dickens Fellowship, and on various annual Dickens festivals. This section is meant as a supplement to the main entry on Dickens, pp. M6-7, and does not appear in other editions of this encyclopedia.

962. Corse, Larry B., and Sandra Corse, comps. "Dickens, Charles." In their *Articles on American and British Literature: An Index to Selected Periodicals, 1950-1977.* Chicago, Athens, OH, and London: Swallow Press, Ohio University Press, 1981, pp. 323-28.

Compiled, as pointed out in the preface, "to assist students using small college libraries with limited collections of literary periodicals." The bibliography of Dickens contains articles found in the forty-eight periodicals selected.

963. Cotton, Gerald B., and Hilda M. McGill. *Fiction Guides. General: British and American.* Readers Guide Series. London: Archon Books and Clive Bingley, 1967, passim.

A bibliographical survey, often evaluative, of guides to the novel and short story from general studies to studies of types of fiction. Cotton and McGill also cover guides to research on the novel, collections of reviews and criticism, bibliographies, biographical dictionaries and bibliographies, dictionaries, library catalogues, etc. There are no sections on individual authors, but a good many of the items listed contain sections or chapters on Dickens.

964. Cushing, Helen G., and Adah V. Morris, eds. "Dickens, Charles." In *Nineteenth Century Readers' Guide to Periodical Literature, 1890-1899, with Supplementary Indexing, 1900-1922.* 2 vols. New York: H. W. Wilson, 1944, I, 725-26.

Lists reviews of primary works as well as secondary periodical studies, including some items from 1900-25 if the periodicals in which they appeared were first added to the list covered by the *Readers' Guide* (**1046**) or other Wilson indexes between 1900 and 1922 (entries are added up to the point of the periodicals' inclusion in the *Readers' Guide*). As a result, a number of Dickens entries are post-1900. Also see entries for Charles Dickens, Jr., and Mary Dickens.

965. David, Deirdre. "Guide to Further Reading." In *The Cambridge Companion to the Victorian Novel.* Ed. Deirdre David. Cambridge, Eng.: Cambridge University Press, 2001, pp. 255-61.

A selective, unannotated list of major, principally book-length studies of all aspects of the Victorian novel.

966. Davis, Paul. "Appendix B: A Select Bibliography about Dickens and His Works." In his *Charles Dickens A to Z: The Essential Reference to His Life and Work.* New York: Facts on File, 1998, pp. 419-21.

A highly selective unannotated list of 1) General Introductions and Reference Works, 2) Bibliographies, 3) Biographies, and 4) Works of Scholarship and Criticism. Some major bibliographies are omitted, including volumes in the Garland Dickens Bibliographies (**13**).

967. Devonshire. M[arian] G. "Chronological List of Articles and Reviews on English Novels or Novelists from 1830 to 1870, with the Name of the Periodical, the Author, the Critic (Where Possible), and the Publisher" and "Bibliography." In her *The English Novel in France, 1830-1870* (**569**), pp. 415-46, 447-48.

The first of these two appendices includes some Dickens items, principally reviews of his works and five 1870 obituaries in French magazines. The "Bibliography" lists general studies of the English novel.

968. Diaz, Alfred J., [et al.], eds. *Guide to Reprints: An International Bibliography of Scholarly Reprints.* Kent, CT: Guide to Reprints, 1967- , passim.

Annually lists a number of reprints available of studies of Dickens and of editions of Dickens's novels and other works. The latest edition seen, *Guide to Reprints, 2002* (2 vols., München: K. G. Saur, 2002) contains, the foreword indicates, "over 71,000 titles from over 500 publishers." The first volume is an author-title index, the second volume a subject index.

969. Dick, Aliki L. "Charles Dickens (1812-1870)." In his *A Student's Guide to British Literature: A Selective Bibliography of 4,128 Titles and Reference Sources from the Anglo-Saxon Period to the Present.* Littleton, CO: Libraries Unlimited, 1972, pp. 198-201.

The section on Dickens in this unannotated, highly selective list of reference works, bibliographies, texts, and studies of criticism is not really useful. Several novels and all of his nonfictional and shorter writings are omitted from the list of his works and only forty-one books are included in an uneven listing of secondary studies. Robert B. Partlow, the first editor of *Dickens Studies Annual,* is misidentified as "R. B. Barlow."

970. Dunn, Richard J. "Charles Dickens." In his *The English Novel: Twentieth Century Criticism.* Vol. 1: *Defoe Through Hardy.* Chicago: Swallow Press, 1976, pp. 33-53.

An unannotated, highly selective listing of predominantly post-1940 studies (books and articles) through 1974 under the headings of the individual novels, general studies, and bibliography (three items only). Dunn excludes dissertations, biographies, reviews, short notes, and explications of text. Also see the useful sections on "General Studies" and on "General Bibliography" of the novel, pp. 171-201 and 201-02.

971. Dyson, A. E. "Select Bibliography." In *Dickens: Modern Judgements.* Ed. A. E. Dyson. London: Macmillan, 1968; Nashville, TN: Aurora Publishers, 1970, pp. 281-82.

A highly selective list of book-length critical studies of Dickens and two collections of critical essays.

972. Faxon, Frederick W., Mary E. Bates, and Anne C. Sutherland, comps. "Dickens, Charles, 1812-70." In their *Cumulated Magazine Subject Index, 1907-1949: A Cumulation of the F. W. Faxon Company's Annual Magazine Subject Index.* 2 vols. Boston: G. K. Hall, 1964, I, 460-61.

A cumulation of the *Annual Magazine Subject Index to American and British Publications* (Boston: G. K. Hall, 1908-49). This is a fairly limited list. Also see listings for members of Dickens's family, I, 461.

973. Fenstermaker, John J., comp. *Charles Dickens, 1940-1975: An Analytical Subject Index to Periodical Criticism of the Novels and Christmas Books.* Boston: G. K. Hall; London: Prior, 1979. xix + 302 pp.

A useful, if perhaps over-categorized, unannotated bibliography of what Fenstermaker terms "post-Wilsonian" criticism of Dickens's novels and the five Christmas Books, intentionally limited to articles "devoted to substantive considerations of *Dickens as a novelist*" in scholarly and critical journals. Under a general "Novels" heading and under the titles of the individual novels, one finds a list of the relevant articles, which are further analyzed under a variety of subject headings, such as characterization, composition, critical assessment, illustrations, influences, language and style, literary influences, plot, point of view, publication, setting, structure/unity, techniques, text, themes, and even subheadings (for example, characterization under *Bleak House* is subdivided into "Anal characters," "Chancery litigants," "Fairy-tale influence," "Grotesque," etc.). Appendices list selected books and their reviews and editions of Dickens's novels and their reviews published 1940-75. There is also an author index. This bibliography is based on Fenstermaker's doctoral dissertation, "Dickens Criticism 1940-70: An Analytical Subject Index." *Dissertation Abstracts International,* 34 (1973/74), 3340A (Ohio State University, 1973).

Reviews: *Choice,* 16 (1979), 992 (a "mine of information"); R. J. Dunn, *Analytical & Enumerative Bibliography,* 4 (1980), 67-73 (an "excellent index, a reliable, well-analyzed survey of some eleven hundred articles," with "lucid" arrangement; an "accurate and useful volume"); N. Heiser, *Library Journal,* 104 (1979), 1551 (a mainly descriptive review); D. Schmidt, *Journal of Popular Culture,* 13 (1979/80), 371-72 ("competently conceived" but with some "idiosyncracies of form"); S. Shatto, *Dickens Studies Newsletter,* 12 (1981), 92-93 ("scrupulous," useful, carefully done, though, as its title indicates, selective).

974. Fenstermaker, John J. "February 7 (175 Years Ago): Charles Dickens, 1812-1870." In *Book of Days, 1987: An Encyclopedia of Information Sources on Historical Figures and Events, Keyed to Calendar Dates.* Ed. C. Edward Wall et al. Ann Arbor, MI: Pierian Press, 1986, pp. 60-62.

A brief, highly selective listing of reference sources (six works), works by Dickens (seven listed), works about him (six), audiovisual productions (seven), and a few other bits of information, minimally useful, perhaps, to someone who knows nothing about Dickens.

975. Fielding, K[enneth] J. "Bibliography." In his *Charles Dickens: A Critical Introduction*. London, New York, and Toronto: Longmans, Green; New York: David Mackay, 1958, pp. 207-11; as "Select Annotated Bibliography." In 2nd ed., enlarged, London: Longmans, Green; Riverside Studies in Literature. Boston: Houghton Mifflin, 1965, pp. 253-61.

A short list of "Dickens's Principal Works" and an even shorter one of "Books about Dickens." In the revised edition Fielding expands his bibliography to include bibliographies and lengthens the sections in the first edition.

976. Fielding, K[enneth] J. "Select Bibliography." In his *Studying Charles Dickens*. York Handbooks. Beirut, Leb.: York Press; Harlow, Eng.: Longman Group, 1986, pp. 121-27.

A sound if highly selective bibliography of book-length studies, with some evaluative guidance, preceded by a short-title list of Dickens's works.

977. Ford, George H., and Lauriat Lane, Jr. "Bibliography." In their *The Dickens Critics*. Ithaca, NY: Cornell University Press, 1961; reprinted in paperback, 1966, pp. 387-410.

An alphabetical listing of principal books, articles, and essays, 1840-1960, of Dickens criticism.

978. Freeman, Ronald E., ed. *Bibliographies of Studies in Victorian Literature for the Ten Years 1965-1974*. New York: AMS Press, 1981, passim.

Photographic reproduction of the annual Victorian bibliography (**1058**), but with new, continuous pagination, as well as the original pagination. See the section on Dickens for each year. Freeman includes a list of errata and a 133-page subject and author index. In the introduction, Freeman notes that the "more than 17,600 entries" in his bibliography suggest "the thriving state of Victorian scholarship between 1965 and 1974." He also reports that Dickens led individual authors with 1,159 entries (Browning was second with 602, Hardy third with 503, Tennyson fourth with 442, and George Eliot fifth with 362; Thackeray only came in twelfth with 187 entries, closely followed by Trollope with 181). Freeman points out that the Dickens entries are larger in number than those of Hardy, Eliot, Thackeray, and Trollope combined and attest to "the variety, vitality, techniques, humor, and the quintessential Victorian world created in his novels." For other volumes in this series, see

Templeman (**1025**), Slack (**1022**), Wright (**1033**), and Tobias (**1026**). For a fuller description of the contents, see **1058**.

979.   Gall, Peter. "Literaturverzeichnis." In his *Die Moderne Kritik über Charles Dickens: Ein Beitrag zum 100 Todestag (9. Juni 1870) von Charles Dickens.* Winterthur, Switzerland: Verlag Hans Schellenberg, 1970, pp. 65-69.

A bibliography of books and articles referred to in this study of modern critical views of Dickens, most from the 1950s and 1960s, with a few older works included, and most studies in English, with several in German and other languages.

980.   Glancy, Ruth. "Bibliography." In her *Student Companion to Charles Dickens.* Student Companions to Classic Writers. Westport, CT, and London: Greenwood Press, 1999, pp. 157-62.

An unannotated, highly selective listing of Dickens periodicals, general book-length studies of Dickens, and book-length studies of *Oliver Twist*, the Christmas Books and Christmas Stories, *David Copperfield, Hard Times, A Tale of Two Cities*, and *Great Expectations*—works to which Glancy devotes individual chapters in her volume.

981.   Gold, Joseph, comp. *Phase 1. Charles Dickens: A Preliminary Checklist of Criticism, Being the First of a Two Part Publication Designed to Bring Together a Comprehensive Listing of Critical Writings about Charles Dickens.* Winnipeg: University of Manitoba Press, 1969. 361 pp.

In many respects an earlier version of Gold's *The Stature of Dickens* (**982**), but with a different organizational structure: 1) selected bibliographic studies, 2) biographies and studies of letters and speeches, 3) articles in periodicals, 4) book-length studies, 5) selected reviews of major critical studies, 6) dissertations and theses, 7) books on the novel with significant Dickens material, and 8) studies of individual Dickens works selected from the above sections. Items are arranged alphabetically within sections and are not annotated.

982.   Gold, Joseph, comp. *The Stature of Dickens: A Centenary Bibliography.* Toronto and Buffalo, NY: Published for University of Manitoba Press by University of Toronto Press, 1971. xxix + 237 pp.

This bibliography largely covers the period 1870-1968/69, with some earlier references. As Gold notes, this is not a definitive listing of Dickens criticism and scholarship, for it omits "the vast majority of peripheral, occasional, and ephemeral items," but a "presentation" of what Gold finds to be "of lasting, scholarly value or interest." The entries are numbered (3,625 items) and listed chronologically in four sections: 1) studies primarily on Dickens (1,948 items); 2) studies of the individual novels (with separate headings for each), *A Christmas Carol*, and the letters (totalling 1,335 items); 3) doctoral dissertations (201 items); and 4) studies with "significant mention of Dickens or with special relevance to the study of Dickens" (141 items). An introduction contains a listing of "general and specific bibliographical aids" (79 items, unnumbered, and thus not in Gold's author index). The work also includes a Dickens chronology and occasionally corrects and obviously updates Miller (**1005**), though Miller is more inclusive for nineteenth-century works, and certainly for peripheral items, and Gold is fuller than Collins (**8**). To give some indication of the selectivity of the bibliography, for the Christmas Books and Christmas Stories Gold only includes studies of *A Christmas Carol* (43 items). Compare this to Ruth Glancy's 610-page volume on the Christmas works and other short fiction in the Garland Dickens Bibliographies (**98**), which lists 669 items for *A Christmas Carol* alone and a total of 2,201 items. Admittedly, many of Glancy's listings fall into the categories that Gold has deliberately excluded from his bibliography. Despite its shortcomings, it is still the most useful bibliography of Dickens studies available for the period 1870-1968/69. It is, of course, projected that when the Dickens Bibliographies series (**12, 13**) is completed, it will supplant every previous Dickens bibliography, including Gold's. Illustrated. See Gold (**981**) for a slightly earlier and differently arranged bibliography, Cohn and Collins (**958**) for a continuation of Gold's bibliography, 1970-79, and Cohn [et al.] (**1037**) for succeeding years.

Reviews: R. D. Altick, *Nineteenth-Century Fiction*, 27 (1972/73), 107-10 (finds a number of flaws in what he characterizes as "a loose baggy monster" of a bibliography, though he also sees it as "quantitatively the best source for the great modern period of Dickens studies, from 1940 onward"); *American Reference Books Annual*, 3 (1972), 520 (highly recommended; praises selectivity); C. R. Andrews, *Library Journal*, 96 (1971), 3312-13 ("based on careful, extensive scholarship"); J. K. Bracken (**1139**), p. 74 (the "most comprehensive single-volume bibliography of works by and about Dickens"); *Choice*, 8 (1971/72), 1317-18 (an "excellent bibliography"; a "big improvement" over earlier ones); D. DeVries, *Dickensian*, 68 (1972), 188-91 (finds merit in the bibliography but, in comparing it with others, notes, with various examples, its selectiveness and its occasional arbitrariness of arrangement, selection, and indexing–still, "an essential reference work"); R. C. Ellsworth, *Queen's Quarterly*, 79 (1972), 108 ("an exemplar of bibliographical scholarship," a "fitting tribute" to Dickens, and a fine example of "book design and production"), reprinted in *Canadian Library Journal*, 29 (1972), 260; K. J. Fielding, *Review of English Studies*, ns 24 (1973), 100-02 (while noting some "imperfections," recognizes the bibliography's "value and convenience"); H. J. Heaney, *Dickens Studies Newsletter*, 3 (1972), 7-12 (offers some minor criticism but generally finds the coverage full, though notes some omissions); R. Partlow, *Dickens Studies Newsletter*, 2 (1971), 103-05 (finds the bibliography logically organized, sees it as a "fine effort" for a selective bibliography, but would like a more "definitive" one); L. Pothet, *Etudes anglaises*, 28 (1975), 233 (in French; despite some reservations finds the bibliography has "les mérites considérables").

983. Grillo, Virgil. "About Dickens and His Other Works: Selected Bibliography of Secondary Sources." In his *Charles Dickens' **Sketches by Boz**: End in the Beginning* (**2502**), pp. 223-30.

Lists 156 studies of Dickens's works other than *Sketches by Boz* to accompany his bibliography of studies of *Sketches by Boz* (**1115**). Also see Grillo (**133**).

984. Guiliano, Edward, and Philip Collins. "Further Reading." In *The Anno-tated Dickens*. Ed. Edward Guiliano and Philip Collins. 2 vols. New York: Clarkson N. Potter; London: Orbis Book Publishing Corp., 1986, I, 1074-75; II, 1120-21.

Guiliano and Collins print the same highly selective but reasonably repre-sentative bibliography at the end of each volume. They list Works (letters, miscellaneous papers, and speeches but not editions of individual novels or collected works), Biographies, Critical Anthologies and Reference Books, Criticism (Books), Periodicals, and Bibliographies. In the last section, they do not, unfortunately, include the early volumes in the Garland Dickens Bibliog-raphies (**13**). For their textual annotations, see Guiliano and Collins (**2299**).

985. Hanham, H. J., comp. and ed. "Dickens." In his *Bibliography of British History, 1851-1914*. Oxford: Clarendon Press, 1976, pp. 942-43 and pas-sim.

A highly selective list, with brief evaluations, of bibliographies, biographies, and critical studies of Dickens. See the index for other references to Dickens.

986. Hawes, Donald. "Bibliography." In his *Who's Who in Dickens*. London and New York: Routledge, 1998, pp. 277-78.

A highly selective bibliography listing fifty-one major studies of Dickens.

987. Helm, W[illiam] H. "A Short Bibliography." In his *Dickens*. Regent's Library. London: Herbert & Daniel, [1912], pp. 539-46.

Lists criticisms, reminiscences, biographies and miscellaneous items, as well as collected editions and separate works.

988. Hobsbaum, Philip. "A Selective Bibliography." In his *A Reader's Guide to Charles Dickens*. London: Thames & Hudson, 1972; New York: Farrar, Straus and Giroux, 1973; reprinted Syracuse, NY: Syracuse University Press, 1998, pp. 294-311.

An unannotated bibliography of general studies of Dickens and critical studies of individual Dickens works that Hobsbaum "found useful" in prepar-ing his guide.

989. Hodgkins, Louise M. "Charles Dickens, 1812-1870." In her *A Guide to the Study of Nineteenth Century Authors*. Boston, New York, and Chicago: D. C. Heath, 1889, pp. 45-48.

A brief student guide prepared for a Wellesley College course of lectures on nineteenth-century authors. Hodgkins lists early biographies (books) and early critical studies (mainly magazine articles and reviews). This work went through various editions through at least 1904 without being updated.

990. Hollington, Michael. "Bibliography: The Critical Response." In his *Charles Dickens: Critical Assessments* (**26**), I, 27-38.

A selective, unannotated listing of biographies, bibliographies, journals of Dickens studies, book-length criticism, and shorter criticism of Dickens.

991. Horsman, Alan. "Select Bibliography." In his *The Victorian Novel*. Oxford History of English Literature. Ed. F. P. Wilson et al. Vol. 11, part 2. Oxford: Clarendon Press, 1990; reprinted as vol. 13. Ibid., 1990, pp. 448-57.

Includes four pages of useful general studies, but, in the section on Dickens, lists only twenty-six (unannotated) items, an eccentric selection of book-length studies—for, example, Horsman lists the Garland Dickens Bibliographies (**13**), Fenstermaker's bibliography (**973**), and Oppenlander's volume on *All the Year Round* (**158**), but not Lohrli's on *Household Words* (**155**), and not Cohn's (**1037**), Cohn's and Collins's (**958**), Gold's (**982**), or, for that matter, any other.

992. Ikeler, A. Abbott. "Dickens Studies Since 1970." *British Studies Monitor*, 9, iii (Winter 1980), 26-48.

Surveys and evaluates some sixty-five or so book-length studies. The footnotes, giving full bibliographical references, are essentially a bibliography of important Dickens studies, 1970-78.

993. Johnson, Edgar. "The Present State of Dickensian Studies." *Victorian Newsletter*, no. 7 (April 1955), 4-9.

A survey—under such headings as bibliography, Dickens originals, topography, critical studies, and biography—of then recent publications in the field of Dickens studies. Johnson often relates the listings to earlier works in the field.

994. Jones, Howard Mumford, et al. "Charles Dickens: 1812-1870." In their *Syllabus and Bibliography of Victorian Literature (Including the Regency Period)*. Ann Arbor, MI: Brumfield and Brumfield, 1934-35, pp. 193-200.

Prepared for students presumably in a course at the University of Michigan. The Dickens entry is a selected list under these headings: Bibliographical and Biographical References, Collected Editions, List of Titles and Editions, and The Dickens Criticism, with occasional brief annotations. Also see "The Background," pp. 1-71, for background studies of the period.

995. Jordan, John O. "Selected Bibliography." In *The Cambridge Companion to Charles Dickens*. Ed. John O. Jordan. Cambridge: Cambridge University Press, 2001, pp. 224-29.

A highly selective, unannotated listing of primary sources, biographies, reference materials, periodicals devoted to Dickens studies, collections of critical studies, and general studies, principally book-length, of Dickens.

996. Kitton, Fred[eric] G. *Dickensiana: A Bibliography of the Literature Relating to Charles Dickens and His Writings*. London: George Redway, 1886; reprinted New York: Haskell House, 1971. xxxii + 511 pp.

A bibliography of secondary works published through 1884, divided into biographical and critical studies with additional sections listing poetic tributes, anthologies, music, plays, plagiarisms, testimonies, "notes and queries" (selections from articles in *Notes and Queries*), and ephemera. One of the earliest bibliographies of Dickens studies, Kitton's volume serves as the basis for any more complete bibliography of nineteenth-century studies of Dickens and his works. It is fully annotated, often with excerpts running from one-half to four pages in length. It is particularly valuable for contemporary reviews of Dickens's novels and articles in rare issues of magazines. Illustrated. For some additions, see Carty (**953**).

Reviews: *Book-Lore*, 3 (1885/86), 181 (a brief notice; "contains information indispensable to all Dickens's collectors and is interesting to all who admire the great novelist"); *Saturday Review*, 61 (1886), 510-11 ("a comprehensive catalogue" of Dickens's writings and of "a good quantity of books written about him," with "copious extracts from reviews of his works and from sermons on his character").

997. Koppershoek, A. M. "A Critical Bibliography of Nineteenth-Century English Literature." *Dutch Quarterly Review of Anglo-American Letters*, 19 (1989), 307-14.

A highly selective, annotated list of works, ca. 1984-88, in paragraph format. The works about Dickens, pp. 312-13, amount to only seven book-length studies.

998. Lane, Lauriat, Jr. "Dickens Studies 1958-1968: An Overview." In "Charles Dickens Special Number." *Studies in the Novel*, 1, ii (Summer 1969), 240-54.

A useful survey of Dickens scholarship and criticism, 1958-68. Also see Vann (**1028**).

999. Lerner, Laurence. "Dickens, Charles, 1812-1870." In *Reader's Guide to Literature in English*. Ed. Mark Hawkins-Dady. London and Chicago: Fitzroy Dearborn, 1996, pp. 178-82.

Following a highly selective list of biographies of Dickens and studies of his works, most from the mid-twentieth century on, Lerner comments in turn on the works listed.

1000. "List of Selected Books on Dickens Still in Print: Not Including Out of Print Books Obtainable Second-hand Only." *Dickensian*, 24 (1927/28), 55-56.

A list of books, published 1906-26, then in print, under several headings: Biography; Criticism; Topography; Readings, Recitations and Plays; Reference; and Miscellaneous.

1001. Magill, Frank, ed., with Stephen L. Hanson and Patricia K. Hanson, assoc. eds. "Charles Dickens (1812-1870)." In *Magill's Bibliography of Literary Criticism: Selected Sources for the Study of More than 2,500 Outstanding Works of Western Literature*. 4 vols. Englewood Cliffs, NJ: Salem Press, 1979, I, 497-517.

Lists a selection of books and articles about Dickens under headings of the individual novels, including *A Christmas Carol* but not the other Christmas Books, principally studies from the 1960s and 1970s. General studies included are listed under each of the novels with which they are concerned.

1002. Marcus, Steven. "Bibliography." In his *Dickens: From Pickwick to Dombey*. New York: Basic Books, 1965, pp. 379-84.

Lists books that he has found "most useful" in his study of Dickens.

1003. Mazzeno, Laurence W. "Charles Dickens." In his *The Victorian Novel: An Annotated Bibliography*. The Magill Bibliographies. Pasadena, CA, and Englewood Cliffs, NJ: Salem Press, 1989, pp. 36-93.

A highly selective annotated bibliography with a brief "General Studies" section as well as a section on each of the novels. Mazzeno includes *A Christmas Carol* but not the other four Christmas Books. The annotations are often evaluative.

1004. Members of English 259a, Harvard University, Spring Term, 1965. "The Novels of Dickens: A Bibliography." Mimeograph copy of typescript manuscript. [Cambridge, MA: Harvard University], 1965. 183 pp. In Dickens House, London.

Annotated bibliography of reviews and critical studies of thirteen Dickens novels (*Dombey and Son* and *Nicholas Nickleby* are not included) by a class of Harvard students. The annotations are not very good, about what might be expected of such a class, though several of the compilers have since become recognized Dickens scholars.

1005. Miller, William. *The Dickens Student and Collector: A List of Writings Relating to Charles Dickens and His Works, 1836-1945.* Cambridge, MA: Harvard University Press, 1946. xii + 351 pp.

The most thorough Dickens bibliography for the period of books, magazine articles, and occasional newspaper articles, though closely rivaled by the "Dickensiana" serial bibliography in the *Dickensian* (**1043**), which includes many newspaper articles not in Miller. But it is not structured usefully nor is it as thorough and as accurate as one would like. See Calhoun and Heaney (**1392**) on the shortcomings of this bibliography. Miller divides the work into twelve parts, largely following the divisions of Kitton (**996**): 1) Personal (biographical), 2-5) Critical, including appreciations and depreciations, reviews of individual works, reviews of *Forster* and reviews of the *Hogarth-Dickens Letters*, 6) Poetical, 7) Dramatic, 8) Musical, 9) Anthological, 10) Plagiaristic, 11) Topographical, and 12) Bibliographical. Within each section, works are arranged in chronological order. The bibliography is largely unannotated. Despite its length, the index (pp. 283-351) is not complete and should be used cautiously. It is primarily an author index but even in this regard is not entirely accurate. While some titles are listed, there is no rationale for the selection; anonymous articles, for example, are not usually listed by title, but seem, instead, to be identified principally by the journal in which they appeared. A brief introduction by Robert H. Haynes lays claim to near completeness for the volume but also suggests that World War II may have been responsible for errors caused by Miller's inability to return to England to consult his notes there. For further evaluation of this work, see the introduction to the present volume, pp. xix-xxi and xli.

Two supplements were published by Miller: *Supplement to "The Dickens Student and Collector: A List of Writings Relating to Charles Dickens and His Works"* (Brighton: Privately printed, 1947, 12 pp.) and *A Second Supplement to "The Dickens Student and Collector: A List of Writings Relating to Charles Dickens and His Works"* (Hove, Sussex: Privately printed, 1953, 15 pp.). These continue the arrangement of the original volume, the first mainly containing works omitted from it, the second largely, though selectively, bringing the entries up to 1952/53. They are not indexed. Miller's typed manuscript (with corrections and paste-ins) entitled "Songs and Other Musical Compositions Founded on or Suggested by the Works of Charles Dickens or Incidents Therein," the subtitle of the "Musical" section of Miller's bibliography and presumably the manuscript for this section, is in the music collection of the Library of Congress. For lists of Miller's own collection of Dickens music, now in the Dickens House, London (**1457C4**), see Lightwood (**1486**) and Hill (**1473**).

Reviews: *Bulletin of Bibliography and Dramatic Index*, 19 (1945), 5 ("a distinguished piece of work"); *Notes and Queries*, 192 (1947), 221 (criticizes the bibliography's lack of completeness and its inadequate index); R. Straus, *Dickensian*, 43 (1946/47), 150-51 (favorable remarks); *Times Literary Supplement*, 12 July 1947, p. 352 (criticizes the arrangement of entries but reserves judgment on the bibliography's completeness). Also see Calhoun and Heaney (**1392**).

1006. Millward, Robin H. "Charles Dickens: A Reading List." In *Charles Dickens, 1812-1870*. London: Westminster City Libraries, [1970], pp. 4-9.

Lists several general studies, bibliographies, and biographies of Dickens.

1007. Monod, Sylvère. "Bibliographie." In his *Dickens romancier: Etude sur la création littéraire dans les romans de Charles Dickens* (**2307**), pp. 493-503.

An annotated selective list of book-length bibliographies, editions, manuscripts (with locations), biographies and collections of letters, and critical studies (general and for individual works) concerning Dickens, as well as a few studies of the history of the novel. The bibliography is omitted from Monod's *Dickens the Novelist*, the revised English version of *Dickens romancier*.

1008. National Council of Teachers of English. *Abstracts of English Studies*. Boulder, CO: National Council of Teachers of English, 1 (1958)-23 (1980); Calgary, Alberta, Can.: University of Calgary, 24 (1981)-34 (1991) , passim.

Contains abstracts of English studies selected from a number of literary journals. To locate those concerned with Dickens see the subject index for each issue as well as the yearly index. Harner (**1147**), p. 63, finds the coverage "erratic" and the subject indexing "inadequate"; to use this series intelligently, one needs to consult the individual issues as well as the annual index. The publication was issued monthly through volume 23 (1979/80) and quarterly thereafter.

1009. Nayder, Lillian. "Wilkie Collins Studies: 1983-1999." *Dickens Studies Annual*, 28 (1999), 257-329.

The "Bibliography," pp. 307-23, lists eight studies in a brief section on "Collins and Dickens," p. 319. For other references to Collins's relationship with Dickens, see the sections on comparative studies, pp. 319-20, and dissertations, pp. 321-23. Dickens is also mentioned occasionally in Nayder's long discussion of Collins scholarship, pp. 257-307.

1010. New York Public Library, New York. "Electronic Resources by Subject [for Home Access]." http://www.nypl.org/branch/eresources.html.

A simplified, limited version of what is available on computers at the library itself, including The Biography Resource Center (a Gale database), Books in Print (an R. R. Bowker database of more than 2.8 million titles), Literature Resource Center ("built on the Gale Group's three trademark author bases: *Contemporary Authors Online, Contemporary Literary Criticism Select*, and the *Dictionary of Literary Biography Online*"), and Gale's Ready Reference Shelf (this is a combination of other Gale databases). Dickens references may be found throughout.

1011. Newsom, Robert. "Selected Bibliography." In his *Charles Dickens Revisited.* Twayne's English Authors Series, 558. New York: Twayne, 2000, pp. 201-12.

A highly selective survey mainly of studies of Dickens under the headings "Bibliographical and Encyclopedic Resources," "Primary Sources," "Biographies," "Historical and Background Studies, Literary History," "Criticism," "Dickens and His Illustrators," and "Electronic Resources." This bibliography is also online, appended to Newsom's bibliography of *Bleak House* (**1228**), at http://humwww.ucsc.edu/dickens/DEA/Bibliographies/BleakHouse.biblio/BH_Biblio.html.

1012. *19th Century Masterfile: A Paratext Resource.* Paratext Electronic Reference Publishing. http://www.paratext.com/19cm_intro.htm.

An online database available through libraries that claims to be "the largest resource for pre-1920 studies, with over 6 million citations online." A keyword search for "Dickens" on 16 January 2003 produced 1,319 records. The database may also be searched by author, title, and periodical.

1013. Nisbet, Ada. "Charles Dickens." In *Victorian Fiction: A Guide to Research.* Ed. Lionel Stevenson. Cambridge, MA: Harvard University Press, 1964, pp. 44-153.

An invaluable guide to Dickens studies prior to 1964. Documenting the "phenomenal rise in the number of ardent scramblers over Dickensian terrain" since 1918, Nisbet surveys the field of Dickensian publishing, criticism, and scholarship under the headings of manuscripts (with locations), bibliography, editions, letters, biography, and criticism, the last of which is subdivided under the headings of social realism, imagination and symbolism, self-revelation, craftsmanship, lure of the theater, precursors and imitators, foreign influence (a particularly valuable and lengthy section), and humor. After taming, as she puts it, the "multitudinous seas of Dickens criticism," Nisbet concludes that few would deny that modern criticism "has brought more mature appreciation of Dickens' multiple and diverse achievements." See the index to the entire volume for references to Dickens in chapters devoted to other Victorian novelists. The introductory chapter, "General Materials," by Bradford A. Booth, pp. 1-20, though unduly brief, notes a few general studies of Victorian literature that may usefully be consulted. Supplemented by Collins (**959**).

Reviews: A. O. J. Cockshut, *Review of English Studies*, ns 17 (1966), 341-42 (in a generally unfavorable review, finds the historical survey of Dickens criticism unbalanced and poorly done); K. J. Fielding, *Dickensian*, 61 (1965), 126-28 (an "entirely reliable" account, covering "everything of importance that has been written about Dickens in the past 30 years"); N. C. Peyrouton, *Dickens Studies*, 1 (1965), 102-03 (an impressive survey); L. Poston, III, *College English*, 26 (1964/65), 244 (the Dickens section by Nisbet is "exhaustive," and Booth's section is "a masterpiece of compressed but judicious comment"); S. M. Smith, *Modern Language Review*, 62 (1967), 120-21 (excellent survey and arrangement of material; discriminating assessments); G. and K. Tillotson, *Nineteenth-Century Fiction*, 19 (1964/65), 405-10 (Nisbet's contribution is a "gargantuan" achievement); *Times Literary Supplement*, 15 April 1965, p. 289 ("all essays provide a sufficient survey of the relevant critical material; no commentary on the Dickens section").

1014. Page, Norman. "Select Bibliography." In his *A Dickens Companion* (**223**), pp. 309-18.

Comments on the locations of Dickens's manuscripts and on a few collected editions of Dickens's works, but this is principally a selective bibliography of Dickens studies.

1015. Palmer, Helen H., and Anne J. Dyson, comps. "Charles Dickens." *English Novel Explication: Criticisms to 1972*. Hamden, CT: Shoe String Press, 1973, pp. 67-84.

Unannotated listings of articles and studies in books, 1958-72, intended as an updating of Bell and Baird (**948**). Palmer and Dyson list, for example, ten items for *Pickwick Papers*, thirty-two for *Our Mutual Friend*. They include indexes of books and journals consulted. For supplements see Abernethy, Kloesel, and Smitten (**941**).

1016. [Pollard, Arthur]. "Bibliography." In *The Victorians*. Ed. Arthur Pollard. Vol. 6 of *The New History of Literature*. New York: Peter Bedrick Books, 1987; reprinted as vol. 6 of *Sphere History of Literature*, London: Sphere, 1988; as vol. 6 of *Penguin History of Literature*, New York: Penguin Books, 1993, pp. 499-543.

See Part 4, "Dickens," pp. 508-09, for a highly selective but annotated bibliography including the Clarendon Dickens, collections of Dickens's letters, and twenty-three full-length studies of Dickens. The original publication of *The Victorians*, as vol. 6 of *The History of Literature in the English Language* (London: Barrie & Jenkins in Association with Sphere Books; New York: Bantam, 1970), does not contain the bibliography.

1017. Price, Martin. "Selected Bibliography." In *Dickens: A Collection of Critical Essays*. Ed. Martin Price. Twentieth Century Views. Englewood Cliffs, NJ: Prentice-Hall, 1967, pp. 182-84.

A brief commentary on collected editions of Dickens's works, followed by a highly selective list of principally book-length biographies and critical studies.

1018. Quinn, Martin. "An Annotated Bibliography of the Writings about Charles Dickens and His Works, 1947 to 1967." Typewritten manuscript. [1967?]. 171 pp. In the Dickens House, London.

Includes 989 books, articles, and doctoral dissertations in English and other languages, with a subject index. Quinn does not include reprints published during the twenty years covered unless they were revisions, excludes articles in the *Dickensian*, and admits in his introduction that he has made no "systematic attempt to gather foreign items" or book reviews, including only those "that found their way to my hands."

1019. Riverside Public Library, Riverside, CA. "Cha[rle]s. Dickens, 1812-1870." In *February Celebrations*. Bulletin 27. Riverside, CA: Riverside Public Library, February 1912, pp. 3-5.

A short-title checklist of biographies and essays, poems and recitations, and magazine articles about Dickens, "not intended as a select or complete list," as a note indicates, but as "an easy, ready reference."

1020. Samuel, Joy, comp. "Dickens, Charles John Huffam (1812-70)." In *From Dickens to Hardy*. Ed. Boris Ford. Pelican Guide to English Literature, 6. Harmondsworth, Eng., Baltimore, MD, etc.: Penguin Books, 1958, p. 473; frequently reprinted with revisions, from 1960 on; listing revised by R. C. Churchill, 1969, pp. 475-76; also new and revised edition, Guide to English Literature, 6 (comp. Joy [Samuel] Groombridge). The Belle Sauvage Library. London: Cassell, 1963, pp. 477-78; listing further revised by Norman Vance in New Pelican Guide to English Literature, 6. Harmondsworth, Eng., New York, etc.: Penguin, 1982, pp. 486-87; reprinted in *A Guide for Readers to the New Pelican Guide to English Literature*. Harmondsworth, Eng., New York, etc.: Penguin, 1984, pp. 400-02.

A one-paragraph summary of Dickens's life followed by an equally brief, highly selective, unannotated list of biographies, editions of collected works, letters, and critical studies. The latest version, Vance's updating for 1984, comprises a random list of biographies (though anchored by *Forster* and *Johnson*), two sets of collected works, the *Pilgrim Letters*, Collins's edition of the *Public Readings* (**652**), and twenty-four secondary studies, the latest of which was published in 1980. The only bibliography listed in the last group is that of Churchill (**956**), who wrote the essay on Dickens that appears in *From Dickens to Hardy*. Also see other parts of the bibliographical section (the whole edited by Samuel and the later compilers listed) of this volume for an unannotated listing of a variety of background studies in Victorian life, literature, and fiction, which is more useful than the Dickens section, though the latter grows slightly longer in successive editions.

1021. Schlicke, Paul. "General Bibliography." In his *Oxford Reader's Companion to Dickens* (**2309**), pp. 605-07 (pp. 619-21 in 2000 paperback edition).

A brief bare-bones list of Dickens's works (titles and dates only), selected reference books, and book-length studies of "works cited frequently in the text."

1022. Slack, Robert C., ed. *Bibliographies of Studies in Victorian Literature for the Ten Years 1955-1964*. Urbana: University of Illinois Press, 1967, passim.

Photographic reproduction of the annual Victorian bibliography (**1058**) in *Modern Philology* (1956-57) and *Victorian Studies* (1958-65), but with new, continuous pagination, as well as the original pagination. See the section on Dickens for each year. In an introduction, Slack discusses the comprehensiveness of the annual bibliography, the divisions of the bibliography, and the great increase in publications in the field. He includes a chart of the number of entries in the various divisions of the bibliography and a statistical analysis of entries, year-by-year, pointing out that Dickens led in the number of entries for the ten years (621 items). He also looks at types of studies of Dickens and compares these to those of Thomas Hardy and the seven other most popular Victorian authors. The volume contains a 61-page index of Victorian authors, authors of entries, and selected subject headings. For other volumes in this series, see Templeman (**1025**), Wright (**1033**), Freeman (**978**), and Tobias (**1026**). For a description of the contents, see **1058**.
Review: M. S[later], *Dickensian*, 64 (1968), 117-18 (Slater finds this a "welcome volume," though he complains about Slack's condescending comment in his introduction on articles in the *Dickensian*).

1023. Slater, Michael. "Dickens, 1812-1870." In *The English Novel: Select Bibliographical Guides*. Ed. A. E. Dyson. London and New York: Oxford University Press, 1974, pp. 179-99.

Contains evaluative commentary on modern editions of Dickens's works and on Dickensian critical studies and commentary, biographies and letters, bibliography, and background reading, followed by a useful if highly selective bibliography (pp. 191-99) under the same headings, largely of book-length studies.

1024. Staples, Leslie C. "Miniature Bibliographies: Some British Novelists. II. Charles Dickens." *British Book News*, no. 73 (August-September 1946), 299-301.

A brief essay-bibliography, summarizing Dickens's career (by way of itemizing his works) and providing a highly selective listing of biographical and critical studies.

1025. Templeman, William D., ed. *Bibliographies of Studies in Victorian Literature for the Thirteen Years 1932-1944*. Urbana: University of Illinois Press, 1945, passim.

Photographic reproduction of the annual Victorian bibliography in *Modern Philology* (**1058**), but with new, continuous pagination. See the section on Dickens for each year. The volume includes a preface by Templeman, a brief foreword by Howard Mumford Jones, and a four-page "Index of Victorian Authors." For continuations, see Wright (**1033**), Slack (**1022**), Freeman (**978**), and Tobias (**1026**). For a description of the contents, see **1058**.

1026. Tobias, Richard C., ed. *Bibliographies of Studies in Victorian Literature for the Ten Years 1975-1984*. New York: AMS Press, 1991, passim.

A reprint of the annual Victorian bibliography in *Victorian Studies* (**1058**) for 1975-84. See the section on Dickens for each year. In a terse introduction, Tobias notes that the nineteen compilers of the bibliography "scanned more than 500 scholarly and popular journals to produce it." In reluctantly, and therefore briefly, surveying literary trends evidenced by the entries, Tobias notes that "Dickens continues to dominate." He also spells out the more elaborate divisions of the bibliography instituted during his editorship and includes a short list of errata, pp. 904-05, and an index, pp. 906-1130, compiled by himself and Barbara N. Tobias. For other volumes in this series, see Templeman (**1025**), Slack (**1022**), Freeman (**978**), and Wright (**1033**). For a description of the contents, see **1058**.

1027. Tower Hamlets Libraries. *Charles Dickens, 1812-1870: A Selected Reading List*. London: Premier Press, [1970]. 10 pp.

A very brief handlist of Dickens's works and secondary studies.

1028. Vann, J. Don. "A Checklist of Dickens Criticism, 1963-1967." In "Charles Dickens Special Number." *Studies in the Novel*, 1, ii (Summer 1969), 255-78.

While not pretending to be comprehensive, this is a reasonably full alphabetical listing of books and articles on Dickens published 1963-67, with a few works from 1961-62. Intended as an updating of Nisbet's Dickens bibliography in Lionel Stevenson's *Victorian Fiction* (**1013**), only a few of the more important studies are missing, though Vann omits most collections of critical commentary and introductions to Dickens's novels. See also Lane (**998**).

1029. Venner, R. H. *Charles Dickens: A Brief Reader's Guide.* [Nottingham, Eng.]: Printed for Nottinghamshire County Council for Leicestershire, Nottingham, Nottinghamshire, Derbyshire and Burton upon Trent Libraries, 1970. 18 pp.

Contains lists of Dickens's works, book-length critical studies of them, book-length biographies and collections of letters of Dickens, and books on the Victorian age. All but the list of Dickens's works contain brief annotations and are quite selective. An introduction by N. V. Tilley traces Dickens's declining and then rising reputation following his death. Illustrated.

1030. Watt, Ian, comp. "Dickens, Charles (1812-1870)." In his *The British Novel: Scott Through Hardy.* Goldentree Bibliographies in Language and Literature. Northbrook, IL: AHM Publishing Corp., 1973, pp. 33-47.

A highly selective but useful, if now somewhat outdated, unannotated beginner's list of bibliographies, editions, letters, biographical and general studies, criticism, and other studies of Dickens's works in general as well as of individual novels.

1031. Wells, Daniel A. "Dickens, Charles (1812-1870), English Novelist." In his *The Literary Index to American Magazines, 1815-1865.* Metuchen, NJ, and London: Scarecrow Press, 1980, pp. 43-45.

In quite abbreviated form, lists articles and book reviews in twenty-four selected American literary magazines.

1032. Wells, Daniel A. "Dickens, Charles (1812-1870), English Novelist." In his *The Literary Index to American Magazines, 1850-1900.* Bibliographies and Indexes in American Literature, 22. Westport, CT, and London: Greenwood Press, 1996, pp. 109-13.

In quite abbreviated form, lists articles and book reviews in thirteen selected American literary magazines.

1033. Wright, Austin, ed. *Bibliographies of Studies in Victorian Literature for the Ten Years 1945-1954.* Urbana: University of Illinois Press, 1956, passim.

Photographic reproduction of the annual Victorian bibliography in *Modern Philology* (**1058**), but with new, continuous pagination, as well as the original pagination. See the section on Dickens for each year. Wright includes a list of errata, and a forty-page index of authors of the listings, Victorian authors mentioned as well as those who are the subjects of the various entries, and a number of subject headings. For other volumes in this series, see Templeman (**1025**), Slack (**1022**), Freeman (**978**), and Tobias (**1026**). For a description of the contents, see **1058**.

1034. Zasadinski, Eugene. "Charles Dickens, 1812-1870." In *Research Guide to Biography and Criticism*. Ed. Walton Beacham. 2 vols. Washington, D. C.: Research Publishing, 1985, I, 337-41.

A brief bibliographical survey of biographies and autobiographical, biographical, and critical sources for the study of Dickens's life and works. Zasadinski singles out *Forster, Johnson,* and R. Shelton MacKenzie's *Life of Charles Dickens* (Philadelphia: T. B. Peterson and Brothers, 1870) as the principal biographies, finding *Johnson* to be still definitive. Also see "Charles Dickens, 1812-1870," in *Research Guide to Biography and Criticism*. Vol. 4: *1990 Update* (Washington, D. C.: Beacham Publishing, 1990), pp. 131-37, for an annotated list of more recent (1985-89) biographical and critical studies of Dickens, and an unannotated list of "Other Sources," concerning Dickens.

3B. SERIAL BIBLIOGRAPHIES CONTAINING DICKENS STUDIES

Note: All of these serial bibliographies should be compared by the researcher since each lists works not included by the others (see **1036-37, 1039, 1042,** and **1058** in particular). For a comparative study of Dickens entries in current serial bibliographies, see Loomis (**1413**). Also see Wortman (**1162**) and **Bibliographies of Dickens studies, serial bibliographies,** in part 2 of the subject index.

1035. *Arts and Humanities Citation Index, 1976[-].* Philadelphia: Institute for Scientific Information, 1978- , passim.

The volumes for each year (increasing from three for 1976 to six for 1982 on) contain three principal indexes. The first, "Citation Index," is "an alphabetical listing by author of all the references (cited items) found in footnotes and bibliographies of journals (citing items) covered" in this reference work. The listings are quite abbreviated; sources need to be identified in the second index, "Source Index," an alphabetical author index. In the third index, "Permuterm® Subject Index," "every significant English word in the titles of the source items indexed . . . is paired with every other significant English word which appears with it in a title." Again, items can be more explicitly identified in the "Source Index." Check under Dickens in the first two indexes and under Dickens or other appropriate subject word in the third. Issued annually through 1988 and semiannually (three volumes each half) thereafter. Harner (**1147**), p. 54, notes that the index is available on CD-ROM and online at http://www.webofscience.com, a pay program. Also see Harner, pp. 54–55, for further details about the index.

1036. Chaudhuri, Brahma, comp. and ed. "Charles Dickens." In his *Annual Bibliography of Victorian Studies [1976-].* Edmonton, Can.: LITIR Database, 1980- , passim.

Lists books (with selected reviews), articles, and dissertations on Dickens under various general headings as well as under his individual works. The complete bibliography is a printed version of the LITIR (Literary Information and Retrieval) Database. It contains sections on 1) General and Reference Works, 2) Fine Arts, 3) Philosophy and Religion, 4) History, 5) Social Sciences, 6) Science and Technology, 7) Language and Literature, and 8) Individual Authors; it includes subject, author, title, and reviewer indexes. Chaudhuri provides brief annotations only where titles are not self-explana-

275

tory. The latest volume seen, for 1999, was compiled and edited by Fred Radford in 2000, with the Dickens entries on pp. 73-78. Harner (**1147**) notes, pp. 293-94, that Chaudhuri "expanded and cumulated" these bibliographies as *A Comprehensive Bibliography of Victorian Studies, 1970-1984*, 3 vols. (Edmonton: LITIR Database, 1984-85), which in turn was "corrected and expanded" as *Cumulative Bibliography of Victorian Studies, 1970-1984*, 2 vols. (Edmonton: Access Elite, 1988). There was also an earlier *Cumulative Bibliography of Victorian Studies: 1976-1980* (Edmonton: LITIR, 1982). Chaudhuri has since published additional five-year cumulations, for 1985-89, 1990-94, and 1995-99 (the last compiled and edited by Brahma Chaudhuri, James Mulvihill, and Fred Radford), as well as *Cumulated Index to Reviews of Books on Victorian Studies, 1975-1989* (Edmonton: LITIR, 1990). Also recently published is *Cumulative Bibliography of Victorian Studies: 1945-1969*, 2 vols. (Edmonton: LITIR, 1999). The bibliography is also available in other forms as *Victorian Database on CD-ROM* (1970-99) and *Victorian Studies on the Web* (http://www.victoriandatabase.com—see **1234**), the last of which, Harner points out, "subsumes [this] confusing array of print and CD-ROM products." A number of author and subject bibliographies, 1970-85/86, drawn from these bibliographies have been made available in a Bibliographies on Demand series, published by Access Elite. For Dickens, see Chaudhuri (**954**).

1037. Cohn, Alan M., [et al.], comps. "The Dickens Checklist." In *Dickens Studies Newsletter*, 1, ii (September 1970)-14, iv (December 1983), passim; continued in *Dickens Quarterly*, 1, i (March 1984)-6, ii (June 1989), passim; continued from June 1989 by, respectively, William G. Wall, Karen Kurt, Diane Hébert, Patricia Matthew, Karen Droisen, and, most recently, Danny Siegel.

An awesome quarterly listing of new editions of Dickens's works, secondary studies (books, reprints, pamphlets, journal articles, doctoral dissertations, and reviews), and audiovisual and miscellaneous materials, by far the most thorough of serial bibliographies. See Paroissien (**1421**) for Cohn's secret to comprehensiveness. Also see Cohn and Collins (**958**). Following Cohn's death in 1989, the bibliography was continued quarterly by others. But Cohn's act has proved hard to follow. The recent listings have not been as thorough as his, and users of them should be aware that several entries in each issue may have been advertised but not yet published. Probably the most notorious example of this bibliographer's nightmare is the listing of Edgar Rosenberg's long anticipated edition of *Great Expectations* in the Norton Critical Editions series (**2401**) in the June 1992 checklist; the work was not published until 1999.

1038. "Dickens, Charles." In *American Humanities Index for 1975[-]*. Troy, NY: Whitston, 1976- , passim.

Indexes articles in "creative, critical, and scholarly journals in the arts and humanities," most of which "are indexed exclusively" by the *American Humanities Index*, though this exclusivity does not seem to be true for the Dickens entries, which, for 1996, for example, are from such journals as *Dickens Quarterly*, *Journal of Narrative Technique*, *Victorian Newsletter*, *Victorians Institute Journal*, and *Nineteenth Century Prose*, which are included in most serial bibliographies. The number of journals covered has increased considerably over the years. For further criticism, see Harner, (**1147**), p. 54.

1039. "Dickens, Charles." In *Annual Bibliography of English Language and Literature for 1920[-]*. Modern Humanities Research Association. Cambridge, Eng.: Bowes and Bowes, 1921-35; Cambridge: Cambridge University Press, 1936-64; London: Modern Humanities Research Association, 1965- , passim.

An annual unannotated list of books (primary and secondary, with reviews), festschriften, proceedings and transactions of academies and learned societies, articles in journals, dissertations, etc., with a stronger emphasis on British and European studies than in the other annual bibliographies of language and literature in English. The Dickens researcher should also examine the general entries for the section on the nineteenth century as well as the even more general sections at the beginning of the bibliography. Various editors have served to organize the scholars who compile the bibliography and to put the bibliography together. The editors of the latest volume (volume 76, for 2001, published 2002) are Gerald Lowe, Jennifer Fellows, James R. Kelly, and Bruce T. Sajdak. The number of journals covered has greatly increased over the years, from slightly over 100 in the first issue to around 1,500 in the latest. For fuller details, see Harner (**1147**), pp. 51-52. This bibliography is also available on CD-ROM and online (http://www.lib.cam.ac.uk/mhra/abell) as part of Chadwyck-Healey's Literature Online Service (http://lion.chadwyck.co.uk:8080), to which libraries may subscribe.

1040. "Dickens, Charles." In *Périodex: Index analytique de périodiques de langue française 1972-1973[-]*. Montreal: La Centrale des bibliothèques, réalisé en collaboration avec Le Service d'informatique du ministère de l'Éducation du Québec (SIMEQ), 1973-83, passim.

Lists Dickens articles published in French.

1041. "Dickens (Charles)." In *Subject Index to Periodicals [1915-1961]*. London: The Library Association, 1916-62, passim; continued as *British Humanities Index [1962-]*. Ed. Peter Ferriday [et al.]. London: The Library Association, 1963-90; London: Melbourne, Munich, and New York: Bowker-Sauer, 1991- , passim.

A subject index that originally included articles published in British, American, and continental periodicals but by the end of World War II had restricted itself to articles in British publications. Book reviews are excluded. The Dickens entries are relatively few in number. Originally an annual list, since 1954 it has been issued quarterly, the last issue each year being the annual cumulation. According to Wortman (**1162**), pp. 18-19, the *British Humanities Index* is available on CD-ROM (Saur, 1985-).

1042. ["Dickens, Charles (1812-1870)"]. In "American Bibliography for 1921[-49]" and "1950[-55] American Bibliography." In *Publications of the Modern Language Association of America*, 37 (1922)-71 (1956), passim; continued as "1956[-62] Annual Bibliography." *Publications of the Modern Language Association of America*, 72 (1957)-78 (1963), passim; reprinted as *1921-25[-1954-55] MLA American Bibliography of Books and Articles on the Modern Languages and Literatures* and *1956[-1962] MLA International Bibliography of Books and Articles on the Modern Languages and Literature*. 8 and 7 vols. Millwood, NY: Kraus Reprint, 1976, passim; further continued as "1963[-82] MLA International Bibliography of Books and Articles on the Modern Languages and Literatures." *Publications of the Modern Language Association of America*, 79 (1964)-83 (1968), passim; also published separately as *1963[-] MLA International Bibliography of Books and Articles on the Modern Languages and Literatures*. New York: New York University Press, 1964-68; New York: Modern Language Association of America, 1969- , passim.

Currently published each year in five volumes, with volume 1 containing the entries for British authors, among others. The bibliography lists books, articles (found, in recent years, in over 3,000 journals), and dissertation abstracts, but not reviews of books, with an author index (from 1951 on). The section on Dickens is, accordingly, reasonably thorough. Prior to 1956, the entries were limited to works by American scholars. For the first five years, the bibliography was in essay form, but thereafter it appeared in list form. From 1981 on, there is brief annotation for each entry, identifying principal subjects (up to three) covered by the reference that are used in the new, elaborate subject index in each volume.

Also see *1970[-1975] MLA Abstracts of Articles in Scholarly Journals*, comp. John H. Fisher and Walter S. Achtert, 3 vols. each year (New York: Modern Language Association of America, 1972-77). These volumes were intended to supplement the annual bibliography "and thus provide for the scholar and student additional access to current scholarship," but the project did not last long. See the section on Dickens in volume 1 of each year's publication.

The bibliographies for 1963 to the present are available online through OCLC (Online Computer Library Center, Dublin, OH), updated ten times a year, and other sources (see the Modern Language Association Web site, http://www. mla.org). The bibliographies for 1981-date are also available on CD-

ROM through Wilsondisc (H. W. Wilson Co., Bronx, NY) and SilverPlatter (SilverPlatter Information, Inc., Newton Lower Falls, MA), both updated quarterly. See Harner, (**1147**), pp. 46-50, and Wortman (**1162**), pp. 13-15, for fuller details and database availability.

1043. "Dickensiana Month by Month." *Dickensian*, 1 (1905)-14 (1918), passim; "Dickensiana of the Quarter," 15 (1919)-37 (1940/41), passim; "Recent Dickensiana" or "Dickensiana," 38 (1941/42)-64 (1968), passim.

The titles vary somewhat over the years, and occasionally the bibliography is missing from an issue. It lists books, magazine and newspaper articles, and a variety of other Dickensiana, much of it ephemeral in nature. Yet for the years preceding the now standard annual bibliographies, this is certainly the serial Dickens bibliography of record. Succeeded by Michael Slater [et al.], "The Year's Work in Dickens Studies" (**1052**).

1044. Dietrich, F[elix], [et al.], comps. *Bibliographie der Zeitschriftenliteratur mit Einschluss von Sammelmerken.* Vols. 1-128. Osnabrück, etc.: Dietrich, [etc.], 1896-1964; continued as *IBZ: Internationale Bibliographie der Zeitschriftenliteratur aus allen Gebeiten des Wissens/ International Bibliography of Periodical Literature Covering All Fields of Knowledge/ Bibliographie internationale de la littérature périodique dans tous les domaines de la conaissance [1965-].* Osnabrück: Felix Diedrich, 1965- ; vols 1-70 (1896-1932) reprinted New York: Kraus Reprint, 1961-?, passim.

Lists German periodical literature, non-German periodical literature (beginning 1911), and book reviews (beginning 1925). The latest publication seen, for 1999, consists of two half-year parts of six volumes each, edited by Otto and Wolfram Zeller. According to Harner, (**1147**), p. 57, the coverage of this bibliography, "now extending to several thousand serials published worldwide, emphasizes those in English and German and excludes only those in Oriental languages"; nevertheless, its coverage of articles on Dickens is not as extensive as the serial bibliographies published by the Modern Humanities Research Association (**1039**) and the Modern Language Association (**1042**) and in *Victorian Studies* (**1058**) and *Dickens Quarterly* (**1037**). Wortman (**1162**), p. 20, notes that the work is also available on CD-ROM (Zeller, 1986-).

1045. *FRANCIS bulletin signalétique 523. Histoire et sciences de la littérature.* Vandœuvres-lès-Nancy: Institut de l'Information Scientifique et Technique (later Paris: Centre nationale de la recherche scientifique/centre de documentation sciences humaines), 1948- , passim.

A list of articles, briefly annotated in French, including occasional studies of Dickens. According to Wortman (**1162**), p. 16, the list is compiled from "about 600 international periodicals, reports, dissertations, congress and colloquium publications, and Festschriften," arranged by literary period. The publication appears quarterly, with author and subject indexes, which are cumulated annually. The latest index seen, 48 (1994), lists forty studies of Dickens. According to Wortman, the publication is also available on CD-ROM (Centre nationale de la recherche scientifique, 1984-).

1046. Guthrie, Anna L., [et al.]. "Dickens, Charles." In *Readers' Guide to Periodical Literature, 1900-* . Vols. 1- . Minneapolis [and, later, New York]: H. W. Wilson, 1901- , passim.

Lists articles on Dickens in relatively general and popular magazines of the time–from ninety-nine magazines for 1900 to about 250 for recent issues–as well as reviews of books by or about Dickens, though through volume 2 (1905-09) it also indexed over 400 books and reports as a supplement to the second edition of the *A. L. A. Index* (**944**). The bibliography is also issued roughly every three weeks and in quarterly as well as annual cumulations and for the earlier years of the series in cumulative volumes first of five years, then four, three, and two years, and finally one year as warranted by the growing number of entries. See entries for other members of the Dickens family. Supplemented by *Poole's Index* and its continuations (**1049**) and by *Nineteenth Century Readers' Guide* (**964**). Harner (**1147**), p. 59, notes that from 1983 on listings can be searched online and on CD-ROM.

1047. Kaplan, Fred, [et al.]. "Recent Dickens Studies." In *Dickens Studies Annual: Essays on Victorian Fiction*. Vols. 8- . New York: AMS Press, 1980- , passim.

A useful annual essay-bibliography (with some variations in title) surveying and evaluating recent Dickens studies (books, chapters in books, and articles), by Fred Kaplan for 1977-78, 8 (1980), 299-324; by Robert Newsom for 1979, 9 (1981), 265-86; by Sylvia Manning for 1980, 10 (1982), 241-62; by Sylvère Monod for 1981, 12 (1983), 357-85; by Robert Patten for 1982, 13 (1984), 283-322; by Richard Dunn for 1983, 14 (1985), 359-87; by Edwin Eigner for 1984, 15 (1986), 381-412; by Jerome Meckier for 1985, 16 (1987), 305-75; by David Paroissien for 1986, 17 (1988), 317-71; by George J. Worth for 1987, 18 (1989), 403-35; by Susan R. Horton for 1988, 19 (1990), 301-43; by John Kucich for 1989, 20 (1991), 313-60; by Chris R. Vanden Bossche for 1990, 21 (1992), 253-79; by William J. Palmer for 1991, 22 (1993), 331-68; by Stanley Friedman for 1992, 23 (1994), 337-401; by Barry V. Qualls for 1993, 24 (1996), 275-91; by Joel J. Brattin for 1994, 25 (1996), 327-72; by Joseph W. Childers for 1995, 26 (1998), 335-53; by Trey Philpotts for 1996, 27 (1998), 307-63; by Elisabeth G. Gitter for 1997, 28 (1999), 197-224; by Harland S. Nelson for 1998, 29 (2000), 387-464; by Michael Lund for 1999, 30 (2001), 343-72; by David Garlock for 2000, 31 (2002), 305-36; and by Goldie Morgentaler for 2001, 33 (2003), forthcoming. For a comparative study of Dickens entries in current serial bibliographies, see Loomis (**1413**).

1048. Kline, Sims, ed. *Literary Criticism Register: A Monthly Listing of Studies in English & American Literature.* DeLand, FL: *Literary Criticism Register*, 1983- , passim.

Lists the contents of a number of literary journals (by journal), recently published books, and dissertations. For the Dickens items, see the "Annual Index Issue," the last issue for the year. In his first edition, p. 51, Harner (**1147**) is quite critical of this series; he does not even list the work in his 2nd, 3rd, and 4th editions, though a reference to it remains in their indexes.

1049. Poole, William F., and William I. Fletcher, eds. "Dickens, Charles." In *Poole's Index to Periodical Literature, 1802-81.* 2 vols. Boston: Houghton, Mifflin, 1882; revised 1891; also five supplementary volumes that continue the index to January 1907. Boston: Houghton, Mifflin, 1888-1908; reprinted in 6 vols. (actually 7, with the 2 vols. for 1802-81 designated as vol. 1, parts 1 and 2). Gloucester, MA: Peter Smith, 1963, passim; continued as "Dickens, Charles (1812-1870)." In *International Index to Periodicals.* Vols. 1 (1907-15)-18 (April 1964-March 1965). New York: H. W. Wilson, 1916-65, passim; further continued in *Social Sciences & Humanities Index (Formerly International Index).* Ed. J. Doris Bart [et al.]. Vols. 19 (April 1965-March 1966)-27 (April 1973-March 1974). New York: H. W. Wilson, 1966-74, passim; further continued in *Humanities Index.* Ed. Elizabeth E. Pingree [et al.]. Vols. 1 (April 1974-March 1975)- . New York: H. W. Wilson Co., 1975- (issued monthly as well as in annual cumulations), passim.

Poole's Index is an author and subject index that contains the briefest of information about the entries (usually only the journal title, volume number and beginning page number of each article). Still, though by no means complete, it is useful in locating nineteenth-century pieces about Dickens in the more intellectual journals and early twentieth-century articles not covered by the *Readers' Guide* (**1046**). To compensate for the brevity and incompleteness of the listings, three belated supplementary works have been published: 1) *Poole's Index: Date and Volume Key,* ed. Marion V. Bell and Jean C. Bacon, ACRL Monographs, 19 (Chicago: Association of College and Reference Libraries, 1957, 61 pp.), which provides dates to go with the volume numbers listed in 2) *Poole's Index; Transfer Vectors for Poole's Index to Periodical Literature: Number One: Titles, Volumes, and Dates,* compiled by Vinton A. Dearing (Los Angeles: Pison, 1967, 95 pp.), which gives additional publication information for entries, but volume 2 of which (a "projected key to subject headings"), according to Harner (**1147**), p. 477, was never published, and 3) *Cumulative Author Index for Poole's Index to Periodical Literature, 1802-1906,* comp.

C. Edward Wall (Ann Arbor, MI: Pierian Press, 1971, 488 pp.), which lists the authors of articles included in *Poole's Index* and, in cryptic form, the location of the articles in the six-volume 1888-1908 edition. Also see Harner (**1147**), pp. 476-77, and Marcuse (**1152**), pp. 50-51, for published additions and corrections; *Nineteenth Century Readers' Guide* (**964**); and *19th Century Masterfile* (**1012**).

The entries in the continuations supplement those in the *Readers' Guide to Periodical Literature* (**1046**). The *International Index* began as a continuation of the *A. L. A. Index* (**944**) as well and took over some of the magazines being indexed in the *Readers' Guide* that were of more special interest to the fields of the social sciences and the humanities and added a number of others in these fields not formerly included. The entries in the continuations contain fuller bibliographical information (titles *are* included, for example), and the *International Index* is useful for the early years of the twentieth century not covered by the standard serial bibliographies, such as the annual Modern Language Association of America (**1042**), Modern Humanities Research Association (**1039**), and Victorian bibliographies (**1058**), and the quarterly Dickens bibliography in the *Dickens Studies Newsletter* and its continuation the *Dickens Quarterly* (**1037**). But even as early as the 1920s the *International Index*, and its subsequent continuations, simply could not compete with these more specialized bibliographies, even though they were and continue to be issued monthly as well as annually. According to Wortman (**1162**), p. 18, the *Humanities Index* is available on CD-ROM (Wilson, 1983-) and online (OCLC and Wilson, 1983-).

1050. Rouse, H. Blair, ed. "A Selective and Critical Bibliography of Studies in Prose Fiction for the Year 1948[-1951]." *Journal of English and Germanic Philology*, 48 (1949), 259-84; 49 (1950), 358-87; 50 (1951), 376-407; 51 (1952), 364-92.

An annual selective listing of four-years' duration of studies in prose fiction, arranged by author of article or book, including, of course, studies of Dickens. A subject index identifies studies of a particular author. For later studies, see Bell and Baird (**948**) and supplements.

1051. Sears, Minnie E., and Marian Shaw [et al.], eds. "Dickens, Charles." In *Essay and General Literature Index, 1900-1933[-1985-1989]*. 11 "Permanent Cumulations" vols. New York: H. W. Wilson, 1934-90, passim; continued thereafter in half-yearly and yearly accumulations, 1990- . New York: H. W. Wilson, 1991- , passim.

Lists chapters in books and the contents of essay collections. Originally published as *Essay and General Literature Index, 1900-1933: An Index to about 40,000 Essays in 2,144 Volumes of Collections of Essays and Miscellaneous Works*, comp. Minnie E. Sears and Marian Shaw (New York: H. W. Wilson, 1934), and continued annually thereafter, with periodic cumulations. Also see *Essay and General Literature Index: Works Indexed 1900-1969*. New York: H. W. Wilson, 1972. Wortman (**1162**), p. 19, indicates that the *Index* is available on CD-ROM (Wilson, 1983-) and online (OCLC and Wilson, 1983-).

1052. S[later], M[ichael], [et al.]. "The Year's Work in Dickens Studies, 1967[-1976]." *Dickensian*, 64 (1968)-73 (1977), passim; "The Year's Work in Dickens Studies, 1977[-81]: A Survey of Periodical Literature." *Dickensian*, 75 (1979)-79 (1983), passim.

Continues the serial bibliography begun in the first issue of the *Dickensian* in 1905 (**1043**). Edited by Slater for 1967-69, Malcolm Andrews for 1970-77, and Jean Elliott for 1978-81. The yearly summary lists editions of Dickens's works (for 1967-76) and books (for 1967-76) and dissertations (for 1967-72) on Dickens, followed by an essay survey of selected periodical literature published during the year in question. For 1977-81, the bibliography is limited to a survey of periodical literature. For a fuller annual evaluative survey of Dickens criticism and scholarship, 1977-date, see "Recent Dickens Studies," in *Dickens Studies Annual* (**1047**).

1053. Stange, G. Robert, [et al.]. "Recent Studies in Nineteenth-Century Literature." *Studies in English Literature, 1500-1900*, 1 (1961)- , passim.

An annual review article in the Autumn issue by various authors, since volume 6 (1966) entitled "Recent Studies in the Nineteenth Century," containing comments on selected book-length studies of nineteenth-century English authors. Usually a page or two of each survey is devoted to studies of Dickens.

1054. Summers, Montague, [et al.], comps. "The Nineteenth Century and After." In *The Year's Work in English Studies [for 1919-1920-]*. Ed. Sir Sidney Lee [et al.]. Published for the English Association. Vols. 1- . London: Oxford University Press, 1921-63; London: John Murray, 1964 (for 1962)-83 (for 1980); London: John Murray, and Atlantic Highlands, NJ: Humanities Press, 1984 (for 1981)-89 (for 1986); Oxford, Eng., and Cambridge, MA: Blackwell, and Atlantic Highlands, NJ: Humanities Press, 1990 (for 1987)-95 (for 1992); Oxford, Eng., and Cambridge, MA: Blackwell Publishers, 1996 (for 1993)- , passim. Vols. 1-32 (1919-51), reprinted New York and London: Johnson Reprint, 1966, passim; vols. 1-43 (1919-62), reprinted New York and London: Johnson Reprint, 1970, passim.

An annual evaluative survey, always with a paragraph or more devoted to important books and journal articles on Dickens. The title of the section in which Dickens is included varies, and the editors change regularly, Summers being only the first of many. In the latest volume seen, volume 81, for 2000 (published in 2002), which was edited by William Baker and Kenneth

Womack, pp. 704-07 are devoted to Dickens studies, as compared to the one brief paragraph in the first volume.

1055. Townsend, Francis G., [et al.], comps. "Recent Publications." *Victorian Newsletter*, no. 2 (November 1952)-no. 53 (Spring 1978), passim.

A briefly annotated, highly selective listing of general studies of the Victorian period and studies of Victorian authors, including Dickens. Continued semi-annually through Spring 1978, except for Nos. 26 (Fall 1964), 27 (Spring 1965), and 44 (Fall 1973). The title from no. 3 on is "Recent Publications: A Selected List." Compilers include Townsend, Nos. 2 (November 1952)-7 (Fall 1955); Oscar Mauer, Nos. 8 (Spring 1956)-17 (Spring 1960); Robert A. Greenberg, Nos. 18 (Fall 1960)-25 (Spring 1964); and Arthur F. Minerof, Nos. 28 (Fall 1965)-53 (Spring 1978).

1056. Valk, Barbara G., and Ana María Cobos, eds. *Hapi: Hispanic American Periodicals Index, 1970-1974[-]: Authors.* Los Angeles: UCLA Latin American Center Publications, University of California, Los Angeles, 1977- , passim.

Lists occasional Dickens entries.

1057. Vann, J. Don, [et al.]. "Victorian Periodicals, 1971-72[-]: A Checklist of Criticism." *Victorian Periodicals Newsletter*, 6 (1973)-11 (1978); *Victorian Periodicals Review*, 12 (1979)- , passim.

See entries under Dickens in the subject index. Since the bibliography for 1992, published in 27 (1994), the bibliography has ceased to be published annually; that for 1993 was published in 29 (1996), that for 1994-97 in 31 (1998), and that for 1997-99 in 33 (2000), all edited by Solveig C. Robinson. There are occasional brief annotations. Titles vary. The bibliographies for 1971/72-1987 were cumulated, with additions, by Uffelman, Madden, and Dixon (**1185**).

1058. "Victorian Bibliography for 1932[-]." Ed. W. D. Templeman, *Modern Philology*, 30 (1932/33)-42 (1944/45); ed. Charles F. Harrold, *Modern Philology*, 43 (1945/46); ed. Austin Wright, *Modern Philology*, 44 (1946/47)-53 (1955/56); ed. Francis G. Townsend, *Modern Philology*, 54 (1956/57), and *Victorian Studies*, 1 (1957/58)-2 (1958/59); ed. Robert C. Slack, *Victorian Studies*, 3 (1959/60)-8 (1964/65); ed. Ronald E. Freeman, *Victorian Studies*, 9 (1965/66)-18 (1974/75); ed. Richard C. Tobias, *Victorian Studies*, 19 (1975/76)-28 (1984/85); ed. Edward H. Cohen, *Victorian Studies*, 29 (1985/86)- , passim.

These annual bibliographies are compiled by a committee of the Victorian Division of the Modern Language Association; the scholar listed as editor serves as chairman of the committee and is responsible for the final compilation. Whether published in *Modern Philology* or *Victorian Studies*, the bibliography for each year has always appeared in the June issue of the following year, though in more recent years that June issue has sometimes been a long time in making its appearance. It lists books, essays in books, articles from an extensive list of journals, and reviews of books (listed under the book itself). Occasionally the editors provide annotation, more in the earlier years than the more recent, when the length of the bibliography has pretty much precluded any but the most necessary explanatory annotation.

Dropping a fifth heading, "Continental Material," after the first year, the bibliography (through that for 1975) listed items under these four headings: 1) Bibliographical Material; 2) Economic, Political, Religious, and Social Environment; 3) Movements of Ideas and Literary Forms; and 4) Individual Authors. Beginning with the bibliography for 1975, six headings are used: 1) Bibliographical Material; 2) Histories, Biographies, Autobiographies, and Historical Documents; 3) Economic, Educational, Political, Religious, Scientific, and Social Environment; 4) Fine Arts, Music, Photography, Architecture, City Planning, Performing Arts; 5) Literary History, Literary Forms, Literary Ideas; and 6) Individual Authors. The Individual Authors section of each year's bibliography is where one will find the principal Dickens entries. One should consult the other sections of the bibliography as well for background studies relevant to Dickens and for other works that may deal in part with Dickens.

To give a rough idea of the increase in Dickens scholarship, the 1932 bibliography contained twenty-nine items on Dickens in the Individual Authors section, while the 1997 bibliography listed 106 new items under Dickens and another twenty-two elsewhere in the bibliography, as well as reviews for twenty-nine items previously listed in the 1996 bibliography. For collections of these bibliographies in volume form, see Templeman (**1025**) for 1932-1944, Wright (**1033**) for 1945-1954, Slack (**1022**) for 1955-1964, Freeman (**978**) for 1965-1974, and Tobias (**1026**) for 1975-1984.

1059. Wodehouse, Margaret E., and Marion C. Wilson [et al.]. *Canadian Periodical Index: An Author and Subject Index/Index de périodiques canadiens: Auteurs & sujets, 1964[-]*. Ottawa: Canadian Library Association and National Library of Ottawa, 1965- , passim.

There are no Dickens entries in the volumes for the first two years, but there is usually at least one entry per year thereafter. Cumulated annually from monthly issues. This bibliography continues the *Canadian Index: A Guide to Canadian Periodicals and Films 1948[-1963]* (later title: *Canadian Index to Periodicals and Documentary Films*), ed. Dorothy B. Chatwin and Margaret E. Wodehouse [et al.]. (Ottawa: Canadian Library Association and, later, National Library of Canada, 1949-64).

3C. BIBLIOGRAPHIES OF STUDIES OF INDIVIDUAL DICKENS WORKS

Note: Also see **Bibliographies of Dickens Studies, bibliographies of studies of individual works**, in part 2 of the subject index and **critical and special studies, bibliographies** under the individual work in part 1 of the subject index.

Barnaby Rudge

Note: See Rice (**93**).

Bleak House

1060. Bloom, Harold. "Bibliography." In *Charles Dickens's **Bleak House**. Ed. Harold Bloom. Modern Critical Interpretations. New York, New Haven, CT, and Philadelphia: Chelsea House, 1987, pp. 163-65.

A selected bibliography of sixty-one books and articles about *Bleak House*.

1061. DeVries, Duane. "Selected Bibliography." In Dickens's *Bleak House*. Ed. Duane DeVries (**2324**), pp. 1073-80.

Divided into "Bibliographical Materials" and "Criticism and Special Studies Relevant to *Bleak House*," the latter of which lists 108 studies, in addition to the fourteen included in the "Selected Criticism" section (pp. 921-1071).

1062. Dyson, A. E. "Select Bibliography." In *Dickens: **Bleak House:** A Casebook*. Ed. A. E. Dyson. London: Macmillan, 1969; Nashville, TN: Aurora, 1970, pp. 274-76.

A highly selective, highly personal list of books on Dickens and *Bleak House*.

1063. Ford, George, and Sylvère Monod. "Bibliography." In Dickens's **Bleak House:** *An Authoritative and Annotated Text, Illustrations, a Note on the Text, Genesis and Composition, Backgrounds, Criticism* Ed. George Ford and Sylvère Monod (**2327**), pp. 985-86.

A quite selective bibliography, though focused on *Bleak House*. It is an expansion and updating of the shorter bibliography to be found in Ford and Monod's critical edition of *Hard Times* (**2411**), with a small section on criticism of that novel replaced by a considerably longer section of critical studies of *Bleak House*.

1064. Hawthorn, Jeremy. "References." In his ***Bleak House:*** *The Critics Debate*. London: Macmillan; Atlantic Highlands, NJ: Humanities Press International, 1987, pp. 83-87.

Lists a number of studies of *Bleak House* referred to in the text.

1065. Page, Norman. "Selected Bibliography." In his ***Bleak House:*** *A Novel of Connections*. Twayne's Masterworks Studies. Boston: Twayne, 1990, pp. 97-99.

An unannotated and highly selective list of biographies, general critical studies, and twelve articles concerning *Bleak House*.

1066. Shatto, Susan. "Selected Bibliography." In her *The Companion to **Bleak House*** (**2331**), pp. 302-12.

Lists articles by others in *Household Words* and *All the Year Round* relevant to *Bleak House* and books and articles of particular value for the notes provided; it is not really a bibliography of criticism and other studies of this novel.

1067. Tambling, Jeremy. "Further Reading." In *Bleak House*. Ed. Jeremy Tambling. New Casebooks. Basingstoke, Eng., and London: Macmillan; New York: St. Martin's Press, 1998, pp. 246-49.

Selective, unannotated lists of books and articles on *Bleak House*, followed by a brief list of "General Studies."

Christmas Books, Christmas Stories, and Other Shorter Fiction

Note: Also see Glancy (**98**). In section 1 of part 1 of the subject index, see **Christmas Books, Christmas Numbers, Christmas Stories, Shorter fiction, The Battle of Life, The Chimes, A Christmas Carol, The Cricket on the Hearth,** and **The Haunted Man and the Ghost's Bargain**.

1068. Baldwin, Dean, and Gregory L. Morris. *The Short Story in English: Britain and North America: An Annotated Bibliography*. Magill Bibliographies. Metuchen, NJ, and London: Scarecrow Press; Pasadena, CA, and Englewood Cliffs, NJ: Salem Press, 1994, passim.

Baldwin and Morris do not include studies of specific works by Dickens, but do have useful sections on "Reference Works," pp. 7-9; "Histories of the Short Story," pp. 10-18; and "Short Story Theory," pp. 19-26. The entries are well annotated.

1069. Karson, Jill. "For Further Research." In Readings on **A Christmas Carol**. Ed. Jill Karson. San Diego, CA: Greenhaven Press, 2000, pp. 168-69.

Lists nineteenth book-length studies of *A Christmas Carol*.

1070. Thomas, Deborah A. "Select Bibliography." In Dickens's *Selected Short Fiction*. Ed. Deborah A. Thomas. Penguin English Library. London, Baltimore, MD, etc.: Penguin Books, 1976, pp. 31-34.

Lists several general studies of Dickens and studies of Dickens's short fiction, with occasional brief annotation. In an appendix, pp. 407-10, Thomas lists the headlines from the relevant volumes in the Charles Dickens Edition (1867-68) that Dickens wrote to accompany the selections included here.

1071. Thomas, Deborah A. "Selected Bibliography." In her *Dickens and the Short Story*. Philadelphia: University of Pennsylvania Press, 1982, pp. 183-87.

Lists a number of studies, most post-World War II, that, as Thomas indicates, were "especially useful in contributing to my thinking about Dickens' short stories."

1072. Walker, Warren S., comp. "Charles Dickens." In his *Twentieth-Century Short Story Explication. Interpretations, 1900-1975, of Short Fiction since 1800*. 3rd ed. Hamden, CT: Shoe String Press, 1977, p. 169.

Not a particularly good source for studies of Dickens's short stories. Walker lists only one item for each of four short stories by Dickens. Also see Walker's *Twentieth-Century Short Story Explication. Supplement II to Third Edition. With Checklist of Books and Journals Used* (Hamden, CT: Shoe String Press, 1984), covering 1981-84, p. 87 (one reference); *Supplement III* (1987), covering 1981-84, p. 107 (eight references); *Supplement IV* (1989), covering 1985-86, p. 77 (three references); *Supplement V* (1991), covering 1987-88, p. 95 (two references). Unannotated. *Supplement I* (1980), covering 1976-79, contains no Dickens references. *Twentieth-Century Short Story Explication. An Index to the Third Edition and Its Five Supplements, 1961-1991*, by Warren S. Walker and Barbara K. Walker (Hamden, CT: Shoe String Press, 1992), p. 63, lists the Dickens items but misses the reference in *Supplement II*. The first edition of Walker's checklist was published as *Twentieth-Century Short Story Explication. Interpretations, 1900-1960 Inclusive, of Short Fiction Since 1800* (Hamden, CT: Shoe String Press, 1961) and was followed by two supplements (1963, 1965), updating the checklist through 1964. A second edition, covering 1900-66, was published in 1967. These bibliographies are based on the annual "Bibliography" in *Studies in Short Fiction* (**1074**).

1073. Wessinger, Deborah W., with Debra C. Adams and Mary J. Richardson, comps. "A Cumulative 32-Year Index to *Studies in Short Fiction* (1963-1995)." A special issue of *Studies in Short Fiction*, 32, iv (Fall 1995). vii + pp. 521-713.

Under "Dickens, Charles," pp. 543-44, the compilers list eleven studies and two book reviews.

1074. Wright, Elizabeth, [et al.]. "Short Fiction Criticism since 1960" (later, "Annual Bibliography of Short Fiction Interpretation"). *Studies in Short Fiction*, 1 (1964)-31 (1994), passim.

An annual unannotated list of criticism arranged by author of the fiction, including Dickens, and then by title. The editors change over the years. The first bibliography is continued by Wright and George Hendrick (volumes 2-7), by her and Eugene B. Vest (volumes 8-9), by Warren S. Walker (volumes 10-29), and by Wendell M. Aycock (volumes 30-31). In the first volume, Wright indicates that the bibliography continued the work begun by Jarvis Thurston et al., in *Short Fiction Criticism: A Checklist of Interpretations Since 1925 of Stories and Novelettes (American, British, Continental) 1800-1958* (Denver, CO: Alan Swallow, 1960). Inexplicably, this volume does not include Dickens's short fiction.

David Copperfield

Note. Also see Bauer (**101**), Dunn (**103**), and Dunn and Tandy (**104**).

1075. Bloom, Harold. "Bibliography." In *Charles Dickens's **David Copperfield**. Ed. Harold Bloom. Modern Critical Interpretations. New York, New Haven, CT, and Philadelphia: Chelsea House, 1987, pp. 125-27.

A selective bibliography of sixty-eight general critical studies and critical studies of *David Copperfield*—in books and articles.

1076. Bloom, Harold. "Bibliography." In *Major Literary Characters: David Copperfield*. Ed. Harold Bloom. New York and Philadelphia: Chelsea House, 1992, pp. 239-43.

Contains some 109 items, 1938-88, most from the 1970s and 1980s, relevant to *David Copperfield*.

1077. Buckley, Jerome H. "Selected Bibliography." In *David Copperfield: Authoritative Text, Backgrounds, Criticism*. Ed. Jerome H. Buckley (**2357**), pp. 853-54.

Lists forty-six studies of *David Copperfield*. Buckley also includes Dickens's number plans for *David Copperfield*, his autobiographical fragment, and a Dickens chronology.

1078. "'David Copperfield' in the 'Dickensian': An Index to Twenty-Five Volumes." *Dickensian*, 27 (1930/31), 130-31.

An index of references to *David Copperfield* in the *Dickensian*.

1079. Dunn, Richard J. "Part One: Materials" and "Works Cited." In *Approaches to Teaching Dickens' David Copperfield*. Ed. Richard J. Dunn. Approaches to Teaching Masterpieces of World Literature, 5. New York: Modern Language Association, 1984, pp. 1-16, 152-59.

In "Materials," Dunn surveys inexpensive editions of *David Copperfield* in print and bibliographical, textual, biographical, critical, and background studies of use to students and instructors. Despite the limitations suggested by the title of "Works Cited," this section is actually a relatively full listing of studies of *David Copperfield*. Also see Dunn (**103**) and Dunn and Tandy (**104**).

1080. Hollington, Michael. "Bibliography." In his *David Copperfield by Charles Dickens*. Collection CNED-Didier Concours. [Paris]: Didier Érudition, CNED, 1996, pp. 161-70.

A selective checklist mainly of books and articles about *David Copperfield*.

1081. Hollington, Michael, and Anny Sadrin. "Capes/Agregation 1997: Charles Dickens: *David Copperfield*." *Cahiers victoriens et edouardiens*, no. 44 (October 1996), 185-201.

Using a system of stars "style Guides Michelin," Hollington and Sadrin list and comment on editions of *David Copperfield* and, under a variety of headings, on bibliographical, biographical, and critical studies of the novel published for the most part since the 1970s.

1082. Peck, John. "Further Reading." In *David Copperfield and Hard Times: Charles Dickens*. Ed. John Peck. New Casebooks. Basingstoke, Eng.: Macmillan; New York: St. Martin's Press, 1995, pp. 255-62.

Lightly annotated and highly selective, this bibliography lists books and articles specifically on *David Copperfield* and *Hard Times*, as well as more general studies—with occasional annotations.

1083. Storey, Graham. "Bibliography." In his *David Copperfield: Interweaving Truth and Fiction*. Twayne's Masterwork Studies, 68. Boston: Twayne, 1991, pp. 105-08.

Lists a few editions of *David Copperfield*, a few other works by Dickens (collected letters, public readings), and, in a section of "Secondary Sources," forty-four books and articles dealing in whole or in part with *David Copperfield*. For the last, Storey provides brief annotations.

Dombey and Son

Note: Also see Litvack (**106**).

1084. Sadrin, Anny. "Charles Dickens: *Dombey and Son*, Bibliographie sélective." *Cahiers victoriens & edouardiens*, no. 32 (October 1990), 146-60.

An unannotated listing of bibliographical sources, selected editions, textual studies, correspondence, a few biographies and biographical studies, and 130 or so critical studies.

Great Expectations

Note: Also see Worth (**109**) and Diedrick (**2385**).

1085. Bloom, Harold. "Bibliography." In *Charles Dickens's* **Great Expectations**. Modern Critical Interpretations. Ed. Harold Bloom. Philadelphia: Chelsea House, 2000, pp. 297-98.

A highly selective bibliography listing forty-four books and articles about Dickens, some specific to *Great Expectations*.

1086. Bloom, Harold. "Works about Charles Dickens and *Great Expectations*." In *Charles Dickens's* **Great Expectations**: *Bloom's Notes*. Ed. Harold Bloom. A Contemporary Literary Views Book. Broomall, PA: Chelsea House, 1996, pp. 74-78.

Lists seventy-two books and articles about Dickens and *Great Expectations* and contains "Books by Charles Dickens" (**4**), pp. 69-73.

1087. Bradbury, Nicola. "Select Bibliography." In her *Charles Dickens'* **Great Expectations**. Critical Studies of Key Texts. London, etc.: Harvester/Wheatsheaf; New York: St. Martin's Press, 1990, pp. 117-20.

Lists fifty-three works, predominantly book-length studies.

1088. Crompton, Louis. "Bibliography." In Dickens's *Great Expectations*. Ed. Louis Crompton (**1088**), pp. xxiii-xxv.

Lists, with brief annotations, the principal books and magazine articles about *Great Expectations*, 1911-63, as well as several major biographical and general critical studies.

1089. Hollington, Michael. "Capes/Agregation 2000: Bibliographie: Charles
Dickens: *Great Expectations.*" *Cahiers victoriens et edouardiens,* no. 50 (October 1999), 219-32.

Using a system of stars "style Guides Michelin," Hollington lists and annotates selected editions of *Great Expectations* and, under a variety of headings,
bibliographical, biographical, and critical studies of the novel, principally studies in English and mainly from the 1960s on.

1090. Kappel, Lawrence. "For Further Research." In *Readings on **Great Expectations.*** Ed. Lawrence Kappel. San Diego, CA: Greenhaven Press,
1999, pp. 133-34.

Lists fourteen book-length general studies of Dickens and twenty books
and articles on *Great Expectations.*

1091. Paroissien, David. "Select Bibliography." In his *The Companion to **Great
Expectations*** (**2398**), pp. 456-80.

An unusually extensive if unannotated list of background material (including some of Dickens's own writings, particularly articles in *Household Words*)
and critical studies of *Great Expectations.*

1092. R[osenberg], E[dgar], and J[ean] C[allahan]. "Selected Bibliography." In
Dickens's ***Great Expectations:*** *Authoritative Text, Backgrounds, Contexts,
Criticism.* Ed. Edgar Rosenberg (**2401**), pp. 729-46.

A solid selective bibliographical survey and evaluation of secondary studies, with only six of fourteen sections—Backgrounds, Special Studies, Full-
Length Critical Studies, Criticism, Closure, and Editions—specifically devoted
to *Great Expectations.* The other sections apply more generally to Dickens: Periodicals, Bibliographies, Biographies of Dickens, Biographical Studies and
Reminiscences, Aids to Research, Reference Works, Critical Introductions,
and Collections of Critical Studies. The section on closure lists studies since
1949 on the endings of *Great Expectations,* a field surveyed more fully in
Rosenberg (**2399, 2401**). See also the numerous entries under "Conclusion" in
the subject index to Worth (**109**). In the third printing (2000), the bibliography
is revised and somewhat expanded and updated by two pages. Add to this
bibliography the items included in the "Backgrounds," "Contexts," and "Criticism" sections, pp. 531-720, accompanying the text of the novel, and particularly Rosenberg's own commentary, pp. 361-527.

1093. Sadrin, Anny. "Critical Survey: Prefaces to [Editions Published in Dickens's Lifetime]" and "Bibliography." In her *Great Expectations* (**108**),
pp. 243-75, 281-86.

The first is a valuable survey of criticism of *Great Expectations* through 1986. The second is a useful, selective bibliography, principally of studies of *Great Expectations*. For other supplementary bibliographical and textual material, see Sadrin (**661, 2405**).

1094. Sell, Roger D. "Further Reading." In *Charles Dickens:* ***Great Expectations***. Ed. Roger D. Sell. New Casebooks. Basingstoke, Eng.: Macmillan; New York: St. Martin's Press, 1994, pp. 233-37.

In addition to more general studies, lists, with light evaluative annotation, a number of "Approaches to *Great Expectations*."

1095. Tredell, Nicolas. "Select Bibliography." In *Charles Dickens:* ***Great Expectations*** Ed. Nicolas Tredell (**2410**), pp. 187-97.

An unannotated selective list of Dickens's works, editions of *Great Expectations*, bibliographies of criticism of Dickens's works, biographies, general studies of Dickens's works, and contemporary reviews, studies, and film versions of *Great Expectations*.

Hard Times

Note: Also See Manning (**110**) and Peck (**1082**).

1096. Bloom, Harold. "Bibliography." In *Charles Dickens's* ***Hard Times***. Ed. Harold Bloom. Modern Critical Interpretations. New York, New Haven, CT, and Philadelphia: Chelsea House, 1987, pp. 135-36.

A selected bibliography of forty general critical studies and critical studies of *Hard Times*–in books and articles.

1097. Flint, Kate. "Select Bibliography." In Dickens's *Hard Times for These Times*. Ed. Kate Flint. Penguin Classics. London, New York, etc.: Penguin Books, 1995, pp. xxxv-xxxvii.

An unannotated list of thirty-two books and articles dealing in whole or in part with *Hard Times*.

1098. Ford, George, and Sylvère Monod. "Bibliography." In Dickens's *Hard Times: An Authoritative Text, Backgrounds, Sources, and Contemporary Reactions, Criticism*. Ed. George Ford and Sylvère Monod (**2411**), p. 378; 2nd ed., pp. 429-30; 3rd ed., (ed. Fred Kaplan and Sylvère Monod) pp. 479-80.

A highly selective list of general studies; in the first edition only eight studies of *Hard Times* are listed, apart from the studies reprinted in whole or in part in the critical section of this edition. In the second and third editions the editors revise, update, and somewhat enlarge the bibliography. For textual matters concerning this edition, see Ford and Monod (**2411**). The bibliography in the second edition is reprinted with minor revisions as "Selected Bibliography" in Dickens's *Hard Times: An Authoritative Text*, ed. George Ford and Sylvère Monod, A Norton Anthology Edition (New York and London: W. W. Norton, 1993), pp. 183-84.

1099. Samuels, Allen. "Selected Bibliography." In his *Hard Times: An Introduction to the Variety of Criticism*. Basingstoke and London: Macmillan, 1992, pp. 95-97.

Lists thirty-seven books and articles about *Hard Times*.

1100. Simpson, Margaret. "Select Bibliography." In her *The Companion to Hard Times* (**2415**), pp. 248-66.

A fairly detailed, if unannotated, list of studies of *Hard Times*, numerous background and related studies, and a large number of articles relevant to *Hard Times* from *Household Words* by Dickens and others.

1101. Thomas, Deborah. "Bibliography." In her *Hard Times: A Fable of Fragmentation and Wholeness*. Twayne's Masterworks Studies. New York: Twayne; London, etc.: Prentice Hall International, 1997, pp. 158-64.

An unannotated bibliography, principally of studies of *Hard Times*.

Little Dorrit
Note: See Tony Williams in DeVries (**12**).

Martin Chuzzlewit
Note: Also see Lougy (**113**).

1102. Metz, Nancy A. "Select Bibliography." In her *The Companion to Martin Chuzzlewit* (**2426**), pp. 511-32.

Consists largely of critical and background studies, many not specifically on *Martin Chuzzlewit*.

1103. Monod, Sylvère. "Bibliography." In his *Martin Chuzzlewit* (**2427**), pp. 199-205.

Lists general works on Dickens (bibliographical and biographical), general criticism (fifty studies, many of which contain sections on *Martin Chuzzlewit*), and fifty-one studies specifically about *Martin Chuzzlewit*.

The Mystery of Edwin Drood

Note: Also see Cox (**115**).

1104. Hargrave, Wilfred. "Bibliography of 'Edwin Drood.'" *Notes and Queries*, 6th ser., 11 (1885), 89.

Asks for a list of *Drood* commentary. See responses by G. F. R. B., p. 194, who lists articles in *Poole's Index to Periodical Literature* (**1049**); by W. C. W. and by A. C. B., p. 331, who add articles published in 1884; and by C. H. G., p. 446, who asks about the publishing history of *The Uncommercial Traveller*.

1105. Matz, B. W. "*The Mystery of Edwin Drood*: A Bibliography." *Dickensian*, 7 (1911), 130-33.

A listing of adaptations, continuations, dramatizations, and critical studies of *The Mystery of Edwin Drood*, excluding contemporary reviews. The items for 1905-11 are particularly numerous, deriving from "Dickensiana Month by Month" in the *Dickensian* (**1043**), which, presumably, Matz had a hand in compiling. But one should check both sources as some items in one are not to be found in the other. Slightly updated as "The Mystery of Edwin Drood: A Bibliography" in Nicoll, *The Problem of Edwin Drood* (**2448**), pp. 203-09, and supplemented by Winifred Matz (**1106**).

1106. Matz, Winifred. "A Bibliography of *Edwin Drood*, 1911-28." *Dickensian*, 24 (1927/28), 236, 301-02; 25 (1928/29), 42-44, 185-87.

A listing of books, pamphlets, and newspaper and magazine articles, supplementing the bibliographies by B. W. Matz (**1105**) and Nicoll (**2448**).

1107. Stewart, Richard F. *End Game: A Survey of Selected Writings about **The Mystery of Edwin Drood**.* Shelburne, Ontario, Can., and Sauk City, WI: The Battered Silicon Dispatch Box, George A. Vanderburgh, 1999. 385 pp.

Lists, comments extensively on, and evaluates 163 "principal solutions, completions and commentaries, and many, perhaps too many, of the minor ones as well," in chronological order, from *The Cloven Foot* (1870), by Orpheus C. Kerr (pseudonym for Robert Newell), the first continuation/parody of *Edwin Drood*, to Don R. Cox's 1998 *Drood* bibliography (**115**), which Stewart calls "a monumental achievement" (while offering a few relatively minor criticisms). Stewart does note the Nathan L. Bengis *Drood* Collection in the Wilson Library, University of Minnesota, which, he points out, Cox does not mention. Stewart includes occasional "Intermissions" and an "Afterword" in which he summarizes and comments personally on the items in his survey. "I have no new and startling solution to the mystery," he concludes, though he inclines towards Edwin being alive. Illustrated.

Review: C. Forsyte [Gordon Philo], *Dickensian*, 96 (2000), 158-61 ("an entertaining and useful reference handbook for the library of Droodists," quite different from Don R. Cox's *Drood* bibliography).

1108. Walters, J. Cuming. "Bibliography." In his *The Complete Mystery of Edwin Drood. The History, Continuations, and Solutions (1870-1912)*. London: Chap-man and Hall, 1912; Boston: Dana Estes, 1913; reprinted Folcroft, PA: Folcroft Library Editions, 1974; Norwood, PA: Norwood Editions, 1978, pp. 255-64.

A list of articles, books, continuations, dramatizations, and letters to the editor about *Drood*, but not editions of the work. Also see Walters (**849**).

Nicholas Nickleby

Note: See Paul Schlicke in DeVries (**12**).

The Old Curiosity Shop

Note: See Schlicke and Schlicke (**117**).

Oliver Twist

Note: Also see Paroissien (**118**).

1109. Dunn, Richard J. "Selected Bibliography." In his *Oliver Twist: Whole Heart and Soul*. Twayne's Masterwork Studies, 118. New York: Twayne; Toronto: Maxwell Macmillan Canada; New York, Oxford, Singapore, Sydney: Maxwell Macmillan International, 1993, pp. 109-12.

A brief but annotated bibliography of largely book-length, mainly general studies of Dickens, but with reference, obviously, to *Oliver Twist*.

1110. Paroissien, David. "Select Bibliography." In his *The Companion to Oliver Twist* (**2473**) pp. 312-23.

Lists articles by Dickens and others in *Household Words* relevant to *Oliver Twist*, a few unpublished sources, and books and articles of particular value for the notes provided, many concerned with background information and others with criticism of and commentary on *Oliver Twist*.

Our Mutual Friend

Note: See Brattin and Hornback (**120**).

1111. Cotsell, Michael. "Select Bibliography." In his *The Companion to Our Mutual Friend* (**2482**), pp. 289-94.

Lists articles by others in *Household Words* and *All the Year Round* relevant to *Our Mutual Friend* and books and articles of particular value for the notes provided.

Pickwick Papers

Note: Also see Engel (**125**).

1112. "Books about Pickwick." *Dickensian*, 32 (1935/36), 116.

A list of twenty-five books, 1883-1932.

1113. D[exter], W[alter]. "'The Pickwick Papers' in 'The Dickensian,' 1905-1929." *Dickensian*, 26 (1929/30), 204-06, 273-74.

An index of references to *Pickwick Papers* in the *Dickensian*.

Sketches by Boz

Note: Also see Robert Hanna in DeVries (**12**).

1114. DeVries, Duane. "Bibliography." In his *Dickens's Apprentice Years* (**2499**), pp. 178-84.

A fairly extensive listing of studies of *Sketches by Boz* and of Dickens's early years. Also see DeVries (**132**).

1115. Grillo, Virgil. "Bibliography: Secondary Sources Relating to *Sketches by Boz*" In his *Charles Dickens' **Sketches by Boz**: End in the Beginning* (**2502**), pp. 219-22.

Lists sixty-three studies of *Sketches by Boz*. Also see Grillo (**133, 983**).

A Tale of Two Cities

Note: Also see Glancy (**138**).

1116. Beckwith, Charles E. "Selected Bibliography." In *Twentieth Century Interpretations of **A Tale of Two Cities**: A Collection of Critical Essays.* Ed. Charles E. Beckwith. Englewood Cliffs, NJ: Prentice-Hall, 1972, pp. 120-22.

Annotates fourteen studies of or involving *A Tale of Two Cities*.

1117. Bloom, Harold. "Bibliography." In *Charles Dickens's **A Tale of Two Cities**.* Ed. Harold Bloom. Modern Critical Interpretations. New York, New Haven, CT, and Philadelphia: Chelsea House, 1987, pp. 139-40.

A selected bibliography of thirty-eight critical studies of *A Tale of Two Cities* and general studies—in books and articles.

1118. Bloom, Harold. "Works about Charles Dickens and *A Tale of Two Cities.*" In *Charles Dickens's **A Tale of Two Cities**: Bloom's Notes.* Ed. Harold Bloom; reprinted as *Bloom's Reviews, Comprehensive Research and Study Guides: Charles Dickens's **A Tale of Two Cities**.* Ed. Harold Bloom (**4**), pp. 71-75.

Lists seventy books and articles on the subject.

1119. Glancy, Ruth F. "Selected Bibliography." In her ***A Tale of Two Cities:*** *Dickens's Revolutionary Novel.* Twayne's Masterwork Studies, 89. Boston: Twayne, 1991, pp. 128-32.

Largely a list of reviews and criticism of *A Tale of Two Cities*, with a few general studies.

1120. Nardo, Don. "For Further Research." In *Readings on **A Tale of Two Cities**.* Ed. Don Nardo. San Diego, CA: Greenhaven Press, 1997, pp. 169-71.

Lists twenty-eight book-length general studies of Dickens and eighteen books and articles about *A Tale of Two Cities.*

1121. Newlin, George. "Bibliography." In his *Understanding **A Tale of Two Cities**: A Student Casebook to Issues, Sources, and Historical Documents.* "Literature in Context" Series. Westport, CT, and London: Greenwood Press, 1998, pp. 237-40.

A bibliography of background studies principally relevant to *A Tale of Two Cities.*

1122. Sanders, Andrew. "Select Bibliography." In his *The Companion to **A Tale of Two Cities**.* (**2508**), pp. 168-71.

Lists articles by Dickens and others relevant to *A Tale of Two Cities* and books and articles of value for the notes provided, mainly of background studies.

Nonfictional, Theatrical, and Poetical Works

Note: Also see the section on *Sketches by Boz,* above, Robert Hanna in DeVries (**12**), and Hargrave (**1104**), as well as section 2 of part 1 of the subject index.

1123. Brannan, Robert L. "Bibliography." In his *Under the Management of Mr. Charles Dickens: His Production of "The Frozen Deep"* (**466**), pp. 161-73.

A fairly extensive bibliography of works relevant to Dickens's revisions in and production of Wilkie Collins's play, including background studies.

1124. Flint, Kate. "Further Reading" and "A Note on the Text." In Dickens's *Pictures from Italy*. Ed. Kate Flint. Penguin Classics. London, New York, etc.: Penguin Books, 1998, pp. xxxv, xxxvi-xxxvii.

The bibliography lists eleven studies of *Pictures from Italy*, while the textual note indicates which parts of the work were originally published as "Travelling Letters Written on the Road" in the London *Daily News*, 21 January-11 March 1846. Flint also points out that the manuscripts of a fragment of the seventh and all of the eighth parts are in the Forster Collection, Victoria and Albert Museum.

1125. Lohrli, Anne. "Bibliography." In her *Household Words: A Weekly Journal 1850-1859* (**155**), pp. 519-34.

A valuable list of sources for *Household Words* and its contributors, including Dickens.

1126. Oppenlander, Ella Ann. "List of Sources." In her *Dickens' All the Year Round: Descriptive Index and Contributor List* (**158**), pp. 743-52.

A useful list of sources for *All the Year Round* and its contributors, including Dickens.

1127. Paroissien, David. "Bibliography" In his edition of *Pictures from Italy* (**434**), pp. 258-60.

Lists, ten reviews, two parodies, and fifteen secondary studies of *Pictures from Italy*, as well as the original editions and two Italian translations.

1128. Paroissien, David. "Selected Bibliography." In *Selected Letters of Charles Dickens*. Ed. David Paroissien. Basingstoke and London: Macmillan; Boston: Twayne, 1985, pp. 360-65.

Lists useful works relevant to the letters included under these headings: Biography, Ragged Schools, Urania Cottage and Prostitution, Parliament and Self-Help, and The Profession.

1129. Stone, Harry. "Selective Bibliography." In his *Charles Dickens' Uncollected Writings from Household Words 1850-1859* (**449**), pp. 668-72.

Notes that the bibliography is "highly selective" and includes "works that are essential to any study of Dickens and those works that shed important additional light on *Household Words*, Dickens' editorial procedures, or similar matters."

1130. Sullivan, Alvin, ed. *British Literary Magazines.* [Vol. 3]: *The Victorian and Edwardian Age, 1837-1913.* Westport, CT, and London: Greenwood Press, 1984, passim.

Contains brief commentaries on the origin, aims, characteristics, nature of contents, editorial policies, history, and other information about several magazines edited by Dickens, each of which is followed by a bibliography of studies of the magazine and of the people involved with it. See particularly *"All the Year Round,"* by J. Don Vann, pp. 11-14; *"Bentley's Miscellany,"* by Roger P. Wallins, pp. 34-41; and *"Household Words,"* by Patricia Marks, pp. 170-75. Also see *"The Dickensian,"* by Nancy A. Metz, pp. 110-16. Consult the index for references to Dickens's lesser involvement with other Victorian journals.

1131. White, Robert B., Jr. "Dickens, Charles." In his *The English Literary Journal to 1900: A Guide to Information Sources.* American Literature, English Literature, and World Literatures in English: An Information Guide Series, 8. Detroit, MI: Gale Research, 1977, pp. 222-24.

An unannotated list of eighteen studies (books, articles, dissertations) of Dickens as a journalist and editor. Also see cross references in the Note at the beginning of this section, and see the sections on *All the Year Round,* p. 499; the *Daily News,* pp. 78-79; *Household Words,* pp. 110-11; and the *Morning Chronicle,* pp. 136-37, for studies of publications with which Dickens was closely associated.

3D. BIBLIOGRAPHIES OF SPECIALIZED STUDIES OF DICKENS AND HIS WORKS

Note: In part 2 of the subject index, see **Bibliographies of Dickens studies, bibliographies of studies of Dickens and his works**, and other headings identified in the sections below.

Bibliographies, Reference Works, Textual Studies

Note: Also see **Bibliographies of Dickens studies, bibliographies; Bibliographies of Dickens's works, bibliographies; Reference works (with sections on Dickens), bibliographies;** and **Textual studies of Dickens's works, bibliographies,** in part 2 of the subject index.

1132. Arnim, Max. *Internationale Personalbibliographie, 1800-1943.* 2 vols. Leipzig: Verlag Karl W. Hiersemann, 1944, I, 288; 2nd ed. 2 vols. Stuttgart: Hiersemann Verlag, 1952, I, 288; vol. 3, *[1944-1975].* Comp. Franz Hodes. Issued in parts, Stuttgart: Anton Hiersemann, 1978-81, p. 307.

Volumes 1 and 3 between them list sixteen Dickens bibliographies, three of which are in German publications and one in a Spanish publication.

1133. Balay, Robert, et al., eds. *Guide to Reference Books.* 11th ed. Chicago and London: American Library Association, 1996, passim.

The latest edition of a long series of valuable guides to reference books, beginning in 1907, and often known over the years by the name of its editor–Mudge (Isadore G. Mudge), the 1929 and 1936 editions; Winchell (Constance M. Winchell), the 1951 and 1967 (8th) editions; and Sheehy (Eugene P. Sheehy), the 1976 (9th) and 1986 (10th) editions.

1134. Bell, Inglis F., and Jennifer Gallup. "Dickens, Charles." In their *A Reference Guide to English, American, and Canadian Literature: An Annotated Checklist of Bibliographical and Other Reference Materials.* Vancouver: University of British Columbia Press, 1971, p. 89.

The authors uselessly list, and without annotation, a mere four works on Dickens. The more general sections of their checklist, where entries *are* briefly annotated, are, unfortunately, also very selective.

1135. Besterman, Theodore. "Dickens, Charles John Huffam." In his *A World Bibliography of Bibliographies and of Bibliographical Catalogues, Calendars, Ab-*

stracts, Digests, Indexes, and the Like. 4th ed. 5 vols. Lausanne: Societas Bibliographica, 1965-66, I, cols. 1628-31; reprinted in his *Literature: English & American: A Bibliography of Bibliographies.* Besterman World Bibliographies. Totowa, NJ: Rowman and Littlefield, 1971, pp. 210-16.

Lists thirty-nine major primary and secondary bibliographies, catalogues, and bibliographical studies of Dickens. Also see, passim, Besterman's lists of bibliographies of more general studies of English literature, particularly for the nineteenth century, for bibliographies that would contain sections on Dickens. The fourth edition claims to be "revised and greatly enlarged throughout." Earlier editions were published 1939-40, 1947-49, and 1955-56. For an update of this work that covers 1964-74 publications, see Toomey (**1160**). Howard-Hill's sections on Dickens (**1148**) are more complete, as, not to be immodest, is the volume you now hold in your hands.

1136. *Bibliographische Berichte.* 30 vols. Frankfurt am Main: Vittorio Klosterman, 1959-88.

Published as *Bibliographische Berichte/Bibliographical Bulletin* beginning with volume 4 (1962). Harner (**1147**), pp. 18-19, points out that this annual bibliography of bibliographies in articles and books is an "essential complement for 1956-87" to the *Bibliographic Index* (**1141**) because it provides "extensive coverage of European publications." For Dickens items see the subject index (there are also cumulated subject indexes). Of limited value for Dickens studies.

1137. Biondi, Lee. "The Charles Dickens Reference Shelf." In his "Collecting Charles Dickens" (**2202**), pp. 51-53.

A nicely annotated if highly selective bibliography of works that are bibliographies or deal with bibliographical aspects of Dickens's works, particularly *Sketches by Boz* and *Pickwick Papers.* Biondi also comments on the work that still needs to be done in identifying and evaluating American editions of Dickens's works.

1138. Blazek, Ron, and Elizabeth Aversa. In their *The Humanities: A Selective Guide to Information Sources.* 5th ed. Library Science Text Series. Englewood, CO: Libraries Unlimited, 2000, passim.

Useful annotated lists of "Principal Information Sources" for the various humanistic disciplines, including basic bibliographical works with sections on Dickens. See particularly sections 11 and 12, "Accessing Information in Language and Literature" and "Principal Information Sources in Language and Literature," pp. 391-97, 399-536. Earlier editions are pretty much superseded—the first and second editions, by A. Robert Rogers (1974, 1979), and the third and fourth editions, by Blazek and Aversa (1988, 1994).

1139. Bracken, James K. "Charles Dickens (1812-1870)." In his *Reference Works in British and American Literature.* Vol. 2: *English and American Writers.* Englewood, CO: Libraries Unlimited, 1991, pp. 73-77; slightly revised and updated as "Charles (John Huffam) Dickens, 1812-1870." In his *Reference Works in British and American Literature.* 2nd ed. Englewood, CO: Libraries Unlimited, 1998, pp. 145-50.

Lists and provides extensive evaluative annotation for a highly selective list of bibliographies, handbooks, and Dickens journals.

1140. Chalcraft, Anthony, Ray Prytherch, and Stephen Willis, eds. "Dickens." In *Walford's Guide to Reference Material.* Vol. 3: *Generalia, Language and Literature, the Arts.* 7th ed. London: Library Association, 1998, pp. 778-79, and passim.

An annotated list of several Dickens bibliographies, encyclopedias and dictionaries, and chronologies, as well as a vast array of more general reference works in the fields indicated in the title under a variety of headings and subheadings. Earlier editions, with different editors, were published in 1959 (with a supplement in 1963), 1968, 1975, 1982, 1990, and 1994. Harner (**1147**), p. 9, calls this guide the "British counterpart" to *Guide to Reference Books* (**1133**).

1141. Charles, Dorothy, and Bea Joseph [et al.]. "Dickens, Charles, 1812-1870." In their *Bibliographic Index: A Cumulative Bibliography of Bibliographies, 1937-1942[-].* New York: H. W. Wilson Co., 1945- , passim.

Lists book-length bibliographies, bibliographies in magazines, and bibliographies at ends of books. Published annually and, up to 1969, in cumulations of various numbers of years (the bibliography for 1993 is volume 33). Currently published monthly as well.

1142. Clark, Lucy, Fredson Bowers, and, beginning with the checklist for 1950, Howell J. Heaney, comps. "A Selective Check List of Bibliographical Scholarship for [1949-72]: Part II. Later Renaissance to the Present." *Studies in Bibliography,* 3-27 (1950-74), passim. The checklists for 1949-55 reprinted as *Selective Check Lists of Bibliographical Scholarship, 1949-1955.* Charlottesville: Bibliographical Society of the University of Virginia, 1957, passim. The checklists for 1956-62 reprinted as *Selective Check Lists of Bibliographical Scholarship, Series B, 1956-1962.* Ed. Howell J. Heaney and Rudolf Hirsch. Charlottesville: University Press of Virginia for Bibliographical Society of the University of Virginia, 1966, passim.

See the cumulative index in each volume of the collected checklists for the Dickens items. The annual bibliography contains no index.

1143. Cox, James T., Margaret Putnam, and Marvin Williams. "Textual Studies in the Novel: A Selected Checklist, 1950-74." *Studies in the Novel,*
7 (1975), 445-71.

Divided into general studies, studies of American novelists, and studies of
English novelists. The last section lists forty-four Dickens studies (pp. 462-63)
but misses a number of others and includes a few that are not technically textual studies.

1144. Ensor, Pat. *CD-ROM Research Collections: An Evaluative Guide to Bibliographic and Full-Text CD-ROM Databases.* Westport, CT, and London:
Meckler, 1991, passim.

Identifies, describes, and evaluates a number of major reference guides
available on CD-ROM, including *Bibliographie Nationale Française depuis 1975 sur
CD-ROM* (see **1493**), *Biography Index* (**1247**), *British Library General Catalogue of
Printed Books to 1975* (**1438**), *Cumulative Book Index* (**81**), *Dissertation Abstracts*
(**1195**), *Essay and General Literary Index* (**1051**), *Humanities Index* (**1049**), and the
MLA International Bibliography (**1042**).

1145. Harner, James L. "Databases." In his *Literary Research Guide* (**1147**),
pp. 30-32.

Identifies and comments on two databases available through the Internet
"designed for cataloging, interlibrary loan, serials control, acquisitions, and
production of online catalogs by libraries": OCLC, the Online Union Catalog
(**1155**), and RLIN, the Research Libraries Information Network (**1158**).

1146. Harner, James L. "Internet Resources." In his *Literary Research Guide*
(**1147**), pp. 73-75.

Harner comments on the "phenomenal growth of the Internet and especially the World Wide Web" and its value and potential for researchers. He
further identifies two very useful "metapages," Literary Resources on the
Web, http://andromeda.rutgers.edu/~jlynch/Lit (**1230**), maintained by Jack Lynch at
Rutgers University at Newark, and Voice of the Shuttle: Web Page for Humanities Research, http://humanitas.ucsb.edu, now http://vos.ucsb.edu (**1236**), maintained by Alan Liu, University of California at Santa Barbara—with links to
other Internet sites. In addition, Harner also lists five major database vendors
(access to whose databases may be available in one's local or university
library)—Blaise Line, Ovid Technologies, Dialog, SilverPlatter, and Wilson-
Web. Others are listed in Harner's section on union catalogue databases
(**1145**). In the "metapages" one may navigate to a fascinating variety of Victorian links, including several Dickens pages.

1147. Harner, James L. *Literary Research Guide: An Annotated Listing of Reference Sources in English Literary Studies*. 4th ed. New York: Modern Language Association of America, 2002. x + 802 pp.

A useful listing of reference works for the study of literature in English, with elaborate annotation. In a preface, Harner notes that, in preparing the fourth edition, he "assessed anew each of the works cited in the third edition" (1998) and as a result "deleted 25 entries, added 41, conflated a few existing entries, and revised 568." Comparable revisions were made in the third and the second (1993) editions. The first edition was published in 1989. Harner refers readers to his World Wide Web site (http://www-english.tamu.edu/pubs/lrg) for revisions and additions to be incorporated into his fifth edition. He points out that the fourth edition "includes substantially more electronic resources than previous editions but warns that "the Web remains too unstructured, unregulated, and unstable to offer many free literary reference sources of value." This reference guide is included here not because it contains information about Dickens but because it provides detailed descriptions of the limitations and merits of a number of the more general bibliographical works listed in this section, in reference to which it has been frequently consulted. Also see Marcuse (**1152**) and other works in this section.

1148. Howard-Hill, T[revor] H., comp. *Index to British Literary Bibliography*. 9+ vols. Oxford: Clarendon Press, 1969- , passim.

An impressive multi-volume series in progress, occasionally annotated and with selective reviews of books, but one must be cautious of errors and, where Dickens is concerned, lack of completeness.

Vol. 1: *Bibliography of British Literary Bibliographies*, 1969; 2nd ed., revised and enlarged, 1987.

An unannotated, numbered bibliography of general and individual author bibliographies published 1886-1969 (with some reprints of later date in the second edition). Consult the general section, pp. 1-236 in the first and pp. 1-334 in the second edition, as well as "Dickens, Charles John Huffam, 1812-70," pp. 306-11 in the first and pp. 444-53 in the considerably expanded second edition.

Vol. 2: *Shakespearean Bibliography and Textual Criticism: A Bibliography*, 1971.

See "Index to British Literary Bibliography. I. Bibliography of British Literary Bibliographies: Supplement," pp. 179-322–a supplement to the first edition of volume 1, since incorporated into its second edition. There are only five Dickens items listed in "Dickens, Charles John Huffam, 1817[sic]-1870," pp. 256-57.

Vol. 3: *The Early British Book: A Bibliography to 1890*. In preparation.

Vol. 4: *British Bibliography and Textual Criticism: A Bibliography.* 1979.

This volume lists general studies of bibliographical and textual criticism, 1890-1969, and is the first of a three-volume set within the larger work, of which volume 5 contains bibliographical and textual studies of individual authors, 1890-1969, and volume 6 is the index to volumes 4 and 5, as well as to volumes 1 and 2, which see for the Dickens entries. Howard-Hill notes in his introduction to volume 4 that he includes "some items published before 1890 and some published after the cut-off date of 1969" in volumes 4 and 5.

Vol. 5: *British Bibliography and Textual Criticism: A Bibliography (Authors).* 1979.

"Dickens, Charles John Huffam, 1817[sic]-70." pp. 132-47, lists bibliographical and textual studies (unannotated) of Dickens, 1888-1969, largely supplementing the listings in volume 1, above, though there is occasional overlapping of references—and some serious typographical errors.

Vol. 6: *British Literary Bibliography and Textual Criticism, 1890-1969: An Index.* 1980.

An "Index of Authors, Editors, Compilers, and Titles," pp. 1-119, and "Index of Subjects," pp. 121-409, for volumes 1, 2, 4, and 5. For Dickens, see pp. 199-200. Also see "Corrections to *British Bibliography and Textual Criticism* (volumes 4 and 5)," pp. xvii-xix.

Vol. 7: *British Literary Bibliography, 1970-1979: A Bibliography.* 1992.

In "Dickens, Charles John Huffam, 1817[sic]-70," pp. 439-45, lists bibliographies and bibliographical and textual studies (unannotated) of Dickens for 1970-79. The volume itself updates the listings in volumes 1, 2, 4, and 5, above. See pp. 1-354 for general studies—bibliographical and textual criticism, book production and distribution, forms and genres, etc. Also see the subject index under Dickens for additional entries.

Vol. 8: *British Literary Bibliography, 1980-1989: A Bibliography,* 1999.

A bibliography of general bibliographies and bibliographical and textual studies. See the subject index in volume 9 for Dickens items.

Vol. 9: *British Literary Bibliography, 1980-1989: A Bibliography (Authors),* 1999.

See "Dickens, Charles John Huffam, 1817[sic]-70," pp. 552-57 for bibliographies and bibliographical and textual studies concerning Dickens. There is an index of authors (of the publications listed), editors, publishers, and titles, as well as a subject index for volumes 8 and 9.

1149. Kehler, Dorothea. *Problems in Literary Research: A Guide to Selected Reference Works.* 4th ed., revised. Lanham, MD, and London: Scarecrow Press, 1997, passim.

Intended for beginning graduate students as a "reference guide that teaches," this heavily annotated bibliography provides details for about thirty-six major reference works, a number of which are included in this section (3D). To this list, Kehler adds an "Annotated List of Supplementary Works, Including Sections on Children's Literature, Comparative and World Literature, Film, Literary Theory, and Rhetoric," pp. 151-203, which provides briefer annotation for 177 additional works. The three earlier editions were also published by Scarecrow Press (Metuchen, NJ, and London, 1975, 1981, 1987).

1150. Kennedy, Arthur G., and Donald B. Sands. *A Concise Bibliography for Students of English.* 5th ed. Revised by William E. Colburn. Stanford, CA: Stanford University Press, 1972, passim.

There are no sections on individual authors. See the chapters on British Literature, the Nineteenth Century, and Criticism for works that should include Dickens. This bibliography was originally published in 1940 by Kennedy, with revised editions in 1945 and 1954. The fourth edition was prepared by Sands after Kennedy's death and published in 1960.

1151. Madden, David, and Richard Powers. "Charles Dickens." In their *Writers' Revisions: An Annotated Bibliography of Articles and Books about Writers' Revisions and Their Comments on the Creative Process.* Metuchen, NJ, and London: Scarecrow Press, 1981, pp. 46-47 and 147.

An unnecessarily selective list of six items dealing with Dickens's revisions.

1152. Marcuse, Michael J. *A Reference Guide for English Studies.* Berkeley and Los Angeles, CA, and Oxford, Eng.: University of California Press, 1990. lxxii + 790 pp.

A useful listing of reference works for the study of literature in English, with valuable and elaborate annotation. As with Harner (**1147**), it is included here because it contains detailed descriptions of the limitations and merits of a number of the more general bibliographical works listed in this section. It also contains a brief but unannotated section on "Dickens (1812-1870)," pp. 274-75, that lists journals devoted to Dickens studies and an extremely limited and therefore not very useful listing of books on Dickens.

1153. Meckier, Jerome. "Charles Dickens: Research in Progress (1971)." *Dickens Studies Newsletter,* 2 (1971), 111-21.

Lists research projects in 1970/71 of over 100 scholars around the world.

1154. Northrup, Clark S., et al. "Dickens, Charles, 1812-1870." In their *Register of Bibliographies of the English Language and Literature*. Cornell Studies in English. New Haven, CT: Yale University Press; London: Humphrey Milford, Oxford University Press, 1925, pp. 114-16.

The compilers list, with light annotation, forty-seven books and articles that are bibliographies or bibliographical studies of Dickens, most general in nature but a few devoted to specific works and limited, obviously, by the date of publication.

1155. OCLC. Online Union Catalog (OLUC) or Online Computer Library Center (OCLC). Dublin, Ohio. http://www.oclc.org.

OCLC, as it describes itself online, is "a nonprofit, membership, computer library service and research organization whose public purpose is to further access to the world's information." Access is available, however, only through subscribing libraries. Harner (**1147**), pp. 30-31, points out that this is a database of "several million records for books, journals, manuscripts, audio and video recordings, and software," among which, obviously, one will find information about Dickens. According to Harner it is also available as "WorldCat through the FirstSearch database" (accessible through the Internet), which provides a variety of ways to limit one's search. OCLC WorldCat (**1503**), he points out, is an "invaluable resources for literary and linguistic research" in offering access to other databases besides OLUC, among which are included *Article First* ("an index to the tables of contents of more than 13,000 journals since 1990") *Arts and Humanities Citation Index* (**1035**), *Biography Index* (**1247**), *Book Review Digest* (**1211**), *Books in Print* (**67**), *Dissertation Abstracts Database* (**1195**), *Modern Language Association International Bibliography* (**1042**), and *Readers' Guide* (**1046**).

1156. Patterson, Margaret C. *Literary Research Guide*. Detroit: Gale Research, 1976, passim; 2nd ed. New York: Modern Language Association of America, 1983, passim.

An annotated bibliography of general reference works, a number of which are included in this section (3D). Patterson notes in her preface to the second edition that she has added entries for "about three hundred new titles published during the last five years" and expanded a number of sections of the work.

1157. Research in British Universities, Polytechnics, and Colleges Office, British Library, comp. *Research in British Universities, Polytechnics, and Colleges, 1979[-1984]*. Boston Spa, Eng.: The British Library, 1980-85, passim; continued by British Library Board, as *Current Research in Britain: The*

Humanities [1985-]. Boston Spa [London], Eng.: British Library Lending Division, 1985- , passim.

A list of research in progress in Britain by doctoral students as well as by others. For Dickens projects, see the index. For further details see Marcuse **(1152)**, p. 552.

1158. Research Libraries Information Network (RLIN). Research Libraries Group, Mountain View, CA. http//www.rlg.org.

As its Web site announces, the Research Libraries Group (RLG) is "a not-for-profit membership corporation of over 160 universities, national libraries, archives, historical societies, and other institutions with remarkable collections for research and learning." It "develops and operates information resources used by members and nonmembers around the world" and is available through subscribing libraries. Harner **(1147)**, p. 31, notes that this Internet information-retrieval system "contains several million unique records representing the holdings of participating libraries or included in several special databases." It offers subject and keyword searches, as well as a variety of other ways to limit one's search. While Harner finds RLIN's coverage "not as extensive" as that of OLUC **(1155)**, it has "features of particular importance to literature scholars," including the listings in *Location Register of English Literary Manuscripts and Letters: Eighteenth and Nineteenth Centuries* **(1528)**, *National Union Catalog of Manuscript Collections* **(1480)**, the RLG Conspectus ("a record of collection strengths of RLG member libraries in over 3,000 fields"), the *English Short-Title Catalogue* database **(15)**, and CitaDel, a "collection of individual databases including *BHA: Bibliography of the History of Art, Dissertations Abstracts Online* **(1195)**, *FRANCIS* **(1045)**, and *HAPI: Hispanic American Periodicals Index*" **(1056)**.Through the Eureka interface, a recent check of the RLG Union Catalog (RLIN) for "Dickens" produced 11,958 listings of editions, translations, and adaptations of Dickens's works, with basic bibliographical information, though in no apparent order of arrangement, but refining one's search will make the database easier to work with. A similar search for *David Copperfield* produced 600 items.

1159. Schweik, Robert C., and Dieter Riesner. *Reference Sources in English and American Literature: An Annotated Bibliography.* New York: W. W. Norton, 1977, passim.

Lists and comments on general reference works, many of which one would consult in compiling an annotated Dickens bibliography. See particularly the sections on the Victorian period and fiction.

1160. Toomey, Alice F. "Dickens, Charles." In her *A World Bibliography of Bibliographies, 1964-1974: A List of Works Represented by Library of Congress*

Printed Catalog Cards: A Decennial Supplement to Theodore Besterman, **A World Bibliography of Bibliographies**. 2 vols. Totowa, NJ: Rowman and Littlefield, 1977, I, 285-86.

A listing of separately published primary and secondary bibliographies and exhibition and library catalogues concerning Dickens. See also Besterman (**1135**).

1161. Van Patten, Nathan. "Dickens, Charles, 1812-1870." In his *An Index to Bibliographies and Bibliographical Contributions Relating to the Work of American and British Authors, 1923-1932*. Stanford: Stanford University Press; London: Humphrey Milford, Oxford University Press, 1934, pp. 71-75.

A list of major and minor items, limited, obviously, by the period covered.

1162. Wortman, William A. *A Guide to Serial Bibliographies for Modern Literatures*. Selected Bibliographies in Language and Literature, 3. New York: Modern Language Association of America, 1982; 2nd ed. New York: Modern Language Association of America, 1995, passim.

In the 1995 edition, Dickens is represented only by "The Dickens Checklist" in *Dickens Quarterly*, previously *Dickens Studies Newsletter* (**1037**), by the "Year's Work in Dickens Studies" in *Dickensian* (**1052**), and by the "Recent Dickens Studies" section of *Dickens Studies Annual* (**1047**). This guide is of principal use for its listing and description of more general bibliographies that include sections on Dickens, though the Dickens sections are not noted and are left to the researcher to find.

1163. Wynar, Bohdan S., ed. *American Reference Books Annual, 1970[-]*. Littleton, CO: Libraries Unlimited, 1970- , passim.

See under Dickens in the subject index in individual volumes as well as in the five-year cumulative indexes, but also browse in the sections on "Literature" and "British Literature" in individual volumes. The annotations are fullsome and evaluative. *ARBA*, as it is known, has also been available online since 1997, at http://www.paratext.com/arba_intro.htm, through subscribing libraries, where it currently features, according to its home page, "9,500+ reviews of reference works." It is updated monthly. Also see *ARBA Guide to Biographical Dictionaries* (Littleton, CO: Libraries Unlimited, 1986), passim, also edited by Wynar. This work is a heavily annotated bibliography of sources of biographical information. For works that should contain information on Dickens, see particularly the section on "British Literature: General Works and Fiction."

1164. Wynar, Bohdan S. *Introduction to Bibliography and Reference Work: A Guide to Materials and Sources.* 4th ed. Rochester, NY: Libraries Unlimited, 1967, pp. 67-99.

Useful, though now outdated, for its annotated section on national and trade bibliographies–American, British, German, French, Italian, Soviet, and Spanish. Earlier editions were published in Denver, CO, by the Graduate School of Librarianship, University of Denver, 1963, and in Denver, CO, by the Colorado Bibliographic Institute, 1964, 1966.

Indexes

Note: Also see **Indexes concerning Dickens and his works** in part 2 of the subject index.

1165. Dunn, Frank T., comp. *A Cumulative Analytical Index to* **The Dickensian,** *1905-1974, Together with an Index to the Illustrations, Compiled by Mary Ford and Michael Slater.* Hassocks, Eng.: Harvester Press, 1976. x + 199 pp.

An unannotated author and subject index to articles and notes in the *Dickensian* superseding previous indexes compiled by Doris L. Minards for 1905-34 and 1935-60 (**1167-68**). The index to illustrations (**1350**), pp. 183-99, is an artist/subject index. Also see Dunn (**1404**).

Reviews: M. D. Anderson, *Indexer*, 10 (1976/77), 148-49 (finds that references to "the immense mass of miscellaneous material in the seventy volumes have been most skilfully organized into compact form"); D. DeVries, *Dickensian*, 72 (1976), 173-75 (comments on the variety of information about Dickens scholars, Dickens scholarship, Dickensiana, and illustrations of Dickens and his works that this index provides, and finds the index a major contribution to Dickens scholarship); R. J. Dunn, *Dickens Studies Newsletter*, 7 (1976), 79-80 ("excellent," though a few "slips" are noted); K. J. Fielding, *Modern Language Review*, 72 (1977), 926 ("an extraordinary and even magnificent achievement,"–"clear, exact, and comprehensive"); Mollie Hardwick, *Books and Bookmen*, 21 (March 1976), 42-43 (quite "detailed and exhaustive"; finds that a "gentle meander" through it "brings out the luscious flavour" of the *Dickensian*); G. Storey, *Times Literary Supplement*, 2 April 1976, p. 403 ("admirably comprehensive and discriminating index").

1166. Falk, Byron A., Jr., and Valerie R. Falk. "Dickens, Charles." In their *Personal Name Index to "The New York Times Index," 1851-1974.* 22 vols. Succasunna, NJ: Roxbury Data Interface, 1976-83, VI, 315-16; *1975-1996 Supplement.* 7 vols. Sparks, NV: Roxbury Data Interface, 1998-99, II, 376.

An "index to an index," gives the year and page number of Dickens entries in the annual issue of *The New York Times Index* (**1169**), from 1851 on. Also see entries for other members of the Dickens family.

1167. [Minards, Doris, ed.]. *The Dickensian: A Magazine for Dickens Lovers. Index to the First Thirty Volumes, 1905 to 1934.* London: The Dickens Fellowship, 1935. iv + 97 pp.

An author/subject index to the official publication of the Dickens Fellow-ship. Superseded by Dunn (**1165**).

1168. [Minards, Doris, ed.]. *The Dickensian: Index to Volumes XXXI-LVI, 1935-1960*. London: The Dickens Fellowship, 1961. iv + 66 pp.

An author/subject index, also indicating year of publication and page num-bers for listings. A list of books reviewed, indexed by title, is also included. Superseded by Dunn (**1165**).

1169. *The New York Times Index for the Published News of September 1851-December 1862, [1863-1874, 1875-1879, 1880-1885, 1886-1889, 1890-1893, 1894-1898, 1899-June 1905, July 1905-December 1906, 1907-]*. New York: *New York Times*, 1859- , passim.

See under Dickens for articles concerning him and his works. The multi-year volumes to 1906 are not easy to use, but thereafter the index is a simple alphabetical one, later on issued quarterly or semiannually, and currently bi-weekly, quarterly, and annually.

1170. *Palmer's Index to the Times Newspaper (London), 1790[-1941]*. Corsham, Eng.: Palmer, 1868-1943; reprinted Vaduz, Liechtenstein: Kraus Reprint, 1965, passim; replaced by and (after 1941) continued by *The Annual Index to the Times*. London: Times Office (1907-13) and *The Offi-cial Index to the Times* (1914-60), and *The Times Index* (1972-), passim (publishers vary). Online also.

The gateway to the numerous Dickens news, feature, and critical articles in England's premier newspaper. It is best to go with the online index, which should be available in most research libraries. Simply search for Dickens.

1171. Patterson, Margaret C. "Dickens, Charles (1812-70)." In her *Author Newsletters and Journals: An International Annotated Bibliography of Serial Pub-lications Concerned with the Life and Works of Individual Authors*. American Literature, English Literature, and World Literatures in English: An In-formation Guide Series, 19. Detroit: Gale Research, 1979, pp. 90-94; updated by her "Author Newsletters and Journals: Supplement 1[, 2, and 3]." *Serials Review*, 8, iv (Winter 1982), 61-72; 10, i (Spring 1984), 51-59; 11, iii (Autumn 1985), 31-44.

In the original volume and two of the supplements, lists and describes sev-eral Dickens publications–1) *CDRC Report: A News Letter* (Charles Dickens Reference Center, Lesley College, Boston), superseded by 2) *Dickens Studies*, in turn superseded by 3) *Dickens Studies Annual*; 4) *Dickensian*; 5) *Dickens Studies Newsletter*, superseded by 6) *Dickens Quarterly*. Illustrated.

1172. Slayden, David. "Annotated Checklist: Dickens." *Victorian Studies*, 20, supplement (June 1977), 97-101.

In an annotated checklist of all articles published in *Victorian Studies*, volumes 1-20 (1957-77), includes a section on Dickens that provides annotation (100-150 words per listing) for the twelve articles published on Dickens and reference to two other articles that deal in part with Dickens. Also see the "Cumulative Index," pp. 123-76, which lists all articles published in *Victorian Studies* and all book reviews (under author of the book).

1173. Tennyson, Elizabeth J., and G. B. Tennyson, comps. *An Index to "Nineteenth-Century Fiction," Volumes 1-30, Summer 1945-March 1976*. Berkeley, Los Angeles, and London: University of California Press, 1977, pp. 20-26, 116-20.

The author-subject index lists articles about Dickens published in *Nineteenth-Century Fiction*. The book review index lists reviews of books about Dickens published there.

Publishing, Book and Periodical Production

Note: Also see **Book production, publication, and distribution, bibliographies; Nineteenth-century book and periodical printing and publication, bibliographies of studies of;** and **Publishing, book and periodical publication, bibliographies**, in part 2 of the subject index.

1174. Anderson, Patricia J., and Jonathan Rose. "Checklist for Further Reading." In *British Literary Publishing Houses, 1820-1880*. Ed. Patricia J. Anderson and Jonathan Rose. Dictionary of Literary Biography, 106. Detroit, MI: Gale Research, 1991, pp. 334-37.

A selected list of general studies of British publishers, including Dickens's, for the period indicated.

1175. Bell, Bill. "Some Recent Work in Victorian Publishing History." *Victorian Literature and Culture*, 19 (1991), 361-69.

Surveys a number of studies of Victorian publishing history, ca. 1987-91, with occasional reference to Dickens.

1176. Houghton, Walter E. "British Periodicals of the Victorian Age: Bibliographies and Indexes." *Library Trends*, 7 (1958/59), 554-65.

Identifies, describes, and evaluates the various bibliographies and indexes of articles in Victorian periodicals. Houghton also describes the scope of *The Wellesley Index to Victorian Periodicals, 1824-1900* (**1177**), then in preparation.

1177. Houghton, Walter E., Esther R. Houghton, et al., eds. *The Wellesley Index to Victorian Periodicals, 1824-1900: Table of Contents and Identification of Contributors, with Bibliographies of Their Articles and Stories.* 5 vols. Toronto: University of Toronto Press; London: Routledge & Kegan Paul, 1966, 1972, 1979, 1987, 1989, passim.

The full title tells much of the story of this mammoth scholarly endeavor. Each of the first four volumes takes up eight to fifteen major monthly or quarterly periodicals, for a total of forty-three, itemizes and numbers the articles in them, issue by issue, excluding any poetry. The editors claim this is an extension backwards of the *Nineteenth Century Readers' Guide* (**964**) and a supplement, expansion, and correction of entries in *Poole's Index* (**1049**), but such a characterization scarcely does this project justice. Its principal virtue is the completeness of entries for forty-three important nineteenth-century periodicals and its identification of the authors of the predominantly anonymous or pseudonymous articles and book reviews. For volume 1, for example, the editors supply the name of the author or "suggest a probable or possible one" for 97% of the more than 27,000 articles, stories, and book reviews in eight journals and provide evidence for such identifications, though they are not quite as successful in later volumes, identifying 84.29% of the authors in volume 2, 80% of those in volume 3, and 73% of those in volume 4–still an amazing record. Each of the first four volumes is divided into three parts: Part A, "Table of Contents and Identification of Contributors"; Part B, "Bibliographies of Contributors," which lists the authors alphabetically with a list of their contributions to the journals covered in that volume; and Part C, "Index of Initials and Pseudonyms," which gives or suggests the real name of the author.

Bentley's Miscellany (in volume 4) is the only magazine covered that Dickens edited, so he is scarcely mentioned as an author in the first three volumes. But authors of articles about him in the journals covered in the first four volumes are occasionally identified as are reviewers of his novels and other works; however, there is no subject index to locate these. See volume 4, pp. 5-13, for comments on Dickens's involvement with *Bentley's Miscellany* as its first editor from January 1837 to February 1839 and volume 4, pp. 15-23, for a list of its contents during this period (and see the list of contents through April 1839 for the final installments of *Oliver Twist*). Also check the appendices in volumes 2-5 for corrections and additions to previous volumes. Volume 5, *Epitome and Index: Dated Bibliographies of All Identified Authors and Their Contributions to Major Quarterlies and Monthlies of the Period with a Separate Bibliography of Identified Pseudonyms and Initials*, was edited by Jean Harris Slingerland. Here, the list of Dickens's works is short, mostly those he published in *Bentley's Miscellany*. Also see Houghton (**1411**).

1178. Ingram, Alison. *Index to the Archives of Richard Bentley & Son, 1829-1898.* Cambridge, Eng.: Chadwyck-Healey; Teaneck, NJ: Somerset House, 1977. 127 unnumbered pp.

Indexes the Bentley archives in the British Library, the University of Illinois, and the University of California, Los Angeles, and summarizes the Bentley items in the Bodleian Library, Oxford, and the Berg Collection, New York Public Library. For use with *The Archives of Richard Bentley & Son, 1829-1898* (Cambridge, Eng.: Chadwyck-Healey, 1976), 159 microfilm reels. Dickens items are identified.

1179. Linton, David, and Ray Boston, eds. *The Newspaper Press in Britain: An Annotated Bibliography.* London: Mansell, 1987, passim.

The index identifies twenty-three books and articles concerning Dickens's career as a journalist.

1180. Madden, Lionel, and Diana Dixon. *The Nineteenth-Century Periodical Press in Britain: A Bibliography of Modern Studies, 1901-1971.* Garland Reference Library of the Humanities, 53. New York: Garland Publishing, 1976, passim.

In Section D, "Studies and Memoirs of Proprietors, Editors, Journalists and Contributors," see entries under Dickens, pp. 200-07, and "John Dickens," pp. 207-08. In Section C, "Individual Periodicals and Newspapers," see the entries for the periodicals with which Dickens was affiliated–the *Morning Chronicle,* the *Evening Chronicle, Bentley's Miscellany, Master Humphrey's Clock,* the *Daily News, Household Words,* and *All the Year Round.* Section A, "Bibliographies, Finding Lists and Reports on Bibliographical Projects," and Section B, "General History of Periodicals and Newspapers," also contain studies that refer to Dickens, but one needs to go through these item by item since there is no subject index for the volume. Originally published as a supplement to *Victorian Periodicals Newsletter,* 8, iii (September 1975), 1-76. Continued by Uffelman, Madden, and Dixon (**1185**).

1181. Myers, Robin. *The British Book Trade from Caxton to the Present Day: A Bibliographical Guide Based on the Libraries of the National Book League and St. Bride Institute.* London: André Deutsch, 1973, passim.

Briefly annotated listings of works on various aspects of the book trade. See the index for items specifically related to Dickens, but he is also, obviously, covered in a number of the other, more general works included.

1182. Patten, Robert. "Select Bibliography." In his *Charles Dickens and His Publishers* (**224**), pp. 465-83.

A useful unannotated list of books and articles on Dickens's relationships with his publishers—works Patten consulted in writing this thorough and important study.

1183. Rosenblum, Joseph. *A Bibliographical History of the Book: An Annotated Guide to the Literature*. Magill Bibliographies. Metuchen, NJ, and London: Scarecrow Press; Pasadena, CA, and Englewood Cliffs, NJ: Salem Press, 1995, passim.

A heavily annotated bibliography, with principal sections on resources, technical aspects, history, and miscellaneous aspects (including book collecting, bookselling, and private presses) of the book and book publication. References to Dickens may be found in a number of the items, though Dickens is not listed in the subject index.

1184. Shattock, Joanne. "Sources for the Study of Victorian Writers and Their Publishers." *Browning Institute Studies*, 7 (1979), 93-113.

A useful annotated bibliography in essay form of the primary or archival sources, general background material, and specialized studies concerned with Victorian writers, including Dickens, and their publishers.

1185. Uffelman, Larry K., with Lionel Madden and Diana Dixon. "The Nineteenth-Century Periodical Press in Britain: A Bibliography of Modern Studies 1972-1987." *Victorian Periodicals Review*, 25, ii (Summer 1992), i-iv, 1-124 (special issue, not the regular Summer 1992 issue).

A continuation of Madden and Dixon (**1180**). See entries under Dickens, pp. 79-83, as well as under titles of individual periodicals with which he was affiliated—the *Morning Chronicle*, the *Evening Chronicle, Bentley's Miscellany, Master Humphrey's Clock*, the *Daily News, Household Words*, and *All the Year Round*—in the section on "Individual Periodicals and Newspapers," pp. 37-68. Based on the annual "Victorian Periodicals, 1971-72[-]" (**1057**).

1186. Vervleit, Hendrik D. L., ed. *ABHB: Annual Bibliography of the History of the Printed Book and Libraries*. Vols. 1[-15]: *Publications of 1970[-1984]*. The Hague, etc. (place of publication varies): Martinus Nijhoff, 1973-86, passim; *Publications of 1985[-]*. Vol. 16- . Dordrecht, Neth., Boston, and Lancaster, Eng. (later London): Kluwer Academic Publishers, 1988- , passim.

An unannotated listing, with items arranged by country and century under more general aspects of book printing, book publication, and book collecting—see the sections on nineteenth-century Great Britain for Dickens material. Volume 17A is a *Cumulated Subject Index, Volume One (1970)-Volume 17 (1986)*, ed. Hendrik D. L. Vervleit (Dordrecht, Neth., Boston, and London: Kluwer Academic Publishers, 1989), with a number of Dickens items listed for most years. Since volume 19, the bibliography has been edited by the Department of Special Collections of the Koninklijke Biblotheek, The Hague, Neth.

Dissertations

Note: Also see Gabel and Gabel (**1273**) and Ministère de l'Education Nationale (**1277**). Not included here are lists of dissertations for individual universities and a number of catalogues of foreign language dissertations. For the latter, see Wortman (**1162**), pp. 157-58, and Reynolds (**1206**). Also see **Dissertations on Dickens and related subjects, bibliographies** in part 2 of the subject index and under individual works in part 1 of the subject index.

1187. Altick, Richard D., and William R. Matthews, comps. "Dickens, Charles." In their *Guide to Doctoral Dissertations in Victorian Literature 1886-1958*. Urbana: University of Illinois Press, 1960, pp. 45-49.

Lists eighty-two American, British, and European doctoral dissertations on Dickens, with cross references to fourteen others. Although there is an "Index to Authors of Dissertations," there is no subject index, so one will need to go through the rest of the ninety-six-page list item by item to find other dissertations that probably contain material on Dickens even though he is not mentioned in the title. "Thorough but not exhaustive," Harner (**1147**), p. 296, concludes about Altick and Matthew's work, adding that a supplement "would be welcomed by scholars."

1188. Aslib [Association of Special Libraries and Information Bureaux]. *Index to Theses Accepted for Higher Degrees in the Universities of Great Britain and Ireland*. Vols. 1 (1950-51)-34 (1985). Ed. P[eter] D. Record [et al.]. London: ASLIB, 1953-85; continued as *Index to Theses with Abstracts Accepted for Higher Degrees by the Universities of Great Britain and Ireland and the Council for National Academic Awards*. Ed. Geoffrey M. Paterson [et al.]. Vols. 35 (1986)- . London: Aslib, 1986- .

Issued quarterly and in yearly cumulations, this index covers bachelor's, master's, and doctor's theses in all subjects, giving author, title, university, degree, and year of the dissertation but, until volume 35 (1986/87), as Harner (**1147**), p. 69, notes, not abstracts. For Dickens entries see, obviously, the section on Language and Literature, English. For pre-1950 dissertations, see Bilboul and Kent (**1189**). Available to library subscribers at http://www.theses.com.

1189. Bilboul, Roger R., and Francis L. Kent, eds. "Dickens, Charles." In their *Retrospective Index to Theses of Great Britain and Ireland, 1716-1950*. Vol. 1: *Social Science and Humanities*. Oxford: European Bibliographical Center/Clio Press; Santa Barbara, CA: American Bibliographical Center/Clio Press, 1975. p. 57.

The 1975 edition lists all of twelve master's theses on Dickens. For post-1950 theses, see Aslib's *Index to Theses Accepted for Higher Degrees in the Universities of Great Britain and Ireland* (**1188**). A twenty-six page *Addenda* was published in 1977.

1190. *The Brits Index: An Index to the British Theses Collections (1971-1987) Held at the British Library Document Supply Centre and London University.* 3 vols. Godstone, Eng.: British Theses Service, 1989, passim.

Individual volumes are devoted to author, title, and subject indexes. For the easiest entrée to theses concerned with Dickens, see the section on "English Literature: 19th Century Literature," in the subject index, volume 3, pp. 67-71.

1191. *Canadian Graduate Theses in the Humanities and Social Sciences, 1921-1946 / Thèses des gradués Canadiens dans les humanités et les sciences sociales.* Ottawa: Edmond Cloutier, 1951, passim; continued as *Canadian Theses / Thèses canadiennes, 1947-1960.* 2 vols. Ottawa: National Library of Canada/Bibliothèque nationale du Canada, 1973, passim; further continued as *Canadian Theses / Thèses canadiennes, [1961-].* Ottawa: National Library of Canada/Bibliothèque nationale du Canada, 1963- , passim.

Lists M.A. and Ph.D. theses. The occasional Dickens entry will be found under "Literature, English/Litterature anglaise." See Harner (**1147**), pp. 68-69, for microfiche (only since 1980-81) and online versions.

1192. "Catalogues des thèses." *Cahiers victoriens & edouardiens*, no. 37 (April 1993), 141-63.

Mainly lists French dissertations in progress—a few on Dickens.

1193. "Catalogue des thèses victoriennes et edouardiennes." *Cahiers victoriens & edouardiens*, no. 19 (April 1984), 101-28.

Lists several French dissertations on Dickens, 1975-83.

1194. "Dickens." In *Comprehensive Dissertation Index, 1861-1972.* Vol. 29: *Language and Literature A-L.* Ann Arbor, MI: Xerox University Microfilms, 1973, pp. 350-51. Continued in annual supplements, to date, with *Ten-Year Cumulation, 1973-1982* (1984); *Five-Year Cumulation, 1983-1987* (1989); and *Five Year Cumulation, 1983-1987* (1989), and annually thereafter, passim.

The listings give author, title, number of pages, year, and university but provide no abstracts. Also check under subject headings of "Dicken" (the misspelling of the indexers not the authors of the dissertations), "Dickensian,"

"Nineteenth," "Nineteenth Century," and "Novel." According to the introduction to the 1973 edition, the work contains "virtually all of the dissertations accepted for academic doctoral degrees (not professional or honorary) granted by United States educational institutions" and some accepted by foreign universities. See Harner (**1147**), pp. 67-68, for how to use, for database versions, and for locating abstracts online.

1195. *Dissertation Abstracts International.* Ann Arbor, MI: UMI, 1970- . Also available on the World Wide Web through UMI Proquest Digital Dissertations, at http://wwwlib.umi.com/dissertations.

Lists and provides abstracts (written by their authors) of doctoral dissertations and some master's theses. This series began as *Microfilm Abstracts*, 1938-51, then *Dissertation Abstracts*, 1952-69. Libraries are in the process of discarding the printed volumes since, in recent years in particular, they have occupied an enormous amount of shelf space, and the microfilm, CD-ROM, and now online versions are much more convenient to use. In earlier years, a number of universities did not list their doctoral dissertations (a few still do not). But, annoyingly, the online database does not provide abstracts for dissertations before 1980, and, as a result, as Harner (**1147**), p. 66, indicates, "researchers will frequently find themselves digging through stacks of the printed versions"—if these are even available. The advantage of the online version is that one can search for dissertations by author, title, subject, and a variety of other ways. One will, of course, find many dissertations on Dickens listed. For more details, see Harner, pp. 66-68. While the online database is fully available only through subscribing libraries, a visitor may, as the home page indicates, "freely access the most current two years of citations and abstracts" in the database on a home computer, a gift of obviously limited value.

1196. Gabel, Gernot U., and Gisela R. Gabel, comps. *Dissertations in English and American Literature: Theses Accepted by Austrian, French, and Swiss Universities, 1875-1970.* Hamburg: Gernot Gabel Verlag, 1977, passim; supplemented by *Dissertations in English and American Literature: Theses Accepted by Austrian, French, and Swiss Universities, 1875-1970: Supplement 1971-1975 and Additions.* Köln: Edition Gemini, 1982, passim.

Gives author, title, university, and date of fifteen dissertations on Dickens, with the addition of one in the supplement. A preface notes that this bibliography was intended as something of a supplement to Mummendey (**1203**) and McNamee (**1202**).

1197. Habicht, Werner, and, later, Horst Weinstock, comps. *English and American Studies in German: Summaries of Theses and Monographs: A Supplement to Anglia, 1967/68[-].* Tübingen: Max Niemeyer, 1969- , passim.

Fairly lengthy abstracts in English of dissertations and monographs, principally in German. Occasionally there are Dickens studies but not in every volume. Harner (**1147**), p. 63, points out that since the work "relies on authors and editors for abstracts, coverage is incomplete but does include many studies overlooked in the standard bibliographies." The volumes for 1969-81 were edited by Habicht; that for 1982 by Habicht and Weinstock, and those from 1983 on by Weinstock.

1198. Howard, Patsy C., comp. "Charles Dickens." *Theses in English Literature 1894-1970.* Ann Arbor, MI: Pierian Press, 1973, pp. 88-93.

Lists 148 unpublished baccalaureate and master's theses on Dickens. The list, Howard indicates, is "necessarily incomplete."

1199. *Katalog doctorskikh: kandidatskikh dissertatsii.* . . . Moscow: Biblioteka, 1958- , passim.

Wortman (**1162**), p. 158, indicates that this is a classified catalogue, published twice a month, containing "author and subject indexes of dissertations in all subjects deposited in the Lenin Library and the Central State Library of Medicine" in Moscow.

1200. Litto, Frederic M. *American Dissertations on the Drama and the Theatre: A Bibliography.* Kent, OH: Kent State University Press, 1969, passim.

Contains four dissertations with Dickens's name in the title—see p. 173 of "The Key-Word-in-Context index." Also see the subject index under England, 1800-49 and 1850-99, for dissertations that may make reference to Dickens although his name is not in the title and for related or background studies.

1201. *Masters Abstracts: Abstracts of Selected Masters Theses on Microfilm.* Vols. 1-12. Ann Arbor, MI: University Microfilms (later, Xerox University Microfilms), 1962-74, passim; *Masters Abstracts: A Catalog of Selected Masters Theses on Microfilm.* Vols. 13- 23. Ann Arbor, MI: Xerox University Microfilms (later, University Microfilms International), 1975-85, passim; *Masters Abstracts International.* Vols. 24- . Ann Arbor, MI: University Microfilms International, 1986- , passim.

Issued quarterly (through volume 30) and six times a year thereafter and cumulated annually; contains abstracts of occasional dissertations on Dickens. See the subject index (through the volume for 1987; thereafter omitted). Harner (**1147**), p. 68, notes that this work "abstracts a relatively small percentage of the annual output of master's theses even in the United States."

1202. McNamee, Lawrence F. "Charles Dickens." In his *Dissertations in English and American Literature: Theses Accepted by American, British and German Universities, 1865-1964.* New York and London: R. R. Bowker, 1968, pp. 584-89; continued in his *Dissertations in English and American Literature: Supplement One: Theses Accepted by American, British and German Universities, 1964-1968.* New York and London: R. R. Bowker, 1969, pp. 232-35, and in his *Dissertations in English and American Literature: Supplement Two: Theses Accepted by American, British, British Commonwealth and German Universities, 1969-1973.* New York and London: R. R. Bowker, 1974, pp. 339-45.

Lists author, title, year of degree, and university but does not provide abstracts of doctoral dissertations on Dickens for the years indicated in the titles. See under "Dickens" in the "Cross-Index of Authors" for dissertations dealing in part with Dickens.

1203. Mummendey, Richard. *Language and Literature of the Anglo-Saxon Nations as Presented in German Doctoral Dissertations, 1885-1950/Die Sprache und Literatur der Angelsachsen im Spiegel der deutschen Universitätsschriften, 1885-1950.* Bonn: Bouvier; Charlottesville: Bibliographical Society of the University of Virginia, 1954, passim.

Look under "Dickens" in the index for thirty-five dissertations on Dickens. There are no abstracts or other annotation. Altick and Matthews (**1187**) warn in their preface that Mummendey's bibliography is "seriously deficient," their own listing containing "about 130 titles, in Victorian literature alone, which Mummendey overlooked." For other limitations, see Harner (**1147**), pp. 71-72.

1204. Naaman, Antoine, and Léo A. Brodeur. "Dickens, Charles." In their *Répertoire des thèses littéraires canadiennes de 1921 à 1976.* Collection "Bibliographies," 3. Sherbrooke, Québec: Éditions Naaman, 1978, p. 134.

Lists seventeen M.A. and Ph.D. theses on Dickens (nos. 2578-94). Also see no. 1645 for an eighteenth.

1205. *Nihon hakushiroku.* Tokyo, 1955- , passim.

Wortman (**1162**), p. 158, indicates that this is an annual "compilation of titles and abstracts of Japanese dissertations."

1206. Reynolds, Michael M. *A Guide to Theses and Dissertations: An Annotated Bibliography of Bibliographies.* Detroit: Gale, 1975, passim; revised and enlarged as *Guide to Theses and Dissertations: An International Bibliography of Bibliographies.* Phoenix, AZ: Oryx, 1985, passim.

A useful annotated bibliography of bibliographies of theses and dissertations; see particularly Section B: National and Section I [letter not number]: Languages and Literature. Harner (**1147**), pp. 65-66, indicates that this guide is "the essential, time-saving source for identifying both the well-known and the obscure indexes, bibliographies, and abstracts that must be searched for theses and dissertations relevant to a topic."

1207. Silvey, H[erbert] M., ed. "English and Literature." *Master's Theses in the Arts and Social Sciences, 1976[-1990]*, no. 1[-no. 14]. Cedar Falls, IA: Research Publications, 1977-90, passim; continued as *Master's Theses Directories: The Arts and Social Sciences, no. 15, 1991[-no. 16, 1992]*. Cedar Rapids, IA: Master's Theses Directories, 1991-92, passim; then as *Master's Theses Directories: Education*, no. 40, 1991[-no. 41, 1992]. Ibid., 1991-92, passim; then as *Master's Theses Directories*. Ibid., 1993- , passim.

An unannotated listing of theses. Unfortunately, those concerning Dickens must be culled from the "English and Literature section" in each volume.

1208. *Union List of Higher Degree Theses in Australian University Libraries: Cumulative Edition to 1965*. Hobart: University of Tasmania Library, 1967, passim; supplemented by *Union List of Higher Degree Theses in Australian University Libraries: Supplement, 1966-1968[-1989]*. Hobart: University of Tasmania Library, 1971-91, passim.

Lists a total of four master's theses on Dickens in the two volumes. Harner (**1147**), p. 69-70, reports that supplements were published irregularly.

1209. U. S. Library of Congress. Catalog Division. *A List of American Doctoral Dissertations Printed in 1912[-1938]*. Ed. Charles A. Flagg [et al.]. Washington, D. C.: U. S. Government Printing Office, 1913-40, passim.

Check the subject index for dissertations on Dickens. Lists only dissertations received in the Catalog Division of the Library of Congress.

1210. Vitoux, Pierre. "Catalogue des thèses, en cours, soutenues, inscrites." *Cahiers victoriens et edouardiens*, no. 49 (April 1999), 195-214.

A list, sans summaries, of French dissertations, 1991-97, with occasional Dickens items.

Book Reviews

Note: The standard bibliographies of reviews are included below, and they can provide a starting point for collecting reviews of a particular work, but they are all annoyingly selective in the journals covered. For compiling a more comprehensive list, the scholar might better use the Dickens Bibliographies series (**12, 13**); quarterly *Dickens Studies Newsletter* and *Dickens Studies* bibliographies (**1037**), and the cumulation by Cohn and Collins for 1970-79 (**958**); the annual

Victorian Studies bibliographies (**1058**) and their cumulations (**978, 1022, 1025-26, 1033**); and the MHRA annual bibliographies (**1039**). All of these list reviews of full-length studies of Dickens with greater thoroughness. All but the last also list reviews of editions of Dickens's works. Also see **Book reviews, bibliographies** in part 2 of the subject index.

1211. *The Book Review Digest.* Minneapolis, MN, and later New York: H. W. Wilson, 1905- , passim.

Includes a summary of each volume listed and excerpts from reviews published in a group of "selected" periodicals. Issued monthly and cumulated annually, by various editors. The latest volume seen, for 2001 (March 2001-February 2002) includes reviews from eighty-six journals and has a subject index, title index, and all of three Dickens entries. Also see *Author/Title Index, 1905-1975* (4 vols., New York: H. W. Wilson, 1976); *1975-84* (ibid., 1986); and *1985-1994* (ibid., 1995). Also available on CD-ROM and online (OCLC and Wilson, 1983-) in subscribing libraries.

1212. deVaux, Paula (1976-79), deVaux and Patricia A. Bishop (1980), and Bishop (1981-82), eds. *Current Book Review Citations, 1976[-82].* New York: H. W. Wilson, 1977-83, passim.

Minimal information is provided in author and title indexes, but the editors do include the principal scholarly journals. They list, for example, seven reviews (out of thirteen noted below in section 7B) of DeVries's *Dickens's Apprentice Years* (**2499**).

1213. Farber, Evan I., et al., eds. *Combined Retrospective Index to Book Reviews in Scholarly Journals, 1886-1974.* 15 volumes. Arlington, VA: Carrollton, 1979-82, passim.

Less general than its title suggests, and therefore less valuable to Dickens scholars, this index only lists reviews published in "459 scholarly journals in History, Political Science and Sociology,"

1214. Farber, Evan I., Janice Budeit, and Stanley Schindler, eds. *Combined Retrospective Index to Book Reviews in Humanities Journals, 1802-1974.* 10 vols. Woodbridge, CT, and Reading, Eng.: Research Publications, 1983-84, III, 392-94.

Volumes 1-9 comprise the author index, volume 10 the title index. The list of reviews of Dickens's works is very selective, obviously, given the limits set by the title. For reviews of Dickens studies one will need to know the author or title.

1215. *An Index to Book Reviews in the Humanities, [1961-90].* Detroit (1961-64) and Williamston (1965-91), MI: Phillip Thompson, 1961-91, passim.

A check of several Dickens titles reveals that this index lists some but by no means all of the reviews of the books.

1216. *Internationale Bibliographie der Zeitschriftenliteratur, Abteilung C: Bibliographie der Rezensionen [1900-1943].* 77 vols. Osnabrück, Ger.: Dietrich, 1901-44, passim; continued as *Internationale Bibliographie der Rezensionen wissenschaftlicher Literatur/International Bibliography of Book Reviews of Scholarly Literature/Bibliographie internationale des rescensions de la littérature savante.* Osnabrück: Felix Dietrich, 1971- , passim. Also available on CD-ROM from 1995 on.

For reviews of book-length studies of Dickens and his works, see under Dickens in the "Index Rerum" (classified subject index of book reviews). For more details, see Harner **(1147)**, pp. 62-63. Also see Dietrich **(1044)**.

1217. *The New York Times Book Review Index, 1896-1970.* 5 vols. New York: Arno Press, 1973, passim.

Contains author, title, byline, subject, and category indexes, one per volume, of reviews published in the *New York Times.* For reviews of Dickens's works, including letters, see I, 324; for reviews of Dickens studies, see IV, 307-08. For post-1970 reviews, see *The New York Times Index* **(1169)**.

1218. Oggel, L. Terry, and Rosalie Hewitt [et al.], eds. *Index to Reviews of Bibliographical Publications: An International Annual.* Vol. 1: *1976-*Vol. 10: *1985.* Troy, NY: Whitston, 1978-91, passim.

The editors vary over the ten volumes. They pick up some reviews of books about Dickens but by no means all. They list, for example, only three of at least thirteen reviews of Churchill's *A Bibliography of Dickensian Criticism, 1836-1975* **(956)**.

1219. Tarbert, Gary C., and Barbara Beach, eds. *Book Review Index: A Master Cumulation, 1965-1984.* 10 vols. Detroit: Gale Research, 1985, passim; cumulated annually thereafter, with varying editors. Also available on CD-ROM and online at libraries.

The briefest of listings for each review. See under Dickens for reviews of editions of his writings, including letters, in a mixture of 450-500 general and scholarly periodicals. Volumes 1-7 comprise the author index, volumes 8-10 the title index. The volumes for 2001 and 2002 were edited by Dana Ferguson.

1220. *Times Literary Supplement Index, 1902-1939.* 2 vols. Reading, Eng.:Newspaper Archive Developments, 1978, I, 416-17; *1940-1980.* 3 vols. Reading, Eng.: Research Publications, 1982, I, 704-06; *1981-1985.* Reading, Eng., and Woodbridge, CT: Research Publications, 1986, p. 97, and annually thereafter.

Contains an unannotated list of reviews of Dickens's works and of Dickens studies, bibliographical notes, and reports on auction sales published in the weekly issues of *Times Literary Supplement.* The index is published annually as well, to the present date.

Web Sites

Note: The Web sites listed below and elsewhere in this bibliography seem to be some of the more substantial–and relatively more endurable–of the lot, though the choice of sites and the value attributed to them represent one person's point of view. Web sites are notoriously ephemeral, and the reader should not expect to find all of them where indicated. The ones in this section have been included largely because they provide links to a number of other, perhaps equally valuable, sites, and, in this regard, operate very much as secondary bibliographies. For others, see **Web sites concerning Dickens** in part 2 of the subject index. Two Web sites that do not belong in this section, and will be annotated in volume 4 of *DeVries*, will be useful to Dickens students and scholars in search of texts of Dickens's works. The first is The Online Books Page Web site, University of Pennsylvania (http://digital.library.upenn.edu/books or http://onlinebooks.library.upenn.edu). It provides access to over 18,000 books, as indicated on its home page, from a variety of sources, principally Project Gutenberg, the second Web site, at http://promo.net/pg. The latter is the Internet's "oldest producer of FREE electronic books," as its home page announces, a total of 6,267 as of 27 January 2003. These include seventy Dickens texts that one may download, including Dickens's major and many minor works, as well as speeches and miscellaneous papers and several studies of Dickens now out of copyright. On both sites one may search by author, title, subject, and a small variety of other ways. An author search on 28 January 2003 in the Online Books Page, produced fifty seven Dickens items, with sometimes more than one source available for text.

A philosophically-oriented reader may want to look at the conflicting views about the value of using electronic tools in scholarly editing and textual scholarship in P. Aaron Potter's "Centripetal Textuality" and Jerome McCann's response, "Textual Scholarship, Textual Theory, and the Uses of Electronic Tools: A Brief Report on Current Undertakings," in *Victorian Studies*, 41 (1997/98), 593-607 and 609-19.

1221. The Active Portal Project. University of Wisconsin, Madison, WI. http://www.active-portal.com/dickens.

Provides access to "7200 links to pages found on 467 sites" concerning Dickens (as of 7 September 2003), with listings "ranked according to an estimate of their quality and popularity."

1222. Carlo Dickens: A Site Devoted to Dickens Studies in Italy Web site. Università degli Studi di Milano, Dipartimento di Scienza del Linguaggio e Letterature Straniere Comparate–Sezione di Anglistica. http://users.unimi.it/dickens/dickens.htm.

To some extent a site still under development, as it occasionally acknowledges. Clicking on "Essays" produces a list of ten or so essays in English by Italian scholars, essays on *Pictures from Italy,* or studies of translations (principally into Italian) of Dickens's works, the last including, as of 7 September 2003, Anny Sadrin's "The Tyranny of Words: Reading Dickens in Translation" (**621**) and Francesco M. Casotti's "Italian Translations of Dickens" (**562**). Clicking on "Dissertations" produces one work, Maria G. Rinieri's "A Child's History of England di Charles Dickens" (Università degli Studi di Milano, 2000/01). From the abstract provided by Rinieri the study does not seem to be textual or bibliographical in nature, but the author includes in the abstract a short bibliography of critical studies of *A Child's History of England* international in scope.

1223. Charles Dickens Web site. Ed. Ritva Raesmaa, University of Finland, Helsinki. http://www.helsinki.fi/kasv/nokol/dickens.html.

Provides web links to numerous Dickens sites under the headings of Dickens's Works, Dickens's Life and Family, and Dickens's London.

1224. Concordances of Great Books Web site. William A. Williams, Jr., webmaster. http://www.concordance.com; replaced by Alex Catalogue of Electronic Texts. Conducted by Eric Lease Morgan. South Bend, IN. http://www.infomations.com/alex.

The Dickens portion of the incredible Web site Concordances of Great Books, unfortunately no longer available since the death of Williams in 2003, contained the texts of fifty-five works, many from the Project Gutenberg and The Online Books Page Web sites (see note, above, to this section), links to both of which were provided. This site has since been at least partially replaced by Alex Catalogue of Electronic Texts, which is described on its home page as "a collection of public domain documents from American and English literature as well as Western philosophy." One searches for documents by author, title, or date. As of 7 September 2003, the user can display the text of twenty Dickens works—*American Notes, A Child's History of England, David Copperfield, Dombey and Son, Hard Times, The Mystery of Edwin Drood, The Old Curiosity Shop, Oliver Twist, Pickwick Papers, Pictures from Italy, A Tale of Two Cities,* the five Christmas Books, "A Holiday Romance," "Hunted Down," *Master Humphrey's Clock,* and *Speeches: Literary and Social* (**43**). It is hoped, obviously, that Mr. Morgan will continue to add Dickens texts to his Web site. One may display text and search for words within the text of a single document. One may also create an e-book in Adobe Reader (with some choice of font, font size, and other parameters) and download that to a file folder on one's computer, though a version of Adobe Reader must be on the computer if one wants to read what has been downloaded.

1225. David Perdue's Charles Dickens Page: Dedicated to Bringing the Genius of Dickens to a New Generation of Readers Web site. Ed. David Perdue. http://www.fidnet.com/~dap1995/dickens/index.html.

A section of this Web site entitled "Dickens on the Web" lists a goodly number of useful Web sites under the general headings of Dickens Societies and Organizations, Dickens Scholarly Pages, Places (such as Dickens museums), Performances (of dramatizations of Dickens's works), Books and E-Texts, Dickens Web-Based Activities, and Other Good Dickens Resources. In addition, this site contains a brief biographical sketch of Dickens; brief discussions of his novels in general and individually (with links to other sites as well); an alphabetical list of his characters (with short descriptions); comments on Dickens's original illustrators; a "Timeline," or chronology, of Dickens's life and works; a commentary on Dickens's London, and a map of it; and pieces on Dickens and Christmas, his family and friends, and Dickens in America. Colorfully and effectively illustrated.

1226. The Dickens Fellowship Web site. The Dickens Fellowship, London. http://www.dickensfellowship.btinternet.co.uk.

This useful Web site provides a brief biographical sketch of Dickens in chronology format, descriptions of his fiction and journalism, information about the Dickens Fellowship, and web links to branches of the Fellowship, the Dickens House Museum (**1457**), Gadshill Place (a commercial site), the Charles Dickens Birthplace Museum in Portsmouth (**1580**), the Dickens site of the Active Portal Project of the University of Wisconsin (**1221**), Mitsuharu Matsuoka's The Dickens Page (**1227**), Ritva Raesmaa's Dickens Page in Finland (**1223**), David Perdue's Charles Dickens Page (**1225**), and William A. Williams, Jr.'s Dickens Concordance (**1224**) [now inoperative]. The Web sites for the branches of the fellowship are often useful, with links of their own, as well as colorful photographs and illustrations and information about Dickens's life, works, and world.

1227. The Dickens Page Web site. Ed. Mitsuharu Matsuoka, Nagoya University, Nagoya, Japan. http://www.lang.nagoya-u.ac.jp/~matsuoka/Dickens.html.

An incredibly full Web site, with links to numerous other sites and discussion groups: Index of the Dickens Page, Dickens Fellowship (and the Japan Branch), Dickens Society, Mailing Lists, Dickens Home Pages, Life and Works (a long essay by Alan Shelston), Chronology, Bibliography (lists 445 full-length studies, 1870-2000; some recent editions of Dickens's works; and links to a number of booksellers), Works & E-texts, Conferences, Academic Resources, Recreational Resources, Miscellany, Dickens Discussion Board, The Carol Discussion, the text of *Forster*, George Gissing's *The Immortal Dickens: A Critical Study*, G. K. Chesterton's *Dickens: Appreciations and Criticisms*,

Dickens Family Tree, Dickens Gadshill Appeal, and Dickens Humour. There is also a link to a concordance of twenty Dickens works (**1224**), a Dickens filmography (**697**), and "What's New," a long, eclectic list of other Dickens links. For a quite lengthy list of links to more general Victorian sites, see http://lang.nagoya-u.ac.jp/~matsuoka/Victorian.html. For additional Dickens sites, click on the Nineteenth Century Authors button at this site or go directly to http://lang.nagoya-u.ac.jp/~matsuoka/19th-authors.html.

1228. The Dickens Project Web site. University of California, Santa Cruz, CA. http://humwww.ucsc.edu/dickens.

This valuable Web site identifies itself as "a scholarly consortium devoted to promoting the study and enjoyment of the life, times, and work of Charles Dickens," centered at the Santa Cruz campus of the University of California. The home page provides access to information about the Dickens Project's conferences, publications, members, and fellowships and a brief life of Dickens by Sara Hackenberg and Ryan Johnson. Other links on the home page are of some bibliographical and textual interest. "Other On-line Dickens Resources" lists and evaluates a number of other major and minor Dickens and Victorian Web sites, with links to them. "*Our Mutual Friend:* The Scholarly Pages," edited by Jon M. Varese, contains the text, articles about, and a selected bibliography (no compiler given) of the novel, including editions published in Dickens's lifetime, six "classic" studies, a "Comprehensive Bibliography of Recent Criticism (1988-1998)," and six film and television adaptations (1911-1998). In addition to providing access to a number of resources for teaching and study of Dickens and his works, "The Dickens Electronic Archive" (http://hum.ucsc.edu/dickens/DEA/DEA.index.html) contains selective bibliographies of criticism of *Barnaby Rudge* (by Joss Marsh and John Bowen), *Bleak House* (by Robert Newsom), *Little Dorrit* (by Hillary T. May), *Nicholas Nickleby* (by Hesper Wilson), *Oliver Twist* (by Jon M. Varese), *Our Mutual Friend* (links to the selected bibliography in *Our Mutual Friend:* The Scholarly Pages, above), *Pickwick Papers* (Hillary T. May), and Dickens Filmography (no author given). Newsom's bibliography for *Bleak House* is actually three bibliographies–1) his unannotated list of studies of *Bleak House*, 2) an annotated, evaluative survey of general bibliographies and reference sources, primary sources (letters, public reading versions, etc.), biographies, background studies, general Dickens criticism and studies of his illustrators, and 3) electronic resources, slightly adapted, as he indicates, from the bibliography in his *Charles Dickens Revisited* (**1011**); and a useful selective bibliography of studies of *Bleak House* prepared for the Dickens project by Kelly Hager in 1988. "Dickens Searchworks" (at http://humwww.ucsc.edu/dickens/searchworks/searchworksindex.html) contains the full text of *Bleak House*, which may be searched for the occurrence of specific words and phrases.

Review: N. A. Metz, *Dickens Quarterly*, 18 (2001), 153-56 (finds *"Our Mutual Friend*: The Scholarly Pages" useful, easy and quick of access, "visually appealing," scholarly sound, and a "rich" resource).

1229. Guida, Fred. A Christmas Carol and Its Adaptations Web site. http://www.dickensachristmascarol.com.

Although intended in large part as publicity for this and other works by Guida (it prints the foreword, introduction, and table of contents from the work as well as excerpts from reviews of it and contains icons for ordering the work), this illustrated site also provides links to other major and a few minor Dickens Web sites.

1230. Lynch, Jack. Literary Resources on the Net Web site. English Dept., Rutgers University, Newark. http://www.andromeda.rutgers.edu/~jlynch/Lit.

As announced on its home page, a "collection of links to sites on the Internet dealing especially with English and American Literature." One clicks on "Victorian British" to get to the page "Literary Resources–Victorian British," where one will find links to ninety or more major (and some minor) Victorian Web sites, including four Dickens sites. Many of the links to more general Victorian sites will contain links to still other Dickens sites.

1231. New Books in Nineteenth-Century British Studies Web site. Ed. Kirsten L. Parkinson, Dept. of English, University of Southern California, Los Angeles, CA. http://www.usc.edu/dept/LAS/english/19c/newbooks.html.

Announces on its home page that it "offers complete publication information for scholarly works on the British Romantic and Victorian periods." This site lists works alphabetically by author and by title published in individual years, from 1995 on, as well as works to be published. A "search engine" button is available to allow one to "search the full text of the book listings and reviews" by "author, title words, subject, key words, publisher name, and publication year." A search for "Dickens" on 7 March 2003 produced ninety-five entries. Selecting an individual entry produces full bibliographical information and a brief publisher's description of the work. Reviews are given for some of the works. This Web site also provides a number of links to other nineteenth-century web resources.

1232. NVSA: The Northeast Victorian Studies Association Web site. Ed. Glenn Everett, Dept. of English, University of Tennessee, Martin, TN. http://fmc.utm.edu/nvsa/index.htm.

Provides a variety of information about the Northeast Victorian Studies Association and its annual conferences and awards, as well as a useful list of Victorian Web sites (http://fmc.utm.edu/nvsa/nvsaweb.htm), which Everett believes may be "the most complete list of interdisciplinary Victorian resources on the Web." Included are the major Victorian Web sites, sites for numerous Victorian authors, including Dickens, and a small number of discussions "archived from electronic conference lists."

1233. Victorian Research Web: Scholarly Resources for Victorian Research Web site. Ed. Patrick Leary, History Department, Indiana University, Bloomington. http://www.indiana.edu/~victoria.

This important Web site announces itself as "a collection of resources" dedicated to "the scholarly study of nineteenth-century Britain and to aiding researchers, teachers, and students in their investigations of any and all aspects of this fascinating period." According to The Dickens Project (**1228**), it is "a source for research guides, journals in Victorian studies, on-line discussion groups in various areas of interest, teaching syllabi, and–of course–more links to other on-line resources." This site contains the VICTORIA archives, a search engine giving access to "over eight years' worth of scholarly discussion by Victorianists around the world." The site also offers valuable sections on 1) "Archives: Locating Manuscript Material," a bibliographical discussion and evaluation of a variety of manuscript source materials and a descriptive list of thirty-three libraries with Victorian archives, all with numerous links to other Web sites; 2) "Libraries and Bibliographies: Finding Printed Materials," a discussion and evaluation of a variety of research guides, with links to library catalogues; 3) "Planning the Research Trip: Tips for Working in Britain," a very practical, useful section with links to numerous travel guides, places to stay, Internet and computer access, and "Fun Stuff" (theaters, museums, etc.); 4) "Journals," a list of links to journals on Victorian subjects; 5) "Discussion Groups," a list of links to VICTORIA as well as to a number of smaller sites devoted to individual authors and subjects; 6) "Teaching Resources," a list of links to nearly 100 syllabi of courses at a number of colleges and universities; and 7) "Other Victorian Resources," an evaluation of and links to a number of other sources, including major and minor Web sites.

1234. Victorian Studies on the Web Web site. Ed. Brahma Chaudhuri and Fred Radford, University of Alberta. http://www.victoriandatabase.com.

Correctly describes itself as an "indispensable source of information on every important publication from 1945 to [date] on every field of Victorian studies." This is the home of the LITIR (Literary Information and Retrieval) Database of Victorian studies, based at the University of Alberta, and currently edited by Brahma Chaudhuri, its founder, and Fred Radford. A variety of printed versions have been published (**954, 1036**) and a CD-ROM version is also available, but the online database is more current than these. Libraries may subscribe to the online version, but individuals as well as libraries may register online for a free, one-month trial period. Perhaps not as well known as other Victorian bibliographies, this is more selective than it claims to be (though no more or less selective than the others), but it is prone to typographical and other errors. This Web site also contains a section entitled "What's New," which lists recent and forthcoming books; lists of articles in recent issues of a number of journals on Victorian subjects, including the *Dickens Quarterly*, *Dickens Studies Annual*, and the *Dickensian*, as well as *Notes and Queries*; a variety of "Announcements & Queries"; and "Victoriana on the Web," a short list of links to other major Victorian Web sites.

1235. The Victorian Web Web site. Ed. George P. Landow, Brown University. http://www.victorianweb.org.

A rich site, funded by the University Scholars Programme, National University of Singapore, that offers a variety of information on Victorian matters. According to The Dickens Project (**1228**), it is "similar in scope" to Indiana University's Victorian Research Web (**1233**) "but very different in style and content," and offering "a remarkably comprehensive catalog of Victoriana," including information on twenty topics, such as religion, philosophy, politics, social history, science, art, economics, literature, bibliography (on various Victorian topics), and "Related WWW Resources" (providing links to a long list of Victorian Web sites). For Dickens, click on "Authors" and then "Charles Dickens" or go directly to http://www.victorianweb.org/dickens/dickensov.html. This will produce a variety of sections on Dickens: Biography, Works, Economic Contexts, Political History, Social History, Religion, Science, Genre & Mode, Literary Relations, Visual Arts, Themes, Characterization, Imagery, Narrative, Bibliography, and Related WWW Resources. Clicking on any of these will produce a variety of additional material in the form of articles, chapters from books, and bibliographical lists (many prepared specifically for this Web site) by a variety of authors—students as well as Dickens scholars. Under "Works," one has access to the texts of some of Dickens's works; "overviews" of most, some of which include selected bibliographies; "Bibliography for Dickens's Short Fiction (1833-1868), Including *Sketches by Boz*, Stories from the Christmas Numbers of *Household Words*, and *All the Year Round*, and *A Holiday Romance*," by Philip V. Allingham, a list of studies of Dickens's short fiction; a list of collected editions of Dickens's works, 1847-1990, also by Allingham; and a chronology of the appearance of Dickens's novels in parts, from E. D. H. Johnson's *Charles Dickens: An Introduction to His Novels* (New York: Random House, 1969). Under "Bibliography," one has access to Johnson's "Bibliographical Note" from his volume; "Major Biographies of Dickens—A Critical Overview," by Allingham, a detailed comparison and evaluation of the four major biographies; Allingham's "Bibliography for Dickens's Short Fiction," above; "Great Expectations: Dickens's Treatment of Childhood, and the Child Voice," by M. Bernadette Vergara, a list of studies;"Crime in Victorian Britain: Suggested Readings," by Suzanne Hader; "Charles Dickens's *Hard Times*: Bibliography of Suggested Readings," by Allingham; "Names in Dickens: Scholarly Articles on Dickens and Onomastics," by Glen

Downey;"Great Expectations and Narration," by John Mejia, a list of studies; "Fiction and the Autobiographical Voice: Great Expectations and Charles Dickens," by Judy Rosen, a list of studies; and "*Great Expectations* and Familial Relations," by Amy Larocca, a list of studies; and links to Fred Guida's *Christmas Carol* site (**1229**) and The Dickens Project (**1228**).

1236. Voice of the Shuttle Web site. Ed. Alan Liu et al. English Department, University of California, Santa Barbara. http://vos.ucsb.edu.

An incredible humanities Web site, the Victorian Literature section of which (http://vos.ucsb.edu/browse.asp?id=2751), offers an enormous number of links to Victorian literature in general as well as to a large number of individual authors, among them Charles Dickens. The Dickens links are not numerous, however. They include links to the texts of eight of the novels, to the Dickens Project (**1228**), the Dickens Page (**1227**), and a couple of minor items.

Biography

Note: Also see Stievater (**1356**) and **Biographical studies of Dickens, bibliographies** and **Biographies of Dickens, bibliographies** in part 2 of the subject index.

1237. American Library Association. "Dickens, Charles, 1812-1870." In *A. L. A. Portrait Index: Index to Portraits Contained in Printed Books and Periodicals*. Ed. William C. Lane and Nina E. Browne. Washington, D. C.: Government Printing Office, 1906, p. 413; reprinted in Burt Franklin: Bibliography and Reference Series, 68. 3 vols. New York: Burt Franklin, [1967], I, 413.

Lists a number of magazines and books containing portraits of Dickens and three of his children published 1842-1904.

1238. Bank, David, and Anthony Esposito, eds. *British Biographical Index*. 4 vols. London, Melbourne, Munich, and New York: K. G. Saur, 1990, II, 535; also Bank, David, and Theresa McDonald, eds. *British Biographical Index/Britischer Biographischer Index*. 2nd cumulated and enlarged ed. 5 vols. München: K. G. Saur, 1998, II, 900.

The first edition lists twenty biographical reference works with Dickens entries. Also see other members of the Dickens family, II, 535. All entries, the editors note, are included in the *British Biographical Archive* (1984-89), "a compilation of 324 biographical reference works originally printed between 1601 and 1929, reproduced in a single alphabetical sequence on 1,236 microfiche." Also see *Series 2: A Supplementary Series Gathered from 268 Sources, Complementing the Materials Published in the First Series, and Extending the Coverage to 1960*. London, 1991- , whose references are included in the second edition, which contains twenty-two Dickens entries.

1239. Batts, John S. *British Manuscript Diaries of the Nineteenth Century: An Anno tated Listing.* Fontwell, Eng.: Centaur Press; Totowa, NJ: Rowman and Littlefield, 1976, pp. 78, 217, 225, 233.

Lists Dickens's own diary for January-December 1867 in the Berg Collection, New York Public Library, but also three other diaries with references to Dickens–those of Sophia Lockhart, wife of the critic John Gibson Lockhart (for 1823-53); Thomas Miller, a poet and novelist (for January-September 1861); and Charles William Shirley Brooks, editor of *Punch* (for 1864, 1865-73).

1240. Bell, Peter, comp. "Dickens, Charles (John Huffam), 1812-70, Major Novelist." In his *Victorian Biography: A Checklist of Contemporary Biographies of British Men & Women Dying between 1851 and 1901.* Edinburgh: Peter Bell, 1993, pp. 40-41.

The Dickens scholar may skip this one; it lists only four works–and with some inaccuracies.

1241. *Bibliography of Biography, 1970-1984.* London: British Library Bibliographic Services, 1985, passim.

Check under Dickens in both the bibliography proper and in the "Author/Title Sequence" for biographical studies of Dickens.

1242. *Biographical Books, 1876-1949.* New York and London: R. R. Bowker, 1983, pp. 384-86.

Lists sixty-six biographies and biographical studies of Dickens.

1243. *Biographical Books, 1950-1980.* New York and London: R. R. Bowker, 1980, pp. 325-28.

Lists 101 biographies and biographical studies of Dickens, many of them reprints of earlier works.

1244. Cimbala, Diane J., Jennifer Cargill, and Brian Alley. *Biographical Sources: A Guide to Dictionaries and Reference Works.* Phoenix, AZ: Oryx Press, 1986, passim.

In a section on "Writers," pp. 64-84, the authors list 128 works, a number of which should include brief biographical sketches of Dickens. Also see "General Sources," pp. 1-25.

1245. Herbert, Miranda C., and Barbara McNeil. *Biography and Genealogy Master Index: A Consolidated Index to More than 3,200,000 Biographical Sketches in* *over 350 Current and Retrospective Biographical Dictionaries.* 2nd ed. 8 vols. Gale Biographical Index Series, 1. Detroit: Gale Research, 1980, II, 525.

The title is sufficiently descriptive, and Dickens is one of the persons for whom biographical sketches are listed. The original edition was published in 1975-76 as *Biographical Dictionaries Master Index* by Gale Research. The second edition was followed by two five-year cumulations, *1981-85 Cumulation* (5 volumes, 1985) and *1986-90 Cumulation* (3 volumes, 1990) and one-year, one-volume cumulations thereafter, through 2000. The volumes through 1995 were edited by Barbara McNeil, thereafter by Jennifer Mossman (1996 and 1997 editions), Geri Speace (1998 and 1999 editions), and Frank V. Castronova (2000 edition). *Author Biographies Master Index.* edited by Dennis La Beau (**1249**), and, in later editions, by Barbara McNeil and others (**1250**), is, according to Harner (**1147**), p. 79, a clone of this work. Harner also notes that the second edition has been published in microfiche as *Bio-base* and that entries are available on CD-ROM, and online at http://galenet.gale.com/a/acp/db/bgmi through subscribing libraries.

1246. *International Bibliography of Biography, 1970 to 1987.* 12 vols. London, Munich, New York, and Paris: K. G. Saur, 1988, II, 85-88; VII, 291-92.

Lists 118 books with biographical information about Dickens published 1970-87, many of them reprints of earlier biographies and biographical studies.

1247. Joseph, Bea, and Charlotte W. Squires [et al.], eds. "Dickens, Charles, 1812-1870." In their *Biography Index: A Cumulative Index to Biographical Materials in Books and Magazines, January 1946-July 1949[-].* New York: H. W. Wilson, 1949- , passim.

Lists biographical studies of Dickens. *Biography Index* is published quarterly and in, first, three-year, then two-year, and, since 1992, one-year cumulations. For further details, see Harner (**1147**), pp. 76-77, who notes that since July 1984 entries can be searched online and on CD-ROM.

1248. Kitton, Frederic G. "Catalogue of the Portraits of Charles Dickens." In his *A Supplement to Charles Dickens by Pen and Pencil, Including Anecdotes and Reminiscences Collected from His Friends and Contemporaries.* 5 parts. London: Frank T. Sabin, 1889-90; collected as part of *Charles Dickens by Pen and Pencil and A Supplement to Charles Dickens by Pen and Pencil.* 2 vols. London: Frank T. Sabin, 1890, pp. i-xvi.

Lists drawings and sketches, miniatures, oil paintings, sculptures, daguerreotypes and photographs, and various other portraits and "assumed" portraits of Dickens and provides a variety of information about them.

1249. La Beau, Dennis, ed. *Author Biographies: Master Index: A Consolidated Guide to Biographical Information Concerning Authors Living or Dead as It Appears in a Selection of the Principal Biographical Dictionaries Devoted to Authors, Poets, Journalists, and Other Literary Figures.* 2 vols. Gale Biographical Index Series, 3. Detroit, MI: Gale Research, 1978, I, 281. Also see

The title tells all. La Beau includes forty entries for Dickens and four for his son Charles. Also see Herbert and McNeil (**1245**) and McNeil (**1250**).

1250. McNeil, Barbara, ed. *Author Biographies Master Index: A Consolidated Index to More than 1,030,000 Biographical Sketches Concerning Authors Living and Dead as They Appear in a Selection of the Principal Biographical Dictionaries Devoted to Authors, Poets, Journalists, and Other Literary Figures.* 4th ed. 2 vols. Detroit, etc.: Gale Research, 1994, I, 396.

Based on Herbert and McNeil (**1245**), lists some sixty-five dictionaries containing entries on Dickens. Also see listings for other members of the Dickens family and successors. A fifth edition, edited by Geri Speace, was published in two volumes in 1997 (Gale Biography Index Series, 3, Detroit, etc.: Gale). The Dickens entries are in volume 1, p. 248. Also see LaBeau (**1249**).

1251. Riches, Phyllis M., comp. "Dickens (Charles) 1812-1870, Novelist." In her *An Analytical Bibliography of Universal Collected Biography, Comprising Books Published in the English Tongue in Great Britain and Ireland, America and the British Dominions.* London: The Library Association, 1934; reprinted Detroit: Gale Research, 1980, p. 147.

A more selective list than the title indicates of sixty-nine books containing biographical sketches of Dickens, most little known and ephemeral. Some of the studies listed are predominantly critical rather than biographical, though often superficially so.

1252. Serafin, Steven. "Checklist for Further Reading." In *American Literary Biographers: First Series.* Ed. Steven Serafin. Dictionary of Literary Biography, 103. Detroit, MI, and London: Gale Research, 1991, pp. 320-24; reprinted with variations as "Books for Further Reading." In *American Literary Biographers: Second Series.* Ed. Steven Serafin. Dictionary of Literary Biography, 111. Ibid., 1991, pp. 319-24; as "Checklist of Further Readings." In *Nineteenth-Century British Literary Biographers.* Ed. Steven Serafin. Dictionary of Literary Biography, 144. Ibid., 1994, pp. 317-22; as "Checklist of Further Readings." In *Late Nineteenth and Early Twentieth-Century British Literary Biographers.* Ed. Steven Serafin. Dictionary of Literary Biography, 149. Ibid., 1995, pp. 295-300; as "Checklist of Further Readings." In *Twentieth-Century British Literary Biographers.*

Ed. Steven Serafin. Dictionary of Literary Biography, 155. Ibid., 1995, pp. 339-44.

An unannotated list of studies of biography and biographers. For studies of Dickens biographers included in these volumes, see Murray Baumgarten on Fred Kaplan, in 111, pp. 97-104; Charles Calder on Hugh Kingsmill, in 149, pp. 109-15; Ian Duncan on Edgar Johnson, in 103, pp. 168-74; John J. Fenstermaker on John Forster, in 144, pp. 75-86; Glen M. Johnson on Peter Ackroyd, in 155, pp. 3-12; W. P. Kenney on G. K. Chesterton, in 149, pp. 36-48, and on Julian Symons, in 155, pp. 296-304; James King on Claire Tomalin, in 155, pp. 305-09; and Valerie G. Myer on Angus Wilson, in 155, pp. 328-33.

1253. Slocum, Robert, ed. *Biographical Dictionaries and Related Works: An International Bibliography of More than 16,000 Collective Biographies, Bio-Bibliographies, Collections of Epitaphs, Selected Genealogical Works, Dictionaries of Anonyms and Pseudonyms, Historical and Specialized Dictionaries, Biographical Materials in Government Manuals, Bibliographies of Biography, Biographical Indexes, and Selected Portrait Catalogs.* 2nd ed. 2 vols. Detroit, MI: Gale Research, 1986, passim.

A wide-ranging bibliography of briefly-annotated entries. Persons covered in these works are not identified, however. The best chance of finding works that include Dickens will be in the sections on "National or Area Biography: Great Britain," I, 252-85, and "Biography by Vocation: The Arts: Language and Literature," II, 758-72, 801-10. The original edition was also published by Gale Research (Detroit, 1967), with two supplements (1972, 1976).

1254. Wachter, Phyllis. "Bibliography of Works about Life-Writing for 1984[-]." *Biography*, 8 (1985)- , passim.

In the fall issue of each year, Wachter publishes a briefly annotated bibliography of books, articles, and dissertations about autobiographical writings, though there is rarely a specific reference to Dickens. The bibliography in the 1985 volume was three pages long; the latest seen (for 1997-98), fifty-three pages.

Literary Criticism, Theory, Themes

Note: Also see **Critical and appreciative studies of Dickens's works** in part 2 of the subject index.

1255. Accardi, Bernard, et al. *Recent Studies in Myths and Literature, 1970-1990: An Annotated Bibliography.* Bibliographies and Indexes in World Literature, 29. New York, Westport, CT, and London: Greenwood Press, 1991, passim.

The index identifies some nine studies involving Dickens's works.

1256. Baer, Florence E. *Folklore and Literature of the British Isles: An Annotated Bibliography.* Garland Reference Library of the Humanities, 622; Garland Folklore Bibliographies, 11. New York and London: Garland Publishing, 1986, passim.

Contains a number of references to Dickens. See the General Index.

1257. Baker, William, and Kenneth Womack, comps. *Recent Work in Critical Theory, 1989 1995: An Annotated Bibliography.* Bibliographies and Indexes in World Literature, 51. Westport, CT, and London: Greenwood Press, 1996, passim.

Contains a number of studies about Dickens. See the subject index, p. 536.

1258. Bullock, Chris, and David Peck, comps. "Dickens, Charles." In their *Guide to Marxist Literary Criticism.* Bloomington: Indiana University Press, 1980, pp. 86-87.

An unannotated list of twenty-three items, 1938-78.

1259. Chittick, Kathryn. *The Critical Reception of Charles Dickens, 1833-1841.* New York: Garland Publishing, 1989. xvi + 277 pp.

A most useful volume. The first part contains chronological listings of works that 1) provide an "Overview of English Literature 1814-1841," pp. 1-21, and 2) cover "Reviews of Dickens's Works and Related Topics 1832-1842," pp. 22-87. As Chittick points out in her preface, many of these reviews, particularly those in newspapers, "are often little more than excerpts with a few mindless effusions appended," and others are only brief passing notices, but she rightly includes them because, as she somewhat circumlocutiously explains, "the phenomenon of Dickens's excerptibility becomes a major point of discussion in the reviews of his works." In the second part, pp. 88-150, the reviews are listed under the headings of the individual works, and in part 3 they are listed by periodical, with some additional information for some of the magazines. Part 4 is a bibliography of secondary sources and part 5 a list of the approximately 120 periodicals consulted.

Reviews: J. J. Fenstermaker, *Dickens Quarterly,* 8 (1991), 85-88 (a valuable, "comprehensive survey" of the sources used); L. James, *Dickensian,* 89 (1993), 60-62 (a useful work; readers are indebted to Chittick "not only for the new items she has unearthed but for adding substance to our sense of the way early Dickens permeated English reading matter for the casual reader"); M. B. Lambert, *American Reference Books Annual,* 21 (1990), 499-500 (feels more information is needed about how the volume is formatted but finds the work useful and informative).

1260. Duncan, Joseph E. "Archetypal Criticism in English, 1946-1980." *Bulletin of Bibliography,* 40 (1983), 206-30.

Lists five studies of Dickens, all of specific novels, p. 215.

1261. Ford, George H. "Appendix: Dickens' Awareness of Reviews" and "Bibliography." In his *Dickens and His Readers: Aspects of Novel-Criticism since 1836*. Princeton, NJ: Published for the University of Cincinnati by Princeton University Press; London: Oxford University Press, 1955; reprinted New York: Norton; Toronto: George J. McLeod, 1965 (paperback); New York: Gordian Press, 1974, pp. 263-66, 303-05.

The first is a list of thirty-four reviews and notices of and essays on Dickens's writings to which Dickens made reference principally in his letters, with the source of the reference given. "It is likely," Ford notes, "that his eye fell upon many other notices for which we have no record." The second is a short bibliography divided into three parts: 1) studies of "The Reputation of Novelists and the History of Novel-Criticism," 2) "Studies of Dickens' Reputation," and 3) "Some Victorian Essays on Fiction."

1262. Herget, Winfried, and Udo J. Hebel. "Sentimentality: A Selected Bibliography of Critical Studies." In *Sentimentality in Modern Literature and Popular Culture*. Ed. Winfried Herget. Tübingen, Ger.: Gunter Narr, 1991, pp. 273-312.

Contains a few Dickens items, but the bibliography is a bit too broad in scope and too selective to be of much use to the Dickens student or scholar.

1263. Marshall, Donald G. *Contemporary Critical Theory: A Selective Bibliography*. New York: Modern Language Association of America, 1993, passim.

An unannotated and very selective listing of studies, organized by critical approach. The index lists only four Dickens studies.

1264. [Mony, Robert, et al.]. *Reader's Index to the Twentieth Century Views Literary Criticism Series, Volumes 1-100*. Englewood Cliffs, NJ: Prentice-Hall, 1973, passim.

Provides detailed subject indexes, volume by volume, for the studies in the series (there are no indexes in the volumes themselves). Martin Price's collection of Dickens studies (**1017**) is included, pp. 120-24. Dickens also appears in the indexes for at least forty-eight of the other authors. There is also an "Index to Critics," pp. 641-81.

1265. Newcomb, Mildred. "Bibliographical Essay." In her *The Imagined World of Charles Dickens*. Columbus: Ohio State University Press, 1989, pp. 213-34.

A fully annotated list of twenty-three major studies on the nature of Dickens's imagination. Several of the annotations are over a page long.

1266. Orr, Leonard. *Research in Critical Theory Since 1965: A Classified Bibliography.* Bibliographies and Indexes in World Literature, 21. New York, Westport, CT, and London: Greenwood Press, 1989, passim.

Lists several Dickens studies, but, since the bibliography, which is not annotated, is structured by type of critical theory, Dickens items can be found only by going through the bibliography item by item.

1267. Rajec, Elizabeth M. *The Study of Names in Literature: A Bibliography.* New York: K. G. Saur Publishing, 1978, passim; also *The Study of Names in Literature: A Bibliography: Supplement.* München, New York, London, and Paris: 1981, passim.

Scattered throughout the original volume are twenty works concerned with Dickens's use of names in his works. See the index. The supplement adds eleven more.

1268. von Rosador, Kurt T. "Dickens 1970: 'These Goblin Volumes.'" *Archiv für das Studium der Neueren Sprachen und Literaturen,* 208 (1971/72), 298-309.

Despite its seemingly English title, this review of books and articles on Dickens published in 1970 is in German.

1269. Weiner, Alan R., and Spencer Means. "Dickens, Charles." In their *Literary Criticism Index.* Metuchen, NJ, and London: Scarecrow Press, 1984, p. 158; 2nd ed., 1994, pp. 131-32.

In the first edition, for individual Dickens novels the authors identify which of eighty-six multiple-author bibliographies contain relevant critical studies; in the second edition 146 bibliographies are used.

Comparative Literature

Note: also see **Comparative literature, bibliographies (with studies of Dickens)** in part 2 of the subject index.

1270. Baldensperger, Fernand, and Werner P. Friederich. *Bibliography of Comparative Literature.* Chapel Hill, NC: Studies in Comparative Literature, 1, 1950; reprinted New York: Russell & Russell, 1960, p. 592.

Contains thirty-two Dickens entries, 1867-1947. Continued by Friederich et al. (**1271**).

1271. Friederich, Werner P., et al., and, later, Hugh H. Chapman, Jr., et al., comps. "Bibliography of Comparative Literature, [1949/51-59]." *Yearbook of Comparative and General Literature.* Vols. 1- 9. Chapel Hill: University of North Carolina Studies in Comparative Literature, 1952-60, passim; continued as "Annual Bibliography: 1960[-69]." Ed. Glauco Cambon et al. Vols. 10-12 (for 1960-63). Chapel Hill: University of North Carolina Studies in Comparative Literature, 1961-63, passim; vols. 13-19 (for 1963-69). Bloomington: Published at Indiana University in collaboration with the Comparative Literature Committee for the National Conference of Teachers of English, the American Comparative Literature Association, and the Comparative Literature Section of the Modern Language Association of America, 1964- ; reissued New York: Russell and Russell, 1965-[71?], passim.

An elaborate, multi-headed annual bibliography of comparative literature, including relationships between literature and politics and literature and the arts and sciences, a continuation of Baldensperger and Friederich (**1270**). For Dickens entries, check under his name in "English Contributions: Other English Authors," 1949/51-59, and under "Individual Authors," 1960-69; there is, unfortunately, no index.

Non-English Studies of Dickens

Note: Also see works in section 2A, **Bibliographies and Surveys of Translations of Dickens's Works**, and **Studies of Dickens and his works, non-English bibliographies and surveys** in part 2 of the subject index.

1272. Diakonova, Nina. "Russian Dickens Studies, 1970-1995." *Dickens Quarterly*, 12 (1995), 181-86.

A selective bibliographical survey of Russian critical studies of Dickens and his works.

1273. Gabel, Gernot U., and Gisela R. Gabel. "Dickens, Charles." In their *Catalogue of Austrian and Swiss Dissertations (1875-1995) in English and American Literatures*. Hürth, Ger.: Edition Gemini, 1997, pp. 104-05.

Lists thirteen dissertations. Also see "Nineteenth Century: General," pp. 90-94. Unannotated.

1274. Gummer, Ellis N. "List of German Critical Works on Dickens, 1870-1937," "List of Articles on Dickens in German Periodicals, 1837-1870," "Notes on Some Early German Translators of Dickens' Works," and "General Bibliography." In his *Dickens' Works in Germany, 1837-1937*. Oxford: Clarendon Press; New York: Oxford University Press, 1940; reprinted New York: Octagon Books, 1976, pp. 175-79, 180-84, 185-93, 194-97.

Valuable listings of earlier German criticism and scholarship. Gummer's work, which he notes was originally presented as a thesis for a degree of

Bachelor of Letters at Oxford University, examines the reception of Dickens's novels in Germany and Dickens's influence on several German authors.

1275. Katarsky, I[gor]. [Bibliography]. In his *Dikkens v Rossii: seredina XIX veka.* Moscow: Nauka Press, 1966, pp. 404-07.

Contains a bibliography in Russian of mid-nineteenth-century Russian studies of Dickens's works. See Henry Gifford, "Dickens in Russia," *Forum for Modern Language Studies*, 4 (1968), 45-52, for a study of nineteenth-century Russian criticism based on Katarsky's volume. In a review of Katarsky's study in *Dickensian*, 63 (1967), 120-22, Gifford indicates that Katarsky comments on the influence of early Russian translations of Dickens's works, as well as on critical studies of Dickens in "some forty journals."

Reviews: J.-L. Backes, *Revue de Littérature Comparée*, 45 (1971), 287-89 (in French; generally favorable, though with some qualifications); H. Gifford, *Dickensian*, 63 (1967), 120-22 (an "admirable survey" of the Russian reception of Dickens's works, 1837-61). Also see obituaries for Katarsky in *Dickens Studies Newsletter*, 2 (1971), 99, and in *Dickensian*, 68 (1972), 51-52, both by Mira Perper.

1276. Makowiecki, Stefan, et al., comps. "Dickens, Ch[arles]." In *Bibliografia anglistyki polskiej, 1945-1975/Bibliographies of Writings on English Language and Literature in Poland, 1945-1975.* Ed. Jacek Fisiak. Warsaw: Państwowe Wydawnictwo Naukowe/Polish Scientific Publishers, 1977, pp. 122-24.

Lists twenty-eight studies of Dickens, principally in Polish (though a few are in English), published 1945-75.

1277. Ministère de l'Education Nationale. *Inventaire des thèses de doctorat soutenues devant les universités françaises, 1981[-].* Paris: Université de Paris I, Bibliothèque de la Sorbonne, 1982- , passim.

Annually lists French doctoral dissertations under a fairly elaborate system of subject headings. For the relatively rare studies of Dickens, see heading 22, "Etudes anglaises." Wortman (**1162**), pp. 157-58, notes that this series continues the *Catalogue des thèses de doctorat soutenue devant les universités françaises* (Paris: Cercle de la Librairie, 1885-1984), with author, subject, and university indexes.

1278. Sadrin, Anny. "French Studies of Dickens since 1970." *Dickens Quarterly*, 12 (1995), 187-98.

More a look at the writings of a few recent French critics than a bibliographical survey. Sadrin does include "Translations of Dickens's Novels and Stories, Paris: Gallimard, Collection 'La Pléiade,'" p. 196, about an edition that, for the moment, contains the definitive translations of Dickens's works into French. The section "Works Cited," pp. 196-98, lists the works in English and French mentioned in Sadrin's survey.

1279. *Verzeichnis Lieferbarer Bücher/German Books in Print, 1999/2000. Schlag-
        wort-Verzeichnis.* 22nd ed. 7 vols. Frankfurt am Main: Verlag der Buch-
        händler-Vereinigung GmbH, 1999, II, 2913.

This most recent keyword/subject index to German books in print lists
sixteen book-length studies of Dickens, thirteen in German, three in English,
and is "computed," as the foreword notes, from the *Autoren Titel Stickwörter*
portion (**635**) of this major work.

Works of Individual Dickens Scholars

Note: Also see **Dickens scholars, bibliographies of works by** in part 2 of the subject index.

1280. "Bibliography of F. G. Kitton's Writings on Dickens." *Dickensian*, 1
        (1905), 245-46.

Lists books and magazine and newspaper articles, 1882-1905, including
several not found in other bibliographical lists covering this period. There are
a few errors in dating, however, and at least one omission–"An Old Coach
Road," *Art Journal*, ns 37 (1885), 221-24, 249-52.

1281. Collie, Michael. *"Charles Dickens," "The Immortal Dickens,"* and "Chrono-
        logical List of Gissing's Publications to 1905." In his *George Gissing:
        A Bibliography.* Toronto: University of Toronto Press, 1975, pp. 83-87,
        104-07, 124-26; extensively revised and extended as *"Charles Dickens:
        A Critical Study," "Critical Studies of the Works of Charles Dickens,"* and
        "Appendix I. Select Checklist of Books and Articles about George
        Gissing." In his *George Gissing: A Bibliographical Study.* St. Paul's Bibliog-
        raphies, 12. Winchester, Eng.: St. Paul's Bibliographies, 1985, pp. 80-82,
        107-10, 146-55.

For the sections on Gissing's two book-length studies of Dickens–*Charles
Dickens: A Critical Study*, 1898 (London: Blackie & Son), and *The Immortal Dickens*, 1925 (London: Cecil Palmer), which was published earlier in the United
States (New York: Greenberg, 1924) as *Critical Studies of the Works of Charles
Dickens*–Collie provides full-fledged bibliographical descriptions of their first
English and American editions (but mentions no revised versions or reprints),
and provides valuable background on Gissing's writing of these works. On
p. 107 of the first and pp. 109-10 of the second edition, he also lists Gissing's
shorter writings on Dickens. In the second edition Collie updates, somewhat
expands, and revises the structure of the entries in the first edition, omits the
chronological list of Gissing's publications, and adds the appendix indicated.

1282. Fenwick, Gillian. *Leslie Stephen's Life in Letters: A Bibliographical Study.*
        Aldershot, Eng.: Scolar Press, 1993, p. 310.

Contains a full bibliographical description of Frank Marzials's *Life of Charles Dickens . . . with a Biography of Dickens by Sir Leslie Stephen* (Philadelphia: John D. Morris, 1905), Stephen's contribution to which, Fenwick notes, is "substantially the same" as Stephen's article on Dickens in the *Dictionary of National Biography*, ed. Leslie Stephen and Sidney Lee (London: Smith, Elder, 1888), XV, 20-32, but without the bibliography. The *DNB* article is listed on p. 250 of Fenwick's study.

1283. Fielding, K[enneth] J. *W. J. Carlton: A Tribute, with a List of His Writings on Dickens.* N.p.: Privately printed by K. J. F[ielding], [1973]. 6 pp.

A sixty-item, unannotated list of Carlton's "Writings on Dickens," pp. 4-6, preceded by a brief biographical sketch of Carlton. Also see "William J. Carlton," an obituary by Leslie C. Staples, in *Dickensian*, 69 (1973), 201-03, for a notice of this publication.

1284. Fitzgerald, Percy. "A Bibliography of the Author's Writings." In his *Memoirs of an Author.* 2 vols. London: Richard Bentley and Son, 1895, II, 398-408.

Identifies his own work for *Household Words* and *All the Year Round*, as well as his other writings through 1894. In these memoirs, Fitzgerald comments on Dickens's relationships with a number of literary people of his time, evaluates Dickens as a writer, and discusses his own career as a writer for Dickens's weekly magazines.

1285. Fitzgerald, Percy. *An Output: A List of Writings on Many Diverse Subjects; of Sculptures; Dramas; Music; Lectures; Tours; Collections; Clubs; and Public Donations. Being a Record of Work Done During a Long and Busy Life, 1850-1912.* London: Jarrold & Sons (Printed for private circulation only), [1912]. 40 pp.

Contains a very brief description of Fitzgerald's life, his work for *Household Words* and his friendship with Dickens and his family, with lists of Fitzgerald's writings in the British Museum library ("close on one hundred and twenty works"), sculptures, and other activities in the arts and letters. Illustrated.

1286. Green, Roger L. "Andrew Lang: Critic and Dickensian." *Dickensian*, 41 (1944/45), 10-14.

Contains, in addition to a brief survey of Lang's generally superficial remarks on Dickens, a list of his writings on Dickens.

1287. "K. J. Fielding: Publications." In special issue, "Essays in Honour of K. J. Fielding." *Prose Studies*, 10, iii (December 1987), 324-28.

Lists Fielding's books, articles, and reviews, which are almost entirely on Dickens.

1288. Kincaid, James R., and Albert J. Kuhn. "Bibliography of the Writings of Richard D. Altick." In *Victorian Literature and Society: Essays Presented to Richard D. Altick.* Ed. James R. Kincaid and Albert J. Kuhn. Columbus: Ohio State University Press, 1984, pp. 349-59.

Contains a few Dickens items.

1289. Maack, Annegret. "Angus Wilsons Auseinandersetzung mit Charles Dickens." *Literatur in Wissenschaft und Unterricht,* 12 (1979), 267-86.

A study of Wilson's works on Dickens followed by a bibliography of Wilson's writings and interviews, including several about Dickens, and studies of Wilson's works, pp. 284-86.

1290. Matz, Winifred. "Bibliography of B. W. Matz." *Dickensian,* 21 (1925), 196-98.

Lists books, pamphlets, and magazine and newspaper articles by Matz, a Dickens scholar and first editor of the *Dickensian,* as well as books edited, compiled, or containing notes by him. Most are concerned with Dickens.

1291. Wolff, Joseph J., comp. and ed. *George Gissing: An Annotated Bibliography of Writings about Him.* De Kalb: Northern Illinois University Press, 1974, passim.

See "Index: Primary Titles," pp. 291-93, for studies of Gissing's *Charles Dickens: A Critical Study* (1898).

Influence and Relationship Studies

Note: Also see **Influence and comparative studies concerning Dickens and his works, bibliographies,** and **Charles Dickens, relationships with friends, acquaintances, associates** in part 2 of the subject index.

1292. Beetz, Kirk H. "Part II, Criticism and Scholarship." In his *Wilkie Collins: An Annotated Bibliography, 1889-1976* (**141**), pp. 69-136.

An annotated bibliography of critical studies of Collins, with a number of references to Dickens, Dickens studies, and the relationship of Dickens and Collins. In addition, see "Wilkie Collins's Works, 1843-1890: A Bibliographic Essay," pp. 1-21, and the author and subject indexes for a number of references to studies of the literary and personal relationship of the two authors. Also see Beetz (**1293**), Cordasco (**1295**), Gasson (**1306**), and Nayder (**1316**).

1293. Beetz, Kirk H. "Wilkie Collins Studies, 1972-1983." *Dickens Studies Annual*, 13 (1984), 333-55.

An essay bibliography, something of a supplement to and update of Beetz's book-length bibliography of Collins (**141**), with some commentary on studies dealing with the relationship between Collins and Dickens. Also see Beetz (**1292**), Cordasco (**1295**), Gasson (**1306**), and Nayder (**1316**).

1294. Colby, Robert A. "Thackeray Studies, 1993-2001." *Dickens Studies Annual*, 31 (2002), 365-96.

There are occasional Dickens references in this survey. Also see Flamm (**1303**), Olmsted (**1317**), Goldfarb (**1307**), and Shillingsburg (**1323**).

1295. Cordasco, Francesco, and Kenneth W. Scott. *Wilkie Collins and Charles Reade: A Bibliography of Critical Notices and Studies.* Brooklyn, NY: Long Island University Press, 1949, passim.

This seven-page bibliography includes studies of the relationships of Reade and Collins with Dickens. Also see Beetz (**1292-93**), Gasson (**1306**), and Nayder (**1316**).

1296. Dameron, J. Lasley, and Irby B. Cauthen, Jr. *Edgar Allan Poe: A Bibliography of Criticism, 1827-1967.* A John Cook Wyllie Memorial Publication. Charlottesville: Published for the Bibliographical Society of the University of Virginia by the University Press of Virginia, 1974, passim.

The index identifies some twenty-four studies related to Dickens, a few of which do not show up in Dickens bibliographies. All entries are annotated. Also see Hyneman (**1311**) and Kirby (**1313**).

1297. Davies, James A. "Bibliography." In his *John Forster: A Literary Life.* Leicester, Eng.: Leicester University Press; Totowa, NJ: Barnes & Noble Books, 1983, pp. 291-307.

In this biography of Dickens's biographer and closest friend, the bibliography lists Forster's publications, including articles and reviews, as well as studies of Forster, many concerning his relationship with Dickens. Also see Davies (**1298**) and Fenstermaker (**1301**).

1298. Davies, James A. "Forster Research: A Progress Report." *John Forster Newsletter*, 1, i (May 1978), 21-30.

Comments on then current research on the Dickens-Forster friendship, and includes a "Bibliography (1876-1977)" of Forster studies (pp. 24-30). Also see Davies (**1297**) and Fenstermaker (**1301**).

1299. Davis, Marjorie T. "An Annotated Bibliography of Criticism on Elizabeth Cleghorn Gaskell, 1848-1973." Doctoral Dissertation (University
of Mississippi, 1974).

In his essay on Gaskell in *Victorian Fiction: A Second Guide to Research*, edited
by George H. Ford (**959**), pp. 204-18, James D. Barry characterizes Davis's
dissertation as one of three recent Gaskell bibliographies that "stand out." He
adds that it "contains almost five hundred entries." Also see Hamilton (**1309**),
Selig (**1322**), Tennyson (**1326**), Welch (**1327**), and Weyant (**1328**).

1300. Drake, Dana B. "Charles Dickens." In his *Don Quijote in World Literature:
A Selective Annotated Bibliography*. Garland Reference Library of the Humanities, 187. New York and London: Garland, 1980, pp. 144-49 and
passim.

Annotates some eight works on the influence of Cervantes on Dickens,
mostly in *Pickwick Papers*.

1301. Fenstermaker, John J. "Selected Bibliography." In his *John Forster*.
Twayne's English Authors Series, 379. Boston: Twayne, 1984, pp. 122-
27.

In this study of Forster's literary career, the bibliography lists Forster's
principal works (though not his reviews) and some secondary sources (lightly
annotated), including studies concerning Forster's relationship with Dickens.
Also see Davies (**1297-98**).

1302. Fisher, Benjamin F., IV. *The Gothic's Gothic: Study Aids to the Tradition of
the Tale of Terror*. Garland Reference Library of the Humanities, 567.
New York and London: Garland Publishing, 1988, passim.

Lists a number of Dickens items, with brief annotations (see the index).
Also see Frank (**1304-05**).

1303. Flamm, Dudley. *Thackeray's Critics: An Annotated Bibliography of British and
American Criticism, 1836-1901*. Chapel Hill: University of North Carolina
Press, [1967], passim.

The index lists eighty-eight Dickens items, and there are passing references
to Dickens in Flamm's introduction, mainly to critics' comparisons of Dickens and Thackeray. Flamm's bibliography is continued in Olmsted (**1317**),
Goldfarb (**1307**), Shillingsburg (**1323**), and Colby (**1294**).

1304. Frank, Frederick S. "Charles Dickens (1812-1870)." In his *Guide to the
Gothic: An Annotated Bibliography of Criticism*. Metuchen, NJ, and London:
Scarecrow Press, 1984, pp. 176-79, and *Guide to the Gothic II: An Anno-*

tated Bibliography of Criticism, 1983-1993. Lanham, MD, and London: Scarecrow Press, 1995, pp. 218-21.

The original volume contains an annotated list of twenty-four items on Gothic elements in Dickens's works, the supplement ten items. Also see Fisher (**1302**) and Frank (**1305**).

1305. Frank, Frederick S. *Gothic Fiction: A Master List of Twentieth Century Criticism and Research*. Meckler's Bibliographies on Science Fiction, Fantasy and Horror, 3. Westport, CT, and London: Meckler, 1988, passim.

For this unannotated bibliography, the index notes twenty-eight Dickens items. Also see Fisher (**1302**) and Frank (**1304**).

1306. Gasson, Andrew. "Appendix E: Select Bibliography." In his *Wilkie Collins: An Illustrated Guide*. Oxford, New York, etc.: Oxford University Press, 1998, pp. 185-89.

Includes a number of studies of Collins's relationship with Dickens—see particularly the sections on "The Dickens Connection" and "Theatrical." Also see Beetz (**1292-93**), Cordasco (**1295**), and Nayder (**1316**).

1307. Goldfarb, Sheldon. *William Makepeace Thackeray: An Annotated Bibliography, 1976-1987*. Garland Reference Library of the Humanities, 857. New York and London: Garland Publishing, 1989, passim.

The index lists thirty-nine Dickens items. Also see Colby (**1294**), Flamm (**1303**), Olmsted (**1317**), and Shillingsburg (**1323**).

1308. Green, David B., and Edwin G. Wilson, eds. *Keats, Shelley, Byron, Hunt, and Their Circles, a Bibliography: July 1, 1950-June 30, 1962*. Lincoln: University of Nebraska Press, 1964, passim.

Briefly annotated. For occasional reference to Dickens, particularly to his relationship with Leigh Hunt, see the index. Also see Hartley (**1310**).

1309. Hamilton, Susan. "Ten Years of Gaskell Criticism." *Dickens Studies Annual*, 31 (2002), 397-414.

There are a few references to Dickens in this bibliographical survey. Also see Davis (**1299**), Selig (**1322**), Welch (**1327**), and Weyant (**1328**).

1310. Hartley, Robert A. *Keats, Shelley, Byron, Hunt, and Their Circles, a Bibliography: July 1, 1962-December 31, 1974*. Lincoln: University of Nebraska Press, 1978, passim.

See annotation for Green and Wilson (**1308**).

1311. Hyneman, Esther F. *Edgar Allan Poe: An Annotated Bibliography of Books and Articles in English, 1827-1973.* Boston: G. K. Hall, 1974, passim.

Since this bibliography has no subject index, there is no easy way to identify books and articles with reference to Poe's relationship with Dickens and to their influence on each other except by going through it item by item. Also see Dameron and Cauthen, Jr. (**1296**) and Kirby (**1313**).

1312. Jeffrey, David L., gen. ed. *A Dictionary of Biblical Tradition in English Literature.* Grand Rapids, MI: William B. Eerdmans; Leominster, Eng.: Gracewing, 1992, passim.

In "Use of the Bible by a Single Author or Group of Authors," pp. 937-60, lists (with brief annotations) seventeen studies of the influence of the Bible on Dickens (see pp. 942-43). Also see "The Influence of the Bible on English Literature: Selected General Studies," pp. 929-36.

1313. Kirby, David. "The Victorians." In his *America's Hive of Honey; or, Foreign Influences on American Fiction through Henry James: Essays and Bibliographies.* Metuchen, NJ, and London: Scarecrow Press, 1980, pp. 146-64 and passim.

Primarily an annotated bibliography of studies of influences on American authors. Kirby includes a few studies of Dickens's influence on William Dean Howells, Herman Melville, Edgar Allan Poe, and Mark Twain. See the index for the few other references to Dickens. Also see Dameron and Cauthen, Jr. (**1296**) and Hyneman (**1311**).

1314. Knowles, Owen. *An Annotated Critical Bibliography of Joseph Conrad.* Hemel Hempstead, Eng.: Harvester Press; New York: St. Martin's Press, 1992, passim.

A fairly substantial annotated bibliography. For the twelve items dealing with Dickens's influence on Conrad, see the subject index.

1315. MacPike, Loralee. "Select Bibliography." In her *Dostoevsky's Dickens: A Study of Literary Influence.* Totowa, NJ: Barnes and Noble Books, 1981, pp. 215-23.

A fairly extensive unannotated listing of works dealing with Dickens and Dostoevsky, together and separately.

1316. Nayder, Lillian. "Wilkie Collins Studies: 1983-1999." *Dickens Studies Annual*, 28 (1999), 257-329.

A bibliographical survey followed by an unannotated list of Collins studies, including a brief section on "Collins and Dickens," p. 319, listing eight shorter studies. Also see Beetz (**1292-93**), Cordasco (**1295**), and Gasson (**1306**).

1317. Olmsted, John C. *Thackeray and His Twentieth-Century Critics: An Annotated Bibliography, 1900-1975.* Garland Reference Library of the Humanities, 62. New York and London: Garland Publishing, 1977, passim.

The index lists sixty-four Dickens items, many of which are annotated. Also see Colby (**1294**), Flamm (**1303**), Goldfarb (**1307**), and Shillingsburg (**1323**).

1318. Pangallo, Karen L. *George Eliot: A Reference Guide, 1972-1987.* Boston: G. K. Hall, 1990, passim.

Lists a number of works on the personal and literary relationship of Dickens and Eliot, some of which are not found in Dickens bibliographies. See the subject index for these references.

1319. Robson, John M. "John Stuart Mill." In *Victorian Prose: A Guide to Research.* Ed. David J. DeLaura. New York: Modern Language Association, 1973, pp. 185-218.

Lists and comments on, pp. 217-18, several essays that deal with the question of Mill's influence on Dickens in *Hard Times* and Mill's less than enthusiastic response to Dickens's treatment of women in *Bleak House*.

1320. Rosenberg, Edgar. "The Shaw/Dickens File: 1885 to 1950: Two Checklists." *Shaw Review*, 20 (1977), 148-70; 21 (1978), 2-19.

An unfinished series containing only the first two parts of the first checklist. These itemize Shaw's comments on Dickens, 1885-96 (109 items) and 1896-1915 (166 items), in chronological order, with annotations to place them in context and with all sources fully identified. The second checklist was to have listed the Dickens works to which Shaw alluded, 1885-1950. In an introduction, Rosenberg comments on the great range and frequency of Shaw's Dickensian allusions and the consistency/inconsistency of his views on Dickens's works and points out that Shaw more frequently refers to the Dickens novels he does not like than to those he does. Rosenberg also notes stylistic similarities in the works of Shaw and Dickens but cautions against taking Shaw's own statements about his great indebtedness to Dickens at full face value. For a continuation, see Rosenberg (**1321**)

1321. Rosenberg, Edgar. "The Shaw/Dickens File: 1914 to 1950. An Annotated Checklist (Concluded). Addenda: 1885 to 1919." *Shaw: The Annual
of Bernard Shaw Studies*, 2 (1982), 101-45.

A continuation of the checklist begun in Rosenberg (**1320**): "III. 1914 to
1950," pp. 108-33 (items 277-469), and "IV. Addenda: 1885 to 1913,"
pp. 133-45 (items 470-538). Rosenberg also comments on the sources of the
listings included here and in the earlier publication.

1322. Selig, Robert L. *Elizabeth Gaskell: A Reference Guide*. Boston: G. K. Hall,
1977, passim.

An annotated list of writings about Gaskell, 1848-1974. The index contains
a large number of references to Dickens. Also see Davis (**1299**), Hamilton
(**1309**), Tennyson (**1326**), Welch (**1327**), and Weyant (**1328**).

1323. Shillingsburg, Peter L. "Thackeray Studies, 1983-1992." *Dickens Studies
Annual*, 23 (1994), 303-36.

There are occasional Dickens references in this bibliographical survey.
Also see Flamm (**1303**), Olmsted (**1317**), Goldfarb (**1307**), and Colby (**1294**).

1324. Spilka, Mark. "Bibliography." In his *Dickens and Kafka: A Mutual Interpretation*. London: Dennis Dobson, 1963, pp. 297-308.

Lists thirty-one Dickens and Kafka studies in Part "A. Dickens-Kafka
Comparisons: A List of Specific References," and forty-four studies of gro-
tesque comedy in Part "B. Grotesque Comedy: A Selected Checklist." Part C,
"Works Cited," completes Spilka's bibliography.

1325. Tarr, Rodger. *Thomas Carlyle: A Bibliography of English-Language Criticism,
1824-1974*. Charlottesville: Published for the Bibliographical Society of
the University of Virginia by the University Press of Virginia, 1976, passim.

Lists forty-four items related to Dickens. Also see Tennyson (**1326**).

1326. Tennyson, G. B. "The Carlyles." in *Victorian Prose: A Guide to Research*.
Ed. David J. DeLaura. (**1319**), pp. 31-111.

Includes a brief section, pp. 63-64, listing and evaluating studies of Carlyle's literary relations with and influences on Dickens and, p. 65, the interrela-
tionship of Carlyle, Dickens, Gaskell, and Kingsley. Also see Tarr (**1325**).

1327. Welch, Jeffrey. *Elizabeth Gaskell: An Annotated Bibliography, 1929-1975*.
New York and London: Garland Publishing, 1977, passim.

The subject index lists thirty-four references to Dickens, one to *All the Year Round*, and seven to *Household Words*. Also see Davis (**1299**), Hamilton (**1309**), Selig (**1322**), Tennyson (**1326**), and Weyant (**1328**).

1328. Weyant, Nancy S. *Elizabeth Gaskell: An Annotated Bibliography of English-Language Sources, 1976-1991*. Metuchen, NJ, and London: Scarecrow Press, 1994, passim.

See the subject index for fifteen references to Dickens Also see Davis (**1299**), Hamilton (**1309**), Selig (**1322**), Tennyson (**1326**), and Welch (**1327**).

Background Studies of Nineteenth-Century Life and Literature

Note: Also see Shattock (**1184**) and Gillie (**1351**), as well as **Nineteenth-century life and literature, bibliographies of background studies** in part 2 of the subject index.

1329. Altholz, Josef L., comp. *Victorian England, 1837-1901*. Conference on British Studies Bibliographical Handbooks. Cambridge: Cambridge University Press for the Conference on British Studies, 1970. pp. xi + 100.

An indispensable guide to background bibliographies, catalogues, surveys, guides, and studies of the history of Victorian England, excluding literature, but particularly useful for the cultural, political, and social background of Dickens's novels and other writings. As the editor points out, the work is selective, with an emphasis on more recent studies, largely through 1967.

1330. Madden, Lionel. *How to Find Out about the Victorian Period: A Guide to Sources of Information*. Oxford, Eng., New York, etc.: Pergamon Press, 1970. xiv + 173 pp.

This useful guide for both "the general study of the period and for research into specific areas of Victorian history and achievement" contains chapters dealing very generally with Victorian philosophy, religion, social and economic thought, education, science, the visual arts, music, literature, and history, but not specifically with Dickens or his works. The forty-eight illustrations are of pages of reference works cited to show the format and kind of information supplied. See Storey and Madden (**1335**) and Storey (**1334**) for more specialized research guides.

1331. Modern Language Association Discussion Groups, Literature and Other Arts, General Topic 9, Bibliography. *A Bibliography on the Relations of Literature and the Other Arts, 1952-1958*. Comp. Alfred R. Neumann and ed. David B. Erdman. New York: New York Public Library, 1959, passim; expanded as *A Bibliography on the Relations of Literature and the Other Arts, 1952-1967*. New York: AMS Press, 1968, passim; issued annually for 1959-84, Hanover, NH: Department of German, Dartmouth College, 1959-85, passim; thereafter published as "Bibliography on the Relations of Literature and Other Arts, [1985-]." *YCGL: Yearbook of Comparative and General Literature*, 34 (1985)- , passim.

This bibliography, with some modifications of headings over the years, is basically divided into four parts: Theory and General, Music and Literature, The Visual Arts and Literature, and Film and Literature. The second and third parts have the subsection "1830 to the Present," where one is most likely to find references to Dickens.

1332. Propas, Sharon W. *Victorian Studies: A Research Guide*. Garland Reference Library of the Humanities, 1068. New York and London: Garland Publishing, 1992. xxi + 334 pp.

A useful annotated bibliography of research works on all aspects of the Victorian period though it does not deal with particular authors or other individuals.

1333. Stevenson, Lionel. "The Victorian Period." In *Contemporary Literary Scholarship: A Critical Review*. Ed. Lewis Leary. New York: Appleton-Century-Crofts, 1958, pp. 139-56.

Surveys major studies of the Victorian period, including studies of the novel, and, on pp. 154-55, seven studies of Dickens's works, 1937-55. Also see Booth (**1339**).

1334. Storey, Richard. *Primary Sources for Victorian Studies: An Updating*. Occasional Papers in Bibliography. Leicester, Eng.: Victorian Studies Centre, University of Leicester, 1987. 40 pp.

An updating of Storey and Madden (**1335**), listing, for researchers, primary printed sources in Victorian studies, 1977-87, under various subject headings.

1335. Storey, Richard, and Lionel Madden. *Primary Sources for Victorian Studies: A Guide to the Location and Use of Unpublished Materials*. London and Chichester, Eng.: Phillimore, 1977. 81 pp.

The authors list and comment on what repositories and printed guides should be consulted to lead the research student to appropriate manuscript materials, principally in Britain but also elsewhere, with some practical hints for using these materials. Chapters deal with the Historical Manuscripts Commission and the National Registry of Archives, national and local repositories, general published guides and bibliographical resources for special subject areas. This work is updated by Storey (**1334**).

1336. Vance, Norman. "Part III. Further Reading and Reference." In *The Cambridge Guide to the Arts in Britain*. Vol. 7: *The Later Victorian Age*. Ed. Boris Ford. Cambridge, New York, etc.: Cambridge University Press, 1989, pp. 307-48.

Useful for background on the arts in Victorian England. See also a brief section on Dickens, p. 337, and the novel, pp. 334-35, and Gillie (**1351**).

Craft of Fiction

Note: Also see **Craft of fiction in Dickens's works, bibliographies** in part 2 of the subject index.

1337. Bailey, Richard W., and Dolores M. Burton. *English Stylistics: A Bibliography*. Cambridge, MA, and London: M. I. T. Press, 1968, passim.

Lists eleven studies of Dickens's style under various headings (see the index). Most entries are not annotated.

1338. Bennett, James R. *A Bibliography of Stylistics and Related Criticism, 1967-83*. New York: Modern Language Association, 1986, passim.

Lists and annotates a number of Dickens studies. See Index 2, p. 379.

1339. Booth, Bradford. "The Novel." In *Contemporary Literary Scholarship: A Critical Review*. Ed. Lewis Leary. New York: Appleton-Century-Crofts, 1958, pp. 259-88.

Surveys a number of general studies of the novel, though in a brief section on Dickens comments on three biographies rather than any literary studies. Also see Stevenson (**1333**).

1340. Clark, J[ohn] Scott. "Bibliography on Dickens's Style." In his *A Study of English Prose Writers. A Laboratory Method*. New York: Charles Scribner's Sons, 1898, 1905, pp. 610-12.

A list of critical studies of Dickens's prose style, a part of Clark's chapter on Dickens, pp. 607-47.

1341. Evans, James E. *Comedy: An Annotated Bibliography of Theory and Criticism*. Metuchen, NJ, and London: Scarecrow Press, 1987, passim.

See the subject index for some thirty-nine scattered references to studies of comic elements in Dickens's works.

1342. Koehmstedt, Carol L., comp. *Plot Summary Index*. Metuchen, NJ: Scarecrow Press, 1973; revised by Carol K[oehmstedt] Kolar. *Plot Summary*

Index. 2nd ed., revised and enlarged. Metuchen, NJ, and London: Scare-crow Press, 1981, passim.

In the title index, lists sources of plot summaries for individual Dickens novels. Also see the author index.

1343. Nilsen, Don L. F. "Charles Dickens Bibliography." In his *Humor in Eighteenth- and Nineteenth-Century British Literature: A Reference Guide.* West-port, CT, and London: Greenwood Press, 1998, pp. 195-97.

This unannotated bibliography is the concluding part of "Charles (John Huffam) Dickens (1812-1870)," pp. 177-97, Nilsen's survey of critical studies of humor in Dickens's novels. The bibliography contains only thirty-nine items, missing, obviously, a number of important studies. For more general studies, see "Nineteenth-Century English Humor Bibliography," pp. 99-100, a list of thirty-five studies. Also see Nilsen (**1344**).

1344. Nilsen, Don L. F. *Humor Scholarship: A Research Bibliography.* Bibliogra-phies and Indexes in Popular Culture, 1. Westport, CT, and London: Greenwood Press, 1993, passim.

Although Dickens has only a small listing in the index (for entries in which his name appears in the title), this is an extensive bibliography of studies of humor, many general in nature, in which Dickens may very well be included. Unfortunately, the entries are not annotated, so one can only find this out by consulting each work. It is more useful to use Nilsen's *Humor in Eighteenth- and Nineteenth-Century British Literature: A Reference Guide* (**1343**).

1345. "Stylistics Annotated Bibliography, 1966[-90]." *Style*, 1-25 (1967-91), passim.

See the author index to locate briefly annotated Dickens items—usually sev-eral per year.

1346. Vann, J. Don. "Serialized Novels in Magazines." In *Victorian Periodicals: A Guide to Research.* Vol. 2. Ed. J. Don Vann and Rosemary T. Van-Arsdel. New York: Modern Language Association of America, 1989, pp. 81-90.

An evaluative bibliographical essay. See particularly the section on Dick-ens, pp. 83-84, but the more general sections, pp. 81-83 and 85, are useful, too. In addition, consult the brief sections on Wilkie Collins and Elizabeth Gaskell, pp. 89-90. Volume 1 of this work, also edited by Vann and VanArsdel (New York: Modern Language Association of America, 1978), contains only passing references to Dickens.

Art, Illustration

Note: Also see Vance (**1336**) and **Charles Dickens, and art, illustration, and music** in part 2 of the subject index.

1347. Andrews, Nathalie T., and Margaret M. Bridwell. "Selected Bibliography." In *The Inimitable George Cruikshank* (**1777**), pp. 39-53.

A useful annotated Cruikshank bibliography of catalogues of his works, auction catalogues, catalogues of exhibitions and collections, biographies, biographical sketches, critical studies, exhibition notices, and even obituaries. Most items have some reference to Cruikshank's relationship with Dickens or to his illustrations for Dickens's works.

1348. *Art Index, January 1929-September 1932[-]*. New York: H. W. Wilson, 1932-, passim.

Contains occasional unannotated Dickens references, but should also be used for material on Dickens's illustrators. Currently published monthly and in quarterly and annual cumulations. Also available on CD-ROM, Wilsondisc, September 1984- (New York: H. W. Wilson, 1987-), and online at subscribing libraries. The latest annual volume seen, edited by Christine Milne and Mark L. Ferguson, covered November 1998-October 1999 and was published in 2000.

1349. Cohen, Jane R. "Selected Bibliography." In her *Charles Dickens and His Original Illustrators*. Columbus: Ohio State University Press, 1980, pp. 277-88.

A useful if not always accurate unannotated bibliography of Dickensian illustration.

1350. Ford, Mary, and Michael Slater, comps. "Index to the Illustrations." In Frank T. Dunn's *A Cumulative Index to **The Dickensian**, 1905-1974* (**1165**), pp. 183-99.

Lists the numerous illustrations in the *Dickensian* for the years indicated. Together, these illustrations comprise a fascinating collection of Dickensiana. Many are illustrations to Dickens's works, facsimile reproductions of letters and other manuscript material, photographs and drawings of places in his works, of people and places in his life, and of Dickens himself.

1351. Gillie, Christopher. "Further Reading and Reference." In *Cambridge Guide to the Arts in Britain*. Vol. 6: *Romantic to Early Victorians*. Ed. Boris Ford. Cambridge, Eng., New York, etc.: Cambridge University Press, 1990, pp. 291-319; reprinted in paperback as *The Cambridge Cultural History*. Vol. 6: *The Romantic Age in Britain*. Ibid., pp. 291-313.

The section on Dickens in this bibliography contains a very brief biographical note and a list of major Dickens studies, but the bibliography is really more useful for its general sections on the Cultural and Social Setting, Graphic Satire and Illustration, and Literature. The typography and page setup are somewhat different in the paperback edition, but the text itself seems unaltered. See also Vance (**1336**).

1352. Harris, Elree I., and Shirley R. Scott. *A Gallery of Her Own: An Annotated Bibliography of Women in Victorian Painting.* New York and London: Garland Publishing, 1997, passim.

An annotated bibliography identifying books, articles, and dissertations on women artists of the Victorian period, including Dickens's elder daughter Kate Dickens Perugini. See the index for the relevant publications.

1353. Johnson, William S. "Dickens, Charles (1812-1870)." In his *Nineteenth-Century Photography: An Annotated Bibliography, 1839-1879.* Boston: G. K. Hall, 1990, p. 185.

In this huge bibliography (xv + 962 pp.), Johnson lists six articles on Dickens and photography.

1354. Montgomery, David L. Appendices. In his "William Powell Frith (1819-1909): A Reevaluation of His Artistic Career." *Dissertation Abstracts International,* 59 (1998/99), 2222A (University of Missouri, Columbia, 1997).

In this examination and reevaluation of Frith's artistic career, Montgomery, his abstract indicates, includes an appendix containing photographic reproductions of all of Frith's known paintings. Additional appendices "serve as a catalog of all Frith's paintings," presumably including his portraits of Dickens and his literary paintings of characters in Dickens's works.

1355. Muir, Percy. *Victorian Illustrated Books.* London: B. T. Batsford, 1971, passim.

See the annotated lists of "Books Applicable to This Chapter" and "Selected List of Illustrated Books" at the end of three chapters: chapter 3, "Two Colossi–Thomas Bewick and George Cruikshank," pp. 25-50 and 50-58; chapter 5, "Pickwick, Punch and Other Periodicals," pp. 89-123 and 123-28; and chapter 10, "America," pp. 250-66 and 266-69.

1356. Stievater, Susan M. "Dickens, Charles (1812-70), English Novelist." In *Biographies of Creative Artists: An Annotated Bibliography.* Ed. Susan M. Stievater. Garland Reference Library of the Humanities, 1185. New York and London: Garland Publishing, 1991, pp. 56-57.

Lists and briefly annotates five Dickens biographies (a highly selective, eccentric group) and summarizes Dickens's life in 150 words.

Theater and Films

Note: Also see Brannan (**1123**), and Litto (**1200**), as well as **Theater, film, and Dickens, bibliographies** in part 2 of the subject index.

1357. Aceto, Vincent J., Jane Graves, and Fred Silva, [et al.], eds. *Film Literature Index [1973-]: A Quarterly Author-Subject Periodical Index to the International Literature of Film.* Albany, NY: Filmdex, 1975- , passim.

Published quarterly with annual cumulations, this index occasionally lists articles and reviews concerned with film adaptations of Dickens's works. See a "prototype" online version at http://www.albany.edu/sisp/fatdoc/index.htm.

1358. American Society for Theatre Research and the International Association of Libraries and Museums of the Performing Arts, in Cooperation with the International Federation for Theatre Research. *IBT: International Bibliography of Theatre: 1982[-].* Ed. Benito Ortolani. Brooklyn, NY: Theatre Research Data Center, Brooklyn College, City University of New York, 1985- , passim.

Contains occasional items on Dickens, with brief annotations. See Harner (**1147**), pp. 133-34, for the scope and limitations of this bibliography.

1359. Baker, Blanch M. *Theatre and Allied Arts: A Guide to Books Dealing with the History, Criticism, and Technic of the Drama and Theatre and Related Arts and Crafts.* New York: H. W. Wilson, 1952; reprinted New York: Benjamin Blom, 1967, passim.

Lists and annotates only three studies of Dickens and the theater and three editions of *Memoirs of Joseph Grimaldi*, edited by Dickens. Even so, this work largely supersedes Baker's *Dramatic Bibliography: An Annotated List of Books on the History and Criticism of the Drama and Stage and on the Allied Arts of the Theatre* (New York: H. W. Wilson, 1933; reprinted New York: Benjamin Blom, 1968).

1360. *Bibliographic Guide to Theatre Arts, 1975[-].* Boston (and, later, New York): G. K. Hall, 1976- , passim.

Contains occasional Dickens references, with call numbers for the New York Public Library or the Library of Congress provided.

1361. Connolly, L. W., and J. P. Wearing. "Dickens, Charles (1812-70)." In their *English Drama and Theatre, 1800-1900: A Guide to Information Sources.* American Literature, English Literature, and World Literatures in English Information Guide Series, 12. Detroit, MI: Gale Research, 1978, pp. 149-57 and passim.

Connolly and Wearing list critical studies of Dickens as a dramatist, as well as bibliographical and biographical works with sections on Dickens's plays and theatrical interests, all lightly annotated. They also list Dickens's plays and collected editions containing them. For other entries, see under Dickens in the index. Also see Connolly and Wearing (**1362**).

1362. Connolly, L. W., and J. P. Wearing. "Nineteenth-Century Theatre Research: A Bibliography for 1972[-1981]." *Nineteenth Century Theatre Research*, 1 (1973)-10 (1982), passim.

This annual bibliography includes occasional Dickens items. Wearing edited volumes 6-10 alone. Also see Connolly and Wearing (**1361**).

1363. Faxon, Frederick W., Mary E. Bates, and Anne C. Sutherland, eds. "Dickens, Charles." In their *Cumulated Dramatic Index, 1909-1949: A Cumulation of the F. W. Faxon Company's Dramatic Index*. 2 vols. Boston: G. K. Hall, 1965, I, 332-33.

An unannotated listing of critical studies of Dickens's plays and theatrical interests.

1364. Gentile, John S. "The Performance Career of Charles Dickens: An Annotated Bibliography." *Resources in Education*, 17 (January 1982), 56.

An abstract of an Education Resources Information Center Document, ERIC Doc. Ed 206 020, CS 503 548, available in microfiche or paper document form. The document is a ten-page annotated bibliography of forty resources "concerned with Dickens's success as a performer interpreting his literary works." Check the latest issue of *Resources in Education* for ordering instructions.

1365. Johnson, Claudia D., and Vernon E. Johnson. *Nineteenth-Century Theatrical Memoirs*. Westport, CT, and London: Greenwood Press, 1982, passim.

Annotates thirty-nine books with references to Dickens.

1366. Pointer, Michael. "Bibliography." In his *Charles Dickens on the Screen* (**788**), pp. 195-97.

Lists works that contain information about film adaptations of Dickens's works.

1367. Ross, Harris. "Charles Dickens." In his *Film as Literature, Literature as Film: An Introduction to and Bibliography of Film's Relationship to Literature.* Bibliographics and Indexes in World Literature, 10. New York, Westport, CT, and London: Greenwood Press, 1987, pp. 180-84 and passim.

Lists studies of Dickens and film and studies and reviews of film versions of Dickens's novels. For additional references to Dickens, see the index under Dickens and titles of his individual novels. Dickens is not mentioned in Ross's introductory chapters.

1368. Wearing, J. P. "Dickens, Charles (1812-70)." In his *American and British Theatrical Biography: A Directory.* Metuchen, NJ, and London: Scarecrow Press, 1979, p. 309.

Lists only seven sources for Dickens.

1369. Welch, Jeffrey E. *Literature and Film: An Annotated Bibliography, 1909-1977.* Garland Reference Library of the Humanities, 241. New York and London: Garland Publishing, 1981, passim; continued as *Literature and Film: An Annotated Bibliography, 1978-1988.* Garland Reference Library of the Humanities, 1114. New York: Garland Publishing, 1993, passim.

Both volumes list a number of Dickens studies. See their indexes.

1370. Zambrano, Ana L. "Audio Visual Teaching Materials: A Dickensian Checklist–An Addendum." *Dickens Studies Newsletter,* 8 (1977), 17-19.

Updates her checklist of the previous year (**1371**).

1371. Zambrano, Ana L. "Audio-Visual Teaching Materials: A Dickensian Checklist–Part I" and "Audio-Visual Teaching Materials: A Dickensian Checklist–Part II." *Dickens Studies Newsletter,* 7 (1976), 43-46, 110-13.

Lists educational teaching aids in the form of film, filmstrips, videotape recordings, cassettes, and tapes–with numerous details. Part I lists audio-visual aids on the life and times of Dickens, aids dealing with more than one Dickens work, and aids focusing on *A Christmas Carol.* Part II lists aids devoted to *David Copperfield, Great Expectations,* "The Magic Fishbone," *Oliver Twist, Pickwick Papers,* "The Runaways" ("The Boots," from *The Holly-Tree Inn,* Dickens's Christmas Number for 1855), "The Signal Man" (from *Mugby Junction,* Dickens's Christmas Number for 1866), and *A Tale of Two Cities.* Also see Zambrano's addendum (**1370**).

Science and Psychology

Note: Also see **Science, psychology, technology and Dickens, bibliographies** in part 2 of the subject index.

1372. Dudley, Fred A., et al. *The Relations of Literature and Science: A Selected Bibliography, 1930-1949*. Pullman, WA: Published for "General Topics VII, a Discussion Group of The Modern Language Association of America, by the Department of English of The State College of Washington," 1949, passim; updated as *The Relations of Literature and Science: A Selected Bibliography, 1930-1967*. Ann Arbor, MI: University Microfilms, 1968, passim.

An unannotated listing. In addition to a number of general studies (pp. 9-21), the earlier volume includes only one study specifically of Dickens. The later volume, in addition to a much expanded list of general studies (pp. 1-14, 79-89), includes ten studies of Dickens, though only one, Taylor Stoehr's *Dickens: The Dreamer's Stance* (Ithaca, NY: Cornell University Press, 1965), is a full-length work. An update today would have a considerably larger section on Dickens. Harner (**1147**), p. 718, points out that the bibliography by Schatzberg, Waite, and Johnson (**1377**) "incorporates and expands" Dudley's 1968 volume.

1373. Gaskell, E. "Bibliography." In his *Dickens and Medicine* (**1795**), pp. 13-15.

A checklist of books and articles on Dickens and medicine.

1374. Kiell, Norman, comp. *Psychoanalysis, Psychology, and Literature: A Bibliography*. 2nd ed. 2 vols. Metuchen, NJ, and London: Scarecrow Press, 1982, passim.

Updates the first edition (Madison: University of Wisconsin Press, 1963, 4,460 entries) with over 15,500 new entries. Volume 1 contains the unannotated listings. Volume 2 contains author, title, and subject indexes. See the author index for Dickens, where entry numbers are listed under such subheadings as "alienation," "anality," "fantasy," "identity," "primal scene," and "schizophrenic." Also see *Supplement to the Second Edition* (Metuchen, NJ, and London: Scarecrow Press, 1990), passim, which updates the second edition to 1987 and includes a number of items missed in that edition.

1375. [Manheim, Leonard F., and Eleanor B. Manheim]. "Bibliography." *Literature and Psychology*, 1 (1951)-23 (1973), passim.

An annotated bibliography of books and principally articles on psychological approaches to literature, with occasional reference to studies of Dickens and his works. Originally published in four of the five issues per year, then more or less annually, beginning with the bibliography for 1964/65 in volume

18 (1968; there were no bibliographies in volumes 14-17) through volume 23 (1973), which contained the bibliography for 1970.

1376. Natoli, Joseph, and Frederik L. Rusch, comps. "Dickens, Charles." In their *Psychocriticism: An Annotated Bibliography.* Bibliographies and Indexes in World Literature, 1. Westport, CT: Greenwood Press, 1984, pp. 104-07 and passim.

The compilers list and annotate twenty-five psychoanalytical studies of Dickens's works, principally of individual novels.

1377. Schatzberg, Walter, Ronald A. Waite, and Jonathan K. Johnson, comps. "Charles Dickens (1812-70)." In their *The Relations of Literature and Science: An Annotated Bibliography of Scholarship, 1880-1980.* New York: Modern Language Association of America, 1987, pp. 251-53.

A listing of eleven studies on Dickens's interest in science. Also see "Nineteenth Century: Studies and Surveys," pp. 215-36, for more general studies of the influence of science on literature. Dickens is occasionally mentioned in the annotation. Also see Dudley (**1372**) and Harner (**1147**), pp. 717-18.

1378. van Meurs, Jos, and John Kidd. *Jungian Literary Criticism, 1920-1980: An Annotated Critical Bibliography of Works in English (with a Selection of Titles after 1980).* Metuchen, NJ, and London: Scarecrow Press, 1988, passim.

See the index for the eight Dickens studies listed.

Detective, Crime, and Mystery Studies

Note: Also see **Detective, crime, and mystery studies concerning Dickens, bibliographies** in part 2 of the subject index.

1379. Bleiler, E[verett] F., comp. "Dickens, Charles." In *Detective and Mystery Fiction: An International Bibliography of Secondary Sources.* Comp. Walter Albert. Madison, IN: Brownstone Books, 1985, pp. 415-36.

Principally a selective, annotated bibliography of over 150 studies and continuations of *The Mystery of Edwin Drood.* There is also a much briefer section on "Non-Drood References," pp. 415-17. Continued as "Murder Once Removed: A Continuing Supplement to *Detective and Mystery Fiction* [1984-]." *Armchair Detective,* 20 (1987), 279-92, 386-98; 21 (1988), 70-85; 22 (1989), 48-61, 174-83, 278-89; 24 (1991), 204-18, 324-39, 457-68.

1380. Breen, Jon L. *What about Murder? A Guide to Books about Mystery and Detective Fiction.* Metuchen, NJ, and London: Scarecrow Press, 1981, passim, and *What about Murder? 1981-1991*. Metuchen, NJ, and London: Scarecrow Press, 1993, passim.

The two volumes list, with annotations, a number of studies concerning Dickens's works. According to Harner (**1147**), p. 113, the earlier volume was supplemented by Breen's regular column in *Armchair Detective*, 18 (1984)-30 (1997).

1381. Johnson, Timothy W., and Julia Johnson et al. "Dickens, Charles (1812-1870)." In their *Crime Fiction Criticism: An Annotated Bibliography*. New York and London: Garland Publishing, 1981, pp. 183-202.

A surprisingly extensive annotated listing of studies of Dickens's use of mystery, crime, and detectives, particularly in *Bleak House* and *The Mystery of Edwin Drood*. The authors point out that this bibliography "contains more citations on Charles Dickens than on any other author, including Sir Arthur Conan Doyle."

1382. Skene Melvin, David, and Ann Skene Melvin, comps. *Crime, Detective, Espionage, Mystery, and Thriller Fiction & Film: A Comprehensive Bibliography of Critical Writing through 1979*. Westport, CT, and London: Greenwood Press, 1980, passim.

Lists fourteen unannotated Dickens items in the subject index.

Miscellaneous

1383. F[rewin], L[ouis] B. "Illinois Dickens Bibliography." *Dickensian*, 46 (1949/50), 219.

Lists six articles on Dickens and his family that appeared in the *Journal of the Illinois State Historical Society*.

1384. Grech, Anthony P. "The Library: Law and Society in the Life and Works of Charles Dickens." *The Record of the Association of the Bar of the City of New York*, 27 (1972), 275-86.

An unannotated checklist of books and articles dealing with law and society in Dickens's life and works.

1385. Kiell, Norman. "Food in Literature: A Selective Bibliography." *Mosaic*, 24 (1991), 211-63.

Lists, as one might suspect, some studies of Dickens's use of food in his works.

1386. Rahn, Suzanne. *Children's Literature: An Annotated Bibliography of the History and Criticism.* Garland Reference Library of the Humanities, 263. New York and London: Garland, 1981, passim.

A well-annotated bibliography of studies of children's literature. The index identifies seventeen studies involving Dickens's works.

3E. COMMENTARIES ON BIBLIOGRAPHIES AND BIBLIOGRAPHICAL STUDIES

Note: Also see Fitzgerald (**344, 2229**) and Johnson (**993**), as well as **Bibliographies of Dickens studies, commentaries on**, and **Bibliographical studies of Dickens's works, commentaries on**, in part 2 of the subject index.

1387. Altick, Richard D. "Victorians on the Move; Or, 'Tis Forty Years Since." *Dickens Studies Annual,* 10 (1982), 1-21.

On the rapid rise of Victorian studies in the previous forty years, with references to Dickens. The "high water mark of Dickens scholarship and criticism was reached in the years 1970-72," Altick asserts, when, following upon the commemoration of the centenary of his death, "some eighteen double-columned pages of the Victorian Bibliography [in *Victorian Studies* (**1058**)] were needed to record the output."

1388. Bede, Cuthbert [Edward Bradley]. "A 'Dickens Catalogue.'" *Notes and Queries,* 6th ser., 10 (1884), 44.

Offers a few additions to the items listed in a sale catalogue of J. W. Jarvis & Son, published in 1884 (**2043**), and gives George Frederick Pardon, whose name appears on the title page of the second edition of the work (1856), as the name of the author of *The Faces in the Fire,* which, Bede states, had sometimes been attributed to Dickens. In the preface to that edition, Bede points out, Pardon mentions how flattered he is that the work has been attributed to Dickens but assures his readers that he had not tried to imitate Dickens.

1389. Brattin, Joel J. "A 'Lost' Gissing Manuscript Recovered." *Gissing Newsletter,* 20, iv (October 1984), 15-17.

Reports that the manuscript of Gissing's introduction to *Martin Chuzzlewit,* long thought lost, is in the Kenyon Law Starling Collection, Department of Special Collections, Stanford University Libraries. Brattin describes the four pages of text and points out several interesting differences between manuscript and published text. The essay, originally meant as the introduction to *Martin Chuzzlewit* in the Rochester Edition of Dickens's works (**2302**), was first published in 1924 in Gissing's *Critical Studies of the Works of Charles Dickens* (New York: Greenberg), after the collected edition was abandoned by the publisher because of slow sales. Also see Coustillas (**288**).

1390. Brice, Alec W. "Letter to the Editor." *Dickensian*, 72 (1976), 46-47.

Offers further corroboration of Tillotson and Burgis's identification of reviews by John Forster in the *Examiner* (**540**).

1391. Brice, Alec W. "Reviewers of Dickens in the *Examiner*: Fonblanque, Forster, Hunt, and Morley." *Dickens Studies Newsletter*, 3 (1972), 68-80.

Argues that contrary to accepted opinion–see, for example, Philip Collins's "Dickens's Self-Estimate: Some New Evidence" (**1395**), to which this article is by way of a reply–John Forster did *not* write most of the seventy or more "notices or mentions" of Dickens's works in the *Examiner* between 1836 and 1865 although he quotes from "almost all" of them in *Forster*. Brice offers considerable if not always definitive evidence that Albany Fonblanque wrote the early ones of *Sketches by Boz* and *Pickwick Papers*, except for two of the latter that *were* by Forster; Leigh Hunt those of *Nicholas Nickleby* and the Christmas Books and two of *Oliver Twist*; and Henry Morley probably all the pieces after 1855.

1392. Calhoun, Philo, and Howell J. Heaney. "Dickensiana in the Rough." *Papers of the Bibliographical Society of America*, 41 (1947), 293-320; reprinted separately as *Dickensiana in the Rough*. Portland, ME: Antheonsen Press, 1947. 30 pp.

A devastating criticism of Miller's *Dickens Student and Collector* (**1005**) for claiming to be virtually complete when it is anything but that. The authors note typical omissions and give a long list of bibliographies that Miller had obviously not consulted. They also rightly fault the "mussy and confusing" arrangement of the bibliography, the absence of clarifying annotation, the eccentric and inadequate index, and the errors throughout. No Dickens bibliographer–or any bibliographer, for that matter–can dare to ignore the advice and warnings of Calhoun and Heaney. Also see comments in the introduction to the present bibliography, pp. xix-xxi and xli.

1393. Carter, John. "Books Issued in Parts." In Gordon N. Ray, Carl J. Weber, and John Carter's *Nineteenth-Century English Books: Some Problems in Bibliography*. Urbana: University of Illinois Press, 1952, pp. 65-68; reprinted in his *Books and Book-Collectors*. Cleveland and New York: World, 1957, pp. 168-72.

Notes that Hatton and Cleaver's bibliography of Dickens's part issues (**24**) "provided a more elaborate description" of them "than had ever been attempted before, or is ever likely to be attempted again" and "brought a massive sort of order into the description of text, plates and wrappers." On the other hand, Carter criticizes Hatton and Cleaver for placing too much importance on the advertising material, particularly the inserted slips, in determining the rarity of an issue or edition. He also comments on the bibliographical problems associated with collecting books in parts.

1394. Collins, Philip. "Dickens in America, 1867-68." *Dickens Studies Newsletter*, 4 (1973), 48-50.

Describes a book of press-cuttings from American newspapers covering Dickens's visits to America in 1867-68 now in the Gimbel Collection, Yale University Library—see Podeschi (**1509**), p. 418—and points out its value as evidence of American opinions of Dickens.

1395. Collins, Philip. "Dickens' Self-Estimate: Some New Evidence." In *Dickens the Craftsman: Strategies of Presentation*. Ed. Robert B. Partlow, Jr. Carbondale and Edwardsville: Southern Illinois University; London and Amsterdam: Feffer & Simons, 1970, pp. 21-43.

In investigating Dickens's own estimation of his accomplishments as a novelist, Collins holds that John Forster's evaluations of Dickens's qualities in the reviews he published in the *Examiner* provide "a substantial and apparently unused body of evidence about Dickens' self-awareness and self-estimation," since the two were close friends and must have had conversations about the subject. On the other hand, Collins concedes, the *Examiner* reviews were published anonymously (though Forster was editor of the journal) and, thus, it is not certain how many, if any, of them Forster wrote. Collins believes that there is "entirely convincing evidence that Forster wrote almost all of the *Examiner* reviews of Dickens," principally found in similarities of phrasing in the reviews and in Forster's commentary on Dickens's novels in his *Life of Charles Dickens (Forster)*. He does not offer full evidence here but does include samples of phrasing for eight novels as "specimens" of such proof in a section at the end of the essay entitled "Evidence for Forster's Authorship of the *Examiner* Reviews," pp. 41-43. See response by Alec W. Brice (**1391**).

1396. Collins, Philip, and G. W. Spence. "Letters to the Editors." *Dickens Studies Newsletter*, 2 (1971), 54-55.

In his letter, Collins suggests "a collaborative enterprise" for the editors of the *Dickens Studies Newsletter* and their American colleagues comprising "a collection of press cuttings from American newspapers, magazines, etc., about Dickens's visits of 1842 and 1867-8." He mentions a comparable book of press cuttings on Dickens's public readings in Great Britain compiled by John Greaves to be found in the Dickens House Library. Spence's letter concerns *Barnaby Rudge*.

1397. Coustillas, Pierre. "Gissing's Writings on Dickens: A Bio-Bibliographical Survey." *Dickensian*, 61 (1965), 168-79; reprinted, "with some revisions and corrections," as *Gissing's Writings on Dickens: A Bio-Bibliographical Survey, Together with Two Uncollected Reviews by George Gissing from The Times Literary Supplement.* London: Enitharmon Press, 1969. 25 pp.

A biographical sketch of Gissing covering his involvement with Dickens criticism from 1898 on, particularly in reference to the writing and publication of *Charles Dickens: A Critical Study* (London: Blackie & Son; New York: Dodd, Mead, 1898) and the writing of the introductions for the Rochester Edition of Dickens's novels, 1898-1900 (**2302**). Only six of these introductions were published, Coustillas points out; they and all but two of the remaining introductions (those to *David Copperfield* and *The Christmas Books*) were published as *Critical Studies of the Works of Charles Dickens* (New York: Greenberg, 1924) and as *The Immortal Dickens* (London: Cecil Palmer, 1925). Illustrated. For the introduction to *David Copperfield*, see Dunn (**1405**) and Coustillas (**1398**), and for that to *Martin Chuzzlewit*, see Brattin (**1389**). The volume edition also reprints two uncollected and unsigned reviews by Gissing: "Mr. Swinburne on Dickens," *Times Literary Supplement*, 25 July 1902, p. 243, a review of an article on Dickens in the July 1902 issue of the *Quarterly Review*, and "Mr. Kitton's Life of Dickens," *Times Literary Supplement*, 15 August 1902, p. 243.

Reviews: A. Curtis, *Dickens Studies Newsletter*, 4 (1973), 26-28 (an "intriguing" volume because it reprints two of Gissing's reviews of Dickens studies from the *Times Literary Supplement*); P. J. Keating, *Victorian Studies*, 13 (1969/70), 393-96 (an "excellent" monograph); M. S[later], *Dickensian*, 66 (1970), 253 (finds this an "attractive little volume," but is more interested in the two previously uncollected reviews by Gissing than in Coustillas's survey); *Times Literary Supplement*, 11 June 1970, p. 630 (contains an "illuminating and substantial" introduction).

1398. Coustillas, Pierre. Letter to the Editor. *Dickensian*, 77 (1981), 168-69.

Responding to Richard Dunn's printing (**1405**) of George Gissing's newly discovered and not previously published introduction to *David Copperfield* intended for the Rochester Edition of Dickens's works (**2302**), Coustillas, a noted Gissing scholar, comments that this introduction is quite different from the one Gissing wrote for the Autograph Edition (**2303**). He notes that, though the manuscripts for Gissing's introductions to *Sketches by Boz* and *Dombey and Son* are in the Gimbel Collection, Yale University Library (**1509**), the introduction Gissing presumably wrote for the Christmas Books (which, like the edition of *David Copperfield*, was advertised but never published) is still missing, as are the manuscripts for his introductions to *Martin Chuzzlewit* and *Bleak House*, though the former was sold by Parke-Bernet Galleries in 1944 (**1971**) and the latter by Sotheby and Co., in 1929 (**1982**). Likewise, the manuscripts of Gissing's other introductions to individual novels have not been located. Since Coustillas's letter, however, Brattin (**1389**) has located the manuscript of the introduction to *Martin Chuzzlewit*. Also see Coustillas (**288**).

1399. Cox, Arthur J. Letter to the Editor. *Dickensian*, 88 (1992), 106-09.

Points out a number of errors, some textual in nature, in Jacobson's *The Companion to* **The Mystery of Edwin Drood** (**2444**).

1400. Davis, George W. "First Issue of 'Dombey and Son.'" *Dickensian*, 15 (1919), 50.

A letter to the editor correcting errors concerning *Dombey and Son* in Eckel (**16**). See addenda by R. T. Jupp, pp. 162-63, and Morris F. Cook, pp. 219-20.

1401. Dexter, Walter. "A Necessary Correction: Some Mis-Statements from America." *Dickensian*, 29 (1932/33), 127-30.

Points out two errors in Eckel's revised bibliography (**16**) regarding *Sketches by Boz* and other errors in the Bibliophile Society's edition of *Charles Dickens and Maria Beadnell: Private Correspondence*. George P. Baker (St. Louis: Privately printed for W. K. Bixby, 1908).

1402. "Dickens Part-Issues." *Times Literary Supplement*, 22 March 1934, p. 220.

Praises the "greater detail, the greater clarity of expression and the more convincing arguments" to be found in Hatton and Cleaver's *A Bibliography of the Periodical Works of Charles Dickens* (**24**) than in the second edition of Eckel's *The First Editions of the Writings of Charles Dickens* (**16**) and comments on bibliographical problems connected with using the advertising inserts in the parts editions of Dickens's novels to determine primacy of issue. In response, [Comte] A[lain] de Suzannet, 12 April 1934, p. 268, criticizes some of Hatton and Cleaver's judgments based on the presence or absence of advertising inserts.

1403. Dobrin, David. "A Dickens Concordance? Why Not a Comsurvance?" *Dickens Studies Newsletter*, 11 (1980), 53-54.

Responding to comments by Sylvère Monod (**1419**) and Joseph Gold (**1407**) on the need for a Dickens Concordance, Dobrin proposes a "computer survey concordance," which would save an enormous amount of shelf space by putting the project on tapes or floppy disks. A concordance is now available on the Internet (**1224**).

1404. Dunn, Frank T. "Indexing *The Dickensian* 1905-74." *Dickensian*, 71 (1975), 131-35.

Discusses the problems, joys, and insights involved in doing the then new index (**1165**) to the *Dickensian*.

1405. Dunn, Richard. "Gissing's Introduction to the Rochester *David Copper-field." Dickensian*, 77 (1981), 3-11.

Dunn prints for the first time George Gissing's introduction and F. G. Kitton's "Bibliographical Note" designated for *David Copperfield* for the Rochester Edition of Dickens's works (**2302**). The edition of *David Copperfield* for which these were intended was never published, Dunn points out, because the series was cancelled after only six novels were published. In his bibliographical introduction, p. 3, Dunn notes that he discovered the page proofs for the introduction in a scrapbook (**1575**) in the Dickens House library and that the introduction was not included with those for other Dickens novels in Gissing's *Critical Studies of the Works of Charles Dickens* (New York: Greenberg, 1924). Also see Coustillas (**1398**) for comments on this introduction and the others Gissing wrote for the Rochester Edition.

1406. Fenwick, Gillian. "A Bibliographical Study of the Published and Unpublished Writings of Leslie Stephen." *Dissertation Abstracts International,* 53 (1992/93), 4331A (York University, Canada).

A study of Stephen's writing and publishing career, with various appendices, including, presumably Stephen's entry on Dickens in the *Dictionary of National Biography.*

1407. Gold, Joseph. "The Dickens Concordance." *Dickens Studies Newsletter,* 7 (1976), 65-69.

Discusses a proposed Dickens concordance and some of the problems involved. Unfortunately the project never got beyond the planning stage. Also see Dobrin (**1403**) and Monod (**1419**). An online concordance is now available (**1224**).

1408. Harris, Kevin. "Projects, News, Notes: Dickens Studies: A Comprehensive Bibliography." *Dickens Quarterly*, 1 (1984), 157-59.

A proposal for a comprehensive computerized bibliography.

1409. Haynes, E. B. "Seymour's 'Dying Clown.'" *Dickensian*, 30 (1933/34), 230.

Offers a correction to Hatton and Cleaver (**24**).

1410. Haynes, E. B. "Some Notes on Hatton and Cleaver's Bibliography of Dickens." *Dickensian*, 30 (1933/34), 193-96.

Offers some corrections to Hatton and Cleaver's (**24**) collations of parts issues of *Nicholas Nickleby, Bleak House,* and *Our Mutual Friend.*

1411. Houghton, Walter E. "Reflections on Indexing Victorian Periodicals."
Victorian Studies, 7 (1963/64), 192-96.

Houghton comments on the inadequacy of earlier indexes of Victorian
periodicals and of his and his wife's plans and revised plans for the *Wellesley
Index* **(1177)** as well as the problems they encountered, financial and otherwise.

1412. Hunt, Peter R. "A Note on R. C. Churchill's Defense of Chesterton on
Dickens." *Chesterton Review*, 12 (1986), 83-88.

Defends Churchill's *A Bibliography of Dickensian Criticism*, **(956)** against
Philip Collins's sometimes harsh criticism of it **(956)**.

1413. Loomis, Abigail A. "Dickens Duplications: A Study of Overlap in Serial
Bibliographies in Literature." *RQ* (Reference and Adult Services Division, American Library Association), 25 (1985/86), 348-55.

Concludes that there is no one serial bibliography in the humanities, and
particularly in literature, that "provides ongoing comprehensive coverage"
despite the need for such, though there is much overlapping. This study,
which analyzes the 1980 Dickens entries in the Modern Language Association
bibliography **(1042)**, the Modern Humanities Research Association bibliography **(1039)**, *The Year's Work in English Studies* **(1054)**, "Recent Dickens Studies"
in *Dickens Studies Annual* **(1047)**, "The Year's Work in Dickens Studies" **(1052)**
in the *Dickensian*, "The Dickens Checklist" **(1037)** in *Dickens Studies Newsletter*
(now *Dickens Quarterly*), and the "Victorian Bibliography" **(1058)** in *Victorian
Studies*, confirms statistically the great difficulty that scholars, and particularly
bibliographers, have in locating all the Dickens studies published in a given
year. The *Dickens Studies Newsletter* was found to contain the largest number of
entries and the shortest time lag (though about half were published prior to
1980), and, because highly selective, the *Dickensian* and the *Year's Work in English Studies* the smallest number. Loomis also found a high rate of duplication,
or overlap, and percentages of unique entries ranging from eight to fifteen
percent in the less selective bibliographies. She proposes that greater bibliographical control might be achieved through a consolidation or division of
efforts and certainly through more extensive cross-referencing, fewer retrospective entries, and clearer statements of editorial policies.

1414. Marshall, George. "'History of Pickwick." *Notes and Queries*, 8th ser., 11
(1897), 341-43.

Offers a long list of errors in Percy Fitzgerald's *The History of Pickwick* **(127)**,
occasioned by an earlier notice of an error (non-textual) by J. B. Firman,
p. 225, with further responses by C. C. B., pp. 414-15; by Marshall and also
Charles Green, pp. 473-74; and by John T. Page, 8th ser., 12 (1897), 13-14.

1415. Marshall, George. "'Pickwickian Manners and Customs.'" *Notes and Queries*, 9th ser., 1 (1898), 401-03.

Itemizes numerous errors in Percy Fitzgerald's *Pickwickian Manners and Customs* (**881**). See further contributions to the list by "Nemo," by C. C. B., and by Edward H. Marshall, p. 76, and by George Marshall again, pp. 314-15.

1416. [Matz, B. W]. "When Found." *Dickensian*, 2 (1906), 3-4.

Contains a brief commentary on an eight-volume grangerized copy of *Forster* with "extra plates, portraits, autograph letters, MSS, etc." in the sale of the late Sir Henry Irving's library. This copy is now in the Dickens House Library, London.

1417. Miller, William. "Elihu Burritt and Charles Dickens." *Dickensian*, 12 (1916), 37-39.

Asks for the whereabouts of an unpublished collection of newspaper and magazine obituary notices of Dickens's death collected by Burritt, "the blacksmith poet," in 1870.

1418. Miller, William, and A. de Suzannet. "Hatton and Cleaver's Bibliography." *Dickensian*, 30 (1933/34), 229-30.

The authors offer corrections to Hatton and Cleaver (**24**).

1419. Monod, Sylvère. "The Need for a Dickens Concordance." *Dickens Studies Newsletter*, 9 (1978), 65-69.

Makes a convincing case for the need for a Dickens concordance. Includes an introductory note by Joseph Gold, general editor of the projected concordance. Unfortunately, the project never got beyond the planning stage. Also see Dobrin (**1403**) and Gold (**1407**). A concordance is now available on the Internet (**1224**).

1420. Muir, P. H. "Rare Book Notes: The Blight of Dickens." *Bookseller*, 6 May 1936, p. 443; 4 June 1936, p. 551.

Warns collectors about patched-together collections of parts issues of Dickens's novels. In the 6 May article, Muir criticizes John Eckel, in his *The First Editions of the Writings of Charles Dickens and Their Values: A Bibliography* (**16**) for not being "blessed with a bibliographical turn of mind" in suggesting in his work that "by a little patching here and there from other sets, deficiencies may be supplied." Muir also complains that Eckel and other Dickens collectors pay too much attention to variations in "incidental features" (variations in plates, advertisements, and wrappers, for example) and not enough to textual variations, of which, he believes, many have gone unrecorded. In the 4 June article, Muir notes that Dickens "was vigorously collected in his own life-time," as evidenced by John Dexter's "Hints to Dickens Collectors" (**2216**) in *Dickens Memento* (**1948**); Charles P. Johnson's *Hints to Collectors of Original Editions of the Works of Charles Dickens*, 1885 (**27**); and J. C. Thomson's *Bibliography of the Writings of Charles Dickens*, 1904 (**48**). Where *A Christmas Carol* is concerned, Muir finds Eckel's conclusions about the issues of the first edition "hardly less doubtful" in his 1932 revision than in his 1913 edition; he also takes issue with E. A. Osborne's conclusions in "The Variants of 'The [sic] Christmas Carol'" (**280**).

1421. Paroissien, David. "Alan M. Cohn 1926-1989: In Memoriam." *Dickens Quarterly*, 6 (1989), 126-28.

In his tribute to a dedicated bibliographer, Paroissien, editor of *Dickens Quarterly*, answers the question of how Cohn, Humanities Librarian and Professor of English at Southern Illinois University, Carbondale, achieved such thoroughness of coverage in the quarterly Dickens bibliographies he compiled for *Dickens Studies Newsletter* and its successor, *Dickens Quarterly*, 1970-89 (**1037**): "Every working day he went through a batch of books and humanities journals placed in a box on his library desk and noted down anything of relevance to Dickens. Relevant citations were fed into a data bank stored in a computer, the books and journals left his desk to make their way, through other departments, into circulation for library users, while Dickensians all over the world waited for the publication of his quarterly bibliographies in the journal. Through the summers, through other vacations and even through semesters off he had earned for sabbatical leaves, the same disciplined steps of Al's routine proceeded without much variation."

1422. Patten, Robert L. "Proposal for an Annotated Edition of the Works of Charles Dickens Delivered to a Symposium on Dickens Held During the Modern Language Association of America Convention, 29 December 1969." *Dickens Studies Newsletter*, 2 (1971), 108-11.

Sees a great need to begin work on an annotated edition of the novels to supplement the volumes in the Clarendon Edition, which is strictly a *textual* edition. Patten offers examples of the value of such annotations to Dickens studies. Such a project, in modified form, has since been undertaken by Susan Shatto and colleagues in The Dickens Companions (**2311**).

1423. Prideaux, W. F. "Bibliographical Notes on Dickens and Thackeray." *Notes and Queries*, 10th ser., 3 (14 January 1905), 22-23.

In part a generally favorable commentary on J. C. Thomson's Dickens bibliography (**48**), though noting a couple of errors and misprints and wishing for "a more scientific plan" for the collations and a listing of collected editions. See Robert Pierpont (**436**) for a reply.

1424. Schlicke, Paul. "Editing *The Oxford Reader's Companion to Dickens.*" *Dickensian* 95 (1999), 206-11.

Schlicke comments on the conception, scope, emphasis, and production of this valuable guide (**2309**) that he edited (and much of which he wrote) for Oxford University Press.

1425. Shenker, Israel. "Unpublished Work by Joyce Is Found." *New York Times*, 19 September 1975, pp. 39, 49.

Reports the discovery of "a cache of unpublished writings" by James Joyce, including an essay entitled "The Centenary of Charles Dickens." A photographic facsimile of the first page of Joyce's eight-page manuscript accompanies the article. Shenker quotes Joyce's statement in the essay that Dickens had "few (if any) equals in the art of presenting a character."

1426. Strange, E. H. "Notes on the Bibliography of *Nicholas Nickleby.*" *Dickensian*, 33 (1936/37), 30-33.

Contains minor addenda to Hatton and Cleaver's "excellent collations" (**24**) of *Nicholas Nickleby* concerning the wrappers, advertisements, plates, and text of the monthly numbers.

PART FOUR: CATALOGUES, COLLECTIONS, SCRAPBOOKS, GUIDES, LIBRARY ACCESSIONS

Note: The reader will find a variety of works in this section, from national bibliographies and union catalogues (which, because of their extent, might well have been listed in 1A, above) to short lists of Dickensiana in local libraries. An enormous number of library catalogues are now available on the Internet—see Harner (**1147**) and particularly Libdex (**1522**), Libweb (**1484**), and OCLC WorldCat (**1503**). Printed catalogues of libraries with strong Dickens holdings that are available for consultation on the shelves of other libraries have also been included here. For an annotated list of other printed library catalogues, see Nelson (**1565**). Also see **Dickens collections** in part 2 of the subject index.

4A. LIBRARY CATALOGUES AND CATALOGUES OF DICKENS COLLECTIONS

Note: Also see **Dickens collections, library catalogues and catalogues of Dickens collections** in part 2 of the subject index.

1427. Alston, R. C. *Books with Manuscript: A Short Title Catalogue of Books with Manuscript Notes in the British Library, Including Books with Manuscript Additions, Proofsheets, Illustrations, Corrections, with Indexes of Owners and Books with Authorial Annotations.* London: British Library, 1994, p. 152.

Does not list any notes by Dickens himself, but does include four works by or about Dickens that contain annotations by others.

1428. Bath Municipal Libraries. *Charles Dickens. List of Works, Criticisms, etc., Dickensiana, Biography and Illustrations in Books and Periodicals in the Libraries, September, 1926.* Subject List No. 1. [Bath, Eng.: Bath Municipal Libraries, 1926]. 4 pp.

Lists works in the libraries under these headings: bibliographies, works, criticisms, Dickensiana, topography, Dickens and Bath, poetry on Dickens, biography, and illustrations.

1429. Baughman, Roland. *The Centenary of Arthur Rackham's Birth, September 19, 1867: An Appreciation of His Genius and a Catalogue of His Original Sketches,*

Drawings, and Paintings in the Berol Collection. New York: Columbia University Libraries, 1967, passim.

The catalogue lists and briefly describes several Dickens items in the Berol Collection, Columbia University Library: three original drawings each by Rackham for *A Christmas Carol* (1915) and *The Chimes* (1931), items A113-14, A233-35; line drawings in pen, undated, of "scenes reminiscent of *A Christmas Carol*, including a likeness of Dickens," item E16; and a sketchbook for *A Christmas Carol* and *The Romance of King Arthur and His Knights of the Round Table*, 61 pp., in pencil, item F14. This catalogue also contains an essay, "The Genius of Arthur Rackham," by Baughman, pp. 7-14, but it contains no reference to Rackham's illustrations for the two Christmas Books.

1430. [Bergen University Library, Bergen, Norway]. *Katalog over Jacob Christensens Dickens-samling/Catalogue of the Jacob Christensen Dickens Collection, Bergen University Library*. Bergen, Norway: Universitetsbiblioteket Bergen, 1974. 25 pp.

In a preface, printed in both English and Norwegian, John Brandrud, then director of the Bergen University Library, points out that the collection, donated by the wife of the late Jacob Christensen, a shipowner, contains about 370 books and pamphlets, including novels in parts and volume form, letters, manuscripts, proof sheets, association books, relics, and Dickensiana. The catalogue itself is divided into collected works, selected works and speeches, letters (published volumes not autograph letters), editions of individual works, biography and criticism, illustrations (published rather than original), miscellanea relating to Dickens, and manuscripts. The collection contains parts editions of twelve of Dickens's novels and *Sketches by Boz* and volume editions of major and minor works. The manuscripts include one page of the manuscript of *Dombey and Son*, several letters (one, to Clarkson Stanfield, 21 November 1845, is reproduced in facsimile), and a galley proof for parts of pp. 33 and 34 of *Mugby Junction* with several excisions and other corrections. This portion of the 1866 Christmas Story was written by Charles Collins, so the corrections, it is pointed out, may be by Dickens and show him tightening up Collins's manuscript. For a slightly earlier description of the collection, see Martens (**1678**).

1431. Bibliothèque Nationale de France, Paris. "Dickens (Charles)." In BN-OPALE PLUS Online Catalogue. http://www.bnf.fr.

The site is in French, but an English version may be selected. The catalogue lists books and periodicals in the national library of France in Paris "from the beginnings of printing to these days," amounting to 7,000,000 records, and presumably superseding the incomplete printed catalogues (**1432-33, 1493**). Also available on this home page is the Catalogue collectif de

France (ccfr), which accesses more than 14,000,000 documents from the Catalogue des fonds des bibliothèques municipales rétroconvertis and the Catalogue du système universitaire de documentation, in addition to the Catalogue BN-OPALE PLUS. To give some idea of the extent of these holdings, a "search simple" for editions of *David Copperfield* produced 172 entries from the BN-OPALE PLUS catalogue and 291 from the ccfr, which may be accessed separately at http://www.ccfr.bnf.fr.

1432. Bibliothèque Nationale, Paris. "Dickens (Charles)." In *Catalogue général des livres imprimés: Auteurs, collectivités–auteurs, anonymes, 1960-1969*. Série 1–Caractères Latins. Vol. 6. Paris: Bibliothèque Nationale, 1974, pp. 759-63.

Lists works by Dickens acquired by the library, 1960-69, predominantly works in French but also English editions and editions in other languages. For works acquired prior to 1910, see Ministère de l'Instruction publique et des Beaux-Arts (**1493**). For works acquired 1910-60, see Bibliothèque Nationale (**1433**). Superseded by the BN-OPALE PLUS Online Catalogue (**1431**).

1433. Bibliothèque Nationale, Paris. "Dickens (Charles)." In *Catalogue général des livres imprimés, 1879-1959: Supplément sur fiches, avec corrections et annotations*. Paris: Chadwyck-Healey France, 1986, fiches 258-59.

Lists works by Dickens acquired by the library, 1910-59–predominantly works in French but also English editions and editions in other languages. For works acquired prior to 1910, see Ministère de l'Instruction publique et des Beaux-Arts (**1493**). For works acquired after 1959, see Bibliothèque Nationale (**1432**). Superseded by the BN-OPALE PLUS Online Catalogue (**1431**).

1434. Bilas, Lidia Z. "Literature in the Lincke Collection Translated from the Spanish, French and English into German: A Bibliographic Survey of Translations in the Lincke Collection at the University of Chicago." *Dissertation Abstracts International*, 55 (1994/95), 2377A (University of Chicago, 1994).

The abstract does not mention Dickens, but he is surely represented among the over 15,000 volumes in this collection of works published 1780-1880 in the Lincke Rental Library, Leipzig. The collection, which represents, Bilas indicates, the reading of the middle-class Leipzig reader, contains 901 volumes of translations from the English, mainly narrative prose and novels.

1435. BLPC: The British Library Public Catalogue. http://blpc.bl.uk.

This site provides "simple searching and ordering of documents from the British Library's extensive collections"–by author, title, subject, and other categories. An author search for Dickens on 23 December 2002 produced 3,958 items and a subject search produced 2,589. One can also go to this site by way of the British Library's home page, http://portico.bl.uk, and from there link to the online catalogue, to the COPAC online catalogue (**1452**), or to numerous other British Library sites.

1436. British Library, London. *Charles Dickens: The J. F. Dexter Collection: Accessions to the General Catalogue of Printed Books, Manuscripts, Prints and Drawings.* London: Published for the British Library Board by the British Museum Publications, 1974. 120 columns; reprinted in Storey (**1527**).

Purchased in 1969, the collection contains first and later editions of the novels, speeches, reading editions, piracies and imitations; the autograph manuscript of the preface to the Cheap Edition of *Oliver Twist*; over sixty-eight letters; page proofs of parts of *Little Dorrit, Martin Chuzzlewit, The Old Curiosity Shop*, and lesser works, with Dickens's corrections; albums of original drawings by Cruikshank, Hablot K. Browne, and others; additional illustrations for the novels; and a variety of rare Dickensiana. Volumes in the collection frequently have letters, newspaper cuttings, portraits, and other matter inserted in them. This catalogue is intended as a supplement to the Dickens entries in the *British Library General Catalogue of Printed Books* (**1438**). All items in the collection have been microfilmed as part of the *Charles Dickens Research Collection* put together by an editorial board headed by Graham Storey (**1527**).

Reviews: P. Collins, *Times Literary Supplement*, 5 December 1975, p. 1464 (a descriptive review); K. Tillotson, *Dickensian*, 72 (1976), 101-03 (comments favorably and in some detail on the collection and on Dexter, whom she sees as "the first and greatest English collector of early Dickens editions and Dickensiana" and as a "man of vast knowledge and fine judgment").

1437. British Library, London, Department of Manuscripts. "Dickens, Charles." In *Index of Manuscripts in the British Library*. Vol. 3. Cambridge, Eng.: Chadwyck-Healey, 1984, pp. 290-91.

Lists principally letters but also six leaves of the manuscript of *Pickwick Papers*, letters to and agreements with Richard Bentley, and several minor items. Also see under headings for other members of Dickens's family for a few more items.

1438. British Library, London, Department of Printed Books. "Dickens (Charles)." In *The British Library General Catalogue of Printed Books to 1975*. Vol. 82. London, München, New York, Paris: K. G. Saur, 1981, pp. 349-447; also supplements, *1976 to 1982*. Vol. 12, 1983, pp. 409-13; *1982 to 1985*. Vol. 7, 1983, pp. 487-90; *1986 to 1987*. Vol. 5., 1988, pp. 274-77; *1988 to 1989*. Vol. 7, 1990, pp. 175-77; *1990 to 1992*. Vol. 7, 1993, pp. 77-80; *1993 to 1994*. Vol. 7, 1995, pp. 148-50; *1995 to 1996*. Vol. 7, 1997, pp. 80-82.

A list of the Dickens holdings in the British Library, London, divided into 1) Works, 2) Smaller Collections, 3) Letters, 4) Speeches, 5) Single Works, 6) Selections, Adaptations and Abridgements from Two or More Works, 7) Works Edited with Prefaces by Dickens, 8) Doubtful and Suppositious Works, 9) Bibliographical Appendix, and 10) General Appendix. The last two sections, containing short-form references to entries listed elsewhere in the catalogue under their authors' names, provide useful lists of bibliographical and other secondary studies of Dickens. Also see works by other members of the Dickens family, immediately preceding and following the Charles Dickens entries. The supplements list individual and secondary works separately, but with no subheadings. Further two-year supplements are expected. These printed catalogues are, however, pretty much superseded by the British Library's online catalogue, the British Library Public Catalogue, http://blpc.bl.uk (**1435**), which brings the holdings up to date. Various subject catalogues and supplements of the library's holdings (from 1881 on) are available, but have not been listed here. As Harner (**1147**) indicates, p. 34, the online catalogue, "for the most part, supersedes an unwieldy array of printed catalogs that were frequently difficult to search by anyone unfamiliar with the complex British Library cataloging rules."

1439. British Museum, London. *Charles Dickens. An Excerpt from the General Catalogue of Printed Books in the British Museum.* London: British Museum; printed by William Clowes and Sons, 1926. 29 pp.

Includes all books by and many about Dickens in the British Museum Library (later, the British Library) through 1926; a predecessor of **1440** and the Dickens entries in **1435** and **1438**.

1440. British Museum, London. *Dickens. An Excerpt from the General Catalogue of Printed Books in the British Museum.* London: The Trustees of the British Museum, 1960, cols. 236-378 [72 pp.].

Includes all books by and many about Dickens in the British Museum Library (later, the British Library) through 1955. Updates **1439** and precedes the Dickens entries **1435** and **1438**.

1441. British Museum, London, [Department of Manuscripts]. *Catalogue of Additions to the Manuscripts: Plays Submitted to the Lord Chamberlain, 1824-1851: Additional Manuscripts 42865-43038.* London: Trustees of the British Museum, 1964, pp. 51-54.

Includes copies of Dickens's *The Village Coquettes* (autograph, 1836), *The Strange Gentleman* (autograph, 1836), and *Is She His Wife? or Something Singular* (1837), all now in the British Library. Also consult the title index for dramatizations of Dickens's novels and stories by others. As noted in the preface by

T. C. Skeat, the Licensing Act of 1737 "required copies of all plays intended for performance in Great Britain to be submitted to the Lord Chamberlain for scrutiny." The whole collection, Harner (**1147**) notes, pp. 187-88, is "an unrivaled collection of manuscripts and printed acting copies and editions documenting English theater and drama since the early eighteenth century." Manuscript and printed copies of plays submitted between 1852 and 1967 and plays produced from 1968 on (when licensing was no longer required), he indicates, are in the Department of Manuscripts, British Library, and indexed there.

1442. British Museum, London, [Department of Manuscripts]; later, British Library, [Department of Manuscripts]. "Dickens, (Charles)." In *Catalogue of Additions to the Manuscripts in the British Museum in the Years MDCCCLIV-MDCCCLXXV*. London: British Museum; later, British Library, 1880, passim; continued in six-year, then five-year cumulations thereafter, except for a ten-year cumulation, 1936-45, until the 1951-55 volume (published 1982), passim. The volumes for 1956-75 are in preparation. A new series began with the volume for 1986-90 (published 1993), which was followed by that for 1981-85 (1994) and that for 1976-80 (1995), passim.

The 1880 volume was the first in this monumental series that goes back to acquisitions in 1776 (published 1843) to list and describe manuscripts by and about Dickens, the earliest from 1870 (principally letters and reminiscences about Dickens). An *Index* that gives accession numbers, which may then be consulted for fuller descriptions in the catalogue itself, was usually published with the section on *Descriptions* in a single volume until the 1936-45 and later cumulations, when the two sections were published separately as *Part I: Descriptions* and *Part II: Index*. Dickens items appear regularly.

1443. Brooklyn Public Library, Brooklyn, NY. *Charles Dickens, 1812-1870. A List of Books and of References to Periodicals in the Brooklyn Public Library*. Brooklyn, NY: Brooklyn Public Library, 1912. 68 pp.

An annotated list of bibliographies, editions, plays based upon Dickens's works (six only), and "biography, criticism, etc." (books, parts of books, and periodical pieces)–as of 1912. Unfortunately, a number of these works are now missing from the library's collection.

1444. Bushloper, Lida. "Author-Emended Printed Material in the Huntington Library." *Huntington Library Quarterly*, 57 (1994), 61-78.

Under Dickens (p. 68), lists a reading copy of *Doctor Marigold* with deletions marked, a corrected proof of *New Uncommercial Samples*, and the corrected proof of a speech (no date given).

1445. Carr, Sister Mary Callista, comp. *Catalogue of the Dickens Collection at the University of Texas.* Austin: University of Texas Humanities Research Center, 1961. ix + 195 pp.; revised as *A Catalogue of the VanderPoel Dickens Collection at the University of Texas.* By Sister Lucile Carr. Tower Bibliographical Series, 1. Austin: University of Texas Press, 1968. xi + 274 pp.

An impressive catalogue of 1) "Autograph Manuscripts and Other Original Work" ("The Ivy Green," 137 Dickens letters, and illustrations to his works); 2) "Books and Periodicals" (various parts issues and other editions of Dickens's works, speeches, letters, selections, collected editions, parodies, plagiarizations, and dramatizations, including a previously unrecorded prime *Pickwick* in parts, for which the full collation is given, a set that Sister Carr describes as a "near approach to completeness"); 3) "Extra Illustrations and Portraits"; 4) "Dickensiana" (including association books, songs and music, critiques, and studies); and 5) "Biographies and Bibliographies." Fourteen illustrations.

The expanded catalogue of 1968 notes that the original collection described in the 1961 edition has been supplemented by "the fine collection" of Halstead VanderPoel and named for him, the principal additions being an album of original watercolor and pencil illustrations to *Pickwick Papers* drawn for F. W. Cosens by "Phiz" (Hablot K. Browne), a pre-publication copy of *A Christmas Carol*, and numerous early American editions of Dickens's works. The collection also contains a publisher's proof of volume 1 (containing the first part of *Pickwick Papers*) of the St. Dunstan Illuminated Edition of Dickens's works, meant to be "Printed on Vellum and bound in richly decorated blue morocco," but, the catalogue notes, "so far as we know the projected edition was never published." Plate VII is a photographic facsimile of the title page for volume 1. The items in 1), above, have been increased by twenty-six (but no new Dickens letters or manuscripts), in 2) by 336, in 3) by eighteen, in 4) by 228, and in 5) by seventy-three. Twenty-four illustrations. Also see Genet (**1796**).

Reviews (1961 edition): S. Nowell-Smith, *Library*, 5th ser., 17 (1962), 173-75 (comments favorably on the collection itself but would like more bibliographical detail and commentary in the catalogue); E. A. Osborne, *Book Collector*, 10 (1961), 231-35 ("marred by the bad organization of its material, redundancy, the misuse of established bibliographical terms and the creation of new and vague ones, and insufficient use of available Dickensian research"); [L. S. Thompson], *Papers of the Bibliographical Society of America*, 55 (1961), 408 ("meticulous"); *Times Literary Supplement*, 31 March 1961, p. 208 (a brief description only).

Reviews (1968 edition): *Choice*, 7 (1970/71), 49 (a valuable collection, but the edition itself is "extravagantly handsome . . . puffery"); J. Fletcher, *Library Journal*, 95 (1970), 2157 (a brief notice); S. Nowell-Smith, *Library*, ser. 5, 25 (1970), 170 (briefly notes the expansion of entries in the revised edition—see his earlier review, above); T. d'A. Smith, *Dickensian*, 66 (1970), 251-53 (a highly critical review; finds errors, omissions, a "tacit dismissal of all research," practically no attempt to further "bibliographical knowledge of Dickens"); [L. S. Thompson], *Papers of the Bibliographical Society of America*, 63 (1969), 350 (a brief description); *Times Literary Supplement*, 26 February 1970, p. 232 (finds errors, oversights, and misinformation); R. Vogler, *Dickens Studies Newsletter*, 1, iii (December 1970), 15-18 ("useful though defective"; ultimately "will take its place on the shelf of standard Dickens reference works"); G. Wing, *Ariel: A Review of International English Literature,* 1, iv (October 1970), 56-66 ("attractively produced" and seemingly "admirably organized").

1446. Centro Nazionale per il Catalogo Unico delle Biblioteche Italiane e per le Informazioni Bibliografiche, Rome. *Catalogo cumulativo, 1886-1957, del Bollettino delle Pubblicazioni Italiane ricevute per diritto di stampa dalla Biblioteca Nazionale Centrale di Firenze.* Vol. 13. Nendeln, Liechtenstein: Kraus Reprint, 1968, pp. 77-84.

Lists Dickens's works published in Italy and principally in Italian in the Biblioteca Nazionale Centrale, Florence. Balay (**1133**), p. 81, indicates that for 1886-1957, this is the most complete record of Italian publications based on copyright deposit, and that its annual supplements, from 1958 on, published with the title *Bibliografia Nazionale italiana: Catalogo alfabetico annuale. A cura della Biblioteca nazionale Centrale di Firenze* comprise "an important bibliographical tool for Italian publications." For readers of Italian, more information can be found on the Web site http://iccu.sbn.it/istituto.html.

1447. *Charles Dickens.* Tenri Central Library Photo-Series, 26. Tenri, Japan: Tenri Central Library, n. d.

A catalogue listing two brief autograph Dickens letters, first editions in parts of several of Dickens's works, and a few miscellaneous items acquired by the library. Illustrated.

1448. *Charles Dickens, 1812-1870: A Bibliography.* St. James-Assiniboia, Can.: St. James-Assiniboia Public Library, [1970]. 8 pp.

A very small handlist of standard Dickens works and studies in the library with an introduction by John S. Russell, Chief Librarian.

1449. Clapinson, Mary, and T. D. Rogers. *Summary Catalogue of Post-Medieval Western Manuscripts in the Bodleian Library, Oxford: Acquisitions 1916-1975.* 3 vols. Oxford: Clarendon Press; New York: Oxford University Press, 1991, passim.

See the Dickens entry in the index, III, 1571, where letters by both Dickens and his son Charles are listed, as well as a photograph of Dickens and a manuscript fragment of *Mrs. Lirriper's Lodgings.*

1450. Clark, William A., Jr. *The Library of William Andrews Clark, Jr.:* **The Posthumous Papers of the Pickwick Club,** *by Charles Dickens. The Douglas-Austin Copy Now in the Possession of William Andrews Clark, Jr. A Bibliographical Description.* San Francisco: Printed by J. H. Nash, 1920. 12 pp.

A full number by number collation of the so-called "Douglas" copy of *Pickwick Papers* in parts. An accompanying letter, pp. 9-10, from John C. Eckel to S. H. Austin, Philadelphia, former owner of the set, asserts that this "far excels either in brilliancy and 'points'" the Lapham set (**122**), with which he had compared it. Also included, pp. 10-12 are some notes on the writing, illustrating, and publishing of *Pickwick Papers*. Also see Cowan and Clark (**1453-54**) and University of California (**1536**).

1451. The Club of Odd Volumes, Boston. *The Works of George Cruikshank in Oil, Water Colors, Original Drawings, Etchings, Woodcuts, Lithographs, and Glyphographs, Collected by John B. Gough, with a Facsimile of the Catalogue and Twenty-Eight Original Drawings Reproduced by Photogravure.* Boston: The Club of Odd Volumes, 1890, passim.

Includes an alphabetical list of titles of Cruikshank's illustrations in the twenty-five volumes of Gough's collection, including those for *Sketches by Boz*, *Oliver Twist*, and the *Memoirs of Joseph Grimaldi*, as well as a list of the original sketches included in volume 25, which contains other sketches of Dickens's scenes from *Sketches by Boz* and *Oliver Twist*. Among the illustrations reproduced are a pencil sketch of Dickens at age 26 and a pencil drawing for "Oliver Twist at Mrs. Maylie's Door."

1452. Consortium of University Research Libraries (CURL). COPAC Web catalogue. http://copac.ac.uk/copac.

Provides free access to "the merged online catalogues of 22 of the largest university research libraries in the UK and Ireland *plus* the British Library," with other library catalogues to be added in the future. The catalogues may be searched by author/title, periodical, or subject. An author search for Dickens on 11 November 2002 produced 7,523 entries, while a subject search produced 4,735 entries.

1453. Cowan, Robert E., and William A. Clark, Jr., comps. *The Library of William Andrews Clark, Jr.: Cruikshank and Dickens. In Two Parts: Part I: Cruikshank. Part II: Dickens.* 2 vols. San Francisco, CA: John Henry Nash, 1921-23; reprinted as two vols. in one, New York: Johnson Reprint Corp., 1969. 145 + 94 pp.

Contains full bibliographical descriptions of Clark's collection of miscellaneous works illustrated by Cruikshank and collections of Cruikshank's works (I, 1-77; II, 1-54) and first editions of Dickens's works (I, 79-142; II, 57-90), some in parts. The editions in parts are itemized number by number and with identification of the advertising in them as well. There are also indexes to authors and titles listed for both Cruikshank and Dickens. Volume II includes detailed issue by issue descriptions of the *Bentley's Miscellany* volumes edited by

Dickens and of the Christmas Numbers of *Household Words* and *All the Year Round* and various interesting editions of Dickens's works. Some volumes in the library contain inserted letters or other materials. Also see Clark (**1450**), Cowan and Clark (**1454**), and University of California (**1536**).

1454. Cowan, Robert E., and William A. Clark, Jr., comps. *The Library of William Andrews Clark, Jr.: Index to Authors and Titles.* 2 vols. San Francisco: John H. Nash, 1922-30, I, 33-38 and passim; II, 30-34 and passim.

Contains short entries, giving only author, title, place of publication, imprint, and edition, as well as a reference to the fuller entry in the various volumes of the library's catalogues, including the Dickens-Cruikshank catalogue (**1453**), and the *Pickwick Papers* catalogue (**1450**). Also see University of California (**1536**).

1455. Currie, Barton. "John Forster and the Dickens Manuscripts." In his *Fishers of Books.* Boston: Little, Brown, 1931, pp. 60-85 and passim.

A listing of the manuscripts and page proofs in the Forster Collection, Victoria and Albert Museum Library, London. In a rambling account, Currie locates and comments on other Dickens manuscripts and reprints a then unpublished letter from Dickens to Madame De la Rue (27 September 1845), partly reproduced in photo facsimile. He also indicates problems associated with collecting a prime *Pickwick* in parts and, throughout, gives passing hints to Dickens collectors. Illustrated.

1456. [Dickens, Marie Roche, Lady]. Manuscript Material Forming Part of the Dickens-Roche Gift of Translations of Dickens's Works. In British Library, London. L. R. 106. b. 22. [1935, etc.]. 30 unnumbered pp.

Contains "Catalogue of Translations of Charles Dickens' Works Belonging to Marie Dickens. Begun in 1908," pp. [1]-[7], a handwritten list of fifty-four works, apparently as received since they are not in alphabetical order, written in a small lined notebook of about 4½" x 7", giving title, number of volumes, the language of the translation, and in some instances place of publication. This is followed by "Catalogue. C. D. Translations 1933," pp. [9]-[11]. Alphabetized by language, this is a more organized continuation of the first catalogue, with seventy-six titles. The third catalogue is entitled "C. D. Room," pp. [16]-[27], a list of books, presumably then in the home of Lady Dickens and Sir Henry Fielding Dickens, her husband, identified as in various cupboards, containing editions of Dickens's works as well as bibliographies, published letters, biographies, critical studies, topographical studies, Dickens Fellowship materials, and miscellaneous works. Also included is a list labeled "Auntie's Books," obviously those having belonged to Georgina Hogarth. Bound in with the notebook are numerous letters written to Marie Dickens about translations of Dickens's novels into various languages, some with lists of translations, and all obviously in response to her inquiries.

1457. The Dickens House, now, as of 2003, The Dickens Museum, London. Library Collections.

The Dickens House, 48 Doughty Street, London, the residence of Dickens, his wife, and growing family from late March or early April 1837 to December 1839, became the property of the Dickens House Trust (officially The Dickens House and Dickens House Fund) and was turned into a museum in 1925. Unfortunately, though there are in-house card catalogues and those for some of the collections are currently being generated on the computer, there is no printed or online catalogue of its holdings, nor of the library of manuscripts, editions of Dickens's works, and Dickensiana that developed over the years, largely through gifts from Dickensians, Dickens scholars, and Dickens collectors—except for the Miller and Suzannet collections (see below). Thus a catalogue of its full holdings cannot be consulted elsewhere. A few individual collections have been catalogued. There are plans, however, for a full cataloguing of these collections. The entries here can only give a general view of this excellent collection and are pretty much limited to characterizing the library portion of the museum. For more information about the house itself, its interior, and the collection of furnishings and memorabilia, see Harris and Parker (**1652**), *The Dickens House* (**1579**), "Some Treasures of the Dickens House. 1. Personal Relics" (**1741**), and The Dickens House, Miscellaneous Scrapbooks (**1575**).

The library itself began to form before the opening of the Dickens House, with the creation of the National Dickens Library, built on the collection of Frederic G. Kitton, in 1908, under the aegis of the Corporation of London. At this time, Harris and Parker point out, it consisted of 451 volumes and was housed in the Guildhall until 1925, when, "much augmented by donations, it became the nucleus of the Dickens House Library." A catalogue of the library in 1908 exists in manuscript in the Dickens House, Harris and Parker indicate, but it was never printed, and one started in 1925 was apparently never completed. Also see "A National Dickens Library" (**1687**), Rendall (**1718**), and Ridge (**1720**). The library was considerably expanded by the B. W. Matz Collection in 1925 and by a number of other collections since (see below). See Harris and Parker for fuller details. The present-day library consists of two main divisions: 1) the collection of first and later editions of individual Dickens works and collected editions (some twenty-five sets) and 2) the collection of Dickensiana—bibliographies, textual studies, biographies, biographical studies, critical studies, specialized studies, photographs, slides, and other media. Over the years, numerous manuscripts and letters by Dickens, letters and documents by others (members of the Dickens family, friends, acquaintances, and associates), original drawings for the novels and other art work, playbills, and memorabilia have also been acquired, largely through the generosity of Comte Alain de Suzannet and, following his death in December 1950, the comtesse–see The Suzannet Collection, below. These items comprise, perhaps, a third division of the library–the items on display in the museum itself. Special collections include the following:

A. The Suzannet Collection, completed 1971.

An amazingly rich collection that includes first and early editions, presentation copies (a special feature of the collection), early translations, reading copies (with revisions and often stage directions in Dickens's hand), original drawings for the novels, portraits of Dickens and other paintings, playbills and programs, and a variety of Dickensiana in addition to letters and other manuscripts. Fortunately, a printed catalogue of the Suzannet Collection has been published–Michael Slater's *The Catalogue of the Suzannet Charles Dickens Collection* (**1524**). As Slater indicates in the introduction, scarcely a year passed, from the 1930s on, "without the Dickens House being enriched by the gift of some notable item from the rapidly growing collection" of the comte, the latest being in 1971, some years after the comte's death in December 1950, when, Slater notes, the comtesse presented "a very substantial part of the collection" to the Dickens House, "the most magnificent donation the museum has ever received." Many of these gifts are on exhibition in the Suzannet Rooms at the Dickens House. The manuscripts include a number of Dickens letters and documents (Slater lists 443 items–only eleven or so are not letters–in his catalogue, including a number of letters given by Walter Dexter that had originally been given to him by the comte), Maria Beadnell's album, a page of the manuscript of *Pickwick Papers* (out of the twelve that the comte acquired), chapter 9 of the manuscript of *Nicholas Nickleby*, the manuscripts of "The Schoolboy's Story" and "Our Commission," a set of prompt books for some of Dickens's amateur productions with manuscript notes and stage directions in Dickens's hand, Dickens's own copy of the proofs of Bulwer-Lytton's *Not So Bad as We Seem* with corrections in his and John Forster's hands, and other documents connected with the amateur performances and his reading tours. Also see Collins (**645, 652**), "Gift of Dickens Manuscripts" (**1639**), "Magnificent Gift to the Dickens House" (**1675**), "A Princely Donation: Munificent Gift to the Dickens House" (**1708**), and Suzannet (**1529-30**) for fuller details.

B. The Farrer-Ouvry Papers, 1994.

The most recent collection to enter the Dickens House is the Farrer-Ouvry Papers, on permanent loan from Farrer & Company, London. This is a large metal lawyer's box of papers, labeled "Charles Dickens, Esq.," containing letters and documents associated with the various legal matters handled by the firm for Dickens and his heirs, 1858-1954, in some forty-eight files (from a list supplied by Farrer and Company), as follows:

1. Letters and documents concerning the winding up of *Household Words*, 1858-59.
2. Further letters on *Household Words*, etc., 1859-60, 1868.
3. Letters and papers concerning *All the Year Round* and Dr. Michael M. Laseron, director of the Industrial Orphan Home, April-May 1866.
4. Letters and papers concerning the threatened action against Colin Rae Brown, a journalist, for slander, October 1858 (see *Pilgrim Letters*, VIII, 754).
5. Letters about the death of Walter Savage Landor Dickens, 31 December 1863, 1863-68.
6. Agreement with T. C. Evans (about a series of eighty readings in the United States) and other items, 1867-69.
7. Letters about J. Arnold Cave of the Marylebone Theatre and Dickens, 1866.
8. Correspondence about Charles Fechter, a French actor, 1869-70.
9. Documents concerning publication in New Zealand and Boston of *Our Mutual Friend* and *Edwin Drood*; notes on the sale of Dickens's copyrights to Chapman and Hall.
10. Pocket "Letts Diary" for 1874 belonging to John Forster.
11. Letters of Georgina Hogarth to Frederic Ouvry concerning the business arrangements for her edition of the letters of Charles Dickens and letters from Charles Dickens the Younger to her.
12-17. Letters from John Forster, acting as Dickens's executor, to Farrer & Company, 1870-72.
18. Numerous letters by Forster, Georgina Hogarth, and others, principally to Farrer & Company, and other documents, principally legal, some concerned with the shares of Dickens's children in his estate.
19. Business and legal correspondence connected with the disposal of the Forster estate, 1876-77.
20-21. Letters, largely to Farrer & Company, August-November 1894 and 1870-77.
22. Letters concerning a performance of *A Message from the Sea*, January 1861.
23. Letter to Dickens from H. Buchanan MacPhail, supplementing those concerning Colin Rae Brown (No. 4, above), 1858.
24a. Letters to Farrer & Company concerning King & Company, coach builders, February 1866.
24b. Letters and documents concerning the estate of Henry Austin, Dickens's brother-in-law, 1861-62.
25. Letters connected with the Dickenses' separation, May-July 1858.
26. Documents concerning Dickens's estate.
27. Letters concerning Dickens and his son Sidney, 1869-70.
28. Letters and documents concerning sums received by Dickens's children as legatees, 1870-75.

29. Papers relating to the piracy of *Great Expectations* by the *Eastern Province Herald* of South Africa in 1861.
30. Further papers concerning Charles Fechter, 1868-69.
31. Letters from Charles Dickens the Younger to W. H. Wills, etc., concerning the dispute about Wills's share in *All the Year Round*, 1871.
32. Correspondence concerning the piracy of *The Strange Gentleman*, 1873.
33. Miscellaneous letters and documents unrelated to Dickens, 1870-71.
34. Accounts concerning *Edwin Drood*, 1871.
35. Draft Deed of Separation of Dickens from his wife, 7 June 1858.
36. Letters from Coutts & Company concerning the disposal of Dickens's estate, 1870-72.
37. Fifteen letters from Georgina Hogarth to Farrer & Company, 1871-88.
38-39. Letters to Dickens, letters to and from members of his household, and other letters and documents on various matters, 1868-75.
40-41. Documents concerning the Royal Literary Fund, 1891; the Dickens Centenary Fund, 1912; and documents and letters concerning a variety of other matters, 1869-1934.
42. Deeds relating to Gad's Hill Place, 1817-91.
43. Copies of letters, 1954.
44-45. Documents regarding the Trustees of the Dickens Centenary Trust Fund, 1928-29.
46. K. J. Fielding file concerning a new edition of Dickens's letters, 1950.
47. Arthur A. Adrian file, 1953.

This collection has now been fully cataloged on computer at the Dickens House.

C. Other Special Collections or Bequests (chronologically arranged below).

These collections, originally separate and distinct, have been incorporated into the general collection, either as part of the items on exhibition at the museum or in the library of editions and Dickensiana.

1. The F. G. Kitton Collection, 1908.

First and later editions of Dickens's works, plagiarisms and continuations of his novels, Dickensiana, portraits, autograph letters of Dickens and his friends, original drawings by Kitton and other modern artists for Dickens's works, a variety of Dickensiana, and eighteen volumes of magazine articles and ten volumes of newspaper cuttings—see Dickens House, Miscellaneous Scrapbooks (**1575**). Also see "A National Dickens Library" (**1687**), Ridge (**1720**), and Ward (**1760**).

2. The B. W. Matz Collection, 1925-26.

A collection of numerous editions of Dickens's works, a variety of Dickensiana, and valuable scrapbooks. For the scrapbooks, see Dickens

House, Miscellaneous Scrapbooks (**1575**); for the books and other materials, see Palmer (**1697**) and Ridge (**1720**).

3. The Dr. Howard Duffield Collection of Droodiana, 1937-38.

Various editions, translations, source books, press clippings, continuations, scholarly studies and debates, and dramatic versions. For the catalogue of this collection, see Duffield (**1459**). Also see Carden (**1604**), Hopkins (**1805**), and Roe (**1721**).

4. The William Miller Collection of Dickens Music, 1940.

Nearly 200 pieces of music based on Dickens's works. See Hill (**1473**) for a catalogue of items in this gift to the Dickens House. For a report on the recent conserving of this collection, see "When Found: The Music Collection in the Dickens House" (**1766**). Also see Lightwood (**1486**).

5. The Dr. Sydney A. Henry and Miss M. Henry Collection, 1959.

A collection of first editions, especially in parts. See Harris and Parker (**1652**) and Staples (**1744**).

6. The William J. Carlton Bequest, 1974.

Consists of fifteen autograph letters, thirteen other letters and manuscripts related to Dickens, and a collection of books and pamphlets. See Slater (**1737**).

7. The Noel C. Peyrouton Bequest, 1976.

Over 100 Dickens letters (most then previously unpublished), forty-three letters by people who had known Dickens that were written to F. G. Kitton while he was compiling *Charles Dickens by Pen and Pencil* (**1248**), one page of the autograph manuscript of *Tom Tiddler's Ground*, several volumes from Dickens's own Gad's Hill library, and a variety of Dickensiana. See Slater (**1736**).

8. The Gladys Storey Papers, 1980.

A "rich and fascinating" collection of notes, notebooks, diary transcriptions, newspaper cuttings, photographs, a typescript of Storey's *Dickens and Daughter* (London: Frederick Muller, 1939), and numerous other materials, as reported by Parker and Slater (**1701**).

9. The Philip F. Skottowe Papers, 1980.

Includes Dickensian books and papers and Skottowe's manuscripts of biographies of Thomas N. Talfourd and Clarkson Stanfield. See Slater (**1735**).

10. The Sir Felix Aylmer Papers, 1981.

Connected with Aylmer's research for his *Dickens Incognito* (London: Rupert Hart-Davis, 1959). Mentioned in Harris and Parker (**1652**).

11. The Leslie C. Staples Bequest, 1981.

The gift includes letters (by Dickens, Ellen Ternan, and others), plagiarisms and piracies, and a variety of Dickensiana. See Reynolds (**1719**) and Makinen (**1676**).

D. The Photographic Collection.

Based on the collection of T. W. Tyrrell, this includes photographs of portraits of Dickens (painted and photographic), portraits (painted and photographic) of his family and circle (a strong collection, including Ellen Ternan), topography of London relating to Dickens's novels (mainly photographs), topography of Kent and miscellaneous topography, illustrations (both original and later) of the novels, homes of Dickens from childhood on, and miscellaneous (ranging from social conditions to other topography). Catalogued.

E. Glass Negative and Film Negative Collection.

Some 4,000 glass and 3,000 film negatives including portraits, topography, and illustrations for the novels. Catalogued.

F. 35 mm. Slide Collection.

Duplicates parts of the photographic collection, particularly topography. Catalogued.

G. Magic Lantern Slide Collection.

An extensive collection, in process of being catalogued. It includes portraits of Dickens, his family, and friends; his homes; topography; illustrations to the works; and miscellaneous—quite a rich resource.

H. Post Card Collection.

A mixture of the rare and the commonplace, 1870-date, concentrating on illustrations to the novels, topography, actors in plays based on Dickens's novels, and theatrical productions of his novels. Also see Dickens House, Miscellaneous Scrapbooks (**1575M-N**).

I. Film, Video, and Audio Collection.

A small collection at this time. Some early films unfortunately needed to be destroyed—see Harris and Parker (**1652**).

J. Collection of Minutes of the Executive Committee of the Dickens Fellowship, 1904/05-date.

Some are in shorthand.

K. Collection in Storeroom Boxes.

A miscellaneous collection of storage boxes labeled Dickensian Topography, Dickens Fellowship Events, Birthday Dinners and Programs (2 boxes), Film and Theatre Programs and Posters (3 boxes), Dickensian Music, Exhibition/Auction Catalogues (2 boxes), Dramatizations (film scripts/plays), Dickens's Family and Friends, Illustrations of Dickens's Characters, Research Material and Illustrations Gathered by C. H. Green for an Extra-illustrated Edition of *A Tale of Two Cities*, Productions of Dickens's Works by the Dickens Fellowship Players, Yorkshire Television Production of *Dickens in London*, Cloisterham Mailbag, Part 1 (letters from the Duffield Collection), Literary Articles, Staples Papers, Newspaper Cuttings from the Staples Bequest, and some seventeen additional boxes of even more miscellaneous materials.

L. The Objects Photographic Collection.

A 35 mm. film collection, containing photographs of every object in the Dickens House collection. In progress.

M. The Clippings Collection.

A large collection of loose black-and-white and colored prints and engravings clipped or obtained from a variety of sources. All are in process of being photographed for easy accessibility and use.

N. Nina Burgis Papers.

A collection of materials and notes and copies of original documents, published and unpublished, compiled as part of this eminent scholar's research into nineteenth-century social history.

O. Miscellaneous Audiovisual Materials.

A small collection of uncatalogued video and audio tapes and film stills.

For other items in the Dickens House and the Dickens House library, see **Dickens House, collections** in part 2 of the subject index.

1458. Driver, Clive E., comp. *A Selection from Our Shelves: Books, Manuscripts and Drawings from the Philip H. & A. S. W. Rosenbach Foundation Museum*. Philadelphia: The Museum, 1973. Pages unnumbered.

The Dickens items, numbered 73-75, include a Cruikshank pencil drawing for "The Tuggs's at Ramsgate" (*Sketches by Boz*), twenty-four leaves of the manuscript of *Pickwick Papers* (parts of chapters 13 and 35), and a part of the manuscript of *Nicholas Nickleby* (the complete chapter 10, twenty-six leaves of chapter 16, seventeen leaves of chapter 17, and the complete chapter 20). Illustrated with the Cruikshank drawing and a facsimile of a page of *Pickwick Papers* manuscript.

1459. Duffield, Howard. *A Catalogue of the Curious Literature Created by the Unfinished Novel of Charles Dickens "The Mystery of Edwin Drood". . . . Exhibited at the Grolier Club in the City of New York, State of New York, U. S. A.* Unpublished typescript in the Dickens House, London, 1938. 132 pp.

The annotated catalogue of the Howard Duffield Collection of Edwin Drood Literature in the Dickens House (**1457C3**), listed under the following headings: 1) Starting Points, 2) The Novel, 3) Illustrators and Illustrations, 4) Continuations, 5) Solutions, 6) Dramatizations, 7) Monographs, 8) Periodicals, 9) Newspapers, 10) Allusions and References, 11) Background, 12) Side-Lights. See Hopkins (**1805**). Also see Carden (**1604**) and Roe (**1721**).

1460. Eaton, Seymour, ed. *Charles Dickens: Rare Print Collection.* In 10 parts in paper covers. Connoisseur Edition. Philadelphia: Published for private circulation by R. G. Kennedy, 1900. 75 plates.

The plates, some in color, with no accompanying text apart from captions, include sixty-three paintings, engravings, drawings, and photographs of Dickens, his family, and friends (see Parts I, II, IV, V, VIII, IX, and X). Part III contains reproductions of six playbills and the wrapper cover of the monthly installments of *Pickwick Papers*. Part VI contains reproductions of various documents and items of Dickensiana (Dickens's marriage license, one-half page of the manuscript of *David Copperfield*, a page in Dickens's hand from Ellis and Blackmore's Cash Book of 1828, for example). Part VII contains drawings, mainly by F. G. Kitton, of Dickens's homes. Podeschi (**1509**), who lists two numbered sets of Eaton's collection in the Gimbel collection at Yale University, points out that "this 'rare print collection' was in reality printed in large quantities and widely advertised" (p. 455). A copy in the Brooklyn Public Library, for example, is not identified as the Connoisseur Edition, nor are the place of publication and publisher identified in a volume obviously put together from the ten published parts.

1461. Edwards, Peter, and Andrew Dowling, eds. *The Edmund Yates Papers in the University of Queensland Library: A Catalogue.* Victorian Fiction Research Guides, 21. [St. Lucia, Austral.]: University of Queensland, 1993, passim.

Lists principally letters to and from Yates and his son and from George Augustus Sala to Yates, some of which refer to Dickens. Also listed are letters to Yates concerning his *Edmund Yates: His Recollections and Experiences* (2 vols., London: Richard Bentley and Son, 1884), including one from Georgina Hogarth, some of which also, as Edwards and Dowling note in their introduction (see pp. 6-7), comment on Dickens. The manuscript of Yates's *Recollections and Experiences* is also included (see p. 62). The "Index of Personal Names in Letters, Postcards and Telegrams," pp. 57-72, identifies twenty-three references to Dickens, three to his son Charles, Jr., and two to his brother Frederick Dickens. Unfortunately, while the letters in the collection are itemized, Edwards and Dowling give no indication of their contents.

1462. Field, William B. Osgood. *John Leech on My Shelves.* New York: Privately printed, 1930, passim.

Field, a New York collector, lists books in his library illustrated by John Leech, including first editions of Dickens's five Christmas Books, to all of which Leech contributed illustrations, with full bibliographical descriptions, including lists of illustrations in each work and additional commentary (pp. 76, 107, 122, 123-24, 142). Field also lists a sketch, "Social Miseries, No. 7," that Leech presented to Dickens and that was sold at auction following Dickens's death (p. 231). Leech's illustrations for the Christmas Books are included in "List of Etchings and Woodcuts," pp. 255-94. Also see "A List of Reference Books for John Leech," p. 296. Illustrated.

1463. Folger Shakespeare Library, Washington, D. C. *A Catalog of Manuscripts of the Folger Shakespeare Library, Washington, D. C.* 3 vols. Boston: G. K. Hall, 1971, I, 514-15.

Lists a number of autograph letters by Dickens and other members of his family as well as letters by others about Dickens and his family.

1464. Free Library of Philadelphia. *The Collections of William M. Elkins in The Free Library of Philadelphia: A Brief Description.* Philadelphia: Free Library of Philadelphia, 1949. 14 pp.

Published in connection with the opening of a new Rare Book Room at the library, constructed from the library in Elkins's home, with its furnishings, this small volume provides a brief commentary on Elkins as a collector and on the authors he collected. The author notes that the nucleus of Elkins's Dickens collection was made up of purchases from the sale of the library of Harry B. Smith (**1525, 1918**), to which Elkins added thirty presentation copies, including the parts of *Pickwick Papers* presented to Mary Hogarth prior to her death, with four letters from Dickens regarding her death and two trinkets she had given him, and many other items not further identified. See the catalogue for the library's 1946 exhibition based on Elkins's collection (**1793**) for fuller details.

1465. [Freeman, Arthur, comp.]. *George Gissing, 1857-1903: Books, Manuscripts and Letters: A Chronological Catalogue of the Pforzheimer Collection.* London: Bernard Quaritch, 1992, pp. 20-22, 24, 31-32, 70.

Includes the autograph manuscript of *Charles Dickens: A Critical Study* (London: Blackie & Son, 1898), as well as two leaves of notes on Dickens and a collection of letters and royalty reports concerning the volume, 1897-1903; the Rochester Edition of Dickens's works, 1899-1901 (**2302**), for which Gissing wrote the introductions, with letters and other items connected with its publishing history; Gissing's abridgement of *Forster* (London, Chapman and Hall, 1903 [1902]); and lesser items. Freeman also includes a reference to Gissing's writing of his "love of Dickens" increasing "as the years go by" in a letter he wrote to Percy Fitzgerald, 5 March 1901.

1466. Fulton, Richard D., and C. M. Colee, gen. eds. *Union List of Victorian Serials: A Union List of Selected Nineteenth-Century British Serials Available in the United States and Canadian Libraries.* Garland Reference Library of the Humanities, 530. New York and London: Garland Publishing, 1985, pp. 8-12, 70-71, 329-32.

Locates runs in the United States and Canada of *All the Year Round, Bentley's Miscellany,* and *Household Words.*

1467. Gregory, George. *Index to the Unique Copy of The Life of Charles Dickens, 1812-1870, by John Forster. Chapman & Hall, 1873. Extra Illustrated with Upwards of 2,100 Engravings, Portraits, Autograph Letters, Theatrical Playbills, etc., . . . Now the Property of George Gregory, 4 Daniel Street, Bath, [Eng.].* Bath, Eng.: Privately printed, 1925. iii + 72 pp.

The index proper to the additions in a grangerized edition of *Forster*, pp. 1-49, is followed by "Index to the *American Visits* in preparation for 'American Notes,'" material found chiefly in volumes 3 and 9 of this edition, pp. 50-58; "Portraits of Charles Dickens Contained in Volume X" (161 portraits are listed), pp. 59-66; "The Politics of Charles Dickens," a transcript of part of a letter from Dickens, 7 July 1865, to an unidentified correspondent (actually Percy Fitzgerald–see *Hogarth-Dickens Letters*, II, 234-35) complaining that his daughter was visiting a Conservative family during election week and asking Fitzgerald to "think of *my feelings as a Radical Parent*," p. 66; "Autograph Letters Signed" (111 letters, with two from Dickens, the one mentioned above and the other to Dr. [Thomas] Mayo, 8 May 1850), p. 67; "Small Reproductions" (of plates reproduced in the *Dickensian*, 1905-22), pp. 68-69; "Charles Dickens and *Punch*" (an exchange of letters between George Gregory and "R. C. N." in the *Bristol Daily Press*, February 1926), p. 70; "Addenda" (several items added to the copy, including nine autograph letters, one from Dickens), p. 71; and "Errata et Corrigenda," p. 72. The "Addenda" section is in a copy in the Dickens House library, which also contains a number of inked-in corrections and additions; the copy in the British Library replaces it with "Supplemental Matter added since the Index was printed," pp. 71-72. This lists a number of items, including letters from Dickens to A. C. Lewis, 22 December 1866, and to Samuel Lindley, 25 May 1864. Gregory also prints a transcript of a letter from Dickens to Angus Fletcher, 24 March 1844, before the title page.

1468. Hamilton, Sinclair. *Early American Book Illustrators and Wood Engravers, 1670-1870.* [Vol. I:] *A Catalogue of a Collection of American Books Illustrated for the Most Part with Woodcuts and Wood Engravings in the Princeton University Library.* Princeton, NJ: Princeton University Library, 1958, passim, and *Early American Book Illustrators and Wood Engravers, 1670-1870.* Vol. II: *Supplement. A Supplement to the Main Catalogue, Issued in 1958, of a Collection of American Books Illustrated for the Most Part with Woodcuts and Wood Engravings in the Princeton University Library.* Princeton, NJ: Princeton University Press, 1968, passim.

Lists and gives brief bibliographical descriptions of and occasional commentary on works illustrated by a number of American artists. Those included in volume 1 who illustrated Dickens works are Hammatt Billings, Sol Eytinge, Jr., John McLenan, Thomas Nast, Charles S. Reinhart, William L. Sheppard, Henry L. Stephens, and Thomas Worth. Hamilton adds two more Dickens works illustrated by Sol Eytinge, Jr., in volume 2. Illustrated.

1469. Harvard College Library, Cambridge, MA, Houghton Library. *The Houghton Library, 1942-1967: A Selection of Books and Manuscripts in Harvard Collections.* Cambridge, MA: Harvard College Library, 1967, p. 66.

In a collection of photographic facsimiles of items in various Harvard College Library collections, includes a preliminary study for John Leech's illustration of the Fezziwigs' ball in *A Christmas Carol.*

1470. Harvard University, Cambridge, MA, Houghton Library. "Dickens, Charles, 1812-1870." In *Catalogue of Manuscripts in the Houghton Library, Harvard University.* Vol. 2. Alexandria, VA: Chadwyck-Healey, 1986, pp. 446-48.

Lists principally letters but also the holograph manuscripts of "George Silverman's Explanation," "His Brown Paper Parcel" (one of the Christmas Stories Dickens wrote for *Somebody's Luggage,* 1862), three *Uncommercial Traveller* papers ("A Fly-Leaf in a Life," "A Plea for Total Abstinence," and "City of London Churches"), and "On Mr. Fechter's Acting" (published in the *Atlantic Monthly,* August 1869); thirty-nine water colors by "Kyd" (Joseph Clayton Clarke) of characters in Dickens's early novels (*Pickwick Papers* to *Barnaby Rudge*); several drawings by George Cruikshank for *Oliver Twist;* and drawings by John Leech for *The Haunted Man* and *A Christmas Carol.* For a few items concerned with and by other members of Dickens's family, see pp. 448-49.

1471. Harvard University Library, Cambridge, MA. *English Literature.* 4 vols. Part of *Widener Library Shelflist.* Vols. 35-38. Cambridge, MA: Harvard University Library, 1971, passim.

The Dickens titles in the library are most easily located in volume 3 (Author and Title Listing, A-L), pp. 263-69; the information given is minimal—title and place and date of publication of all the editions of individual Dickens works (no collected or partial editions are listed) as well as studies of Dickens whose titles begin with "Dickens" published through 1970. Possibly useful, depending on what one is looking for and what information one has, are volumes 1 (Classified Listing by Call Number), 2 (Chronological Listing), and 4 (Author and Title Listing, M-Z). Also see volume 18, *Literature: General and Comparative* (1968), for a listing of general works on literature, many of which will contain sections on Dickens.

1472. Harvard University, Pusey Library, Cambridge, MA. Harvard University Theatre Collection, passim.

Not seen, but described in Paroissien (**118**), p. 65, as an "extensive but uncatalogued collection of American and British playbills and newspaper clippings of reviews of Victorian and modern versions of Dickens's novels compiled by an industrious but unscholarly enthusiast," an important—and underused— "resource for the stage historian interested in the adaptations of Dickens's novels."

1473. Hill, T[homas] W. "A Unique Collection of Music." *Dickensian,* 37 (1940/41), 43-54.

Describes the collection given to the Dickens House by William Miller of nearly 200 pieces of music based on Dickens's works, concluding (pp. 48-54) with "A Catalogue of the Miller Collection of Dickens Music at the Dickens House," giving composer, title, and other publication information, arranged by type of music and subdivided by novel. Illustrated. Also see Lightwood (**1486**) for an earlier list of the collection and Dickens House, London, Library Collections (**1457C4**). Section VIII, "Musical: Songs and Other Musical Compositions Founded on or Suggested by the Works of Charles Dickens or Incidents Therein," pp. 202-28 in Miller's *The Dickens Student and Collector* (**1005**), is a bit more extensive, containing fifty or so more items than are in Hill's list, presumably because it also lists works Miller had not been able to acquire for his own collection.

1474. Hughes, William R. *A Week's Tramp in Dickens-Land, Together with Personal Reminiscences of the "Inimitable Boz" Therein Collected.* London: Chapman and Hall, 1891, pp. 412-22.

In the final chapter of this topographical study, Hughes lists and briefly describes the manuscripts and page proofs of Dickens's novels and mentions other Dickens materials in the Forster Collection in the Museum at South Kensington (later the Victoria and Albert Museum) and elsewhere. Hughes also comments briefly on other documents concerning Dickens in London institutions. Illustrated.

1475. Hurst, Clive, ed. *Dickens Playbills in the Bodleian Library*. Oxford: Oxford Microform Publications., 1981. 9 microfiche. vi + 8 pp. introduction and guide.

Copies are available in the Bodleian Library, Oxford, and in the Cambridge University Library.

1476. Juchhoff, Rudolf, comp. "Dickens, Charles, 1837-1896 [sic]." *Sammelt-katalog der biographischen und literarkritischen Werke zu englischen Schriftstellern des 19. und 20. Jahrhunderts (1830-1958): Verzeichnis der Bestände in deutschen Bibliotheken* Krefeld, Ger.: Scherpe Verlag, 1959, pp. 70-78.

Lists nineteenth- and twentieth-century works, including many German studies, about Dickens in German libraries, though Dickens is given his eldest son's vital statistics, Dickens's being, of course, 1812-70.

1477. Kelley, Philip, and Betty A. Coley, comps. *The Browning Collections: A Reconstruction, with Other Memorabilia: The Library, First Works, Presentation Volumes, Manuscripts, Likenesses, Works of Art, Household and Personal Effects, and Other Association Items of Robert and Elizabeth Barrett Browning*. Waco, TX; London; New York; and Winfield, KS: Armstrong Browning Library of Baylor University, The Browning Institute, Mansell Publishing, and Wedgestone Press, 1984, passim.

A finding list for the items dispersed in the 1-6 May 1913 auction sale of the art collection, collection of autograph letters and manuscripts, and library from the estate of Pen Browning, son of Robert and Elizabeth Barrett Browning, principally items formerly in the possession of his parents, but also a finding list for items in other Browning collections as well. For the several items associated with Dickens, see the index.

1478. Klinkenborg, Verlyn, Herbert Cahoon, and Charles Ryskamp. *British Literary Manuscripts: Series II, from 1800 to 1914*. New York: Pierpont Morgan Library, in Association with Dover Publications, 1981, pp. [121-26] and 275.

In this catalogue proper of part of the Pierpont Morgan collection, compiled by Klinkenborg, three Dickens items are reproduced in facsimile with accompanying commentary and transcriptions of the text: a page of the manuscript of *A Christmas Carol* (item 61), two pages of a letter from Dickens to Wilkie Collins, 11 August 1858 (item 62), and a page of the manuscript of *Our Mutual Friend* and the number plan for No. II of that novel (item 63). Klinkenborg notes that the Morgan library has over 1,400 Dickens letters, including most of Dickens's correspondence with Wilkie Collins, William Macready, and Angela Burdett-Coutts. Also see "Complete Checklist of British Literary Manuscripts and Autographs in the Pierpont Morgan Library," compiled by Herbert Cahoon, pp. 263-311. The section on Dickens (p. 275) briefly lists the manuscripts (*A Christmas Carol, The Battle of Life, The Cricket on the Hearth,* "Holiday Romance," "Hunted Down," *Our Mutual Friend,* with its number plans, "Reflections of a Lord Mayor," *Sketches of Young Gentlemen,* "That Other Public," and separate pages of still others), original drawings, and miscellaneous manuscripts and collections of letters associated with Dickens in the library.

1479. Library of Congress, Washington, DC. *National Register of Microform Masters.* 6 vols. Library of Congress Catalogs. Washington, D. C.: Library of Congress, 1976, II, 709-10; then annual volumes for 1970 (published 1971)-1983 (published 1984), passim.

Catalogues and gives locations of materials that have been filmed "and for which masters exist," including individual Dickens works.

1480. Library of Congress, Washington, DC. *The National Union Catalog of Manuscript Collections, Based on Reports from American Repositories of Manuscripts, 1959-1961[-1993].* Ann Arbor, MI: J. W. Edwards, 1962; Hamden, CT: Shoe String Press, 1964; Washington, D. C.: Library of Congress, 1965-94, passim.

Issued annually after the 1964 volume with various cumulative indexes (of two, three, and four years) of names, subjects, and repositories. The last volume published was for 1993 and the last cumulative index for 1991-93 (both published 1994). For Dickens, these volumes contain a description and listing of materials in collections in the United States, arranged only in the order in which a number was assigned to a manuscript collection, so the best way to locate Dickens items is through the cumulative indexes, though there are also indexes at the end of each volume, but only through 1984. Among the more important collections listed are 60-1085, Free Library of Philadelphia, about 800 items, mainly letters, and the manuscripts of three complete and two fragmentary dramatic sketches; 60-1401, the Morris L. Parrish Collection of Victorian Novelists, Princeton University Library; 60-1551, the Fales Collection, New York University Library; 61-2476, Dickens papers consisting of about 1,250 items, Henry E. Huntington Library, San Marino, California, principally correspondence and original illustrations; 62-375, a collection of William Harrison Ainsworth's letters to Dickens, Huntington Library; 68-639, papers of John Forster, Huntington Library; 71-1901, Dickens papers, University of Texas, Austin; 72-880, the William Miller collection, Duke University Library, including scrapbooks of British and American periodical articles and papers; 84-2007, the papers of Annie Fields, Massachusetts Historical Society Library, Boston; and 84-2146, Dickens papers, Pierpont Morgan Library, New York, including some 1,392 letters, manuscripts, publishing agreements, checks, and a catalogue of Dickens's library at Gad's Hill. This Union Catalog is available for 1986/87 onward on the Internet at http://lcweb.loc.gov/coll/nucmc. At that Web site, a search of the NUCMC/RLG Union Catalog-AMC File Easy Search Form for Charles Dickens on 23 April 2003 produced 868 records, mostly individual or small collections of letters and principally from collections in England. Also see the cumulative catalogue, *Index to Personal Names in the National Union Catalog of Manuscript Collections, 1959-1984*, 2 vols. (Alexandria, VA: Chadwyck-Healey, 1988), I, 295, with entries listed for Dickens, his brother Frederick, his sister Letitia, his children Charles, Henry, and Mary, and the Dickens family.

1481. Library of Congress Online Catalogue. http://catalog.loc.gov; or the Library of Congress home page, http://www.lcweb.loc.gov.

Clicking on "About the Library" on the Library of Congress home page (http://www.lcweb.loc.gov) produces a statement by James Billington, the Librarian of Congress, that the library is the largest in the world, with "more than 120 million items on approximately 530 miles of bookshelves"–and, obviously, growing daily. On 24 September 2002 a search for Charles Dickens items produced 1,760 entries of books by Dickens and 1,610 entries of books about him.

1482. Library of Congress and the National Union Catalog Subcommittee of the Resources Committee of the Resources and Technical Services Division, American Library Association. "Dickens, Charles, 1812-1870." In *The National Union Catalog: Pre-1956 Imprints: A Cumulative Author List Representing Library of Congress Printed Cards and Titles Reported by Other American Libraries*. Vols. 142, 143. London and Chicago: Mansell, 1971, CXLII, 574-698; CXLIII, 1-61; *Supplement*, 1980, DCCXVIII, pp. 28-68.

A "reportory" and finding list of "the catalogued holdings of selected portions of the catalogued collections of the major research libraries of the United States and Canada, plus the more rarely held items in the collections of selected smaller and specialized libraries." The Dickens items are arranged under 1) collected editions, followed by collected works in translation; 2) selected works (editions of two or more works); 3) selections, fragments, adaptations, etc.; 4) correspondence; 5) separate works, including editions, translations, extracts, abridgements, adaptations, etc.; and 6) selective index to these entries. See entries, too, for other Dickens family members. Also see cumulations for 1956/67-1982 (various publishers, 1970-83?), passim, and *NUC: Books*, microfiche (Washington, DC: Library of Congress, 1983-), passim. See Harner (**1147**), pp. 32-33, for fuller details.

1483. Library, University of California, Berkeley. "Dickens, Charles, 1812-1870." *Author-Title Catalog*. Vol. 28: *Desc-Dirf*. Boston: G. K. Hall, 1963, pp. 634-48.

Facsimiles of the cards in the card catalogue, listing individual and collected editions of Dickens's works and writings on Dickens by a few of his children in the library to 1963. Now online at either http://www.lib.berkeley.edu or http://sunsite2.berkeley.edu:8000.

1484. Libweb. Library Servers via WWW Web site. Berkeley Digital Library SunSITE. http://sunsite.berkeley.edu/libweb.

An extraordinary Web site, comparable to Peter Scott's Libdex (**1522**). As its home page announces, it "currently lists over 6500 pages from libraries in over 115 countries." One may go into the chosen library's online catalogue and search for books and other library holdings by keyword "for location, library type, name, or other information." To find out which libraries around the world possess a particular book, use OCLC WorldCat (**1503**).

1485. Liebert, Herman W., and Marjorie G. Wynne. "The General Collection of Rare Books and Manuscripts." *Yale University Library Gazette*, 48 (1973/74), 227-40; reprinted with alterations and additions in *The Beinecke Rare Book and Manuscript Library: A Guide to Its Collections*. New Haven, CT: Yale University Library, 1974, pp. 12-26; rev. ed., as *The Beinecke Rare Book and Manuscript Library: A Guide to the Collections*. New Haven, CT: Yale University Library, 1994.

Under Dickens (p. 17 in the 1974 edition), the text briefly notes a "large collection of material by and about Dickens" given by Col. Richard Gimbel in 1970–for details, see Butt (**2287**), Gimbel (**1797**), and Podeschi (**1509, 1705**). While the article in the *Yale University Library Gazette* is not accompanied by illustrations, plate XXXIII of the heavily illustrated 1974 volume is a photographic facsimile of page 135 of a duplicate set of page proofs for *Edwin Drood*, with Dickens's corrections, sent to Luke Fildes, the book's illustrator.

1486. Lightwood, James T. "A List of Vocal and Instrumental Music Associated with Dickens and with the Characters in His Novels." In *Charles Dickens and Music*. London: Charles H. Kelly, 1912, 1916 (Every Age Library), [1920]; reprinted New York: Haskell House, 1970, pp. 172-77.

Notes that all these pieces were then in the collection of William Miller. Lightwood provides only titles and composers—and lyricists for the songs—but no dates or other publication information. See Hill (**1473**) for a later listing of the collection and Dickens House Library Collections (**1457C4**).

1487. Machin, Roger, comp. *Bibliotheca Dickensiana, Being a Catalogue of the First Editions, Complete Works, and Other Editions of the Novels of Charles Dickens, Together with a Representative Selection of Books and Publications Pertaining to the Study Thereof; All Forming a Part of the Collection of English Books in the Library of Kyoto University of Foreign Studies.* Kyoto, Japan: University Library, 1975. lxvii + 191 pp.

In English and Japanese. The title tells virtually all. The bibliography is in three parts. Part 1, "Bibliographies; First Editions," lists seven bibliographies of Dickens's works, first editions in parts of ten of his novels, and other first editions. Part 2, "Later Editions; Studies," includes editions later than the first of a number of the works; collected editions; Dickens's periodical works; stylistic studies; biographies and biographical studies; topographical studies; studies of Dickens's thought and influences on his criticism; the writing of the novels; characters and scenes in the novels; letters, speeches, and public readings; miscellaneous; and illustrations (these are all subheadings). Part 3, "Classified Index to 'The Dickensian,'" lists articles in the *Dickensian* under the same headings used in parts 1 and 2, adding only "Works Based on Dickens, Parodies, etc." An introductory section, pp. vi-lxvii, contains photographs of a number of covers and title pages of volumes in the collection and photographic facsimiles of letters from Dickens, with accompanying text in both Japanese and English about the individual works of Dickens and transcripts in English of the four letters in the collection, to George Cattermole, 15 January 1852; Thomas Dixon, Jr., 4 April 1853; Alfred Dickens, 30 May 1860; and J. H. Nightingale, 25 March 1861, all of which may be found in the appropriate volumes of *Pilgrim Letters.* The volume concludes with "A Chronological Table of Dickens's Life and Writings" and an "Index to Authors." Illustrated.

Review: M. S[later], *Dickensian*, 73 (1977), 52 (praises the "handsomely-produced catalogue" as "useful").

1488. Massachusetts Historical Society, Boston. *Catalog of Manuscripts of the Massachusetts Historical Society.* 7 vols. Boston: G. K. Hall, 1969, II, 546-47.

Lists letters from Dickens and letters by others in which Dickens is mentioned—some thirty-one items.

1489. Maurice, E. Grace, ed. *Union List of Manuscripts in Canadian Repositories/Catalogue collectif des manuscrits des archives canadiennes.* Rev. ed. 2 vols. Ottawa: Public Archives, Canada, 1975, and Supplements (with French title as *Catalogue collectif des manuscrits conservés dans les dépôt d'archives canadiennes*): *1976.* 1976; *1977-1978.*1979; *1979-1980.* 1982; *1981-1982.* Ed. Peter Yurkiw, 1985, passim.

Consult the index for the Dickens items. The 1975 edition lists only seven, principally letters but also proofs and correspondence concerning Hatton and Cleaver's bibliography of Dickens's periodical works (**24**).

1490. McPherson, Brian, comp. *Charles Dickens 1812-1870: Catalogue. Alfred and Isabel Reed Dickens Collection, Dunedin Public Library, New Zealand.* Wellington, NZ: A. H. and A. W. Reed for the Dunedin Public Library, 1965. vii + 64 pp.; also published bound with John S. Ryan, ed. *Charles Dickens and New Zealand: A Colonial Image.* Wellington, Auckland, and Sydney: A. H. and A. W. Reed for the Dunedin Public Library, 1965; San Francisco: Tri-Ocean Books, 1966. 184 + vii + 64 pp.

A catalogue of a collection given by the Reeds to the Dunedin Public Library in 1948. The collection includes a page of the manuscript of *Mrs. Lirriper's Lodgings* (a photographic facsimile is included), letters (with facsimiles), monthly parts and one-volume editions of Dickens's works, and Dicknsiana, including an extra-illustrated copy of *Forster-Ley,* in twenty volumes compiled by A. H. Reed. In a foreword, Reed describes his formation of this collection of Dickensiana. See the revised edition by McPherson, Ronnie, and Fache (**1491**), and the supplement to that by Ronnie (**1515**). Ryan's work is a collection of twenty-four articles from *Household Words* and six from *All the Year Round* relating to New Zealand, with an index.

1491. McPherson, Brian, Mary A. Ronnie, and Ada H. Fache, comps. *Charles Dickens 1812-1870: Catalogue. Centenary Edition. Dunedin Public Library, New Zealand, Alfred and Isabel Reed Collection.* Centenary Edition (second, enlarged, ed.). Ed. Mary A Ronnie. Wellington, Auckland, Sydney, and Melbourne: A. H. and A. W. Reed for the Dunedin Public Library, 1970. 108 pp.

An updating of the 1965 catalogue (**1490**). The editors reprint Reed's original foreword as "Introduction" and add a brief "Introduction to Centenary Edition," also by Reed, in which he notes that it is "gratifying that numerous accessions to the Collection necessitate a second edition so quickly." A foreword by E. A. Horsman characterizes the collection as "of unusual range and interest" and identifies the principal accessions since 1965 as a "full length" Dickens letter to P. W. Banks (misspelled Bankes by Dickens, as noted by the editors of the *Pilgrim Letters*) from early December 1836, given only in part in *Pilgrim Letters,* I, 204; a letter of [11 December 1837] to E. Hill, a physician (the editors of *Pilgrim Letters,* VII, 792, give the recipient as [James B.] Hill and date the letter [?Summer 1838]), asking him to see his "little boy this morning as early as possible"; a letter to Thomas Mitton, 19 April 1860 (dated 19 August 1860 in *Pilgrim Letters*, IX, 289), giving details of the death of his brother Alfred Dickens, who had died on 27 July; a brief letter to Henry Johnston, 26 August 1869, declining an invitation to lecture at the Glasgow Athenaeum, not previously published; and numerous editions and secondary studies, and a few other items. Some of the facsimiles included in the first edition are omitted and new ones added, including the Banks letter, a letter from Catherine Dickens to George Cattermole (9 October [1845?]), and a note from Dickens concerning a reading. Some editorial notes are expanded. Illustrated. Also see the supplementary catalogue edited by Ronnie (**1515**).

Review: *Dickensian*, 66 (1970), 253 ("splendidly edited" by Ronnie).

1492. Metzdorf, Robert F., comp. "Dickens, Charles (1812-1870)." In *The Tinker Library. A Bibliographical Catalogue of the Books and Manuscripts Collected by Chauncey Brewster Tinker*. New Haven, CT: Yale University Library, 1959, pp. 172-74 and passim.

Lists only the first bound edition of several of Dickens's works and contains a few passing references to Dickens.

1493. Ministère de l'Instruction publique et des Beaux-Arts. "Dickens (Charles)." In *Catalogue général des livres imprimés de la Bibliothèque Nationale: Auteurs*. Vol. 40. Paris: Imprimerie Nationale, 1910, pp. 338-67; also available on microfiche, revised, in *Catalogue général des livres imprimés, 1879-1959, avec corrections et annotations*. Paris: Chadwyck-Healey, 1986, and on CD-ROM as *Catalogue général de la Bibliothèque Nationale de France des origines à 1970 sur CD-ROM*. Paris: Bibliothèque Nationale, 1996- , passim.

Lists works by Dickens in the library through 1909, predominantly works translated into French but also English editions and editions translated into other languages. For works acquired 1910-59, see the Bibliothèque Nationale's *Supplément sur fiches* (**1433**); for works acquired 1960-69, see Bibliothèque Nationale (**1432**). Superseded by the BN-OPALE PLUS Online Catalogue (**1431**).

1494. National Portrait Gallery, London. *Catalogue of the National Portrait Gallery, 1856-1947. With an Index of Artists*. London: National Portrait Gallery, 1949, p. 73.

Provides information about portraits of Dickens by Ary Scheffer (1855), Daniel Maclise (1839), and Harry Furniss (pen-and-ink drawings in a series done ca. 1880-1910); a caricature of Sir Henry Fielding Dickens by "Spy" for *Vanity Fair* (1897); and portraits of various friends and associates of Dickens (Wilkie Collins, George Cruikshank, and Daniel Maclise, for example).

1495. New York Public Library, New York. *The Arents Collection of Books in Parts and Associated Literature: A Complete Checklist.* Comp. Sarah A. Dickson, assisted by George Solovieff. New York: New York Public Library, 1957. 88 pp.

The checklist, pp. 21-80, includes a number of Dickens items (pp. 25-35): not only original editions in parts but a variety of other editions published in parts in England, America, and elsewhere, as well as various volume editions of minor and major works; sets of illustrations; imitations; the autograph manuscript of four pages of *Pickwick Papers*; eleven autograph letters; a few original drawings and etchings by Hablot K. Browne for *Nicholas Nickleby*, *David Copperfield*, and *Little Dorrit*; Daniel Maclise's pencil drawing for the title page of *The Cricket on the Hearth*; and 656 watercolor and pen and ink drawings by "Kyd" (Joseph Clayton Clarke) for Dickens's works, as well as the items mentioned in Dickson's "The Arents Collection of Books in Parts and Associated Literature: A Brief Survey" (**1629**), which is here reprinted as "A Brief Survey," pp. 7-20. Indexes of authors and artists are also included. Most of the letters were not included in *Nonesuch Letters* but are included in *Pilgrim Letters*. Also see the supplement (**1496**).

Reviews: T. Bolton, *Papers of the Bibliographical Society of America*, 52 (1958), 224-26 (gives some description of the contents of this attractive and "useful little reference work"); A. D. Wainwright, *Book Collector*, 7 (1958), 435-36 (surveys the collection, finding it an "impressive array" of books in parts).

1496. New York Public Library, New York. *The Arents Collection of Books in Parts and Associated Literature: A Supplement to the Checklist, 1957-1963.* Comp. Perry O'Neil. New York: New York Public Library, 1964, pp. 13, 27-28.

Adds nine Dickens items to those in the original checklist (**1495**).

1497. New York Public Library, New York. CATNYP: The Research Libraries Online Catalog. http://catnyp.nypl.org.

The online catalogue for this great library, "representing a substantial portion of The Research Libraries' collections," including "over 3 million records for titles cataloged since 1972 and more than 2 million records for roman alphabet books cataloged prior to 1972." The Web site cautions, however, that some earlier titles are still to be found only in the 800-volume *Dictionary Catalogue of the Research Libraries* (**1498**). Items may be searched for online by author, title, subject, journal or newspaper, call number, and other number indexes. A search in the author index for Charles Dickens on 10 March 2003 produced 1,420 entries; the subject index produced 893 entries. The online catalogue for the eighty-five branch libraries, LEO: The Branch Libraries Online, will be found at http://webpac.nypl.org/leo.html. Both online catalogues may also be accessed at http://www.nypl.org/catalogues/index.html, where further details about the two catalogues will be found.

1498. New York Public Library, New York. "Dickens, Charles, 1812-1870." In *Dictionary Catalogue of the Research Libraries of the New York Public Library, 1911-1971*. New York: New York Public Library, Astor, Lenox and Tilden Foundations, 1979, vols. CXC, 477-553, and CXCI, 1-22. Also see supplements for 1972-79 (published 1980), vol. XIV, 540-43, and for 1972-88 (published 1989), vol. XVIII, 471-76.

Reproduces cards from the original card catalogue, with all their imperfections resulting from heavy usage over the years–torn-off corners, smears, corrections, etc. The Dickens holdings are impressive, though older volumes, when called for, are sometimes in very bad condition. The entries, lightly annotated from time to time, are arranged under collected works, individual works (including adaptations and studies), collections of letters, selections, bibliographies, general studies, and special studies. The supplements do not reproduce cards but contain essentially the same information. All of these are, however, pretty much superseded by the online catalogue (**1497**).

1499. New York Public Library, New York, Astor, Lenox & Tilden Foundations, The Research Libraries. "Dickens, Charles." In *Dictionary Catalog of the Henry W. and Albert A. Berg Collection of English and American Literature*. 5 vols. Boston: G. K. Hall, 1969, I, 777-812, and passim; also *First Supplement*. 1975, pp. 123-24, 595, 730, and *Second Supplement*. 1983, pp. 138, 544, 673.

This well-known collection contains numerous autograph letters (see I, 787-809), including 113 to Richard Bentley and forty to Émile de la Rue; many letters written by others, including members of his family, that mention Dickens (I, 809-13); and a number of letters *to* Dickens (see Dickens items in the appendix of correspondents, IV, 631-32). An appendix providing provenance for a number of items is also included (for Dickens, see V, 468-71). Another important part of the collection is a full complement of first and other editions of Dickens's works, major and minor (with several sets of parts editions for a number of the novels, for example), including presentation copies, some with letters inserted and numerous variations of the first edition of *A Christmas Carol*. Other gems of the collection include a number of Dickens's reading copies with manuscript corrections and additions, several manuscripts ("A Curious Dance Round a Curious Tree," his Memoranda Book, his 1867 diary, a page from the manuscript of *Martin Chuzzlewit*, three pages from that of *Oliver Twist*, the corrected proofs for *Our Mutual Friend*, various publishing agreements, and other lesser holograph documents–see I, 783-85). In addition, the collection is rich in original drawings for the novels by Hablot K. Browne, George Cattermole, George Cruikshank, John Leech, and Marcus

Stone, among his original illustrators, but also by "Kyd" (Joseph Clayton Clarke), F. A. Fraser, Frederick W. Pailthorpe, Felix O. Darley, James Mahoney, Thomas Sibson, and A. H. Forrester (see I, 777-83), not to mention sets of extra illustrations, adaptations, playbills, relics, bibliographies, and other Dickensiana. The catalogue also lists a number of items connected with John Forster, including some holograph notes and some page proofs with additions for his biography of Dickens and a number of letters, though none to Dickens (see II, 99-103). Also see the entry for Catherine Dickens, I, 746. In the introduction, the late Lola L. Szladits, then curator of the collection, rightfully claims that the Berg Collection is "one of America's most celebrated collections of first editions, rare books, autograph letters, and manuscripts."

The only significant additions regarding Dickens listed in the supplementary volumes are three original drawings by Hablot K. Browne and a letter from Dickens to Thomas A. Trollope. For commentary on the collection, see **Henry W. And Albert A. Berg Collection, New York Public Library**, in part 2 of the subject index.

1500. New York Public Library, New York, Astor, Lenox & Tilden Foundations, The Research Libraries. "Dickens, Charles, 1812-1870." In *Dictionary Catalog of The Rare Book Division.* 21 vols. Boston: G. K. Hall, 1971, VI, 141-51.

The collection contains numerous editions of Dickens's major and minor works (including a two-volume edition of *David Copperfield* bound from the original parts with eighteen original watercolor character sketches for the novel by "Kyd"–Joseph Clayton Clarke), sale catalogues, published collections of letters, editions of extra illustrations, bibliographies, and other Dickensiana.

1501. New York Public Library, New York, Research Libraries. *Dictionary Catalog of the Manuscript Division.* 2 vols. Boston: G. K. Hall, 1967, I, 239.

Lists an autographed portrait of Dickens from 1868; miscellaneous originals, photostats, and facsimiles of manuscripts; clippings; and sale catalogues (otherwise unspecified); thirty-one holograph letters relating to the Boz Ball, 1842 (actually photostat negatives from originals once in the library of Herman LeRoy Edgar); letters by others about Dickens; and a few lesser items.

1502. New York University Libraries, New York, Fales Collection. "Dickens, Charles John." In *Fales Library Checklist.* Rev. and ed. Theodore Grieder. 2 vols. New York: AMS Press, 1970, I, 262-77; *First Supplement*, 1974, pp. 102-03; *Second Supplement*, 1977, pp. 74-75.

An unannotated, alphabetical short-title list of printed works by Dickens and printed volumes of letters and illustrations in the collection, followed by a list of secondary studies alphabetized by author. The collection was donated to New York University by DeCoursey Fales in memory of his father Haliburton Fales. While a short-title catalogue has obvious limitations, this one does give a picture of the scope of the collection. The supplements list works added to the collection through 1971 and then through 1975 For fuller descriptions of some of the items in the collection, see Egerer (**1630**), and Winterich (**1773-74**).

1503. OCLC WorldCat Web site. http://www.oclc.org/worldcat.

A valuable research tool available through libraries, probably best for searching for individual works. It contains, as its home page announces, "the merged catalogs of libraries around the world, making it the world's largest and richest database of bibliographical information," housing "over 48 million bibliographic records," with the number growing by the millions each year. The database is searched through OCLC's FirstSearch service. Searches are possible for author, title, keyword, and a variety of other possibilities. On 30 January 2003, a search for author "Dickens, Charles" produced 17,254 records, though they seemed to be listed in no noticeable order. Using the keyword "Charles Dickens" produced 12,147. A title search for "Great Expectations" produced 1,190 records. The advantage that this database has over Libweb (**1484**) and Peter Scott's LibDex (**1522**) is that it locates libraries that have particular items.

1504. Olsthoorn, J. F. M., and J. M. L. Schoolmeesters. *Catalogus Dickens-Collectie van Godfried Bomans/Catalogue of the Dickens-Collection of Godfried Bomans*. Tilburg, Neth.: Bibliotheek Katholieke Hogeschool Tilburg, 1983. 73 pp.

A listing of works in the collection, now housed in the library of Tilburg University. Bomans, a Dutch author, founded a branch of the Dickens Fellowship in the Netherlands in 1956. In their introduction, the editors point out that the collection has its limitations and is best characterized as "a representative collection of Dickens-literature," containing "most of the important books written on Dickens, some curiosities, plus a few items which might interest bibliophiles."

1505. Ormond, Richard. "Dickens, Charles John Huffam (1812-70)." In his *National Portrait Gallery: Early Victorian Portraits*. 2 vols. London: Her Majesty's Stationery Office, 1973, I, 138-45, and passim.

Lists oil paintings of Dickens by Ary Scheffer (1855-56) and Daniel Maclise (1839) and six pen-and-ink portraits by Harry Furniss owned by the National Portrait Gallery. Ormond provides considerable information about the provenance of the two oils, exhibitions in which they have hung, the literature concerning them, and the occasion of the painting of each portrait, with Dickens's own comments in his letters about the sittings. The portrait by Maclise is reproduced in color (I, 140). Under "Iconography," I, 142-45, Ormond lists numerous other paintings and drawings *not* in the collection and their locations. In volume 2, *Plates*, all eight holdings are reproduced in black and white, along with a few of the portraits listed in "Iconography" (see plates 255-71).

1506. Parkinson, Ronald. *Catalogue of British Oil Paintings, 1820-1860.* London: Her Majesty's Stationery Office, 1990, passim.

A catalogue of paintings in the Victoria and Albert Museum, London, with reproductions in black and white and brief descriptions of and technical information about them, including William Maw Eagley's "Florence Dombey in Captain Cuttle's Parlour" (1888), p. 78; William P. Frith's "Charles Dickens in His Study" (1859), pp. 94-96, and his "Dolly Varden" (1842), pp. 96-99; "Portrait of John Forster" by Daniel Maclise and Thomas Warrington (1830), pp. 184-85; and Edward Matthew Ward's "John Forster in His Study" (ca. 1850), pp. 295-96. In his detailed description of Frith's portrait of Dickens, Parkinson comments on circumstances surrounding the painting of the portrait, which, he notes, Frith himself found "unsuccessful" and Dickens did not much care for, though John Forster, who commissioned the portrait, liked it very much. Parkinson also comments extensively on Frith's painting of Dolly Varden (*Barnaby Rudge*) and the circumstances surrounding his painting of five other portraits of this popular Dickens character.

1507. Parrish, M[orris] L. *A List of the Writings of Charles Dickens.* Philadelphia: Library Company of Philadelphia, 1938. [20 pp.].

Compiled from the collection at Dormy House, Pine Valley, New Jersey, for an exhibition at the Library Company of Philadelphia, 17 February to 10 March 1938. This is a bibliographically sparse list of a number of first and early English and American editions of Dickens's works, minor as well as major, including a few works not by Dickens. Eventually this collection was acquired by the Princeton University Library—see Gerould (**1638**), Clark (**1607**), and Wainwright (**1758-59**).

1508. Parrish, M[orris] L., and Elizabeth V. Miller. *Wilkie Collins and Charles Reade: First Editions (with a Few Exceptions) in the Library at Dormy House, Pine Valley, New Jersey, Described with Notes.* London: Constable, 1940; reprinted New York: Burt Franklin, 1968, passim.

In listing the published versions of Collins's works, Parrish and Miller identify Collins's contributions to Dickens's Christmas Stories and other pieces in *Household Words* and *All the Year Round,* as well as his dramatic collaborations with Dickens. Parrish and Miller also note that, in a copy of the extra Christmas Number for 1867 (*No Thoroughfare*), a brief letter from Dickens to Collins, 28 August 1867, is "laid in," as is a letter from Collins to Harry D. Waller, both noting the collaboration between Dickens and Collins. Both are reproduced in photographic facsimile. Also in the collection are playbills for dramatic productions of *The Frozen Deep* and *The Lighthouse*.

1509. Podeschi, John B. *Dickens and Dickensiana: A Catalogue of the Richard Gimbel Collection in the Yale University Library*. New Haven, CT: Yale University Press, 1980. xxiii + 570 pp.

A beautifully done catalogue of a magnificent Dickens collection bequeathed to Yale University by Colonel Richard Gimbel at his death in 1970. Podeschi points out that Gimbel began the collection in 1925 and that many items in it were purchased at the sales of other great Dickens collections, particularly the Hatton collection in 1927 and 1929 (**1906, 1893**), the Daoust in 1929 (**1905**), and the Hird in 1953 (**1963**). The catalogue is divided into eight sections: 1) major editions of Dickens's works published before 1870, 2) minor editions published during Dickens's lifetime and afterwards, 3) translations and adaptations, 4) collected editions and selections, 5) periodicals containing Dickens's works, 6) manuscripts, 7) autograph letters and documents (399 items), and 8) Dickensiana (1,879 items).

Glancing through the first section, one gets the impression that Gimbel must have cornered the market on early editions of Dickens's works. For example, the collection contains five copies of different states of the first issue of *A Christmas Carol*, nineteen copies of later states of the first edition, twenty-one copies of the second through fourteenth (1860) editions, six copies of the first American edition (Carey and Hart, Philadelphia), four copies of the New York edition (Harper & Brothers), and twelve copies of other editions published before 1870. It contains fifteen copies of *Pickwick* in parts, from a copy with "most of the collectors' points of 'first issue'" to one with extra plates by Thomas Onwhyn. Many of the copies of Dickens's novels are presentation copies; others are extra-illustrated or special copies for other reasons—a veritable collector's heaven. In this section, Podeschi has provided proper bibliographical descriptions, collating the first copy of each edition and transcribing title pages in "a quasi-facsimile manner," and giving information about contents, printer, plates, binding, and other matters.

The other sections of the catalogue are less fully descriptive, but special features are indicated. The manuscript section contains thirty items, including early drawings attributed to Dickens; manuscript fragments of "O'Thello," *Oliver Twist*, "Tom Tiddler's Ground," and "Aboard Ship"; complete manuscripts of the "Full Report" of the first and second meetings of "the Mudfog Association for the Advancement of Everything," "Mr. Robert Bolton," "The Perils of Certain English Prisoners" (Dickens and Wilkie Collins), several addresses, and two prologues; and a complete set of corrected proofs of *The Mystery of Edwin Drood* that Dickens gave to Luke Fildes for guidance in illustrating the novel, as well as other fragments of proofs, more fully described in Cardwell (**2434**), and several minor pieces.

Interesting non-Dickens manuscripts in the collection include Wilkie Collins's autograph manuscript of *No Thoroughfare*, with two versions of Act V and the "manuscript prompt-book for the role of Obenreizer in the play"; a three-page autograph manuscript of an autobiographical sketch by Wilkie Collins in which Collins writes that the play *No Thoroughfare* was "written as a collaboration with Dickens and [the actor Charles] Fechter"; the manuscript of an adaptation of *The Chimes* by Samuel Atkins; a 152-page typescript entitled "Charles Dickens: *The Pickwick Papers*: Comparative Description of the Parts Represented in Certain Notable Sets"; Gimbel's own manuscripts, typescripts, notebooks, and correspondence relating to Dickens and to his collection; the autograph manuscripts of George Gissing's introductions to *Dombey and Son* and *Sketches by Boz* intended for the Rochester Edition of Dickens's works but published instead in his *Critical Studies of the Works of Charles Dickens* (New York: Greenberg, 1924); William Dean Howells's autograph manuscript of his review of the *Hogarth-Dickens Letters*, published in the *Atlantic Monthly*, 45 (February 1880), 280-82; Andrew Lang's autograph manuscript of "The Puzzle of Edwin Drood," published in an unidentified source–it was Arthur Eckersley, "The Drood Mystery: Extracts from an Unpublished Article by Andrew Lang," *Book Monthly*, 9 (1912), pp. 833-36, as indicated in Don Richard Cox, *The Mystery of Edwin Drood: An Annotated Bibliography* (**115**), item 871); Morris L. Parrish's typescript "Collation of *Pickwick Papers* in Parts"; Richard Herne Shepherd's autograph manuscript, in three notebooks, of "A Monograph on *Sketches by Boz* 1833-1836," never published, tracing textual differences between original magazine or newspaper publication and book publication; and Algernon Swinburne's corrected typescript of his "Charles Dickens," originally published in the *Quarterly Review*, 196 (July 1902), 20-39, and expanded as *Charles Dickens*, ed. Theodore Watts-Dunton (London: Chatto and Windus, 1913).

Reviews: *American Notes and Queries*, 21 (1982/83), 195-96 ("meticulous" bibliographical descriptions of an "incomparable" collection); K. J. Fielding, *Dickens Studies Newsletter*, 13 (1982), 54–57 (notes the richness and importance of the collection–and some errors in the catalogue); R. L. Patten, *Papers of the Bibliographical Society of America*, 77 (1983), 209-17 ("exemplary"; put together with "admirable rigor and good sense," with "much fuller descriptions of American editions than previous authorities" and "full bibliographical descriptions of the major editions"); T. Rice (**93**), p. 50 (an "[i]ncoherently organized volume that neither catalogs the Gimbel collection very effectively nor collates the editions of C[harles] D[ickens]'s works very clearly," but useful until better bibliographies appear).

1510. Pratt Institute, Brooklyn, NY, School of Library Service. *English Literature. XLIV. Dickens.* General Literature, Lecture 76. Brooklyn, NY: Pratt Institute, n. d., pp. 624-28.

A mimeographed short-title list of works by Dickens and bibliographical, biographical, and critical studies of Dickens, presumably in the Pratt Institute Library.

1511. Quinn, Mary, comp. *Elizabeth Gaskell and Nineteenth Century Literature: Manuscripts from the John Rylands University Library, Manchester: A Listing and Guide to the Research Publications Microfilm Collection.* Reading, Eng., and Woodbridge, CT: Research Publications, 1989, pp. 5-7, 61-74.

An index for the thirteen-reel microfilm collection of the same title. On pp. 5-7, Quinn lists the letters from Dickens to Elizabeth and William Gaskell to be found on Reel 2. On pp. 61-74, she lists an extra-illustrated edition of *Forster* in thirteen volumes and describes "all manuscript enclosures and substantial printed items but not the numerous portraits and views" in the volumes. Included are thirty-five Dickens letters, some Dickens family letters (including a letter written by John Dickens), one of Dickens's shorthand books, the manuscript of a speech he delivered to the Royal Academy, various illustrations and playbills "concerning his involvement in amateur theatricals," a "rare collection" of dramatizations of Dickens's works, clippings, and numerous lesser items to be found on Reels 9-11. The collection also includes the manuscript of Dickens's *A Child's Dream of a Star* (Reel 12), which he gave to Elizabeth Gaskell. For further details of the Gaskell Collection, see Dexter (**1612**), John Rylands University Library (**1658**), Lingard (**1671**), "Notes and News [Gaskell Collection]" (**1694**), and Tyson (**1533-34**).

1512. Reid, George W. *A Descriptive Catalogue of the Works of George Cruikshank: Etchings, Woodcuts, Lithographs, and Glyphographs, with a List of Books Illustrated by Him, Chiefly Compiled from the Collections of Mr. Thomas Morson, Mr. Edmund Story Maskelyne, and Mr. Edwin Truman. With an Essay on His Genius and Works by Edward Bell, M. A., and Three Hundred and Thirteen Illustrations.* 3 vols. London: Bell & Daldy, 1871, passim.

The catalogue (in volume 1) lists the illustrations that Cruikshank did for Dickens's early works. See particularly pp. 145-46, 149-58, 163, 195-204, 326-29, and 333. Volumes 2 and 3 contain plates of a number of the items in the catalogue. The illustrations for Dickens's works, all in volume 3 and identified by the numbers given them in the catalogue, are only from *Oliver Twist* (numbers 1850-73). In his essay, Bell comments on Cruikshank's illustrations, including a brief reference to those for Dickens's novels, but not on the artist's relationship with Dickens.

1513. Robinson, F[rank] W. *The Library of George W. Childs.* Philadelphia: Collins, Printer, 1882. 46 pp.

In this small pamphlet, Robinson notes that Childs's library contained several presentation volumes from other authors that were originally in Dickens's library and the holograph manuscript and number plans of *Our Mutual Friend*, which he briefly describes. He quotes excerpts from the number plan for the first installment of the novel; prints a letter from Dickens to Childs, 4 November 1868, welcoming Childs to England and inviting him and his wife to Gad's Hill Place; and mentions a seven-page letter from Mamie Dickens, 6 February 1874, giving an account "of the family and their movements," both letters inserted into the manuscript. Robinson also refers to Childs's expanded copy of the Osgood edition of Dickens's works (he is not more specific) in fifty-six volumes, into each volume of which, he notes, "is inserted an autograph letter from Mr. Dickens to Mr. Childs, the first dated 1855," but he provides no additional information about these letters. While nine letters to Childs and one to Mrs. Childs from Dickens are in the *Pilgrim Letters*, the earliest is dated 31 July 1865. Also see Childs (**2480**) and "A Library of Rarities" (**1669**).

1514. Rolfe, Franklin P. "The Dickens Letters in the Huntington Library." *Huntington Library Quarterly*, 1 (1937/38), 335-63.

Itemizes a "notable store of Dickens material" in the Henry E. Huntington Library, San Marino, CA—over 1,350 letters "to, from, or pertaining to" Dickens, more than 900 of which were then unpublished, ranging from 1832 to 1870. The collection, Rolfe indicates, includes letters from Dickens to Maria Beadnell/Mrs. Winter, 1833, 1855-62; to Thomas Mitton, 1833-61 (ninety-two); to the Hon. Mr. and Mrs. Richard Watson, 1846-70 (fifty-five); to W. H. Wills, including not only most of the letters published in R[udolph] C. Lehmann's *Charles Dickens as Editor, Being Letters Written by Him to William Henry Wills, His Sub-Editor* (London: Smith, Elder; New York: Sturgis & Walton, 1912) but also 125 not then previously published; to Frederic Ouvry, Dickens's lawyer from 1858 on, 1858-70 (eighty-two); to Georgina Hogarth, 1845-70 (a two-and-one-half-page list); and to Mr. and Mrs. James T. Fields, most previously published in Fields's *Yesterdays with Authors* (Boston: James R. Osgood; London: Sampson Low, Marston, Low, and Searle, 1872), pp. 125-250. The collection also includes the letter book for *All the Year Round*; Georgina Hogarth's correspondence with Annie Fields, 1869-1913; and a large collection of letters written to Charles Kent by numerous literary and political figures invited to a public banquet for Dickens, 2 November 1867, prior to his departure for America, and for which Kent served as secretary.

1515. Ronnic, Mary A., comp. *Charles Dickens, 1812-1870: Supplementary Catalogue, 1971, of the Alfred and Isabel Reed Collection*. Wellington, Auckland, Sydney, Melbourne: A. H. & A. W. Reed, for the Dunedin Public Library, 1971. 27 pp.

In an introduction, A. H. Reed notes that the 1970 catalogue (**1491**), to which this is a supplement, contained 1) twenty-one items of manuscript material, 2) 482 printed items, and 3) 245 autograph letters of people in the Dickens circle or referred to in *Forster*, and that the items in this 1971 supplement include an autograph letter of Dickens to a Mr. Friend (possibly John Friend, according to the editors of *Pilgrim Letters*, VII, 716), 5 October 1855, in the third person, declining an invitation to deliver a lecture, and 102 printed or microfilmed items. Two essays are also included: 1) "Frederic G. Kitton and His Bibliography," by A. H. R[eed], a tribute in honor of the copy of *Dickensiana: A Bibliography of the Literature Relating to Charles Dickens and His Writings* (**996**) in the Dunedin Library, which was Kitton's own corrected and supplemented proof copy, with an addenda of thirty manuscript pages, and 2) "Pickwick in America," on Pickwick plagiarisms.

Review: *Dickensian*, 68 (1972), 131 (briefly descriptive only).

1516. Rosenbach, A. S. W. *A Catalogue of the Books and Manuscripts of Harry Elkins Widener.* 2 vols. Philadelphia: Privately printed, 1918, II, 50-51.

Does not itemize the Dickens or Cruikshank works in the Widener collection since the catalogues of these items were published separately—see Rosenbach (**1517-18**), Widener (**1546**), and "The Widener Dickens Collection" (**1768**). Under "The Paxton Album" in the catalogue, however, Rosenbach lists and prints three letters in regard to a charitable subscription for a Miss Marguerite Power—a circular letter from Thackeray, Dickens, and John Forster, 24 December 1857; a letter from Dickens to Thackeray, 4 December 1857; and a letter from Thackeray to Dickens, 7 December [1857].

1517. Rosenbach, A. S. W. *A Catalogue of the Works Illustrated by George Cruikshank and Isaac and Robert Cruikshank in the Library of Harry Elkins Widener.* Philadelphia: Privately printed, 1918, passim.

In addition to various editions of works by Dickens with illustrations by George Cruikshank, some being presentation copies or having other special characteristics, the Widener collection, now in the Harvard University Library, also contains three original Cruikshank drawings for *Sketches by Boz* and nine for *Oliver Twist*, Cruikshank's own set of proofs of his twelve etchings for *Memoirs of Joseph Grimaldi*, and an edition of *Oliver Twist* containing two original drawings for the novel and a page of pencil studies on which, Rosenbach notes, Cruikshank "afterwards based his claim to be considered the joint author of the work." The collection also contains a set of forty-eight original drawings and a title page by F. W. Pailthorpe for *Memoirs of Joseph Grimaldi* and a copy of *The Pic Nic Papers*, edited by Dickens and containing an inscription in his hand.

1518. Rosenbach, A. S. W. *A Catalogue of the Writings of Charles Dickens in the Library of Harry Elkins Widener.* Philadelphia: Privately Printed, 1918; reprinted New York: Arno Press, [1968]. vii + 111 pp.

An introductory piece on "The Charles Dickens Collection" by Rosenbach notes the "fastidious standards" of Widener as collector and bibliographer, requiring, for example, not only *Pickwick Papers* in parts, not only an inscribed copy, but the one inscribed to Thomas Noon Talfourd, to whom the work was dedicated (this is in the collection). The collection, Rosenbach points out, is not complete, Widener having died before reaching that point, but it has "wonderful things" hidden in it, such as twenty-six letters to Charles Lever, since published in Flora V. Livingston's *Charles Dickens's Letters to Charles Lever* (Cambridge, MA: Harvard University Press; London: Humphrey Milford, Oxford University Press, 1933). The items in the collection are too numerous to be listed here but include publishing agreements with John Macrone and with Chapman and Hall (including that for *Pickwick Papers*), the petty cash book kept by Dickens as a law clerk in 1827, original editions of minor as well as parts editions and other editions of Dickens's major works (many being presentation copies), and associated items for many of them, including letters bound with particular sets. The principal editions are fully collated and the text of the letters and publishing agreements furnished. The collection also includes playbills and the autograph manuscript of Dickens's early parody of Gray's "Elegy Written in a Country Churchyard," various books from Dickens's library, Dickensiana, parodies of Dickens's works, and original drawings for Dickens's novels by Hablot K. Browne, "Kyd" (Joseph Clayton Clarke), George Cruikshank, Luke Fildes, Robert Seymour, and Clarkson Stanfield. This is a truly impressive collection. This volume incorporates descriptions and annotations for items in Widener (**1546**), with occasional revisions, but of course includes many additional items. Also see the Widener catalogue on the works of George Cruikshank (**1517**) and Rosenbach's *A Catalogue of the Books and Manuscripts of Harry Elkins Widener* (**1516**).

Review: G. P. Winship, *Library*, 4th ser., 1 (June 1920), 49 (a brief notice).

1519. Sadleir, Michael. "Dickens, Charles (1812-1870)." In his *XIX Century Fiction: A Bibliographical Record Based on His Own Collection.* 2 vols. Cambridge: Printed at Cambridge University Press and published London: Constable; Berkeley and Los Angeles: University of California Press, 1951; reprinted New York: Cooper Square Publishers, 1969; New York: James Cummins, 1992, I, 104-09.

The catalogue of the library of one of the great collectors of the nineteenth-century novel. The collection is, however, weak on Dickens and several other major authors because, as Sadleir explains in his preface, "Passage from the Autobiography of a Bibliomaniac," collecting Dickens and other major authors was "such easy game" if one had the money. He characterizes his Dickens collection as "insignificant" but lists as its one "claim to distinction" its "complete series of Dickens' 8vo fictions (except *Master Humphrey's Clock*) *in cloth* and mostly in fine condition." Sadleir provides descriptive bibliographical details for these volumes and for a few other items. Illustrated.

Reviews: H. G. Dick, *Nineteenth-Century Fiction*, 6 (1951/52), 209-17 (notes that what Sadleir has to say about first editions in cloth of Dickens's works "will electrify traditional collectors"—see annotation above); P. H. Muir, *Spectator*, 186 (1951), 530 (despite some limitations, "an indispensable work of reference," though with "no pretension to completeness"; no comment on Dickens items); *Times Literary Supplement*, 13 April 1951, p. 234 (honors Sadleir as a collector and praises the value and rarity of his collection of Dickens's first editions in cloth).

1520. Saumarez Smith, Charles. *The National Portrait Gallery*. London: National Portrait Gallery, 1997, pp. 122-23.

Included in this catalogue is a color illustration of Dickens's portrait by Daniel Maclise, 1839, with color close-ups of the face and the left hand. Saumarez Smith briefly describes the occasion of the painting and the reactions of Dickens and Thackeray to the portrait.

1521. Saunders, W. H., comp. *List of Books, Prints, Portraits, Autograph Letters & Memorials Exhibited at Dickens' Birthplace Museum, 393 Commercial Road, Portsmouth; Also a Summary of the Writings of Charles Dickens Together with a Review of the Life of the Great Novelist*. Portsmouth, Eng.: W. H. Barrell, 1904; reprinted Folcroft, PA: Folcroft Library Editions, 1975. 61 pp.; revised ed., Portsmouth, Eng.: W. H. Barrell, 1910. 63 pp.

The first of a series of guides to the Charles Dickens Birthplace Museum, located in the house where Dickens was born (originally 387 Mile End Terrace, Portsmouth). The 1904 edition lists 108 editions and studies of Dickens's works, with several errors in dating, and fifty-one portraits and other items. After establishing that the house was indeed Dickens's birthplace, Saunders's "Life" of Dickens is very short on biographical details and not very well written, with superficial commentary on his works and an obvious preference for Dickens's pathos over his other qualities though, surprisingly, finding much merit in *Bleak House* and *Little Dorrit*, and ending with a series of notes on Dickens's religious faith (reverent), Dickens as a reader (marvelous), his visits to Portsmouth, and his fondness for children. Illustrated. For later guides to the museum, see Seale (**1523**) and Portsmouth City Museums (**1580**).

1522. Scott, Peter, ed. LibDex: The Library Index. http://www.libdex.com.

An astonishing, impressive, and obviously important and useful "worldwide directory of library home pages, web-based OPACs, Friends of the Library pages, and library e-commerce affiliate links," according to this Web site's own home page. It offers the user 16,835 online library catalogues to browse through, along with the other uses indicated. One may search "across millions of documents within Electronic Library" or by country or university. Public libraries are also included. Also see the comparable Libweb (**1484**). To find out which libraries around the world possess a particular book, use OCLC WorldCat (**1503**).

1523. Seale, Alfred A., comp. *List of Books, Prints, Portraits, Autograph Letters and Memorials Exhibited at Dickens' Birthplace Museum, 393 Commercial Road, Portsmouth; Also a Review of the Life of the Great Novelist, Together with a Summary of the Writings of Charles Dickens.* Portsmouth, Eng.: W. H. Barrell, 1914; revised 1923; reprinted Folcroft, PA: Folcroft Library Editions, 1975; Norwood, PA: Norwood Editions, 1975; Philadelphia: R. West, 1977. 71 pp.

Updatings of the *List* originally compiled by W. H. Saunders (**1521**) in 1904. By 1914, the list of books numbered 202, the portraits and other materials, sixty-six, and an additional set of portraits and books presented or loaned by Seale, who was then curator of the museum, ninety-seven. The 1923 edition lists the books, magazines, prints, relics, autograph letters, portraits, and other items in the collection at Portsmouth, as well as a collection of Dickensiana and review and magazine articles about Dickens, 1837-1912, loaned by Seale. The list is preceded by Saunders's rather poorly written sketch of Dickens's life, dated "Portsmouth, 1904." This work also contains a genealogical table compiled by Seale and a list of Dickens's works, with several errors in dating. Illustrated. For a later guide to the museum, see Portsmouth City Museums (**1580**).

1524. Slater, Michael, ed. *The Catalogue of the Suzannet Charles Dickens Collection.* London and New York: Sotheby Parke Bernet Publications in Association with the Trustees of the Dickens House, 1975. xvi + 299 pp.

The first section of this compilation (pp. 1-167) comprises the catalogue of the Suzannet Collection at the Dickens House (with sixty-eight illustrations) and is an annotated itemization of the impressive number of gifts (713 items) given over the years to the Dickens House first by Comte Alain de Suzannet and, some years after his death in December 1950, by the comtesse in 1971. The introduction by Slater is a fascinating history of the comte's building of his Dickens collection, which Slater characterizes as "one of the three finest private collections of Dickensiana assembled in this century." Slater also mentions a number of fine items in Suzannet's collection that did *not* make their way into the Dickens House collection and were sold at auction. The catalogue is organized under twelve headings: 1) First and Early Editions, 2) Dickens's Reading Copies (some six items, all of which have alterations in Dickens's hand and two of which—*The Haunted Man and the Ghost's Bargain* and *The Bastille Prisoner*, from *A Tale of Two Cities*—were never given as readings),

3) Dickens's Speeches (Printed Texts), 4) Collected Editions, 5) Dickensiana, Biography and Criticism, 6) Playbills and Programmes, 7) Paintings, Prints and Drawings (including important portraits of Dickens as well as numerous drawings for his works), 8) Autograph Letters and Documents (443 items, 1831-70), 9) Literary Manuscripts (including Maria Beadnell's album, a page of *Pickwick Papers*, chapter 9 of *Nicholas Nickleby*, "The Schoolboy's Story," and "Our Commission"), 10) Manuscript Dickensiana (mainly letters written by family and friends), 11) Varia (including Dickens's marriage license), and 12) Letters and Documents Relating to the Suzannet Collection.

The second section of this work (pp. 169-287) is a reprinting of the Sotheby sale catalogue (**1977**) of the remaining items in the Suzannet Collection, with sixteen illustrations and an appended price list identifying purchasers as well as prices paid. Slater has also included an index to the entire volume. See Suzannet (**1529-30**) for the comte's own earlier catalogues, Slater (**1819**), and Sotheby & Co. (**1976**).

Reviews: P. Collins, *Times Literary Supplement*, 5 December 1975, p. 1464 (a descriptive notice with commentary on Suzannet as a Dickens collector); Mollie Hardwick, *Books and Bookmen*, 21, vi (March 1976), 42-43 (praises both the Suzannet collection and Slater's annotations); T. d'A. Smith, *Dickensian*, 72 (1976), 38-39 (a "lavishly illustrated and absorbingly annotated" catalogue, done with "impeccable scholarship," though Smith has some minor criticism); H. Stone, *Dickens Studies Newsletter*, 7 (1976), 51-53 (praises the catalogue as a "handsome" volume, edited with "grace and skill," with an "informative introduction," a "fitting tribute to a great collector," and an "elegant entrée to a great collection"; also surveys the high quality and importance of the comte's generous gifts to the Dickens House).

1525. Smith, Harry B. "Charles Dickens." In his *A Sentimental Library, Comprising Books Formerly Owned by Famous Writers, Presentation Copies, Manuscripts, and Drawings.* [New York]: Privately printed, 1914, pp. 66-108.

A heavily annotated, handsomely and lavishly prepared bibliography of Dickens items in Smith's collection, including volumes from Dickens's own library as well as parts and volume first editions. Smith gives provenance where known and notes where letters or (in the case of *Nicholas Nickleby*) instructions to the illustrator are bound in. The collection also contains an autograph album of Priscilla Horton, an actress, containing an unpublished poem, "To Ariel," by Dickens, with a drawing also by him; the manuscript of Algernon Swinburne's essay on *Oliver Twist*, written as an introduction to the novel for the aborted Autograph Edition of Dickens's works (**2303**) and first published as part of Swinburne's *Charles Dickens*, ed. Theodore Watts-Dunton (London: Chatto and Windus, 1913), as Paroissien (**118**) indicates (p. 191); several Cattermole drawings for *Master Humphrey's Clock*; eight pages of proofs for *Martin Chuzzlewit* with extensive revisions; financial statements for *Household Words* and *All the Year Round*; the manuscript for "Song of the Wreck" for Wilkie Collins's play *The Lighthouse*; and W. P. Frith's well-known portrait of Dickens. In "An Appreciation" (pp. xvii-xxvi), Luther S. Livingston notes that Smith amassed a nearly complete "*set* of presentation or inscribed copies" of

Dickens's works, including the presentation copies of the first fourteen numbers of *Pickwick Papers* to Mary Hogarth prior to her early death. He also indicates that there are "nearly one hundred" Dickens letters in the collection, including twenty-two to Henry Kolle, and that the rarest item is "Proof, Private and Confidential," the pamphlet Dickens had privately published "giving particulars of the life and habits of an American, Thomas Powell, who had published libelous, or at least objectionable statements about various English writers." Sometimes the complete text of letters is provided, sometimes excerpts. Numerous illustrations.

1526. State University of New York, Lockwood Memorial Library, Buffalo, NY. *Charles Dickens: A Preliminary Catalogue of His Works and Books Related to Him in the Rare Book Room Collection, Lockwood Memorial Library, State University of New York at Buffalo.* Buffalo: The Library, 1970. i + 26 pp.

Listed in Cohn and Collins (**958**). A copy is available in The Poetry/Rare Books Collection at the library.

1527. Storey, Graham, et al., editorial board. *The Charles Dickens Research Collection from the J. F. Dexter Collection in The British Library and Other Major Holdings in Great Britain and the United States of America.* Cambridge, Eng., and Alexandria, VA: Chadwyck-Healey, 1990. ix + 116 pp.

A catalogue to accompany a major microfilm project, the photographing of all pages of the 324 items in the Dexter Collection (**1436**) in addition to 216 items in other collections. Part I (pp. 1-27) is a reel by reel list of the collection willed by Dexter to the British Library of bibliographies and secondary studies of Dickens as well as editions of Dickens's works and illustrations to them. It includes a grangerized copy of *Forster* in fourteen boxes that contains letters, playbills, portraits, etc., and Forster's own presentation copy of the work. The British Library catalogue itself of the Dexter collection is reprinted on pp. 28-88. Items from other collections are listed on pp. 89-116 and considerably expand the secondary studies and to some extent the editions of Dickens's works beyond those in the Dexter collection and include additional manuscripts, particularly of minor works, and the diary of Mrs. John Forster. Unfortunately, locations of these manuscripts are not indicated in the catalogue itself.

1528. Sutton, David C., ed. "Dickens, Charles, 1812-1870." In his *Location Register of English Literary Manuscripts and Letters: Eighteenth and Nineteenth Centuries.* 2 vols. London: British Library, 1995, I, 293-306.

Lists manuscripts and proofs of Dickens's novels and other works, contracts, diaries, notebooks, prefaces, prompt books, speeches, and letters (a large section, pp. 296-306), giving the location of each manuscript, its accession or call number, and information about access to the library in which it is to be found. As the editor notes, this work is essentially a print-out of the Location Register of English Manuscripts and Letters database (**1158**).

1529. Suzannet, A[lain] de. *Catalogue des manuscrits, livres imprimés et lettres autographes composant la bibliothèque de la Petite Chardière. Oeuvres de Charles Dickens.* 3 vols. Lausanne: Imprimeries Réunies, 1934. 94 + 244 + 239 pp.

An incredible collection of Dickens materials by one of the great international collectors of the twentieth century. The bibliographical descriptions are modest but are accompanied by full explanatory notes. Volume 1 lists manuscripts and books, volume 2 autograph letters, 1832-48, and volume 3 autograph letters, 1849-70. Manuscript materials include page 81 of the *Pickwick Papers* manuscript, Ellen Beard's album (containing poems by Dickens), "The Ivy Green," thirty-nine pages of the *Nicholas Nickleby* manuscript (chapter 9), a page of the manuscript of "Tom Tiddler's Ground," and the manuscripts of "Our Commission" and "The Schoolboy's Story." Other items include some original drawings and an excellent collection of parts, first, and other editions of Dickens's works. The letters, including some 637 by Dickens and a number concerned with Dickens (III, 211-28) by family and friends, are listed individually with lengthy excerpts from them and explanatory notes. Many were previously unpublished but destined to be included in the *Nonesuch Letters* four years later and, ultimately, in the *Pilgrim Letters*. See Suzannet (**1530**), Slater (**1524, 1819**), and Sotheby & Co. (**1976-77**) for other catalogues of the collection.

1530. Suzannet, A[lain] de. *Oeuvres de Charles Dickens.* In his *Catalogue d'un choix de livres, imprimés et manuscrits, lettres, autographes, dessins originaux et gravures, provenant de ma bibliothèque de Biarritz.* Vol. I. Biarritz: Privately printed, 1925. 83 pp.

Only fifty-six copies were printed of this listing of the parts, first, and other rare editions of Dickens's works (with frequent explanatory notes and excerpts from the novels); autograph letters (many previously unpublished); and some Dickensiana. For later catalogues of the Suzannet collection, see Suzannet (**1529**), Slater (**1524, 1819**), and Sotheby & Co. (**1976-77**).

1531. Thirsk, James W., comp. *Charles Dickens, 1812-1870: A Centenary Reading List of Books in Ealing Public Libraries.* London: Ealing Public Libraries, 1970. 15 pp.

A list of books by and about Dickens, with brief introductory remarks and quotations from and about Dickens.

1532. Tillotson, Kathleen, and Nina Burgis, eds. "[Appendix] C. Inventory of Contents of 1 Devonshire Terrace, May 1854." In *Pilgrim Letters*, IV, 704-26.

An inventory, partly in Dickens's hand and partly in his wife's, that itemizes the contents of the Dickens residence, room by room—carpets, fire irons, waste paper baskets, paintings, curtains, furniture, china, and coal scuttles—giving a valuable look at the daily life of the Dickenses. Of particular value is the "Inventory of the Books," which itemizes every book in Dickens's library at the time (pp. 711-26).

1533. Tyson, Moses, comp. "Hand-List of Additions to the Collection of English Manuscripts in the John Rylands Library." *Bulletin of the John Rylands University Library*, 19 (1935), 458-85.

Items 725, 726, and 729 (pp. 464-66) are the Dickens additions. Item 725 is a grangerized edition of *Forster* containing 35 autograph letters by Dickens; letters from various people to Mrs. Dickens and Helen Hogarth, her youngest sister; a shorthand exercise book in Dickens's hand; a holograph manuscript of a review by Dickens of Lord Londonderry's *A Letter to Lord Ashley, M. P., on the Mines and Collieries Bill* (**457**); and a holograph manuscript of Dickens's speech at the Royal Academy dinner, 30 April 1870. Item 726 is a "much corrected" holograph manuscript of *A Child's Dream of a Star* (from the Gaskell Collection). Item 729 consists of twenty-six letters from Dickens to Elizabeth Gaskell, three to her husband, the Reverend William Gaskell, and one from W. H. Wills to Elizabeth Gaskell (also from the Gaskell Collection). For further details of the Gaskell collection, see Quinn (**1511**) and the cross-references there and Tyson (**1534**).

1534. Tyson, Moses, ed. "A List of the Letters and Manuscripts of Charles Dickens Which Are Now in The John Rylands Library." Appended to Tyson (**457**), pp. 192-96.

This list includes thirty letters in the Elizabeth Gaskell Collection (twenty-seven to her, all but one from Dickens, and three from Dickens to her husband); thirty-five other letters and the manuscript of the Londonderry review, Dickens's shorthand exercise book, and the manuscript of a speech given at the Royal Academy dinner, 30 April 1870, all bound into an extra-illustrated edition of *Forster*; and three other letters and a check in Dickens's hand. Also in the extra-illustrated volume are a letter from John Dickens to J. P. Harley, four letters to Mrs. Charles Dickens, four letters to Helen Hogarth (Catherine's youngest sister), and a letter from Bulwer-Lytton to the Dickenses, as well as portraits and a variety of Dickensiana. Some of these were earlier listed in Tyson (**1533**), and some are printed in the article to which this list is appended.

1535. University Library, University of Illinois, Urbana-Champaign. *Catalogue of the Rare Book Room, University Library, University of Illinois, Urbana-Champaign.* 11 vols. Boston: Hall, 1972, III, 384-89; also *First Supplement.* 2 vols. Ibid., 1978, I, 350.

Includes parts editions and other editions of Dickens's novels, editions of Dickens's other writings, collections of letters, and Dickensiana.

1536. University of California, Los Angeles. "Dickens, Charles." In *Dictionary Catalog of the William Andrews Clark Memorial Library, University of California, Los Angeles.* 15 vols. Boston: G. K. Hall, 1974, IV, 630-44.

Lists parts and other editions of Dickens's novels and other works in the collection, printed collections of letters and speeches, studies of individual works, and general studies. The catalogue also includes a Dickens-Thackeray Scrap Book, bound in red cloth, containing "clippings and extracts from newspapers, periodicals, and books pasted on, or inserted between, approximately 56 leaves." Also see Clark (**1450**) and Cowan and Clark (**1453-54**).

1537. University of the State of New York, The State Education Department, New York State Library, Albany, NY. "Dickens, Charles." In *The Gotshall Collection in the New York State Library.* New York State Library Bibliography Bulletin, 84. Albany: New York State Library, 1960, pp. 42-57.

Itemizes a collection formed by William Charles Gotshall of first editions of Dickens's works in parts and volume form, Dickensiana, and one manuscript—a note from Dickens to "Kent" (presumably William Charles Kent), 29 October 1866 (the text of which is not included in *Pilgrim Letters*, XI, 259), mounted in a volume of *Great Expectations* in parts. In an introduction, "The Gotshall Collection," pp. 7-13, Charles F. Gosnell, State Librarian, notes that the Dickens collection of some 120 volumes, most bound in ornate leather, "is outstanding" and includes "practically all of Dickens's works in first edition form plus other items in which he had a minor interest or which concern him in some way." Illustrated.

1538. Victoria and Albert Museum, Dyce and Forster Auxiliary Collection, National Art Library, London. "MS Accounts of Sales of Works of Charles Dickens: 1. Bradbury & Evans, 1845-1861; 2. Chapman & Hall, 1846-1861 (with 3 Loose Letters); 3. Chapman & Hall, 1862-1870 (with 2 Letters & 1 Undated Account, Loose)." Catalogue Nos. FD.18.1-3, passim.

In his AMS Press bibliography of *Dombey and Son* (**106**), p. 11, Leon Litvack notes that these documents, which he has himself used, "provide the primary source material" for Robert Patten's *Charles Dickens and His Publishers* (**224**).

1539. Victoria and Albert Museum, Forster and Dyce Collections, London. *The Forster and Dyce Collections from the National Art Library at the Victoria and Albert Museum, London.* Brighton: Harvester Microform, 1987, II, 97-124.

According to the "The Dickens Checklist" in *Dickens Quarterly*, 5 (1988), 40, this is a printed inventory of the contents, "minor literary manuscripts, diaries, theatrical records," and correspondence, included in *Manuscripts, Correspondence, and Papers of Charles Dickens from the Forster Collection, Victoria and Albert Museum* (Brighton: Harvester Microform, 1987), 4 reels.

1540. Victoria and Albert Museum, National Art Library, London. *National Art Library Catalogue, Victoria and Albert Museum, London, England: Author Catalogue.* 10 vols. Boston: G. K. Hall, 1972, III, 165-67; X, 127.

Lists principally a rather hodgepodge collection of editions of Dickens's works with illustrations, as well as some letters.

1541. [Victoria and Albert Museum, London]. South Kensington Museum. "The Forster Collection." In *Handbook of the Dyce and Forster Collections in the South Kensington Museum.* South Kensington Museum Art Handbooks. London: Published for the Committee of Council on Education by Chapman and Hall, 1880, pp. 53-94.

In the chapters of this volume devoted to the Forster Collection, chapter 5, "Biographical Sketch of Mr. Forster," by Henry Morley, pp. 53-73, touches only in passing on John Forster's relationship with Dickens. Chapter 6, "The Library," pp. 74-83, is concerned with the range of the collection, referring briefly to Forster's collection of original editions of Dickens's works. Chapter 7, "Autographs," pp. 84-91, itemizes the original manuscripts of Dickens's novels in the collection–*Oliver Twist* (incomplete), *Sketches of Young Couples, The Old Curiosity Shop, Barnaby Rudge, American Notes, The Chimes, Dombey and Son, David Copperfield, Bleak House, Hard Times, Little Dorrit, A Tale of Two Cities,* and *The Mystery of Edwin Drood*–with notes about the letters, notes, and other matters connected with each manuscript, and also "a few other separate leaves and smaller collections in the autograph of Charles Dickens, containing dedications, prefaces, and memoranda for his novels and some articles and travelling letters contributed to 'the Examiner' and 'the Daily News.'" Also mentioned are the corrected proofs for *Dombey and Son, David Copperfield, Bleak House,* and *Little Dorrit,* portions of proofs for other works, including proofs for a part of *Pickwick Papers,* and "a considerable number of letters and notes, nearly all written by Dickens to Mr. Forster," as well as the original invitations to a public dinner and ball given for Dickens in New York in 1842. These are available on microfilm as *Manuscripts of the Works of Charles Dickens: From the Forster Collection in the Victoria and Albert Museum, London* (Wakefield, Eng.: Micro Methods, 1970), on ten reels, and *Manuscripts, Correspondence, and Papers of Charles Dickens from the Forster Collection, V&A Museum* (Brighton: Harvester Microform, 1987), on four reels. See *The Forster and Dyce Collections from the National Art Library of the Victoria and Albert Museum, London* (**1539**), II, 97-124, for a detailed list of contents. Chapter 8, "Paintings and Drawings," pp. 92-94, notes Frith's portrait of Dickens and of "Dolly Varden," Maclise's drawing of Dickens and Forster in Jonson's *Every Man in His Humour*, and others. Appendix 3, pp. 104-05, lists the playbill for 20 September 1845 of *Every Man in His Humour*. Illustrated. Also see Victoria and Albert Museum (**1542-43**). A brief description of the Forster Collection may be found on the Internet at http://www.nal.vam.ac.uk/nalforst.html.

1542. [Victoria and Albert Museum, London]. South Kensington Museum, Science and Art Department of the Committee of Council on Education. "Dickens (Charles)." In *Forster Collection. A Catalogue of the Printed Books Bequeathed by John Forster, Esq., LL.D.* London: Printed for Her Majesty's Stationery Office by Eyre and Spottiswoode, 1888, pp. 138-41.

The lists of collected editions, individual editions, and page proofs of Dickens's novels in the collection fill only three pages of this 710-page catalogue. "John Forster," the introduction by Rev. W. Elwin, pp. vii-xxviii, makes only passing reference to Forster's relationship with Dickens. Also see Victoria and Albert Museum (**1541, 1543**). One may also search for the Dickens items in the collection in the online catalogue of the National Art Library at the Victoria and Albert Museum, http://www.nal.vam.ac.uk.

1543. [Victoria and Albert Museum, London]. South Kensington Museum, Science and Art Department of the Committee of Council on Education. *Forster Collection. A Catalogue of the Paintings, Manuscripts, Autograph Letters, Pamphlets, Etc., Bequeathed by John Forster, Esq., LL.D.* London: Printed for Her Majesty's Stationery Office by Eyre and Spottiswoode, 1893. 261 pp.

Part I includes paintings, watercolors, and drawings by Frith (a portrait of Dickens and a painting of "Dolly Varden"), Daniel Maclise, George Cattermole, Luke Fildes, Clarkson Stanfield, and an unknown artist of Dickens, his family and friends, and characters from his works. Part II lists 1) Dickens's letters to Forster and other materials connected with Dickens's amateur theatrical production of Ben Jonson's *Every Man in His Humour* and other productions; 2) Dickens's manuscripts, working plans, and notes for *Oliver Twist* (in part), *The Lamplighter* (not in Dickens's hand), *The Old Curiosity Shop, Sketches of Young Couples, Barnaby Rudge, American Notes, Martin Chuzzlewit, The Chimes,*

"Travelling Letters Written on the Road" (Numbers VII and VIII only of the newspaper articles expanded into *Pictures from Italy*), *Dombey and Son*, *David Copperfield*, *Bleak House*, *Hard Times*, *A Child's History of England* (chapters II and VI only), *Little Dorrit*, *A Tale of Two Cities*, *The Mystery of Edwin Drood*, the dedication and prefaces to *Master Humphrey's Clock*, the dedication to the 1847 edition to *Pickwick Papers*, the 1848 preface to *Nicholas Nickleby*, the 1849 preface to *Martin Chuzzlewit*, the manuscripts of twenty magazine and newspaper pieces, proofs for some of the novels and articles, 137 letters to Forster and a few to other correspondents, and a series of Dickensiana, including items concerning Dickens's 1842 American trip and some playbills. In Part III, "Modern Pamphlets," a number of relevant items are included under the Dickens heading (see p. 122). Also see Victoria and Albert Museum (**1541-42**). One may also search for the Dickens items in the John Forster collection in the online catalogue of the National Art Library, at the Victoria and Albert Museum, http://www.nal.vam.ac.uk.

1544. Watt, John Y. "Catalogue of the Books and Papers in the Fitzgerald Collection, Eastgate House, Rochester [England]." Typescript (Carbon). 1935. 145 pp. In the Dickens House, London.

An unannotated listing of items in the collection: Dickens's works; plays by others based on them; periodicals, pamphlets, and newspaper cuttings; sale catalogues; music and theatrical materials related to Dickens's works; personalia; autograph, catalogued, or copied letters; miscellaneous studies; art works and illustrations, including portraits, illustrators of and illustrations to his works; and calendars, cartoons, prints, and photographs.

1545. Weedon, Alexis, and Michael Bott. *British Book Trade Archives, 1830-1939: A Location Register*. History of the Book-On-Demand Series, 5. Bristol: Eliot & Michael Turner, 1996, pp. 9, 35.

Lists holdings in the Victoria and Albert Museum concerning the relationship of Dickens with Chapman and Hall. Also see miscellaneous records for notes from Dickens and Thackeray to William Raymond Sams, publisher.

1546. Widener, Harry Elkins, [and A. S. W. Rosenbach]. *A Catalogue of Some of the More Important Books, Manuscripts and Drawings in the Library of Harry Elkins Widener*. Philadelphia: Privately printed, 1910, passim.

A magnificently produced volume on special paper and with numerous reproductions of title pages and other illustrations. The Dickens items include three Cruikshank drawings for *Sketches by Boz* (one illustrated); the petty cash book Dickens kept as a law clerk for Edward Blackmore; *Pickwick Papers* in parts and other editions; the original agreements between Dickens and John Macrone for *Sketches by Boz*; first bound editions of a number of the novels and other works, including some presentation copies; the autograph manuscript of Dickens's parody of Gray's "Elegy Written in a Country Churchyard"; and several letters from Dickens inserted in some of these volumes. All are extensively annotated and described, with letters and inscriptions fully recorded. See Rosenbach (**1518**) for the full catalogue of Widener's Dickens collection.

1547. [Williamson, Edmund S.], comp. *Dickensiana: Illustrated Catalogue of Works by and Literature Relating to Charles Dickens in Library of E. S. Williamson, 118 Spencer Avenue, Toronto, Canada.* [Toronto]: Privately printed, 1896. [30 pp.]; reprinted, with additions, 1906. [33 pp.].

An undistinguished list, largely of secondary references, interspersed with seven illustrations. The 1906 edition contains the seven illustrations and a poem by "Sam. Kent," entitled "A Writer Chap Like Dickens." See also Williamson (**1548**).

1548. Williamson, E[dmund] S. *Glimpses of Charles Dickens, and Catalogue of Dickens Literature in Library of E. S. Williamson.* Toronto: Bryant Press, 1898. 56 pp.

A list of the editions of Dickens's works and Dickensiana in the library of E. S. Williamson, interspersed with brief comments on a variety of subjects— F. Edwin Elwell's statues of Dickens and Little Nell; Francis Jeffrey Dickens in Canada; a letter to Williamson from a Canadian journalist; the homes of Dickens (illustrated); "A Reverie in Dickens" (a poem by John Arbory); brief excerpts from Dickens's diary of 1838; a transcript of a shorthand copy of a letter that Dickens wrote to Richard Bentley on 14 July 1837; the unauthentic Old Curiosity Shop in London; an excerpt from "The Lounger," in *The Month* (New York), 1 (1897), pp. 213-35, on Williamson's Dickens bookplate (see p. 230–the bookplate shows Mr. Pickwick sitting at his desk, with a portrait of Dickens on the wall); a letter to the editor reprinted from the *Toronto Mail and Empire* of 1895 (no more specific date given) by G. W. Johnson denouncing attribution of a poem "The Children" to Dickens; "Memorials of Chuzzlewit"; and brief notes on three other Dickens collectors. The contents of Williamson's library are grouped under these headings: Works of Dickens; Pickwickiana; Biographical; Speeches, Letters, and Readings; Anthological; Bibliographical; Topographical, etc.; Plagiaristic; Dedications; Miscellaneous; Illustrated Works, etc.; Magazine Articles; and Framed Pictures. Twenty-two illustrations. Also see Williamson (**1547**). For earlier notice by Dickens's eldest son that "The Children" was not by his father, see Dickinson (**498**).

1549. Wise, Thomas J. *The Ashley Library: A Catalogue of Printed Books, Manuscripts, and Autograph Letters Collected by Thomas J. Wise.* 11 vols. First printed for private circulation only, 1922-36; reprinted Folkestone, Eng., and London: Dawsons of Pall Mall, 1971, II, 37-47.

The Dickens items in the library include various first editions of Dickens's minor works (*Sunday under Three Heads, The Village Coquettes,* the five Christmas Books, *A Curious Dance Round a Curious Tree,* and the forged 1852 edition of *To Be Read at Dusk*); two four-page letters from Dickens to Leigh Hunt (12 May 1840 and 31 January 1855), both reproduced in facsimile; editions of Dickens's letters and speeches; and a variety of Dickensiana. Collations and other information are provided. See the Dickens entries in the indexes, IX, 219, and XI, 168, and a few additional items in IX, 67; X, 95; XI, 56-57. A preface by Simon Nowell-Smith in volume 1 of the 1971 edition gives information about Wise and his library.

1550. Wolff, Robert L., [Katharine F. Bruner, and Mary A. Wolff], comps. "Dickens, Charles (1812-1870)." In their *Nineteenth-Century Fiction: A Bibliographical Catalogue Based on the Collection Formed by Robert Lee Wolff.* Vol. 2: *D-K.* Garland Reference Library of the Humanities, 331. New York and London: Garland, 1982, pp. 16-19.

In a five-volume work intended to augment and supplement Sadleir's *XIX Century Fiction* (**1519**) with more than four times as many entries, Wolff lists only a small collection of various editions of Dickens's works, with some annotation, but, as noted in a "Publisher's Note" in volume 1: *A C* (1981), echoing Sadleir's own disclaimer, the Dickens holdings in Wolff's collection are "relatively meagre" because so many other collectors of Dickens's works had preceded him in this field. The volume includes photographs of the bindings of the three-volume edition of *Oliver Twist* and of one-volume editions of other works by Dickens. The only edition in parts in the collection is of *David Copperfield.*

1551. Wright, R. Glenn, assisted by Barbara E. Rosenbaum. *Author Bibliography of English Language Fiction in the Library of Congress through 1950.* 8 vols. Boston: G. K. Hall, 1973, I, 669-97; also *Chronological Bibliography of English Language Fiction in the Library of Congress through 1950.* 8 vols. Boston: G. K. Hall, 1974, I-III, passim, and *Title Bibliography of English Language Fiction in the Library of Congress through 1950.* 9 vols. Boston: G. K. Hall, 1976, I-III, passim.

A reproduction of cards (with many handwritten notations) in the PZ3 section (works of authors whose first work was published before 1950) of the Library of Congress. The Dickens listings, most accessible in the author bibliography, include editions of collected and individual works published through late spring 1970. The works in the chronological bibliography are arranged first by country of author, then by year of publication, and then by author.

The United Kingdom of Great Britain authors are in volumes 1-3. The works in the title bibliography are arranged first by nationality of author, then title of work, then date of publication. Here, too, the United Kingdom of Great Britain authors are in volumes 1-3. While the Library of Congress collection is useful, it is not comprehensive and, obviously, oriented towards American editions.

4B. GUIDES TO COLLECTIONS

Note: Also see **Dickens collections, guides**, in part 2 of the subject index.

1552. Ash, Lee, and William G. Miller et al., comps. "Dickens, Charles, 1812-1870." In their *Subject Collections: A Guide to Special Book Collections and Subject Emphases as Reported by University, College, Public, and Special Libraries and Museums in the United States and Canada.* 7th ed., rev. and enl. 2 vols. New Providence, NJ: R. R. Bowker, 1993, pp. 622-23.

Lists twenty-nine libraries with Dickens collections and provides a few general details about their holdings, principally the number of volumes, letters, manuscripts, playbills, prints, and ephemera, besides giving addresses and telephone and fax numbers of the libraries.

1553. Bell, Barbara L. *An Annotated Guide to Current National Bibliographies.* Government Documents Bibliographies. Alexandria, VA: Chadwyck-Healey, 1986, passim.

Lists and provides considerable information about national bibliographies of Afghanistan to Zimbabwe that one could consult for publications by and about Dickens.

1554. DeWitt, Donald L., comp. *Articles Describing Archives and Manuscript Collections in the United States: An Annotated Bibliography.* Bibliographies and Indexes in Library and Information Science, 11. Westport, CT, and London: Greenwood Press, 1997, p. 152.

Lists only Franklin P. Rolfe's "The Dickens Letters in the Huntington Library" (**1514**).

1555. DeWitt, Donald L., comp. *Guides to Archives and Manuscript Collections in the United States: An Annotated Bibliography.* Bibliographies and Indexes in Library and Information Science, 8. Westport, CT, and London: Greenwood Press, 1994, passim.

See the index for seven collections with Dickens items—the Henry E. Huntington Library, San Marino, CA; the Boston Public Library; The Houghton Library, Harvard University; the Princeton University Library; the Pierpont Morgan Library, New York; the Free Library of Philadelphia; and the University of Texas Library. The entries themselves identify the years covered by each collection and the number of Dickens items therein. The list is obviously incomplete. See section 4A, above, particularly items **1453**, **1458**, **1463**, **1488**, **1495-96**, **1499**, **1501**, **1509**, and **1630**.

1556. [Dexter, Walter]. "Unique Items in Famous Dickens Collections." *Dickensian*, 30 (1933/34), 63-67, 112-16, 204-06, 292-96; 31 (1934/35), 31-34; 32 (1935/36), 264-65.

Itemizes manuscripts, proofs, letters, presentation copies, special editions, illustrations, and Dickensiana in the collections of 1) the Pierpont Morgan Library, New York, and the library of William M. Elkins, Philadelphia; 2) the library of the Comte de Suzannet, Lausanne; 3) the Henry E. Huntington Library, San Marino, CA, and the Dickens House library, London; 4) the Harry Elkins Widener Library, Harvard University, Cambridge, MA; 5) The Forster Collection, the Victoria and Albert Museum Library, London; and 6) the library of the late Charles J. Sawyer, then in the possession of his son.

1557. Downs, Robert B. *American Library Resources: A Bibliographical Guide*. Chicago: American Library Association, 1951, passim; also *Supplement, 1950-1961* (1962), *Supplement, 1961-1970* (1972), and *Supplement, 1971-1980* (1981), passim.

Lists books and principally articles concerning Dickens collections and Dickensiana in libraries. See the index for Dickens items. Also see *Cumulative Index, 1870-1970*, compiled by Clara D. Keller (Chicago: American Library Association, 1981).

1558. Downs, Robert B., and Elizabeth C. Downs. *British Library Resources: A Bibliographical Guide*. Chicago: American Library Association; London: Mansell, 1973; revised, updated, and expanded as *British and Irish Library Resources: A Bibliographical Guide*. London: Mansell; Bronx, NY: Distributed in the United States and Canada by H. W. Wilson, 1981, p. 338.

Quite incomplete, listing only twelve Dickens items, mainly books dealing with library collections of Dickensiana or exhibition catalogues.

1559. Gallico, Alison, ed. *Directory of Special Collections in Western Europe*. London, Melbourne, Munich, New York: Bowker-Saur, 1993, p. 69.

The only Dickens collection mentioned is the Tilburg University Library Dickens Collection, Tilburg, the Netherlands (**1504**), which, it is noted, contains 500 monographs and serials, a printed catalogue of which may be obtained from the library. The collection is identified by Gallico as "inconsistent owing to its private origin."

1560. Harner, James L. "Research Libraries." In his *Literary Research Guide* (**1147**), pp. 23-25.

Provides a list of thirty-four major research libraries, for most of which Web sites are given and most of which would have sizeable collections of Dickens materials.

1561. "Illustrations to Dickens in the Market." *Bookworm*, 2 (1889), 345-48.

Itemizes the locations in 1889 of collections of original drawings for Dickens's works and gives auction prices for some.

1562. Jones, Dolores B., ed. "Dickens, Charles." In her *Special Collections in Children's Literature: An International Directory*. 3rd ed. Chicago and London: American Library Association, 1995, p. 122.

Lists seven collections of Dickens materials—the University of Florida Library, Gainesville; the Huntington Library, San Marino, CA; the Newberry Library, Chicago; the Fales Library, New York University; the William A. Clark Memorial Library, University of California, Los Angeles; the Gimbel Collection, Beinecke Library, Yale University; and the University of Texas Library, Austin. The second edition, edited by Carolyn W. Field (Chicago: American Library Association, 1982) lists the last three and the University Research Center, University of California, Los Angeles, and the San Diego, CA, Public Library. The first edition, edited by Carolyn W. Field, as *Subject Collections in Children's Literature* (New York and London: R. R. Bowker, 1969) does not include Dickens collections.

1563. [Kitton, Frederic G.]. "Dickens's Mss." *Literature*, 5 (1899), 22.

A listing of the owners (museums and collectors) of the manuscripts of all of Dickens's principal and some of his minor works in 1899.

1564. National Historical Publications and Records Commission. *A Guide to Archives and Manuscripts in the United States*. Ed. Philip M. Hamer. New Haven, CT: Yale University Press, 1961, passim.

See the index for Dickens collections at the Henry E. Huntington Library, San Marino, CA (1,250 items); the Boston Public Library (60 items); the Houghton Library, Harvard University (71 letters and two literary manuscripts); the Princeton University Library (letters, the number unspecified); the Pierpont Morgan Library, New York (600 letters to Angela Burdett-Coutts); the Free Library of Philadelphia (800 letters), and the University of Texas Library (129 items). Succeeded by the less useful *Directory of Archives and Manuscript Repositories in the United States* (Washington, DC: National Historical Publications and Records Commission, National Archives and Records Service,

General Services Administration, 1978; 2nd ed. Phoenix, NM, and New York: Oryx Press, 1988), in both editions of which the collections are listed but with no details.

1565. Nelson, Bonnie R. *A Guide to Published Library Catalogs.* Metuchen, NJ, and London: Scarecrow Press, 1982, pp. 113-22 and passim.

Lists, in 429 numbered entries, with frequently extensive annotation, published catalogues of general and specialized libraries and of special divisions of libraries under various categories of specialization, including "English and American Literature," pp. 113-22. While this guide is not useful for locating Dickens collections, obviously many of the libraries listed have extensive Dickens holdings.

1566. Reynard, Keith W., ed. *The Aslib Directory of Literary and Historical Collections in the UK.* London: Aslib, the Association for Information Management, 1993, passim.

Lists and provides brief information about Dickens items in the Cuming Museum, London; the Dickens House Museum, London; the Keats House Museum, London; the Portsmouth Central Library; the Rochester upon Medway Studies Center, Rochester; and the Victoria and Albert Museum, London.

1567. Reynard, Keith W., and Jeremy M. E. Reynard, eds. *The Aslib Directory of Information Sources in the United Kingdom.* 10th ed. London: Aslib, the Association for Information Management, 1998, passim.

Provides telephone and fax numbers, address, type of organization, scholarly connections, subject coverage, special collections, and printed publications of four collections–the Dickens Fellowship, the Dickens House Museum Library, the Great Yarmouth Central Library in Norfolk, and the Medway Archives and Local Studies Centre in Strood, Rochester. The Hampshire County Library in Portsmouth and the Charles Dickens Birthplace Museum, Portsmouth, were mentioned in other recent editions. The directory also covers such establishments as the British Library without reference to their Dickens collections. The first edition of this directory was published in 1928 and later editions in 1957, 1968 (reprinted with minor corrections, 1970), 1977, 1982, 1990, 1992, 1994, and 1996.

1568. Sheppard, Roger, ed. *Directory of Literary Societies and Author Collections.* London: Library Association Publishing, 1994, passim.

Gives the scheme and scope, the terms of access, and other practical information about collections containing Dickens material in the Bath Central Library, the Portsmouth Central Library, the John Rylands University Library of Manchester, the Dickens House Museum (London), the Dickens Library in Thomas Carlyle's House (London), and the Wisbech Museum (Wisbech, Cambridgeshire). Sheppard also provides information about the aims, officers, and other practical matters of the Dickens Fellowship.

1569. Turecki, Gwen E., and John Krol, eds. *Directory of Special Libraries and Information Centers: A Guide to More than 22,110 Special Libraries, Research Libraries, Information Centers, Archives, and Data Centers Maintained by Government Agencies, Business, Industry, Newspapers, Educational Institutions, Nonprofit Organizations, and Societies in the Fields of Science and Engineering, Medicine, Law, Art, Religion, the Social Sciences, and Humanities. 1996.* 19th ed. New York, etc.: Gale Research, 1996 [1995], passim.

Identifies fifteen libraries with special Dickens collections but misses many others. The only English library listed, for example, is that in the Dickens House, London. The editors give no details of the holdings in these collections. Harner (**1147**), p. 26, notes that this series began in 1963.

1570. Williams, Moelwyn I., ed. *A Directory of Rare Books and Special Collections in the United Kingdom and the Republic of Ireland.* London: Library Association, 1985, pp. 38, 73, 89, 122, 175-77, 366; revised by B. C. Bloomfield, with the assistance of Karen Potts. 2nd ed. London: Library Association Publishing, 1997, pp. 41, 87, 109, 149-50, 207-08, 410, 558, 577.

The first edition lists and comments on six Dickens collections, as well as providing information about library hours, restrictions, and catalogues. The collections include 1) the collection of first and early editions of Dickens's works, including the manuscript of *Great Expectations*, in the Rev. Chauncey Hare Townshend collection in the Wisbech and Fenland Museum Library, Wisbech; 2) the collection in the Portsmouth Central Library, which was formerly in the Dickens Birthplace Museum, including editions, Dickensiana, and scrapbooks; 3) The Percy Fitzgerald Dickens Library in the Rochester Museum, containing editions, translations, personal letters and papers of Dickens, scrapbooks, plagiarisms, and other items; 4) the John Dexter Library and the Lady Dickens Library of translations of Dickens's works, along with a file of letters to Lady Dickens, the wife of Sir Henry Fielding Dickens, in connection with the translations, in the British Library; 5) the Dickens House Museum and its library, London; and 6) the John Forster Collection of manuscripts, proofs, and editions of Dickens's works in the Victoria and Albert Museum, London. Bloomfield and Potts's revised edition adds the University of Sussex Library, Brighton, and various collections in the Brotherton Library, University of Leeds.

4C. DICKENS SCRAPBOOKS

Note: There are more Dickens scrapbooks in libraries than are included here. These are ones the author has encountered in the libraries he has used in compiling this bibliography. References to others will be found under **Dickens collections, Dickens scrapbooks**, in part 2 of the subject index.

1571. Berg Collection, New York Public Library, New York. *The Dickens Fellowship. Vol. 1, 1902-3; vol. 2, 1903-4; vol. 3, 1904-5; vol. 4, 1905-6; vol. 5, 1906-7; vol. 6, 1907-8.* 6 scrapbooks, with bookplate of "W. Miller, Dickensiana."

Contains clippings of newspaper and magazine articles, as well as Dickens Fellowship publications and other items concerning the Dickens Fellowship for the years indicated. The first scrapbook is particularly valuable because items concern the founding of the organization in 1902. The scrapbooks also contain letters and postcards to William Miller, an early Dickens scholar, from various fellow Dickensians; tickets to Fellowship dinners and other events; posters for Fellowship events; and programs, announcements, and photographs.

1572. Berg Collection, New York Public Library, New York. *Scrapbook of Clippings, Letters, Facsimiles, Portraits, etc., Relating to Dickens and Other 19th Century Writers.* N. d., with bookplate of W. T. H. Howe.

Principally illustrations from magazines, books, and advertisements. About one-half of this thick album contains Dickens-related items.

1573. British Library, London. *E. R. Moran. Collections Relating to C. Dickens, etc.* [Cuttings from Newspapers Relating to Dickens, etc.]. Egerton MSS. 2154/Farnborough, n. d., pp. [1-18].

A bound scrapbook of principally newspaper clippings containing reviews of books, reports of speeches, and a few biographical and critical sketches of Dickens, Douglas Jerrold, and others, ca. 1842-44, the source of most, unfortunately, not indicated. The first eighteen pages are devoted to Dickens materials. This scrapbook, acquired in 1870, is one of the earliest entries in *Catalogue of Additions to the Manuscripts in the British Museum in the Years MDCCCLIV-MDCCCLXXV* (**1442**).

1574. Dexter, J[ohn] F., comp. A Collection of Newspapers, Press-Cuttings, Portraits, Title Pages, Wrappers, Illustrations and Other Material Relating to the Works of Charles Dickens. [1837-1919?]. In the John F. Dexter Collection, British Library (**1436**), Dex. 310 (18).

This collection is predominantly but not exclusively concerned with *Pickwick Papers* and also includes advertisements for Dickens's works and studies of his characters. See British Library (**1436**), col. 57, from which the title, above, is taken.

1575. The Dickens House, now, as of 2003, The Dickens Museum, London. Miscellaneous Scrapbooks.

The Dickens House contains a number of scrapbooks and collections of newspaper and magazine articles, pamphlets, and other materials of considerable interest and importance to any Dickens scholar, as itemized below. The more important of the general items will be found listed and annotated elsewhere in this bibliography; the more ephemeral, trivial, and insignificant items, as well as any item concerning individual works, will not.

A. [Greaves, John]. [*Charles Dickens's Readings*]. Two volumes bound in brown/green cloth. 71 + 60 pp.

Two scrapbooks of clippings, photostats, and typed transcripts of announcements, advertisements, reports, and reviews of Dickens's readings; letters of inquiry about the readings; and some miscellaneous information, largely about the rooms, halls, and theaters in which Dickens read. Volume 1 contains materials for Dickens's first and second series of public readings, 2 August 1858 to 27 October 1859 and 28 October 1861 to 27 June 1862. Volume 2 covers the third series of readings, 23 March 1866 to 13 May 1867, and the farewell readings, 6 October 1868 to 20 April 1869. The contents are arranged sequentially by place and date of readings, with some exceptions, and the volumes contain tables of contents listing each reading. The American readings are not included.

B. *Dickens Studies–Newspaper Cuttings*. Five cardboard folders of clippings pasted on cardboard.

This material is accompanied by information about the collection and some of its more interesting aspects. As the information indicates, the "ten bundles," now in five folders, are organized as follows:

Folder I, Bundle 1. Articles on the opening of the Dickens House Museum in 1925, on the theft of letters from the House shortly thereafter, and on various Dickens exhibits. 24 pp.

Folder 1, Bundle 2. Commentary on and largely newspaper reviews of Ralph Straus's *Charles Dickens, a Portrait in Pencil* (London: Gollancz,

1928), Carl E. Bechhofer Roberts's *This Side Idolatry* (London: Mills and Book; Indianapolis, IN: Bobbs-Merrill, 1928), Robert Graves's *The Real David Copperfield* (London: Arthur Baker, 1933), Dickens's *The Life of Our Lord* (1934), *Forster-Ley*, and a few other works that were published 1928-34. 64 pp.

Folder II, Bundle 3. Contemporary reviews of *Forster*, Percy Fitzgerald's *The Life of Charles Dickens as Revealed in His Writings* (2 vols., London: Chatto and Windus, 1905), F. G. Kitton's *Charles Dickens: His Life, Writings, and Personality* (London and Edinburgh: T. C. & E. C. Jack, 1902), *Forster-Ley*, George A. Sala's *Charles Dickens* (London: George Routledge, [1870]), and others, 1870-1928. 103 pp.

Folder III, Bundle 4. Personal recollections of Dickens; Dickens in various places—readings, speeches; notices of his death, 1870-1931. 110 pp.

Folder IV, Bundle 5. Articles on *David Copperfield*, 1869-1938. 73 pp.

Folder IV, Bundle 6. Articles on Dickens's family and descendants. 16 pp.

Folder IV, Bundle 7. Miscellaneous notes, articles. 52 pp.

Folder V, Bundle 8. Journalistic *jeux d'esprit* (competitions, exam papers, etc.), 1888-1918. 15 pp.

Folder V, Bundle 9. Articles about the Dickens Fellowship's activities, the *Dickensian*, and Bransby Williams's recreations of Dickens characters. 32 pp.

Folder V, Bundle 10. Articles on local coverage of a Dickens conference in Bath, England, 1903. 12 pp. Also includes an envelope of additional miscellaneous clippings.

C. Kitton, F. G., comp. *Dickens Ana*. 7 bound scrapbooks.

An amazing collection of materials. The first four volumes, titled as indicated above and numbered, contain original letters, drawings and reproductions of drawings by Kitton and others, proofs of illustrations to various works by Kitton and others, and thousands of other items of Dickensiana, including newspaper and magazine cuttings, photostats of Dickens documents and manuscripts, photographs, advertisements for Warren's Blacking, obituary notices for Dickens's family, friends, and acquaintances, a section containing information about Dickens's letters (from sale catalogues and newspaper notices), reviews of books about Dickens, a few original playbills, reproductions of many Dickens portraits, advertisements featuring Dickens or his characters, Christmas cards, and a variety of other memorabilia and Dickensiana. Most items are from the 1890s and through 1903, though a few are earlier, even from before Dickens's death in 1870.

The last three volumes are slightly smaller in size and their being covered in brown wrapping paper to protect their leather covers prevents one from seeing what name or volume number may be embossed on their spines, but they are obviously part of this series of bound scrapbooks. Somewhat more specialized, they contain a comparable variety of materials on the works indicated:

> Vol. [5]. Dickens's early writings (pp. 1-3), *Sketches by Boz* (pp. 5-11), *Pickwick Papers* (pp. 12-159), *Oliver Twist* (pp. 161-83).

> Vol. [6]. *Nicholas Nickleby* (pp. 1-38), *Master Humphrey's Clock* (pp. 40-44), *The Old Curiosity Shop* (pp. 46-66), *Barnaby Rudge* (pp. 67-85), *American Notes* (pp. 86-88), *Martin Chuzzlewit* (pp. 90-114), *A Christmas Carol* (pp. 116-30), *Dombey and Son* (pp. 132-50), the five Christmas Books (pp. 154-62), the *Daily News* (pp. 164-66), *David Copperfield* (pp. 152, 168-98).

> Vol. [7]. *Bleak House* (pp. 1-48), *Little Dorrit* (pp. 49-60), *Great Expectations* (pp. 62-66), *A Tale of Two Cities* (pp. 68-74), *Our Mutual Friend* (pp. 75-82), *The Mystery of Edwin Drood* (pp. 84-98), the Christmas Stories (pp. 100-16), "Hunted Down" (p. 118), *Pictures from Italy* (p. 120), *Household Words* and *All the Year Round* (pp. 122-32), Dickens Ana (pp. 134-40), Criticisms (pp. 142-66), Illustrations (pp. 168-88).

The collection shows just how much Dickensiana has been published in obscure local newspapers of the British Isles, the United States, Canada, Australia, India, and elsewhere that has never been recorded anywhere—and no doubt never will be. Almost all of these pieces are ephemeral and even trite, though a number are by well-known Dickensians of the time. They do, however, document the great and continuing interest in Dickens and all things Dickensian in the later nineteenth and early twentieth century.

D. Kitton, F. G., comp. *Dickens Ana: Magazine Articles*. 17 vols.

A collection of magazine articles and a few newspaper articles, pamphlets, and introductions to Kitton's and other authors' books, 1837-1904, many listed in Kitton's *Dickensiana* (**996**). An Access database, "The Kitton and Matz Dickensiana Collection," available at the library, provides information about author, title, and other publication details for the magazine articles in this collection and the Matz collection of magazine articles listed in item H, below. An index has been compiled by Florian Schweizer, the current Assistant Curator.

E. [Kitton, F. G., comp.]. *Dickens Ana: Pamphlets*. 4 vols.

A collection of forty-five rare and obscure pamphlets, some directly related to Dickens, others tangential at best.

F. Matz, B. W. [*Dickensiana*]. 15 bound scrapbooks.

Largely a collection of newspaper and magazine cuttings, with interspersed items of Dickensiana and other memorabilia. All volumes are covered in brown wrapping paper to protect their leather bindings, which prevents one from seeing what may be embossed on their covers and spines by way of title or volume number. The information supplied about title and volume is hand-written on the wrappers. The material is loosely organized as follows:

Vols. 1-4 and 6, labeled "Miscellaneous," contain cuttings almost exclusively from 1905-08. Vols. 1 and 2 contain a variety of material. Vol. 3 is devoted largely to *Edwin Drood*, pp. 1-24, 94-101; reviews of G. K. Chesterton's *Charles Dickens* (London: Methuen, 1906) and Percy Fitzgerald's *The Life of Charles Dickens as Revealed in His Writings* (2 vols., London: Chatto and Windus, 1905), pp. 25-46; and Dickens and the Stage (pp. 64-92). Vol. 4 contains cuttings from 1905-06 on J. Comyns Carr's dramatization of *Oliver Twist* with Herbert Beerbohm Tree as Fagin (1905), pp. 1-50, and "Dickens-land," pp. 52-110. In addition to miscellaneous items, vol. 6 contains sections on Dickens Societies and Clubs, pp. 100-03, and Political and Topical Cartoons and Illustrations, pp. 104-10.

Vol. 5, labeled "Dickens Fellowship Material," contains announcements published in *Household Words*, 1902-08, about the Fellowship, as well as programs for various activities, tickets, dance cards, menus and programs for banquets, posters, playbills, and publications connected with Fellowship activities.

Vols. 7-11 are labeled "Newspaper Articles." With occasional exceptions, vol. 7 contains articles from 1907 to 1909, vol. 8 from 1910 to 1911, vol. 9 from April 1911 to January 1912, vol. 10 from January to August 1912, and vol. 11 from August 1912 to December 1913, with a concluding section on dramatizations of Dickens's works.

[Vol. 12], labeled "The Charles Dickens Centenary, 1912, Cuttings," contains newspaper cuttings from that year.

[Vol. 13], labeled "Cartoons and Illustrations to Dickens," contains cartoons from *Punch* and elsewhere, series of character sketches, other illustrations, and calendars from 1844 to 1912 (selected years).

[Vol. 14], labeled simply "Matz," contains illustrations, calendars, cigarette cards, advertisements, transfers, and series of character sketches, but no cartoons, of Dickens and particularly his characters.

[Vol. 15], labeled "The Trial of John Jasper for the Murder of Edwin Drood," contains letters, tickets, programs, playbills, scenarios, scripts, photographs, and newspaper and magazine reviews of the trial sponsored by the Dickens Fellowship and performed in London on 7 January 1914. Some material concerning an American version in Philadelphia, 29 April 1914, is also included, as are associated items.

G. Matz, B. W., comp. *Charles Dickens*. 1 vol.

A bound scrapbook (269 pp.) of newspaper cuttings, largely of obituaries and eulogies of Dickens with some reviews of early biographies and reminiscences of Dickens and illustrations from these newspaper clippings, all pasted in but, unfortunately, with rare exception, with no indication of the newspapers in which these pieces appeared. A few covers of monthly parts numbers of Dickens's novels are bound in.

H. [Matz, B. W., comp.]. *Magazine Articles on Charles Dickens.* 14 vols.

A collection of magazine articles, dating from 1836-1912, arranged chronologically in each volume but not throughout the set. There is no other discernable arrangement. Some are from obscure magazines of the period.

I. *Magazine Articles (Continuation).* Two folders.

Folder 1 contains articles mainly from 1912-17 with a few of earlier date. Folder 2 contains articles mainly from 1917-24 with a few of earlier date.

J. *Newspaper Cuttings Relating to Charles Dickens, 1911, 1912, 1913, 1914, 1915, 1916, 1917-18, 1919-21.* 8 bound scrapbooks. Originally in Guildhall Library, London. Presented by the Dickens Fellowship.

Newspaper clippings from a variety of sources, predominantly British, London and provincial, for the years indicated.

K. Newspaper Clipping Files Collection.

Based on the Leslie C. Staples collection of press cuttings, with Miscellaneous Cuttings, 1936-69, in one volume, and Press Cuttings, 1970 date, in one volume per year.

L. Matz, B. W. Dickensiana: Bransby Williams (Character Actor) Album. 1 vol.

Contains professional photographs of Williams in various Dickens and non-Dickens roles.

M. Matz, B. W. Dickensiana: Dickens Post Card Album. 3 vols.

A collection of post cards containing Dickensiana of every variety.

N. Wellesman, Walter. Scrapbook. 1 vol.

Presented to the Dickens House by his granddaughter Eveleen Poperwell, 14 September 1977. Contains a few pasted-in articles (the source usually not identified), illustrations, and post cards.

1576. New York Public Library, New York. *Charles Dickens, 1812-1870: Scrapbook. Clippings, Photographs, Pictures.* [1927?]. In New York Public Library, New York.

A scrapbook, compiled ca. 1927, largely of clippings of illustrations from magazine articles and books about Dickens but also including title pages of editions, illustrations from the novels, sets of extra illustrations, and photographs. Many of these are illustrations of places in Dickens's novels. A large number of magazines and books were obviously destroyed to make the scrapbook.

4D. DICKENS MUSEUM GUIDES

Note: Also see **Dickens collections, Dickens museum guides,** in part 2 of the subject index.

1577. *Charles Dickens and His Bleak House: A Story and a Guide.* Canterbury: Gibbs and Son, n. d. [1959?]. 20 pp.; revised as *Bleak House, Broadstairs, Kent.* N. p.: N. p., [1970?]. 18 pp.

Provides something of a history of Dickens's stay at the house "high up on the cliffs at Broadstairs," his summer seaside residence, known then as "Fort House" and now as "Bleak House," several rooms of which were opened as a museum in 1959. The guide is to the rooms of the house, the study of which, it is noted in the earlier edition, "contains a number of interesting mementoes and souvenirs of Dickens which are well worth the visitor's close inspection," the most important being "a fragment of proof [not further specified] with corrections in Dickens's own handwriting " In the later edition the guide to the rooms has been expanded and the contents more specifically noted and the fragment of proof, still unspecified, moved to the Billiards Room with the other Dickens mementoes. Both editions are illustrated with photographs of the rooms and the exterior of the house, those in the later edition being newer. Also see the museum's Web site, http://www.bleakhouse.ndo.co.uk, which provides a brief illustrated history of the house and a description and photographs of the museum and its grounds. For a sale of items from the collection, see Sotheby's (**2014**).

1578. *Dickens House, Broadstairs.* [Broadstairs, Eng.: Dickens House Museum, Broadstairs], 1949. 12 pp.; revised and enlarged as *Souvenir Guide to the House on the Cliff Immortalised by Charles Dickens as the Home of Betsey Trotwood in the Novel David Copperfield.* Broadstairs: Dickens House Museum, Broadstairs, 1974. 15 pp.

The guidebook to the house—not to be confused with Bleak House, also at Broadstairs (**1577**)—that apparently served as the model for Miss Trotwood's home in *David Copperfield,* with a brief description of its contents. Illustrated.

1579. The Dickens House, London. *The Dickens House.* [London: The Dickens Fellowship, 1926]. 16 unnumbered pages; also several later editions, with varying titles.

Contains "The Dickens House: How It Was Bought by the Dickens Fellowship and Given to London," a brief history of the acquisition of the house that Dickens lived in from 1837-39; "Notes on Dickens's Residence at 48, Doughty Street"; "Work Done by Dickens at 48, Doughty Street," a list of nine works Dickens wrote there; and numerous illustrations and facsimiles of pages from various manuscripts of Dickens's writings. The brochure was considerably revised in 1929 as *A Souvenir Guide to the Dickens House and Its Treasures* (London: The Dickens Fellowship, [1929], 16 pp.). The "Notes on Dickens's Residence at 48 Doughty Street," pp. 3-7, is here identified as by Walter Dexter; it is still part of the latest publication of the guide, now entitled *The Dickens House Museum, 48 Doughty St., London WC1*, though the attribution of the article to Dexter was dropped with the second of several intervening editions. The 1929 edition also contains "A Walk Through the Dickens House," by A. W. Edwards, pp. 8-13, identifying the Dickens artifacts in the collection. This section has changed considerably over the years, particularly in the 1971 and later editions, and now includes a description of the two Suzannet Rooms, which house a selection of materials from the famous Suzannet collection, including such items as Maria Beadnell's album, a variety of Dickens letters, and Count D'Orsay's 1841 and 1842 portraits of Dickens. The concluding section, listing first editions of Dickens's works written at 48 Doughty Street, increases the number of works to twelve in the 1929 edition, but this section was dropped thereafter until restored in the handsome *Dickens House Museum Guide* (ca. 1986), in which the Dexter essay was modified and the section on "A Visit to the Dickens House" further expanded. The latest edition of the work, *The Dickens House Museum, 48 Doughty St., London WC1* (London: Dickens House, [1990], 20 pp.), is illustrated throughout, with color illustrations on both sides of both covers, and contains "Dickens's Life and Writings at 48 Doughty Street," pp. 1-6, and "A Visit to the Dickens House," pp. 7-19, a room-by-room guided tour. It is considerably changed from earlier editions. A new guide is being issued in 2003. Also see the museum's Web site, http://www.dickensmuseum.com, where one can click on icons that provide a brief history of the Dickens House, details of temporary exhibitions there, and information about the research library and photograph library. Also available is a "virtual tour," a series of descriptions of the contents of the rooms in the museum. Another icon on the home page offers web links to the headquarters and several branches of the Dickens Fellowship (**1226**), Mitsuharu Matsuoka's Dickens Page (**1227**), the Dickens Project of the University of California, Santa Cruz campus (**1228**), David Perdue's Charles Dickens Page (**1225**), the Bleak House Museum (**1577**), and a few other sites.

1580. Portsmouth City Museums. *A Guide to the Charles Dickens Birthplace Museum*. Portsmouth City Museums Publication No. 3. Portsmouth: Portsmouth City Museums, 1970. 13 pp.

Notes that the building has been newly restored. The pamphlet consists of short articles on "Landport in 1812" by Barbara Walker, pp. 3-4; "'I Was Born on a Friday,'" by J[ohn] Greaves, pp. 5-8; and "Dickens Birthplace Museum" by A. J. Howath, pp. 9-12. Illustrated. For earlier guides to the museum, see Saunders (**1521**) and Seale (**1523**). Also see the museum's Web site, http://www.charlesdickensbirthplace.co.uk, for a brief illustrated description of the house and brief commentary on the Dickens family's life there. Another Web site, http://www.portsmouth-guide.co.uk/local/cdbthp, devotes a page to a brief description of the museum, accompanied by a color photograph of the exterior of the house.

1581. Taylor, J. C., comp. *Eastgate House Museum, Rochester, with a Short Guide to the Collections*. Jubilee Edition. Rochester, Eng.: Museum Committee, 1953. 16 pp.

The museum, it is explained, is in the building that served as the model for the Nun's House in *The Mystery of Edwin Drood* and possibly for Westgate House, the school for young ladies where Mr. Pickwick had one of his misadventures in *Pickwick Papers*, though Dickens there placed the school in Bury St. Edmunds rather than Rochester. The museum, the Guide points out, has a Charles Dickens Room with an exhibition of letters, programs, portraits, mementoes, and a library of over 400 volumes of Dickensiana presented to it by Percy Fitzgerald. Illustrated. Also see Blount (**1837**).

4E. REPORTS ON COLLECTIONS AND LIBRARY ACCESSIONS

Note: Also see **Dickens collections, reports on collections and library accessions**, and **Collecting Dickens** in part 2 of the subject index.

1582. "About this Edition." In Dickens's *Great Expectations*. Collector's Edition, the New York Public Library. New York, London, etc.: Doubleday, 1997, pp. xxiii-xxxvi.

Comments on an edition based on materials in the Berg Collection, New York Public Library, particularly an extra-illustrated copy of *Great Expectations*, Dickens's Memoranda Book (**2530**), portraits of Dickens, and various relics, some of which are illustrated in the edition.

1583. "Accessions to the Dickens House Museum." *Dickensian*, 70 (1974), 121-23.

Announces the accession by the Dickens House Museum, London, of four playbills and an engraved silver-plated goblet presented to Dickens in 1837 by the *Morning Chronicle* staff, and the loan from the Eastbourne Public Library of the Gilbert Foyle (of Foyle's Bookshop, London) Collection of Dickens First Editions (since returned to Eastbourne). Illustrated.

1584. "Accessions to the V. & A. Library." *Dickensian*, 67 (1971), 34.

Describes a volume of letters sent to John Forster by "grateful readers" of *Forster* and a deed box "containing various Forster papers preserved by his executors," among other items added to the Victoria and Albert Museum Library, London.

1585. A[dams], E[lizabeth] L. "First Editions of Dickens." *More Books: The Bulletin of the Boston Public Library*, 6th ser, 14 (1939), 457.

On the purchase by the Boston Public Library of original editions of *Oliver Twist*, *Master Humphrey's Clock*, and *A Christmas Carol*, with brief descriptions of the volumes and some commentary on the origins of the works.

1586. Agate, James. "In the Matter of Dickens: A Pavement Meditation in Doughty Street." *T. P.'s and Cassell's Weekly*, ns 4 (1925), 364.

On the formal opening of the Dickens House Museum.

1587. Altick, Richard D. *The Art of Literary Research* (**172**), passim.

Comments in passing on the collection of Dickens manuscripts in the Victoria and Albert Museum, London (**1541-43**), p. 62 in the first edition, pp. 70-71 in the second, pp. 75-76 in the third, and p. 83 in the fourth.

1588. Andrew, Nigel. "Triumph and Tears of a Tireless Genius." *Times* (London), 18 January 1986, p. 34.

Comments on Dickens's life in the house at 48 Doughty Street, London, and on the Dickens House Museum now occupying it, "full almost to bursting with Dickensiana." Illustrated.

1589. [Andrews, Malcolm]. "Editorial." *Dickensian*, 97 (2001), 3.

Notes that the Dickens Archive, offered for auction by Sotheby's in 1999 (**2014**), with most items going unsold—see Patten (**2149**)—was eventually purchased "substantially intact" by a London dealer and recently sold to the British Library. Andrews notes an article by John Sutherland in the *Guardian*, 7 February 2001, that "outlined the history of the acquisition and speculated interestingly on the value of such second-order archival material." The *Guardian* article can be read online in the archives at the newspaper's Web site, http://www.guardian.co.uk. Sutherland believes that the purchase of the Dickens Archive by the British Library was "a well-conceived purchase" and "signals a strategic intention to invest in infrastructure."

1590. Barrett, Daniel. "Recent Collections of Nineteenth-Century Theatre Materials on Microfilm." *Nineteenth Century Theatre*, 17 (1989), 66-81.

Surveys what is available, mentioning in passing that most of the materials in the Forster and Dyce Collection in the Victoria and Albert Museum have been filmed by Harvester Press but that "the diaries and theatrical records of Charles Dickens," along with other items, "have not been published in a separate series."

1591. Basbanes, Nicholas A. "Continental Drift." In his *A Gentle Madness: Bibliophiles, Bibliomanes, and the Eternal Passion for Books.* New York: Henry Holt, 1995, pp. 410-64.

Briefly characterizes, pp. 420-26, the collection of William Self, a producer of television series and films, as "arguably the world's leading collection of Charles Dickens books to be found in private hands." The high point of the collection, Basbanes indicates, is a group of twenty-three presentation copies

of Dickens's novels. Basbanes also mentions the collection of Kenyon Starling of Dayton, Ohio, who willed his Dickens collection to Self at his death in
1983.

1592. Beazell, William P. "Some Rare Dickens Play Bills." *Index* (Pittsburgh,
PA), 17, xxvi (28 December 1907), 6.

Comments on William Glyde Wilkins's collection of over fifty playbills of
dramatizations of Dickens's novels, 1837-70. Illustrated. See Anderson Galleries (**1930**).

1593. Betjeman, John, et al. "Dickensian Heritage." *Times* (London), 20 June
1980, p. 2.

A letter to the editor by Betjeman and a number of distinguished British
Dickens scholars and members of the Dickens family in opposition to the
proposed demolition of Ordnance Terrace in Rochester and, with it, the
home in which Dickens was born. The letter achieved its end. As reported in
"Fellowship News and Notes: When Found: Ordnance Terrace Reprieved,"
Dickensian, 76 (1980), pp. 178-79, the houses there were saved from destruc-
tion and the Medway Borough Council's intent was to purchase No. 11, Dickens's birthplace, and open the house as a museum, as well as to improve the
rest of the area.

1594. Brattin, Joel. "Fellman, Dickens, and Illustration." In *Illustrating Dickens:
Selected Works from the Robert D. Fellman Collection* (**1779**), pp. 25-31.

Describes Robert D. Fellman and the collection of autograph letters, drawings and illustrations, and other related items that he bequeathed to the
George C. Gordon Library, Worcester Polytechnic Institute, in 1996. Brattin
also gives something of a history of Dickens's "collaborative work," as he
characterizes it, with his original illustrators, coordinated to a large extent with
the illustrations from the collection accompanying his text. He also comments
on illustrations in the collection (and catalogue) by later artists, among them
seventy-five drawings by "Kyd" (Joseph Clayton Clarke) and a "substantial
portfolio of original pen and ink illustrations" by Donald McKay, done for
The Dickens Digest (New York and London: McGraw-Hill, 1943).

1595. Brattin, Joel. "The Robert D. Fellman Collection at WPI." *Dickensian*,
92 (1996), 80.

A brief description of the collection donated by Fellman to Worcester
Polytechnic Institute, Worcester, MA. Also see Jean Shurtleff's obituary of
Fellman, "In Memoriam: Robert D. Fellman 1923-1996," pp. 79-80.

1596. "Breach in Dickens Vault Fails to Save Films." *Times* (London), 1 June 1973, p. 5.

Reports that the steel door of a recently discovered vault that contained early films based on Dickens's works was forced open, but it was discovered that the seventeen cans of film stored there for twenty-five years were "damaged beyond repair."

1597. Brock, H. I. "Dickens Spirit Returns to Old Home." *New York Times Magazine*, 1 March 1925, p. 13.

On turning the house at 48 Doughty Street, London, into the Dickens House Museum. Brock comments on the changes in the house and its occupants over the years, on Dickens's early married life there from 1837 to 1839, and on the initial collection of books and artifacts to be housed in the museum. Illustrated.

1598. Brown, Norman B., and William H. Huff. "Notable Acquisitions, 1980/1981." *Non Solus*, No. 8 (1981), 37-44.

Describes on p. 44 John E. Velde, Jr.'s gift to the University of Illinois Library of Eaton's *Charles Dickens Rare Print Collection* (**1460**) and Velde's leatherbound collection of *The Works of Charles Dickens* (Philadelphia, ca. 1900) in eighty-six volumes and six supplementary volumes of plays, poems, and speeches, including 621 original watercolor sketches of Dickens characters by "Kyd" (Joseph Clayton Clarke), a two-page letter from Dickens to Charles M. Kent, 3 January 1857, and numerous hand-colored illustrations.

1599. Bump, Jerome. "Parody and the Dickens-Collins Collaboration in 'No Thoroughfare.'" *Library Chronicle of the University of Texas*, 37 (1986), 38-53.

Describes and comments on a copy of the published version of *No Thoroughfare* in the Wolff Collection of the Harry Ransom Humanities Research Center, University of Texas, Austin, with "interleaved annotations" and an introduction by Richard Herne Shepherd (ten handwritten pages). The notes, Bump reports, correct misprints (Bump gives no examples), reveal "how the work differs from a Dickens short story of the same name," and identify "which scenes were written by whom." Bump believes that in the drama Dickens and Collins were deliberately parodying the genre of melodrama.

1600. Burton, Anthony. "The Forster Library as a Dickens Collection." *Dickens Studies Newsletter*, 9 (1978), 33-37.

Describes the John Forster Collection in the Victoria and Albert Museum Library, London. A "frozen" collection, it consists, Burton points out, of the

10,000 volumes and other materials in the donor's library at his death, including the manuscripts, number plans, and proofs of most of Dickens's novels, which Dickens had earlier bequeathed to Forster. Burton also reminds scholars what the collection does not contain and provides useful information about using the collection.

1601. Burton, Anthony. "Literary Shrines: The Dickens House and Other Writers' House Museums." *Dickensian*, 73 (1977), 138-46.

Comments (pp. 142-44) on how the Dickens House Museum, London, is linked "by the bonds of common interest" to other such writers' house museums, particularly in recreating "something of the atmosphere and appearance" of the house when the author lived there. The Dickens House, "like most of the others, started out bare," Burton notes, though it soon "filled up," not only with memorabilia but, unlike the others, with an excellent library formed by the collections of a number of Dickens scholars and collectors. It is trying, Burton indicates, to build "the finest and most comprehensive Dickens library extant" and make it available to Dickens students and scholars, as well as make itself the "meeting place for all lovers of Dickens throughout the world." Dickens himself, Burton reminds the reader, put on a series of amateur theatricals in 1848 to raise funds for a curator for the Shakespeare Birthplace Museum at Stratford.

1602. Burton, Anthony. "Some Recent Work on the Forster Collection." *John Forster Newsletter*, 1, i (May 1978), 10-20.

Describes the Dyce and Forster collections at the Victoria and Albert Museum, London (**1543**), concentrating mainly on the non-Dickens portion of the Forster collection. Illustrated with an etching of Forster's library at Palace Gate, Kensington.

1603. Cahoon, Herbert, ed. "News and Notes." *Papers of the Bibliographical Society of America*, 53 (1959), 78, 274.

Two notes locating eight original copies of the broadside about the Great International Walking Match that took place in Boston on 29 February 1868.

1604. Carden, Percy T. "Secrets of the Dickens House." *Dickensian*, 34 (1937/38), 232-34.

Contains a brief account of the then newly acquired Howard Duffield Collection of *Edwin Drood* literature (**1457C3, 1459**) by the Dickens House, London, briefly referred to in the previous issue, p. 211. See Hopkins (**1805**) and Roe (**1721**).

1605. Carver, A. Llewellyn. "The Portsmouth Public Libraries and the Dickens Birthplace Museum." *Library World*, 40 (1937/38), 230-33.

A very brief description of the collection in the Dickens Birthplace Museum in Portsmouth, consisting of some 400 books and pamphlets, as well as paintings, drawings, and sketches relative to Dickens's life and works–and also the sofa on which he died, among other artifacts. Illustrated.

1606. "'A Christmas Carol.' Dickens Inscription in First Edition." *Times* (London), 21 December 1951, p. 5.

Reports the discovery of a presentation copy of *A Christmas Carol* in a gift of books to the Columbia University Library. The copy contained a lengthy inscription (quoted here in full) in Dickens's hand to Frank Powell, a young boy.

1607. Clark, Alexander P. "The Manuscript Collections of the Princeton University Library." *Princeton University Library Chronicle*, 19 (1957/58), 159-90.

In a survey of manuscripts in the Princeton University library, mentions in passing a "significant" group of letters and manuscripts of Dickens in the Morris L. Parrish Collection, but gives no details. For fuller information about the Parrish Collection, See Parrish (**1507**), Gerould (**1638**), and Wainwright (**1758-59**).

1608. Collins, Philip. "Dickens Editions." *Times Literary Supplement*, 16 April 1970, p. 430.

Collins expresses his dismay that the great British research libraries do not contain complete sets of the original parts editions in which most of Dickens's novels were published. See the responses by I. G. Philip, Keeper of Printed Books, Bodleian Library; A. H. Chaplin, Principal Keeper of British Books, British Museum; and A. G. S. Ensor, Borough Librarian, Eastbourne, 30 April 1970, p. 480. Also see a reply by Joan M. Gladstone, University Library, University of Newcastle upon Tyne, 14 May 1970, p. 539. The responders, as one might suspect, defend the holdings of their libraries.

1609. Dempster, Carolyn. "Dickens of a Job." *Times Higher Education Supplement*, 29 August 1986, p. 10.

An interview with Kevin Harris, creator of a new classification system for the Dickens House Library and author of *The Dickens House Classification* (**1650**). Harris points out the need for such a system and the difficulties of producing one that could also be used for comparable collections of other authors.

1610. [Dexter, Walter]. "Dr. Duffield's *Drood* Collection." *Dickensian*, 34 (1937/38), 211.

Notes that Duffield has given his collection of Droodiana to the Dickens House, London. See Dickens House (**1457C3, 1459**).

1611. [Dexter, Walter]. "When Found—Another 'Morning Chronicle' Post-script." *Dickensian*, 33 (1936/37), 151.

Photograph and description of a silver goblet presented to Dickens by the staff of the London *Morning Chronicle* in 1837 on his resignation from the newspaper. Dexter believes this to be an item not previously recorded, though it was, he notes, in the sale of the Jupp collection, Anderson Galleries, 1922 (**1929**). See **1583** for an announcement of its acquisition by the Dickens House, London.

1612. [Dexter, Walter]. "When Found—Dickens Manuscripts in the Rylands Library, Manchester." *Dickensian*, 30 (1933/34), 159-62.

Announces the publication of an article by Moses Tyson in the *Bulletin of the John Rylands Library* (**457**) on the holdings in the Rylands library and includes the facsimile reproductions of two pages of a book on shorthand in the collection that Dickens apparently put together in the late 1850s, "probably for one of his children"—undoubtedly his son Henry, who describes his father's attempts to teach him shorthand in *Memories of My Father* (London: V. Gallancz, 1928; New York: Duffield, 1929). Dexter points out that the library's collection also includes a number of letters, an extra-illustrated edition of *Forster*, the manuscripts of *A Child's Dream of a Star* (1850) and of a speech of 30 April 1870, and the corrected proofs of a review of *A Letter to Lord Ashley, M. P., on the Mines and Collieries Bill*, a pamphlet by the Marquis of Londonderry. Dexter notes that, though Tyson asserts that the review was not published, it appeared in the *Morning Chronicle* in 1842. The editors of *Pilgrim Letters*, III, note (p. 351) that the review appeared there on 20 October. Also see Quinn (**1511**) and the cross-references there.

1613. "The Dexter Bust." *Dickensian*, 58 (1962), 149-50.

Notes that the bust of Dickens done by Henry Dexter in the United States in 1842 is now in the Dickens House, London.

1614. [Dickens, Peter]. "Opening of the Suzannet Rooms." *Dickensian*, 67 (1971), 188-91.

Consists of the remarks of Captain Peter Dickens, a great-grandson of Dickens, at the opening of a permanent exhibition at the Dickens House,

London, of an extraordinary collection of Dickensiana donated to the museum by the Comtesse de Suzannet. Illustrated.

1615. "Dickens and Handel. Manuscripts for British Museum." *Glasgow Herald*, 15 January 1916, p. 4.

Records Lady Wernher's gift of five pages of *Pickwick Papers* (chapter 19, pp. 47-51, of the manuscript) to the British Museum.

1616. "Dickens Find Made at Columbia." *New York Times*, 20 December 1951, p. 40.

Prints a long inscription by Dickens, in the form of a comical dialogue, to a boy, Frank Powell, in a copy of the first edition of *A Christmas Carol* newly acquired by Columbia University, New York, and gives the provenance of the volume. The inscription, dated 13 March 1844, is reprinted in *Pilgrim Letters*, IV, 71-72, with useful notes (the editors indicate, for example, that Powell was later killed in the American Civil War).

1617. *The Dickens House Library, Classification & Cataloguing Project: An Occasional Newsletter*, no. 1 (May 1983)-no. 5 (November 1985), passim.

Concerned with matters connected with the project. No. 2 contains the primary classification system for the arrangement of volumes and materials in the library in the Dickens House, London. See also Harris (**1649-51**).

1618. "The Dickens House Reopened." *Times* (London), 6 December 1937, p. 9.

Describes the museum after "redecoration and the rearrangement of its contents," and gives something of its history. Accompanied by a photograph of Lady Dickens (Henry Fielding Dickens's widow) at the reopening ceremonies.

1619. "Dickens. Interesting Facts Gathered by a Collector." *New York Times*, Saturday Review of Books and Art section, 9 December 1899, p. 862.

Describes the E. S. Williamson collection of Dickensiana, Toronto, Canada, and passes along other information from a fifty-six-page brochure published by Williamson (**1548**). Also see Williamson (**1547**).

1620. "Dickens Letters. The British Museum Collection. Forthcoming Release to Students." *Times* (London), 15 January 1934, p. 9.

Indicates the approaching accessibility of 136 letters from Dickens to his wife Catherine, some written before their marriage, which their daughter Kate

Perugini had deposited to the British Museum on condition that they not be released to scholars until her and her brother Henry Fielding Dickens's deaths. Some summaries of the letters are given.

1621. "Dickens Library. Celebrations of the Great Novelist's Birthday." *Daily News* (London), 7 February 1907, p. 11.

Comments on the "fine" Kitton Collection of Dickensiana then being purchased for £300 by the nation and to be placed in the London Guildhall and held in trust for the nation by the Council of the Dickens Fellowship (it would ultimately end up in the Dickens House Museum, London). The collection included editions of Dickens's works, plagiarisms and imitations, portraits of Dickens, and other items, the reporter indicates. Illustrated.

1622. "Dickens Library for Rochester." *Times* (London), 27 January 1913, p. 8.

Brief notice of Percy Fitzgerald's gift of nearly 200 volumes to the Rochester, England, library.

1623. "The Dickens Reference Library." *T. P.'s Weekly*, 12 (1908), 764.

Notes that J. W. T. Ley and William Miller have indexed the Walter Dexter collection, to which other works and collections have been added, the total coming to over 10,000 items, and that Henry J. Glaisher contributed a "large collection of newspaper cuttings related to the death of Dickens." The Dexter Collection is now in the British Library (**1436**).

1624. "A Dickens Shrine. 48, Doughty-Street to Be Opened Today" and "A Dickens Shrine. 48, Doughty-Street Opened to the Public." *Times* (London), 9 June 1925, p. 13, and 10 June 1925, p. 12.

The earlier article is a brief report on the purchase and furbishment of the London house Dickens lived in from 1837 to 1839, the later a report of the opening ceremonies and the speech by Lord Birkenhead on the occasion of the building's dedication as a museum, the Dickens House.

1625. "A Dickens Souvenir." *Harvard Library Notes*, no. 14 (March 1925), 37-38.

Records a gift of "a handful of books" from Mrs. Cornelius C. Felton from her husband's library, including a first edition of *A Christmas Carol* inscribed to him by Dickens. The report also records a letter in the Sumner collection of the library from Dickens to Charles Sumner, March 1842, in which he mentions that he misses Felton, whom he had met in Boston earlier that year (the editors of *Pilgrim Letters*, III, 126-28, date the letter 13 March 1842, from

Washington, D. C.). The anonymous author of this article also quotes from a manuscript diary (further details not given), 3 May-20 June 1853, kept by Felton in London and Paris, about two dinners with Dickens in London after not having seen him for eleven years, at which Dickens, for comic purposes of his own, introduced him to his friends, including John Forster and George Cruikshank, as "Professor Stowe."

1626. "Dickens's Birthday. A Glance Through a 'Dickens Collection.'" *Pall Mall Gazette*, 47 (7 February 1888), 5.

Describes the collection of W. R. Hughes of Birmingham, England, which contained over 2,000 items, including sixteen portraits of Dickens and other art work; books from Dickens's library; letters, speeches, readings, and other Dickensiana; playbills; editions of Dickens's works; and books, pamphlets, and articles about him. For a number of clippings on Hughes and his collection that appeared in various newspapers, see Dickens House Scrapbooks (**1575C**), III, 70, 72-75, 82-83. Also see "Chronicle and Comment" (**2084**), "An Interesting Dickens Collection" (**1656**), Van Noorden (**1756**), and Wright (**1776**).

1627. "Dickens' 'Life of Our Lord.'" *American Book Collector*, 15, iii (November 1964), 24.

Notes that an anonymous donor has given the original forty-six-page manuscript of Dickens's *Life of Our Lord* to the Philadelphia Free Library in memory of D. Jacques Benoliel, a Philadelphia industrialist. Dickens willed the manuscript that he had written for his children in 1846 to Georgina Hogarth, his sister-in-law, and it was sold at Sotheby's, 25 July 1939 (**1981**), where it was purchased by the Rosenbach firm, Philadelphia, for a client, it is reported here. Also see Weart (**1762**).

1628. Dickinson, Donald C. *Henry E. Huntington's Library of Libraries*. San Marino, CA: Huntington Library Press, 1995, pp. 95-98 and passim.

A biography of Huntington, with passing references to his collecting of Dickens, particularly his letters—see the index. Dickinson comments in somewhat greater detail (pp. 95-98) on Dickens's works and letters purchased by Huntington at the two Coggeshall sales in 1916—see Anderson Galleries (**1931**).

1629. Dickson, Sarah A. "The Arents Collection of Books in Parts and Associated Literature: A Brief Survey." *Bulletin of the New York Public Library*, 61 (1957), 267-80; reprinted as "A Brief Survey." In her *The Arents Collection of Books in Parts and Associated Literature: A Complete Checklist* (**1495**), pp. 7-20.

In describing the rich collection of George Arents in the New York Public Library, Dickson mentions in passing *Sketches by Boz* in parts; a number of editions of *Pickwick Papers*, including one of "the fourteen 'Prime Pickwicks,'" and two very rare American editions, 1836-37 and 1836-38; all the English as well as twelve American parts issues of Dickens's longer novels; and autograph letters (not here identified). Illustrated.

1630. Egerer, J[oel] W. *The Fales Library: Charles Dickens in the Fales Library*. New York University Libraries Bibliographical Series, 3. New York: New York University Libraries, 1965. 44 pp.

Egerer, then the curator of the Fales Library, justifiably claims that the library's Dickens collection is "one of the best-rounded collections of Dickens editions, Dickens manuscripts, and Dickensiana in this hemisphere." In a running commentary mixing details of Dickens's professional life as a writer with the library's Dickens holdings, Egerer describes in some detail the highlights of the collection—the printed editions, American as well as English; translations and dramatizations of and songs and music based on Dickens's works; manuscripts, including 104 Dickens letters, a couple of prologues to dramatic presentations, a "portion of the corrected manuscripts of pieces reprinted in *The Uncommercial Traveller*," and more minor items; Dickensiana, including letters by George Cruikshank (150), Douglas Jerrold (50), John Forster (47), Mark Lemon (4), Catherine Dickens ("a few"), John Dickens (1), and Georgina Hogarth ("a few"), and drawings by Cruikshank (50) and Hablot K. Browne ("some"), as well as a collection of bibliographical, biographical, and critical materials and illustrations and sets of extra illustrations for Dickens's works. Illustrated. For fuller details of the collection, see its catalogue (**1502**). Also see Winterich (**1773-74**).

1631. Fielding, K[enneth] J. "A Guide to Research Materials on the Major Victorians (Part III): Charles Dickens." *Victorian Newsletter*, no. 14 (Fall 1958), 22-23.

Briefly notes the locations of Dickens's chief manuscripts, large collections of letters, and private papers.

1632. "50 Dickens Letters. Gift to Philadelphia Library." *Times* (London), 3 February 1958, p. 6.

Reports that a gift from Mrs. Katherine K. Benoliel to the Philadelphia Free Library of fifty Dickens letters, 1835-70, more than half of which "have never been published," is the "final instalment" of her larger gift of 513 Dickens letters, bringing the total collection of Dickens letters in the library to 750.

1633. Fitzgerald, Percy. "Boz and Music." *Dickensian*, 4 (1908), 173-77.

Describes items in Fitzgerald's collection of sheet music based on Dickens's characters and works. See corrections by William Miller, p. 222. Illustrated.

1634. Fitzgerald, Percy. "Dickens's Editorial Home and Birthplace." *Times* (London), 3 September 1903, p. 5.

A letter to the editor concerning two Dickens locations lamentably scheduled for demolition—the offices of *Household Words*, Wellington Street, Strand, and Dickens's birthplace, in Mile-End Terrace, Landport, Portsmouth. The latter survived, ultimately purchased by the Corporation of Portsmouth for a Dickens Museum for £1,125 at auction. See the *Times* for 5 September, p. 4; 9 September, p. 7; 25 September, p. 4; and 1 October, p. 10.

1635. Foster, Peter. "A Radiant Mrs Dickens Returns to London Home." *Times* (London), 7 October 1995, p. 8.

Comments on and gives the provenance for two long-lost portraits of Catherine Dickens by Daniel Maclise, a watercolor and an oil, painted in 1846/47, to be exhibited at the Dickens House Museum, London. Illustrated. Also see a second article in the same issue of the *Times*, by Edward Gorman, "Doomed Love Story of the 'Biggest Ego in England' and His Pet Mouse," p. 8, which gives a thumbnail sketch of Catherine's life and her fall from Dickens's grace.

1636. Frost, Bill. "Happy Broadstairs Days Helped Dickens to Dispel Childhood Demons." *Times* (London), 10 August 1995, p. 6.

On Fort House, since renamed Bleak House, Broadstairs, Kent, where Dickens and his family spent summers, 1839-51, and now a museum. Frost briefly describes some of the items in the museum and, equally briefly, comments on Dickens's life there. He also notes Dickensian associations with other places in Broadstairs. Illustrated.

1637. "Gems of the South Kensington Collection." *Strand Magazine*, 33 (1907), 243-50.

Contains a brief description by W. P. Frith of the painting of "Dolly Varden" that he did for Dickens and prints the brief letter from Dickens, 15 November 1842, commissioning him to do both it and a companion picture of Kate Nickleby. Illustrated.

1638. Gerould, Gordon H. "The Dickens Collection." *Princeton University Library Chronicle*, 8, i (November 1946), 21-23.

In a special issue devoted to the Morris L. Parrish Collection of Victorian Literature, Princeton University Library, Gerould's contribution briefly notes that nearly 700 items comprise the Dickens holdings (**1507**) in the collection, including some Dickens letters, a variety of printed Dickensiana, and, most prominently, "beautiful copies" of the parts issues, the first volume editions, and early American as well as British editions of Dickens's major novels. For later reports on the collection, see Wainwright (**1758-59**). Also see Clark (**1607**).

1639. "Gift of Dickens Manuscripts. French Ambassador's Tribute. 'Pioneer of the Entente Cordiale.'" *Times* (London), 9 July 1938, p. 9.

Covers the presentation by the French ambassador, M. Corbin, of a gift from the Comte de Suzannet of sixty pages of Dickens manuscripts to the Dickens House Museum, and gives the gist of the ambassador's speech in which he refers to Dickens as the "pioneer of the entente Cordiale." The gift consisted of thirty-nine pages of the manuscript of *Nicholas Nickleby* (chapter 9), ten pages of "The Schoolboy's Story" from *Another Round of Stories* (the *Household Words* Christmas issue, 1853), and "Our Commission" (11 pp.), from *Household Words*, 11 August 1855. Also see "A Princely Donation" (**1708**).

1640. "Gift to Dickens Museum. Letters and Portrait." *Times* (London), 31 March 1927, p. 12.

Announces a gift from Major and Mrs. James Knowles of an eight-volume Grangerized copy of *Forster* that had originally been given to the actor Henry Irving by J. L. Toole in 1891, which contained twenty-eight Dickens letters as well as 272 other letters and various portraits, playbills, sketches, and other memorabilia.

1641. Gilbert, Francis. "The Dickens Museum." *Times* (London), 27 September 1997, Weekend Travel Section, p. 24.

Finds the Dickens House Museum, London, "a serious and scholarly museum," and "worth several visits."

1642. Gordan, John D. "New in the Berg Collection: 1952-1956." *Bulletin of the New York Public Library*, 61 (1957), 303-11, 353-63.

Notes two new Dickens items in the collection: a first edition of *A Christmas Carol* in one of its variants (p. 311) and the reading (or "prompt") copy of *The Cricket on the Hearth*, which joins, Gordan indicates, "a dozen other prompt copies corrected and used by Dickens" already in the collection (p. 353). See Collins (**652**) for an updated count.

1643. Greaves, John. "Dickens at Doughty Street." *Times Educational Supplement*, 18 July 1975, p. 14.

In response to a favorable review by Phillip Venning (*Times Educational Supplement*, 20 June 1975, p. 22) of Greaves's *Dickens at Doughty Street* (London: Elm Tree Books, Hamish Hamilton, 1975), Greaves objects angrily to Venning's characterization of the Dickens House Museum as a "clutter of bogus Dickensiana," insisting, quite correctly, that it is "possibly the finest collection of Dickensiana in the world."

1644. Greaves, John. "The Dickens House, London." *Dickens Studies Newsletter*, 6 (1975), 38-42.

On the fiftieth anniversary of the opening of the Dickens House Museum, London, gives a brief history of Dickens's life in the house at 48 Doughty Street, London, and of the building's transformation into a museum in 1925.

1645. Greaves, John. "Historic Additions to the Dickens House Museum." *Dickensian*, 63 (1967), 81, 130.

Announces the "long loan" to the Dickens House, London, of Dickens's desk, the original "empty chair," ink stand, and gavel. Only the ink stand is currently in the Dickens House. The desk and chair are now in the possession of Jeanne-Marie Dickens, Hartford, Connecticut—see Charles Dickens Heritage Foundation (**1785**). Illustrated.

1646. Guckert, Diane. "Dickens Museum No Longer a Bleak House." *Times* (London), 22 September 1983, p. 12.

Reports on ceremonies marking the restoration of the drawing room in the Dickens House, with a description of the wallpaper, color scheme, and furnishings.

1647. Haraszti, Zoltán. "A Gift of Rare Books." *Boston Public Library Quarterly*, 4 (1952), 67-87.

Refers on pp. 82-85 to parts editions of four novels by Dickens—*Dombey and Son*, *Bleak House*, *Little Dorrit*, and *Our Mutual Friend*—in the collection of Lee M. Friedman donated to the Boston Public Library and provides a few details about the production of these serializations.

1648. Hardwick, Michael, and Mollie Hardwick. "Dickens House, Doughty Street, Bloomsbury, London." In their *Writers' Houses: A Literary Journey in England*. London: Phoenix House (J. M. Dent), 1968, pp. 11-15.

Briefly describes Dickens's life at 48 Doughty Street, 1837-39, and the interior as it was then and is now, as home of the Dickens House Museum. Illustrated.

1649. Harris, Kevin. "Bibliographic Classification and Cataloguing in Dickens Studies." *Dickensian*, 80 (1984), 163-64.

A note on a plan to produce a "working system for organizing and retrieving material in the field of Dickens studies," specifically for cataloguing the collection in the Dickens House library, London. Also see Harris (**1650-51**) and *The Dickens House Library, Classification & Cataloguing Project: An Occasional Newsletter* (**1617**).

1650. Harris, Kevin. *The Dickens House Classification, Prepared for the Library of the Dickens House, London.* SOLIS Research Reports, 18. London: School of Librarianship and Information Studies, Polytechnic of North London, 1986. 98 pp.

A report on and a detailed outline of a library classification system developed for the Dickens House Museum and its library, London, not only for books and manuscripts, with which a library normally deals, but also for its "collections of visual images," which range from films to postcard collections, from clippings to jigsaw puzzles. Since it is not a familiar classification system, such as the Library of Congress or the Dewey Decimal, it seems unnecessarily strange and arbitrary, to which one who has tried to use it can testify. Still, other libraries use comparably exotic systems, including the British Library and the New York Public Library, and continued use should make it sufficiently familiar and bearable, whatever one's philosophical position on the degree to which knowledge need be categorized. Practically speaking, for the printed texts themselves, a less complex outline might very well be sufficient for a researcher or cataloguer, particularly for a library that numbers its holdings in the thousands rather than in the millions. However, for the diverse visual materials in which the Dickens House is especially rich, such categorization is indeed useful and necessary. An alphabetical "Index to the Dickens House Classification," pp. 75-98, provides specific call numbers for a variety of subjects. Also see Harris (**1649, 1651**) and *The Dickens House Library, Classification & Cataloguing Project: An Occasional Newsletter* (**1617**).

1651. Harris, Kevin. "A Faceted Classification for Special Literature Collections: The Dickens House Classification." *International Library Review*, 19 (1987), 335-44.

Describes in some detail the Dickens House Classification (DHC), a cataloguing system designed for author-based collections of books and other ma-

terials. Also see Harris (**1649-50**) and *The Dickens House Library, Classification &*
Cataloguing Project: An Occasional Newsletter (**1617**).

1652. Harris, Kevin, and David Parker. "The Dickens House, London." *Dickens Studies Newsletter*, 14 (1983), 129-35.

Gives details of the appearance of the house at 48 Doughty Street, London, and its interior decoration when Dickens lived there and the extent to which this is preserved in the house today. Harris and Parker also comment on the growth of the collection of books and manuscripts since the establishment of the museum in 1925, briefly note the special classification designed for recataloging the collection, and record that the film collection mentioned in "When Found—Our Film Library," *Dickensian*, 44 (1947/48), 60, a list of six films (1923-1947) and several newsreels (1927-1936), was destroyed as unsafe because of deterioration. See **1457I**.

1653. Haysom, G., et al. *National Dickens Library Report. Library Committee, Presented 9th April, 1908.* [London: Privately printed, 1908]. 3 pp.

On the presentation of the National Dickens Library to the City of London's Guildhall Library by the Dickens Fellowship. The report points out that the library is based on Frederic G. Kitton's collection of Dickensiana, which consisted of "451 volumes, by or relating to Charles Dickens," and included "many first editions of the novels, four volumes illustrating the author's life, eighteen volumes of magazine articles, three volumes dealing with the scenes and characters of the novels, 250 portraits, two volumes of illustrations, a number of original sketches by Jacomb Hood, W. Raincy and J. H. Bacon, autograph letters, &c." The library would eventually come back to the Fellowship when the Dickens House opened in 1925—see The Dickens House, London (**1457, 1579**) and Ridge (**1720**). For fuller descriptions of some of the items in the collection, see The Dickens House, London, Miscellaneous Scrapbooks (**1575**). For a description of the collection in 1908, see "A National Dickens Library" (**1687**). A copy of the 1908 report may be found in volume 6 of the Dickens Fellowship scrapbooks in the Berg Collection, New York Public Library (**1571**).

1654. "Hobby Hitching Post." *Rotarian*, 63, vi (December 1943), 60-61.

On the collecting of Dickensiana by Lewis A. Hird, a past president of the New York City Rotary Club, including first editions, letters, association volumes, and drawings by George Cruikshank, Hablot K. Browne, and John Leech, as well as Dickens's office chair, his folding reading lamp, and other relics. Illustrated. See the Parke-Bernet sale catalogue for Hird's collection (**1963**).

1655. Hogan, J. F. "Dickens: Unpublished Letters." *Notes and Queries,* 11th ser., 5 (1912), 86-87.

Mentions a collection of letters in the Melbourne University library between Dickens and G. W. Rusden, who "was for a long time the highest Parliamentary official in Melbourne" and who "published histories of Australia and New Zealand, and various other works." Hogan expresses his hope that the correspondence, which is of a "personal and intimate character," will nevertheless be made available for publication. The letters were first published in 1972/73–see Mary Lazarus's "The Problem of Plorn: Edward Dickens's First Days in Australia." *Dickensian,* 68 (1972), 90-99; reprinted with other letters in her *A Tale of Two Brothers: Charles Dickens's Sons in Australia* (Sydney and London: Angus and Robertson, 1973). Hogan notes that the library also owns a complete set of his novels that Dickens presented to Rusden.

1656. "An Interesting Dickens Collection." *Birmingham Daily Mail,* 26 May 1887, p. [2]; reprinted as *An Interesting Dickens Collection, Reprinted from the "Birmingham Daily Mail," May 26, 1887.* [Birmingham, Eng.: *Birmingham Daily Mail*], 9 June 1887. 11 pp.

Describes in some detail the collection of W. R. Hughes of Birmingham, consisting of 1,117 items at the time of writing–books about Dickens, paintings, engravings, music, playbills, and other Dickensiana, but no original letters or manuscripts. Also see "Chronicle and Comment" (**2084**), "Dickens's Birthday. A Glance Through a 'Dickens Collection'" (**1626**), Van Noorden (**1756**), and Wright (**1776**).

1657. "Interesting Gift to the Nottingham Mechanics' Institution. A Farewell Dinner." *Nottingham Daily Express,* 13 January 1912. In Dickens House Scrapbooks (**1575J**).

Records a gift to the institution from Mrs. James Ward of a volume of newspaper cuttings relating to Dickens, dating from about the time of his death in 1870 to 1899, and an autograph letter from Dickens to a Mr. Teakes (identified as William Jeakes in *Pilgrim Letters,* VII, 528n), 9 February 1855, indicating Dickens's interest in seeing a drying machine on its completion and mentioning a forthcoming visit to France.

1658. John Rylands University Library, Manchester, Eng. *English Studies: A Guide to Research Resources.* Manchester, Eng.: John Rylands University Library, 1989, p. 15.

Mentions that the Gaskell Collection contains letters from Dickens and that a collection in the Deansgate Building "holds an important group of letters and manuscripts relating to Dickens" inserted in an extra-illustrated copy of *Forster*, as well as a manuscript copy of an edition of *A Christmas Carol* designed by Alan Tabor, a Manchester artist, for George G. Harrap & Co., publishers. For further details of the collection, see Quinn (**1511**) and the cross-references there.

1659. Johnson, E. D. H. "The George Cruikshank Collection at Princeton." In *George Cruikshank: A Revaluation*. Ed. Robert L. Patten. Special issue of *Princeton University Library Chronicle*, 35, i/ii (Autumn/Winter, 1973/74), 1-33.

Notes that the collection contains several drawings and pencil sketches for early editions of *Oliver Twist* and *Sketches by Boz* (pp. 16-17). Illustrated.

1660. Johnston, William R. "Alfred Jacob Miller—Would-Be Illustrator." *Walters Art Gallery Bulletin*, 30, iii (December 1977), [2]-[3].

Notes that Miller's "abiding interest in literary genre is manifested in his private sketch-books," presented to the Walters Art Gallery, Baltimore, MD, by Mr. and Mrs. J. William Middendorf, II. These sketchbooks include drawings of "a number of incidents" from Dickens's novels. Johnston also points out that a finished painting based on one of the sketches—a scene from *The Old Curiosity Shop* involving the Marchioness—was recently given to the Gallery by Margaret Hodges.

1661. Kelley, H. Gilbert. "Notes from the Library: 'Book in Shilling Numbers.'" *Journal of the Rutgers University Library*, 10, ii (June 1947), 59-60.

In announcing the presentation to the Rutgers University Library by Stanley R. March of *Dombey and Son* in complete unbound parts, comments on Dickens's publication of most of his novels in monthly parts for a shilling each—and his barely keeping ahead of his monthly deadlines. Illustrated.

1662. Kenyon, Karen. "The Dickens House Museum." *British Heritage*, 16, 1 (December 1994/January 1995), 54-57.

A brief description of the museum and its contents, accompanied by several color photographs of the exterior and interior of the building.

1663. Lane, Lauriat, Jr. *The Collings-Mennen Extra-Illustrated Copy of John Forster's Life of Charles Dickens, Given by William G. Mennen, '08.* Ithaca, NY: Cornell Library Associates, 1955. 19 pp.; reprinted, with revisions, as "The Mennen Copy of Forster's *Life of Dickens*." *Cornell Library Journal*, No. 8 (Spring 1969), 20-34.

Describes a grangerized copy of the original edition of *Forster* presented to the library by William G. Mennen, class of 1908, in six leather-bound volumes. Lane, noting certain errors in illustrations, believes the copy was largely put together by Edward J. Collings, assisted by Alexander Ireland. It contains 440 portraits, over 200 autograph letters (six by Dickens, three by Forster, others by Gladstone, Thackeray, Carlyle, Thomas Hood, Thomas Moore, Longfellow, and Wilkie Collins), numerous illustrations of localities with Dickensian associations, and eight pencil drawings by Fred Barnard. It does not, Lane indicates, match in fullness the grangerized *Life* compiled by Thomas [sic, William?] Wright in twelve volumes, with 119 autograph letters by Dickens himself, that was sold at Sotheby's (**2008**) in June 1899. Illustrated. Also see Kitton (**2124**), "Notes of the Day" (**1695**), "A Unique Dickens Collection" (**2188**), and "Wright Collection" (**2196**).

1664. "The Latest Gifts to the Dickens House: Important Letters and Association Books." *Dickensian*, 25 (1928/29), 141-42.

Lists seven letters, several first editions, a presentation copy of *The Haunted Man*, and other books and memorabilia from various donors given to the Dickens House, London.

1665. Layard, S. S. "Robert Seymour." *Times Literary Supplement*, 9 June 1921, p. 373.

Layard describes rough pencil drawings by Seymour for *Pickwick Papers* sold at auction and others in his own possession and mentions two of Seymour's sketchbooks donated to the Victoria and Albert Museum, London.

1666. Leach, Elizabeth. "Playbills and Programmes." *Manchester Review*, 11, i (Spring/Summer 1966), 7-22.

In a survey of a collection of theater programs and playbills in the Central Library, Manchester, Leach mentions a playbill for a performance on 26 July 1847 of Ben Jonson's *Everyman in His Humour*, with a cast of Dickens, John Forster, and others.

1667. Lehmann-Haupt, Hellmut. "English Illustrators in the Collection of George Arents." *Colophon*, New Graphic Series, 1, iv (1940), [23]-[46].

Mentions "the beautiful collection of 'Phiz' drawings" in Arents's collection (**1495**), including a watercolor sketch for *David Copperfield* (illustrated), which, Lehmann-Haupt notes, varies some from Dickens's text although the etching (the original steel plate for this is also in the collection) Browne made based on it does not.

1668. "Library Notes & Queries." *Princeton University Library Chronicle,* 8 (1946/47), 90.

A four-line note announcing a gift to the Princeton University Library of a pastel portrait of Dickens done by E. Goodwyn Lewis in 1869.

1669. "A Library of Rarities." *Walford's Antiquarian,* 12 (1887), 282-86.

Commenting on the extensive library of George Washington Childs, the author notes that the treasure of the collection was the manuscript (with its number plans) of *Our Mutual Friend* (now in the Pierpont Morgan Library, New York) and that a study of it "reveals Dickens's method of going about his story writing." The author also looks briefly at the numerous corrections in the manuscript, noting the small hand in which Dickens wrote the number plans and the manuscript, every inch of paper of which, he observes, is covered "as though paper was dear or scarce." Also see Robinson (**1513**).

1670. "Library Receives More of Dickens." *New York Times,* 2 February 1958, p. 39.

Notes that a gift from Katherine K. Benoliel in memory of her husband, D. Jacques Benoliel, to the Free Library of Philadelphia of fifty letters by Dickens, written between 1835 and 1870, brings the total number of Dickens letters in the Benoliel Collection to 533. No excerpts from the letters are given.

1671. Lingard, Christine. "The Gaskell Collection in Manchester Central Library." *Gaskell Society Journal,* 2 (1988), 59-75.

Prints an autograph letter from Dickens to Elizabeth Gaskell, 6 December 1852, referring to her contribution, "The Old Nurse's Story," to the Christmas number of *All the Year Round* for that year, also printed in 1988 in *Pilgrim Letters,* VI, 817. Other items with Dickens associations in the collection mentioned by Lingard are Gaskell's manuscript of "How the First Floor Came to Crowley Castle," part of *Mrs. Lirriper's Lodgings,* the *All the Year Round* Christmas Number for 1863, and the manuscript of a short story, "Helena Matthewson," by Meta (Margaret) Gaskell, daughter of Elizabeth and William Gaskell, printed in *Household Words,* 4 July 1857. For further details, see Quinn (**1511**) and the cross-references there.

1672. Lohf, Kenneth A. "Our Growing Collections: Sherwin Gift." *Columbia Library Columns,* 33, i (November 1983), 42.

Briefly announces that Mrs. Judith Johnson Sherwin, daughter of Edgar Johnson, has donated her father's papers, including his notes, manuscripts, and proofs of *Johnson,* to the Columbia University Library.

1673. MacColl, Margaret. "Dickens at the Free Library: William M. Elkins Collection Opens to Public, Featuring Dickens Manuscripts, Illustrations and Personal Effects." *Philadelphia*, 36, iv (April 1949), 17-19.

A brief description of the Elkins bequest of over 8,000 books and manuscripts to the Philadelphia Free Library and the bequest by Elkins's family of his study itself, which was reassembled at the library to house the collection. Most of the three pages of the article are taken up by twelve illustrations of items in the collection. Also see Free Library of Philadelphia (**1464**, **1793**), Sargent (**1726**), Shaffer (**1730**), Stevenson (**1748**), and Dexter (**1556**).

1674. Maclean [actually McLean], Robert S. "William Pleater Davidge Presents an 'Evening with Charles Dickens': Some Newly Discovered Manuscripts of the First Dickens Reader." *Dickensian*, 92 (1996), 195-207.

Maclean provides useful details about a well-known nineteenth-century actor's public readings from Dickens's works, 1845-58, based on the Davidge collection, Harvard College Library, Cambridge, MA, which includes two manuscripts of Davidge's lecture notes on Dickens. Illustrated.

1675. "Magnificent Gift to the Dickens House." *Dickensian*, 67 (1971), 67-69.

Describes gifts to the Dickens House, London, from the Comtesse de Suzannet, including more than ninety letters; various portraits and playbills; a copy of the trial issue of *A Christmas Carol*; Dr. Frank Beard's notes on Dickens's pulse beats during his readings in 1870; twenty-five original drawings for Dickens's books by Robert Seymour, Hablot K. Browne, Clarkson Stanfield, John Leech, and Marcus Stone; Maria Beadnell's album, with verses by the young Dickens; and Dickens's own copies of seven of his public readings, with various corrections and stage directions.

1676. Makinen, M. A. "Parodies of Dickens." *Antiquarian Book Monthly Review*, 10 (1983), 62.

A brief letter to the editor noting that numerous parodies of Dickens's novels are in the Dickens House collection, London, most in the Leslie Staples Bequest (**1457C11**).

1677. "The Manuscript of the 'Battle of Life.'" *Dickensian*, 1 (1905), 122.

Notes that J. Pierpont Morgan had recently acquired the manuscripts of "Hunted Down" and *The Battle of Life*, the latter of which the commentator, presumably B. W. Matz, the editor, asserts "would have found a much more fitting home" in England.

1678. Martens, Johanne. "Gustav Brosings samlinger av bergensiana og Jacob Christensens Dickens-samlingtil Universitetsbiblioteket i Bergen." *Biblio-tek ogforskning Arbok*, 19 (1973), 113-29.

The summary in English, "Gustav Brosing's Collection of Local History and Jacob Christensen's Dickens Collection in the Bergen University Library," pp. 128-29, notes that the second part of the article (pp. 122-27) describes a "magnificent Dickens collection" donated by the wife of the deceased Christensen, a wealthy Bergen shipowner—about 370 books and pamphlets by and about Dickens, including first editions in parts and volume form of most of Dickens's novels, Dickensiana, sets of extra illustrations, nine autograph Dickens letters, the manuscript for Dickens's obituary of Clarkson Stanfield (published as "The Late Mr. Stanfield," in *All the Year Round*, 1 June 1867), the manuscript of twenty-one lines from *Dombey and Son*, two proof sheets with Dickens's corrections, and a watercolor by John Leech of the comedian John Pritt Harley as the Strange Gentleman in Dickens's early play (1836) of the same title. For the catalogue of Christensen's collection, see *Katalog over Jacob Christensens Dickens-samling* (**1430**).

1679. Matz, B. W. "Some Original Studies by 'Phiz.'" *Dickensian*, 2 (1906), 299.

Describes a collection of pencil studies by Hablot K. Browne. The few for Dickens's works are reproduced in this and later issues—see 2 (1906), 282, and 3 (1907), 9, 30, 58, 99, 114, and 162.

1680. Miller, A. G. Schaw. "Dickens's 'The Battle of Life.'" *Times Literary Supplement*, 31 July 1937, p. 564.

Notes that in his private collection he has copies of all four issues of the first edition of *The Battle of Life* noted in the second edition of Eckel (**16**).

1681. Miller, W[illiam]. "Another Magnificent Gift to the Dickens House." *Dickensian*, 23 (1926/27), 180.

Describes an eight-volume, extra-illustrated copy of *Forster* presented to the Dickens House Museum, London, containing letters, original drawings for the novels, and a multitudinous array of other materials.

1682. Miller, W[illiam]. "First Editions of the Works Written at 48 Doughty St. Presented to the Dickens House by Sir George Sutton, Bar[one]t." *Dickensian*, 24 (1927/28), 101-02.

Brief bibliographical descriptions of first editions of twelve works presented to the Dickens House, London, by Sutton that Dickens wrote while residing at 48 Doughty Street.

1683. "Missing Dickens Relics. Supposed Theft from Doughty-Street House."
   Times (London), 22 June 1931, p. 14.

Reports that a man has been detained for the "disappearance . . . of a number of autograph letters and other manuscripts associated with Charles Dickens." Subsequent articles report (23 June, p. 5) that the man was a John Bostock, a freelance journalist, and (30 June, p. 11) that he stole manuscripts, letters, and books to a value of £1,100, for which he received a sentence of twelve months at hard labor.

1684. "More Gifts to the Dickens House." *Dickensian*, 34 (1937/38), 224.

The gifts to the Dickens House, London, include thirty-four letters from Dickens to Bradbury and Evans, forty-five letters to Georgina Hogarth, and the manuscript of Dickens's youthful poem, "The Bill of Fare."

1685. Munby, A. N. L. *The Cult of the Autograph Letter in England.* London: University of London, Athlone Press, 1962, passim.

Comments briefly (pp. 68-70) on the "great collection of books and manuscripts" that John Forster bequeathed to the Victoria and Albert Museum in 1872, including numerous literary autographs, among them Dickens's, of course. Munby also mentions the library that Chauncey Hare Townshend (who died in 1865) bequeathed to the Wisbech Museum and Literary Institute. Townshend's library included the manuscript of *Great Expectations*, which Dickens had presented to Townshend after dedicating the novel to him. Munby also notes a Sotheby sale of 27 May 1875 that included the manuscript of *A Christmas Carol* (it is merely listed in the catalogue with no bibliographical description) and one of 18 June 1890 that included manuscripts of Dickens and Wilkie Collins (**2004**). He also mentions letters by Dickens in the Reference Library of Manchester Central Library (**1671**).

1686. Munford, W. A. "A New Dickens Library." *Dickensian*, 32 (1935/36),
   56.

A brief, general description of a collection of secondary works in the Dover, England, Public Library.

1687. "A National Dickens Library." *T. P.'s Weekly*, 9 (1907), 177.

A formal announcement of a room in the Guildhall Library for a Dickens collection, the nucleus of which would be the collection of the late F. G. Kitton, which is briefly described, of first and later editions of Dickens's works, plagiarisms and continuations of his novels, Dickensiana, portraits, eighteen volumes of magazine articles, ten volumes of newspaper cuttings (four dealing with Dickens's life, three with his works, and three with his illustrations), autograph letters of Dickens and his friends, plays and pamphlets, speeches, original drawings by Kitton and other modern artists for Dickens's works, and other items. These were later incorporated into the Dickens House Museum library, London. See Dickens House Scrapbooks (**1575**) and Ridge (**1720**).

1688. "The National Dickens Library." *Times* (London), 8 February 1908, p. 10.

Report of the dedication on Dickens's birthday (7 February) of the National Dickens Library, installed in Guildhall, London, and composed of the "library collected by the late Mr. Frederic G. Kitton," which had been purchased by funds raised by the Dickens Fellowship (this library would later be transferred to the Dickens House Museum).

1689. "New and Notable: Charles Dickens." *Princeton University Library Chronicle*, 20 (1958/59), 158-60.

Records a gift to the Princeton University library by Robert H. Taylor of over twenty first editions of Dickens's books, "the majority of which contain inscriptions in the hand of the author." One of the contributions (no inscription) is the Jupp-Kern-Bandler prime *Pickwick* in parts.

1690. "New Dickens Letters. Correspondence with W. P. Frith, R. A.: The Cattermole Case." and "Two Victorians." *Times* (London), 6 March 1922, pp. 6, 13.

Both articles note the donation by the two daughters of Frith of 220 letters to the Victoria and Albert Museum. Most of the letters are "addressed to Frith by his numerous friends." Among them, it is pointed out, are a number of letters from Dickens, including letters concerned with helping the widow of George Cattermole, one of Dickens's artist friends. The first article gives brief excerpts from a few of Dickens's letters and indicates that there are also letters from John Forster and Wilkie Collins, some of which discuss Dickens. The second article comments on Frith's relationship with Dickens and asserts that Frith's "crowded canvases" (such as "Derby Day" and "Railway Station") are "as full of life as any chapter in Dickens's novels."

1691. "News from the Field: Acquisitions, Gifts, Collections." *College and Research Libraries*, 17 (1956), 85-87.

Briefly notes (p. 87) "a valuable Dickens collection" given to Cornell University by William G. Mennen containing Dickens letters, first editions, a six-volume grangerized copy of the first edition of *Forster* with 440 engravings and

235 autograph letters by Dickens and other eminent writers, and other items. See Lane (**1663**) for a description of the grangerized volume.

1692. Nisbet, Ada. "Introduction." In *Charles Dickens and George Cruikshank: Papers Read at a Clark Library Seminar on May 9, 1970*. By J. Hillis Miller and David Borowitz. Los Angeles: William Andrews Clark Memorial Library, University of California, 1971, pp. v-vi.

Refers to the Dickens and Cruikshank materials in the collection given to the library by William Andrews Clark, Jr., and mentions the exhibition of rarities from the collection with which the two lectures in this volume are associated. The collection, Nisbet notes, includes a prime *Pickwick* in parts and various editions of Dickens's novels, Cruikshank drawings, and a seven-volume grangerized copy of Thackeray's *Essay on the Genius of George Cruikshank* (London: Henry Hooper, 1840), with "autographs, manuscript letters, sheets of original drawings, additional memoirs and 1,700 illustrations, including original caricatures, etchings, and woodcuts."

1693. "Notable Purchase by The Dickens House." *Dickensian*, 68 (1972), 89.

Records the acquisition by the Dickens House, London, of a letter from Dickens to Maria Beadnell, subsequently printed in Michael Slater's "David to Dora: A New Dickens Letter." *Dickensian*, 68 (1972), 162-66.

1694. "Notes and News [The Gaskell Collection]." *Bulletin of the John Rylands University Library*, 17 (1933), 193-94.

Announces the acquisition by the John Rylands Library, Manchester, England, of Mrs. Elizabeth Gaskell's collection of letters, mainly from Victorian literati, including thirty from Dickens. For further details, see Quinn (**1511**) and the cross-references there.

1695. "Notes of the Day." *Literature*, 9 (1901/02), 569-71.

Among other information, comments on the location of some of Dickens's manuscripts, items in the William Wright collection, and a "Boz Club" in London. For more information about the Wright collection, see Kitton (**2124**), Lane (**1663**), Sotheby, Wilkinson, and Hodge (**2008**), "A Unique Dickens Collection" (**2188**), and "Wright Collection" (**2196**).

1696. "Opening of the Suzannet Rooms." *Dickensian*, 67 (1971), 188-91.

A transcription of Captain Peter Dickens's address at the opening of the Suzannet Rooms in the Dickens House, London, 11 June 1971.

1697. Palmer, Cecil. "The B. W. Matz Loan Collection Now at the Dickens House." *Dickensian*, 21 (1925), 193-95.

Sees the Matz collection in the Dickens House, London, as, "in many respects, the most valuable collection that has been accumulated by one man." The collection includes "books, pictures, pamphlets, portraits, magazine and newspaper articles, and other items" that "provide a complete and comprehensive record of all that has appeared in print of the works of Dickens and his commentators." More specifically, the collection includes 1,300 books and pamphlets, numerous editions of Dickens's works, 113 editions of *A Christmas Carol* and the other Christmas Books, fifty studies of *Pickwick Papers*, thirty studies of *The Mystery of Edwin Drood*, eighty-six volumes and sixty pamphlets of topographical studies, a large variety of other studies, twenty bound volumes of magazine articles, fifteen scrapbooks of newspaper cuttings, a collection of 387 portraits of Dickens, and a variety of relics. See also Palmer (**1698**) and Dickens House (**1457C2, 1575**).

1698. Palmer, Cecil. "A Dickens Shrine for London: Mr. B. W. Matz's Loan of Priceless Relics." *T. P.'s and Cassell's Weekly*, 3 (1924/25), 578.

A collection "presented as a loan collection" to the Dickens House Museum, London, including Dickens's reading table and other "relics," numerous editions of Dickens's works, books and pamphlets about him, twenty bound volumes of magazine articles (though it is not certain which twenty volumes are referred to), and 387 mounted portraits of Dickens. See also Palmer (**1697**) and Dickens House (**1457C2, 1575**).

1699. Parker, David. "The Future of the Dickens House." *Dickensian*, 88 (1992), 179-84.

A report on possible refurbishment, reorganization, and expansion of the London museum–a detailed accounting, with financial projections.

1700. Parker, David. "The Reconstruction of Dickens's Drawing-Room." *Dickensian*, 78 (1982), 9-18.

Describes a project sponsored by a grant from the Heritage of London Trust to reconstruct the drawing-room at 48 Doughty Street (Dickens's home from 1837 to 1839 and now the Dickens House Museum) "to a state as closely resembling its condition before Dickens left for Devonshire Terrace in late 1839 as all the available evidence assists us to determine." As Parker shows, considerable information about details of the room and its furnishings is available. Three illustrations, one on p. 8.

1701. Parker, David, and Michael Slater. "The Gladys Storey Papers." *Dickensian*, 76 (1980), 3-16.

An examination of the "notebooks, loose-leaf notes, transcriptions from diaries, newspaper cuttings, letters to Miss Storey, copies of letters written by her, copies of Dickens family letters, Miss Storey's diary for 1937, a typescript of *Dickens and Daughter* not quite identical to the published text, photographs, sketches, and other miscellaneous material." These items, all part of the Storey papers now in the Dickens House Museum, London (**1457C8**), reveal, among other things, the authors indicate, that Storey was more circumspect about Dickens's relationship with Ellen Ternan than critics have suggested. Parker and Slater rightfully see the Storey papers as "a rich and fascinating addition to the Dickens House collections." Illustrated. Also see Katherine M. Longley's response, pp. 17-19, in which she comments on her examination of the Gladys Storey papers and takes some issue with Parker and Slater, and Parker's further response, "The Gladys Storey Papers: A Footnote," pp. 158-59.

1702. Persson, Allan. "Dickens-museer." *Bokvännen* (Stockholm), 42 (1987), 119.

A brief account, in Swedish, of the Dickens Museum, London.

1703. Philips, Hartley M. "Pittsburgher Owns Finest Collection of Dickens Mementoes in the United States. William Glyde Wilkins, an Enthusiast in 'Dickensiana,' Possesses Rare Portraits, Original Letters and Priceless Editions of the Great Novelist." *Pittsburgh Gazette Times*, 17 October 1909. In Dickens House Scrapbooks (**1575F**).

Describes the collection. For details, see Beazell (**1592**) and Anderson Galleries (**1930**).

1704. Pierpont Morgan Library, New York. *In August Company: The Collections of the Pierpont Morgan Library*. New York: Pierpont Morgan Library in Association with Harry N. Abrams, 1993, pp. 209-11.

Comments on the manuscript of *A Christmas Carol* in the Pierpont Morgan Library and reproduces its opening page and a caricature of Dickens and Thackeray (in color).

1705. Podeschi, John. "Gimbel Collection." *Times Literary Supplement*, 7 January 1972, p. 15.

A letter to the editor inspired by "A French Collector of Dickens" (**2111**) briefly describing the Gimbel Dickens Collection at Yale University and noting the forthcoming catalogue of the collection, compiled by Podeschi (**1509**). Also see the response by the anonymous writer of the original article, *Times*

Literary Supplement, 14 January 1972, p. 40, welcoming Podeschi's catalogue and expressing the need for a full bibliography of Dickens's works.

1706. Preston, Edward. "When Found: The Dickens Bust at Canterbury." *Dickensian*, 93 (1997), pp. 223-24.

Gives the provenance of a bust made in 1870 by John Adams-Acton, on view in the Canterbury Heritage Museum. Illustrated with a photograph of David Dickens, a descendant, with the bust.

1707. Price, Cecil. "The Hendre Theatre." *National Library of Wales Journal*, 11 (1959), 103-04.

Describes a "most valuable" collection of playbills purchased by the National Library of Wales, apparently put together by John Rolls of the Hendre Theatre, Monmouth, Wales, including three programs for performances by Dickens's company of amateur actors.

1708. "A Princely Donation: Munificent Gift to the Dickens House." *Dickensian*, 34 (1937/38), 221-24.

An account of the presentation ceremony for a gift from Comte Alain de Suzannet to the Dickens House, London, of sixty pages of manuscript—chapter 9 of *Nicholas Nickleby* (39 pp.), "The Schoolboy's Story" (10 pp.), and "Our Commission" (11 pp.). Also see "Gift of Dickens Manuscripts" (**1639**).

1709. "Proposed Dickens Museum." *Times* (London), 19 June 1922, p. 5.

Briefly notes that the Dickens Fellowship has "secured the option to purchase" 48 Doughty Street, London, Dickens's home between 1837 and 1839, for the purpose of establishing a national Dickens museum. A later article, "A Dickens Shrine," 20 July, p. 13, adds that the Fellowship has acquired the property and comments briefly on Dickens's life there.

1710. Pym, Horace N. "Chapter II. On Charles Dickens." In his *A Tour Round My Book-Shelves*. [Edinburgh]: Privately Printed for Author by Ballantyne, Hanson, 1891, pp. 7-14.

Pym comments on the Dickens rarities in his collection—two checks signed by Dickens, Samuel Laurence's crayon drawings of Dickens and his wife, a grangerized copy of *Pickwick Papers*, twenty-four original watercolor drawings for *Pickwick Papers* by F. W. Pailthorpe and drawings by others also for *Pickwick Papers*, and several Dickens letters. Two of these letters, both to Wilkie Collins, are first published here: one, dated 4 October 1862, gives the outline of stories for *Somebody's Luggage*, the *All the Year Round* Christmas number for 1862; in the other, dated 8 October 1862, Dickens responds to Collins's suggestions for this Christmas number, comments on a story he has written for the number, and describes a visit to the ailing John Poole. Both are printed from manuscript in *Pilgrim Letters*, X, 134, 137-38. Also see Sotheby's (**2016**).

1711. Ramsaur, Edmund George, Jr. "Evaluation of the Charles Dickens Materials (in the William A. Whitaker Collection of Charles Dickens and George Cruikshank in the University of North Carolina Library)." Unpublished Master's Thesis (School of Library Science, University of North Carolina, 1955). 52 pp.

Listed in Downs (**1557**). Available in the University of North Carolina Library, Chapel Hill.

1712. "Rare Books." *Library of Congress Quarterly Journal of Current Acquisitions*, 4, iii (May 1947), 95-102.

Among other acquisitions, notes a Dickens collection presented by Leonard Kebler, including twenty-five first editions, ten of which are in original parts, various other editions of several Dickens works, and a letter from Dickens to Edward Chapman dated 11 May 1859. Illustrated.

1713. Ray, Gordon N. *Bibliographical Resources for the Study of Nineteenth-Century English Fiction*. Los Angeles, CA: School of Library Science, University of California, Los Angeles, 1964, passim.

In this printing of a lecture on the availability in research libraries and private collections of first and other editions of nineteenth-century novels and of magazines in which some of them were originally serialized, Ray occasionally refers to novels by Dickens. The essay is based, he points out, on a survey he conducted. Its data is tabulated as "A Survey of Holdings in Nineteenth Century English Fiction in 29 Collections," pp. 22-31.

1714. Ray, Gordon N. "Contemporary Collectors XVIII: A 19th-Century Collection." *Book Collector*, 13 (1964), 33-44, 171-84.

Ray describes his own collection of nineteenth-century books, which included sets of monthly numbers of Dickens's novels and *Sketches by Boz*. In his collection, "Dickens is complete," Ray writes, "except for the part issues of *David Copperfield*." Dickens is mentioned only on pp. 39 and 41. Illustrated.

1715. Reed, A[lfred] H. " Charles Dickens." In his *Rare Books and Manuscripts: The Story of The Dunedin Public Library's Alfred and Isabel Reed Collection*. Reed Fund Publications, 10. Wellington, NZ, Auckland, NZ, and Syd-

ney, Austral.: Published by A. H. & A. W. Reed for the Dunedin Public
Library, 1968, pp. 35-37.

Comments on Dickens's relationship with Thomas Mitton and Mitton's
sister Mary Anne, who married William Cooper, Reed's great-uncle. Reed
notes his own acquisition of a letter from Dickens to Mitton, 19 August 1860.
He also writes about the extra-illustrated copy he compiled of *Forster-Ley*
(**1717**) that ultimately grew to twenty-two volumes containing not only "portraits, cuttings, etc.," but also "hundreds of letters" by "people in the Dickens
circle, or by people referred to in Forster's biography," as well as some by
Dickens himself and by "most of his intimate friends." Reed also comments
on volumes in the library's collection from Dickens's own library and on
other items in the collection. An appendix, "An Early and Interesting Letter
of Charles Dickens," pp. 51-54, contains a facsimile of a previously unpublished Dickens letter.

1716. Reed, A[lfred] H. *Charles Dickens: A Centenary Tribute*. Wellington, NZ,
      Auckland, NZ, Sydney, Austral., Melbourne, Austral.: A. H. & A. W.
      Reed for the Dunedin Public Library, 1970. 30 pp.

An illustrated pamphlet containing a series of brief pieces occasioned by
some of the Dickens items in the Dunedin Public Library, characterized here
as "the most comprehensive Dickens collection in the Southern Hemisphere."
The articles include "Charles Dickens: Shorthand-Writer," pp. 7-9 (on an edition of Joseph Gurney's *Brachygraphy*, a similar copy of which was used by
young Dickens to teach himself shorthand); "A 'Sikes and Nancy' Reading,"
pp. 10-11 (on an admission card to Dickens's reading of this work, 14 November 1868); "A Dickens Manuscript: Mrs. Lirriper Comes to Dunedin,"
pp. 12-15 (a page from the holograph manuscript of chapter 1 of *Mrs.
Lirriper's Lodgings*, here reproduced in photographic facsimile); "Charles Dickens in Japanese," pp. 16-19 (on ten volumes of translations of Dickens's
works into Japanese); "Dickens in New York: A Presentation Copy of *Sketches
by Boz*," pp. 20-22; "Dickens Letters Discovered in New Zealand: Dickens in
London, circa 1837," pp. 23-25; and "Dickens in Glasgow," pp. 26-27.

1717. Reed, A[lfred] H. "Dickensiana in the Dunedin Library." In *From the
      Black Rocks, on Friday, and A Gold Digger's Notes* (**529**), pp. 57-61.

Refers to an extra-illustrated edition of *Forster-Ley* with over 200 autograph
letters, including letters by Dickens, among many others; a few books from
Dickens's library, and runs of *Household Words*, *All the Year Round*, and the
Dickensian. Reed reproduces a one-line note, with Dickens's signature, to
Frederick Chapman and the last page of "From the Black Rocks, on Friday,"
as it appeared in *All the Year Round*, 17 May 1862, not by Dickens but perhaps

edited by him—see Reed (**529**) and Ross and Bagnall (**532**). Also see Reed (**1715**).

1718. Rendall, Vernon. "Dickens in Doughty Street." *New Statesman*, 25 (1925), 630-31.

On the then newly-opened Dickens House Museum, London, and the value of as well as the gaps in its collection of Dickensiana.

1719. Reynolds, Margaret. "The Leslie C. Staples Bequest." *Dickensian*, 77 (1981), 125-27.

Itemizes a collection (**1457C11**) bequeathed to the Dickens House, London, that comprises "11 autograph Dickens letters, 21 other manuscript letters (including a series of autograph letters of Ellen Ternan), a unique collection of 80 Dickens plagiarisms and piracies, over a hundred books, many miscellaneous papers and an engraved silver snuff box." The bequest also included a fragment of the proofs, heavily marked by Dickens, of Percy Fitzgerald's "Schooldays at Saxonhurst," published in *All the Year Round*, 1 and 8 September 1866. Some of the miscellaneous papers referred to are copies of legal documents relating to *Household Words* and *All the Year Round.*

1720. Ridge, W. Pett. "The National Dickens Library." *John o' London's Weekly*, 14 (1925/26), 881-82.

On the combining of the Dickens House collection, London, with the Matz and the Kitton collections of books and other materials. Ridge comments briefly on the letters, portraits, and memorabilia then in the Dickens House. See The Dickens House Library Collections (**1457C1-C2**).

1721. Roe, F. Gordon. "The Edwin Drood Mystery: An American Gift to London." *Connoisseur*, 104 (1939), 227-31.

Describes Dr. Howard Duffield's collection of Droodiana (**1457C3, 1459**) acquired by the Dickens House, London, including various editions, translations, source books, press clippings, continuations, scholarly studies and debates, and dramatic versions. See Carden (**1604**) and Hopkins (**1805**).

1722. Rust, S. J. "At the Dickens House: Legal Documents Relating to the Piracy of *A Christmas Carol.*" *Dickensian*, 34 (1937/38), 41-44.

A brief history of the legal maneuvering involved in Dickens's attempt to suppress the piracy of *A Christmas Carol* in Parley's Illuminated Library and a listing of five documents relevant thereto in the Dickens House, London. One of them, a letter from Serjeant Talfourd to Thomas Mitton, 28 February

1844, on various legal matters, is printed in full. In it, Talfourd expresses the hope that "some means may be found to deliver our friend [Dickens] from the penalty which will await on success—the payment of his own costs of an action against Bankrupt Robbers," some 700 pounds as it turned out, Rust notes.

1723. Rust, S. J. "Treasures at the Dickens House: Education at Shaw's Academy, Bowes." *Dickensian*, 35 (1938/39), 32-36.

Publishes four letters (written in the most correct style and "copper-plate" handwriting) from one of Shaw's pupils to his mother and uncle and describes two copybooks kept by other students—all these items now, as Rust points out, are in the Dickens House collection, London, and relevant to Squeers's Dotheboys Hall in *Nicholas Nickleby*. Illustrated. See a brief addendum on p. 64 and also "More Letters from Bowes Academy," pp. 111-12, which supplements Rust's account with a poem intended to be engraved on a gravestone, another letter from a pupil of Shaw to his parents, and a letter from Shaw announcing the imminent death (three months later) of this boy.

1724. Rust, S. J. "Treasures at the Dickens House: The First Number of the 'Daily News.'" *Dickensian*, 34 (1937/38), 119-21.

Describes the first number of the *Daily News* (21 January 1846), a copy of which is in the Dickens House, London, comments on Dickens's written contributions to it, and prints excerpts from some of them.

1725. [Sanders, Andrew]. "When Found: A New Acquisition." *Dickensian*, 78 (1982), 57.

Briefly itemizes the acquisition by the Dickens House Museum, London, of documents and a group of some forty-eight letters (by various people) concerned with the *Daily News* and the Guild of Literature and Art. Material from this collection particularly relevant to Dickens is discussed in Kathleen Tillotson's "New Light on Dickens and the *Daily News*," *Dickensian*, 78 (1982), 89-92.

1726. Sargent, George H. "Dickensiana in America." *Bookman's Journal and Print Collector*, 6 (1922), 23-24.

Notes the acquisition by William M. Elkins of the A. S. W. Rosenbach Dickens collection (formerly the collection of Harry B. Smith) and describes the important presentation copies of first editions of various novels and "nearly a hundred autograph letters," including twenty-two to Henry W. Kolle, in the collection. See Free Library of Philadelphia (**1464, 1793**), MacColl (**1673**), Shaffer (**1730**), Stevenson (**1748**), and Dexter (**1556**). Sargent also mentions the sale of the Dickens collections of Frederick Corder of London (**1896**) and William Glyde Wilkins of Pittsburgh (**1930**), as well as various individual sale items—editions in parts, an 1867 diary by Dickens, the Book of Memoranda, various relics, the W. P. Frith painting of Dolly Varden (*Barnaby Rudge*), and several letters.

1727. Schlicke, Paul, ed. Collections of Dickensiana. *Oxford Reader's Companion to Dickens* (**2309**), passim.

Contains several entries by various contributors on collections of Dickensiana. See particularly J[oel] J. B[rattin], "Collections of Dickens Materials," pp. 109-10; [Anon.], "Dexter Collection," p. 152, and "Forster Collection," p. 240; D[avid] P[arker], "Dickens Birthplace Museum," p. 173, and "Dickens House Museum," pp. 176-77; M[ichael] S[later], "Dickens Fellowship," p. 176; and A[nthony] P. B[urton], "Victoria & Albert Museum," p. 583. Except for Brattin's entry, these are brief descriptions of the museums and their holdings. Brattin's piece identifies and briefly describes the holdings of the "most important repositories" of Dickens's manuscripts, letters, and other unique materials. The pagination varies somewhat in the 2000 paperback edition—see, respectively, pp. 113-14, 158, 248, 175-76, 180, 179-80, and 595.

1728. Schlicke, Paul. "Letter to the Editor." *Dickensian*, 74 (1978), 54.

Notes that Dickens's set of the Collected Edition of Douglas Jerrold's works (8 volumes, London: Bradbury and Evans, 1851-54), with Dickens's bookplates but no marginal annotations, is in the Aberdeen University Library, Aberdeen, Scotland.

1729. "Secrets of the Author and the Actress." *Times* (London), 2 April 1980, p. 16.

Reports on the discovery of papers in the back of a wardrobe when movers were removing the effects of Gladys Storey two years after her death. The papers were given to the Dickens House Museum, London, whose curator, David Parker, when interviewed, said that there is documentary evidence in the papers that Dickens "kept a house for Ellen Ternan at Peckham" and that Henry Fielding Dickens, one of Dickens's sons, revealed that Dickens's relationship with Ternan "produced a son, who died in infancy."

1730. Shaffer, Ellen. "The Rare Book Department of the Free Library of Philadelphia." *College and Research Libraries*, 18 (1957), 284-89.

In a brief history and description of the rare book collections of the Free Library, provides information about the Dickens collection in the William M. Elkins Library, based on the Harry B. Smith collection (**1525**). The collection contains thirty presentation copies of Dickens's works, including the *Pickwick* in parts, the early numbers of which Dickens presented to Mary Hogarth; original drawings by "Phiz" (Hablot K. Browne) for *Dombey and Son*, *David Copperfield*, and *Bleak House*; and "a wealth of association material." Shaffer also describes the D. Jacques Benoliel Collection of 402 Dickens letters, including "long runs of correspondence" with Frank Stone, Mark Lemon, John Leech, Arthur Rylands, Frederick Dickens, Lady Blessington, and Daniel Maclise, and with some emphasis on Dickens's love for the theater. Many of these letters, Shaffer notes, were unpublished in 1957. Also see Free Library of Philadelphia (**1464**, **1793**), MacColl (**1673**), Sargent (**1726**), Stevenson (**1748**), and Dexter (**1556**).

1731. Shatto, Susan. "Tennyson's Library." *Book Collector*, 27 (1978), 494-513.

Toward the end of this article (pp. 512-13), Shatto contrasts Tennyson's library as it would have been in 1838 with G. H. Lewes's description, in "Dickens in Relation to Criticism." *Fortnightly Review*, 19 (1872), 141-54, of Dickens's in 1838 and finds Tennyson's a far superior collection of "the classics, the poets, the sciences, history, philosophy and religion." Shatto adds that, unlike Dickens in later life, Tennyson was not "a displayer of books as a symbol of success and status." She also notes that there is no trace of the set of his novels that Dickens presented to Tennyson in 1843. See Kathleen Tillotson's response (**1751**).

1732. Shipman, Carolyn. "A Poet's Library." *Critic*, 4 (1903), 315-23.

Itemizes some of the treasures in the library of Richard Henry Stoddard, including page forty of the manuscript of *Oliver Twist*, with an accompanying letter from Dickens to Charles Edward Lester, 19 July 1840. Dickens's letter is printed here along with a facsimile of the manuscript page, which Dickens sent to him later at Lester's request, with a remark that it is authentic, "a portion of the original and only draught–I never copy."

1733. "Sir Frederick Macmillan's Gift of Personal Relics of Dickens." *Dickensian*, 27 (1930/31), 234.

Briefly describes a gift to the Dickens House, London, of various personal items originally given at Dickens's death to a page boy at Gad's Hill who helped attend Dickens on his last night alive.

1734. S[later], M[ichael]. "The Birthplace Museum." *Dickensian*, 66 (1970), 264-66.

On the restoration and reopening of the museum in Portsmouth, England, in the house where Dickens was born. Illustrated.

1735. S[later], M[ichael]. "In Memoriam: Mr. Philip Skottowe." *Dickensian*, 76 (1980), 127.

In a brief obituary, Slater notes that Skottowe bequeathed to the Dickens House, London, his Dickensian books and papers, including the manuscripts of his unpublished studies of Thomas N. Talfourd and Clarkson Stanfield. See **1457C9**.

1736. Slater, Michael. "The Peyrouton Bequest." *Dickensian*, 72 (1976), 98-100.

The bequest (**1457C7**) includes several volumes from Dickens's own Gad's Hill library, etchings and other volumes not presently in the Dickens House library, London, over 100 Dickens letters (most previously unpublished), forty-three letters by people who had known Dickens that were written to F. G. Kitton while he was compiling *Charles Dickens by Pen and Pencil* (**1248**), and one page of the autograph manuscript of *Tom Tiddler's Ground*, the 1861 Christmas number of *All the Year Round*.

1737. S[later], M[ichael]. "The W. J. Carlton Bequest." *Dickensian*, 70 (1974), 46-47.

Describes the fifteen autograph letters, thirteen other letters and manuscripts related to Dickens, and the collection of books and pamphlets bequeathed to the Dickens House, London, by an eminent Dickensian (**1457C6**).

1738. [Slater, Michael]. "When Found: Souvenir of Christmas at Gad's Hill." *Dickensian*, 68 (1972), 136.

Describes a poster (reproduced on p. 135) then recently acquired by the Dickens House Museum that advertises sporting events at Gad's Hill, Christmas 1866.

1739. Smetham, Henry. "Dickens Libraries." *Dickensian*, 32 (1935/36), 150.

Briefly and generally describes the collection of 430 volumes and "70 odd" portfolios of clippings, advertisements, notices, reviews, pamphlets, lectures, sale catalogues, etc., bequeathed by Percy Fitzgerald to the city of Rochester. The collection, Smetham indicates, had been recently organized by the Eastgate House Museum, Rochester, England, where it resides.

1740. Smith, M. A. "Autograph Letters." *Manchester Review*, 11, iv (Spring/Summer 1967), 97-120.

In commenting on autograph letters in the various collections of the Manchester public libraries, notes that there are eleven Dickens letters (none reprinted or specifically identified in the article) scattered among six collections. On pp. 100-01 Smith prints a letter from William Harrison Ainsworth to James Crossley, a Manchester lawyer, dated 25 October 1838, introducing Dickens to Crossley and stating, among other pleasantries, that he rather suspects Dickens is visiting Manchester because he "is reconnoitreing for character."

1741. "Some Treasures of the Dickens House. 1. Personal Relics." *Dickensian*, 24 (1927/28), 233-35.

Descriptions of personal items, furniture, and furnishings of Dickens in the Dickens House, London. Illustrated.

1742. Spielmann, M. H. "Frith's Portraits of Charles Dickens." *Times Literary Supplement*, 6 March 1919, p. 125.

In a letter to the editor, Spielmann comments on and gives the provenance of William P. Frith's original portrait of Dickens (in the Forster Collection, Victoria and Albert Museum, London, painted 1859) and three copies he made of it. Also see the reply, by B. W. Matz, 20 March 1919, pp. 152-53, who notes that there is a fourth copy extant, done in 1898.

1743. Staples, Leslie C. "When Found—." *Dickensian*, 43 (1946/47), 113-17.

In items on pp. 113-14, reports Arnold N. Palmer's gift to the Dickens House, London, of a page of the manuscript of *Oliver Twist* (from chapter X), inherited by Palmer from his grandfather, Alderman G. S. Nottage, who bought it at the Gad's Hill sale in 1870. Staples notes that the extant portion of the manuscript (chapters XII-XLIII) is in the Forster Collection of the Victoria and Albert Museum, London, and four other pages (all from chapter X) in other collections. He also briefly describes two other gifts to the Dickens House: the manuscript of "The Influence Exercised by Women in the Home," given by Frank S. Johnson, which was originally printed in the *Dickensian* in 1927 (**548**), but according to Fielding (**500**) is not by Dickens, and the original Special Marriage License of Dickens and Catherine Hogarth, presented by the Comte de Suzannet, which is reproduced (p. 114) along with the page of the *Oliver Twist* manuscript (facing p. 111).

1744. Staples, Leslie C. "When Found—Munificent Gift." *Dickensian*, 55 (1959), 132.

Notes the gift of Dr. Sydney A. Henry of his "wonderful collection of first editions of Dickens" to the Dickens House, London (**1457C5**). Most of the novels, Staples points out, are "represented in sets of the monthly parts in pristine condition, not only of the first issues but with the numerous variants," as well as "other notable first editions in the original cloth."

1745. Staples, Leslie C. "When Found–Notable Additions to the Dickens House." *Dickensian*, 45 (1948/49), 172-74.

The additions to the Dickens House, London, include the Dickens family Bible with entries in Dickens's hand recording the births of his children, Millais's famous drawing of the dead Dickens, and a chair owned by Dickens as a young man. Illustrated.

1746. Staples, Leslie C. "When Found–The MS. of *Great Expectations*," "When Found–The MS. of *Our Mutual Friend*," and "When Found–And [the MS. of] *Titbull's Almshouses*." *Dickensian*, 43 (1946/47), 60-61, 61, 61-62.

Notes in passing that the manuscript of *Great Expectations* was presented by Dickens to the Reverend Chauncey Hare Townshend in 1861, and, when Townshend died seven years later, he bequeathed it to the town of Wisbech in Cambridgeshire. Staples also indicates that the manuscript of *Our Mutual Friend* later passed into the collection of the Pierpont Morgan Library, New York, and that the manuscript of "Titbull's Almshouses," an *Uncommercial Traveller* paper, published in *All the Year Round*, 24 October 1863, was then in the possession of Mrs. E. C. Wayland of Comox, British Columbia.

1747. Stark, Lewis M., and Robert W. Hill. "The Bequest of Mary Stillman Harkness." *Bulletin of the New York Public Library*, 55 (1951), 213-24.

On pages 214-15 lists the Dickens items in a collection bequeathed to the New York Public Library: first editions of *A Christmas Carol* and a number of Dickens's minor works, bound collections of the original parts of several of Dickens's works, and Richard Herne Shepherd's copy of *Pictures from Italy*, "interleaved and annotated" with notes on the differences between the first edition and the earlier "Travelling Letters Written on the Road," published in the London *Daily News*, January-March 1846.

1748. Stevenson, Lionel. "The Elkins Collection, Philadelphia Free Library." *Victorian Newsletter*, no. 3 (April 1953), 6.

A brief note to the effect that the William M. Elkins Collection in the Philadelphia Free Library contains first editions, letters, corrected proofs, and other matter–including original drawings for illustrations to Dickens's works, many items from the Harry B. Smith library (**1525**), and *Pickwick Papers* in parts with the earlier numbers inscribed by Dickens to Mary Hogarth. Also see Free Library of Philadelphia (**1464, 1793**), MacColl (**1673**), Sargent (**1726**), Shaffer (**1730**), and Dexter (**1556**).

1749. Szladits, Lola L. *Brothers: The Origins of the Henry W. and Albert A. Berg Collection of English and American Literature, the New York Public Library.* New York: New York Public Library, 1985, passim.

Comments in passing on Dickens items in the collection—various relics, annotated texts for his readings, the travel diary for his second trip to America in 1867-68, the manuscript of Wilkie Collins's *The Lighthouse*, and the prompt-book for Collins's *The Frozen Deep*, with many changes in Dickens's hand.

1750. "Tells of New Dickens Manuscript." *New York Times*, 19 January 1912, p. 4.

Notes that the eight-page autograph manuscript of "Ecclesiastical Regis-tries," part of "The Doom of English Wills," published in *Household Words*, 28 September 1850, was then in the possession of Charles Sessler, a Philadel-phia bookseller.

1751. Tillotson, Kathleen. "Bibliographical Notes & Queries: Note 424. Charles Dickens's Library." *Book Collector*, 28 (1979), 436.

Responding to Shatto's contrast of Tennyson's library to Dickens's (**1731**), Tillotson points out in this seven-line note that the list of books in Dickens's library included in an appendix (**1532**) that she and Nina Burgis printed in *Pil-grim Letters*, IV, shows that the collections of Dickens and Tennyson were actually "comparable in size and range."

1752. "A Treasure of the Dickens House." *Dickensian*, 25 (1928/29), 225.

A facsimile reproduction of Dickens's handwritten presentation of a copy of *The Haunted Man* to C. R. Leslie—in the collection of the Dickens House, London.

1753. "Treasure Trove for Dickensians." *New York Times Magazine*, 28 Sep-tember 1924, p. 6.

Comments on the discovery of minutes of meetings and other documents of the Guild of Literature and Art in the hand of Dickens, then in the collec-tion of Edward L. Dean, New York; prints a letter from Dickens to Joseph I. Jenkins, 13 May 1851, complimenting him on his design of an engraved card of invitation to the benefit theatrical performances that Dickens was then act-ing in and directing; and reproduces a facsimile of a page in Dickens's hand from the Book of Chairman's Agenda, a rare pen-and-ink sketch of Dickens from 1837, and a photograph of Dickens from about 1860.

1754. Turner, Ginny. "C. Dickens, Author, 48 Doughty St., London." *Travel & Leisure*, 12, iii (March 1982), 172.

A brief description for tourists of the interior and contents of the Dickens House Museum, London. Illustrated.

1755. van der Merwe, Pieter. "Sketches for Scenery by Clarkson Stanfield: New Finds, 1980-84." *Theatre Notebook*, 40 (1986), 22-29.

Mentions the "cut-down central portion of the act drop for Dickens's amateur production of Wilkie Collins's *The Lighthouse*, which Stanfield executed in 1855," now in the Dickens House, London, as "one of the earliest surviving pieces of English scene painting by any artist, let alone one of the most eminent."

1756. [Van Noorden, Charles]. "Some Dickens Relics." *Sketch*, 30 (1900), 314.

Refers to paintings in the W. R. Hughes collection, Birmingham, England: Dickens as Captain Bobadil by Charles R. Leslie and William P. Frith's painting of Dolly Varden. Illustrated. Also see "Chronicle and Comment" (**2084**), "Dickens's Birthday. A Glance Through a 'Dickens Collection'" (**1626**), "An Interesting Dickens Collection" (**1656**), and Wright (**1776**).

1757. Wade, David. "Dickens Month." *Times* (London), 20 June 1970, Books, p. III.

Comments on some British radio programs to honor Dickens on the centenary of his death. Also see Peter Vansittart, "Radio," 29 August, p. 6, for a review of another radio program.

1758. Wainwright, Alexander D. "Morris L. Parrish Collection of Victorian Novelists." *Princeton University Library Chronicle*, 57 (1995/96), 177-81.

Lists acquisitions, 1994-95, including a few French and one German translation of works by Dickens and a copy of *The Frozen Deep* (London, 1866), with corrections by Wilkie Collins. For earlier reports on the Parrish Collection (**1507**), see Gerould (**1637**) and Wainwright (**1759**).

1759. Wainwright, Alexander D. "The Morris L. Parrish Collection of Victorian Novelists: A Summary Report and an Introduction." Special Issue: Parrish Collection–II. *Princeton University Library Chronicle*, 17, ii (Winter 1956), 59-67.

In this follow-up on Gordon H. Gerould's 1946 report (**1637**) on the Dickens collection (**1507**), Wainwright records that the Dickens collection has been enlarged from various sources by seventeen letters (thirteen to Peter

Cunningham, April-October 1848, concerning a theatrical benefit for Sheridan Knowles), more than eighty printed items (including a number of first English and American editions of several of Dickens's works), and a pastel portrait of Dickens done by E. Goodwyn Lewis in 1869 (pp. 64-65). Wainwright also records (p. 62) manuscript additions to the Wilkie Collins collection of interest to Dickens scholars: the corrected page proof of Collins's 1861 edition of *The Woman in White* (serialized in *All the Year Round*, 26 November 1859-25 August 1860), a packet of notes and other material gathered by Collins in preparation for the writing of *The Moonstone* (serialized in *All the Year Round*, 4 January-8 August 1868), and an acting copy of *The Frozen Deep* (1866). For further details of additions to the Collins collection, see Robert P. Ashley, "The Wilkie Collins Collection," in the same issue, pp. 81-84. Also see Wainwright (**1758**).

1760. Ward, H. Snowden. "A Peep into the Kitton Collection." *T. P.'s Weekly*, 9 (1907), 778.

A brief survey of some of the items in the collection, largely for the purpose of soliciting contributions for the National Dickens Library Fund—see "A National Dickens Library" (**1688**).

1761. Warman, Christopher. "Dickens Relics on Show in His London House." *Times* (London), 12 June 1971, p. 2.

Finds the exhibition at the Dickens House Museum, London, of an "important collection of Dickensiana," the gift of the Comtesse de Suzannet, "fascinating." For the catalogue of the Dickens House's Suzannet collection, see Slater (**1524**).

1762. Weart, William G. "Dickens Ms. Given to Philadelphia." *New York Times*, 2 October 1964, p. 31.

Mentions the presentation by an anonymous donor of the manuscript of *The Life of Our Lord* to the Free Library of Philadelphia in memory of D. Jacques Benoliel. A part of the first page of the manuscript is reproduced in facsimile. Also see "Dickens' 'Life of Our Lord'" (**1627**).

1763. [Weber, Carl J.]. "Dickens and Bewick." *Colby Library Quarterly*, ser. 2, No. 15 (August 1950), 242-44.

Announces the acquisition by the Colby Library of the copy of Bewick's *History of English Birds* (1804) presented to Dickens by Chauncey Hare Townshend in July 1864 and comments on the relationship of the two men.

1764. Wells, John. "Papers of Eighteenth and Nineteenth-Century Literary Authors in Durham Libraries: A Brief Survey." *Durham University Journal*, 85 (1993), 111-13.

Mentions two letters from Dickens, 1851-52, in the papers of Maria, Third Countess Grey, but gives no other details. For two letters to the countess from this period, see *Pilgrim Letters*, VI, 432, and VII, 906-07, probably the ones to which Wells refers.

1765. Wheeler, Michael D. "Mrs. Gaskell's Reading, and the Gaskell Sale Catalogue in Manchester Central Library." *Notes and Queries*, ns 24 (1977), 25-30.

Notes that in the catalogue of the auction sale of the possessions of the Gaskell's second daughter, which contained the library of Elizabeth Gaskell and her husband, Dickens is represented only by the first edition of his collected Christmas Books and by volumes of *Household Words*, though obviously the Gaskells had read other Dickens novels.

1766. "When Found: The Music Collection at Dickens House." *Dickensian*, 86 (1990), 57.

A report from David Parker, then curator of the Dickens House, London, on the conserving of the music collection at the Dickens House, through the industriousness of Maggie Maranto of the Dickens Fellowship, New York.

1767. Wickham, D. E. "The A. Edward Newton Catalogues." *Private Library: Quarterly Journal of the Private Libraries Association*, 2 (1989), 82-92.

Describes the contents of Newton's library—for details of the Dickens items, see Parke-Bernet Galleries (**1970**). Newton himself (1863-1940), Wickham notes, was seen by some who knew him as a twentieth-century Mr. Pickwick and by others as "the living personification of Ned Cheeryble" (*Nicholas Nickleby*). Also see Newton (**2250-51**) and "The A. Edward Newton Library" (**2071**).

1768. "The Widener Dickens Collection: An Unpublished Poem by the Novelist." *Dickensian*, 16 (1920), 83-85.

A reprint of an article from the *Boston Evening Transcript* (date not given) that describes the Widener collection and reproduces the first five stanzas of the manuscript of the poem by the youthful Dickens entitled "Elegy Written in a Country Churchyard," a parody of Thomas Gray's more famous poem. See Rosenbach (**1516-18**) and Widener (**1546**).

1769. Williams, Hugo. "Freelance." *Times Literary Supplement*, 4 October 1996, p. 20.

Describes a visit to the Dickens House Museum (London), Dickens's life in the house, and present-day restorations of the rooms. See the response in a letter to the editor from Arthur J. Cox, who calls Williams's account a "poisoned-pen description."

1770. W[illiams], K. S[heila]. "Dickens in Parts in the Library." *Turnbull Library Record*, ns 3 (1970), 152.

Notes that the Turnbull Library in Wellington, NZ, possesses the original parts of seven of Dickens's novels—*Pickwick Papers, Master Humphrey's Clock, Dombey and Son, David Copperfield, Bleak House, Little Dorrit*, and *Our Mutual Friend*.

1771. Williamson, George C. "Dickens for Collectors." *Weekly Dispatch* (London), 21 May 1922, p. 6.

Notes that a recent "recrudescence" of interest in Dickens was due to the sale of the Baroness Burdett-Coutts's collection of letters, books, and manuscripts. Williamson provides descriptions of some valuable Dickens editions. For the sale, see Sotheby, Wilkinson and Hodge (**1996**). For the later sale of Dickens's letters to the Baroness in particular, see Parke, Bernet Galleries (**1958**). These letters are now in the Pierpont Morgan Library, New York. Most were printed in Edgar Johnson's *The Heart of Charles Dickens, as Revealed in His Letters to Angela Burdett-Coutts* (New York: Duell, Sloan and Pearce; Boston: Little, Brown, 1952), and all should be in the volumes of the *Pilgrim Letters*.

1772. Wilson, R. A. "Translations of the Works of Charles Dickens." *British Museum Quarterly*, 14 (1940), 59-60.

Announces the gift to the British Museum of "nearly a hundred volumes" of translations of Dickens's works into other languages originally collected by the wife of Sir Henry Fielding Dickens, including a file of letters to Lady Dickens connected with compiling the collection. See Lady Marie Roche Dickens (**1456**).

1773. Winterich, John T. *The Fales Collection: A Record of Growth*. [New York University Libraries Bibliographical Series, 2]. New York: New York University Libraries, 1963, passim.

In a follow-up to his earlier report on the collection (**1774**), Winterich notes that photostats of some seventy-five previously unpublished Dickens letters in the collection had been provided to the editors of the then forthcoming Pilgrim Edition of the letters. He also notes that a number of additional books from Dickens's library and presentation copies of his novels had been added to the collection. He also prints another item in the collection—Dickens's recipe, handwritten for Mr. and Mrs. James T. Fields, for champagne cup. For further details of this collection, see its catalogue (**1502**), Egerer (**1630**), and Winterich (**1774**).

1774. Winterich, John T. *The Fales Collection: An Appreciation.* [New York University Libraries Bibliographical Series, 1]. New York: New York University Libraries, 1959, pp. 14-17.

Notes that in the collection of DeCoursey Fales of the British and American novel from mid-eighteenth century on, now in the New York University Library, New York, "Dickens's novels, major and minor, are here in the full variety of forms in which they were originally issued, largely in paper-wrapped parts" as well as a great variety of important "peripheral material," some of which is described. For further details of this collection, see its catalogue (**1502**), Winterich (**1773**), and Egerer (**1630**).

1775. Witherow, John. "Cash Plea by Dickens Museum." *Times* (London), 16 July 1984, p. 3.

Indicates that the Dickens House Museum, London, is seeking funds for the cost of cataloguing its collection of 8,000 slides and photographs. Illustrated.

1776. Wright, Thomas. "A Famous Book Lover." In *The Olney Almanac for 1900.* In Dickens House Scrapbooks (**1575D**), II, 18.

Briefly describes W. R. Hughes's collection of Dickensiana by way of a eulogy. Also see "Chronicle and Comment" (**2084**), "Dickens's Birthday. A Glance Through a 'Dickens Collection'" (**1626**), "An Interesting Dickens Collection" (**1656**), and Van Noorden (**1756**).

PART FIVE: EXHIBITIONS

5A. EXHIBITION CATALOGUES

Note: Also see Edgar, Vail, and Cavanaugh (**17**) and Duffield (**1459**) and **Exhibitions, catalogues**, in part 2 of the subject index.

1777. Andrews, Nathalie T., and Margaret M. Bridwell, comps. *The Inimitable George Cruikshank: An Exhibition of Illustrated Books, Prints, Drawings and Manuscripts from the Collection of David Borowitz*. Louisville, KY: University of Louisville Libraries, 1968, passim.

In this catalogue for an exhibition at the J. B. Speed Art Museum, University of Louisville, 12 October-15 November 1968, the compilers list twenty-eight proofs of Cruikshank's illustrations for *Sketches by Boz*, a set of *Oliver Twist* in parts (1846) with his illustrations, and a four-volume grangerized copy of Blanchard Jerrold's *The Life of George Cruikshank, in Two Epochs* (**891**). An introductory essay by Richard A. Vogler, "The Inimitable George Cruikshank: 1792-1878," pp. 1-17, generally discusses Cruikshank's work and career, but with only passing allusion to his relationship with Dickens and to his illustrations for Dickens's works. The catalogue also contains an annotated "Selected Bibliography" (**1347**), pp. 39-53, of works about Cruikshank. Illustrated.

1778. "Anniversaries: An Exhibition of Books Published in 1648, 1748, 1848." *Bulletin of the New York Public Library*, 52 (1948), 289-99.

For Dickens, lists three presentation copies of *The Haunted Man and the Ghost's Bargain*, a set of unbound sheets of this Christmas Book, and an autograph letter to Mary Boyle, 16 September 1850, concerning a performance of Ben Jonson's *Every Man in His Humour* at Knebworth, Edward Bulwer-Lytton's estate, in November 1850.

1779. Brattin, Joel J., and Rodney G. Obien, eds. *Illustrating Dickens: Selected Works from the Robert D. Fellman Collection*. Worcester, MA: George C. Gordon Library, Worcester Polytechnic Institute, 2002. 56 pp.

A beautifully illustrated catalogue for an exhibition of "Selected Works from the Robert D. Fellman Collection," 24 March-14 April 2002 at the Whistler House Museum of Art, Lowell, Massachusetts (the Fellman Collection is housed in the Gordon Library, Worcester Polytechnic Institute). Included are three essays, Robert L. Patten's "Dickensian Words and Images," pp. 9-15, which is a thumbnail history of the illustrating of Dickens's novels and Dickens's relationship with his illustrators; Bert G. Hornback's "Illustrating the Inimitable," pp. 17-23, which comments on the visual nature of Dickens's descriptions and their attractiveness to his illustrators; and Joel J. Brattin's "Fellman, Dickens, and Illustration" (**1594**), pp. 25-31, which describes Fellman, the collection, and a number of items in it. In a brief preface, p. 5, Rodney G. Obien, archivist and Special Collections Librarian of the Gordon Library, comments on the collection and notes that the exhibition was mounted in conjunction with a conference, "Dickens and America: Literature, Industry, and Culture," held in Lowell, Massachusetts, 4-6 April 2002. The "List of Figures," pp. 6-7, and the numerous illustrations, indicate that the exhibition contained autograph letters by Dickens and others, portraits of Dickens and his wife, wrapper designs for and illustrations from his novels, original pencil and pen and ink sketches by his illustrators, the attendance book for the Guild of Literature and Art with the signatures of Dickens and his friends, and other items.

1780. British Council. *Charles Dickens 1812-1870*. London: British Council, 1970. 22 pp.

A pamphlet to accompany a "centenary book exhibition" prepared by British publishers. It lists mainly volumes of Dickens's works, criticisms and biographies, study guides, abridgements, editions for students, and studies of the social and intellectual background of the nineteenth century available in 1970. It also contains a brief list of rare and out-of-print books in the exhibition and a one-page preface by Margaret Lane, then President of the Dickens Fellowship, emphasizing Dickens's "genius for communication," which she finds "second only" to Shakespeare's.

1781. British Museum, King's Library, London. *Charles Dickens, 1812-1870*. London: British Museum, 1970.

Not seen. In reviewing this centenary exhibition for the *Dickensian* (and its "brief catalogue"), Trevor Blount (**1837**) indicated that it was based on "a notable assemblage of material" from the then recently acquired John F. Dexter Collection (**1436**), and contained a selection of autograph letters, original drawings by George Cruikshank and Hablot K. Browne, part of the manuscript of *Pickwick Papers*, the manuscript of the preface to the Cheap Edition, and corrected page proofs of *The Old Curiosity Shop*, *Martin Chuzzlewit*, *Hard Times*, *Little Dorrit*, and *A Tale of Two Cities*. Also see **1834** and **1837**.

1782. *A Catalogue of a Selection from the Works of George Cruikshank, Extending over a Period of Upwards of Sixty Years [from 1799 to 1863], Now Exhibiting at Exeter Hall. Consisting of Upwards of One Hundred Oil Paintings, Water-Colour Drawings, and Original Sketches; Together with over a Thousand Proof Etchings, from His Most Popular Works, Caricatures, Scrap Books, Song Headings, etc., and the* **Worship of Bacchus.** London: George Bell, [1863], passim.

Includes eleven illustrations from *Sketches by Boz*, twenty-four from *Oliver Twist*, and six from *Memoirs of Joseph Grimaldi*. A second edition [1863] contains a brief preface by Cruikshank in which he expresses his gratitude for the exhibition.

1783. *Charles Dickens, 1812-1870: An Exhibition of His Works Held at the Wahlert Memorial Library, October 18 to November 20, 1970.* Dubuque, IA: Loras College, 1970. 15 pp.

More a brief sketch of Dickens's life and career than the catalogue of an exhibition at Loras College, though boldfaced numbers in the margins apparently refer to items in the collection.

1784. *Charles Dickens, 1812-1870: Exposition organisée par le British Council en commémoration du centième anniversaire de la mort de Dickens du 18 mars au 27 mars 1970.* Liège: Bibliothèque Générale de l'Université de Liège, [1970]. 16 unnumbered pp.

Lists and briefly describes the fifty-four items in an exhibition honoring the centenary of Dickens's death, including portraits of Dickens and others, illustrations of places relevant to Dickens's life and works, letters, some original illustrations for the novels, and a page each of the manuscripts of *Oliver Twist*, *The Old Curiosity Shop*, and *A Tale of Two Cities*.

1785. Charles Dickens Heritage Foundation, Hartford, CT. *Charles Dickens Heritage Journal*, no. 4 (Winter 1996). 21 pp.

Published in connection with a Dickens exhibition, Hartford, CT, November-December 1996, that included the desk and chair that were in Dickens's library at Tavistock House in London and at Gad's Hill, as well as other memorabilia. A good bit of the issue advertises the foundation and reproductions of the desk and chair, but it also contains a partial Dickens family tree and three brief articles: Wilson H. Faude's "Dickens in Hartford," p. 4; Lynne Benedict's "Dickens's Spirit Alive Today: The Story of Jeanne-Marie Dickens and The Charles Dickens Heritage Foundation," p. 5; and David Parker's "The Empty Chair," pp. 6-7. Illustrated.

1786. *Christmas with Charles Dickens: An Exhibition Presented by The House of Bewlay in Conjunction with the Dickens Fellowship from 2 December 1954 to 1 January 1955 at 138 Park Lane, London W1.* [London: House of Bewlay and the Dickens Fellowship, 1954]. 7 pp.

An exhibition of some fifty items consisting of portraits, photostats of pages of manuscripts, letters, parts and first editions, relics, and Dickensiana, each briefly noted.

1787. Dickens Fellowship, London. *Catalogue of a Pickwick Exhibition Held at the Dickens House, 48 Doughty Street, London, W. C. 1, March-April, 1936, under the Auspices of the Pickwick Centenary Celebrations Committee.* Arr. William Miller. London: The Dickens Fellowship, [1936]. 47 pp.

Gives frequently full descriptions of the 234 items in the exhibition, followed by a listing of ninety-five English editions of *Pickwick Papers*–also to be found in "English Editions of Pickwick" (**126**). Items in the exhibition include a page of the manuscript, letters, editions, relics, original drawings, extra illustrations, paintings, and a variety of related items. A one-page introduction by William Miller comments generally on the collection. Illustrated. Also see **1836, 1845,** and **1880**.

1788. Dickens Fellowship, London. *The Pickwick Exhibition, Held at the New Dudley Gallery, 169 Piccadilly, W., from July 22nd to August 28th, 1907, under the Auspices of the Dickens Fellowship: Catalogue of Exhibits.* Comp. and ed. B. W. Matz and J. W. T. Ley. London: The Dickens Fellowship, [1907]. 116 pp.

With an introductory essay, "Pickwick the Immortal! What It Is and What It Contains," by Percy Fitzgerald. The "List of Exhibits," pp. 23-116, itemizes English, American, and other foreign editions and translations of *Pickwick Papers;* plagiarisms, parodies, plays, playbills, and music; Pickwickiana; relics and mementoes; political cartoons and caricatures; postcards, calendars, posters, advertisements; portraits and biographies of Dickens; autograph letters; and a number of other items. Some items are extensively described, most only briefly. Illustrated. Also see **1878-79**.
Review: *Athenaeum,* no. 4161 (27 July 1907), 97-98 (highly favorable).

1789. Dickens Fellowship, London. *The Second Dickens Exhibition, Held under the Auspices of the Dickens Fellowship, at the New Dudley Gallery, 169, Piccadilly, London, W. 1, July 29th to September 19th, 1908: Catalogue of Exhibits.* London: New Dudley Gallery, [1908]. 48 pp.

The illustrated catalogue of an exhibition of pictures (forty-six items), prints (fourteen items), relics (fourteen items), autograph letters (forty-three items), signatures, plagiarisms of *Edwin Drood*, and all of Dickens's major and some of his minor works in various editions. An introduction by J. W. T. Ley, pp. 7-9, notes that "today Dickens is the most popular and most beloved novelist" and that the object of the organizers of the exhibition was to make it "as comprehensive as possible." An insignificant foreword by Percy Fitzgerald is also included. The *Dickensian*, 4 (1908), lists a number of newspaper accounts of the exhibition (p. 252) and reviews the exhibition itself (pp. 234-36). For the first and third exhibitions, see Kitton (**1806**) and New Dudley Gallery (**1813**). Also see **1852** and **1881**.

1790. *A Dickens Library: Exhibition Catalogue of the Sawyer Collection of the Works of Charles Dickens, Comprising Manuscripts, Autograph Letters, Presentation Copies, the Issues in Original Parts, Dickensiana, Etc.* Letchworth, Eng.: Privately Printed by the Garden City Press, 1936. 108 pp.

A descriptive listing of the items in the collection of the late Charles J. Sawyer, exhibited 27 March-4 April 1936, at Messrs. C. J. Sawyer, London, divided into 1) original manuscripts and autograph letters, 2) presentation copies, 3) the novels in parts, 4) first editions of the works, 5) extra illustrations, and 6) Dickensiana. The collection contained the original autograph manuscripts of "The Condition of the Working Class"–Dickens's revision of part of a preface that Angela Burdett-Coutts wrote for her *Common Things*, as noted in K. K. Collins and Alan M. Cohn, "Charles Dickens, Harriet Martineau, and Angela Burdett Coutts's *Common Things*," *Modern Philology*, 79 (1981/82), 407-13–and "Emigration" (the latter, previously unpublished, has since been published in *Pilgrim Letters*, VI, 858-60). It also contained Dickens's exchange of letters with Mrs. Eliza Davis over his depiction of Jews and other important Dickens letters, as well as a series of forty letters, 1868-1902, between the Dickens family and Edward Bulwer Lytton Dickens (Plorn), Dickens's youngest child, in Australia; Daniel Maclise's portrait of Dickens as a young man; and Dickens's meerschaum pipe. A detailed description of the parts of the MacGeorge-Sawyer copy of *Pickwick Papers* in parts is also included. Illustrated. Also see **1836** and **1864**.

1791. Dutton, E. P., and Co., Old Book Department, New York. *An Exhibition of Relics and Furniture Belonging to Charles Dickens*. New York: E. P. Dutton, Old Book Department, [1927].

Podeschi (**1509**), p. 369, notes that the items in the catalogue were for sale.

1792. Franklin Club, St. Louis. *An Exhibition of Books, Prints, Drawings, Manuscripts & Letters Commemorative of the Centenary of Charles Dickens*. St. Louis: Franklin Club, 1912. vi + 49 pp.

Moderately brief descriptions of items in an exhibition, 7-12 February 1912, of first editions, letters, drawings, sets of extra illustrations, original portraits, manuscripts, and other items, including Dickensiana.

1793. Free Library of Philadelphia. *The Life and Works of Charles Dickens, 1812-1870: An Exhibition from the Collection of William M. Elkins, Esq., of Philadelphia, Held at The Free Library, June-July, 1946.* Philadelphia: Free Library of Philadelphia, 1946. xiii + 58 pp.

Lists items from one of the famous Dickens collections, selected to present chronologically Dickens's life and works. The exhibition contained first editions, bound and in parts; autograph letters; thirty presentation copies; playbills; memorabilia and relics; Priscilla Horton's autograph album; original drawings for the illustrations to Dickens's works (Hablot K. Browne's for *Dombey and Son, David Copperfield,* and *Bleak House,* and others by George Cruikshank, George Cattermole, and Joseph Clayton Clarke ["Kyd"]); paintings; thirty pages of corrected proof sheets for *Martin Chuzzlewit;* proof sheets for Dickens's eulogy of Thackeray published in the *Cornhill Magazine,* 9 (February 1864), 129-32; a page of manuscript for *Nicholas Nickleby;* and other items—all with commentary and introductions to the numerous sections of the exhibition. In "A Note on this Collection," pp. ix-xi, Elkins characterizes his collection as sentimentally rather than bibliographically motivated. It contains, for example, the set of *Pickwick Papers* in parts whose first fourteen numbers are inscribed to Mary Hogarth, originally in the Harry B. Smith collection (**1525**). Eight illustrations. See Stevenson (**1748**). For the catalogue of the collection, see Free Library of Philadelphia (**1464**).

1794. Freeman, Arthur. *George Gissing (1857-1903): An Exhibition of Books, Manuscripts and Letters from the Pforzheimer Collection in the Lilly Library.* Bloomington: Lilly Library, Indiana University, 1994, passim.

Apart from first editions of two of Gissing's works on Dickens, the exhibition catalogue describes the autograph manuscript of his *Charles Dickens, a Critical Study* (London: Blackie & Son, 1898), with many revisions; and his autograph notes on Dickens (two leaves) concerning *Martin Chuzzlewit* and several Christmas tales for that edition. Also in the exhibition were letters from Gissing to Frederic G. Kitton, 1898-1903, concerning their individual works on Dickens and their collaboration on the Rochester Edition of Dickens's Works (**2302**). Freeman provides valuable annotations (see items 37-39, 60, 84). See Freeman (**1465**) for the catalogue of the collection.

1795. Gaskell, E. *Dickens and Medicine: An Exhibition of Books, Manuscripts and Prints to Mark the Centenary of His Death: With an Introduction and Bibliography.* Exhibition Catalogues of the Wellcome Institute, 5. London: The

Library, The Wellcome Institute of the History of Medicine, 1970. 32 pp.

Among the items listed in this exhibition catalogue, pp. 17-32, are an autograph letter (reproduced in photographic facsimile) from Dickens to Georgina Hogarth, 7 August 1857, on his health; material largely in the form of books and prints on Dr. John Elliotson and animal magnetism, phrenology, Dr. Southwood Smith, the Metropolitan Sanitary Association, and hospitals with which Dickens was acquainted; and George Cruikshank's illustrated books on alcoholism, *The Bottle* (1847) and *The Drunkard's Children* (1848). Also included is a checklist of books and articles on Dickens and medicine (**1373**), pp. 13-15. In the introduction, pp. 3-11, Gaskell, the librarian of the Wellcome Institute, comments on Dickens's interest in and involvement with medical matters and practitioners. Illustrated. Also see **1837**.

Reviews: T. Blount, *Dickensian*, 66 (1970), 231-35 (the catalogue's introduction is helpful, the exhibition itself "engrossing"); *Book Collector*, 19 (1970), 515-16, 519 ("admirably complementary" to the Victoria and Albert Museum 1970 Exhibition [**1827**]); D. Taylor, *Punch*, 259 (1970), 880 ("a more unlikely combination for an exhibition it would be hard to find").

1796. Genet, Malcolm. *Charles Dickens, 1812-1870: An Exhibition of Books and Manuscripts from the VanderPoel Dickens Collection, Miriam Lutcher Stark Library, The University of Texas at Austin, Texas, 15 September-31 December 1970.* [Austin: Humanities Research Center, University of Texas, 1970]. 48 pp.

An illustrated catalogue for an exhibition honoring the centenary of Dickens's death based on the VanderPoel Collection, University of Texas (**1445**). The items are listed, with description and commentary, according to 1) The Major Novels (editions and letters concerning them), 2) Pickwick and Pickwickiana, 3) Dickens and Christmas, 4) Secondary Works (*Sketches by Boz, American Notes, A Child's History of England, The Uncommercial Traveller*, Dickens's plays, *Pictures from Italy*, and others), 5) Dramatizations, 6) Dickens in America, and 7) Dickens's journalism and editorial work. Also see **1888**.

1797. Gimbel, Richard. "An Exhibition of 150 Manuscripts, Illustrations, and First Editions of Charles Dickens to Commemorate the 150th Anniversary of His Birth Selected from His Collection and Described by Colonel Richard Gimbel, 1920." *Yale University Library Gazette*, 37 (October 1962), 46-93.

The entire issue is given over to the descriptive catalogue of the exhibition that opened on 6 February 1962 in the Sterling Memorial Library at Yale. The exhibition included parts and other editions of the novels, reading editions, some corrected galley proofs of *Edwin Drood* and other shorter works, original drawings for the novels, paintings and portraits, autograph letters, relics and ephemera, the manuscripts of "Mr. Robert Bolton" and *The Perils of Certain*

English Prisoners, fragments of manuscripts from "O'Thello," *Pickwick Papers*, and *Oliver Twist*, and other interesting related items. Illustrated. For a complete catalogue of Gimbel's collection, see Podeschi (**1509**).

1798. Gordan, John D. "First Fruits: An Exhibition of First Editions of First Books by English Authors in the Henry W. and Albert A. Berg Collection." *Bulletin of the New York Public Library*, 53 (1949), 159-72, 227-47; also as *First Fruits: An Exhibition of First Editions of First Books by the English Authors in the Henry W. and Albert A. Berg Collection*. New York: New York Public Library, 1949. 36 pp.

Dickens works in the exhibition include the first series of *Sketches by Boz* and three letters from 1835-36. The comments about these are not bibliographical in nature. For the Berg collection catalogue, see New York Public Library (**1499**).

1799. Gordan, John D. *George Gissing, 1857-1903: An Exhibition from the Berg Collection*. New York: New York Public Library, 1954, pp. 34-35.

Contains heavily annotated entries on English and American editions of *Charles Dickens: A Critical Study* (1898) and of *The Immortal Dickens* (1925), as well as an autograph letter from Gissing to James B. Pinker, 13 October 1901, on Gissing's 1902 abridged version of *Forster*. For the Berg collection catalogue, see New York Public Library (**1499**).

1800. Gordan, John D. "Reading for Profit: The Other Career of Charles Dickens." *Bulletin of the New York Public Library*, 62 (1958), 425-42, 515-22; also as *Reading for Profit: The Other Career of Charles Dickens: An Exhibition from the Berg Collection*. New York: New York Public Library, 1958. 28 pp.

Gives fairly detailed descriptions of items in an exhibition, drawn mainly from the Henry W. and Albert A. Berg collection, New York Public Library, on Dickens's public readings, including twelve of the prompt books for the readings, letters, announcements of readings, photographs, manuscripts, and other materials. Illustrated. For the Berg collection catalogue, see New York Public Library (**1499**). Also see **1861** and **1869**.

1801. Grolier Club, New York. "Case VI. 'A Christmas Carol,'" "Case VII. Other Dickens Christmas Books," and "Case VIII. Holiday Books." In *A Ha! Christmas: An Exhibition at the Grolier Club of Jock Elliott's Christmas Books, 6 December 1999 through 29 January 2000*. [Comp. Jock Elliott]. New York: Grolier Club, 1999, pp. 55-65, 66-72, 73-82.

In a handsome catalogue of an exhibition at the Grolier Club, lavishly illustrated in full color and with well-annotated entries, described case by case, Elliott presents the highlights of his collection of Christmas books through the ages. Case VI contains principally a first edition each of *Sketches by Boz* and *Pickwick Papers*, and several states of the first edition of *A Christmas Carol*, including one with a defective title page, as well as later editions. It also includes broadsides advertising dramatizations of *A Christmas Carol*, and a letter from Dickens to George Lovejoy, 24 October 1843 (in *Pilgrim Letters*, VII, 854), reproduced in photographic facsimile (p. 59). Case VII contains editions of Dickens's other Christmas Books and Christmas Stories, as well as a pencil sketch (reproduced on p. 68) of an illustration by John Leech for *The Cricket on the Hearth*, an original painting in color (reproduced on p. 72) by Arthur Rackham for a 1915 edition of *A Christmas Carol* (London: William Heinemann), and a letter from Dickens to the Reverend William Tennant, 23 December 1854 (in *Pilgrim Letters*, VII, 488). Case VIII contains nineteenth-century Christmas books by others, including Thackeray. The exhibition catalogue, as well as the exhibition itself, concludes with item 147 (see p. 95), an edition of *A Christmas Carol*, illustrated by Everett Shinn (Philadelphia: John C. Winston, 1938), one illustration from which is reproduced on the cover of the catalogue.

1802. Grolier Club, New York. *Catalogue of an Exhibition of the Works of Charles Dickens*. New York: Grolier Club, 1913; reprinted Folcroft, PA: Folcroft Library Editions, 1973. xxvi + 230 pp.

Items in the catalogue are arranged chronologically, with detailed descriptions of first and later editions, original sketches for some works, thirty-two pages of the manuscript of *Pickwick Papers*, extra illustrations, related items, original manuscripts of *A Christmas Carol* and other shorter works, letters, playbills, relics, and other materials. The catalogue contains an introduction by Royal Cortissoz that praises Dickens as a genius who "touched our hearts" because of his "happy faith in mankind" and an index (pp. 221-30). Although there is no indication in the volume itself, "News for Bibliophiles" (**1873**) and Northrup (**1154**) state that the catalogue was compiled by Ruth S. Grannis. Illustrated. A smaller-sized edition, omitting the illustrations, Cortissoz's introduction, and the index, was also published, with the title *Catalogue of an Exhibition of the Works of Charles Dickens, January 23rd to March 8th* (New York: Grolier Club, 1913, 220 pp). Also see **1858**, **1873**, and **1882**.

Review: *Nation*, 96 (1913), 102-03 (describes some of the rarer items in the collection, including a new issue of the first edition of *The Battle of Life*, and finds the catalogue "the best printed guide for the Dickens collector thus far issued").

1803. Grolier Club, New York. *Catalogue of an Exhibition of Works by John Leech (1817-1864) Held at the Grolier Club from January 22 until March 8, 1914*. New York: Grolier Club, 1914, passim.

Lists works in the exhibition in chronological order by year, including the drawing Leech did in connection with his unsuccessful application to illustrate *Pickwick Papers* following Robert Seymour's suicide, first published in the Victoria Edition of *Pickwick Papers* (2 vols., London: Chapman and Hall, 1887), I, facing p. 203; an original watercolor sketch for *A Christmas Carol*; and original pencil sketches for all but one of Leech's illustrations for *The Chimes*, as well as editions of the Christmas Books by Dickens that he illustrated. See items 15, 110-12, 132-34, 141-43, and 159. The catalogue also lists (item 300) a scrapbook containing 175 autograph letters concerning John Leech, addressed to George Evans, written between 1882 and 1888 by Robert Browning, John Millais, George Du Maurier, Caroline Leech, Georgina Hogarth, and many others. The catalogue entry notes that, in the twenty-fourth chapter of his *John Leech: His Life and Work* (2 vols., London: Richard Bentley and Son, 1891), W. P. Frith "tells of Evans's attempt to write a life of Leech, and acknowledges his indebtedness to the quantity of material which, on the death of Mr Evans, fell into his hands, and from which he drew largely for his work." In an introduction, pp. vii-xxii, Stanley K. Wilson asserts that Leech "rose to his moment" in the illustrations he did for Dickens's Christmas Books. Also see "Books and Magazine Articles about John Leech," pp. 170-74. Illustrated.

1804. Guildhall Art Gallery, London. *Charles Dickens and His London: An Exhibition of Pictures, Prints, Drawings and Relics Arranged by the Guildhall Art Gallery in Collaboration with Dickens Fellowship, 16 May to 31 May 1962.* London: Guildhall Art Gallery, 1962. 32 pp.

The illustrations in the exhibition are of London and not from Dickens's books. An introduction by Leslie C. Staples, pp. 3-7, comments on Dickens's London, particularly its "tremendous variety." Also see **1887**.

1805. Hopkins, Albert A. "A Notable 'Drood' Collection." *Dickensian*, 28 (1931/32), 231-34.

Lists some 450 items (editions and secondary works) in an exhibition held at the Grolier Club, New York, from the collection of Dr. Howard Duffield, with descriptions of the more important items. Illustrated. Also see Carden (**1604**), The Dickens House Library Collections (**1457C3**), Duffield (**1459**), and Roe (**1721**).

1806. Kitton, F[rederic] G., comp. and ed. *The Dickens Exhibition Held at the Memorial Hall, London, March 25th, 26th, and 27th, 1903: Catalogue of Exhibits.* London: Dickens Fellowship, [1903]. 67 pp.

Lists the first parts issues and volume editions of Dickens's works, extra illustrations, music, plays, imitations, Dickensiana, presentation copies, letters, various "relics" (with some description), numerous paintings and drawings (portraits of Dickens as well as illustrations for his novels), photographs, manuscripts, and autograph letters included in the exhibition. In his introduction, Kitton claims that this is the first exhibition "absolutely restricted to Dickens." For the second and third exhibitions, see Dickens Fellowship (**1789**), and New Dudley Gallery (**1813**). Also see **1851**.

Review: *Athenaeum*, 121 (1903), 530 ("an excellent piece of bibliography, which may well become important to collectors").

1807. Knebworth House, Hertfordshire, Eng.. *Dickens Centenary Exhibition of Letters and Other Items Resulting from the Lifelong Friendship between Charles Dickens and Edward Bulwer Lytton and the Story of the Guild of Literature and Art at Knebworth House.* Hertfordshire, Eng.: Knebworth House, [1970]. 42 pp.

Provides notes and commentary on the nineteen "Panels" that comprised this exhibition, which traced the developing friendship of the two men and their mutual acquaintances as well as their involvement in amateur theatrical productions in support of the Guild of Literature and Art. Also see **1837**.

1808. Kubiak, Richard, comp. *George Cruikshank: Printmaker (1792-1878). Selections from the Richard Vogler Collection.* Santa Barbara, CA: Santa Barbara Museum of Art, 1978, pp. 39-44 and passim.

In this well-annotated catalogue for an exhibition at the Santa Barbara Museum of Art, April-May 1978, Kubiak lists and describes five illustrations that Cruikshank did for *Sketches by Boz* and nine that he did for *Oliver Twist*. Illustrated. Also see Vogler's preface to this catalogue, "Some Personal Remarks about Collecting Cruikshank," pp. 6-9, where he gives his background as a collector (from age six). He did not start collecting Cruikshank until 1952, when he was an undergraduate at Washington and Lee University, and did not specialize in him until graduate school at UCLA. There, encouraged by Professor Ada Nisbet, he points out, he became a "champion" of Cruikshank in the controversy over how much the artist contributed to the content of *Oliver Twist*, though he does not feel so strongly on the subject now. Illustrated.

1809. Laurence, Dan H., with Lois B. Garcia. *Shaw: An Exhibition.* Austin: Humanities Research Center, University of Texas at Austin, 1977, passim.

Catalogue of an exhibition, 11 September 1977-28 February 1978, that contained a few items, principally letters and other manuscripts, on Dickens as a writer and his influence on Bernard Shaw. See particularly items 85 (Shaw's comments on the title page of the Limited Editions Club edition of *Great Expectations*, for which he wrote the introduction), 126 (the manuscript of an unpublished paper on the greater realism of Dickens's later novels),

242 (a letter asserting Dickens "doesn't dramatize well"), and 623 (a letter from 1912 attesting that his works "are all over Dickens"). See the index for all other Dickens references.

1810. "Letters of English Authors, from the Collection of Robert H. Taylor: A Catalogue of an Exhibition in the Princeton University Library, May 13 to September 30, 1960." *Princeton University Library Chronicle*, 21, iv (Summer 1960), 200-36; printed with same title, Princeton, NJ: Princeton University Library, 1960. 34 pp.

Lists and gives excerpts from three Dickens letters (nos. 99-101 in the catalogue): 1) to an unidentified correspondent, ca. 1836/37, printed in *Pilgrim Letters*, I, 199-200, as written to F. Crewe, [?27 November 1836]; 2) to Henry W. Longfellow, 29 December 1842; and 3) to Esther Elton (whom the editors of *Pilgrim Letters*, IX, 388, note was then Mrs. Nash), 5 March 1861, a gossipy letter about his daughter Kate, her husband Charles Collins, and Collins's mother, "old Mrs. Collins."

1811. Liverpool University, Harold Cohen Library, Liverpool, Eng. *Pickwick and Pickwickiana*. A dittoed list. Liverpool, Eng.: Liverpool University Library, 1970. 7 typewritten pp.

Richard A. Vogler reports (**1888**) that the list "gives evidence of a display drawn from the collection, not necessarily of a wealthy, but certainly of a devoted and astute collector," and one that has "the kind of depth (including a wide variety of editions and ephemera) that results from years of collecting and study in one's chosen speciality." Malcolm Andrews (**1834**) praises the exhibition as "one of the most interesting" exhibitions of Dickens produced in 1970.

1812. National Book League, London. *Victorian Fiction: An Exhibition of Original Editions at 7 Albemarle Street, London, January to February 1947*. Arr. by John Carter and Michael Sadleir. Cambridge: Published for the National Book League by Cambridge University Press, 1947, passim.

The exhibition was designed, Carter notes in his introduction, "to show what Victorian fiction looked like and how it was published" and "to show not only the diversity of Victorian fiction but also the strongly marked tradition found in certain categories." *Pickwick Papers* is included as one illustration of works issued in parts, *Oliver Twist* as an example of Cruikshank as an illustrator, the 1866 edition of *Pickwick Papers* with Dickens's presentation inscription to Queen Victoria to illustrate that Dickens was one of the "Giants" of Victorian fiction, and the one-volume first edition of *Nicholas Nickleby* as an example of a novel of social protest. Bibliographical descriptions of the items are minimal. Illustrated.

1813. New Dudley Gallery, London. *The Third Dickens Exhibition. Scenes from His Life, Works & Characters. Illustrated by Well-Known Artists. Also a Collection of Portraits (at Various Periods of His Life). His Homes and Haunts.* London: New Dudley Gallery, 1909. 79 pp.

The paper cover to this exhibition catalogue reads: *The Third Dickens Exhibition at the New Dudley Gallery, 169, Piccadilly, London, W. 1, August 7th to September 30th, 1909: Catalogue of Exhibits.* The catalogue lists and provides occasional explanatory notes about portraits of Dickens and characters from his novels, paintings of scenes from his life and works, personal relics, letters, manuscript fragments, first and parts editions of the novels and other works, illustrations to the novels, and other items. Some of the items were for sale. An introduction by Percy Fitzgerald is insignificant. Illustrated. For the first and second exhibitions, see Kitton (**1806**) and the Dickens Fellowship (**1789**). Also see **1850**.

1814. New York Public Library, Henry W. & Albert A. Berg Collection, New York. *Charles Dickens: The First Exhibition from the Collection, December 16, 1941.* New York: New York Public Library, 1941. 4 pp.

A brief, general account of the items in the exhibition. For the Berg Collection catalogue, see New York Public Library (**1499**). Also see **1838**.

1815. "One Hundred Treasures: An Exhibition to Mark the One-Hundredth Anniversary of the New York Public Library." *Bulletin of the New York Public Library*, 53 (1949), 277-89.

The only Dickens work included in the exhibition was the reading copy in the Berg Collection of *A Christmas Carol*, which includes written directions and other notes.

1816. Ormond, Richard, and John Turpin. *Daniel Maclise, 1806-1870. National Portrait Gallery, 3 March-16 April 1972; National Gallery of Ireland, Dublin, 5 May-18 June 1972.* London: Arts Council of Great Britain, 1972, passim.

This well-annotated exhibition catalogue includes Maclise's drawings of Dickens, his wife Catherine, and Georgina Hogarth (1843); his well-known painting of Dickens (1839); *Waterfall at St. Nighton's Kieve, Near Tintagel*, his painting of a woman at a waterfall for which Georgina Hogarth served as model (1842); his painting of John Forster as Kitely in Ben Jonson's *Every Man in His Humour* (ca. 1848); and his illustrations for *The Chimes* and *The Cricket on the Hearth*. In his introduction, pp. 3-15, Ormond asserts that it was Maclise's "great natural charm," his amiability, his carefreeness, and his "instinctive zest for life" that "endeared him to Dickens" and to John Forster, though they were both saddened when, in later life, Maclise drifted into "depression and inaction." However, Ormond observes, "by a curious irony," in this later period Maclise's art work "remained his one salvation," deepening and maturing "as he himself sank into lethargy." Ormond and Turpin include a chronology for Maclise, pp. 16-18, with occasional references to his relationship with Dickens. Also see **1841**.

1817. Public Library, Museums, and National Gallery of Victoria, Victoria, Australia. *Dickens Exhibition, 1936. Guide to the Books, Autographs, Letters, and Pictures Exhibited in Celebration of the Centenary of the Publication of The Pickwick Papers on March 31, 1836.* Melbourne: Printed for the Trustees by Fraser & Jenkinson, 1936. 18 pp.

Lists items in the exhibition, including an edition in parts and other editions of *Pickwick Papers*, illustrations for the novel, editions of other Dickens novels in parts or volume form, and several of Dickens's letters, some forty-seven items in all. The writer comments on the difficulty of putting together a set of first issues of the parts of *Pickwick Papers*.

1818. Ray, Gordon N. *The Illustrator and the Book in England from 1790 to 1914.* New York and London: Pierpont Morgan Library/Oxford University Press, 1976, passim.

An elaborately illustrated volume for an exhibition at the Pierpont Morgan Library, New York, March-April 1976, based "almost entirely" on Ray's own collection. It includes several original illustrations to Dickens's works (with commentary by Ray) by Daniel Maclise (no. 28), George Cattermole (no. 60), Thomas Sibson (no. 78–to *Master Humphrey's Clock*, unauthorized, 1842), George Cruikshank (nos. 114-16), Hablot K. Browne (nos. 125, 128, 131), John Leech (no. 135), Richard Doyle (no. 140), and James Mahoney (nos. 212-13–to *Little Dorrit* and *Our Mutual Friend* for the Household Edition). For references to Dickens in the bibliographical descriptions accompanying the items, see the index.

1819. Slater, Michael, comp. *Catalogue of Treasures from the Dickens Collection Formed by the Late Comte Alain de Suzannet on Exhibition at the Dickens House 1 June-12 September 1970.* London: The Dickens Fellowship, [1970]. 42 pp.

Provides information about the ninety-four items (letters, playbills, drawings and sketches, rare editions, manuscripts, and other materials) exhibited from the collection of one of the great Dickens collectors. Slater also includes items presented to the Dickens House by the comte (1930-50) and by his wife (1966). A foreword by Leslie Staples provides a brief account of Suzannet as a collector, Dickensian, and scholar. Many of the items in the collection were later donated by the comtesse to the Dickens House and others sold at Sotheby's in 1971; see Slater (**1524**), and Sotheby & Co. (**1976-77**). Illustrated. See Suzannet (**1529-30**) for the comte's own earlier catalogues of his collection. Also see **1834, 1837, 1866,** and **1888.**

Reviews: M. Y. Andrews, *Dickens Studies Newsletter*, 1, ii (September 1970), 11-12 (an "admirable catalogue" and "one of the most intimate and refreshing exhibitions" of the centenary year); T. Blount, *Dickensian*, 66 (1970), 231-35 (the catalogue provides "full and helpful documentation" for a "useful" and "striking" exhibition); R. Vogler, *Dickens Studies Newsletter*, 1, iii (December 1970), 15-18 (an excellent "memento of a collector's collection").

1820. Southwark Public Libraries and Cuming Museum, London. *Catalogue of Books, Portraits, Illustrations and Miscellaneous Exhibits. An Exhibition Arranged to Commemorate Publication of Pickwick Papers by Charles Dickens in 1836. Inaugurated by Walter Dexter, Esq., 19th March, 1936.* London: Southwark Public Libraries and Cuming Museum, 1936. 27 pp.

An exhibition of mainly bound editions of Dickens's novels (not just of *Pickwick Papers*), various associated items, and Dickensiana, all listed chronologically, 1836-1936, ending with Miller and Strange's *A Centenary Bibliography of the Pickwick Papers* (**129**), followed by lists of autographs and portraits, Dickens's illustrators, playbills, prints and illustrations, and miscellaneous items in the exhibition. With preface by F. Helliwell, Chief Librarian and Curator. Also see **1836** and **1843.**

1821. Spiers, John, and Pierre Coustillas. "X. Charles Dickens." In their *The Rediscovery of George Gissing: A Reader's Guide.* London: National Book League, 1971, pp. 120-27.

In this heavily annotated catalogue of an exhibition at the National Book League, London, 23 June-7 July 1971, the section on Dickens contains descriptions of various editions of Gissing's studies of Dickens.

1822. Steinberg, Norma S. *Monstrosities and Inconveniences: Works by George Cruikshank from the Worcester Art Museum.* Worcester, MA: Worcester Art Museum, 1986, passim.

A catalogue of an exhibition at the Worcester Art Museum, 10 November 1986-23 January 1987, from the Samuel B. Woodward collection, that reproduces two of Cruikshank's illustrations for *Oliver Twist.* Steinberg comments in an accompanying paragraph on the artist's "persistent" imagery in them and notes that many of the figures in Cruikshank's illustrations for *Oliver Twist* are his "typical London characters—the old-clothes man, the burglar, the beadle." As to the extent of Cruikshank's influence on the novel, she adds: "It would be difficult to say that Dickens did not write his text to fit such characters, but the story is certainly his."

1823. Szladits, Lola L., ed. *Charles Dickens 1812-1870: An Anthology*. New York: New York Public Library and Arno Press, 1970. 166 pp.; 2nd ed., as *Charles Dickens 1812-1870: An Anthology from the Berg Collection*. New York: New York Public Library, 1990. ix + 179 pp.

Contains excerpts from letters, studies of Dickens, and Dickens's works in loosely chronological order and numerous illustrations (drawings, plates, page proofs, manuscripts, playbills, title pages, monthly wrapper illustrations), all taken from materials in the Berg Collection, New York Public Library, and originally published in association with the Berg Collection's centenary exhibition of Dickensiana. The second edition contains the same text and illustrations as the original edition, but, as pointed out in a new foreword by Francis O. Mattson, it was redesigned and rearranged in connection with a 1990 exhibition at the New York Public Library that was a revival, in memory of Szladits, of the 1970 exhibition that had been prepared by her. Also see **1834**, **1848**, **1876**, and **1888**.

Reviews of the first edition: M. Y. Andrews, *Dickens Studies Newsletter*, 1, ii (September 1970), 10-12 (a brief description); *American Reference Books Annual*, 2 (1971), 458 ("well-produced"); *Choice*, 7 (1970/71), 1372 (contains some interesting items, but this is mainly a "visual" book designed "to bombard the reader with a flood of Dickensiana"); T. J. Galvin, *Library Journal*, 95 (1970), 3462 (a brief, mainly descriptive notice); E. Lloyd, *Wall Street Journal*, 21 August 1970, p. 6 (a descriptive notice); [L. S. Thompson], *Papers of the Bibliographical Society of America*, 64 (1970), 481 (briefly notes that this is an "effective publication"); *Times Literary Supplement*, 14 August 1970, p. 906 (a useful collection); R. Vogler, *Dickens Studies Newsletter*, 1, iii (December 1970), 17 ("disappointing").

Reviews of the second edition: S. Monod, *Etudes anglaises*, 46 (1993), 88-89 (in French; a useful volume for most); [W. S. Peterson], *Papers of the Bibliographical Society of America*, 84 (1990), 195 (briefly notes that this is a "fitting tribute to both the Dickensian riches of the Berg Collection and the energy of its second curator").

1824. Timm, Regine, ed. *The Art of Illustration: Englische illustrierte Bücher des 19. Jahrhunderts aus der Sammlung Dr. Ulrich von Kritter: Eine Ausstellung im Zeughaus der Herzog August Bibliothek, Wolfenbüttel, 1 Dezember 1984 bis 21 April 1985*. Ausstellungskataloge der Herzog August Bibliothek, 44. Wolfenbüttel, Ger.: Herzog August Bibliothek, 1984, passim.

This illustrated exhibition catalogue contains some listings of Dickens's illustrated works—see the index.

1825. Tussaud, Madame, and Sons, London. *Exhibition Catalogue Containing Biographical and Descriptive Sketches of the Distinguished Characters Which Compose Their Exhibition and Historical Gallery*. London: Printed by Ben George for Madame Tussaud and Sons, 1881, p. 3.

Listed in Podeschi (**1509**), p. 395, and therefore in the Gimbel Collection, Yale University Library, New Haven, CT. Dickens, Podeschi indicates, is treated on page 3 in what is obviously a bibliographical curiosity.

1826. van der Merwe, Pieter T. *The Spectacular Career of Clarkson Stanfield, 1793-1867: Seaman, Scene-Painter, Royal Academician.* [Newcastle-upon-Tyne]: Tyne and Wear County Council Museums, 1979, passim.

A joint exhibition and catalogue put together by van der Merwe for the Tyne and Wear County Council Museums and the Rheinisches Landesmuseum, Bonn, in 1979, "largely based on research undertaken for a postgraduate thesis" by van der Merwe at the University of Bristol, December 1978. In England the exhibition was housed in the Sunderland Museum and Art Gallery, Sunderland. The catalogue contains two sections relevant to Stanfield's relationship with Dickens: "Family and a Few Friends: The Dickens Circle," pp. 148-55, and "The Dickens Theatricals," pp. 156-61. Included in these sections, with much commentary on the relationship of Dickens, Stanfield, John Forster, Daniel Maclise, Thackeray, and others, are various drawings and paintings by Maclise, Thackeray, Stanfield, and others, several containing depictions of Dickens; a Stanfield drawing for *The Cricket on the Hearth*; portraits of various friends of Dickens; letters; and playbills. Only a few of the items in these two sections of the catalogue are illustrated, however. Also see the useful "Select Bibliography," pp. 175-76. In the biographical sketch at the beginning of the catalogue, van der Merwe comments on Dickens's relationship with Stanfield. The German version of the catalogue, which differs in some respects from the English version and lists somewhat fewer items, was published as *Clarkson Stanfield (1793-1867): die erstaunliche Karriere eines viktorianischen Malers: Seemann, Bühnenmaler, Landschafts- und Marinemaler, Mitglied der Royal Academy* (Köln: Rheinland-Verlag in Kommission bei Rudolf Habeit Verlag, Bonn, 1979).

1827. Victoria and Albert Museum, London. *Charles Dickens: An Exhibition to Commemorate the Centenary of His Death, June-September, 1970.* London: Victoria and Albert Museum, 1970. 123 pp.

The aim of this spectacular exhibition and this heavily illustrated exhibition catalogue, which lists and describes an impressive body of Dickens material, was, as Graham Reynolds, Keeper of the Department of Prints & Drawings and Paintings at the V & A, notes in the introduction, "to illustrate the many and varied contacts Charles Dickens had with the life of his times." Well-annotated listings of over 612 items, in good part from the V & A's own collections, are grouped under some sixteen headings, arranged in a loosely chronological pattern, but including "Dickens and the Theatre," "Dickens as Editor," "Dickens at Work," "Personalia," "Portraits of Dickens," and "Dickens's Friends," as well. The centerpieces of the exhibition are the manuscripts from the Forster Collection of the V & A (**1539, 1541-43**), number parts and other editions of the works, original drawings by Dickens's illustrators, and Dickens's letters. Also see **1834, 1837, 1848, 1865, 1875,** and **1888.**

Reviews: T. Blount, *Dickensian*, 66 (1970), 231-35 (an "admirable" exhibition; the catalogue is "a mine of interesting information," recorded with "admirable scholarship"); *Book Collector*, 19 (1970), 515-16, 519 ("the best the V&A have ever mounted," revealing "the real Dickens, in all his grandeur and pettiness"); D. Coombes, *Connoisseur*, 175 (September 1970), 75 ("fully annotated" and "well-illustrated" catalogue); D. DeVries, *Dickens Studies Newsletter*, 1, ii (September 1970), 12-16 (more a review of the exhibition than the catalogue; a "major cultural event," a rich and enlightening show, a "major contribution to Dickens scholarship"); W. Gaunt, *Times* (London), 17 June 1970, p. 8 (a largely descriptive notice, but points out that the paintings, drawings, prints, and photographs in the collection "not only trace out a visual biography but re-create the social atmosphere of the times in those aspects that interested Dickens most"); G. Smith, *Victorian Studies*, 14 (1970/71), 459-62 ("informative and attractive"); *Times Literary Supplement*, 14 and 21 August 1970, p. 906 (high praise for "the imagination of the organizers" of the exhibition and for "the team that produced the catalogue"); K. Tetzeli von Rosador, *Archiv für das Studium der neueren Sprachen und Literaturen*, 208 (1971/72), 298-309 (in German; does not really review the exhibition); R. A. Vogler, *Dickens Studies Newsletter*, 1, iii (December 1970), 15-18 (a "handsome catalogue" with "universal appeal"); M. Webster, *Pantheon*, 28 (1970), 533 (descriptive); G. S. Whittet, *Art and Artists*, 5, vi (September 1970), 36-38 (an "evocative exhibition," telling the story of Dickens's life and career "in a striking sequence of displays").

1828. Victoria and Albert Museum, London. *Dickens Exhibition, March to October, 1912*. London: H. M. Stationery Office, 1912. 63 pp.

A nicely descriptive catalogue (with eight illustrations) of the exhibition commemorating the centennial of Dickens's birth based on the Forster Collection in the V & A library of manuscripts, letters, and editions, as well as pictures, drawings, prints, and photographs. There is also an edition without the illustrations. For the catalogue of the Forster Collection, see Victoria and Albert Museum (**1539, 1541-43**). Also see **1854**.

Reviews: *Dickensian*, 8 (1912), 131-32 (favorable); A. W. P[ollard], *Library*, 3rd ser., 3 (1912), 343-44 (an "excellent" exhibition; the catalogue "will be valued by all who care for Dickens").

1829. Victoria and Albert Museum, London. *George Cruikshank*. London: Arts Council of Great Britain, 1974, passim.

The illustrated catalogue of an exhibition, 28 February-28 April 1974. It also provides a chronology for Cruikshank that includes his associations with Dickens (pp. 34-44) and a selective bibliography (p. 45). See pp. 45-59 of the "Catalogue," for Cruikshank's original pencil drawings and etchings for *Sketches by Boz*, *Oliver Twist*, *The Loving Ballad of Lord Bateman*, and *Memoirs of Joseph Grimaldi*. In his introductory essay, "Cruikshank: The Artist's Role," pp. 5-30, William Feaver comments on the relationship of Cruikshank and Dickens. Also see **1840**.

1830. Victoria and Albert Museum, London, Department of Engraving, Illustration and Design. *Catalogue of an Exhibition of Drawings, Etchings, & Woodcuts by Samuel Palmer and Other Disciples of William Blake, October 20-December 31, 1926*. London: Published under the authority of the Board of Education, 1926, passim.

The catalogue includes and describes an engraver's proof of Palmer's sketch of the Villa D'Este for *Pictures from Italy*, with Palmer's notes in pencil for the engraver (no. 93), and Palmer's original drawing of the Campagna for *Pictures from Italy*, again with his notes for the engraver, which are quoted (no. 98). Also see black-and-white reproductions (plates XIX, XIV) of two watercolors—of the Villa D'Este and of the cypresses at the Villa D'Este—done in 1837 (nos. 127, 92). A "Biographical Introduction" by A. H. Palmer, pp. 1-20, contains no mention of Dickens.

1831. Vogler, Richard A. *An Oliver Twist Exhibition: A Memento for the Dickens Centennial, 1970: An Essay.* Los Angeles: University Research Library, University of California, 1970. 16 pp.

The catalogue for an exhibition, 7 May-15 June 1970. In his essay Vogler comments on editions of *Oliver Twist*, the illustrations by Cruikshank, and the Dickens-Cruikshank controversy over how much influence the artist had on Dickens's writing of the novel. Illustrated.

Reviews: M. Y. Andrews, *Dickens Studies Newsletter*, 1, ii (September 1970), 10-12 ("an important contribution to scholarship"); [L. Ash], *American Notes and Queries*, 9 (1970/71), 27 (finds the catalogue useful).

1832. Wardroper, John. *Cruikshank 200: An Exhibition to Celebrate the Bicentenary of the Artist George Cruikshank.* [London]: John Wardroper, 1992, passim.

Catalogue of an exhibition at the Museum of the Order of St. John, Clerkenwell, London, 30 September-21 October 1992 and later, through 3 April 1993, elsewhere, principally of drawings, watercolors, paintings, etchings, book illustrations, and pamphlets by George Cruikshank. Included are a pencil portrait of Dickens from about 1837 (item 72); a proof of an etching, "The Streets, Morning," for *Sketches by Boz* (item 73); a pencil and watercolor sketch for *Oliver Twist* (item 74); four etched plates for *Oliver Twist* (item 75); a copy of *Memoirs of Joseph Grimaldi*, which was illustrated by Cruikshank (item 77); a photographic enlargement of a plate from that work (item 78); and a playbill for two performances of Dickens's amateur acting company at Theatre Royal, Haymarket, 15 and 17 May 1848. The plate from *Memoirs of Joseph Grimaldi* and two plates from Oliver Twist are reproduced on pp. 45 and 46. In his introduction, pp. 5-16, a sketch of Cruikshank's life and artistic career, Wardroper comments briefly on Cruikshank's sometimes smooth, sometimes stormy collaboration with Dickens. Also see **1839**.

5B. REPORTS AND COMMENTARIES
ON EXHIBITIONS

Note: See reviews listed in section 5A and **Exhibitions, reports and commentaries, Exhibitions honoring centenary of Dickens's birth, Exhibitions honoring centenary of Dickens's death**, and **Exhibitions honoring centenary of publication of Pickwick Papers** in part 2 of the subject index.

1833. Andrews, Malcolm Y. "Museum Exhibitions." *Dickens Studies Newsletter*, 1, ii (September 1970), 10-12.

Reviews centenary exhibitions in the United States and England.

1834. Andrews, Malcolm Y., and Duane DeVries. "Museum Exhibitions." *Dickens Studies Newsletter*, 1, ii (September 1970), 10-16.

Reviews of exhibitions in honor of the centenary of Dickens's death–at the Pierpont Morgan Library, New York; the Berg Collection, New York Public Library (**1823**); the British Museum, London (**1781**); the Dickens House, London (**1819**); the Liverpool University Library (**1811**); and the Victoria and Albert Museum, London (**1827**).

1835. Atkinson, Brooks. "Critic at Large: Library Display Recalls Some of the Furor Dickens Caused Here in the 1840's." *New York Times*, 15 March 1962, p. 24.

Comments on a display at the Pierpont Morgan Library, New York, of some of its Dickens holdings, in connection with which Atkinson notes the development of Dickens's dislike of America during his 1842 visit. He suggests that Dickens may have been too thin-skinned–and a bit vindictive as well.

1836. "Bibliographical Notes: Pickwick Centenary Exhibitions." *Times Literary Supplement*, 4 April 1936, p. 304.

Comments on and describes exhibitions of manuscripts and proofs of several of Dickens's works from the Forster Collection, Victoria and Albert Museum, London; a Dickens exhibition at the bookshop of Messrs. Sawyer, London, of a collection built, in turn, by Thomas Wilson, Cumberland Clark, and Charles J. Sawyer (**1790**); an exhibition of editions, piracies, playbills, etc., at the Southwark Central Library, London (**1820**); and an exhibition devoted to *Pickwick Papers* at the Dickens House, London (**1787**).

1837. Blount, Trevor. "'Inimitable' Exhibitions." *Dickensian*, 66 (1970), 231-35.

Reports on six centennial exhibitions—at the Victoria and Albert Museum (**1827**), the Dickens House Museum(**1819**), the Wellcome Institute of the History of Medicine (**1795**), the British Museum (**1781**), Knebworth House (**1807**), and Eastgate House (**1581**). For other exhibitions, see Slater (**1884**).

1838. Brooks, Philip. "Notes on Rare Books." *New York Times Book Review*, 22 February 1942, p. 20.

A favorable commentary on a Dickens exhibition in the New York Public Library (**1814**) of material in the Henry W. and Albert A. Berg Collection, including manuscripts, letters, drawings, editions, playbills, and ephemera. Brooks describes a number of items in the exhibition.

1839. Burton, Anthony. "'Cruikshank 200': An Exhibition Celebrating the Bicentenary of George Cruikshank." *Dickensian*, 89 (1993), 64-65.

A description/review of a travelling exhibition—London, Burnley, Maidstone, Sheffield, and Twickenham—that included illustrations George Cruikshank provided for *Oliver Twist* and *Memoirs of Joseph Grimaldi*. Illustrated. For the exhibition catalogue, see Wardroper (**1832**).

1840. B[urton], A[nthony]. "Things Seen: The Cruikshank Exhibition." *Dickensian*, 70 (1974), 124-26.

A description/review of an exhibition of works by George Cruikshank at the Victoria and Albert Museum, 28 February-28 April 1974 (**1829**), and then at various other locations. Illustrated.

1841. B[urton], A[nthony]. "Things Seen: The Maclise Exhibition." *Dickensian*, 68 (1972), 116-17.

Notice of the Arts Council exhibition of the works of the painter Daniel Maclise at the National Gallery, London, March-April 1972 (**1816**), including Dickens items. The exhibition catalogue contains "interesting background information," Burton notes.

1842. Byrne, Dymphna. "A Tale of Two Cities." *History Today*, 39, v (May 1989), 62.

A description of an exhibition that opened first in Brighton (4 May-1 July 1989), then in London (24 July-15 September 1989), and eventually in Paris "concerned with contemporary life in London and Paris during and just after the [French] Revolution." Organized by the Manorial Society, the exhibition included the manuscript of *A Tale of Two Cities* from the Victoria and Albert Museum, London, and the reading copy of the novel (never performed) from the Dickens House, London. Also see a briefer description of "Shadow of the Guillotine: Britain and the French Revolution," the exhibition at the British Museum, 12 May-9 September 1989, p. 63.

1843. "The Centenary of Mr. Pickwick. Dickens Relics on Exhibition." *Times* (London), 20 March 1936, p. 12.

A description of an exhibition at the Southwark Central Library in London (**1820**) celebrating the centenary of the publication of *Pickwick Papers*, with excerpts from a speech by Walter Dexter at the opening ceremonies.

1844. Chandler, G. "Liverpool Dickens Exhibition." In *Dickens and Fame 1870-1970: Essays on the Author's Reputation.* Ed. Michael Slater. Centenary Number of *Dickensian*, 66, ii (May 1970), 187.

A report by the librarian of the Liverpool City Library of an exhibition there of Dickens's novels in parts, first editions, and holograph letters from various Liverpool public and private collections.

1845. Clarke, Alan. "One Page of Dickens—£2000. Sam Weller Relic to Be Shown at Pickwick Centenary." *Sunday Dispatch* (London), 1 March 1936, p. 7.

Reports that a page of the original manuscript of *Pickwick Papers*, presented to the Dickens Fellowship by Comte Alain de Suzannet, would be part of an exhibition of Pickwickian relics at the Dickens House, London (**1787**). Clark also describes other events planned for the centenary of the publication of *Pickwick Papers* and mentions that only forty-four manuscript pages of the novel are known to exist—Engel (**125**) locates forty-six pages.

1846. "Commentary." *Times Literary Supplement*, 11 June 1971, p. 674.

In part describes an exhibition at the Dickens House based on items recently given to the museum by the Comtesse de Suzannet (**1819**).

1847. "David Copperfield Centenary. Two London Exhibitions." *Times* (London), 30 April 1949, p. 4.

Briefly notes two small exhibitions of *David Copperfield* items at the Victoria and Albert Museum and the Dickens House Museum. No catalogues seem to have been issued.

1848. "Dickens and Others in New York." *Times Literary Supplement*, 9 July 1970, p. 756.

A brief review of exhibitions at the Victoria and Albert Museum, London (**1827**), the Berg Collection, New York Public Library (**1823**); and the Pierpont Morgan Library, New York, in honor of the centenary of Dickens's death.

1849. "Dickens Birthplace. 'Pickwick' Exhibition at Portsmouth." *Times* (London), 27 March 1936, p. 19.

Notes an exhibition celebrating the centenary of the publication of *Pickwick Papers*, but comments more on the museum itself than the exhibition. No catalogue seems to have been issued.

1850. "A Dickens Exhibition." *Times* (London), 14 August 1909, p. 10.

A brief review of the third New Dudley Gallery exhibition (**1813**), a show that "will please Dickens collectors."

1851. "The Dickens Exhibition." *Times* (London), 26 March, 1903, p. 5.

The reviewer finds that the exhibition at Memorial Hall, London (**1806**), provides " convincing evidence of Dickens's immense hold upon the feelings and the hearts of the people." Also see "A Dickens Exhibition," 25 March 1903, p. 11, for a description of the exhibition opening that day.

1852. "The Dickens Exhibition." *Times* (London), 30 July 1908, p. 11.

Report on and a description of items in the second Dickens exhibition at the New Dudley Gallery (**1789**)–"an exhibition of great interest and importance to all lovers of Dickens."

1853. "A Dickens Exhibition in the Treasure Room." *Boston Public Library Quarterly*, 11 (1959), 147–48.

Describes a Dickens exhibition of first editions and autograph letters in the Boston Public Library in honor of the fortieth anniversary of the Boston Branch of the Dickens Fellowship.

1854. "A Dickens Exhibition. Interesting Relics at South Kensington." *Times* (London), 19 March 1912, p. 6.

This laudatory and descriptive review notes that "every phase of Dickens's activities is represented in the Exhibition" (**1828**).

1855. "Dickens Illustrations at the Victoria Galleries." *Times* (London), 27 March 1912, p. 5.

A laudatory review of the "accomplished drawings" of Charles Green—fourteen watercolors done between the 1860s and the 1890s of scenes from various Dickens novels.

1856. "Dickens in 3-D." *New York Times*, 1 March 1959, Magazine Section, p. 54.

Photographs of five of twenty-four Royal Doulton china figurines of Dickens characters in an exhibition at the Brooklyn Children's Museum, New York.

1857. "Dickens on Public Executions. Letters to 'The Times' on Exhibition." *Times* (London), 1 February 1949, p. 6.

A notice of a Dickens exhibition at the Southwark Central Library, London, but principally a reprinting of Dickens's letter of 13 November 1849, published the following day in the *Times*.

1858. "Dickens Relics in New York." *Dickensian*, 9 (1913), 96-97.

A review of the Grolier Club exhibition of 1913 (**1802**).

1859. "A Dickens Tableau at Tussaud's." *Times* (London), 1 February 1912, p. 10.

A brief announcement of a centenary "tableau" at Madame Tussaud's of the interior of Dickens's study based on Luke Fildes's famous painting "The Empty Chair," done after Dickens's death. The tableau, however, would have a wax figure of Dickens sitting in the chair.

1860. "Dickens's Paris." *T. P.'s Weekly*, 12 (1908), 68.

A description of an exhibition at the Paris Municipal Library of old prints and drawings of places in Paris associated with Dickens and his works.

1861. Edwards, Oliver. "Talking of Books: When Dickens Read." *Times* (London), 6 November 1958, p. 13.

On an exhibition, "Reading for Profit: The Other Career of Charles Dickens," at the Berg Collection, New York Public Library. Edwards finds the exhibition catalogue (**1800**) "extremely interesting" and notes that twelve of Dickens's sixteen prompt books are in the Berg Collection there and in the exhibition. The exhibition itself, he adds, gives a satisfying account of how Dickens "plied his trade."

1862. "Exhibition of Dickensiana" and "A Dickens Exhibition at Olympia." *Dickensian*, 10 (1914), 94, 122.

Brief notes on a collection of Dickensiana from various sources arranged by William Miller for the Children's Welfare Exhibition, London, 1914.

1863. "Exhibition of Dickensiana in America: A Famous Pickwick." *Dickensian*, 19 (1923), 140-41.

Description of some items in the Harry F. Marks exhibition in New York City of first editions, letters, and Dickensiana, with praise for the Lapham-Wallace copy (**122**) of *Pickwick Papers* in parts.

1864. "Exhibition of Dickensiana. Rare Editions and Letters. The Sawyer Collection." *Times* (London), 27 March 1936, p. 19.

Description of an exhibition at Messrs. C. J. Sawyer, London, 27 March-4 April 1936 (**1790**), of Charles J. Sawyer's collection of Dickens manuscripts, letters, first editions, and Dickensiana.

1865. Gaunt, William. "Dickens's World." *Times* (London), 17 June 1970, p. 8.

A highly favorable review of the Dickens exhibition (**1827**) in the Victoria and Albert Museum to honor the centenary of Dickens's death.

1866. Greaves, J[ohn]. "Dickensiana." *Times Literary Supplement*, 21 August 1970, p. 927.

A letter to the editor briefly describing a Dickens centenary exhibition at the Dickens House, 1 June-12 September 1970 (**1819**), of treasures from the Suzannet collection.

1867. Honour, Hugh, ed. *The European Vision of America.* Cleveland, OH: Cleveland Museum of Art, 1975, passim.

Catalogue of an exhibition to honor the Bicentennial of the United States organized by the Cleveland Museum of Art; the National Gallery of Art, Washington, DC; and the Réunion des Musées nationaux, Paris, at each of which the exhibition was shown, 1975-77. Plates 328 and 329 of the catalogue are two of Hablot K. Browne's illustrations of the fictitious city of Eden for *Martin Chuzzlewit*. Honour comments on Dickens's 1842 visit to the United

States, refers to the "close collaboration" between Dickens and his illustrator, and points out that Browne had never visited America, his view of Eden deriving "from Dickens's text, aided, perhaps, by anti-emigration prints, of which several were published during the previous decade."

1868. Jacobs, Leonard. "A Dickens Exhibition." *Dickensian*, 93 (1997), 230.

A brief description of an exhibition principally for teenagers of illustrations for and editions of *Oliver Twist*, *A Christmas Carol*, and *David Copperfield* at Helmond Castle near Eindhoven, The Netherlands, 22 November 1997-12 March 1998. Illustrated.

1869. Knox, Sanka. "Library Revives Big Hit of 1858 in Exhibition on Dickens as a Reader." *New York Times*, 1 August 1958, p. 9.

Notes the opening of an exhibition, "Reading for Profit: The Other Career of Charles Dickens," at the Berg Collection, New York Public Library and describes some of the exhibits. For the catalogue of the exhibition, see Gordan (**1800**).

1870. Lecker, Barbara. "Reports." *Dickensian*, 66 (1970), 186-92.

Reports on a number of exhibitions and meetings in England and the United States in commemoration of the one-hundredth anniversary of Dickens's death.

1871. Leybourne, Winifred. "'By Speech and Pen: The Life and Writings of Charles Dickens': Central Library, Liverpool, 23 June-25 August 1995." *Dickensian*, 91 (1995), 227.

A description of an exhibition commemorating the 125th anniversary of Dickens's death, consisting mainly of parts, first, and other editions of various Dickens works and many studies of Dickens's life and writings, as well as materials connected with the Liverpool Branch of the Dickens Fellowship.

1872. "Mr. Harry Furniss's Dickens." *Times* (London), 22 February 1912, p. 11.

A laudatory review of an exhibition of Furniss's drawings at the Doré Gallery, London, "some in pen and ink, and some coloured, of scenes from Dickens's novels"–200 drawings illustrating seven novels (*Pickwick Papers*, *Oliver Twist*, *Nicholas Nickleby*, *Martin Chuzzlewit*, *Dombey and Son*, *David Copperfield*, and *Bleak House*).

1873. "News for Bibliophiles." *Nation*, 96 (1913), 102-03.

Praises the catalogue for the Dickens exhibition at the Grolier Club, New York (**1802**), 23 January to 8 March 1913, as "the best printed guide for the Dickens collector thus far issued" and comments principally on rare and previously unrecorded editions of several minor works, mainly plays by Dickens, in the collection. The anonymous author states that the catalogue was compiled by Ruth S. Grannis.

1874. "Notes and News: Dickens Exhibition." *Bulletin of the John Rylands University Library*, 45 (1962/63), 7-9.

Describes an exhibition at the library of manuscripts, autograph letters, editions of Dickens's works, and books of Dickensiana to honor the 150th anniversary of Dickens's birth and the Diamond Jubilee of the Dickens Fellowship. The manuscripts included those of "A Child's Dream of a Star," Dickens's review of the Marquess of Londonderry's *Letter to Lord Ashley, M. P., on the Mines and Collieries Bill*, a shorthand notebook, and his last public speech, delivered at the Royal Academy dinner, 2 May 1870.

1875. Panter-Downes, Mollie. "Letter from London." *New Yorker*, 46 (25 July 1970), 74-76.

Briefly describes the Dickens centenary stamps and the "exhaustively complete" centenary exhibition at the Victoria and Albert Museum, London (**1827**).

1876. P[aroissien], D[avid]. "Announcements: Dickens in New York." *Dickens Quarterly*, 8 (1991), 50-51.

A brief description of the Dickens exhibition in the Berg Collection, New York Public Library, 12 October 1990-13 April 1991 (**1823**).

1877. "Pickwick Centenary Exhibitions." *Times Literary Supplement*, 4 April 1936, p. 304.

Briefly describes several London exhibitions honoring the centenary of the publication of *Pickwick Papers*.

1878. "The Pickwick Exhibition." *Dickensian*, 3 (1907), 201-04.

Describes items in the exhibition at the New Dudley Gallery (**1788**). Illustrated.

1879. "A Pickwick Exhibition." *Times* (London), 22 July 1907, p. 12.

Characterizes an exhibition centered on *Pickwick Papers* at the New Dudley Gallery, London, as "a remarkable view of the popularity of the immortal work" and of the "permanence of the book's charm." The reviewer also notes the "good and elaborate catalogue, prepared by Mr. B. W. Matz and Mr. J. W. T. Ley" (**1788**). For a further report, see "The Pickwick Exhibition," 23 July, p. 10.

1880. "'Posthumous Papers.' A Pickwick Exhibition in London." *Times* (London), 26 March 1936, p. 12.

A description of numerous items in an exhibition celebrating the centenary of the publication of *Pickwick Papers* at the Dickens House Museum, London (**1787**), including "manuscripts, printed books, drawings and paintings, personal relics, and a wide variety of other things connected with the novel."

1881. R., A. C. "An Interesting Dickens Exhibition." *Lady's Pictorial*, 29 August 1908, p. 324.

Favorable, descriptive review of an exhibition organized by the Dickens Fellowship at the New Dudley Gallery (**1789**). Illustrated.

1882. Roberts, W[illiam]. "Dickens in America." *Bookman* (London), 44 (1913), 119-20.

A review and description of the exhibition of manuscripts, portraits, parts and other editions, and personal relics of Dickens at the Grolier Club, New York, in January 1913 (**1802**).

1883. "Show Dickensiana Valued at $100,000." *New York Times*, 15 May 1923, p. 31.

A report on an exhibition at Harry F. Marks's bookstore, New York, including editions, letters, relics, and mementoes of Dickens.

1884. [Slater, Michael]. "Editorial Note on Exhibitions." *Dickensian*, 66 (1970), 235-36.

Brief description of two centenary exhibitions in Britain–1) "Charles Dickens and Some of His Contemporaries," Shakespeare Birthplace Trust, Stratford, and 2) "Pickwick and Pickwickiana," Liverpool University Library–and even briefer mention of several exhibitions in the United States.

1885. S[taples], L[eslie] C. "Things Seen: Dickens in Camden." *Dickensian*, 71 (1975), 157-58.

A description/review of a Dickens exhibition in the Camden Central Library, June 1975, marking the fiftieth anniversary of the Dickens House Museum, Doughty Street, London. Illustrated.

1886. "The Talk of the Town: Dip into Dickens." *New Yorker*, 38 (7 July 1962), 17.

Briefly describes the exhibition at the Pierpont Morgan Library, New York, honoring the 150th anniversary of Dickens's birth and touches upon the depth of the library's collection of Dickens's letters and manuscripts.

1887. "Things Seen: The London Dickens Knew." *Times* (London), 22 May 1962, p. 15.

A review of a Dickens exhibition at Guildhall Art Gallery, London (**1804**), commemorating the 150th anniversary of Dickens's birth. The reviewer particularly recommends the topographical watercolors and prints in the exhibition, a number of which are described, as of "absorbing interest," though mainly of documentary rather than artistic value. Illustrated.

1888. Vogler, Richard A. "Exhibition Catalogues." *Dickens Studies Newsletter*, 1, iii (December 1970), 15-18.

Briefly evaluates five catalogues of exhibitions honoring the centenary of Dickens's death—those of the Victoria and Albert Museum, London (**1827**); the Dickens House Museum, London (**1819**); the Berg Collection, New York Public Library (**1823**); the University of Texas (**1796**); and the Liverpool University Library (**1811**)—seven dittoed pages containing an "annotated list comprised largely of items lent by an unidentified local collector to the library for its exhibition of 'Pickwick and Pickwickiana.'"

PART SIX: COLLECTING DICKENS
6A. AUCTION SALE CATALOGUES

Note: Where auction sale and booksellers' catalogues are concerned, no attempt has been made to trace items that moved from one collection to another; doing so might, however, make for an interesting and valuable research project. Nor can it be claimed that this is a complete listing of such catalogues containing collections of Dickens's works and Dickensiana. Sale catalogues for all the major and many minor collections should be here, but undoubtedly some of the more minor sales have not been recorded (or, for that matter, located). The note, below (**2010**), about the Sotheby sale catalogues in the Dickens House, could very well apply to the sale catalogues of other auction houses as well. In this section the term "Dickensiana" is used to refer both to materials related to Dickens, often of an ephemeral nature, and to biographical studies and critical and other studies of his works. Also see **Auction sales (with Dickens items), catalogues**, in part 2 of the subject index.

1889. American Art Association, New York. *Catalogue of the Private Library of Dr. Dudley Tenney, of New York City, Comprising a Notable Collection of Dickensiana: First Editions of Books Illustrated by Cruikshank, Leech, Seymour and Other Artists, Many of the Volumes Extra-Illustrated.* New York: American Art Association, [1922], passim.

Catalogue of a sale, 22 November 1922, listing many extra-illustrated volumes of biographies and other studies of Dickens as well as of the novels themselves. It also lists illustrated and extra-illustrated editions of works by other authors. A copy in the Fales Collection, New York University Library, notes sale prices for about half of the items.

1890. American Art Association, New York. *Catalogue of the Valuable Library Formed by the Late M. C. D. Borden, Esq.* New York: American Art Association, 1913, passim.

Catalogue of a sale, 17-19 February 1913. The Dickens items, lots 193 (sixty-three separately-described items) and 194, filling twenty pages of the catalogue, include a set of parts and first volume editions of Dickens's works, some with autograph letters and many with original drawings added and extra illustrations; the original manuscripts of *The Perils of Certain English Prisoners and Their Treasures* in Dickens's and Wilkie Collins's hands and of "A Curious Dance Round a Curious Tree" in Dickens's hand; and Dickensiana, including extra-illustrated copies of the three-volume *Hogarth-Dickens Letters* and of the *Memoirs of Joseph Grimaldi*. Entries are fully annotated.

1891. American Art Association, New York. "Charles Dickens: Magnificent Series of Autograph Letters, Rare First Editions, Extra-Illustration Material and Other Dickensiana." In *Rare First Editions, Inscribed Copies, Original Manuscripts . . ., Including the More Important Volumes from the Library of The Late Carlotta Russell Lowell . . ., the Remaining Portion of the Library of the Late Dr. Dudley Tenney . . ., the Collection of Louise Van Dyke. . . .* New York: American Art Association, 1925, lots 152-79 (unnumbered pages).

Catalogue of a sale, 4-5 May 1925, including eight brief autograph letters, quoted apparently in full; an eclectic variety of first editions; sets of extra illustrations; and Dickensiana.

1892. American Art Association, New York. *Collectors' Items from the Library of Dr. George C. F. Williams of Hartford, Connecticut: First Editions of Standard British and American Authors in Unusually Fine Condition.* New York: American Art Association, 1925, passim.

Catalogue of a sale, 23-24 April 1925. The Dickens items, lots 115-40, include parts and first volume editions of Dickens's works and some Dickensiana.

1893. American Art Association, New York. *First Editions of Charles Dickens and Modern Authors—Barrie, Galsworthy, Shaw, Trollope, and Others; a Series of Gissing A. L. S.; and a Superb Unpublished Dickens Letter [from the Library of Thomas Hatton of Leicester, England].* New York: American Art Association, 1929, pp. 5-27.

The illustrated catalogue of a sale, 26 February 1929, including (lots 23-137) numerous parts and volume editions of Dickens's works, playbills, sets of extra illustrations, proofs of illustrations, and a few letters. The then unpublished letter referred to in the title was to Madame De La Rue, 27 September 1845 (a long letter from which several substantial excerpts are printed; the full letter is in *Pilgrim Letters*, IV, 387-91). The others, also then unpublished, were to Charles Manby (24 October 1848—summarized here, as it is in *Pilgrim Letters*, V, 429), to Mrs. Manby (20 November 1865—summarized here as it is in *Pilgrim Letters*, XI, 111), and to Charles Hicks, a reader for Bradbury and Evans ([London 1838]—excerpted). The copy in the New York Public Library has sale prices written in. For other sales of Hatton's collections, see American Art Association (**1906**), Parke-Bernet Galleries (**1972**) and Sotheby & Co. (**1978-79, 1981**).

1894. American Art Association, New York. *First Editions of Esteemed Nineteenth Century Authors Mainly in Original Bindings, Inscribed Copies and Desirable Autographs, Including the Henry Alexander Collection of the Writings of*

Charles Dickens and the Balance of the Charles Meeker Kozlay Collection of the Writings of Bret Harte. New York: American Art Association, 1926, passim.

The illustrated catalogue of a sale, 1 April 1926, devoted in part to Alexander's Dickens collection, lots 111-332, including various parts and other first and later volume editions of Dickens's works (among them many American editions), a few books from Dickens's library, a variety of Dickensiana, sets of extra illustrations, and memorabilia. A featured item is a portrait of Dickens in 1867 by William Barksdale Myers, a Philadelphia artist, painted "from sketches made from life" and reproduced as the frontispiece to the catalogue. It is noted that it was earlier reproduced in color in *Century Magazine*, 83, iii (January 1912), 322. The New York Public Library copy of this catalogue has prices written in.

1895. American Art Association, New York. *The Herman L. R. Edgar Collection of First Editions of W. M. Thackeray* . . . . New York: American Art Association, 1924, passim.

Catalogue of a sale, 30 January-1 February 1924. The Dickens items, lots 162-210, comprising twelve pages, include parts, first volume, and many American editions of numerous Dickens works; oil paintings of "Little Nell" by Hablot K. Browne and of "Little Nell's Grandfather" by George Cattermole; and Dickensiana. Illustrated.

1896. American Art Association, New York. *Illustrated Catalogue of a Notable Collection of First Editions, Costume and Colored Plate Books, Manuscripts and Association Items of Superlative Interest from Various Collections, Including Those of Mr. Frederick Corder of London, England, Mr. David G. Joyce of Chicago, Illinois, Captain E. W. Martindell of Ashford, England*. New York: American Art Association, 1922, passim.

In this catalogue of a sale, 26-27 January 1922, lots 288-334 include numerous parts and volume editions of Dickens's novels, his 1867 diary, and Dickensiana, with all items fairly heavily annotated.

1897. American Art Association, New York. *Illustrated Catalogue of First Editions of Rare Books and Handsomely Bound Sets of Esteemed Authors, the Property of Sydney Herbert, Esq., of London and New York, and Other Owners as Herein Designated*. New York: American Art Association, 1916, passim.

Catalogue of a sale, 16-18 February 1916. The Dickens items, lots 262-304, consist of parts and volume editions of Dickens's works (including a number of early issues of first editions) and printed collections of illustrations.

1898. American Art Association, New York. *Illustrated Catalogue of Rare Books, Manuscripts, Broadsides and Autographs, Comprising Americana, Association Items and Standard Sets, and an Extensive Collection of Colored-Plate Books.* New York: American Art Association, 1916, passim.

Catalogue of a sale, 13-15 December 1916, principally of the collection of John Henry Osborne, according to Podeschi (**1509**), p. 358. The Dickens items, lots 182 and 360-69, include twenty-one unpublished drawings by Hablot K. Browne of characters from Dickens's works, done for F. W. Cosens; parts and volume editions of various Dickens works, including a prime *Pickwick Papers* in parts (with a five-page part by part bibliographical description); and Dickensiana.

1899. American Art Association, New York. *Illustrated Catalogue of the Important Library of the Late Samuel H. Austin, of Philadelphia: Books, Manuscripts, Drawings, Unique and Notable Cruikshankiana, Famous Dickens and Thackeray Items.* New York: American Art Association, 1917, passim.

This catalogue of a sale, 23-24 April 1917, includes several relevant Cruikshank items: a pencil sketch of Dickens at age 26, a pencil sketch possibly intended for *Oliver Twist*, a pencil sketch of Dickens used in *Forster* and three pencil sketches for *Oliver Twist*, one with Dickens's hand-written remark ("Rose & Oliver Twist too old") scratched out by Cruikshank (illustrated). The Dickens items include the Captain R. J. H. Douglas set of *Pickwick Papers* in parts, which John C. Eckel, in a letter accompanying the set, calls "the finest and most perfect copy of an original issue it has ever been my fortune to handle"; a number of parts issues and original issues of Dickens's other works; an autograph letter to the Countess of Blessington, 13 October 1845; and a "Corrected Copy" of *The Frozen Deep* with corrections in Wilkie Collins's hand. Illustrated.

1900. American Art Association, New York. *Illustrated Catalogue of the Literary Treasures of Walter Thomas Wallace of South Orange, New Jersey.* New York: American Art Association, 1920, passim.

An illustrated, well-annotated catalogue of a sale, 22-25 March 1920. The Dickens items, lots 313-97, include a variety of Dickensiana and parts and first volume editions of individual works, several with Dickens letters laid in. These letters are to George Cattermole, 12 September 1841, concerning the illustrations for *Barnaby Rudge* (transcription provided, but the letter is printed from manuscript in *Pilgrim Letters*, II, 378-79); to William Day, 19 January 1843; to Messrs. Chapman and Hall, 7 May 1870, concerning proofreading of *A Child's History of England*, undoubtedly for the Charles Dickens Edition (transcription provided, but the letter is printed from manuscript in *Pilgrim Letters*, XII, 522); to an unnamed recipient, 24 November 1856, concerning proofreading for *Little Dorrit* (transcription provided; the editors of *Pilgrim Letters*, VIII, 226, suggest that it was probably to William Bradbury or one of his printers); and to Mr. Ecles (actually Eeles–see the letters in *Pilgrim Letters*, VI, 524-25), 21 and 22 October 1851, concerning the fake book backs for Dickens's study (transcription provided; the fake titles are also listed in *Pilgrim Letters*, VI, 851). The last was earlier printed in *Hogarth-Dickens Letters*, as addressed to Mr. Eeles).

1901. American Art Association, New York. *The Important Library of Alexander M. Hudnut of New York City.* . . . New York: American Art Association, 1926, passim.

Catalogue of a sale, 3-4 November 1926. The Dickens items, lots 132-90, include parts and first volume editions of Dickens's works, collections of plates of illustrations, Dickensiana, and Dickens's letter to "The Ladies and Gentlemen, my correspondents, through Mr. Clarke," 24 March 1869, concerning the schedule of his readings, a transcription of which is provided (but the letter is printed from manuscript in *Pilgrim Letters*, XII, 316-17).

1902. American Art Association, New York. *The Private Library of Herbert L. Rothchild of San Francisco, California.* . . . New York: American Art Association, 1924, passim.

Catalogue of a sale, 30 April-2 May 1924. The Dickens items, lots 367-81, comprising five pages, include parts and first volume editions of Dickens's works.

1903. American Art Association, New York. *The Renowned Collection of First Editions of Charles Dickens and William Makepeace Thackeray Formed by George Barr McCutcheon.* New York: American Art Association, [1926]; reissued New York: G. A. Baker, [1930?], passim.

Catalogue of a sale, 21-22 April 1926, listing 512 items (329 for Dickens, 183 for Thackeray). The catalogue contains numerous illustrations and often detailed descriptions of the items, which include a collection of *Pickwick Papers* in parts (characterized in the catalogue as "one of the finest in existence"; a full, thirteen-page collation is included), the original autograph manuscript of a page of Dickens's early parody of *Othello*, twelve numbers and two supplements of the *Gadshill Gazette*, in addition to parts and various volume editions of Dickens's major and minor works (including some dedication copies), sets of extra illustrations, playbills, music, adaptations, and several autograph letters. In the copy in the Fales Collection, New York University Library, auction prices have been written in. Also see **2114, 2116,** and **2138.**

1904. American Art Association, New York. *The Renowned Collection of the Late William F. Gable of Altoona, Pennsylvania.* 8 parts. New York: American Art Association, 1923-25, passim.

Catalogue of an eight-part sale extending over a year and a half, five parts of which contain Dickens items. In *Part One: First Editions, Autograph Manuscripts and Letters of English and American Authors*, a sale of 5-6 November 1923, the Dickens items, lots 296-312, consist of a few parts and first volume editions, a collection of plates for *Pickwick Papers*, seven autograph letters (with substantial excerpts given), books from Dickens's library, and some Dickensiana. One of the letters, to George Scott, 20 June 1848, is not in *Pilgrim Letters*; in it, according to the catalogue, Dickens mentions conflicts between Italians and Austrians and Chartist agitation in London.

In *Part Three: Autographs and Manuscripts. . . .*, a sale of 13-14 February 1924, the Dickens items, lots 330-39, include ten autograph letters, with excerpts given. Those incorrectly dated here are to Antonio Gallenga, 13 May 1852 (correctly dated 20 May 1852 and printed in *Pilgrim Letters*, VI, 678); to William Cullenford, misdated 2 August 1857 (dated 2 August 1851 and included in *Pilgrim Letters*, VI, 453); and an undated one to Sir Edwin Landseer (dated [?July 1850-14 May 1851] in *Pilgrim Letters*, VI, 389).

In *Part Four: Autograph Manuscripts, Inscribed Copies, First Editions, Letters. . . .*, a sale of 10-11 March 1924, Dickens items include lot 279, a letter from Hablot K. Browne to Dickens, no place or date given, but about the frontispiece for *Master Humphrey's Clock*, which Browne was doing for Chapman and Hall because, as he writes, George Cattermole was "hors de combat"–dated [?7 March] 1841 in *Pilgrim Letters*, II, 218n-19n, where it is quoted from Kitton's *"Phiz" (Hablot Knight Browne). A Memoir* (London: George Redway, 1882), p. 23. Other Dickens items, lots 749-60, consist of eleven autograph letters, with excerpts given. The only letter not printed in *Pilgrim Letters* is to John Hollingshead, 16 December 1868 (unless this is the letter dated 15 December 1868 in *Pilgrim Letters*, XII, 246).

In *Part Five: English & American Writers, Rare Historical Americana. . . .*, a sale of 24-25 November 1924, lot 129 is a letter from George Cruikshank to Dickens, 3 April 1841, with excerpt given. Other Dickens items, lots 154-70, include editions of Dickens's works, some Dickensiana, and six autograph letters, with excerpts given. Those published in *Pilgrim Letters* with corrected information are to J. Hoskins, 18 November 1842 (*Pilgrim Letters* notes, III, 377, that this is L. Hoskins but gives no excerpt, adding that it was mentioned in *Nonesuch Letters*, I, 490; the catalogue excerpt quotes Dickens as regretting he was not home when Hoskins called but that "Mr. Cruikshank will be happy to consent to the publication of his name as a member of the committee, but not as a receiver of subscriptions"); to an unnamed correspondent (half of the first page is cut away), 29 December 1850 (*Pilgrim Letters*, VI, 250, dates it [28] December 1850); and to "my dear Goaden," 24 July 1851 (*Pilgrim Letters*, VI, 442, suggests the correspondent was J. T. Gordon, not Goaden).

In *Part Seven: Rare First Editions and Inscribed Volumes, Original Manuscripts and Autographs of Famous Authors and Statesmen. . . .*, a sale of 3-4 March 1925, Dickens items, lots 137-49, include a facsimile of a brief letter from Dickens to Francis Smedley, 19 April 1841; three autograph letters by George Hogarth, Dickens's father-in-law, mentioning Dickens; a few editions of Dickens's works; and Dickensiana.

1905. American Art Association, New York. *The Renowned Collection of the Works of Charles Dickens Formed by Mr. and Mrs. Edward C. Daoust.* New York: American Art Association, [1929]. 45 pp.

Illustrated catalogue of the 8 April 1929 sale of first and subsequent editions of Dickens's works, the original manuscripts of a page of Dickens's early parody of *Othello* and of the poem "The Song of the Wreck," Dickensiana, various relics, and other items, 245 in all. Also see **2094**.

1906. American Art Association, New York. *The Renowned Collection of the Works of Charles Dickens Formed by Thomas Hatton of Leicester, England.* New York: American Art Association, [1927]. Pages unnumbered.

Sale catalogue of 254 items sold 7 December 1927, including parts, first volume, and subsequent editions of Dickens's works (including "a matchless copy" of *Pickwick Papers* in parts), letters, parodies and imitations, and a variety of Dickensiana. Descriptions are moderate in length, with a few quite detailed. For further sales of the Hatton collection, see American Art Association (**1893**), Parke-Bernet Galleries (**1972**) and Sotheby & Co. (**1978-79, 1981**). Also see **2118** and **2154**.

1907. American Art Association, New York. *Selections from the Libraries of Roland R. Conklin of Huntington, Long Island, and Charles F. Kennedy of Brewer, Maine, Together with Several Other Properties. Rare First Editions, Some Hitherto Undescribed, of Nineteenth Century English & American Authors, including Dickens . . . .* New York: American Art Association, 1924, passim.

Catalogue of a sale, 12-13 May 1924. The Dickens items, lots 168 and 180-218, comprising seven pages, include first and American editions of Dickens's works, Dickensiana, and playbills for adaptations of Dickens's works.

1908. American Art Association, Anderson Galleries, New York. *A Charles Dickens Collection of Superlative Merit and Equally Fine First Editions of American and English Authors: The Library of the Honorable Frederick W. Lehmann, St. Louis, Mo.* New York: American Art Association, Anderson Galleries, Inc., 1930, pp. 39-65.

Out of a total of 1,052 items, the Dickens entries, lots 233-336, include unused "Buss" plates, numerous first and important later editions in parts and volume form, corrected galley-proofs of a speech Dickens gave at the anniversary dinner of the Royal Free Hospital, 6 May 1863, a few letters, three pen-and-ink drawings presumably by Dickens, drawings by others, secondary works, and a variety of Dickensiana. The copy in the Library of Congress, a gift from Charles H. Butler, has prices noted in pencil. Also see **2115** and **2169**.

1909. American Art Association, Anderson Galleries, New York. "Dickens (Charles)." In *The Library of John C. Eckel, Author of The First Editions of the Writings of Charles Dickens, Etc.* New York: American Art Association, Anderson Galleries, 1935, pp. 15-22 and passim.

Lists a collection, sold 15-16 January 1935, of parts, first volume and other editions of many of Dickens's works, a set of corrected galley proofs of Eckel's *The First Editions of the Writings of Charles Dickens and Their Values: A Bibliography* (**16**), and a few Dickensiana, some listed under their authors' names. Annotations point our the special features of the items.

1910. American Art Association, Anderson Galleries, New York. "A Fine Series of Dickens Items." In *English and American First Editions, Autograph Letters, and Manuscripts, Including Selections from the Libraries of Francis K. Swartley [and Others] . . . [and Including] Remarkable Dickens Mementos, and Fine Sets, from the Library of Edward C. Daoust, Cleveland, Ohio. . . .* New York: American Art Association, 1936, pp. 95-104.

Catalogue of a sale, 9-10 December 1936. The Dickens items, lots 247-65, include three autograph letters–to Miss Doner, 8 April 1856; Wilkie Collins, 25 March 1862; and Andrew W. Tuer, 10 March 1869–with excerpts given, various parts and first volume editions, and relics. The editors of *Pilgrim Letters*, VIII, 84-85, note that the sale catalogue is "clearly in error" in identifying the recipient of the 1856 letter as Miss Doner; the contents of the letter indicate that the recipient was Miss Marguerite Power.

1911. American Art Association, Anderson Galleries, New York. *First Editions, Autograph Letters, Manuscripts, and Standard Sets Including Dickens and Thackeray Collections of J. Macy Willets. . . .* New York: American Art Association, Anderson Galleries, 1937, pp. 47-54.

Catalogue of a sale, 11-12 November 1937, which included, in addition to numerous items by numerous other authors, parts and volume editions of Dickens's works, as well as one Dickens letter, to Mrs. Hurnell, 14 January 1850 (in *Pilgrim Letters*, VI, 9-10). The items by other authors in Willets's collection are much more interesting.

1912. American Art Association, Anderson Galleries, New York. "A Large and Attractive Group of Works by Charles Dickens." In *Early English Literature; Incunabula and Americana; First Editions of Works by Dickens and Thackeray; Bibliographies: The Splendid Library of the Late Honorable Frederick Spiegelberg, New York, N. Y.* New York: American Art Association, Anderson Galleries, 1937, pp. 58-73.

Catalogue of a sale, 3-4 November 1937, offering numerous parts, first volume, and other editions of Dickens's works, including American editions and minor works (lots 213-71). Illustrated.

1913. American Art Association, Anderson Galleries, New York. *The Library of George Ulizio, Pine Valley, N. J. Part I. First Editions of English Authors.* New York: American Art Association, Anderson Galleries, 1931, pp. 26-50.

Catalogue of a sale, 28-30 January 1931, of parts and first volume editions of Dickens's works, including the first McCutcheon copy, improved, of *Pickwick Papers* in parts, with a fragment containing four lines of page 398 of the original manuscript inserted, three letters, and a few other items. Illustrated. Also see **2223** and **2237**.

1914. American Art Association, Anderson Galleries, New York. *The Library of the Late Rev. Dr. Roderick Terry of Newport, Rhode Island,* Part I. . . . New York: American Art Association, Anderson Galleries, 1934, pp. 71-74.

Catalogue of a sale, 2-3 May 1934, with just three Dickens items: two letters (both in *Pilgrim Letters*) and a page containing autograph poems by Dickens, Robert Southey, Leigh Hunt, and others, dated "22 Oct. 1836." Dickens's poem is six lines long and signed "Boz.": "Now, if I don't make/The completest mistakes/That ever put man in a rage,/This bird of two weathers/Has moulted his feathers/And left them in some older cage." The side of the page containing Dickens's and Southey's poems is reproduced in facsimile.

1915. American Art Association, Anderson Galleries, New York. *Rare & Valuable Colored Plate Books & an Extensive Cruikshank Collection from the Library of the Late Sir David Lionel Goldsmid-Stern Salomons, Bart., Broomhill, Tunbridge Wells.* Part One, A-G; Part Two, H-Z. New York: American Art Association, Anderson Galleries, 1930, passim.

Catalogue of a sale, 16-17 and 29-30 January 1930, that lists, among many Cruikshank items, I, 70-84, twenty-nine India proofs before letters of illustrations for *Sketches by Boz* and twelve for *The Loving Ballad of Lord Bateman*, originally from Cruikshank's own collection (lot no. 385). Also included are a number of editions of Dickens's works illustrated by others as well as by

Cruikshank (lots 437-96), I, 90-102, including an edition of *Pickwick Papers* containing two Dickens letters, 15 October 1860, arranging dates for a reading, "the nearer Christmas time the better, I suppose" (noted in *Pilgrim Letters*, IX, 327, as to H. G. Adams, but with only this excerpt from the catalogue; the letter itself has not been located), and (lot 440) 27 December 1866 (in *Pilgrim Letters*, XI, 288). Also see lot 1254, II, 245, a grangerized edition (in four volumes) of Thackeray's *An Essay on the Genius of George Cruikshank* (London, 1840). All items are annotated and include bibliographical descriptions. Illustrated. Sale prices are given for most items in the copy in the New York Public Library.

1916. American Art Association, Anderson Galleries, New York. "A Superb Collection of A. L. s. and First Editions by Charles Dickens, Together with a Splendid Series of Original Watercolor Drawings by Hablot Knight Browne ('Phiz'), John Leech, and F. W. Pailthorpe, Numbers 137-192 [actually 194]." In *The Library of the Late Ogden Goelet of New York. Part Two. Public Sale January 24 and 25*. New York: American Art Association, Anderson Galleries, 1935, pp. 59-86.

As in the earlier sale (**1917**), Browne's watercolor drawings were done for Frederick Cosens, these being based on Browne's original etchings for *Nicholas Nickleby*, *Dombey and Son*, and *Bleak House*. The sale also included five pen and sepia wash drawings for *Martin Chuzzlewit* and seven for *Sketches of Young Ladies* by "Quiz" that Browne did in preparation for doing the etchings for these works, seven pencil drawings by John Leech for *A Christmas Carol*, and Pailthorpe's watercolor drawings for *Pickwick Papers*, *Great Expectations*, and other works and his pencil drawings for *Great Expectations*. Dickens letters in the sale included eight to H. G. Adams, nine to Peter Cunningham. three to Alexander Ireland (publisher of the *Manchester Examiner*), four to J. P. Harley, twenty-three to John Forster, and a number to various other correspondents. Also in the sale were numerous first and other editions of Dickens's works and a collection of portraits, playbills, and photographs. All items are fully annotated, with excerpts from many of the letters. The New York Public Library rare book collection contains a copy of this sale catalogue with many sale prices written in. Also see p. 172 for a Thackeray drawing of Dickens, himself, and others.

1917. American Art Association, Anderson Galleries, New York. "A Superb Collection of Autograph Letters, Drawings, and First Editions by Charles Dickens, Together with a Splendid Series of Original Watercolor Drawings by Hablot Knight Browne ('Phiz'), Numbers 109-146." In *The Library of the Late Ogden Goelet of New York. Part One. Public Sale January 3 and 4*. New York: American Art Association, Anderson Galleries, 1935, pp. 54-83.

The watercolor drawings by Browne are copies of the etched illustrations he and Robert Seymour did for *Pickwick Papers* and that he did for *Martin Chuzzlewit, David Copperfield,* and *Little Dorrit,* all done in the late 1860s for Frederick W. Cosens. The sale also included a collection of twenty-one original pencil drawings by F. W. Pailthorpe for *Oliver Twist;* various first editions of Dickens's works; a collection of thirty-three letters, most from Dickens to Edmund Yates; ten letters from Dickens to Thomas Mitton, twelve to Shirley Brooks, three to Georgina Hogarth, ten to Thomas Adolphus Trollope, fourteen to Mrs. Mary Sargeant Gove Nichols, and several others to various correspondents. All items are fully annotated, with excerpts from many of the letters. Also see p. 89 for a grangerized copy, extended from one to nine volumes, of Graham Everitt's *English Caricaturists and Graphic Humourists of the Nineteenth Century* (1893) and p. 135 for drawings by John Leech published in *Punch* magazine. The New York Public Library rare book collection contains a copy of this sale catalogue with many sale prices written in. Also see **1916** and **2186**.

1918. American Art Association, Anderson Galleries, New York. "A Superb Collection of First Editions, Autograph Manuscripts, Autograph Letters, and Ephemera by or Relating to Charles Dickens." In *First Editions, Association Books, Autograph Letters and Manuscripts by the Brownings, Dickens, Byron, Thackeray, Swinburne, Lamb, and Other Esteemed Nineteenth Century English and French Authors . . . Collected and Catalogued by the Late Harry B. Smith.* New York, American Art Association, Anderson Galleries, 1936, pp. 88-117.

The Dickens portion of this catalogue for a sale, 8-9 April 1936, includes ninety-one lots, among them parts and first volume editions of all of Dickens's novels except *Great Expectations,* major non-fiction, and other minor works; some Dickensiana; an extra-illustrated *Memoirs of Joseph Grimaldi;* forty autograph letters (enumerated); and a two-page memorandum by Dickens to W. H. Wills, his sub-editor for *Household Words* and *All the Year Round,* concerning "financial arrangements to be made" by Wills for Ellen Ternan and others while Dickens was in America in 1867-68. In regard to Ternan, Dickens reminded Wills that John Forster had his power of attorney: "He knows Nelly as you do and will do anything for her." Excerpts from a number of the letters are given, and three are reproduced in facsimile. Prices are written in by hand in a copy of the catalogue in the Library of Congress. Also see a *New York Times* report on the first half of the sale (**2147**).

1919. American Art Galleries, New York. *Catalogue of the Valuable Literary and Art Property Gathered by the Late Augustin Daly, Part II: Books.* New York: American Art Galleries, 1900, pp. 74-91.

Catalogue of a sale, 20-27 March 1900. The Dickens items, lots 811-972, include parts and first volume editions of Dickens's works and Dickensiana. A few special items, more fully annotated, include the Victoria Edition of *Pickwick Papers* (1887) with extra illustrations; materials concerned with the origin of *Pickwick Papers* and Robert Seymour's claims thereto, including a long letter by Mrs. Seymour and a letter from Dickens to Seymour about Seymour's drawings for *Pickwick Papers*; grangerized copies of the *Memoirs of Joseph Grimaldi*, *Forster* (nine volumes), and the *Hogarth-Dickens Letters*; the original manuscript of "His Brown Paper Parcel" (*Somebody's Luggage*); 100 letters from Dickens to George Cattermole, Henry Kolle, and Dickens's publishers; and other letters from and to Dickens.

1920. American Art Galleries, New York. *Illustrated Catalogue of Notable Library Sets; Cruikshankiana, Occasional Drawings and Caricatures Collected by the Late Richard Waln Meirs of Philadelphia, Pennsylvania.* New York: American Art Galleries, 1919, passim.

Catalogue of a sale, 19 November 1919, of drawings by and works illustrated by Isaac Cruikshank and his sons George and Robert, including a number of editions of Dickens's works illustrated by George Cruikshank. Illustrated.

1921. Anderson Auction Co., New York. *Catalogue of Rare Books, Manuscripts, and Autograph Letters, Mostly from Private Sources and Including Some Choice Items from the Collection of Evert Jansen Wendell . . . .* New York: Anderson Auction Co., 1905, pp. 21-25.

Catalogue of a sale, 19 May 1905. Dickens items, lots 84-109, include parts and first volume editions of many of Dickens's works; two Dickens letters, with excerpts given (to Lewis Gaylord Clark, 30 July 1845, as noted in *Pilgrim Letters*, IV, 343, where it is printed in full, and to Sol Eytinge, 15 May 1869 [actually 14 May, as pointed out in *Pilgrim Letters*, XII, 354, where the letter is printed from manuscript]); the proof sheets for the Charles Dickens Edition of *A Child's History of England* (1870 or 1871), with "copious" corrections and additions in Dickens's hand and the running headlines written in; the autograph manuscript of *Sketches of Young Gentlemen*, with many corrections and additions; a portion of the original manuscript of *No Thoroughfare* in Wilkie Collins's hand with some manuscript notes by Dickens; and a few items of Dickensiana.

1922. Anderson Auction Co., New York. *Catalogue of the Library of Edwin M. Lapham of Chicago, Ill. A Remarkable Collection, Principally of English Authors of the Georgian and Victorian Eras, in Specially Choice Condition, with a*

Number of Autograph Letters and Original Manuscripts. New York: Anderson
Auction Co., [1908], pp. 38-47.

Catalogue of a sale, 1-3 December 1908. The descriptions of the Dickens
items (pp. 38-41) are brief except for an extensive collation of *Pickwick Papers*
in parts, what would later become known as the "Lapham-Wallace" set, here
described as "one of the finest copies" in existence (for a collation of this set,
see **122**).

1923. Anderson Auction Co., New York. "Dickensiana." In *A Collection of
Excessively Rare Books, Letters and Illuminated Manuscripts.* New York: Anderson Auction Co., [1909], pp. 71-88.

Catalogue of a sale, 14 and 15 December 1909, including parts and first
volume editions of a number of Dickens's novels, rare first editions of many
of his minor works and bound first and other editions of his novels, presentation copies, sets of extra illustrations, playbills, a set of F. W. Pailthorpe's original drawings in color for *Pickwick Papers*, and an edition of Thomas
Woolnoth's *Facts and Faces* (London, 1852) with a four-line poem written on
the first fly-leaf by Dickens, dated Gad's Hill, 9 December 1860, and signed
by him: "Man's face–the index to his soul/Shows what may be found
within./The broad brow has a heavenly goal,/The narrow a haven of sin."
Also see **2190**.

1924. Anderson Auction Co., New York. "The Writings of Charles Dickens."
In *Catalogue of the Library of the Late Wilhelmus Mynderse of Brooklyn, N.Y.*
New York: Anderson Auction Co., 1909, pp. 23-30.

Catalogue of a sale, 28-29 October 1909, including parts, first volume, and
other early editions of Dickens's works; a letter; and some Dickensiana.

1925. Anderson Galleries, New York. *Association Books Collected by Edwin W.
Coggeshall of New York City.* New York: Anderson Galleries, 1920, pp. 7-
19, 26.

Catalogue of a sale, 4 November 1920. The Dickens items, lots 14-30 and
67, include several presentation copies of individual Dickens works (with facsimiles of the inscriptions provided); a few volumes from Dickens's library;
Luke Fildes's pencil and chalk drawing of "The Empty Chair"; ten letters
from Mamie Dickens and Georgina Hogarth to Edward Bulwer Lytton Dickens (Dickens's youngest child), 1869-79; and a bound volume containing
sixty-nine letters by Dickens and letters by other authors, together with "original sketches and designs for illustrations of Characters and Episodes in Dickens's Novels by Charles Green, R. I., George Cruikshank, and Augustus Egg,
R. A." The sixty-nine Dickens letters are enumerated and excerpts are given

from a number of them. The catalogue also includes a presentation copy of *Vanity Fair* with a dedication from Thackeray to Dickens and an autograph letter from Thackeray to Dickens, 30 March (no year given), turning down an invitation because he is otherwise engaged. In his edition of *The Letters and Private Papers of William Makepeace Thackeray* (4 vols. Cambridge, MA: Harvard University Press, 1945-46), IV, 322, Gordon N. Ray assigns it vaguely to 1836-58. Also see **2181**.

1926. Anderson Galleries, New York. *Books, Autographs and Manuscripts of Extreme Rarity from the Library of Mrs. Luther S. Livingston of Cambridge, Mass., with a Few Important Books from the Library of the Late Commodore E. C. Benedict of Greenwich, Conn., and Other Collections . . . .* New York: Anderson Galleries, 1923, pp. 33-36.

Catalogue of a sale, 5-6 March 1923. The Dickens items, lots 128-33, include a few parts and first volume editions of Dickens works; the original manuscript of a poem of eight lines in Dickens's hand, dated 14 April 1857, written in a collector's album (a facsimile is included); and a letter from Dickens to Professor C. C. Felton, 2 January 1844, signed "The Proscribed One" (printed in full in *Pilgrim Letters*, IV, 2-5).

1927. Anderson Galleries, New York. *Catalogue of a Most Unusual Collection of Books and Manuscripts, Many in Superb Bindings; Books from the Library of the Late Frederick R. Hulsey; Selections and Duplicates from Mr. Henry S. Van Duzer; Important Books and Manuscripts Sold by Order of A. Mitchell Palmer, Alien Property Custodian.* New York: Anderson Galleries, 1919, pp. 88-95.

Catalogue of a sale, 17-18 February 1919. The Dickens items, lots 340-62, include various editions of his works, a grangerized copy of *Forster/Hogarth-Dickens Letters*, four autograph letters, and a portrait of Dickens by W. P. Frith (which sold for $1,700 according to a pencilled-in note in a copy in the New York Public Library) done "at about the same time as the one commissioned by John Forster" (now in the Victoria and Albert Museum, London) and essentially a replica of that painting. A black-and-white reproduction of the painting serves as a frontispiece to the catalogue. Also see **2153**.

1928. Anderson Galleries, New York. *Catalogue of the William Harris Arnold Collection of Manuscripts, Books & Autograph Letters to Be Sold by Order of Gertrude Weld Arnold.* New York: Anderson Galleries, 1924, pp. 56-63.

Catalogue of a sale, 10-11 November, 1924, that included, lots 259-63, several presentation copies of Dickens's works, the autograph manuscript of Dickens's "Address to the Readers of *Household Words* on His Discontinuing that Publication and Beginning *All the Year Round*," and eleven Dickens letters, with excerpts, all of which have been published in *Pilgrim Letters*. Illustrated.

1929. Anderson Galleries, New York. *The Dickens Collection Formed by the Late R[alph] T. Jupp of London.* New York: Anderson Galleries, 1922. 74 pp.

Illustrated catalogue of a sale, 1-2 February 1922 of first editions of Dickens's works (including a *Pickwick Papers* in parts), the Memoranda Book (a page of which is illustrated), letters by Dickens and others (including twenty from members of the Dickens family and over 100 letters from John Forster to William Johnson Fox), personal relics, and two extra-illustrated editions of *Forster.* Descriptions of many items are fairly detailed. The copy in the Fales Collection, New York University Library, has prices written in. See the Sotheran catalogue (**2056**). Also see **2080, 2104, 2108**, and **2163**.

1930. Anderson Galleries, New York. *The Dickens Collection of the Late William Glyde Wilkins of Pittsburgh, Pa.* New York: Anderson Galleries, 1922. 65 pp.

Catalogue of a sale, 13-14 February 1922, of a valuable collection of first editions in parts and book form (English, American, French, German, Dutch), extra illustrations, autograph letters, playbills, and other items. Notes point out special features of individual items. The catalogue lists two interesting editions of *Forster.* One is a grangerized version of the 1911 Memorial Edition (2 vols., London: Chapman and Hall), edited by B. W. Matz, with "500 portraits, facsimiles, and other illustrations"–inlaid with twelve autograph letters by or about Dickens or about Forster's biography. The other is an undated edition accompanied by a large collection of illustrations meant to go into an extra-illustrated edition, including "over 150 mounted photographic reproductions of Dickens' portraits at various periods of his life; 60 reproductions of photographs of Dickens's various residences; and nearly 500 miscellaneous plates, these latter unmounted." Editions of Dickens's works in this collection are also often accompanied by collections of extra illustrations and other related materials, including a copy of *Pickwick Papers* with nearly 1,000 additional plates. The Fales Collection, New York University Library, has a copy of the catalogue with selling prices noted in pencil. Also see **2105**.

1931. Anderson Galleries, New York. *Dickens Collection, Thackeray Collection, and Other Rare Books and Autographs from the Library of Mr. Edwin W. Coggeshall of New York.* 2 vols. New York: Anderson Galleries, 1916, passim.

Illustrated catalogues of a two-part sale, 25-27 April and 15-17 May 1916. The first catalogue, pp. 22-63 and 65, itemizes a collection of first editions of Dickens's works in parts (including a particularly fine *Pickwick Papers*) and in volume form, presentation copies, sixty-six autograph letters with excerpts from most, drawings, Dickens's copy of George Eliot's *Scenes from Clerical Life*, Dickensiana, extra-illustrations, playbills, and even furniture, often with detailed descriptions of the items. The second catalogue lists Dickensiana (pp. 14-16) and itemizes about 600 Dickens letters (pp. 36-105), 425 to W. H. Wills, 125 of them then previously unpublished, and 131 to Georgina Hogarth, most previously unpublished. The catalogue frequently quotes from individual letters. Also see **2148**.

1932. Anderson Galleries, New York. *Early English Literature, Modern First Editions & Association Copies, Important Original Manuscripts of Robert Louis Stevenson & Other Modern Authors, Collected by Mr. Harry Glemby, New York.* New York: Anderson Galleries, 1926, passim.

Catalogue of a sale, 15-16 November 1926. The Dickens items, lots 172-99, comprising six pages, include parts and first volume editions of Dickens works, a few items of Dickensiana, thirty-nine Dickens letters, and letters by John and Mamie Dickens.

1933. Anderson Galleries, New York. *The Fine Private Library of the Hon. John M. Patterson of Philadelphia.* . . . New York: Anderson Galleries, 1922, pp. 23-55.

Catalogue of a sale, 15 May 1922, including, among other items, first editions of Dickens bound and in parts, other editions, numerous variants of the Christmas Books, an original pencil portrait of Dickens by John Leech, the manuscript of the prologue to John Westland Marston's *The Patrician's Daughter*, presentation copies to and from Dickens, original drawings by various artists, sixteen letters from Dickens to fifteen correspondents, and Dickensiana. A copy in the New York Public Library has sale prices pencilled in.

1934. Anderson Galleries, New York. *The Library of Jerome Kern, Part I, A-J.* New York: Anderson Galleries, 1929, pp. 114-61.

A heavily illustrated catalogue of a sale, 7-10 January 1929, of the library of one of the great modern American composers. Kern's impressive collection of Dickens materials included Dickens's marriage license, the Jupp-Kern collection of *Pickwick Papers* in parts, original drawings by Hablot K. Browne and Robert Seymour for *Pickwick Papers*, original watercolors by "Kyd" (Joseph Clayton Clarke) for several novels, playbills, first editions in parts and volume form, other drawings by Browne, three pages of the manuscript of *Oliver Twist*, presentation copies, page proofs of forty-eight pages of the Cheap Edition of *Christmas Books*, several letters, ten pages of the manuscript of *A Curious Dance Round A Curious Tree*, a proof copy of "Report of the Select Committee [of the Guild of Literature and Art] with corrections in Dickens's hand, a page of the manuscript of "O'Thello," Dickens's Book of Memoranda, a grangerized copy (the Broadley copy) of *Forster*, and the complete manuscript of *The Perils of Certain English Prisoners* by Dickens and Wilkie Collins. A copy of the catalogue in the New York Public Library has sale prices and purchasers written in. Also see **2077-78**, **2119**, and **2123**.

1935. Anderson Galleries, New York. "A Portion of the Library of Newbury Frost Read" and "Original Drawings for the Works of Charles Dickens, Rare Issues of Tennyson, Etc., Etc., the Property of an English Baronet." In *First Editions of Byron, First Editions, Original Manuscripts of Charles Dickens & Original Drawings for His Works, Etc., Etc.* New York: Anderson Galleries, 1925, pp. 47-68, 68-83.

In this catalogue of a sale, 8 December 1925, the Read library includes parts editions of several of Dickens's novels, rare first editions of a number of minor works, ten pages of manuscript of *A Curious Dance Round a Curious Tree* in Dickens's hand (one page is illustrated in facsimile), the manuscript of *The Perils of Certain English Prisoners* in the hands of Dickens and Wilkie Collins with Dickens's inscription to Collins and additional notes and letters relevant to the work, the manuscript of Dickens's prologue to John Westland Marston's *The Patrician's Daughter* (one page of which is illustrated in facsimile), a page of the manuscript of Dickens's early Shakespeare travesty "O'Thello," Dickens's autograph draft of the title-page for *Oliver Twist*, page-proofs of pp. 161-208 of the Cheap Edition of the Christmas Books with revisions and running-heads added in Dickens's hand, the original contract with Chapman and Hall for *Our Mutual Friend*, over twenty Dickens letters, forty original drawings and their proofs by Marcus Stone for *Our Mutual Friend*, original portraits of Dickens by George Cruikshank and John Leech, twenty-one unpublished drawings by "Phiz" (Hablot K. Browne) of characters in the works of Dickens, 648 original illustrations in color of Dickens characters by "Kyd" (Joseph Clayton Clarke), playbills, Dickensiana, and a few other items. The collection of an "English Baronet," whom Podeschi (**1509**), p. 359, identifies as Stuart Samuel, includes original drawings by George Cruikshank, Hablot K. Browne, Robert Seymour, John Leech, and George Cattermole for Dickens's works, one of which, by Browne for *Pickwick Papers*, contains hand-written criticism by Dickens. Also see **2117** and **2137**.

1936. Anderson Galleries, New York. *The Private Library of the Late Stanisias Gorski . . .; First Editions of Charles Dickens Collected by Mrs. R. K. Mygatt, New York City. . . .* New York: Anderson Galleries, 1924, pp. 17-23.

Catalogue of an auction, 25 March 1924. The Mygatt collection, lots 166-222, included parts and volume editions of Dickens's works and some Dickensiana.

1937. Anderson Galleries, New York. *The Splendid Library of the Late Theodore N. Vail of New York, Comprising a Large Variety of the Choicest Colored Plate*

Books by Aiken, Cruikshank, and Rowlandson; an Extensive Collection of the First Editions of Dickens and Thackeray, the Former with Manuscripts and Original Drawings. . . . New York: Anderson Galleries, 1922, pp. 66-79.

A catalogue of sale, 2-6 May 1922. The Dickens items, lots 430-510, include editions in parts (some enhanced with a variety of extra illustrations); numerous first editions of minor Dickens works; original drawings by known and unknown artists (*Pickwick Papers*, for example, is represented by original drawings by Hablot K. Browne, F. W. Pailthorpe, and Alfred Crowquill [Alfred H. Forrester], as well as several sets of printed extra illustrations); the original manuscript of *The Perils of Certain English Prisoners*; ten pages of the manuscript of *A Curious Dance Round a Curious Tree*, in Dickens's hand, showing his share in the authorship of the piece; two grangerized editions of *Forster* and one of the *Hogarth-Dickens Letters*; and some Dickensiana. A copy in the New York Public Library has sale prices pencilled in. See a brief report on the two manuscripts in "Notes on Sales: Dickens's Manuscripts" (**2144**).

1938. Anderson Galleries, New York. *Two Fine Collections of First Editions: Charles Dickens Collected by Mr. Harold Hartshorne, New York City; Oscar Wilde Collected by Mr. Arthur C. Rhodes, Cedarhurst, L. I.; The Bibliographical Library of a New England Collector; and Other Collections.* New York: Anderson Galleries, 1924, pp. 5, 17-31.

Catalogue of a sale, 4-5 March 1924. Of the Dickens items, lots 35-38 are bibliographical Dickensiana. The Hartshorne collection, lots 140-217, includes parts, first volume and other editions of various Dickens works; a prompter's copy of Dickens's early play *The Strange Gentleman* (1836); several sets of extra illustrations for several Dickens works; imitations; a collection of 240 watercolors of Dickens characters by "Kyd" (Joseph Clayton Clarke); thirty-nine autograph letters from Dickens, his father, and his daughter Mamie, 1840-70, to various correspondents (not identified in detail, but some excerpts are given, and the catalogue notes that "58 pages of Dickens' letters in all" are here), a grangerized copy of Edgar Browne's *Phiz and Dickens* (**857**) in two volumes, with numerous added illustrations, portraits, and twenty-one autograph letters of Dickens and his friends and associates, including two by Dickens himself; and Dickensiana.

1939. Bangs & Co., New York. *Catalogue of the Library and Autographs of William F. Johnson, Esq., of Boston, Mass.* New York: Bangs & Co., 1890, pp. 54-55, 126-27.

The Dickens items, numbered 468-76 and 1117-19, include a few first editions; some Dickensiana; the manuscript in Dickens's hand of the "Articles of Agreement" for a walking match between Dickens, George Dolby, J. R. Osgood, and James T. Fields in Boston, 3 February 1868; the manuscript in

Dickens's hand of a series of punch recipes; and an autograph letter from Dickens to an unnamed correspondent, 4 August 1866–identified as Thomas Headland in *Pilgrim Letters*, XI, 230.

1940. Cameron, Kenneth W. "American and British Authors in F. B. Sanborn's Papers." *American Transcendental Quarterly*, no. 6, iv (1970), 2-53.

Reprints an auction catalogue, part of which contains items from the library of F. B. Sanborn. The Dickens items consist of the manuscript of the 1868 postscript to *American Notes* (item 313) and two letters: item 312, to J[ohn] Watkins, 25 November 1866 (in *Pilgrim Letters*, XI, 277), and item 469, to Thomas Mitton, no date, but with the brief text given in full–the letter is printed in *Pilgrim Letters*, I, 611, with an estimated date of early December 1839.

1941. Christie and Manson, Messrs., London. *Catalogue of the Library of the Late Samuel Rogers, Esq.* London: Christie and Manson, 1856. 86 pp.; reprinted in facsimile in *Sale Catalogues of Libraries of Eminent Persons. Volume 2: Poets and Men of Letters.* Ed. A. N. L. Munby. London: Mansell, 1971, pp. 217-340.

A catalogue of a sale, 12-18 May 1856, possibly the earliest sale of Dickens items. These include eleven of Dickens's works, among them three presentation copies to Rogers (*American Notes*, *Nicholas Nickleby*, and *Master Humphrey's Clock*), the last with "an autograph letter from the author" (no date or other details given). These items are listed on pp. 14, 73, and 81 in the original edition and on pp. 230, 289, and 297, in the reprint. The facsimile is of a copy of the catalogue that has sale prices written in.

1942. Christie, Manson & Woods, International. *The Estelle Doheny Memorial Library, St. John's Seminary, Camarillo California, Sold on Behalf of the Archdiocese of Los Angeles. Part III. Printed Books and Manuscripts, Including Western Americana.* New York: Christie, Manson & Woods, [1988], pp. 161-66.

A handsomely illustrated catalogue of a sale, 1-2 February 1988, including Dickens editions in parts and volume form, miscellanea, and autograph Dickens letters–to George Cattermole, 12 September 1841; [Felix] Joyce, of Bradbury and Evans, 5 April 1852; Reverend Charles de la Pryme, 17 July 1852 (the excerpt given here is in *Pilgrim Letters*, VI, 716, but listed, from an earlier sale catalogue, as to an "Unknown Correspondent"; it has since been published, *Pilgrim Letters*, VIII, 378, from manuscript as to De la Pryme, under the date of 17 July 1857); George Dolby, 6 January 1867; to Mrs. George Cattermole, 10 April 1869); and to William Charles Kent, 30 April 1869. The annotations are useful, and excerpts from the letters are provided.

1943. Christie, Manson, & Woods, London. *Catalogue of the Beautiful Collection of Modern Pictures, Water-colour Drawings, and Objects of Art, of Charles Dickens, Deceased.* London: Christie, Manson, and Woods, [1870]. 11 pp.; reprinted, "with the names of the Purchasers and Prices realised appended to each lot." London: Field and Tuer, 1870, 1885; also reprinted in *Dickens Memento* (**1948**), 1884, and *Catalogue of the Library of Charles Dickens from Gadshill, Reprinted from Sotheran's "Price Current of Literature," Nos. CLXXIV and CLXXV; Catalogue of His Pictures and Objects of Art, Sold by Messrs. Christie, Manson & Woods, July 9, 1870; Catalogue of the Library of W. M. Thackeray Sold by Messrs. Christie, Manson & Woods, March 18,1864; and Relics from His Library, Comprising Books Enriched with His Characteristic Drawings, Reprinted from Sotheran's "Price Current of Literature," No. CLXXVII.* London: Piccadilly Fountain Press, 1935; reprinted London: Sotheran, 1936, pp. 121-32.

Lists forty paintings and drawings and twenty-eight objects of art sold at auction on 9 July 1870. All reprints give the prices realized and the purchasers. For a report on this sale, see "Charles Dickens' Art Relics" (**2083**). Also see Messrs. Thomas & Homan, auctioneers (**2019**), and Henry Sotheran & Co. (**2055**) for other sales of Dickens's possessions. Also see **2073**, **2082**, and **2125**.

1944. Christie, Manson & Woods, London. *Catalogue of the Collection of Works of Art Presented to the British Red Cross Society and the Order of the Hospital of St. John of Jerusalem in England to Be Sold for the Benefit of Their Funds.* [London: Christie, Manson & Woods, 1918], pp. 218-23.

Catalogue of a sale, 8 April 1918, including a number of Dickens letters contributed by various donors, among them Henry F. Dickens–three letters to Henry F. Dickens, 7 October 1867, 11 February 1868, 9 August 1869 (the last not in *Pilgrim Letters*); one to Charles Fechter, 30 April 1862; one to John Forster, no date given, but concerning a reading of *Little Dombey* (probably to Daniel Maclise, according to the editors of *Pilgrim Letters*, VIII, 584, with a suggested date of 11 June 1858). Also included was Dickens's Book of Memoranda (**2530**), contributed by Mrs. Comyns Carr, which a pencilled note in the copy of the catalogue in the Dickens House, London, indicates was sold for £325. Entries are accompanied by descriptive commentary, and excerpts from the twenty letters itemized are given. In the Dickens House copy, prices for most items are pencilled in. Also see **2107**.

1945. Christie, Manson, & Woods, London. *Catalogue of the Library of William Charles Macready, Esq., Deceased. . . .* London: Christie, Manson, & Woods, 1873, p. 7; reprinted in facsimile in *Sale Catalogues of Libraries of Eminent Persons. Volume 12: Actors.* Ed. James F. Arnott. London: Mansell, 1975, p. 437.

A catalogue of a sale, 8-9 July 1873, which lists eight Dickens novels, four of which are presentation copies to Macready and one (*The Haunted Man and the Ghost's Bargain*) to his wife. The facsimile is of a copy of the catalogue that has sale prices written in.

1946. Christie, Manson & Woods, London. "The Property of Lord Gawain Douglas." In *Valuable Printed Books, the Properties of Lord Gawain Douglas, [etc.].* London: Christie, Manson & Woods, 1972, pp. 41-47.

Catalogue of a sale, 29 November 1972, of the Dickens collection inherited by Lord Gawain Douglas from his father, the Marquess of Queensberry, of editions in parts and volume form, as well as eleven autograph Dickens letters, with brief excerpts, 1837-66, all reprinted in *Pilgrim Letters*. Also see **2182**.

1947. Christie, Manson & Woods, London. *Valuable Autograph Letters, Historical Documents and Music Manuscripts, with Some Music Reference Books, the Properties of the Late Baron Hatvany . . . and Various Other Owners.* London: Christie, Manson & Woods, 1980, pp. 57-62.

Catalogue of a sale, 22 October 1980. The Dickens items, lots 137-55, include sixteen Dickens letters, mainly to the Duke of Devonshire (two), Charles Coote (ten), and Clarkson Stanfield (three). One letter, to Mrs. [James] Hulkes, 18 June 1865, published, as the catalogue notes, only in a "heavily edited version" in *Nonesuch Letters* (but from manuscript in *Pilgrim Letters*, XII, 61-62), contains Dickens's elaboration on the account in the *Examiner* of the Staplehurst railway accident. The sale also included letters to Mrs. Hulkes from Mamie Dickens, 18 June 1870 (on her father's death); Georgina Hogarth, 1 November 1870; and Charles Dickens, Jr., 19 April 1872. Illustrated.

1948. *Dickens Memento, with Introduction by Francis Phillimore [Wilfred Meynell?], and "Hints to Dickens Collectors" by John F. Dexter, [and] Catalogue with Purchasers' Names & Prices Realised of the Pictures, Drawings, and Objects of Art of the Late Charles Dickens, Sold by Auction in London by Messrs. Christie, Manson, & Woods on July 9th, 1870.* London: Field & Tuer; New York: Scribner & Welford, [1884]; reprinted Folcroft, PA: Folcroft Library Editions, 1978. 47 pp.

A reprint of the eleven-page catalogue of the Dickens sale (**1943**), with the names of purchasers of the items in the sale and the prices paid. In the introduction, pp. 1-5, "Phillimore" comments on Dickens's fame and on the sale of Dickens's pictures, drawings, and objects of art, describing the "intense excitement" and frenzied bidding for objects associated with Dickens and noting that the "great prize" was the set of silver Pickwick ladles presented to

Dickens by Chapman and Hall on the completion of *Pickwick Papers*. See Dexter (**2216**) for the hints to collectors.

1949. Fenner, Robin A., & Co., The Stannard Gallery, Tavistock, Devon, Eng. *Catalogue [of a Sale of the Estate Contents of "Norstead," the Tavistock Home of Miss Judith Hughes. . .]*. Tavistock, Devon, Eng.: Robin A. Fenner & Co., The Stannard Gallery, 2001, passim.

Catalogue of a sale, 9 July 2001, of the effects of a descendant of Mrs. Georgiana Morson, governess of Urania Cottage, the home for fallen women that Dickens helped Angela Burdett-Coutts set up and run. Lots 357-73 consist of two letters from Georgina Hogarth to Mrs. Morson, undated, but presumably written in the early 1850s during the tenure of Mrs. Morson; thirteen letters from Dickens to Mrs. Morson; and three covers to her in Dickens's hand—all previously unpublished. The letters appear to be quoted in full, though there are errors in dating that are corrected in an "Amendments" sheet (other errors remain). Most of the letters are very brief and concerned with appointments or finances (12 April 1849, 8 April 1850, 9 May 1851, 22 November 1851, 18 December 1851, 11 December 1852, 12 January 1853, 13 January 1854). Five, however, the more interesting of the lot, contain Dickens's comments on women in the home. A letter of 31 October 1852 instructs Mrs. Morson to provide underclothing, a dress and bonnet, and a warm bath, preferably two of the last, for an Eliza Wilkin, "that she may be perfectly clean and wholesome." In one of 14 July 1850, Dickens asks Mrs. Morson to tell "the girls" who were immigrating the next day that he hopes they "will do well, marry honest men and be happy." In one of 3 January 1853, of which a photographic facsimile is provided, Dickens informs Mrs. Morson that he has accepted Elizabeth Macklin for the home and asks her to send clothing for Miss Macklin, the daughter of one of the wardens of Coldbath Field Prison. In one of 27 December 1849, he notes that Maria Cridge "is to go to Bartholomew's Hospital." In the longest letter, dated 4 January 1854, Dickens reluctantly agrees to Mrs. Morson's plea to give Rhena Dolland, who has, to his great disbelief, expressed a desire to leave the home, a second chance because it is a "forgiving Christmas time." But, he sternly insists, if Mrs. Morson ever hears from her "<u>one word expressive of discontent and an intention to leave the home</u>" she must at "<u>that instant put the dress upon her and shut the gate upon her for ever</u>" (Dickens's underlining). He adds that this strict attitude toward those who are "indifferent to their own misery and degradation" should be conveyed to the other women, that the woman who deserves pity is the one who "would try hard to do well," a "grateful girl sincerely trying to reform herself." All of these letters have been printed in *Pilgrim Letters*, XII, Appendix A. See also **2089** and **2187**.

1950. Henkels, Stan. V., comp. *The Magnificent Library of Mr. A. S. Whiton of New York City, Embracing an Unequalled Collection of First Editions of Dickens, Thackeray, Lever, Lover and Ainsworth. Many of Them in the Original Parts as Well as First Editions of All the Popular English and American Authors. Cruikshankiana and Colored Sporting Books.* Philadelphia: Samuel T. Freeman & Co., Auctioneers, 1911, pp. 37-53.

A sale of 17-18 February 1911. The Dickens items, lots 167-248, consist of parts editions of some of the novels and volume editions of the novels and many minor works (with some bibliographical descriptions and annotations of these items), and some Dickensiana. Illustrated.

1951. Hodgson & Co., London. *Catalogue of Exceedingly Rare & Valuable Books from the Library of the Rt. Hon. C. G. Milnes Gaskell of Thornes House, Wakefield . . . [Including] Interesting Autograph Letters of Charles Dickens, W. M. Thackeray, W. H. Ainsworth, George Cruikshank, and Other Literary Men of the Period.* London: Messrs. Hodgson & Co., 1924, pp. 41-46.

Catalogue of a sale, 28-29 February 1924, including three letters from Dickens to William Harrison Ainsworth, with excerpts (to be found in full in *Pilgrim Letters*, I, 384, 498, and VII, 494); letters (with excerpts given) to Ainsworth from Catherine Dickens, Georgina Hogarth, R. H. Barham, and John Forster, some of which make reference to Dickens; and the draft of a letter from George Cruikshank to John Macrone regarding Cruikshank's drawings for *Sketches by Boz* in which Cruikshank complains that Dickens had not lived up to the arrangement with him "that I was to have an early & regular supply of MS. in order that the work might not be hurried." Also see **2167**.

1952. Hodgson & Co., London. *A Catalogue of Interesting Autograph Letters and Manuscripts from the Collection of the Late Richard Bentley, Esq., of Upton Park, Slough (Sold by Order of the Trustees), Including an Important Series of Over One Hundred Autograph Letters of Charles Dickens. With Several Signed Agreements. . . .* London: Hodgson & Co., 1938, passim.

In the Bentley sale, 8 July 1938, pp. 19-27, the relevant lot is no. 232. It contains the correspondence between Dickens and Richard Bentley, 1836-68, concerning *Bentley's Miscellany*, *Oliver Twist*, and *Memoirs of Joseph Grimaldi*, amounting, it is pointed out, to about 190 pages of writing paper. Also included are seven of the original agreements between Dickens and Bentley regarding *Bentley's Miscellany*, *Oliver Twist*, and *Barnaby Rudge* and two letters from Dickens to his solicitors, Smithson and Mitton. The collection of letters, it is noted, throws light on the early years of Dickens's literary career, on his relations with one of his publishers, and on Dickens's "violence of expression" in his dealings with Bentley, though the later letters reveal that "all ill-feeling was subsequently forgiven and forgotten on both sides." Illustrated with facsimiles. Also see **2072** and **2161**.

1953. Hodgson & Co., London. *A Catalogue of Rare and Beautiful Books . . . Including Autograph Letters from Dickens to Cruikshank. . . .* London: Hodgson & Co., 1937, passim.

The catalogue of a sale, 9-10 December 1937. In addition to various editions of Dickens's novels (lots 360-68 and 512-14), the catalogue lists an "exceptionally interesting series of forty autograph letters to George Cruikshank" from Dickens, 1837-48, regarding Cruikshank's illustrations for *Oliver Twist*. The cataloguer notes that two of the letters refer to *The Loving Ballad of Lord Bateman* (1839), in one of which Dickens notes that he has altered "a word here and there" in the song and "added some notes"; in the other he reminds Cruikshank that he is "particularly–*most particularly*–anxious to remain unknown . . . for weighty reasons" as having had a hand in the work (lot 573). Lots 574-78 comprise two more letters from Dickens to Cruikshank (both undated), one from John Forster (17 June 1840) inviting him to "a small private Dinner to Dickens," and other items. Also see another part of the sale, "Interesting Autograph Letters, Etc., Referring to Charles Dickens and George Cruikshank. In Their Collaboration as Author and Illustrator. The Property of a Lady," pp. 45-48. Also see **2095** and **2179**.

1954. Hodgson & Co., London. *A Catalogue of Rare and Valuable Books Including the Library of W[illia]m Roots, Esq., M. D., F. S. A. . . .* London: Hodgson and Co., 1907, passim.

Catalogue of a sale, 20 March 1907, containing Hablot K. Browne's original drawing of the trial scene in *Pickwick Papers* and a few other Dickens items.

1955. Hodgson & Co., London. *A Catalogue of the Valuable Modern Library of the Late Captain James Stewart . . . To Which Are Added Rare Books and Interesting Manuscripts from Various Sources, Including . . . Original Mss. of Two Sketches by Charles Dickens and Autograph Presentation Copies of The Pickwick Papers, 1842, with Five Other Inscribed Philadelphia Editions of His Novels. . . .* London: Hodgson and Co., 1927, pp. 10-12, 21-23.

Catalogue of a sale, 24-25 November 1927. Dickens items, lots 122-45 and 242-49, include various editions of Dickens's works, though nothing particularly distinctive; several presentation copies, as indicated in the title; and the manuscripts of "The Friends of the Lions" (*Household Words*, 2 February 1856) and "Our Commission" (*Household Words*, 11 August 1855). A facsimile of the first page of the manuscript of the former serves as the frontispiece to the catalogue. Also see **2173**.

1956. Knight, Frank & Rutley, Messrs., London, etc. *The Singularly Interesting Freehold Residential Property Known as Gadshill Place, the Home of Charles Dickens from 1857 to 1870.* London, etc.: Messrs. Knight, Frank & Rutley, 1923. 16 pp. + fold-out plan of the property.

Illustrated catalogue of a sale, 26 July 1923, of Dickens's last home. A brief account of Dickens's life, pp. 2-4, is followed by descriptions of the rooms in the house (with dimensions given) and of the other buildings on the property.

1957. Merwin-Clayton Sales Co., New York. *First Editions and Association Copies from the Library of a Prominent New York Lawyer . . . .* New York: Merwin-Clayton Sales Co., 1911, p. 14.

Catalogue of a sale, 27 October 1911, included here only because it is listed in Podeschi (**1509**); the Dickens items, lots 118-24, comprise minor Dickensiana only.

1958. Parke-Bernet Galleries, New York. *Autograph Letters, Manuscripts, and Documents of Three Centuries: Adams, André, Blake, Browne, Burns, Dickens, Eliot, Emerson, Queen Elizabeth, Franklin, Jefferson, Keats, Poe, Washington, and Many Others, Comprising Selections from the Collection of the Late Oliver R. Barrett.* New York: Parke-Bernet Galleries, 1950, pp. 70-81.

Catalogue of a sale, 30 October-1 November 1950. Lot 312 is the Baroness Burdett-Coutts's collection of 554 letters, most from Dickens to herself, 1 July 1839-11 June 1865, originally sold in 1922 (**1996**) with about fifty letters to Mr. or Mrs. Brown (her companion) and a few to other correspondents, as well as ten letters from Catherine Dickens, one from John Dickens to Burdett-Coutts, and about fifty from various correspondents to Dickens, Burdett-Coutts, and others. The collection is itemized, with excerpts from many of the letters, and three facsimile reproductions. Lots 313-15 comprise five other Dickens letters. Also see **2096-97**.

1959. Parke-Bernet Galleries, New York. *Books, Autographs, Drawings, Paintings, Illuminated and Other Manuscripts, etc., Collected by the Late Henry S. Borneman, Philadelphia.* New York: Parke-Bernet Galleries, 1955, pp. 75-77.

Catalogue of a sale, 1-2 November 1955. Dickens items, lots 368-82, include an original oil portrait and alabaster bust of Dickens (artists unknown), and parts and volume editions of various Dickens works.

1960. Parke-Bernet Galleries, New York. *Books from Two Private Libraries . . . Belonging to Mrs. Louis Samter Levy . . . and a New York Collector.* New York: Parke-Bernet Galleries, 1953, pp. 16-23.

Catalogue of a sale, 17-18 February 1953. Dickens items, lots 140-81, include nineteen letters (itemized, with excerpts) to Arthur Ryland, 24 January 1844 to 6 September 1869, and various parts and first editions of Dickens's works, minor as well as major, including one presentation copy.

1961. Parke-Bernet Galleries, New York. "Charles Dickens." In *English and American Books and Manuscripts: The Library of the Late Barton W. Currie of Philadelphia.* New York: Parke-Bernet Galleries, 1963, pp. 29-38.

Catalogue of a sale, 7-8 May 1963. Dickens items, lots 116-47, include a letter to Thomas Chapman, 27 December 1842, along with a heavily corrected four-page manuscript on The Sanatorium, a subscription hospital, apparently the conclusion to an article by Chapman, chairman of Lloyd's Register of Shipping and of the Sanatorium Committee, published, according to the editors of *Pilgrim Letters*, III, 384, in the *Morning Chronicle*, 29 November 1942. The letter and the manuscript have obviously not been located because the editors of *Pilgrim Letters*, III, 402, print only the excerpt given in this sale catalogue (see a photograph, p. 31, of the opened manuscript). Another item listed is a copy in Dickens's hand of three paragraphs from *The Old Curiosity Shop* describing the death of Little Nell's grandfather, addressed to Miss Mary L. Plumb, of Oswego, New York, 16 February 1842, sent to be sold at a fair, "for which Dickens sent his good wishes as well as the Ms." This item is not mentioned in *Pilgrim Letters*. Other items include a two-paragraph passage from *The Old Curiosity Shop* describing the death of Little Nell that Dickens had written out for Mrs. Cornelius C. Felton, undated, apparently sent in a letter to her husband, 20 June 1859; various parts and volume editions of Dickens's works; playbills; three presentation copies; five original pen-and-ink drawings for *Little Dorrit* by J. Mahoney; and Dickensiana. Illustrated. The New York Public Library copy has sale prices written in.

1962. Parke-Bernet Galleries, New York. "Charles Dickens Items." In *Sets in Fine Bindings, [etc.].* New York: Parke-Bernet Galleries, 1938, pp. 36-39.

Catalogue of a sale, 4-5 May 1938, lots 121-29, including Dickens's three-page manuscript of "The Song of the Wreck," his prologue to Wilkie Collins's play *The Lighthouse* (the first page of the prologue is reproduced in facsimile); four Dickens letters (excerpts given, but all in *Pilgrim Letters*); and a hand-painted miniature portrait of Dickens.

1963. Parke-Bernet Galleries, New York. *The Distinguished Collection of First Editions, Autographs, Manuscripts, Original Drawings by and Relating to Dickens Formed by Lewis A. Hird, Englewood, New Jersey.* New York: Parke-Bernet Galleries, 1953. 55 pp.

This catalogue of a sale, 17 November 1953, includes many of Dickens's novels in parts; original drawings for *Pickwick Papers*, *A Tale of Two Cities*, and *A Christmas Carol*; groups of letters to John Leech, Clarkson Stanfield, George Cruikshank, and others; autograph manuscripts of "New Uncommercial Samples: On an Amateur Beat" and of an apology to the American people for opinions expressed in *American Notes* and *Martin Chuzzlewit*; and various mementoes, one-volume first editions, playbills, Dickensiana, and other items. The catalogue contains fifteen illustrations and detailed descriptions of many items.

1964. Parke-Bernet Galleries, New York. *The Eldridge R. Johnson Collection. Part I. Manuscripts, Books and Drawings, Including the Famous Original "Alice" Manuscript and Two Copies of the Rare First [1865] Edition and Other Carroll Books and Autographs; Important Cruikshank Books and Drawings*. New York: Parke-Bernet Galleries, Inc., 1946, pp. 66-69.

This catalogue of a sale, 3-4 April 1946, includes two Dickens letters to George Cruikshank—one, said to be from 1837 (the editors of *Pilgrim Letters*, I, date it [?20 October 1838], p. 441), is about the manuscript of *Oliver Twist* and contains rough sketches on the back for that novel; the other, "probably 1839" (though convincingly dated [16 September 1837] by the editors of *Pilgrim Letters*, I, p. 309) has apparently to do with Dickens's thoughts of resigning from the editorship of *Bentley's Miscellany*, something he did not do until January 1839 (and hence the date attributed to it in this catalogue). Other Dickens items are a pencil drawing by Cruikshank for the front wrappers of the first edition in parts of *Oliver Twist* (illustrated in the catalogue), some sketches by Cruikshank for *Oliver Twist*, a pencil sketch of Dickens as a young man, an incredible nine-volume collection of extra illustrations to Dickens's novels by various artists, and a first edition of *Sketches by Boz* with a pencil tracing by Cruikshank.

1965. Parke-Bernet Galleries, New York. *First Editions, Autograph Manuscripts, Byrne, Byron, Carroll, Dickens, . . . from the Library of Walter P. Chrysler, Jr., New York and Warrenton, Va*. New York: Parke-Bernet Galleries, 1952, pp. 22-37.

Catalogue of a sale, 26-27 February 1952. Dickens items, lots 102-45, fully annotated, include the nine-page autograph manuscript of "On an Amateur Beat" (*The Uncommercial Traveller*), with a facsimile of the first page; a letter on the religious education of children to an unnamed correspondent, 25 July 1839, which the catalogue attributes to Sarah Flower Adams and the editors of *Pilgrim Letters*, I, 567-68, probably correctly, to a Mrs. Godfrey; the original proof sheets of the first edition of *A Christmas Carol*; Dickens's own reading copy of *The Cricket on the Hearth*, with numerous alterations; several presentation copies; numerous parts and volume editions of Dickens's works, minor as well as major; a playbill; an original pen-and-ink sketch for *Martin Chuz-zlewit* by Fred Barnard; and miscellaneous items.

1966. Parke-Bernet Galleries, New York. *First Editions, Incunabula, Bibles, French Illustrated Books, Armorial Bindings, . . . A Remarkable Dickens Collection of Autograph Letters . . . Property of Jacob J. Podell . . . [and] Estate of Mrs. Henry Ford.* New York: Parke-Bernet Galleries, 1952, pp. 54-72.

Catalogue of a sale, 29-30 January 1952. Dickens items, lots 166-84, include eighty-four letters to Mark Lemon, 21 June 1847-25 May 1870; fifty-eight letters to various correspondents; minor manuscripts; twelve original pencil sketches by Hablot K. Browne, George Cruikshank, and other artists; and a variety of mementoes. Entries are heavily annotated and a number of the letters are excerpted. Illustrations include photographs of some mementoes and facsimiles of some letters and manuscripts.

1967. Parke-Bernet Galleries, New York. *First Editions, Manuscripts, Autograph Letters of Charles Dickens: The Renowned Collection Formed by the Late Herman LeRoy Edgar, Dobbs Ferry, New York [Together with Another Collection].* New York: Parke-Bernet Galleries, 1944, pp. 30-114.

Dickens items in this heavily-illustrated catalogue of a sale, 18-19 April 1944, include the manuscript of the Prologue to John Westland Marston's *The Patrician's Daughter*, letters, first and early editions, drawings, playbills, and Dickensiana.

1968. Parke-Bernet Galleries, New York. *First Editions of Charles Dickens . . . from the Library of the Late the Vice-Chancellor Maja Leon Berry . . . and from Other Sources. . . .* New York: Parke-Bernet Galleries, 1963, pp. 31-44.

Catalogue of a sale, 5 February 1963. Dickens items, lots 135-73, are fully annotated and include four letters, an original pencil drawing by Hablot K. Browne, parts and volume editions of Dickens's works, an extra-illustrated *Pickwick Papers* (with two additional letters bound in), and Dickensiana.

1969. Parke-Bernet Galleries, New York. *Rare and Valuable Books, Important Autograph Letters & MSS, Drawings and Paintings: Final Liquidation of the Stock of the Late Gabriel Wells, New York City.* New York: Parke-Bernet Galleries, 1951, pp. 30-41.

Catalogue of a sale, 12-13 November 1951. Dickens items, lots 135-72, are fully annotated and include an autograph manuscript of three dramatic sketches and parts of two others (about 1,300 words) that appears to comprise parts of "a burlesque of the 'Great Exhibition' of 1850," with excerpts and a facsimile of a page of it included; an autograph manuscript of quotations from

The Old Curiosity Shop (about 170 words) that Dickens wrote out for Miss Lucretia Bancroft, Worcester, MA, 6 February 1842; thirty-nine autograph letters from Dickens to various correspondents; parts and volume editions of Dickens's works, with two presentation copies; and a plaster bust of Dickens (artist unknown). Illustrated.

1970. Parke-Bernet Galleries, New York. *Rare Books, Original Drawings, Autograph Letters and Manuscripts Collected by the Late A. Edward Newton, Removed From His Home, Oak Knoll, Daylesford, Pa.* 3 vols. New York: Parke-Bernet Galleries, 1941, I, 185-223.

The Dickens items, lots 485-560, in this annotated and lavishly illustrated catalogue of a sale, 16-18 April 1941, include letters, presentation copies of his works, two drawings for *A Christmas Carol* by John Leech, the Bruton-Patterson copy of *Pickwick* in parts, other rare parts and volume editions of Dickens's works, the proof sheets and "trial" issues of *A Christmas Carol*, watercolor paintings by "Kyd" (Joseph Clayton Clarke) of Dickens characters, and other items. An advanced prospectus for the sale, *The Rare Books and Manuscripts Collected by the Late A. Edward Newton*, was issued by Parke-Bernet Galleries in early 1941. It contains biographical sketches of Newton, particularly as a collector, and lists the principal authors and alludes to the principal items in the collection, including some of the Dickens items mentioned above. Also see **1767** and **2071.**

1971. Parke-Bernet Galleries, New York. *Rare First Editions, Autograph Letters and Manuscripts . . .: The Distinguished Library of Howard J. Sachs, Stamford, Conn.* New York: Parke-Bernet Galleries, 1944, pp. 10-11.

While this catalogue for a sale of 1 February 1944 contains nothing by Dickens himself, it lists (lots 23-26) three autograph manuscripts, George Gissing's introductions to *Martin Chuzzlewit*, *Sketches by Boz*, and *Dombey and Son*, written for the Rochester Edition of Dickens's works (London: Methuen, 1900-01), with autograph corrections, and two letters, one bound into the manuscript of the introduction to *Dombey and Son*, from Gissing to a Mr. Colles, regarding remuneration for the introductions and the Rochester Edition, the other concerning his remuneration for "Prefaces to Dickens's Christmas Books," which have not yet been located. The volumes on *Martin Chuzzlewit*, *Sketches by Boz*, and *Dombey and Son* were never published, the introductions first appearing in Gissing's *Critical Studies of the Works of Charles Dickens* (New York: Greenberg, 1924).

1972. Parke-Bernet Galleries, New York. "Splendid Collection of the Writings of Charles Dickens." In *A Complete Set of "Annals of Sporting," First Editions of English Authors, Dickens, Including "Pickwick Papers," Surtees,*

Ainsworth, Lever, Thackeray, and Others, Mainly in Original Parts or Cloth, Property of Thomas Hatton, Leicester, England. New York: Parke-Bernet Galleries, 1938, pp. 19-42.

Catalogue of a sale, 20 April 1938, of a portion of Hatton's library. Hatton notes in a foreword to the catalogue that his "first *Pickwick* which is included in the sale must rank very high in quality and for unusual 'points,'" the collation of which reveals "numerous elusive points of earliest issue which were previously unknown." The catalogue includes collations for two sets of *Pickwick Papers* in parts, with notes on their special features. One is characterized as "a very fine copy" (lot 64) and the other as "an exceptionally fine copy" (lot 65). Also listed are parts and cloth editions of other Dickens novels; a collection of fifty-nine plays based on Dickens's works (lot 68); a pen and ink sketch by Frederick Barnard for *Martin Chuzzlewit* (lot 79); a "unique copy" of *The Cricket on the Hearth*, with a pink insert advertising the then forthcoming publication of the *Daily News*; the "original autograph manuscript" of George Gissing's introduction to *Bleak House* for the Rochester Edition (1900); and sets of extra illustrations. Illustrated. For other Hatton sales, see American Art Association (**1893, 1906**) and Sotheby & Co. (**1978-79, 1981**). Also see **2151**.

1973. Phillips, International Auctioneers & Valuers, London. *Books, Maps & Manuscripts.* London: Phillips, 2000, p. 58.

Catalogue of a sale, 24 March 2000, that includes item 218, an "Album of carte-de-visite photographs and autographs compiled by Catherine Dickens," including the autographs of Hans Christian Andersen, Wilkie Collins, Harriet Beecher Stowe, Thackeray, Tennyson, and others. Each autograph is mounted beneath the appropriate card, it is indicated, and the autographs were "evidently cut from letters addressed to her." The album is described as a "vivid record of Dickens's circle" and as "a roll-call of those who remained on friendly terms" with Catherine after her separation from Dickens.

1974. Puttick & Simpson, London. "Autograph Letters and Documents." In *Catalogue of Valuable Books, Including the Library of the Late Rev. H. Clementi-Smith . . . and . . . Also an Important Collection of Autograph Letters & Documents.* London: Puttick & Simpson, 1905, pp. 35-44.

Catalogue of a sale, 7-8 June 1905, including seven Dickens letters (lots 465, 467-71, and 502), all to be found in *Pilgrim Letters*, and a note from Thackeray to William Harrison Ainsworth referring to Dickens (lot 562). Also see **2098**.

1975. Puttick & Simpson, London. *Catalogue of Valuable Books . . . , Also Autographs, etc., . . . Also Three Leaves of the Original MS. of Oliver Twist.* London: Puttick and Simpson, 1921, p. 21.

Catalogue of a sale, 22 July 1921. The only Dickens item in the catalogue, lot 330, consists of pp. 17, 18, and 23 of the manuscript of chapter 10 of *Oliver Twist*, containing "many deletions and additions, but varying from the printed text" and "doubtless the first draft." The catalogue notes that Dickens gave these pages to Mrs. Rebecca Ball Wilson, a first cousin on his mother's side, and that they are being sold by "the present representative of the family." A copy of the catalogue in the British Library, London, indicates that the pages were sold to [Charles] Sessler (a Philadelphia bookseller) for £150. Also see **2140**.

1976. Sotheby & Co., London. *Catalogue of a Further Portion of the Well-Known Library, the Property of the Comte de Suzannet, La Petite Chardière, Lausanne, Comprising the Celebrated Collection of Material Concerning Charles Dickens, Including Upwards of One Thousand Autograph Letters, Several Autograph Manuscripts, Letters Relating to Him, Presentation Copies of His Works, and the Earliest Known Portrait of Him.* London: Sotheby & Co., 1938. 111 pp.

A nicely descriptive catalogue, with ten illustrations, for the sale on 11 July 1938 of a portion of the justly famous collection of one of the great Dickens collectors, principally letters that Suzannet had amassed. The collection included 175 letters from Dickens to Thomas Beard, thirty-one to Edmund Yates, seventy-two to John Leech, and forty-five to Georgina Hogarth, as well as Maria Beadnell's album containing early poems by Dickens. The catalogue contains quotations from many of the letters. See **2072, 2092, 2128,** and **2165**.

1977. Sotheby & Co., London. *Catalogue of Autograph Manuscripts and Letters, Original Drawings and First Editions of Charles Dickens, from the Collection of the Late Comte Alain de Suzannet (Removed from La Petite Chardière, Lausanne), the Property of the Comtesse de Suzannet.* London: Sotheby & Co., [1971]. 121 pp.

The sale catalogue of the remaining portion of a magnificent collection, much of which had already been presented to the Dickens House—see Slater (**1524**), who includes this sale catalogue as well as a price list. The sale, 22-23 November 1971, consisted of 325 lots. The catalogue is divided into 1) First and Early Editions of Dickens's Works, 2) Collected Editions, 3) Dickensiana, Biography and Criticism, 4) Bibliography, 5) Original Drawings, 6) Autograph Letters of Dickens, 7) Literary Manuscripts of Dickens, and 8) Manuscripts of Dickensiana (letters and writing by others mentioning Dickens or with Dickensian associations). In a foreword, Michael Slater notes that, while a number of valuable items in the Suzannet collection had been presented to the Dickens House, the sale still contains a number of "great jewels," including manuscript pages of *Pickwick Papers* and *Nicholas Nickleby*, "fine sets" of *Pickwick* in parts, important letters and sets of letters, many original drawings by Hablot K. Browne and other Dickens illustrators, various presentation copies of Dickens's works, and the latest revisions of Dickens's reading version of "Mrs. Gamp." Sixteen illustrations. Also see **2081, 2111,** and **2134.**

1978. Sotheby & Co., London. *Catalogue of the Important Collections Mainly of the Writings of Charles Dickens and of Other XIX Century Authors Forming a Part of the Library of Thomas Hatton, Esq., at Anstey Pastures, Leicester.* London: Sotheby & Co., 1931, pp. 8-23.

The Dickens items in this catalogue of the sale, 30 November-1 December 1931, of the library of a famous collector include parts, first volumes, and later editions of Dickens's work (with an elaborate bibliographical description of a *Pickwick* in parts) and Dickensiana. The copy in the Fales Collection, New York University Library, contains a printed list of prices and purchasers. For other sales of the Hatton collection, see American Art Association (**1893, 1906**), Parke-Bernet Galleries (**1972**), and Sotheby & Co. (**1979, 1981**). Also see **2177.**

1979. Sotheby & Co., London. *Catalogue of the Remaining Library of Thomas Hatton, Esq., Removed from Anstey Pastures, Leicester.* London: Sotheby & Co., 1933, pp. 8-18.

Catalogue of a sale, 20-21 February 1933, of a collection of parts, first volume, and later editions of Dickens's works, Dickensiana, and a few portraits, photographs, and playbills. The copy in the Dickens House Museum, London, has many sale prices written in. Some sale prices are also given in "Mr. T. Hatton's Collection," *Times Literary Supplement,* 9 March 1933, p. 172, where it is also noted that a number of the items sold had originally been in Hatton's 1931 sale (**1978**) but had since "found their way back into his collection." For other sales of the Hatton collection, see American Art Association (**1893, 1906**), Parke-Bernet Galleries (**1972**), and Sotheby & Co. (**1978, 1981**). Also see **2164.**

1980. Sotheby & Co., London. *Catalogue of the Valuable Library and Collection of Drawings and Engravings by George Cruikshank, the Property of J[oseph] H. White, Esq., Comprising English Books of the XIX Century, Particularly Those Illustrated by George Cruikshank and H. K. Browne; . . . A Remarkably Extensive Series of Book Illustrations and Other Engravings by Cruikshank; And an Important Collection of His Original Drawings. . . .* London: Sotheby & Co., 1931, passim.

An auction catalogue of a sale, 2 November 1931, that includes a few first editions of Dickens's works; sets of Cruikshank's illustrations for *Sketches by Boz, Oliver Twist,* and *The Loving Ballad of Lord Bateman;* and an original drawing for *Oliver Twist* with a small pencil portrait of Dickens (lot 311), which is reproduced as the frontispiece to the catalogue. Illustrated. A handwritten note in the margin of the copy in the John F. Dexter Collection (Dex. 197b)–see British Library (**1436**)–indicates that the drawing was sold to A. S. W. Rosenbach for £45. Also see **2176**.

1981. Sotheby & Co., London. *Catalogue of the Valuable Printed Books, Autograph Letters & Historical Documents, Etc., Comprising . . . the Property of Thomas Hatton, Esq. . . . and the Holograph Manuscript of Dickens' Life of Our Lord, the Property of Lady Dickens and of Her Children.* London: Sotheby & Co., 1939, pp. 49-54, 79-80.

Catalogue of a sale of 24-25 July 1939. The Dickens items in the Hatton collection, lots 258-75, include parts and volume editions of several Dickens novels and a copy of *Bleak House* (Rochester Edition) in two volumes with the holograph manuscript of George Gissing's introduction, containing a number of corrections and alterations, a facsimile of a page of which is included. The forty-six-page autograph manuscript of Dickens's *Life of Our Lord* (lot 413) is described in great detail, with a facsimile of the last page of the manuscript and with an explanation, written by Lady Dickens (Henry Fielding Dickens's wife), as to why the work was not published until 1934. The manuscript was sold for £1,400–see "Dickens Ms. Brings £1,400 in London" (**2101**) and "The Sale Room. Dickens's 'Life of Our Lord'" (**2175**). For other sales of the Hatton collection, see American Art Association (**1893, 1906**), Parke-Bernet Galleries (**1972**), and Sotheby & Co. (**1978-79**). Also see **2106** and **2175**.

1982. Sotheby & Co., London. *Catalogue of Valuable Printed Books & Manuscripts, Fine Bindings, Autograph Letters and Historical Documents, &c. . . . .* London: Sotheby & Co., 1929, pp. 38-43, 51-60, 119, 122, 128, 130-31, 169.

An auction catalogue of a sale, 3-7 June 1929, of a number of collections; scattered throughout are first editions, bound and in parts, of Dickens's works, sets of extra illustrations, and Dickensiana. In the copy in the New York Public Library, prices are pencilled in, though there is also a printed list of the sale prices. Other items include a presentation copy of *Oliver Twist* to William C. Macready; nineteen letters from Dickens to some seventeen different correspondents (ca. 1841-70), with excerpts from or summaries of them; an original pencil sketch of Dickens from life by Edward Sheil; a portrait in oils (unsigned); and George Gissing's autograph manuscript, with numerous corrections, of his introduction to Dickens's *Bleak House*, written for the Rochester Edition of Dickens's works but first published in his *Critical Studies of the Works of Charles Dickens* (New York: Greenberg, 1924). A facsimile of the first page of the manuscript is included. Illustrated. Also see **2143** and **2166**.

1983. Sotheby & Co., London. *Catalogue of Valuable Printed Books [and Other Properties]. Also Works of Charles Dickens in the Original Parts, Proof Sheets Corrected by Him, Annotated and Presentation Copies, Including the Property of Miss F. M. Sterling, Home Wood, Hartfield, and the Property of Miss B. M. Orford, Prestatyn, N. Wales,* . . . [etc.]. London: Sotheby & Co., 1926, passim.

Catalogue of a sale, 14-16 June 1926, including corrected page proofs (incomplete) for *Our Mutual Friend*, sold for Miss F. M. Sterling, niece of Marcus Stone, to whom, the catalogue notes, Dickens presented the proofs (lot 635); Dickens's acting copy of J. B. Buckstone's *Uncle John* (lot 636), with both the names of the performers in Dickens's amateur acting company (including his own) and some modifications of the text inserted in Dickens's hand (also sold for Miss Sterling), of which a photographic facsimile of a page is included; first editions in parts (lots 638-47); a few playbills; and letters (excerpts given) to Lady and Sir Joseph Oliffe (lots 741-50), all since printed, as well as editions of Dickens's works inscribed to Lady Oliffe (lots 630-34). Also see **2171**.

1984. Sotheby & Co., London. *Catalogue of Valuable Printed Books, Illuminated and Other Manuscripts, Autograph Letters and Historical Documents, etc.* London: Sotheby & Co., 1930, passim.

Auction catalogue of a sale, 16-19 June 1930, containing various editions of Dickens's works, mainly in parts (pp. 62-64, 90-91, 97-100); letters and undated notes (1845-65) from Dickens to John Thompson, his personal servant, which include, as excerpts indicate, instructions for serving dinner, handling wines, providing theatrical properties, and other matters; four short letters to W. H. Wills (1857-58); an autograph manuscript of seventeen lines on two pages about Mrs. Gamp (*Martin Chuzzlewit*); a page of proof containing revisions and thirty-seven lines entirely rewritten for *Dombey and Son* (pp. 101-04); and other collections of autograph letters by Dickens too numerous to list here (pp. 29, 105-12). Two of the letters and a hand written program for an amateur production of Shakespeare's *The Merry Wives of Windsor* by Dickens's company of amateurs are reproduced in the catalogue. Also see **2142** and **2172**.

1985. Sotheby & Co., London. *Catalogue of Valuable Printed Books, Illuminated & Other Manuscripts, Autograph Letters & Historical Documents, etc. [Comprising Various Properties].* London: Sotheby & Co., 1931, passim.

Catalogue of a sale, 27-28 April 1931, including (lot 503) one page of the autograph manuscript of *Tom Tiddler's Ground* (illustrated in photographic facsimile); a letter (lot 502) from Dickens to Hugh Tilsey, 1 October 1841 (in *Pilgrim Letters*, II, 400); a leaflet advertising the first number of *Pickwick Papers* (lot 372); and several first editions in parts and volume form (lots 373-76). Also see **2091** and **2168**.

1986. Sotheby & Co., London. *Catalogue of Valuable Printed Books, Illuminated Manuscripts, Autograph Letters and Historical Documents, etc., Comprising a Very Interesting Collection of Autograph Letters and Relics of Charles Dickens, Formerly the Property of His Housekeeper, Anne Browne; Presentation Copies of Forster's Life of Charles Dickens . . . , Dickens's Letters . . ., [etc.], the Property of Miss Fannie Crosbie (Deceased), Niece of the Late John Forster, Esq.; Mamie Dickens's Manuscript Copy of Dickens's The Life of Christ. . . .* London: Sotheby & Co., 1935, pp. 24, 27-37, 40-43.

Catalogue of a sale, 22-24 July 1935. Dickens items include various editions of individual works of Dickens; the manuscript of *The Life of Christ* (published as *The Life of Our Lord* in 1934) in Mamie Dickens's hand; Dickensiana; various relics; photographs; letters to Dickens's housekeeper (then Mrs. Cornelius) from Dickens and other members of his family; other Dickens letters; letters of Dickens and John Forster to each other; and letters of Forster to others and others to him. Also see **2156** and **2174**.

1987. Sotheby & Co., London. *Catalogue of Valuable Printed Books, Music, Autograph Letters and Historical Documents . . . .* London: Sotheby & Co., 1964, passim.

Catalogue of a sale, 15-17 December 1964. For Dickens items see lots 16-56, 143-74, 178-80, 556, 560-61, 611-98, and 701-02. These include parts and first volume editions of Dickens's works, Hablot K. Browne's original drawing for an illustration for *Dombey and Son,* a number of Dickens letters, a collection of letters and documents concerning the General Theatrical Fund Association (including the manuscript of Dickens's speech to the organization, 29 March 1847), a tenancy agreement for 1 Devonshire Terrace, Dickens's revised draft of an announcement for *Master Humphrey's Clock,* the holograph manuscript of a playbill for his amateur company's performances of *The Merry Wives of Windsor,* letters written by members of Dickens's family, several letters from John Forster to others (including one to Dickens, early February 1841, praising the death of little Nell as a "literary masterpiece"), nine letters from Dickens and three from Georgina Hogarth to Henry Morley, two other Dickens letters, photographs of Dickens, and Dickensiana. Excerpts are given from some of the letters, and some entries are annotated.

1988. Sotheby & Co., London. "Property of a Gentleman." In *Catalogue of Travel, Navigation and Other Valuable Printed Books, Autograph Letters & Historical Documents . . . [including] A Collection of First Editions of Dickens . . . [and Other Collections] Which Will Be Sold by Auction . . . on Monday,* *the 26th February, 1962, and the Following Day.* . . . London: Sotheby & Co., 1962, pp. 59-63.

Important principally for its incidental reference to an issue of the first edition of Dickens's *The Battle of Life* as a forgery (Lot 266, p. 61), and thus characterized by John Carter (**253**) as Round Two in the establishment of the earliest published version of that Christmas book.

1989. Sotheby & Co., London. "The Property of Miss A. C. Dexter." In *Catalogue of Printed Books, Autograph Letters, etc., . . . and a Collection of Letters of Charles Dickens, the Property of Miss A. C. Dexter.* London: Sotheby & Co., 1945, pp. 33-34.

In this catalogue of a sale, 28-30 May 1945, Miss Dexter's collection, lots 461-72, comprises twenty letters to Peter Cunningham and sixteen letters to other correspondents from Dickens, with brief excerpts from some or brief summaries, all now in *Pilgrim Letters*.

1990. Sotheby & Co., London. "The Property of Mrs. A. Pitt Jones." In *Catalogue of Valuable Printed Books, Autographs Letters and Historical Documents.* . . . London: Sotheby & Co., 1969, p. 68.

Catalogue of a sale, 24 November 1969, of fourteen autograph Dickens letters, 1841-51 and 5 August 1868, and one from 1871 written by Charles Dickens, Jr., to Henry P. Smith. The contents of the letters are summarized. Also see **2160**.

1991. Sotheby Parke Bernet & Co., London. *Catalogue of Autograph Letters, Literary Manuscripts and Historical Documents.* London: Sotheby Parke Bernet & Co., 1979, pp. 110-16.

Catalogue of a sale, 18 and 20 June 1979, including thirty-two letters from Dickens, principally to his solicitors Frederic Ouvry and William J. Farrer, with brief summaries or excerpts, and a few other items—autograph checks, envelopes, etc. (lots 593-636).

1992. Sotheby Parke Bernet & Co., London. *Catalogue of Valuable Autograph Letters, Literary Manuscripts and Historical Documents, Including Sections of Continental and Music Manuscripts.* London: Sotheby Parke Bernet & Co., 1982, pp. 178-79.

Includes three letters (all reprinted in volumes of the *Pilgrim Letters*), and a mahogany occasional table that Dickens used as a prompt table for his amateur theatrical productions. A photograph of the table is reproduced on p. 178.

1993. Sotheby Parke Bernet & Co., London. *Catalogue of Valuable Autograph Letters, Literary Manuscripts & Historical Documents, Volume II.* London: Sotheby Parke Bernet & Co., 1979, pp. 286-97.

Catalogue of a sale, 14 March 1979, including eleven autograph letters from Dickens to various correspondents, with numerous excerpts and photographic facsimiles, as well as a few other items of Dickensiana, including the certificate of his burial in Westminster Abbey.

1994. Sotheby Parke Bernet & Co., London. "Dickens (Charles)." In *Catalogue of Valuable Autograph Letters, Literary Manuscripts, Historical Documents and Literary Relics and Portraits.* [London: Sotheby Parke Bernet & Co., 1977], pp. 176-84.

Lots 323-46 of a sale, 5 and 6 July 1977, comprise a photograph of Dickens, various relics, and eleven letters, facsimiles of and quotations from portions of which are included. These letters are all in *Pilgrim Letters*. One, to Mr. (?) Brinely, 27 July 1841, is corrected in *Pilgrim Letters*, VII, Addenda, as to J. C, Prince, but only an eleven-line excerpt is quoted; a fuller extract is given in XII, 577. Another, to T. J. Thompson, no date, is in *Pilgrim Letters*, VII, Addenda, where it is dated [?21 August 1846].

1995. Sotheby Parke Bernet & Co., London. "Letters by Charles Dickens" and "Dickens (Charles)." In *English Literature Comprising Printed Books, Autograph Letters and Manuscripts, 21-22 July 1983.* [London: Sotheby Parke Bernet & Co., 1983], pp. 66-77, 89-91.

Lots 171-206 (with numerous facsimile reproductions) include fifty-one letters by Dickens, three signed royalty checks, a printed prospectus for his Farewell Readings in St. James's Hall beginning on 11 January 1870, three letters by John Dickens, and an extra-illustrated copy of *Forster* (three volumes expanded to six), which contains 160 autograph letters, seven of which are by Dickens. The catalogue prints excerpts from the letters and indicates previous publication, though some had not then been previously published. Lots 244-49 include first editions of *Master Humphrey's Clock, American Notes, Bleak House* (in parts), two autograph letters, and a silver-plated inkstand.

1996. Sotheby, Wilkinson & Hodge, London. *The Burdett Coutts Library. Catalogue of the Valuable Library, the Property of the Late Baroness Burdett Coutts.* London: Dryden Press: J. Davy & Sons, 1922, passim.

The Dickens items in this sale of 15-17 May 1922 include some presentation copies with inscriptions, the autograph manuscript of *The Haunted Man and the Ghost's Bargain* (with a title page and four pages of memoranda), and a collection of "upwards of six hundred letters from Charles Dickens," 1839-66, addressed to Miss Coutts, each listed individually with excerpts, and a few from her, along with fifty-one letters from Dickens to Mr. or Mrs. Brown, 1843-65, and two to Edward Marjoribanks (1840-41), as well as letters from Catherine Dickens, John Dickens, Charles Dickens, Jr., and Francis Jeffrey Dickens to Miss Coutts. The Coutts letters reappear in a Parke-Bernet Galleries sale in 1950 (**1958**). Most of the letters are now in the Pierpont Morgan Library (**1478**). For descriptions of the sale, see **2079, 2102,** and **2130**.

1997. Sotheby, Wilkinson & Hodge, London. *Catalogue of an Extensive and Interesting Collection of Works by and Relating to Charles Dickens, Formed by J. A. Clark, Esq., the Broadway, London Fields, Comprising First & Other Editions of His Writings, Works by Various Authors, Illustrating His Life and Novels; Extensive Collections of Portraits, Engravings, Play Bills and Magazine Articles; Illustrations to His Works; Autograph Letters, the Rare Music to the Village Coquettes, and Various Memorials Relating to Him, etc.* London: Dryden Press: J. Davy & Sons, 1895. 18 pp.

Catalogue of a sale, 27 April 1895, that included 256 lots of the items described in the extensive title, including thirteen autograph letters (no excerpts given) and the manuscript of "That Other Public," an article by Dickens in *Household Words*, 3 February 1855.

1998. Sotheby, Wilkinson & Hodge, London. *Catalogue of Autograph Letters and Manuscripts, Comprising Original Manuscripts in the Autograph of the Late Wilkie Collins; . . . Autograph Letters of Charles Lamb, Dickens, Thackeray . . . &c; Also two Original Agreements between Charles Dickens & Richard Bentley for Publishing "Barnaby Rudge," &c.* London: Sotheby, Wilkinson & Hodge, 1891, pp. 3-8.

Catalogue of a sale, 3-4 June 1891, containing numerous manuscripts and printed versions (some with revisions in Collins's hand) of Collins's plays and novels; twelve "long and interesting" letters from John Forster to William Harrison Ainsworth, 1842-54, "on literary and other matters," in some of which Forster mentions Dickens; and two agreements between Dickens and Richard Bentley concerning *Barnaby Rudge*, both dated 28 January 1839, as well as a note by Dickens in reference to these agreements. The catalogue also offers six letters from Dickens to Ainsworth, 1841-49.

1999. Sotheby, Wilkinson & Hodge, London. *Catalogue of the Collection of the Works of George Cruikshank, the Property of H. W. Bruton, Esq. (of Gloucester). Comprising a Most Extensive Series of Books Illustrated by Him, in Fine Condition, and Many Handsomely Bound by Celebrated Binders; Proofs before Letters of All His Important Works, Many Being in Unique State; Original Drawings, Including Those Intended to Illustrate His Autobiography; an Almost Complete*

Collection of His Caricatures and Broadsides, Forming a Satirical History of the Early Part of the Present Century, &c. London: Sotheby, Wilkinson & Hodge, 1897, passim.

Catalogue of a sale, 10-12 June 1897, that includes proofs for pretty much everything by Dickens that Cruikshank illustrated as well as the original drawing for the title-page of the second series of *Sketches by Boz*.

2000. Sotheby, Wilkinson & Hodge, London. *Catalogue of the Complete Series of Original Water-Colour Drawings to Charles Dickens' "Old Curiosity Shop," & "Barnaby Rudge," by Hablôt [sic] K. Browne (Phiz), Together with a Fine Series of Original Drawings & Sketches by George Cruikshank, T. Rowlandson, J. Leech, C. Keene and R. Caldecott, &c., from the Collection of a Gentleman.* London: Sotheby, Wilkinson & Hodge, 1897, passim.

Catalogue of a sale, 14 June 1897, including sixty-one of Browne's drawings for *The Old Curiosity Shop* and sixty for *Barnaby Rudge*.

2001. Sotheby, Wilkinson & Hodge, London. *Catalogue of the Important & Valuable Collection of Autograph Letters of the Late F. W. Cosens, Esq. F. S. A.* London: Sotheby, Wilkinson & Hodge, 1890, pp. 4, 8-10.

Catalogue of a sale, 24 July 1890, including a number of Dickens letters (117 to a variety of correspondents, nineteen to Mrs. Trollope or Thomas A. Trollope, and eight to Richard H. Horne), the contents of a few of which are summarized; a few letters by friends of Dickens (one from Hablot K. Browne to an unnamed correspondent asserts that he has "made a bonfire of shoals of Dickens' letters"), and eleven letters from Browne to Cosens concerning the commissioned illustrations to *Little Dorrit, Bleak House,* and *Dombey and Son* that he did for Cosens, 1866-69 (see **1916-17, 2006**).

2002. Sotheby, Wilkinson & Hodge, London. *Catalogue of the Library of the Late Edmund Yates, . . . [With] Works by Tennyson, Thackeray, and Dickens, Including a Portion of Charles Dickens' Correspondence with Edmund Yates. . . .* Sotheby, Wilkinson & Hodge, 1895, passim.

Catalogue of a sale, 21-22 January 1895, of numerous volume editions of Dickens's works and some Dickensiana (lots 109-137, pp. 10-11); thirty-four unitemized letters from Dickens to Yates (lot 200, p. 15); and Dickens's "Writing-Slope" (lot 229, p. 17), given to Yates by Georgina Hogarth after Dickens's death. Also see **2126**.

2003. Sotheby, Wilkinson & Hodge, London. *Catalogue of the Original Drawings to Martin Chuzzlewit, and Other Valuable Drawings, Books & Manuscripts.* London: Dryden Press, 1889. 14 pp.

An annotated catalogue of a sale, 9 July 1889, including the forty drawings by Hablot K. Browne for *Martin Chuzzlewit* and six watercolor drawings illustrating Dickens's works; an original manuscript by Thackeray in prose and verse addressed to "Dear Gamp and Harris" (*Martin Chuzzlewit*); the original proofs of forty-three etchings by Browne for *Pickwick Papers*; the original manuscript of Dickens's only contribution to *Punch* ("Dreadful Hardships, Endured by the Shipwrecked Crew of the 'London' Chiefly for Want of Water"), never published; the manuscript diary of Shirley Brooks for 1864 containing references to Dickens, George Eliot, and others, but mainly to Thackeray and John Leech; three Dickens letters; proofs of fifty-two illustrations to works of Dickens by F. O. C. Darley and Sir John Gilbert; and other items. The copy in the Dickens House Museum, London, has the names of most buyers and the sale prices pencilled in. Also see **2162**.

2004. Sotheby, Wilkinson & Hodge, London. *Catalogue of the Original Manuscripts of Charles Dickens and Wilkie Collins.* London: Dryden Press: J. Davy & Sons, 1890. 16 pp.

A heavily annotated catalogue of a sale, 18 June 1890, including two manuscripts of *The Frozen Deep*—the original, with additions in Dickens's hand, and the prompt-book for the production, with many pages in Dickens's hand. The catalogue also lists manuscripts of Dickens's Prologue to and his "The Song of the Wreck" for Collins's *The Lighthouse*; the manuscript of *The Perils of Certain English Prisoners* by Dickens and Collins, with the original sketch and plans for the story; several playbills for Dickens's amateur productions for charity; and various Collins manuscripts, including those of his major works. Illustrated.

2005. Sotheby, Wilkinson & Hodge, London. *Catalogue of the Splendid and Unique Collection of the Works of George Cruikshank Formed by Captain R. J. H. Douglas, R. N.* London: Sotheby, Wilkinson & Hodge, 1911, passim.

Catalogue of a sale, 9-10 and 13-16 February 1911, including a number of editions of Dickens's works illustrated by Cruikshank.

2006. Sotheby, Wilkinson & Hodge, London. *Catalogue of the Valuable and Extensive Library of Printed Books, Engravings & Drawings of Frederick William Cosens, Esq., Deceased.* . . . London: Sotheby, Wilkinson & Hodge, 1890, pp. 37-38, 87-90.

Catalogue of a sale, 11-22 November 1890, of editions of Dickens's works and Dickensiana (lots 1510-60) but, more importantly, of drawings of Dickens characters by "Kyd" (Joseph Clayton Clarke), lot 1560, and large sets of extra illustrations (forty to sixty-one per novel) made by Hablot K. Browne expressly for Cosens for *Barnaby Rudge, Bleak House, David Copperfield, Dombey and Son, Little Dorrit, Martin Chuzzlewit, Nicholas Nickleby, The Old Curiosity Shop,* and *Pickwick Papers,* lots 661-69, most with Browne's receipts for the payment of £100-£120 for each set of drawings. Sale prices noted in a copy of the catalogue in the New York Public Library indicate that these sold for less than they originally cost—from £48 (for *Little Dorrit*) to £105 (for *Pickwick Papers*).

2007. Sotheby, Wilkinson & Hodge, London. *Catalogue of the Valuable Collection of the Works of George Cruikshank, the Property of the Late William Hughes Hilton, Esq.* London: Sotheby, Wilkinson & Hodge, 1911, passim.

Catalogue of a 377-item sale, 28 July 1911, of works illustrated by Cruikshank, including many of his own, listing various editions of Dickens works illustrated by Cruikshank (items 153-63) and a letter from Dickens to George Cattermole (item 321), concerning Barnaby Rudge's raven, from which an excerpt is quoted (no date given, but the entire letter, dated 28 January 1841, is printed in *Pilgrim Letters,* II, 197-98).

2008. Sotheby, Wilkinson & Hodge, London. *Catalogue of the Valuable Library and Collections of Engraved & Other Portraits and Autograph Letters, the Property of the Well-Known Amateur William Wright, Esq.* London: Dryden Press: J. Davy & Sons, 1899, passim.

The preface to this three-part catalogue of a sale, 12-18 June 1899, claims that the Dickens collection is "the finest and most complete" ever offered for sale, which was perhaps true in 1899. The Dickens section, lots 289-510 (pp. 28-52 of the first part of the catalogue), contains numerous presentation copies, some accompanied by letters of presentation, including the parts of *Pickwick Papers* presented to Mary Hogarth prior to her death; many editions in parts, first bound editions, later editions, and extra-illustrated editions of Dickens's works; the autograph manuscripts of *The Battle of Life* and "Mrs. Gamp with the Strolling Players"; a page of the manuscript of Dickens's early travesty of *Othello;* a one-page manuscript of his contribution to *Punch* entitled "Dreadful Hardships Endured by the Shipwrecked Crew of 'The London' Chiefly for Want of Water" (but never published there); several agreements with publishers; many sets of extra illustrations; original drawings by George Cruikshank, John Leech, George Cattermole, Hablot K. Browne, and "Kyd" (Joseph Clayton Clarke); a portrait of Dickens by W. P. Frith (1859); a couple of Dickens letters; the petty cashbook kept by Dickens while working as a clerk for Edward Blackmore; playbills; a collection of music based on Dickens's works; scrapbooks; relics; and Dickensiana. Among the last are a grangerized copy of *Forster* extended to twelve volumes and containing 119 Dickens letters (not enumerated), letters by others, portraits, playbills, views, and yet more Dickensiana; a grangerized copy of Kitton's *Dickens by Pen and Pencil* (London: Frank T. Sabin, 1889-90), with seven more Dickens letters (not enumerated), portraits, original drawings, playbills, and other items; and a grangerized copy of *Macready's Reminiscences*, edited by Sir Frederick Pollock (2 vols., London: Macmillan, 1875) containing a letter by Dickens.

The third part of the catalogue, "The Collection of Autograph Letters," lists and gives excerpts from four Dickens letters (lots 1147-50), to Chapman & Hall, 28 May 1846; to Edward Chapman, 26 April 1847; to Mark Lemon, 2 July 1856; and to Edward Chapman, n. d. (correctly dated [7 May 1837] in *Pilgrim Letters*, I, 256). Lot 1151 is a set of verses by Dickens, entitled "The Response," addressed to Mark Lemon (text given). In a copy of the catalogue in the New York Public Library, prices and buyers are written in. Also see **1663**, **1695**, **2124**, **2188**, and **2196**.

2009. Sotheby, Wilkinson & Hodge, London. *Catalogue of Valuable & Rare Books and Important Illuminated and Other Manuscripts . . . [and] A Collection of 155 Autograph Letters of Charles Dickens, 1836-1870. . . .* London: Sotheby, Wilkinson & Hodge, 1898, passim.

Catalogue of a sale, 27-31 June 1898. A number of Dickens items were offered on the second day of the sale, principally first editions (lots 324-43), pp. 27-28, but the main collection, "Another Property," pp. 77-81, was auctioned on the fourth day as lot 927, a "highly important collection" of letters from Dickens to various correspondents, all but three of which, the catalogue indicates, were believed to be previously unpublished. Excerpts from several letters are given. Also see **2127**.

2010. Sotheby, Wilkinson & Hodge, London. *Catalogue of Valuable Books and Manuscripts.* A series of catalogues [titles and form of auction house name vary]. London: Dryden Press: J. Davy & Sons, 1905-24; London: Sotheby & Co., 1924- .

Sale catalogues of various private libraries, often several per sale volume, and often including at least a few Dickens items, sometimes illustrated. Occasionally private collections are offered for sale that are significantly or exclusively devoted to first and later editions of Dickens's writings, his autograph letters, manuscripts, and Dickensiana. All listings are decently annotated, with listings of letters usually accompanied by excerpts. The Dickens House library, London, has a good set of the Sotheby sale catalogues, 1905-85, on open shelves, often with sale prices written in, as have the British Library, the New York Public Library, the Library of Congress, and other major research libraries. Among the Sotheby catalogues in the Dickens House will be found the following more important sales:

"The Choice Library of John Neville Cross, Esq.," 29 June-1 July 1905, pp. 8-21.

"A Fine Series of Autograph Letters by Charles Dickens, the Property of Mrs. Walton," and "Relics of Charles Dickens, for Many Years in Use at His Residence at Gad's Hill, the Property of Henry F. Dickens, Esq., K. C." (six items), 13-17 August 1917, pp. 93-95, 109. Also see **2159**.

"The Property of Mrs. C. L. Agnew" (a number of Dickens's letters to Bradbury and Evans, 1840-54), "The Property of M. R. Dawkins, Esq." (six letters from Dickens to John Easthope, 1836 and 1844), "The Property of G. C. Whiteley, Esq." (five pages of Chapter 39 of the manuscript of *Pickwick Papers*), and "Other Properties" (seven additional letters from Dickens to various correspondents), 17-21 December 1928, pp. 34-43. Also see **2119**, **2146**, and **2178**.

For 15-17 December 1930, pp. 3, 31, 82-83, 98-100, 101-02, 109 (various Dickens letters, including nine to Emily Jolly, and editions).

For 15-17 February 1932, pp. 60-63, 68, 70 (first editions), 67 (an oil painting of Dickens bowling), and 71-74 and 78 (letters to various correspondents, including nine to Ainsworth, 1837-42, and several from other members of the Dickens circle to Ainsworth).

"The Property of Admiral Sir Gerald Dickens, K. C. V. O., C. B., C. M. G.," 30-31 May 1949, p. 34 (Charles Dickens's marked prompt books for Boucicault's *Used Up*, Mrs. Inchbald's *Animal Magnetism*, and Charles Dance's *A Wonderful Woman*).

"The Property of Miss Gladys Storey, O. B. E.," 20-21 May 1968, pp. 91-99 (nine letters, twenty-two checks, and the autograph manuscript of Dickens's prospectus for *The Wits' Miscellany*, published as *Bentley's Miscellany*, with Dickens as its first editor). Also see **2180**.

For 5-6 July 1977, pp. 176-84 (various properties, including several relics and letters to various correspondents).

For 24-25 July 1978, pp. 278-86 (various properties, including an autograph inventory of the library and contents of Dickens's house at 1 Devonshire Terrace, May 1844, published in *Pilgrim Letters*, IV, 704-26, and letters to various correspondents, checks, and other items).

For 22-23 July 1985, lot numbers 79-117 (first editions, letters, Dickensiana, and two autograph household account books kept by Dickens for Gad's Hill Place, April 1866-April 1870).

2011. Sotheby, Wilkinson & Hodge, London. *Catalogue of Valuable Printed Books, Illuminated Manuscripts, Autograph Letters and Historical Documents Comprising the Important Collection of the Writings of Charles Dickens, Including an Exceedingly Fine Set of the Pickwick Papers Formed by the Late E. H. Cox, Esq., of Stourbridge, Worcestershire, and Sold by Order of the Executrix . . . [and Other Properties]*. London: Sotheby, Wilkinson & Hodge, 1924, pp. 10-23.

Catalogue of a sale, 15-17 December 1924. The Dickens items, lots 88-176, include numerous parts and first volume editions of his works and feature five complete sets of *Pickwick Papers* in parts, one set of which (lot 98) is collated part by part. Also included are sets of extra illustrations to Dickens's novels, a complete set of proofs of George Cruikshank's illustrations for *Oliver Twist* (lot 118), and playbills. Also see **2170**.

2012. Sotheby, Wilkinson & Hodge, London. *The H. W. Bruton Collections. Catalogue of the Very Choice Collection of Printed Books, Autograph Letters and Book Illustrations, the Property of the Late Henry William Bruton, Esq., Bewick House, Gloucester.* . . . London: Sotheby, Wilkinson & Hodge, 1921, pp. 21-34 and passim.

Catalogue of a sale, 9-10 June 1921, partly of Dickens items (lots 146-212), including parts, first volume, and other editions of Dickens's major and minor writings; several George Cruikshank letters regarding the illustrations for *Sketches by Boz* (excerpts provided) and proofs of his illustrations for *Sketches by Boz* and *Oliver Twist*; a detailed collation of a fine copy of *Pickwick Papers* in parts (the Bruton copy); sets of extra illustrations; copies of various states of the first edition of *A Christmas Carol*; and Dickensiana. Also see lots 393-96 for more Cruikshank illustrations to Dickens's novels. Illustrated.

2013. Sotheby, Wilkinson & Hodge, London. *The Truman Collections: Catalogue of the Collection of the Works of George Cruikshank, the Property of the Late Edwin Truman, Esq., M. R. C. S.* London: Sotheby, Wilkinson & Hodge, 1906, passim.

Catalogue of a sale, 7-12 May 1906, that includes editions of Dickens's works illustrated by Cruikshank, sets of proofs for editions of *Sketches by Boz*, and "Miscellaneous Proofs to Dickens, Ainsworth, etc.," not otherwise explained.

2014. Sotheby's, London. "Session Two." In *English Literature and History, Including The Charles Dickens Archive.* London: Sotheby's, 1999, pp. 81-240.

A sale of 15 July 1999 with several sections of Dickens items. "The Charles Dickens Archive," pp. 81-141 was also published separately as *The Dickens Archive* (London: Sotheby's, 1999, 84 unnumbered pages). Lots 160-87, many multi-itemed, consist mainly of legal papers that had remained in the Dickens family's possession. The documents reveal, the introduction notes, "a portrait of a man of genius equally at home as a man of business or (for all his qualms about it) as a man of law, driven by the need for money and security." It also represents a man determined to have his own way and who, "for the first time in literary history, establishes agreements for authors giving them a share of the copyright of their work and adequately rewarding them for the commercial success of their products." Most of the documents, it is pointed out, have not been published, but many are reproduced in black-and-white or color facsimile in the catalogue, The items are described in considerable detail under three headings: I, "Publishing Agreements and Related Papers" (for *Sketches by*

Boz, Pickwick Papers, Bentley's Miscellany and *Oliver Twist, Memoirs of Joseph Grimaldi, Pic Nic Papers, Master Humphrey's Clock, Barnaby Rudge, Household Words* and its dissolution, *A Tale of Two Cities, All the Year Round, Great Expectations, Our Mutual Friend,* the 1867-68 American reading tour, *Edwin Drood,* and lesser works); II, "Domestic Papers" (such as life insurance policies and papers relating to the Gad's Hill property); and III, "Posthumous Papers" (including documents connected with the *Hogarth-Dickens Letters* and the estate of Mamie Dickens). Prices of the items that sold are noted in a copy of the catalogue in the Dickens House, but there is a further handwritten note in this copy stating that a "majority of the papers failed to reach their reserve and were unsold." Nevertheless, the detailed annotation of the documents is valuable in giving a good idea of the contents of the papers, as are the numerous photographs of them.

Another section, "[William] Charles Kent," pp. 142-47, lots 188-93, itemizes "the surviving archive and library" of Kent, a journalist and editor and one of Dickens's writer's for *Household Words.* Included are numerous letters to Kent from Georgina Hogarth, W. H. Wills, John Forster, Henry Fielding Dickens, Charles Dickens, Jr., Mamie Dickens, Kate Dickens, other members of the Dickens family, Blanchard Jerrold and others, some with reference to Dickens. "Other Properties," pp. 148-56, lots 194-210, includes bound editions of individual Dickens works and collected editions, two previously published letters, and watercolor drawings of Dickens characters by "Kyd" (Joseph Clayton Clarke) for a deck of playing cards. "The Bleak House Museum, Broadstairs," pp. 157-65, lots 211-30, includes items from the museum's collection—various relics (a chair, a shirt, an inkstand and a pen tray, a walking stick, spoons, etc.), a page of proof for a periodical article (not identified, but probably by Percy Fitzgerald; a photographic facsimile is reproduced on p. 158), books by and about Dickens, letters by Georgina Hogarth and three children of Dickens, a photograph of Ellen Ternan, and a collection of playbills and theater programs.

Also see Patten (**2149**), Williams (**2192**), and Woudhuysen (**2195**). The archive was eventually sold to the British Library, London—see Andrews (**1589**).

2015. Sotheby's, London. *English Literature and History.* London: Sotheby's, 2000, pp. 36-41.

Catalogue of a sale, 24 February 2000. Lots 49-58 include an autograph letter from Dickens to Joseph Crook, 10 December 1856 (lot 49), included in *Pilgrim Letters,* XII, Appendix A, pp. 673-74. Lot 52 is a proof page with numerous corrections and revisions in Dickens's hand of a periodical article by another author, unidentified, but with a note (obviously not in Dickens's hand) that it was "Given me by Percy Fitzgerald June 1889." Also listed are some Dickens relics (lots 53-54, 56-58) and a small portrait of Catherine Dickens (lot 55) "in pencil and wash," dated 1836.

2016. Sotheby's, London. *The Library of Horace N. Pym (1844-1896)*. London: Sotheby's, 1996, passim.

Catalogue of a sale, 23 April 1996. In the introduction, "Horace N. Pym: Aspects of a Victorian Bookman," pp. 11-15, John Pym, a descendent, indicates that Pym's love of Dickens, whom he never had a chance to meet, "was his abiding passion." Pym did become a friend of Georgina Hogarth and Mamie Dickens, however, with both of whom he "conducted an animated correspondence." The Dickens items in the catalogue, pp. 23-29, include a few volumes from Dickens's library; a letter from Wilkie Collins to Pym, 5 December 1887, mentioning that Dickens was one of the first subscribers to Collins's life of his father (lot 32); four preliminary pencil sketches by George Cattermole for *Master Humphrey's Clock* (lot 40); a letter from Mamie Dickens to Pym, 26 October (no year), thanking him for his condolences on the death of one of her brothers (lot 43); an extra-illustrated *Pickwick Papers*, compiled by Pym, with watercolor drawings by F. W. Pailthorpe (lot 44); portraits of young Dickens and his wife by Samuel Laurence (lot 45—reproduced in black and white); and a variety of lesser items and Dickensiana. Illustrated. Also see **1710, 2191**, and **2194**.

2017. Sotheby's, London. "The Property of Various Owners." In *English Literature and History, Comprising Printed Books, Autograph Letters and Manuscripts.* . . . London: Sotheby's, 1987, pp. 38-51.

Catalogue of a sale, 23-24 July 1987. The Dickens items, lots 47-63, which include several editions of individual works, are principally letters, with excerpts given. All are reprinted in *Pilgrim Letters* (and a few, earlier, in *Nonesuch Letters*). Illustrated.

2018. Sotheby's, New York. *The Library of Richard Manney*. New York: Sotheby's, [1991], passim.

A handsome, hard-cover catalogue of the library of a collector who describes his collection, auctioned off on 11 October 1991, as "a very personal one" in his introduction. The Dickens items, lots 75-105, include the manuscript of *The Haunted Man and the Ghost's Bargain*, bound along with "four pages of outline notes" and a letter to Angela Burdett Coutts, 13 February 1850, that accompanied the manuscript when Dickens sent it to her (this item sold for $308,000); the manuscript of Dickens's "In Memoriam," his eulogy of Thackeray, published in the *Cornhill Magazine*, 9 (February 1864), 129-32, along with his letter to George Smith, 15 January 1864, presenting him with the manuscript (this lot sold for $23,100); and numerous editions of Dickens's works in parts issue or volume form, all with scholarly bibliographical descriptions and other information. The catalogue contains a number of color illustrations, including two pages of the manuscript of *The Haunted Man*, one of the manuscript of "In Memoriam," and the letter to Miss Coutts. Reported by William Rees-Moog in "The Return of the Folios," *Times Literary Supplement*, 11 October 1991, p. 31, and Edward Preston in "When Found: 'The Haunted Man' Goes under the Hammer," *Dickensian*, 87 (1991), 183.

2019. Thomas & Homan, Messrs., auctioneers, Rochester, Eng. *Catalogue of the Household Furniture, Linen, about 200 Dozen of Superior Wines and Liquors, China, Glass, Horse, Carriages, Green-house Plants, and Other Effects of the Late Charles Dickens*. Rochester, Eng.: Messrs. Thomas and Homan, [1870]. 40 pp.

Catalogue of the 10-13 August 1870 sale of many of the Dickens household possessions, everything from birch brooms and flower pots to bottles of old port. The contents are organized by locations—the yard, meadow, garden, conservatory, coach house and stables, chalet, kitchen and adjoining rooms, servants and family bedrooms, dining room, billiard room, drawing room, library, halls, bathroom, servants' hall, and wine cellar, with special sections on plate, wine, china, and linens. Collins (**8**) notes that a copy in the British Library has the buyers' names and prices written in. See Christie, Manson & Woods (**1943**) and Henry Sotheran & Co. (**2055**) for other sales of Dickens's possessions. Also see **2110**, **2113**, and **2158**.

6B. BOOKSELLERS' CATALOGUES

Note: Also see **Booksellers' catalogues** in part 2 of the subject index.

2020. Argosy Book Stores, New York. *Charles Dickens: First Editions.* New York: Argosy Book Stores, [ca. 1950?].

Podeschi (**1509**), p. 360, notes that items in the catalogue were for sale.

2021. Borg, James M., and Kathleen Lamb. *A Dickens Miscellany.* Chicago: James M. Borg, Antiquarian Bookseller, 1978. 97 pp.

A bookseller's catalogue (with prices) of various editions of Dickens's works, including some in parts, and also of letters and association items, illustrations and pictorial Dickensiana, biographical and critical studies, parodies and satires, and bibliographies and other reference works.

2022. Dawson's Book Shop, Los Angeles. *Books from the Library of Charles Dickens, Together with Autograph Letters, Books and Pamphlets by Charles Dickens and Other Books of the Dickens Period from the Langstroth Collections.* Catalogue 323. Los Angeles: Dawson's Book Shop, [1961]. [32 pp.].

Notes that Charles and James Langstroth were book collectors who had been classmates of A. S. W. Rosenbach, the noted Dickens collector, at the University of Pennsylvania. The catalogue lists some forty-eight works from Dickens's library; twelve autograph letters from Dickens and letters written by Frederick Dickens, John Forster, and others; a set of prime *Pickwick* in parts, originally compiled by Thomas Hatton; various editions of Dickens's works, many in parts; sets of extra illustrations; playbills; a copy of B. W. Matz's two-volume *The Life of Charles Dickens* (London: Chapman and Hall, 1911), with original letters bound in; Dickensiana; and several George Cruikshank and William Harrison Ainsworth items.

2023. "Dickensiana." Tavistock Books Web site, Almeida, CA.
   http://www.tavbooks.com.

The Web site of Tavistock Books, a firm specializing in editions and studies of Dickens. As of 17 March 2003, the Web site lists 987 Dickens items, with prices.

2024. Dodd, Robert H., bookseller, New York. *Cruikshankiana: A Choice Collection of Books Illustrated by George Cruikshank, Together with Original Water-Colors, Pen and Pencil Drawings, Etchings, Caricatures and Original Proofs.* Catalogue 22. New York: Robert H. Dodd, December 1916, pp. 28-29, 40.

Includes first editions of *Sketches by Boz,* first and second series, and a complete set of twenty-eight plates of proofs for *Sketches by Boz.* Illustrated. The catalogue begins with an essay, "Cruikshank in America," by Arthur B. Maurice, pp. 3-9.

2025. Dutton, E. P., and Company, New York. *A Catalogue of First Editions of the Works of Charles Dickens and Dickensiana from the Library of a Discriminating Collector Including the Famous "Coggeshall" Pickwick Papers.* New York: E. P. Dutton and Company, n. d. 13 pp.

Fairly brief descriptions of a number of editions in parts, presentation copies, and Dickensiana, with prices.

2026. Edwards, Francis, bookseller, London. *George Cruikshank: Books, Drawings, Prints.* London: Francis Edwards, bookseller, 1907, passim.

There are seven Dickens items in this book catalogue with prices.

2027. Heartman, Charles F. *Americana . . . [and] An Unusual Collection of Dickensiana.* Catalogue 151. New Orleans, LA: Charles F. Heartman, 1952.

Podeschi (**1509**), p. 376, notes that items 168-204 concern Dickens.

2028. Heritage Book Shop, Inc., Los Angeles. *Charles Dickens.* Comp. Christina Michaud and Lee Biondi. Catalogue 206. Los Angeles: Heritage Book Shop, Inc., [October 1999]. 108 pp.

A beautifully illustrated bookseller's catalogue of 227 numbered items, 178 of which consist of various editions, including a number of copies of editions in parts and others in the original cloth bindings, as well as translations, of major works, selected minor works, and sets, with numerous bibliographical and publication details. The catalogue also includes four Dickens letters (items 179-81, 183). Two previously unpublished—to Thomas Mitton, 31 January 1843, and to John Overs, 20 May 1844—have since been published in *Pilgrim Letters,* XII, Appendix A, pp. 585 and 590-91. In a third letter, to Thomas Adolphus Trollope, 8 November 1867, not in *Pilgrim Letters,* Dickens, as paraphrased in the catalogue, "thanks Trollope for his 'kind note' and reminds him he has already sent his love via Trollope's (now more famous) brother Anthony." Item 184 consists of 131 autograph letters "by and to Charles Dickens, his friends, and his family," varying "from personal reminiscences of Dickens to matters of routine correspondence," though none apparently is actually by Dickens himself. Highlighted is "a twelve-page letter from R. W. Buss to John Forster, reflecting on Dickens's involvement in The Pickwick Papers and his rejection of Buss's illustrations for that work," with substantial excerpts provided. In addition, the catalogue offers some Dickensiana, reference works, and original art, the last consisting of a pencil drawing of "Mr. Pecksniff on His Mission" for *Martin Chuzzlewit* (item 189); seven drypoint etchings by Gerald M. Burn of Dickensian places (item 190); oil portraits of Dickens by Samuel Drummond, ca. 1836-37 (item 197), and Henry Woodhouse, ca. 1860s (item 218), illustrated in color on, respectively, the front and back covers of the catalogue; eleven original drawings for the Household Edition (1877-80) of *Little Dorrit* by Charles Green and J. Mahoney (item 201); a number of drawings by F. W. Pailthorpe for *Pickwick Papers* and *Great Expectations* (items 208, 209); and a collection of thirty-seven "mostly original" photographs of Dickens covering forty-years There is also a list of "References Cited." This Dickens catalogue was posted online at http://www.heritagebookshop.com but is no longer available there, though a successor may be now or at some future date. On this Web site, a search for "Dickens" on 17 March 2003 produced 193 Dickens works and twenty studies of Dickens.

2029. Heritage Book Shop, Los Angeles. *Charles Dickens.* Comp. Lee Biondi. Catalogue 181. Los Angeles: Heritage Book Shop, [1991]. 36 pp.

The volumes listed include collected editions, various editions of individual works, including some editions in parts, and one letter, with descriptions and useful notes. Illustrated with portraits of Dickens.

2030. Heritage Book Shop, Inc., Los Angeles. *Charles Dickens.* Comp. Lee Biondi. Catalogue 192. Los Angeles: Heritage Book Shop, Inc., [1993]. 62 pp.

Includes collected editions, various editions of individual works, Dickensiana, reference works, and a few letters, including one to an unnamed correspondent, 23 October 1865, identified in *Pilgrim Letters*, XI, 101, as Frederick Lehmann, thanking him for a gift of a "noble dog"; and another to an unnamed correspondent, 4 May 1869, identified in *Pilgrim Letters*, XII, 349, as Messrs. Banton & Mackrell, about his son Sidney's debts. Annotations are full. Illustrated.

2031. Jarndyce Antiquarian Booksellers, London. *Charles Dickens.* Comp. Brian Lake and Janet Nassau, in association with Christopher Johnson. Catalogue XLV. London: Jarndyce Antiquarian Booksellers, Summer 1986. 90 unnumbered pp.

Lists 788 items, most with only brief descriptions, including collected editions, various editions of individual works (some in parts or original cloth), translations, adaptations of every sort, sets of extra illustrations, photographs of Dickens, playbills, music based on Dickens's works, and a variety of memorabilia, Dickensiana, and ephemera. Also included are a copy of *A Christmas Carol* with illustrations by Arthur Rackham (1915), with "a signed sketch in ink by Rackham of a version of the Marley door knocker different from that reproduced in the edition" (item 193) and illustrated two pages on in the catalogue; a manuscript by William R. Hughes of an essay, "Notes of a Dickens Collector," describing his "early pleasure in reading Dickens' works and in building up his collection" (item 656); a grangerized copy (item 670) of J. W. T. Ley's *The Dickens Circle* (London: Chapman and Hall, 1918); and the W. H. Collis Dickens Collection, an album "indexed and containing cuttings, notes and correspondence with other Dickens scholars and collectors, including Thomas Hatton, A. H. Cleaver, and E. H. Strange, discussing points of Dickens bibliography," the whole containing, the catalogue notes, "a wealth of unpublished bibliographical information," and a set of exercise books recording advertisements in parts issues of Dickens's novels (items 715, 716). Illustrated.

2032. Jarndyce Antiquarian Booksellers, London. *Charles Dickens: A Selection of First and Early Editions.* Comp. Brian Lake and Janet Nassau. Catalogue LXXIX. London: Jarndyce Antiquarian Booksellers, Summer 1991. 22 unnumbered pp.

Lists seventy-one items, with useful descriptions, principally first and early bound editions of Dickens works, along with some Dickensiana.

2033. Jarndyce Antiquarian Booksellers, London. *Charles Dickens in Original Cloth.* Comp. Brian Lake and Janet Nassau. Catalogue 50. London: Jarndyce Antiquarian Booksellers, Summer 1987. 42 pp.

A bookseller's catalogue of 107 numbered items, almost entirely volumes of individual Dickens works in the original cloth bindings of the volume editions, with brief bibliographical descriptions. In an introduction, pp. 7-9, the compilers comment on the scarcity of volumes of Dickens's works "in the original cloth." Illustrated.

2034. Jarndyce Antiquarian Booksellers, London. *Dickens.* Comp. Brian Lake and Janet Nassau, in association with Christopher Johnson. Catalogue 33. London: Jarndyce Antiquarian Booksellers, Spring-Summer 1984. 63 unnumbered pp.

Lists 605 items, briefly described, including collected editions, various editions of individual works (some in parts or original cloth), a variety of adaptations, sets of extra illustrations, playbills, memorabilia, Dickensiana, and ephemera. Also included are drawings for *Oliver Twist* done by George Cruikshank in 1866 for, as Cruikshank indicates, a "Mr Cousens" (undoubtedly

F. W. Cosens–see **1916-17, 2001, 2006**), for which Cruikshank was to be paid 100 guineas (item 94), the three volumes of the *Nonesuch Letters* with notes and corrections (partially erased) by the editors of the *Pilgrim Letters* in the preparation of that edition (item 350), and a set of eleven original water-color sketches of Dickens characters (item 369) by "Kyd" (Joseph Clayton Clarke). Illustrated.

2035. Jarndyce Antiquarian Booksellers, London. *The Dickens Catalogue*. Comp. Brian Lake and Janet Nassau. Catalogue LXI. London: Jarndyce Antiquarian Booksellers, Spring 1989. 142 unnumbered pp.

A bookseller's catalogue of 1,008 numbered items, comprising collected editions, parts and volume editions (many in the original cloth) of individual works, translations, a variety of adaptations, original drawings (see items 226, 366), proofs of illustrations, sets of extra illustrations, theater programs and playbills, music based on Dickens's works, photographs of Dickens, memorabilia, and a huge variety of Dickensiana. The catalogue contains several "Kyd" (Joseph Clayton Clarke) items: a first edition of *Martin Chuzzlewit* with seven of his watercolor drawings of characters from the novel bound in (312), an unpublished illustrated manuscript (ca. 1912) by the same artist of a sequel to *A Christmas Carol* (item 684, with illustrations from it reproduced on the previous and following page) entitled "Afterwards: Being a Somewhat Unexpected Sequel to 'A Christmas Carol'" (for its publication in a facsimile edition, see **2038**), and a number of his original illustrations of characters in Dickens's works (items 685-703). The catalogue also lists a manuscript by William R. Hughes (see **2031**); the W. H. Collis Dickens Collection, (see **2031**); three original drawings by Hablot K. Browne for *Martin Chuzzlewit* (items 991-93)and one for *Nicholas Nickleby* (item 182) and six original drawings by John Leech for *Cricket on the Hearth* (items 994-99). Illustrated.

2036. Jarndyce Antiquarian Booksellers, London. *The Dickens Catalogue*. Comp. Brian Lake and Janet Nassau. Catalogue LXXI. London: Jarndyce Antiquarian Booksellers, Autumn 1990. 130 unnumbered pp.

A bookseller's catalogue of 800 numbered items, usually briefly described, comprising collected editions, parts and volume editions (some in the original cloth) of individual works, translations, various adaptations, sets of extra illustrations and proofs of illustrations, photographs of Dickens, theater programs and playbills, music based on Dickens's works, and a large quantity of Dickensiana. The catalogue also offers a few original drawings of Dickens characters (items 599-605) by "Kyd" (Joseph Clayton Clarke); a carbon fair copy typescript of Charles Dickens Jr.'s "Personal Reminiscences of Charles Dickens" (item 642), the "text of a lecture probably delivered in the early 1890s," according to the catalogue; and a manuscript by William R. Hughes (see **2031**) of which a facsimile of the first page is included (item 776). Illustrated.

2037. Jarndyce Antiquarian Booksellers, London. *The Dickens Catalogue.* Comp. Brian Lake and Janet Nassau. Catalogue LXXXIII. London: Jarndyce Antiquarian Booksellers, Winter, 1991-92. 142 unnumbered pp.

A bookseller's catalogue of 879 numbered items, usually briefly described, comprising collected editions, parts and volume editions (some in the original cloth) of individual works, translations, a variety of adaptations, sets of extra illustrations and proofs of illustrations, photographs of Dickens, theater programs and playbills, music based on Dickens's works, and many items of Dickensiana. The catalogue also lists three original unpublished drawings by Frederick W. Pailthorpe for *Pickwick Papers* (items 69-71), original watercolors (items 570-71) by "Kyd" (Joseph Clayton Clarke), four original illustrations by an unknown artist for *Great Expectations* (item 358) inserted into an 1866 edition of the novel, a typescript of reminiscences of his father by Charles Dickens, Jr. (see **2036**), a manuscript of a 1917 lecture on Gabriel Grubb (*Pickwick Papers*) by William Glossip (item 95), a manuscript of an apparently unpublished essay (ca. 1920) by Cumberland Clark entitled "Charles Dickens as an Essayist" (item 602), two files of working notes and clippings for a biography and bibliography of Frederic G. Kitton by Grenville Cook (item 711), and the W. H. Collis Dickens Collection (see **2031**). Illustrated.

2038. Jarndyce Antiquarian Booksellers, London. *The Dickens Catalogue.* Comp. Brian Lake and Janet Nassau. Catalogue XCVI. London: Jarndyce Antiquarian Booksellers, Winter 1993/94. 100 unnumbered pp.

Lists 691 items for sale–a variety of collected editions, editions of individual works (some in parts or original cloth), translations, adaptations of every sort, sets of extra illustrations and proofs of illustrations, music based on Dickens's works, photographs of Dickens, a watercolor sketch (item 402) of Nancy (*Oliver Twist*) by "Kyd" (Joseph Clayton Clarke), the original well-known watercolor caricature of Dickens (item 408) by "Spy" (Leslie Ward), a watercolor portrait of Dickens (1889) by James Wallace (item 412), the W. H. Collis Dickens Collection (see **2031**), and a large variety of Dickensiana. The catalogue also lists (451) and advertises (on the inside back cover) a facsimile limited edition of *Afterwards: Being a Somewhat Unexpected Sequel to "A Christmas Carol,"* by "Kyd" (Joseph Clayton Clarke), the two illustrations for which are reproduced on the back cover and the final page of the catalogue. The manuscript itself was offered for sale in an earlier and in later Jarndyce catalogues(see **2035, 2039, 2041**). Illustrated.

2039. Jarndyce Antiquarian Booksellers, London. *The Dickens Catalogue.* Comp. Brian Lake and Janet Nassau. Catalogue CXXXI. London: Jarndyce Antiquarian Booksellers, Summer 1999. 196 unnumbered pp.

A bookseller's catalogue of 1,811 numbered items, usually briefly described, comprising collected editions, parts and volume editions (some in the original cloth) of individual works, translations, a variety of adaptations, sets of extra illustrations and proofs of illustrations, photographs of Dickens, theater programs and playbills, music based on Dickens's works, and a variety of Dickensiana and ephemera. Original works of art include six pencil drawings by Hablot K. Browne for *Nicholas Nickleby* (items 216-21), two by John Leech for *The Cricket on the Hearth* (items 360, 361), four (items 95, 264, 457, 511) by "Kyd" (Joseph Clayton Clarke) and the "Kyd" manuscript (see **2035**), the three by Pailthorpe for *Pickwick Papers* (see **2037**), and one by Edward Dalziel for *Little Dorrit* (item 549). Also included are a sketch of Fort House (Broadstairs) by Joseph Pettit (item 895), a pencil sketch of Dickens by George Cruikshank signed by both him and Dickens, ca. 1838 (item 931), and lesser works (932, 933, 935). Other items include John Dighton's duplicated post-production typescript for the 1947 film of *Nicholas Nickleby* (item 226), the Dickens-Jerrold archive (see **2041**), the manuscript by William Glossip (see **2037**), and a British Museum Library book application slip filled out by Dickens (item 908) for *Women: Thoughts on the Times but Chiefly on the Profligacy of Our Women* (1779), a facsimile of which is included.

The catalogue offers several Dickens letters, with excerpts given and a few facsimile reproductions. Six of these letters had not been previously published when the catalogue was issued, but all are included in Appendix A in volume XII of *Pilgrim Letters*. These include letters to the Reverend Sydney Smith, 16 April 1841; to Charles Manby, 7 February 1850; to Joseph Langford, 2 July 1857 (reproduced in facsimile) and 23 November 1857; to Professor [David T.] Ansted, 28 February 1860; and to Mrs. John Forster, 18 July 1861–see *Pilgrim Letters*, XII, 575, 621, 678-79, 680, 689-90, and 691.

The catalogue also offers a few letters regarding Dickens written by others, with excerpts or summaries provided, including a letter from Georgina Hogarth to a Miss Greville, 8 February 1851 (item 921) on amateur theatrical matters and mentioning the illness of Dickens's daughter Dora; a letter from Luke Fildes to Frederick Chapman, 30 July 1870, on a drawing for the frontispiece to *Edwin Drood* (item 927); a letter from Joseph W. Chitty to Frederick Chapman about the copyright of *Forster*, 10 July 1876 (item 928); and a letter from Daniel Maclise to Messrs. Chapman & Hall, 23 May 1839, acknowledging payment for his well-known portrait of Dickens (item 930). Illustrated.

2040. Jarndyce Antiquarian Booksellers, London. *The Dickens Catalogue.* Comp. Helen Smith. Catalogue CXLV. London: Jarndyce Antiquarian Booksellers, Winter, 2001-02. 208 unnumbered pp.

A bookseller's catalogue of 1,842 numbered items, usually briefly described, and, like earlier Jarndyce catalogues, comprising collected editions, parts and volume editions (some in the original cloth) of individual works, translations, a variety of adaptations, sets of extra illustrations and proofs of illustrations, photographs of Dickens, theater programs and playbills, music based on Dickens's works, and a variety of Dickensiana and ephemera. Original works of art include drawings by George Cruikshank, including a pencil sketch of Dickens signed by both him and Dickens, ca. 1838, as well as drawings by John Leech, "Kyd" (Joseph Clayton Clarke), Frederick W. Pailthorpe, and H. B. Andrews.

The catalogue offers several Dickens letters, with excerpts given. Some have been included in the twelve volumes of the *Pilgrim Letters*, but others are still unpublished. The latter include a letter to J. Palgrave Simpson, 8 October 1855 (item 9, here paraphrased); another to William Kelly, 3 October 1858 (item 11, reproduced in facsimile); and yet another to Peter Royal, 11 May 1863 (item 16, summarized here).

Other manuscripts not included in previous Jarndyce catalogues include the articles of agreement between Edward Blackmore and Charles Potter, one of his clerks, 10 March 1827, signed, as witnesses, by George Lear and Dickens, fellow clerks at Ellis and Blackmore, solicitors (item 2); the Gad's Hill cellar book, a list of casks of wine, brandy, and whiskey, begun by Dickens on 6 June 1870, three days before his death (item 3); and an anonymous lecture entitled "Charles Dickens, His Social & Religious Message" (item 1077). Three other interesting items are also offered for sale. The first is an album kept by Mary Boyle (item 1079), a close friend of Dickens from late 1849 on. The second is an archive of scripts, posters, and other memorabilia connected with a number of productions of plays based on Dickens's works by the Dickensian Tabard Players, founded by Ross Barrington in 1925 (item 1082). Only one of these productions is recorded in Bolton (**676**), the cataloguer points out. The third is an archive consisting of a number of manuscripts and notes for articles and books about Dickens by John Cuming Walters, 1907-33, as well as ephemera concerning the Dickens Fellowship (of which Walters became president in 1910), 1908-20 (items 1088-1113). Illustrated.

2041. Jarndyce Antiquarian Booksellers, London. *The Dickens Catalogue.* Comp. Kate Hunter with the assistance of Helen Smith and Brian Lake. Catalogue CXIII. London: Jarndyce Antiquarian Booksellers, Summer 1996. 185 unnumbered pp.

A bookseller's catalogue of 1,766 numbered items, usually briefly described, comprising collected editions, parts and volume editions (some in the original cloth) of individual works, translations, adaptations of every sort, sets of extra illustrations and proofs of illustrations, photographs of Dickens, theater programs and playbills, music based on Dickens's works, the "Kyd" manuscript (see **2035**) and other "Kyd" (Joseph Clayton Clarke) drawings (items 150, 408, 929), the Pailthorpe drawings for *Pickwick Papers* (see **2037**), the remaining three of John Leech's drawings for *The Cricket on the Hearth* (see **2035**), other original drawings (see items 925, 926, 940, 1751), a first edition of Wilkie Collins's *The Frozen Deep* (1866) with corrections in a hand other than Collins's but "clearly authorial" (item 795) a page of which is included in facsimile, the typescript of Charles Dickens Jr.'s "Personal Reminiscences of Charles Dickens" (see **2036**), a "Collection of 180 Typewritten Copies of Letters" (item 771) from Dickens to Chapman and Hall and to Wilkie Collins and from John Dickens to Chapman and Hall (of which "one or two," the catalogue compilers claim, "have escaped publication" in *Pilgrim Letters*), and a huge variety of Dickensiana.

Also included are two Dickens letters, with excerpts or summaries provided. The first is to John Major, 3 November 1840 (item 955), the last page of which is reproduced (the letter appears in full in *Pilgrim Letters*, II, 145). The second, to Mrs. Richard Johns, 18 November 1854 (item 956), is included in *Pilgrim Letters*, XII, Appendix A, pp. 659-60. There are also letters concerning Dickens, all with excerpts or summaries provided, from Wilkie Collins, Georgina Hogarth, Henry Fielding Dickens, Daniel Maclise, W. H. Wills, and Edmund Yates to various correspondents (items 798, 957, 959, 961, 963, 964); a letter from Leigh Hunt to Dickens, 16 August [1852], offering a poem for publication in *Household Words* (item 960); an "archive of material" relating to John Cuming Walters's notes for and manuscripts of a number of his writings on Dickens (items 1616-45); and a collection of material, "Dickens & the Jerrolds: An Archive" (item 954), including the manuscript of all but two pages of Dickens's recollections of his last meeting with Douglas Jerrold, nineteen letters from Douglas Jerrold to Dickens (1843-49), thirty-three letters from William Blanchard Jerrold to various correspondents, and forty-seven letters from a number of other correspondents. The archive also contains three letters from Dickens—to Samuel Laman Blanchard, 9 February 1839; to Douglas Jerrold, 9 July 1845; and to William Blanchard Jerrold, 11 January 1859, with excerpts given (all are in *Pilgrim Letters* volumes).

An "Introductory Note on the Collected Editions of Dickens' Works Published During His Lifetime" describes and lists the individual volumes, with publication dates, in the Cheap Edition (1847-64), the Library Edition (1858-59), the Illustrated Library Edition (1861-74), the Charles Dickens Edition (1867-75), and the People's Edition (1865-67). Illustrated.

2042. Jarndyce Antiquarian Booksellers, London. *The Essential Edwin Drood: A Bibliographical Catalogue.* Comp. Brian Lake and Janet Nassau. Catalogue CIV. London: Jarndyce Antiquarian Booksellers, 1995. 73 unnumbered pp.

Lists 210 well-annotated items, including six editions in parts, nine editions in the original cloth, and numerous other editions of *The Mystery of Edwin Drood*; a variety of adaptations and continuations; a three-page letter from Harper and Brothers to Dickens, 5 March 1870, on a misunderstanding regarding the American publication of *Edwin Drood* (item 48), a facsimile of the first page of which is included; a two-page letter from Luke Fildes to Frederick Chapman, 30 July 1870, concerning the illustrations (item 49), a facsimile of the first page of which is likewise provided; and the manuscript notes, a corrected manuscript of the preface, proofs, etc., for the second edition of J. Cuming Walters's *Clues to Dickens's "Mystery of Edwin Drood"* (1905), and the manuscript (ca. 1906?) of one of Walters's articles or talks on the novel (items 75, 80).

The catalogue also includes the working notes and typewritten drafts of Sir William Robertson Nicoll's *The Problem of Edwin Drood* (1912), as well as letters and other matter concerning it (item 99), including a letter from Hugh Thomson, the book's illustrator, to Hodder Williams, its publisher, "analysing the wrapper design for Drood," the first page of which is reproduced in the catalogue; a three-page letter from Edmund Gosse to Nicoll "concerning an 1884 interview he had undertaken with Luke Fildes"; and a series of letters from J. Cuming Walters to Nicoll, including six pages of corrections to and comments on the typescript.

There are also four original drawings for the Waverley Edition of *Drood* (1912) by Charles Pears (item 102); albums compiled by F. S. Johnson and Grenville Cook of materials concerned with the Trial of John Jasper, held by the Dickens Fellowship in London, 7 January 1914, as well as correspondence by others about the trial and about collecting artifacts of it (item 113); J. Cuming Walters's collection of the notes he prepared for his role as prosecuting attorney for the trial and other materials (item 124); a typescript of an unpublished article by Katherine Kelly on the conclusion of the novel (item 147); a draft corrected typescript of a bibliography of *Edwin Drood* by Grenville Cook, along with a file of newspaper cuttings, correspondence, etc. (item 179); and numerous items of Droodiana.

A preface to the catalogue by Grenville Cook contains his views on how Dickens meant to end the novel and brief comments on some continuations and studies of the novel. A "Bibliographical Introduction" provides publishing information about the original parts edition, the original cloth edition (with considerable information about the cloth variants), and the text and illustrations. A brief list of eight bibliographical studies relevant to the novel is also included. Illustrated.

2043. Jarvis, J[ohn] W., & Son, London. *Dickens Catalogue.* London: J. W. Jarvis & Son, 1884. 40 pp.

An early bookseller's catalogue of editions of Dickens's works, extra illustrations, portraits, autograph letters, playbills, music, and other Dickensiana. Roberts (**2157**) claims this is the earliest Dickens catalogue. Also see Bede (**490**).

2044. Maggs Bros., London. "Charles Dickens." In their *Charles Dickens and Walter Scott.* Maggs Catalogue 1120. London: Maggs Bros., 1990, pp. 3-56.

An extensive listing of various editions of works by Dickens, including a number of editions in parts, many from the former Suzannet collection, as well as several autograph letters, Dickensiana, and biographies and critical studies, with their prices and useful descriptions and notes. Numerous facsimiles of title pages or covers of items for sale are included.

2045. Maggs Bros., London. *English Literature of the 19th & 20th Centuries, Being a Selection of First and Early Editions of the Works of Esteemed Authors & Book Illustrators.* . . . London: Maggs Bros. Catalogues 511 (1928), pp. 129‑41; 531 (1930), pp. 113-30; 548 (1930), pp. 91-108; 588 (1933), pp. 60-68; 599 (1934), pp. 55-62; 607 (1935), pp. 52-60; and 649 (1937), pp. 32-35.

Book catalogues, with prices. In addition to numerous editions of Dickens's works, sometimes presentation or other special copies, they offer sets of extra illustrations, Dickensiana, and autograph letters (with excerpts).

2046. Maggs Bros., London. *Original Manuscripts and Collections of Autograph Letters of Celebrated Authors to Which Are Appended Autograph Letters of Lady Hamilton and Lord Nelson.* Catalogue 436. London: Maggs Bros., 1923, pp. 70‑74.

A bookseller's catalogue, with prices, containing the manuscript of Dickens's 14-line prologue to a play by Beaumont and Fletcher written for Fanny Kelly, the actress, beginning "A Play by Fletcher; Written in that age/When the deep-hearted and strong-worded Stage/Had life in England . . ." (the full text is in *Pilgrim Letters*, IV, 458n), accompanied by four letters from Dickens to her concerned with his amateur productions of Shakespeare's *The Merry Wives of Windsor* and Ben Jonson's *Every Man in His Humour*, dated between 24 May and 11 July 1848 (all in *Pilgrim Letters*). The prologue is reproduced in photographic facsimile facing p. 56. The catalogue also includes a "remarkable series" of autograph letters by Dickens written between 1839 and 1870. Of these, one, to Oliver Wendell Holmes, 26 March 1862 (summarized in the catalogue as "inviting him to a reading"), was given the probable date of 26 March 1868 in *Pilgrim Letters*, XII, 84, but the letter itself remains unlocated, and two were not published in *Pilgrim Letters*: to son Henry F. Dickens, 9 August 1869 (on family matters); and to J. S. Le Fanu, 7 April 1870 (concerning a proposed contribution by Le Fanu to *All the Year Round*). Further items include a brief quotation from *A Christmas Carol* in Dickens's hand, the manuscript of an early version (before it was altered by Dickens) of Mark Lemon's play *Mr. Nightingale's Diary* in "an unknown hand," and the proof sheets of Algernon Swinburne's essay on Dickens (published in the *Quarterly Review* in July 1902), with corrections and additions by Swinburne.

2047. Quaritch, Bernard, bookseller, London. *A Catalogue of Books in English Literature and History.* London: Bernard Quaritch, 1915, pp. 95-103.

A bookseller's catalogue that includes first and other editions of Dickens's works, with occasional annotation, as well as various secondary studies and sets of etchings and proofs of plates for the novels.

2048. Robson & Co., London. *A Catalogue of Rare Books, Manuscripts and Drawings, Including . . . Sets of Thackeray and Dickens, Sporting Subjects, Cruikshankiana. . . .* London: Robson & Co., [1897?], pp. 36-37.

A handwritten notation in a copy of this bookseller's catalogue in the Library of Congress indicates that the catalogue was issued or received 3 August 1897. The Dickens items consist of a forty-eight volume set of first editions of Dickens's works, a presentation copy to Edmund Yates of *The Uncommercial Traveller* (1861), a first edition of *A Holiday Romance*, and a "special copy" of Frederic Kitton's *Charles Dickens by Pen and Pencil* (London: Frank T. Sabin, 1889-90). There are no Dickens-related items in the "Cruikshankiana" portion of the catalogue.

2049. Sawyer, Charles J., Ltd., London. *Charles Dickens, 1812-70: First & Collected Editions, Autograph Letters, Personal Relics.* Catalogue 103. London: Charles J. Sawyer, Ltd., 1931. 32 pp.

A catalogue, with limited annotation, of various collected works, novels in the original parts, and some novels and other works in first bound editions, a few with autograph letters bound in. Other items include some of the original steel plates by Hablot K. Browne for *Martin Chuzzlewit* and *Nicholas Nickleby*, some Dickensiana, a few autograph letters, and a small number of personal relics. Illustrated.

2050. Sawyer, Charles J., Ltd., London. *A Collection of First Editions of the Works of Charles Dickens: Autograph Letters, Personal Relics, and Dickensiana.* Catalogue 129. London: Charles J. Sawyer, Ltd., 1936. 44 pp.

A well-annotated listing of parts, first volume, and later editions of various Dickens works; a few autograph letters with excerpts; Dickensiana; illustrations, portraits, etc., including over 200 original water-color drawings by "Kyd" (Joseph Clayton Clarke), a colored drawing by George Cruikshank for *A Christmas Carol*, two "wash" drawings by Hablot K. Browne for *Dombey and Son*, and several photographs of Dickens; and personal relics. Illustrated. Also see **2150.**

2051. Sawyer, Charles J., Ltd., London. *A Remarkable Dickens Collection, Comprising Original Manuscripts, Presentation Copies, a Complete Set of the Issues in Origi-*

nal Parts [of His Novels], Bound Copies of First Editions, Dickensiana, Etc. Catalogue 145. London: Charles J. Sawyer, Ltd., 1938. ii + 56 pp.

A heavily-annotated book catalogue of 285 items, with prices. In addition to editions of Dickens's works, the catalogue contains a number of autograph letters (with excerpts); sets of extra illustrations; the manuscript of "Emigration" (then unpublished but since published in *Pilgrim Letters*, VI, 858-60); the manuscript of Dickens's epitaph for the gravestone of Mrs. Katherine Thomson, his wife's grandmother; extra-illustrated copies of various Dickens novels; a "trial edition" of *A Christmas Carol*; grangerized editions of *Forster* and *Hogarth-Dickens Letters*; playbills; and a few books from Dickens's library. Illustrated. Also see **2093**.

2052. Schwartz, Dr. J., bookseller, New York. *A Collection of Letters of Charles Dickens, the Greatest of the Great English Novelists and the Finest Letter-Writer of Them All, of Unusual Interest and Priced Much Beneath Their Real Worth, A Selection from the Stock of Dr. J. Schwartz, Dealer in Rare Books.* Catalogue 39. New York: Dr. J. Schwartz, Spring 1939. 27 pp.

A bookseller's catalogue, with prices for all items (ranging from $12-$125), of thirty-eight letters, all printed, apparently in full, and Dickens's copy of Lockhart's *Life of Scott* (7 vols), with Dickens's bookplates.

2053. Slatter, A. J. *A List of Books on Charles Dickens and Dickensiana Offered for Cash by A. J. Slatter.* London: A. J. Slatter, [1926].

Listed in Podeschi (**1509**), p. 391, as simply a "bookseller's catalogue."

2054. Smith, Fuller d'Arch Limited, London. *Charles Dickens: Books from the Library of the Late Leslie C. Staples.* London: Fuller d'Arch Smith Limited, n. d. [1981]. 63 unnumbered pp.

A preface notes that this is "the greater part" of Staples's library. Missing are a number of bequests to personal friends and others, as well as a bequest of his "unparalleled collection of Dickens piracies and plagiarisms" to the library of the Dickens House Museum, "to which he had devoted so much of his life." Included are a number of first and later editions of Dickens's works, including some translations; some plagiarisms, piracies, dramatizations, and imitations (presumably duplicates); printed collections of Dickens letters; numerous bibliographical, biographical, and critical works; and sets of extra illustrations—some 698 numbered items in all. On Staples's bequest to the Dickens House, see Dickens House Collections (**1457C11**).

2055. Sotheran, Henry, & Co., London. "Catalogue of the Library of Charles Dickens, Esq., Author of *The Pickwick Papers*, Etc., Comprehending His

Entire Library as Existing at His Decease," and "Charles Dickens's Library (Continued from Preceding Catalogue)." In *Sotheran's Price Current of Literature: A Catalogue of Second Hand Books, Ancient and Modern, in All Classes of Literature.* . . . Nos. 174 and 175 (November and December 1878), 9-27 and 1-18; reprinted in *Catalogue of the Library of Charles Dickens from Gadshill, Reprinted from Sotheran's "Price Current of Literature," Nos. CLXXIV and CLXXV; Catalogue of His Pictures and Objects of Art, Sold by Messrs. Christie, Manson & Woods, July 9, 1870; Catalogue of the Library of W. M. Thackeray Sold by Messrs. Christie, Manson & Woods, March 18, 1864; and Relics from His Library, Comprising Books Enriched with His Characteristic Drawings, Reprinted from Sotheran's "Price Current of Literature," No. CLXXVII.* Ed. J. H. Stonehouse. London: Piccadilly Fountain Press, 1935; reprinted London: Sotheran, 1936, pp. 1-120.

The two-part catalogue of Dickens's library lists the books in his library at his death and gives publication information along with occasional notes about the contents and special characteristics—some, for example, contain annotations in Dickens's hand. Among the most notable items, as Stonehouse indicates in his preface to the reprint, were Dickens's own copies of six of his readings from his works, with his autograph notations, additions, and excisions, and numerous editions of his own works, including translations into many languages. There is also a collection of old playbills, cuttings, drawings, engravings, and other miscellanea concerning Ben Jonson's *Bartholomew Fair,* "evidently intended by Dickens," it is noted, to be used in some projected work. The list is also valuable because it gives scholars a view of the extent of Dickens's reading (though one does not know how many of the volumes he may actually have read) and shows the large number of books sent to him by their authors—there are numerous presentation copies. In the reprint, Thackeray's library, pp. 133-60, contained, of Dickens's works, only a copy of *A Christmas Carol,* with an autograph inscription by Dickens, and a copy of *Master Humphrey's Clock,* containing *The Old Curiosity Shop* and *Barnaby Rudge.* The catalogue of Thackeray relics, pp. 161-82, lists the "Original Autograph Draught of the Letter Addressed by Thackeray to Charles Dickens, on the Subject of the Dispute with a Member of the Garrick Club" (that is, Edmund Yates), containing alterations and interlineations (p. 179). Also see Christie, Manson and Woods (**1943**) and Thomas & Homan, Messrs., auctioneers (**2019**) for other sales of Dickens's possessions. For comments on these sales, see "At Dickens's Sale" (**2073**), "The Charles Dickens Sale" (**2082**), "Charles Dickens' Art Relics" (**2083**), "Gad's Hill Place" (**2113**), and "The Sale at Gad's Hill" (**2158**). Also see **2099, 2135,** and **2184.**

2056. Sotheran, Henry, & Co., London. *Illustrated Catalogue of Books in Beautiful Old Bindings; The Dr. R[alph] T. Jupp Collection of Charles Dickens's Works: Autographs, Mss., Etc.: Also of a Collection of Letters and Relics of the Original*

Dora of David Copperfield. . . . Sotheran's Price Current of Literature, 775. London: Henry Sotheran & Co., 1920, passim.

"The Dr. R. T. Jupp Collection . . .," pp. 35-42, contains various editions of Dickens's works, including parts editions (sometimes more than one set); various pamphlets, speeches, imitations, portraits, and playbills; two grangerized editions of *Forster;* extra illustrations and miscellaneous illustrations, as well as original drawings by Fred Barnard, F. W. Pailthorpe, and Hablot K. Browne; 116 autograph letters from Dickens to various correspondents, sixteen letters by members of the Dickens family, and eighteen letters by others (including William H. Ainsworth, Robert Buss and his son Alfred, Lewis Carroll, Robert L. Stevenson, William M. Thackeray, John Forster, Edward Fitzgerald, W. P. Frith, Algernon Swinburne, and G. W. Thornberry) referring to Dickens; and several Dickens manuscripts–his Book of Memoranda, two unpublished verses written for Christiana Weller, a draft of a handbill for farewell readings at Manchester in 1867, a page from a hotel register, and the prompt-book and call-plot for Richard B. Peake's *Comfortable Lodgings.* Illustrated with a facsimile of a page from the Memoranda Book. "Relics of the Original 'Dora' of *David Copperfield* . . .," pp. 43-45, lists, with some annotation and some excerpts, letters from Maria Beadnell Winter's brothers, her husband, her father, Georgina Hogarth, and others to her, as well as two of Dickens's visiting cards, and a few other items. Illustrated with a photograph of Mrs. Winter. "Charles Dickens: Browning Gift-Copies," pp. 45-46, lists only several copies of Dickens's novels presented by Robert Browning to his son Pen on various birthdays. See also Anderson Galleries (**1929**) and **2057, 2080, 2129,** and **2139.**

2057. Sotheran, Henry, Ltd., London. *A Choice of Books Old and New: The Charles Dickens Number, Comprising First Editions of His Works, Autograph Letters by Him and His Circle.* . . . Sotheran's Price Current of Literature, 822. London: Henry Sotheran, Ltd., 1931, pp. 2-28.

A catalogue, with prices, of autograph letters by Dickens (items 1-16, with brief excerpts given from some) and his circle (items 17-153) to various correspondents (the letters from members of the Dickens circle are unfortunately not about Dickens); some editions in parts and bound first editions of Dickens's works and some of his readings (items 154-278); a few collected editions (items 279-89); Dickensiana (items 290-331); and imitations (items 332-33). The catalogue notes, p. 28, that particulars of "A Collection of Autograph Letters by, or addressed to, Mrs. Winter (formerly Miss Maria Sarah Beadnell), the original 'Dora' of *David Copperfield,* and of Some Personal Relics Relating to Her Engagement to Charles Dickens and Her After Career" would "be sent on application." Also see **2056** and **2141.**

2058. Sumner & Stillman, booksellers, Yarmouth, ME. *First American Editions of Charles Dickens: The Allan D. McGuire Collection.* Catalogue 36. Yarmouth, ME: Sumner & Stillman, 1991. 41 pp.

Provides descriptions and elaborate notes for the eighty-seven items in the sale, principally first American editions of Dickens's works, with some Dickensiana (six additional items). In a two-page preface, McGuire comments on his collecting of Dickens first editions. Illustrated principally with photographs of title pages and covers of works in the sale.

2059. Vandoros, T. S., Middleton, WI. *Rare Books.* Catalogue 4. Middleton, WI: T. S. Vandoros, n. d., pp. 5-13.

Lists a number of first and other editions of Dickens's works and paraphrases and gives excerpts from a letter from Dickens to Hepworth Dixon, dated only Thursday Afternoon 1859, which was subsequently printed from manuscript in *Pilgrim Letters*, IX, 186, where it is no more precisely dated.

6C. AUCTION AND BOOKSELLERS' RECORDS

Note: Also see **Auction sales, auction and booksellers' records**, in part 2 of the subject index.

2060. *Book-Auction Records (Formerly Known as "Sales Records"): A Priced and Annotated Record of London, Book Auctions*; later entitled *Book-Auction Records: A Priced and Annotated Annual Record of London, New York and Edinburgh Book-Auctions, Comprising Books from the Invention of Printing to the Current Year, Bindings, Early Manuscripts, and Rare Sets of Engravings*. London: Karslake, 1903-19; succeeded by Henry Stevens, Son, & Styles, 1920-68, and then by Dawson's of Pall Mall, 1969- , passim.

Always numerous Dickens entries, with auction house and selling price but not purchaser given. Harner (**1147**), p. 616, notes that originally the index covered only London, then Great Britain, the United States (1915-21 and since 1940), and other countries (since 1968); otherwise, the title is reasonably descriptive. There are a number of cumulative indexes. Also available on the Internet at http://www.dawson.co.uk/bathp.htm.

2061. *Book-Prices Current: A Record of the Prices at Which Books Have Been Sold at Auction From December, 1886, to November 1887[-August 1956]*. 64 vols. London: Elliot Stock [succeeded by other publishers], 1888-1957, passim.

Always numerous Dickens entries, with auction house, date of sale, selling price, and frequently purchaser given. The title is nearly sufficiently descriptive. Harner (**1147**), p. 616, notes that this publication began with English sales, added American ones with volume 30 (1916), and some manuscripts with volume 35 (1921); he finds *American Book-Prices Current* (**2065**) and *Book-Auction Records* (**2060**) to be "superior indexes to sales covered in common" because of the frequently-truncated entries in *Book-Prices Current*. The arrangement of entries varies; see the index if necessary. There are cumulative indexes for volumes 1-10, 11-20, and 21-31.

2062. Editors of Collector Books. *The Standard Old Book Value Guide*. Paducah, KY: Collector Books, 1978, pp. 72-73.

Gives then current prices for a number of Dickens's works.

2063. *List of Catalogues of English Book Sales, 1676-1900, Now in the British Museum.* London: British Museum, 1915; reprinted Mansfield Centre, CT: Martino Fine Books, 1995, passim.

Lists sales virtually day by day, with some indication of the contents, but the index does not particularly pick up on this—at least there are no Dickens entries in the index. To make effective use of this volume one really needs to be interested in a particular sale whose date and auction company are known.

2064. Livingston, Luther S., ed. "Dickens (Charles)." *Auction Prices of Books: A Representative Record Arranged in Alphabetical Order from the Commencement of the English Book-Prices Current in 1886 and the American Book-Prices Current in 1894 to 1904 and Including Some Thousands of Important Auction Quotations of Earlier Date.* 4 vols. New York: Dodd, Mead, 1905, II, 1-17.

Lists the auction house, date of sale, and price realized for editions of Dickens's works sold during the period indicated in the title.

Review: *Athenaeum*, no. 4061 (26 August 1905), 264-65 (devotes two long paragraphs to the Dickens items).

2065. Livingston, Luther S., [et al.], comps. *American Book-Prices Current: A Record of Books, Manuscripts and Autographs Sold at Auction in New York, Boston and Philadelphia, from September 1st, 1894, to September 1st, 1895[-], with the Prices Realized.* New York: Mead [later, other publishers], 1895- , passim. Also on the Internet, http://lola.olywa.net/abpc/index.cfm.

Numerous Dickens items. The selling price is noted but not the seller or purchaser, so this compilation is not particularly useful in tracking anything down. The entries are separated into 1) autographs and manuscripts, including letters, and 2) books and other items. The title varies, the most recent seen being *American Book-Prices Current, 2002. Volume 108: The Auction Season September 2001-August 2002* (Washington, CT: Bancroft-Parkman, 2003). The organization varies, too, the more recent volumes listing entries alphabetically by author under two headings: "Autographs & Manuscripts" and "Books, Broadsides, Maps & Charts." Cumulative indexes are also issued, the latest being for 1991-95. A search on 16 January 2003 of the Internet database, available in libraries, produced 917 Dickens records of autograph and manuscript sales and 3,748 records of book sales, with information about the auction house, the date of sale, the lot number, and the selling price. The database may be searched by author, title, editor/publisher, year of sale, and date of sale.

2066. Mandeville, Mildred S., comp. *The Used Book Price Guide: An Aid in Ascertaining Current Prices: Retail Prices of Rare, Scarce, Used and Out-of-Print Books.* Kenmore, WA: Price Guide Publishers. Part 1 (1962), Part 2 (1963), Part 3 (1964); revised editions, 1977 (with supplement), 1983; as *Mandeville's Used Price Guide: Five Year 1989 Edition*, Ed. Richard L. Collins. Kenmore,

WA: Price Guide Publishers, 1988; revised editions as *Five Year, 1994 Edition*, 1983, and *Three Year Edition*, 1998 (the last two edited by Richard L. Collins and Alea Collins), passim.

A number of Dickens works are listed.

2067. McGrath, Daniel F. [succeeded by Anne F. McGrath]. *Bookman's Price Index: An Annual Guide to the Values of Rare and Other Out-of-Print Books and Sets of Periodicals*. Detroit: Gale Research, 1964- , passim.

Annually gives prices listed in book catalogues published "in the previous year by leading antiquarian and specialist dealers in the United States, England, and Western Europe," frequently mentioning Dickens items. There are also periodic cumulative indexes.

2068. McKay, George L., comp. *American Book Auction Catalogues, 1917-1934: A Union List*. New York: New York Public Library, 1937, passim.

A chronological list that provides brief annotations for the contents of each sale and notes the libraries in which copies of each catalogue may be found (from a limited list of repositories). Unfortunately, this work is only valuable if you know the collector or the date of the sale since there is an index of owners but no subject index. Details are pretty much limited to a short title of each catalogue, the name of the auction house, date of sale, the number of lots, and total pages.

2069. Shapiro, S. R., ed. *United States Cumulative Book Auction Records, 1940-45[-1950-51]*. New York: [Walter N. Dennis]: 1946-51, passim.

Has substantial sections on Dickens.

2070. Sotheby & Co., London. *Catalogues of Sales: A Guide to the Microfilm Collection*. [Ann Arbor, MI]: Xerox University Microfilms in Association with Sotheby Parke-Bernet Publications, 1973- , passim.

The catalogues, published in individual volumes for 1734-1850, 1851-1900, 1901-45, 1946-70, and 1971-80 (the last seen), are of limited use since the sales are identified only by their date and general content, such as Art (Objects), Art (Pictorial), Books, Documents and Mss. The microfilm reel number or (for 1971-80) the microfiche number is also given.

6D. REPORTS ON AUCTION SALES
AND BOOKSELLERS' CATALOGUES

Note: See **Auction sales (with Dickens items), reports on auction sales and booksellers' catalogues**, in part 2 of the subject index for other items. For scholars wishing to do a thorough examination of Dickens items in auction and booksellers' catalogues, three recent articles in *Papers of the Bibliographical Society of America*, 89 (1995), may provide something of a starting point: Lenore Coral's "Toward the Bibliography of British Book Auction Catalogues, 1801-1900," pp. 419-25; Karen Nipps's "PACSCL's [Philadelphia Area Consortium of Special Collections Libraries] Auction and Dealer Catalogue Project," pp. 427-33; and Eric Holzenberg's "Book Catalogue Collections in Selected American Libraries," pp. 465-67.

2071. "The A. Edward Newton Library." *Dickensian*, 37 (1940/41), 221-22.

Describes a sale at Parke-Bernet Galleries, New York, April 1941 (**1970**), that included twenty-one presentation copies of Dickens's novels, here listed, noting bindings, inscriptions, and sale prices.

2072. "Antiquarian Notes." *Times Literary Supplement*, 23 July 1938, p. 500.

Describes 1) items in the "notably important" Suzannet sale at Sotheby's, 11 July 1938 (**1976**), largely of a thousand Dickens letters but also of Maria Beadnell's album and a number of presentation copies of the novels, and 2) a sale at Hodgson's, 8 July 1938 (**1952**), of a number of letters and manuscripts from the collection of the late Richard Bentley (one of Dickens's early publishers), including 112 letters from Dickens to Bentley and agreements concerning *Bentley's Miscellany*, *Memoirs of Joseph Grimaldi*, *Oliver Twist*, and *Barnaby Rudge*.

2073. "At Dickens's Sale." *Chambers's Journal*, 47 (August 1870), 502-05; reprinted in *Every Saturday*, 9, ns 1 (27 August 1870), 557-58, and *Hobbies*, 61, vii (September 1956), 106-07; viii (October 1956), 106-07, 125.

Describes the crowded auction room, the "motley" assemblage, the frantic scene, and the hectic bidding and other proceedings at the sale of Dickens's pictures, drawings, and objects of art by Messrs. Christie and Manson. The article also lists a number of the items sold and their selling prices. See the sale catalogue (**1943**). Also see Oliver D. Savage, "The First Dickens Sale," *Dickensian*, 37 (1940/41), 227-29, for an excerpt from the report in *Chambers's Journal* describing the crowd and excitement at the sale of Dickens's possessions.

2074. Bean, Andrew [now Andrew Xavier]. "Dickens's Portrait." *Times Literary Supplement*, 5 January 1996, p. 15.

In a letter to the editor, Bean (now Xavier), then deputy curator of the Dickens House Museum, London, and now curator, regrets that the museum was unable to purchase Samuel Drummond's painting of Dickens as a young man at a Sotheby's sale, 18 December 1995, because needed financial support was not forthcoming, largely because of concern about the authenticity of the portrait. Bean also comments on what he and Catherine Griffey reveal about the provenance and legitimacy of the portrait in their then forthcoming article, "The Samuel Drummond Portrait of Charles Dickens," *Dickensian*, 92 (1996), 25-30, where they provide strong evidence that the painting is authentic.

2075. "The Book Market: Dickens and Thackeray: Sales and Editions." *Academy*, 52 (1897), 454-55.

Prints reports from booksellers around England about sales of editions of Dickens and Thackeray. Usually Dickens's works sell better than Thackeray's, and better editions are available, they report, though Birmingham and Oxford had better sales of Thackeray—with Dickens, according to the Birmingham correspondent, "on the wane for a considerable time."

2076. "Bookworm" (pseud.). "The Hunt for Old Books: First Editions of Dickens." *Daily Report* (London), 4 October 1906, p. 8.

Some hints to collectors of Dickens's works.

2077. Bruccoli, Matthew J. *The Fortunes of Mitchell Kennerley, Bookman*. San Diego, CA, New York, and London: Harcourt, Brace, Jovanovich, 1986, passim.

Gives some details of auction sales of Dickens items in the 1921/22 season, p. 147; the 1925/26 season, pp. 171-72; the 1928/29 season, principally the Jerome Kern sale (**1934**), pp. 204-05; and the 1937/38 season, p. 233.

2078. Bruccoli, Matthew J. "The Kern Sale." *American Book Collector*, ns 7, xi (November 1986), 11-17.

A detailed account of the sale, 7-10 and 21-24 January 1929, of Jerome Kern's famous collection (**1934**). Bruccoli notes that the Dickens items in the collection, auctioned on 8 January, sold for a total of $252,540, including $28,000 for a "perfect" copy of *Pickwick Papers* in parts, $15,000 for the manuscript of *The Perils of Certain English Prisoners*, and $10,250 for an inscribed copy of *A Tale of Two Cities*. Bruccoli includes this account in his *The Fortunes of Mitchell Kennerley, Bookman* (**2077**).

2079. "Burdett-Coutts Sale." *Times* (London), 30 March 1922, p. 7.

Quotes from several letters that Dickens wrote to Angela Burdett-Coutts, in a collection that included the manuscript of *The Haunted Man and the Ghost's Bargain*, as well as hundreds of letters, to be sold at auction at Sotheby's, 15-17 May (**1996**). For reports on the sale, see "The Burdett-Coutts Library. £3,700 for Dickens Ms." (i.e., of *The Haunted Man and the Ghost's Bargain*), 16 May, p. 13, and "Dickens Letters for America. Burdett-Coutts Sale Ended," 18 May, p. 18 (sale of "upwards of 600 letters" from Dickens to Miss Burdett-Coutts to O. R. Barrett, a "well-known Chicago lawyer," for £2,150).

2080. Bushnell, George H. "A Famous Dickens Library." In his *From Bricks to Books: A Miscellany*. London: Grafton, 1949, pp. 149-55.

On the collection of Ralph T. Jupp, Bushnell's cousin, offered for sale intact in 1920 by Henry Sotheran & Co. (**2056**). When no buyer materialized, Bushnell reports, the collection was sent to the United States for sale of the items individually by Anderson Galleries, New York, in February 1922 (**1929**). Bushnell notes that Jupp had purchased much of the collection from or through Walter T. Spencer, a London bookseller. He identifies and comments on a number of the rarer items in it. Jupp himself, Bushnell adds, had hoped to found a permanent Dickens library and museum in London but had not lived to carry out this project.

2081. Carter, John. "The Suzannet Sale at Sotheby's." *Dickensian*, 68 (1972), 43-47.

Gives buyers and prices of many lots at the 22-23 November 1971 sale. See the catalogue (**1977**) for detailed descriptions of the items.

2082. "The Charles Dickens Sale (By Our Own Reporter)." *Era*, 32 (17 July 1870), 14.

A detailed report on the Christie, Manson & Woods sale (**1943**) of Dickens's art.

2083. "Charles Dickens' Art Relics. The Sale of the Great Novelist's Household Art Relics—Interesting Sketches of Objects Associated with the Author. From a Special Correspondent." *New York Times*, 25 July 1870, p. 5.

In an account of the sale (**1943**), datelined London, 12 July 1870, the *Times* correspondent notes that John Forster, who"—the *Daily News* tells us—is by common consent spoken of as [Dickens's] biographer," was present. Some of the items sold, some of the purchasers, and some of the prices realized are mentioned. The reporter also comments on Dickens's role in the Staplehurst railway accident, the deleterious effect of Dickens's public readings on his health, Dickens's reception by Queen Victoria in 1869, and Dickens's grave in Westminster Abbey.

2084. "Chronicle and Comment." *Bookman* (New York), 11 (1900), 501-10.

On pp. 502-05 comments on a few items in a then recent sale of the Dickens collection of W. R. Hughes of Birmingham, including a painting of Dickens as Captain Bobadil, a character in Ben Jonson's *Every Man in His Humour*, and on a few paintings by W. P. Frith in the Forster Collection, Victoria and Albert Museum, London. Also see "Dickens's Birthday. A Glance Through a 'Dickens Collection'" (**1626**), "An Interesting Dickens Collection" (**1656**), Van Noorden (**1756**), and Wright (**1776**).

2085. "Cigarette Papers for After-Dinner Smoking: Dickens Cheques: No Bid!" *People*, 12 July 1908, p. 2.

Notes that, at a theatrical fête in the Botanic Gardens, Regents Park, London, there were no bids on "dead" checks made out and signed by Dickens.

2086. "The Continuing Craze for Dickens: Interview with Mr. Walter T. Spencer." *Dickensian*, 19 (1923), 23.

Reprints a New York *World* account of a sale of Dickens manuscripts and first editions in London. Spencer comments on the eagerness of collectors to purchase Dickens items.

2087. "Copy of 'Pickwick' Sells for $13,000." *New York Times*, 29 January 1931, p. 11.

A report on the sale of the library of George Ulizio (**1913**), giving prices and buyers for the more important and expensive items in the sale.

2088. Davalle, Peter. "Old Curiosity Shopping: Brian Lake Specialises in Old Books by the Writer Who Virtually Invented Christmas." *Times* (London), 8 December 1990, p. 16.

An article on the Jarndyce Bookshop, London, and its collection of Dickens editions for sale. Davalle interviews Lake, who, with his wife Janet Nassau, owns the shop. Illustrated. For Jarndyce catalogues, see **2031-42**.

2089. de Bruxelles, Simon. "Fallen Women Were All Right in Dickens's Book." *Times* (London), 8 June 2001, p. 11.

Reports on fourteen newly-discovered letters that Dickens wrote to Georgina Morson, who ran Urania Cottage, Angela Burdett-Coutts's home for fallen women, to be sold in Robin Fenner's auction rooms (**1949**) in Tavistock, Devon, on 9 July 2001.

2090. Dexter, Walter. "When Found–A Rare Copy of 'Bleak House.'" *Dickensian*, 26 (1929/30), 253.

Notes a copy of *Bleak House* sold at Sotheby's in May 1930 "to which Dickens had added descriptive page headings that do not appear in any published edition."

2091. Dexter, Walter. "When Found–Sale Notes." *Dickensian*, 27 (1930/31), 250.

Records auction prices from a Sotheby's sale, 27-28 April 1931 (**1985**), of a page of the manuscript of *Tom Tiddler's Ground*, an original drawing by Hablot K. Browne for *Pickwick Papers*, and a few other items.

2092. "Dickens & His Dreams. Haunted by One for a Year. Notable Mss. to Be Sold." *Times* (London), 10 July 1938, p. 26.

On the sale of nearly 840 letters from the Suzannet collection (**1976**) at Sotheby's, 11 July 1938. The reporter quotes from several of Dickens's letters, including one on his dreams (the full letter, to Dr. Thomas Stone, 2 February 1851, is in *Pilgrim Letters*, VI, 276-79).

2093. "A Dickens Catalogue." *Times* (London), 11 July 1938, p. 10.

Notes the publication of a Charles J. Sawyer catalogue, 1938 (**2051**), devoted to Dickens and mentions some of the items in the catalogue.

2094. "Dickens Collection Is Sold for $27,005." *New York Times*, 9 April 1929, p. 28.

A report on the sale of the Mr. and Mrs. Edward C. Daoust collection (**1905**) on 8 April, giving the names of some buyers and some of the sale prices.

2095. "Dickens Letters at Hodgson's." *Times Literary Supplement*, 27 November 1937, p. 916.

Describes the sale of forty letters, 1837-48, from Dickens to George Cruikshank, several dealing with the illustrations for *Oliver Twist* and others verifying that Dickens wrote the notes for *The Loving Ballad of Lord Bateman* and made minor alterations in this poem. See Hodgson & Co. (**1953**).

2096. "Dickens Letters Bought for $8,000." *New York Times*, 2 November 1950, p. 29.

Notes that at a Parke-Bernet Galleries sale, New York, 1 November 1950 (**1958**), of the collection of the late Oliver R. Barrett 550 letters from Dickens to Angela Burdett-Coutts, most not previously published, went to the Carnegie Bookstore. Excerpts from a few are given. The letters are now in the Pierpont Morgan Library.

2097. "Dickens Letters Sold in New York." *Times* (London), 4 November 1950, p. 5.

Reports that, in the Oliver Barrett sale at the Parke-Bernet Galleries, New York, 1 November 1950 (**1958**), the Carnegie Bookshop was the purchaser of 450 Dickens letters for $8,000.

2098. "Dickens Letters: The Novelist's Reproof of Harrison Ainsworth." *Daily Mail* (London), 9 June 1905, p. 3.

On a Puttick and Simpson sale (**1974**), 8 June 1905, of Dickens letters. The reporter quotes from two Dickens letters since published.

2099. [Dickens Library]. *New York Times*, 25 March 1879, p. 4.

An untitled piece noting that a London bookseller, Henry Sotheran (**2055**), has listed in his monthly catalogue over 2,000 volumes from Dickens's Gad's Hill library, which the *Times* writer characterizes as a "common-place collection" except for a number of presentation copies that Dickens received from other authors, the copies of his public readings with manuscript notes and alterations in his own hand, and his own copies of first editions of his works.

2100. "Dickens MS. Brings $17,000 at Auction." *New York Times*, 18 October 1944, p. 19.

Reports the sale of the manuscript of *Our Mutual Friend* by Drexel Institute of Technology to the Rosenbach Company and briefly describes the manuscript. Also see Fynmore (**2112**).

2101. "Dickens Ms. Brings £1,400 in London." *New York Times*, 26 July 1939, p. 21.

Notes that in a Sotheby's sale, 25 July 1939 (**1981**), the manuscript of *The Life of Our Lord* was purchased by Philip Rosenbach, brother of A. S. W. Rosenbach.

2102. "Dickens Rarities Are Sold" and "Dickens Letters Sell for £2,150." *New York Times*, 16 May 1922, p. 19, and 18 May 1922, p. 19.

News reports of a two-day sale, 15-17 May 1922, at Sotheby's of the Burdett-Coutts collection (**1996**), including 600 letters.

2103. "Dickens Rarities in America." *Dickensian*, 13 (1917), 46-47.

Mentions a number of collections of Dickensiana for sale in the United States in 1916.

2104. "Dickens Sale Nets $11,613." *New York Times*, 2 February 1922, p. 6.

A brief news report on the R. T. Jupp sale (**1929**), Anderson Galleries, 1 February 1922.

2105. "Dickens Sale Nets $4,535 on First Day" and "Dickens Sale Ends with $9,669 Total." *New York Times*, 14 February 1922, p. 22, and 15 February 1922, p. 16.

News reports of the two-day sale of the William Glyde Wilkins collection (**1930**) at the Anderson Galleries, 13-14 February 1922.

2106. "Dickens's Life of Christ." *Times Literary Supplement*, 29 July 1939, p. 460.

A nine-line announcement that Dickens's manuscript of *The Life of Our Lord* sold for £1,400 at Sotheby's (**1981**) on 25 July 1939.

2107. "Dickens' Method of Writing." *Great Thoughts*, 72, 8th ser., 8 (1919/20), 388.

An account of a Red Cross sale at which three Dickens letters (two contributed by Henry F. Dickens) and Dickens's Book of Memoranda (**2530**) were sold. The Book of Memoranda is briefly described and excerpts from the letters are included. For more details of the sale, which included a number of Dickens letters, see Christie, Manson & Woods (**1944**).

2108. "Dickens's Raven Here to Be Sold." *New York Times*, 4 December 1921, Sect. 2, p. 1.

Comments and to some extent itemizes the Dr. R. T. Jupp collection (**1929**) to be sold at the Anderson Galleries, 1-2 February 1922, which included a letter about Grip the raven, as well as the stuffed form of the bird.

2109. "Eff" (pseud.). "A Wonderful Piece of Work." *The World* (London), 10 July 1878, pp. 16-17.

A detailed description of a grangerized copy of *Forster* as a "portentous set of thirteen huge folio volumes," sixteen inches by twelve, "superbly bound in red morocco and gold," and filled with "a mass of illustrative portraits, sketches, views, autograph letters, and other cognate matters," including the manuscript of Dickens's review of Lord Londonderry's *A Letter to Lord Ashley, M. P., on the Mines and Collieries Bill.* A number of these additions are described and excerpts given from several of the Dickens letters.

2110. "The Effects of the Late Charles Dickens." *Times* (London), 16 August 1870, p. 10.

Reports on the sale of Dickens's household furniture and other possessions by Messrs. Thomas & Homan, Rochester, 13 August 1870 (**2019**), giving sale prices for a number of items.

2111. "A French Collector of Dickens." *Times Literary Supplement*, 10 December 1971, p. 1561.

Describes the sale of a large part of the Dickens collection of the Comte de Suzannet at Sotheby's, 22-23 November 1971, and gives prices and purchasers for a number of the more important items—drawings by Dickens's illustrators, parts issues of the novels, letters, twelve consecutive pages of the manuscript of *Pickwick Papers*, and twenty-two pages of the manuscript of *Nicholas Nickleby*. See the catalogue of the sale (**1977**) and Podeschi (**1509**)

2112. Fynmore, A. H. W. "A Dickens Manuscript." *Notes and Queries*, 187 (1944), 255.

Reports the sale of the manuscript of *Our Mutual Friend* to the Rosenbach Foundation for $17,000. Also see "Dickens MS. Brings $17,000 at Auction" (**2100**).

2113. "Gad's Hill Place." *Birmingham Daily Post*, 11 August 1870. In Dickens House Scrapbooks (**1575C**), III, 42.

In connection with the four-day sale at Gad's Hill of Dickens's household effects, carriages, etc. (**2019**), describes Gad's Hill Place as it appeared shortly after Dickens's death and provides some details of the sale itself. Comparable accounts can be found in many other papers of about the same date. See Dickens House Scrapbooks (**1575C**), III, 42 and 44, for clippings of a number of these.

2114. "High Price at Dickens Sale. £1,400 for a 'Pickwick' First Edition." *Times* (London), 23 April 1926, p. 13.

A report on the first-day sale of the George Barr McCutcheon library, American Art Association, New York (**1903**), with some prices noted.

2115. Hopkins, A[lbert] A. "The Frederick W. Lehmann Sale." *Dickensian*, 27 (1930/31), 140-41.

Report of a sale, with prices. For details see American Art Association, Anderson Galleries (**1908**).

2116. Hopkins, A[lbert] A. "The George Barr McCutcheon Sale." *Dickensian*, 22 (1926), 169-72.

Describes items in the sale of a well-known collection, which included a prime *Pickwick* and a prime *Vanity Fair* in parts (**1903**), with auction prices. Illustrated.

2117. Hopkins, A[lbert] A. "An Important Sale of Dickens Manuscripts." *Dickensian*, 22 (1926), 113-15.

Describes the Newbury Frost Read sale, 8 December 1925, at the Anderson Galleries, New York (**1935**), which included the manuscripts of *The Perils of Certain English Prisoners*, "A Curious Dance Round a Curious Tree" (with ten pages in Dickens's hand, evidence that it was *not* by W. H. Wills), the title page (in Dickens's hand) for *Oliver Twist* in monthly parts, the prologue to John Weston Marston's play *The Patrician's Daughter*, and a page of "O'Thello." Read's collection also included first editions and the page proofs of pp. 161-208 of the Cheap Edition of *The Christmas Books*, with corrections, changes, and running heads in Dickens's hand. Other items in the sale not from the Read collection are also listed, including some original drawings for *Pickwick Papers* (one with notes by Dickens) and *A Christmas Carol*. Illustrated.

2118. Hopkins, A[lbert] A. "Notes on the Thomas Hatton Sale." *Dickensian*, 24 (1927/28), 116-18.

Describes and gives prices of a sale on 7 December 1927 of a well-known collection (**1906**). Illustrated.

2119. Hopkins, A[lbert] A., and W[illiam] Miller. "Two Important Sales." *Dickensian*, 25 (1928/29), 98-99.

Hopkins gives a brief account, with prices, of the Jerome Kern sale (**1934**) in New York and Miller of a sale at Sotheby's in London (**2010**) that included five pages of the manuscript of *Pickwick Papers*. A further listing of items and prices in the Kern sale is given on p. 244.

2120. Hopkins, Frederick M. "Rare Book Notes." *Publisher's Weekly*, 125 (17 February 1934), 796-97.

Notes that the publication rights to the 14,000 word manuscript of Dickens's *Life of Our Lord* were sold for $210,000 to the London *Daily Mail*.

2121. "In an Auction Room." *New York Times*, 31 July 1880, p. 2.

Notes the sale, at Robinson & Fisher's, Bond Street, London, of thirty-seven original sketches by Hablot K. Browne for *Nicholas Nickleby* and works by other illustrators of Dickens's books in the possession of the late Frederick Chapman of Chapman and Hall.

2122. Jerrold, Sidney. "Dickens and E. L. Blanchard." *Times Literary Supplement*, 3 July 1930, p. 554.

Notes a confusion between E. L. Blanchard and Laman Blanchard in the attribution of letters referred to in "Notes on Sales: Dickens and Barrie Manuscripts" (**2142**).

2123. "Kern Library Sale. High Prices for Dickens, Byron, and Conrad." *Times* (London), 10 January 1929, p. 14.

Gives prices and buyers for a number of the Dickens items in the sale at the Anderson Galleries, New York (**1934**).

2124. Kitton, F[rederic] G. "Notes on the Dickens Sale." *Literature*, 4 (1899), 668-69.

Kitton notes his disappointment in the less than immaculate first editions and a grangerized edition of *Forster* in the sale of the library of William Wright (**2008**). He provides brief quotations from a few of the letters in the sale and mentions that among other items were some portraits and illustrations by W. P. Frith and John Leech and the manuscript of *The Battle of Life*. For earlier notes on the Wright sale, see pp. 552 and 636. Also see Lane (**1663**), "Notes of the Day" (**1695**), "A Unique Dickens Collection" (**2188**), and "Wright Collection" (**2196**).

2125. "The Late Mr. Charles Dickens." *Times* (London), 11 July 1870, p. 8.

Reports on the sale at Christie, Manson, & Woods, 9 July 1870 (**1943**) of Dickens's pictures and other objects of art, noting the "overwhelming attendance of the friends of the deceased, and other patrons of literature and art," with nearly every lot "keenly contested." The reporter lists 118 items with sale prices and purchasers. Also see reports in the *Times* for 22 June 1970, p. 11 (lists some of the items in the then forthcoming sale), and 12 July, p. 12 (quotes from an account of the sale in *Pall Mall Gazette* in which the reporter marvels at–and laments–the prices fetched for perfectly ordinary items such as a Chinese gong).

2126. "Letters from Charles Dickens to Edmund Yates." *The World* (London), 23 January 1895, pp. 23-24.

Describes a volume of about three dozen autograph letters written by Dickens between 1837 and 1870 from the estate of Edmund Yates, a friend and one of the young writers for *All the Year Round*, being sold by Sotheby, Wilkinson and Hodge (**2002**). The reporter comments on Dickens's relationship with Yates and prints excerpts from some of the letters.

2127. "Letters of Charles Dickens." *Times* (London), 30 June 1898, p. 11.

Announces the Sotheby, Wilkinson, and Hodge sale, 30 June 1898 (**2009**), of 135 Dickens letters, 1836-70, almost all of which were then unpublished, a number of which are briefly described and excerpted.

2128. "Letters of Charles Dickens." *Times Literary Supplement*, 23 July 1938, p. 500.

Describes the sale of part of the Dickens collection of Comte de Suzannet at Sotheby's, 11 July 1938 (**1976**), including, among other items, Maria Beadnell's album, the manuscript of "The Ivy Green," and 1,000 Dickens letters (175 to Thomas Beard, thirty-seven to George Cruikshank, eleven to Bradbury and Evans, thirty-eight to Edmund Yates, fifteen to Thomas Mitton, seventy-two to John Leech, twenty-two to Mark Lemon, twenty-eight to Peter Cunningham, forty-five to Georgina Hogarth, and over 500 other letters).

2129. Matz, B. W. "A Notable Dickens Collection." *Dickensian*, 16 (1920), 198-200.

Describes the R. T. Jupp collection for sale (**2056**), including Dickens's Book of Memoranda, a page of which is reproduced in facsimile. Bushnell (**2080**) reports that the collection did not sell and was later auctioned off by the Anderson Galleries, New York in 1922 (**1929**).

2130. [Matz, B. W.]. "When Found." *Dickensian*, 18 (1922), 115-21.

On pp. 118-19, describes the sale of Angela Burdett-Coutts's library at Sotheby's, 15-17 May 1922 (**1996**), noting that the manuscript of *The Haunted Man*, one of Dickens's Christmas Books, was sold to Philip Rosenbach, a Philadelphia collector, and Burdett-Coutts's collection of over 600 letters from Dickens to her to O. R. Barrett, a Chicago lawyer, which he subsequently sold through Parke-Bernet Galleries, New York (**1958**; also see **2096-97**). The manuscript comprised five octavo pages and sixty-nine quarto ones and was accompanied by a letter from Dickens to Angela Burdett-Coutts (13 February 1850) presenting her with the manuscript in which, he notes, she "took a kind interest."

2131. "Missing Dickensiana." *Dickensian*, 69 (1973), 101.

Describes two items from the Suzannet sale (**1977**) lost or stolen: a four-page letter from Dickens to W. H. Wills, 18 June 1853, and a copy of *Mrs. Lirriper's Lodgings* with page 22 of the manuscript bound in.

2132. "New Auction Records for 'Pickwick Papers.'" *Dickensian*, 13 (1917), 192.

Reports that a prime *Pickwick* in parts, originally sold in 1894 for £34 and resold in 1914 for £495, was sold in America in 1917 for $4,500.

2133. Norman, Geraldine. "Collector to Sell Early Love Letter by Dickens." *Times* (London), 11 March 1972, p. 1, and "Dickens Love Letter Sold at Auction for £1,200." *Times* (London), 29 March 1972, p. 16.

Notes in the earlier report that a hitherto unknown letter from Dickens to Maria Beadnell, his early love, written apparently in 1831, was to be auctioned off at Sotheby's, 28 March 1972, and gives excerpts from the letter. The later report reveals that the letter was purchased by the Dickens House Museum. The letter has since been printed in its entirety by Michael Slater, "David to Dora: A New Dickens Letter," *Dickensian*, 68 (1972), 162-64, with explanatory commentary, and in *Pilgrim Letters*, VII, 777-78, in both of which a date of late 1831 is given.

2134. Norman, Geraldine. "A Two-Day Feast for Dickens Lovers." *Times* (London), 23 November 1971, p. 17, and "British Museum Buys Original Dickens Manuscript for £12,000." *Times* (London), 24 November 1971, p. 16.

In her report of the first day of a two-day sale of the Suzannet collection at Sotheby's (**1977**), Norman gives sale prices for a number of items in what she characterizes as "the most important [Dickens] collection remaining in private hands." Illustrated. In her report of the second day of the sale, Norman gives the purchase prices for a number of items, including the sale of the manuscript of chapter 15 of *Nicholas Nickleby* to the British Museum for £12,000.

2135. "Notes." *Literature*, 5 (1899), 74-78.

One note (pp. 74-75) concerns the sale of William Makepeace Thackeray's library in 1864 (**2055**), following his death. One item in the sale, an inscribed copy of *A Christmas Carol* from Dickens, was thought to have been purchased at the sale for Queen Victoria, 18 March 1864, (for £25 10s), a story discounted in a letter quoted from F. G. Kitton who investigated the matter. He traced the volume to other hands, but could not locate the actual volume in 1899. In a second excerpt from his letter, Kitton offers an explanation for Dickens's inscription—"W. M. Thackeray from Charles Dickens (whom he made very happy once a long way from home)." It refers, Kitton asserts, to favorable remarks about Dickens in Thackeray's "Dickens in France," which Dickens undoubtedly saw in the March 1842 issue of *Fraser's Magazine* while he was in America in that year.

2136. "Notes on Rare Books." *New York Times Book Review*, 10 May 1925, p. 27.

Comments on the Lapham-Wallace set of *Pickwick Papers* in parts (**122**), then once again coming up for sale. Also see **1863** and **1922**.

2137. "Notes on Rare Books." *New York Times Book Review*, 6 December 1925, pp. 30, 32.

Reports on the collections of Newbury Frost Read and an unnamed English baronet (**1935**) then about to be sold at the Anderson Galleries, New York, including original illustrations and drawings for Dickens's novels, presentation copies, a fragment of his youthful "O'Thello" travesty, the manuscript of *The Perils of Certain English Prisoners*, and other autograph documents and letters.

2138. "Notes on Rare Books." *New York Times Book Review*, 11 April 1926, p. 25.

On the then forthcoming sale of George B. McCutcheon's collection of Dickens and Thackeray rarities (**1903**), 21-22 April 1926, at the American Art Association, including first editions, letters, an excerpt from the manuscript of "O'Thello," and an edition of *Pickwick Papers* in parts with three original drawings by Hablot K. Browne. See the *New York Times*, 18 April, Sect. 2, p. 9, and 22 April, p. 7, for accounts of the sale itself.

2139. "Notes on Sales." *Times Literary Supplement*, 29 July 1920, p. 491.

Comments on the sale of R. T. Jupp's Dickens collection by Sotheran's (**2056**).

2140. "Notes on Sales." *Times Literary Supplement*, 4 August 1921, p. 504.

Comments briefly on a sale at Puttick and Simpson's, 22 July 1921 (**1975**), of three pages of *Oliver Twist* manuscript, "possibly" from the first draft of the beginning of chapter 10, with "many deletions and additions." Dickens, it is reported, gave these pages to Mrs. Rebecca Ball Wilson, his first cousin.

2141. "Notes on Sales: A Dickens Catalogue." *Times Literary Supplement*, 5 February 1931, p. 104.

Briefly reviews a then recent Sotheran Dickens catalogue (**2057**), but more fully describes the contents of, gives some prices for, and comments on the "modest prices" asked for volumes in Dickens's library, sold by Sotheran's in 1878 (**2055**).

2142. "Notes on Sales: Dickens and Barrie Manuscripts." *Times Literary Supplement*, 26 June 1930, p. 540.

Notes a sale at Sotheby's (**1984**) of twenty-one Dickens letters to various correspondents, 1836-65 (brief excerpts are quoted); a series of notes, 1845-65, to John Thompson, Dickens's butler; a few manuscript pages; and other items. Also see Jerrold (**2122**).

2143. "Notes on Sales: Dickens and Others." *Times Literary Supplement*, 20 June 1929, p. 500.

Reports on a sale at Sotheby's (**1982**) including presentation copies and editions in parts (with prices) of several Dickens novels.

2144. "Notes on Sales: Dickens Manuscripts." *Times Literary Supplement*, 1 June 1922, p. 368.

Notes sale of the library of Theodore N. Vail at the Anderson Galleries, New York, 2-6 May 1922 (**1937**), which included ten pages of the manuscript of "A Curious Dance Round a Curious Tree," showing, it is asserted, that Dickens was the coauthor with W. H. Wills. The sale also included the manuscript of *The Perils of Certain English Prisoners and Their Treasures*, with the title page and chapters 1 and 3 in Dickens's hand and chapter 2 in the hand of Wilkie Collins.

2145. "Notes on Sales: Dickens's Imitators." *Times Literary Supplement*, 13 April 1922, p. 248.

Provides some details of serialized imitations of Dickens's early works (*Sketches by Boz* through *Barnaby Rudge*) published by Edward Lloyd and others—based on items in a 1922 sale at the American Art Galleries, New York.

2146. "Notes on Sales: Pickwick and Others." *Times Literary Supplement*, 20 December 1928, p. 1016 (see **277**).

Notes the appearance in current sales of two fragments of the manuscript of *Pickwick Papers*, one of one and one-half pages, the other of five pages (**2010**), and comments on other extant fragments of the manuscript. Also see a letter to the editor by J. P. Gilson, 3 January 1929, p. 12, who reminds readers of five pages of the manuscript not mentioned in the article then (and now) in the British Library. Also see Clarke (**1845**). In his bibliography of *Pickwick Papers* (**125**), pp. 14-16, Elliot Engel locates forty-six pages of the manuscript.

2147. "$1,450 Paid for Book Inscribed by Dickens." *New York Times*, 9 April 1936, p. 19.

Reports prices paid for some of the items in a sale at the Anderson Galleries, New York (**1918**), of the library of Harry B. Smith, including a number of Dickens items.

2148. "Original Dickens Sale in New York." *Dickensian*, 12 (1916), 156.

Notes that the sale of the library of Edwin M. Coggeshall, Anderson Galleries, New York, 25 April 1916 (**1931**), included presentation copies and first editions of Dickens, a copy of *Pickwick Papers* in parts with a page of the original manuscript (a part of the chapter describing the wedding breakfast and old Mrs. Wardle's reminiscences), the original manuscript of *The Village Coquettes*, and the manuscript of a speech Dickens delivered at Gore House to the Metropolitan Sanitary Association, 10 May 1851. A further note on page 191 mentions that the sale also included some 600 Dickens letters, about one-half of which were to W. H. Wills and the rest mainly to Georgina Hogarth.

2149. Patten, Robert. "The Dickens Archive and the Sotheby's Sale." *Dickensian*, 95 (1999), 257-58.

Comments on the importance of items from three sources: family papers, the archives of Charles Kent, and the Bleak House Museum, Broadstairs. Patten notes that, of the twenty-eight lots in the Dickens archives, only three sold, but that most of the items in the Kent and Bleak House archives found buyers. Also see Williams (**2192**) and Sotheby's (**2014**).

2150. "The Pickwick Centenary. Dickens Items Offered by Booksellers." *Times* (London), 18 March 1936, p. 17.

Briefly notes Dickens items in catalogue no. 129 of Charles J. Sawyer, London (**2050**), and Catalogue no. 188 of Thomas Thorp, London.

2151. "'Pickwick' in Parts." *Times* (London), 8 April 1938, p. 21.

A notice of a then forthcoming sale at Parke-Bernet Galleries of the Thomas Hatton library, 20 April 1938 (**1972**), including two sets of "Pickwick" in parts. The writer comments on various sets of "Pickwick" in parts, indicating that the copy sold at the Kern sale (**1934**) is the finest of the lot.

2152. Pope-Hennessy, Una. "Charles Dickens and His Wine Cellar." *Food and Wine*, no. 45 (Spring 1945), 1-6.

Largely about the sale at auction of Dickens's wine cellar after his death (**2019**), describing the wines, as well as such related items as the Pickwick punch ladles and a leather traveling case of wine glasses, and giving their sale prices. Pope-Hennessy also comments on Dickens's relationship with Josef Valckenberg, whom he had met at Mainz, Germany, on his way to Switzerland with his family in May 1846. Valckenberg introduced his brother, a wine merchant, to Dickens, she points out, and Dickens apparently purchased wine from him then and later, for some bottles of German wine from that area were in the sale.

2153. "Portrait of Dickens to Be Sold Here." *New York Times Magazine*, 16 February 1919, p. 9.

Notes that the 1859 painting of Dickens by William P. Frith would be sold at the Anderson Galleries sale, 17 February 1919 (**1927**). The painting, an illustration of which accompanies the article, was sold for $1,700, as reported 18 February, p. 11.

2154. "Rare Books." *New York Times Book Review*, 4 December 1927, pp. 40, 42.

Contains a brief description of the Thomas Hatton collection (**1906**) of Dickens editions and other materials to be sold at the American Art Gallery, 7 December 1927. The prices of a few of the items sold are given in a report of the sale, *New York Times*, 8 December 1927, p. 22.

2155. "Red Cross Sale. 'Pickwick' Ms. for the Nation." *Times* (London), 27 April 1915, p. 11.

A report of a sale for charity of five pages of the autograph manuscript of *Pickwick Papers*, donated by Mrs. Frank Gielgud and sold to Lady Wernher for £450, "who authorizes us to state that this MS. is to become the property of the nation."

2156. "Relics of Dickens Sold." *New York Times*, 24 July 1935, p. 15.

Notes a Sotheby's sale (**1986**), 23 July 1935, of a number of relics, including some clothing and an armchair, the former property of one of Dickens's servants, as well as Edward Bulwer Lytton Dickens's manuscript copy of "The Life of Our Lord," and a draft of the first part of the "violated letter"–Dickens's letter to Arthur Smith, 25 March 1858, giving him permission to explain Dickens's marital breakup to others. Prices are given.

2157. Roberts, W. "The First Dickens Catalogue. Jarvis's Bookshop." *Times* (London), 3 April 1936, p. 12.

A letter to the editor reminiscing about the London Bookshop and the first Dickens catalogue (**2043**), which it issued in 1884, and describing some of the items in the catalogue, principally editions in parts, bound first editions, and Dickensiana.

2158. "The Sale at Gad's Hill." *Era*, 32 (14 August 1870), 5.

A report on the sale of Dickens's household furniture by Messrs. Thomas and Homan, auctioneers (**2019**), giving prices paid for a number of the items.

2159. "Sale of Dickens Relics. Agreement for Publication of 'Our Mutual Friend.'" *Times* (London), 17 August 1917, p. 10.

Brief report of a sale at Sotheby, Wilkinson, and Hodge, 16 August 1917 (**2010**), of Dickens's autograph letters to Clarkson Stanfield, an agreement between Dickens and Chapman and Hall for publication of *Our Mutual Friend*, and some Dickens relics from Gadshill, previously owned by the late Georgina Hogarth and sold by Henry Fielding Dickens, consisting of several pieces of furniture.

2160. "Sale of Dickens's Letters at Sotheby's." *Dickensian*, 65 (1969), 99; 66 (1970), 236.

The earlier report is a brief note of a sale of thirteen Dickens letters, only two of which, it is noted, are in the *Nonesuch Letters*. The reporter quotes briefly from one to Elizabeth Gaskell, 27 March 1854, the full text of which was subsequently published in *Pilgrim Letters*, VII, 299. By now most if not all of the other letters have also been published in subsequent volumes of *Pilgrim Letters*. The later report is a very brief description of a sale of fourteen Dickens letters on 24 November 1969 (**1990**).

2161. "Sale of Dickens's Letters. Light on His Early Career." *Times* (London), 9 July 1938, p. 9.

Comments on a sale at Hodgson's, 8 July 1938 (**1952**), p. 9, of 112 letters from Dickens to Richard Bentley, 1836-68, and several of the original publishing agreements between the two. The early letters, the reporter notes, convey much of Dickens's anger over Bentley's treatment of him, while the later ones show that those old wounds have been healed.

2162. "Sale of Manuscripts and Drawings." *Times* (London), 18 July 1889, p. 13.

A report of a sale at Sotheby, Wilkinson and Hodge, 9 July 1889 (**2003**), of numerous drawings by Hablot K. Browne for *Martin Chuzzlewit*, as well as manuscripts of two minor Dickens works.

2163. "The Sale Room." *Times* (London), 15 February 1922, p. 13.

Gives the prices of some items in the R. T. Jupp sale, 1-2 February, at the Anderson Galleries, New York (**1929**).

2164. "The Sale Room. A Dickensian's Library." *Times* (London), 22 February 1933, p. 11.

A brief report of the Sotheby sale, 20-21 February 1933 (**1979**), of the remaining library of Thomas Hatton, realizing £3,148. But see also Parke-Bernet Galleries (**1972**) and Sotheby & Co. (**1981**) for later Hatton sales and American Art Association (**1893, 1906**) and Sotheby & Co. (**1978, 1981**) for earlier sales.

2165. "The Sale Room. A Notable Dickens Collection. Disposal of Letters and Manuscripts." *Times* (London), 16 June 1938, p. 13.

Comments on the then forthcoming sale at Sotheby's, July 11 1938 (**1976**), of a further portion of the Suzannet Dickens collection of "more than 1,000 autograph letters, several manuscripts, presentation copies of his works, and what is claimed to be the earliest known portrait of Dickens" (a small reproduction of which accompanies the article), painted by an aunt, Janet Barrow, in 1830. In the post-sale report, "The Sale Room. £3,687 for Relics of Charles Dickens," 12 July, p. 13, the reporter indicates that there was "keen bidding" for this "remarkable" collection, gives prices for the principal sets of letters, and mentions that the 1830 Barrow painting went for only £30.

2166. "The Sale Room. 'A Tale of Two Cities.'" *Times* (London), 5 June 1929, p. 11.

Reports on a sale at Sotheby's, 4 June 1929 (**1982**), of principally Dickens items, the star of which was a presentation copy of *A Tale of Two Cities* to George Eliot that sold for £1,180.

2167. "The Sale Room. Dickens and Ainsworth." *Times* (London), 27 February 1924, p. 11.

On a then forthcoming sale at Hodgson's, 28-29 February 1924 (**1951**), of letters and documents of Dickens, Ainsworth, and others, with brief excerpts from two of Dickens's letters.

2168. "The Sale Room. Dickens, Browning, and Dr. Johnson." *Times* (London), 29 April 1931, p. 11.

Contains a brief description of the Dickens items, with purchasers and prices, of a sale at Sotheby's, 28 April 1931 (**1985**).

2169. "The Sale Room. Dickens Collection in America." *Times* (London), 22 November 1930, p. 9.

A brief report on the then forthcoming sale of the Frederick W. Lehmann collection (**1908**), at American Art Association, Anderson Galleries, New York, 2-3 December 1930.

2170. "The Sale Room. Dickens First Editions." *Times* (London), 16 December 1924, p. 11.

Report of a Sotheby, Wilkinson, and Hodge sale, 15-17 December 1924 (**2011**), of the property of E. H. Cox, including five sets of *Pickwick Papers* in parts.

2171. "The Sale Room. Dickens First Editions." *Times* (London), 17 June 1926, p. 9.

Report of a sale at Sotheby, Wilkinson and Hodge, 16 June 1926 (**1983**), including corrected proofs of *Our Mutual Friend*, Dickens's acting copy of J. B. Buckstone's *Uncle John* (1833), and numerous parts and volume editions of individual Dickens works. Prices are given for the items mentioned in the report.

2172. "The Sale Room. Dickens Letters and Mss." *Times* (London), 20 June 1930, p. 13.

Gives purchasers and prices for a number of Dickens letters and a few minor manuscripts sold at Sotheby's, 16-19 June 1930 (**1984**).

2173. "The Sale Room. Dickens Mss." *Times* (London), 25 November 1927, p. 13.

A report, with auction prices given, of Hodgson's sale, 24 November 1927 (**1955**), of the manuscripts of two of Dickens's articles for *Household Words*,

"Our Commission" (£800) and "The Friends of the Lions" (£590), and various editions of Dickens's works. The sale was announced in the *Times*, 9 November, p. 11.

2174. "The Sale Room. Dickens's Life of Christ." *Times* (London), 24 July 1935, p. 12.

Report of a sale at Sotheby's, 23 July 1935 (**1986**), of a number of letters and relics of Dickens, including a twelve-page letter from Robert W. Buss giving his account of his work on *Pickwick Papers* and Edward Bulwer Lytton Dickens's copy of his father's *Life of Christ*, written in the hand of his sister Mamie.

2175. "The Sale Room. Dickens's 'Life of Our Lord.'" *Times* (London), 10 July 1939, p. 15.

Notes publication of the catalogue for the then forthcoming Sotheby sale, 24 July 1939 (**1981**). The sale itself is reported in "The Sale Room. £1,400 Paid for Dickens's 'Life of Our Lord,'" 26 July, p. 11. The autograph manuscript was purchased by Philip Rosenbach, it is reported, after some spirited bidding.

2176. "The Sale Room. High Prices for Cruikshank Drawings." *Times* (London), 3 November 1931, p. 15.

A brief report of a sale at Sotheby's, 2 November 1931 (**1980**), listing some purchasers and prices.

2177. "The Sale Room. 'Pickwick' in Parts." *Times* (London), 1 December 1931, p. 19.

A brief report of a sale at Sotheby's, 30 November 1931 (**1978**), with purchasers and prices given for several Dickens items.

2178. "The Sale Room. £7,500 for 'Pickwick' Fragment." *Times* (London), 18 December 1928, p. 8.

A report on a sale at Sotheby's, 17 December 1928 (**2010**), with purchasers and prices of several items noted, including five pages of the manuscript of *Pickwick Papers* (to the Rosenbach Company, New York City for £7,500) and a number of Dickens's letters.

2179. "Sales and Bibliography: Dickens's Letters at Hodgson's." *Times Literary Supplement*, 27 November 1937, p. 916.

Comments on a forthcoming sale at Hodgson & Co., London, 9-10 December 1937 (**1953**), involving forty letters from Dickens to Cruikshank, 1837-48, several concerned with Cruikshank's illustrations for *Oliver Twist* and two others revealing Dickens's hand in *The Loving Ballad of Lord Bateman*, from which the article quotes.

2180. "Sales of Dickens's Letters at Sotheby's, April and May 1968." *Dickensian*, 64 (1968), 163.

Identifies letters (most the property of Gladys Storey), prices paid, and purchasers. See **2010**.

2181. "69 Dickens Letters are Sold for $3,000." *New York Times*, 5 November 1920, p. 15.

A report of the sale of the Edwin W. Coggeshall collection (**1925**) at the Anderson Galleries, 4 November, including a volume of autograph Dickens letters, first editions, and presentation copies. Some of the items are listed and prices and purchasers given.

2182. S[later], M[ichael]. "Dickens at Christie's." *Dickensian*, 70 (1974), 48.

A brief description of the sale of the Dickens collection of the late Marquess of Queensberry, 29 November 1972, by his son, Lord Gawain Douglas (**1946**), with the sale prices for a few of the items.

2183. [Slater, Michael]. "Dickens at Sotheby's." *Dickensian*, 66 (1970), 29; 67 (1971), 20, 44, 90, 159; 68 (1972), 108; 69 (1973), 46-47; 70 (1974), 30, 96, 120; 71 (1975), 102-03; 72 (1976), 47-49; 73 (1977), 163-64; 75 (1979), 53-55.

These brief entries are particularly important for noting sales of letters not then included in published volumes of *Pilgrim Letters* and earlier editions of Dickens's letters, occasionally with brief excerpts from the letters, as well as of other important Dickens material. By now, probably all of these letters have been printed in volumes of *Pilgrim Letters* published subsequently.

2184. Stonehouse, J[ohn] H. "Dickens's Library." *Times Literary Supplement*, 21 June 1934, p. 443.

Corrects a statement in Sir Henry Dickens's *Recollections* (2 vols., London: William Heinemann, 1934) that his father's library (**2055**) was sold by public auction. It was sold, Stonehouse asserts, by "private treaty, and bought by Henry Sotheran and Co." Stonehouse also refers to two books on the battlefields of the American Civil War that Dickens had in his library and had read.

2185. "Taking a New Look at Dickens." *Times* (London), 14 March 2001, p. 14.

Reproduces a newly discovered photograph of Dickens taken by John Jabez Edwin Mayall, to be sold at Sotheby's, 11 May 2001. It shows a clean-shaven Dickens with a "weak chin," according to the accompanying text. A brief note, 12 May 2001, p. 10, indicates that the photograph, taken between 1853 and 1855, sold for £39,950 to a "private British collector."

2186. "33 Dickens Letters Bought for $6,000." *New York Times*, 4 January 1935, p. 19.

A report on the sale of the library of Ogden Goelet (**1916-17**), which, the reporter writes, "has been described as one of the last of the great American libraries of the nineteenth century." The thirty-three letters, it is noted, mainly written to Edmund Yates, were sold to Dr. A. S. W. Rosenbach and shed some light on Dickens's marital problems.

2187. Trump, Simon. "Dickens Kept a Keen Eye on Fallen Women." *Sunday Times* (London), 1 July 2001, section 1, p. 12.

A report on the fourteen letters discovered by Robin Fenner, an auctioneer, and to be sold by him (**1949**), that Dickens wrote between 1849 and 1854 to Georgina Morson, governess of Urania Cottage, Angela Burdett-Coutts's home for fallen women. In interviews, Michael Slater and Margaret Brown, the associate editor of *Pilgrim Letters*, XII, speculate about the darker side of Dickens reflected in these letters. Illustrated.

2188. "A Unique Dickens Collection." *Birmingham Daily Gazette*, 6 June 1899. In Dickens House Scrapbooks (**1575**), C, III, 72.

Describes the collection of William Wright then up for sale (**2008**). It included "rare and extremely scarce" editions of Dickens's works, among them presentation copies, the manuscript of *The Battle of Life*, autographs, specially illustrated books, a portion of the manuscript of "O'Thello," the petty cash book kept by Dickens while a clerk for Ellis and Blackmore, and Wright's own grangerized edition of *Forster*, which is described in some detail. For other descriptions of the collection see Kitton (**2124**), Lane (**1663**), "Notes of the Day" (**1695**), and "Wright Collection" (**2196**), as well as the *Daily News*, 10 June 1899; the *Daily Graphic*, 10 and 14 June 1899; the *Morning Post*, 14 June 1899; the *Daily Chronicle*, 14 June 1899, and other papers in Dickens House Scrapbooks (**1575C**), III, 84.

2189. "Unique Items in the Sale Rooms." *Dickensian*, 31 (1934/35), 91, 230.

Brief descriptions of seven presentation copies of Dickens's novels.

2190. "Unpublished Dickens Poem." *New York Times*, 19 December 1909, p. 16.

A report of a sale at the Anderson Galleries (**1923**) on 15 December 1909, including first editions, editions in parts, presentation copies, sets of extra illustrations, original drawings, and, as the title of the article indicates, an edition of Thomas Woolnoth's *Facts and Faces* (London, 1852) with a four-line poem written on the first flyleaf by Dickens, dated Gad's Hill, 9 December 1860, and signed by him.

2191. Vincent, John. "Dickens Memorabilia to Be Sold at Auction." *Times* (London), 15 April 1996, p. 20.

A description of items in a forthcoming sale at Sotheby's, 23 April 1996 (**2016**), from the collection of Horace Pym, a Victorian London solicitor, which includes a "vast collection of rare first editions, portraits and memorabilia relating to Charles Dickens and many other great literary figures." Also see a further, illustrated, report, 23 April 1996, p. 20, and Woudhuysen (**2194**).

2192. Williams, Tony. "When Found: Sale of Dickens Items." *Dickensian*, 95 (1999), 175.

Mentions the then forthcoming sale of "an unusually important archive of papers relating to Charles Dickens" at Sotheby's, London (**2014**). Two photographs of items in the sale are on pp. 98 and 176. Also see Patten (**2149**).

2193. Windsor, John. "Victorian Secrets at Sotheby's Leverhulme Sale." *Art and Auction*, 23, vi (June 2001), 74.

Notes that the then forthcoming sale of the contents of Thornton Manor, home of the Viscounts Leverhulme, would include "a collection of Charles Dickens memorabilia–books, autograph letters, and a wine cooler presented to Dickens after a rapturous public reading of *A Christmas Carol* in Edinburgh in 1858."

2194. Woudhuysen, H. R. "Horace and His Novels." *Times Literary Supplement*, 19 April 1996, p. 23.

Comments on a then forthcoming sale at Sotheby's, 23 April 1996 (**2016**), of the library of Horace N. Pym (1844-96), a Victorian solicitor whose "literary tastes centred on Dickens," and who was a friend of Georgina Hogarth. Woudhuysen provides little information about the items in the sale, however. Also see Vincent (**2191**).

2195. Woudhuysen, H. R. "Tassels and Hock Glasses." *Times Literary Supplement*, 9 July 1999, p. 34.

Mentions Dickens items in a then forthcoming sale at Sotheby's, 15 July 1999 (**2014**), including family legal papers, items from the Bleak House Museum (Broadstairs), and the archive and library of Charles Kent (1823-1902), who wrote for *Household Words* and *All the Year Round*. The sale, Woudhuysen notes, would include 120 letters from Georgina Hogarth to Kent, 1867-97, in which she "often referred to their shared admiration for Dickens."

2196. "Wright Collection. Great Prices for Dickens Books and Others in London." *New York Times*, Saturday Review of Books and Art Sect., 1 July 1899, p. 444.

Notes that the Wright collection (**2008**) includes a number of Dickens items—particularly a grangerized copy of an edition of *Forster* that included 482 letters, including 119 by Dickens, and 445 portraits, including 100 of Dickens, as well as playbills and other Dickensiana. The collection also includes the petty cash book kept by Dickens while a young law clerk at Ellis and Blackmore's that shows his salary as 13s. 6d. per week, various presentation copies of his novels, the manuscript of *The Battle of Life*, some first and early editions of his novels, and the manuscript of "Mrs. Gamp with the Strolling Players." Also see Kitton (**2124**), Lane (**1663**), "Notes of the Day" (**1695**), and "A Unique Dickens Collection" (**2188**).

2197. Young, John. "Dickens Saw Through Novelist's Cover Story." *Times* (London), 31 May 1995, p. 3.

Comments on a brief letter, dated 18 January 1858, then coming up for auction at Phillips's, 15 June 1995, from Dickens to Joseph Langford, the London manager of Blackwood's, the publisher of George Eliot's *Scenes of Clerical Life*, January 1858. In the letter Dickens correctly insists that the author of the work is a woman. The letter (in *Pilgrim Letters*, VIII, 507) was expected to sell for up to £6,000. Illustrated.

6E. COLLECTING DICKENS

Note: Also see **Collecting Dickens** in part 2 of the subject index.

2198. Adams, Frederick B., Jr. *The Uses of Provenance*. Berkeley: School of Librarianship, University of California; Los Angeles: School of Library Service, University of California, 1969, pp. 19-20.

Contains a brief reference to the authentic stuffed pet raven of Dickens in the collection of Colonel Richard Gimbel—see Podeschi (**1509**). Adams adds that, for Dickens relics, "an accompanying certificate of provenance by his sister-in-law, Georgina Hogarth, is recommended as a safeguard."

2199. Ahearn, Allen, and Patricia Ahearn. *Collected Books: The Guide to Values*. New York: G. P. Putnam's Sons, 1991, pp. 167-69; revised as *Collected Books: The Guide to Values, 1998 Edition*. New York: G. P. Putnam's Sons, 1997, pp. 195-98.

The intent of this work is to "provide a basis for identifying and pricing the English-language first editions of books by collected authors," as the authors do for Dickens's works in parts and volume form. Their estimates of prices for Dickens's works rise considerably in the second edition. For example, the price of a copy of *Bleak House* in parts is given as $1,500 in the 1991 edition and $2,500 in the 1998; the price of the 23-volume Nonesuch Edition of Dickens's works is listed as $4,000 in 1991 and $7,500 in 1998.

2200. Arnold, William H. *Ventures in Book Collecting*. New York: Charles Scribner's Sons, 1923, pp. 62-74, 84-86, 314-17, and passim.

Arnold comments on Dickens rarities he has collected over the years; prints several notes and letters in his collection from Dickens to Thomas Noon Talfourd (6 May 1847), to Walter Savage Landor (26 July 1840), to George P. Putnam (24 July 1851), and to Mary Boyle (25 December 1852); and includes some facsimile reproductions of Dickens's signature and book dedications. He also quotes from a letter by Sir Theodore Martin, written more than forty years later, describing the reconciliation between Thackeray and Dickens in 1863, just a few days before Thackeray's death, and reprints a letter from Elizabeth Gaskell to Geraldine Endsor Jewsbury, dated 21 July 1854, detailing her annoyance with herself in her handling of an agreement with Dickens to do a serialized novel for *Household Words*.

2201. Benjamin, Mary. *Autographs: A Key to Collecting.* New York: R. R. Bowker, 1946; corrected and revised, New York: Walter R. Benjamin Autographs, 1963; reprinted New York: Dover Publications, 1986, passim.

Comments in passing on Dickens's autograph. See the index.

2202. Biondi, Lee. "Collecting Charles Dickens." In "Charles Dickens Special" issue of *Firsts: The Book Collector's Magazine*, 7, ix (September 1997), 24-57.

Consists of five articles on Dickens by Biondi, all of which deal, at least in part, with advice for beginning Dickens collectors: "Strategies of Collecting" (**2203**), pp. 24-39; "In the Beginning . . . Charles Dickens Makes a Pseudonym for Himself: A Bibliographical Background to Dickens' *Sketches by Boz*" (**359**), pp. 40-46; "Rise to Fame: *Pickwick* Triumphant" (**341**), pp. 47-50; "The Charles Dickens Reference Shelf" (**1137**), pp. 51-53; and "Great Complications" (**298**), pp. 54-57. Fully illustrated.

2203. Biondi, Lee. "Strategies of Collecting." In his "Collecting Charles Dickens" (**2202**), pp. 24-39.

Beginning with the premise that "a nice 'Dickens Collection' is do-able at various paces and price levels, and with a reasonable degree of difficulty," Biondi surveys the bibliographic points needed by collectors of editions of Dickens's major works from *Sketches by Boz* to *The Mystery of Edwin Drood*. For each work he indicates the "problems, complications and acceptable compromises" of collecting significant editions and comments on each work's availability in the rare book market and the range of prices a collector might expect to pay. This is practical advice from an experienced bookseller who, as he notes, deals with Dickens phone calls "every day I go to work." His advice on collecting *A Christmas Carol*, for example, is to find a copy in good condition "that you *like*," for he has seen copies with almost every variety of points possible. "We know," he points out, "that there was a rush to the public with this immediately successful book and copies were thrown together with whatever was at hand at the printers and case-binders when demand rose." Heavily illustrated.

2204. Brewer, Reginald. *The Delightful Diversion: The Whys and Wherefores of Book Collecting.* New York: Macmillan, 1935, passim.

Contains several references to collecting Dickens.

2205. Brown, T. J. "English Literary Autographs, XV: Charles Dickens, 1812-1870." *Book Collector*, 4 (1955), 237.

A brief technical analysis of Dickens's handwriting and the small changes in it over the years, accompanied by photographic facsimiles of his handwriting in 1837/38 and 1859, facing p. 236.

2206. Cannon, Carl L. *American Book Collectors and Collecting, from Colonial Times to the Present*. New York: H. W. Wilson, 1941, passim.

Contains numerous references to collecting Dickens and to collectors of Dickens.

2207. Carlton, W[illiam] J. "Alex. Hair Galloway on Dickens." *Notes and Queries*, 197 (1952), 522.

Notes his acquisition of a small volume by Galloway not found in Dickens bibliographies (and not in the British Library): *A Critical Dissertation on Some of the Writings of Charles Dickens, Esq., with Illustrative Extracts* (Liverpool: Edward Howell, n. d. [ca. 1850], 48 pp.). The work was subsequently listed in the 1953 supplement to Miller (**1005**), where it is given a date of 1846, and in the 1969 *New Cambridge Bibliography of English Literature* (**8**), and Churchill (**956**), in both of which it is given a suggested date of 1862. A copy of the work is in the Dickens House library.

2208. Carter, John. *Taste & Technique in Book Collecting: A Study of Recent Developments in Great Britain and the United States*. Cambridge: Cambridge University Press, 1948, 1949; New York: R. R. Bowker, 1948, passim; reprinted with corrections, notes, and an epilogue as *Taste & Technique in Book Collecting. With an Epilogue*. London: Private Libraries Association, 1970, passim.

Comments in passing on the difficulties of collecting Dickens, as well as other Victorian authors, because of the complexities of publication and republication practices. See, for example, pp. 98, 100-01, 159, and 161. Other references to Dickens are noted in the index.

2209. Chancellor, E. Beresford. "First Editions of Dickens." In his *Literary Diversions*. London: Dulau, 1925, pp. 14-19.

On the early joy of collecting almost anything in any state by Dickens and the later pleasure in being able to discriminate between the useless and the valuable in collecting truly rare Dickens items, with notes on "points" to watch for in collecting some of the works.

2210. "Charles Dickens in Pottery and Pictures." *Sphere*, 39 (1909), 174.

A page of photographs of nine Royal Doulton pottery pieces and two illustrations of inns mentioned in *Pickwick Papers*.

2211. Claverton, Douglas. "Big Money in First Editions of Dickens." *Collector's Weekly*, 26 September 1970, p. 8.

Comments that no author of English literature could be a greater attraction to a collector than Charles Dickens and that any first or early edition in good condition of one of his novels would be a sound investment.

2212. Clendening, Logan. "The Bibliography of *Pickwick Papers.*" In his *A Handbook to Pickwick Papers.* New York and London: Alfred A. Knopf, 1936, pp. 137-49.

Discusses some of the problems connected with collecting a prime *Pickwick* in parts and briefly comments on seven book-length studies of *Pickwick Papers.* Illustrated.

2213. "The Collecting World: The Old Curiosity Shop." *Collecting,* 1 (1907), 186.

Notes that the London building known as "The Old Curiosity Shop" probably was not Dickens's source for the eponymous building in *The Old Curiosity Shop.* The anonymous author also mentions some features of editions of Dickens and sets of extra illustrations for his novels. Illustrated.

2214. Cooper, T. P. "The Crest of Dickens." *Dickensian,* 13 (1917), 298.

Contains a reproduction of the crest Dickens used on his bookplates, silverplate, and tableware. Cooper queries whether the crest was spurious or authorized. See Cooper (**2215**), Dexter (**2217**), Hoefnagel (**2235**), and Lee (**2241**).

2215. Cooper, T. P. "Dickens and His 'Heraldic Crest.'" *Dickensian,* 18 (1922), 194-96.

Points out that Dickens used a sham heraldic emblem on his dinner service, silverplate, and bookplates, apparently one originally granted by the College of Arms in 1625 to one William Dickens, a citizen of London. Illustrated. See Cooper (**2214**), Dexter (**2217**), Hoefnagel (**2235**), and Lee (**2241**).

2216. Dexter, John F. "Hints to Dickens Collectors." In *Dickens Memento* (**1948**), pp. 7-35.

Advises collectors of Dickens's works about which editions are valuable and rare, what to look for in authentic first and later editions, and what to expect to pay in 1884/85. Dexter also comments on various items of Dickensiana, manuscripts, and manuscript fragments that were either in his possession or had passed through his hands since Dickens's death.

2217. Dexter, Walter. "When Found—Dickens's Crest." *Dickensian*, 27 (1930/31), 3, 80.

A brief note (p. 3) on Dickens's use on his plates, cutlery, and bookplates of a coat of arms granted in 1625 to a family named Dickens that came from West Stoke in Sussex. On p. 80 Dexter prints a brief letter from Dickens, 5 April 1869, to a Mr. J. O. Marples, referring to his restricted use of the crest. See a letter to the editor from T. P. Cooper, pp. 236-37, pointing out that Dickens had no right to use this crest. Also see Cooper (**2214-15**) for earlier and Hoefnagel (**2235**) and Lee (**2241**) for later information and commentary on this subject.

2218. Dickens, David, and Norman M. Jacoby. "Charles Dickens's Travelling Medicine Chest." *Dickensian*, 92 (1996), 19-24.

The authors describe and examine the contents of the leather-bound travelling medicine chest that Dickens took to America in 1867-68, newly rediscovered in a private collection (not identified). While the authors discovered the chest in a search for evidence that Dickens suffered from asthma, the contents of the chest, they announce, did not provide the proof they had hoped for. Illustrated with photographs of the medicine chest and a handwritten inventory of its contents, with brief annotations in Dickens's hand. Also see the frontispiece to the issue of the *Dickensian* and a response by Joel J. Brattin, p. 129, noting references in *Martin Chuzzlewit* to asthma and a portable medicine kit.

2219. "The Dickens Collector." *Dickensian*, 2 (1906), 68.

Summary of an interview with Walter T. Spencer in the *Manchester Guardian* (**2222**) about collecting Dickens.

2220. "Dickens in Pottery." *Chambers's Journal*, 88, 7th ser., 1 (1910/11), 350.

A brief description of the 1910/11 pieces of Doulton china (plates, bowls, tankards, jugs, vases) with scenes from Dickens's novels on them.

2221. "Dickens Rarities." *Globe and Traveller* (London), 7 February 1912, pp. 1-2.

On the joys of collecting rare Dickens editions and issues of editions.

2222. "Dickens' Collectors." *Manchester Guardian*, 7 February 1906, p. 12.

An interview with Walter T. Spencer, a London rare book dealer, who provides descriptions of Dickens collectors (good and bad) and collectibles. Summarized in "The Dickens Collector" (**2219**).

2223. Dickinson, Donald C. *Dictionary of American Book Collectors.* New York, Westport, CT, and London: Greenwood Press, 1986, passim.

Contains biographical sketches and information about the collections of well-known American book collectors, with brief bibliographies of books by and about them. See, for example, the sections on William M. Elkins, pp. 104-05; DeCoursey Fales, pp. 111-12; Richard Gimbel, pp. 137-38; Ogden Goelet, pp. 138-39; Jerome Kern, pp. 190-91; Frederick Lehmann, pp. 199-200; George B. McCutcheon, pp. 224-25; and B. George Ulizio, pp. 317-18. Other well-known collectors of Dickens's works are included, such as A. S. W. Rosenbach, Harry B. Smith, Harry E. Widener, and William A. Clark, Jr., with no or but passing reference to their Dickens collections.

2224. Doulton & Co., Burslem, England. *A Tribute in Pottery to the Genius of Charles Dickens.* Burslem, Eng.: Doulton & Co., Royal Doulton Pottery, [1911]. 50 unnumbered pp.

A text full of praise for Dickens and his works is accompanied by twenty-six full-page illustrations of characters from his works (with brief descriptions of the characters in Dickens's own words) that are painted on various pieces of Royal Doulton china. A letter from Alfred Tennyson Dickens, dated 23 May 1911, expressing his "high appreciation" of the "Charles Dickens" Doulton Pottery Ware, is reproduced.

2225. E., E. J. M. "Dickens Knockers." *Notes and Queries,* 11th ser., 5 (1912), 111.

On bedroom door knockers with characters from Dickens's novels imprinted on them.

2226. "Early Dickens Editions." *New York Times,* 7 June 1908, sect. 2, p. 4.

Briefly describes the first American edition of *Pickwick Papers* and Cuthbert Bede's (Edward Bradley's) edition of the Christmas Books to be sold at an Anderson Gallery sale.

2227. F., F. D. "Dickens's Autographs." *Notes and Queries,* 5th ser., 11 (1879), 87.

Notes that a Dickens edition with an inscription in Dickens's hand and his signature increases its value at an auction sale.

2228. Fielding, K[enneth] J. "The Manuscript of the 'Cricket on the Hearth.'" *Notes and Queries,* 197 (1952), 324-25, 329.

Traces the provenance of the manuscript, largely with reference to Walter T. Spencer's *Forty Years in My Bookshop* (**2271**), with some corrections to Spencer's account. The manuscript is now in the Pierpont Morgan Library, New York.

2229. [Fitzgerald, Percy]. "The Romance of Old Books." *Tinsley's Magazine*, 36 (1885), 446-67; somewhat expanded as part of "Of Grangerising and Dickensiana." In his *The Book Fancier or The Romance of Book Collecting*. London: Sampson Low, Marston, Searle, & Rivington, 1886; New York: Scribner & Welford, 1887, pp. 168-92.

In the section on Dickens, pp. 458-67 in the article and pp. 178-92 of *The Book Fancier*, notes that "within the last two or three years" an "eager quest for early copies and first editions of Dickens' works has developed to an extraordinary degree." Fitzgerald thinks that this would have amused Dickens, for "he had little toleration for the 'fads' of the bibliophilist." Fitzgerald nevertheless proceeds to mention various rarities among Dickens's works, sometimes giving then current sale prices, and some of the studies and continuations of Dickens's works, including topographical volumes on the market, sets of extra illustrations for Dickens's works, and portraits. He also describes the extraordinary grangerized copy of *Forster* that a Mr. Harvey expanded into thirteen large folio volumes.

2230. Gamut, David. "The Bibliophile Rambles." *New York Times*, 5 February 1888, p. 12.

Contains some information for early collectors about collecting Dickens's works.

2231. Grubb, G. H. "Old Books and New: No. 4.–Collecting Dickens' Works: A Beautifully-Bound Modern Edition of 'The Pickwick Papers' for £25." *Bazaar, Exchange and Mart*, 9 July 1927, p. 33.

Notes that the library of the late B. W. Batz (sic–should be Matz) was recently acquired by the Dickens Fellowship and is in the Dickens House, London. Grubb also mentions a number of valuable editions of Dickens's works that he saw at Charles J. Sawyer's bookshop in London, including the *Pickwick Papers* noted in the title, and works that are available at Messrs. Maggs, another bookshop.

2232. Hamilton, Charles. *Collecting Autographs and Manuscripts*. Norman: University of Oklahoma Press, 1961, 1970, 1974, pp. 130-32.

Prints a page of Dickens's autographs from 1831, 1832, 1838, 1859, and 1870 to show changes from the "bold, forceful, and clear" early signatures to the "more and more crabbed" signatures of the later years. Hamilton also prints a facsimile of part of a letter from Dickens to David C. Colden from America 1842 (10 March 1842, in *Pilgrim Letters*, III, 109-12). A paperback edition was published in 1993 (Santa Monica: Modoc), with fourteen additional chapters.

2233. "Handsworthy" (pseud.). "A Birmingham Dickens Souvenir and Other Reminiscences." *Birmingham Weekly Post*, 18 February 1905, p. 1.

A letter to the editor describing a lithographed ticket designed by E. M. Ward for a performance of Bulwer-Lytton's *Not So Bad as We Seem* by Dickens's company of amateur actors at the Birmingham Town Hall, 12 May 1852. A reproduction of the front of the ticket accompanies the letter, which also contains information about the play, the town hall, and other visits by Dickens to Birmingham.

2234. Hills, Gertrude. "Pursuing a Perfect Pickwick in Parts." *American Book Collector*, 1 (1932), 346-52.

A flippant narrative, probably fictional, of a bookseller pursuing a *Pickwick* in parts, supposedly locked in a bank vault in Greensborough, Virginia, that she never saw since the owner only wanted to know what the set of parts was worth before she contributed it to a university.

2235. Hoefnagel, Dick. "Bibliographical Notes & Queries: Note 453. The Bookplate of Charles Dickens." *Book Collector*, 32 (1983), 349-51.

Notes that there are two variants of Dickens's bookplate, as the accompanying illustration shows. Also see Cooper (**2214-15**), Dexter (**2217**), and Lee (**2241**).

2236. Johnson, Charles P. "First Editions. Charles Dickens." *Bookworm*, 1 (1888), 81-83, 132-33.

Largely for the beginning book collector, comments on what to look for in buying first editions of Dickens's works and what prices to expect to pay (in 1888). Johnson covers mainly the minor works but also *Sketches by Boz*, *Oliver Twist*, *Nicholas Nickleby*, and *Pickwick Papers*.

2237. Keller, Dean H., and Matthew J. Bruccoli. "B. George Ulizio (2 February 1889-29 September 1969)." In Rosenblum (**2261**), pp. 282-88.

Comments briefly on Ulizio as a Dickens collector. Illustrated. See the catalogue for the sale of Ulizio's library (**1913**).

2238. Klappholz, David. "Charles Sessler (5 November 1854 to 4 September 1935)." In Rosenblum (**2262**), pp. 272-78.

In this sketch of the life and collecting career of Sessler, a Philadelphia publisher and bookseller, Klappholz mentions Sessler's great interest in collecting Dickens and notes that Colonel William Gimbel consulted Sessler when he started collecting Dickens. Illustrated. For Gimbel's collection, see Gimbel (**1797**) and Podeschi (**1509**).

2239. Lake, Brian. "English Literature of the Nineteenth Century." In *Antiquarian Books: A Companion for Booksellers, Librarians and Collectors.* Comp. and ed. Philippa Bernard, with Leo Bernard and Angus O'Neill. Philadelphia: University of Pennsylvania Press, 1994, pp. 203-08.

Comments on Jarndyce Booksellers' catalogues of literature (**2031-42**), published after the firm started in the late 1960s, and notes that for those early days the "Dickens prices look quite reasonable," *Little Dorrit* in parts selling for a mere £52, for example. Now, Lake indicates, prices for scarcer items have gone "through the roof." Illustrated.

2240. Lang, Andrew. *The Library. With a Chapter on Modern English Illustrated Books by Austin Dobson.* London: Macmillan, 1881; 2nd ed., 1892, pp. 57-58.

Mentions that purchasing anything by and about Dickens is a "sound investment" for a beginning book collector; comments briefly on a nine-volume grangerized copy of *Forster* with "some eight hundred engravings, portraits, views, playbills, title pages, catalogues, proof illustrations from Dickens's works, a set of the Onwhyn plates, rare engravings by Cruikshank and 'Phiz,' and autograph letters"; and notes the rarity of early editions of Dickens's works, brought on, Lang remarks in a footnote, by their "being hacked to pieces by Grangerites." Also see Dobson (**876**).

2241. Lee, Brian N. "Charles Dickens." In his *British Bookplates: A Pictorial History.* Newton Abbot, Eng., London, and North Pomfret, VT: David & Charles, 1979, p. 102.

Comments briefly on the bookplate Dickens used, "adopting without entitlement the crest granted to William Dickens in 1625." Lee states that it is not generally known that there is a variant of this. He also mentions the label designed after Dickens's death and placed by the auctioneers of his library in the books sold. One version of Dickens's own bookplate is reproduced on p. 103. See also Cooper (**2214-15**), Dexter (**2217**), and Hoefnagel (**2235**).

2242. Lemperly, Paul. *Books and I.* Cleveland, OH: Rowfant Club, 1938, pp. 38-39.

Mentions a copy of *Master Humphrey's Clock*, inscribed to Frederick Salmon by Dickens and including an autograph note to Salmon from Dickens (dated 25 October 1841 in *Pilgrim Letters*, II, 408-09), as an example of a true "association copy" of a book, from a collector's point of view, and gives both the inscription and the note as well as a photographic facsimile of both.

2243. "Literary Notes and News." *Westminster Gazette*, 13 September 1909, p. 4.

For collectors, comments on the difficulty of forging Dickens's autograph and on Dickens's use of blue paper and blue ink for his letters after "the Pickwick period."

2244. McGovern, J. B. "The Brontë Poems." *Notes and Queries*, 12th ser., 8 (1921), 450.

Prints a query from the *Manchester Guardian*, 2 May 1921, about Dickens's copy of a first edition of *Poems by Currer, Acton, and Ellis Bell* (1846) that came up for sale, presumably in 1921. McGovern is curious about how Dickens came into possession of it since Charlotte Brontë complained about its poor sales at the time of publication. McGovern received no responses to his query.

2245. McKendrick, Russ. "Numismatics: Christmas Carol Time." *New York Times*, 11 December 1977, Section II, p. 47.

Describes a bronze medal issued in 1912 with Dickens's face on one side and Bob Cratchit carrying Tiny Tim on his shoulders on the other side. McKendrick also notes the circumstances of the medal's issue. Illustrated.

2246. Miller, W[illiam]. "The Value of First Editions." *Dickensian*, 33 (1936/37), 38-39.

Gives prices one might pay for editions in 1) parts, 2) original cloth, and 3) rebound half-leather for the various works of Dickens. The information is quite dated, obviously, but of some historic interest. For example, in 1936 one could have picked up *Bleak House* in parts for £10-£18, *David Copperfield* for £50-£75, and *Pickwick Papers* for £45 or more.

2247. Morris, Leslie A. "A. S W. Rosenbach (22 July 1876-1 July 1952)." In Rosenblum (**2261**), pp. 220-29.

Biographical sketch of an important bookseller and Dickens collector. Illustrated. For Rosenbach's collection, see Driver (**1458**), Sargeant (**1726**), Morris (**2249**), Rosenbach (**2260**), and Wolf and Fleming (**2281**).

2248. Morris, Leslie A. "Harry Elkins Widener (3 January 1885-15 April 1912)." In Rosenblum (**2261**), pp. 311-18.

In a sketch of Widener's life and career as a book collector, Morris comments in passing on Widener's acquisition of Dickens items (**2249**). Illustrated. For Widener's Dickens collection, see Rosenbach (**1518**).

2249. Morris, Leslie A. "Harry Elkins Widener and A. S. W. Rosenbach: Of Books and Friendship." *Harvard Library Bulletin*, 6 (1995), 7-28.

This biographical sketch of two major American collectors, the latter a Philadelphia bookseller, touches upon the role Rosenbach played in Widener's acquisition of works by Dickens, George Cruikshank, and others. Morris notes that, following Widener's death in the sinking of the Titanic, his mother, Eleanor Elkins Widener, a survivor of the tragic event, inherited the collection and expanded it. Ultimately, he adds, she had Rosenbach compile the catalogues of the collection, one on Robert L. Stevenson, one on Cruikshank (**1517**), one on Dickens (**1518**), and two volumes "for everything else." In 1915 she deposited the collection in the Harry Elkins Widener Memorial Library at Harvard University.

2250. Newton, A[lfred] Edward. *The Amenities of Book Collecting, and Kindred Affections*. Boston: Atlantic Monthly Press, 1918; 2nd ed., 1919; 3rd ed., 1920; reprinted in Essay and General Literature Index Reprint Series. Port Washington, NY: Kennikat Press, 1969, passim.

Makes numerous passing references to presentation copies and editions of Dickens's works in his collection and to the joys and anguishes of a book collector. Newton includes a facsimile reproduction of a three-paragraph dedication by Dickens to J. P. Harley (the actor) in a copy of *The Village Coquettes*. A useful index was added and minor corrections made in the second edition.

2251. Newton, A[lfred] Edward. *This Book-Collecting Game*. Boston: Little, Brown, 1928, passim.

Contains bits of information about collecting Dickens. See the index.

2252. Nikirk, Robert. "Looking into Provenance." In *A Miscellany for Bibliophiles*. Ed. H. George Fletcher. New York: Grastorf & Lang, 1979, pp. 15-45.

In commenting on the use of a bookseller's catalogue devoted entirely to the library of one person as a means of determining provenance, Nikirk uses the catalogue of Dickens's own library issued by Sotheran in 1878 (**2055**) as an example. Nikirk warns that, since modern restrikes of Dickens's bookplate have been made, one cannot be certain that a volume containing his bookplate was actually part of his library at his death without checking the Sotheran cata-logue.

2253. Overmier, Judith A. "Harry B. Smith (28 December 1860-1 January 1936)." In Rosenblum (**2262**), pp. 278-85.

In this sketch of Smith's life and collecting career, Overmier mentions Smith's collection of presentation copies of Dickens's novels and Droodiana, among other Dickens items. Illustrated. For the catalogue of Smith's "Senti-mental" collection, see Smith (**1525**).

2254. Preston, Edward. "When Found: 'This Is the Pass.'" *Dickensian*, 94 (1998), 150-51.

Reports on a recent acquisition by Alan Newton, a collector of autograph manuscripts, of a list in Dickens's hand of people (principally the actors) to be allowed backstage without a pass for a performance of *The Frozen Deep* by Dick-ens's amateur company, 4 July 1857, when Queen Victoria attended the perfor-mance. The list is headed by a note that no one is to be admitted at the stage door without a pass or an order from Dickens or Arthur Smith. A photograph of the document accompanies the text.

2255. Purser, Charles. "Dickens's Calligraphy." *Times* (London), 11 July 1939, p. 10.

In a letter to the editor, Purser comments on the difficulty of reading Dick-ens's handwriting, noting that, when he (Purser) was a boy working in his fa-ther's printing office, "journeyman printers from London used to tell me they had seen compositors burst into tears when they had to set up Dickens's 'copy'" because they were paid on the basis of their productivity, and Dickens's manuscripts were not conducive to that.

2256. Quayle, Eric. "Charles Dickens and Wilkie Collins." In his *The Collector's Book of Detective Fiction*. London: Studio Vista, 1972, pp. 42-50.

Provides basic information about collecting the works of these two authors, particularly those, such as *Oliver Twist, Bleak House, Barnaby Rudge, The Moonstone,* and *The Woman in White,* containing murders or elements of detective fiction. Illustrated.

2257. Roberts, W[illiam]. *Rare Books and Their Prices. With Chapters on Pictures, Pottery, Porcelain and Postage Stamps.* London: George Redway, 1896, pp. 29-34.

Notes a decline in interest in collecting first editions of Dickens and Thackeray unless they contain "some extraneous matter" or are in the original wrappers with the advertising inserts, or have the requirements for the earliest issue. Roberts gives examples of what to look for with such works as *Oliver Twist, Memoirs of Grimaldi, Martin Chuzzlewit,* and particularly *Pickwick Papers.*

2258. Roe, F. Gordon. "Queen Victoria Meets Mr. Pickwick, and Some Bogus Pickwickiana." *Connoisseur,* 114 (1944), 105-07.

Provides information of use to collectors about some of the imitations or plagiarisms of *Pickwick Papers.* Illustrated.

2259. Roland, Paul. "Collecting the Everyman's Library." *Book and Magazine Collector,* no. 103 (October 1992), 50-57.

Notes that the twenty-two volumes of Dickens's works "caused the most problems" in producing the Everyman's Library because of their length.

2260. Rosenbach, A. S. W. *A Book Hunter's Holiday: Adventures with Books and Manuscripts.* Boston and New York: Houghton Mifflin, the Riverside Press, Cambridge, 1936; reprinted in facsimile in Essay Index Reprint Series. Freeport, NY: Books for Libraries Press, 1968, pp. 18-19, 64-67.

This well-known book collector comments on his collection; on pages of the manuscript of *Pickwick Papers;* on Dickens's interest in murder and horror, particularly in *Bleak House* and *Edwin Drood* (Rosenbach especially regrets that the manuscript of the latter novel, in the Forster Collection, Victoria and Albert Museum, London, will never be his); and on Edgar Allen Poe's anticipation of the plot of *Barnaby Rudge.* Illustrations include the frontispiece for *A Christmas Carol* and Dickens's inscription in a copy of *A Christmas Carol* presented to Mrs. Henry Austin, 22 December 1843 (facing p. 242).

2261. Rosenblum, Joseph, ed. *American Book-Collectors and Bibliographers, First Series.* Dictionary of Literary Biography, 140. Detroit, Washington, DC, and London: A Bruccoli Clark Layman Book, Gale Research, 1994, passim.

A collection of biographical sketches and bibliographies of and about a number of well-known American collectors and scholars. For those whose Dickens collections are mentioned, see Leslie A. Morris on A. S. W. Rosenbach (**2247**), pp. 220-29, and on Harry Elkins Widener (**2248**), pp. 311-18, and Dean H. Keller and Matthew J. Bruccoli on B. George Ulizio (**2237**), pp. 282-88. Illustrated. Also see Rosenblum (**2262**).

2262. Rosenblum, Joseph, ed. *American Book-Collectors and Bibliographers, Second Series.* Dictionary of Literary Biography, 187. Detroit, Washington, DC, and London: A Bruccoli Clark Layman Book, Gale Research, 1997, passim.

A second collection of biographical sketches and bibliographies of and about a number of well-known American collectors and scholars. For those whose Dickens collections are mentioned, see Joseph Rosenblum on William Andrews Clark, Jr. (**2263**), pp. 30-39; Theodore Spahn on Jerome Kern (**2270**), pp. 185-91; David Klappholz on Charles Sessler (**2238**), pp. 272-78; and Judith A. Overmier on Harry B. Smith (**2253**), pp. 279-85. Illustrated. Also see Rosenblum (**2261**).

2263. Rosenblum, Joseph. "William Andrews Clark, Jr. (29 March 1877-14 June 1934)." In Rosenblum (**2262**), pp. 30-39.

In this sketch of Clark's life and collecting career, Rosenblum comments on the Dickens items in Clark's collection, principally Dickens's works published in monthly parts (p. 37). Illustrated. See the catalogue of Clark's Dickens collection (**1453, 1536**).

2264. Rostenberg, Leona, and Madeleine Stern. *Old Books, Rare Friends: Two Literary Sleuths and Their Shared Passion.* New York, London, etc.: Doubleday, 1997, pp. 136-38.

Two booksellers's account of discovering a set of *Master Humphrey's Clock* in parts in an old barn.

2265. Sawyer, Charles J., and F. J. Harvey Darton. "Charles Dickens." In their *English Books, 1475-1900: A Signpost for Collectors.* 2 vols. London: Charles J. Sawyer, 1927, II, 237-92.

In this introduction to book collecting, the authors point out that book collectors see Dickens as "not only the most eminent of all the Victorians, but . . . one of the most eminent figures in all their booty." In a running description, the authors provide basic information about editions, manner of publication, illustrators, principal bibliographical problems, and related matters concerning Dickens's major and minor works. They tell the collector what to look for, comment on the relative rarity of various editions, and give some prices current in 1927. Among other illustrations, they reproduce the first page of the manuscript (not in Dickens's hand) of "The Stratagems of Rozanza," an early piece from about 1828, identified as "by C. J. H. Dickens." They also provide a full bibliographical description of what they describe as "the rarest and most expensive of Dickens's books," the monthly serialization of *A Tale of Two Cities* in eight (as seven) parts in blue wrappers (1859), and give details about the various states of the first editions of *A Christmas Carol* and *The Battle of Life*. For other commentary on the states of the first edition of *A Christmas Carol*, see Calhoun and Heaney (**252**) and the cross references listed there.

2266. Schooling, J. Holt. "The Signatures of Charles Dickens (with Portraits), from 1825 to 1870." *Strand Magazine*, 7 (1894), 80-89.

Reproduces facsimiles of some thirty-one signatures of Dickens, often strikingly different, and eighteen portraits, with running commentary, largely descriptive, on the handwriting, which Schooling believes shows the influence of Dickens's state of mind and state of health.

2267. Shaffer, Ellen. "Portrait of a Philadelphia Collector: William McIntyre Elkins (1882-1947)." *Papers of the Bibliographical Society of America*, 50 (1956), 115-68.

While this article is almost entirely devoted to Elkins's collection of Americana, Shaffer briefly mentions, pp. 119-20, some of his Dickens holdings in connection with works from Harry B. Smith's "Sentimental Library" (**1525**). Also see Free Library of Philadelphia (**1793**).

2268. Slater, J[ohn] H. "First Editions of Dickens." *Connoisseur*, 1 (1901), 176-78.

Notes the "great demand for really good copies" of first issues of first editions of Dickens's works in original wrappers or cloth binding and gives the points for identifying such issues of *Sketches by Boz*, *Sunday under Three Heads*, *The Village Coquettes*, *Is She His Wife?*, and, inevitably, *Pickwick Papers*. Illustrated.

2269. "Some Furnishing Relics of Charles Dickens." *The House* (London), 1 September 1897, 20-21.

Contains sketches and brief descriptions of some chairs and desks used by Dickens.

2270. Spahn, Theodore. "Jerome Kern (27 January 1885-11 November 1945)." In Rosenblum (**2262**), pp. 185-91.

In this sketch of Kern's life and collecting career, Spahn notes the preponderance of Dickens items in Kern's collection of literary works and manuscripts. Illustrated. See the sale catalogue of Kern's collection (**1934**).

2271. Spencer, Walter T. "Dickensiana." In his *Forty Years in My Bookshop*. Ed. Thomas Moult. London: Constable; Boston and New York: Houghton Mifflin, 1923; London: Constable, 1927, pp. 89-161 and passim.

Spencer, a London bookseller, comments on a variety of Dickensiana that passed through his hands—various manuscripts (Georgina Hogarth sold him the manuscript for *The Cricket on the Hearth*, he states, when she needed money) and letters (at the time of writing, he notes, he had "not less than two hundred" unpublished Dickens letters in his possession, from some of which he quotes). He also comments on some of Dickens's illustrators, among them F. W. Pailthorpe, and claims that Joseph Grego was the author of *Charles Dickens: The Story of His Life* (London: John Camden Hotten; New York: Harper & Brothers, 1870) and *Thackeray, the Humourist and Man of Letters* (London: John Camden Hotten; New York: D. Appleton, 1864), writing them for Hotten under the pseudonym of "Theodore Taylor." Illustrated.

2272. Spencer, W[alter] T. "'A Page from My Life': Adventures with Dickens." *Graphic*, 118 (1927), 103.

Spencer, a London bookseller, notes that he began reading Dickens as a boy and recalls some of the rare Dickens items on hand in his shop in 1927 or that had passed through his hands earlier, including some 500 Dickens letters, the manuscript of *The Cricket on the Hearth* (sold to him by Georgina Hogarth), three pages of the manuscript of *Oliver Twist*, one page of the manuscript of *Dombey and Son*, Dickens's costume for Captain Bobadil in Ben Jonson's *Every Man in His Humour*, and various relics.

2273. Stone, Harry. "Dickens." *Notes and Queries*, ns 6 (1959), 233-34.

An unanswered request for any other extant call slips that Dickens filled out as a reader in the British Museum library besides the six printed in Kitton's *Charles Dickens by Pen and Pencil* (London: Frank T. Sabin, 1889-90). Kitton indicated there that many others were in the hands of collectors, Stone notes, though no others have ever been reproduced.

2274. Storm, Colton, and Howard Peckham. *Invitation to Book Collecting, Its Pleasures and Practices, with Kindred Discussions of Manuscripts, Maps, and Prints.* New York: R. R. Bowker, 1947, pp. 175-83.

In a section on how to use bibliographical works to determine the rarity and value of a book, the authors use *Pickwick Papers* in parts as an example.

2275. "Tariff on Dickens's Hair. One Lock Holds Up Case of Books at Custom House." *New York Times*, 10 December 1913, p. 1.

Points up the difficulty of collecting Dickens relics. Custom House officials, it is reported, insisted that a duty of about $70 was due on a lock of Dickens's hair since it was not considered an "antiquity." Also reported in *Times* (London), 11 December 1913, p. 8.

2276. Trela, D. J. "John Forster (2 April 1812-1 February 1876)." In *Nineteenth-Century British Book-Collectors and Bibliographers*. Ed. William Baker and Kenneth Womack. Dictionary of Literary Biography, 184. Detroit, Washington, DC, and London: A Bruccoli Clark Layman Book, Gale Research, 1997, pp. 104-11.

A sketch of Forster's life and literary career with frequent reference to his personal and professional relationship with Dickens. Trela comments on the collection Forster left in his will to the Victoria and Albert Museum, London, a collection with major Dickens holdings, "perhaps its chief glory." Trela adds bibliographies of Forster's writings and writings about him. Illustrated. For catalogues of the Forster Collection, see **1539, 1541-43**.

2277. Winterich, John T. *Collector's Choice*. New York: Greenberg, 1928, passim.

Contains several comments on what to look for in collecting Dickens, with some reference to the usefulness of bibliographies of Dickens.

2278. Winterich, John T. *A Primer of Book Collecting*. New York: Greenberg Press, 1926; London: G. Allen and Unwin, 1928, pp. 15-16, 40-41, 84-86, 169-71; revised and enlarged ed., New York: Greenberg Press 1935, pp. 19-21, 44-45, 97-08, 198-200.

Offers advice to the collector of Dickens—confine collecting to minor "spheres of Dickensian research," such as imitations, dramatic adaptations, sheet music, and every edition of a single title. Winterich also comment on the inception of *Pickwick Papers*, on the eighty-five page collation of *Pickwick* in parts in Hatton and Cleaver (**24**), and on artist errors in illustrations for *Pickwick Papers*, *Nicholas Nickleby*, *Martin Chuzzlewit*, and *Dombey and Son*. Two of the four sections on Dickens in the first edition are expanded in the 1935 edition. Also see **2279**, below.

2279. Winterich, John T., and David A. Randall. *A Primer of Book Collecting*. Newly revised and enlarged ed. New York: Greenberg Press, 1946, pp. 15-16, 33-34, 73-74, 149-50; 3rd revised ed. New York: Crown; London: George Allen & Unwin, 1966, pp. 19-20, 43-44, 92, 171-72.

Although changes are made elsewhere in these two revised editions of the volume originally prepared by Winterich alone (**2278**), no further revisions were made in the sections on Dickens.

2280. Wise, Thomas J., ed. *A Reference Catalogue of British and Foreign Autographs and Manuscripts. Part III: The Autograph of Charles Dickens*. London: Printed for distribution to members of the Society of Archivists, 1894. 6 unnumbered pp.

Consists of large folio-sized photographic reproductions of two Dickens letters to Henry Austin, his brother-in-law, dated "Wednesday Evening" ("Early 1835" in *Pilgrim Letters*, I, 56-57) and 1 May 1842. In a brief preface, Wise comments on changes in Dickens's signature.

2281. Wolf, Edwin, 2nd, with John F. Fleming. *Rosenbach, a Biography*. Cleveland and New York: World Publishing Co., 1960; London: Weidenfeld and Nicholson, 1961, passim.

A fascinating biography of the famous Philadelphia antiquarian book dealer and collector, Dr. A. S. W. Rosenbach, and his wheeling and dealing in the world of rare books. There are numerous references to the Dickensiana that passed through his hands and to the numerous sales of libraries of great collectors that he attended. Much of Rosenbach's Dickens collection, the authors indicate, was sold to William Elkins, ultimately making its way to the Free Library of Philadelphia. Rosenbach also sold many Dickens items to Jerome Kern and Comte Alain de Suzannet.

PART SEVEN: MANUSCRIPTS AND TEXTUAL CHANGES: DICKENS AT WORK

7A. GENERAL TEXTUAL STUDIES

Note: Also see part 2B, **Bibliographies and Bibliographical Studies of Dickens's Reading Versions of His Works**, above, and **Craft of fiction in Dickens's works; Charles Dickens, as editor; Manuscripts of Dickens's works; Number plans, notes, and memoranda for Dickens's novels; Proofs of Dickens's works;** and **Textual studies of Dickens's works** in part 2 of the subject index, as well as comparable headings under individual works in part 1 of the subject index.

2282. [Andrews, Malcolm]. "Editorial." *Dickensian*, 90 (1994), 82-84.

Comments on the re-conservation of Dickens's manuscripts in the Forster Collection, Victoria and Albert Museum, London (**1539, 1541-43**). They will be rebound, Andrews notes, into seventy-four rather than the present thirty-eight volumes and the manuscript leaves removed from their current backings to reveal cancelled text previously inaccessible on about 500 pages. Andrews also comments on the "elusive pleasure," in the computer age, of being "in direct contact with manuscript material of this value" and being able to sense Dickens at work on his novels. Illustrated with photographs of the old and new binding of the manuscript of *American Notes*. Other works have been rebound more recently–see Low (**2304**).

2283. B[rattin], J[oel] J. "Composition, Dickens's Methods of." In *Oxford Reader's Companion to Dickens*. Ed. Paul Schlicke (**2309**), pp. 111-19 (pp. 116-23 in 2000 paperback ed.).

A concise yet detailed, knowledgeable description of Dickens at work, with frequent reference to his own comments on how he wrote. Illustrated with a photographic facsimile of a page of the manuscript of *Nicholas Nickleby* and the last page of the manuscript of *The Mystery of Edwin Drood*.

2284. Brattin, Joel J. "A Map of the Labyrinth: Editing Dickens's Manuscripts." *Dickens Quarterly*, 2 (1985), 3-11.

Makes a case not only for using the manuscript of a Dickens novel as the copy-text for the most authoritative edition but, perhaps more importantly, for preparing transcriptions of all the manuscripts with cancellations and additions indicated as clearly and accurately as possible. To show the value of such a transcription to an understanding of Dickens's "aesthetic and human values and his rhetorical and compositional strategies," Brattin provides both a facsimile and his transcription of a page of the manuscript of *Martin Chuzzlewit*. He then does a close analysis of what the revisions reveal of Dickens's craft. He acknowledges the difficulty of making an accurate transcription, particularly of the manuscripts of the later novels, which are more heavily revised than the page from *Martin Chuzzlewit*.

2285. Brattin, Joel J. "Reading between the Lines: Interpreting Dickens's Later Manuscripts." *Dissertation Abstracts International*, 47 (1986/87), 534A (Stanford University, 1986).

Examines the manuscripts of *Little Dorrit, A Tale of Two Cities, Great Expectations*, and *Our Mutual Friend*, describing them as "extraordinary complex tangles of interlineations, deletions and substitutions" that "record the great bulk of Dickens's creative and practical decisions about the shape and purpose of his fiction." Individual chapters look at "Structure and Plot in *Little Dorrit*," "The Creating of Flora Finching" (*Little Dorrit*), "Doubles and Doubling in *A Tale of Two Cities*," "Affection in *Great Expectations*," "The Creation of Bradley Headstone" (*Our Mutual Friend*), and "Constancy and Change, and the Dust Mounds of *Our Mutual Friend*."

2286. Butt, John. "Dickens at Work." *Durham University Journal*, 40, ns 9 (1947/48), 65-77.

Comments on and offers examples of Dickens's sometimes varying practices in publishing his novels serially, focusing on what Dickens's manuscripts, number plans, and letters reveal about how he managed "to write a consistent story and divide it into equal self contained portions without finishing his work before publication started," at least from *Martin Chuzzlewit* on, though such instalment-by-instalment notes do not exist for *Great Expectations* and *A Tale of Two Cities*. The extant notes reveal, Butt asserts, "the care with which Dickens planned his instalments" and–particularly from 1850 on–a "very remarkable" interest in plotting. Butt prints for the first time the page of notes for the final instalment attached to the manuscript of *Great Expectations*, which here, he states, Dickens drew up before writing the last instalment–but see House (**2391**) and Butt's later retraction (**2378**). Although the opening sentences of this article are virtually the same as those in the first chapter of Butt and Tillotson's *Dickens at Work* (**2291**), the article and the chapter are not otherwise similar.

2287. Butt, John. "Dickens's Manuscripts." *Yale University Library Gazette,* 36 (1961/62), 149-61.

In this printing of an address given at the opening of the Dickens exhibition at the Yale University Library in February 1962–see Gimbel (**1797**)–Butt comments on the location and completeness of the manuscripts of Dickens's novels, Dickens's revisions in page proof, and even Dickens's own errors in the page proofs caused by his not always consulting the manuscript, leaving the manuscript, in Butt's opinion, with "limited textual authority." The manuscript corrections, Butt notes, reveal "something about Dickens's habits of work," the later manuscripts, for example, containing far more extensive revisions than the earlier ones. Butt also gives some indication of Dickens's working notes for many of his novels, comments on the huge number of Dickens's letters (another category of manuscripts), mentions the then forthcoming *Pilgrim Letters,* and praises Dickens's ability as a letter writer.

2288. Butt, John. "Dickens's Notes for His Serial Parts." *Dickensian,* 45 (1948/49), 129-38.

Finds that Dickens's earliest notes for his novels are the fragmentary ones for *Martin Chuzzlewit.* From *Dombey and Son* on, however, his notes for the novels that were published in monthly installments are "uniform in appearance," and thorough, with a sheet of notes for each monthly part. A close study of these number plans, including notice of changes in ink, reveals, Butt indicates, that the right-hand side of each sheet, which contains chapter-by-chapter headings, was sometimes done after each chapter was completed, sometimes before–serving as a "rough plan of the direction" each chapter "was to take," when done beforehand, and, when done afterwards, as a chapter-by-chapter summary "to refresh his memory of the details of the preceding part before embarking upon the next." The notes on the left-hand side, far more informally arranged, were usually done, Butt surmises, before Dickens wrote an installment and show him planning the contents of his chapters. Six pages (three sheets) of the number plans (for parts III, IV, and VII) for *David Copperfield* are reproduced in photo facsimile. This article, with minor revisions, was incorporated as part V of "Dickens as a Serial Novelist," the first chapter of *Dickens at Work* (**2291**).

2289. Butt, John. "New Light on Charles Dickens." *Listener,* 47 (1952), 341-42.

Comments on Dickens's manuscripts and number plans for his novels, citing examples of excisions and revisions in them (including a facsimile reproduction of the number plan for no. VI of *Dombey and Son*) to illustrate how Dickens planned his monthly numbers and how his mind worked as he manipulated the plot, characters, and theme of a novel. See Butt and Tillotson (**2291**) for a much more fully developed discussion of these matters.

2290. Butt, John. "The Serial Publication of Dickens's Novels: *Martin Chuzzlewit* and *Little Dorrit.*" In his *Pope, Dickens and Others: Essays and Addresses.* Edinburgh: Edinburgh University Press, 1969, pp. 149-64.

An address to a summer school at Madingley Hall, Cambridge, 1958, published posthumously, on how Dickens constructed the monthly numbers of his novels for effect and to develop his plot to expound a theme. Butt comments on a number of the novels in passing. For *Little Dorrit* he consults the number plans to show Dickens "designing each Number."

2291. Butt, John, and Kathleen Tillotson. *Dickens at Work.* London: Methuen, 1957; Fair Lawn, NJ: Essential Books, 1958; new ed. University Paperbacks, 257. London: Methuen, 1968; reprinted London and New York: Methuen, 1982, 238 pp.

While this thoroughly scholarly and fascinating work, by now a classic in its field, is predominantly a study of Dickens as a craftsman of serial publication of a novel, it is also rich in textual information, principally about the eight works to which chapters are devoted: *Sketches by Boz, Pickwick Papers, Barnaby Rudge, Dombey and Son, David Copperfield, Bleak House, Hard Times,* and *Little Dorrit.* The volume is based to a considerable extent on work both authors had done in the late 1940s and early 1950s (**2286, 2288-89, 2360-61, 2373,** and **2378**; also see **2287, 2290,** and **2377** for three later studies). In examining the number plans, manuscripts, proof sheets, and editions of these works, Butt and Tillotson trace innumerable textual changes made during each work's progress from manuscript to published work. Illustrated. The 1968 edition contains the same text and pagination, but in a "Preface to the 1968 edition" Tillotson lists a few addenda and notes the death of John Butt and the commencement of the Clarendon Edition of Dickens's works (**176**) and the *Pilgrim Letters.*

The introductory chapter, "Dickens as a Serial Novelist," written largely by Butt, examines Dickens's "habits at the desk," developed mostly from his letters and his memoranda, in producing the mainly monthly installments of his novels (only six of fifteen were not published this way). Chapter 2, "*Sketches by Boz:* Collection and Revision," largely by Tillotson, compares the text of the various magazine and newspaper pieces that Dickens wrote between 1833 and 1836 with his revisions and arrangements of them when he included them in subsequent editions of *Sketches by Boz* (no manuscripts have survived). Chapter 3, "From Sketches to Novel: *Pickwick Papers* (1836-7)," also principally by Tillotson, examines, "largely by inference," since only a few pages of manuscript, no proofs or number plans and very few letters on the subject exist, how Dickens wrote his first novel. The evidence for the writing of *Barnaby*

Rudge, the subject of chapter 4 (Tillotson's), "*Barnaby Rudge*: The First Projected Novel," comes largely from Dickens's letters and some comparison of the text of the manuscript with that of the earliest printed text, since, according to Tillotson, proof sheets have not survived (Rice [93] points out, however, that proofs for two chapters are in the Forster Collection, Victoria and Albert Museum, London, though they show "very few corrections").

Chapter 5, "*Dombey and Son*: Design and Execution," a major chapter in the work, explores the writing of the first novel with extant number plans, showing that, at least from this point on, Dickens "planned each instalment on paper before he began writing." Here Butt and Tillotson, working together–the chapter originally appeared "in substantially its present form" in *Essays and Studies 1951* (**2373**)–use the title, the design of the monthly cover, Dickens's letters to John Forster, the manuscript and number plans, and the proof sheets to "throw light" on Dickens's design for the novel and the "degree of consistency with which he maintained his purpose."

Chapter 6, "*David Copperfield* Month by Month" (largely Butt's), is a close, and fascinating, examination of a full set of number plans, with a month by month transcription of them included, and accompanied by a month by month explanation of what they reveal of Dickens's interweaving of the strands of the novel into the finished text. In chapter 7, "The Topicality of *Bleak House*," Tillotson, this time *without* consulting any of the available textual apparatus, studies the integration by Dickens of a "diversity of detail," social and political in nature, "into a single view of society." In the next chapter, "*Hard Times*: The Problems of a Weekly Serial" (largely Butt's), attention turns to the problems of weekly publication of the parts of the novel, though Butt indicates that Dickens actually planned the novel more as five monthly installments than as twenty weekly ones, a scheme that did not work well in practice because he found the frame and space of a weekly installment restricting and frustrating. At the same time, it reveals, Butt illustrates, with a number of excerpts from the number plans, "the attention which Dickens was now paying to construction." In the final chapter, "From 'Nobody's Fault' to *Little Dorrit*," Tillotson, the principal author, again illustrates her interest in the "conditions of publication of Victorian fiction" (as noted in the preface), in the connection between text and social problems, particularly, as she illustrates, between planning (in the number plans) and dominant "political, social, and ethical themes."

Reviews: G. Banyard, *Contemporary Review*, 192 (1957), 239-40 ("endlessly fascinating" material); G. Carnall, *Modern Language Review*, 53 (1958), 574-75 (of "unquestionable" value); P. A. W. Collins, *Universities Quarterly*, 12 (1957/58), 104-10 (finds the volume useful and important if somewhat limited in scope); M. Engel, *Victorian Studies*, 1 (1957/58), 288-89 ("an extremely valuable but incomplete consideration" of Dickens at work); DeL. Ferguson, *New York Times Book Review*, 27 April 1958, p. 14 (mainly reviews Dickens's writing practices but finds that the study "will interest other audiences besides specialists" and casts "fresh light on the eternal mystery of creative art"); H. Gifford, *Durham University Journal*, 50 (1957/58), 85-88; E. Gillett, *National and English Review*, 149 (1957), 79-82 ("consistently helpful and easy to read," a book for the Dickens specialist); D. F. Howard, *Kenyon Review*, 21 (1959), 309-20 ("excellent analysis" of Dickens's art and his "habits as a writer"); E. Johnson, *Saturday Review*, 29 March 1958, p. 19 (Butt and Tillotson's evidence documents "beyond question" Dickens's "constant and growing preoccupation with structure and design, his concern for style and atmosphere, and his steadily increasing mastery of them all," a most "useful work of textual criticism"); J. D. Jump, *Review of English Studies*, ns 10 (1959), 98-100 ("scrupulous scholarship," presented with "elegance and occasionally with wit"); L. Lane, Jr., *Modern Language Notes*, 74 (1959), 543-46 (generally favorable); C. J. McCann, *Thought*, 34 (1959), 313-14 (generally favorable); S. Monod, *Etudes Anglaises*, 11 (1958), 166-67; A. Nisbet, *Nineteenth-Century Fiction*, 12 (1957/58), 239-45 ("a significant contribution to Dickens studies"); W. W. Robson, *Spectator*, 2 August 1957, p. 168 ("an intelligently done piece of scholarly collaboration"); C.P. Snow, *New Statesman and Nation*, 27 July 1957, pp. 119-20 (comments on the surprises revealed in this study of how much Dickens was a conscious, careful craftsman in rapport with his reading audience and sees Butt and Tillotson as "public benefactors" in this "limited and precise" investigation into Dickens's "working methods"); *Times Literary Supplement*, 26 July 1957, p. 459 (comments on Dickens's writing practices and asserts that Butt and Tillotson are "the first English scholars to make full intelligent use of the wealth of material in the Forster collection," Victoria and Albert Museum, the chapter on *Bleak House* being "a masterpiece of interpretive criticism"); E. F. Walbridge, *Library Journal*, 83 (1958), 1078-79 (for "all Dickens collections").

2292. "Charles Dickens's Manuscripts." *Chambers's Journal*, 54 (1877), 710-12; reprinted in *Eclectic Magazine*, ns 27 (1878), 80-82; *Littell's Living Age*, 136, 5th ser., 21 (1878), 252-54; and, with minor variations, *Potter's American Monthly*, 10 (1878), 156-58.

Lists the manuscripts and page proofs in the Forster Collection, Victoria and Albert Museum Library, London, and comments on the "number of alterations and interlineations with which the pages abound" and the "anxious thought, care, and elaboration" such corrections indicate. The author also notes the increasing amount of revision over the years and describes a number of changes in manuscript and proof. The reprint in *Potter's American Monthly* adds a paragraph criticizing the way in which the manuscripts and page proofs of Dickens's novels are displayed in cases in the library.

2293. Coolidge, Archibald C., Jr. "Appendix 1: The Installment Divisions." In his *Charles Dickens as Serial Novelist*. Ames, IA: Iowa State University Press, 1967, pp. 183-86.

Itemizes the installment divisions (with chapters indicated) for the monthly and weekly serializations of Dickens's novels.

2294. Dartle, R. (pseud.?). "Dickens: Page Headings." *Notes and Queries*, 12th ser., 9 (1921), 208.

Queries whether or not page headings in Chapman and Hall's editions of Dickens's works are by Dickens himself. In a response, pp. 515-16, T. W. Tyrrell quotes from Arthur Waugh's introduction to Dickens's *Collected Papers* in the Biographical Edition (vol. 19, London: Chapman and Hall, 1902-03) to the effect that Dickens wrote the headings for the volumes in the Charles Dickens Edition (London: Chapman and Hall, 1867-[75]), and that they were used by Chapman and Hall in subsequent editions, but that any changes in later editions or in works in the Charles Dickens Edition published after his death would not, obviously, have been by Dickens.

2295. Dickens, Charles, Jr. "Introduction." In individual volumes in Dickens's *The Works of Charles Dickens* [Macmillan Edition] (**185**), passim.

The individual works are identified on each title page as "A Reprint of the First Edition, with the Illustrations, and an Introduction, Biographical and Bibliographical, by Charles Dickens the Younger." The claim that the texts are those of the first editions should be taken with several grains of salt, however. In each introduction, Dickens's eldest son comments on the work in question, emphasizing bibliographical and biographical elements rather than providing critical commentary.

2296. Dooley, Allan C. "Varieties of Textual Change in the Victorian Era." *Text: Transactions of the Society for Textual Scholarship*, 6 (1994), 225-47.

Not about Dickens specifically, but a useful commentary on the importance of examining textual changes in literary works.

2297. Everson, Philip A. "Proof Revisions in Three Novels by Charles Dickens: *Dombey and Son, David Copperfield,* and *Bleak House.*" *Dissertation Abstracts International,* 48 (1987/88), 1459A (University of Delaware, 1987).

Examines "the effects of monthly serial publication" on three Dickens novels through revisions Dickens made in selected page proofs, more often for length than for aesthetic considerations. In doing so, Everson indicates in the abstract, Dickens often created "new and often inadvertent meanings in the unrevised passages which surround them." In his concluding chapter, Everson argues that, over his career, "Dickens refined his techniques as a serial writer" and that, "as his novels became more complex, his proof revisions became increasingly significant."

2298. Forster, John. *The Life of Charles Dickens.* Ed. J. W. T. Ley. London: Cecil Palmer, 1928, passim.

The manuscripts and page proofs of Dickens's novels are strong presences in Forster's biography—in letters to Forster, from which Forster quotes, Dickens writes that he is enclosing chapters of a manuscript or a set of page proofs for Forster's perusal, criticism, and correction, or he writes Forster of his difficulties with a chapter or a character, or mentions correcting proofs or changing chapters around, or the difficulty of making copy fit a required number of pages or of getting an illustrator to get a character right. But there are only occasional references to textual changes as such. Forster does include some manuscript fragments of interest: the autobiographical fragment given him by Dickens (pp. 23-36, 339-40); "An Account of a late Expedition into the North, for an Amateur Theatrical Benefit, written by Mrs. Gamp (who was an eye-witness), Inscribed to Mrs. Harris, Edited by Charles Dickens," which Dickens began as a means of raising money for his amateur theater group, but of which just this fragment was apparently completed, pp. 459-63; the original manuscript ending to *Great Expectations* (pp. 737-38); excerpts from Dickens's Book of Memoranda (**2530**), pp. 292-93, 747-60; and the fragment entitled "How Mr. Sapsea Ceased to Be a Member of the Eight Club," the "detached slips" of which, Forster recounts, were found within "the leaves of one of Dickens's other manuscripts." Forster speculates that this is a scene that Dickens wrote for *Edwin Drood,* in which Mr. Sapsea is a character, but decided not to use, pp. 811-14 (also see **2433-38, 2442,** and **2449**).

Forster does comment in passing on changes Dickens made in the text of *The Old Curiosity Shop* (pp. 149-50), *Barnaby Rudge* (pp. 166-69), *Dombey and Son* (pp. 431, 473-74, 477-79, 482), *David Copperfield* (p. 503), *Bleak House* (pp. 550), and *Edwin Drood* (pp. 809-10), and discusses Dickens's insistence that his illustrators modify drawings, Cruikshank for *Oliver Twist* (pp. 477-78; Dickens's letter to Cruikshank is produced in facsimile) and Hablot K. Browne for *Dombey and Son* (pp. 475-76), a page of whose attempts at drawing the face of Mr. Dombey are reproduced (facing p. 475). He also records Dickens's attempts at titles for *Martin Chuzzlewit* (p. 290), *Household Words* (pp. 512-13), *David Copperfield* (pp. 524-25), *Bleak House* (p. 565), *Little Dorrit* (p. 623), *All the Year Round* (pp. 671-72), and *A Tale of Two Cities* (p. 729) and reproduces in facsimile the number plans for the first number of *Bleak House* and *Little Dorrit* (facing pp. 624 and 625), the last page of the manuscript of *Edwin Drood,* and a part of a page from the manuscript of *Martin Chuzzlewit* (facing pp. 809 and 810). At the point in the text where Forster reproduces the two pages of number plans already mentioned, he indicates that Dickens's notes for some of the novels are in his possession (p. 624), and he later mentions a number plan for *Edwin Drood* (p. 810). Forster does not use any of this material, however, for studying Dickens's craftsmanship or creativity or his development as a writer. This information will also be found in the original and all later editions of Forster's *Life of Charles Dickens* (**19**), but *Forster-Ley* has been used here and page numbers indicated because the edition is easiest to come by in libraries.

2299. Guiliano, Edward, and Philip Collins. Annotations. In *The Annotated Dickens.* Ed. Edward Guiliano and Philip Collins. 2 vols. New York: Clarkson N. Potter; London: Orbis Book Publishing Corp., 1986, passim.

As the editors indicate in their preface, the extensive annotation in these two volumes "records some significant textual variations which occur in the manuscript, proofsheets, or earlier published editions." Volume 1 contains *Pickwick Papers, Oliver Twist, A Christmas Carol,* and *Hard Times;* volume 2 contains *David Copperfield, A Tale of Two Cities,* and *Great Expectations.* For their bibliography see Guiliano and Collins (**984**).

2300.   Hoefnagel, Dick. "Charles Dickens's Annotated Copy of Pepys's *Memoirs.*" *Dickensian,* 85 (1989), 162-66.

Briefly comments on and prints Dickens's notations in the front of four of the five volumes of his set of Samuel Pepys's diary, now in the Dartmouth College Library. The notations, Hoefnagel indicates, identify possible passages Dickens intended to use for later quotation. Illustrated with a photograph of the notations in volume 1.

2301.   Hornback, Bert G. *"The Hero of My Life": Essays on Dickens.* Athens, OH: Ohio University Press, 1981, passim.

Largely a critical study of *David Copperfield, Our Mutual Friend,* and *The Mystery of Edwin Drood.* Hornback prints the trial titles Dickens wrote down in his notes for *David Copperfield,* pp. 1-3, and bases parts of his discussion of this novel (pp. 1-85) on what the titles reveal about Dickens's artistic intentions for the work. Hornback also prints excerpts from the manuscripts of *Our Mutual Friend* and *The Mystery of Edwin Drood,* but principally of *David Copperfield* with additions and deletions indicated to show Dickens the craftsman at work.

2302.   Kitton, F[rederic] G. "Bibliographical Note." In the initial volume of each of the six novels published in *The Works of Charles Dickens.* Rochester Edition. 11 vols. London: Methuen, 1900-01, passim.

These notes provide information about the manuscript, parts publication, illustrations, and other matters concerning the writing and initial publication of each of the six novels published in this incomplete collected edition: *Pickwick Papers,* 2 vols. (1899), I, xx; *Nicholas Nickleby,* 2 vols. (1900), I, xxi; *Bleak House,* 2 vols. (1900), I, xxiii-xxiv; *Oliver Twist* (1900), pp. xxiii-xxiv; *The Old Curiosity Shop,* 2 vols. (1901), I, xxiii-xxiv; and *Barnaby Rudge,* 2 vols. (1901), I, xxiii. Also see Kitton's bibliographical notes for the Autograph Edition (**2303**).

2303.   Kitton, Frederic G. "Bibliographical Note." In the initial volume of each of the six works published in *The Complete Works of Charles Dickens.* Edited with Annotations, Bibliography and Topography by Frederic G. Kitton [and Introductions by Various Critics]. Autograph Edition. 15 vols. [of 56 projected]. New York and London: George D. Sproul, 1902-05, passim.

Kitton's notes for the six works published–*Pickwick Papers* (three volumes), *David Copperfield* (three volumes), *The Old Curiosity Shop* (two volumes), *Reprinted Pieces* (one volume), *Barnaby Rudge* (three volumes), and *Dombey and Son* (three volumes)–are concerned largely with the writing and initial publication of the works. This edition is particularly noteworthy for its numerous illustrations, the original ones being supplemented by hundreds of more modern ones. Kitton's notes for *Pickwick Papers*, *The Old Curiosity Shop*, and *Barnaby Rudge* follow roughly the outlines of the bibliographical commentary in the Rochester Edition volumes of these novels (**2302**) but are more extensive. The text of this collected edition was also intended to be issued as the St. Dunstan Edition in 130 volumes (fifteen copies printed on parchment) and the Bibliophiles' Edition in 112 volumes (fifty copies "on a special hand-made paper with ornamental border in color"). But volumes in these editions were apparently never issued–see Carr (**1445**) and *Prospectus of the Autograph Edition* (**226**).

2304. Low, Annette. "The Conservation of Charles Dickens' Manuscripts." *V&A Conservation Journal*, no. 9 (October 1993), 4-7.

Notes that the method used in 1965-66 to rebind the manuscripts of Dickens's novels in the Forster Collection at the Victoria and Albert Museum library had "led to severe warping of the leaves." Low describes the latest project to rebind the manuscripts and summarizes the conclusions reached about how best to preserve them for the future. She points out that in the more elaborate and cautious binding that followed, removal of the backing from the manuscript leaves revealed cancelled passages on the back of about 500 pages of text. As of 1993 only two novels had been rebound though Low projects (unfortunately inaccurately) that all the novels in the collection would have been rebound by 1995. Illustrated. This fascinating article may be retrieved (and printed) from Internet Web site http://www.nal.vam.ac.uk/pubs/lowecons.html, where a postscript has been added that, as of May 1996, seven of the twelve manuscripts in the collection had been rebound–*Oliver Twist*, *The Old Curiosity Shop*, *Barnaby Rudge*, *American Notes*, *Martin Chuzzlewit* (half done), *Bleak House*, and *Hard Times*–with the rest expected to be done by the end of 1997 and stored in "permanent drop-back boxes lined with MicroChamber© papers as a precaution against the polluted London environment." Also see Andrews (**2282**).

2305. "Marginalia: Where the Manuscripts of Dickens Are." *Bookman's Journal*, ser. 3, 15 (1927), 221.

Quotes a letter from Walter Dexter in the London *Daily Telegraph* (no date given) to the effect that most manuscripts of Dickens's novels and of many of his journalistic pieces are in the Victoria and Albert Museum along with the corrected proofs of most of the novels but that the manuscripts of six pages of *Pickwick Papers*, six chapters of *Nicholas Nickleby*, all of *Our Mutual Friend*, and all of the Christmas Books except for *The Chimes* (which is in the Victoria and Albert Museum) are in the United States.

2306. McGann, Jerome J. "The Socialization of Texts." In his *The Textual Condition*. Princeton Studies in Culture/Power/History. Princeton, NJ: Princeton University Press, 1991, pp. 69-87.

In chapter 3 of this work, McGann discusses the importance of authorial intention in editing a text, particularly, in Dickens's case, where illustrations are concerned. McGann sees illustrated Dickens novels as "works of composite art." He also notes that different forms of publication of a Dickens work required that the work be *"written* differently," *"produced* differently," and have different "aesthetic effects." Even more different, he argues, are modern scholarly editions, which are often composites, such as Kathleen Tillotson's *Oliver Twist* (**2474**), and perhaps arguably "not the work of Charles Dickens," though still part of what McGann terms "the continuous socialization of the texts."

2307. Monod, Sylvère. *Dickens the Novelist*. Norman: University of Oklahoma Press, 1968, passim; translated and revised from his *Dickens romancier: Etude sur la création littéraire dans les romans de Charles Dickens*. Paris: Hachette, 1953, passim.

In the course of this study of the way in which Dickens's novels were "conceived, constructed, and written," Monod makes frequent references to Dickens's revisions in the manuscripts and page proofs of his novels from *Oliver Twist* on and to the number plans where they are extant. See particularly pp. 126-29 (*Oliver Twist*), 178-79 and 446 (*The Old Curiosity Shop*), 187-88 (*Barnaby Rudge*), 199-210 (*The Old Curiosity Shop* and *Barnaby Rudge*), 229 and 238-39 (*Martin Chuzzlewit*), 257-68 (*Dombey and Son*), 277-98 (*David Copperfield*), 399 and 422-23 (*Little Dorrit*), 423-40 (*Bleak House, Little Dorrit*, and *Our Mutual Friend*), 441-42 and 447-48 (*Hard Times*), 463-65 (*Hard Times* and *A Tale of Two Cities*), and 491-93 and 500-02 (*The Mystery of Edwin Drood*). These materials, Monod concludes, "provide evidence of Dickens' earnest, conscientious, even anxious work, and particularly of his passionate, lifelong interest in language and style, an interest abundantly reflected in the evolution of his own handling of written English." The passages indicated above are all direct translations from the earlier French edition. The French version, however, has appendices, pp. 481-91, that Monod did not include in the English version, and these contain longer cancelled passages from *Martin Chuzzlewit, David Copperfield*, and *The Old Curiosity Shop*, and excerpts from memoranda for *Dombey and Son, Little Dorrit*, and *Our Mutual Friend*.

2308. Page, Norman. "Appendix E: The Number-plans." In his *A Dickens Companion* (**223**), pp. 353-56.

Prints brief excerpts from Dickens's number plans for *Bleak House, Our Mutual Friend,* and *Edwin Drood* to show the kind of information they contain.

2309. S[chlicke], P[aul] V. W. Entries for all of Dickens's novels, other major works, and most of his minor works, excluding individual Christmas Stories. In *Oxford Reader's Companion to Dickens.* Ed. Paul Schlicke. Oxford and New York: Oxford University Press, 1999; paperback ed., 2000, passim.

For each work, Schlicke comments intelligently if, of necessity, concisely on the "Inception and Composition," "Contract, Text, and Publication History," and "Illustrations," providing broadly relevant bibliographical and textual information. The sections for the lesser works are smaller in scope, and occasionally by authors other than Schlicke. In "Note to Paperback Edition," Schlicke indicates that a "small number of errors and infelicities" in the original edition have been corrected. For a list of all the works with entries in the guide, see "Dickens's Works," pp. xviii-xix, in the "Classified Contents List." Also see Brattin (**2283**), Russell (**227**), Schlicke (**1021**, **798**, **1727**), and Vann and Sadrin (**238**), as well as Schlicke's interesting account, "Editing the *Oxford Reader's Companion to Dickens*" (**1424**).

Reviews: P. Ackroyd, *Times* (London), 4 March 1999, p. 40 ("invaluable to scholars, readers and admirers of Dickens into the next century and beyond"); P. J. McCarthy, *Dickensian,* 95 (1999), 243-45 ("a singular and thorough success", the "result of reading this splendid book is a renewed and heightened sense of Dickens's importance to his world and astonishment once more at his range of friendships, activities, and the number and variety of lines he had out to life"); A. Poole, *Times Higher Education Supplement,* 28 May 1999, p. 25 ("magnificent," a "necessary possession for all Dickensians"); M. Reynolds, *Times Literary Supplement,* 23 April 1999, p. 24 ("a dense compendium of scholarship," but "leavened with delightful details"; "scrupulous, encyclopaedic and useful"); G. J. Worth, *Dickens Quarterly,* 17 (2000), 51-55 (despite some quibbles, praises Schlicke for his "masterful job of pulling together what must have started out as a disparate conglomeration of submitted materials without however stifling individual viewpoints and perceptions" and for making the volume "reader-friendly"; "a treasure" that will give "much delight, as well as much instruction to everyone who spends time with it").

2310. Schooling, J. Holt. "Charles Dickens's Manuscripts." *Strand Magazine,* 11 (1896), 29-40.

This article is accompanied by twenty-six illustrations of pages from Dickens's manuscripts, proof pages, number plans, and illustrations for various works and is based on research done in the principal repository of these materials—the Forster Collection, Victoria and Albert Museum Library, London. The commentary points out some of the interesting alterations and unusual characteristics of the collection.

2311. Shatto, Susan, gen. ed. The Dickens Companions. London, Boston, and Sydney: Allen & Unwin (and, later, Edinburgh: Edinburgh University Press, and then Mountfield, Eng.: Helm Information; Westport, CT: Greenwood Press), 1986- .

A useful series of detailed notes to individual novels of Dickens, with entries on the number plans and other textual matters. Eight volumes have been published to date—see Michael Cotsell on *Our Mutual Friend* (**2482**), Wendy S. Jacobson on *The Mystery of Edwin Drood* (**2444**), Nancy A. Metz on *Martin Chuzzlewit* (**2426**), David Paroissien on *Great Expectations* (**2398**) and *Oliver Twist* (**2473**), Andrew Sanders on *A Tale of Two Cities* (**2508**), Susan Shatto on *Bleak House* (**2331**), and Margaret Simpson on *Hard Times* (**2415**). A forthcoming volume on *Little Dorrit*, by Trey Philpotts, has been advertised. Michael Cotsell served as associate editor for the early volumes in the series. For the later volumes, Shatto and David Paroissien are listed as "Series Editors." In "General Preface by the Editors," which appears in all volumes, the editors announce that the series will provide "the most comprehensive annotation of the works of Dickens ever undertaken," including "material from Dickens manuscripts and proofs . . . when it is of major significance," though the notes are intended to be largely explanatory.

2312. Spielmann, M. H. "How Dickens Improved His Style: His Tell-Tale Manuscripts." *Graphic* (London), 81 (1910), 360.

The text revolves around accompanying photographic facsimiles of pages from the manuscripts of *Oliver Twist, Martin Chuzzlewit, David Copperfield*, and *Bleak House*, with Spielmann commenting on what the illustrations reveal—Dickens's increasingly smaller, increasingly cramped hand and the increasingly larger number of corrections. These show the more careful craftsman, Spielmann indicates, "putting down his first thoughts in spontaneous expression, quickly modifying what seemed to him incomplete, or, at all events, unsatisfying, and then returning to polish and touch up, with infinite conscientiousness and ungrudged labour, and with a loving hand."

2313. [Staples, Leslie C.]. "Shavings from Dickens's Workshop: Unpublished Fragments from the Novels." *Dickensian*, 48 (1951/52), 158-61 (*David Copperfield*); 49 (1952/53), 37-43, 65-68 (*Dombey and Son*), 169-74 (*Little Dorrit*); 50 (1953/54), 17-23, 63-66, 132-36 (*The Old Curiosity Shop*), 188-91 (*Bleak House*).

Prints passages that, for a variety of reasons, though largely because of space restrictions in his monthly or, in the case of *The Old Curiosity Shop*, weekly parts of the novels, Dickens cancelled in proof. For additional cancellations in the *Bleak House* proofs, see DeVries (**2323**).

2314. Stone, Harry, ed. *Dickens' Working Notes for His Novels.* Chicago and London: University of Chicago Press, 1987. xxxv + 393 pp.

A coffee table-sized volume that provides photographic facsimiles (most in actual size) as well as transcriptions of all Dickens's extant working notes for *The Old Curiosity Shop* (fragmentary), *Martin Chuzzlewit* (fragment), *Dombey and Son, David Copperfield, Bleak House, Hard Times, Little Dorrit, Great Expectations* (only general notes), *Our Mutual Friend,* and *The Mystery of Edwin Drood.* In an informative introduction, Stone emphasizes the "unflagging intellectual concentration that invariably accompanied the writing process for Dickens." He notes that, while Dickens's own comments about his writing are "intermittent, often sketchy, and largely a matter of happenstance" (the most important being his communications to John Forster), the other major sources are the Book of Memoranda (**2530**), the manuscripts and page proofs, and the number plans and other working notes that are the subject of this volume. Stone's description of how Dickens conceived his number plans and his discussion of what they reveal about how Dickens's imagination worked and how he structured his novels are valuable, though Stone is chary with credit to other scholars who have preceded him in this field, apart from a brief listing of four such. Each set of Dickens's working notes is preceded by an introduction providing details about the publication of the novel involved and about its manuscript and working notes. For Dickens's notes for *The Haunted Man,* not in this volume, see Glancy (**2338**); for his notes for *The Cricket on the Hearth,* also not here, see Klinkenborg (**2345**); and for his plot summary for *The Chimes,* originally printed in *Forster,* see *Pilgrim Letters,* IV, 203-05.

Reviews: *AB Bookman's Weekly,* 79 (1987), 2091-92; R. Altick, *Times Literary Supplement,* 7 August 1987, pp. 841-42 ("a masterly collection of Dickens's working notes"; Altick further comments on Dickens's working methods, concluding that Dickens "may have been an inspired improviser, but he was also a careful planner"); M. Y. Andrews, *Dickensian,* 88 (1992), 110-12 (excellent photographic reproduction of Dickens's notes and "scrupulous transcriptions" of them; a "sumptuous volume," with "lovingly and scrupulously performed" editorial work); J. J. Brattin, *Dickens Quarterly,* 6 (1989), 17-22 (notes a few errors and inconsistencies and finds the introduction "unfortunately quirky in its emphasis," but still finds this an "enormously useful" and valuable addition to "the Dickens bookshelf" with "consistently excellent" photographic reproductions of the notes); J. H. Brown, *Humanities* (National Endowment for the Humanities), 7, vi (November-December 1986), 8-9 (favorable; illustrated); W. Burgan, *Victorian Studies,* 33 (1989/90), 501-03 (praises the edition and Stone's commentary); J. Carey, *Sunday Times* (London), 9 August 1987, p. 43 (thinks Dickens was not as methodical a constructor of novels as Stone portrays him, but finds this a "beautiful," valuable volume); P. Collins, *Times Higher Education Supplement,* 10 July 1987, p. 18 (a "welcome addition" to Dickens studies, with a "well-argued introduction," though Collins regrets that Stone did not discuss more fully "the problems presented by serialization"); H. Gifford, *Durham University Journal,* 50 (1957/58), 85-88 (material explored "with admirable care and thoroughness"); L. Hartveit, *English Studies,* 70 (1989), 93-94 ("indispensable to the student of Dickens, on any level, for the teacher as well as the scholar," with an "illuminating and very readable introduction"); D. Hewitt, *Notes and Queries,* ns 36 (1989), 252-53 (a "sumptuous edition"); L. Menand, *New Republic,* 197, xi-xii (14-21 September 1987), 55-57 (reviews the history of Dickens's serial publication of his novels and his method for creating his working notes; finds that Stone's volume meets its scholarly purpose "magnificently," though doubts the value of the notes per se for providing evidence that Dickens was, as Stone asserts, "a consummate artist and totally dedicated to his craft"); S. Monod, *Etudes anglaises,* 42 (1989), 221-22 (in French; praises); J. Mortimer, *Spectator,* 259 (25 July 1987), 30-31 (describes the number plans as Dickens's "endless telegrams to himself," and Stone's volume as a "fascinating compilation"); M. Rubin, *Christian Science Monitor*, 11 September 1987, p. 20 ("superbly edited and produced edition," Dickens's notes revealing that he was "a highly conscious, conscientious artist who took great pains to achieve his effects"); J. Sutherland (**2316**), p. 26 (comments on the working notes of other Victorian novelists as well as Dickens's, and concludes that this is a "sumptuous" and scholarly volume, with "formidably knowledgeable" introductions to the sets of working notes; see letter from M. Bapp, 29 October 1987, p. 4, on Dickensian names in the London telephone directory); J. D. Vann, *Choice*, 25 (1987/88), 120 ("eminently usable," a "beautifully presented" and "important research source for studying Dickens's process of composition"); D. Walder, *Listener*, 117 (18 June 1987), 22-23 (praises Stone's editorial work).

2315. Sucksmith, Harvey P. *The Narrative Art of Charles Dickens: The Rhetoric of Sympathy and Irony in His Novels*. Oxford: Clarendon Press, Oxford University Press, 1970, passim.

Frequently refers to Dickens's manuscript revisions, his number plans, the corrected proofs, and textual changes in editions published in Dickens's lifetime to develop his study of Dickens's "conscious and rhetorical art" from *Sketches by Boz* through *The Mystery of Edwin Drood*. Sucksmith also includes "A Complete Transcript of the Alternative Titles in the Original Manuscript of *Hard Times*" as an appendix, p. 358, and a "Bibliography" (**47**). He notes that parts of Chapter IX "appeared in a slightly different form in *Renaissance and Modern Studies*" (**2332**).

2316. Sutherland, John. "Martin Chuzzlewig." *London Review of Books*, 15 October 1987, p. 26.

Ostensibly a review of Harry Stone's *Dickens' Working Notes for His Novels* (**2314**), but Sutherland takes time to comment on the nature and variety of Dickens's working notes (as well as those of other Victorian novelists). He finds that "almost exclusively" Dickens's notes "deal with tactical rather than long-term strategic problems." While Dickens's construction of his working notes remained "remarkably the same" over "the twenty years of his maturity," Sutherland finds that "there is a growing sense of 'art' from novel to novel," with Dickens's earlier written directions to himself tending "to be logistical" and later ones "stressing theme and symbol." Sutherland points out that two "features" dominate the notes: 1) a "sensitivity to names" and 2) a "habitual dualism," particularly when Dickens "chattered so incessantly and profitably to himself" in the notes.

2317. Watt, Alexander. "Literary Methods of Charles Dickens." *People's Friend*, 29 June 1896, pp. 423-24.

Uses both his examination of Dickens's manuscripts and material in *Forster* to show the great care Dickens took in writing, revising, and authenticating details in his manuscripts. Watt mentions the book of memoranda (**2530**) that Dickens kept later in his career but not the number plans for the novels.

7B. TEXTUAL STUDIES OF INDIVIDUAL WORKS

Note: Also see relevant subheadings under individual works in part 1 of the subject index.

Barnaby Rudge

Note: Also see Hargreaves (**2466**).

2318. Brattin, Joel J. "'Secrets Inside . . . to Strike to Your Heart': New Readings from Dickens's Manuscript of *Barnaby Rudge*, Chapter 75." *Dickens Quarterly*, 8 (1991), 15-28.

Notes that Dickens deleted about fifteen percent of chapter 75 of *Barnaby Rudge* in order to make the text fit into the "precisely twelve pages of text" that he used for each weekly number of *Master Humphrey's Clock*, in which he serialized the novel, and that none of the cancelled passages was used in any edition of the novel.

Bleak House

2319. Blount, Trevor. "A Revised Image in the Opening Chapter of Dickens's 'Bleak House.'" *Notes and Queries*, ns 9 (1962), 303-04.

Notes Dickens's cancellation of a dependent clause somewhere between manuscript and page proof in the opening paragraph of *Bleak House*—a reference to the deposits of mud on London pavements as like "layers upon layers of barnacles" sticking to a ship's keel, which Blount characterizes as an "ill-suited" image.

2320. Bradbury, Nicola. "Appendix 3: Dickens's Number Plans for *Bleak House*." In Dickens's *Bleak House*. Ed. Nicola Bradbury. Penguin Classics. London, New York, etc.: Penguin Books, 1996, pp. 992-1011.

Prints, with some indication of underlining and other markings, the complete number plans for the novel.
Review: J. J. Brattin, *Dickens Quarterly*, 16 (1999), 42-48 (a "serviceable" introduction, some inconsistencies in textual matters, confusing and occasionally inaccurate transcription of number plans, most notes "accurate and useful").

2321. Brattin, Joel. "'All the Fine Gentlemen . . . Down to Zoodle': Alphabets and Alphabetical Order in *Bleak House*." *Dickensian*, 98 (2002), 113-18.

Comments in parts of this study on changes Dickens made in the manuscript of *Bleak House* in the list of names of "gentlemen" and in the names of Miss Flite's birds.

2322. Chaudhuri, Brahma. "The Interpolated Chapter in *Bleak House*." *Dickensian*, 81 (1985), 103-04.

Notes that Dickens wrote chapter 2 of *Bleak House* as "the result of an exigency of serial publication," adding it when the three chapters he had written for the first number turned out to be short of the thirty-two printed pages needed. A "careful reading" of the chapter shows, Chaudhuri asserts, "its inconsistency and superfluity," though, on the other hand, it did introduce the Dedlocks, thereby raising "a great deal of curiosity in the readers." Illustrated.

2323. DeVries, Duane. "The *Bleak House* Page-Proofs: More Shavings from Dickens's Workshop." *Dickensian*, 66 (1970), 3-7.

Prints passages overlooked by Staples (**2313**) that were cancelled by Dickens principally in the first of two sets of page proofs for installment no. 2 of *Bleak House.*

2324. DeVries, Duane. "Introduction," "The Discarded Titles of *Bleak House*," and "The Number Plans for *Bleak House*." In Dickens's *Bleak House*. Ed. Duane DeVries. The Crowell Critical Library. New York: Thomas Y. Crowell, 1971, pp. xiii-xix, 833-35, 837-75.

Prints transcriptions of and comments briefly on the discarded titles and the number plans of *Bleak House*. In the introduction DeVries explains why he chose the first edition in parts as the copy-text for this edition and indicates the parts divisions in the text. He also describes what the individual monthly part looked like and what it contained, and he comments generally on minor revisions that Dickens made in later editions of the novel and passages that Dickens deleted in proof but which, in this edition, are included within brackets in the text. DeVries includes a "Selected Bibliography" (**1061**), pp. 1073-80.
Review: T. Blount, *Dickensian*, 67 (1971), 168-72 ("lavish ancillary aids," "very well chosen bibliography," "modest" introduction, "admirably balanced anthology of scholarly and critical excerpts"; an "immensely useful compendium, notable for its judicious discrimination").

2325. Edgecombe, Rodney S. "A Variant Reading in *Bleak House*." *Notes and Queries*, ns 40 (1993), 479.

Notes a textual variant between the manuscript and corrected proof of *Bleak House.*

2326. Ford, George H. "The Titles for *Bleak House.*" *Dickensian*, 65 (1969), 84–89.

Prints the various titles that Dickens wrote down as possibilities for the work that eventually became *Bleak House* and speculates about what the unused ones reveal of Dickens's intentions for the work. Also see Ford and Monod (**2327**).

2327. Ford, George, and Sylvère Monod. "A Note on the Text" and "Textual Notes." In Dickens's *Bleak House: An Authoritative and Annotated Text, Illustrations, a Note on the Text, Genesis and Composition, Backgrounds, Criticism.* Ed. George Ford and Sylvère Monod. Norton Critical Edition. New York: W. W. Norton, 1977, pp. 773-813, 815-80.

In "A Note on the Text" the editors print and comment on the list of titles that Dickens considered for the novel, the number plans, and the running headlines that Dickens wrote for the Charles Dickens Edition (1868) of the novel. They also discuss the manuscript, proofs, and the various editions of the novel published in Dickens's lifetime, as well as their choice of the text of the first volume edition (1853) as the copy-text for the Norton Edition. They indicate that there are 462 passages where they have found differences between the 1853 and 1868 editions, some of which they have incorporated in their edition, as well as eighty-three readings from the manuscript itself. Many of these are recorded in the "Textual Notes" that follow, particularly, as Ford and Monod point out, for one "specimen chapter," chapter 5. Also see Ford and Monod (**1063**), Ford (**2326**), and Monod (**2329**).

Reviews: *Choice*, 15 (1978), 1214 (along with their edition of *Hard Times* [**2411**], a "superb and thorough work, a "touchstone for critical editions," with much helpful background material; "the evolution of the composition of *Bleak House* is carefully developed, and the text is established by authority by a thorough study of Dickens's working plans and the extant versions of the novel"); P. Collins, *Dickens Studies Newsletter*, 13 (1982), 19-21 ((an "admirable achievement," though regrets that only nine original illustrations were used); P. Coustillas, *Etudes anglaises*, 33 (1980), 88-90 (in French; favorable); C. Dawson, *Studies in English Literature*, 18 (1978), 750 ("almost indispensable"); M. Slater, *Times Literary Supplement*, 20 June 1980, p. 716 ("handsomely supplies an imposing textual apparatus," with "extensive and meticulous annotation"; "crushingly demonstrates the corruption of the Charles Dickens Edition on which most modern reprints are based"); H. P. Sucksmith, *Dickensian*, 75 (1979), 107-08 (authoritative text, a "wealth of material" about the novel, "by far the best edition at present available"); K. Tillotson, *Nineteenth-Century Fiction*, 34 (1979/80), 220-24 (praises choice of first edition as copy-text, the extensive textual notes, and the supplementary apparatus, offering only minor corrections).

2328. Gill, Stephen. "Note on the Composition and Text." In Dickens's *Bleak House*. Ed. Stephen Gill. World's Classics. Oxford and New York: Oxford University Press, 1996, 1998, xxiii-xxv.

Gives dates and chapters for the publication of the monthly parts of the novel and notes that there "is at present no authoritative text" of *Bleak House*, although he finds the edition that Ford and Monod did for the Norton Critical Editions (**2327**) the closest to it. Gill also acknowledges his own indebtedness to the Norton Edition in preparing this World's Classics Edition. In addition, he comments briefly on the number plans for the novel and the original illustrations by Hablot K. Browne.

Review: J. J. Brattin, *Dickens Quarterly*, 16 (1999), 42-48 (points out a few textual flaws in the edition but finds the table of publication dates in "Note on the Composition and Text" useful).

2329. Monod, Sylvère. "'When the Battle's Lost and Won . . . ': Dickens *v.* the Compositors of *Bleak House.*" *Dickensian*, 69 (1973), 3-12.

As much a warning to future editors of *Bleak House* as a study of textual changes, this article examines in some detail Dickens's corrections in proof of over 700 errors incurred by at least forty different compositors who originally set up the novel in type from Dickens's manuscript. Monod also notes 159 errors Dickens did *not* catch in proof and briefly comments on 160 changes in the Cheap Edition, seventy of which he thinks "were for the worse"; twenty-six in the Library Edition; and 265 in the Charles Dickens Edition, "148 of which are regrettable." Monod believes that most if not all of these changes were compositors' errors not approved by Dickens.

2330. Page, Norman. "Appendix: Dickens's Number-Plans for *Bleak House.*" In Dickens's *Bleak House*. Ed. Norman Page. Penguin English Library. Harmondsworth, Eng., Baltimore, MD, and Ringwood, Austral., 1971, pp. 936-52.

Prints a transcription of the page of tentative titles and the complete number plans for the novel, with underlining and other marks indicated, but with no clear indication of where one page of notes ends and another begins.

Review: T. Blount, *Dickensian*, 67 (1971), 168-72 ("adequately printed; includes all of Hablot K. Browne's original illustrations but a "rather arbitrary" and short bibliography).

2331. Shatto, Susan. *The Companion to **Bleak House***. The Dickens Companions. London: Unwin Hyman, 1988, passim.

In the notes to the novel, with which most of the volume is concerned, Shatto includes Dickens's part by part number plans for *Bleak House*, with some reference to where the printed text of the novel differs from the manuscript and page proofs. Shatto also includes a "Selected Bibliography" (**1066**), pp. 302-12. Illustrated.

Reviews: T. Braun, *Notes and Queries*, 36 (1989), 408 (so rich it "can be read almost in its own right as a commentary on Dickens's world"–"a 'must' for students and scholars alike"); J. Childers, *Dickens Quarterly*, 7 (1990), 395-98 ("a model of scholarship, not only making *Bleak House* "more accessible to late-twentieth century readers" but providing "insights into aspects of Victorian culture that would escape many of even the most informed scholars of Dickens's works and the period"); S. Gill, *Review of English Studies*, 41 (1990), 158 (high praise); D. Hawes, *Times Higher Education Supplement*, 15 July 1988, p. 18 ("some fascinating material here, enabling the reader "to understand more precisely than before the extent to which *Bleak House* is a text permeated with the values and facts of mid-Victorian England"); S. Monod, *Victorian Studies*, 33 (1989/90), 513-15 (while taking exception to a few of Shatto's notes, finds the volume filled with "excellent material," with an introduction that "brilliantly demonstrates the contemporaneity of *Bleak House*"); J. M. Parker, *Choice*, 26 (1988/89), 468 ("interesting and informative," with "a good bibliography and a useful index"); A. Sadrin, *Etudes anglaises*, 43 (1990), 348-49 (in French; praises).

2332. Sucksmith, H[arvey] P. "Dickens at Work on *Bleak House*: A Critical Examination of His Memoranda and Number Plans." *Renaissance and Modern Studies*, 9 (1965), 47-85.

Prints a transcription (with some minor errors) of Dickens's number plans for *Bleak House* and comments at some length on their appearance and how Dickens created and used them in planning and writing his novel, particularly to create pathos, "moral sympathy," and irony in the novel, which in turn produce a rhetoric that structures and deepens the complex tragic vision of the work. Incorporated in "a slightly different form" in his *The Narrative Art of Charles Dickens: The Rhetoric of Sympathy and Irony in His Novels* (**2315**).

2333. Watson, J. L. "Dickens at Work on Manuscript and Proof: 'Bleak House' and 'Little Dorrit.'" *Journal of the Australasian Universities Language and Literature Association*, 45 (May 1976), 54-68.

In this study of Dickens's manuscript, number plans, and page proofs for *Bleak House* and *Little Dorrit*, Watson finds that Dickens's great concern with imagery in his plans and revisions provides a strong "sense of artistic control." He illustrates Dickens's changes by providing a number of transcriptions from the number plans and manuscripts of these two novels.

Christmas Books, Christmas Stories, and Other Shorter Fiction

Note: Also see Stone (**450**), Kitton (**267**), and, for *Master Humphrey's Clock*, Brennan (**2460-61**), and Patten (**2467**), as well as sections on the individual works in part 1 of the subject index. For other commentary on the states of the first edition of *A Christmas Carol*, see **A Christmas Carol, states of the first edition**, in section 1 of part 1 of the subject index.

2334. Adams, Frederick B., Jr. "Preface." In Dickens's **A Christmas Carol: A Facsimile of the Manuscript in the Pierpont Morgan Library**. Ed. Frederick B. Adams, Jr. New York: James H. Heineman, 1967; reprinted London: Folio Press, 1970; New York: Dover; London: Constable, 1971, pp. v-vii.

Comments briefly on the manuscript. The text itself consists of a photographic facsimile of the manuscript (including John Leech's woodcuts) and the text of the first edition on facing pages, with the color illustrations by Leech inserted on separate pages.

Review: M. Slater, *Dickensian*, 67 (1971), 118 (prefers the facsimile to the introductory matter).

2335. Andrews, Malcolm, "Introducing Master Humphrey." *Dickensian*, 67 (1971), 70-86.

An examination of the first eleven numbers of *Master Humphrey's Clock*, which included the early installments of *The Old Curiosity Shop* along with other pieces by Dickens (the novel completely took over with the twelfth number). In investigating the "evolution" of *Master Humphrey's Clock*, Andrews prints two entries regarding the title from Dickens's 1840 diary and reproduces a pencil drawing by Hablot K. Browne for one of the illustrations of Master Humphrey himself with remarks written on it by Dickens ("Master Humphrey <u>admirable</u>," followed by suggested revisions to the drawing).

2336. Batterson, Richard F. "The Manuscript and Text of Dickens's 'George Silverman's Explanation.'" *Papers of the Bibliographical Society of America*, 73 (1979), 473-76.

Describes the present state of the manuscript, which is in the Houghton Library, Harvard University, and notes minor changes in text between the American printing in the *Atlantic Monthly* and the English printing in *All the Year Round*, involving 244 accidental differences, mainly in spelling, and fifty-two largely stylistic changes between the manuscript and the published versions that reveal Dickens "curbing his tendency to wordiness," "restraining a propensity to overemphasize," and giving additional stress to a point. Batterson also suggests a change Dickens ought to have made and speculates about the changes made in proof (the proof sheets themselves seem not to have survived).

2337. Glancy, Ruth F. "Dickens and the Framed Tale." *Index to Theses* (**1188**), 27, ii (1980), 180 (University of London, Queen Mary College), 1978.

No abstract included. According to Glancy's summary elsewhere (**98**), p. 493, chapters IV-VI "discuss Dickens's editing of the Christmas numbers" of *Household Words* and *All the Year Round*.

2338. Glancy, Ruth. "Dickens at Work on *The Haunted Man*." *Dickens Studies Annual*, 15 (1986), 65-85.

A fascinating, detailed study of Dickens's fifth and last Christmas Book. In discussing Dickens's planning and writing of this work, Glancy looks at his comments on the work in his letters, the three pages of notes he made for the story (with further notes on the title page of the manuscript), and the sixty-nine-page manuscript itself (now in the Carl H. Pforzheimer Library, New York Public Library). She also notes textual differences between the manuscript and the printed version of the novel. She concludes that Dickens "had *The Haunted Man* well planned from the start."

2339. Glancy, Ruth. "The Shaping of *The Battle of Life*: Dickens' Manuscript Revisions." *Dickens Studies Annual*, 17 (1988), 67-89.

A detailed study of the manuscript (in the Pierpont Morgan Library, New York) and the changes Dickens must have made in the proofs, determined by comparing the manuscript with the text of the first edition since the proofs themselves are apparently not extant. For the provenance of the manuscript, see Arthur A. Adrian, *Georgina Hogarth and the Dickens Circle* (London: Oxford University Press, 1957), pp. 21, 203-04.

2340. Hearn, Michael P., ed. *The Annotated Christmas Carol: A Christmas Carol by Charles Dickens*. New York: Clarkson N. Potter, distributed by Crown Publishers, 1976; reprinted as *A Christmas Carol*. New York: Crown, 1989. 182 pp.

In his introduction, pp. 1-51, Hearn comments on the writing and publication of Dickens's first Christmas Book, the various foreign editions, piracies (and resulting law suits), and other Christmas works by Dickens and others. The text itself, pp. 53-172, is a reproduction of "the first, uncorrected printing" of *A Christmas Carol* (1843), with comments in Hearn's marginal notes on "significant textual differences in the many states of the story." Hearn also includes a bibliography (**99**), pp. 174-80. Contains the original illustrations by John Leech and other illustrations in the introductory section. Cohn and Collins (**958**) list a paperback edition (New York: Avon, 1977).

Reviews: *Choice*, 13 (1976/77), 1594 (an "attractive volume," a "worthwhile addition to any library serving either the general reader or the specialist"); E. Herman, *Chicago Tribune*, 23 December 1976, section 2, pp. 1, 3 (not so much a review as Herman's views on Dickens's revival of Christmas customs while at the same time presenting Dickens's "growing concern for the plight of the poor and the evils of child labor in industrial England"); R. Kirsch, *Los Angeles Times*, 5 December 1976, "The Book Review" section, pp. 1, 24 (a "lovely volume"); J. G. Schiller, *AB Bookman's Weekly*, 58 (8 November 1976), 2537-38 (contains "an authoritative study of the text"); B. Weeks, *Washington Post*, 25 December 1976, pp. C1, C6 (an "intriguing and inviting volume"; Hearn's list of editions and illustrations is "awesome in length although it makes no claim to be definitive"); G. J. Worth, *Nineteenth-Century Fiction*, 32 (1977/78), 348-51 (a "handsome" but "pretentious and bloated" volume).

2341. Johnson, Edgar. "Introduction." In Dickens's *A Christmas Carol*. New York: Columbia University Press, 1956; reprinted 1967 (**265**), pp. iii-vi.

Notes that the manuscript of the novel is "scored with corrections and deletions and with entire redrafts of many pages, to a degree unusual with Dickens at this stage of his career." For bibliographical notes to this edition, pp. vii-xii, see Johnson (**264**).

2342. Kent, W. "Tiny Tim Again." *Dickensian*, 30 (1933/34), 151.

In a letter to the editor, points out that, since there is no reference to the fate of Tiny Tim in the manuscript of *A Christmas Carol*, this must have been added in page proof.

2343. Kinnane, John. "Facsimile of 'A Christmas Carol' Manuscript." *Antiquarian Book Monthly*, December 1993, p. 22.

Praises a facsimile of the manuscript (**2346**) as "elegantly produced" and traces the provenance of the manuscript, now in the Pierpont Morgan Library, New York. Illustrated.

2344. Kitton, F[rederic] G. "Some Famous Christmas Stories." *Library Review*, 1 (1892/93), 705-17.

In what is ostensibly a review of Dickens's *Christmas Books* in the Macmillan Edition (**2295**), with an introduction by Dickens's eldest son, Kitton comments on various bibliographical matters concerning the five Christmas Books—manuscripts, adaptations, genesis, and publication details.

2345. Klinkenborg, Verlyn. "A Note on the Manuscript." In Dickens's *The Cricket on the Hearth: A Fairy Tale of Home* (**2350**), p. 19.

Gives the provenance of the manuscript, now in the Pierpont Morgan Library, New York, and describes the manuscript's physical state. The manuscript of the novel, with numerous cancellations, corrections, and additions, is reproduced in facsimile, pp. [23-96], and includes three pages of Dickens's notes—a page of tentative titles and two pages on which Dickens experimented with names of characters.

2346. Mortimer, John. "Meeting the Manuscript." In Dickens's *A Christmas Carol: A Facsimile Edition of the Autograph Manuscript in the Pierpont Morgan Library*. New York: Pierpont Morgan Library; New Haven, CT: Yale University Press, 1993, pp. ix-xiii.

Describes the manuscript of *A Christmas Carol*, comments on what the textual changes reveal about Dickens's working methods, and gives something of the history of the writing and the publication of the work. The text itself consists of a photographic facsimile of each page with a transcription of the text on the facing page. An "Appendix," pp. 138-39, contains photographic facsimiles of seven cancelled passages found on the versos of pages of the manuscript. Also see Charles E. Pierce, Jr.'s "Foreword" (**2349**), pp. vii-viii; David Tatham's "John Leech's Illustrations," pp. xv-xxiii; Mortimer (**2347**); and Kinnane (**2343**).
Review: M. Y. A[ndrews], *Dickensian*, 89 (1993), 235 (a "handsome facsimile" but one lacking full scholarly apparatus and not always accurate, though watching Dickens at work in the manuscript "is a fascinating experience").

2347. Mortimer, John. "Poorhouses, Pamphlets and Marley's Ghost." *New York Times*, 24 December 1993, p. A27.

Comments on the manuscript of *A Christmas Carol* and the circumstances of the writing and publication of the novel. An accompanying note indicates that this article is "adapted from the introduction " to the Pierpont Morgan Library's facsimile reproduction of the novel (**2346**).

2348. "Mr. Morgan Owns Manuscript of 'A Christmas Carol.' Original in Dickens's Handwriting of the Most Famous Yuletide Story Ever Written Is in the Private Library of the Financier and Collector." *New York Times Magazine*, 8 December 1912, p. 3.

A brief journalistic history of the writing, publication, and reception of *A Christmas Carol*, with briefer description of the manuscript. Illustrated with facsimiles of three pages of the manuscript and a photograph of Dickens.

2349. Pierce, Charles E., Jr. "Foreword." In Dickens's *A Christmas Carol: A Facsimile Edition of the Autograph Manuscript in the Pierpont Morgan Library.* (**2346**), pp. vii-viii.

Comments on the provenance of the manuscript.

2350. Sanders, Andrew. "Introduction." In Dickens's *The Cricket on the Hearth: A Fairy Tale of Home.* Guildford, Eng.: Genesis Publications, 1981, pp. 11-17.

Comments on the origin, writing, publication, and reception of the work and briefly on the work itself, which here consists of a facsimile of the manuscript in the Pierpont Morgan Library, New York, with the original illustrations, four in color. For "A Note on the Manuscript," p. 19, see Klinkenborg (**2345**).

Review: D. Paroissien, *Dickens Quarterly*, 2 (1985), 144-47 (complains about the price–£75–of this luxurious limited edition).

2351. Sibley, Brian. *A Christmas Carol: The Unsung Story* (**800**), pp. 127-28.

Contains a brief section on the provenance of the manuscript of *A Christmas Carol*, now in the Pierpont Morgan Library, New York.

2352. Slater, Michael. "Appendix A: The Deleted 'Young England' Passages from *The Chimes*," "Appendix B: The Descriptive Headlines Added to *A Christmas Carol* and *The Chimes*, in the Charles Dickens Edition, 1868," and "Appendix D: The Descriptive Headlines Added to the *Cricket [on the Hearth]*, the *Battle [of Life]* and *The Haunted Man* in the Charles Dickens Edition 1868." In Dickens's *The Christmas Books.*

Ed. Michael Slater. 2 vols. Penguin English Library. Harmondsworth, Eng., Baltimore, MD, and Ringwood, Austral.: Penguin Books, 1971, I, 247-52, 253-55; II, 359-61.

Appendix A contains six paragraphs of political satire deleted in the manuscript of *The Chimes* at John Forster's suggestion. Appendixes B and D list the headlines that Dickens's added in the Charles Dickens Edition of the *Christmas Books* (1868). For "Appendix C: Dickens's Readings from the *Christmas Books*," see Collins (**644**).

Reviews: A. Easson, *Dickens Studies Newsletter*, 4 (1973), 68-71 ("a very handsome piece of work," "excellently introduced and annotated," with illustrations "in approximately their original places in the text"); S. Monod, *Dickensian*, 68 (1972), 122-24 ("truly first-rate" editing, with the introduction supplying "an excellent and balanced appraisal of each book"; useful supplementary material, "reasonable" textual choices, but "a sparse handful of trifling misprints").

2353. Slater, Michael. "*The Chimes*: Its Materials, Making, and Public Reception; With an Assessment of Its Importance as a Turning-Point in the Works of Dickens." *Index to Theses* (**1188**), 15 (1964/65), 16 (Balliol College, Oxford University, 1965).

No abstract provided, but the title makes the contents sufficiently clear. Glancy (**98**), p. 189, calls this a definitive study "of all aspects of the book's conception, writing, social criticism, and contemporary response." Some of this material is incorporated in Slater (**2354**).

2354. Slater, Michael. "Dickens (and Forster) at Work on *The Chimes*." *Dickens Studies*, 2 (1966), 106-40.

An examination of the manuscript of *The Chimes*, two sets of page proofs, an outline of the general idea of the story, and Dickens's letters to Forster about the work. The result is a fascinating, detailed study of Dickens at work on one of his Christmas Books, with help in the editing stage from John Forster. Slater also traces further minor changes in the Cheap Edition (1852) and the Charles Dickens Edition (1868). Also see Slater's doctoral dissertation (**2353**).

2355. Stone, Harry. "A Note on the Text." In Dickens's *George Silverman's Explanation*. Ed. Harry Stone. Northridge: California State University Northridge Libraries, Santa Susana Press, 1984, pp. xxxiv-xxxv.

Notes that virtually all the versions of this work contain numerous changes in spelling, capitalization, hyphenation, punctuation, and other incidentals. It is here published from the text of the original version in the *Atlantic Monthly*, January-March 1868.

David Copperfield

2356. Brattin, Joel J. "'Let Me Pause Once More': Dickens' Manuscript Revisions in the Retrospective Chapters of *David Copperfield*." *Dickens Studies Annual*, 26 (1998), 73-90.

Comments on manuscript revisions in the four chapters of *David Copperfield* in which Copperfield "looks back over significant phases of his life"—chapters 18, 43, 53, and 64. Illustrated.

2357. Buckley, Jerome H. "Number Plans for *David Copperfield*." In Dickens's ***David Copperfield**: Authoritative Text, Backgrounds, Criticism*. Ed. by Jerome H. Buckley. New York and London: W. W. Norton, 1990, pp. 741-62.

Buckley accompanies his transcription of the number plans with brief comments on Dickens's development and use of them. He also includes Dickens's autobiographical fragment, a Dickens chronology, and a bibliography of studies of *David Copperfield* (**1077**).

Reviews: J. J. Brattin, *Dickens Quarterly*, 8 (1991), 179-87 (contains "valuable critical and historical materials"; while most of the annotations are useful, the work is "filled with dozens and dozens of typographical errors"); J. A. Davies, *Notes and Queries*, ns 38 (1991), 244-45 (notes a few misprints, criticizes some editorial choices, finds the selection of critical essays not "adventurous," and concludes that this is a "useful working edition" for undergraduates that needs to be "handled with care").

2358. Burgis, Nina. "Appendix B: The Trial Titles" and "Appendix C: The Number Plans." In Dickens's *David Copperfield*. Ed. Nina Burgis. World's Classics. Oxford and New York: Oxford University Press, 1983, pp. 719-21, 722-37; reprinted as "Appendix C: The Trial Titles" and "Appendix D: The Number Plans." In Dickens's *David Copperfield*. Ed. Nina Burgis. With Introduction and Notes by Andrew Sanders. World's Classics. Oxford and New York: Oxford University Press, 1997, 1999, pp. 871-73, 874-89.

Comments on the text, which is that of the Clarendon *David Copperfield* (**2359**), and prints the variations on the title that Dickens jotted down as well as the complete number plans for the novel.

Review: J. J. Brattin, *Dickens Quarterly*, 16 (1999), 42-48 (finds Sanders's introduction "useful," but "seriously underestimating" the extent of Dickens's manuscript revisions, and his notes "clear, succinct, and useful").

2359. Burgis, Nina. "Introduction." In Dickens's *David Copperfield*. Ed. Nina Burgis. Clarendon Edition. Oxford: Clarendon Press; Oxford, London, Glasgow, New York, etc.: Oxford University Press, 1981, pp. xv-lxii.

Notes that the "complete manuscript, including trial titles and number plans, corrected proofs of the first edition and texts of three further substantive editions published in Dickens's lifetime (1858, 1859, and 1867) are available for the establishment of the text and history of composition and publication" of *David Copperfield.* The manuscript and number plans and their relationship to the text of the first edition are fully discussed on pp. liii-lxii. Burgis also comments at some length on the relationship of Dickens's autobiographical fragment to *David Copperfield.* In addition, she discusses other aspects of the development and composition of this novel, the relationship between the novel and the number plans, and the textual differences between the editions of the novel published in Dickens's lifetime, changes fully recorded in footnotes in the text of the novel. Elsewhere in the volume she includes a "Descriptive List of Editions 1849-1867" (**102**), Dickens's 1850 and 1867 prefaces (pp. lxxi and 752), and the trial titles, number plans, and descriptive headlines added in the 1867 edition (pp. 753-81). Also see Butt and Tillotson, "Preface by the General Editors" (**176**).

Reviews: E. Blishen, *Manchester Guardian Weekly,* 3 May 1981, p. 22 (a "marvel" of "tireless editing"); J. H. Buckley, *Dickensian,* 77 (1981), 172-73 (a "scholarly achievement of the first magnitude," drawing on "an abundance of primary sources"; also praises Burgis's textual decisions and notes); *Choice,* 19 (1981/82), 237 ("highly recommended"); R. J. Dunn, *Review,* 4 (1982), 97-111 (a lengthy, intelligent review; finds the introduction "one of the most complete and lucid discussions of [Dickens's] progress" with *David Copperfield,* but has some reservations about occasional textual choices); S. Gill, *Review of English Studies,* ns 34 (1983), 352-53 (a fine edition, with a solid introduction); R. Gilmour, *Times Education Supplement,* 24 April 1981, p. 21 (superbly edited; "quite simply, the best and fullest edition of the novel we have or are likely to have"); L. Hartveit, *English Studies,* 63 (1982), 471-73 (the work "bears throughout the stamp of a careful and authoritative editor"); W. Igoe, *Month,* 262 (1981), 288; S. Manning, *Nineteenth-Century Fiction,* 38 (1983/84), 101-04 (a "superb" edition, particularly where textual matters are concerned); P. J. McCarthy, *Victorian Studies,* 25 (1981/82), 517-19 (praises the textual work and finds the introduction "masterful"); S. Monod, *Modern Language Review,* 77 (1982), 932-36 (a "superb" job; a substantial, interesting, and informative introduction; excellent textual apparatus); A. Sadrin, *Etudes anglaises,* 36 (1983), 98-100 (in French; praises the introduction and editing but regrets the absence of explanatory notes–in this and other volumes in the Clarendon Edition); A. Sanders, *Times Literary Supplement,* 1 May 1981, p. 482 (a "truly scholarly," authoritative edition; "Dr. Burgis is to be congratulated for the ease with which she takes us through the complex evidence of the novel's inspiration and composition in her introduction"); D. M. Slater, *British Book News,* July 1981, pp. 438-39 (carefully edited, with an introduction of "admirable lucidity and eloquence"–a "splendid edition"); J. Stillinger, *Journal of English and Germanic Philology,* 81 (1982), 579-83 (Stillinger examines Burgis's text choices in some detail and indicates some disagreement with her and with the practices of the Clarendon editors in general); H. Stone, *Dickens Studies Newsletter,* 14 (1983), 22-28 (praises what the textual apparatus and introduction reveal about the writing and revising of the novel, but finds some discrepancies in the text and textual notes, and particularly in the transcription of the number plans, whose "literally hundreds" of small errors are "not trivial but subversive"); J. Sutherland, *London Review of Books,* 17 February-2 March 1983, pp. 11-12 ("copious and lucid introduction"); A. Welsh, *Yale Review,* 71 (1981/82), 149-57 (agrees with Burgis's choice of copy-text but not with her inclusion of readings from the manuscript).

2360. Butt, John. "The Composition of *David Copperfield.*" *Dickensian,* 46 (1949/50), 90-94, 128-35, 176-80; 47 (1950/51), 33-38.

This is Butt's early version of the chapter on *David Copperfield* in *Dickens at Work* (**2291**), which is a considerable revision and expansion of this series of articles. Here Butt does not reproduce the number plans, only quoting from them in his explanatory remarks about the month by month writing of the novel; in *Dickens at Work*, each number plan for the novel is given in full, followed by more extensive explanatory remarks, though Butt uses there what he can from these *Dickensian* pieces.

2361. Butt, John. "*David Copperfield*: From Manuscript to Print." *Review of English Studies*, ns 1 (1950), 247-51.

Butt comments on the heavily corrected state of Dickens's manuscripts and the difficulties the printers must have had in deciphering them, which he illustrates with reference to the manuscript and page proofs of *David Copperfield*. Butt also comments on deletions and additions that Dickens made in proof to fit the copy into the requisite thirty-two pages of each monthly number for many of his novels—and prints, by way of illustration, a one-half-page passage that Dickens cancelled in the proof near the end of chapter 21 of *David Copperfield*.

2362. Cowden, Roy W. "Dickens at Work." *Michigan Quarterly Review*, 9 (1970), 125-32.

A posthumous study, edited by Sheridan Baker, of Dickens's writing methods in *David Copperfield*, based principally on significant revisions Dickens made in the manuscript and page proofs of the novel.

2363. Ford, George H. "Appendix: Passages Omitted from the Proof Sheets of *David Copperfield*." In Dickens's *David Copperfield*. Ed. George H. Ford. Riverside Editions. Boston: Houghton Mifflin, Riverside Press, Cambridge, MA, 1958, pp. 673-78.

Prints twelve passages cancelled in the monthly proof sheets.

2364. Gaskell, Philip. "Dickens, *David Copperfield*, 1850." In his *From Writer to Reader: Studies in Editorial Method*. Oxford: Clarendon Press, 1978, pp. 142-55.

An examination of Dickens's writing and publishing of *David Copperfield*, with considerable reference to the manuscript, proofs, and printed editions of the novel, from an editorial point of view. Gaskell also comments on (and diagrams) alterations in the text in the six editions of the work published in Dickens's lifetime. He traces a few changes in part of chapter 4 from manuscript to first edition, prints facsimiles of a page from chapter 4 as it appeared in the manuscript, corrected page proofs, and first edition; analyzes in detail changes Dickens made in this page; and considers which version an editor should choose for a modern edition of the work, though he concedes that, in making textual choices, no editor is "going to please everybody." Looking briefly at Alan Horsman's edition of *Dombey and Son* (**2376**), Gaskell calls it an "estimable edition," by far the best to date of that novel, though he quibbles about the decision (for the Clarendon Edition of Dickens's works as a whole) to regularize "inconsistent spelling, capitalization, hyphenation, etc., of the copy-text."

2365. Gaskell, Philip. "The Textual History of *David Copperfield*." In his *A New Introduction to Bibliography*. New York and Oxford: Oxford University Press, 1972, pp. 384-91 and passim.

In this appendix to his study, Gaskell traces in some detail the process involved in Dickens's writing, proofreading, and publishing of *David Copperfield*, including the six editions published in his lifetime. Gaskell also examines the changes Dickens made in a brief portion (one-third page) of chapter 54 from manuscript through the sixth edition, illustrated with facsimile copies of the passage in manuscript, page proof, and the published editions. Scattered throughout Gaskell's introduction to bibliography are references to Dickens's serialization of his novels and his editing of galleys and page proofs of them—see the index.

2366. Hawes, Donald. "David Copperfield's Names." *Dickensian*, 74 (1978), 81-87.

Comments on the names Dickens tried out for *David Copperfield* and reproduces (p. 80) the page of Dickens's notes on which he wrote them all down.

2367. "How Dickens Corrected His Proofs." *Dickensian*, 3 (1907), 297-98.

Facsimiles of a proof page of *David Copperfield* and one of *Nicholas Nickleby* showing extensive corrections by Dickens.

2368. Kidson, Frank. "The King Charles's Head Allusion in *David Copperfield*." *Dickensian*, 2 (1906), 44.

Notes that in the page proofs for *David Copperfield* Dickens changed Mr. Dick's obsession with a bull in a china shop to one with King Charles's head.

2369. "King Charles in the China Shop." *Dickensian*, 45 (1948/49), 158.

A photographic facsimile of Dickens's proof corrections for p. 145 of *David Copperfield*, showing that Mr. Dick's obsession was originally with a bull in a china shop rather than King Charles's head. The page was earlier reproduced by Stuart-Young (**2370**). Also see Kidson (**2368**).

2370. Stuart-Young, J. M. "The Head of King Charles—and the Bull in the China Shop." *Dickensian*, 24 (1927/28), 119-21.

Prints a facsimile reproduction of the page of proof for *David Copperfield* on which Dickens changed Mr. Dick's obsession with a bull in a china shop to a comparable obsession with King Charles's head. The page was later reproduced in "King Charles in the China Shop" (**2369**). Also see Kidson (**2368**).

2371. Tambling, Jeremy. "Appendix A: The Descriptive Headlines Added in 1867 Charles Dickens Edition" and "Appendix B: The Number Plans." In Dickens's *David Copperfield.* Ed. Jeremy Tambling. Penguin Classics. London and New York: Penguin Books, 1996, pp. 807-13, 814-55.

Lists the headlines that Dickens added to the 1867 edition of the novel and prints the complete number plans, with underlining and other markings indicated.
Review: J. J. Brattin, *Dickens Quarterly*, 16 (1999), 42-48 (criticizes everything about the edition and the editing).

2372. Thorpe, James. "The Establishment of the Text." In his *Principles of Textual Criticism.* San Marino, CA: Huntington Library, 1972, pp. 171-202.

Comments on the difficulty of determining which readings of a text are "authorial," with a brief reference to the manuscript and proofs of *David Copperfield* and noting that in the proofs for the novel Dickens excised or added passages to contain the text within the required thirty-two pages per installment. "It is not easy to decide," Thorpe asserts, "which of these variant readings should be regarded as the fulfillment of Dickens' intentions." Also see Thorpe (**2408**).

Dombey and Son

2373. Butt, John, and Kathleen Tillotson. "Dickens at Work on *Dombey and Son.*" *Essays and Studies, 1951,* ns 4 (1951), 70-93; reprinted, with minor revisions, as Chapter 5, "*Dombey and Son:* Design and Execution," of *Dickens at Work* (**2291**), pp. 90-113.

Examines in fascinating detail the title, the parts cover design, the manuscript, the number plans, and the proof sheets of *Dombey and Son,* as well as Dickens's comments on the novel in his letters, to show Dickens keeping, in his own words, "a steadier eye upon the general purpose and design" of his novel. Illustrated.

2374. Herring, Paul D. "The Number Plans for *Dombey and Son*: Some Further Observations." *Modern Philology*, 68 (1970/71), 151-87.

Intended as a supplement to the discussion in Butt and Tillotson's "*Dombey and Son*: Design and Execution," in their *Dickens at Work* (**2291**), where the number plans are quoted from but a transcription is not given. Herring provides a complete transcription of the number plans for the novel, part by part, with interspersed commentary on how Dickens used them in crafting the novel. Herring believes that the number plans represent "the first time Dickens had so elaborately planned (on paper) each serial part" and so was not entirely consistent as he was later in his career in how he structured them. They reveal, Herring asserts, "Dickens's growing awareness of the necessity for skillful craftsmanship in the planning and composition of his novels."

2375. Horsman, Alan. "Appendix B: The Number Plans." In Dickens's *Dombey and Son*. Ed. Alan Horsman. World's Classics. Oxford and New York: Oxford University Press, 1982, pp. 737-51.

Prints a complete set of the number plans for the novel, with underlining and cancellations indicated.

2376. Horsman, Alan. "Introduction." In Dickens's *Dombey and Son*. Ed. Alan Horsman. Clarendon Edition. Oxford: Clarendon Press; Oxford, London, Glasgow, New York, etc.: Oxford University Press, 1974, pp. xiii-xlvi.

Discusses the conception, problems in writing, and design of *Dombey and Son* and examines textual differences in the various editions of the novel published in Dickens's lifetime (more fully itemized in footnotes in the text of the novel). Horsman also describes the manuscript and proofs of the novel. Elsewhere in the volume, he includes a "Descriptive List of Editions 1846-1867" (**105**), all Dickens's prefaces to *Dombey and Son* (pp. lv, 834), and appendices containing the number plans, descriptive headlines added in the 1867 Charles Dickens Edition, information about Dickens's reading editions of the novel, and commentary on Hablot K. Browne's illustrations for the novel. Illustrated. Also see Butt and Tillotson, "Preface by the General Editors" (**176**), and Gaskell (**2364**).

Reviews: C. C. Barfoot, *English Studies*, 56 (1975), 443 ("superbly presented, with full critical apparatus"); *British Book News*, October 1974, pp. 695-96 (finds the introduction "lucid" and "magnificent," but regrets the exclusion of "explanatory annotation"); *Choice*, 11 (1974/75), 1628 ("useful mainly to textual scholars"); T. Cribb, *Review of English Studies*, ns 27 (1976), 93-96 (while noting a few imperfections, praises the volume's high editorial standards); R. J. Dunn, *Dickensian*, 71 (1975), 47-49 (congratulates Horsman for providing "an illuminating and authoritative text," showing "the kind of creative energy Dickens poured into *Dombey and Son*," and praises the introduction and "editorial apparatus"); K. J. Fielding, *Durham University Journal*, 67 (1974/75), 249-51 (high praise for bringing the reader "so much closer to Dickens in every way"); Mollie Hardwick, *Books and Bookmen*, 19, xi (August 1974), 30-32 ("everything here for the serious Dickens scholar," including a "lucid" introduction, rich footnotes, and excellently reproduced illustrations); A. Ikeler, *British Studies Monitor*, 9, iii (Winter 1980), 26-48 (scholarly); J. Maxwell, *Notes and Queries*, ns 23 (1976), 86-89 (has some reservations about several textual choices, here enumerated, and notes a few misprints); S. Monod, *Etudes anglaises*, 28 (1975), 101-03 (in French; an excellent introduction and textual notes); N. Page, *Dickens Studies Newsletter*, 6 (1975), 19-23 (a "fine edition," characterized by "meticulous and judicious scholarship, allied to an admirable clarity of presentation"); M. Slater, *Times Literary Supplement*, 20 September 1974, p. 1020 (a "superb edition," with valuable appendices, but regrettably lacking explanatory annotation; the introduction, of "exemplary precision," makes an "irrefutable case" for using the first edition as copy-text and provides a detailed account of the inception and writing of *Dombey and Son*).

2377. Tillotson, Kathleen. "New Readings in *Dombey and Son*." In *Imagined Worlds: Essays on some English Novels and Novelists in Honour of John Butt*. Ed. Maynard Mack and Ian Gregor. London: Methuen, 1968, pp. 173-82.

A detailed examination of Dickens's revisions in the manuscript and proofs of No. 4 (January 1847, chapters 11-13) of *Dombey and Son*. Tillotson also comments on misreadings that persisted through various editions.

Great Expectations

Note: Most studies of the two (or more) endings of *Great Expectations* have been omitted here because they are primarily concerned with which of the endings is the more valid, more honest one for the novel rather than with textual changes. For these references, see the numerous entries under "Conclusion" in the subject index to Worth (**109**).

2378. Butt, John. "Dickens's Plan for the Conclusion of *Great Expectations*." *Dickensian*, 45 (1948/49), 78-80.

Responding to criticism by Humphry House (**2391**), Butt corrects information in his earlier article, "Dickens at Work" (**2286**), concerning Dickens's notes for the final number of *Great Expectations*. He believes now, he asserts, that these notes were made *after* Dickens wrote chapter 53 rather than at the beginning of the final stage of Pip's expectations (chapter 40).

2379. Calder, Angus. "Appendix A: The End of the Novel," "Appendix B: 'Dates,'" and "Appendix C: Biddy's Letter." In Dickens's *Great Expectations*. Ed. Angus Calder. Penguin English Library, EL3. Harmondsworth, Eng., and Baltimore, MD: Penguin Books, 1965, etc., pp. 494-96, 497, 498.

In Appendix A, Calder reprints Dickens's working notes for the ending he originally intended for *Great Expectations* and the ending itself, as preserved in *Forster*. The revised ending, that used in the serialization of the novel in *All the*

Year Round, in which Pip is happily, though with melancholy overtones, re-united with Estella, "muffles the moral lesson which Dickens wished to draw most forcibly from the tale–that Pip's one unselfish use of his good fortune is the only source of future blessing to him," Calder asserts. Calder also traces the minor changes that Dickens made in the ending in subsequent editions. In Appendix B, Calder comments on the manuscript list of dates Dickens worked out for the novel, and, in Appendix C, he comments on revisions that Dickens made between the 1861 and 1868 editions in Biddy's letter to Pip in chapter 27.

2380.   Cardwell, Margaret. "Appendix A: The Original Ending," "Appendix B: Dickens's Working Notes," and "Appendix C: *All the Year Round* Instalments and Chapter-Numbering in Different Editions." In Dick-ens's *Great Expectations*. Ed. Margaret Cardwell. World's Classics. Ox-ford and New York: Oxford University Press, 1994, pp. 481-82, 483-86, 487-89.

In Appendix A Cardwell prints the original ending to *Great Expectations* from the manuscript, in Appendix B the three brief sets of notes extant for the novel, and in Appendix C the dates and contents of the weekly install-ments of the novel in *All the Year Round.*

Review: A. Dilnot, *Dickensian*, 90 (1994), 138-39 (praises the "superior text and the low price").

2381.   Cardwell, Margaret. "Introduction." In Dickens's *Great Expectations*. Ed. Margaret Cardwell. Clarendon Edition. Oxford: Clarendon Press; Oxford, New York, etc.: Oxford University Press, 1993, pp. xiii-lxiii.

Discusses in considerable detail the conception, writing, revision, and re-ception of *Great Expectations* as it was serialized in *All the Year Round* and ex-amines the textual differences between the manuscript and the various edi-tions of the novel published in Dickens's lifetime (more fully itemized in foot-notes to the text of the novel). Cardwell also comments on Dickens's unper-formed reading version of the novel and on a dramatized version of the novel, presumably not by Dickens, prepared "with a view to safeguarding dramatic copyright." She also provides useful information about her emendations to the 1861 edition (her copy-text) taken from the manuscript, about the manu-script of the novel, and about the extant proofs. Elsewhere in the volume, Cardwell includes a "Descriptive List of Editions 1861-1868" (**107**) and ap-pendices containing Dickens's original ending for the novel, his working notes, a list of the *All the Year Round* installments and the chapter numbering in the different editions, technical commentary on the five impressions of the 1861 English edition, a note on the texts of the 1862 and 1864 editions, a list of the eight illustrations that Marcus Stone did for the Library and later edi-tions (which are reproduced along with the vignette title page of the 1862 edition), and the descriptive headlines that Dickens added in the 1868 edition. Also see Butt and Tillotson, "Preface by the General Editors" (**176**).

Reviews: M. Y. Andrews, *Dickensian*, 89 (1993), 226-30 (an "excellent edition," maintaining "the high standards of scholarship established by the Clarendon Dickens," with an "absorbing introduction" that traces "the genesis, composition and weekly publication of *Great Expectations*"); J. J. Brattin, *Dickens Quarterly*, 11 (1994), 138-47–see Brattin (**299**); T. Cribb, *Review of English Studies*, ns 47 (1996), 105-06 (finds Cardwell's case for the three-volume 1861 edition as copy-text "admirably made," though has some doubts about the choice); M. Demoor, *English Studies* (Lisse, Netherlands), 76 (1995), 293-95 (Cardwell's "expertise is . . . indisputable"); D. Hewitt, *Notes and Queries*, ns 41 (1994), 259-60 (high praise); B. Lake, *Antiquarian Book Monthly*, 21, i (January 1994), pp. 30-31 (a "definitive edition" that straightens out the sequence of the impressions of the first three-volume edition); D. Mehl, *Archiv für das Studium der neueren Sprachen und Litteraturen*, 233 (1996), 180-81 (in German); A. Sadrin, *Etudes anglaises*, 48 (1995), 98-99 (highly favorable); W. P. Williams, *Analytical & Enumerative Bibliography*, ns 8 (1994), 84-85 (an excellent scholarly edition excellently edited).

2382. Collins, Philip. "Novel on Blue Paper." *Times Literary Supplement*, 22 September 1978, p. 1063.

In a review of the Scolar Press's production (London, 1977) of a color microfilm of the manuscript, number plans, and other memoranda of *Great Expectations*, Collins provides a brief history of the manuscript and finds the microfilm technically a "pleasing and efficient production," though he complains about the cost of it. In his bibliography of the novel (**109**), p. 5, George J. Worth points out that the manuscript, written "in blue ink on blue paper, with many cancellations and insertions" is "very difficult to read" and the color microfilm of it "almost impossible to decipher." Prepublication notices may be found in *Scolar Newsletter*, no. 9 (8 May 1975), 6, and no. 10 (23 April 1976), 803, and in *Times Literary Supplement*, 25 June 1976, p. 803.

2383. Crompton, Louis. "Dickens's Plan for *Great Expectations*" and "How *Great Expectations* Was Published." In Dickens's *Great Expectations*. Ed. Louis Crompton. Indianapolis and New York: Bobbs-Merrill, 1964, pp. xxvii-xxviii, xxix-xxx.

Dickens's "Plan" is an excerpt from *Forster* (Book Ninth, Part III) on Dickens's writing of the novel. The second piece provides some details about the serial publication of the novel in *All the Year Round*. Crompton also prints the first ending (from the galley proofs) and the revised ending (in all editions), pp. 522-26. Crompton includes a "Bibliography (**1088**), pp. xxiii-xxv.

Reviews: T. Boyle, *College English*, 27 (1965/66), 650-51 ("outstanding" introduction; editing is "amazingly detailed and always intelligent"); D. DeVries, *Dickens Studies Newsletter*, 5 (1974), 56-61 (reasonably full editorial apparatus, well footnoted, textually sound, readable).

2384. Dexter, Walter. "When Found–The End of 'Great Expectations.'" *Dickensian*, 34 (1937/38), 82.

A one-paragraph comment on the difference between the original ending printed in *Forster* and the ending to the serialization in *All the Year Round*.

2385. Diedrick, James K. "The Endings of *Great Expectations*: A Critical Bibliography." Typescript. Dickens House Museum. 5 pp.

In his bibliography of *Great Expectations*, (**109**), George Worth indicates, p. 308, that Diedrick's typescript contains sixty-one items "published between 1899 and 1974 pertaining to the endings of *Great Expectations* and to more general considerations of closure in Victorian fiction" but that the entries are not annotated. Worth himself identifies 99 entries on the conclusion of the work in his subject index, p. 337.

2386. Dunn, Albert A. "The Altered Endings of *Great Expectations*: A Note on Bibliography and First-Person Narrative." *Dickens Studies Newsletter*, 9 (1978), 40-42.

On Dickens's revisions of the ending of *Great Expectations* and the "ambiguity of the phrasing" in the "third" ending, printed in the 1868 Charles Dickens Edition. Such ambiguity, Dunn believes, maintained "both the novel's design and the integrity of its vision of life."

2387. Greenberg, Robert A. "On Ending *Great Expectations*." *Papers on Language & Literature*, 6 (1970), 152-62.

Compares the original and revised endings of the novel, preferring the latter for giving greater import to Dickens's emphasis on Pip's and Estella's self-discoveries. Greenberg also surveys earlier studies of this subject.

2388. Hargrave, Wilfred. "A Trifle Light as Air, Being the Strange Story of a Dickens Misprint." *Connoisseur*, 4 (1902), 188-91.

On a misprint of "air" for "hair" in the fourteenth paragraph of chapter 26 of *Great Expectations* in editions after the first (3 vols., 1861). A photographic facsimile of the relevant page of the manuscript of the novel is included to show, Hargrave indicates, that Dickens clearly wrote the word "hair."

2389. Harkness, Bruce. "Bibliography and the Novelistic Fallacy." *Studies in Bibliography: Papers of the Bibliographical Society of the University of Virginia*, 12 (1960), 59-73.

On the need for critics to be aware of a book's textual characteristics. Using Dickens's *Great Expectations* as one of his examples (see pp. 65-67), Harkness points out that knowing it was published serially in thirty-six weekly parts is important to understanding the nature of its plot complications and developments.

2390. Hoefnagel, Dick. "An Early Hint of *Great Expectations*." *Dickensian*, 82 (1986), 82-84.

Prints a photographic facsimile of the flyleaf of Dickens's copy of Samuel Johnson's *Dictionary of the English Language*, an edition published in 1825 and now in the Dartmouth College library, which, Hoefnagel maintains, contains in Dickens's hand the words "Great Expectations" and "Magwitch," among several other last names, along with the date "Christmas-Day 1856." This may be evidence, Hoefnagel suggests, that nearly four years before he began to write it Dickens was doing some meditating about *Great Expectations*. But see the responses by Kathleen Tillotson (**2409**) and Jerome Meckier (**2395**).

2391. House, Humphry. "G. B. S. on *Great Expectations*." *Dickensian*, 44 (1947/48), 63-70, 183-86.

In an interlude in his study of George Bernard Shaw's comments on *Great Expectations*, House summarizes John Butt's assertion in "Dickens at Work" in the *Durham University Journal* (**2286**) that, at the end of the thirty-ninth chapter (the end of the Second Stage of Pip's expectations), Dickens "seems to have paused to decide what to do next" (quoting Butt), as Dickens's notes for *Great Expectations* seemed to indicate and that he generally "*tended* not to plan ahead for each novel as a whole" (House's paraphrase). But House argues that just because an overall plan for the novel was not written down by Dickens does not mean it never existed in the author's head for *Great Expectations* and other novels. He refers to other entries in Dickens's notes to suggest that Dickens had indeed done some planning ahead. See Butt's reply (**2378**).

2392. Law, Graham, and Adrian J. Pinnington. "A Note on the Text" and "Appendix A1: Dickens's Working Memoranda." In Dickens's *Great Expectations*. Ed. Graham Law and Adrian J. Pinnington. Broadview Literary Texts. Peterborough, Can., and Orchard Park, NY: Broadview Press, 1998, pp. 29-32, 513-15.

In "A Note on the Text," the editors comment on Dickens's writing of the novel, the provenance of the manuscript, details of the novel's serial publication in *All the Year Round*, and textual choices they made in preparing this edition. In Appendix A1, the editors print the relatively sparse notes that are extant for *Great Expectations*, with Dickens's cancellations and underlining indicated.

2393. Macy, George, Blanche Patch, George Bernard Shaw, and William Maxwell. *The Mystery of the Unhappy Ending [of **Great Expectations**]: A Correspondence.* [New York: Limited Editions Club, 1937]. 15 unnumbered pages.

An exchange of letters occasioned by Shaw's desire to reproduce the "original" and what he remembered as the more unhappy ending to *Great Expectations* in the edition being prepared for the Limited Editions Club (1937)–only to discover that the original ending in *All the Year Round* was not that. See Shaw (**2406**) for the resolution to the matter.

2394. Maxwell, William. "[Query] 229. Dickens: *Great Expectations.*" *Bibliographical Notes and Queries*, 2, viii (February 1937), 7.

A query about the different endings Dickens wrote for *Great Expectations*.

2395. Meckier, Jerome. "Dickens, *Great Expectations*, and the Dartmouth College Notes." *Papers on Language and Literature*, 28 (1992), 111-32.

Finds the notes attributed to Dickens on the flyleaf of Dickens's copy of Samuel Johnson's *Dictionary of the English Language* in the Dartmouth College library indeed spurious, after reviewing in detail the arguments of Hoefnagel (**2390**) and Tillotson (**2409**) on the matter. Meckier also reviews earlier uses by other authors of the term "great expectations"–and Dickens's own use of it in *Martin Chuzzlewit*–and looks at Dickens's authentic notes in the Book of Memoranda (**2530**) relevant to *Great Expectations*, including a list of possible names for characters.

2396. Millhauser, Milton. "*Great Expectations*: The Three Endings." *Dickens Studies Annual*, 2 (1972), 267-77, 372-73.

More a critical than a textual study of the ending(s) of the novel ("one at the forge, one in Cairo, and one in London settling romantic accounts with Estella"), since the three endings referred to in the title are in all editions of the novel. It is only the third ending, which Millhauser terms the "Post Scriptum" of the novel that Dickens revised at Bulwer-Lytton's suggestion. Millhauser does, however, examine (and print, pp. 276-77) Dickens's working notes for the novel's conclusion and finds there that Dickens had planned the first two endings "well in advance." Millhauser does not really deal with the textual variants of the third ending.

2397. Mitchell, Charlotte. "Appendix A: The Ending as Originally Conceived" and "Appendix B: Dickens's Working Notes." In Dickens's *Great Expectations*. Ed. Charlotte Mitchell. Penguin Classics. New York: Viking Penguin Books, 1996, pp. 508-09, 510-12.

Prints the original ending that Dickens wrote and the notes he used in writing the novel.

2398. Paroissien, David. *The Companion to Great Expectations.* The Dickens Companions. Mountfield, Eng.: Helm Information; Westport, CT: Greenwood Press, 2000, passim.

In his notes to *Great Expectations*, with which most of the volume is concerned, Paroissien includes a "small selection" (as he indicates in "A Note on the Text," p. 15) of the variant readings between manuscript and printed text, indicates the weekly installments by date, and prints a transcript of the five pages of Dickens's working notes for the novel, with corrections indicated (pp. 344-48). In his introduction, pp. 1-14, while discussing Dickens's writing of the novel for serial publication in *All the Year Round*, Paroissien comments briefly on Dickens's use of entries from his Book of Memoranda (**2530**) and the working notes (see p. 5). He also examines the textual differences in the ending for the novel in the manuscript, corrected proofs, serial version and first edition, and the 1868 Charles Dickens Edition (pp. 11-13). In an appendix, "Serial Installments in *All the Year Round*," pp. 453-55, he comments on and provides details about the thirty-six weekly numbers of the novel. Illustrated. Also see the "Select Bibliography" (**1091**), pp. 456-80.

Reviews: A. Christensen, *RSV: Revisti di Studi Vittoriani*, 6, xi (Gennaio 2001), 131-36 (praises the bibliography and index and acknowledges that the commentary "sometimes dazzles us" with Paroissien's knowledge of the period); A. Dilnot, *Dickensian*, 98 (2002), 54-56 (a fine work of scholarship; Paroissien "seems to have a comprehensive knowledge of Dickens at his fingertips"); S. Gill, *Review of English Studies*, 53 (2002), 456-47 ("There is much to praise in this book," including "the judicious use made of textual details from manuscript, proof, and printing history" and the bibliography); D. Parker, *Dickens Quarterly*, 18 (2001), 55-59 ("valuable information and commentary," much of which Parker surveys); and S. Thornton, *Etudes anglaises*, 53 (2000), 500-01 (in French; "un travail remarquable," "indispensable").

2399. Rosenberg, Edgar. "Last Words on *Great Expectations*: A Textual Brief on the Six Endings." *Dickens Studies Annual*, 9 (1981), 87-115.

Once again examines the–now *six*–possible endings for *Great Expectations*, preferring the original ending Dickens wrote but reluctantly deciding that the ending printed in the first edition should be the one used in an authoritative edition. Rosenberg also surveys the debate about the primacy of the endings and goes over the evidence of the manuscript and proofs. For an expanded version of this essay, see Rosenberg (**2401**).

2400. Rosenberg, Edgar. "'Murder' 'Shot!' 'Drowned!': A Note on Dickens's Descriptive Headlines." *Q/W/E/R/T/Y*, 9 (October 1999), 87-95.

An engrossing examination of how Dickens used the running headlines that he wrote for the volumes in the Charles Dickens Edition of his novels, with emphasis on those for *Great Expectations*. Rosenberg is particularly intrigued by Dickens's frequent reference to Magwitch in the headlines as "he" rather than using his name, a discussion pretty much borrowed from his earlier "A Preface to *Great Expectations*: The Pale Usher Dusts His Lexicons" **(2402)**.

2401.   Rosenberg, Edgar. "Preface," "The Original Ending," "Adopted Readings," "Textual Notes," "Launching *Great Expectations*," "Writing *Great Expectations*," "A Note on Dickens's Working Plans," "The Descriptive Headlines," and "Putting an End to *Great Expectations*." In Dickens's ***Great Expectations***: *Authoritative Text, Backgrounds, Contexts, Criticism*. Ed. Edgar Rosenberg. Norton Critical Edition. New York and London: W. W. Norton, 1999, pp. xi-xix, 359, 361-66, 367-88, 389-423, 427-68, 469-88, 489-90, 491-527.

In the stunningly scholarly and intelligent accoutrements to the authoritative text of *Great Expectations*, Rosenberg provides what must be the ultimate commentary on textual matters and the creative process involved in the writing of the novel. In addition, he supplements his own commentary with Jean Callahan's "The (Unread) Reading Version of *Great Expectations*" **(643)**, pp. 543-56.

Rosenberg's "Preface" is a delight to read (do not miss footnote 1, or, for that matter, his "Acknowledgments," pp. xiii-xiv) and its content is valuable; he comments on his choice of copy-text–the serialization in *All the Year Round*–and his rare departures from it, as well as on the extent to which his own contributions to this volume are indebted to earlier publications of his. [Collectors should take note that this annotation is based on the third reprint of this edition in which, as Christa Grenawalt, a Norton editorial assistant, notes in a letter accompanying a complimentary copy, "we have corrected the thirty-two (!) pages of errata he brought to our notice."]

In "Adopted Readings," Rosenberg lists all the substantive changes in phrasing from the manuscript and from the editions of 1861 (three-volume edition), 1862 (Library Edition), and 1868 (Charles Dickens Edition) that he made in the text of the serialization in *All the Year Round*. His "Textual Notes" is a "table of variant readings . . . meant to be selective, not exhaustive" from the manuscript, three sets of corrected proofs, and all published versions through 1868. With fewer than a dozen exceptions, the footnotes to the text itself are explanatory rather than textual.

"Launching *Great Expectations*" is a detailed accounting of Dickens's writing of the novel over nine months and its publication in serial and three-volume format, with charts detailing weekly (in America and England), monthly (though the novel was not ultimately published in monthly parts), and volume publication. Rosenberg also comments briefly on other early editions of *Great Expectations*. See the photographic facsimiles of the first page of both the American and English serialized versions, pp. 424-25, and of the top part of the first page of the manuscript itself, p. 426.

"Writing *Great Expectations*" is a fascinating, inspired study of Dickens's writing habits and his writing of *Great Expectations*, with much reference to manuscript and page proof revisions and what they reveal of Dickens's editorial genius (here applied to his own writing). Rosenberg also comments perceptively, as well as wittily, on Dickens's handwriting and the difficulty of reading it–with praise for the compositors who somehow managed to do so much of the time. There is one *faux pas*, however: on page 434 Rosenberg seems to blame the American compositors at *Harper's Weekly* for inexperience in reading Dickens's hand, when, as he notes elsewhere, they were working from uncorrected page proofs sent from England–and therefore never glimpsed the manuscript.

In "A Note on Dickens's Working Plans," Rosenberg comments on and includes photographic facsimiles and transcripts of four of the "scant five half sheets" of notes for the novel that "evidently guided Dickens in composing the final chapters of the novel." In this section he includes "A Note on Antecedents," pp. 476-79, a summary of his findings in "Towards *Great Expectations*: From Notebook to Novel" (**2404**). In "The Descriptive Headlines," he lists the headlines that Dickens wrote for the Charles Dickens Edition (1868), though he fails to indicate their source.

"Putting an End to *Great Expectations*" is a considerable expansion of his "Last Words on *Great Expectations*: A Textual Brief on the Six Endings" (**2399**). Here he expands his commentary on Bulwer-Lytton's *A Strange Story*, the dreariness of which (in Dickens's opinion, at least) forced him to begin serializing *Great Expectations* in *All the Year Round* before *A Strange Story* was finished. Rosenberg also fills out his examination of the variant endings and indicates his preference for the earliest, least happy ending. In a new concluding section entitled "A Note on Bulwer's Meddling," pp. 518-27, he greatly expands his examination of Bulwer-Lytton's part in Dickens's revision of his original ending, including a survey of critical commentaries on the endings–by more than 100 commentators, Rosenberg notes, though he finds only three of the commentaries substantial.

Rosenberg also includes "Charles Dickens: A Chronology," pp. 721-27, with parallel columns for his "Life" and "Works"; "Selected Bibliography" (**1092**), pp. 729-46, by himself and Jean Callahan, revised, somewhat expanded, and updated from the first printing, where it occupied pp. 729-44; and "Dickens's Letters on *Great Expectations*," pp. 531-36, containing Dickens's comments on the creation of the novel. Illustrated.

Review: J.-C. A[malric], *Cahiers victoriens et edouardiens*, no. 49 (April 1999), 230 (in French; a remarkable edition); A. Christensen, *RSV: Revisti di Studi Vittoriani*, 6, xi (Gennaio 2001), 131-36 (praises Rosenberg's editorial work in "this authoritative new edition," the "richness" of the "contextual material, and a bibliography that "masterfully surveys" its subject); *Contemporary Review*, 275 (1999), 110 (a "superb edition of the text" and "all that is essential to a full understanding" of the novel); A. Dilnot, *Dickensian*, 95 (1999), 246-47 ("a triumph of painstaking professionalism which is nevertheless regularly witty and stimulating"); *Forum for Modern Language Studies*, 37 (2001), 339-40 (the volume includes an "illuminating and detailed account of the different endings" and "frequent but nicely judged" footnotes); S. Monod, *Etudes anglaises*, 52 (1999), 505-06 (in French; praises the editorial work and finds the edition of considerable value, much dominated by "une puissante vitalité" in the personal style of Rosenberg).

2402. Rosenberg, Edgar. "A Preface to *Great Expectations*: The Pale Usher Dusts His Lexicons." *Dickens Studies Annual*, 2 (1972), 294-335, 374-78.

Rosenberg elucidates his "editorial practices" and the problems involved in preparing an edition for Norton of *Great Expectations* (**2401**) finally published in 1999. He comments on the annotation, Dickens's Book of Memoranda (**2530**), the running headlines that Dickens wrote for the Charles Dickens Edition (1868), his letters on the writing of the novel (most quoted or misquoted in *Forster*), the relationship of the novel to Dickens's personal life, Dickens's planning of the work as a monthly serial though he published it finally in weekly installments, and the "Wisbech Memoranda," Dickens's extant sheets of notes for the novel (bound with the manuscript and now in the Wisbech Museum). Rosenberg does not comment much here on textual matters—for these see the introductory matter in his 1999 edition.

2403. Rosenberg, Edgar. "Small Talk in Hammersmith: Chapter 23 of *Great Expectations*." *Dickensian*, 69 (1973), 90-101.

Comments thoroughly on changes Dickens made in the manuscript, page proofs, and printed editions of Chapter 23 in the characters of Mrs. Coiler and Mrs. Pocket, minor figures in the novel. Rosenberg reprints this essay, somewhat condensed and tightened up, as part IX of "Writing *Great Expectations*" in the Norton Edition of the novel (**2401**), pp. 455-61.

2404. Rosenberg, Edgar. "Towards *Great Expectations*: From Notebook to Novel." *Q/W/E/R/T/Y*, 9 (October 1999), 69-85.

In this rich study of the sources (in Dickens's own writings) of *Great Expectations*, Rosenberg begins, pp. 70-73, with entries Dickens made in the Book of Memoranda (**2530**) that he kept, 1855-65, that are relevant to *Great Expectations*. Several of these have not been linked previously to the novel. Rosenberg finds other sources in a few of the Christmas Stories in Dickens's journals *Household Words* and *All the Year Round* and several of the "Uncommercial Traveller" essays in *All the Year Round*. He summarizes all these findings in the sub-section entitled "A Note on Antecedents" in the Norton Edition of *Great Expectations* (**2401**), pp. 476-79.

2405. Sadrin, Anny. "Manuscript and Memoranda." In her *Great Expectations* (**108**), pp. 18-25.

Notes that the microfilm distributed by Scolar Press (1977) of the manuscript of *Great Expectations*, which is in the Wisbech and Fenland Museum,

Wisbech, Cambridgeshire, is "blurred and unreadable." Sadrin also describes the manuscript and prints and comments on the memoranda that accompany it. For other supplementary bibliographical and textual material in this edition, see Sadrin (**661, 1093**).

2406. Shaw, George Bernard. "Preface." In Dickens's *Great Expectations*. Edinburgh: R. & R. Clark for Limited Editions Club, 1937, pp. v-xxii.

Shaw notes that he is printing the original ending to *Great Expectations* for the first time (from the manuscript), but in an "Editor's Postscript," pp. xxiii-xxvi, he prints the ending that Dickens published in *All the Year Round* for readers "who still like all their stories to end at the altar rails." Also see Macy, Patch, Shaw, and Maxwell (**2393**).

2407. Staples, Leslie C. "When Found–the Manuscript of *Great Expectations* [and] the Manuscript of *Our Mutual Friend*." *Dickensian*, 43 (1946/47), 60-61.

These are brief notes, the latter incidental, the former about a projected sale of the manuscript of *Great Expectations* that never took place.

2408. Thorpe, James. "The Aesthetics of Textual Criticism." *PMLA: Publica tions of the Modern Language Association of America*, 80 (1965), 465-82; reprinted in *Bibliography and Textual Criticism: English and American Literature, 1700 to the Present*. Ed. O M Brack, Jr., and Warner Barnes. Chicago: University of Chicago Press, 1969, pp. 102-38; revised slightly under the same title as Chapter 5 of his *Principles of Textual Criticism* (**2372**), pp. 3-49.

In commenting in section III of the essay on the different endings that Dickens wrote for *Great Expectations*, finds that the only "real" ending is the one that Dickens published. In the revision, Thorpe adds a footnote expanding on which ending various critics preferred.

2409. Tillotson, Kathleen. "*Great Expectations* and the Dartmouth College Notes." *Dickensian*, 83 (1987), 17-18.

Responding to Hoefnagel (**2390**), Tillotson asserts that the monogram "CD," the address, and the date on the upper part of the flyleaf of Dickens's copy of Samuel Johnson's *Dictionary of the English Language* "are clearly the additions of an imitator, skilful enough to deceive anyone not closely familiar" with Dickens's handwriting in 1856. Also see Meckier (**2395**)

2410. Tredell, Nicolas. "Appendix A" and "Appendix B." In *Charles Dickens: Great Expectations*. Ed. Nicolas Tredell. Icon Critical Guides. Cambridge, Eng.: Icon Books; St. Leonards, NSW, Aus.: Allen & Unwin, 1998; reprinted in Columbia Critical Guides. New York: Columbia University Press, 2000, pp. 168, 169-70.

Appendix A reprints the "proof" version of the original ending. Appendix B compares the volume and chapter numbers of the three-volume edition (1861) with the consecutive chapter numbers of a typical one-volume edition of the novel. Tredell also includes a "Select Bibliography" (**1095**).

Hard Times

Note: Also see Terauchi (**308-09**).

2411. Ford, George, and Sylvère Monod. "A Note on the Text," "Dickens' Working Plans," "The Running Headlines," and "Textual Notes." In Dickens's *Hard Times: An Authoritative Text, Backgrounds, Sources, and Contemporary Reactions, Criticism.* Ed. George Ford and Sylvère Monod. Norton Critical Editions. New York: W. W. Norton, 1966, pp. 228-30, 231-40, 241-42, 243-68; as "A Note on the Text" (with sub-sections "Dickens' Working Plans," "Textual History," "The Running Headlines," and "Our Text") and "Textual Notes." 2nd ed. New York and London: W. W. Norton, 1990, pp. 221-36, 237-64; as "A Note on the Text" (with sub-sections "The Genesis of *Hard Times*: A History of the Text," "Dickens' Working Plans," "The Running Headlines," and "Our Text"), "Textual Notes," and "Emendations List." 3rd ed. Ed. Fred Kaplan and Sylvère Monod. New York and London: W. W. Norton, 2001, pp. 223-41, 243-71, 273-74.

In the first edition, "A Note on the Text" comments on the six sources consulted by the editors—the original manuscript, the number plans, the corrected proofs, the weekly serialization in *Household Words*, the first edition in book form (1854), and the Charles Dickens Edition (1868)—in determining the text for this edition, using the 1868 edition as copy-text. "Dickens' Working Plans" comments briefly on and provides a transcription of the plans. "The Running Headlines" are those Dickens wrote for the 1868 edition. "The Textual Notes" section identifies significant differences between the six sources used for the text.

In the second edition, the editors bring the text closer to that of the 1854 rather than the 1868 edition, enlarge the critical section and revise and extend the annotations and textual modifications and notes.

In the third edition the editors use the 1854 edition as the copy-text, with only "downright mistakes" corrected. They rearrange parts of the "Notes on the Text" section; expand and modify the "Textual Notes" to reflect their change in copy-text; add an "Emendations List," pp. 273-74, of alterations to the 1854 text, "mostly corrections of accidental mistakes"; and add several essays and omit a few in the "Contexts" and "Criticism" sections of the volume. Also see Ford and Monod (**1098**).

Reviews (first edition): [P. Collins], *Times Literary Supplement*, 6 April 1967, p. 285 (rivals the Clarendon Edition in "textual authority" and includes explanatory annotation, "enterprising" editorial matter, and "judicious" selections of criticism); K. J. Fielding, *Dickensian*, 63 (1967), 149-52 (praises all aspects of the volume and its editorial apparatus); A. Smith (**307**) (reviewing paperback editions of *Hard Times*, Smith finds this "a Dickensian feast of an edition" and by far the best of the lot).

Review (second edition): J. J. Brattin, *Dickens Quarterly*, 8 (1991), 179-87 ("a significant improvement over the 1966 edition," though with "serious flaws rendering it unreliable as a source for scholarly citation," some of which Brattin comments on).

2412. Monod, Sylvère. "Dickens at Work on the Text of *Hard Times*." *Dickensian*, 64 (1968), 86-99.

Monod comments extensively on his study of Dickens's changes in the text between the manuscript (including his working notes) and editions through the 1868 Charles Dickens Edition for the preparation of the Norton Edition of *Hard Times* (**2411**), which he coedited with George Ford. Monod gives numerous examples of intentional and unintentional changes in the text, particularly stylistic changes and changes that Dickens made for "various artistic purposes," such as consistency of characterization, unified tone, and audience appeal. Illustrated with a facsimile of a page of the manuscript.

2413. Murray, J. A. H. "Various Readings in Dickens." *Notes and Queries*, 6th ser., 12 (1885), 289.

Notes a variant reading in editions of *Hard Times* and queries whether or not there are more such variants in Dickens's works.

2414. Schlicke, Paul. "Note on the Text" and "Appendix D: Dickens's Working Notes for *Hard Times*." In Dickens's *Hard Times*. Ed. Paul Schlicke. World's Classics. Oxford and New York: Oxford University Press, 1989, pp. xxiii, 399-408.

Notes that the edition is based on the original World's Classics Edition of the novel published by Oxford University Press in 1924. In the Appendix, Schlicke prints a transcription of the number plans for the novel, with Dickens's underlining and other markings indicated.

Review: S. Monod, *Etudes anglaises*, 43 (1990), 350-51 (in French; generally favorable).

2415. Simpson, Margaret. *The Companion to **Hard Times***. Mountfield, Eng.: Helm Information; Westport, CT: Greenwood Press, 1997, passim.

In the notes proper, with which most of the volume is concerned, Simpson, as she indicates in a brief "A Note on the Text" (p. 13), includes a selection of variant readings from the autograph manuscript and the corrected proofs, as well as a transcription of Dickens's working notes for the novel. In the introduction, pp. 1-11, Simpson comments briefly on the genesis of *Hard Times* and more fully on the various themes and social "topics" of the novel. There are also a "Select Bibliography" (**1100**), pp. 248-66, and a useful subject index. Illustrated. See Simpson's doctoral dissertation "The Companion to *Hard Times*," with abstracts in *Index to Theses* (**1188**), 45, v (1996), 1798 (Queen's University, Belfast, 1995), and *Dissertation Abstracts International*, 57 (1996/97), 1079C.

Reviews: M. Y. A[ndrews], *Dickensian*, 94 (1998), 141-43 ("a reference book of copious proportions," the "depth and range of research . . . very impressive"; in its own right, this is "a fragmentary social and cultural history oriented around a single fictional text," making for "fascinating reading"); K. J. Fielding, *Dickens Quarterly*, 15 (1998), 184-86 ("encyclopaedic," the informative annotations showing "how ambitious and dense the novel is, how far beyond the full comprehension of even most of its contemporary readers, and how we need well-informed help to rise to the challenge of understanding it"); S. Gill, *Review of English Studies*, 50 (1999), 399-400 ("a cornucopia of interest and delight, the result of a great deal of resourceful and imaginative research"); D. Hawes, *Analytical & Enumerative Bibliography*, 11 (2000), 95-97 ("wonderfully comprehensive," "an indispensable fund of information"); S. Thornton, *Etudes anglaises*, 52 (1999), 97-98 (in French; favorable).

2416.   Woodings, R. B. "A Cancelled Passage in *Hard Times*." *Dickensian*, 60 (1964), 42-43.

Actually on *three* brief passages that Dickens cancelled in the proof sheets of *Hard Times*.

Little Dorrit

Note: Also see Butt (**2290**) and Watson (**2333**).

2417.   Easson, Angus. "Introduction" and "Notes on the Text." In Dickens's *Little Dorrit*. Ed. Angus Easson. Everyman Dickens. London: J. M. Dent; Rutland, VT: Charles E. Tuttle, 1999, pp. xxiii-xxxv, xxxvi-xxxvii.

In his introduction, Easson briefly describes Dickens's writing of this novel and, in "Notes on the Text," comments on the manuscript and number plans for it and provides some publication details. Easson also includes "Dickens and His Critics," pp. 911-18, in which he surveys critical views of the novel from the early reviews to 1960, and "Suggestions for Further Reading," pp. 919-21, in which he lists post-1960 studies of *Little Dorrit*, as well as some more general studies of Dickens and his works.

Reviews: P. J. McCarthy, *Dickensian*, 97 (2001), 66-69 ("rich in scholarship," with a "brilliant introductory essay," "copious notes," and "notably rich appendix on Dickens and his critics"); T. Philpotts, *Dickens Quarterly*, 17 (2000), 94-97 ("consistently accurate" annotations, "informative appendices and other supplementary material, but poorly reproduced illustrations).

2418.   Herring, Paul D. "Dickens' Monthly Number Plans for *Little Dorrit*." *Modern Philology*, 64 (1966/67), 22-63.

Prints a transcription of Dickens's number plans for *Little Dorrit*, part by part, interspersed with commentary pointing out how Dickens used them both to develop and to keep track of the intricate "interlocking plots" and the numerous characters he needed for an effective, comprehensive portrayal of the society of the early 1850s as a world of imprisonment. Also see Herring's doctoral dissertation, "The Background of Charles Dickens's 'Little Dorrit'" (University of Chicago, 1964).

2419. Sucksmith, Harvey P. "Appendix: The Number Plans." In Dickens's *Little Dorrit*. Ed. Harvey P. Sucksmith. World's Classics. Oxford and New York: Oxford University Press, 1982, pp. 692-714.

Includes a transcription of the complete number plans for the novel with underlining and other markings indicated.

Review: M. Reynolds, *Dickensian*, 79 (1983), 110-13 (generally favorable).

2420. Sucksmith, Harvey P. "Introduction." In Dickens's *Little Dorrit*. Ed. Harvey P. Sucksmith. Clarendon Edition. Oxford: Clarendon Press; Oxford, London, Glasgow, New York, etc.: Oxford University Press, 1979, pp. xiii-xlix.

Looks in considerable detail at Dickens's difficulties in the planning and composition of *Little Dorrit* and his "concern for details of organic structure, for continuity and foreshadowing." Sucksmith also comments on the textual changes in the various editions published in Dickens's lifetime (fully listed in the footnotes in the text of the novel) and describes in considerable detail the manuscript and page proofs. Elsewhere in the volume, he includes a "Descriptive List of Editions 1855-1868" (**111**), the 1857 preface (pp. lix-lx), and appendices containing excerpts from Dickens's notebook of memoranda (**2530**) relating to *Little Dorrit*, a reproduction of the number plans, and the descriptive headlines added in the 1868 edition (pp. 801-35). Also see Butt and Tillotson, "Preface by the General Editors" (**176**).

Reviews: *Choice*, 17 (1980/81), 219 ("definitive," with a "valuable introduction"; "essential for serious Dickensian study"); T. Davis, *Journal of English and Germanic Philology*, 80 (1981), 585-90 (finds the introduction knowledgeable but confusing, the editorial textual choices questionable, and "unduly selective"); M. Dodsworth, *English*, 29 (1981), 186-87(a brief notice; is skeptical of its value); K J. Fielding, *Yearbook of English Studies*, 11 (1981), 321-22 (praises the editorial work and the introduction as fine examples of "the editor's characteristic insight and scrupulousness"); J. Gattégno, *Etudes anglaises*, 34 (1981), 349 (in French; an excellent edition); S. Gill, *Review of English Studies*, ns 32 (1981), 468-69 (Sucksmith has produced a text "closer to the author's intentions than any other that has ever appeared," with a praiseworthy introduction); C. Lamont, *Notes and Queries*, ns 28 (1981), 352-53 (praises Sucksmith's "critical sensitivity" and "succinctness," but finds the illustrations of poor quality); S. Monod, *Dickensian*, 76 (1980), 106-07 (an "excellent edition"); A. Shelston, *Critical Quarterly*, 22, ii (Summer 1980), 87-88 (Sucksmith's editorial work "contributes substantially to our understanding of the novel's narrative and thematic development"); M. Slater, *British Book News*, April 1980, pp. 246, 248 (praises Sucksmith's "splendid" scholarship and his detailed, "fascinating," and "enlightening" introduction–a "superb achievement and a major contribution to Dickens studies"); M. Slater, *Times Literary Supplement*, 20 June 1980, p. 716 ("elegantly written" with an "illuminating" introduction); J. Stillinger, *Nineteenth-Century Fiction*, 35 (1980/81), 543-47 (has some quibbles about Sucksmith's textual choices but agrees with his choice of copy-text and finds the volume, "considered altogether, a very valuable piece of scholarship"); J. Sudrann, *Dickens Studies Newsletter*, 13 (1982), 80-84 (Sucksmith "presents a text and apparatus which, if not faultless, certainly comes as close as scholarly possible to giving us both a true sense of the novel as Dickens wrote it and exciting glimpses of the tact, craftsmanship, and artistry of the novelist at work"; regrets more of the manuscript revisions were not included, but otherwise has high praise for the textual apparatus, the appendices, and the introduction).

2421. Wall, Stephen, and Helen Small. "Appendix B: The Number Plans." In Dickens's *Little Dorrit*. Ed. Stephen Wall and Helen Small. Penguin Classics. London, New York, etc.: Penguin Books, 1998, pp. 791-833.

Comments briefly on Dickens's working notes for the novel and prints them, with underlining, cross-outs, and other markings indicated, in a rough approximation of the handwritten notes.

Review: T. Philpotts, *Dickens Quarterly*, 17 (2000), 94-97 (a "beautifully produced" scholarly edition but with some mistakes, several of which are noted, in the annotations).

Martin Chuzzlewit

Note: Also see Butt (**2290**).

2422. Cardwell, Margaret. "Appendix B: Preliminaries and Number Plans." In Dickens's *Martin Chuzzlewit*. Ed. Margaret Cardwell. World's Classics. Oxford and New York: Oxford University Press, 1984, pp. 723-26.

Cardwell prints variations in title and names of characters that Dickens jotted down as well as the only extant number plans for *Martin Chuzzlewit*–those for numbers 4 and 6.

2423. Cardwell, Margaret. "Introduction." In Dickens's *Martin Chuzzlewit*. Ed. Margaret Cardwell. Clarendon Edition. Oxford: Clarendon Press; Oxford, London, Glasgow, New York, etc.: Oxford University Press, 1982, pp. xv-lx.

Discusses the conception, problems in writing, and design of *Martin Chuzzlewit* and examines textual differences in the various editions of the novel published in Dickens's lifetime (more fully itemized in footnotes in the text of the novel). Cardwell also describes the manuscript and proofs of the novel. Elsewhere in the volume, she includes a "Descriptive List of Editions 1843-1867" (**112**), all Dickens's prefaces (pp. lxix and 846-48), and appendices containing preliminaries and number plans, discarded passages from chapter 6, Dickens's instructions to the illustrator, descriptive headlines added in the 1867 edition, the postscript added in the 1868 edition, and the manuscript fragment "A New Piljians Projiss." Also see Butt and Tillotson, "Preface by the General Editors" (**176**).

Reviews: *Choice*, 20 (1982/83), 1595 (a "fine introduction," an "indispensable" volume in a "monumental" series); M. J. Drummond, *Times Education Supplement*, 24 June 1983, p. 29 (an anti-scholarly put-down); L. Hartveit, *English Studies*, 65 (1984), 83-85 (an excellent introduction and edition); D. Mehl, *Anglia*, 103 (1985), 508-11(in German; favorable); S. Monod, *Modern Language Review*, 79 (1984), 159-62 (questions editorial judgment in occasional textual notes, criticizes the poor quality of the illustrations, but otherwise finds this an excellent "definitive" edition, with an "absorbing" introduction); A. Sadrin, *Etudes anglaises*, 37 (1984), 469-70 (in French; praises the intro-duction and textual apparatus); A. Sanders, *Dickensian*, 80 (1984), 46-47 (an admirable introduction and "scrupulously established" text); S. Shatto, *Dickens Quarterly*, 2 (1985), 22-25 (finds Cardwell "on firm ground with textual matters" but criticizes the "high-handed and eclectic" handling of accidentals); A. Shelston, *Critical Quarterly*, 26, iii (Autumn 1984), 87-89 (while praising the assiduity of Cardwell's work, regrets the deliberate omission of critical appraisal); J. Sutherland, *London Review of Books*, 17 February-2 March 1983, pp. 11-12 (favorable).

2424. Furbank, P. N. "Appendix A: Rejected Beginning to Chapter 6." In Dickens's *The Life and Adventures of Martin Chuzzlewit*. Ed. P. N. Fur-bank. Penguin English Library. Harmondsworth, Eng., Baltimore, MD, and Ringwood, Austral.: Penguin Books, 1968, pp. 921-25.

Prints, with minimal commentary, a lengthy passage from the manuscript of the novel that is "a rejected draft of the opening of chapter 6" of *Martin Chuzzlewit*.

2425. Ingham, Patricia. "A Note on the Text and Its History," "Appendix B: Some of Dickens's Working Papers for *Martin Chuzzlewit*," and "Notes." In Dickens's *The Life and Adventures of Martin Chuzzlewit*. Ed. Patricia Ingham. Penguin Classics. London, New York, etc.: Pen-guin Books, 1999, pp. xxx-xxxiii, 785-88, 793-826.

Comments briefly on the manuscript and, at greater length, on the changes between manuscript and first edition and the first and later editions of this novel. In appendix B, Ingham transcribes seven pages of Dickens's notes for the novel, excluding a few pages in which he experimented with the lengthy title of the parts edition. In "Further Reading," pp. xxvii-xxix, she lists twenty articles on *Martin Chuzzlewit*, 1969-94, and several book length works on Dick-ens.

2426. Metz, Nancy A. *The Companion to Martin Chuzzlewit.* The Dickens Companions. Mountfield, Eng.: Helm Information; Westport, CT: Greenwood Press, 2001, passim.

In the notes to the novel, with which most of the volume is concerned, Metz includes occasional textual notes, largely, as she indicates, from Margaret Cardwell's Clarendon Edition of the work (**2423**), on which this volume is based. In an appendix, "Preliminaries and Number Plans," pp. 499-502, Metz provides "transcripts of the brief memoranda on which Dickens sketched out his ideas for numbers 4 and 6, as well as the preliminary slips on which he experimented with the title and names of characters." She adds a "Select Bibliography" (**1102**), pp. 511-32. Illustrated.

Reviews: J. Bowen, *Times Literary Supplement,* 8 March 2002, p. 31 ("an indispensable guide"); K. Flint, *Dickens Quarterly,* 19 (2002), 170-74 ("marvellously rich," "compendious"; it "elucidates all kinds of social, literary, and culinary obscurities through referencing a very wide range of sources, and in doing so, gives a solid materiality to the world imaginatively plotted and vivified by the novelist himself").

2427. Monod, Sylvère. "Chapter 2: The Text and Its Variations" and "Chapter 11: External and Additional Material." In his *Martin Chuzzlewit.* London, Boston, and Sydney: George Allen & Unwin, 1985, pp. 9-17, 173-85.

In chapter 2, Monod comments on the manuscript of *Martin Chuzzlewit* and the two sheets of "crude 'mems'" for numbers 4 and 6 of the novel and briefly compares the texts of editions of the novel published in Dickens's lifetime. In chapter 11, he compares and contrasts Dickens's three prefaces to the novel and examines what critics have had to say about Hablot K. Browne's illustrations. Also see his "Bibliography" (**1103**), pp. 199-205.

The Mystery of Edwin Drood

2428. Aylmer, Felix. *The Drood Case.* London: Rupert Hart-Davis, 1964; New York: Barnes & Noble, 1965. x + 218 pp.

Contains some examination of the manuscript of and Dickens's notes for *Edwin Drood,* and Aylmer reprints, in "Appendix C: The Notes," pp. 187-99, a page by page transcription of Dickens's working notes. The seventeen illustrations include facsimiles of pages of the manuscript and the notes, the monthly parts cover, preliminary drawings, Charles Collins's rejected sketches, and some of Luke Fildes's published illustrations.

Reviews: D. Birch, *Dickensian,* 61 (1965), 36-39 (praises, with minor criticisms); *Economist,* 213 (1964), 713 (contains "much that is ingenious and even acceptable," but generally Aylmer's "arguments will not hold"); K. J. Fielding, *Nineteenth-Century Fiction,* 20 (1965/66), 410-12 (has many weaknesses but is still "an exciting attempt to solve a mystery no one has succeeded in solving"); B. Kreissman, *Library Journal,* 90 (1965), 3044-45 (finds the argument "sometimes labored" but nevertheless establishing a case that "must be reckoned with in future solutions of the *Mystery*"); N. C. Peyrouton, *Dickens Studies,* 1 (1965), 104-06 (has a number of objections to Aylmer's argument); *Times Literary Supplement,* 5 November 1964, p. 1000 (criticizes Aylmer's solution as "no more convincing" than other such solutions and does not find his supporting evidence "impeccable"), with replies by Aylmer, 12 November, p. 1026, and the reviewer, 19 November, p. 1039; F. T. Wood, *English Studies,* 46 (1965), 516 (Aylmer "argues his case cogently and with considerable skill," but, like other *Drood* theories, his is highly speculative).

2429. Beer, John. "*Edwin Drood* and the Mystery of Apartness." *Dickens Studies Annual,* 13 (1984), 143-91.

Makes reference to Dickens's notes and textual revisions for *The Mystery of Edwin Drood* in commenting on where studies from *Forster* on thought Dickens meant to go with the plot of the novel.

2430. Burgan, William M. "The Refinement of Contrast: Manuscript Revision in *Edwin Drood*." *Dickens Studies Annual*, 6 (1977), 167-82, 198-99.

Studies a number of revisions in *Drood* to show that in his revisions in manuscript Dickens was primarily "engaged in augmenting rather than curbing his initial ideas," resulting in five kinds of significant revision to refine contrast in the novel: "1) the augmenting of symbolism; 2) the enhancement of stylistic tension through paradox and unconventional figurative language; 3) the control of tone; 4) the elaboration of simple images through analysis into discrete components, or through reinforcement by other, parallel images; and 5) the isolation of contrasting aspects in closely similar phenomena." The revisions, fewer in number than in earlier manuscripts such as *Little Dorrit* ("a printer's nightmare"), "bear no trace of self-doubt," Burgan concludes; "they are acts of discovery."

2431. Carden, P|ercy| T. "Dickens's 'Number Plans' for *The Mystery of Edwin Drood*." *Dickensian*, 27 (1930/31), 183-85, 200-01, 266-69, 284-85, 300-01.

Facsimile reproductions of Dickens's notes for his unfinished novel, with brief explanatory remarks by Carden.

2432. Carden, Percy T. *The Murder of Edwin Drood Recounted by John Jasper, Being an Attempted Solution of the Mystery Based on Dickens' Manuscript and Memoranda.* London: Cecil Palmer, 1920, passim.

A retelling and completion of the story, based on the assumption that Jasper killed Drood, and with Jasper's execution at the end. Carden provides occasional evidence from the manuscript (not as much, however, as the title suggests) in footnotes and brief appendices to support some of his contentions about the plot.

2433. Cardwell, Margaret. "Appendix A: Manuscript List of Projected Names and Titles," "Appendix B: The Number Plans," and "Appendix C: The Sapsea Fragment." In Dickens's *The Mystery of Edwin Drood*. Ed. Margaret Cardwell. World's Classics. Oxford and New York: Oxford University Press, 1982, pp. 218, 219-31, 232-33.

In the appendices, Cardwell prints Dickens's experiments with names and titles, the extant number plans, and the "Sapsea Fragment." For the last, see

Forsyte (**2442**). Also see this title under *The Mystery of Edwin Drood* in section 1 of part 1 of the subject index.

2434. Cardwell, Margaret. "Introduction." In Dickens's *The Mystery of Edwin Drood.* Ed. Margaret Cardwell. Clarendon Edition. Oxford: Clarendon Press; Oxford, London, Glasgow, New York, etc.: Oxford University Press, 1972, pp. xiii-l.

Discusses the conception and the pressure of writing the six numbers of *Edwin Drood* that Dickens completed before his death and examines at considerable length the differences in text between the manuscript and the published version (more fully itemized in footnotes in the text of the novel). Cardwell also describes the manuscript and proofs of the novel. Elsewhere in the volume, she includes a "Descriptive List of Editions 1870-1875" (**114**) and appendices containing a manuscript list of projected names and titles, the number plans, the so-called "Sapsea Fragment," descriptive headlines added in the 1875 edition (probably by W. H. Wills), commentary on the illustrations, information about an American edition of 1870, the novel's "After-History" (speculations about the possible ending of the novel and completions of the novel by others, 1870-78), and a discussion of the proof sent to Luke Fildes, the illustrator. Illustrated.

The Sapsea Fragment was originally printed in *Forster.* For useful comment on it, see Forsyte (**2442**) and see this title under *The Mystery of Edwin Drood* in section 1 of part 1 of the subject index. Also see Butt and Tillotson, "Preface by the General Editors" (**176**). In a review in the *Dickensian,* 79 (1983), 110-13, of the World's Classics Edition of *The Mystery of Edwin Drood* (**2433**), based on the Clarendon Edition, Margaret Reynolds, the reviewer, indicates that, although the textual notes of the Clarendon Edition, on which this edition is based, are not included, the World's Classics Edition contains "minor emendations" and incorporates a few new readings based on the "Fildes proofs" of *Edwin Drood,* an important set of early proofs (**1485, 2439**). These proofs, in the Gimbel Collection, Yale University Library (**1509**), were not available to Cardwell when preparing the Clarendon Edition. Also see Cardwell's doctoral dissertation, "*Edwin Drood*: A Critical and Textual Study" (Bedford College, University of London, 1968/69), listed in *Index to Theses* (**1188**), 19 (1968/69), 18.

Reviews: C. C. Barfoot, *English Studies,* 54 (1973), 367 (a "superb edition"); J. F. Burrows, *Journal of the Australasian Universities Language and Literature Association,* no. 44 (November 1975), 275-77 ("scrupulous attention to detail"; the introduction gives a "full account of editorial problems and procedures"); *Choice,* 10 (1973/74), 92 (the "definitive edition"); A. J. Cox, *Mystery and Detection Annual,[1973],* pp. 307-12 (finds it a "definitive edition" but disagrees with some remarks made in the introduction about sources for the novel and the dating of the "Sapsea Fragment"); B. F. Fisher, IV, *Nineteenth-Century Fiction,* 28 (1973/74), 229-32 (praises Cardwell's "magisterially imposing editorial labor," particularly with manuscript, proofs, and early editions); A. Ikeler, *British Studies Monitor,* 9, iii (Winter 1980), 26-48 (scholarly); G. Joseph, *Studies in English Literature, 1500-1900,* 13 (1973), 720-21 ("meticulously edited"); J. C. Maxwell, *Notes and Queries,* ns 23 (1976), 86-89 ("full textual details, but no commentary"; questions a few textual choices); D. Mehl, *Archiv für das Studium der neueren Sprachen und Literaturen*, 210, (1973), 419-20 (in German; praises); S. Monod, *Etudes anglaises*, 25 (1972), 567-68 (in French; praises); E. Rosenberg, *Dickens Studies Newsletter*, 5 (1974), 70-84 (despite "a few pet peeves and donnish remonstrances," calls this a "splendid edition," with an introduction that is "first-rate" and "may be fairly regarded as the most succinctly comprehensive record we now have of the evolution of *Drood*" and finds that "virtually all of [Cardwell's] substantive emendations improve on the hitherto accepted . . . readings" and her recording of Dickens's manuscript "cancellations, afterthoughts, oversights" is equally "instructive"); T. A. Shippey, *Library*, 5th ser, 28 (1973), 255-57 (comments on a variety of textual matters and on Cardwell's carefulness in providing a "reliable text"); H. P. Sucksmith, *Yearbook of English Studies*, 4 (1974), 326-28 (an excellent edition, "painstakingly and lavishly annotated"); *Times Literary Supplement*, 11 August 1972, p. 946 (finds Cardwell, if anything, "too reverential" towards the manuscript copy, though generally praises the textual work and introductory matter), and see a letter from Stanley Bayliss, 18 August, p. 970, and reply by the reviewer, 25 August, pp. 996-97; A. Wilson, *Dickensian*, 69 (1973), 48-51 (praises the "thoroughness, the complexity, and the rare intelligence" of Cardwell's "meticulous scholarship" and is pleased to have many readings restored from the manuscript, though quibbles a bit about one kind of editorial decision; still, a "splendid volume").

2435. Connor, Steven. "Notes on the Text and Illustrations" and "Appendix A: The 'Sapsea Fragment.'" In Dickens's *The Mystery of Edwin Drood*. Ed. Steven Connor. Everyman Library. London: Dent, 1996, pp. xxxvii-xxxix, 275-80.

In the first, Connor comments on variations from the manuscript in early published editions of *Drood*, with only one short paragraph on the illustrations for the novel. In the second, he describes the manuscript of the Sapsea Fragment and favors a suggestion by Charles Forsyte (**2442**) that the fragment was written prior to the start of *Edwin Drood* and reprints the fragment. Also see this title under *The Mystery of Edwin Drood* in section 1 of part 1 of the subject index and see Connor (**831**).

2436. Cox, Arthur J. "The *Drood* Remains." *Dickens Studies*, 2 (1966), 33-44.

An examination of changes in the manuscript of *The Mystery of Edwin Drood* to show problems Dickens had with writing to length. Cox also comments on the Sapsea Fragment, which he thinks Dickens wrote to fill up the first two numbers and then discarded. Also see this title under *The Mystery of Edwin Drood* in section 1 of part 1 of the subject index.

2437. Cox, Arthur J. "Introduction." "Appendix A: Dickens's Notes and Number Plans," "Appendix B: The 'Sapsea Fragment,'" and "Notes." In Dickens's *The Mystery of Edwin Drood*. Ed. Arthur J. Cox. Penguin English Library. Harmondsworth, Eng.: Penguin Books, 1974, 1985, pp. 11-30, 281-95, 296-301, 302-14, and passim.

In the introduction, Cox comments on the "inception and construction" of this novel, touching upon Dickens's use of items in his Book of Memoranda (**2530**), the cover designs, and, briefly, the excisions and corrections in the page proofs. He also includes a transcription of Dickens's notes and number plans for the novel, as well as the unused scene known as the "Sapsea Fragment" (also see this title under *The Mystery of Edwin Drood* in section 1 of part 1 of the subject index). His notes detail significant changes between manuscript, proofs, and printed text.

2438. Cox, Arthur J. "A Note on the Text," "Appendix A: Dickens's Notes and Number Plans," and "Appendix B: The 'Sapsea Fragment.'" In Dickens's *The Mystery of Edwin Drood*. Ed. Arthur J. Cox. London: Folio Society, 1982, pp. xvii-xviii, 231-45, 246-51.

In the textual note, Cox describes Dickens's initial plan for the length of *Edwin Drood* and comments briefly on the manuscript. In Appendix A, he comments generally on Dickens's practice in preparing the number plans for his novels and more specifically on those for *Drood*, which are here transcribed. In Appendix B, Cox comments on and describes the manuscript fragment, which was first printed in *Forster*, noting that John Forster himself, not Dickens, titled the fragment "How Mr. Sapsea Ceased to be a Member of the Eight Club. Told by Himself." Cox believes the fragment to be a discarded piece of manuscript in which Dickens was "merely trying out an idea," perhaps in December 1869, after being warned by his printers that the first two numbers were too short. Also see this title under *The Mystery of Edwin Drood* in section 1 of part 1 of the subject index.

2439. Cox, Don R. "The *Every Saturday* Page Proofs for *The Mystery of Edwin Drood*." *Dickensian*, 90 (1994), 95-101.

An important supplement to Margaret Cardwell's introduction in the Clarendon Edition of *the Mystery of Edwin Drood* (**2434**). Cox describes and gives the provenance of a previously unnoted if incomplete set of page proofs for *The Mystery of Edwin Drood* in the Harvard University Library. This is a set that Dickens sent to Boston as advance sheets for the serialization of the novel in *Every Saturday*. The set contains chapters 10, 11, and 12 (no. 3 of the monthly parts). Cox points out that, since the *Every Saturday* published version "matches the 1870 English published version" more closely than it does this set of proofs, Dickens must have sent "a second stage of proof" to Boston, probably no longer extant. Cox also provides a list of "variant readings found in the published *Every Saturday* version (keyed to the pagination of the Clarendon Edition), and the justification (if it exists) for these readings that may be found in the *Every Saturday* proofs." The proofs, Cox concludes, "verify some of the changes we know took place between the first version (as represented by the manuscript and the subsequent Fildes proofs in the Gimbel Collection, Yale University) and the final printed version (as represented by either *Every Saturday* or the London publication)."

2440. Ford, George H. "Dickens's Notebook and 'Edwin Drood.'" *Nineteenth-Century Fiction,* 6 (1951/52), 275-80.

Includes one excerpt from Dickens's Book of Memoranda (**2530**) not previously published. Ford indicates, largely from previously published information, that, contrary to *Forster,* Dickens *did* consult this notebook a number of occasions while working on *Edwin Drood.* He also notes that the version of the Book of Memoranda printed in *Nonesuch Letters,* III, 785-96, was compiled by publishing the excerpts from it in *Forster* in the order in which Forster quoted them, but omitting three.

2441. Forsyte, Charles [Gordon Philo]. "An Ancient Cathedral Town?" *Notes and Queries,* ns 31 (1984), 66-69.

Using a manuscript reading as evidence, argues against emendations made in the opening paragraph of *Edwin Drood* in the Clarendon Edition (**2434**).

2442. Forsyte, Charles [Gordon Philo]. "The Sapsea Fragment–Fragment of What?" *Dickensian,* 82 (1986), 12-26.

A detailed description and close examination of a manuscript in the Forster Collection, Victoria and Albert Museum, London, about Mr. Sapsea, a character in *The Mystery of Edwin Drood,* a fragment that was not included in that novel. Forsyte believes it to be "part of an autonomous piece, written before *Edwin Drood,* and in origin having no connection with it whatever." Letters to the editor follow, offering a variety of other explanations of Dickens's intentions. See Katherine M. Longley, pp. 84-85; Arthur J. Cox, pp. 178-79; and Forsyte again, 83 (1987), 48-49, 110. Both Forsyte and Longley are fascinated by the unprovable possibility that the uncharacteristic black ink–in which part of the Sapsea Fragment and a part of *Drood* were written–was the ink available in the house at Peckham, where Dickens settled Ellen Ternan, his mistress, and quote passages written in the black ink that would be ironically significant. No one here believes that it was a rejected portion of *Edwin Drood.* Also see this title under *The Mystery of Edwin Drood* in section 1 of part 1 of the subject index.

2443. J[ackson], H[enry]. "The Manuscript." In his *About Edwin Drood.* Cambridge: Cambridge University Press, 1911; reprinted Folcroft, PA: Folcroft Library Editions, 1974; New York: Haskell House, 1974; Norwood, PA: Norwood Editions, 1976; Philadelphia: R. West, 1977, pp. 73-87.

Describes the number plans and the chapter modifications and a few incidental changes in the text of the manuscript of Dickens's unfinished novel.

2444. Jacobson, Wendy S. *The Companion to **The Mystery of Edwin Drood**.* The Dickens Companions. London: Allen & Unwin, 1986, pp. 185-92 and passim.

In the notes to the novel, with which most of the volume is concerned, Jacobson includes Dickens's part by part number plans for the six numbers completed, with some references to where the printed text of the novel differs from the manuscript. The "Selected Bibliography," pp. 185-92, lists articles by others in *Household Words* and *All the Year Round* relevant to *The Mystery of Edwin Drood* and books and articles of value for the notes provided; it is not a bibliography of criticism and other studies of this novel. Illustrated. Arthur J. Cox (**1399**) notes some errors in this work. Also see Jacobson's doctoral dissertation, "A Commentary on Dickens's *The Mystery of Edwin Drood*" (University of Birmingham, 1975), listed in *Index to Theses* (**1188**), 26, ii (1978), 6.

Reviews: L. Černy, *Anglia*, 107 (1989), 241-44 (in German; generally favorable); P. Collins, *Times Literary Supplement*, 16 January 1987, p. 66 (a volume in an "invaluable" series); T. J. Cribb, *Review of English Studies*, 39 (1988), 136-38 ("useful," if "not as thorough as might be wished"); E. Lauterbach, *Modern Fiction Studies*, 33 (1987), 367-71 ("a well-researched and provocative book," with a "cogent introduction"); S. Monod, *Modern Language Review*, 83 (1988), 979-80 (generally favorable; a "first-rate" bibliography and index); P. Preston, *Notes and Queries*, 35 (1988), 389-91 (praises); A. Shelston, *Critical Quarterly*, 29, iii (Autumn 1987), 84-87 (contains "a wealth of information" that will make it "an invaluable adjunct" to the reading of the novel); and M. Slater, *Times Higher Education Supplement*, 5 December 1986, p. 18 (finds the volume useful but with omissions).

2445. Lehmann-Haupt, C. F. "Studies on Edwin Drood." *Dickensian*, 31 (1934/35), 299-305; 32 (1935/36), 29-34, 135-37, 219-20, 301-06; 33 (1936/37), 57-62.

Makes passing comments on Dickens's changes in the manuscript and proof of his last work.

2446. "Marginalia: The Minor Mystery of Edwin Drood." *Bookman's Journal*, ser. 3, 16 (1928), 393.

Briefly describes the appearance of the manuscript of *The Mystery of Edwin Drood* in the Victoria and Albert Museum—the "minor mystery" having to do with some misapprehension about what had been pasted over in it (see **2447**) or with an apparently nonexistent "rough MS. outline" of the novel.

2447. "The Mystery of Edwin Drood: Secret of the Pasted Manuscript. Museum Quest." *Daily Chronicle* (London), 13 April 1928, p. 9.

Describes an examination at the South Kensington Museum (now the Victoria and Albert Museum) of pasted-over passages in the manuscript of *Edwin Drood*. Though the brief passages discovered are quoted, they are, the author laments, only passages that Dickens had later altered, rather than a "key to the mystery" of how Dickens meant to continue and end his unfinished novel. Also see **2446**.

2448. Nicoll, W[illiam] Robertson. "The Text of 'Edwin Drood,'" "Notes for the Novel," and "The Illustrations on the Wrapper." In his *The Problem of "Edwin Drood": A Study in the Methods of Dickens*. London, New York, and Toronto: Hodder and Stoughton, 1912; reprinted New York: Haskell House, 1972, pp. 3-19, 56-68, 69-81.

Comments on the revisions in the manuscript and page proofs, prints "now for the first time" the complete number plans for parts 1-6 and a general page of notes in Dickens's hand containing various characters' names and several proposed titles for the novel. Nicoll examines the wrapper illustrations for the monthly parts. He indicates that, after Dickens's death, John Forster "had in every case ignored Dickens's erasures and had replaced all the omitted passages in the text," passages that Nicoll identifies by printing them here. Nicoll also includes a "Bibliography," pp. 203-09, compiled by B. W. Matz, which updates his earlier bibliography of continuations and studies of *Edwin Drood* (**841**). One illustration (a reproduction of the wrapper for No. 1 of the monthly parts).

2449. Paroissien, David. "Introduction," "A Note on the Text," "Appendix 1: The 'Sapsea Fragment,'" "Appendix 2: The Number Plans," and "Notes." In Dickens's *The Mystery of Edwin Drood*. Ed. David Paroissien. Penguin Classics. London, New York, etc.: Penguin Books, 2002, pp. xiii-xxxvi, xlii-xliii, 273-78, 279-93, 321-81.

A number of sections of Paroissien's edition of this novel are concerned with textual matters. In the introduction, he comments on Dickens's use of his Book of Memoranda (**2530**) and his number plans in planning and writing this novel. He also explores the influence of Wilkie Collins on Dickens. In "A Note on the Text," he provides details about the original publication of the novel and his own edition. His section of "Notes" contains numerous references to the manuscript, the number plans, and the Book of Memoranda. In the first two appendices, Paroissien reprints the number plans for the novel and the "Sapsea Fragment." For the latter, see Cox (**2438**) and see this title under *The Mystery of Edwin Drood* in section 1 of part 1 of the subject index. Paroissien also includes "Appendix 3: The Illustrations," pp. 294-99, a brief history of the illustrating of the novel, and prints reproductions of the original title page and the drawing that Charles Collins originally did for the monthly wrapper cover before illness prevented him from continuing work on the novel and he was replaced by Luke Fildes. In "Further Reading," pp. xxxvii-xli, Paroissien lists and lightly annotates twenty-six studies of this novel and twelve reference works of importance to it.

2450. Reece, Benny R. "The Notes" and "Appendix D: The Notes." In his *The Mystery of Edwin Drood Solved.* New York, Los Angeles, and Chicago: Vantage Press, 1989, pp. 43-45, 61-69.

Prints Dickens's number plans and notes for *The Mystery of Edwin Drood* in Appendix D and describes and comments on them in "The Notes."

2451. Rosenberg, Edgar. "Dating *Edwin Drood.*" *Dickensian*, 76 (1980), 42-43.

Argues that an entry in Dickens's Book of Memoranda (**2530**), Dickens's first reference to an idea that developed into *Edwin Drood*, was recorded "as early as autumn or winter 1860."

2452. Saunders, Montagu. *The Mystery in the Drood Family.* Cambridge: Cambridge University Press, 1914; reprinted Folcroft, PA: Folcroft Library Editions, 1974; New York: Haskell House, 1974; Norwood, PA: Norwood Editions, 1978, pp. 5-17 and passim.

Comments in passing on some of Dickens's notes for *Edwin Drood.*

Nicholas Nickleby

Note: Also see "How Dickens Corrected his Proofs" (**2367**).

2453. Ford, Mark. "A Note on the Text," "Appendix 2: Running Titles Added in 1867," and "Appendix 3: Significant Revisions Made in the 1848 and 1867 Editions." In Dickens's *Nicholas Nickleby.* Ed. Mark Ford. Penguin Classics. London, New York, etc.: Penguin Books, 1999, pp. xxxii-xxxiii, 783-88, 789-96.

In the textual note Ford comments briefly on changes that Dickens made in the text, mainly in the 1848 Cheap Edition, including cuts of "some of the original's more melodramatic flourishes," and prints a number of these in Appendix 3. Appendix 2 lists the running heads that Dickens added in the 1867 Charles Dickens Edition.

2454. Gawthorp, Walter E. "'Nicholas Nickleby': A Strange Misprint." *Notes and Queries*, 155 (1928), 365.

Corrects a misprint in some editions of *Nicholas Nickleby* in the first paragraph of chapter 10.

2455. Schlicke, Paul. "Appendix A: The *Nickleby* Proclamation," "Appendix B: Running Heads for the 1867 Edition," and "Textual Notes." In Dickens's *Nicholas Nickleby.* Ed. Paul Schlicke. World's Classics. Oxford and New York: Oxford University Press, 1990, pp. 832-34, 835-43, 865-70.

Appendix A is a warning Dickens issued to potential pirate printers, Appendix B contains the heads that Dickens wrote for the 1867 edition, and the textual notes indicate changes in text between the 1838-39 parts edition, the 1848 Cheap Edition, and the 1867 Charles Dickens Edition.

Review: S. Monod, *Etudes anglaises*, 44 (1991), 349 (in French; favorable).

2456. Slater, Michael. *The Composition and Monthly Publication of* **Nicholas Nickleby**. Menston, Eng.: Scolar Press, 1973; also published as the final installment of *The Life and Adventures of Nicholas Nickleby. Reproduced in Facsimile from the Original Monthly Parts of 1838-9*. Menston, Eng.: Scolar Press, 1972-73. iv + 43 pp.; also published as part of a boxed set; reprinted as "The Composition and Monthly Publication of *Nicholas Nickleby*." In Dickens's *The Life and Adventures of Nicholas Nickleby*. 2 vols. London: Scolar Press; Philadelphia: University of Pennsylvania Press, 1982, I, vii-lxxxvi.

Contains occasional commentary about textual modifications by Dickens during the writing of this novel and provides photographic reproductions of three pages of the manuscript and two drawings by Hablot K. Browne, who illustrated the novel. Slater also comments briefly on textual alterations in Dickens's reading version of a portion of the novel, *Nicholas Nickleby at the Yorkshire School*, a page of which is reproduced. In "A Bibliographical Note," pp. i-iv (pp. lxxxv-lxxxvi in the 1982 reprint), Slater comments on textual variants in the text and in the advertising supplements to the monthly parts of *Nicholas Nickleby*. For "Appendix: The Extra Illustrations to *Nicholas Nickleby*," p. 43 (I, xxxv, in the 1982 reprint), see Slater (**926**).

Reviews: *American Book Collector*, ns 4, iii (May/June 1983), 50 ("a lively, , exhaustive, and well-illustrated introduction"); E. M. Brennan, *Dickensian*, 69 (1973), 187-89 (an "excellent facsimile set and scholarly introduction to it," the latter being "a rich and valuable distillation of scholarly knowledge about the novel's genesis and progress"); *British Book News*, September 1973, p. 616 (a "superb facsimile reprint"; Slater's introduction is "a well-documented and fascinating account of the background of the novel"); *Choice*, 20 (1982/83), 1288 ("authoritative" introduction); T. C. Holyoke, *Antioch Review*, 41 (1983), 247-48 (Slater's introduction is "a valuable addition" to the facsimile edition); J. Meckier, *Dickens Studies Newsletter*, 6 (1975), 96-98 (Slater's introduction is "a thorough exploration of how the novel came to be written," though it does not cover all aspects of the subject, particularly not "serialization as a structural technique"); *Times Literary Supplement*, 22 June 1973, p. 723 ("an extremely valuable introduction," "comprehensive, sound and cogent," "valuable and authoritative in much the same way as John Butt's and Kathleen Tillotson's *Dickens at Work*").

2457. Slater, Michael. "A Note on the Text," "Appendix A: The Manuscript of *Nicholas Nickleby*," and "Appendix C: Descriptive Headlines Added in 1867." In Dickens's *Nicholas Nickleby*. Ed. Michael Slater. Penguin English Library. Harmondsworth, Eng., New York, etc.: Penguin Books, 1978, pp. 35-37, 935-39, 943-51.

In his note on the text Slater comments briefly, with some examples, on the "450 substantial alterations" that Dickens made to the 1839 text in subsequent editions published in his lifetime–but he notes that he has followed the 1839 text "exactly as printed" with a few noted exceptions. In Appendix A, Slater gives the location of the six extant chapters of the novel and identifies and quotes some of the revisions Dickens made in them. Appendix C lists the descriptive headlines that Dickens added in the Charles Dickens Edition of the novel.

Review: P. Collins, *Times Literary Supplement*, 21 April 1978, p. 446 (finds the introduction "a model of how such tasks should be accomplished"); S. Monod, *Etudes anglaises*, 32 (1979), 485-86 (high praise for the edition and its introduction); A. Wilson, *Dickensian*, 74 (1978), 110-11 (an "excellent, perspicacious introduction").

2458. Suzannet, Alain de. "The Original Manuscript of *Nicholas Nickleby*." *Dickensian*, 43 (1946/47), 189-92.

Describes the extant portions of the manuscript and includes facsimiles of three manuscript pages.

The Old Curiosity Shop

Note: Also see Andrews (**2335**).

2459. Brattin, Joel J. "Some Old Curiosities from *The Old Curiosity Shop* Manuscript." *Dickens Quarterly*, 7 (1990), 218-34.

A huge compilation of passages cancelled or revised in manuscript and page proofs of the novel, with Brattin's hypotheses as to why Dickens made these changes. These are new examples–to be added to those in Staples (**2313**), Easson (**2462-64**), and Tick (**2468**). Also see Brennan (**2460**).

2460. Brennan, Elizabeth M. "Introduction." In Dickens's *The Old Curiosity Shop*. Ed. Elizabeth M. Brennan. Clarendon Edition. Oxford: Clarendon Press; Oxford, New York, etc.: Oxford University Press, 1997, pp. xiii-xcv.

Discusses the conception and writing of the early numbers of *Master Humphrey's Clock* in considerable and fascinating detail, number by number, and, in particular, the development of *The Old Curiosity Shop* "from a short tale . . . to an independent novel," which became, with issue no. 12, the sole publication in the magazine. In doing so, Brennan makes frequent reference to the manuscript and proofs and to Dickens's letters commenting on the writing of the novel. Brennan also discusses the variations in binding of the first volume edition of *The Old Curiosity Shop*, studies the textual differences between the first and later editions, and comments on the manuscript and proofs as well. She uses the first (1841) edition as her copy-text for the Clarendon Edition and notes in detail any departures from that (there are corrected galley proofs for "all or part of 32 chapters of the 73" in the novel). She appends a "Descriptive List of Editions" (**116**) to the introduction and, in Appendix A, "Additional Apparatus (pp. 577-90), includes additional, longer textual variations, apart from the numerous and shorter ones footnoted in the text itself. She also appends Dickens's number plans and memoranda for chapters 41-44 (pp. 591-95); a detailed listing of information about the weekly and monthly parts of the first eighty-eight numbers of *Master Humphrey's Clock* (pp. 596-98); a list of compositors (pp. 599-605); the various prefaces Dickens wrote (pp. 606-10); "Master Humphrey from His Clock Side in the Chimney-Corner," the transitional chapter Dickens wrote in passing from *The Old Curiosity Shop* to *Barnaby Rudge,* the novel that succeeded the former in *Master Humphrey's Clock* (pp. 611-16); a list of variant issues of the first edition of *The Old Curiosity Shop* (pp. 617-18); the descriptive headlines added to the Charles Dickens Edition, 1867 (pp. 619-23); a "Finding List of Illustrations" (pp. 624-29); a section on "Little Nell on Stage, 1840-1841" (**677**), pp. 630-34; and a listing of the contents of the first eighty-eight numbers of *Master Humphrey's Clock* (pp. 635-38). Illustrated. Also see Butt and Tillotson, "Preface by the General Editors" (**176**).

Reviews: M. Y. A[ndrews], *Dickensian,* 94 (1998), 133-35 (an "admirable edition"; Andrews offers additional evidence for when Dickens decided Little Nell should die); J. A. Davies, *Notes and Queries,* 46 (1999), 144-45 ("exemplary textual scholarship" and superb reproduction of the illustrative elements of the original publication as part of *Master Humphrey's Clock*); M. DeMoor, *English Studies* (Amsterdam), 80 (1999), 572-73 (Brennan's "extensive introduction does not only hold the key to the different manuscripts used, it presents a fascinating account of the genesis of the novel"); P. Schlicke, *Dickens Quarterly,* 16 (1999), 203-09 (with the introduction, useful appendices, and authoritative text, "provides scholars with substantially more detailed information about *The Old Curiosity Shop* than has ever been available up to now"); M. Slater, *Review of English Studies,* ns 50 (1999), 254-56 ("deftly written introduction"; generally favorable comments on the extensive textual apparatus).

2461. Brennan, Elizabeth M. "Note on the Text," "Appendix A: Passages Deleted from MS and Proofs," and "Appendix B: Dickens's Number Plans and Memoranda." In Dickens's *The Old Curiosity Shop.* World's Classics. Ed. Elizabeth M. Brennan. Oxford and New York: Oxford University Press, 1998, pp. xxxiii-xxxvii, 555-68, 569-73.

In "Notes on the Text," Brennan comments on the novel's publication as part of *Master Humphrey's Clock,* the manuscript and proofs, and selected restorations made in this and the Clarendon Edition (**2460**), on which the text of this edition is based. In Appendix A, Brennan prints thirty-eight passages deleted from the manuscript and page proofs, a selection of the more substantial passages from Brennan's "Additional Apparatus," pp. 577-90, in the Clarendon Edition. In Appendix B, she prints the extant number plans, for chapters 41-44 only, and two memoranda Dickens wrote concerning the novel. Also see "Appendix E: Little Nell on Stage, 1840-41 (**677**), pp. 580-84.

Reviews: M. Y. A[ndrews], *Dickensian,* 94 (1998), 133-35 (an "exceptionally good value," taking "full advantage" of Brennan's work on the Clarendon Edition, but also "providing generous explanatory notes"); A. Sadrin, *Etudes anglaises,* 52 (1999), 120 (in French; favorable); P. Schlicke, *Dickens Quarterly,* 16 (1999), 203-09 (praises the "thoroughness and accuracy" of the explanatory notes and the "judiciousness" of the introduction).

2462. Easson, Angus. "Dickens's Marchioness Again." *Modern Language Review,* 65 (1970), 517-18.

Prints two passages, from chapters 51 and 66, that Dickens's added in the page proofs for *The Old Curiosity Shop.* Along with the cancellation noted in Grubb (**2465**), they show, Easson indicates, that Dickens was strongly hinting that Quilp was the Marchioness's father and Sally Brass her mother.

2463. Easson, Angus. "Notes." In Dickens's *The Old Curiosity Shop.* Ed. Angus Easson. With an Introduction by Malcolm Andrews. Penguin English Library. Harmondsworth, Eng.: Penguin Books, 1972; reprinted 1983, pp. 681-720.

Includes passages Dickens cancelled in manuscript and proofs.
Reviews: *Times Literary Supplement,.* 11 August 1972, p. 946 (more descriptive than evaluative); R. L. Patten, *Dickensian,* 69 (1973), 54-56 (finds Andrews's introduction "tactful and balanced" but Easson's discussion of the text "a little over-casual and simplistic, even for the general reader" and believes he might have devoted more space to "the complex evolution of the novel's periodical structure").

2464. Easson, Angus. "*The Old Curiosity Shop*: From Manuscript to Print." *Dickens Studies Annual,* 1 (1970), 93-128, 286-87.

A detailed if necessarily selective examination of the four extant number plans and other notes, as well as of revisions in the complete manuscript and in the proofs for twenty-three complete chapters and parts of eight others in the Forster Collection, Victoria and Albert Museum, London. Easson deals not only with changes in grammar, punctuation, and style but also changes in the manuscript as Dickens was writing it that show "the way his imagination was fired," his active creativity, and the developing comedic element in the work. Easson also identifies several additions in manuscript and proofs to fill space; quotes numerous substantial passages, particularly comic ones, cancelled in proof for lack of space; and notes a few instances in which portions of such cancelled passages were incorporated into later numbers of the novel. The revisions show, Easson concludes, the limitations on Dickens imposed by serial publication and Dickens's wrestling "with the Protean shape of his material." Also see Staples (**2313**).

2465. Grubb, Gerald G. "Dickens's Marchioness Identified." *Modern Language Notes,* 68 (1953), 162-65.

Responds to an article by William C. Bennett, "The Mystery of the Marchioness," in *Dickensian,* 36 (1939/40), 205-08, in which Bennett summons convincing hints from *The Old Curiosity Shop* to prove that the Marchioness was the child of Sally Brass and Daniel Quilp. Grubb prints a cancelled passage from the corrected page proofs in the Victoria and Albert Museum, London, to show that Dickens originally had Sally Brass actually confess that she was the Marchioness's mother. See the response by Angus Easson (**2462**).

2466. Hargreaves, G. D. "British Printers on Galley Proofs." *Library*, ser. 6, 1 (1979), 380-83.

In a letter to the editor, Hargreaves notes in response to John B. Jones's "British Printers on Galley Proofs: A Chronological Reconsideration," *Library*, ser. 5, 31 (1976), 105-17 (which makes no reference to Dickens), that there are a number of surviving galley proofs of novels, among which Hargreaves lists proofs for "as many as 32 chapters" of Dickens's *Master Humphrey's Clock*, containing *The Old Curiosity Shop* and *Barnaby Rudge*.

2467. Patten, Robert. "'The Story-Weaver at His Loom': Dickens and the Beginning of *The Old Curiosity Shop*." In *Dickens the Craftsman: Strategies of Presentation*. Ed. Robert B. Partlow, Jr. Carbondale and Edwardsville: Southern Illinois University Press; London and Amsterdam: Feffer & Simons, 1970, pp. 44-64, 191-93.

Studies what Dickens's letters and the manuscript and published text of *The Old Curiosity Shop* reveal of Dickens's modification of his original plans for *Master Humphrey's Clock* in his expansion of *The Old Curiosity Shop* from a short tale into a long serial.

2468. Tick, Stanley. "The Decline and Fall of Little Nell: Some Evidence from the Manuscripts." *Pacific Coast Philology*, 9 (April 1974), 62-72.

Finds evidence in the revisions in the manuscript and proofs of *The Old Curiosity Shop* that, long before John Forster suggested to Dickens that Little Nell might die, Dickens was already considering her death as a possible conclusion to the novel and that, once he had decided on her death, he kept that concealed as much as possible from his readers until the last moment.

Oliver Twist

2469. Horne, Philip. "A Note on the Text" and "Selected Textual Variants." In Dickens's *Oliver Twist, or, The Parish Boy's Progress*. Ed. Philip Horne. Penguin Classics. London, New York, etc.: Penguin Books, 2002, pp. l-liii, 530-54.

In "A Note on the Text," Horne argues convincingly for his choice of copy-text, the serial publication of the novel in *Bentley's Miscellany*, February 1837 to April 1839. It is a longer version than later editions, he points out, and thus, in his Penguin edition, "some long passages" that Dickens excised in the three-volume 1838 edition "now appear in the novel for the first time in a critical edition." In "Selected Textual Variants," Horne first describes and speculates about the reasons for cuts Dickens made between the manuscript and the serialized version, between the latter and the 1838 edition, and between the 1838 and 1846 editions. Then he lists the variants between all of these in a chapter by chapter compilation; a number of them are quite substantial. Horne also includes, in "Further Reading," pp. xlv-xlix, a list of commentaries by a number of Dickens's contemporaries and a list of forty-one books and articles on *Oliver Twist* by "later scholars and critics."

2470. Lane, Lauriat, Jr. "'Oliver Twist': A Revision." *Times Literary Supplement*, 20 July 1951, p. 460.

Looking principally at chapter 52 of *Oliver Twist*, notes Dickens's substitution of "Fagin" for "the Jew" in the Charles Dickens Edition, 1867, at the instigation of Mrs. Eliza Davis, to whose husband he had sold his home, Tavistock House, in 1860 and who had written to him on 10 July 1863 to protest his treatment of Jews in *Oliver Twist*. See replies by Hugh Harris, 27 July, p. 469, and Cecil Roth, 3 August, p. 485, who notes that the "full story of Dickens's revision of *Oliver Twist* is rather more complicated" than Lane indicates. Roth also points out that, in the manuscript of a page of chapter 10, Dickens scratched out a reference to Fagin as the "old gentleman" and substituted the word "Jew."

2471. Miller, William. "Charles Dickens and C. Edwards Lester." *Dickensian*, 8 (1912), 295-96.

Points out that a letter from Dickens to Lester, 19 July 1840, was accompanied by a page of the manuscript of *Oliver Twist*, sent, as Dickens writes in the letter, "in compliance with your request" and with "much pleasure in doing so." Page 40 (part of chapter 15) of the manuscript, the page sent to Lester, is reproduced in facsimile. Also see Miller (**2472**).

2472. Miller, W[illiam]. "The Manuscript of *Oliver Twist*." *Dickensian*, 11 (1915), 222-23.

A letter to the editor querying the number of pages extant of the manuscript of *Oliver Twist*. Miller points out that a portion (chapter 12 of Book 1 to chapter 6 of Book 3) is in the Forster collection, Victoria and Albert Museum Library, London, and that page forty of the manuscript (part of chapter 15) was given by Dickens to C. Edwards Lester in 1840, reproduced in facsimile earlier by Miller (**2471**). These and two other small fragments of manuscript are described by Paroissien (**118**), p. 6, Shipman (**1732**), and more fully by Tillotson (**2474**), pp. xlv-xlvii.

2473. Paroissien, David. *The Companion to **Oliver Twist***. The Dickens Companions. Edinburgh: Edinburgh University Press, 1992, passim.

In the notes proper, with which most of the volume is concerned, Paroissien comments from time to time, as he points out in a brief note on the text, p. 9, on variant readings collated in Tillotson's Clarendon Edition of the novel (**2474**) that he considers significant. Illustrated. Paroissien also includes a "Select Bibliography" (**1110**), pp. 312-23.

Reviews: P. Faulkner, *Review of English Studies*, 46 (1995), 111-12 (annotations are "thorough and often illuminating"); F. Kaplan, *Dickensian*, 89 (1993), 54-56 (praises the annotations, illustrations, bibliography, and appendices; this volume "exemplifies the high quality and practical usefulness of the series as a whole," and Paroissien "has done his job . . . with exemplary assiduousness"); A. Sadrin, *Etudes anglaises*, 47 (1994), 91 (in French; an "indispensable" volume); G. Smith, *Notes and Queries*, ns 40 (1993), 111-13 (criticizes the Dickens Companions series in general as "dominated by history to the exclusion of literary criticism"); G. J. Worth, *Dickens Quarterly*, 10 (1993), 171-73 (provides "invaluable assistance" for the student, with a "useful introduction").

2474. Tillotson, Kathleen. "Introduction." In Dickens's *Oliver Twist*. Ed. Kathleen Tillotson. Clarendon Edition. Oxford: Clarendon Press; Oxford, London, Glasgow, New York, etc.: Oxford University Press, 1966, pp. xv-xlvii.

Discusses the composition, publication, and reception of *Oliver Twist* and examines textual differences in the various editions of the novel published in Dickens's lifetime (more fully itemized in footnotes in the text of the novel). Tillotson also describes the incomplete manuscript of the novel. Elsewhere in the volume, she includes a "Descriptive List of Editions 1838-1867" (**119**), Dickens's prefaces to the 1841 (third) and the 1850 ("Cheap") editions of the novel (pp. lxi-lxv, 382-84). She also adds appendices containing details about the Philadelphia editions of 1838-39, the descriptive headlines added in the 1867 edition, information about "Sikes and Nancy" (Dickens's reading version of a part of the novel), commentary on the illustrations, and a discussion of the reception of the novel, 1837-46. Tillotson also includes a glossary of thieves' cant and slang and an 1837 map of London. Much controversy was generated by her choice of the 1846 edition of the novel, published in ten parts from January to October 1846 and then in one volume (essentially the fourth edition), as her copy-text, as some of the reviews below indicate. Fredson Bowers's lengthy review in *Nineteenth-Century Fiction* is particularly important. Illustrated. Also see Butt and Tillotson, "Preface by the General Editors" (**176**).

Reviews: R. D. Altick, *Victorian Studies*, 11 (1967/68), 415-16 (praises the quality of the volume, though would have preferred an earlier copy-text and finds the care lavished on textual changes not productive of substantial new information); C. A. Bodelson, *English Studies*, 48 (1967), 466-67 ("an impressive piece of scholarship," though something "has gone wrong" in the printing of Cruikshank's illustrations; the introduction is "a very full account of the writing and publication" of the novel); F. Bowers, *Nineteenth-Century Fiction*, 23 (1968/69), 226-39 (a carefully reasoned argument against Tillotson's choice of copy-text—see Paroissien (**118**), pp. 27-34, for further commentary; A. Burgess, *Spectator*, 217 (1966), 817 (does not comment on the edition; rather, finds the novel, with its "fantastic style" and its Cruikshank illustrations, a "composite entertainment"); [P. Collins], *Times Literary Supplement*, 6 April 1967, p. 285 (offers high praise for Tillotson's editing and the variety of valuable appendices, finds the introduction "an excellent account of the circumstances of the novel's composition," but regrets the lack of explanatory annotation); T. Cribb, *Review of English*

Studies, ns 19 (1968), 87-91 (finds the introduction and textual apparatus most valuable though disputes some of the decisions about variants); *Economist*, 221 (1966), 1037 (Tillotson's work is "massive, authoritative and excellent"); K. J. Fielding, *Dickensian*, 63 (1967), 14-16 (calls it a "splendid new edition," *Oliver Twist* "as Dickens meant us to read it," with the introduction and appendices providing "valuable insights into Dickens as a novelist," but makes no comment on choice of copytext); P. N. Furbank, *Listener*, 76 (1966), 935 ("a splendid achievement"; Tillotson's choice of the 1846 edition as her copy-text "makes perfect sense"); B. G. Hornback, *Michigan Quarterly Review*, 7 (1968), 65-67 (disagrees at length with Tillotson's choice of copy-text, but praises the introduction for being "long and informed"); R. D. McMaster, *Dalhousie Review*, 47 (1967/68), 100-01 ("done with that thoroughness and skill one has come to expect from Mrs. Tillotson"); S. Monod, *Etudes anglaises*, 20 (1967), 195-97 (in French; praises the introduction, textual apparatus, and appendices); K. Muir, *Modern Language Review*, 63 (1968), 687-88 (finds this an "austere edition," but "within the limits she has set herself [Tillotson] has succeeded brilliantly"); S. Nowell-Smith, *Library*, 5th ser., 23 (1968), 83-85 (in regard to "research, precision, and lucidity," Tillotson has "set a dauntingly high standard for editors of the other novels" in the series); R. L. Patten, *Dickens Studies*, 3 (1967), 160-68 (a long, informative review; after surveying editions of the novel, Patten concludes that Tillotson's choice of copy-text "seems irrefutable"; he praises her inclusion of the Cruikshank illustrations, wishes her introduction were longer and fuller, but sees the volume as a "distinguished achievement"); G. Tillotson, *Sewanee Review*, 75 (1967), 325-37 (a personal account by the editor's husband); W. Waring, *Library Journal*, 92 (1967), 1492 (a volume "of unusually high quality," with a "clear" introduction and thorough documentation).

2475. Wheeler, Burton M. "The Text and Plan of *Oliver Twist*." *Dickens Studies Annual*, 12 (1983), 41-61.

Commenting on the development, writing, and revision of *Oliver Twist*, Wheeler indicates that, in revising the work in 1838, Dickens "deleted or emended more than 260 passages that had appeared in *[Bentley's] Miscellany* in the first eighteen installments" of the novel. Most of these changes were "minor" linguistic adjustments, Wheeler points out, and some were "mere curiosities" (such as the height of the Artful Dodger), but a number "are related to Dickens' never resolved difficulties in controlling the time frame of the novel," and others are concerned with the divisions of the novel. But Wheeler believes that the deletions were the most important changes—fourteen of which he finds "significant." Five were made to rid the text of passages that indicated it was not intended to be a novel. Others were made to avoid strikingly similar phrasing in two passages, to "tone down dialogue or descriptive passages," and to get rid of "multiple-option" passages that originally left Dickens room to explore different plot directions. Generally speaking, Wheeler concludes, *Oliver Twist* "is the product of a radical change of plans," not unexpected from a "novice, a uniquely talented and ambitious young writer determined to overcome his own 'adverse circumstances.'"

Our Mutual Friend

2476. Boll, Ernest. "The Plotting of *Our Mutual Friend*." *Modern Philology*, 42 (1944/45), 96-122.

Describes and prints a transcription of the number plans for *Our Mutual Friend* and comments on what they reveal about Dickens's working methods, craftsmanship, and artistry in "the weaving of the story." See Winslow (**2491**) for corrections.

2477. Brattin, Joel J. "Dickens' Creation of Bradley Headstone." *Dickens Studies Annual*, 14 (1985), 147-65.

Examines Dickens's creation of a character in *Our Mutual Friend* in the number plans and the manuscript revisions. When read together, Brattin observes, the plans and the revisions "reveal Dickens's imagination in the process of creating a complex, hauntingly memorable character"—more specifically, they show changes in the character's name; changes in the presentation of his behavior, manners, and emotions (the last particularly through gestures); and changes in his speech and actions. Illustrated with numerous photographic facsimiles of passages in the manuscript.

2478. Brattin, Joel J. "'I Will Not Have My Words Misconstrued': The Text of *Our Mutual Friend*." *Dickens Quarterly*, 15 (1998), 167-76.

Brattin notes that, in preparing *Our Mutual Friend* for the Everyman Paperback Classics Edition, he found 2,203 textual variants between the first edition in parts (1864-65) and the Charles Dickens Edition (1868) of the novel. He analyzes the different kinds of variants (in punctuation, spelling, capitalization, formatting, and, of greater importance, wording). While Brattin finds many of the changes to be improvements, he concludes that, apart from the running heads that Dickens added in the later edition, "every single one of the 2,203 textual corrections, alterations, and mistakes in the Charles Dickens Edition might have been made by someone other than Dickens himself." Brattin suspects that, therefore, Dickens probably did not make the changes himself. He concludes that, unfortunately, "the light" the 1868 text "sheds on Dickens's creative process is at best a diffuse and weak one." He includes a table of "Categories of Variants" between the two editions.

2479. Brattin, Joel J. "Introduction," "Notes on the Text and Illustrations," "Notes," "Appendix A: *Our Mutual Friend* and Dickens's Book of Memoranda," and "Appendix B: Running Titles in the Charles Dickens Edition." In Dickens's *Our Mutual Friend*. Ed. Joel J. Brattin. Everyman Dickens. London: J. M. Dent; Rutland, VT: Charles E. Tuttle, 2000, pp. xxiii-xxxi, xxxii-xxxviii, 875-904, 905-07, 908-13.

In the introduction, Brattin comments briefly on Dickens's Book of Memoranda (**2530**) and on his number plans for the novel, and, in Appendix A, he prints passages from this notebook that are relevant to *Our Mutual Friend*. His section of "Notes" contains a number of references to variants in words and short passages in the text. In "Notes on the Text and the Illustrations," he gives the publication history of the novel in Dickens's lifetime, describes his own preparation of the text for the Everyman Dickens, notes that there were 2,200 variants in the text of the Charles Dickens Edition (1868), provides a list of "Emendations to the Text of 1868, from the First Edition of 1864-5" and a few other emendations, and comments on Marcus Stone's illustrations for the novel. Appendix B is self-explanatory. Brattin also includes "Dickens and His Critics," pp. 914-20, a brief survey of critical opinion of the novel from its earliest reviewers to studies published as late as 1998, and "Suggestions for Further Reading," pp. 921-22, in which he lists twenty-one additional studies, all published since 1982, and a few general works on Dickens.

Review: P. J. McCarthy, *Dickensian*, 97 (2001), 66-69 (for Brattin, "establishing the text" was "a primary obligation," though thinks he may respect his copy-text *too* much; still, a "meticulously done and carefully thought through" edition "rich in scholarship").

2480. Childs, George W. "Recollections of George W. Childs. III." *Lippincott's Monthly Magazine*, 44 (1889), 216-20; reprinted in his *Recollections*. Philadelphia: J. B. Lippincott, 1890, etc., pp. 33-36.

Among other reminiscences of Dickens, Childs, a Philadelphia publisher and collector, records that Dickens told him that "before beginning any one of his works he thought out the plot fully, and then made a skeleton from which he elaborated it." Childs mentions owning the manuscript and number plans (presumably the "skeleton" referred to) of *Our Mutual Friend*, describes the manuscript, and provides a transcription of the number plan for the first number of the novel. The manuscript and number plans of *Our Mutual Friend* are now in the Pierpont Morgan Library, New York City (**1478**). Also see Robinson (**1513**).

2481. Cotsell, Michael. "A Commentary on Dickens's *Our Mutual Friend.*" *Index to Theses* (**1188**), 27, i (1979), 9 (Birmingham University, 1976-77).

No abstract included, but Brattin and Hornback (**120**), pp. 160-61, indicate that, in providing "a full and comprehensive commentary on *Our Mutual Friend*," Cotsell uses information from "Dickens's letters, work plans, and manuscript to reveal the processes of composition." They add that the dissertation, "much revised and shortened to about 86,000 words," would comprise Cotsell's then forthcoming volume on the novel in the Dickens Companion series (**2482**).

2482. Cotsell, Michael. *The Companion to* **Our Mutual Friend**. The Dickens Companions. London: Allen and Unwin, 1986, pp. 1-7 and passim.

In the introduction, pp. 1-7, Cotsell touches upon some of the changes that Dickens made in the manuscript and proof of *Our Mutual Friend*, particularly cuts necessitated by his having written too much copy for most of the early numbers of the novel. In the notes to the novel, with which most of the volume is concerned, Cotsell includes Dickens's part by part number plans, passages excised in the proofs and other revisions, and references to relevant entries in Dickens's Book of Memoranda (**2530**). Cotsell includes a "Select Bibliography" (**1111**), pp. 289-94, Illustrated. Also see his doctoral dissertation, "A Commentary on Dickens's *Our Mutual Friend*" (**2481**).

Reviews: J. J. Brattin, *Dickens Quarterly*, 5 (1988), 31-33 (generally favorably review, with a few useful criticisms); L. Černy, *Anglia*, 107 (1989), 241-44 (in German; generally favorable); L. J. Clipper, *Choice*, 24 (1986/87), 622-23 ("an impressive collection of information"); P. Collins, *Times Literary Supplement*, 16 January 1987, p. 66 (provides "extensive and fascinating information" on a variety of matters); T. J. Cribb, *Review of English Studies*, ns 39 (1988), 136-37 ("useful," if "not as thorough as might be wished"); S. Monod, *Modern Language Review*, 83 (1988), 979-80 (generally favorable; "first-rate" bibliography and index); P. Preston, *Notes and Queries*, 35 (1988), 389-91 (praises); A. Sadrin, *Etudes anglaises*, 40 (1987), 475-76 (in French; indispensable); A. Shelston, *Critical Quarterly*, 29, iii (Autumn 1987), 84-87 (contains "a wealth of information" that will make it "an invaluable adjunct" to the reading of the novel); M. Slater, *Times Higher Education Supplement*, 5 December 1986, p. 18 (finds the volume useful but with omissions).

2483. [Field, Kate]. "'Our Mutual Friend' in Manuscript." *Scribner's Monthly*, 8 (1874), 472-75.

Provides an informal description of the appearance of the manuscript of *Our Mutual Friend*, then in the possession of George W. Childs of Philadelphia, including information about the ink, the revisions, and the soiled portion that was with Dickens in the Staplehurst railway accident. Field also describes and prints transcriptions of portions of the number plans and reproduces facsimiles of two fragments of the number plans.

2484. Hawthorne, Julian. "The Recollection of a Famous Editor." *Pall Mall Gazette*, 52 (18 May 1891), 6.

An interview with George W. Childs of Philadelphia, containing a brief description of the manuscript of *Our Mutual Friend*, then in Childs's possession. The manuscript is "loaded," it is noted, "with erasures and interlineations." "It was in this way," Child is quoted as remarking, "that that astonishing imagination first began to indicate its misgivings of its own power." Childs adds that Dickens told him that *David Copperfield* was his favorite novel.

2485. "The Ms. of 'Our Mutual Friend,' by Charles Dickens." *Notes and Queries*, 5th ser., 2 (1874), 139.

Notes that the manuscript that Dickens gave to E. S. Dallas for his favorable review of *Our Mutual Friend* in the London *Times* was quickly sold by Dallas to George W. Childs of Philadelphia. Excerpts from Kate Field's *Scribner's Monthly* article (**2483**) are given that describe the manuscript. See Fynmore (**2112**) for further details of the sale of the manuscript, which is now in the Pierpont Morgan Library, New York (**1478**).

2486. Poole, Adrian. "Appendix 1: The Illustrations" and "Appendix 2: The Number Plans." In Dickens's *Our Mutual Friend*. Ed. Adrian Poole. Penguin Classics. London, New York, etc.: Penguin Books, 1997, pp. 841-43, 845-84.

Briefly comments on Marcus Stone's illustrations and his relationship with Dickens and prints the number plans for the novel.

2487. S., J. B. "The Skeleton of 'Our Mutual Friend.'" *Notes and Queries*, 7th ser., 11 (1891), 65.

Gives Dickens's number plans for chapters 1 and 2 of *Our Mutual Friend* and quotes George W. Childs (**2480**) on how Dickens wrote his novels, particularly *Our Mutual Friend*, the manuscript of which Childs then owned.

2488. Shea, F[rancis] X. "Mr. Venus Observed: The Plot Change in *Our Mutual Friend*." *Papers on Language & Literature*, 4 (1968), 170-81.

Uses evidence from the manuscript and number plans of *Our Mutual Friend* to argue that Dickens made a major change in the projected plot of the novel early on in his writing of it that weakened the social criticism in the work.

2489. Shea, F[rancis] X. "No Change of Intention in *Our Mutual Friend*." *Dickensian*, 63 (1967), 37-40.

Examines the working notes and corrections in the manuscript of the novel to show that, Chesterton's comments to the contrary in his *Charles Dickens: A Critical Study* (London: Methuen, 1906, etc.), Dickens did *not* intend originally for Mr. Boffin to be corrupted by his inherited wealth.

2490. Shea, Francis X. "The Text of *Our Mutual Friend*: A Study of the Variations between the Copy Text and the First Printed Edition." *Dissertation Abstracts International*, 22 (1961/62), 2007 (University of Minnesota, 1961).

Compares the manuscript (copy-text) with the first printed edition, but not with the proof sheets. The textual variations are "very substantial," Shea indicates in the abstract, "especially in those first five numbers of the monthly parts which Dickens had prepared before serial publication began." In addition to studying these variations, an introduction "also gives a history of the composition of the novel," the publishing history of the novel, and an account of Dickens's working methods.

2491. Winslow, Joan D. "The Number Plans for *Our Mutual Friend*." *Dickens Studies Newsletter*, 9 (1978), 106-09.

Corrects inaccuracies in Boll's transcription (**2476**) of the number plans for *Our Mutual Friend*.

Pickwick Papers

2492. Dickens, Charles. Facsimiles. In his *The Posthumous Papers of the Pickwick Club*. Lombard Street Edition. 2 vols. in 20 monthly parts. With Introduction by John H. Stonehouse. London: Piccadilly Fountain Press, 1932, between pp. x and xi and pp. xxii and xxiii.

Includes photographic facsimiles of a page of the proof for Dickens's introduction to the Cheap Edition (1847), with handwritten additions, and of the five pages of the manuscript of *Pickwick Papers* in the British Museum. The text itself is a reprint of the original text issued in monthly parts. Stonehouse's introduction is largely a history of the inception and writing of *Pickwick Papers*.

2493. Kinsley, James. "Introduction." In Dickens's *The Pickwick Papers*. Ed. James Kinsley. Clarendon Dickens. Oxford: Clarendon Press; Oxford, New York, etc.: Oxford University Press, 1986, pp. xv-lxxxv.

Comments at considerable length on Dickens's initial scheme for and the composition of *Pickwick Papers*, on textual variations in the editions published in Dickens's lifetime (more fully itemized in the footnotes in the text of the novel), and on the extant fragments of the manuscript, including their present locations. Kinsley also includes "Descriptive List of Editions 1837-1867" (**128**), all Dickens's prefaces (pp. xcix-c and 883-88), the addresses to readers in the monthly numbers (pp. 879-82), the descriptive headlines in the 1867 edition (pp. 889-95), and "The Reception of the Novel in 1836-1840" (pp. 896-98), which lists reviews of the novel, early critical commentary, and references in contemporary diaries and letters. Also see Butt and Tillotson, "Preface by the General Editors" (**176**).

Reviews: A. Bewlay, *British Book News*, October 1986, pp. 606-07 (a "model of scholarly enterprise and erudition," with a "lucid" introduction); S. Monod, *Etudes anglaises*, 40 (1987), 473-74 (in French; "superbe"); P. Preston, *Notes and Queries*, ns 35 (1988), 389-91 ("meticulously edited and beautifully produced"); M. Reynolds, *Dickensian*, 83 (1987), 54-56 (high praise for the introduction and the editorial apparatus); A. Sanders, *Times Literary Supplement*, 16 January 1987, p. 66 ("lucid introduction," a fine edition); A. Shelston, *Critical Quarterly*, 29, iii (Autumn 1987), 84-87 (praises Kinsley's "very detailed consideration of both the literary and social contexts of the writing process"); M. Slater, *Times Higher Education Supplement*, 17 October 1986, p. 18 (high praise for Kinsley's introduction and choice of copy-text; overall, "a most splendid edition"); K. Sørensen, *English Studies*, 68 (1987), 292-93 (an "indispensable" edition, a "meticulous" editing job); J. Sutherland, *Review of English Studies*, ns 39 (1988), 311-13 (agrees with Kinsley's choice of the 1837 original edition as copy-text and finds the introduction "a concisely informative account of the novel's complex evolution"); K. T. von Rosador, *Archiv für das Studium der neueren Sprachen und Literaturen*, 225 (1988), 403-04 (the introduction is "a fine abstract of the present state of research" on *Pickwick Papers*–and "embellished by new insights"); W. P. Williams, *Analytical & Enumerative Bibliography*, ns 2 (1988), 182-83 (a "magnificent volume," with "careful and sensitive editing").

2494.   Merry, W. "The Pickwick Manuscripts." *Dickensian*, 11 (1915), 162-63.

A letter to the editor referring to a note in *All the Year Round*, 22 May 1866, whose author claimed to have seen the "whole of the original manuscript of the *Pickwick Papers*," and wondering where the rest of the pages might now be since so few seem to have surfaced. Unfortunately, there was no such issue of *All the Year Round* (the closest were for 19 and 26 May), and it is most unlikely that Dickens would have allowed such a personal reference in his magazine. Leslie C. Staples, p. 194, points out that the British Museum, London, has six pages of the manuscript of *Pickwick Papers*. Also see Suzannet (**2497**) and Kinsley (**2493**), for a listing of these and other extant manuscript pages. Engel (**125**), pp. 14-16, locates forty-six manuscript pages, out of what he estimates must have been "probably more than 1500" pages. The other 1,454 or more pages have not turned up.

2495.   Patten, Robert L. "The Interpolated Tales in *Pickwick Papers*." *Dickens Studies*, 1 (1965), 86-89.

From a study of pages of the manuscript of *Pickwick Papers* in the Rosenbach Foundation Library, Philadelphia (**1458**), Patten argues convincingly that the interpolated story entitled "The True Legend of Prince Bladud" was written at the same time as the surrounding text and was not a story that Dickens had on hand for possible publication in the *Morning Chronicle* or *Bell's Life in London*, as other critics have thought. Photographic facsimiles of four pages of the manuscript are included.

2496.   Patten, Robert. "A Note on the Text and Illustrations," "Appendix A: Addresses to the Reader, 1836-7," and "Appendix B: Descriptive Headings, 1867." In Dickens's *The Posthumous Papers of the Pickwick Club*. Ed. Robert Patten. Penguin English Library. Harmondsworth, Eng., Baltimore, MD, and Ringwood, Austral.: Penguin Books, 1972, pp. 31-32, 899-903, 905-17.

In the textual note, Patten comments briefly on the extant manuscript fragments and minor revisions in early editions of the novel and on his own textual choices for the Penguin edition. Appendix A includes a pre-publication advertisement that appeared in the *Athenaeum* and four addresses to the reader published in the monthly parts. Appendix B contains the descriptive page headings that Dickens added in the 1867 Charles Dickens Edition of the work.

Reviews: P. Shillingsburg, *Dickens Studies Newsletter*, 3 (1972), 119-23 (comments on both the virtues and shortcomings of what is characterized as "the only available paperback edition of *Pickwick* for classroom use"); *Times Literary Supplement*, 11 August 1972, p. 946 ("no other available edition of *Pickwick Papers* assembles so much material"); R. Trickett, *Dickensian*, 69 (1973), 119-21 (does not comment on textual or bibliographical matters, does not much care for Patten's approach to Dickens in his introduction, and finds the illustrations poorly reproduced, but notes rather condescendingly that there is "much accidental pleasure to be had from this edition").

2497. S[uzannet], A[lain de]. "The Original Manuscript of 'The Pickwick Papers.'" *Dickensian*, 28 (1931/32), 193-96.

Points out that only forty-four pages of the manuscript of *Pickwick Papers* have been located and identifies and describes them. Includes a facsimile reproduction of page 81 of the manuscript. Also see Kinsley (**2493**) and Merry (**2494**).

Sketches by Boz

2498. Darton, F. J. Harvey. "The Performance: A Dinner at Poplar Walk" and "Epilogue: After the Performance. I. The Revised Version: Second Thoughts in 1836." In his *Dickens, Positively the First Appearance: A Centenary Review, with a Bibliography of* **Sketches by Boz**. London: Argonaut Press, 1933, pp. 51-68, 69-77.

Prints the text of the original version of Dickens's first published story, "A Dinner at Poplar Walk," from the *Monthly Magazine*, December 1833, and comments on the revisions Dickens made in the tale when he reprinted it as "Mr. Minns and His Cousin" in the second series of *Sketches by Boz* (1836). For more detailed studies of these changes, see DeVries (**2499-2501**) and Grillo (**2502**). Also see Sawyer and Darton (**135**) and "'In All the Glory of Print'" (**2503**).

2499. DeVries, Duane. *Dickens's Apprentice Years: The Making of a Novelist.* Hassocks, Eng.: Harvester Press; New York: Barnes & Noble Books/Harper & Row, 1976. iv + 195 pp.

Throughout traces revisions that Dickens made in his early published articles and tales when he collected them for publication in the various editions of *Sketches by Boz*. Textual changes are emphasized in the portion of chapter 2 (see particularly pp. 32-41) reprinted, with modifications, from "Two Glimpses of Dickens' Early Development as a Writer of Fiction" (**2501**) and in two appendices, "'Hackney Cabs and Their Drivers': A 'New' Sketch by 'Boz,'" pp. 158-66, and "Three Canceled Introductory Sections," pp. 167-69. Also see Grillo (**2502**).

Reviews: M. Y. Andrews, *British Book News*, August 1976, p. 609 ("useful, intelligent and well-researched study," but too much of the "dutiful academic 'thesis'"), and *Journal of English and Germanic Philology*, 76 (1978), 463-64 (De Vries's scholarship is "scrupulous and substantial"; the critical writing is "somewhat dull," but the chronological approach works well and the book as a whole has "an illuminating thoroughness"); *Choice*, 13 (1976/77), 1594 ("examines every shred of extant information about Dickens to try to answer the question of the sudden flowering of talent"); E. Costigan, *Review of English Studies*, ns 29 (1978), 495-97 (takes exception to practically every aspect of DeVries's approach); E. Engel, *Modern Philology*, 77 (1979/80), 102-05 ("sharply focused" and carefully developed, an "invaluable aid in furthering the appreciation" of the early Dickens); A. Ikeler, *British Studies Monitor*, 9, iii (Winter 1980), 26-48 ("modest and sensible" conclusions); J. Lucas, *Literature & History*, 5 (1979), 132-33 (highly unfavorable); R. Maxwell, *Victorian Studies*, 22 (1978/79), 216-19 ("not quite satisfactory as either a critical or an historical work; nonetheless, students of the early Dickens will need it as a basis for further work"); J. Meckier, *Studies in Short Fiction*, 14 (1977), 410-12 (has some reservations about DeVries's method of analysis but finds the study "readable" and the criticism "meticulous"); R. L. Patten, *Dickens Studies Newsletter*, 8 (1977), 48-51 ("exemplary scholarship"); P. Preston, *Notes and Queries*, ns 26 (1979), 352-53 (limited in places, the focus too narrow, but the study of Dickens's development as a craftsman is "illuminating and convincing"); A. Sanders, *Times Higher Education Supplement*, 30 July 1976, p. 16 (finds much wrong with the work); F. S. Schwarzbach, *Dickensian*, 72 (1976), 106-08 (finds the work a "massive compilation of research," a "careful reading of the original texts," but regrets the author "did not give freer rein to his critical abilities"–still, "a book which every student and admirer of Dickens will profit from and enjoy").

2500. DeVries, Duane. "Dickens's *Sketches by Boz*, Exercises in the Craft of Fiction." *Dissertation Abstracts International*, 25 (1965), 5273-74 (Michigan State University, 1964).

In studying Dickens's development as a writer in the fifty-nine sketches and tales that he published between 1833 and 1836 and collected as *Sketches by Boz*, DeVries occasionally pays attention to the revisions Dickens made in these pieces when he collected them as *Sketches by Boz*. When DeVries revised this dissertation as *Dickens's Apprentice Years: The Making of a Novelist* (**2499**), he expanded and added sections dealing with Dickens's revisions.

2501. DeVries, Duane. "Two Glimpses of Dickens's Early Development as a Writer of Fiction." *Dickens Studies Annual*, 1 (1970), 55-64, 282; reprinted, with revisions, in his *Dickens's Apprentice Years: The Making of a Novelist* (**2499**), pp. 32-41.

In this study of Dickens's early development as a craftsman, DeVries traces the extensive revisions that Dickens made in "A Dinner at Poplar Walk," his first published tale (*Monthly Magazine*, December 1833), when he republished it as "Mr. Minns and His Cousin" in *Sketches by Boz* in 1836 and shows that Dickens's fourth published tale, "The Bloomsbury Christening" (*Monthly Magazine*, April 1834), similar in a number of ways to the first tale, is a distinct improvement upon it in Dickens's conscious search for "effective style and form."

2502. Grillo, Virgil. "Chapter Five: Revisions for Synthesis." In his *Charles Dickens' **Sketches by Boz**: End in the Beginning*. Boulder: Colorado Associated University Press, 1974, pp. 85-117.

Traces some of the revisions Dickens made in his early sketches and tales when he republished them in *Sketches by Boz* and provides lists of their original publication. Grillo also traces, through comparable lists, the arrangement of the pieces in the first editions of the two series of *Sketches by Boz* and their rearrangement in the monthly parts reissue, 1837-39. He uses all this information to show something of Dickens's experimentation with literary types and techniques, his development as a writer between 1833 and 1836, and, in conformity with a thesis Grillo develops in the earlier chapters of his study, Dickens's attempt, in his revisions and his arrangement of pieces in the editions of *Sketches by Boz*, "to reconcile divergent attitudes of his stories and sketches, to transform himself from the sardonic promulgator of an absurdist view into the mythic apologist for his own society." Grillo's comments about "The Last Cab-driver, and the First Omnibus Cad," need to be modified, however, in the light of the discovery by DeVries (**2499**) that this piece is a combination of two earlier essays and not the expansion of one of them. Grillo also comments in the concluding sections of the chapter on the relationship of Cruikshank's illustrations to Dickens's text and the generally favorable critical reception of *Sketches by Boz*. Grillo includes two bibliographies: "Bibliography: Secondary Sources Relating to *Sketches by Boz*" (**1115**) pp. 219-22, and "About Dickens and His Other Works: Selected Bibliography of Secondary Sources" (**983**), pp. 223-30.

2503. "'In All the Glory of Print.'" *Dickensian*, 30 (1933/34), 1-10.

Facsimile reproductions of "A Dinner at Poplar Walk" (revised and collected as "Mr. Minns and His Cousin" in *Sketches by Boz* in 1836), Dickens's first tale, from the *Monthly Magazine*, December 1833, and of the corrected page proof of the second page of the preface to the 1847 edition of *Pickwick Papers* in which Dickens describes his feelings both upon submitting the piece and after its publication. Also reprinted in Darton (**2498**).

2504. Loughlin, M. Clare. "Revisions to 'A Visit to Newgate' and Dickens's Experience of the Mannings' Execution." *Dickensian*, 93 (1997), 92-94.

Comments on how three minor changes in the text of "A Visit to Newgate" in the Cheap Edition of Dickens's *Sketches by Boz* (1850) were influenced by Dickens's attendance at the execution of Frederick and Maria Manning on 13 November 1849.

2505. Ser, Cary D. "*Sketches by Boz*: A Collated Edition." *Dissertation Abstracts International*, 40 (1979/80), 4013A (University of Florida, 1974).

In his abstract, Ser indicates that his edition of *Sketches by Boz* "synthesizes the major texts" of the work published in Dickens's lifetime–the individual sketches and tales published in various magazines and newspapers, 1833-36, and the collected editions of 1836, 1837, 1839, 1850, 1858, and 1868. The preface to the dissertation, Ser notes, traces the history of the publication of the work, comments on Dickens's relationships with the publishers John Macrone and Richard Bentley and the illustrator George Cruikshank, and depicts Dickens's frustrating search for financial security through his publication of the work. Ser uses the 1839 edition as the "basic reading text for the collation," he points out, "not only because Dickens carefully revised it, restructuring the work in its entirety, but also because subsequent editions of the text suffered from the contemptuous attitude which Dickens had formed towards it."

2506. Slater, Michael. "Introduction," "Dickens's Prefaces to *Sketches by Boz*," and Headnotes. In Dickens's *Sketches by Boz and Other Early Papers, 1833-39.* Ed. Michael Slater. Dent Uniform Edition of Dickens' Journalism. [Vol. 1]. London: J. M. Dent; Columbus: Ohio State University Press, 1994, pp. xi-xxii, xxxix-xlii, and passim.

In his informative introduction, Slater comments on the writing, revising, and publication of the works included in this volume. The collection of prefaces is useful in tracing Dickens's changing attitude toward these early pieces. Slater also gives further bibliographical and textual information in the headnotes to individual sketches and includes a list of "The First Publication of Dickens's Sketches in Serial and Volume Form" (**136**).

Reviews: M. Y. A[ndrews], *Dickensian*, 90 (1994), 136-37 (a "handsome" edition, "expertly annotated," with a clear historical introduction, but with illustrations of "variable quality"); R. Bennett, *Review of English Studies*, ns 47 (1996), 434-35 (valuable introduction, scholarly apparatus, and annotations); L. Brake, *Studies in Newspaper and Periodical History 1994 Annual*, pp. 210-12 ("informative, learned, and attractive," with "effective editing," though incomplete index; a "splendid project"); J. J. Brattin, *Nineteenth-Century Prose*, 23, i (Spring 1996), 116-19 (commends the "brief but serviceable introduction," useful headnotes, and "informative annotation," the volume's "best feature," but wishes there were more textual notes, less selectivity, better placement of illustrations and notes, and fewer "flat-out errors"); W. M. Burgan, *Victorian Periodicals Review*, 29 (1996), 338-39 (praises "cogency" of annotation); J. Carey, *Sunday Times* (London), 27 February 1994, pp. 6.4-6.5 (comments more on the vividness and reality of Dickens's early journalistic pieces than on Slater's editing of them); K. J. Fielding, *Carlyle Studies Annual*, 18 (1998), 187-89 (though the focus of the review is a comparison of Dickens and Carlyle, notes that the volume contains "a valuable new edition of *Sketches by Boz* and is a "handsome, readable, helpful, and indispensable" volume); P. Foot, *Spectator*, 272 (12 March 1994), 26-27 (finds "there is a lot to be said for the raw young journalist Dickens" but does not comment on the editing or textual concerns of the volume); J. Gross, *Times Literary Supplement*, 23 February 1996, p. 12 (generally favorable); S. Monod, *Etudes anglaises*, 48 (1995), 233-34 (in French; favorable); R. Patten, *American Notes and Queries*, 9, iv (Fall 1996), 52-56 (commends the edition and four-volume project and comments on Dickens's early writing and the influences on it); A. Roberts, *English*, 43 (1994), 271-73 (a "handsome," welcome volume with "excellent" editorial material but with "occasional misprints"); P. Schlicke, *Dickens Quarterly*, 11 (1994), 197-99 (comments on Dickens's excellence as a journalist and finds Slater's first volume in a four-volume collection of Dickens's journalism "cause for enthusiastic rejoicing," with a "useful" introduction and valuable supplementary material); J. D. Vann, *Albion*, 27 (1995), 328-29 (a "valuable work," with an introduction that gives "a good overview of Dickens' writing activities during the seven-year period" covered in the volume, and "very useful" headnotes to the selections and index/glossary).

A Tale of Two Cities

2507. Maxwell, Richard. "A Note on the Text." In Dickens's *A Tale of Two Cities*. Ed. Richard Maxwell. Penguin Classics. London, New York, etc.: Penguin Books, 2000, pp. xlvii-li.

Defends his choice of the weekly serialization in *All the Year Round*, 30 April to 26 November 1859, as his copy-text and, despite this choice, his inclusion of the illustrations that Hablot K. Browne did for the monthly publication of the novel. Maxwell also notes a few variants between early editions of the work. In "Further Reading," pp. xli–xlvi, he comments on thirty-six critical studies of this novel, 1962-99, that he found "particularly useful." He also includes a comparable section on historical studies of the French Revolution.

2508. Sanders, Andrew. *The Companion to* **A Tale of Two Cities**. The Dickens Companions. London, etc.: Unwin; Boston: Unwin Hyman, 1988, passim.

In the notes to the novel, with which most of this volume is concerned, Sanders mentions some of the significant textual differences between manuscript, weekly serialization, and the first volume edition. Sanders also includes a "Select Bibliography" (**1122**), pp. 168-71.

Reviews: T. J. Cribb, *Review of English Studies*, 45 (1994), 123-24 (finds a number of careless errors); D. Gervais in *Modern Language Review*, 86 (1991), 181-82 ("meticulously done," with a "useful" introduction); S. Monod in *Etudes anglaises*, 43 (1990), 349-50 (in French; finds some flaws in a volume that is "solide et parfois brillant"–substantial and occasionally brilliant); G. Storey in *Times Literary Supplement*, 17-23 February 1989, p. 173 (favorable).

2509. Tucker, David. "Dickens at Work on the MS of *A Tale of Two Cities*." *Etudes anglaises*, 32 (1979), 449-57.

Examines three passages that Dickens cancelled in manuscript by pasting slips of paper over them that contained his revisions of those passages. The cancellations were recently revealed, Tucker points out, during conservation work on the manuscript at the Victoria and Albert Museum and showed interesting changes in style, emphasis, and characterization (for example, Mme. Defarge is changed from a "little woman" with "little bright eyes" to "a stout woman" with "a watchful eye"). The revisions, Tucker concludes, were "a considerable improvement" over the original drafts and provide evidence that Dickens "took considerable pains with *A Tale of Two Cities*."

2510. Tucker, David. "The Text of the Oxford Illustrated Dickens. 'A Tale of Two Cities': Some Shortcomings Noted." *Notes and Queries*, ns 25 (1978), 311-13.

Asserts that textually the Oxford Illustrated Dickens is "a far from perfect edition," for which Tucker provides ample evidence, noting particular changes between the text of the weekly and monthly parts of the novel.

Nonfictional, Theatrical, and Poetical Works

Note: Also see the section on *Sketches by Boz*, above, and Flint (**1124**).

2511. Fisher, Leona W. *Lemon, Dickens, and Mr. Nightingale's Diary: A Victorian Farce.* ELS Monograph Series, 41. Victoria, B. C.: English Literary Studies, University of Victoria, 1988. 244 pp.

Prints for the first time—in typographic form, with insertions and deletions indicated—the earliest surviving manuscript of Mark Lemon's play *Mr. Nightingale's Diary* and also reprints the text of the 1851 edition of the work. These are preceded by a historical and bibliographical section in which Lemon's writing of the play, Dickens's hand in its revision, Dickens's production of the play with his amateur company of actors, its reception, and a comparison of the two versions are fully covered.
Review: K. Tillotson, *Dickensian*, 86 (1990), 116-17 (with a few reservations, finds the work a "service to Dickens studies").

2512. Hanna, Robert C. "*The Life of Our Lord*: New Notes of Explication." *Dickensian*, 95 (1999), 197-205.

Summarizes criticism of and commentary on the work, comments on the manuscript and early references to it, and notes (but does not list) the forty editions published since its original posthumous publication in 1934.

2513. Harvey, P. D. A. "Charles Dickens as Playwright." *British Museum Quarterly*, 24 (1961), 22-25.

Describes revisions that Dickens made in copies of three of his plays—*The Village Coquettes, The Strange Gentleman,* and *Is She His Wife?*—filed with the Lord Chamberlain for purposes of licensing, and now in the British Museum.

2514. Haywood, Charles. "Charles Dickens and Shakespeare; or, The Irish Moor of Venice, *O'Thello* with Music." *Dickensian*, 73 (1977), 67-88.

Draws together the four manuscript pages of the sides of John Dickens's part ("The Great Unpaid") for "O'Thello," Dickens's youthful travesty of Shakespeare's tragedy. These pages, Haywood believes, comprise the entire part. He provides photographic facsimiles, a printed transcription, the music to which the airs were set, extensive bibliographical and explanatory notes, and eight illustrations. Also see "'O'Thello: Dickens's Earliest Known Manuscript" (**2518**).

2515. Ingham, Patricia. "A Note on the Text" and "Appendix I: Dickens's Unpublished Introduction of 1842." In Dickens's *American Notes for General Circulation.* Ed. Patricia Ingham. Penguin Classics. London, New York, etc.: Penguin Books, 2000, pp. xxxv-xxxvi, 275-77.

Textual matters are covered in "A Note on the Text," where Ingham comments on the manuscript of the novel and on her collation of the first edition (her copy-text) with the Cheap Edition (1850) and the Charles Dickens Edition (1868), the changes being "few and minor," however. She also comments on the "contentious piece" that Dickens planned as the introduction to the first edition (1842), but which John Forster persuaded him not to print, only to print it himself after Dickens's death in *Forster*. Ingham reprints this introduction in Appendix I. In her introduction, pp. xi-xxxi, she notes some of the pirated American editions of the work, and in "Further Reading," pp. xxxii-xxxiv, she provides a list of eighteen studies of *American Notes*.

2516. J., W. H. "The Dead Hand: Dickens and Scott." *Notes and Queries*, 184 (1943), 191-92.

On Dickens's and Sir Walter Scott's editing of the posthumous works of others—in Dickens's case *Religious Opinions of the Late Reverend Chauncy Hare Townshend* (1869).

2517. Nayder, Lillian. "The Cannibal, the Nurse, and the Cook: Variants of *The Frozen Deep*." Chapter 3 in her *Unequal Partners: Charles Dickens, Wilkie Collins, and Victorian Authorship* (**156**), pp. 60-99.

Examines the revisions that Dickens made in Collins's play *The Frozen Deep*.

2518. "'O'Thello': Dickens's Earliest Known Manuscript." *Dickensian*, 26 (1929/30), 9-12.

Facsimile reproduction of four pages of the sides for the part of The Great Unpaid, a character played by John Dickens in his son's burlesque version of Shakespeare's tragedy. Also see Haywood (**2514**).

2519. Paroissien, David H. "A Critical Edition of Charles Dickens's *Pictures from Italy*." *Dissertation Abstracts International*, 29 (1968/69), 1876A-77A (UCLA, 1968).

As his abstract indicates, in a lengthy "Textual Introduction," Paroissien examines the differences between the extant manuscript of part of the seventh and all of the eighth "Travelling Letters Written on the Road" (as this earlier version of *Pictures from Italy* was titled when it was serialized as eight "letters" in the London *Daily News*) and the first book edition (1846). Paroissien also comments on the textual problems involved in preparing a critical edition of this work and looks at the genesis and composition of the work apart from textual changes.

2520. Paroissien, David H. "Dickens's 'Pictures from Italy': Stages of the Work's Development and Dickens's Methods of Composition." *English Miscellany*, 22 (1971), 243-62.

Discusses how Dickens came to write and put together *Pictures from Italy*.

2521. Slater, Michael. "Note on the Provenance, Selection and Treatment of the Text," "Appendix A: Descriptive Headlines Added by Dickens to Articles in this Volume from *HW [Household Words]* Which Were Included in *RP [Reprinted Pieces]*," and Headnotes. In Dickens's *"The Amusements of the People" and Other Papers: Reports, Essays and Reviews, 1834-51*. Ed. Michael Slater. Dent Uniform Edition of Dickens' Journalism. Vol. 2. London: J. M. Dent; Columbus: Ohio State University Press, 1996, pp. xxvii-xxviii, 370-71, and passim.

In the first section, Slater comments on the sources from which the pieces in this volume come, his criteria for selecting them, and his editorial decisions in determining the text for the selections (for example, he standardizes spelling and punctuation, silently corrects misprints, but, with one exception noted, uses the text of the earliest published version of each piece). In Appendix A, for the articles he includes from *Household Words*, Slater gives the descriptive headlines Dickens used to them when he reprinted them in the Charles Dickens Edition of *Reprinted Pieces* (1858). In the headnotes to many individual pieces, Slater provides information about the present location of known manuscripts and notes differences between manuscript (or page proofs) and printed text. Also see "Appendix B: Complete Listing of Dickens's Known Journalism, December 1833-June 1851" **(159)**.

Reviews: M. Y. A[ndrews], *Dickensian*, 93 (1997), 49-50 (commends Slater's editing and surveys the journalistic pieces selected by Slater, regretting the absence of a few); J. J. Brattin, *Nineteenth-Century Prose*, 24, ii (Fall 1997), 180 ("a fine introduction, useful notes and annotations," and a "splendidly informative and accurate index and glossary"); J. Carey, *Sunday Times* (London), 8 December 1996, pp. 7.1-7.2 ("splendidly edited," the volume's interest lying in Dickens's "persistent engagement with social problems"); J. A. Davies, *Notes and Queries*, ns 44 (1997), 564-65 (commends for "detailed scholarly apparatus" that provides context and explains contemporary references"); K. J. Fielding, *Carlyle Studies Annual*, 18 (1998), 87-89 (though the focus of the review is a comparison of Dickens and Carlyle, notes that this is a "handsome, readable, helpful, and indispensable" volume); A. Hayter, *Times Literary Supplement*, 17 January 1997, p. 18 (comments more on Dickens's "extraordinary powers of observation and description" than anything else, but does mention Slater's "admirable head-notes and summaries of Dickens's activities," 1834-51); L. H. Jackson, *Albion*, 29 (1997), 696-97 (an "important work," with "helpful and informative" introductory and other supplementary matter); J. Mortimer, *Spectator*, 14 December 1996, p. 61 ("admirably edited and annotated"); L. Nayder, *Victorian Periodicals Review*, 30 (1997), 292-94 (mainly descriptive, occasionally critical); M. Rogers, *Library Journal*, 122 (1 April 1997), 134 ("for academic collections supporting serious Dickens scholars"); P. Schlicke, *Dickens Quarterly*, 15 (1998), 62-64 (comments on Dickens's journalistic career, 1836-50, and the "developing skill and maturing outlook" reflected in the pieces in this volume, which is "graced by the exemplary editing" of Slater, particularly his choice of essays, his "highly informative" and succinct headnotes, a detailed index/glossary, and "crisp and accurate annotation").

2522. Slater, Michael, "Textual Note," "Appendix B: Descriptive Headlines Added by Dickens to Articles in this Volume Which Were included in *RP [Reprinted Pieces]*," and Headnotes. In Dickens's *"Gone Astray" and Other Papers from Household Words, 1851-59*. Ed. Michael Slater. Dent Uniform Edition of Dickens' Journalism. Vol. 3. London: J. M. Dent; Columbus: Ohio State University Press, 1998, pp. xxiii, 507-08, and passim.

In the textual note, Slater comments briefly on his silent emendations to the text, the sources of the text, and manuscript locations. In Appendix B, he lists the descriptive headlines that Dickens added to the *Household Words* articles included in the Charles Dickens Edition of *Reprinted Pieces*. In the headnotes for eight of the sixty-five pieces that Slater includes, he gives the location of the manuscript and comments briefly on corrections (always minor) that Dickens made in the published version. Also see "Appendix C: Complete Listing of Dickens's Known Journalism (All in *Household Words*), July 1851-January 1859" (**160**).

M. Y. A[ndrews], *Dickensian*, 95 (1999), 248-50 (Andrews finds the volume "scrupulously edited and annotated" and himself surveys Dickens's writings of the period, their "dominant themes," and their "exhilarating" quality); J. Bowen, *Times Literary Supplement*, 21 May 1999, p. 25 ("a handsome edition: diverting and discreetly informative," with "thorough and tactful annotation"); J. Boylan, *Columbia Journalism Review*, 38, iii (September/October 1999), 61 (an "ample volume"); J. Carey, *Sunday Times* (London), 3 January 1999, Books section, pp. 6.1-6.2 (edited "with matchless expertise"); J. A. Davies, *Notes and Queries*, ns 47 (2000), 380-81 (this and the other volumes in the series comprise "a worthy companion" to *Pilgrim Letters* and the Clarendon Edition of Dickens's works, particularly in their "invariably exemplary" annotation); L. Nayder, *Victorian Periodicals Review*, 32 (1999), 364-66 (an "important" volume for Dickens's social and political views); D. Rainsford, *Dickens Quarterly*, 17 (2000), 246-49 (Slater's introduction, notes, appendices, and glossary make "a permanent and admirable contribution to Dickens scholarship").

2523. Slater, Michael, and John Drew. "Note on the Text and Illustrations," "Appendix C: Descriptive Headlines Added by Dickens to Articles in this Volume Which Were Included in *UT1 [The Uncommercial Traveller (1868)]*," and Headnotes. In Dickens's *The Uncommercial Traveller and Other Papers, 1859-70*. Ed. Michael Slater and John Drew. Dent Uniform Edition of Dickens' Journalism. Vol. 4. London: J. M. Dent; Columbus: Ohio State University Press, 2000, pp. xxvii, 432-35, and passim.

In the note on the text and illustrations, Slater and Drew list silent emendations in the text and the sources of the text and illustrations. In Appendix C, they list the descriptive headlines that Dickens added to twenty-seven *All the Year Round* papers that he included as twenty-eight papers in the Charles Dickens Edition of *The Uncommercial Traveller* (London: Chapman and Hall, 1868). In the headnotes for twenty-five of the fifty-one pieces reprinted in this volume, Slater and Drew comment briefly on matters concerning the manuscript or text. Also see "Appendix D: Complete Listing of Dickens's Known Journalism, December 1833-August 1869" (**161**).

Reviews: M. Y. A[ndrews], *Dickensian*, 97 (2001), 162-64 (a "fine introduction," a valuable volume, the last of four volumes of "splendidly edited journalism"); P. J. McCarthy, *Dickens Quarterly*, 19 (2002), 31-34 ("wonderfully detailed notes," a "most welcome edition").; D. J. Taylor, *Times Literary Supplement*, 5 January 2001, p. 32a (a decade's work on Dickens's journalism brought "to a triumphant conclusion"); C. R. Vanden Bossche, *Albion*, 34 (2002), 523-24 (along with volumes 1-3 of the series, "enables us to see the development and scope of Dickens' non-fiction writing from *Sketches by Boz* to the end of his career"; a "useful" introduction" and headnotes).

2524. Whitley, John S., and Arnold Goldman. "Appendix 1: Dickens's Discarded Introduction" and "Textual Notes." In Dickens's *American Notes for General Circulation*. Ed. John S. Whitley and Arnold Goldman. Penguin English Library. Harmondsworth, Eng., Baltimore, MD, and Ringwood, Austral.: Penguin Books, 1972, pp. 297-300, 359-61.

In Appendix 1, the editors reprint the tough-talking introduction that Dickens originally wrote for *American Notes* and reluctantly cancelled, presumably largely at John Forster's insistence. It was first published in *Forster* as per Forster's agreement, as he announced there, "to undertake for its publication when a more fitting time should come." The textual notes identify eighty-one minor changes made in the Cheap Edition (1850) and the Charles Dickens Edition (1868) of the work.

Review: *Times Literary Supplement*, 11 August 1972, p. 946 (more descriptive than evaluative, though complains about the copy-text)—see reply by Goldman and Whitley, 18 August, p. 970, and the reviewer's response, 25 August, pp. 996-97, and Goldman's further comment, 15 September, p. 1060).

Book of Memoranda

Note: As Fred Kaplan indicates (**2530**), Dickens made entries in what has become known as his Book of Memoranda between 1855 and 1865. He left the notebook in his will to Georgina Hogarth, who, Kaplan states, probably traded it with John Forster for the manuscript of *The Cricket on the Hearth*. Forster, in turn, left it to Dickens's daughter Kate, who gave it to Alice and Joseph W. Comyns Carr (**2527**), who donated it to a Red Cross drive in 1918 (**1944**). After passing through the hands of several collectors, including Jerome Kern (**1934**), it is now in the Henry W. And Albert A. Berg Collection, New York Public Library (**1499**). Although this notebook is not technically part of Dickens's published works, it has been included here because of its impact on textual studies of Dickens's later works—see, for example works listed in this section and Brattin (**2479**), Cotsell (**2482**), Cox (**2437**), Ford (**2440**), Forster (**2298**), Meckier (**2395**), Paroissien (**2398, 2449**), Rosenberg (**2402, 2404, 2451**), Stone (**2314**), and Sucksmith (**2420**).

2525. Aylmer, Felix. "John Forster and Dickens's Book of Memoranda." *Dickensian*, 51 (1954/55), 19-23.

Reviews the provenance of the Book of Memoranda (**2530**) and the excerpts published in *Forster*, in the appendix to the *Nonesuch Letters*, and in Mrs. Comyns Carr's *Reminiscences* (**2527**). Aylmer notes how Forster frequently modified the arrangement of material he quoted and sometimes thereby misrepresented it. See reply by Pakenham (**2532**).

2526. Chittick, Kathryn. "The Meaning of a Literary Idea: Dickens's Memoranda Notebook." *Dalhousie Review*, 62 (1982/83), 473-84.

Explores the creative ways in which Dickens used notes on characterization and images and on various philosophic ideas jotted down in his Book of Memoranda (**2530**) for stories.

2527. Comyns Carr, Mrs. J[oseph W.]. "The Dickens Note-Book." In *Mrs. J. Comyns Carr's Reminiscences*. Ed. Eve Adam. London: Hutchinson, 1926, pp. 280-95.

Mrs. Comyns Carr notes that Dickens's memorandum notebook was given to her and her husband by Kate Dickens Perugini, Dickens's second daughter, and gives a number of excerpts from it. See Kaplan (**2530**) for the complete notebook and a comparative study of what portions of this notebook were published where prior to his edition. Illustrated.

2528. Dexter, Walter. "When Found–Dickens's Memorandum Book." *Dickensian*, 29 (1932/33), 86-87.

Comments on and provides a facsimile reproduction of a page of the manuscript of Dickens's Book of Memoranda. For publication of the entire manuscript, see Kaplan (**2530**).

2529. Forster, John. "Hints for Books Written and Unwritten." In *Forster-Ley* (**2298**), pp. 747-60.

Quotes extensively from Dickens's Book of Memoranda (**2530**), which was then obviously in his possession, and indicates where "hints or suggestions" jotted down were later used by Dickens in the stories and novels that he wrote between 1855 and 1865. In a footnote J. W. T. Ley adds other items from the notebook printed in Comyns Carr (**2527**). This information, except for Ley's addendum, will also be found in the original editions of Forster's *Life of Charles Dickens* (**19**), but the edition edited by Ley is easier to come by in libraries. According to Rosenberg (**2404**), p. 70, Forster printed all but twenty-five of the entries, though he "ignored the chronology of the entries" he printed.

2530. Kaplan, Fred, ed. *Charles Dickens' Book of Memoranda: A Photographic and Typographic Facsimile of the Notebook Begun in January 1855*. New York: New York Public Library, 1981. x + 107 pp.

The first complete publication of Dickens's Book of Memoranda, with photographic facsimile and printed transcription on facing pages of the thirty-one-page manuscript. In his introduction, Kaplan describes the notebook and its provenance and lists the previous publication of excerpts from the manuscript. He includes elaborate editorial notes (pp. 79-107), numbers the entries from 1 to 117, and provides information about where and how Dickens used entries in his writings.

Reviews: R. Beddow, *Book World* (supplement to the *Washington Post*), 15 Aug. 1982, p. 9 ("absolutely useless except as a curio," but "a beautifully printed curio" that "will delight lovers of literature and writers who want to see a master's method"); *BRH: Bulletin of Research in the Humanities*, 84 (1981), 271-72 (essentially a notice of publication, not a review–describes the contents); R. Caserio, *Nineteenth-Century Fiction*, 38 (1983/84), 337-47 (not a review but a post-structuralist or neo-Marxist take on Dickens's note-taking); K. Chittick, *Victorian Periodicals Review*, 16 (1983), 67-68 (finds the notes "generally concise and informative"); *Choice*, 20 (1982/83), 1136 (an "important book for Dickens scholars"); R. J. Dunn, *Modern Language Studies*, 16, ii (Spring 1986), 80-82 (praises Kaplan's editorial work and comments on Dickens's use of the memoranda); G. Ford, *Nineteenth-Century Fiction*, 37 (1982/83), 214-20 ("commendable," an "admirably prepared edition"); S. Monod, *Etudes anglaises*, 36 (1983), 101-02 (in French; praises Kaplan's introduction, editing, and notes–an essential volume for the Dickens scholar); A. Sanders, *Dickensian*, 82 (1986), 180-81 ("admirably edited," a "valuable addition to Dickens scholarship").

2531. Page, Norman. "Appendix D: The Berg Notebook." In his *A Dickens Companion* (**223**), pp. 349-51.

Provides information about Dickens's Book of Memoranda (**2530**).

2532. Pakenham, Pansy. "The Memorandum Book, Forster & *Edwin Drood*." *Dickensian*, 51 (1954/55), 117-21.

Finds some "mis-statements" in Felix Aylmer's account (**2525**) of Dickens's Book of Memoranda (**2530**) and notes that nineteenth-century biographers "had [no] reverence for their subject's literary remains and did not hesitate to cut, alter and amalgamate letters as it suited their editorial purposes." In Dickens's case, she indicates, this involved a book of memoranda, particularly where items relevant to *The Mystery of Edwin Drood* were concerned.

2533. Smith, Harry B. "How Charles Dickens Wrote His Books: Leaves from a Hitherto Unpublished Notebook." *Harper's Magazine*, 150 (1924/25), 50-60; reprinted in *Strand Magazine*, 69 (1925), 128-36.

Gives the provenance of the Book of Memoranda (**2530**) that Dickens kept during the last twenty years of his life, reproduces four of its pages in facsimile, and provides a number of details about its contents–lists of names, titles for stories, notes about incidents, and story ideas, among others. Smith comments generally on the closeness of Dickens's observations of character, his orderliness and methodicalness, and how he used casually recorded notes to develop a story. More specifically, Smith notes some items in the memoranda that Dickens used in writing *Little Dorrit, Our Mutual Friend*, and *The*

Mystery of Edwin Drood. For a complete printing of the Book of Memoranda, see Kaplan (**2530**), who, pp. 3-4, more accurately describes the notebook as consisting of "176 leaves of unwatermarked off-white paper," all but thirty-one of which are blank.

2534. Spencer, T. J. B. "A Case in the State Trials." *Dickensian*, 72 (1976), 141-47.

Identifies the source of an incident about a daughter's poisoning of her father recorded in Dickens's Book of Memoranda (**2530**), one, Spencer notes, that Dickens "never made full use of," but that, according to *Forster*, "struck him greatly by its capabilities."

AUTHOR INDEX

Note: In this and the subject index, below, references to pages in the text are listed first and are always preceded by "p." or "pp." They are followed by small Roman numerals (without "p." or "pp."), which refer to page numbers in the Introduction, and then by arabic numbers, which refer to entry numbers in the bibliography.

Part 1. Anonymous Works

Part 2. Authors

A

Abernethy, Peter L. 941

Accardi, Bernard 1255

Aceto, Vincent J. 1357

Achert, Walter S. 1042

Ackroyd, Peter p. 248, 942, 961, 1251
review by 2309

Adam, Eve (pseud.?) 2527

Adams, Debra C. 1073

Adams, Elizabeth L. 1585

Adams, Frederick B., Jr. lxi, 2198, 2334

Adamson, Lynda G. 162

Adrian, Arthur A. 2339

Agate, James 1586

Ahearn, Allen liii, 2199

Ahearn, Patricia liii, 2199

Aken, R. A., review by 93

Albert, Walter 1379

Albu, R., review by 634

Alderson, Brian 851

Alexandrescu, Sorin 564, 571-72

Allbut, Charles 250

Alley, Brian 1244

Allingham, Philip V. 665, 852, 1235

Allombert, Guy 666

Alston, R. C. 1427

Altholz, Josef L. 1329

Altick, Richard D. 171-72, 725, 943, 959, 1187, 1203, 1288, 1387, 1587
reviews by 982, 2314, 2474

Amalric, Jean-Claude, review by 2401

American Antiquarian Society and the Research Libraries Group, Inc. xxx-xxxi, 65

American Art Association li-lii, 17, 1509, 1726, 1889-1907, 1972, 1978-79, 1981, 2094, 2114, 2116, 2118, 2138, 2154, 2164

American Art Association, Anderson Galleries xlv, li-lii, 1464, 1908-18, 2001, 2034, 2087, 2115, 2147, 2169, 2186, 2237

American Art Galleries li, 1919-20, 2145, 2154

American Library Association 70, 944, 1046, 1049, 1237, 1482

American Society for Theatre Research and the International Association of Libraries and Museums of the Performing Arts 1358

Anderson, John P. xxv, xxix, xxxix-xl, 1, 48

Anderson, M. D., review by 1165

Anderson, Patricia J. 1174

Anderson Auction Co. li, 1921-24, 2136, 2190

Anderson Galleries p. 702, li-lii, 1592, 1611, 1628, 1703, 1726, 1925-38, 2056, 2077-78, 2080, 2104-05, 2108, 2117, 2119, 2123, 2129, 2137, 2144, 2148, 2151, 2153, 2163, 2270

Andrew, Nigel 1588

Andrew, Ray V. 464

Andrews, Charles R., review by 982

Andrews, Malcolm Y. p. 680, lii, 668, 945, 1052, 1589, 1781, 1811, 1819, 1823, 1827, 1833-34, 2014, 2282, 2304, 2335
reviews by 113, 117, 125, 1819, 1823, 1831, 2314, 2346, 2381, 2415, 2460-61, 2463, 2499, 2506, 2521-23

Andrews, Nathalie T. 1347, 1777

Anikst, Alexander 549

Ardagh, J. 251

Argosy Book Stores 2020

Arnim, Max 1132

Arnold, William H. liii, 2200

Arnott, James F. 139, 680, 1945

Aronstein, P., review by 29

Aros, Andrew A. 669, 700

Ash, Lee xlvi, 1552
review by 1831

Ashley, Robert P. 1759

Aslib (Association of Special Libraries and Information Bureaux) 580, 843, 1188-89, 2337, 2353, 2415, 2434, 2444, 2481

Associazione Italiana Editori p. 153, 550

Atkinson, Brooks 1835

Atkinson, David 140, 148, 161

Attwooll, David 182

Austin, Roland 338-39

Avadenei, S., review by 634

Aversa, Elizabeth 1138

Avery, Gillian 798

Axon, William E. A. 551

Aycock, Wendell M. 1074

Aylmer, Felix lxvi, 2428, 2525, 2532

B

B., A. C. 1104

B., C. C. 339, 1414-15

B., C. T. 377

B., G. F. R. 488, 491, 508, 890, 1104

B., I. X. 489

B., W. C. 848

Bachman, Maria 552

Harries, J. M. 347

Harris, Elree I. 1352

Harris, Hugh 2470

Harris, Kevin 1408, 1457, 1609, 1617, 1649-52

Harris, Michael 2506

Harrison, William H. 319

Harrold, Charles F. 1058 *also see* "Victorian Bibliography" *in part 1 of the author index, above*

Hartley, Robert A. 1310

Hartveit, Lars, reviews by 958, 2314, 2359, 2423

Harvard College Library, Houghton Library xlvi, 1469-70

Harvard University, Pusey Library xlvi, 1472

Harvard University Library xlvi, 1471

Harvey, P. D. A. 2513

Haskell, Grace C. 898-99

Hatton, Thomas p. 34, xxvii, xxix-xxx, xxiv, xxxvii-xxxviii, 24, 140, 206, 218, 363, 408, 460, 469, 885, 929, 1393, 1402, 1409-10, 1418, 1426, 1489, 2278

Hawes, Donald 986, 2366
    reviews by 2331, 2415

Hawkins Dady, Mark 999

Hawthorn, Jeremy 1064

Hawthorne, Julian liv, 2484

Haynes, E. B. 24, 1409-10

Haynes, Robert H. 1005

Hays, J. J. 520

Haysom, G. 1653

Hayter, Alethea, review by 2521

Haywood, Charles 2514, 2518

Heaman, Robert xxxii, 12, 120

Heaney, Howell J. xx, xxxiv, xli, lxvii, 193, 252, 263-64, 1005, 1142, 1392, 2265
    review by 982

Hearn, Michael P. lxi, 99, 2340
    review by 46

Heartman, Charles F. 2027

Hebel, Udo J. 1262

Hébert, Diane 1037

Heichen, Paul 25

Heiser, Nancy, review by 973

Helliwell, F. 1820

Helm, William H. 987

Hendrick, George 1074

Henkels, Stanislaus V. 1950

Herbert, Miranda C. 1245, 1249-50

Herget, Winfried 1262

Heritage Book Shop, Inc. 2028-30

Herman, E., review by 2340

Herring, Paul D. lxii, lxiv, 2374, 2418

Hewitt, David, reviews by 2314, 2381

Hewitt, Rosalie 1218

Hicken, Mandy 673

Hill, Holly 733

Hill, Robert W. 1747

Hill, Rowland 646

Hill, Thomas W. xxi, 34, 195, 289, 360, 1005, 1457C4, 1473, 1486

Hills, Gertrude 2234

Hirsch, Rudolf 1142

Hobsbaum, Philip 988

Hodgkins, Louise M. 989

Hodgson, S. 535

Hodgson & Co. lii, 475, 1951-55, 2072, 2095, 2161, 2167, 2173, 2179

Hodnett, Edward 886

Hoefnagel, Dick 2214-15, 2217, 2235, 2241, 2300, 2390, 2395, 2409

Hoffman, Hester R. 955

Hogan, J. F. 1655

Hogarth, Georgina, *Hogarth-Dickens Letters*, ed. Hogarth and Mary (Mamie) Dickens xxiv, xxvi, xxxix, 29, 42, 48, 471, 1005, 1467, 1509, 1890, 1900, 1919, 1927, 1937, 2014, 2051

Hoggart, Paul xxxvii, 835-36

Hollington, Michael 26, 990, 1080-81, 1089

Holloway, John, review by 449

Holyoke, T. C., review by 2456

Holzenberg, Eric p. 580

Honour, Hugh 1867

Hopkins, Albert A. 122, 1457C3, 1459, 1604, 1721, 1805, 1903, 1906, 1908, 1934-35, 2010, 2115-19

Hopkins, Frederick M. 2120

Hornát, Jaroslav 579

Hornback, Bert G. p. 296, xxxii, lvii-lviii, lxv, 12, 13, 120, 1779, 2301, 2481
    review by 2474

Horne, Philip lix, 2469

Horsman, Alan xxxii, 105, 176, 234, 249, 991, 2364, 2375-76

Horsman, E. A. 1491

Horton, Susan R. 1047

Hotten, John C. 42, 43

Houfe, Simon 887

Houghton, Esther R. 1176-77, 1411

Houghton, Walter E. 1176-77, 1411

House, Humphry 2286, 2378, 2391

House, Madeline 134
    Pilgrim Letters, vol. I, ed. House and Graham Storey 134, 237, 412, 475, 1491,

SUBJECT INDEX

Part 1: Dickens's Works

Note: Dickens's fifteen novels and five Christmas Books will be found listed alphabetically under their titles in section 1, below. Shorter works of fiction are listed under **Christmas Stories** or **Shorter fiction**. Dickens's other works are listed first by category–**Attributions and collaborations**, **Nonfiction** (used here to refer to essays, book-length and shorter, and journalistic pieces), **Poetry**, **Public readings**, **Speeches**, and **Theatrical works**– and then alphabetically in section 2, below. Shorter nonfictional works will be found either under the journal in which they were published (*All the Year Round, Examiner,* or *Household Words*) or under the heading **Shorter nonfictional writings**. It has been difficult to index works, principally articles in *Household Words* and *All the Year Round,* erroneously attributed solely to Dickens but on which he may have collaborated or which he may have edited extensively. Even those who have studied these works do not always agree on the extent of Dickens's involvement. They will be found below in section 2 under the heading of **Attributions and collaborations**. Abridgments, anthologies, editions and collected editions have been listed separately in section 3, and Dickens's writings of a personal nature–his autobiographical writings, diaries, letters, and notebooks, unpublished in his lifetime, except for a few letters–form a fourth section of this part of the subject index.

1. INDIVIDUAL WORKS: FICTION

Barnaby Rudge p. 286, xxiv, xxxv, xxix, 36, 93, 162-63, 168, 191, 203, 205, 226, 540, 1396, 1506, 1575C, 1726, 1952, 1998, 2055, 2256, 2260, 2291, 2303
  adaptations 93, 699, 724, 757, 769, 791
  as historical novel 93, 162-63, 168
  bibliographical studies 93, 203, 240-44, 2302-03
  bibliographies of editions 24, 55, 62, 93, 203
  characters
    Grip the raven 2007, 2108
    Rudge, Barnaby 2007
    Varden, Dolly, portrait of 1506, 1541, 1543, 1726, 1756
  critical and special studies 93, 203, 244
  bibliographies p. 286, 93, 1228
  doctoral dissertations 93
  illustrations xxxviii, 24, 93, 637, 857, 927, 933, 1470, 1900, 2000, 2006, 2302-03
  manuscript lx, 93, 1541, 1543, 2302, 2304, 2307, 2318

plagiarisms, imitations, etc. 2145
proofs lx, 1543, 2291, 2466
publication and publishing agreements lx, 162, 168, 205, 226, 243-44, 1952, 1998, 2014, 2072
reviews 540
serial publication 24, 55, 192, 241, 2302-03, 2318
textual studies lx, 2291, 2298, 2307, 2318, 2460, 2466
  bibliographies 93
translations 572, 617, 637
also see Gabriel Vardon, below

Battle of Life, The xxx, 1802
  adaptations 753, 779
  bibliographical studies xxvii, xxix, 46, 253, 286, 1680, 1988, 2265
  bibliographies of editions 46, 98
  critical and special studies, bibliography 98
  forgery 1988
  illustrations 879, 900

2. INDIVIDUAL WORKS: ATTRIBUTIONS AND COLLABORATIONS, NONFICTION, POETRY, PUBLIC READINGS, SPEECHES, THEATRICAL WORKS

manuscript 432, 1962, 2004

"Response, The," addressed to Mark Lemon, manuscript 2008

"Song of the Wreck," from Wilkie Collins's *The Lighthouse*

manuscript 1525, 1905, 1962, 2004

songs by Dickens 154

"To Ariel" 1525

untitled poems (1836), manuscript 1914; (1857), manuscript 1926; (1860), manuscript 1923

verses for Christiana Weller, manuscript 2056

verses on fly-leaf of Thomas Woolnoth's *Facts and Faces* 2190

verses on Leigh Hunt 433

Public readings

Public reading versions of Dickens's works 15, 36, 40-41, 97, 408, 422, 529, 641-64, 668, 676, 704, 745, 780, 800, 1000, 1020, 1083, 1228, 1396, 1436, 1444, 1457A, 1457B6, 1487, 1491, 1499, 1524, 1548, 1575A-B, 1626, 1642, 1675, 1716, 1749, 1797, 1800, 1815, 1842, 1861, 1869, 1901, 1915, 1944, 1965, 1977, 1995, 2014, 2046, 2055-57, 2083, 2099, 2193, 2376, 2381, 2401, 2456, 2474

bibliographies and bibliographical and textual studies xlii, 15, 641-64

also see titles of works for which Dickens created individual readings in section 1 of part 1 of the subject index, above and Charles Dickens, public reading tours *in part 2 of the subject index, below*

Speeches

Speeches (general references) p. 325, xxiii, xxvii, xxix, xxxiii, xlii, 42-43, 150, 226, 393, 408, 422, 460, 984, 1430, 1436, 1438, 1444-45, 1487, 1524, 1528, 1536, 1548-49, 1573, 1575B, 1598, 1626, 1687, 2056; (specific references) 408, 421, 440, 458, 1444, 1511, 1612, 1874, 1908, 1987, 2148

bibliographies 4, 8, 11, 15-16, 28, 35, 40-43, 48, 150, 393, 408, 422, 984, 1438

corrected galley proofs 1908

critical and special studies, bibliography 981

manuscripts 1511, 1533-34, 1874, 1987, 2148

reports of speeches 1573

textual studies 408

Theatrical works

Theatrical writings xxvii, lxvii, 8, 11, 16-17, 40-42, 48, 425, 431, 443, 460, 670, 784, 806, 1005, 1796

bibliography 147

Lord Chamberlain's copies of Dickens's plays 134

burlesque of the Great Exposition, manuscript of portions of 1969

comic dialogue for Frank Powell 1616

comic duologues, attributed to Dickens 394

Frozen Deep, by Wilkie Collins, with revisions by Dickens *see* Wilkie Collins *in part 2 of the subject index, below*

Is She His Wife? xxiii, 134, 398, 405, 412, 436, 444, 447, 775, 1441, 2268, 2513

"Cross Purposes" (not extant), probably earlier version of *Is She His Wife?* 412

Lamplighter, The 398, 1543

Mr. Nightingale's Diary, by Mark Lemon, with revisions by Dickens *see* Mark Lemon *in part 2 of the subject index, below*

No Thoroughfare, by Wilkie Collins with revisions by Dickens *see* Wilkie Collins *in part 2 of the subject index, below*

O'Thello xxvii, 34, 460, 1509, 1797, 1903, 1905, 1934-35, 2008, 2117, 2137-38, 2188, 2514, 2518

manuscript fragments 1509, 1797, 1903, 1905, 1934-35, 2008, 2117, 2137-89, 2188

Strange Gentleman, The 134, 398, 900, 1441, 1457B32, 1678, 1938, 2513

"Stratagems of Rozanza" 2265

Village Coquettes, The 134, 142, 320, 398, 1441, 1549, 1997, 2250, 2268, 2513

manuscript 2148

3. ABRIDGEMENTS, ANTHOLOGIES, EDITIONS, COLLECTED EDITIONS

Abridgements of Dickens works 602, 619, 798, 837, 851, 873

bibliographies 584, 1780

collections 1438, 1482

2411-12

Odyssey Press Edition (New York) 302, 310

Oxford Illustrated Dickens (Oxford University Press) 182, 2510

Oxford India Paper Edition (Chapman and Hall, London) 33

Penguin Edition (Penguin Books, Harmondsworth, Eng., and New York) lix, lxi, lxiv-lxvii, 137, 182, 208, 245, 295, 302, 310, 315, 318, 337, 355, 373, 923, 1070, 1097, 1124, 2320, 2330, 2352, 2371, 2379, 2397, 2421, 2424-25, 2437, 2449, 2453, 2457, 2463, 2469, 2486, 2496, 2507, 2515, 2524

People's Edition (Chapman and Hall, London), xxiii, 184, 2041

People's Edition (Estes and Lauriat, Boston) 201

Peterson, T. B., editions (Philadelphia) 220, 352

Popular Library Edition (Chapman and Hall, London) xxiii

Rinehart Editions (Holt, Rinehart, and Winston, New York) 333

Riverside Edition (Houghton Mifflin, Boston) lxii, 2363

Riverside Edition (Hurd & Houghton, New York) 173, 220

Rochester Edition (Methuen, London) lv, 1389, 1397-98, 1404, 1465, 1509, 1794,

1971-72, 1981-82, 2302-03

Shilling Edition (Chapman and Hall, London) xxiii, 31, 33

Signet Classic Edition (New American Library, New York) 295, 337, 373

Sixpenny Edition (Chapman and Hall, London) xxiii

St. Dunstan's (Millionaire's) Edition (George Sproul, New York) 202, 228, 230-31, 1445, 2303

Standard Library Edition (Houghton Mifflin, Boston) 39

Tauchnitz edition (in Collection of British Authors, Leipzig) 91, 214, 222, 255, 285, 291, 461, 625

Ticknor and Fields Edition (Boston) 239

Two-Shilling Edition (Chapman and Hall, London) 31, 33

Universal Edition (Chapman and Hall, London) 195

University Edition (Estes and Lauriat, Boston) 201

Victoria Edition (Chapman and Hall, London) 863, 1803, 1919

Waverley Edition (Waverley Book Co., London) 2042

World's Classics Edition (Oxford University Press) lix, lxi-lxii, lxv-lxvi, 38, 182, 323, 375, 651, 677, 2328, 2358, 2375, 2380, 2414, 2419, 2422, 2433-34, 2455, 2461

4. PERSONAL WRITINGS

Autobiographies, diaries

autobiographies
autobiographical fragment liv, 1077, 2298, 2357, 2359
bibliographies 1034, 1254
commentaries on Dickens's autobiographical writings 104, 584, 1235, 2359
diaries 1239, 1499, 1539, 1548, 1590, 1726, 1749, 1896, 2335
bibliographies 14, 40, 954, 1528

Letters

letters (general references) xix, xxii-xxv, xxix, xlv, li, lx-lxi, lxvi, lxix, 17, 40, 42-43, 129, 199, 252, 325, 336, 387-88, 392, 394-95, 406, 412, 416, 443, 457, 469, 475, 484, 494, 501, 511, 521, 531, 575, 594, 658, 833, 857, 913, 923, 935, 1128, 1228, 1261, 1350,

1416, 1430, 1447, 1453, 1467, 1487, 1505, 1513, 1515, 1525, 1575B-C, 1655, 1683, 2131, 2161, 2186-87, 2197, 2200, 2217, 2232, 2240, 2242-43, 2271-72, 2280, 2286-87, 2298, 2338, 2354, 2373, 2401-02, 2460, 2467, 2471, 2481
bibliographies 12, 42

collected editions of letters 185, 226, 237, 1128, 1456, 1655, 1771, 2054
bibliographies xlii, 4, 8, 11-12, 14-15, 28, 35, 41-42, 47, 70, 101, 103-04, 125, 575, 955-56, 984, 1007, 1016, 1020, 1023, 1029-30, 1083, 1228, 1487, 1500, 1502, 1535-36
reviews 237

Hogarth-Dickens Letters see Georgina Hogarth *in part 2 of the author index, above*

Nonesuch Letters see Walter Dexter *in part 2 of*

Part 2: Subject Headings

Note: This part of the subject index is largely Dickens-oriented. Accordingly, such headings as **English literature** or, for that matter, **Nineteenth-Century English literature** have been omitted. Thus a work such as the volume on the nineteenth-century in *The Cambridge Bibliography of English Literature*, will be indexed under its Dickens section as **Bibliographies of Dickens's works** and **Bibliographies of Dickens studies** instead of such more general headings. A few general headings have remained and will be found under **Nineteenth-century** (rather than **Victorian period**) headings. Items relevant to Dickens dealing with the period in which he lived will likewise be found under **Nineteenth-century** rather than **Victorian period**. Entries dealing in general with the novel and other types of fiction will be found under **Nineteenth-century prose fiction**, but, again, only with reference to their Dickens connections.

2171-73, 2176-78, 2180-82, 2196, 2199, 2203, 2227, 2229, 2236, 2239, 2246, 2257, 2265
reports on auction sales and booksellers' catalogues lii-liii, 1220, 1416, 1509, 1538, 1589, 1628, 1634, 1665, 1765, 2071-2197
also see Collecting Dickens
Austen, John 886
Austin, Henry, brother-in-law of Dickens 395, 1457B24b, 2260
Dickens's letters to 2280
Austin, Letitia Dickens (Mrs. Henry), sister of Dickens 1480, 2260
Austin, Samuel H., sale catalogue of library 1450, 1899
Australasian, The 225
Autobiographical voice in Dickens's works 1235
Autobiographies and autobiographical writings of Dickens *see* Autobiographies, diaries *in section 4 of part 1 of the subject index, above*
Aylmer, Sir Felix
papers, Dickens House 1457C10
Dickens Incognito 1457C10

B

Bacon, Francis 547
Bacon, J. H. 1653
Bancroft, Lucretia 1969
Bangs & Co., sale catalogue 1939
Banks, P. W. 1491
Banton & Mackrell, Messrs., Dickens's letter to 2030
Barham, R. H. 1951
Barnard, Frederick 886, 894, 897, 906, 1663, 1965, 1972, 2056
Barrett, Oliver R. 2079, 2130
sale catalogue of collection 1958
sale of collection 2096-97, 2130
Barrington, Ross 2040
Barrow, Janet, aunt of Dickens 2165
Bartholomew, Freddie 696
Bartholomew's Hospital, London 1949
Bath, Eng.
Dickens and 1428
Dickens conference (1903) 1575B
Bath Central Library 1568
Beadnell, Maria 2056-57
album 395, 400, 455, 1457A, 1524, 1579, 1675, 1976, 2072, 2128
Dickens's letters to 1401, 1514, 1693, 2133
also see Mrs. Maria Beadnell Winter
Beard, Ellen, album 1529

Beard, Frank 1675
Beard, Thomas, Dickens's letters to 1976, 2128
Beardsley, John E. 515
Beaumont, Francis, and John Fletcher 2046
Bede, Cuthbert (pseud.) *see* Edward Bradley
Bedford, Francis D. 897, 905-06
Bedroom door knockers imprinted with characters from Dickens's novels 2225
Beinecke Rare Book and Manuscript Library, Yale University Library 647, 1485, 1562
Bell, Currer, Acton, and Ellis (pseuds.) *see* Charlotte, Anne, and Emily Brontë
Bell's Life in London 2495
Bell's Weekly Magazine 359, 372
Benedict, Commodore E. C., sale catalogue of library 1926
Bengis, Nathan L., *Drood* Collection in Wilson Library, University of Minnesota 1107
Benjamin, Park 522
Bennett, James Gordon 381
Benoliel, D. Jacques 1627, 1670, 1762
Benoliel, D. Jacques, Collection, Free Library of Philadelphia 394, 1730
Benoliel, Katherine K. 1632, 1670
Benson, Elaine 696
Bentley, George 144, 890
Bentley, Richard 416, 890, 1952
Dickens's letters to lii, 1437, 1499, 1548, 1952, 2072, 2161
Dickens's personal relationship with 144, 1952, 2161, 2505
Dickens's publishing agreements with lii, 244, 329, 336, 1437, 1952, 1998, 2014, 2072
sale catalogue of collection lii, 1952
Bentley, Thomas 724
Bentley, Richard, & Son 54, 142-45, 446, 1178
Bentley's Miscellany xxvii, 142-45, 240, 396, 403, 442, 492, 1177, 1180, 1185, 1453, 1466, 1952, 2014, 2072
bibliography of articles on crime in 169
contributors to 142-45
Dickens's editorship of 142-43, 145, 396, 449, 1130, 1177, 1453, 1964, 2010
publication of *Oliver Twist* in lix, 144, 327-28, 334-35, 1177, 2469, 2475
Berg, Henry W. and Albert A., Collection, New York Public Library p. 702, lxv, 16, 124, 450, 520, 646-47, 649, 653-54, 659, 664, 1178, 1239, 1571-72, 1582, 1642, 1653, 1749, 2531

1827, 1904, 2040, 2291, 2352-53, 2415, 2418, 2426, 2488, 2493, 2502, 2522
popularity among critics 1022, 1026, 1058
public reading tours xxxvi, 408, 422, 529, 641-64, 686, 704, 780, 1396, 1457A, 1457B6, 1491, 1575A-B, 1654, 1675, 1698, 1716, 1749, 1800, 1861, 1869, 1901, 1915, 1944, 1995, 2014, 2046, 2056, 2083, 2193
  deleterious effect of on his health 2083
reading, extent of 2055
reception by Queen Victoria 2083
reception in Europe 625
recipes (handwritten) for champagne cup and punch 1773, 1939
relationships with friends, acquaintances, associates
  Elihu Burritt 1417
  Robert Buss 2028, 2174
  Thomas Carlyle 1326
  George W. Childs 1513, 2480, 2484
  George Eliot (Mary Ann Evans) 1318
  Thomas C. Evans 658
  William P. Frith 1690
  Leigh Hunt 1308
  his illustrators 218, 857, 864, 883, 1525, 1779, 1867, 1953, 2298, 2335
  Charles Kingsley 1326
  Thomas and Mary Anne Mitton 1715
  Edgar Allan Poe 522, 1296, 1311
  Thomas Powell 1525
  Charles Reade 1295
  Robert Seymour 129, 340, 1919
  Clarkson Stanfield 1826
  Bernhard Tauchnitz 214, 222, 285, 291, 625
  Ellen Ternan 481, 1701, 1729, 1918, 2442
  Josef Valkenberg and his brother 2152
  Edmund Yates 2126
  also see Richard Bentley, Biographical studies of Dickens, Biographies of Dickens, Bradbury and Evans, Hablot K. Brown, Edward Bulwer-Lytton, Angela Burdett-Coutts, Chapman and Hall, Wilkie Collins, *and* George Cruikshank, *above, and* Percy Fitzgerald, John Forster, Elizabeth Gaskell, Daniel Maclise, Publishers of Dickens's works, *and* William Makepiece Thackeray, *be-*

low
relics (furniture, personal effects, etc.) xxii, xlvii-xlviii, l, li, 17, 1583, 1605, 1611, 1645, 1654, 1698, 1719, 1733, 1741, 1745, 1756, 1761, 1785, 1787-91, 1793, 1797, 1802, 1813, 1880, 1882-83, 1905, 1929, 1931, 1948, 1963, 1966, 1986, 1992, 1995, 2002, 2010, 2049-50, 2110, 2113, 2125, 2152, 2156, 2165, 2214-15, 2217-18, 2269, 2272, 2275
religious views, faith 437, 1235, 1521, 1965, 2040
representations of
  busts 1248, 1613, 1706, 1959, 1969
  caricatures xlvii, 1704, 1788, 2038
  photographs l, 1248, 1350, 1353, 1449, 1457, 1457C8, 1457D, 1457F, 1457L, 1460, 1544, 1575C, 1576, 1753, 1800, 1806, 1828, 1916, 1930, 1979, 1986-87, 1994, 2028, 2031, 2035-41, 2050, 2185, 2348
  political and topical cartoons and illustrations xlvii, 1575F
  portraits xxv, xxxviii-xxxix, xlvii, 10, 27, 142, 894, 900, 1237, 1248, 1350, 1354, 1416, 1436, 1445, 1457A, 1457C1, 1457D-E, 1457G, 1467, 1494, 1501, 1505-06, 1511, 1520-21, 1523-25, 1527, 1534, 1541, 1543-44, 1548, 1572, 1574, 1575C, 1579, 1581-82, 1621, 1626, 1640, 1653, 1663, 1668, 1675, 1687, 1697-98, 1703, 1710, 1715, 1720, 1742, 1753, 1756, 1759, 1779, 1784, 1786, 1788, 1790, 1792, 1797, 1806, 1813, 1816, 1820, 1827, 1832, 1882, 1894, 1899, 1917, 1927, 1930, 1933, 1935, 1938, 1959, 1962, 1964, 1976, 1979-80, 1982, 1994, 1997, 2008, 2016, 2028-29, 2038-39, 2043, 2050, 2056, 2074, 2109, 2124, 2153, 2165, 2191, 2196, 2229, 2240, 2245, 2266
  statue 1548
reputation *see* Critical and appreciative studies of Dickens, surveys of studies of Dickens's reception and reputation, *above*
residences 1457, 1457D, 1457G, 1460, 1548, 1813, 1930
  1 Devonshire Terrace, London 1532, 1700, 1987, 2010
  48 Doughty Street, London 1457, 1579,

1748, 1779, 1801, 1803, 1816-18, 1823, 1827-28, 1832, 1855, 1916-17, 1925, 1935, 1937-38, 1963-64, 1966, 1977, 1980, 1987, 1999, 2003, 2006, 2028, 2034-42, 2050, 2056, 2111, 2137, 2335, 2428, 2449, 2456

Illustrators of Dickens's works xxxviii, xlii, 19, 41, 56, 61, 218, 226, 257, 301, 564, 851-940, 1011, 1225, 1228, 1348, 1459, 1468, 1485, 1499, 1525, 1544, 1594, 1660, 1667, 1779, 1818, 1820, 1827, 1867, 1977, 2045, 2111, 2121, 2265, 2271, 2298, 2423, 2434, 2456, 2505

catalogues of illustrators 865-66, 886

Dickens's relationships with 218, 857, 864, 1525, 1779, 1867, 1953, 2298, 2335

instructions and criticism regarding illustrations 857, 860, 864, 875, 923, 931, 933, 935, 1525, 2335, 2423

also see individual illustrators, particularly Hablot K. Browne, Robert Buss, George Cruikshank, John Leech, Robert Seymour, Marcus Stone

Imagery, allusion, and symbolism in Dickens's works 127, 1013, 1235, 1459, 1779, 2316, 2319, 2333, 2368-70, 2430, 2526

Inchbald, Elizabeth, *Animal Magnetism*, Dickens's marked prompt book of for an amateur production 2010

Index Translationum p. 153

Indexes concerning Dickens and his works 39-40, 55, 68-69, 72, 94-96, 140, 149, 151, 150, 166, 583, 585, 681-82, 685, 718, 727, 730, 786, 815, 820, 944, 962, 972-73, 1031-32, 1035, 1038, 1040-41, 1049, 1051, 1056, 1059, 1078, 1113, 1126, 1148, 1165-73, 1178, 1342, 1427, 1437, 1454, 1467, 1494, 1511, 1522, 2067

Influence and comparative studies concerning Dickens and his works xxii, 129, 301, 372, 410, 503, 549, 571, 588, 590, 594, 600-01, 606, 617, 625, 628, 632, 634, 792, 806, 868, 1009, 1013, 1274, 1809, 1822, 1831, 2266, 2449

bibliographies 973, 1292-1328, 1487

Dickens's influence on

Auguste Blanche 594

I. L. Caragiale 571

Chinese writers 588

Wilkie Collins 1009, 1292

Joseph Conrad, bibliography of 1314

Feodor Dostoevsky 590, 625, 1315

bibliography of 1315

Emilie Flygare-Carlén 594

German writers 625

William Dean Howells 1313

Italian writers 562

Japanese writers 600-01

Franz Kafka, bibliography of 1324

Herman Melville 1313

Joseph C. Neal 503

Norwegian writers 559

Edgar Allan Poe 1311, 1313

Romanian writers and critics 571

Russian writers and critics 549

Serbo-Croatian novelists 606

George Bernard Shaw 1320, 1809

Swedish writers 594

William Makepeace Thackeray 228, 274

Leo Tolstoy 625

Mark Twain 1313

Alexandru Vlahuță 571

writers in both Modern Yiddish and Modern Hebrew 617

influence on Dickens

Bible, bibliography of 1312

Cervantes, bibliography of 1300

Wilkie Collins 1009, 1292, 2449

George Cruikshank, claims of 325, 858, 1517, 1808, 1822, 1829, 1831

eighteenth-century and early-nineteenth-century essayists 372

Gothic tale of terror, bibliography of studies of 1302-04

John Stuart Mill 1319

Edgar Allan Poe 1311

Romantic poets and essayists 1308, 1310

the theater 806

"Influence Exercised by Women in the Home, The" *see* "Women in the Home"

Insurance Times 439

International copyright law, Dickens's unsuccessful crusade for 173, 189-90, 222, 235, 387

International Magazine 219

Internet resources concerning Dickens xxxvi, xliii-xlv, lxix, 1145-47, 1155, 1158 *also see* E-texts of Dickens's works, *above, and* Web sites concerning Dickens, *below*

invitations to a public dinner and ball given

for Dickens in New York (1842) 1541
Ireland, Alexander 1663
  Dickens's letters to 1916
Irony and satire in Dickens's works lvi, lxiii, 47, 413, 415, 452, 617, 783, 2021, 2315, 2332, 2352
  also see Parody in Dickens's works *below*
Irving, Henry 1640
  sale of library 1416

J

Jackson, Mr. 362
Jacobsen, Eric 608
Jacobson, Wendy, *The Companion to The Mystery of Edwin Drood*, criticism of 1399
James, Henry 1313
Jarndyce Antiquarian Booksellers, catalogues 2031-42, 2088
Jarvis, John W., & Son
  catalogue 1388, 2043
  catalogue sale 2157
Jeakes, William, Dickens's letter to 1657
Jeffrey, Lord (Francis) 242
Jenkins, Joseph I., Dickens's letter to 1753
Jerome, Jerome K. 314
Jerrold, Blanchard, *The Life of George Cruikshank*, grangerized copy of 1777
Jerrold, Douglas 399, 519, 1573, 1630, 1728, 2039, 2041
  collected edition of works 1728
  Dickens's letters to 2041
  letters to Dickens 2041
  The Housekeeper 399
Jerrold, William Blanchard 2041
  Dickens's letters to 2041
Jews, Dickens's depiction of 1790, 2470
Jewsbury, Geraldine Endsor 2200
Johannsen, Albert, *Phiz: Illustrations from the Novels of Charles Dickens* 929
John Jasper's Secret see Henry Morford, *below*
Johns, Mrs. Richard, Dickens's letter to 2041
Johnson, Charles P., *Hints to Collectors of Original Editions of the Works of Charles Dickens* 1420
Johnson, Edgar 1252, 1672 *also see* Edgar Johnson *in part 2 of author index, above*
Johnson, Eldridge R., sale catalogue of collection 1964
Johnson, Frank S. 1743, 2042
Johnson, G. W. 1548

Johnson, Samuel 2168
  Dictionary of the English Language, Dickens's copy of 2390, 2395, 2409
Johnson, William F., sale catalogue of library 1939
Johnston, Henry 1491
Jolly, Emily, Dickens's letters to 2010
Jones, Mrs. A. Pitt, sale catalogue of library 1990
Jones-Evans, Eric 752
Jonson, Ben 887, 1541, 1543, 1666, 1778, 1816, 2039, 2046, 2055, 2084, 2272
  Bartholomew Fair, Dickens's collection of miscellanea concerning 2055
  Every Man in His Humour, Dickens's amateur production of 887, 1541, 1543, 1666, 1778, 1816, 2039, 2046, 2084
    Captain Bobadil, Dickens's portrait as 1756, 2084
    Dickens's costume for 2272
Journal of Narrative Technique 1038
Journal of the Illinois State Historical Society 1383
Joyce, David G., sale catalogue of collection 1896
Joyce, Felix, Dickens's letter to 1942
Joyce, James
  unpublished writings of, discovered 1425
  "Centenary of Charles Dickens, The" 1425
Jung, Carl Gustav, Jungian criticism of Dickens's works 1378
Jupp, Ralph T. 1400, 1611, 1689, 1929, 1934, 2056, 2080, 2104, 2108, 2129, 2139, 2163
  bookseller's catalogue of library li, 2056
  sale catalogue of Dickens collection 1929
  sale of library 2104, 2108, 2119, 2123, 2129, 2139, 2151, 2163
  Jupp-Kern prime *Pickwick Papers* in parts 1934
  Jupp-Kern-Bandler prime *Pickwick Papers* in parts 1689

K

Kafka, Franz, influence of Dickens on, bibliography of 1324
Kaplan, Fred 1252
Katarsky, Igor, obituaries 1275
Keats, John 1308, 1310
Keats House Museum 1566
Kebler, Leonard, Dickens collection, Library of Congress 1712